46th Power Sources Conference 2014

Orlando, Florida, USA
9 – 12 June 2014

ISBN: 978-1-5108-5234-1

Printed from e-media with permission by:

Curran Associates, Inc.
57 Morehouse Lane
Red Hook, NY 12571

Some format issues inherent in the e-media version may also appear in this print version.

Printed by Curran Associates, Inc. (2018)

For permission requests, please contact Power Sources Conference
at the address below.

Power Sources Conference
Palisades Convention Management
411 Lafayette Street, Suite 201
New York, NY 10003

Phone: (212) 460-8090 x 202
Fax: (212) 460-5460

mgoldfarb@pcm411.com

Additional copies of this publication are available from:

Curran Associates, Inc.
57 Morehouse Lane
Red Hook, NY 12571 USA
Phone: 845-758-0400
Fax: 845-758-2633
Email: curran@proceedings.com
Web: www.proceedings.com

PROCEEDINGS OF THE

46th POWER SOURCES CONFERENCE

9–12 JUNE 2014

Chairs' Welcome

Welcome to the Power Sources Conference 2014

You are cordially invited to attend the Power Sources Conference which this year is moving to Orlando Wyndham Resort, Orlando, Florida. The Power Sources Conference will focus on energy-generation and storage technology (largely, but not exclusively, electrochemical) that is of interest to the Department of Defense, other government agencies, and to the civilian marketplace. The conference will comprise the technical program, a poster session, and an exhibition. Also as usual, the technical program is strongly oriented toward technology that is relevant to Government applications.

This year's technical program reflects continued strong interest in high-energy batteries, fuel cells, and other portable and mobile power sources. We're sure that you will also enjoy the exhibit, hospitality suites, and social mixer.

We're hoping to see you in June.

Table of Contents

Table of Contents

Table of Contents

Table of Contents

Table of Contents

Table of Contents

Table of Contents

Table of Contents

Table of Contents

Table of Contents

Table of Contents

Table of Contents

Table of Contents

Author Index

Author Index

Author Index

Author Index

Author Index

Author Index

In-situ Optical Visualization of Li Dendrite Growth at Sub-Ambient Temperatures

Olga Baturina, Corey Love, Benjamin Gould and Karen Swider-Lyons
Chemistry Division, Naval Research Laboratory
Washington DC, USA, 20375
olga.baturina@nrl.navy.mil

Abstract: *Li dendritic growth at -10, 5 and 20°C is visualized by optical imaging of Li vs Li symmetric electrochemical cells in galvanostatic conditions. The temperature and current density range were chosen in order to verify predictions of Akolkar's model [1] with respect to Li dendrite propagation and growth. Our results support predictions of the model. If additional instabilities are introduced at the surface, which are not accounted by the model, uncontrolled dendritic growth may be observed at temperatures at which a suppressed dendritic growth is predicted.*

Keywords: Lithium ion battery; dendrite; Li deposition; nucleation and growth; electrochemical energy conversion

Introduction

Recent safety incidents involving the Boeing 787 Dreamliner and the Navy's Advanced Seal Delivery System highlight the lack of fundamental understanding of the root cause of lithium ion battery (LIB) failures. Failure modes leading to thermal runaway in LIBs (overcharge, overheat, internal short, etc.) are well established; however, the underlying link between the origins of instability at the electrode/electrolyte interfaces leading to nucleation and growth of lithium dendrites and susceptibility to failure is unclear.

Recent modeling of Li dendrite growth [1] predicts accelerated growth of Li dendrites with decreasing temperature. The model accounts for temperature effects on lithium ion transport and Li electrodeposition rate, which is a function of the curvature of the surface (i.e.is different for a flat surface vs. the tip of dendrite). The ratio of Li electrodeposition rates on a flat surface to that of the tip of dendrite determines three well defined regions of Li dendrite growth: uncontrolled dendritic growth, suppressed dendrite growth and intermediate dendritic growth. Depending on current density in LIB, the temperatures at which transition between three regions occur can be determined. For example, at 10 mA cm^{-2}, uncontrolled dendritic growth is expected below 0°C, while it is expected to be suppressed above 13°C. To verify modeling results, three temperatures were selected in order to observe Li dendrite growth at three different regimes: -10°C, 5°C and 20°C. The paper discusses the effects of current density and electrolyte concentration on Li dendrite propagation, nucleation and growth at three different temperature regions.

Experimental

Experiments are conducted in optically transparent symmetric (Li vs. Li) home-made electrochemical cells held at -10, 5 and 20°C in galvanostatic conditions. Li electrodes (both anode and cathode) were prepared by pressing Li foil against the 5 mm wide Cu strips serving as current collectors. The cells were filled with non-aqueous electrolyte containing 1M $LiPF_6$ either in EC:DMC (1:1 by weight) or EC:PC:DEC (1:1:2 by weight) and placed in Tenney environmental chambers, maintained at -10, 5 and 20°C. The constant current in the cells was maintained using Maccor battery test equipment. The current was interrupted when the cells were taken out of the chambers for optical imaging.

Results and Discussion

Figure 1 shows the cell voltage vs. time curves measured in the cells held at -10, 5 and 20°C. When current is applied, metallic Li from the cathode is oxidized to Li^+ ions, that are reduced to Li metal at the anode.

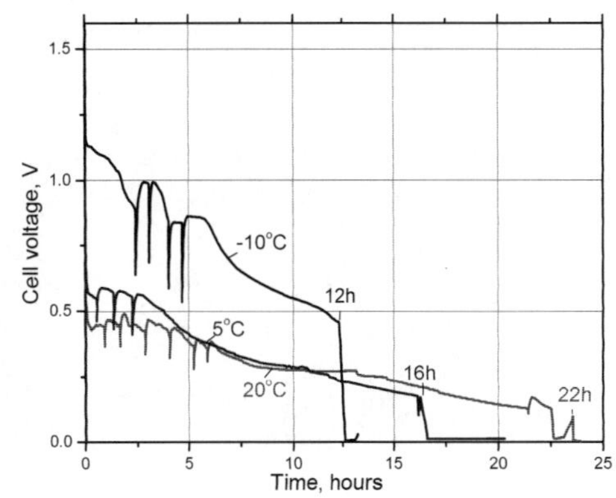

Figure 1. Cell voltage vs time curves for Li optical cells held at -10 (black), 5 (blue) and 20°C (red) at current density of 5 mA cm^{-2}. 1M LiPF6 in EC:PC:DEC (1:1:2). Spikes on the curves are due to interruptions for optical imaging.

Li deposition at the anode may lead to dendrite formation and growth. If this is a case, a dendrite eventually causes electrical short between the anode and cathode, resulting in sudden drop of cell voltage to zero. It can be seen from Figure 1 that time required for shorting the cells decreases with decreasing the cell temperature. This indirect indication of faster dendrite growth with decreasing the cell temperature is confirmed by optical imaging of the cells held at three different temperatures. Figure 2 shows progression in dendrite growth for the cell held at -10°C vs the one held at 20°C. While dendrite formation is first observed at 30 min in cells held at -10°C, no dendrite formation is seen up to 240 min in cells held at 20°C, in agreement with the suppressed dendrite growth predicted by Alkokar model [1]. Figure 3 shows unraveling of dendritic structure in the cell held at 20°C at 10 mA cm^{-2} in 1M $LiPF_6$ in EC:DMC. The dendrite formation starts much earlier (80 min vs 240 min) as we double current density (10 vs 5 mA cm^{-2}) and switch to an EC:DMC solvent. At 160 min from the beginning of the test, the dendrite approaches an opposite electrode. Note, that the dendrite formation in Figure 2 started at the spot previously occupied by a tiny air bubble that became a source of instability in this particular situation.

The dendrite development shown in Figure 2 varies from the Akolkar model [1], as suppressed dendritic growth is expected at 20°C. The reason for disagreement is likely instability caused by an air bubble on the surface of Li electrode.

Conclusions

Li dendritic growth at -10, 5 and 20°C is visualized by optical imaging of Li vs Li symmetric electrochemical cells in galvanostatic conditions. The temperature and current density range were chosen in order to verify predictions of Akolkar's model [1] with respect to dendrite propagation and growth. Our results support predictions of the model. If additional instabilities are introduced at the surface, which are not accounted by the model, uncontrolled dendritic growth may be observed at temperatures at which a suppressed dendritic growth is predicted.

Acknowledgements

Authors are grateful to the Office of Naval Research for financial support of this project.

Reference

1. Akolkar, R. "Modeling dendrite growth during lithium electrodeposition at sub-ambient temperature". *Journal of Power Sources*, vol. 246, pp. 84-89, 2014.

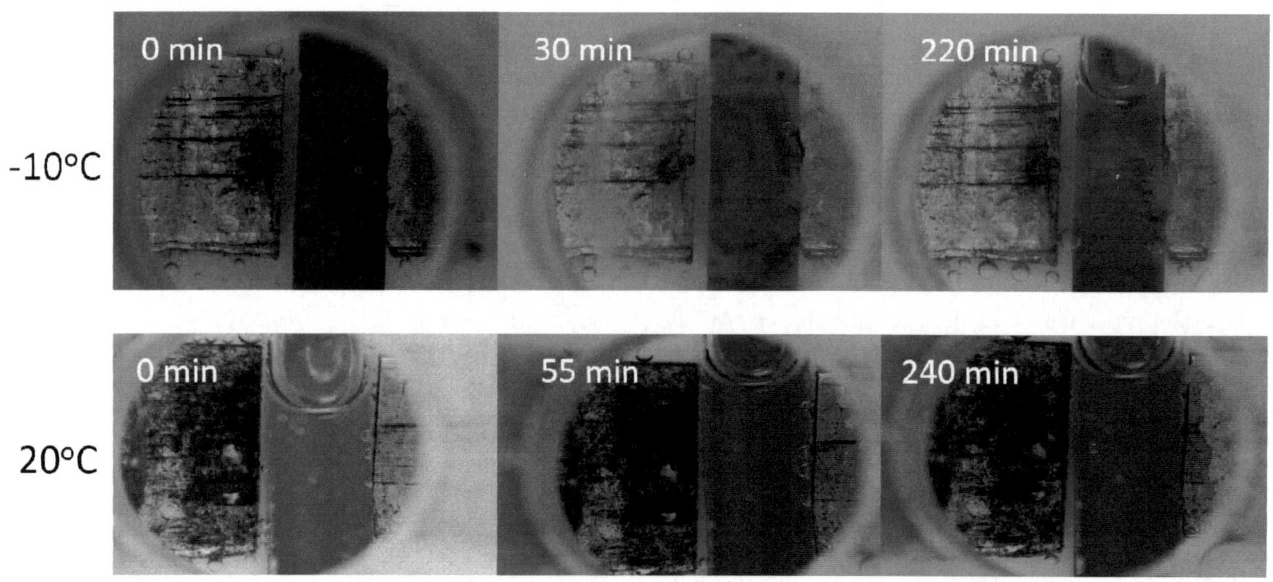

Figure 2. Dendrite growth observed in Li optical cells held at -10 and 20°C at current density of 5 mA cm^{-2}. 1M $LiPF_6$ in EC:PC:DEC (1:1:2)

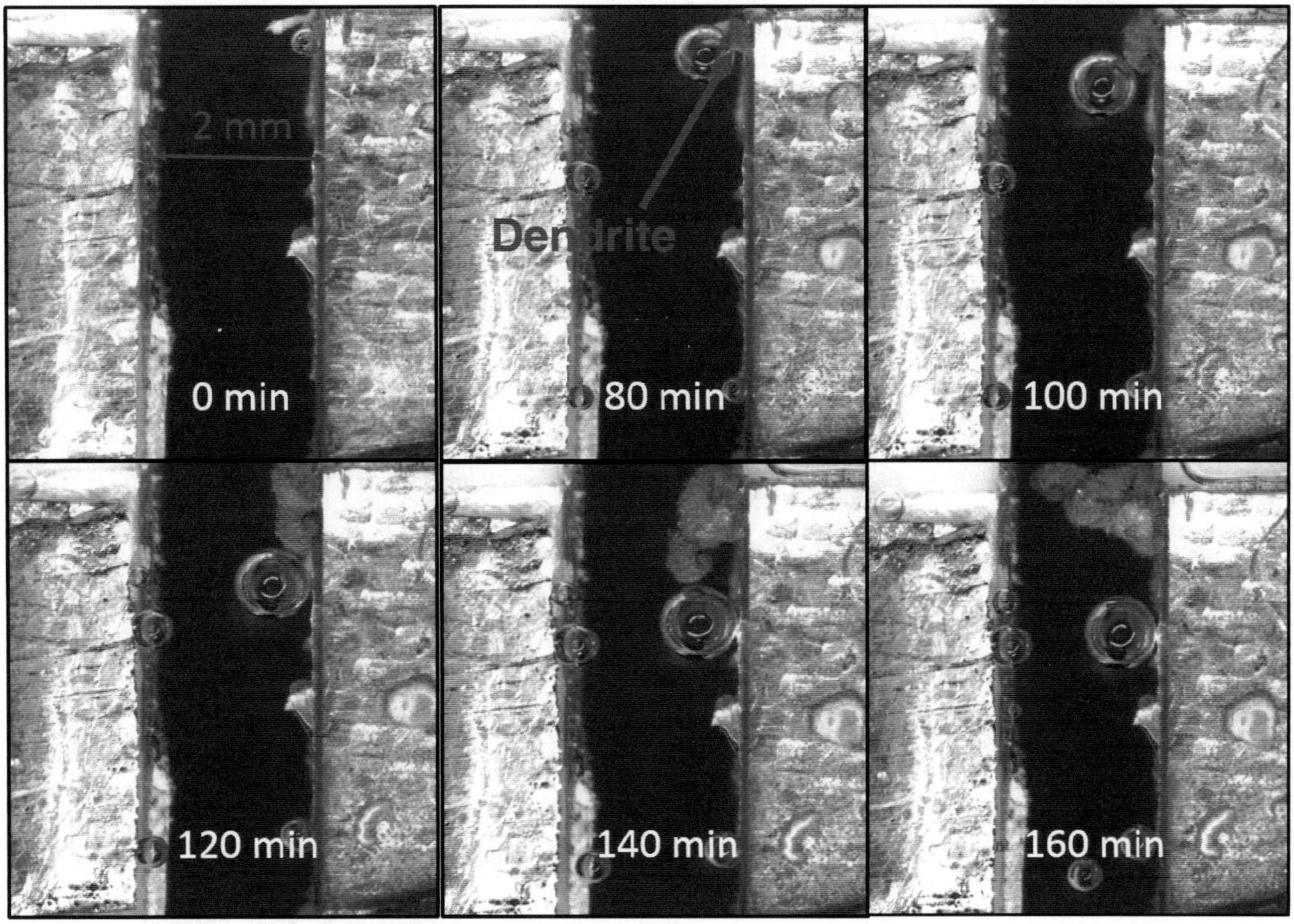

Figure 3. Online dendrite growth observation (without current interruption) in Li optical cells held at 20°C at current density of 10 mA cm^{-2}. 1M $LiPF_6$ in EC:DMC.

On-Demand Cell Internal Short Circuit Device

Eric Darcy[1] and Matthew Keyser[2]

[1]NASA-Johnson Space Center
Mail Code EP5
Houston, TX 77058 USA

[2]National Renewable Energy Laboratories
1617 Cole Blvd
Golden, CO 80401 USA

Contact Author Email: eric.c.darcy@nasa.gov

Abstract: A device implantable in Li-ion cells that can generate a hard internal short circuit on-demand by exposing the cell to 60°C has been demonstrated to be valuable for expanding our understanding of cell responses. The device provides a negligible impact to cell performance and enables the instigation of the 4 general categories of cell internal shorts to determine relative severity and cell design susceptibility. Tests with a 18650 cell design indicates that the anode active material short to the aluminum cathode current collector tends to be more catastrophic than the 3 other types of internal shorts. Advanced safety features (such as shutdown separators) to prevent or mitigate the severity of cell internal shorts can be verified with this device. The hard short success rate achieved to date in 18650 cells is about 80%, which is sufficient for using these cells in battery assemblies for field-failure-relevant, cell-cell thermal runaway propagation verification tests.

Keywords: cell internal short circuit; Li-ion; safety; thermal runaway; on-demand shorting device.

Introduction

Despite significant design maturity and extensive quality controls measures taken during manufacture since the commercialization of Li-ion cells, catastrophic cell internal shorts still occur periodically even in cells from reputable manufacturers. To replicate this, the Battery Association of Japan[1] has established a cell internal short circuit test that involves disassembling a charged 18650 cell and implanting a strategically placed metallic defect, rewinding the jellyroll, closing the cell, and cycling it to induce the short circuit. In addition, Barnett[2] has demonstrated the latency potential of defect induced cell internal shorts at escaping detection during cell screening and becoming catastrophic with more cycling. Quee[3] has reported on prolonged mechanical stress studies that cell void volume declines with repeated cycling as the density of the electrodes degrades. Therefore, sole reliance on prevention measures to mitigate the hazards of cell internal shorts is not sufficient for NASA. In battery designs over 80Wh, NASA battery safety requirements[4] for manned applications require an assessment by tests and analyses of the severity of a single cell thermal runaway event, and if catastrophic, a scoping of the design changes that could be implemented to appreciably reduce severity.

The challenge that our device addresses is how to induce a cell internal short circuit on-demand inside a battery in a way that is relevant to the conditions of such field failures. Traditional cell abuse tests, that electrically overcharge or thermally overheat cells, generally provide a uniform temperature distribution that is not present during a defect induced cell internal short. Cell abuse tests that mechanically crush or penetrate the cell enclosure yield a more localized and relevant internal short, however, these methods often breach the cell enclosure and are difficult to implement in a battery without significant alterations to the design and departure from relevant field failure conditions.

Design

The key feature of our device is an insulating wax layer compatible with Li-ion electrolytes and which melts at about 60 °C. The resulting low profile device shown in Fig.1 can be implanted in wound and in parallel electrode during cell assembly without impacting cell formation or subsequent acceptance testing.

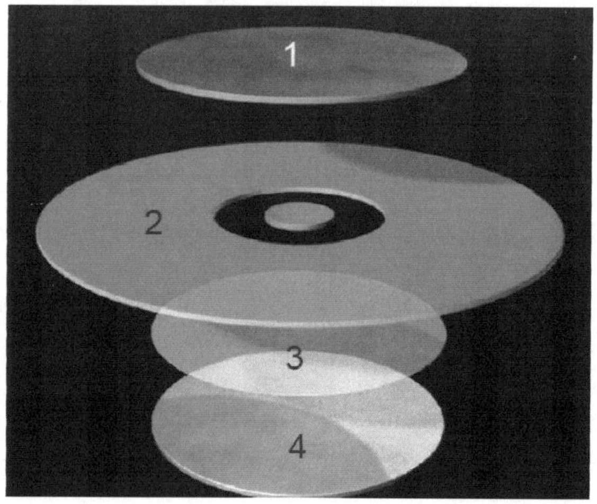

Figure 1. On-Demand Internal Short Circuit Device Design

Using conventional foils, the device thickness is less than 100 microns. As currently designed, the diameters of the metal pads are 11mm. For implantation, a hole > 11mmm is made in the native cell separator to allow a place for the device between anode and cathode materials. The device's and cell's separator layers overlap and are bonded together to secure the location of the device. With a good estimation of the wet electrode thickness and thicker pads, the design of the device can be optimized to achieve current collector-to-current collection shorts or electrode active material-to-current collection shorts, with the former shown in Fig. 2. This allows the 4 internals short circuit combinations to be achieved. The size of the copper puck determines the resistance and current carrying capacity of the device during the initial stages of the short.

The key component of the device is a thin, uniform, and complete wax layer in contact area of the copper puck and aluminum pad. These coated layers are achieved with a spin coating process developed at NREL. During the activation of the device, the thin liquid wax layer is wicked into the separator away from the path of the short. The wound radial pressure of jellyroll electrodes along with the interference fit of the copper puck help ensure good contact between the layers of the device and with the electrodes. With stacked electrode cell designs as in the pouch cells tested, external pressure is required to be maintained on the cell stack to reliably achieved hard shorts.

One caution in assembling these devices is preventing metallic burrs on the pads and the puck. These were found in earlier versions of our device and believed to have caused cell formation charge failures or premature activations. Using chemically etched metallic pads with edges that are free of burrs resolved this issue.

Experimental

To date, our device has been implanted in one 18650 and two pouch cell designs with nominal capacities of 2.4, 3.0, and 8.0Ah. After implantation and prior to electrolyte filling, insulation resistance tests are done to ensure the device is properly insulated. In addition, we find it prudent to perform a destructive device activation test on a sample of dry cells to verify that the device will achieve the anticipated hard short resistance.

Our latest trials with the 18650 cell design had less than 10% formation or cell acceptance failures. Subsequent capacity cycling for 20 cycles at C/10, C/2 and C-rates found negligible capacity or DC resistance impact of the device in comparison to nominal control cells.

To achieve current collector shorts, the active material of the electrode you want to bypass is manually removed in a circular spot with a solvent to expose the underlying current collector. The exposed area needs to be large enough to accommodate the diameter of the thicker pad of the device to ensure good device pad-to-collector contact.

Our latest trials with the 18650 cell design were done with two separator designs (shutdown and non-shutdown) and two short types (collector-to-collector (as shown in Fig.2) and anode active material-to-aluminum collector).

Results

Fig.3 shows typical cell voltage and temperature profiles from a hard short achieved during device activation that lead to thermal runaway. This result was achieved with a collector-to-collector short with a non-shutdown separator. The cell was fully charged and placed in an oven where its temperature was raised about 1 °C per minute. We have found that higher ramp rates lead to less consistent device activations, presumably due to uneven wax melting resulting from large temperature gradients in the cell. Once the cell and device are soaked at > 60°C, activation of the device typically causes a very steep cell voltage decline to near zero and very rapid cell skin temperature rise to the 600-700°C range or gets there with an intermediate pause at the 120-150°C range where separator meltdown occurs. Heating causes cell pressure to rise, open the cell current interrupt device (CID), the cell vent ruptures, and violent venting with flames, sparks, and electrolyte and electrode material venting results.

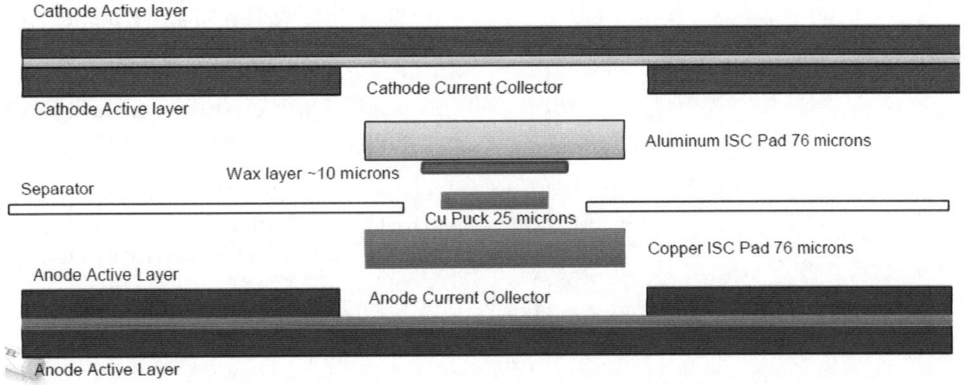

Figure 2. Design of ISC Device for a collector-to-collector cell internal short circuit.

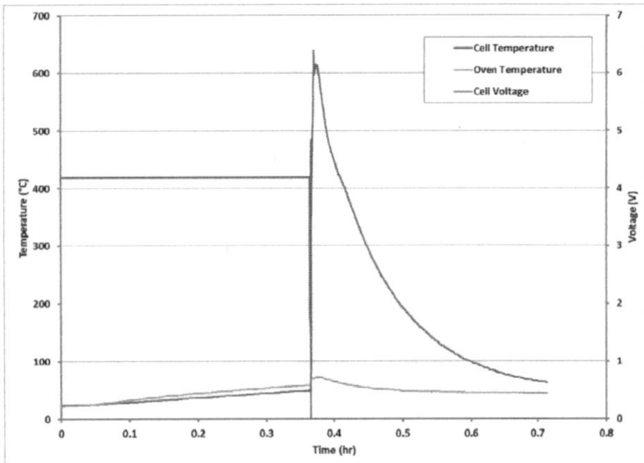

Figure 3. Typical voltage and temperature profiles during a cell hard short activation with collector-collector device[5]

In contrast, Fig.4 shows the typical cell voltage and temperature profiles with the same type of short circuit device but with the cell design equipped with a shutdown separator. Once the device activates the short, the cell voltage immediately drops and cell skin temperature rises abruptly to about 120°C and then safely cools down. Upon destructive disassembly of the cell jellyroll, we found significant portions of the anode were fully charged (Fig.5).

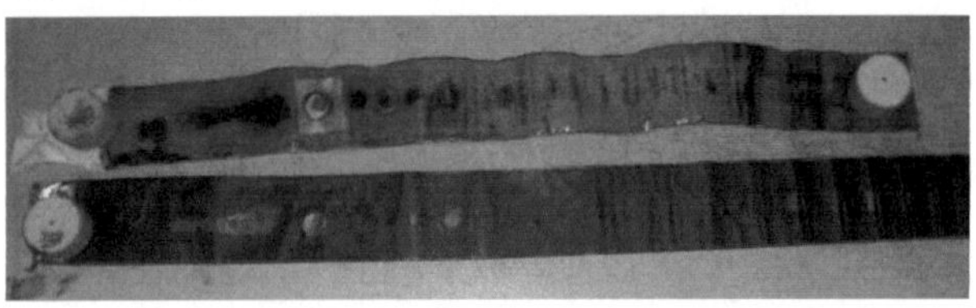

Figure 5. Unwound jellyroll showing significant portions of anode to be still charged (gold spots).[5]

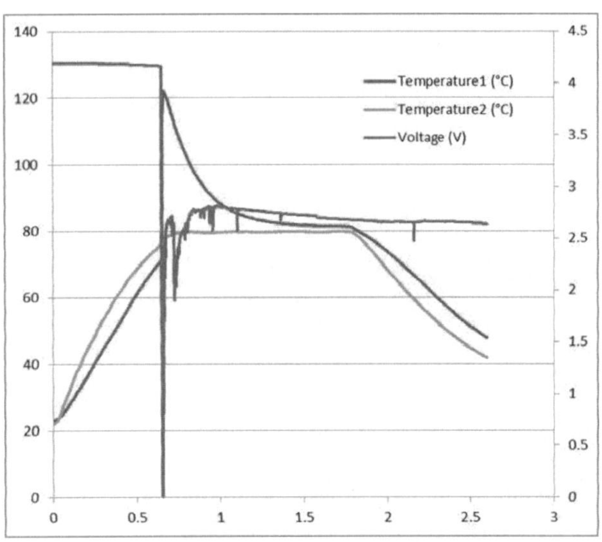

Figure 4. Typical profiles for cell with shutdown separator[5]

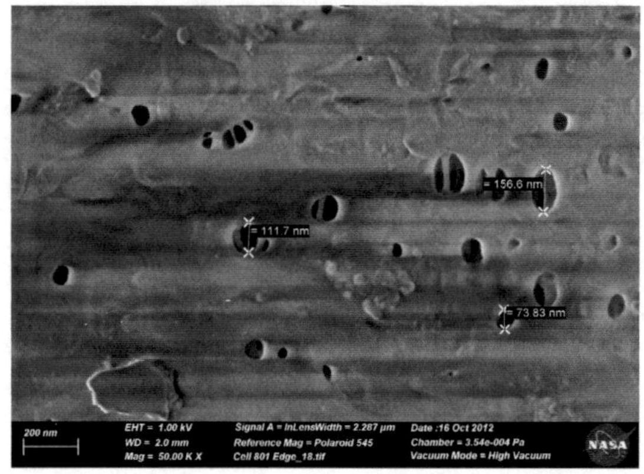

Figure 6. SEM micrograph of separator after shutdown.

Subsequent examination of the separator adjacent to the charged portions of the anode showed very significant porosity loss when compared to nominal separator by scanning electron microscope (Fig.6). The shutdown feature of the separator activates at about 130°C and restricted enough ion flow to shut down the short circuit and prevent the cell from going into thermal runaway. This result was confirmed on numerous repeat runs.

When testing the anode active material-to-cathode collector short, the shutdown separator did not prevent the cell from going into thermal runaway. The catastrophic result was the same with both types of separators. This result was confirmed with multiple repeated runs.

Furthermore, our testing of shorts that involved the cathode active material indicates that these types of shorts lead to benign soft shorts and are typically not hazardous. This is due to the lower electrical conductivity of the cathode.

Discussion

Why are anode-to-aluminum shorts not impeded from driving the cell into thermal runaway by the shutdown separator? This is consistent with the fact that the shutdown separator has been widely used in the industry for over a decade and cell lot recalls are still happening. Case in point is the Sony recall of 2006 which was attributed to this type of short[6]. The BAJ then adopted this short as a method for testing worst case cell internal shorts. Many manufacturers have since then implemented the best practice of insulating as much of their exposed aluminum collectors as practical. Santhanagopalan et. al.[7], were the first to compare the four different types of cell internal shorts with inserting shorting particles and their results agree with ours. Similarly, Barnett et. al.[8] used this type of short to demonstrate the latency potential of cell internal shorts.

Conclusions

The on-demand internal short circuit device has been demonstrated to be very useful in determining which types of short circuits are most hazardous and the effectiveness and limitations of cell safety features (like shutdown separator). Note that the results herein should not be taken as a guarantee that shutdown separator will prevent thermal runaway in all cases of collector to collector shorts.

Furthermore, when a manufacturer determines that in his designs active-active shorts are less hazardous than cathode collector shorts, this suggests that metallic defects embedded in the active electrode material to be more important to mitigate than defects that rests on the surface of the electrodes. This implies that a manufacturer should focus more on having defect-free mixing, coating, and calendaring processes to prevent building cells with embedded metallic defects that could lead to latent catastrophic cell internal shorts. After the calendaring process, the electrode active material has solidified and any metallic defect that gets into the cell assembly processes is less likely to get embedded and bridge to the current collector. Conversely, these results also indicate that embedded metallic defects in the cathode that could bridge to the aluminum collector present the most risk.

Acknowledgements

Authors wish to acknowledge NASA Engineering and Safety Center and the Department of Energy for sponsoring this joint NASA/NREL effort. Also, thanks are due for device implantation and testing contributions of Mark Shoesmith at E-one Moli Energy.

References

1. Battery Association of Japan, Nov 11, 2008 presentation on website.
2. Barnett, B., Power Sources Conference, Las Vegas, NV, 2012.
3. Quee, E., Bang, H.J., and Thillaiyan, R., NASA Aerospace Battery Workshop, Huntsville, AL, 2013.
4. Crewed Space Vehicle Battery Safety Requirements, JSC-20793 Rev. C, Feb 2014.
5. Shoesmith, M., Keyser, M., and Darcy, E., Aerospace Battery Workshop, Huntsville, AL, 2013.
6. Nikkei Electronics, Nov. 6, 2006.
7. Santhanagopalan, S., Ramadass, P., and Zhang, J., J. of Power Sources, 194 (2009) 550-557
8. Barnett, B., McCoy, C., Stringfellow, R., and Sriramulu, S., 31st International Battery Seminar & Exhibit, 2014.

Using COTS Parts for High Reliability Batteries

Daniel E. Wesolowski*, Ashley N. Allen and Hans W. Papenguth
*Power Sources Technology Group
Sandia National Laboratories
Albuquerque, NM 87185-0614, USA
dewesol@sandia.gov

Abstract

High reliability (high-rel) batteries have often used piece parts designated as "high reliability" (e.g. hi-rel fuses and diodes) to achieve the target performance. In this paper, an approach for the acceptance of standard COTS parts is presented. Several statistical techniques (response surface modeling, probit, and the Neyer method) were applied to limit the number of samples required for lot level testing. Tests capable of discriminating outlier parts were established for fuses, diodes, and cells.

Keywords: commercial off the shelf; PTC; MnO_2

Introduction

The use of commercial components in high reliability applications requires special attention to quality assurance. One approach is to perform supplier qualification and use only parts from custom orders. This approach may be cost effective if the component order is large but it becomes prohibitively expensive for low volume production. The use of supplier designated "high reliability" products can incur significant premiums. A particular hi-rel fuse was recently priced at over $150/fuse, while a mil-spec equivalent was $8. The commercial fuse was $0.31, meaning the high reliability fuse was nearly 500 times more expensive than the commercial fuse, despite having nominally the same construction (all met the same MIL-PRF-202 tests). High reliability version of many battery cells are not available, which leads to inconsistency in reliability screening among different battery components.

The focus of this work was to create a series of time-efficient 100% and destructive component-level lot sampling tests capable of assessing key safety and functionality aspects. Screening techniques were developed for diodes, fuses and cells. In this paper, the methodology is demonstrated on a lithium primary battery fabricated at Sandia National Laboratories (SNL).

Battery Safety Architecture

The battery contains a fuse and a set of four diodes (two series/two parallel) on each of several parallel strings. The diode and fuse both have plastic packages. Each cell has an integral positive-temperature-coefficient resettable fuse (PTC) installed by the manufacturer. The diode configuration is designed to prevent charging if any one diode fails short and to ensure reliability if any one diode fails open. Fuses are included on each string to ensure that an internal failure (e.g. PTC activation) will not cause overcurrent on another string. The battery case contains a frustum reverse buckling burst disk to prevent catastrophic over-pressurization in the event of a thermal runaway. The burst disk evaluation is not discussed here.

Methodology

Primary cells and fuses are consumed if tested for functionality, and activation of a PTC results in an unacceptable increase in impedance in some applications. 100% screening techniques for these parts therefore cannot fully test the functionality. Diodes can be 100% checked for breakdown voltage and leakage current (the critical parameters in this application), but passing excessive current through diodes may alter their behavior.

SNL has a standard practice for screening COTS diodes, similar to that in MIL-PRF-19500. Destructive physical analysis (DPA) is used to check for cracks, voids, and other manufacturing defects in a small sample of parts. DPA may include radiography, de-encapsulation, cross-sectioning, and wire pull. Additional samples are subjected to marking-permanency and solderability testing. A total of 154 samples are then subjected to accelerated testing. All units are tested for leakage current and forward bias response, then half the samples are exposed to temperature cycling (MIL-STD-883 Method 1010) and half exposed to temperature and humidity stress testing (JESD-22-A110).

SNL typically uses supplier-designated high-rel fuses without further screening for batteries. A similar screening process was adopted in this work for fuses as is used in diodes. Evaluation was performed according to MIL-PRF-23419 and included temperature cycling, vibration, shock, and moisture resistance testing.

Fuses have a 100% resistance measurement as required by MIL-PRF-23419. Fuse resistance should correlate to blow time at a critical current. However, this test is generally inadequate because very small perturbations in wire manufacturing can have negligible differences in resistance but significant effects on blow time [1]. Some

MIL-PRF specifications for fuses suggest that they may be screened by a long-term test, with current passing through the fuse at 100% or even higher. This test is time consuming to conduct. More importantly, however, an evaluation using X-ray imaging showed that the test may damage the fuse and should be avoided (Figure 1). Fuses exposed to a current level that caused some (two of four) fuses to open showed small beads on the fuse wire, similar to that of metal filaments annealed at temperatures near their melting point [2]. The large cross-sectional areas compensate for the high resistance areas making it difficult to use resistance to identify fuses damaged in this way. This example also illustrates the potential variability in fusing performance in soft shorts.

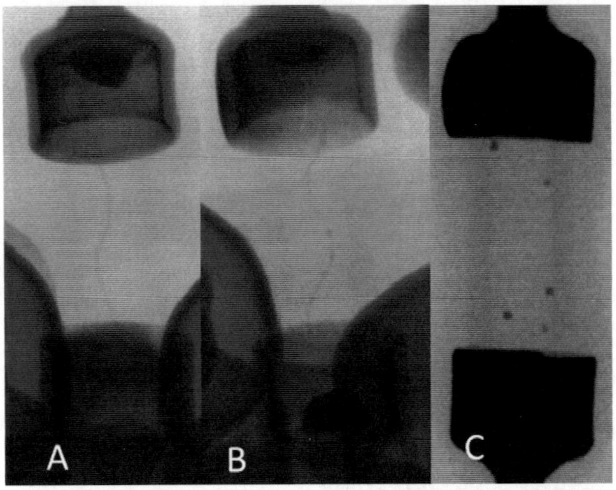

Figure 1. X-ray images of fuses. A) undamaged; B) damaged by high current exposure; and C) blown.

"All-fuse" and "no-fuse" current levels must be known to ensure safety, but for reliability predictions, confidence intervals must be known. The nominal time to fuse is provided by manufacturers, but the distribution of fuse times is not. Two techniques were used to determine the all-fuse and no-fuse current levels. A Neyer d-Optimal series [3] was used to quickly assess these values. This series requires assumption of a distribution. Previous fuse testing at SNL has shown that a log normal distribution is a good fit for the blow time [4]:

$$\log_{10} t = \beta_0 + \frac{\beta_1}{c - \beta_2 + \beta_3 I} + \epsilon \qquad \text{(Eqn. 1)}$$

In eqn. 1 t is time, I is current, ε is the error, and the other terms are fit constants. Testing was subsequently performed at the nominal blow current and a pertinent delta above and below this value to determine the variability in time to blow. Additionally, a probit-type experiment was used to validate the use of the Neyer series for evaluation of the tails of the current-to-blow probability distribution. The Neyer series is designed to consume a fraction of the units required to build a full time-to-blow distribution using probit-type testing.

Quality and reliability may be assessed per MIL-STD-810 at the battery level, but the evaluation of cells is generally done by the cell manufacturer. SNL has taken an approach similar to that for the fuses to screen cells. Cells were assessed for mass, open circuit voltage (OCV), and closed circuit voltage (CCV). Mass provides a qualitative surrogate for capacity. OCV indicates if the active materials are chemically correct and CCV provides insight on cell impedance and PTC condition. Destructive, lot-level cell tests were performed to assess the cell capacity. These were conducted at loads on the manufacturer's data sheet and loads scaled to the battery. Results were compared to a capacity vs. temperature and current model developed from broader testing. Reliability of the cell lot to meet capacity requirements was assessed by comparing cell and lot margin with model predictions.

Destructive, lot-level testing was determined to be the only technique for rigorously assessing PTC performance. A Neyer d-Optimal series was used to minimize the number of units required to assess the PTC activation temperature.

Experimental Procedures

100% fuse screening was performed using a micro-ohmmeter. 2A fast-blow fuses, removed from a single piece of cut tape, were assumed to be from a single lot. Fuses were connected to individual channels in a multi-channel battery tester, preconditioned to test temperatures of 25, 70, or 90°C, and then subjected to a load. Current levels were first selected using the Neyer series. Approximately 20 fuses were used to determine the mid-point current for time to fire at 10s. Probit-type testing was performed using 8 fuses, each at 0.1A increments from 2.4 to 3.4A. Probit testing was performed at 25, 70, and 90°C, and repeated at 25°C with fuses hand-selected based on resistance.

Lithium/MnO_2 primary cells (CR123A size) were selected for this work. All cells were screened on OCV, mass, and the following CCV test. Cells were preconditioned to 25°C then tested according to a screening profile: 10s OCV, 1s 0.5A pulse, 10s OCV rest, and 1s 1A pulse. The first pulse was intended to remove possible passivation within the cell and the second pulse probes the cell impedance. Destructive, lot-level testing was done by discharging selected cells at 20 mA with a voltage cutoff of 1.8V for capacity measurement. Cell PTC destructive testing was performed after simulating cell conditions in the battery. Cells were partially discharged to the capacity required at end-of-mission. Cells were then equilibrated (while at zero load) to the end-of-mission temperature determined by a Neyer series (normal distribution) of 70-110°C and loaded to simulate the end-of-mission discharge rate. PTC activation was indicated by an abrupt drop in cell voltage. Discharge continued to extract a time-to-blow curve from the same data set.

Results: Fuse Screening

A normal probability plot of fuse resistance revealed 2 sub-populations with mean resistances of 44.8 mΩ (σ=2.4 mΩ) and 37.0 mΩ (σ=2.9 mΩ). Probit testing was performed to establish a mean and standard deviation for the lot (the entire cut tape) by selecting fuses at random, and by hand-selecting low resistance fuses. The mean current to blow was nearly identical (2.92 A vs. 2.89 A for selected fuses), but the variability was much lower for the hand-selected fuses (σ=0.14 A vs. 0.08 A for selected fuses). Identifying the subpopulation significantly reduced variability, demonstrating that resistance screening is effective in improving margin.

Neyer testing was used to initially establish the probability of fuse blow within a fixed time period of 10s. The probability of fusing was assumed to be proportional to the current. 27 units were tested. This limited number of tests was able to reveal a 0.001 probability of opening of 2.26±0.13A and a 0.999 reliability of 3.49±0.13A (50% confidence), as shown in Figure 2. The results were verified with a probit approach with 96 tests (2.36±0.06 A at p=0.001 and 3.47±0.06 A at p=0.999). The Neyer series may converge to a low standard deviation in fewer units, but the probit approach is more efficiently conducted, because a multichannel tester can be used for tests in parallel. Probit was used for further fuse work.

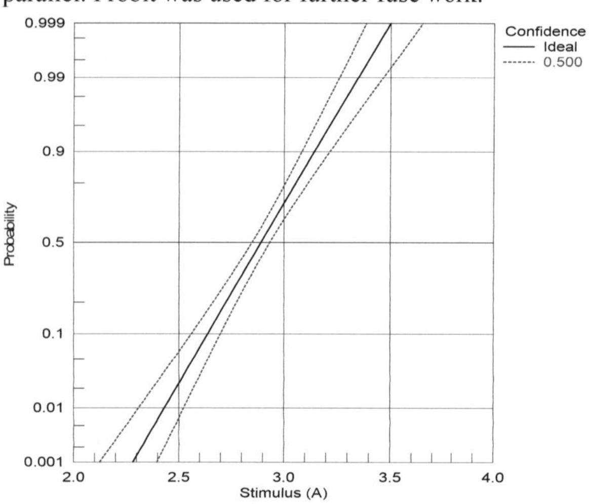

Figure 2. Fuse blow probability as a function of current (Neyer d-Optimal determination)

It is important to know the time-to-blow so that battery reliability and safety can be assessed at pertinent fuse durations. The safety metric is that the fuse should activate in about 10s so that during a short circuit, current is limited before the PTCs activate. This is determined readily from the Neyer or probit testing. The fuse also must not activate at the rated current (about 80% of the fuse value) for the expected life of the battery. This was estimated using parameters derived from the manufacturer's fuse specifications, which indicates the time-to-blow for various current levels. The functional dependence is described by Eqn. 1. Blow time was measured with millisecond resolution up to 2 minutes. The results were poorly correlated to this model, with an R^2 value of 0.15. It is hypothesized that a lengthier test is necessary to account for fuse to fuse variability (e.g. 1 hour or longer). This testing is planned.

Fuse resistance increases with temperature. This increase in resistance reduces the blow current. The temperature dependence of fuse blow current was established with probit testing at 25, 70, and 90°C. Testing verified the expected trend with the mean blow current of 2.92A at 25°C shifting to 2.79A at 70°C and 2.73A at 90°C.

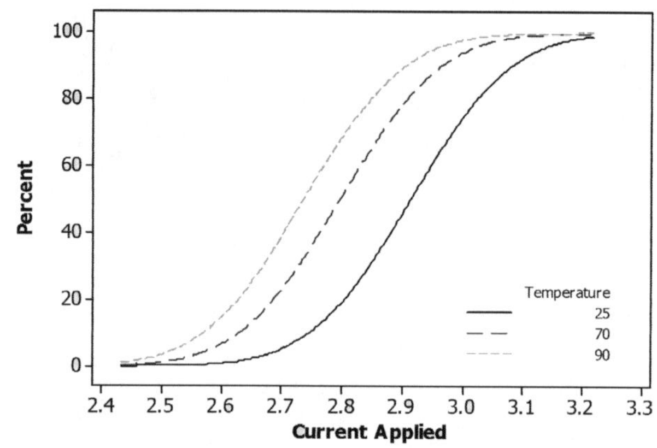

Figure 3. Cum. probability of fusing, by temperature

Results: PTC Screening

Neyer testing indicated that the PTCs activate over a very tight range of conditions. A total of 41 cells were included in the analysis. The mean measured temperature to open under test current conditions was 89.1°C (σ=0.85°C). The 0.0001 probability of opening level was 85.9°C, or 84.7°C at the lower end of a 50% confidence interval. This probability of opening must be multiplied by every cell in the pack to assess battery reliability since none of the PTC can open and still meet requirements. This drives the assessment at very low probability of failure.

Response surface modeling was used to calculate probability of PTC activation as a way to validate the Neyer testing. The cell impedance is in series with the PTC series, since the PTC is an integral part of the cell. Testing showed that the cell voltage behavior qualitatively changes at 85°C. Below this temperature, the rate of change of voltage is consistent with normal discharge, where cell polarization reaches steady state, then increases slowly. The PTC activates above 85°C, leading to a rapid increase in cell impedance and causing a sharp drop in voltage. Only 3 test cells were suitable for performing an analysis of the transition between these two states, because it occurs quickly. Assuming that the voltage has a local-linear relationship with temperature, the 3 cells near 85°C were used to develop a regression that could be extrapolated to 85°C (Figure 4). The predicted cell voltage at 85°C is 2.52V. The cells have a 0.0001 probability of having a voltage below 2.01V, with 95% confidence. This value is nearly identical to the easier to implement Neyer series results.

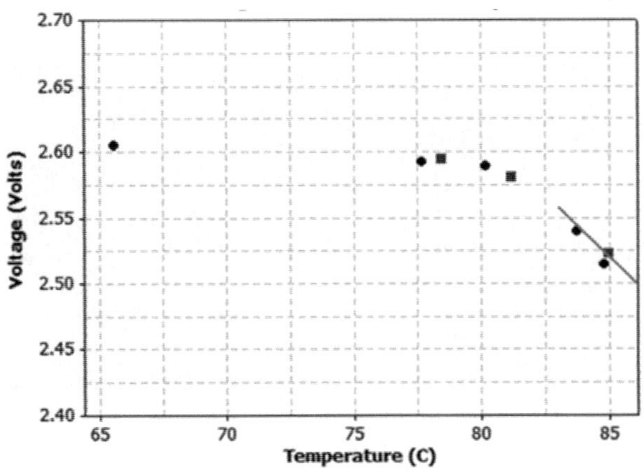

Figure 4. Voltage vs. Temperature at 60s under 1.35A.

Results: Cell Screening

The COTS cells used in this study do not have a readily accessible lot number. A fill date code on the label (month/year) was used as an analog for lot. Sets of 5 cells stored at room temperature for up to 12 years were tested with a 20 mA discharge rate to determine capacity. Lot-to-lot variability in performance is highly significant (Figure 5), but note that the capacity of cells stored from as far back as the year 2000 is within the lot-to-lot variation of recently procured cells. Analysis of data from the same lot indicates that capacity loss in 12 years of real-time aging is statistically zero, but manufacturing variability changes capacity by over 10%.

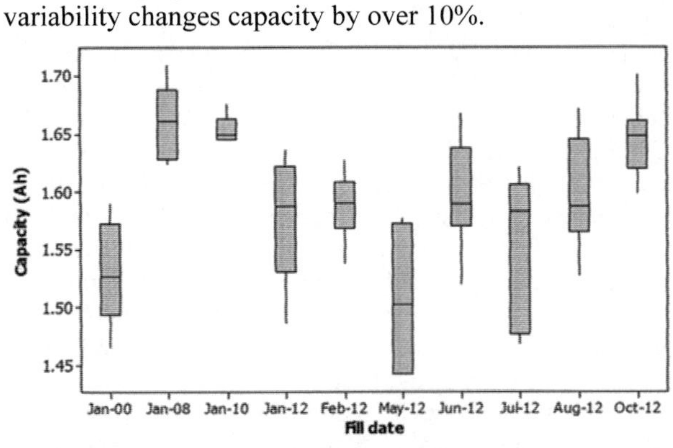

Figure 5. Cell capacity (20 mA discharge rate) by label fill date. All tests performed in 2012.

Cell capacity does not strongly correlate to any of the 100% screening parameters. However, as with fuse testing the goal of the screening process is to improve the selection of consistent cells, rather than to identify high performers. The 100% screening is effective at identifying month-to-month variability in the cells. In particular, the CCV and resistance measurements are immediately useful for battery design and strongly affected by manufacturing variability, as shown in Figure 6.

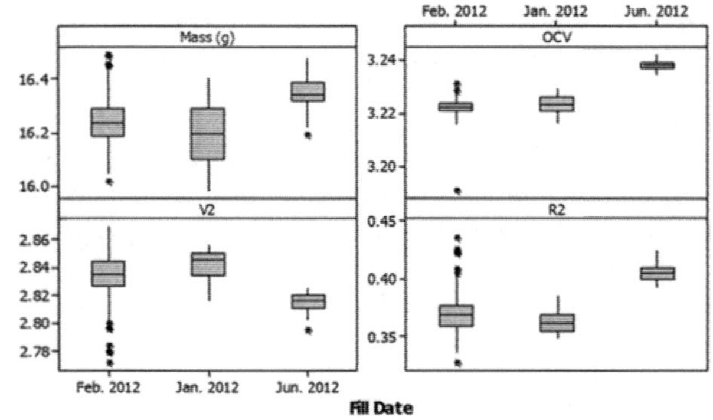

Figure 6. 100% cell screening results, by label fill date.

Conclusions

The 100% screening tests examined here had generally poor correlation to pertinent performance characteristics, but were valuable for reducing variability in that performance. Screening tests allow for identification of subpopulations that improve consistency, as demonstrated by using resistance testing to select fuses. Efficient lot level screening tests (such as Neyer d-Optimal testing for PTCs and probit testing for fuses) provide confidence of sufficient margin with limited testing. Real-time aging indicates that Li/MnO_2 cells have excellent capacity retention.

Acknowledgements

Sandia National Laboratories is a multi-program laboratory operated by Sandia Corporation, a wholly owned subsidiary of Lockheed Martin Company, for the U.S. Department of Energy's National Nuclear Security Administration under contract DE-AC04-94AL85000.

References

1. http://www.nrel.gov/docs/fy13osti/58371.pdf, accessed 3/2014
2. Sandim et al. Scr. Mat. 51, 11, 1099-1104 (2004).
3. B. T. Neyer Technometrics, 36, 61-70 (1994).
4. Personal Communication, Edward V. Thomas, Sandia National Laboratories (2012).
5. Cooper Power Systems. "I2t Testing for Current-Limiting Fuses." (1995).

Screening of COTS Cells for Advanced Li-Ion Batteries

Eivind Listerud, Jay Rhuems and Kris Pritchard
EaglePicher Technologies, LLC
3220 Industrial Road, Joplin, Mo., USA, 64801

Abstract: *This paper includes a discussion on the background and purpose of cell screening applied to commercially available Li-Ion cells used in advanced batteries. Screening data of cells is used to show distributions of selected metrics and how this is applied to eliminate weak cells and better understand variance in the product. An example detailing the insufficiency of only conducting capacity matching for high rate applications will be discussed.*

Keywords: Li-Ion; Li-Ion Testing; Li-Ion Safety; Li-Ion Cell Screening.

Introduction

EaglePicher Technologies (EPT) has a line of advanced Li-Ion batteries for military and commercial applications. Typical use of these batteries would be for engine starts and auxiliary power needs in both aircraft and ground transportation. Examples of these types of batteries can be seen in Figure 1. Engine starts usually require high power loads and are relatively demanding applications, often pushing cells to perform outside their comfort zone when constrained to customer weight and volume demands. A common approach when building these large advanced Li-Ion batteries is to build the cell stack from a sizeable quantity of small capacity, commercially available Li-Ion cells. Several factors are instrumental in determining the right cell product for each application. The selection criteria are determined by the voltage, capacity, energy and power that are demanded by the application, as well as weight, volume, and cost. Safety considerations greatly impact the chemistry selection. $LiCoO_2$, NCA, NMC, and $LiFePO_4$ are evaluated against their energy density and acceptable risk tolerances. Geometric cell features also play an important role. Extensive testing and cell characterization is then performed before a cell product is selected for a specific application. These cells are then constructed in series and/or parallel configurations to deliver the required voltage, capacity, energy and power, as called out in customer supplied specifications. The use of commercial of-the-shelf (COTS) cells is attractive because of availability and cost. However, efforts must be taken to certify that the cells perform as expected. Screening, selection, and matching of cells are critical steps in the battery build process to ensure a robust, high quality, and safe battery. This paper will cover cell screening for advanced batteries and how it relates to cell selection and matching for specific battery applications. The first part will discuss the necessity and the approach to cell screening that is used by EPT. The second part will give examples based on actual screening data.

Figure 1: Advanced Li-Ion batteries for engine starts and auxiliary power.

Necessity of Cell Screening

There are three major reasons for undertaking cell screening as a part of the production of these batteries. The first is to eliminate weak and inconsistent cells. While there typically is a screening process at the manufacturer level that will eliminate some cells, it is not considered adequate in light of the high power load levels to be seen in the starter applications. Also, some manufacturers rely to a large extent on process control and, considering the usage location and size of these batteries, EPT feels that additional screening of cells is prudent. The specific application determines the metric and the threshold used when eliminating cells. Statistical tools such as distribution and scatter plots and a cell ranking method are utilized in this process. This approach enhances both the safety and the performance of the battery. The second reason for undertaking cell screening is to gain a greater understanding of the variance in the cell product and the reliability of the cell supplier. This can help determine the supplier's process capability with regard to EPT's requirement and find new potential suppliers. The third reason is to enable matching of cells for balancing of modules and batteries. All of these batteries have a battery management system (BMS) that will control and balance cell and module voltages. However, in a series configuration there could be limitations to the BMS if the cells diverge too much. Additionally, for high voltage batteries, it sometimes is impractical to implement robust BMS control at the cell level. A well balanced set of cells at the module level is therefore critical for these high voltage batteries.

Approach to Cell Screening

There are two components to the actual screening of cells. The first part is a sequence of charge and discharge cycles at various rates. The cells are initially exposed to a few capacity cycles at a nominal C-rate. This serves a couple of purposes. In addition to being a general baseline check on manufacturers' claims and establishing a distribution profile of actual capacity and energy, it also generates data that can be used to look for soft shorts. Relatively large charge capacities compared to the sequential discharge capacities can be indicative of such an issue[1]. Similar considerations must be given to cells that exhibit a relatively long tapper charge segment or are reaching the upper voltage limit at a faster rate than typical. By normalizing the data, the set of nominal C-rate cycles also allows for a direct comparison of capacity variance between different types of cells from various manufacturers. The cells are also exposed to a set of application specific cycles. This usually involves higher current levels and sometimes lower temperatures. The idea is to stress the cells to some extent and more clearly separate the poor from the good performers. It is worth noting that what is deemed poor performance for one application is not necessarily poor performance for another set of requirements. The final set of testing consists of open circuit voltage (OCV) monitoring over a time period. An accelerated drop in OCV over time is usually indicative of a soft short. An example of this can be seen in Figure 2. The OCV was monitored over a 4 month span for a set of cells and two of these cells exhibit behavior that is indicative of soft shorts.

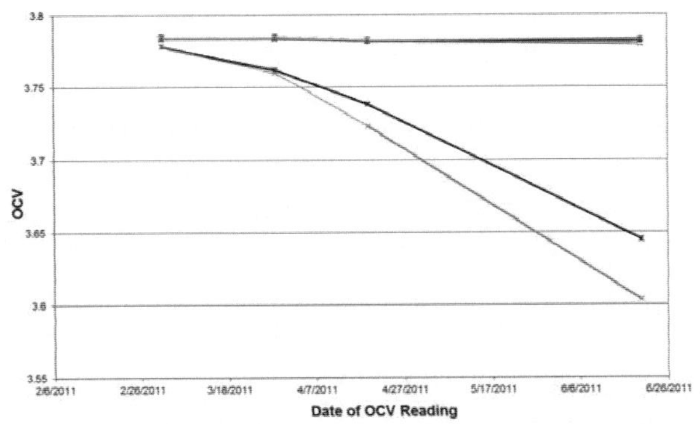

Figure 2: OCV readings of a set of Li-Ion cells being monitored over a 4 month span.

The second component of the screening process is the analysis of the data. Outliers are identified and overall variance in the product is determined by using probability distribution and scatter plots. Cells are also ranked and grouped based on configuration and balancing needs. Finally, the cells are selected for a specific application based on the respective criteria. The following part of the paper will give some examples of screening efforts and cell distributions for various cell types and applications, covering specific issues like cell variance related to manufacturing dates and the potential downside of only performing capacity matching.

Screening to Eliminate Weak Cells

Figure 3 shows a screening overview of a set of more than 3000 Li-Ion type cells that have been subjected to a series of 1C-rate cycles and some high rate pulse loads. Each dot represents a cell and the 1C-rate discharge capacity is represented along the x-axis and the lowest voltage observed during the pulse loads are represented along the y-axis. Typically the cells are categorized into four categories. In Figure 3 this is represented by the four quadrants separated by the green vertical line for a specific capacity criteria and the green horizontal line for a minimum voltage. Each quadrant contains cells that are better suited for different applications, depending on whether the applications have tougher demands on rate capability, capacity, or both. The lower left quadrant has a subcategory, depicted in red, which contains cells that are not to be considered for a set of customer applications. The data in Figure 3 shows that there is no significant correlation between improved capacity and improved rate capability in these specific cells. This underscores the necessity of performing application specific cycles during screening when the requirements demand higher power. When the capacity and the pulse data in Figure 3 are studied separately, it appears that the capacity data follows a normal distribution, as seen in Figure 4. This notion is confirmed by looking at the data in the normal probability plot in Figure 5. The blue dots represent the whole data set and it fits a linear trend reasonably well, having a R^2-value of more than 0.97. Figure 5 also have data separated by the manufacturing dates of the various cells and it is clear that the set of cells designated Date 4 is clearly out of family compared to the rest of the cell population. While this subset has a normal distribution with a higher mean capacity, thus not raising any concerns, it shows how cell performance can be sensitive to manufacturing dates for a given cell type. This requires attention during the screening process. This type of normal capacity distribution for the1C-rate is also observed in other cells made by different manufacturers. By standardizing the capacity values, using the mean and the standard deviation, a comparison of different types of cells from different manufacturers can be generated. This is shown in Figure 6 and is a useful tool when comparing variance in metrics across cell lines and manufacturers' capabilities. While the capacity data in Figure 3 follows a normal distribution, the high rate pulse data distribution is skewed distinctly to one side of the mean value, as seen in Figure 7. Lack of normal distribution in a complex system can often be attributed to just one or a few factors of many dominating the behavior of the system. Since we are exposing these cells to a fairly demanding load in this case, it is reasonable to assume that a single factor, like diffusion, is limiting the cell performance. This is then reflected in an asymmetry of the distributed data.

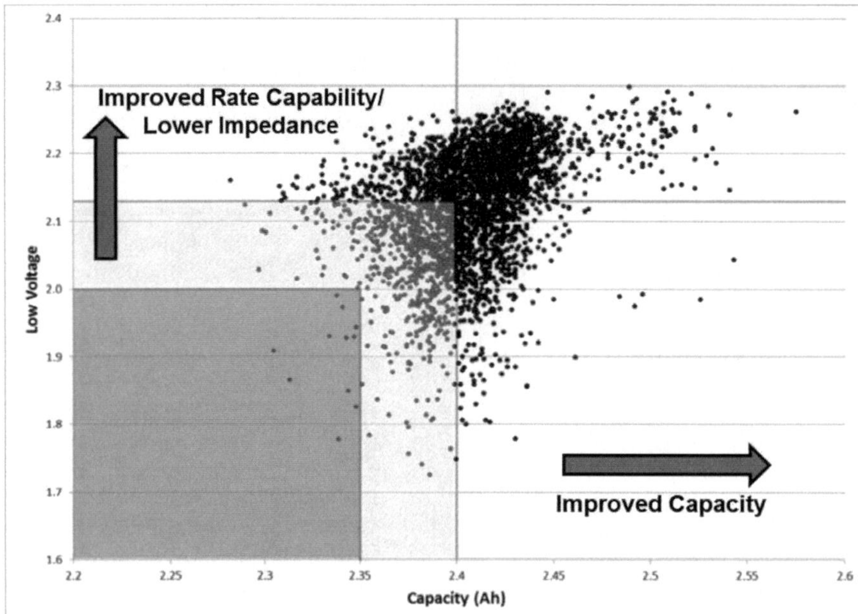

Figure 3: Scatter plot of more than 3000 cells subjected to 1C-rate cycles and subsequent high rate pulse loads. Each dot represents a cell and the 1C-rate capacity is plotted along the x-axis while the low voltage during a specific pulse profile is plotted along the y-axis.

Screening to Match Cells

Different applications require different matching needs. There is some flexibility when using high-end battery management and cell balance architecture. Matching of cells become mainly a performance issue in that a set of unbalanced cells will stress the electronics more, create thermal gradients across the battery and negatively impact the life performance of the cells. Modules of parallel cells will also perform better with matched cells. If only a low-end battery management system is incorporated and there is no individual cell balancing, matching becomes critical for both performance and safety reasons. Divergence of cell voltages during charging could have a detrimental impact on the battery. When screening cells for matching purposes so-called capacity matching has typically been employed in the battery industry. A large set of cells are discharged to a nominal rate and the cells are grouped and ranked according to the capacity they deliver at a certain voltage cut-off. An example of this can be seen in the left graph of Figure 8, where more than 200 cells have been discharged at a 1C-rate and appears to have a tight range of capacities. While this may be adequate if the application requires loads that are well within the performance envelope of the cells, it would be insufficient for applications that require more demanding loads. The cells need to be subjected to loads that are comparable to what the application requires. This will significantly expand the range in performance seen among the cells and more clearly allow for a proper ranking. In addition, it is critical to not only consider capacity as the ranking metric. The pitfall of not doing this can be seen in the right graph of Figure 8. The same cells that are shown with their 1C-rate discharge profiles on the left are now shown with their 22C-rate discharge profiles on the right. Not only is there a greater range in capacity values, there is also a greater discrepancy in average voltage during discharge. What is disconcerting is that two of the cells showing degraded voltage curves still have capacities that match the rest of group. These cells need to be identified and capacity matching is not adequate for that purpose.

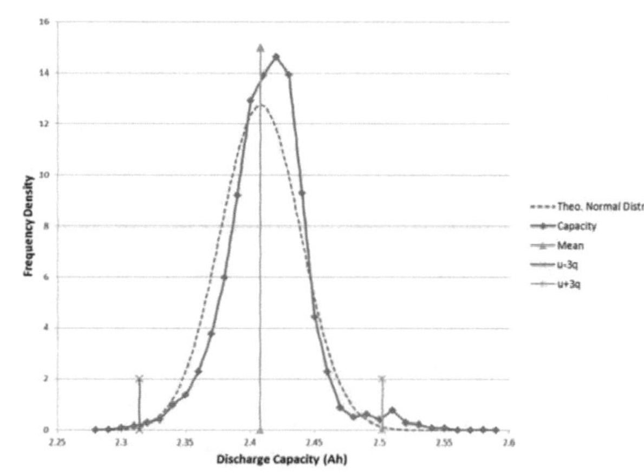

Figure 4: Probability distribution of discharge capacity for more than 3000 cells.

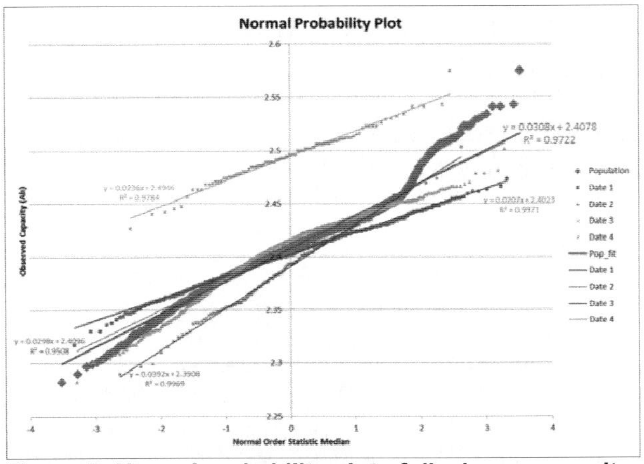

Figure 5: Normal probability plot of discharge capacity data shown in Figure 4.

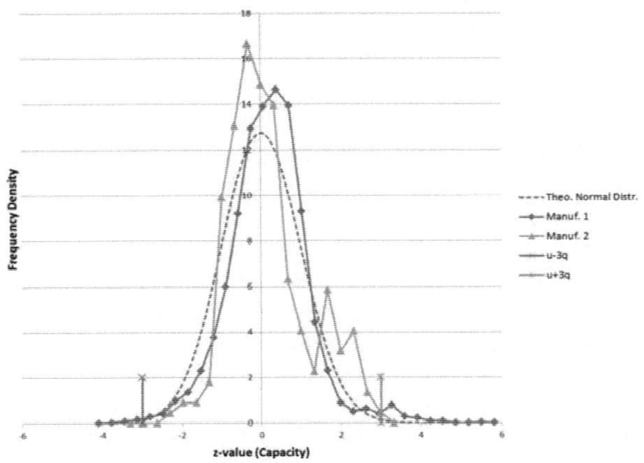

Figure 6: Standardized probability distribution of discharge capacity for cells from two different manufacturers.

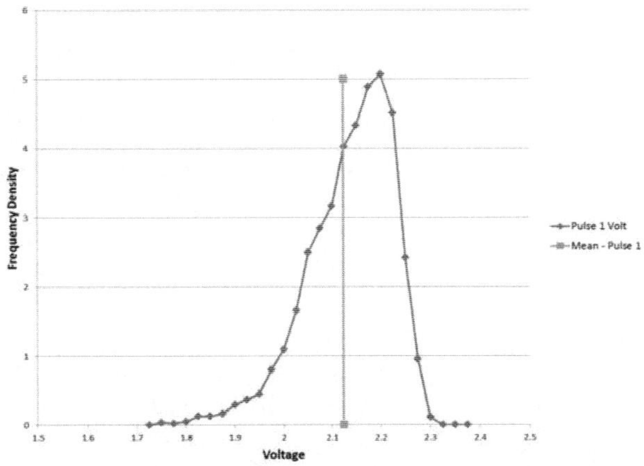

Figure 7: Probability distribution of low voltage during high rate pulse test for more than 3000 cells.

Conclusion

To ensure the performance and safety of the line of advanced Li-Ion batteries EaglePicher Technologies screen all cells used in these batteries. The process eliminates weak cells, gives a greater understanding of the variance in the product, and ensures proper cell matching for greater safety and reliability.

Acknowledgement

Kevin Ames and his group made significant contributions to this effort. This material is released to the public domain in accordance with ITAR 22 CFR 120.11.

Reference

1. Mikolajczak, C., Harmon, J., White, K., Horn, Q., Wu, M., and Shah, K., "Detecting Lithium-Ion Cell Internal Faults in real Time", *Power Electronics*, March 10th 2010.

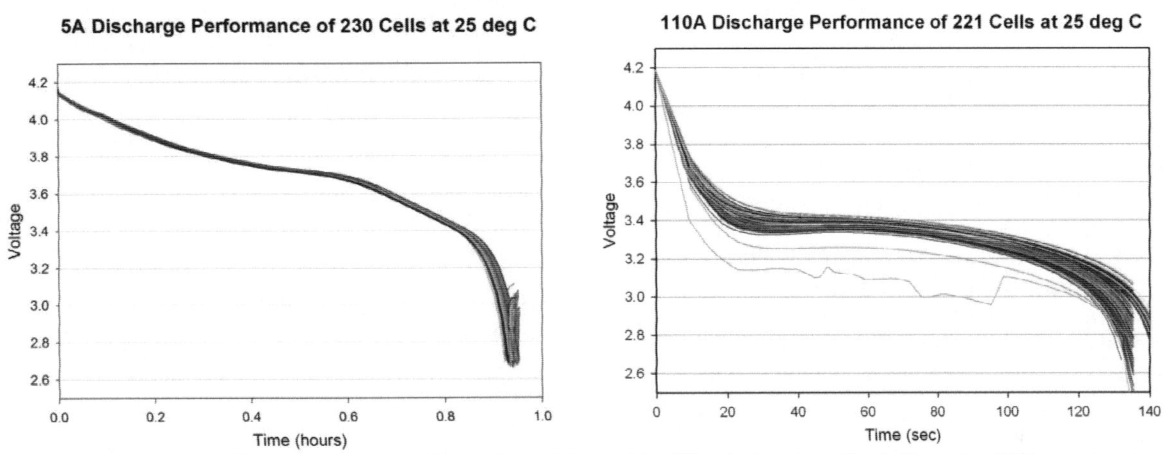

Figure 8: Discharge profiles of more than 200 cells subjected to 1C-rate load on the left and a 22C-rate load on the right.

Low Temperature Improvements for Lithium MnO2 Systems for Military Applications

Carlos R Negrete and Allan J. Davenport
Saft America, Inc, 313 Crescent Street, Valdese, NC 28690
carlos.negrete@saftbatteries.com or www.saftbatteries.com

Abstract: *Saft is an industry leader in the development and manufacturing of both primary and rechargeable portable power solutions with a record of proven reliability across a wide range of applications. Saft has proudly served the United States warfighter providing the most comprehensive range of battery systems to deliver power capability for every mission. Saft continues to offer the ability to deliver solutions in all field proven primary chemistries including Lithium Sulfur Dioxide, Lithium MnO2, and Lithium Thionyl Chloride, and now Lithium MnO2/CFx.*

Saft's LiMnO2 program has delivered over the last 10 years proven battery designs to meet the requirements of the MIL-PRF 49471B and now the MIL-PRF 32271 specifications. Over this time, Saft's commitment to continuous improvement has resulted in increased performance of the chemistry to deliver products with higher energy densities, safety, and reliability. As such, Saft has carried out extensive testing and qualified a new cell design to improve the low temperature performance of MnO2 systems by modifying cathode base materials, processing conditions, and electrolyte formulation optimization. The results have been a significant increase in low temperature discharge capacity and reduction in variability without loss of performance at higher temperatures or long term stability. The work included in this paper summarizes recent improvements to low temperature performance of the chemistry.

Keywords: lithium; manganese dioxide low temperature, primary chemistry

Introduction and Background

LiMnO2 battery systems are widely used for military primary portable power applications. The chemistry is well suited for high capacity and high current discharge applications across a wide temperature range. Today the chemistry is incorporated into various battery applications including the BA5390, BA5380, BA5360, BA5372, BA5388, BA5368, and BA5367 delivering a typical 12 Ampere-hours of capacity for a battery utilizing the standard D cell format. In recent years, the chemistry application has been expanded to create a hybrid cathode chemistry combining MnO2 with carbon monofluoride to further increase the energy density. Along with LiSO2 systems, LiMnO2 has become a standard for military and industrial applications requiring high discharge rate and high energy densities.

LiMnO2 systems provide advantages and disadvantages when compared to LiSO2. As an overall comparison, LiMnO2 provides higher energy densities and lower startup voltage delay at the expense of higher cost per Watt hour delivered and lower extreme cold temperature operating voltage and capacity. In systems where a battery can benefit from self-heating generated during discharge, this phenomenon is improved. However, it is important to note that the self-heating benefit is only observed if the battery is discharged continuously and at sufficiently high rate to raise the temperature of the battery-a distinction to highlight when comparing data generated in the lab when tested per methods spelled out in specifications and actual use in the field where continuous high current discharge is not guaranteed or expected. To exemplify this fact, a comparison of the capacity delivered between a BA5X90 battery where 10 cells insulated in a plastic case deliver a different result versus a single cell (more likely to represent a battery in the field with intermittent use without self heating advantage.

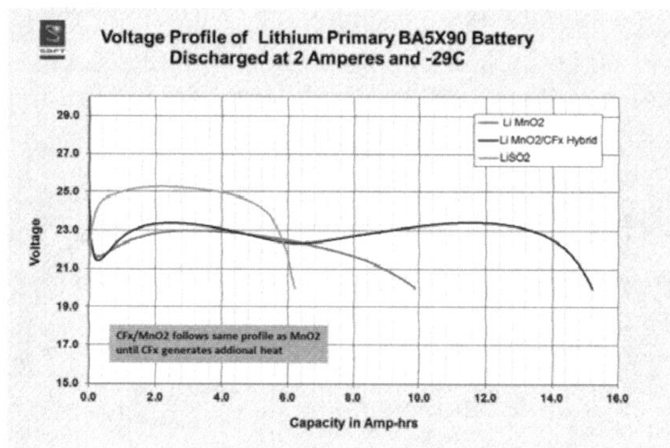

Figure 1

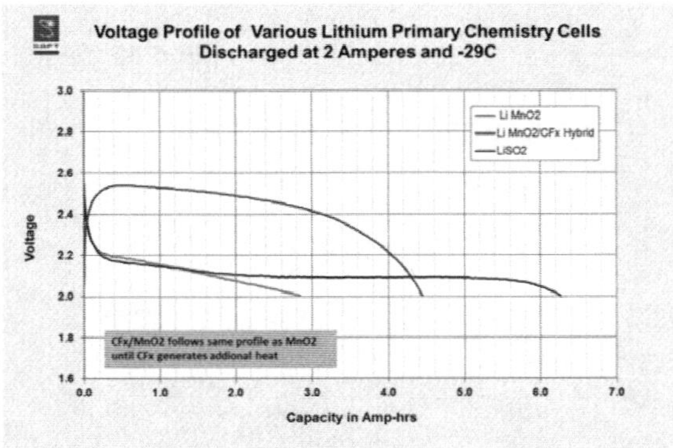

Figure 2

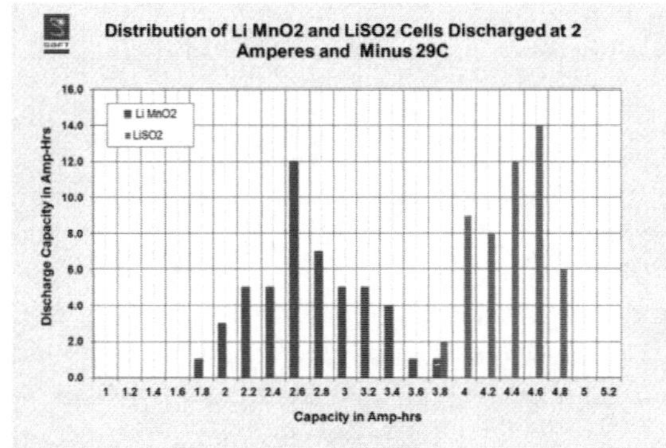

Figure 3

Capacity Delivered at 2 Amperes -29C Discharge

Chemistry	BA5X90	D Cell	Reduction
LiSO2	6.2	4.4	29%
LiMnO2	9.8	2.8	71%
LiMnO2/CFx	15.2	6.3	58%

Table 1

As exemplified in the performance reduction between a battery benefiting from self-heating during a continuous high rate discharge and a single cell with a reduction in this advantage, the performance of a battery used in the field can vary drastically depending on the discharge rate and frequency of use. If the actual use in the field is intermittent rather than continuous and lower discharge rate rather higher, then the actual performance can be expected to be closer to the performance observed for single cells. In this situation, LiSO2 systems deliver the best performance and LiMnO2 suffer the worst loss in capacity. Additionally, LiSO2 systems are further preferred due to the higher operating voltage if the application depends on constant power rather than current.

To further evaluate the chemistries performance in low temperature, the distribution of delivered capacity must be taken into account as this can vary widely -29C. At extreme low temperatures, all chemistries experience significantly wider distribution variability in capacity delivered. For both LiMnO2 and LiSO2, typical capacity at ambient and higher temperatures vary within +/- 5% but at -29C that variation increases significantly with LiMnO2 having the widest distribution near +/- 40%.

Experimental

Extensive work was carried out in the Saft Valdese NC facility with the aim of improving low temperature performance without creating a negative impact in the chemistry performance at higher temperatures or long term storage stability. Typical means to improve low temperature performance often come with a detrimental effect to energy density such as increasing conductive cathode diluents, higher low temperature conductivity electrolyte solvents, or higher electrode surface area.

Saft focused on optimizing the use of various raw material components and processing conditions to increase the performance at low temperature without impacting the electrodes energy density and long terms stability. The resulting cell chemistry maintains the same proven, robust, hermetic cell design and has undergone a successful qualification to the new MIL-PRF 32271 BA5380 and BA5360 battery designs.

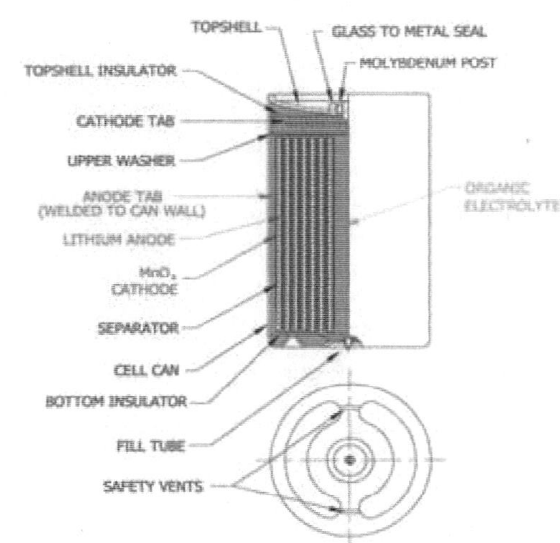

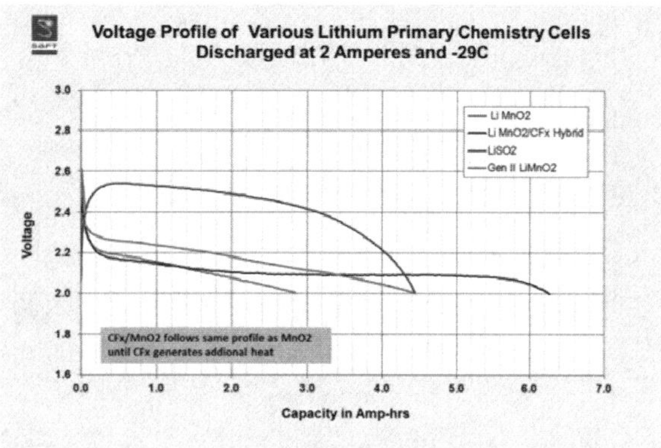

Figure 4

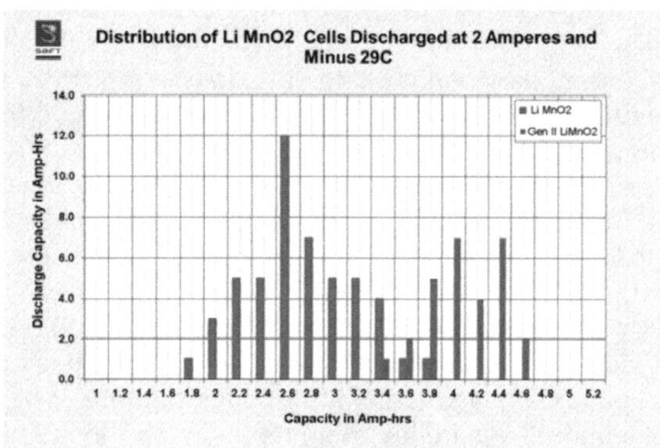

Figure 5

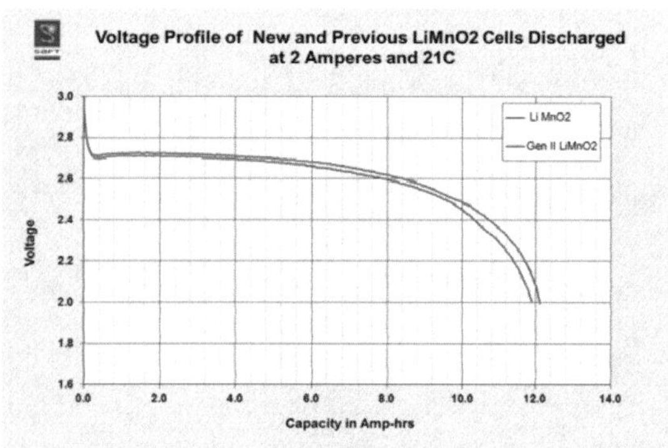

Figure 6

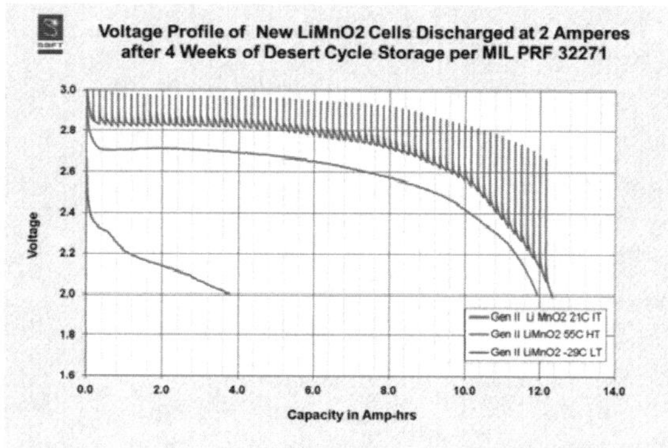

Figure 7

Conclusion

SAFT America has developed a primary Lithium MnO2 battery system technology capable of delivering increased low temperature performance while delivering the highest energy densities at ambient, high temperatures, and after long term storage. The design incorporates all the safety, function, and reliability required to meet the demands of a standard battery specification MIL-PRF 32271. The new cell design delivers capacities similar to LiSO2 systems although at significantly lower operating voltages (thus lower operating time at constant power applications). Thus, for high energy density applications requiring use at low temperatures, LiSO2 is still preferable due to higher operating voltage and significantly lower cost. However, for applications with higher capacity requirements with potential use at low temperatures, the new Lithium MnO2 system provide equally longer performance at ambient and higher temperatures as previously and now with improved discharge performance at lower temperatures.

Acknowledgement

The authors wish to thank the following individuals for their continuous valuable technical assistance including analysis done on materials and cathode samples

Dr. Patrick Bernard, Dr. Robert Staniewicz, NS Raman, Blia Vang, John Burdette, Don Mishue

References

1. 42-44 Proceedings of Power Sources Conference
2. David Linden, "Hand book of Batteries" Second Edition

1,000 Wh/L High Rate Li-CFx D Size Cell Achieved

William C. Bushong, Terrence W. Gurrie, Gregory J. Davidson, Sarah L. Westcott, Tony M. Rubsam, Matthew D. Hennek
Spectrum Brands, Inc. 8123 Forsythia Street, Middleton, WI 53562
(608) 275-3340 Tel.; (608) 288-7459 fax; Bushong@Rayovac.com

Abstract: *Demonstrated to provide both high gravimetric (>700 Wh/Kg) and high volumetric (>1,000 Wh/L) energy density, the recently developed aluminum cased D-size Li-CFx cell is capable of safe, high rate discharge. The cell provides over 19 Ah capacity at room temperature at 50 mA rates and is capable of up to 3 A continuous discharge and 20A pulses.*

Keywords: primary battery; lithium carbon mono fluoride; CFx; CF(n); gravimetric energy density; volumetric energy density; temperature stability; high rate capability

Introduction

Demonstrated to provide both high gravimetric (>700 Wh/Kg) and high volumetric (>1,000 Wh/L) energy density, the recently developed aluminum cased D-size Li-CFx cell is capable of safe, high rate discharge. Its hermetic enclosure allows long-term storage and discharge at elevated temperatures. Over three years of development went into advancing the typical low rate capabilities of Li-CFx chemistry into this safe, high rate capable cell that is useful in multiple applications.

This project succeeded in its purpose to retain the traditional advantages of Li-CFx based cells while safely improving the cell's rate capability across a wide range of operating temperatures. With a mass of 69 grams this cell provides over 19 Ah of capacity at room temperature and 17Ah of capacity at 0 °C or 90 °C, increasing the state of the art for a Li-CFx cell design that meets ANSI D cell specifications. It passes all required UN transportation safety tests and has a built-in Positive Temperature Coefficient device (PTC) for additional safety protection. This cell is ideal for single-cell applications, but is also easily configurable for use in multi-cell batteries for applications such as underground sensors, unmanned underwater vehicles, and emergency transponders.

During the development of this cell a low profile feedthrough was designed and optimized that enabled an increase in useable internal volume of the cell, leading to increased cell capacity. This aluminum D size cell is capable of 3 A continuous discharge with up to 20 A pulse capabilities.

Manufactured in our new 20,000 sq.ft. battery assembly facility using robotically controlled laser welding equipment, the cells are hermetically sealed. Cells are currently helium leak tested to a pass point of 10^{-8} atm-cc/sec then 100% 3D X-ray inspected as part of a stringent quality control process.

This development accomplished a higher rate capable D cell than previously reported for CFx cell chemistry. Compared to state of the art, this advance in technology provides the highest known energy density in a rate capable ANSI primary D cell as measured both gravimetrically and volumetrically.

Advantages of the Li/CFx System

The Li/CFx system has several significant advantages over other 3 V lithium systems:

- Highest specific capacity among 3 volt materials
- Flat voltage discharge profile
- Lowest self-discharge & longest shelf life of 3 V systems
- Operation temperature range from –40 °C to 125 °C

The theoretical specific capacity for CFx is 2.8 times higher than that of MnO_2 and over two times higher than that of SO_2. Theoretical capacity is never attained with any chemistry due to the practical constraints of assembling an actual cell which also includes anode, separator, electrolyte and enclosure, but in practice the Li/CFx cells have much higher capacity than the other 3 volt lithium chemistries.

Rayovac Li/CFx D cells demonstrate greater energy density than competing primary technologies. Rayovac Li/CFx D cells have historically had a gravimetric energy density of > 630 Wh/kg, but by changing the can material from steel to aluminum the gravimetric energy density has been increased to >750 Wh/kg. This is >2x the energy density of a similar sized commercially available Li/MnO_2 cells.

Description of the Li/CFx Cell Chemistry

The cathode is a fluorinated carbon with a general formula of (CFx)n where x*n can be anywhere from 0.25 to 1.35 or more commonly referred to as CFx. The anode is lithium metal.

The simplified discharge reaction is represented as:

Anode Reaction: $Li \rightarrow Li^+ + e^-$

Cathode Reaction: $CF + e^- \rightarrow C + F^-$

Overall Reaction: $Li + CF \rightarrow LiF + C$

During the electrochemical reaction, fluorinated carbon reduces to carbon, which is more conductive than CFx. The CFx is thermally stable to >400 °C and is typically considered chemically inert toward the electrolyte solution. The discharge products, including LiF and carbon, are considered safer than those of other discharged lithium cell chemistries. Li/CFx cells have been commercially manufactured and sold since the 1970's and have a long safety record.

This system chemistry can be readily manufactured into numerous sizes and configurations including flat, coin, button, cylindrical and rectangular shapes.

Rayovac Manufacturing

Rayovac is one of only a few companies manufacturing Li/CFx cells. Rayovac has manufactured coin cells for electronic applications since the early 1980's. Rayovac has been developing Li/CFx cylindrical cell since 1995.

Rayovac recently opened a 20,000 sq.ft. battery assembly facility for Li/CFx cells. Automated coaters, slitters, and calenders produce cathode with a tight tolerance on deposition density and thickness. Improved cathode consistency leads to improved quality of the jellyrolls produced by our automated winder. Advances in cathode processing and jellyroll winding techniques have increased the active material in the cell.

Coin cells use relatively thick separator materials to protect against shorting. This increases the separation between anode and cathode, limiting the peak rate at which the cell can be discharged. Advances in separator materials allow much thinner separator material to provide protection against mechanical and dendrite shorting. The thinner separator provides room for additional active material in the cell. This improves cell capacity and increases electrode interfacial area. Increased interfacial area and a relatively short path length between the anode and the cathode allow the cells to support higher discharge rates not historically associated with the Li/CFx chemistry.

In the past, the steel cans of cylindrical cells have been closed with a crimped seal. The crimped seal required a strong steel can to make a tight seal and required some height at the top of the cell to accommodate the crimp. Leakage around the gasket material used in the crimp limited the high temperature and long term storage capability. Laser welding allows the construction of hermetically sealed cells and allows the use of aluminum cans to reduce weight or magnetic signature. During the development of the D cell a low profile feedthrough was designed and optimized to improve reliability and increase the useable internal volume of the cell, leading to increased cell capacity. This feedthrough design eliminates the need for expensive and fragile glass to metal seals. The headers are welded to the cans using robotically controlled laser welding equipment. Helium leak testing confirms that the cells are hermetically sealed to a pass point of 10^{-8} atm-cc/sec. 3-dimensional X-ray images of the cells are part of a stringent quality control process.

High Capacity and Rate Capability

Testing at different rates was carried out to characterize the room temperature performance of the D cell. Cells were discharged at rates from 0.185 A to 3 A (Figure 1).

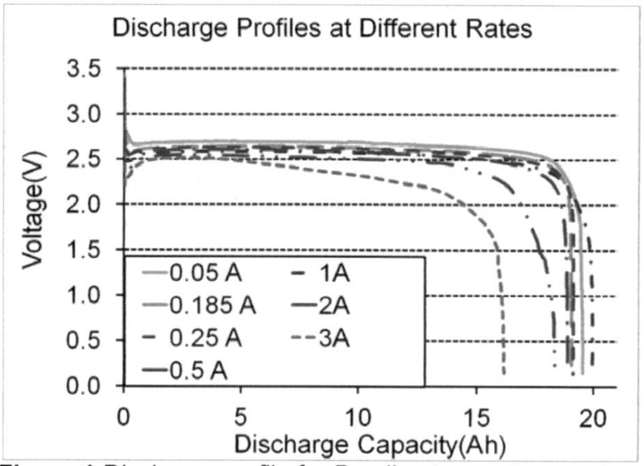

Figure 1 Discharge profile for D cells at room temperature discharged at 0.050 A, 0.185 A, 0.25 A, 0.5 A, 1 A, 2 A, and 3 A rates.

Capacity was measured at a cut off voltage of 2 V. The cells performed similarly, with similar capacity of 18.5 to 19.3 Ah at rates as high as 1 A (Table 1). The PTC built in for safety protection may restrict operation at higher rates. The cells still have capacity of 14.3 Ah at a 3A rate and are capable of up to 20 A pulses.

Table 1 Capacity of D cells at room temperature

Discharge Rate (A)	Capacity @ 2V (Ah)	Standard Deviation (Ah)	Specific Capacity (Ah/g CFx)
0.050	19.3	0.3	0.78
0.185	19.0	0.3	0.76
0.250	19.0	0.04	0.75
0.500	18.8	0.3	0.76
1.0	19.3	0.01	0.77
2.0	16.7	0.5	0.67
3.0	14.3	0.4	0.57

Temperature Operation

Li/CFx cells are especially suited for applications where safety, high temperature stability and reliability are of primary importance to the user. These cylindrical cells have demonstrated good low temperature performance down to –20 °C and high temperature performance up to 90 °C.

These D cells were optimized for operation near freezing temperatures in Unmanned Underwater Vehicles (UUVs). Figure 2 shows the discharge profile at 0 °C of D cells discharged at alternating rates typical for UUVs. An average capacity of 16.4 Ah was achieved to a 2 V cut off.

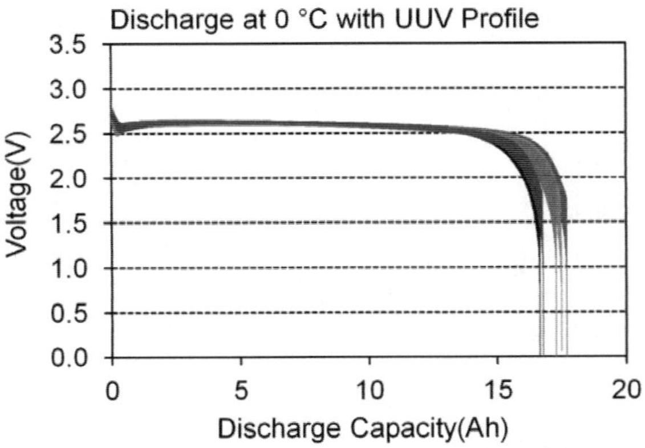

Figure 2 Discharge profile of D cells at 0 °C using a series of lower and higher power pulses mimicking the discharge profile of an Unmanned Underwater Vehicle (UUV).

For a more general comparison, cells were discharged at 50 mA at 0 °C, 22 °C (room temperature), and 90 °C (Figure 3). At 22 °C, the average capacity to a 2V cut off was 19.3 Ah. At 90 °C, the capacity was 90% of that or 17.4 Ah. At 0 °C, the capacity was 84% of that or 16.3 Ah.

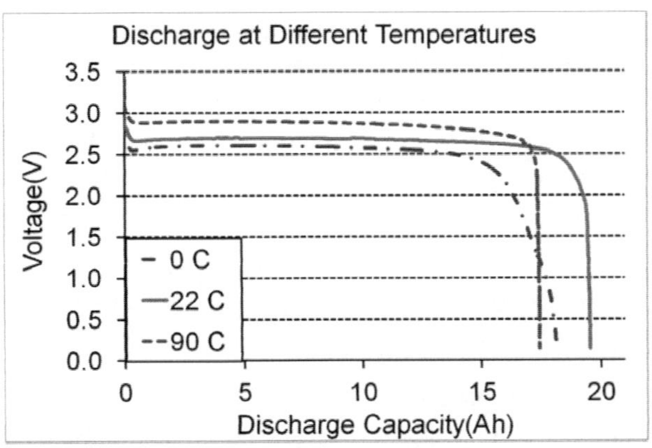

Figure 3 Discharge profile of D cells at 50 mA at 0 °C, room temperature, and 90 °C.

Stability

Stable shelf life depends both on low leakage of electrolyte from the cells and low self discharge. The excellent shelf-life capacity retention of cells with the Li/CFx chemistry is well documented. Typical shelf life for Li/CFx crimped cells is greater than 10 years. Sealing the cells by laser welding rather than crimping allows the construction of hermetically sealed cells greatly reducing electrolyte leakage. The D cells are currently helium leak tested to a pass point of 10^{-8} atm-cc/sec.

Cells are being stored at both room temperature and elevated temperature (60 °C) to test shelf life. After approximately 18 months at room temperature, the cells showed negligible weight loss. Cells stored at 60 °C had a maximum weight loss of less than 40 mg (Figure 4). The oscillation seen in weight is believed to be a seasonal effect due to atmospheric moisture absorption on the external cell surfaces. A fit to the weight loss data predicts a 10 year 60 °C storage weight loss of 110 mg or less than 1% of the total electrolyte mass. Cells were also stored for shorter periods at 90 °C and 110 °C. There was not an increased rate of mass loss at these temperatures.

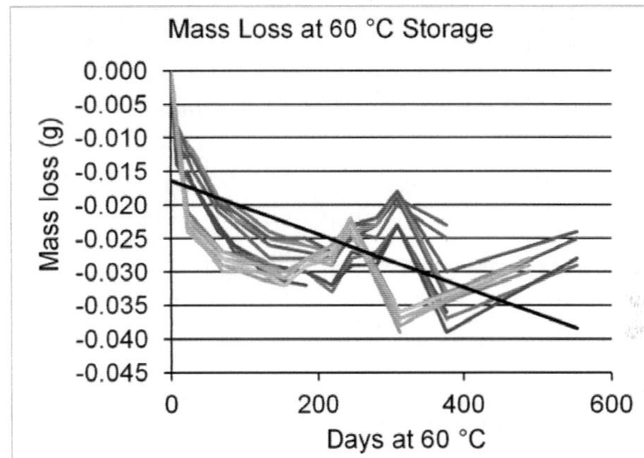

Figure 4 Mass loss over time of cells stored at 60 °C.

Cells have also periodically been removed from storage and discharged at room temperature with a current of 1 A. The initial average capacity of these cells discharged at 1 A to a cutoff voltage of 2 V was 18.5 Ah with a standard deviation of 0.5 Ah or 2.7% of the capacity. For cells stored at room temperature (Figure 5), the variation in capacity with storage time has been less than 1% (Table 2). This is less than the variation in capacity measured between cells. The OCV at room temperature has also been stable.

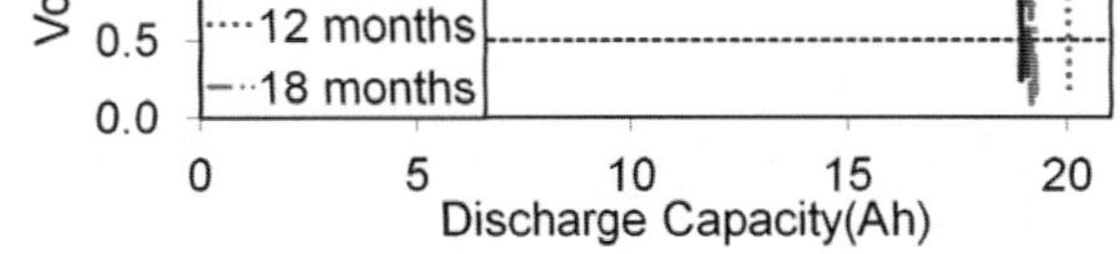

Figure 5 Room temperature (22 °C) discharge profile of D cells at 1 A initially and after 3, 6, 12, and 18 months storage at room temperature (22 °C).

For cells stored at 60 °C, capacity decreased by less than 6% after 18 months (Figure 6). The cells were allowed to return to room temperature for at least 4 hours before being discharged.

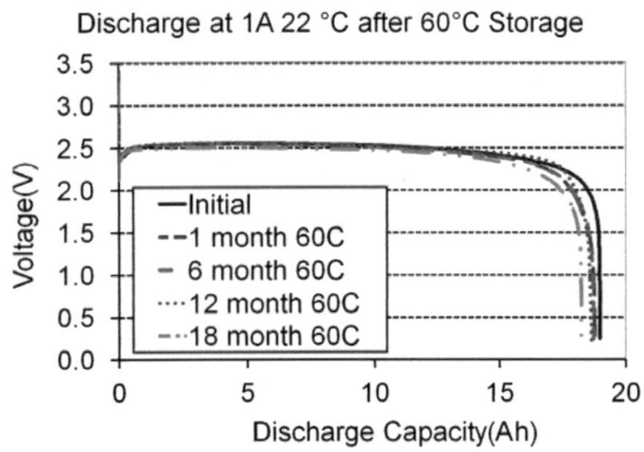

Figure 6 Discharge profile of D cells at 22 °C and 1 A initially and after being stored for 1, 6, 12, and 18 months at 60 °C.

Table 2 Capacity of D cells at 1A discharge rate at 22 °C after storage at 22 °C or 60 °C

	Capacity after 22°C Storage (Ah)	% Drop	Capacity after 60°C Storage (Ah)	% Drop
Initial	18.5		18.5	
1 month	18.5	0.2%	18.2	1.6%
6 months	18.6	-0.3%	18.2	1.4%
12 months	18.5	-0.3%	18.0	2.9%
18 months	18.4	0.8%	17.4	5.8%

Cells have also been stored at 70 °C for 4 weeks or 90 °C for 1 week. After returning to room temperature, the cells were then discharged at a 1 A rate. There was 99% capacity retention at 70 °C and 92% at 90 °C (Figure 7).

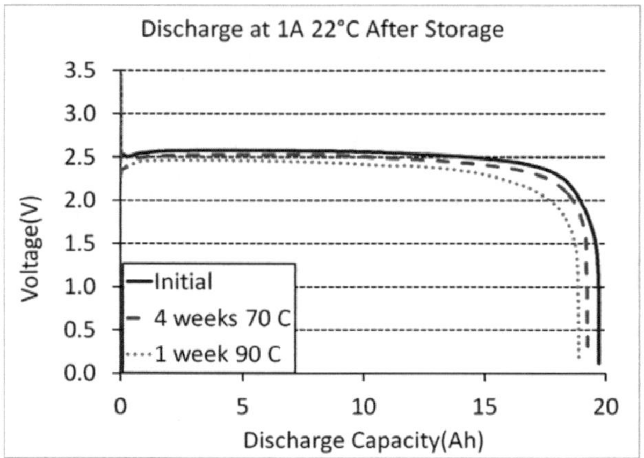

Figure 7 Discharge profile of cells discharged at 1 A at room temperature (22 °C) initially and after storage for 1 week at 90 °C or 4 weeks at 70 °C.

Other Cell Sizes

The wound cell construction and laser welded designs have been applied to both smaller and larger cell sizes (Table 3). Prismatic cells can also be made in almost any form factor using laser welded construction which results in cells with much higher operating temperature capability than pouch cells. Using custom-developed modeling software, some of these cells have been optimized for capacity at lower rates, using thicker cathodes and anodes, while other cells are optimized for their rate capability, using thinner cathodes and anodes for greater surface area in the cell. The choice of electrolyte can also be optimized for the intended operating temperature range.

Much of this work was done under government contracts. Rayovac's government contract work has led to the development of advanced high energy, high rate primary Li/CFx wound cell designs which provide an effective battery system for soldiers. This work has disproved the historical misperception that the Li/CFx system is only capable of low rate discharge.

Acknowledgements

The authors wish to acknowledge the funding received from the US government, particularly the ONR (N00014-11-C-0282).

Table 3 Properties of Li/CFx cells of several sizes

	1/3 N	AAAA	AAA	AA	D	Tall D
Capacity (Ah)	0.27	0.6	1	2.5	19	41
Nominal Rate (A)	0.0005	0.006	0.02	0.05	0.05	0.8
Continuous Rate (A)	0.06	0.06	0.5	1	3	2
Volumetric Energy Density (Wh/L)	665	683	697	850	1001	992

Development of a High Temperature Li/CFx Battery for Downhole Applications

Umamaheswari Janakiraman, Ernest Ndzebet, Mario Destephen, Joe Edington and Greg Miller
Research and Development
Eagle Picher Technologies
3220 Industrial Road
Joplin, MO 64801
Phone: (417) 623-8333
Fax: (417) 206-4708
Contact Author: Mario Destephen
Email: Mario.destephen@eaglepicher.com

Abstract: *Eagle Picher Technologies has developed a high temperature Li/CFx cell that operates efficiently over a temperature range of -20 to 160°C. This technology is suitable for applications requiring high temperature operation such as downhole in the oil and gas industries. CFx is a thermally stable material, which provides improved safety compared to other primary batteries such as Lithium Thionyl Chloride. EPT high temperature D size cell offers 20% more capacity than Thionyl Chloride cells. The observed performance and safety improvements were achieved by using unique cell design that includes our proprietary electrolyte formulation.*

Keywords: Downhole batteries, wide temperature operation range, electrolyte, thermal stability, carbon monofluoride (CFx).

Introduction

There is an increasing demand for the high-temperature batteries to power the deep sea drilling devices. Batteries used in the oil field industries are particularly important given the remote environment, and they must be able to withstand an enormous variety of operating temperatures, ranging anywhere from about -30°C to over 250°C. The batteries also must last long enough to be of practical use in these industries. The remote settings and difficulties presented when operating downhole in an oil well require a high energy density battery with good thermal stability. The challenges of the industries also require a battery that is safe to operate in these extreme conditions.

Current batteries do not operate effectively over an extended temperature window. Some batteries, such as the lithium/copper oxyphosphate, operate effectively at high temperatures but are less effective at low temperatures (≤ 25°C). [1] On the other hand, it is a challenge for many lithium batteries with liquid electrolytes to operate at high temperatures (≥ 180°C).

Current batteries designed to be used in the oil and gas industries such as the lithium thionyl chloride battery use a liquid electrolyte as the cathode active material. These cells are very corrosive, and their use can result in safety issues.

Early Li/CFx batteries[2] which operate at 150°C were unstable at higher temperatures due to excessive pressure generation. Moreover, it has been reported that with some high temperature batteries, the oil rig operators are forced to heat the tool containing the batteries on the surface prior to going downhole. This tends to be a burdensome process and potentially dangerous since the batteries can explode. Therefore, a high energy density and safe battery with consistent performance predictability over a wide temperature range is needed for downhole applications.

The development of battery for oil and gas industry involves selection of materials with good thermal stability, which includes anode, cathode, separator, cell case material and electrolyte. The CFx cathode active material is inherently safe because it is stable and inert up to 400°C. Moreover, the Lithium carbon monofluoride (Li/CFx) is an attractive 3 V system and offered the highest theoretical energy density (~2180 Wh/kg) among the primary lithium chemistries. The theoretical energy density of lithium thionyl chloride is relatively lower (1470 Wh/kg) than the Li/CFx. Due to its high energy density, Li/CFx technology has the potential to replace the current lithium thionyl chloride technology. In addition, Li/CFx has a flat discharge profile, a wide operating temperature range, low self-discharge and long shelf life (> 10 years). Therefore there is increasing interest in developing a CFx based primary battery for downhole applications.

However lithium CFx batteries commonly use organic electrolytes which are flammable. Considering the high temperature requirement for the downhole applications it is imperative to design the cell to ensure safety at high temperature operations. The development of high temperature CFx battery required an electrolyte system with good thermal stability and electrochemical stability. Electrolyte development and cell design optimization were the key enablers for the development of the EPT high temperature CFx cell with improved safety.

In this paper, we report the discharge performance of EPT CFx D cell that can safely operate in a wide temperature range (-20°C to 160°C) with good rate capability.

Experimental

Carbon monofluoride (CFx) was first mixed well with specific amount of commercial carbon. Binder was added to the above mix to make slurry which was then applied on a current collector to form the cathode. EPT proprietary electrolyte was prepared by dissolving Lithium salt and suitable additives in solvents. A cylindrical D size cell was constructed with the CFx cathode, separator, electrolyte and lithium or lithium alloy anode.

The developed D size CFx cells were discharged from open circuit voltage (OCV) down to 1 V at a rate of $\geq$ 0.23 A using an Arbin battery cycler. Cells were tested in an environmental chamber between -20°C and 160°C. The electrochemical stability of the electrolytes was investigated through Cyclic voltammetry measurements using Solartron potentiostat (model SI 1287). Differential scanning calorimetry measurements (Netzsch DSC 200F3) were done with $\leq$ 50mg of sample in a nitrogen flow at a rate of 10 K/min to evaluate the thermal stability of the electrolyte.

Results and discussion

The battery developed for the downhole application is a spirally wound D size cell, which is shown in Figure 1.

Figure 1. EPT high temperature Li/CFx battery.

The CFx D cells were initially tested at a relatively lower rate of 0.23 A in environmental chambers to evaluate its capacity at different temperatures. Figure 2 illustrates the discharge curves of a CFx D size cells at different temperatures. These cells used the EPT proprietary electrolyte. As can be seen in Figure 2, the developed electrolyte enabled the cells to discharge over a wide temperature window (-20°C to 160°C). EPT cells showed a high discharge capacity of 19 Ah at 150°C with an operating voltage of about 2.9 V. Moreover, the cells showed a high volumetric energy density of about 1127 Wh/L. A comparison with the existing thionyl chloride D size cells in the market shows EPT cells offering at least 20% higher capacity than the former over a temperature range from 21°C to 150°C when tested under similar conditions. Further EPT cells show nearly 100% discharge efficiency even at 160°C (18.8 Ah). In addition to the impressive performance at high temperatures, the cells also showed good discharge efficiency at temperatures as low as -20°C. It is to be noted that the D cells were able to get discharged at low temperature without requiring a heater.

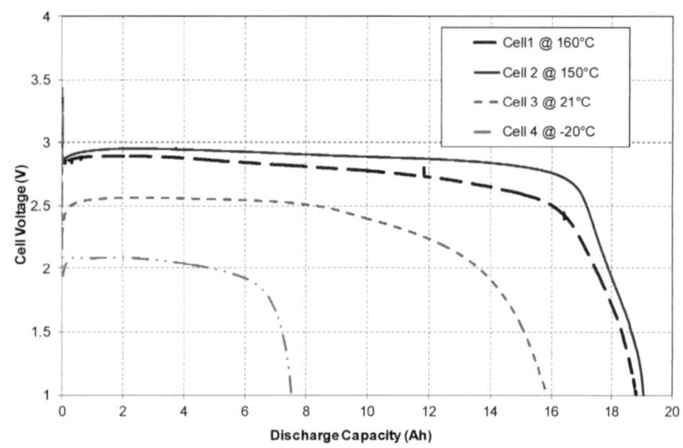

Figure 2. Discharge of EPT CFx D cells at 0.23 A between -20°C and 160°C.

Besides the wide temperature window of operation, EPT CFx cells also show high rate capability. Indeed, the cells were able to discharge at currents ranging from 0.2 A up to 1.75 A at high temperatures. The intermittent discharge of CFx D size cell at 1A at 155°C is shown in Figure 3. As can be seen, these cells delivered 10 Ah. The increase in cell skin temperature was only about 5°C during the test. As the heat output of a cell is proportional to i^2R (i-current, R-resistance), the observed low temperature raise point out to the low impedance of the EPT cells during the high rate discharge.[3]

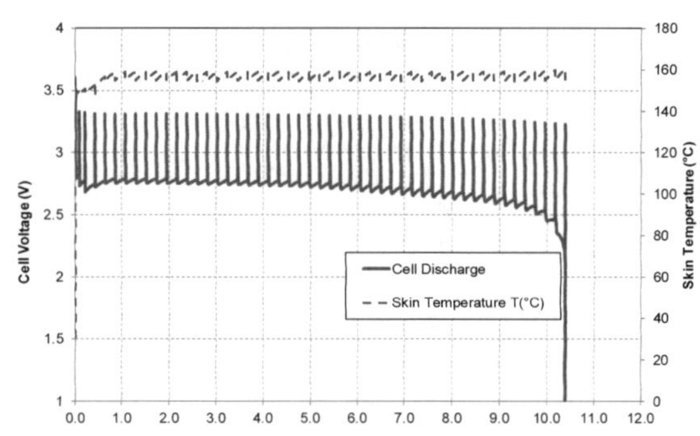

Figure 3. High rate intermittent discharge of EPT CFx D cells at 155°C.

The EPT high temperature CFx battery showed good shelf life upon storage up to 4 weeks at 60°C. As illustrated in Figure 4, no loss in capacity was observed when the stored cells were tested @ 0.23 A at room temperature (RT, 21°C).

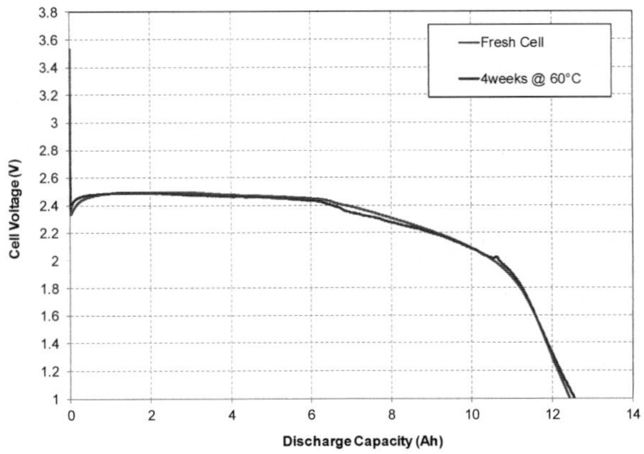

Figure 4. Discharge of EPT CFx D cells at 0.23 A after 4 weeks of storage at 60°C.

The observed good shelf life of EPT cells was attributed to the electrochemical and thermal stability of our proprietary electrolyte as shown in Figures 5 and 6, respectively.

As can be seen in Figure 5, the conventional electrolyte has an oxidation peak of 3.6 V and a reduction peak of 0.5 V vs. Li/Li^+ reference. EPT electrolyte is stable in the cathode potential and displays 10 times higher stability in the anode potential. The extended window of electrochemical stability of an electrolyte is critical in improving the shelf life. It is expected that a lower oxidative/reductive decomposition of electrolyte will improve the shelf life of the battery. Care was taken in the choice of electrolyte components with appropriate physicochemical properties to impart electrochemical and thermal stability of the electrolyte. In addition to the observed electrochemical stability, the EPT electrolyte showed good thermal stability up to 280°C, as illustrated in Figure 6. The electrolyte was also tested with the co-existence of lithium metal by differential scanning calorimetry (DSC) (see Figure 6). The endothermic peak appearing at 180°C is due to the melting of lithium metal.[4]However the electrolyte showed good thermal stability in spite of the molten lithium and showed decomposition only at 250°C. The higher thermal stability of EPT electrolyte associated with that of the cathode and anode material enables EPT CFx battery to safely operate at high temperatures. We have developed another electrolyte system with stability over 300°C for further extending the high temperature operation beyond 160°C.

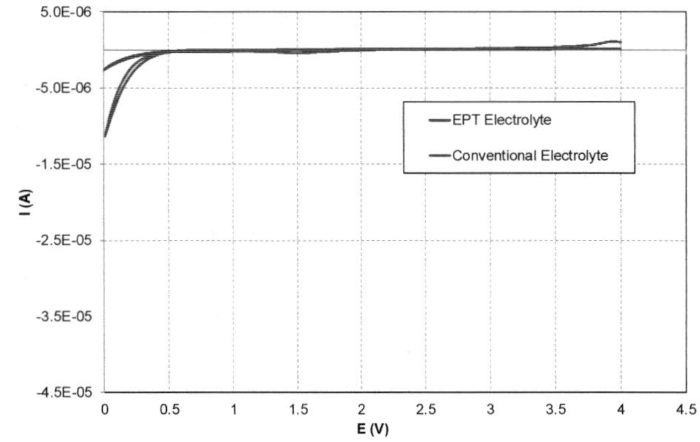

Figure 5. Cyclic voltammogram of electrolytes.

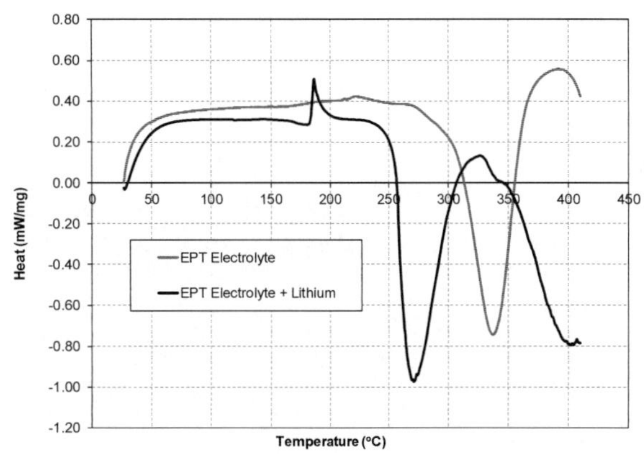

Figure 6. Differential Scanning Calorimetry (DSC) of electrolytes.

Aside from the exceptional discharge characteristics such as wide temperature operation range, high rate capability and good shelf life, the EPT cells also passed the safety tests required for transportation and downhole drilling operations. The tests include shock, vibration, short circuit, forced discharge, and thermal cycling. A typical short circuit test of the EPT cell performed at 55°C is shown in Figure 7. As can be seen, the cell skin temperature stayed below 100°C during the entire duration of the external short circuit test. It is generally considered that the thermal runaway of lithium cells occurs if the heat output exceeds the thermal diffusion.[3] EPT CFx cells were able to pass the recommended safety tests due to the improvements in cell design. The cells passed all the safety tests, without a leak, vent or fire. Further, the cells were able to safely get discharged after shock and vibration testing.

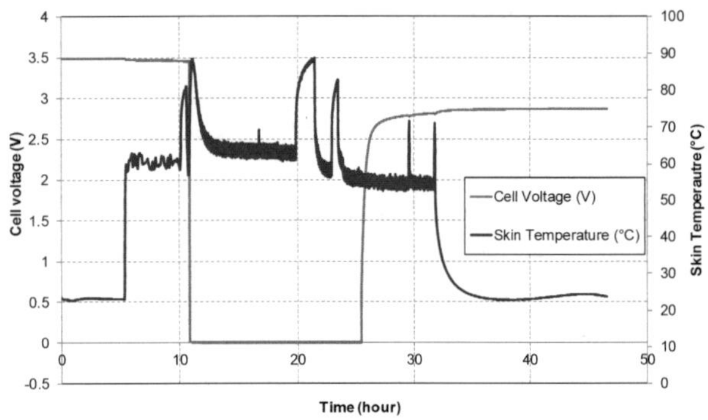

Figure 7. Short circuit test of EPT CFx D cell.

Nail penetration test was done in addition to the above safety tests on the undischarged cells. As shown in Figure 8, the cell didn't catch fire even after 48 hours following the nail penetration. Safety tests further affirm the readiness of EPT CFx battery for downhole applications.

Figure 8. Nail penetration test of EPT CFx D cell.

Conclusion

Eagle Picher Technology has successfully developed a Li/CFx battery which shows wide temperature discharge capability ranging from -20°C to 160°C. Further, the cells show high rate capability and show good shelf life. The developed D size Li/CFx battery passed all the recommended safety testing for transportation and operation in the oil field industry. The new EPT CFx battery is thus a promising technology for downhole application. Further development is under way to extend the operation temperature beyond 160°C.

Acknowledgements

This material is released to the public domain in accordance with ITAR 22 CFR 120.11.

References

1. D. Hensley, M. Milewits, and W. Zhang, "Oilfield Review," *Autumn* (1998) 1- 57.
2. Y. Toyoguchi, T. Lijima, and M. Fukuda, "Active material for positive electrode of battery," *US patent,* no. 4271242, June 2, 1981.
3. S. Tobishima and J. Yamaki, "A consideration of lithium cell safety," *J. Power Sources,* 81-82 (1999) 882.
4. N. Katayama et al, "Thermal stability of propylene carbonate and ethylene carbonate-propylene carbonate-based electrolytes for use in Li cells," J. Power Sources, 109 (2002) 321-326.

Optimization of CF_x and CF_x-MnO_2 Blends for Lithium Batteries

Paula C Latorre and Terrill B Atwater
US Army RDECOM
Communications, Electronics, Research, Development and Engineering Center
Aberdeen Proving Ground, MD 21005

Abstract: *Batteries are typically the limiting factor in the performance of most commercial and military portable electronic equipment. This is due to the restrictions on the size, weight, and configuration placed by the equipment on the power source. One of the most promising electrochemical systems is lithium carbon mono-fluoride (CF_x) batteries, due to their high energy density. Blending the CF_x chemistry has also become very popular in order to achieve high capacities in a wide temperature range. Li/CF_x and Li/CF_x-MnO_2 button cells were fabricated in varying ratios to evaluate the electrochemical properties of both electrochemical systems. Higher number of carbon to fluorine bonds increase the operating voltage at the expense of slightly decreasing the capacity of the cell. The pulse capabilities of these cells reveal the thermodynamic and kinetic properties of the system. Optimal CF_x blends should therefore have an operating discharge potential between 2.0-2.5 volts (i.e. similar thermodynamics and kinetics) in order to have uniform integrated hybrid chemistry. The goal of this effort was to identify and evaluate the optimal blend of Li/CF_x-MnO_2 that would operate in a C4ISR environment.*

Keywords: Li/CF_x; Li/CF_x-MnO_2; Lithium batteries

Introduction

The military continues to need reliable, safe, and efficient power sources with high energy densities, high power, and low weight that will operate over a wide temperature range. The US Army is currently relying on Li/SO_2 and Li/MnO_2 for primary portable power sources. These chemistries have relatively limited energy densities and with increasing technology-driven requirements, the need for a higher energy power source has become more prevalent. Li/CF_x systems are known to have a high theoretical capacity when compared to other primary chemistries. This chemistry has been demonstrated to have double the capacity and energy of Li/SO_2 systems; however it has limited operability at low temperatures and it requires a high level of heat mitigation. Hybridization of this chemistry focuses on retaining the chemistry's high performance characteristics while removing or mitigating its weaknesses. The objective of this effort focuses on varying fluorine content in CF_x to determine its optimal electrochemical performance and its potential for hybridization. This effort is split into two distinct sections. The first section focuses on analyzing the fluorine content of CF_x to determine electrochemical performance. The second section focuses on the hybridization of CF_x.

Background

Graphite is known to react with fluorine compounds at very high temperatures and yield $(CF_x)_n$. The fluorine to carbon ratio highly depends on the fluorination temperature, the fluorine partial pressure, and other physical characteristics of the graphite.[1-3]

The chemical compositions of the various commercial CF_x materials typically range in fluorine content from $0.95 < x < 1.15$. CF_x is prepared from different starting materials, which leads to different physical properties such as particle size, surface area, and decomposition temperature.[3] In addition to having various physical properties among manufacturers, it has been suggested that CF_x where $0.5 < x < 1$ consists of a mixture of two phases, $(CF_{0.5})_n$ and $(CF_1)_n$.[1] For higher CF_x fluorination where $1 < x < 1.3$, the resultant compounds consist of $(CF_1)_n$ with additional prefluorinated CF_2 surface groups.[1] Therefore the reproduction of this effort using varying raw material sources can be done; however data inconsistency is possible. To help minimize these possible inconsistencies, a single source of commercially available CF_x materials with ranging fluorine content was evaluated in this work.

The overall discharge reaction of the Li/CF_x cell is expressed in Equation 1.

$$CF_x + xLi \rightarrow C + xLiF \tag{1}$$

According to this reaction, the higher the fluorine content x, the higher the theoretical specific discharge capacity of the cell. The theoretical discharge capacity, Q, is calculated based on Equation 2, where x is the fluorine constant present in the cathode, F is the Faraday constant, and 3.6 is a unit conversion constant.[1]

$$Q_{th} = \frac{xF}{3.6(12+19x)} \tag{2}$$

Therefore, the theoretical discharge capacity for CF_x is between 100 mAh/g < Q < 950 mAh/g for $0.05 < x < 1.3$, as shown in Figure 1.

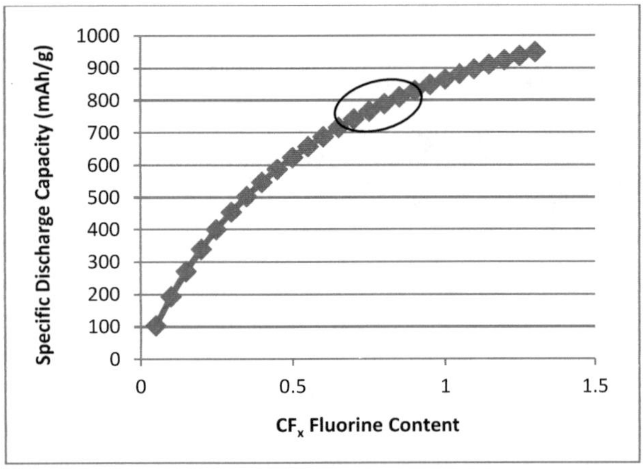

Figure 1. The theoretical specific discharge capacities of Li/CF_x with increasing fluorine content.

In this effort, the fluorine content present in CF_x will be between $0.69 < x < 0.95$. At these elevated fluorine concentrations, the theoretical specific discharge capacity delivered is 2-3 times the specific capacity delivered in $LiMnO_2$, $LiSOCl_2$, and Li/$SOCl_2$ batteries, as shown in Figure 2.

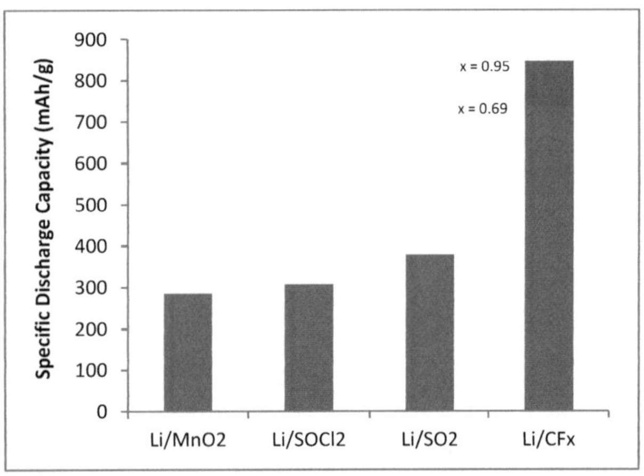

Figure 2. The comparison of the theoretical specific discharge capacities of common primary military batteries with Li/CF_x where $0.69 < x < 0.95$.[8]

Previous work on the analysis of CF_x at low fluorine concentrations has demonstrated that at low discharge rates the energy density increases with fluorine content, however at higher rates, subfluorinated compounds performed better than commercial CF_x.[1] This work proposes to evaluate the CF_x cell performance at higher fluorine concentrations to demonstrate and utilize optimal CF_x materials in hybridization.

The hybridization of CF_x-MnO_2 has been a common practice in industry in the attempt to produce primary lithium safe and reliable high capacity batteries with a wide temperature range. Some disadvantages of pure Li/CF_x batteries include their low-medium discharge rates, initial voltage delays at low temperatures, and their high cost. Hybridization of CF_x with MnO_2 would be advantageous to mitigate these risks without losing CF_x's high performance characteristics.

In the military, batteries will more commonly experience a various current or pulse type load. Common military batteries are not hybridized and thrive in continuous load applications; however, with the advancement in technology and the push for a common power architecture and power management, varying loads are becoming more prevalent. During a continuous discharge, a hybrid battery would be underutilized; however, a hybridized battery can more efficiently distribute a pulse or sporadic type load.

This effort proposes to commence the evaluation of the hybridization of CF_x due to its high energy characteristics. This office and its colleagues have been investigating hybrids for many years.[5-7]

For a known duty cycle, a hybrid battery will recover right before it is asked to continue doing "work." In Li/CF_x-MnO_2, the power piece (MnO_2) needs to recover after a heavy discharge. CF_x will act as the buffer for lower current distributions until MnO_2 returns to its full potential.

Experimental

In the first set of cells, CF_x was used as the active cathode material where x varied from $0.69 < x < 0.95$. CF_x where x varied from $0.69 < x < 0.95$ was hybridized with MnO_2 and used as an active material for the second set of cells. These materials were evaluated for their viability as cathode materials for primary lithium batteries.

Conventional button cells with a surface area of 2.85 cm^2, a lithium anode, and an organic electrolyte were fabricated to evaluate the thermodynamic and kinetic properties of the Li/CF_x electrochemical systems.

The experimental cells were composed of a lithium anode separated from the cathode by a nonwoven glass separator. The CF_x cathode was fabricated by mixing together the active material, carbon, and polytetrafluoroethylene (PTFE) with an 85:10:5 by weight ratio, respectively. The cathode mixture was rolled to 0.04 cm and dried in a vacuum oven. A 0.075 cm thick lithium foil was cut using a 12.7 mm or 19.0 mm diameter hole punch. The cathode was cut into 2.85 cm^2 discs, resulting in a 0.075 g cathode for the button cells. A 0.01 cm nonwoven glass separator was utilized for the separator and as a wick. The electrolyte used was 1 molar $LiPF_6$ in proportional mixtures of diethyl carbonate, dimethyl carbonate, and ethylene carbonate or $LiClO_4$ in proportional mixtures of ethylene carbonate, propylene carbonate, and dimethoxyethane.

Cell impedance and OCV was measured for each cell before being placed on test. Cells were discharged with an ARBIN MSTAT4 battery cycler system controlled by

MITS Pro software. All tests were performed at room temperature. The cells were discharged to 1.0 V. Discharge rates were determined by scaling down cell loading in a battery pack. The discharge rates were maintained at 0.4 to 3.0 mA/cm^2 for Li/CF_x cells. Li/CFx-MnO_2 cells were discharged at 0.4 to 3.0 mA/cm^2 pulses. A minimum of three cells were used for each test condition.

Results

Li/CF_x button cells were fabricated with a fluorine content of 0.69, 0.73, 0.75, 0.77, 0.80, or 0.95. These cells were then discharged at ambient temperature at a continuous current of 1 mA, 2 mA, 5 mA, or 8 mA until a 1 volt cutoff. Voltage and load distributions were determined based on the scale down from cell loading in a typical pack level Li/CF_x.

Figures 3-4 show the electrochemical characterization of the Li/CF_x cell at varying fluorine concentrations. Figure 3 shows that the specific discharge capacities of the cells at the highest continuous load were in the range of 0.70 to 0.82 mA/g. The major difference between Li/CF_x cells where $0.69 < x < 0.95$ is its OCV, regardless of load. Li/CF_x containing higher fluorine concentrations will typically have a higher initial and nominal operating voltage, as shown in Figure 3. These cells also exhibit a shorter initial delay time and the operating voltage does not decrease as significantly as with Li/CF_x cells containing lower fluorine concentrations.

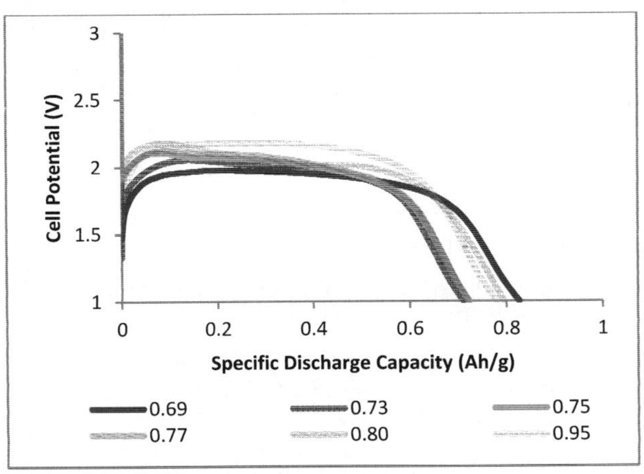

Figure 3. The discharge profiles of Li/CF_x button cells tested at 8 mA continuously where $0.69 < x < 0.95$.

Figure 4 shows the average specific discharge capacities at varying fluorine concentrations and under varying load distributions. It is clearly evident that increasing discharge rate decreases the overall electrochemical performance of the cell. All cells performed as expected and their capacities were comparable.

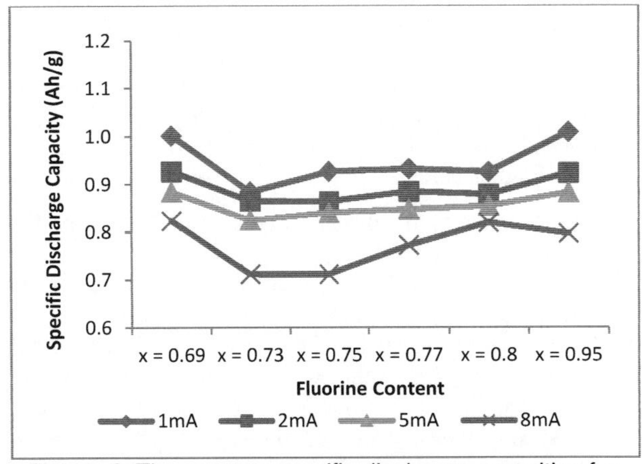

Figure 4. The average specific discharge capacities for Li/CF_x button cells where $0.69 < x < 0.95$ at various current distributions.

Li/CF_x cells were discharged in a pulse profile to determine the system's thermodynamics and kinetics. The pulse discharge consisted of an 8 mA high discharge for 1 minute followed by a 1 mA "rest" for 7 minutes. The average current distribution across the cell was 1.87 mA. During a duty cycle, the kinetics of the cell is attributed to the high discharge rate, whereas under no current or low discharge rates, the cell recovery is attributed to thermodynamics.

Figure 5 shows the pulse discharge profile of the Li/CF_x cells at varying fluorine concentrations to a 1 volt cutoff. The differential potential between high and low discharge was approximately 0.25 volts. Therefore the thermodynamics and kinetics of Li/CF_x were balanced and consistent throughout the life of the cells. Additionally, the electrochemical performance of cells with varying fluorine content discharged under a duty cycle was comparable.

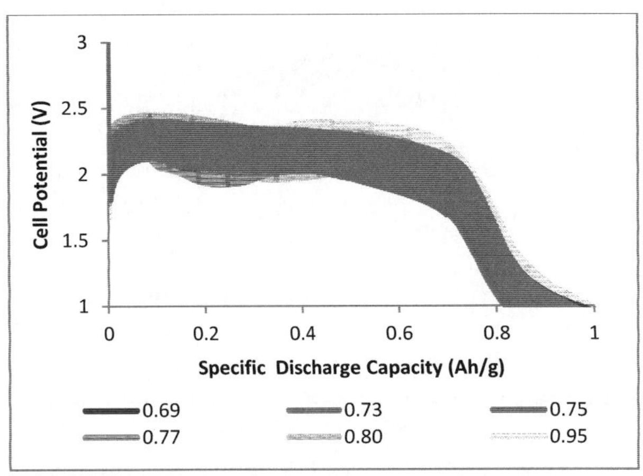

Figure 5. The discharge profiles of Li/CF_x button cells discharged at 8 mA for 1 minutes followed by 1 mA for 7 minutes, where $0.69 < x < 0.95$.

A series of electrochemical hybrid Li/CF_x-MnO_2 cells were fabricated and analyzed. The cathode consisted of a 50:50 ratio of CF_x where x = 0.95 (due to its elevated nominal operating potential) and heat treated MnO_2. Additional Li/CF_x-MnO_2 cells were fabricated where x = 0.69 for comparison.

Figures 6-7 show the discharge profiles of the Li/CF_x-MnO_2 cell using x = 0.95 and x = 0.69, respectively. In both figures, the discharge profiles demonstrate two voltage plateaus; the first occurs with the activation of MnO_2 and the second is the CF_x activation. The nominal operating potential is higher with higher fluorine content, as expected. The reduction in capacity between Li/CF_xMnO_2 where x = 0.69 and x = 0.95 is approximately 11%.

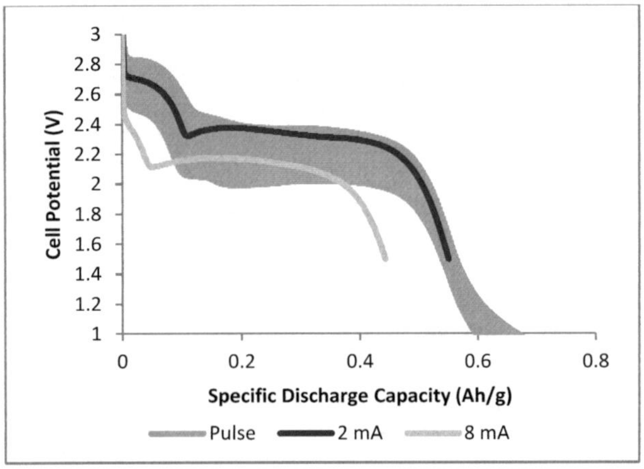

Figure 6. The discharge profile of Li/CF_x-MnO_2 button cells where x = 0.95.

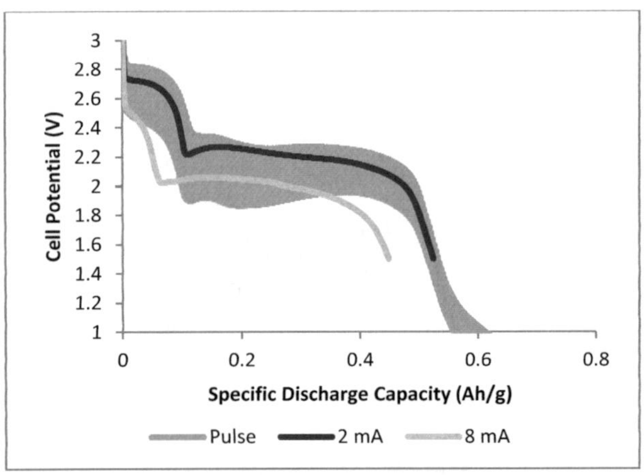

Figure 7. The discharge profile of Li/CF_x-MnO_2 button cells where x = 0.69.

The primary difference between the Li/CF_x cells and the hybridized Li/CF_x-MnO_2 cells is the disappearance of the initial delay and the reduction in specific capacity. The reduction in specific discharge capacity between Li/CF_x to Li/CF_x-MnO_2 is approximately 29%. The differential potential throughout the life of the hybrid Li/CF_x-MnO_2 cells is higher than the Li/CF_x cells at approximately 0.4 volts. Although Li/CF_x-MnO_2 is thermodynamically and kinetically stable and a good hybrid, the elevated differential potential between Li/CF_x and the MnO_2 hybrid suggests that it may not be the ideal solution. An ideal candidate for cathode hybridization should have a discharge profile within the thermodynamic and kinetic profile of the primary material. The resultant hybrid would have equal or narrower differential discharge potentials demonstrating similar thermodynamics and kinetics.

Conclusion

Li/CF_x and Li/CF_x-MnO_2 button cells were fabricated in varying ratios to evaluate the electrochemical properties of both electrochemical systems. The carbon to fluorine ratios in CF_x analyzed in this effort was between $0.69 < x < 0.95$. Although the electrochemical performance of these cells was comparable regardless of the fluorine content present in the Li/CF_x cells, cells containing higher fluorine concentrations typically featured higher initial and nominal operating voltages.

The pulse capabilities of these cells reveal the thermodynamic and kinetic properties of the system. Li/CF_x where x = 0.95 was identified as the optimal CF_x cathode material for hybridization. The Li/CF_x-MnO_2 demonstrated good hybrid characteristics including mitigating the initial delay setback of Li/CF_x cells; however a 29% loss of capacity was observed.

Follow-on work would include the determination of the electrochemical performance at varying CF_x to MnO_2 ratios as well as the hybridization of CF_x with other cathode materials.

References:

1. Lam, P., and R. Yazami. *Journal of power sources* 153.2 (2006): 354-359.
2. Zhang, Sheng S., et al. *Journal of Power Sources* 187.1 (2009): 233-237.
3. J. Read, M. Marx, J. Wolfenstine, S. Zhang, and D. Foster, *Proc. Of the 44th Power Sources Conf.*, Las Vegas, NV, 2010: 167-170
4. Zhang, Xulong, and Xinrong Wang. U.S. Patent Application 12/145,665.
5. Atwater, Terrill B., Peter J. Cygan, and Fee Chan Leung. *Journal of Power Sources* 91.1 (2000): 27-36.
6. Jarvis, Louis P., Terrill B. Atwater, and Peter J Cygan. *Journal of power Sources* 79.1 (1999): 60-63.
7. Jarvis, Louis P., Terrill B. Atwater, and Peter J. Cygan. *Aerospace and Electronic Systems Magazine, IEEE* 15.9 (2000): 37-41.
8. Reddy, Thomas B. *Linden's Handbook of Batteries.* Vol. 4. New York: McGraw-Hill, 2011.

Exfoliated, Nitrogen-Doped Graphene Nanosheet Cathode for Lithium-Oxygen Batteries

Padmakar Kichambare and Stanley Rodrigues

Air Force Research Laboratory, Aerospace Systems Directorate

Wright-Patterson Air Force Base, Ohio 45433-7252.

Abstract: *Cathodes prepared using graphene nanosheets (GNSs), nitrogen-doped graphene nanosheets (N-GNSs), exfoliated nitrogen-doped graphene nanosheets (Ex-N-GNSs) as well as composite of Ex-N-GNSs with lithium aluminum germanium phosphate (LAGP) have been explored for application in lithium-oxygen batteries. These cathodes exhibit remarkable enhancement in cell capacity in comparison to conventional carbon cathodes. This enhancement is ascribed to the unique morphology of GNSs, higher oxygen reduction and oxygen evolution activity as well as fast lithium ion conduction of LAGP. These results demonstrate a strong potential of GNSs as cathodes for rechargeable lithium-oxygen batteries.*

Keywords: Nitrogen-doped graphene nanosheets; scanning electron microscopy; oxygen reduction reaction; cyclic voltammetry; lithium-oxygen battery.

Introduction

The continuous increase in demand for energy as well as global concerns over the depletion of fossil fuels has led to the exploration of high density energy storage systems [1]. Among these energy systems, lithium-oxygen battery holds a great potential, as this battery has a theoretical energy density [2] comparable to gasoline [3]. A typical lithium-oxygen battery is composed of lithium metal anode, porous carbon based cathode exposed to gaseous oxygen, and lithium ion conducting electrolyte. During discharge, lithium is oxidized at the anode and oxygen is reduced at the cathode to produce discharge products. Subsequent charging causes the decomposition of discharge products and the generation of oxygen. Although these batteries operate on a simple chemical reaction between lithium ions and oxygen molecules, there are many technical challenges that need to be overcome for realization of practical lithium-oxygen battery operating in an ambient environment. Several factors dictate the performance of these batteries such as oxygen cathode, electrolyte composition, relative humidity, and cell design [4-7]. In particular, the material architecture of oxygen cathodes play a key role in governing the electrochemical performance of lithium-oxygen battery.

Abraham and Jiang [8] pioneered the lithium-oxygen battery technology. They reported cell capacity of 1410 mAh/g in pure oxygen atmosphere. Following this work, significant efforts have been focused on cathode formulations [9-13], efficient oxygen reduction catalysts [16-17], electrolyte compositions [14-15], effect of moisture [18], etc. In spite of these efforts to improve the sluggish kinetics of oxygen reduction reaction (ORR) as well as oxygen evolution reaction (OER) at the cathode, lithium-oxygen cells still exhibit significantly lower discharge capacity than the theoretical cell capacity, and high overpotential with limited cycle life. To this end, it is important to develop oxygen cathodes with a highly efficient ORR and OER catalyst that have significant impact on the desired energy densities of these cells. Recently, graphene nanosheets (GNSs) have been investigated as electrocatalyst for energy storage applications [19] because of its excellent electrical conductivity, distinct morphology, large surface area, and outstanding electrocatalytic activity. GNSs have been employed as oxygen cathode in fuel cells and show a higher discharge voltage under acidic condition [20]. GNSs, nitrogen-doped graphene nanosheets (N-GNSs) were also exploited in non-aqueous lithium-oxygen cells as cathode material that demonstrated an exceptionally high discharge cell capacity [21].

In continuation of our work on a fully solid-state, rechargeable lithium-oxygen cells [22-25], we report here the use of GNSs, N-GNSs, exfoliated nitrogen-doped graphene nanosheets (Ex-N-GNSs) and composite cathode prepared from mixture of Ex-N-GNSs and lithium aluminum germanium phosphate (LAGP) in a solid-state lithium-oxygen cell and compared the cell performance with cells using cathodes prepared from mesoporous carbon. Furthermore, the role of porosity, surface area and electro-catalytic activity of GNSs on the electrochemical performance is also discussed.

Experimental Details

Commercially available GNSs (Angstron Materials, Inc.) were heated in a vacuum oven at 250 °C to remove any residual surfactant. These GNSs were used for further work. N-GNSs and Ex-N-GNSs were prepared using procedure described in the literature [19]. LAGP was prepared by solid-state sintering technique.

A scanning electron microscope (SEM), (JEOL JSM-6060) equipped with energy dispersive X-ray (EDX) spectroscopy assembly was used to observe the morphologies of the specimens. Structure and purity of these materials were performed by powder X-ray diffraction (XRD) on a Bruker D8 Discover diffractometer operated at 40 kV, 40 mA current with CuKα in the 2θ range of 15 to 80° at an increment of 0.05°. The surface areas of the specimens were determined by nitrogen adsorption / desorption measurements at 77 K (Micromeritics ASAP 2020). The porosity of cathode material was characterized by a gas pycnometer (Micromeritis, Accu Pyc II 1340). Cyclic voltammetry (CV) and galvanostatic charge-discharge measurements of the specimens were conducted using a computer controlled VersaSTAT 4 (Princeton Applied Research) electrochemical workstation. CV measurements were performed in a standard three-electrode cell configuration using 0.1 M KOH as the electrolyte at 25 °C with a scan rate of 5 mV/sec. The working electrode for CV measurement was prepared by applying the paste of specimens and Nafion (tetrafluoroethylene based fluoropolymer-copolymer) on the tip of a graphite rod. A Pt wire was used as the counter electrode. All potentials were measured with respect to saturated calomel electrode (SCE).

Powders of GNSs, N-GNSs, Ex-N-GNSs, and composite **1** (mixture of Ex-N-GNSs with 5 wt % LAGP) were used to fabricate the oxygen cathode. These powders were mixed with de-ionized water and polytetrafluoroethylene (PTFE) to obtain a viscous solution. A nickel foam was then suspended in this solution with sonication for 2 hours. This process was carried to load GNSs in the open voids of nickel foam. Subsequently, the cathode specimen was dried overnight at 100 °C under vacuum. A solid-state lithium-oxygen cell with a 1 cm^2 area was fabricated using a Swagelok type cell in a dry room with controlled moisture content. Nickel foam with GNSs/N-GNSs/Ex-N-GNSs/composite **1** were used as working cathodes along with lithium metal as anode and LAGP as electrolyte.

Electrochemical impedance spectroscopy (EIS) measurements on the lithium-oxygen cells were conducted over a frequency range of 0.1 Hz to 10^6 Hz before and after discharge/charge measurements. All electrochemical tests on these cells were carried under oxygen atmosphere.

Figure 1. SEM image of composite **1** (Ex-N-GNSs and 5 wt % LAGP).

Results and Discussion

The morphology of the working cathode was examined under SEM. Figure 1 shows the SEM micrograph of composite **1** that contains wrinkled, porous, 3D architectures with interconnected pore channels of Ex-N-GNSs and crystals of LAGP (shown by arrows). This favorable morphology facilitates oxygen transport, enhances electrocatalytic activity and provides enough void to accommodate discharge products. EDX conducted on these samples revealed the nitrogen content to be 3-4 at. wt. %.

A typical nitrogen adsorption – desorption isotherm at 77 K for composite **1** is shown in Figure 2. Isotherm shows adsorption hysteresis indicating the presence of micropores The Brunauer-Emmett-Teller (BET) surface

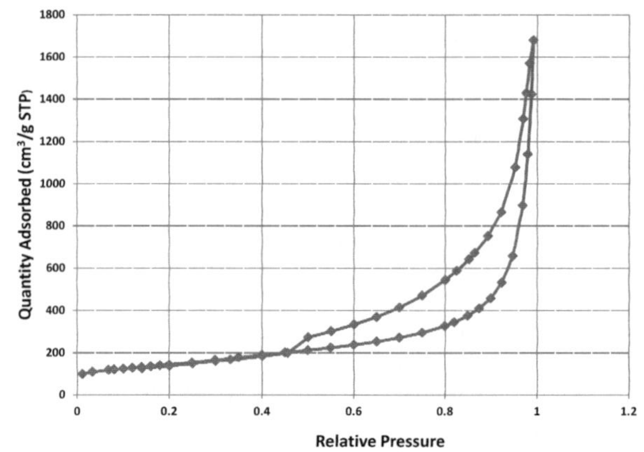

Figure 2. N_2 adsorption - desorption isotherm for composite **1** (Ex-N-GNSs and 5 wt % LAGP).

area of GNSs, N-GNSs, Ex-N-GNSs, and composite **1** were found to be 482, 583, 685, 470 m^2/g, respectively The remarkable nitrogen uptake above the relative pressure ratio of 0.40 has been observed in BET isotherm and is due to the condensation of nitrogen in mesoporous GNSs.

The CV curves recorded for GNSs, N-GNSs, Ex-N-GNSs, and composite **1** in oxygen saturated aqueous solution of 0.1 M KOH are presented in Figure 3. Well defined ORR peaks at around -0.389 V, -0.449 V, -0.397 V, and -0.478 V (vs. SCE) were observed for GNSs, N-GNSs, Ex-N-GNSs, and composite **1**, respectively, with highest reduction current density of 0.0032 A/cm^2 for composite **1.** Figure 3 also shows OER peaks at around 0.466 V, 0.496 V, 0.525 V, and 0.895 V (vs. SCE) for GNSs, N-GNSs, Ex-N-GNSs, and composite **1**, respectively. This indicates that loading of LAGP particles on Ex-N-GNSs helps improve electro-catalytic activity. No electro-catalytic activity was observed for all these cathode materials when the electrolyte was saturated with nitrogen.

Based on the high surface area, porous structure as well as electro-catalytic activity towards oxygen reduction and oxygen evolution of GNSs, N-GNSs, Ex-N-GNSs, and composite **1**, solid-state lithium-oxygen cells with 1 cm^2 active area were fabricated. The cathode side of the cell has perforations to access oxygen. The lithium anode was coupled to an oxygen cathode through a solid electrolyte laminate, described in our previous work [22]. The solid electrolyte laminate provides very high ionic conductivity for transport of lithium ions from lithium anode to oxygen cathode. In addition, the electrolyte laminate improves lithium-electrolyte interfacial stability and passivates the lithium surface.

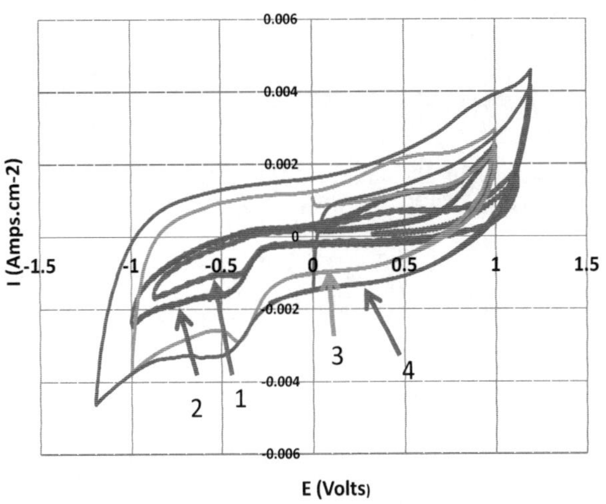

Figure 3. CV of (1) GNSs, (2) N-GNSs, (3) Ex-N-GNSs) and (4) composite **1** in oxygen saturated 0.1 M KOH at a scan rate of 5 mV/sec at 25 °C.

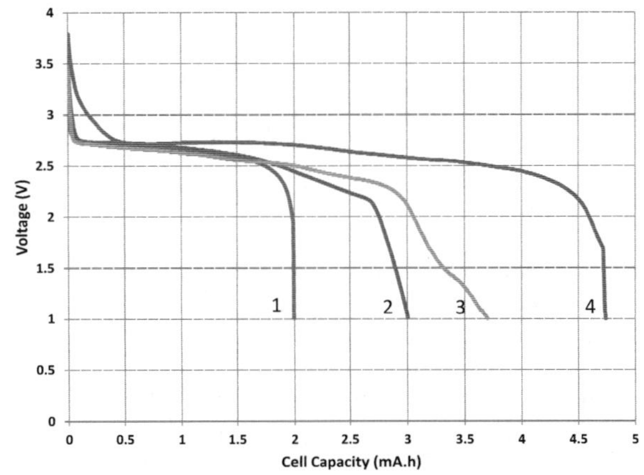

Figure 4. Discharge profiles for a lithium-oxygen cell at 75 °C using (1) GNSs, (2) N-GNSs, (3) Ex-N-GNSs) and (4) composite **1** as cathode in oxygen atmosphere.

The electrochemical performance of GNSs, N-GNSs, Ex-N-GNSs, and composite **1** was evaluated as cathodes in lithium-oxygen cell in oxygen atmosphere. Figure 4 shows the first discharge profiles of the lithium-oxygen cells with GNSs, N-GNSs, Ex-N-GNSs, and composite **1** cathodes using discharge current of 0.2 mA at 75 °C. Cell with composite **1** as cathode delivers 4.75 mAh discharge cell capacity. On the other hand, cells composed of GNSs, N-GNSs, and Ex-N-GNSs as cathodes delivered 1.95 mAh, 3.0 mAh and 3.7 mAh discharge capacities, respectively. In comparison to the discharge cell capacity of GNSs, cathode composed of N-GNSs and Ex-N-GNSs demonstrated significantly improved discharge cell capacity. In our previous work on cells composed of carbon blend (mixture of Ketjenblack and Calgon activated carbon) and nitrogen-doped carbon blend under identical conditions delivered 0.7 mAh and 1.44 mAh cell capacity. Thus, cell capacity enhancement is more than two times when the carbon blend is replaced by graphene in the cathode of lithium-oxygen cells; while nitrogen doping in GNSs and exfoliation of nanosheets has further improved the cell capacity by more than two times. Cell based on composite **1** exhibits highest discharge cell capacity among all cathodes studied in this work. This enhancement in cell capacity is due to improved electro-catalytic activity of composite **1** and fast lithium ion transport deep inside the cathode due to superionic conducting LAGP. A gradual decrease in cell discharge from 2.8 to 2.4 V is also observed in Figure 4 for composite **1**. A sharp cell discharge is observed at around 2.1 V for N-GNSs and Ex-N-GNSs; while GNSs show a sharp cell discharge at around 2.5 V. These results are consistent with our previous work wherein, an incremental increase of up to 20 wt% of LAGP in cathode formulation (N-C blend) is reported. It is noticed from Figure 4 that although open circuit voltage (OCV) of all cells are high, there is a significant potential drop during the initial stage of discharge. This potential drop is due to both an activation barrier of cathode chemistry that includes sluggish kinetics, and series resistances between various cell components. Further research work to tailor cathode architecture and improve the cell performance of lithium-oxygen batteries is currently underway.

Conclusion

In conclusion, this work demonstrates excellent cell performance of lithium-oxygen cell with cathode formulation based on GNSs. The discharge cell capacity of the cell with cathode of Ex-N-GNSs with LAGP is 4.75 mAh. This work highlights the importance of novel cathode architecture and opens up a promising approach to develop highly efficient oxygen electrodes for lithium-oxygen cells.

Acknowledgements

This research was supported by the Air Force Research Laboratory, Wright-Patterson Air Force Base, Ohio.

References:

1. Van Noorden, R., *Nature,* vol. **507**, pp. 26-28, 2014.

2. Bruce, P.G., S.A. Freunberger, L.J. Hardwick, and J.M. Tarascon, *Nat. Mater.,* vol. **11**, pp. 19-29, 2012.

3. Handbook of Batteries and Fuel Cells, 2nd ed., (Ed: Linden, D.), McGraw-Hill, New York, Chap. 38, 1984.

4. Girishkumar, G., B. McCloskey, A.C. Luntz, SD. Swanson, and W.J. Wilcke, *J. Phys. Chem. Lett.*, vol. **1**, pp. 2193-2203, 2010.

5. Zhang, T., and H.B. Zhou, *Nature Commun.*, DOI: 10.1038/ncomms2855, 2013.

6. Oh, D., J. Qi, Y.C. Lu, Y. Zhang, Y. Shao-Horn, and A.M. Belcher, *Nature Commun,* DOI: 10.1038/ncomms3756, 2013.

7. Lim, H.D., H. Song, J. Kim, H. Gwon, Y. Bae, K.Y. Park, J. Hong, H. Kim, T., Kim, Y.H., Kim, X. Lepro, R. Ovalle-Robles, R.H. Baughman, and K. Kang, *Angew. Chem. Int. Ed., DOI: 10.1002/anie.201400711*, 2014.

8. Abraham, K.M. and Z. Jiang, *J. Electrochem. Soc.,* vol. **143**, pp. 1-5, 1996.

9. Zhang, S.S., D. Foster, and J. Read, *J. Power Sources,* vol. **195**, pp. 1235-1240, 2010.

10. Beattie, S.D., D.M. Manolescu, and S.L. Blair, *J. Electrochem. Soc.,* vol. **156**, pp. A44-A47, 2009.

11. Wang, D., J. Xiao, W. Xu, and J.-G. Zhang, *J. Electrochem. Soc.,* vol. **157**, pp. A760-A764, 2010.

12. Eswaran, M., N. Munichandraiah, and L.G. Scanlon, *Electrochem. Solid State Lett.,* vol. **13**, pp. A121-A124, 2010.

13. Trahey, L., C.S. Johnson, J.T. Vaughey, S.H. Kang, L.J. Hardwick, S.A. Freunberger, P.G. Bruce, and M.M. Thackeray, *Electrochem. Solid State Lett.,* vol. **14**, pp. A64-A66, 2011.

14. Lu, Y.C., Z. Xu, H.A. Gasteiger, S. Chen, K. Hamad-Schifferli, and Y. Shao-Horn, *J. Am. Chem. Soc.,* vol. **132**, pp. 12170-12171, 2010.

15. Ren, X., S.S. Zhang, D.T. Tran, and J. Read, *J. Mater. Chem.,* vol. **21**, pp. 10118-10125, 2011.

16. Laoire, C.O., S. Mukerjee, E.J. Plichta, M.A. Hendrickson, and K.M. Abraham, *J. Electrochem. Soc.,* vol. **158**, pp. 12170-12171, 2010.

17. Freunberger, S.A., Y. Chen, Z. Peng, J.M. Griffin, L.J. Hardwick, F. Barde, P. Novak, and P.G. Bruce, *J. Am. Chem. Soc.,* vol. **133**, pp. 8040-8047, 2011.

18. Meini, S., M. Piana, N. Tsiouvaras, A. Garsuch, and H.A. Gasteiger, *Electrohem. Solid State Lett.,* vol. **15**, pp. A45-A48, 2012.

19. Kim, H., H.D. Lim, J. Kim, and K. Kang, *J.Mater.Chem. A.,* vol. **2**, pp. 33-47, 2014.

20. Yoo, E., J. Nakamura, and H. Zhou, *Energy Environ. Sci.,* vol. **5**, pp. 6928-6932, 2012.

21. Li, Y., J. Wang, X. Li, D. Geng, R. Li, and X. Sun, *Chem. Commun.,* vol. **47,** pp. 9438-9440, 2011.

22. Kumar, B., J. Kumar, R. Leese, J.P. Fellner, S.J. Rodrigues, and K.M. Abraham, *J. Electrochem. Soc.,* vol. **157,** pp. A50-A54, 2010.

23. Kichambare, P., J. Kumar, S. Rodrigues and B. Kumar, *J. Power Sources,* vol. **196**, pp. 3310-3316, 2011.

24. Kichambare, P., S. Rodrigues, and J. Kumar, *ACS Appl. Mater. Interfaces,* vol. **4**, pp. 49-52, 2012.

25. Kichambare, P., and S. Rodrigues, *Energy Technol.,* vol. **1**, pp. 209-211, 2013.

Activated Carbons from Hypersaline Hydrothermal Synthesis for Electrochemical Double Layer Capacitors

Stephen M. Lipka, Christopher R. Swartz, Rong Chen, Fon Rogers, Uschi M. Graham
Electrochemical Power Sources Group, Center for Applied Energy Research
University of Kentucky
2582 Research Park Drive, Lexington, KY 40511
Email:steve.lipka@uky.edu

Abstract: Activated carbons with high surface area are widely used as electrode materials for electrochemical double layer capacitors. In this study, carbon material was derived hydrothermally from glucose under hypersaline conditions. After physical activation in steam the activated carbon achieved a high surface area of 1939 m^2/g. The microporosity of the carbon significantly increased compared to the as-synthesized carbon. The activated carbon exhibited high capacitive performance in both organic and aqueous electrolytes.

Keywords: Activated carbon; electrochemical double layer capacitor; surface area; steam activation; hydrothermal synthesis; hypersaline.

Introduction

Electrochemical double layer capacitors (EDLCs) are energy storage devices featuring many advantages, including long cycle life, low internal resistance, and high power densities, and have been applied to electric/hybrid vehicles, heavy-construction equipment, electronics, and grid utility storage [1,2]. Typical electrode materials for EDLCs are porous activated carbons (ACs), metal oxides, graphene, carbon nanotubes, carbon aerogels, carbide-derived carbons, and conductive polymers [2,3].

Hydrothermal synthesis of carbon from carbohydrates and biomass-based precursors has drawn much attention recently due to the fact that it is an environmentally friendly and low cost process [4-7]. The as-synthesized hydrothermal carbon typically exhibits very low Brunauer-Emmett-Teller (BET) surface area (< 10 m^2/g). However, after physical activation the surface area can increase to ~ 1000 m^2/g. Recently, Fechler et al. reported the use of a hypersaline-based hydrothermal synthesis of carbon which resulted in a high surface area of 650 m^2/g for the as-produced hypersaline material, which is much higher than conventional hydrothermal carbons [4]

In the present study porous carbons were derived from glucose using hydrothermal processing under a $NaCl/ZnCl_2$ hypersaline environment as outlined by Fechler's process [4]. The as-synthesized hydrothermal carbon was further activated in steam at 850°C. The activated carbon achieved a surface area of 1939 m^2/g, which is significantly higher than conventional physically activated carbons (~1000 m^2/g). The activated hypersaline carbon was tested as an electrode material for EDLCs in 1.8M $TEMABF_4/PC$ and 38 wt.% H_2SO_4 electrolytes. The activated hypersaline carbons showed excellent capacitive performance in both electrolytes.

Experimental

Following Fechler's process [4], 3.1 g of NaCl, 9.9 g of $ZnCl_2$, 6 g of glucose, and 3 ml of DI water were mixed in a sonicating bath to form an over-saturated slurry. The mixture was then sealed in a 50 ml Teflon lined Parr pressure vessel and heated in an oven at 180°C for 24 hours. After cooling down the black solid product was collected and washed with DI water several times, in order to rinse off the extra salt, and was then dried in a vacuum oven at 120°C over night. This sample was labelled as green carbon (GC). The green carbon was activated in steam at 850°C to increase the surface area. For comparison the green carbon was also carbonized in nitrogen at 850°C. The activated carbon and carbonized carbon were labelled as AC and CC, respectively. The morphology of the GC was investigated using a Hitachi-4800 SEM. The nitrogen adsorption/desorption isothermal tests were performed on a Micromeritics ASAP 2020 to study the surface area, pore volume, and pore size distribution of the carbon powders.

The AC powder was mixed with 3 wt.% polytetrafluoroethylene and rolled to a thickness of 80µm. Electrodes of 12 mm diameter were punched out from the sheet as the electrodes for symmetric EDLC cells. Electrochemical characterization was performed using cyclic voltammetry (CV) and constant current discharge-charge performance tests on a Gamry 750 potentiostat. The electrochemical performance of the AC was investigated in both 1.8M $TEMABF_4/PC$ and 38 wt.% H_2SO_4 electrolytes. For H_2SO_4 electrolyte, cycle life testing was performed on a Maccor 4300 battery cycler using a constant current of 0.5 A/g, between 0 and 1 V for 2000 cycles.

Results and Discussions

Table 1 shows the nitrogen adsorption/desorption isothermal results. Figure 1 shows the pore size distribution of the 3 samples. The GC has a surface area of 448.5 m^2/g, which is much higher than that of conventional glucose-derived hydrothermal carbon (< 10 m^2/g) produced by non-hypersaline hydrothermal synthesis. This may be due to the unique cross-linking structure of carbon formed under hypersaline hydrothermal conditions, which will be discussed in the following section. For the CC sample the surface area and pore volume did not change much, as the pore size distribution of the CC sample was similar to the GC sample. This indicates that the carbonization step did not have a strong effect on the pore structure of the carbon. However, the surface area and pore volume of the AC significantly increased compared to the GC. Figure 1 demonstrated that the pore volumes for the meso and macro pores increased and additional peaks appeared at the micro pore range. The steam activation enlarged the meso and macro pores and created new micro pores on the surface of the carbon, which contribute to capacitive double layer charge storage.

Table 1. Nitrogen adsorption/desorption isothermal results

	surface area (m^2/g)	Volume in pore (cc/g)	Porosity %		
			Micro <2 nm	Meso 2~50 nm	Macro >50 nm
GC	448.5	0.8357	12.8	78.7	8.5
CC	504.4	0.6305	25.1	72.3	2.6
AC	1939.6	2.0193	34.9	59.4	5.7

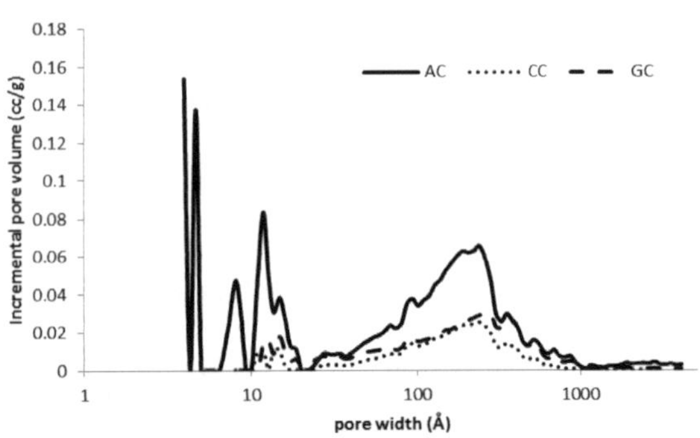

Figure 1. Pore size distribution of the 3 samples

Figure 2 shows the SEM image of the GC sample. Instead of spherical carbon that is typically obtained from pure glucose, the hypersaline condition yielded irregular shaped carbon with higher surface area. It may be presumed that he irregular morphology results when high concentration of ions stabilized the surface of the newly nucleated nano particles, increased surface energy and prohibits further particle growth [4] Instead of growing into larger spherical particles the nuclei formed a cross-linking structure to a porous final product. The high surface area and high meso porous structure of the GC support this assumption.

Fig. 3 and Fig. 4 show the CV and DC performance of the AC in 1.8M $TEMABF_4/PC$ and 38 wt.% H_2SO_4, respectively. The CV and DC curves demonstrated excellent capacitor characteristics especially in 1.8M $TEMABF_4/PC$. The CV data showed a near rectangular shape, indicative of capacitive charge storage. The DC data showed linear charge and discharge curves. The AC exhibited a gravimetric capacitance of 101 F/g and a volumetric capacitance of 40 F/cm^3 in 1.8M $TEMABF_4/PC$. In 38 wt% H_2SO_4, the performance was 130 F/g and 52 F/cm^3. The IR drop was less than 20 mV from the DC curve.

Figure 2. SEM image of GC

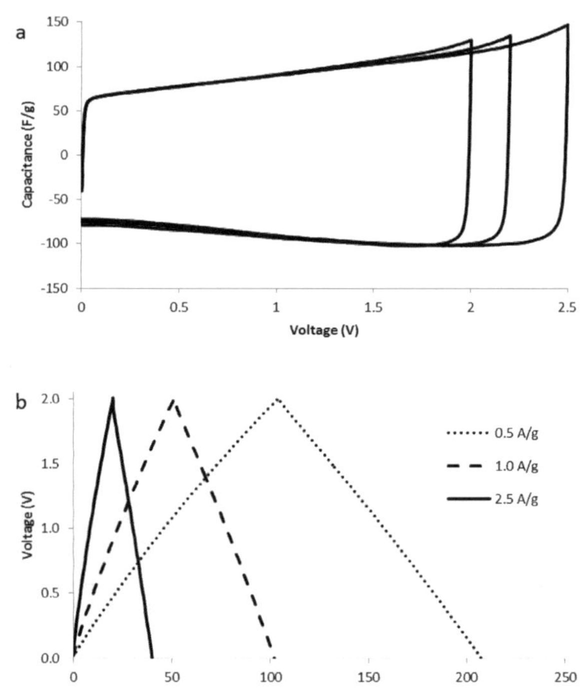

Figure 3. Electrochemical performance of AC in 1.8M $TEMABF_4/PC$. a) CV performance (sweep rate = 20 mV/s), and b) constant current charge/discharge performance.

Figure 5 showed the dependence of capacity on the cycle numbers during a cycle test. The cell was discharging and charging between 0 and 1 V under the constant current of 0.5 A/g for 2000 cycles. The capacitance of the AC only dropped 4% after 2000 cycles.

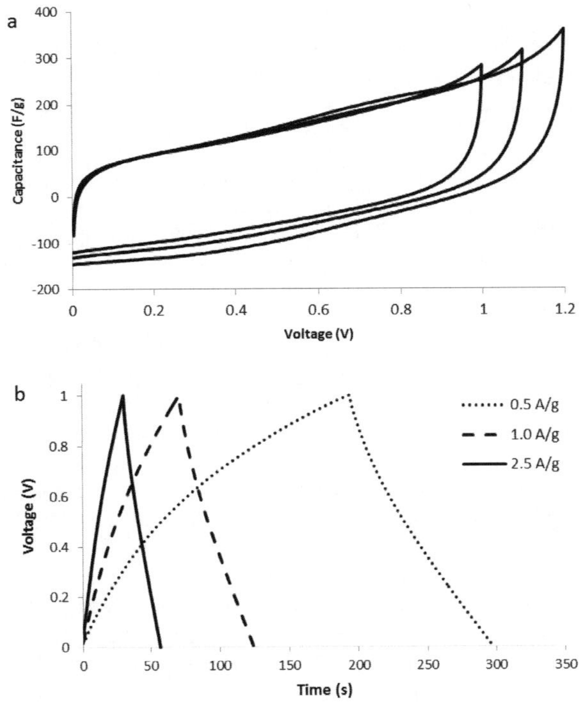

Figure 4. Electrochemical performance of AC in 38 wt.% H_2SO_4. a) CV performance (sweep rate = 20 mV/s), and b) constant current charge/discharge performance.

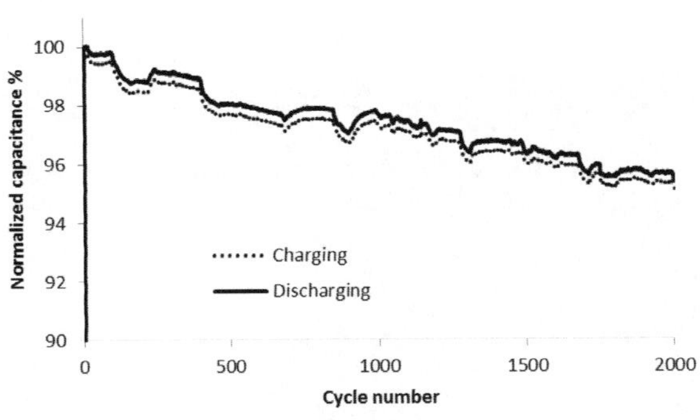

Figure 5. Cycle performance of AC in H_2SO_4.

Conclusions

In summary, high surface area carbon was synthesized using a hypersaline hydrothermal process. The saturated salt contributed to the high surface area and cross-linking structure of the carbon. The as-synthesized carbon was further activated to increase surface area and micro porosity for EDLC applications. The activated carbon showed promising electrochemical performance as electrode materials for EDLCs. Both gravimetric and volumetric capacitance was greatly improved, when compared to conventional activated carbons.

Acknowledgements

The authors wish to acknowledge Ifedi Anyaegbunam and Artashes Ter-Isahakyan for assistance with experimental work.

References

1. Miller J, Simon P. Electrochemical capacitors for energy storage. Science 2008; 321(5889): 651-652.
2. Simon P, Gogotsi Y. Materials for electrochemical capacitors. Nature Materials 2008; 7(11): 845-854.
3. Inagaki M, Konno H, Tanaike O. Carbon materials for electrochemical capacitors. Journal of Power Sources 2010; 195(24): 7880-7903.
4. Fechler N, et al. Salt and sugar: direct synthesis of high surface area carbon materials at low temperature via hydrothermal carbonization of glucose under hypersaline conditions. Joural of Materials Chemistry A 2013; 1: 9418-9421.
5. Hu B, et al. Engineering carbon materials from the hydrothermal carbonization process of biomass. Advanced Materials 2010; 22 (7): 813-828.
6. Sevilla M, Fuertes, A B. The production of carbon materials by hydrothermal carbonization of cellulose. Carbon 2009; 47(9): 2281-2289.
7. Titirici M, Antonietti M, Baccile N. Hydrothermal carbon from biomass: a comparison of the local structure from poly- to monosaccharides and pentoses/hexoses. Green Chemistry 2008; 10(11): 1204-1212.

High Energy Density Ultracapacitors Based on GUITAR-Nanospring Composites

***I. Francis Cheng*[1]*, Isaiah Gyan*[1]*, Haoyu Zhu*[1]*, David N. McIlroy*[2]*, Herbert Hess*[3]**

[1]Department of Chemistry, University of Idaho, Moscow, ID USA
[2]Department of Physics University of Idaho, Moscow, ID USA
[3]Department of Electrical and Computer Engineering University of Idaho,, Moscow, ID 83844-1023
Contact Author Email: hhess@uidaho.edu

Abstract: *The maximum cell voltages in ultracapacitors are limited to the breakdown potential of the electrolyte. Organic electrolyte ultracapacitors are able to produce cell voltages of 3 V or greater. However, manufacturing costs, flammability, and lower ion conductivity makes aqueous systems more preferable. Aqueous systems are limited by the 1.23 V break down of water to hydrogen and oxygen. This limits the practical range for aqueous ultracapacitors to about 1 V cell potential.*

We demonstrate a system capable of a cell potential to 2 V, thereby increasing energy and power densities by nearly 2 orders of magnitude. This disruptive technology will be based on a graphene-like material has been discovered at the University of Idaho that has remarkable electrochemical features.[i-iii] *Graphene from the University of Idaho Thermoylzed Asphalt Reaction (GUITAR) has electrochemical properties that indicate it will surpass present materials. GUITAR itself has visual and microscopic characteristics similar to that of highly oriented pyrolytic graphite (HOPG) which include a metal sheen, and layered characteristics. The figure below summarizes these features.*

Keywords: Composite materials, graphene, ultracapacitors.

Introduction

Despite similarities in appearance, electrochemical studies reveal that GUITAR has physico-chemical properties that distinguish it from other carbon materials. These include (1) rapid electron transfer with redox species ($Fe(CN)_6^{3-/4-}$ and $Ru(NH_3)_6^{3+/2+}$) of 10^{-2} cm/s, and (2) an exceptionally large aqueous potential window of 2 volts in 1 M H_2SO_4. As points of comparison, graphene and HOPG electrodes have rate constants of 10^{-5} to 10^{-9} cm/s with the same redox species and activated carbon has a 1 volt potential window in 1 M H_2SO_4. Faster electron transfer indicates that GUITAR has a higher density of states near the Fermi-level than HOPG or graphene. Other advantages of GUITAR is relatively inexpensive as it can be formed from roofing tar in a controlled combustion procedure and that it produces conformal coatings. An example of the coating process is the deposition of GUITAR on silica nanosprings in the figure below. The area of these composites is 200 m^2/g.

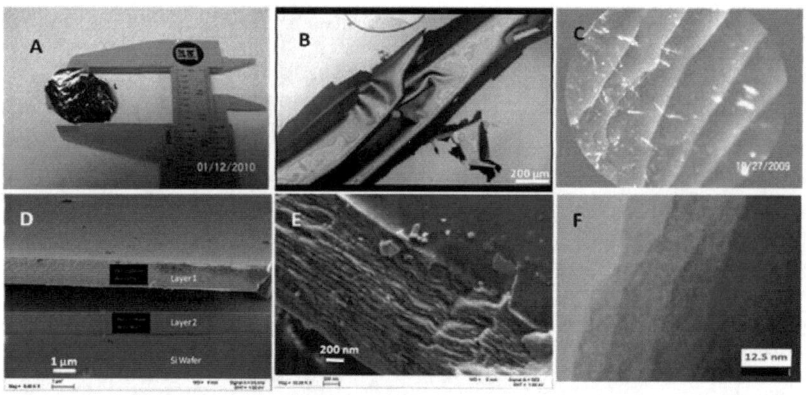

Figure 1. GUITAR graphene, A-a photograph of a flake approximately 25mm in diameter, B-an opticcal micrograph (400x) in water, C-graphene layers (400x), D-9.45K x SEM of microtomed layers on Si, E-23.08K x SEM showing layered characteristics, F-A TEM showing layered characteristics on the nanometer scale.

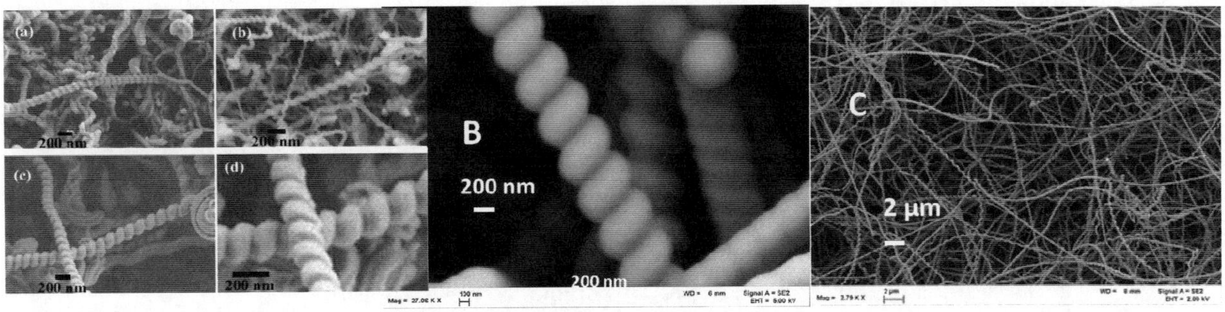

Figure 2. A-Bare Silica nanosprings, B-D Silica nanosprings coated with GUITAR. The process produces evenconformal coatings of 50 nm.

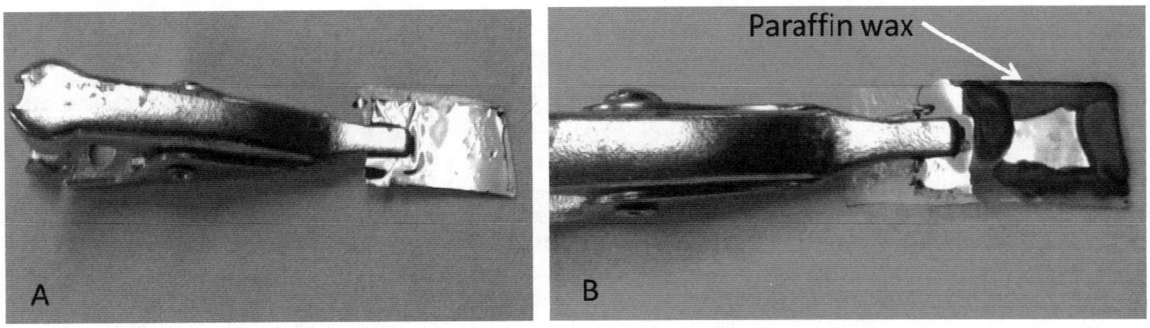

Figure 3. A flat GUITAR mounted electrode, B-Edges sealed in wax.

The combination of properties above indicate that GUITAR has immediate applications in energy storage applications. Ultracapacitors are one such example. The energy stored in these devices ($E = \frac{1}{2} CV^2$), depends on the applied voltage window (V) and the capacitive charge stored.

Preliminary Results.

In order to assess performance flat 0.08 cm^2 electrodes GUITAR and a reference material pyrolytic graphite, were fabricated (see below).Cyclic voltammetric (CV's) analyses in 1 M H_2SO_4 where conducted in a 3 electrode configuration. The aqueous electrochemical window is shown below. The GUITAR electrode can be scanned (50 mV/s) between 1.2 to -0.8 volts in 1 M $H_2SO_4(aq)$ exhibiting primarily only capacitive behavior. The total aqueous windows is 2 volts for GUITAR. On the other hand, the reference materials, pyrolytic graphite and glassy carbon have windows of 0.8 V and 1.3 volts respectively. These windows are shown below in the following cyclic voltammograms. Activated carbon (not shown), is the predominate material in commercial ultracapacitors has potential window of 0.8 V in sulfuric acid. The double layer capacitance can also be obtained from the CV curves as capacitance $C = \frac{i}{dV/dt}$ is obtained from the ration of current (i) and the potential sweep rate (dV/dt).

The capacitance of GUITAR of 640 $\mu F/cm^2$ at 0.1 V in sulfuric acid far exceeds glassy carbon (50 $\mu F/cm^2$) , pyrolytic graphite (7 $\mu F/cm^2$) and literature values of activated carbon (10 - 20 $\mu F/cm^2$).

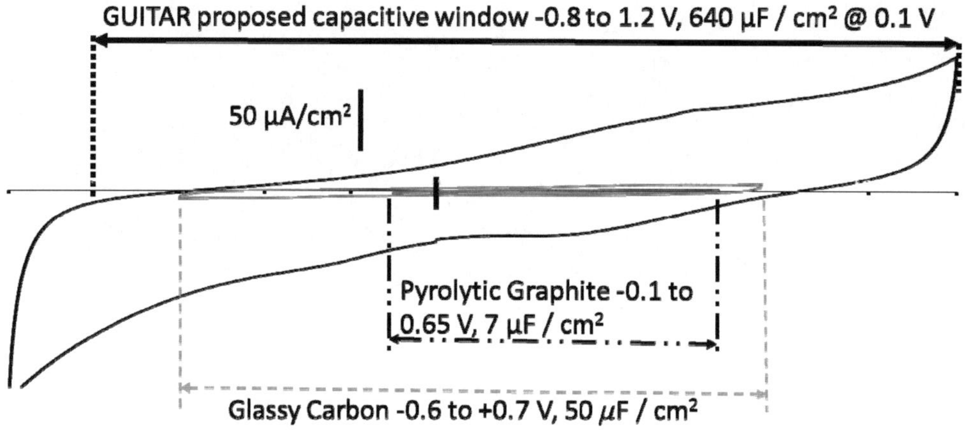

Figure 4. Cyclic voltammetric behavior of GUITAR, pyrolytic graphite, and glassy carbon in 1 M H_2SO_4.

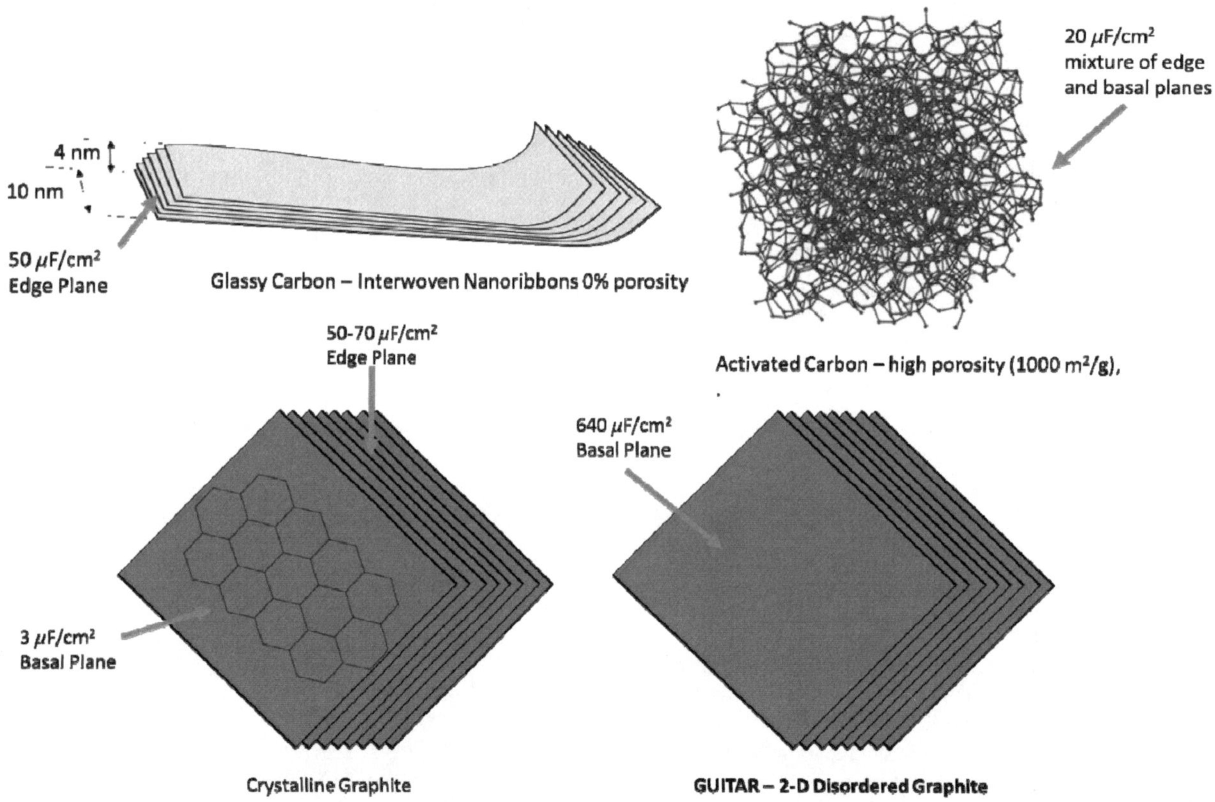

Figure 5. Summary of the capacitive characteristic of glassy carbon, actiavted carbon, crystalline graphites and GUITAR.

Notable, is the comparison of GUITAR with graphite where the basal planes (see below) give a capacitance of 3 μF/cm^2 and the edge plane gives 50-70 μF/cm^2. The following diagram illustrates the capacitive behavior of GUITAR with other carbon materials.

The edge planes of glassy carbon equivalent to those of crystalline graphites (including HOPG). Glassy carbon is a series of tightly woven graphitic nanoribbons with zero porosity and significant exposure of edge planes towards the electrolyte solution. Activated carbon is a porous high surface area (1000 m^2/g) particulate with a mixture of exposed basal and edge planes. It therefore has a capacitance (10-20 μF/cm^2) intermediate of the edge and basal planes of crystalline graphite. However in this sequence, GUITAR has the unexpected behavior of capacitance of 640 μF/cm^2 on its basal plane. Notably, basal planes of GUITAR exceed the capacitance of the edge planes of graphite and glassy carbon by an order of maginitude. We attribute this behavior to the relative disorder of the GUITAR carbon lattice.

Another significant consideration is the applicable potential window of the electrode materials. In terms of energy applications GUITAR on nanosprings have a surface area deficit when compared to activated carbon (200 vs. 1000 m^2/g). However, when increased capacitance and cell voltage is considered GUITAR-based devices will have specific energies that will be nearly two orders of magnitude greater than present ultracapacitors. We expect that GUITAR is a breakthrough material for this application. We will report on preliminary results with the GUITAR on nanospring device.

Summary

GUITAR-nanospring composites are a breakthrough material for aqueous ultracapacitors. Both cell potentials and capacitances are dramatically improved over conventional materials. Increases of cell potential from 1V to 2V and capacitances from 10 μF/cm^2 to 640 μF/cm^2 are demonstrated. The calculated specific energy of the GUITAR-nanospring composite is expected to be 2600 J/g as compared to 30-50 J/g for present designs.

References

1. "Synthesis of graphene paper from pyrolyzed asphalt" I. Francis Cheng, Yuqun Xie, R. Allen Gonzales, Przemysław R. Brejna, Jency Pricilla Sundararajan, B.A. Fouetio Kengne, D. Eric Aston, David N. McIlroy, Jeremy D. Foutch, Peter R. Griffiths, Carbon, 2011, 49, 2852-2861.
2. "Sulfur as an important co-factor in the formation of multilayer graphene in the thermolyzed asphalt reaction" Yuqun Xie, Simon D. McAllister, Seth A. Hyde, Jency Pricilla Sundararajan, B. A. Fouetio Kengne, David N. McIlroy and I. Francis Cheng, *J. Mater. Chem.* **2012**, 22, 5723-5729.
3. "Highest measured anodic stability in aqueous solutions: graphenic electrodes from the thermolyzed asphalt reaction" I. Francis Cheng, Yuqun Xie, Isaiah Owusu Gyan and Nolan W. Nicholas, *RSC Advances*, **2013**, 3, 2379-2384..

Improved Capacitance Using Vertical Arrays of Ag Nanowires

Ke Xu, Daniel K. Choi, Herbert L. Hess, L. Ryan Litzko, Amrit Dahal
University of Idaho
875 Perimeter Drive, Moscow, Idaho USA 83844

Abstract: In recent years, one-dimensional nanostructured materials have brought wide scientific and commercial attentions due to their novel physical and chemical properties for their potential applications in the areas of electronics, photonics, energies, and medicine. In this work, a complementary metal-oxide-semiconductor (CMOS) compatible process has been designed and demonstrated for fabricating on-chip capacitors based on silver (Ag) nanowires as electrodes for integrated circuits (IC). Both an electrodeposition-based process and a soft-solution process for synthesizing Ag nanowires using anodized aluminum oxide (AAO) nanoporous templates were examined. Vertical arrays of Ag nanowires were grown in the pores of high aspect-ratio AAO templates which were already grown on titanium (Ti)/silicon oxide (SiO_2)/silicon (Si) substrates. A thin-film of bismuth ferric oxide (BFO) was deposited by electrodeposition as a high dielectric constant material between a Ag nanowire electrode and a Ag thin-film electrode. The Ag thin-film was deposited as the second electrode on the BFO by DC sputtering. It was found that Ag nanowires-based capacitor possessed approximately one-order of magnitude higher capacitance than Ag thin-film capacitor. The capacitance value of Ag nanowires-based capacitor was measured and was found to be $0.72nF/mm^2$ at 1MHz. Morphology of Ag nanowire electrodes was investigated by field emission scanning electron microscopy (FESEM). [1]

Keywords: nanowires; capacitor fabrication

Introduction

Decreasing the size of materials to nanometer scales has application in various fields. The properties of materials at these scales are different from bulk amount of the material in question. In recent years, one dimension (1D) nanostructured materials have generated interest due to their novel physical and chemical properties and potential applications. The following paper details the development of a three dimensional (3D) nanowire structure in order to increase capacitance per volume.

To design a nanowire based capacitor a short description of the materials used is given. Silver (Ag) has some nice properties that are advantageous in nanoparticle design, such as:

1. They provide a large surface to volume ratio since they have a diameter less than 100nm.
2. They can be used as conductive electrode by using it with highly conductive percolation pathways. [2]
3. They are electromagnetically robust, having good mechanical flexibility. [3]
4. Due to their mechanical properties, they can be used as transparent conductive electrodes as their aspect ratio can be controlled during synthesis, [4]
5. They serve as a unique class of physical and chemical templates for fabricating metal/dielectric core/shell, and metal nanotubes. [3]

Anodized Aluminum Oxide (AAO) has tunable pore dimensions, mechanical strength and thermal stability and can achieve uniform hexagonally ordered, high pore density channels. [5] [6] Unlike track-etched membranes, the anodized alumina has little tiles on the pores relative to the surface normal, resulting in an isolating, non-connecting pore structure. [7] Since template synthesis is considered a common nanowire fabrication method, the AAO template which is widely used for fabricating conductive polymers, metallic and semiconductor nanowires inexpensively and reliably, was selected. [8]

Bismuth Ferric Oxide ($BiFeO_3$ or BFO) is a high dielectric material selected for an on-chip CMOS microcapacitor because BFO is easily deposited by electrodeposition using a room-temperature process. [9]

Formation Process

The nanowire structure was done on a silicon substrate employing electrodeposition. The substrate had to be prepped before depositing Ag and processed afterward to have a solid electric connection. The process is shown in Figure 1 and a description of each step is given below.

1. Substrate Preparation: Layers of 2 μm thick Al and 100 nm thick Ti were deposited on Si02(100nm thick)/Si substrate by DC sputtering after which the fine aluminum coated wafer was sliced into little pieces and mounted on a glass slide with a copper type attached to it.
2. Anodization: Growth of regular self-ordered cylindrical pores from the surface of Al layer was initiated, and the pore diameter controlled, by applying anodizing conditions of 20V at 20^0C in 0.3M oxalic acid electrolyte where platinum (Pt) acted as a cathode and the pre-sputtered Al layer acted as anode.
3. Pore-Widening: Pore widening thins out the barrier layer at the bottom of the AAO pore array and improves conductivity for the metal during the electrodeposition process, and was done by immersing the sample into 5% phosphoric acid (H_3PO_4).

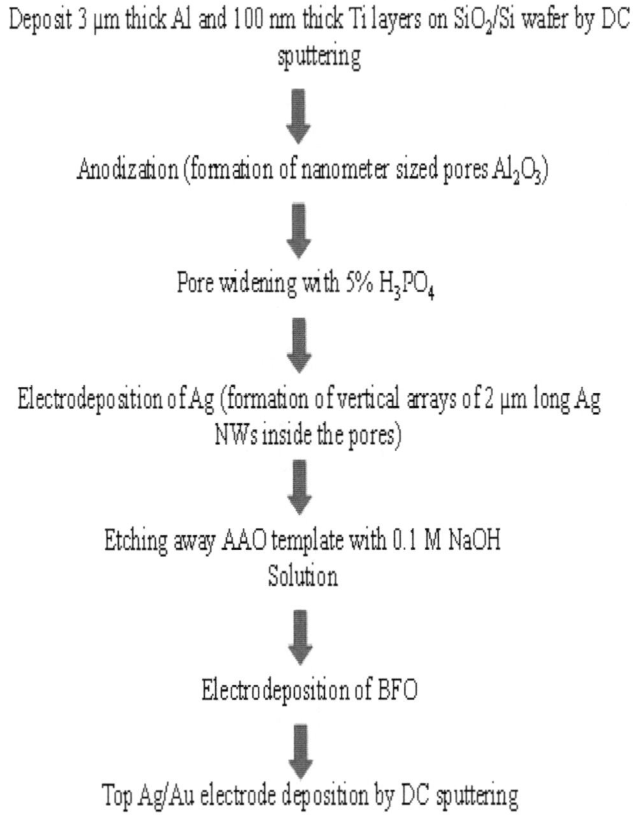

Figure 1. The fabrication process of Ag nanowires based on an on-chip capacitor

4. Electrodeposition of Ag: An Niobium (Nb) anode and sample chip as cathode were immersed in a commercial silver plating solution (1025 RTU@4.5 Troy/Gallon, respectively; Technic Inc., Cranston, RI), and Ag was deposited to the cathode by applying a constant current density of 10 mA/cm^2 using potentiostat/galvanostat model VersaSTAT MC-4 of Princeton Applied Research. Care had to be taken to ensure that the Ag nanowire length was less than the AAO layer thickness, and this was controlled by the electrodeposition timing. For 2 µm long Ag nanowires grown inside 3 µm AAO pores, the applicable parameters are presented in Table 1.
5. Etching AAO Template: The sample was immersed in 0.1M sodium hydroxide (NaOH) solution for 30 minutes during the wet etching process to remove the AA0 template on the substrate and expose the vertical arrays of Ag nanowires.

Table 1. The parameters for Ag electrodeposition

Parameters	Containing and values
Bath solution	Silver plating solution (1025 RTU, Tech Inc.)
Current density	10 mA/cm^2
Deposition rate	0.6 µm /minute
Deposition time	200 seconds
Bath temperature	300K

6. Electrodeposition of bismuth ferric oxide (BFO): A thin film of BFO was deposited on the sample, again using electrodeposition with an Nb plate anode in a solution of 0.1 M $Bi(NO_3)_2$ and 0.1 M $Fe(NO_3)_2$. A thickness greater than the Ag nanowire length was required and thus 4 µm thick layer BFO was deposited by implementing the parameters presented in Table 2.

Table 2. Parameters for electrodeposition of BFO film

Parameters	Containing and values
Bath composition	(150 mL) 0.1 M Bi $(NO_3)_2$ + (100 mL) 0.1 M Fe $(NO_3)_2$
Current density	6 mA/cm^2
Deposition rate	100 nm/minute
Deposition time	40 minutes
Bath temperature	300K

7. Top Electrode Deposition: The topside electrode was deposited on the Ag nanowire embedded BFO dielectric layer using the sputtering process which was selected because electrodeposition couldn't precisely control the deposition thickness.

An illustration of the fabrication process with the resulting intermediate structure formation is shown in Figure 2.

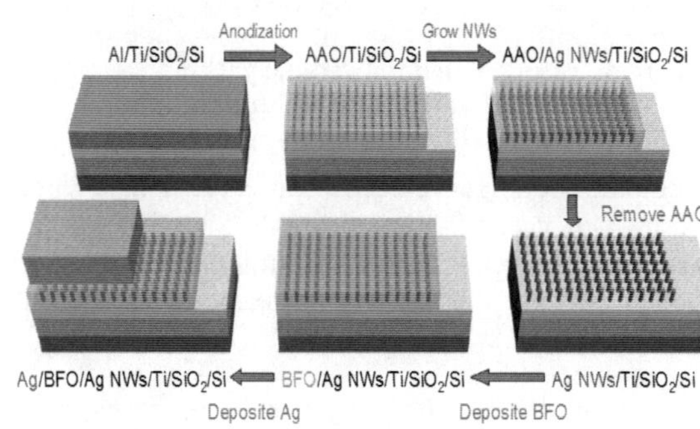

Figure 2. Illustrated fabrication process of Ag nanowires for an on-chip capacitor

Results

Figure 3 shows the schematic and composition of the variable components in the nanowire sample.

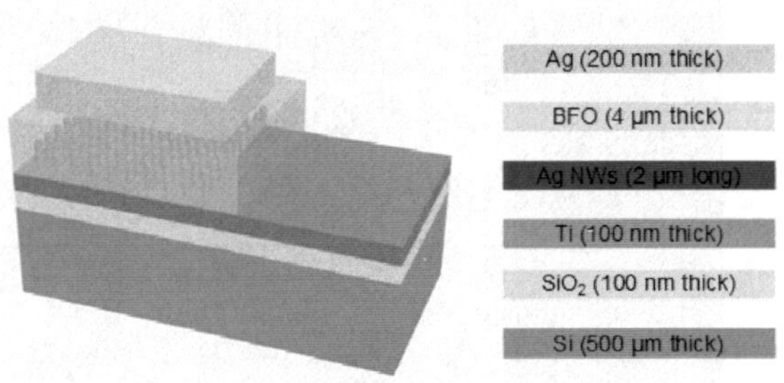

Figure 3. Schematic of Ag nanowires-based on-chip capacitor. The thickness of each layer is listed.

Figure 4 shows the Ag nanowire on the fabricated sample. The exposed nanowires are seen slightly bent, this was caused during the wet etching process when the exposed nanowires stuck together to minimize energy in the system. Regardless of this nanowire bending, the surface area of the cathode electrode was dramatically increased by the dense arrays of Ag nanowires.

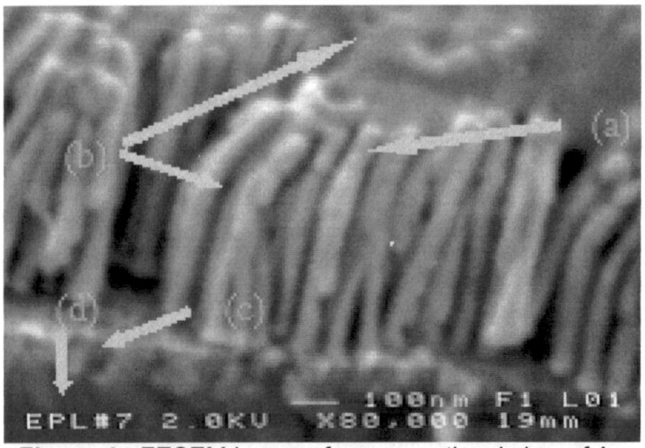

Figure 4.: FESEM image of cross-sectional view of Ag nanowires embedded in BFO films on a silicon substrate at high magnification. The arrows (a), (b), (c), (d) indicate 'Ag nanowires', 'BFO', 'Titanium', 'SiO_2', respectively. The Ag nanowires are aligned vertically with an average diameter of 30-40 nm.

To compare the improved capacitance using nanowire, an Ag thin film capacitor was on a $Pt/SiO_2/Si$ chip using similar processes as 4, 6 and 7 from above. The resulting capacitances were measured at frequencies ranging from 100Hz to 1000 MHz. The results are seen in Figure 5.

Measured at 1MHz, the capacitance for the nanowire design was measured to be $0.72nF/mm^2$ and for thin-film it was measured to be $0.07nF/mm^2$. The results clearly show that using Ag nanowire capacitor provides superior performance than its thin-film counterpart.

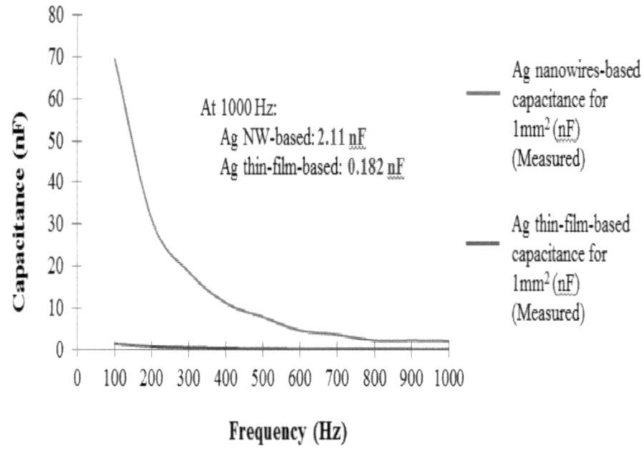

Figure 5: Plot of capacitance vs. frequency for the both Ag nanowires-based and Ag thin-film-based capacitor.

Application in CMOS IC On-Chip Power Supplies

Ag nanowire can be used for on-chip capacitors in CMOS integrated circuit (IC) design. The capacitance improvement gained by this technology enables larger values of capacitance to be placed on the chip. The large frequency-dependent capacitance provides important advantages in nonlinear filtering of power supply outputs. These are an important step toward the eventual goal of an on-chip power supply. .

Conclusions

An array of silver nanowires has been fabricated and verified experimentally as an electrode for a capacitor in a CMOS compatible process. The dielectric is Bismuth Ferric Oxide, a material easily deposited in an electrodeposition process at room temperature. These capacitors exhibit about ten times the capacitance per unit area as the incumbent on-chip capacitance technology. Capacitance values decrease significantly at higher frequencies, though they still greatly exceed current technology.

References

1. K. Xu, "Fabrication and Characterization of Vertical Arrays of Ag Nanowires Grown on Silicon Substrates and Its Application as Electrode Materials in On-chip Capacitors for Integrated Circuits," University of Idaho, Moscow, Idaho, 2012.
2. L. Hu, D. Hecht and G. Gruner, "Percolation in Transparent and Conducting Carbon Nanotube Networks," *Nano Lett,* vol. 4, pp. 2513-2517, 2004.
3. S. Yuyang, "Silver Nanowires- Unique Templates for Functional Nanostructure," *Nanoscale,* vol. 2, pp. 1626-1642, 2010.
4. H. Liangbing, S. K. Han, Y. L. Jung, P. Peter and C. Yi, "Scalable Coating and Properties of Transparent,

Flexible, Silver Nanowire Electrode," *ACS Nano* , vol. 4, pp. 2955-2963, 2010.

5. X. Sun, F. Xu, Z. Li and W. Zhang, "Cyclic Voltammetry for the Fabrication of High Dense Silver Nanowire Arrays with the Assistance of AAO Template," *Material Chemistry and Physics,* vol. 90, pp. 69-72, 2005.
6. Z. Hu, T. Xu, R. Liu and H. Li, "Template Preparation of High-Density and Large-Area Ag Nanowire Array by Acetaldehyde Reduction," *Materials Science and Engineering A,* vol. 371, pp. 236-240, 2004.
7. N. Myung, J. Lim, J. Fleurial, M. Yun, W. West and D. Choi, "Alumina Nanotemplate Fabrication on Silicon Substrate," *Nanotechnology,* vol. 15, pp. 833-838, 2004.
8. J. Chen, "Fabrication of Nanomaterial using Porous Templates," University of Massachusetts, Ann Arbor, 2009.
9. S. Jo, S. Lee and S. Lee, "Structural and Pyroelectric Properties of Sol-Gel Derived Multiferroic BFO Thin-Films," *Materials Research Bulletin,* vol. 47, pp. 409-412, 2012.

Differential Capacity-Based Modeling for In-Use Battery Diagnostics, Prognostics, and Quality Assurance

Lauren M. Marzocca and Terrill B. Atwater
U.S. Army RDECOM
Communications, Electronics, Research, Development and Engineering Center
Aberdeen Proving Ground, MD 21005

Abstract: *A reliable diagnostic/prognostic indicator for electrochemical systems would allow for the prediction of cell failures, a function that would improve battery safety, efficiency, and quality assurance. The technique of differential capacity has proven to be a useful tool in the pursuit of this type of diagnostic/prognostic device. The plots resulting from the differential capacity technique provide a "fingerprint" of a battery system that can be tracked throughout its life, and changes in these plots give insight into the future behavior of the system. The results of several cell-level galvanostatic experiments – performed on several different chemistry types – will be discussed with respect to differential capacity. This type of galvanostatic cell data was analyzed in order to develop a differential capacity-based model for use in a diagnostic/prognostic device.*

Keywords: state of health; safety; rechargeable lithium-ion battery

Introduction

Differential capacity tracks an electrochemical system's capacity increase on charge or decrease on discharge as a function of potential. Plotting differential capacity versus potential creates a snapshot "fingerprint" of the system that can be tracked throughout the system's life. These fingerprints show how characteristic features of the curve change and, unlike the traditional potential versus time curves, give information regarding both the underlying thermodynamics and kinetics of the system. Figure 1 gives a visual comparison between a standard potential versus time discharge plot and a differential capacity plot generated from the same test data. Monitoring the changes in a system's electrochemical properties through differential capacity can help predict failure. This prognostic capability would be useful in preventing safety incidents while also ensuring that a cell or battery is removed from service only after being used to its fullest extent.

Background

Through the Capability Needs Analysis (CNA) process, the U.S. Army derives a list of specific Warfighter requirements that are not currently being met. These requirements are known as CNA gaps. Two power- and energy-related CNA gaps state that "forces lack ability to accurately monitor and manage power demand and supply processes" and that "forces lack comprehensive, institutional awareness of the impact of energy use on operational effectiveness and need to consider efficient use of energy as a mission enabler."[1] The development of an effective battery diagnostic/prognostic device directly addresses both of these gaps.

A paper investigating the usefulness of the differential capacity technique as a fingerprinting tool for electrochemical systems was presented at the 44th Power Sources Conference.[2] This paper discussed the establishment of the fingerprinting method and included experiments to determine charge/discharge rates (Figure 2) and potential integration periods (Figure 3) to optimize data fidelity while maintaining test efficiency. To date, the differential capacity technique has been successfully used to study electrochemical systems of varying chemistries, sizes, and configurations.

Differential capacity was initially investigated as a quality assurance tool. Generating the differential capacity curves of two identical cells will yield nearly identical curves; therefore, the technique can be used to indentify inconsistencies in a production environment. Analysis of this quality assurance data revealed the possibility for using differential capacity as a prognostic tool. Any changes made to the components of an electrochemical system (different electrodes, electrolyte, material ratios, etc.) as well as any changes in testing conditions (different rates, temperatures, abusive conditions, etc.) will cause changes in that system's fingerprint. This aspect of the differential capacity technique has inherent predictive capabilities which could be leveraged in a diagnostic/prognostic device.

Failure Prognosis

Experimental: An experiment was designed to bring out cell failure through high-rate charging. The goal was to monitor changes in the differential capacity curve with each cycle of the test and to observe which characteristic feature(s) of the curve changes as a result of performance degradation. A 3.4 Ah NMC 18650 cell was subjected to a cycle life test with a 2 A constant current charge, a 0.8 A constant current discharge, a potential range of 2.5-4.4 V, and a potential integration period of 10 mV. The differential capacity curves were tracked as the cell was cycled (Figures 4-6).

Results: The cell experienced significant potential fluctuation during cycles 9 and 10 but was able to recover for the latter portion of the test, which was stopped at cycle 17. A differential capacity curve was created for each cycle of the test. The curve progression is shown in Figure 4. The blue curves indicate the cycles before the potential fluctuation, the green curves indicate the cycles during which the fluctuation occurred, and the red curves indicate the cycles after the fluctuation.

Discussion: Figure 5 shows the charge curves for cycles 2-8 (before the potential fluctuation), and Figure 6 shows the charge curves for cycles 11-17 (after the potential fluctuation). The characteristic feature of note for this cell is the second charge peak that appears at approximately 3.8 V. As the cycle number increases, in addition to the expected rightward shift, the second charge peak begins to fade. Immediately after the potential fluctuation, the peak has disappeared entirely. This experiment shows that, for this chemistry, the second charge peak is an indicator of the cell's overall state of health and can therefore be used to predict cell failure in a prognostic device.

Modeling

Experimental: Once the concept of using the differential capacity curve as an indicator for state of health was established, a method of quantifying changes in the curve had to be developed. The Gaussian curve was used as the basis for the differential capacity model. The first experiment that was modeled featured a representative spinel button cell of approximately 10 mAh that was subjected to a 3.5-4.75 V cycle at a rate of 1 mA. A Gaussian curve was used to model the experimental data manually. The general equation for a Gaussian function is given by

$$f(x) = ae^{-\frac{(x-b)^2}{2c^2}} + d. \quad (1)$$

For this particular application, *f(x)* equals the differential capacity at potential x. Coefficients a, b, and c are the curve-defining parameters and were adjusted manually until the best fit was achieved. Table 1 shows the relationship of each coefficient to its corresponding peak and details what physical values or processes dictate the coefficient values.

Table 1. Gaussian curve-defining coefficients.

Coefficient	Effect on Curve	Function of...
a	Height	Theoretical capacity
b	Position	Theoretical potential (impedance, activation energy, polarization)
c	Width	Diffusion

Results and Discussion: The first attempt evaluated the accuracy of a two-curve model to simulate the behavior of the spinel button cell, as shown in Figure 7. This method captured the main features of the experimental data but allowed for significant error in certain areas, namely the flat portions of the curve at low and high potential and the area between the two peaks. To account for this, a third Gaussian curve was added to the model, as shown in Figure 8.

Figures 9-11 show the differential capacity curves and corresponding three-curve Gaussian models at three points – cycles 10, 80, and 130 – during the cycle life test of the aforementioned spinel button cell. Visual inspection of the experimental data indicates a slight change in several of the characteristic features as cycle number increases, especially from cycle 80 to cycle 130. However, if differential capacity curves are to be used in a practical state of health device, these feature changes must be quantified. This can be accomplished by monitoring changes in model curve coefficients a, b, and c throughout the life of the cell.

Figures 12 and 13 show the values of coefficients a, b, and c for each of the three Gaussian curves in the model over the life cycle of the cell. Data was analyzed at 10-cycle intervals from cycle 10 to cycle 130. The b and c coefficients, shown in Figure 12, follow fairly constant trends throughout the life of the cell. The a coefficients, however, shown in Figure 13, begin straying from their respective trends at cycle 80 and then do so more evidently beginning at cycle 110. Monitoring the changes in the coefficients brings out subtle performance degradation in the cell that might not be noticed with only visual inspection of the differential capacity curves. With further testing of different chemistries, a tolerance can be established for each coefficient, which can then be implemented into a diagnostic/prognostic device.

Figure 14 shows the differential capacity curves and the corresponding three-curve Gaussian models (charge only) for cycles 2-5, 10, and 15 of a silicon anode pouch cell. The success of this model indicates that the three-curve Gaussian model is transferrable to other chemistries and cell types. Additionally, this model data shows that, by breaking the experimental data down into three base Gaussian curves and monitoring how each of these curves changes as the cell is cycled, the source of the degradation – in this case, the low charge peak – can be pinpointed. With a more thorough knowledge of the physical relevance of each individual Gaussian curve, the model will allow degradation to be pinpointed to a particular component or chemical process within the cell. This capability would be advantageous for both the research and testing communities, where it could be used to more efficiently target recurring issues with new chemistries and manufactured cells.

Conclusion

The results of this work show that the differential capacity method enhances the ability to predict cell failure and that differential capacity curves can be accurately modeled using Gaussian curves. This type of model utilizes a, b, and c coefficients to quantify and monitor curve changes, which is important if this technique is to be implemented in an in-use battery diagnostic/prognostic device. Future work will include the investigation of other types of failure modes in order to increase the robustness of the method and obtain the necessary data for device implementation.

The three-curve Gaussian model was able to be transferred to a different chemistry and cell type. In the future, more chemistries and cell types will be modeled using the three-curve method to determine whether other types of models will need to be explored. It is also important to understand the physical relevance of each of the model curves in order to better identify the precise causes of cell failure.

References

1. DiGiosaffatte, M. "Capability Needs Analysis." *Army Capabilities Integration Center.* http://www.arcic.army.mil/Articles/aid-Capability-Needs-Analysis.aspx.
2. Atwater, T.B., P.C. Tavares, and L.M. Marzocca. *P. 44th Power Sources Conference*, 2010.
3. Wright, R.B., et al. *P. 201st Meeting of the Electrochemical Society*, 2002.
4. Bloom, I., et al. *P. 204th Meeting of the Electrochemical Society*, 2003.

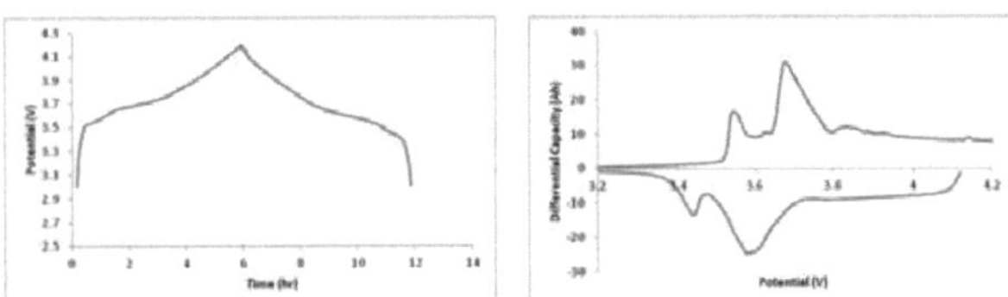

Figure 1. Standard potential vs. time discharge curve compared with corresponding differential capacity curve for a 2.4 Ah NMC 18650 cell.

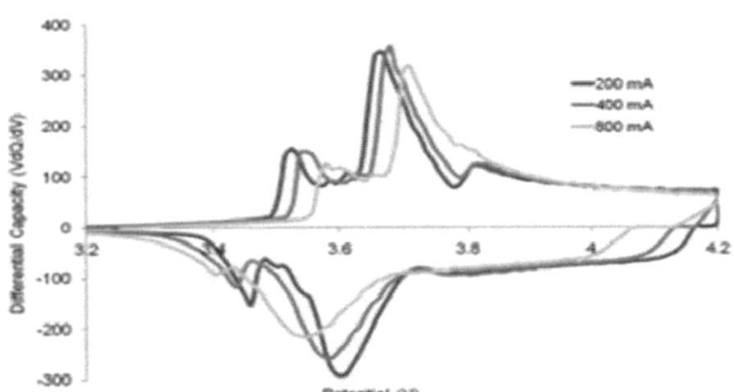

Figure 2. Differential capacity curves comparing data fidelity at varying charge/discharge rates for a 2.4 Ah NMC 18650 cell.

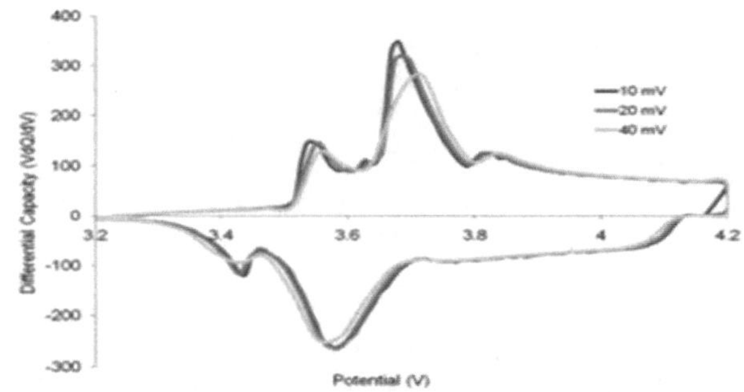

Figure 3. Differential capacity curves comparing data fidelity at varying potential integration periods for a 2.4 Ah NMC 18650 cell.

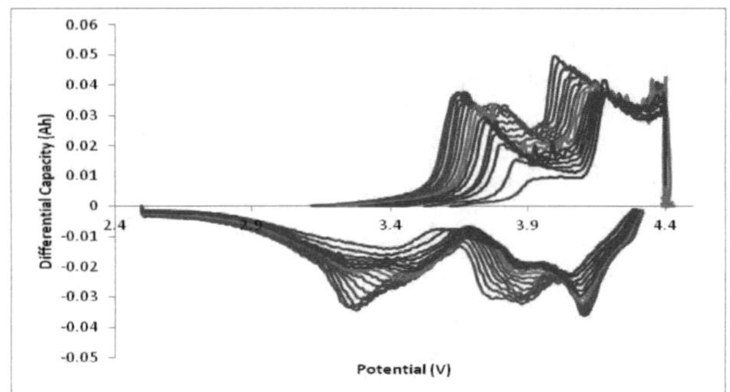

Figure 4. Progression of differential capacity curves during cycle life test for a 3.4 Ah NMC 18650 cell.

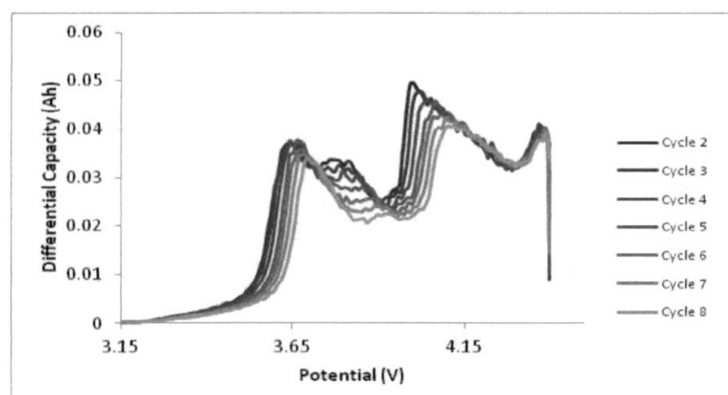

Figure 5. Charge curves before potential fluctuation for a 3.4 Ah NMC 18650 cell.

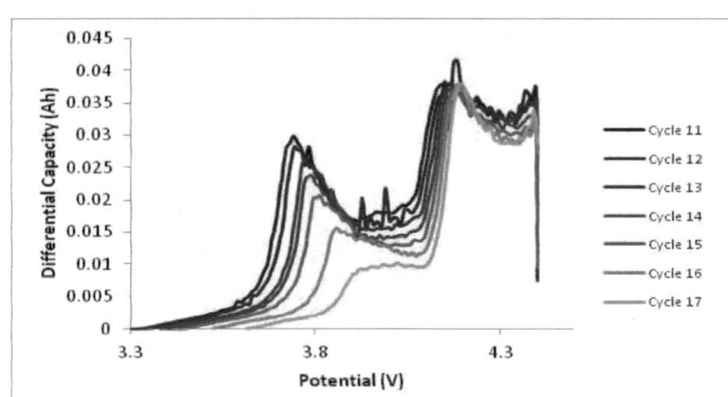

Figure 6. Charge curves after potential fluctuation for a 3.4 Ah NMC 18650 cell.

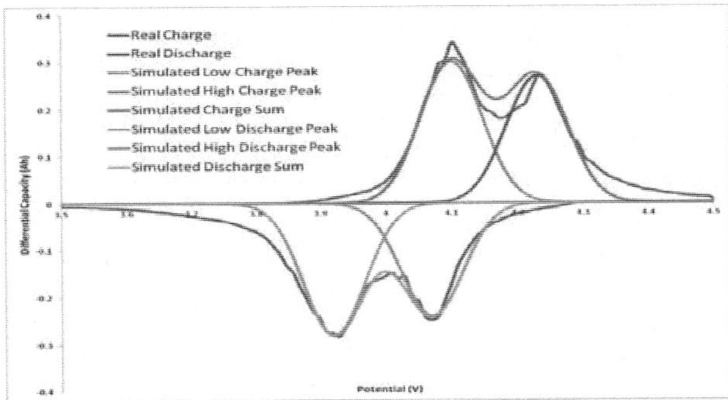

Figure 7. Differential capacity curve with its two-curve Gaussian model for a spinel button cell.

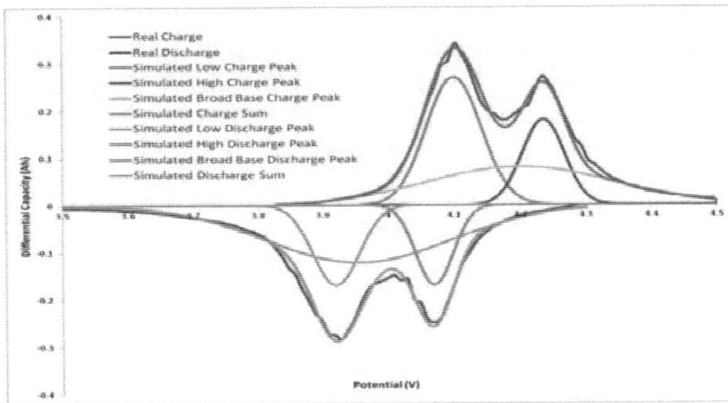

Figure 8. Differential capacity curve with its three-curve Gaussian model for a spinel button cell.

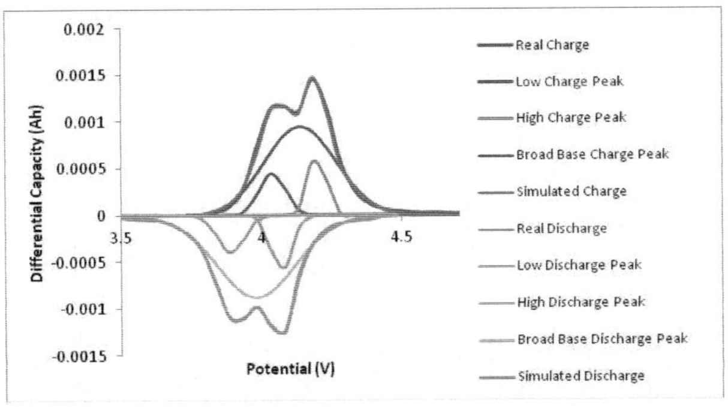

Figure 9. Differential capacity curve with three-curve Gaussian model for a spinel button cell at cycle 10.

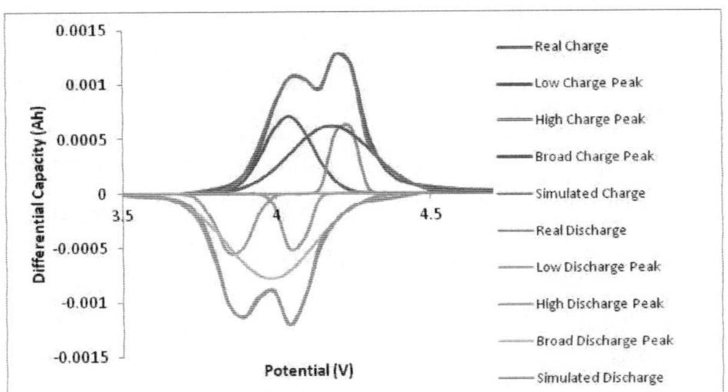

Figure 10. Differential capacity curve with three-curve Gaussian model for a spinel button cell at cycle 80.

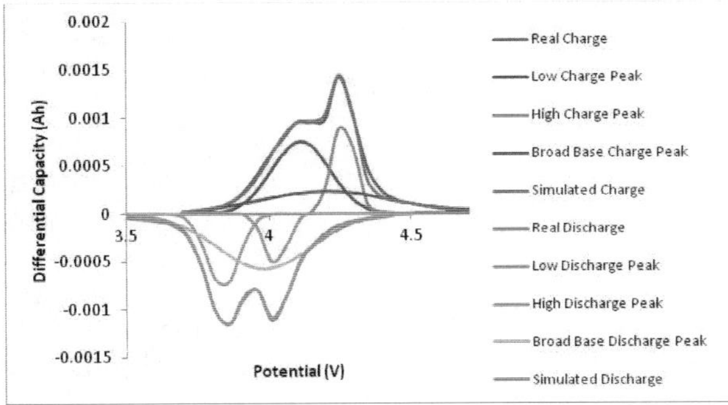

Figure 11. Differential capacity curve with three-curve Gaussian model for a spinel button cell at cycle 130.

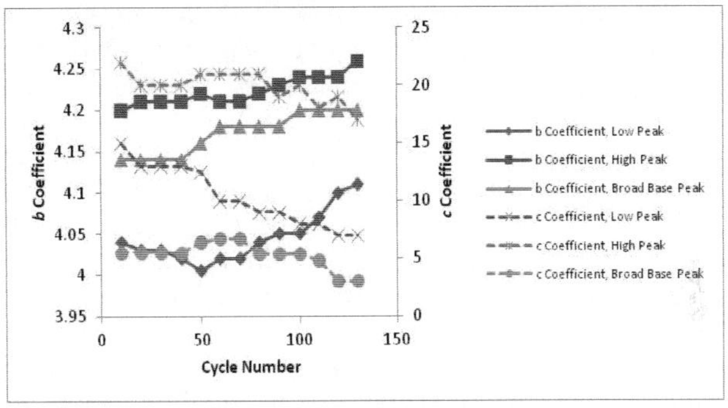

Figure 12. The "*b*" and "*c*" charge coefficients for the three-curve Gaussian model over the life cycle a spinel button cell. The "*b*" coefficients correspond to the primary axis, and the "*c*" coefficients correspond to the secondary axis.

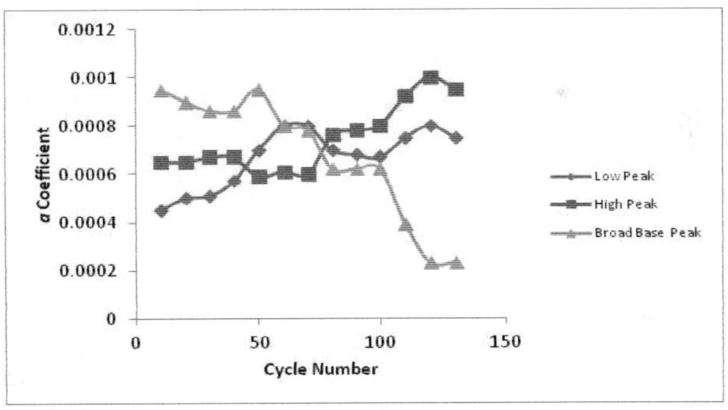

Figure 13. The "*a*" charge coefficients for the three-curve Gaussian model over the life cycle of a spinel button cell.

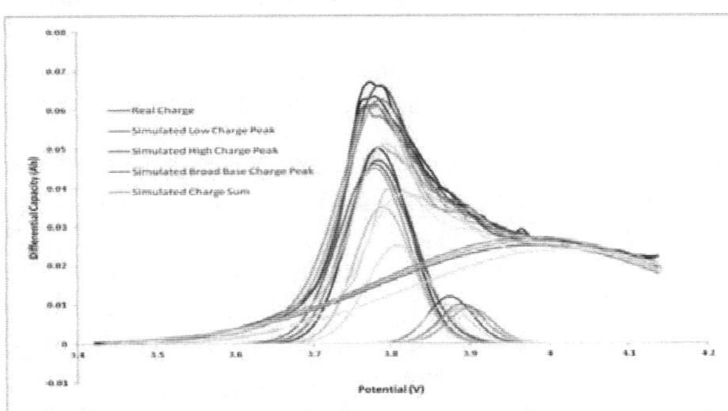

Figure 14. Differential capacity charge curve over the life cycle of a silicon anode pouch cell.

Performance Evaluation of Lithium Ion and Lithium Polymer Batteries Subjected to a High-Impact Shock Event

Edward F. Bukowski
Guidance Technologies Branch / Lethality Division
Weapons Materials Research Directorate
U.S. Army Research Laboratory
Aberdeen Proving Ground, Maryland, USA, 21005
edward.f.bukowski4.civ@mail.mil

Abstract: *An investigation of the survivability and performance of rechargeable lithium batteries subjected to a high-G impact event was recently conducted as part of a research effort into the development of an advanced lethality and accuracy system for a medium caliber 30-mm projectile. Instrumentation of these 30-mm projectiles required a reliable proven power source that could survive the harsh ballistic launch environment. Gun-launched munitions of this type experience setback accelerations which can range from several thousand to tens of thousands of G's during launch. High-G impact experiments were conducted using the U.S. Army Research Laboratory's air-gun facility to achieve shock levels in excess of 60,000G's. The scope of the experiments was limited to lithium-ion cylindrical (model CR2) and lithium-ion polymer (80mAh to 200mAh) cells evaluated in different orientations. Post-impact analysis produced mixed results, with multiple cells exhibiting reduced capacity or complete electrical failure. Several cells were disassembled, and structural anomalies, most likely due to impact, were noted. This paper provides details on experiment execution and individual cell performance.*

Keywords: lithium ion polymer; high-G; munitions

Introduction

The Guidance Technologies Branch (GTB) of the U.S. Army Research Laboratory (ARL) has been actively involved in the research and development of advanced concepts which are contributing to the demonstration of gun-launched precision-fired munitions. These concepts have led to the design and implementation of a variety of diagnostic and guidance, navigation and control systems for a wide range of ballistic projectiles [1][2].

GTB was recently tasked by the Armament Research, Development and Engineering Center (ARDEC) to design and fabricate an instrumented 30-mm projectile as part of their Advanced Lethality and Accuracy System for Medium Caliber (ALAS-MC) program [3]. Execution of this effort presented several unique challenges as the space available for instrumentation was very limited and the projectile launch acceleration was estimated to be anywhere in the range of 60,000G's (60kG) to 85,000G's (85kG). The final design incorporated a miniaturized sensor suite and telemetry package that provided real-time in-flight inertial measurements. These on-board electronics had a minimum operating voltage of 3 volts (V) and current draw of 500 milliamps (mA), which allowed for the use of a single lithium ion (Li-Ion) cell to power the system. A volume having a 22-mm diameter (D) and 28-mm height (H) was allocated for this power source. Rechargeability was also a requirement since the cell was embedded within the projectile and could not be replaced once the unit was assembled. A CR2 model Li-Ion rechargeable cylindrical cell was the first choice due to its standard size of 15.6-mm D by 27-mm H and 3.6-V nominal voltage. It was also chosen based on results from a previous GTB study that evaluated the high-G performance of similar CR2 lithium primary cells. These cells survived accelerations up to 30kG, but significant reductions in performance were noted at levels around 65kG [4]. 400 milliamp-hour (mAh) and 600mAh Li-Ion CR2 cells were chosen for evaluation at higher acceleration levels.

Several lithium ion polymer (LiPo) pouch cells were also chosen for evaluation, but choices were limited due to the small space available and typical rectangular shape of most commercial LiPo cells. 80mAh, 125mAh and 200mAh models were chosen for evaluation. The 80mAh cells were small enough to lay flat within the battery cavity (table 1). The 125mAh and 200mAh models would only fit if mounted in a vertical orientation. This presented a problem as these cells have been shown to potentially fail at high-G levels when mounted vertically [5].

Table 1. Cells chosen for high-G evaluation

Lithium Ion CR2 Cylindrical Cells		
Capacity	**Dimensions (mm)**	**Orientation**
600mAh	15.6(D) x 27(H)	vertical
400mAh	15.6(D) x 27(H)	vertical
Lithium Polymer Pouch Cells		
80mAh	21(L) x 12(W) x 5(H)	flat
125mAh	34(L) x 11(W) x 5.5(H)	vertical
200mAh	35(L) x 12(W) x 6.5(H)	vertical

High-G Air-Gun Experimentation

The high-G impact results obtained in this study were acquired through the use of the 4 inch air-gun located at ARL's Adelphi Laboratory Center (ALC). This facility provided an effective launch simulation platform for evaluating high-G survivability. Shock acceleration was achieved when the kinetic energy of a high-G projectile was absorbed by an aluminum honeycomb mitigator and momentum exchange mass during projectile impact. The mitigator was also used to tailor the duration and magnitude of the acceleration pulse. During this study, the cells were housed in a custom high-G carrier (figure 1) and mounted in either a vertical or horizontal orientation with respect to the direction of acceleration (figure 2). The cells were also encapsulated to provide structural support and cycled multiple times to verify electrical performance.

Figure 1. High-G air-gun carrier

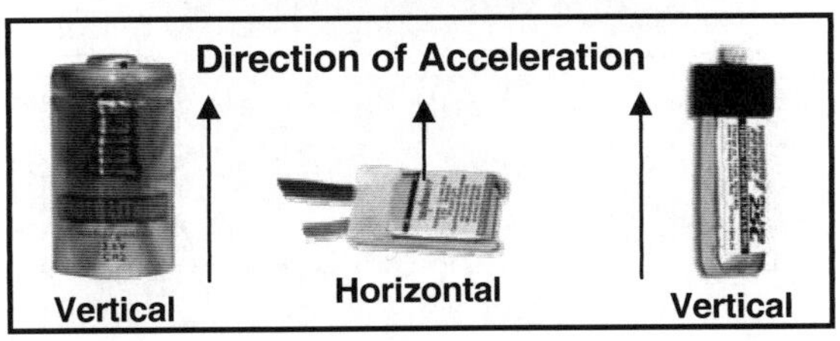

Figure 2. Orientation of cells with respect to acceleration

A total of six air-gun shots were conducted over a four month period. Maximum impact accelerations varied from 50kG up to 80kG (figure 3) and none of the cells were shot more than once. The open circuit voltage (OCV) of each cell was measured before and after each shot. The cells were then cycled post-impact and any changes in electrical performance were noted. Several cells were extracted from the encapsulation material and disassembled to identify potential sources of failure.

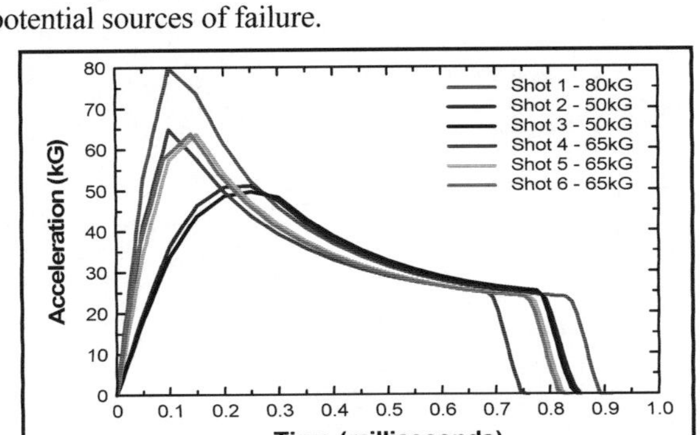

Figure 3. Air-gun impact accelerations

Study Results

600mAh Li-Ion Cylindrical Cells: None of the eight 600mAh cells evaluated during this study survived. Single cells were included on shots 1 (80kG) and 2 (50kG). Shots 3 (50kG) and 4 (65kG) included three cells each. All of the cells were in a vertical orientation and no cells were shot more than once. Post-impact OCV measurements were all below 1V and increases in cell temperature were common.

Several cells were disassembled post-impact and compression of the internal 'jelly-roll' of cathode and anode material was seen in each cell (figure 4). Significant delamination of the cathode and/or anode, especially toward the bottom of the cell, was also common (figure 5).

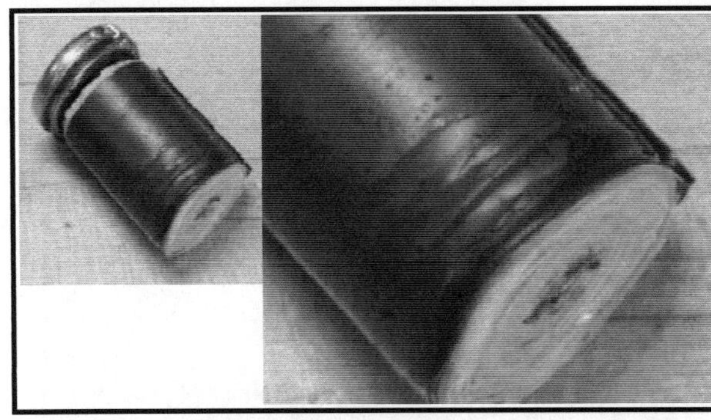

Figure 4. Internal 'jelly-roll' compression from high-G impact

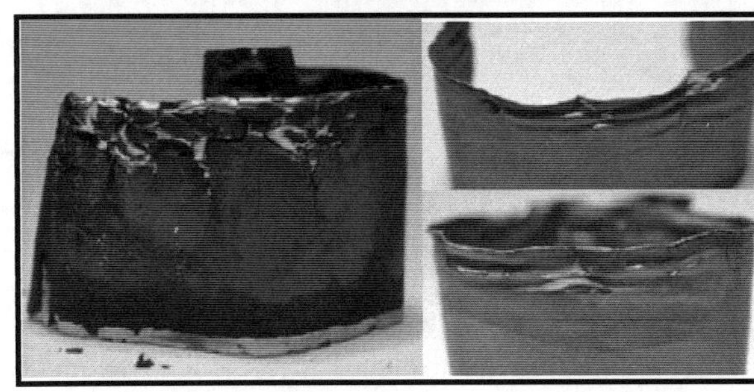

Figure 5. Damaged sections of anode and cathode

400mAh Li-Ion Cylindrical Cells: While the 400mAh cylindrical cells did perform better than their 600mAh counterparts, significant failures did occur. Overall four of the eight cells evaluated did not survive impact. Single cells on shots 1 (80kG) and 2 (50kG) both had post-impact OCV measurements below 1V. One of four cells on shot 5 (65kG) and one of two cells on shot 6 (65kG) suffered a slow decrease in OCV over time to around 0.5V. None of these four cells could be recharged and were no longer operational. The surviving four cells were cycled several times post-impact and a decrease in performance could be seen in all of the cells. Significant reductions in runtime ($\approx$ 6 to 17 minutes) and discharge voltage ($\approx$ 0.2 to 0.35V) were common when compared to pre-impact measurements (figure 6). Once again, cell disassembly routinely revealed considerable compression of the internal 'jelly-roll', with the majority of the damage isolated to the bottom sections of the cells (figure 7).

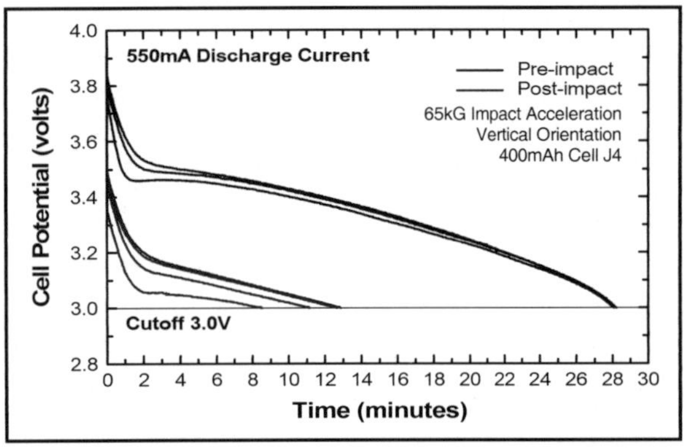

Figure 6. Typical discharge curves of a 400mAh Li-Ion cell

Figure 7. Damage to the internal components of a 400mAh cell can be seen when compared to an un-shocked cell

80mAh LiPo Pouch Cells: A total of 24 80mAh cells were evaluated and no failures occurred. Shots 3 (50kG) and 4 (65kG) each included three cells, shot 5 (65kG) had 12 cells and shot 6 (65kG) had six cells. OCV measurements taken on all 24 cells indicated no differences between pre and post impact. Electrical discharges also showed that any changes in voltage and runtime were negligible in the majority of cells (figure 8). Minor variations were noticed in around 5 of the 21 cells evaluated at 65kG. Worst case, these variations resulted in roughly a 2 minute decrease in runtime and 0.15V decrease in discharge voltage (figure 9). However, overall performance is still considered to be successful with respect to high-G survivability.

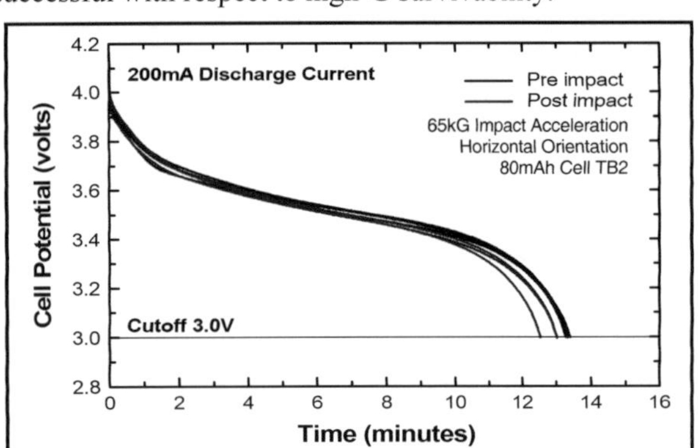

Figure 8. Typical discharge curves of an 80mAh LiPo cell

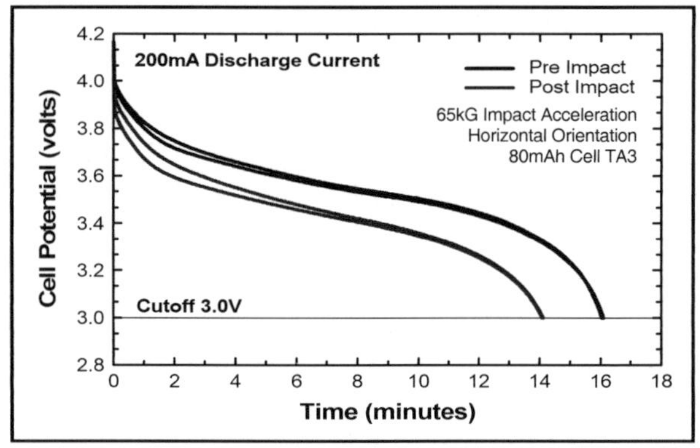

Figure 9. Worst case discharge curves of an 80mAh cell

Although no failures occurred, several cells were still disassembled for comparison to an un-shocked control cell. No noteworthy effects due to the high-G impact event were seen. The internal anode and cathode materials showed no signs of damage or major differences when compared to the control cell (figure 10).

Figure 10. Internal materials of an 80mAh cell post impact

125mAh LiPo Pouch Cells: Shot 3 (50kG) included four 125mAh cells in a vertical orientation. No immediate failures occurred as no changes in OCV were measured. However, changes were observed during post-impact discharges. Three of four cells had decreases of roughly 30 seconds (s) in runtime and 0.15V of potential (figure 11). The 4th cell faired slightly worse with about a 90s decrease in runtime and ≈ 0.3V reduction in potential.

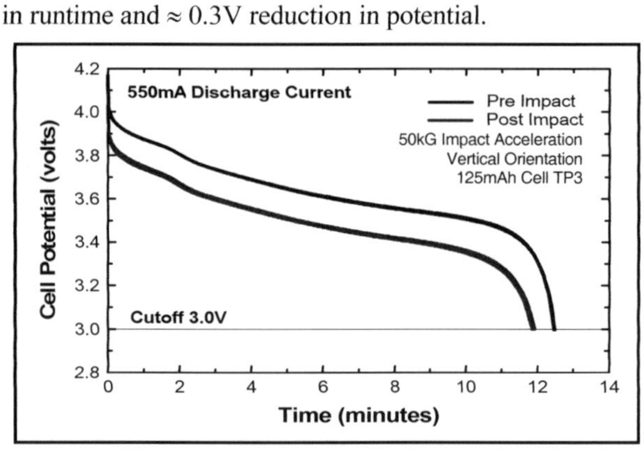

Figure 11. Discharge curves of a 125mAh LiPo cell (50kG)

Shot 4 (65kG) included four 125mAh cells. In this case only three of four cells survived. Post-impact discharges showed common decreases of around 4 minutes in runtime and ≈ 0.35V of potential in the surviving 3 cells (figure 12).

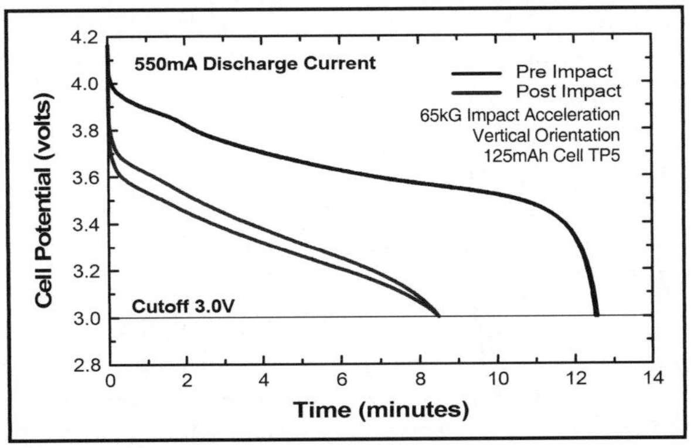

Figure 12. Discharge curves of a 125mAh LiPo cell (65kG)

200mAh LiPo Pouch Cells: Four 200mAh cells were included on shot 6 (65kG), with two of the cells suffering an immediate failure. Post-impact discharges of the remaining two cells displayed considerable decreases in runtime of 10 to 16 minutes (figure 13).

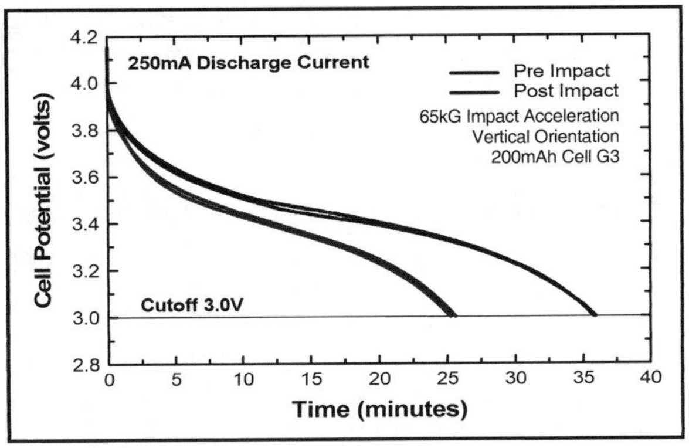

Figure 13. Discharge curves of a 200mAh LiPo cell (65kG)

An internal examination of the 200mAh cells indicated considerable compression of the internal materials (figure 14). Additional damage to the anode and cathode was seen in the bottom portions of the cell.

Figure 14. Internal damage to a 200mAh LiPo cell

Conclusions

All of the Li-Ion cylindrical cells proved to be unreliable at high-G levels of 50kG and above when evaluated in a vertical orientation. The 600mAh cells had a 100% failure rate and the 400mAh cells had a 50% failure rate (4 of 8). Significant decreases in performance were noted in the surviving cells when compared to pre-impact data. Movement of internal components during impact is the most likely cause of these failures and reductions in performance. Compression of the internal 'jelly-roll' and damage to the anode and cathode was routinely noted during post-impact cell disassembly. These results prove that cells of this type, if used in a vertical orientation, are very susceptible to high-G shock and are not reliable or robust enough to be used in certain ballistic applications.

The vertically oriented LiPo pouch cells proved unreliable at 65kG. Two of four 200mAh cells and one of four 125mAh cells failed. The remaining cells displayed considerable reductions in performance. Compression and damage to the internal anode and cathode materials was routinely noted during post-impact cell disassembly.

Vertically oriented 125mAh LiPo cells shocked at 50kG were somewhat more dependable. No failures occurred, and while there were reductions in performance, almost certainly due to the high-G impact, the cells did function well enough to be considered for ballistic use. Further investigation needs to be completed in order to assess the consistency of cell performance at 50kG before reliable use in certain ballistic applications.

The horizontally oriented 80mAh LiPo cells successfully survived high-G impacts up to 65kG. No failures occurred and post-impact analysis showed limited to no changes in performance. No evident anomalies were noted during cell disassembly. These cells were approved for use at 65kG and used as the power source for the sensor and telemetry systems used in the ALAS-MC surrogate 30-mm projectile.

Acknowledgements

The author wishes to thank Dave Grzybowski, ARL, for his contributions to the preparation and execution of this study.

References

1. Fresconi, F., Celmins, I., Ilg, M., Maley, J., "Projectile Roll Dynamics and Control with a Low-Cost Skid-to-Turn Maneuver System," *U.S. ARL*, ARL-TR-6363, March 2013.
2. Grzybowski, D., Peregino, P., Davis, B., "Development of a Telemetry-Enabled High-G Projectile Carrier," *U.S. Army Research Laboratory*, ARL-TR-6099, September 2012.
3. Hart, J. A., "Advanced Lethality and Accuracy System for Medium Caliber (ALAS-MC)," *2012 Joint Armaments Conference*, May 2012.
4. Bukowski, E., "Evaluation of Commercial-off-the-Shelf Lithium Batteries for use in Ballistic Telemetry Systems," *U.S. Army Research Laboratory,* ARL-TR-4840, June 2009.
5. Bukowski, E., "High Impact Shock Survivability Study of Lithium Ion Polymer Cells for use in Ballistic Applications," *44th Power Sources Conference*, June 2010.

High Capacity, High Power, Bullet Robust Lithium-Ion Polymer Cells Using Nano Si or Graphite Negative for Military Conformal and UPS Applications

Denguo Wu and Jiang Fan
American Lithium Energy Corporation (ALE)
1485 Poinsettia Avenue Suite 118, Vista, CA 92081
Tel & Fax: 760-599-7388; jfan@americanlithiumenergy.com

Abstract: *The performance of ALE's polymer lithium-ion cell using nano Si negative and the conventional graphite negative was studied as a potentially strong candidate for military conformal and UPS applications according to the military specifications such as MIL-PRF-32383-4 [1] and industry standards such as the UL1642 standard [2]. For the high capacity polymer cell using nano Si negative, the specific energy is >250 wh/kg while the tested cells passed UL crush, impact and ALE nail tests. However, there is still a need to improve the cell robustness toward the bullet penetration since the cell does not pass this test reliable. For the high capacity polymer cell using graphite negative, the cell shows not only high specific energy about 200 Wh/kg and >500 cycle life but also very robust against the nail and bullet penetration besides UL crush and impact tests. The cell developed in ALE will greatly simplify the design and fabrication of the conformal batteries because the bullet penetration has been considered at the cell level, which could reduce the conformal battery cost substantially. Also, the cell does not generate any significant heat during the normal operation, which is another superior feature for ALE polymer cells for the conformal application because the heat is not good to the human body. Finally, the studied polymer cell from ALE can be produced in a wide range of sizes and shapes depending on the requirements of the target applications, providing flexibility in designing and manufacturing a range of military batteries including the conformal, unmanned air plane, UPSs.*

Keywords: High Energy; High Power; Polymer Li-Ion Cell; conformal Batteries

Introduction

The military conformal and UPS batteries have a requirement to be very versatile in providing the power source for multiple numbers and types of devices and performing in a range of austere and challenging environments. ALE's thin lithium-ion polymer cell is a strong candidate for this application because it not only provides high energy and high power, but also has proven tolerance to mechanical abuse according to both military and industrial standards, besides performance at low temperatures down to -30°C. ALE's polymer lithium-ion cell has great flexibility in its design as it can be produced in a wide range of sizes and shapes to comply with the unique requirements of a given application because of ALE's manufacturing methodology. Here are the details

Results and Discussion

Cell capacity at different currents and room temperature:

Figure 1 presents the cell discharge voltage profiles of a) graphite negative based cell at rates of 0.2C, 0.5C, 1C, 2C and 5C at room temperature, b) nano Si negative based cell at the discharge currents 0.35A, 0.5A, 1A and 2A and at 50°C. The specific energy of lithium ion polymer cell is ~200 Wh/kg for graphite based cell and >250 Wh/kg for Nano Si based cell. The cell can deliver >80% capacity at 5C rate, which corresponds to >500 W/kg for graphite based cell. The power for nano Si based cell is >200 W/kg up to this point. For the graphite based cell, the test protocols are: i) charge to 4.2 V for 3 hours at 0.8C, ii) rest for 30 minutes, iii) discharge to 2.7 V at a specified current rate. For the nano Si based cell, the testing protocols are: i) charge to 4.2 V for 3 hours at 0.3C, ii) rest for 30 minutes, iii) discharge to 2.0 V at a specified current rate

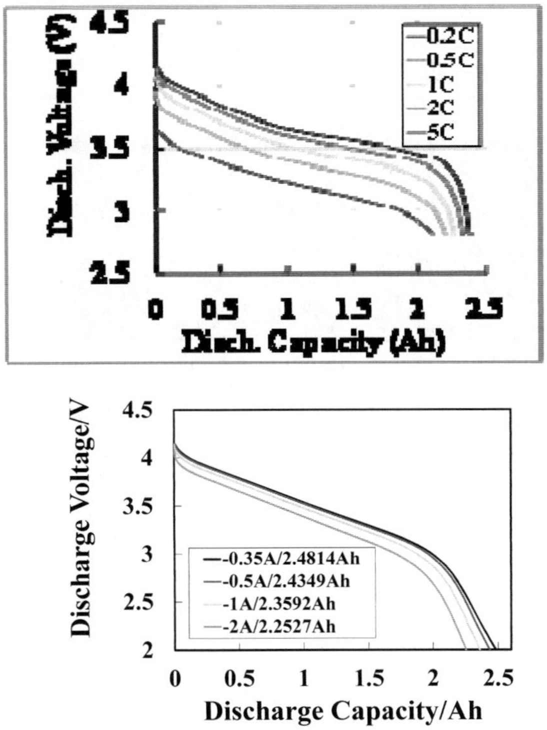

Figure 1 - Cell discharge voltage profiles for a) graphite based cell at different C rates and room temperature and b) nano Si negative based cell at different current and 50°C.

***Cell Performance at Low Temperature*:**

Table 1 lists the ALE's cell capacities at 0.2C rate at room temperature and -30°C. Our graphite based cell was charged at 0.8C at room temperature and then discharged at lower temperatures after the fully charged cell or battery was stored at the low tmperature for two hours. The cell delivered >60% of its initial capacity at room temperature, which should meet the military UPS reqirement. Commercially-available, lithium-ion polymer cells can barely if at all meet the millitary's low temperature performance requirement. This is because the commercial market only requires performance at -20°C, while the military requires performance at -30 to -40°C.

Table 1- Cell Capacity At Room Temperature and -30 °C

Temperature	Cell capacity (Ah)
Room temp.	2.4
-30°C	>1.5

***Cell Cycle Life*:**

Figure 2 shows the graphite based cell capacity vs. the cycle number at room temperature. The cell lost about 20% after 700 cycles, which is very good and should exceed the cycle life requirement in view of the fact that the UPS battery is stand-by for most of its life time and the military requires about 224 cycles. The cell cycle life was evaluated at 100% depth of discharge (100% DOD) and at 0.8C charging and 0.8C discharging at room temperature. Nano Si based cell lost about 25% after 220 cycles which barely meets the military specification (not shown).

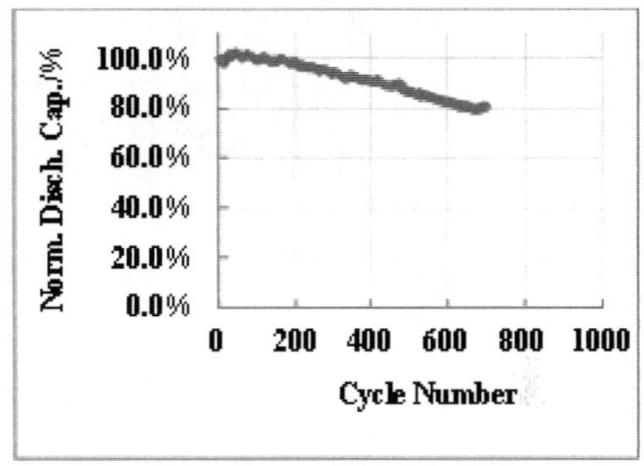

Figure 2 Cell capacity versus cycle number at 100% DOD and at room temperature with 0.8C charging and 0.8C discharging.

***Bullet and Nail Tests*:**

Figure 3 shows the picture of a) the gun (0.22" bullet at the speed over 900 miles per hour), b) the fully charged nano Si based cell after one shot from 50 feet, and c) the fully charged graphite based cell after several shots from 50 feet. Graphite based cell did not catch the fire even after several shots while nano Si cell caught fire in the second shot. It should be pointed out that the nano Si based cell could not pass the bullet test reliably. The graphite based cell is very resistive to bullet and can even sustain 0.17'' bullet penetration at the speed >2000 miles per hour. This capability differentiates our cell from any commercial cell now available in the market and would greatly simplify the conformal battery design and manufacturing. Figure 4 shows a) the nano Si based cell voltage and temperature profiles during the nail test and b) cells after the nail test. In the nail test, the fully charged cell was placed on a flat plate with an open space (1cm wide, 1 cm deep, and 5 cm long) under the cell, and then was manually penetrated by a 3mm diameter nail from the top of the cell at about 1 mm per minute. The cell voltage and temperature were measured accordingly. The graphite based cell can pass the nail test nicely also (not shown).

a)
b)
c)

Figure 3 Bullet tests a) Gun utlized in test b) Graphite based cell after mutiple shots and c) Nano Si negative based cell after one shot

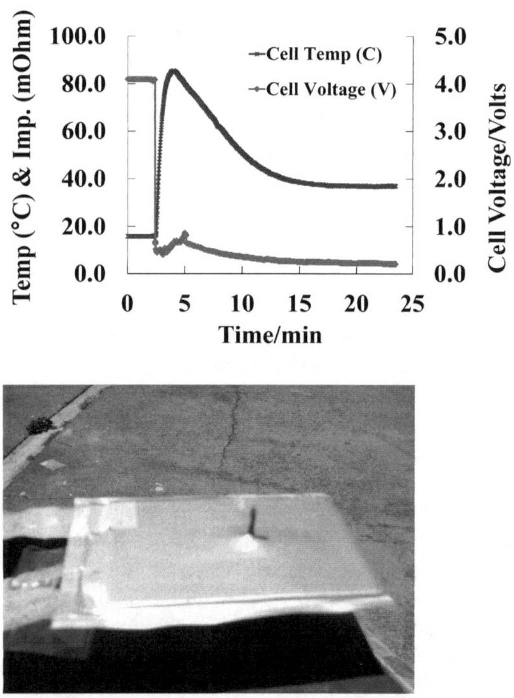

a)
b)

Figure 4 Cell nail test results. (a) Cell temperature, impedance and volt versus test time profile. Cell temperature was increased about 70°C after the nail test. (b) Picture after the nail test, cell is no fire.

***UL Impact and Crush Tests*:**

All tested cells including nano Si and graphite negatives passed UL impact and crush tests without any fire and explosion. Figure 5 shows the picture of nano Si based cell a) before the crush on side and b) after the crush on side. The cell is very robust against mechanical abuse again. For the crush test, the fully charged cell was placed between two flat plates and crushed by a 3000 lb force. For the impact test, the fully charged cell was placed on a flat surface with a metal rod (1.5 cm in diameter) on the top (center) of the cell, and was then impacted by a 9.1 kg metal rod freely dropped to the 1.5 cm metal rod.

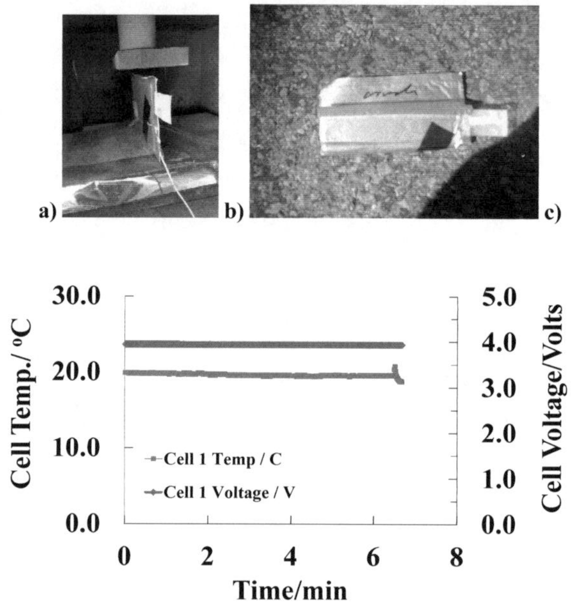

Figure 5 UL Impact and Crush Tests a) before the crush test along the side direction, b) after the crush test, c) Cell temperature, impedance and volt versus test time profiles.

Conclusions

ALE's lithium-ion polymer cell provides high-energy, high-power and >500 cycle life. The cell exhibits outstanding mechanical abuse tolerance, in contrast to cells available on the commercial market, ALE's graphite based cell passes nails tests and are very resistive to the bullet. ALE's lithium-ion polymer cell can be designed and physically configured to comply with any military conformal and UPS battery specification.

Reference

[1] MIL-PRF-32383-4
[2] UL 1642-2012

Acknowledgement

Authors will like to thank Deanna Y. Tyler, Christopher Hurley, Michael T. Brundage, Ed Plichta, US Army, CERDEC, Aberdeen, MD 21005 for their partial financial support for the work per contract W15P7T-13-C-A502; Authors will also like to thank Frank Ashe and Kailash Shukla, US Army, NSRDEC, TSPID, SNPLI for their partial financial support per contract W911QY-11-C-0059 (Phase II)

Electrolytes Based On Imide Salt Solutions in Fluorinated Solvents

Konstantin Tikhonov, Ka Ki Yip, Marc Juzkow
Leyden Energy, Inc.
46840 Lakeview Blvd, Fremont, CA 94538

Abstract: *Performance and safety of the NFi™ family of electrolytes developed by Leyden Energy is discussed. The electrolytes are based on solutions of Li imide salts in non-flammable fluorinated ethers. Non-flammable components constitute up to 85% of the electrolytes by weight and result in significantly improved cell safety under abuse conditions.*

Keywords: Li imide; LiBETI, LiTFSI, fluorinated solvents; ethers; esters; non-flammable; electrolyte; cell safety; abuse conditions

Introduction

Regular Li-ion cells use highly flammable electrolytes based on solutions of $LiPF_6$ in organic solvents. Under abuse conditions, the electrolyte is often expelled from the case in a form of a mist and may easily ignite, often resulting in a battery fire or explosion.

Previous attempts to formulate non-flammable electrolytes included ionic liquid formulations or addition of a flame retardant to traditional flammable solvents. Both approaches generally failed to combine in one formulation good safety and fast lithium transport that enables charge and discharge over a wide temperature range. The ionic liquids are too viscous and cannot meet the operating temperature range requirements of most applications unless they are diluted with carbonate solvents, which undermines the safety. Flame-retardants tend to participate in oxidation and reduction processes negatively affecting cycle life. In addition, their concentration in electrolyte reduces with time affecting safety over life.

Background

Leyden Energy's approach was to formulate electrolytes solutions with as high of a percentage of non-flammable components as possible. One group of fluorinated solvents available on the market in bulk, at a reasonable cost and battery-grade purity are 3M Novec™ fluorinated fluids. These solvents have low viscosity and melting points, are non-flammable and non-toxic. However, their miscibility with organic carbonates and ability to solubilize common lithium salts presents a challenge. Leyden's solution was to use lithium imide salts such as LiBETI and LiTFSI. Imide salts with their large anions containing fluorinated alkyl groups have excellent affinity to fluorinated solvents. They have significantly higher solubility compared to regular salts such as $LiPF_6$, $LiBF_4$ and LiBOB. As a matter of fact, in large concentrations, most fluorinated solvents we have evaluated are not capable of solubilizing any of the other salts except for LiBETI in concentrations needed for good Li transport. Use of LiBETI allowed Leyden to formulate electrolytes with up to 85% non-flammable components by weight. The electrolytes still contain flammable components: small amounts of carbonates are preserved in the electrolyte for efficient SEI formation; addition esters or linear carbonates assist rate and low temperature performance. NFi™ electrolytes are hard to ignite and if ignited they quickly self-extinguish.

Experimental

Electrolytes were prepared in an MBraun glove box from battery-grade solvents, salts and additives. The solvents were pre-dried to a moisture level of less than 20ppm. The salts were separately dried under vacuum prior to use.

Electrolyte characterization included electrochemical measurements carried out on Gamry and Solartron potentiostats, conductivity measurements and custom self-extinguishing time (SET) tests. SET measurements were found to have limited use and were abandoned as they did not correlate well with full cell safety tests results.

NFi™ electrolytes were extensively tested in 18650 cylindrical and pouch cells with a graphite anode and a range of cathode materials that included LFP, NCM and LCO. In this paper we will focus on testing results obtained with graphite-NCM 2.2Ah 18650 cylindrical cells and graphite-NCM 2.0Ah pouch cells. The cells were made from commercially available active materials and manufactured on Leyden's pilot line in Fremont, CA. The performance and safety testing was done at Leyden's battery safety lab capable of a full range of UN and UL safety tests. The safety results were independently confirmed by Mobile Power Solutions test lab near Portland, OR.

Cone calorimetry testing was performed by Exponent Failure Analysis.

The work was performed under DOE SBIR contract number DE-SC0005117.

Results

The conductivity of NFi™ electrolytes varies from 2mS/cm to 5.5mS/cm depending on the fluorinated ether and its concentration and a choice of a carbonate and esters used in the formulation. Interestingly, the conductivity of the electrolytes did not always correlate with the performance at different rates and temperatures, for examples, addition of methylpropyl pyrrolidinium ionic liquids in amount of 5-

10% did not have a significant impact on conductivity but results in drastically reduced rate performance.

Electrolyte formulations with percentages of non-flammable components between 70% and 85% demonstrated long cycle life at up to 60°C, discharge performance at as low as -30°C, and rate capability up to 5C. Figure 1 shows the rate test of an 18650 2.2Ah graphite-NCM cell at 20°C. The average discharge voltage at high rates is lower than the voltage of cells filled with regular carbonate electrolyte, however, the capacity delivered at 2C discharge is similar. Higher rates were not tested due to the PTC device in the cell which limits the maximum current to 2C.

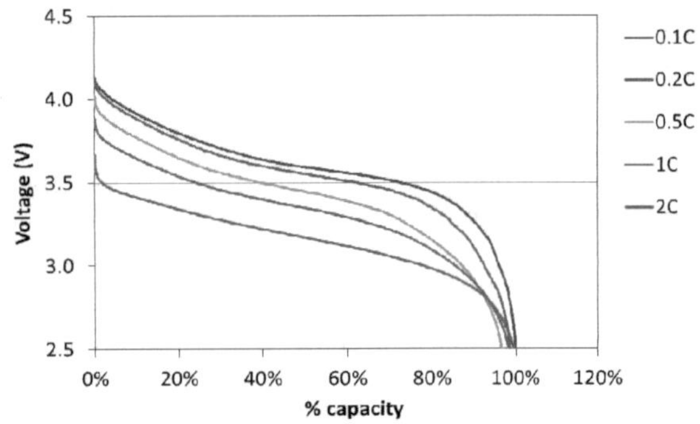

Figure 1. Rate capability of 18650 2.2Ah NCM cell filled with NFi™ electrolyte

Cycle life of the 2.2Ah cell was found to depend on the charge cut-off voltage. This and other experiments indicate that lower charge acceptance rate of the cells with NFi™ electrolytes should be taken into account to be able to achieve long cycle life.

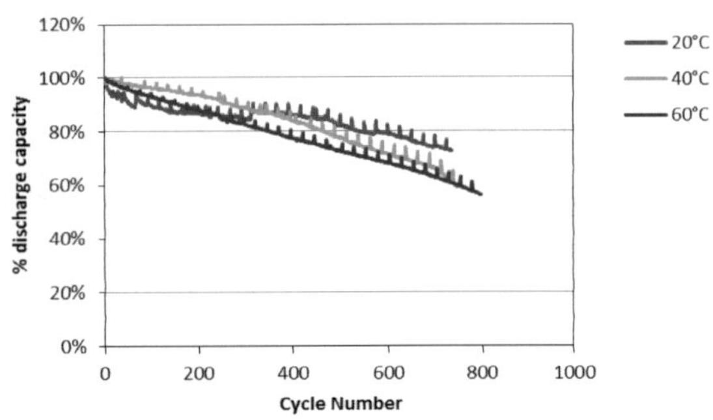

Figure 2. Cycle life of 18650 2.2Ah NCM cells filled with NFi™ electrolyte at 0.5C/0.5C rate from 3.0V to 4.2V

Figures 2 and 3 compare the cycle life of the 2.2Ah NCM cells filled with NFi™ electrolyte at 20, 40 and 60°C to 4.2V and 4.0V charge voltage respectively. The cycle life is significantly improved at lower charge voltage achieving 1000 cycles at room temperature. Cycling tests at lower charge rate of 0.2C showed that the cycle life is charge current dependent indicating diffusion limitations resulting from NFi™ electrolyte use.

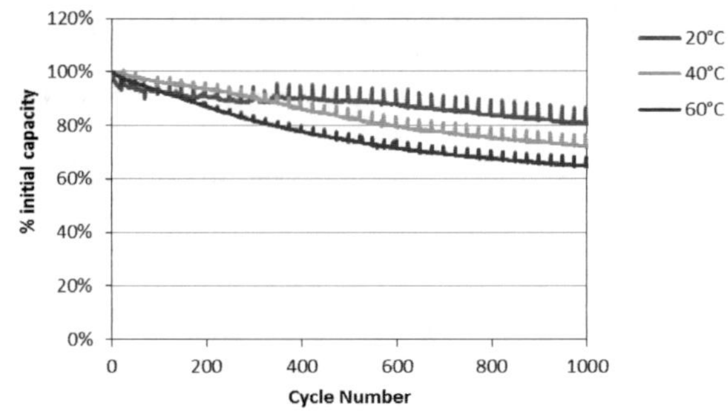

Figure 3. Cycle life of 18650 2.2Ah NCM cells filled with NFi™ electrolyte at 0.5C/0.5C rate from 3.0V to 4.0V

Abuse testing of NFi™ electrolyte in 18650 cells highlighted the degree to which non-flammability of electrolyte has an impact on overall cell safety. On a custom ignition test, which involves increasing cell temperature with a heating wire until it vents through the designed vent in the header and having an ignition source near the cell vent, the cells with NFi™ electrolytes demonstrated no fire while commercially available NCM and even LFP 18650 cells vented with fire. Significant safety benefits were also observed during the Federal Aviation Administration (FAA) alcohol fire test where the cell is exposed to 50ml of ethanol set on fire 4 inches below the cell.

Test	NFi™	1M $LiPF_6$ EC:EMC:DMC (1:2:2) 2%VC
Ignition	No flames 	Flames 
Heating	TRT: 236°C 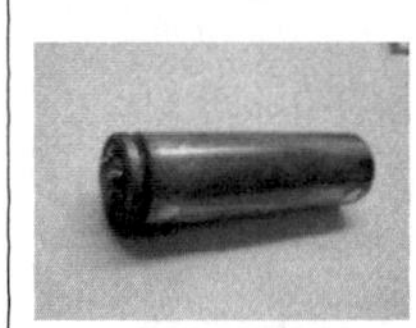	TRT 210°C 
Nail	The cells tested vented sparks and flames. 	The cells tested vented sparks, smoke, and fire. 

Figure 4. Abuse summary on 18650 2.2Ah NCM cells filled with NFi™ and regular electrolyte.

However, in spite of often expressed believe that the non-flammable electrolyte would result in ultimately safe cell, we found that not being the case. When exposed to very high temperature (>220°C), the cells still went to thermal runaway. Similarly, cells failed on nail penetration test. Li-ion cell cathode generates oxygen at high temperature and even in the virtual absence of flammable solvents, it contains large amounts of other "fuel": graphite, separator, etc. Therefore, the benefits of safer electrolyte are most pronounced in events when it is sprayed out of the cell container or with the materials that do not generate significant amount of oxygen under the majority of abusive conditions, such as LFP or LMO.

The NFi™ electrolyte formulations for pouch cells were based on the same fluorinated solvents and salts as formulations for 18650 cells, however, the carbonate and ester solvents were adjusted to lower the vapor pressure and enable pouch cell performance at high temperatures. The cells showed long cycle life at up to 50°C as shown on Figure 5 and high rate capability presented on Figure 6.

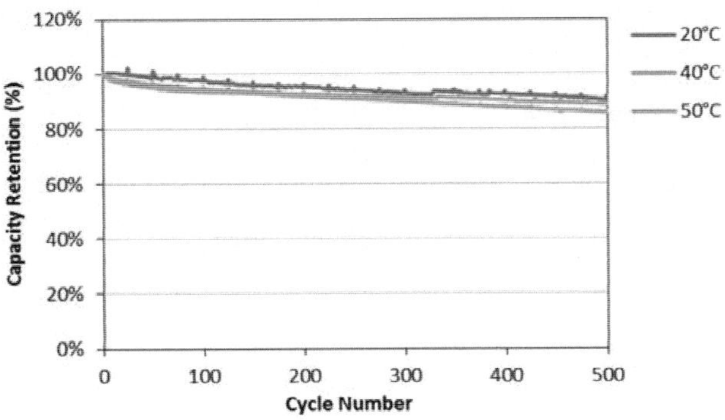

Figure 5. Cycle life of 2.0Ah NCM pouch cell filled with NFi™ electrolyte; 0.5C/0.5C 3.0-4.2V.

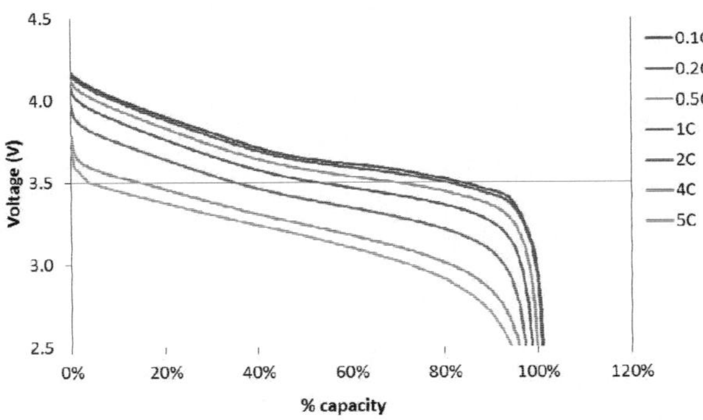

Figure 6. Rate capability of 2.0Ah NCM pouch cell filled with NFi™ electrolyte

The electrolytes also have remarkably good performance at low temperatures, which is largely attributed to the properties of fluorinated ethers with their melting points of as low as -100°C.

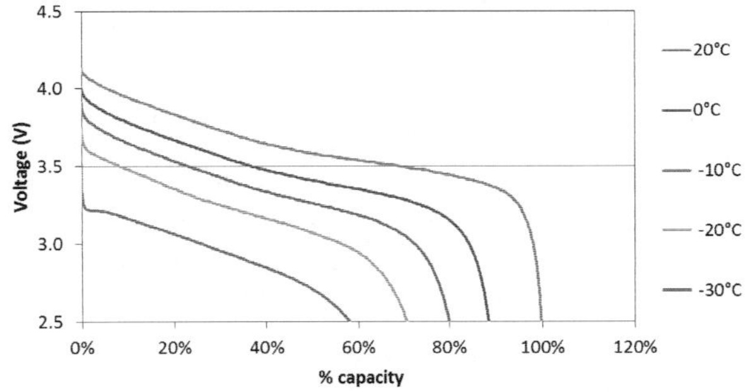

Figure 7. Low temperature performance of 2.0Ah NCM pouch cell filled with NFi™ electrolyte

Safety tests conducted on the NCM pouch cells showed significantly improved safety, most notably on overcharge test with ignition sources. The safety results are summarized on Figure 8.

Electrolyte	1M $LiPF_6$ / EC:DEC 1:2 2% VC	NFi™
Overcharge without plates	The cell swelled and ruptured venting flames. 	The cell swelled and ruptured. No flames 
Overcharge with plates	The cell slightly swelled. 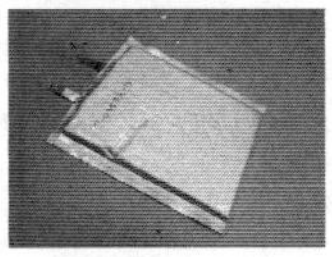	The cell slightly swelled and leaked electrolyte at positive tab. 
Heating without plates	TRT 187.8°C The cell swelled and ruptured. The cell caught fire. 	TRT 200.6°C The cell swelled and ruptured. The cell had sparks and flash. 
Heating with plates	The cell vented electrolyte. No thermal runaway at a max temperature of 250°C. 	The cell vented electrolyte. No thermal runaway at a max temperature of 250°C. 
Impact	Max temperature 93.1°C The impact generated a hard short. 	Max temperature 350°C The cell vented smoke. 

Figure 8. Safety of 2.0Ah NCM pouch cell filled with NFi™ electrolyte

Leyden findings and results of the development were independently verified by Mobile Power Solutions test lab.

In addition to UN and UL testing, Exponent Failure Analysis conducted cone calorimetry measurements. Cone calorimetry is widely used in the field of fire safety engineering. The fully charged battery is ignited and burned using a cone-shaped heater and both heat release rate and total thermal output are measured.

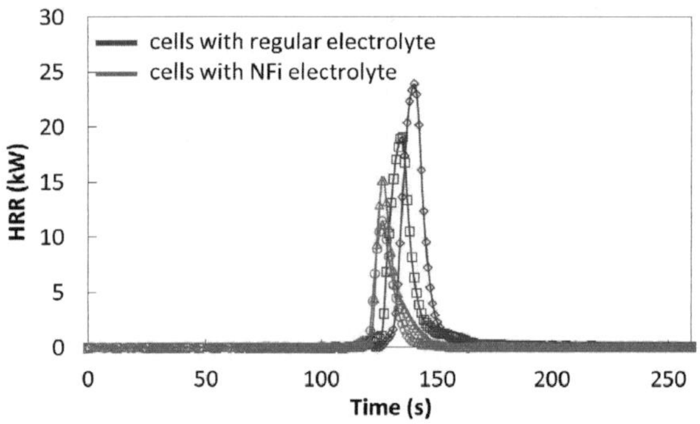

Figure 9. Heat release rate measured by cone calorimetry in 2.0Ah NCM cells.

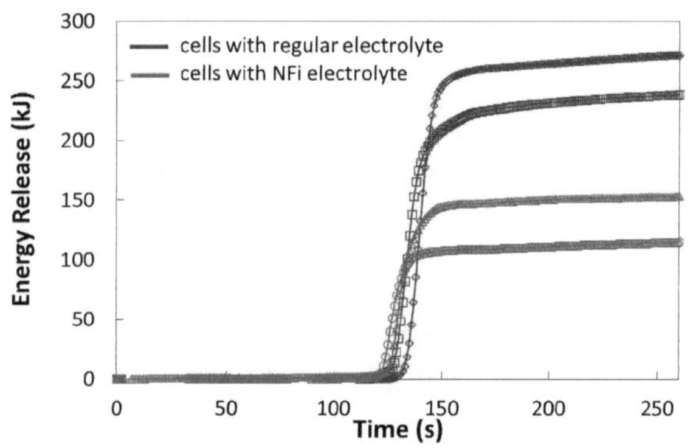

Figure 10. Total heat release measured by cone calorimetry in 2.0Ah NCM cells.

Remarkably, the total heat release is about half of the heat compared to the same cell with a regular electrolyte such as 1M $LiPF_6$ /EC:DEC 1:2 and the peak heat release is about 30% lower. These findings are very significant. Heat generation is a major consideration for pack design since the lower heat release means that heat propagation from cell to cell or to other pack components when non-flammable electrolyte is used is much less of an issue. This has the potential to greatly simplify pack design and reduce the pack cost.

Conclusion

NFi™ electrolytes based on Li imide salt solutions in fluorinated ethers show good performance and improved abuse tolerance under a variety of conditions. The safety of the electrolyte alone, however, is not sufficient to prevent thermal runaway if initiated by the unstable, oxygen releasing cathode. The total thermal heat released will be significantly lower but a cell filled with NFi™ may still undergo thermal runaway. Use of these new electrolytes is advantageous in preventing or reducing the hazard level of the safety events when electrolyte is vented or leaks from a cell in the presence of a heat or ignition source.

Acknowledgements

The work was performed under DOE SBIR program under a contract number DE-SC0005117. Authors want to thank Brian Cunningham, James Barnes and DOE staff for their guidance and discussions. We also would like to thank Mobile Power Solutions and Exponent Failure Analysis for their testing.

Lithium-Ion Battery Safety: Detection of Developing Internal Shorts and Suppression of Thermal Runaway

Christopher McCoy, Suresh Sriramulu, Richard Stringfellow, David Ofer and Brian Barnett
TIAX LLC, 35 Hartwell Avenue, Lexington, MA, USA 02421
barnett.b@TIAXLLC.com

Abstract: *Li-ion batteries are attractive for diverse applications owing to their high energy density and power capability. However, safety concerns are limiting their use in important DoD applications. Among the various triggers of thermal runaway of Li-ion cells, the internal short circuit is the least studied but most dangerous, because it can occur with little warning during normal cell operation. Here we report on two exciting approaches to manage the internal short trigger. The first is a non-invasive, chemistry agnostic technology for detecting growing internal short circuits. The second is a method to intervene and eliminate thermal runaway once the internal short is detected.*

Keywords: Li-ion batteries; Li-ion safety; thermal runaway; internal short-circuits

Introduction

Li-ion batteries find use in diverse DoD applications owing to their high energy density and power capability. However, concerns regarding the safety of Li-ion technology may be limiting its use in many important DoD applications. Essentially, certain "triggers" can stimulate the release of a significant amount of thermal energy in the cell, in the worst case resulting in thermal runaway, typically accompanied by venting of combustible vapors, smoke, sparks, and flame.[1]

Among the various triggers of thermal runaway of Li-ion cells, the internal short circuit trigger is the least studied but most dangerous, because it can occur with little warning with cell operation appearing normal.[2] Indeed, the internal short trigger has led to highly publicized, widespread recalls of Li-ion battery packs used in consumer laptops. In this type of trigger, metal particle contaminants inadvertently introduced into the cell during manufacturing create an internal short that grows and matures during normal operation, and in some cases results in thermal runaway. Even though manufacturers have installed stringent QC measures to minimize metal particle contaminants in cells, the continuing recalls of Li-ion consumer batteries shows that such defects can never be eliminated.[3]

TIAX has been at the forefront of research on internal short circuits in Li-ion cells. Our research, spanning more than seven years, has shown that the primary mechanism by which metal particles induce internal shorts in cells is through a stripping and plating mechanism, in which metal particles present on the cathode of a Li-ion cell dissolve and subsequently plate on the anode.[4] Continued deposition on the anode can result in the formation of a dendrite that eventually grows sufficiently to contact the cathode and short the cell. If the short resistance reaches a critical value, the cell discharge through this internal short results in increasing localized joule heating and temperature rise, which then can stimulate exothermic anode and cathode decomposition reactions. Thermal runaway ensues when heat generation from these sources exceeds the ability of the cell to shed the heat for a sufficiently prolonged period of time.

TIAX is developing technologies to manage the internal short trigger. The function of the various safety technologies being developed at TIAX is summarized in Figure 1. Pre-emption encompasses several technologies, one example of which is electrolyte additives that suppress the dissolution and plating of metals. Containment includes, for example, approaches to prevent flaming outside the battery pack. Specific examples of technologies for detecting internal short circuits and for intervening to suppress thermal runaway (following the detection) are described in this submission.

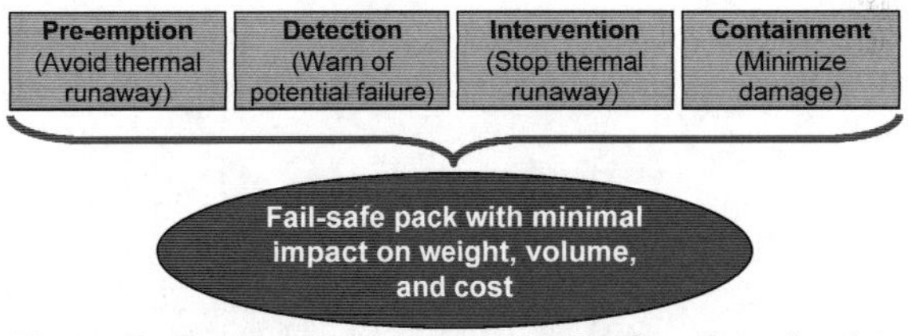

Figure 1: Schematic summarizing the function of safety technologies being developed at TIAX.

Challenges in Internal Short Detection

TIAX has developed approaches to deliberately induce internal short circuits in Li-ion cells by strategic placement of metal particles. During normal charge/discharge cycling, appropriately placed metal particles can eventually induce internal shorts. The resistance of such shorts initially starts at a high value, but gradually decreases during cycling. Figure 2 shows sample experimental data illustrating the evolution of the internal short resistance from an implanted metal particle during continued charge-discharge cycling.

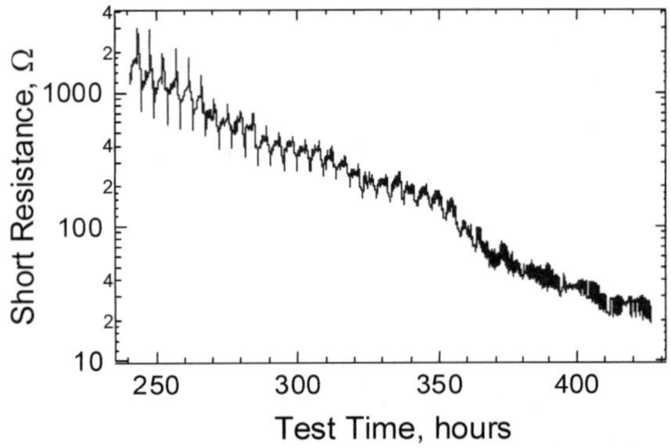

Figure 2: Representative experimental data of the evolution of the internal short resistance in a Li-ion cell with an implanted metal particle during normal charge/discharge cycling. The resistance of the short starts high, but decreases with cycling.

Detecting such shorts (for example when the resistance is 100Ω) is not possible with conventional BMU monitoring employed today. Figure 3 shows the normal voltage and current measured during charge and discharge of an 18650 cell with a surrogate 100Ω short. As can be seen by comparing the top and bottom graphs, there is no noticeable difference in the curves indicating the presence of the 100Ω internal short circuit. In addition, any approach to directly interrogate the cell will only measure the cell's internal impedance, which is more than three orders of magnitude lower (e.g., 50mΩ for a typical 18650 cell) than that of the surrogate short.

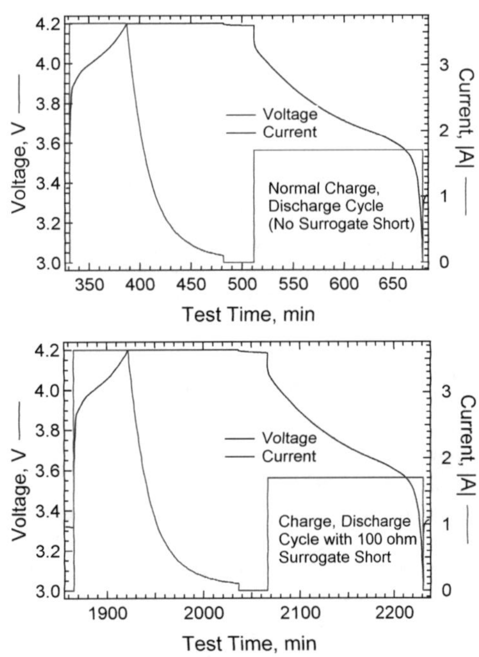

Figure 3: Experimental data for 18650 cell without (top) and with (bottom) 100Ω surrogate internal short. Conventional voltage and current monitoring cannot infer the presence of such a high resistance internal short circuit.

TIAX Internal Short Detection Technologies

TIAX has developed two distinct, patent-pending technologies to detect internal shorts in Li-ion cells. These non-invasive, chemistry agnostic technologies are based on strategically placed sensors and signal processing algorithms. Both technologies have been demonstrated on a wide range of cell sizes from small cells (e.g., 18650 cells with capacity < 2.8 Ah) to large cells (e.g., ~75 Ah), and over the temperature range of -30ºC to 55ºC. The two technologies require significantly different implementation approaches, and provide different pack-level benefits.

Experimental data for one of the two technologies is shown in Figure 4. For this experiment, surrogate internal shorts were used. The magnitude of the surrogate short resistance was separately tuned, and the detection system output was monitored. The results show that a 100Ω short can be easily detected, with excellent signal-to-noise ratio. For context, prior simulation work at TIAX showed that internal short resistance less than 4Ω was needed to cause thermal runaway under the test conditions. Therefore, the detection technology can infer the presence of the internal short, even when the short is 25 times weaker than the critical value and poses no thermal runaway risk. The time to detection of these surrogate shorts was less than 20 s.

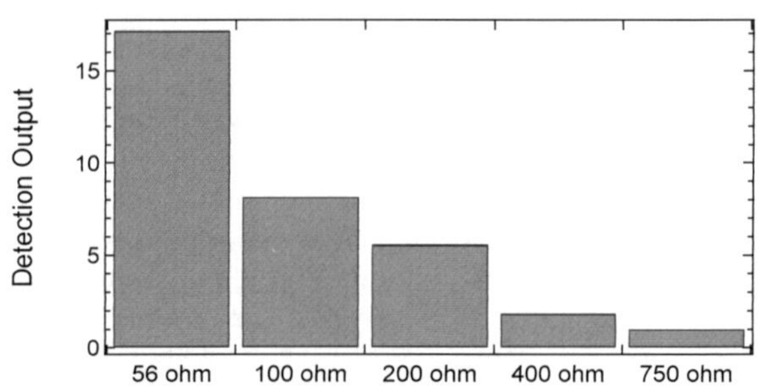

Figure 4: Experimental data showing the sensitivity of a detection system to the internal short resistance.

This internal short detection technology is versatile. It can be applied to any chemistry, and configured for any battery pack. The implementation of this technology requires only minimum modifications to the Battery Management Unit (BMU). It can be implemented with minimal cost impact because only a few additional inexpensive components are needed in addition to the standard components in the battery pack. This technology is presently being adapted for a large-format cell-pack for a major automotive OEM.

Intervention to suppress thermal runaway

For internal shorts that are detected early, a number of technical approaches are available to suppress thermal runaway. Here we describe one example; an experimentally verified approach of increasing the external heat transfer rates to suppress thermal runaway.

Simulation and experimental work at TIAX has shown that the heat transfer environment plays a crucial role in dictating whether or not thermal runaway results from an internal short circuit.[5] We constructed a wind tunnel that was mounted in a fume hood for thermal runaway experiments, such that the surface heat transfer coefficient can be controlled by adjusting the velocity of air flow over the cell. Figure 5 shows a photograph of the wind tunnel and below the photograph, representative experimental heat transfer coefficient data. The wind tunnel includes a chamber with transparent plexiglass windows. The chamber houses a test 18650 cell (fully charged to 4.2 V) and a reference 18650 cell (fully discharged). A miniature hole is drilled at the bottom of each cell and a heater (rated to 30 W) is inserted. The heater power can be independently controlled and simulates localized heat dissipation from an internal short circuit. The external heat transfer coefficient is controlled by manipulating the flow rate of air over the cells.

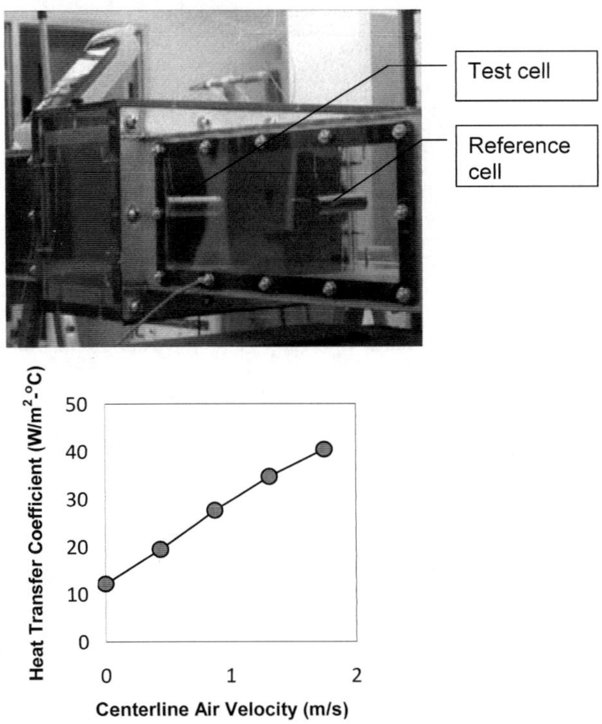

Figure 5: Photograph of the wind tunnel used for thermal runaway experiments (top) and measured surface heat transfer coefficient data (bottom) as a function of air flow rate in the wind tunnel.

Example thermal runaway data generated in the wind tunnel are shown in Figure 6. 18650 cells fabricated at TIAX were used for this experiment. From time t = 0 to t =~700s, the temperature of the test cell and dead cell increase because of internal heating by the heater. However at around 700s, the voltage of the test cell (which is fully charged) dropped to zero and it experienced a violent thermal runaway with the cell surface temperature exceeding 700°C in a very short period of time. In contrast, the dead cell's temperature does not increase as rapidly, and cools down once the heater power is turned off at 900s.

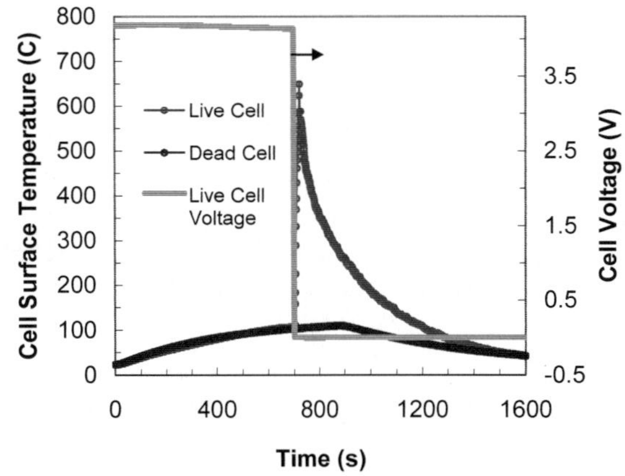

Figure 6: Experimental thermal runaway data generated in the wind tunnel with the heater method. The cells employed for this experiment were 18650 cells fabricated at TIAX. The heater power dissipation was set to 10 W and the heat transfer coefficient was set to 12 W/m^2-K.

Such experimental data were also used to validate an FEA model for simulating thermal runaway of Li-ion cells. The model, which has been described in detail in ref. [1], includes measured cell dimensions, physical properties of cell components, and models for the kinetics of heat release from anode and cathode decomposition reactions. The model is able to match experimental measurements, as is illustrated in Figure 7.

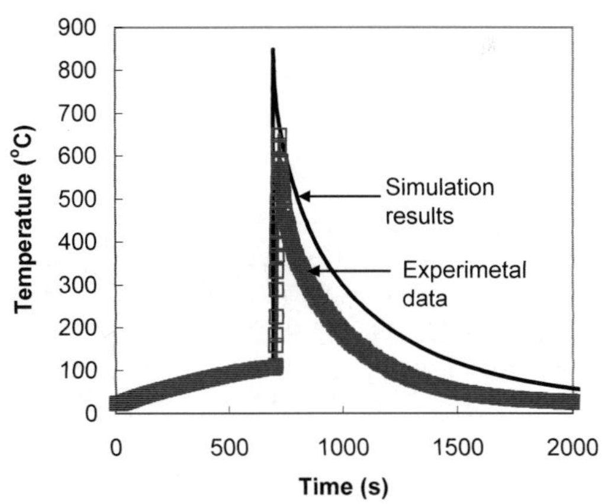

Figure 7: Comparison of cell surface temperatures from thermal runaway experiment (from Figure 6) and simulation results. Only one adjustable parameter was used for the simulation results.

Using the same experimental set-up, we evaluated whether it would be possible to suppress thermal runaway by increasing the external heat transfer coefficient. Figure 8 shows results from these experiments. Two separate experiments were conducted using the heater method with **initially** identical heat transfer coefficient of 12 W/m^2-K. Figure 8 shows the 18650 live cell temperature data for the two experiments. In the first experiment, the heat transfer rate was held constant (solid line) in one experiment, the cell experienced thermal runaway at ~800s. In the second experiment (dashed line), the heat transfer coefficient was increased by a factor of five to 50 W/m^2-K when the cell surface temperature exceeded 130ºC, and this cell did not experience thermal runaway even though the heater continued to dissipate heat within the cell. This experimental result, which matched our model predictions, shows that it is possible to 'kill' thermal runaway by controlling the external heat transfer coefficient, illustrating the value of internal short circuit detection technology.

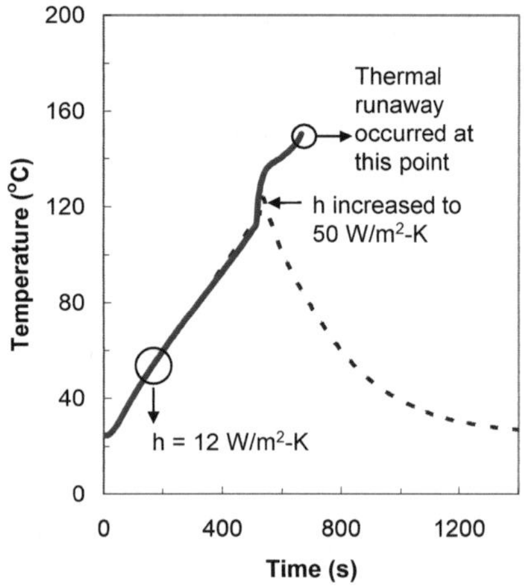

Figure 8: Experimental data showing suppression of thermal runaway by judiciously increasing the external heat transfer coefficient just prior to thermal runaway. Two experiments were conducted with the heater method using 18650 cells. The live cell temperatures for these experiments are shown here.

Summary

The internal short circuit trigger of thermal runaway is not managed today, but has resulted (and is continuing to result) in major battery recalls in consumer electronics and vehicle applications. Internal short circuits can never be completely eliminated, even given significant advances in quality control methods employed by the battery companies. At TIAX, we are developing a wide range of technologies to manage the internal short trigger. Here we reported on two exciting technologies — a non-invasive, chemistry- and cell-size-independent technology to detect internal short circuits, and an approach to 'kill' thermal runaway by controlling the external heat transfer coefficient. The internal short circuit detection technology is being presently adapted for large-format cells on behalf of a major automotive OEM.

TIAX's internal short detection technologies and intervention approaches can be combined to significantly improve the safety profile of Li-ion battery packs, especially for DoD applications.

Acknowledgements

We gratefully acknowledge funding from the US Department of Energy for the thermal runaway experiments and simulations reported here.

[1] B. Barnett, D. Ofer, R. Stringfellow, S. Sriramulu (Safety Issues in Li-Ion Batteries) in: Robert A. Meyers (Ed.), Encyclopedia of Sustainability Science and Technology, Springer Science, 2012

[2] J. Zhang, Li-Ion in EDV and Safety Perspectives, 28th International Battery Seminar, Ft. Lauderdale, Florida, March 2011

[3] B. Barnett, S. Sriramulu, R. Stringfellow, C. McCoy and D. Ofer, Mechanisms of Safety, Predictions of Impending Thermal Runaway and Integrity of Safety Testing, 16th International Meeting on Lithium Batteries (IMLB-16), Jeju Island, Korea, June 2012

[4] C. McCoy, D. Ofer, B. Barnett and S. Sriramulu, Safety Technologies for Lithium-Ion Cells, 45th Power Sources Meting, Las Vegas, NV, 2012

[5] S. Sriramulu, R. Stringfellow, C. McCoy, J. Rempel, Y-E. Hyung and B. Barnett, Perspectives on Factors Controlling Thermal Runaway of Lithium-Ion Batteries, 224th Meeting of the Electrochmical Society, San Francisco, CA, 2013

Advanced Li/CF_x-MnO_2 Hybrid Technology Development

Mario Destephen, Dong Zhang, HyunJoo Bang, and Ernest Ndzebet
EaglePicher Technologies, LLC
3220 Industrial Road, Joplin, MO 64801

Abstract: *This paper describes the work at EaglePicher Technologies on the development of a high performance Li/MnO_2-CF_x technology capable of delivering high capacity at high discharge rates over wide operating temperature range. Performance of the hybrid chemistry has been validated at up to 1.5C rate and at temperatures between -40°C and 85°C. A general overview of recent developments in hybrid chemistry at EaglePicher is presented. Performance of the hybrid chemistry in various cell formats (cylindrical, prismatic, and pouch cells) is presented. The paper covers several applications with emphasis on portable power.*

Keywords: carbon fluoride; manganese dioxide; battery.

Introduction

Lithium/Carbon fluoride (Li/CFx) is an attractive primary power source, because of its high specific energy and energy density, low self-discharge (less than 1% a year), excellent thermal stability, wide operating temperature range (-40 to 85°C), and improved abuse tolerance over other lithium systems. However, the road blocks that prevent a wider market penetration of Li/CFx chemistry are its initial voltage delay at low temperature, thermal management issue at high discharge rates, and its material cost. Several approaches have been used to address these issues including a partial substitution of CF_x by manganese dioxide to form hybrid cathode [1-2]. Using web-coating process, EPT has developed CF_x-MnO_2 hybrid cathode, which not only maintains all the favorable advantages of Li/CF_x but also provides the highest specific energy density and excellent performance in wide temperature range as compared to other lithium primary chemistries.

This paper deals with the development of an advanced CFx hybrid chemistry that uses a mixture of CF_x and MnO_2 as cathode material. The cathode composition, cell design, and battery design were optimized for various applications including portable power, high rate batteries and high energy batteries.

Experimental

Materials and cathode process were described previously [3-4]. Carbon fluoride (CF_x) and electrolytic manganese dioxide (MnO_2) used in this work were commercially available materials. The hybrid cathodes were processed using EPT advanced web coating equipment similar to that used in lithium ion technology. The cathode composition and formulation were optimized to achieve high electrode density without sacrificing the rate capability. The cells incorporate a separator with shutdown technology. The electrolyte is a mixture of organic solvents with a lithium inorganic salt.

Results and Discussion

Through extensive effort of several years, EPT has developed a high energy lithium primary cell technology that includes a CFx/MnO_2 hybrid cathode, a web coating process for the hybrid cathode, and proper electrolyte formulations. Among these features, MnO_2 helps reduce the heat generation, eliminate voltage delay and lower the material cost, while the web coating process provides a thin electrode that allows high rate capability. In this section, we will discuss the performance of the hybrid chemistry in different cell and battery formats for various applications.

D Size Cell Development

The initial efforts in the hybrid chemistry were focused on the development of a D size cell for the BA-XX90 battery application. The target was to develop a cell with twice the capacity and specific energy of the Li/SO_2 cell. Figure 1 shows the discharge profile at 2A of our Li/CFx-MnO_2 cell. Data for the Li/SO_2 and CFx cells are provided for comparison. As can be seen in the figure, the hybrid cells delivered 15.5Ah without the initial voltage delay that is characteristic of CFx cells. This is twice the capacity of Li/SO_2. A lighter aluminum can was incorporated to replace the mild steel container to achieve the specific energy goal.

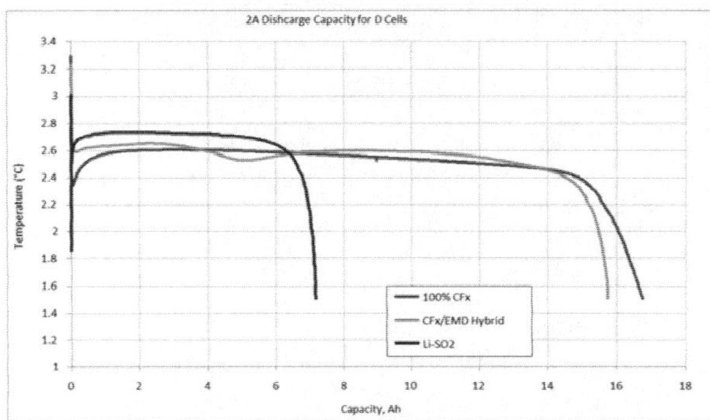

Figure 1. Discharge performance of hybrid D size cell at 2A and room temperature

The cathode and electrolyte formulations were optimized to deliver the rate capability over the wide operating temperature range that was needed for the application. Figure 2 shows the performance of the D cell at 2A and different temperatures. As can be seen in the figure, the cell delivered more than 13 Ah at -40°C.

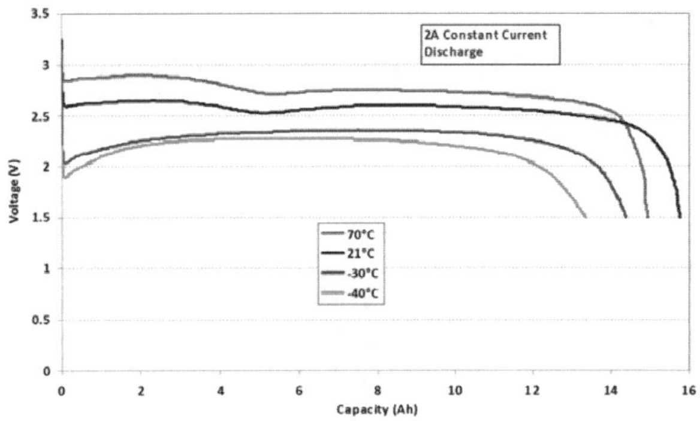

Figure 2. Discharge performance of hybrid D size cells at 2A and different temperatures

BA-XX90 Battery Performance

The hybrid D size cell was incorporated into the BA-XX90 battery for evaluation. In addition to the advantages in capacity and specific energy, the hybrid chemistry provides significant reduction in heat generation during discharge compared to the pure CFx chemistry. A contoured battery case geometry was developed to increase heat conduction to the exterior of the battery. The new BA-XX90 battery case also included a high thermal conductivity case material to further help with heat conduction. Figure 3 shows a picture of the contoured battery case.

Figure 3. Contoured BA-XX90 battery design

Figure 4 shows the discharge performance at 2A of the Li/CFx-MnO_2 hybrid battery. As can be seen, the hybrid cell delivered 16.0Ah above 20.0V and without voltage delay. This is twice the capacity of Li/SO_2. The maximum battery skin temperature was 62°C.

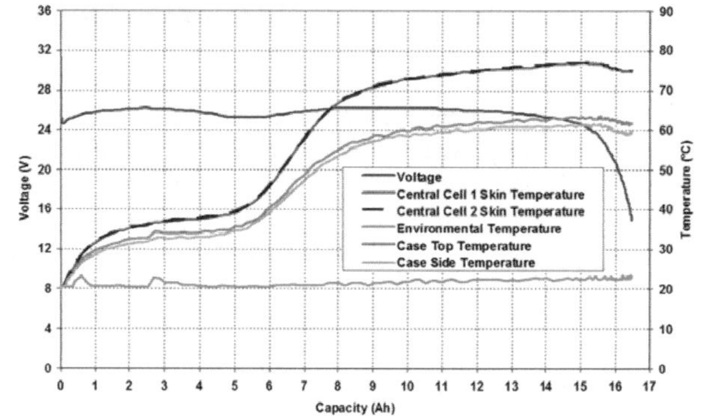

Figure 4. Discharge performance of hybrid battery at 2A

High Rate Hybrid Technology Development

The hybrid cathode was further optimized to improve rate capability for higher rate applications. High conductivity carbon additives were incorporated to improve rate capability. Electrolyte formulation was optimized for low temperature applications. CR123 cells were used as test vehicle for this development.

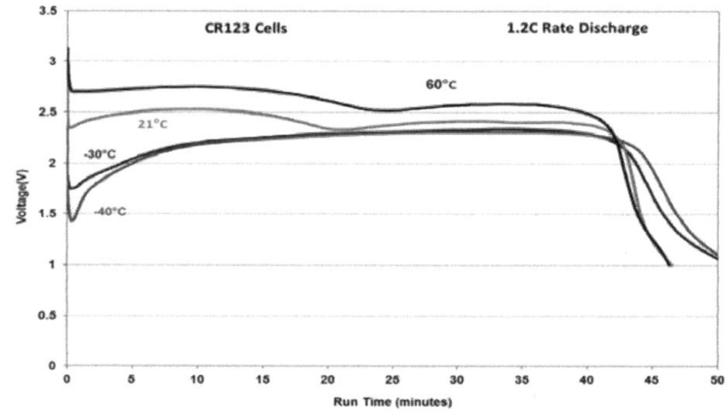

Figure 5. Discharge performance of hybrid CR123 cells

Figure 5 illustrates the discharge profiles of the hybrid CR123 cells at 1.2C rate at different temperatures. As can be seen, the cells exhibit good discharge performance between -40°C and 60°C. It should also be noted that hybrid cells demonstrated good shelf life performance.

Hybrid Pouch Cell Development

Pouch cell with hybrid chemistry was developed to maximize energy density. Pouch cell format offers opportunities for better performance with reduced weight burden in portable power applications. The major challenge for hybrid pouch cell is cell swelling due to the well-known swelling behavior of CF_x during discharge. The higher the amount of CF_x in the hybrid cathode, the higher the extent of swelling was. The swelling will not only affect the battery integrity, but also will negatively impact the battery discharge performance in the pouch cell format. Figure 6 shows a picture of the hybrid pouch cell developed at EaglePicher.

Figure 6. Li/CFx-MnO2 Pouch Cell

The chemistry and design of the pouch cells were optimized by selecting proper cathode active material, cathode composition, carbon conductive additives, and binder. Also, for the active materials, the ratio of the amount of MnO_2 to CF_x was optimized in terms of its effect on swelling, heat generation, and energy density requirement for the conformal battery. The cathode loading was optimized according to the process capability, energy density and power requirements for the battery. Cathode porosity was also optimized based on its effect on cathode swelling and energy density requirement for the battery. Figure 7 illustrates the effect of electrode formulation on pouch cell swelling at different temperatures. As can be seen in the figure, electrode composition B showed less swelling compared to electrode composition A. The lower swelling in electrode B resulted in significant improvements in cell performance.

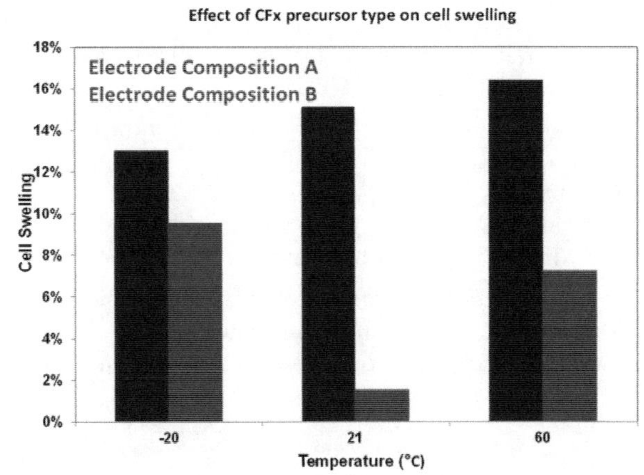

Figure 7. The effect of electrode composition on pouch cell swelling

Performance of the hybrid pouch cell was validated at up to 1.5C rate for a wide range of temperatures. Figure 8 illustrates the performance of pouch cells at different temperatures. As can be seen, the pouch cells were able to deliver high efficiency from -40°C to 60°C. The development of advanced conformal batteries containing these pouch cells is underway at EPT.

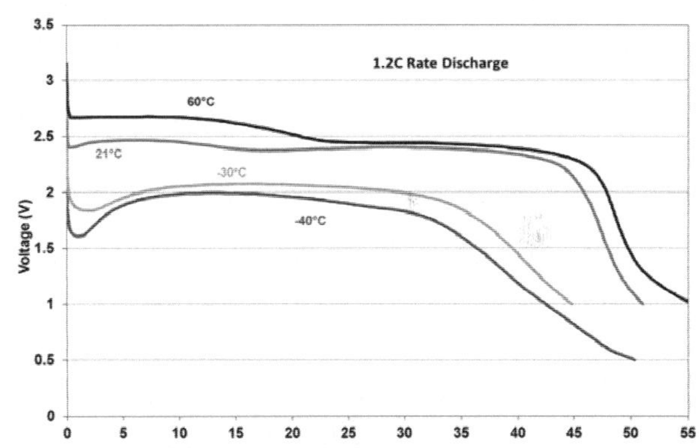

Figure 8. Discharge performance of pouch cells

In conclusion, EaglePicher Technologies has successfully developed high capacity and high rate primary batteries capable of operating in wide range of temperature. The BA-XX90 battery developed with this chemistry provided twice the service life compared to current Li/SO_2 batteries. The hybrid electrode developed for the BA-XX90 battery was further optimized to improve rate capability and low temperature performance for higher rate applications. Performance of the high rate design was demonstrated at up to 1.5C rate and temperatures between -40°C to 60°C. Pouch cells with hybrid chemistry were developed to maximize energy density. The pouch cells offer a good opportunity for conformal power sources.

Acknowledgement

This material is released to the public domain in accordance with ITAR 22 CFR 120.11.

References

1. Marple, J. W., "Performance characteristics of Li/MnO_2-CFx hybrid cathode jellyroll cells" *Journal of Powers Sources*, vol. 19, pp.325-335, 1987.
2. Leger, V. Z., "Non aqueous cell having a MnO_2/polycarbon fluoride cathode," US patent 4327166, April 1982.
3. Zhang, D., E. Ndzebet, M. Yang, "Advanced Battery Chemistry for Portable Power," *Proceeding of the 44th Power Sources Conference*, Las Vegas, Nevada, 14-17 June 2010.
4. Destephen, M., D. Zhang, H. Bang, J. Wang, U. Viswanathan, E. Ndzebet, "Advanced Hybrid Battery Chemistry for Portable Power," *Proceeding of the 45th Power Sources Conference*, Las Vegas, Nevada, 11-14 June 2012.
5. Read, J., D. Foster, J. Wolfenstine, and S. Zhang, "Microcalorimetry of Li/CFx Cells and Discharge Mechanism", *www.arl.army.mil/arlreports/2009/ARL-TR-5043.pdf*, 2009.

Discharge Capacity Improvements for Lithium MnO2 Systems in Military Applications

Carlos R Negrete and Allan J. Davenport
Saft America, Inc, 313 Crescent Street, Valdese, NC 28690
carlos.negrete@saftbatteries.com or www.saftbatteries.com

Abstract: *Saft is an industry leader in the development and manufacturing of both primary and rechargeable portable power solutions with a record of proven reliability across a wide range of applications. Saft has proudly served the United States warfighter providing the most comprehensive range of battery systems to deliver power capability for every mission. Saft continues to offer the ability to deliver solutions in all field proven primary chemistries including Lithium Sulfur Dioxide, Lithium MnO2, and Lithium Thionyl Chloride, and now Lithium MnO2/CFx.*

Saft's LiMnO2 program has delivered over the last 10 years proven battery designs to meet the requirements of the MIL-PRF 49471B and now the MIL-PRF 32271 specifications. Over this time Saft's has incorporated the Lithium Manganese Dioxide and more recently the Mixed Oxide (combining MnO2 and CFx cathode materials) battery technology into multiple battery systems and demonstrated the ability to meet and exceed the requirements of the military.

Saft America continues to develop new cell designs with the aim of increasing overall energy densities while delivering a chemistry platform capable of meeting the robust performance and safety requirements for the military. This paper presents the latest results in cell designs to increase the capacity and energy densities and compares against currently available LiMnO2 and Mixed Oxide systems.

Keywords: lithium; manganese dioxide, primary chemistry, high capacity, BA5X90

Introduction and Background

LiMnO2 battery systems are widely used for military primary portable power applications. The chemistry is well suited for high capacity and high current discharge applications across a wide temperature range. Today the chemistry is incorporated into multiple cell sizes for batteries specified under the MIL-PRF 32271 requirements. With the current Saft D cell (LM33550) design, the chemistry delivers 12.0 ampere hrs (under 2 ampere constant current discharge) and is in current use for the BA5390, BA5380, and BA5360 batteries.

In recent years, the chemistry application has been expanded to create a hybrid cathode chemistry systems combining MnO2 with carbon monofluoride to increase the capacity of the chemistry. After extensive work carried out, a new D sized mixed oxide cell design (Saft's LH33550) containing 20-30% CFx in the cathode has been demonstrated to deliver 15.5 to 16 ampere hours when discharged at 2 amperes constant current. The increase in capacity was achieved through extensive work to develop an efficient high density cathode and overall process and design improvements of other internal components and assemblies to increase the cells active material content. The new mixed oxide cell design has since been tested to demonstrate compliance to the MIL PRF 32271 when utilized in a BA5X90 battery format.

As previously indicated by several sources in the industry, the use of CFx to increase the capacity of a mixed oxide cell also creates several disadvantages to the overall performance of chemistry. When compared to pure MnO2 systems, cells containing CFx have lower operating voltages, significant self heating during the time CFx discharge occurs, lower temperature performance, and significantly higher cost in terms of Whr/$ as the cost of CFx is still substantially higher than MnO2.

Through the development of the mixed oxide LH33550 cell, several cell design modifications and processing improvements were carried out than can also be applied to standard MnO2 systems. Saft has now begun implementing such changes to create a new cell design with significantly higher capacity with all the functionality of previous MnO2 systems and none of the disadvantages of systems containing CFx.

Experimental

The cell is of a spiral wound electrode design using a metallic lithium foil as anode and EMD MnO2 as cathode coated on a current collector screen. The cell utilizes all standard safety features including a separator with "shutdown", specially formulated electrolyte, safety vent mechanism, proven steel housing, and hermetic seal using a positive (Molybdenum) post insulated by TA-23 glass.

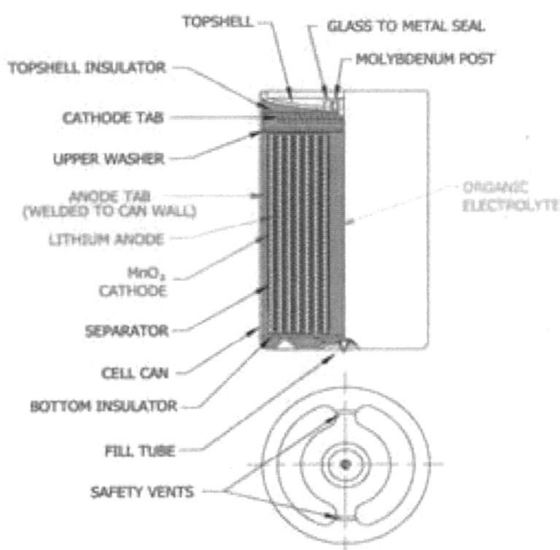

Figure 1

The cells were tested for capacity at 2 ampere constant discharge rate at 21C and compared against existing cell designs of pure MnO2 and MnO2/CFx cells. As results show, the test cells delivered a capacity above 2.0 volts of 13.8 Amp hrs or a 15% increase over the standard 12.0 Amp Hr cell. As with pure MnO2 systems, the operating voltage follows a single discharge profile which is higher than the standard dual plateau profile observed with the mixed oxide system.

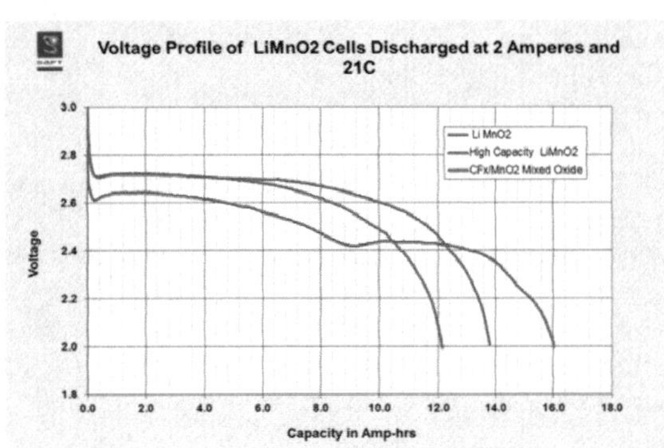

Figure 2

The cells were used to prepare BA5390 batteries in accordance to MIL PRF 32271 requirements. Sample BA5390 batteries were tested for capacity at ambient temperature and under the SICGARS constant power discharge profile. As Figure 2 shows, the MnO2 cells delivered and additional 1 ampere hour of capacity while the mixed oxide cell battery delivered 0.4 of additional capacity versus the results obtained when tested under constant current discharge. The difference in additional delivered capacity under constant power discharge conditions is due to the higher operating voltage of standard MnO2 systems which in turn reduce the current draw requirements.

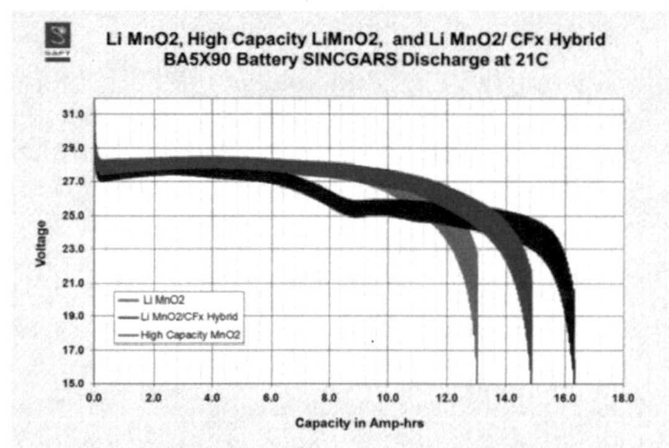

Figure 3

Conclusion

SAFT America has developed a primary Lithium MnO2 battery system technology capable of delivering increased capacities and higher energy densities. Under constant current and constant power discharge conditions such as the SINCGARS profile, the new cell can deliver significantly higher running time without any of the disadvantages observed on battery systems utilizing CFx to increase cell performance. The design incorporates all the safety, function, and reliability required to meet the demands of a standard battery specification MIL-PRF 32271. In this manner, the new technology will serve to provide the end user the option of selecting a battery system with the benefits of significantly higher capacity versus standard MnO2 systems available today without sacrificing performance or substantially higher costs associated with using CFx materials.

References

1. 42-45 Proceedings of Power Sources Conference
2. David Linden, "Hand book of Batteries" Second Edition

CF_x Hybrid Commercialization and Process Automation

Brian Schupbach
EaglePicher Technologies, LLC
Joplin, MO 64801

Abstract: *EaglePicher Technologies has transitioned its Li/CF_x-MnO_2 Hybrid "D" cell and XX90 battery platform to production, including investment in state-of-the-art automation equipment to package the technology in a wide range of cell and battery sizes. This paper will provide an overview of the production product designs, manufacturing capability, and performance data from the D cell and XX90 battery.*

Keywords: Primary; Lithium; Battery; Cell; CFx; Hybrid; Li/CF_x-MnO_2; LCF-XX90-03; LCF-133; BA-5790; Portable Power; Military

Introduction

EaglePicher Technologies, LLC has been aggressively developing and improving its Li/CF_x primary battery chemistry for the past several years. EaglePicher's CF_x Hybrid technology delivers twice the capacity of legacy SO_2 systems in the same volume at the same weight, and nearly 1.4X the capacity of MnO_2 at a much lower weight. The end goal of this effort is production of the next generation primary battery platform to support the Warfighter. This is expected to be a significant improvement for a variety of portable power applications.

In a clear demonstration of confidence and commitment to this technology, EaglePicher has invested in a low-rate-initial-production line dedicated to packaging this technology in a wide range of cell and battery sizes. The production line is fully operational, producing D size cells and assembly capability into the XX90 battery form factor. The LCF-133 D cell and LCF-XX90-03 battery are the first products to be produced on the line. The LCF-XX90-03 battery will meet the requirements of the BA-5790 which is currently being added as a new Type IV Lithium Battery to MIL-PRF-32271A which is the US ARMY performance specification for Lithium Batteries. This cell and battery are currently in testing and on track to complete qualification in 2014.

LCF-133 CF_x Hybrid D Cell

The D size cell is the first form factor to be produced on the production line. The design has been scaled-up for the transition to production and is currently undergoing validation testing with qualification planned for 2014. The cell has been developed to meet the requirements of MIL-PRF-32271A and MIL-PRF-32271-1A draft specifications.

The weight savings from the CF_x material combined with an additional 20% weight reduction by utilizing an aluminum cell container (as opposed to steel), results in a cell weight just under 80 grams. This is an impressive weight for a cell that delivers 15Ah of capacity under a 3A load at 21°C. The cell is capable of operating over a wide temperature range from -40°C to 60°C as shown in Figure 2. It achieves >95% of full capacity at -30°C under a 2A load, without any voltage delay. Additionally, the cell boasts excellent rate capability for a lithium primary cell, handling up to a 4A continuous load with ease, and providing pulse capability up to 10 Amps. The combination of high energy and rate capability make this cell an ideal alterative to Li-Ion for applications where a rechargeable solution is not practical.

Figure 1. LCF-133 CF_x Hybrid D Cell

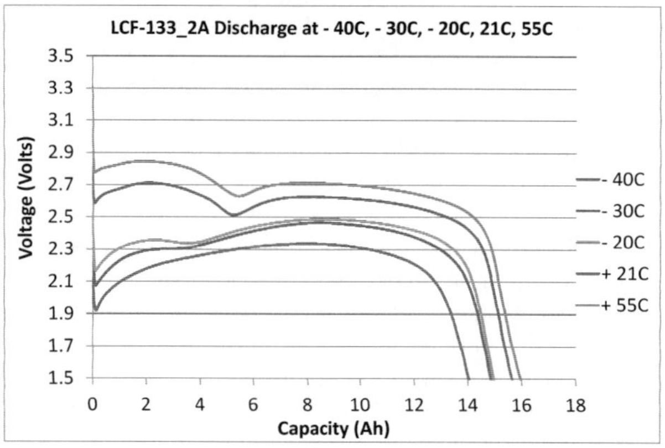

Figure 2. LCF-133, 2A load at various temperatures

LCF-XX90-03 CF_x Hybrid Battery

The LCF-XX90-03 is the first battery being produced on the line. This battery is comprised of 10 LCF-133 D cells and is specifically targeted for the BA-5790 battery defined in the new MIL-PRF-32271A and MIL-PRF-32271-1A draft specifications. The design has been scaled up for production, and prototype testing is currently in process. Validation testing and qualification is scheduled for completion in 2014. The battery fits in the same envelope as the legacy XX90 designs such as the BA-5590 and BA-5390 batteries, but EaglePicher has revamped the design to making handling easier and improve thermal management. Like many other XX90 designs, this battery operates in both 15V and 30V modes. It also incorporates SMBus which can be used to monitor the battery, providing valuable information to devices and the end-user.

Figure 3. LCF-XX90-03 CF_x Hybrid Battery

Weighing in at 1.0 kg, the battery meets the SO_2 max weight specification of 1.06 kg while delivering 15Ah or 2X the capacity of SO_2. This weight is far below the MnO_2 max weight requirement of 1.41 kg and significantly less than the preliminary max weight of 1.27 kg for the CF_x Type IV battery as defined in the draft specification. This doubling of energy density is a significant advantage for the Warfighter, providing twice the mission life for the same weight and volume.

All of the advantages of the LCF-133 cell design translate to exceptional performance at the battery level as well. The battery can support up to a 4A discharge rate in 30V mode and an 8A rate in 15V mode. The low temperature performance is even better at the battery level, with the ability to achieve full 15Ah capacity at -30°C under a 2A load in 30V (series) mode. This is shown in Figure 4. This is a vast improvement over Type I MnO_2 batteries where a significant reduction in capacity is seen at lower temperatures. The improvement in mission time is particularly evident when testing the battery per the IDC (SINCGARS) profile. The CF_x Hybrid battery run time is nearly 60 hours (see Figure 5) as compared to the 40 hour MnO_2 and 30 hour SO_2 requirements.

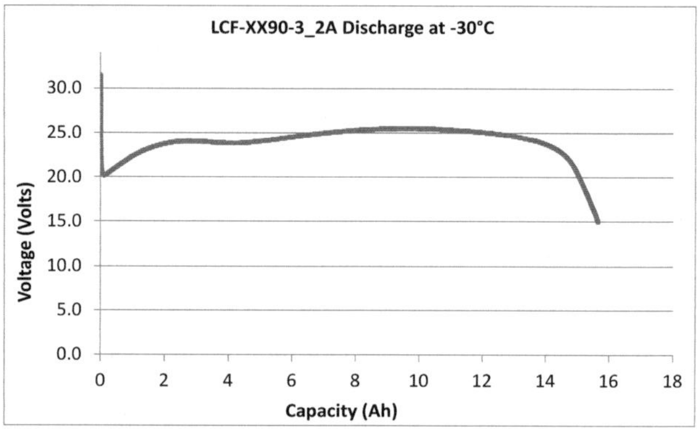

Figure 4. LCF-XX90-03, 2A -30°C

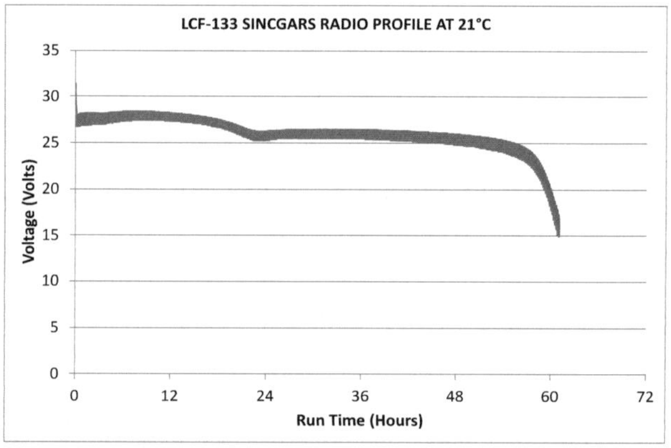

Figure 5. LCF-XX90-03, SINCGARS Radio Profile Ran at 21°C

Manufacturing Capability

EaglePicher has made a significant investment in a dedicated line to produce CF_x cells and batteries. This important step clearly demonstrates the commitment at EaglePicher to move this technology beyond R&D to commercialization. The investment covers equipment from cathode processing through assembly and testing of cells and batteries. The initial startup of the line was geared around production of the D cell and XX90 battery. However, a key requirement for the line was to provide flexibility to produce a wide range of cylindrical cell sizes. Ultimately, the equipment was specked to accommodate 2/3A through DD size cylindrical cells. This capability to produce a large range of cell diameters, heights, and capacities, strongly positions EaglePicher to meet many new application needs as the technology becomes more widely adopted.

In addition to flexibility, the state-of-the-art equipment utilizes a high degree of automation for all core processes. Not only does the automation increase throughput and drive down labor costs, but built-in process controls provide real-time measurements of key process indicators to ensure robust and repeatable processes. The equipment utilizes PLC and HMI driven recipes to manage all the parameters for a specific cell. These recipes simplify product change-overs by automatically configuring all the parameters on the machine when the cell recipe is selected. A list and overview of the core equipment is as follows.

- Powder Mixer – Prepares powders to achieve the right particle size distribution
- Slurry Mixer – Large mixer to prepare cathode slurry. PLC and HMI defined mix sequence with automated execution
- Coater – Applies cathode slurry to substrate.
- Calender – Compresses cathode material to target thickness to achieve desired porosity.
- Slitter – Slits master cathode roll into multiple lanes sized for the applicable cell.
- Winder – Fully automated winder produces jelly roll comprised of cathode, lithium, separator, and tabs. This machine incorporates inline dimensional and electrical checks on each jelly roll to verify conformance.
- Assembly equipment – Jelly roll insertion, internal tab welds, and header to can seating.
- Header welder – Automated weld of header to can that utilizes a vision system to define weld path for each cell position.
- Filling machine – Automated electrolyte filling and sealing of cell. Performs electrical check and pre and post weights on every cell.
- Testing equipment – Test systems to perform pre-discharge, OCV/CCV checks, and lot acceptance testing.
- Cell packaging – Equipment for labeling, heat sleeving, and tabbing.
- Battery packaging – Equipment for tab welding and case assembly.

In addition to the equipment investment, a new dry room with environmental monitoring system was built specifically for assembly of CF_x cells. The dry room with equipment can be seen in Figure 6 below. The cathode processing is also located in a controlled dry room environment.

Conclusion

In conclusion, EaglePicher regards the Li/CF_x-MnO_2 chemistry as the next generation primary battery system with significant advantages over existing lithium-based chemistries. EaglePicher fully expects this technology to be a key solution in meeting the ever increasing demand for more power in a large range of military applications. EaglePicher has made the strategic decision to move this technology forward by investing in a production line that is already full operational and producing the D cell and XX90 battery, both of which will achieve production-readiness in 2014.

Acknowledgement

Thanks to the R&D team at EaglePicher who developed this technology as well as the New Product Development and Operations teams who scaled it up for production. Special thanks to CERDEC for supporting the CF_x development efforts for the last several years and BATTNET for supporting the transition to production. This material is released to the public domain in accordance with ITAR 22 CFR 120.11.

Figure 6. CF_x **Cell Assembly Dry Room**

Fast Activating Miniature Lithium Thionyl Chloride Reserve Battery

Harald Wich, Roland Hein and Sergio Moreno-Lechado
Diehl & Eagle Picher GmbH
Fischbachstr. 20, 90552 Roethenbach a.d. Pegnitz, Germany

Abstract: *A miniature Lithium Thionyl Chloride Reserve Battery (MLRB) with a very fast activation time – single digit milliseconds – was developed. A smaller design as the current Liquid Reserve Batteries (LRB) was achieved. The miniaturization of all subsystems and the improvement of the activation time were possible due to the use of CAD Software as well as FEM and CFD Software. These simulations results were compared with first firing tests.*

Keywords: Electrical fuze; Lithium Thionyl Chloride Reserve Battery; Electrolyte; Unit cell

Introduction

LRB, whose activation time is in the order of hundreds of milliseconds, are commonly used as electrical fuzes for artillery and mortars. Actual LRB have dimensions of about ø32x25 mm but the new generation of fuzes requires smaller batteries. Diehl & Eagle Picher GmbH has designed a MLRB with dimensions of about ø10x10 mm, which is activated in the order of milliseconds, and can be used in medium and smaller caliber.

Design of MLRB

MLRB contains a Lithium cell which is activated by an electrolyte. This electrolyte is stored in a hermetic sealed glass ampoule due to the required long storage time of the ammunition. Between anode and cathode a glass fleece of fibers is placed as separator which is also a medium to retain the electrolyte after the activation. See figure 1.

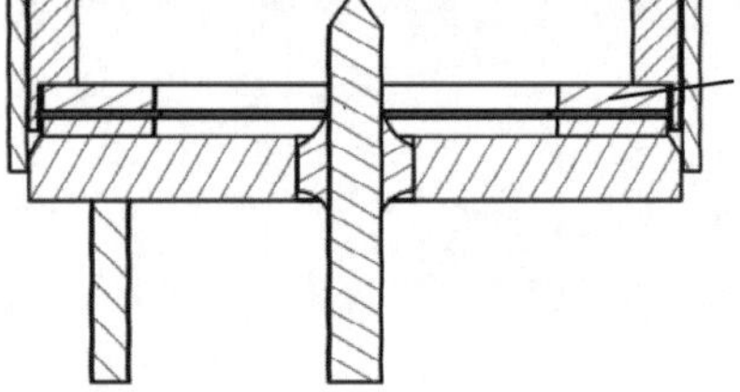

Figure 1. Sketch of MLRB

The challenge here is the activation, due to the breaking of the ampoule, during the launch and not during drop tests. To satisfy this important requirement, an activation mechanism (AM) is designed. The AM consists of a small structure of synthetic material which supports the ampoule. Bridges, which support a disc of the AM, should be broken during the launch and therefore, the ampoule. That is possible due to the extremely high acceleration during the firing of the munition. The acceleration in the axial axis (z) is shown in figure 2 ($1\ g = 9.81\ m/s^2$). The battery is required to activate within less than 5 ms after maximum acceleration.

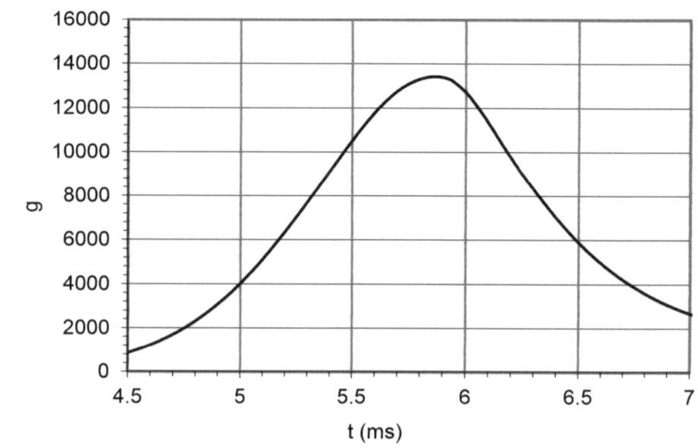

Figure 2. Launch acceleration

Cell design

The simplified load profile, which fulfills all the battery specifications, can be seen in figure 3. The required capacity in this case is 0.0126 mAh.

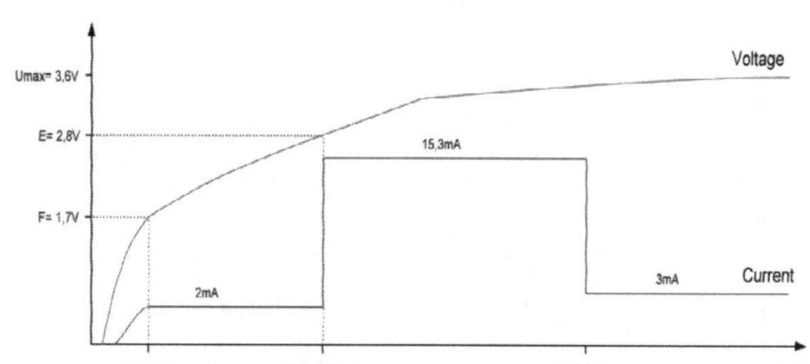

Figure 3. Load profile

Under these conditions, one Lithium cell with a 60 mm^2 surface is designed. The theoretical capacity of the electrolyte is 19.5 mAh and the capacity of the lithium is 23.4 mAh. The nominal voltage of the $SOCl_2$ system is 3.6 V. Thus, the required values of capacity and voltage are reached.

Activation mechanism design

Due to the launch acceleration, an axial force F_z in all the components of the battery is built up. The reaction force (N) supported by the bridges is given by equation 1:

$$F_z^{Bridges} = a \cdot (m_{Amp} + m_{Electr} + m_{Sup\ Disc}) \quad (1)$$

Where a is the acceleration of the system (m/s²), m_{Amp}, m_{Electr} and $m_{Sup\ Disc}$ are the masses of the ampoule, electrolyte and the support disc (kg).

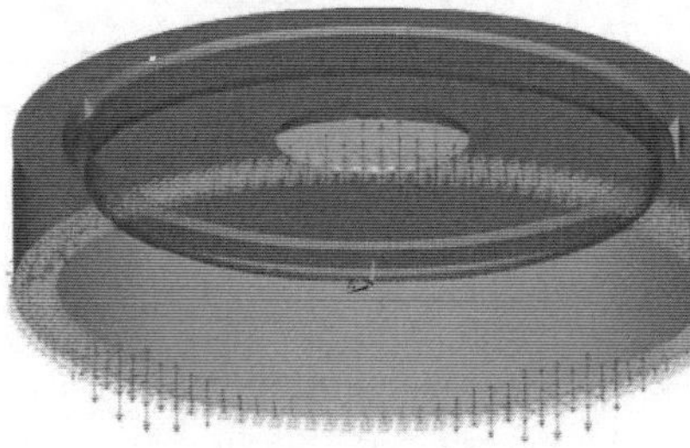

Figure 4. Applied forces on the AM

A finite element analysis was developed to calculate the stress on the AM, especially on the bridges. As a result of the simulations, the bridges were dimensioned and optimized. The bridges were designed to break at roughly $a_0 = 5600$ g´s which occurs at $t_0 = 5.120$ ms after the ignition.

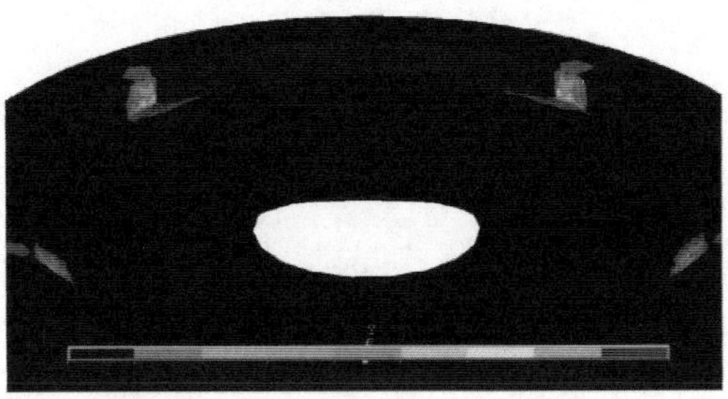

Figure 5. Stress on the AM

Glass ampoule design

The thickness of the glass was also optimized. As it was pointed out, the AM should be broken at $t_0 = 5.120$ ms. After approximately 0.130 ms ($t_1 = 5.250$ ms, $a_1 = 7233$ g), the ampoule collides with the top of the metal pin. The force on the ampoule at this time is:

$$F_z^{Amp} = a_1 \cdot (m_{Amp} + m_{Electr}) \quad (2)$$

The ampoule is designed to be broken when this force is applied on the ampoule bottom. A linear pressure test method was used to select a glass thickness and analyze the breaking behavior. Ampoules were pressed against a metal pin. The force and the deformation in the ampoule were registered when the ampoules were broken. The results in figure 6 belong to an ampoule with 0.5 mm glass thickness.

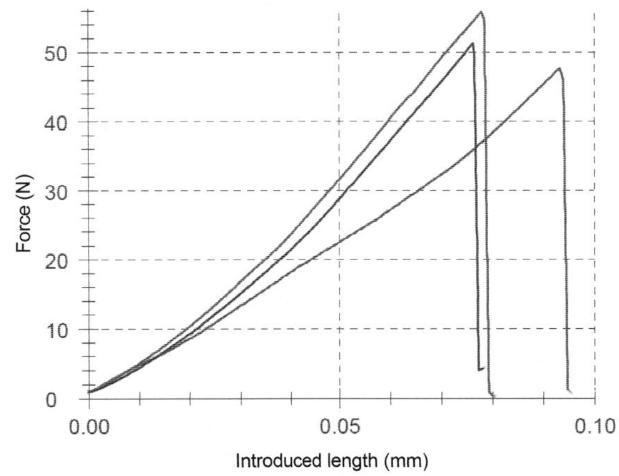

Figure 6. Linear pressure test

A comparison between some tests with different glass thickness is shown in the figure 7. As can be seen, the thicker the ampoule bottom, the higher forces are necessary to break the ampoule.

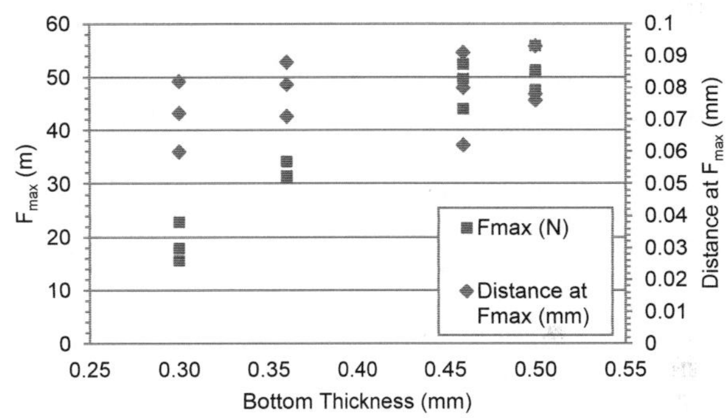

Figure 7. Glass ampoule breaking

The linear pressure test method is somewhat conservative compared with the real situation where the dynamic force F_z^{Amp} is superimposed by the impact after 0.13 ms of the "free flight".

CFD Simulation

At this point, a simulation to analyze the behavior of the electrolyte under launch acceleration was developed. The electrolyte must flood the glass fleece. Apparently this process is very complex and the extreme conditions of the battery must be analyzed. In short, the electrolyte is axially accelerated when the ampoule is shattered at $t_2 = 5.250$ ms, displaces the air under the ampoule and flows through the glass fleece. The axial force on the electrolyte is described in equation 3.

$$F_z^{Electr} = V_{Electr} \cdot a_2 \cdot \rho_{Electr} \quad (3)$$

Where V_{Electr} is the volume of electrolyte (m³), a_2 is the acceleration of the system (m/s²) at t_2 = 5.250 ms and ρ_{Electr} is the density of electrolyte (kg/m³). This CFD simulation is based on the Darcy´s law (equation 4), which explains the behavior of a fluid in an isotropic porous media.

$$\frac{\partial}{\partial t}\left(\rho_{\text{Electr}} \cdot \varepsilon_p\right) + \nabla \cdot \rho_{\text{Electr}} \left(-\frac{\kappa}{\mu}\nabla p\right) = 0 \qquad (4)$$

Where: t is time (s), p is the pressure (Pa), μ is the dynamic viscosity (Pa·s) of electrolyte, ε_p is the porosity, κ the permeability (m^2) of the glass fleece. Due to the appearance of electrolyte and air in the glass fleece during the launch, relative permeability in multiphase flow in porous media is considered [1, 2]. This consideration needs a relative permeability model. See figure 8. Because of the extreme acceleration of the system and the materials used, it is not possible to find similar information sources to compare the model. However, a plausible model for these conditions is considered. As can be seen, this model supposes that the electrolyte can occupy a maximum of 90% of the pores. In this case, the remaining 10% of the pores would be blocked with immobile air. This would be only possible due to the high acceleration which forces the electrolyte to impregnate the glass fleece and displaces the air.

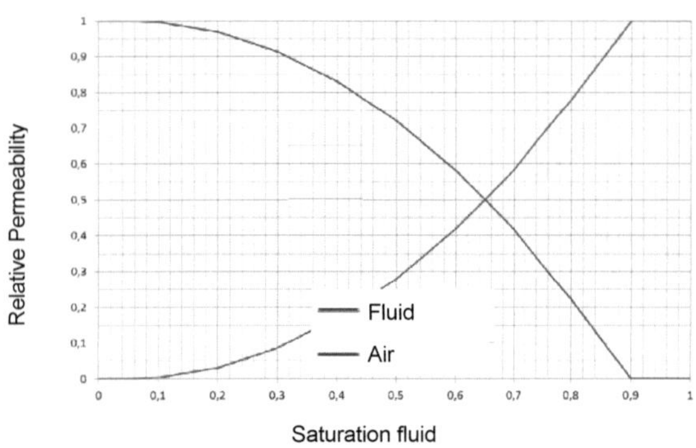

Figure 8. Relative permeability model

On the other hand, the mass transfer equation in porous media is:

$$\frac{\partial}{\partial t}\left(c_1 \varepsilon_p\right) + \nabla \cdot \left(c_1 \cdot \vec{u}\right) = \nabla \cdot D_c \cdot \nabla c_1 \qquad (5)$$

Where: C_l is the concentration of the liquid phase, $\vec{u}$ is the Darcy velocity (m/s) and D_c is the capillary diffusion (m^2/s). The introduced model in the simulation software is shown in figure 9. In order to make easier the reading of the simulation results, three observation points (a, b, c) were introduced in the glass fleece through the radial coordinate.

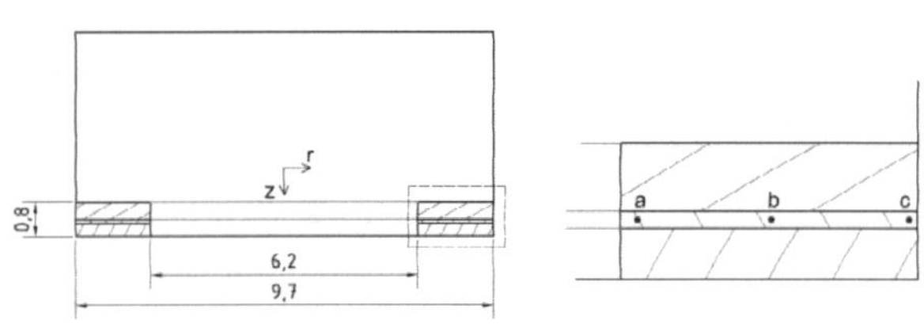

Figure 9. Model for the simulation and observation points

The simulation results are shown in figures 10 and 11. The electrolyte flows after the shattering of the ampoule and occupies the volume inside the cylindrical cell in only 0.001 ms. As it was pointed out according to the supposed model, only a maximal saturation of 90% is possible. The observation points show that the electrolyte flows through the glass fleece and the maximum saturation is reached in the pores.

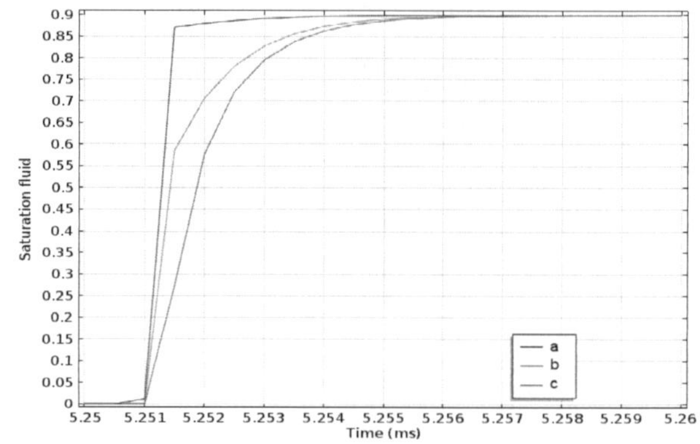

Figure 10. Electrolyte saturation in the observation points

At 5.254 ms, the 85% of the saturation is reached. At 5.256 ms, the 99%. Thanks to the results of the CFD simulation, it can be considered that the electrolyte impregnates the glass fleece at only 5.256 ms. And subsequently the battery is activated.

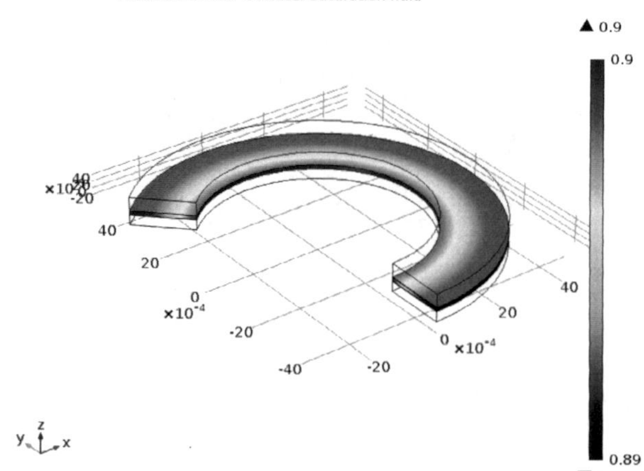

Figure 11. Electrolyte saturation at 5.256 ms

Experimental

The experimental results are shown in figures 12 and 13. Figure 12 represents a firing test where voltage was recorded on a flight recorder. The temporal axis is identical to the temporal axis of figure 2. The voltage levels "E" and "F" are reached before the required times "B" and "C". See figure 3. The load-change at approximately 20 ms indicates the low internal impedance of the load. The activation time in the simulation results is about 5.25 ms whereas the test data show that the voltage is 3 V after 7.68 ms. This difference is not significant. The simulation models simplify the firing process and, for example, do not take into account the time-depending chemical reactions which occur in anode and cathode.

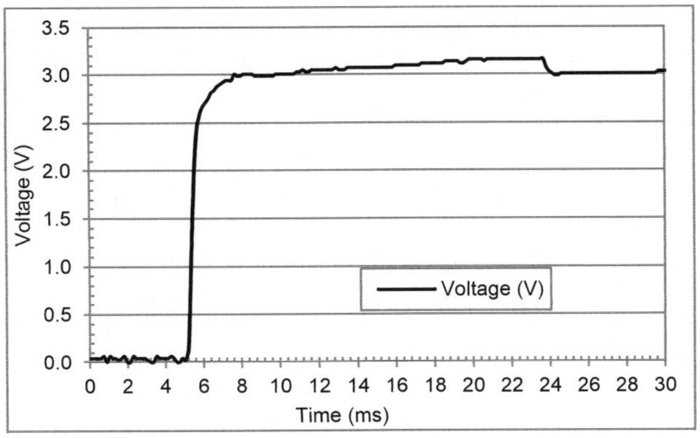

Figure 12. Firing rest result – 30 ms

Figure 13 shows the result of a drop-tower test in order to demonstrate the voltage over lifetime. The load-pulse at around 24 s demonstrates again the internal impedance of battery.

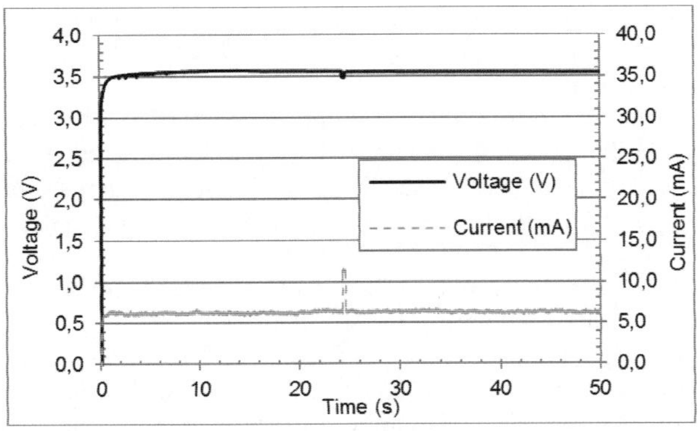

Figure 13. Drop-tower result - 50 s

Conclusions

Several models for different phases of the firing process were designed and simulated to calculate the activation time. The experimental results agree with the simulation results.

The test results show that the designed MLRB achieves the required specifications.

Figure 14. MLRB made by Diehl & Eagle Picher GmbH

References

1. Le Bars, M., M.G. Worster, "Interfacial conditions between a pure fluid and a porous medium: Implications for binary alloy solidification", Journal of fluid mechanics, vol. 550, pp. 149-173, 2006
2. Nield, D., A. Bejan, "Convection in porous media", Springer 2013.
3. Linden, D., T. B. Reddy, "Handbook of Batteries," Mc-Graw Hill, 2001

Properties of the Solid Ionic Conductor: $Li_7La_3Zr_2O_{12}$

Jeff Wolfenstine[1], Jan L. Allen[1], Jeff Read[1], Travis Thompson[2] and Jeff Sakamoto[2]

[1]Army Research Laboratory
2800 Powder Mill Road
Adelphi, MD 20783
[2]Michigan State University
Dept of Chem Engr & Mat Sci
East Lansing, MI 48824

Abstract: Cubic garnet of nominal composition $Li_7La_3Zr_2O_{12}$ (LLZO) is of interest as a possible electrolyte in a Li-metal halide battery composed of molten Li and an insoluble metal halide as electrodes operating in the temperature range ~300-350°C. As a consequence the chemical stability of LLZO with molten Li in this temperature range was investigated. After heating in molten Li the LLZO surface had undergone chemical coloration. X-diffraction, x-ray photoemission spectroscopy, electron paramagnetic resonance and heat-treatment experiments suggest that chemical coloration is a result of the formation of color centers, composed of an electron trapped at an oxygen vacancy. It was also observed that after immersion in molten Li that LLZO exhibited intergranular cracking..

Keywords: garnet; $Li_7La_3Zr_2O_{12;}$ color centers, cracking

Introduction

Cubic garnet of nominal composition $Li_7La_3Zr_2O_{12}$ (LLZO) is of interest as a possible electrolyte and physical barrier in Li-metal halide batteries composed of a molten Li anode and an insoluble metal halide cathode operating at temperatures of 300-350°C. If LLZO is to be used in this application, one important requirement is the chemical stability of LLZO with molten Li in this temperature range. It is the purpose of this paper to investigate the chemical stability of LLZO with molten Li in the temperature range 300-350°C, where it is anticipated to be used in molten Li-metal halide batteries.

Experimental

The cubic LLZO garnet material used in this study was prepared by a solid-state powder processing method and consolidated by uniaxial hot-pressing, as described previously [1]. The exact composition of the material is $Li_{6.28}Zr_2La_3Al_{0.24}O_{12}$. The LLZO material had a relative density of 97% with an equiaxed grain morphology and mean grain size of ~5μm. All chemical stability testing, including the standardizing heat-treatment, was conducted in a glove box under argon with an oxygen and water content less than 1 ppm. All samples were heated at 800°C for 2-4 h to standardize the specimens prior to testing. The purpose of this heat-treatment was to remove any surface films prior to testing. It has been shown for the case of Na wetting on beta-alumina that heating at high temperature enhanced Na wetting. It was suggested that the enhanced wetting was a result of the removal of surface films such as; water, carbonates or hydroxides [1]. It was observed by infrared spectroscopy that LLZO samples left in ambient air over time developed a Li_2CO_3 surface layer on them. The Li_2CO_3 layer could be removed by heating at 800°C for 2-4 h. The Li_2CO_3 layer did not reform as long as the sample was not exposed to ambient air. For chemical stability testing a LLZO sample was wrapped in Li foil, after which the wrapped sample was placed into a stainless tube, which was subsequently sealed at both ends by stainless steel end caps, tightened with a wrench. The sealed tube was heated in a furnace at temperatures of 300-350°C for a period of time ranging from 24 to 168 h. The sealed stainless steel tube was furnace cooled to room temperature, after which the sample was removed from the stainless steel tube, placed into a glass bottle sealed, then removed from the glove box to a dry room. In the dry room the sample was placed in a beaker of dry methanol to remove any adhering metallic Li on the surface, after which it was then stored in the dry room in a sealed pouch until it was analyzed.

The phase(s) present in the LLZO samples prior to and after chemical stability testing were determined using X-ray diffraction with a Rigaku Ultima III x-ray diffractometer in a parallel beam geometry. The surface composition of LLZO samples prior to and after chemical stability testing was determined using x-ray photoemission spectroscopy (XPS). The microstructure of the of LLZO samples prior to and after chemical stability testing was examined using scanning electron microscopy (SEM). In addition, the chemical composition of several LLZO samples after chemical stability testing were investigated in the SEM using energy dispersive X-ray spectroscopy (EDS).

Results and Discussion

The hot-pressed LLZO samples were tan-white colored after heat-treatment at 800°C. After heating in molten Li at 300-350°C the LLZO surface had undergone chemical coloration and become grey-black. The reacted layer was estimated to be ~ 300 nm after 168 h at 300°C. The x-ray diffraction patterns of the LLZO samples before and after immersion in molten Li at 300°C for 196 h are shown in Fig. 1. From Fig. 1 it is seen that the diffraction patterns look similar, before and after immersion in molten Li. For all chemical stability tests the diffraction patterns looked similar before and after testing, suggesting that no new phases formed during immersion. All patterns are predominantly single phase of cubic symmetry with space group $Ia\bar{3}d$.

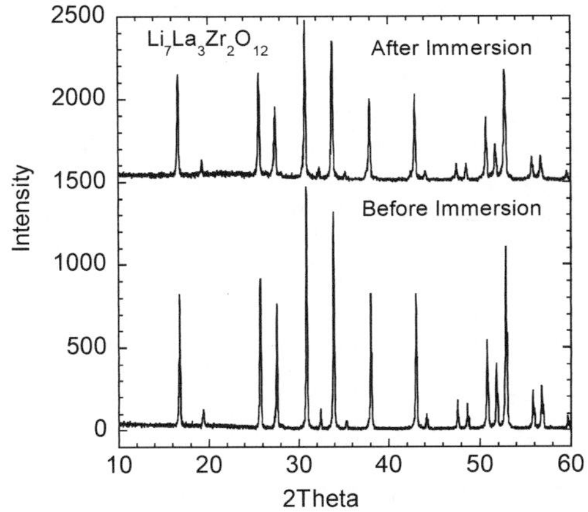

Fig. 1. X-ray diffraction patterns of $Li_7La_3Zr_2O_{12}$ before and after immersion in molten Li for 168 h at 300°C.

XPS spectra of the Li 1s core level electron in LLZO before and after immersion with molten Li at 300°C for 168 h. revealed that the binding energy for the Li 1s electron in LLZO before and after immersion is the same (55.0 eV). This suggests that only one oxidation state for Li is present in both materials, Li^+, no metallic Li is detected in the LLZO material after immersion. In addition, from Fig. 2 it is observed that the relative intensity of the Li^+ 1s electron peak is higher in the LLZO material after immersion compared to the as-received material, suggesting that during immersion with molten Li the Li^+ content of LLZO has increased. This was confirmed by XPS sputtering profiles of LLZO samples after immersion. XPS analysis revealed no shift in the binding energy of the La 3d, Zr 3d and Al 2p electrons before and after immersion with molten Li, suggesting that there was no valence change of La^{+3}, Zr^{+4} and Al^{+3} in LLZO after immersion in molten Li.

Figure 2 is an SEM image of the LLZO sample after immersion in molten Li at 300°C for 92 h. From Fig. 2 it can be observed that the sample exhibits cracks, that are nearly perpendicular to each other. Figure 3 is a high magnification image of a cracked region, revealing that fracture mode is entirely intergranular. Cracks were observed in all samples after immersion testing. No cracks were observed on the sample surface prior to immersion.

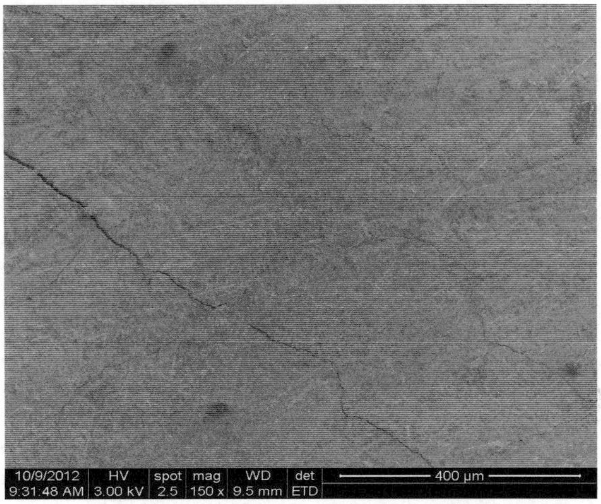

Fig. 2. Scanning electron micrograph of $Li_7La_3Zr_2O_{12}$ after immersion in molten Li for 92 h at 300°C.

Fig. 3. High magnification scanning electron image of $Li_7La_3Zr_2O_{12}$ after immersion in molten Li for 92 h at 300°C.

Several possible explanations may explain the origin of the chemical coloration in LLZO [2,3]. These include: 1] metallic Li in LLZO, 2] transition metal impurities in LLZO and 3] Li atoms diffuse interstitially in LLZO then dissociate to form Li ions and electrons, which is followed by trapping of the electrons by oxygen vacancies to form color centers. For the case of LLZO explanation number 1] can be ruled out since, no metallic Li was observed following immersion of LLZO in molten Li. Explanation 2] can also be ruled out as a possible reason since, LLZO contains no transition metal cations and XPS analysis revealed that La, Zr and Al did not change valence state after immersion. However, during chemical stability testing LLZO was placed inside a stainless steel tube. To check if LLZO picked up any transition metal impurities from the stainless steel tube EDS was conducted using the SEM for Ni, Fe and Cr on LLZO tested for 92 and 168 h. No transition metal impurities were found. Also XPS analysis of the immersed 168 h sample also revealed no transition metal impurities. Thus, explanation seems the most likely. For the case of explanation three an in Li^+ content should be observed in the reacted LLZO region compared to the as-received LLZO. This is in agreement with the experimental XPS results, which reveal an enhanced Li^+ content in the reacted LLZO region compared to the as-received LLZO region. For the case of color centers in should be able to be they could be bleached (change color from grey-black to the original tan-white as a consequence of the destruction of the color centers) as result of heating at high temperatures in an oxidizing atmosphere [3,4]. It was observed that when the grey-black colored reacted LLZO was heated in air at 800°C for 2-4 h it became tan-white colored. The same color as the as-received material. This result is also consistent with suggestion that the grey-black color in LLZO after Li immersion is associated with the formation of color centers.

The observation that LLZO cracked after immersion in molten Li at temperatures ranging from 300-350°C is in agreement with the results of H. Schmid et al. [4] who observed a similar effect with Nasicon, in that it cracked after exposure to molten sodium. Schmid et al. [4] suggested that the cracking of Nasicon was due to stresses generated as a result of volume changes associated with the addition of Na^+ gained during immersion. Owing to the similarity of the crack pattern for LLZO with that for Nasicon and the fact that x-ray diffraction and XPS analysis of the reacted LLZO material confirmed the presence of increased lattice volume and enhanced Li^+ compared to the as-received material respectively, it is highly likely that the cracking in LLZO is a result of stresses generated by volume changes due to additional Li^+ gained during immersion. Preliminary calculations for the stress generated by a volume expansion for LLZO are in close agreement with measured fracture stress values for and other solid state electrolytes, which may suggest in first approximation that LLZO cracking is indeed a result of the volume expansion due additional Li^+ gained during immersion. In order to conclusively confirm this suggestion the fracture stress of LLZO and the elastic constants such as Young's modulus as a function of temperature are required.

Summary

The chemical stability of cubic $Li_7La_3Zr_2O_{12}$ in molten Li in the temperature range 300-350°C, where a molten Li-metal halide battery is anticipated to operate in was investigated. After heating, the LLZO surface had undergone chemical coloration, changing from an initial tan-white color to grey-black. X-diffraction, x-ray photoemission spectroscopy, and heat-treatment experiments suggest that chemical coloration is a result of the formation of color centers, an electron trapped at an oxygen vacancy..

It was also observed that after immersion in molten Li that LLZO exhibited cracks, where as no cracks were observed in the samples prior to immersion. The fracture mode is entirely intergranular. Based on the nature of the LLZO cracking pattern and the close agreement of the predicted stresses with experimental fracture stress values for other cubic garnets and other solid Li- and Na-ion conductors, it is believed that the fracture of LLZO is a result of the stresses generated as a consequence of extra Li^+ gained during immersion.
.

Acknowledgements

JW and JLA would like to acknowledge support of the U. S. Army Research Laboratory (ARL). JS would like to acknowledge the support of the U.S. Army Research Office (ARO).

References

1, J. Wolfenstine, J. L. Allen, J. Read, J. Sakamoto (2013) J Mat Sci 48:5846..

2. L. C. De Jonghe, A. Buechele A (1982) J Mater Sci 17:885.

3. L. C. De Jonghe, A. Buechele, M. Armand (1983) Solid State Ionics 9&10:165.

4. H. Scmid, L. C. Jonghe, C. Cameron (1982) Solid State Ionics 6:57.

Enhanced Performance Flexible Batteries Based on Composite Electrodes

Zhiqian Wang, Natalia Bramnik, Sagar Roy, Somenath Mitra
Department of Chemistry and Environmental Science
New Jersey Institute of Technology
161 Warren St, Newark, NJ, USA, 07102
E-mail: somenath.mitra@njit.edu

Giuseppe L. Di Benedetto, James L. Zunino III
Advanced Materials Technology Branch
U.S. Army Armament Research, Development and Engineering Center
Picatinny Arsenal, NJ, USA, 07806
E-mail: giuseppe.l.dibenedetto.civ@mail.mil

Abstract: *Thin and flexible energy storage devices have been developed using nanostructured materials based composite electrodes to increase current military power and sensing capabilities. This paper will discuss current efforts to develop formulations aimed at optimizing a zinc-carbon battery design. Several polymer nano composite electrodes were fabricated and conducting polymers were added to enhance conductivity. We found that a cathode comprised of a multiwalled carbon nanotubes (MWCNTs) composite showed improved conductivity. The replacement of graphite with MWCNTs provides a longer battery life while reducing internal resistance. The battery also shows good performance under bent conditions. In summary, this battery structure shows great flexibility, portability and easy manufacturability.*

Keywords: flexible battery; multiwalled carbon nanotube; PEDOT:PSS

Introduction

The increasing interest to flexible/bendable electronics requires the development of flexible energy storage devices which can be implemented in products such as smart cards, memory chips, radio frequency identification tags as well as pharmaceutical and cosmetic transdermal delivery patches. Many of these applications can adopt primary zinc-carbon batteries, with zinc as anode active material and manganese dioxide as cathode active material, implemented in thin, flexible substrates. The production costs of such power sources are relatively low due to water-based electrolyte as well as inexpensive and environmentally friendly electrode materials. Moreover, these flexible batteries can be manufactured by cost-effective printing techniques that are compatible with printable electronics [1, 2]. Recent publications [3-5] have focused on the development of different aspects of the flexible zinc-manganese dioxide battery manufacturing processes, including design of the cells, current collectors, electrodes ink as well as electrolyte formulations. The development of highly conductive electrode formulations with minimal amount of inactive components (conductive additive, binder) is particularly important for obtaining higher discharge efficiency.

Due to their high electrical conductivity and large surface area, carbon nanotubes (CNTs) have attracted much attention as effective conductive additives for composite electrodes in electrochemical energy storage devices such as lithium ion batteries and supercapacitors [6-11]. On the other hand, the extraordinary mechanical properties, such as high strength and flexibility, make CNTs a potential key component for engineering of thin and flexible electrodes. Carbon nanotubes films (for example, "bucky" paper) have been proposed as lightweight bendable mechanical support/current collector for a composite electrode [12]. Recently, singlewalled carbon nanotubes (SWCNTs) have been utilized as conductive additive for MnO_2-based electrodes in Zn/MnO_2 flexible batteries [13, 14]. The efficient conductive network of CNTs resulted in significant enhancement of the discharge capacity compared to conventional carbon black additives [13]. However, SWCNTs are still too expensive to be applied as conductive additives and/ or materials for current collectors in commercial batteries.

Since MnO_2 is known to be a poor electrical conductor, a significant amount of conductive additives (usually, graphite or carbon black) are added to the composite cathode in zinc-carbon batteries. There is also the possibility of adding other conducting polymers to enhance conductivity. For example, poly(3,4-ethylenedioxythiophene)-poly(styrenesulfonate) (PEDOT:PSS), PEDOT is known to be a stable conductive polymer which has been successfully applied as an electrode material for organic solar cells [15], supercapacitors [16-17], and a MWCNT polystyrene composite coated with PEDOT and functionalized in-situ with MnO_2 has been used as an electrode in supercapacitors [18].

The objective of this paper is to develop flexible batteries with potential military applications and explore the use of multiwalled carbon nanotubes (MWCNTs) and electroconductive polymer PEDOT:PSS to create highly conductive composite electrodes for flexible zinc-carbon batteries.

Experimental

The cathode paste was prepared by mixing MnO_2 powder, polyvinylpyrrolidone (PVP), aqueous dispersion of poly(3,4-ethylenedioxythiophene)-poly(styrenesulfonate) (PEDOT:PSS, Aldrich) and MWCNTs. For comparison, the cathode mixture with synthetic graphite instead of MWCNTs was prepared as well. The MWCNTs used were as received or functionalized prior to the electrode preparation to improve their dispersibility in the solvent/electrode matrix. The functionalization of MWCNTs was performed in a Microwave Accelerated Reaction System using an experimental procedure previously published by our laboratory [19, 20]. The MnO_2:MWCNTs ratios in the cathode mixture were varied for formulation optimization.

The anode mixture for flexible batteries was made of zinc powder mixed with PVP and PEDOT:PSS aqueous solution. Zinc acetate was also added to provide an excess of Zn cations in the mixture and, therefore, to increase the conductivity of the electrode paste [1]. The anode after drying contained Zn, PVP, rest being PEDOT:PSS and Zn acetate.

The flexible electrodes were prepared by casting the electrode slurry onto the silver coated carbon tape current collector. The typical electrode area was 4cm × 5cm. Copper foil strips stuck to the carbon tape served as electrode tabs.

After applying the slurry onto the current collector, the electrodes were allowed to dry to remove water. The typical weights of the cathode and anode after drying were 0.5 and 1 g, respectively. The electrodes were assembled co-facially with the craft paper separator in between, which had been previously soaked in saturated zinc acetate electrolyte. The battery was finally thermally sealed. The Structure of a flexible cell has been shown in Figure 1.

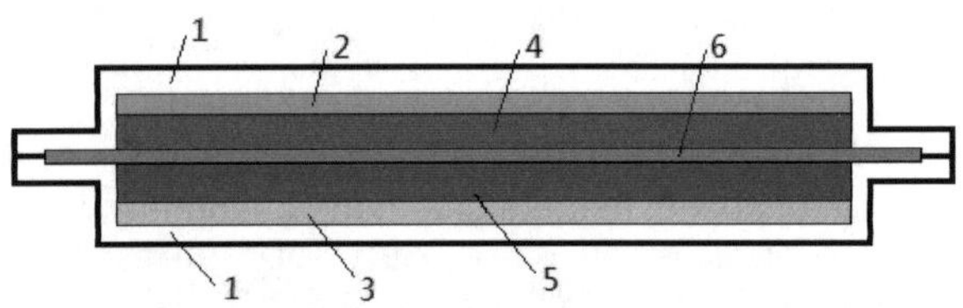

Figure 1. Cross sectional view of flexible printed battery: 1. Laminated Substrate; 2. Cathode Current Collector; 3. Anode current collector; 4. Pasted Cathode; 5. Pasted Anode; 6. Separator.

The electrochemical performance of MnO_2 cathodes was also measured in metal cells with Zn-foil as anode to optimize the formulation. In this case the cathode slurry was cast directly onto the stainless steel current collector and dried. The typical weight of the cathode paste after drying was 0.1 g. For both "rigid" and flexible cells, the Zn anode was taken in excess in respect to MnO_2 cathode.

The electrochemical performance of the battery was measured by discharging in a constant resistance mode (2640 Ω) using Battery Analyzer. Thus discharge current dropped with time. For the electrochemical performance measurement under bending conditions, the battery was firmly attached over a cylindrical solid substrate of different diameters to provide the required curvature.

Results and Discussion

The surface resistance of the cathode composed of MnO_2, graphite and PVP was 3.26 KΩ (see Table 1). In addition, PEDOT:PSS was added to increase the overall conductivity of the MnO_2 cathode. The addition of 1% PEDOT:PSS significantly reduced the resistance of the cathode down to 0.86 KΩ. The internal resistance of the electrodes may have contributed to lowering the operation voltages compared to the theoretical value. The addition of PEDOT:PSS to our composite electrode had a strong impact on the electrochemical performance (Figure1).

Table 1. Surface resistance of MnO2 cathodes with different electrode formulations

Sample	Surface Resistance of 1 cm^2 area (KΩ)	Description of the sample
1	3.26	PVP/MnO_2/Graphite
2	0.86	PVP/PEDOT:PSS/MnO_2/Graphite
3	0.37	PVP/PEDOT:PSS/MnO_2/CNTs (raw)
4	0.54	PVP/PEDOT:PSS/MnO_2/CNTs (functionalized)

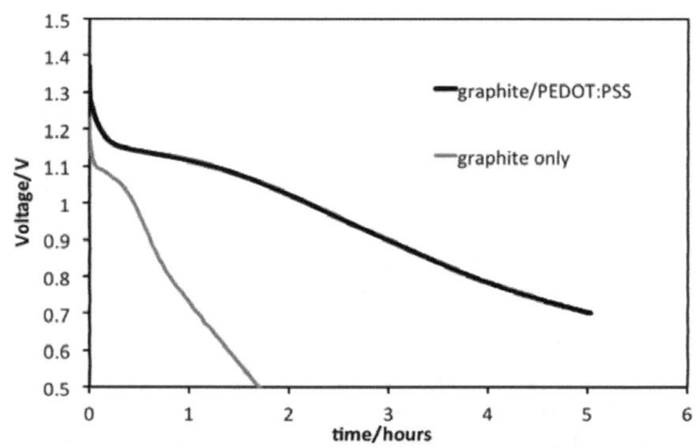

Figure 2. Discharge curves of cathodes prepared with and without PEDOT:PSS. Graphite (8.6% w/w) was added as the conductive additive. The discharge was performed in constant resistance mode in a metal cell with Zn-foil anode

Besides being a conductive polymer [21-23], the PEDOT:PSS showed poor solubility in the electrolyte. It is inferred that the PEDOT:PSS formed a conductive layer on the electrode surface during drying and remained stable in presence of the electrolyte after the battery was assembled, thus forming more stable electrodes. PEDOT layer could bridge MWCNT and MnO_2 as it has been reported to do in supercapacitor electrodes [18]. As shown in Figure 2, when the conductive polymer was added to the cathode together with graphite, the discharge plateau was more pronounced and was located in higher voltage range. In general, the improvement in electrochemical performance upon the addition of the PEDOT:PSS was attributed to the presence of highly conductive and stable binder, which increased the overall conductivity of the cathode.

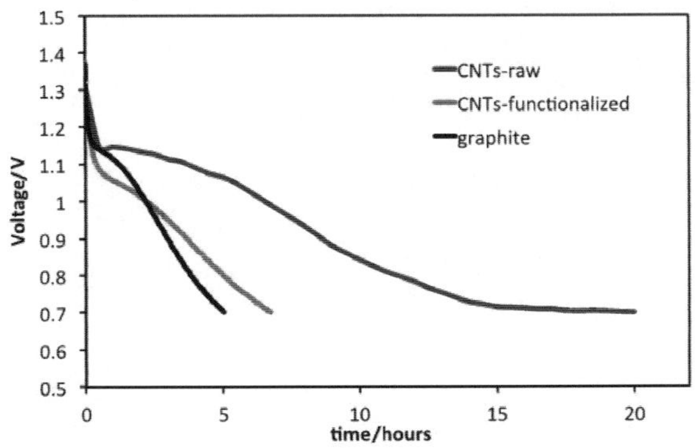

Figure 3. Discharge curves for the electrochemical cells with different carbons (8.6% w/w). The discharges were performed in constant resistance mode in a metal cell with Zn-foil anode.

As compared to graphite, the MWCNTs decreased the resistance of the cathode from 0.86 to 0.37 KΩ. This indicated that MWCNTs were more effective in creating the conductive network. The electrode prepared with functionalized MWCNTs demonstrated slightly higher resistance (0.54 KΩ) than the ones with raw MWCNTs. The hydrophilic carboxylation usually leads to improved wettability and dispersibility [24]. Therefore, carboxylation may significantly enhance the electrical conductivity of CNT composites by promoting better interfacial interactions [25-27]. On the other hand, the covalent functionalization can create large number of defects on the surface of CNTs and decrease electron mobility and conductivity. In this case, it appears that the improvement in dispersibility did not outweigh the increase in resistivity.

The electrochemical performance of MnO_2 cathodes prepared with PEDOT:PSS and different carbon conductive additives, namely, graphite, raw MWCNTs and COOH-functionalized MWCNTs (Figure 2) were measured. Upon discharge down to 0.7 V, the cathode with raw MWCNTs exhibited the highest operation voltage and longest operation time (see Figure 3). The superior performance of raw MWCNTs compared to the graphite is in good agreement with the results of the resistance measurements. The presence of the conductive additive and the more efficient network of the MWCNTs resulted in higher conductivity and a higher discharge voltage. Increasing the concentration of raw MWCNTs resulted in the higher operation voltage and higher discharge capacity. This is seen from Figure 4.

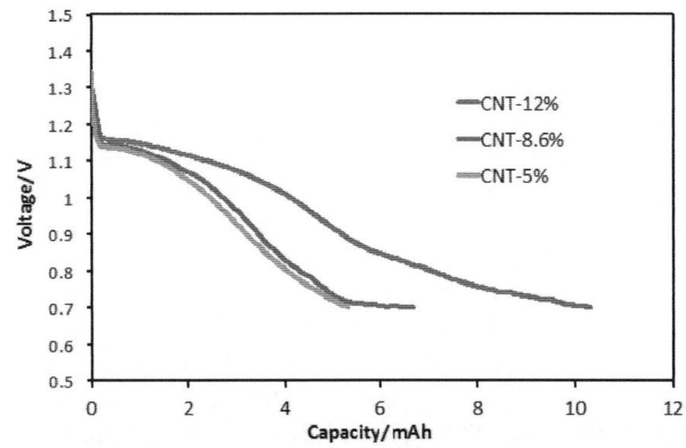

Figure 4. Voltage-capacity curves for Zn/MnO_2 cells with different concentrations of raw CNTs in the cathode. The discharge was performed in constant resistance mode in a metal cell with Zn-foil anode.

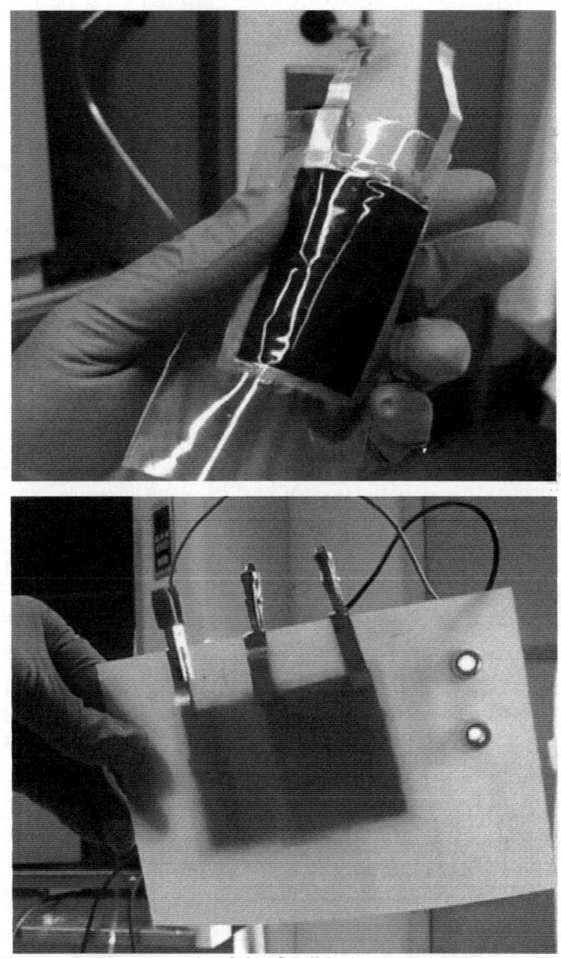

Figure 5. Photograph of the flexible battery (top) and LEDs powered by the flexible batteries (bottom).

The flexible battery prepared with composite cathode and Zn-powder anode is shown in Figure 5. Upon discharge at a constant resistance of 2640 Ω, the flexible battery delivered about 15mAh capacity before significant voltage drop occurred. Typically, bending of the flexible battery can induce a compression of the cell stacking enhancing inter-particle contact and can also vary the contact adhesion between the electrodes and the separator. Bending may also result in cracking in some areas due to the stress on the composite especially in the case of MnO_2. These factors are known to cause variation in performance [14]. Testing the batteries under bending conditions revealed that for the most part the batteries retained their function, though there were some relatively small fluctuations and alterations in the performance. This is presented in Figure 6. In our opinion, the bending performance can be further improved by further optimization of the electrode composition, improving its mechanical properties and packaging process, and by the utilization of more conductive current collectors.

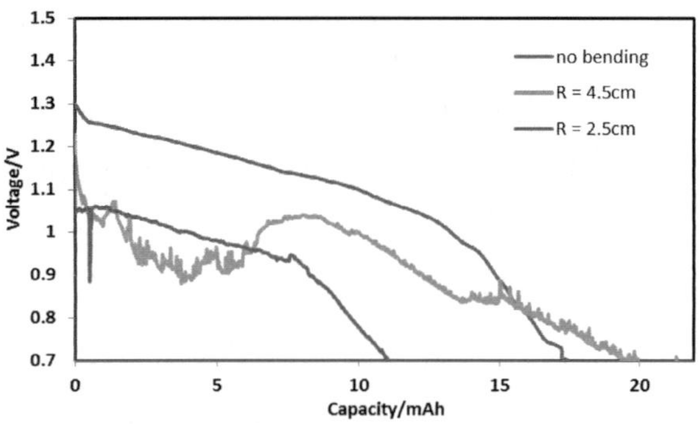

Figure 6. Voltage-capacity curves for flexible batteries under different bending conditions.

Conclusions

We have demonstrated a new approach to the fabrication of MnO_2 composite cathodes based on simultaneous use of conductive polymer PEDOT:PSS and MWCNTs as conductive additives. MWCNTs were found to be more effective in creating conductive networks compared to graphite. The relatively inexpensive raw MWCNTs represent an advantageous alternative to significantly more expensive SWCNTs or less effective graphite in composite MnO_2 cathode.

Overall, these developments have led to the fabrication of flexible batteries with potential military applications. Current efforts are underway to develop alkaline and lithium batteries as well as supercapacitors.

References

1. Bailey, J. C., A. Hilmi, M. A. Schubert, J. Zhang, G. Zheng, US Patent Application 20100209756 A1, 2010.
2. R. Tucholski, G. R., US Patent Application 20110311857 A1, 2011.
3. Southee, D., G. I. Hay, P. S. A. Evans, D. J. Harrison, "Lithographically Printed Voltaic Cells – A Feasibility Study," *Circuit World*, vol. 33, pp. 31-35, 2007.
4. Y.G. Lee, M. G. Choi, K. Y. Kang, K. M. Kim, J. Electrochem. Sci. and Tech. 1 (2010) 39
5. M. Choi, K. M. Kim, Y. G. Lee, Curr. Appl. Phys. 10 (2010) e92
6. G. Wang, Q. Zhang, Z. Yu, M. Qu, Solid State Ionics 179 (2008) 263
7. Y. Feng, Mat. Chem. Phys. 121 (2010) 302
8. Y. J. Kim, Y. A. Kim, T. Chino, H. Suezaki, M. Endo, M. S. Dresselhaus, Small 2 (2006) 339
9. G. Wang, Z. Shao, Z. Yu, Nanotechnology 18 (2007) 205705
10. C. Meng, C. Liu, S. Fan, Electrochem. Commun. 11 (2009) 186
11. X. Jia, C. Yan, Z. Chen, R. Wang, Q. Zhang, L. Guo, F. Wei, Y. Lu, Chem. Commun. 47 (2011) 9669
12. L. Hu, H. Wu, F. La Mantia, Y. Yang, Y. Cul, ACS Nano 4 (2010) 5843
13. A. Kiebele, G. Gruner, Appl. Phys. Lett. 91 (2007) 144104
14. P. Hiraral, S. Imaizumi, H. E. Unalan, H. Matsumoto, M. Minagawa, M. Rouvala, A. Tanioka, G. Amaratunga, ACS Nano 4 (2010) 2730
15. Y. H. Kim, C. Sachse, M. Machala, C. May, L. Mueller-Meskamp, K. Leo, Adv. Func. Mat. 21 (2011) 1076
16. C. Lei, P. Wilson, C. Lekakou, J. Power Sources, 196 (2011) 7823
17. A. Laforgue, J. Power Sources 196 (2011) 559
18. R. K. Sharma and L. Zhai, Electrochimica. Acta 54 (2009) 7148-7155
19. Y. Chen, Z. Iqbal and S. Mitra, Adv. Funct. Mater. 17 (2007) 3946
20. Y. Chen and S. Mitra, J. Nanosci. Nanotechnology 8 (2008) 5770
21. C. Ionescu-Zanetti, A. Mechler, S. A. Carter, R. Lal, Adv. Mat. 16 (2004) 385
22. Z. Hu, J. Zhang, Z. Hao, Y. Zhao, Solar Energy Materials & Solar Cells 95 (2011) 2763
23. Y. Kim, J. Lee, H. Kang, G. Kim, N. Kim, K. Lee, Solar Energy Materials & Solar Cells 98 (2012) 39
24. T. W. Chou, L. Gao, E. Thostenson, Z. Zhang, J. H. Byun, Comp. Sci. Tech. 70 (2010) 1
25. Y. Liu, L. Gao, Carbon 43 (2005) 47
26. Z. Spytalsky, C. Krontiras, S. Georga, C. Gallotis, Composites Part A: Appl. Sci. and Manufact. 40 (2009) 778
27. Q. Li, Y. Li, X. Zhang, S. Chikkannanavar, Y. Zhao, A. Dangelewicz, L. Zheng, S. Doorn, Q. Jia, D. Peterson, P. Arendt, Y. Zhu, Adv. Mat. 19 (2007) 335

Thermal Behavior of Lithium Ion Battery Separators

Brian Morin, PhD
Dreamweaver International
Brian.Morin@Dreamweaverintl.com
2 Parkway Commons Way, Greer, SC, 29650 USA

Abstract: *Thermal behavior of battery separators used in lithium ion batteries are compared. Dry-type polyolefin separators are compared to nanofiber based nonwoven separators. Behavior is similar below about 70 C, but above that temperature the polyolefin separators begin to shrink and then melt. Nonwoven separators that have not been dried show a water elution between 50 and 150 C. Separators also show very different behavior under exposure to flame while saturated with electrolyte, with the polyolefin separators catching fire and burning, eventually being reduced in size by >50%, while the nonwoven separators retain their shape and size, but do char in some areas. In summary, the nanofiber-based battery separators produced by Dreamweaver show dramatically higher thermal stability as well as greatly improved behavior when exposed to flame.*

Keywords: lithium ion; membrane; battery separator; nanofiber.

Introduction

There have been several instances of thermal events in lithium ion batteries that have recently achieved a high profile in the media. These events make improved safety to prevent and mitigate the damage from thermal events in lithium ion batteries of considerable importance. This study compares the thermal properties of commercial dry-processed separators for lithium ion batteries made from polypropylene and from a tri-layer of polypropylene and polyethylene to separators made from wet-laid combinations of nanofibers and microfibers.

Methods

Five commercial separators were obtained, including:

1. Dry Process PP, 25 micron, obtained from MTI.
2. Trilayer Dry Process PP/PE, 25 micron, obtained from MTI
3. Dreamweaver Gold, 25 micron
4. Dreamweaver Silver, 25 micron
5. Dreamweaver Silver AR, 30 micron

Each of these separators were tested at the Clemson Materials Science and Engineering Department for TMA, DSC, and TGA, with the following condtions.

TMA: Sample size 22 mm length x 10 mm width, tested in air with static force 0.001 N (1 gf), tested in both machine direction and cross direction from 25 – 300 C

DSC: Sample size ~4 mg tested under Helium gas, ramped from 0 to 300 C at 10 C/min, hold 0.5 min, then ramp 300 to 0 C at 10 C/min.

TGA: Sample size ~2.5 mg, tested under Nitrogen gas, ramped from 25 to 1000 C at 10 C/min.

For flame exposure, three separators were tested, the dry process PP, 25 micron, the Dreamweaver Silver and the Dreamweaver Gold. Roughly 3" squares were cut from each, and saturated in lithium ion electrolyte (mixture of EC, DEC and DMC at equal ratios with 1M $LiPF_6$). These were then laid on a piece of aluminum foil with an excess of electrolyte, and the electrolyte was lit and allowed to burn until the flames self-extinguished.

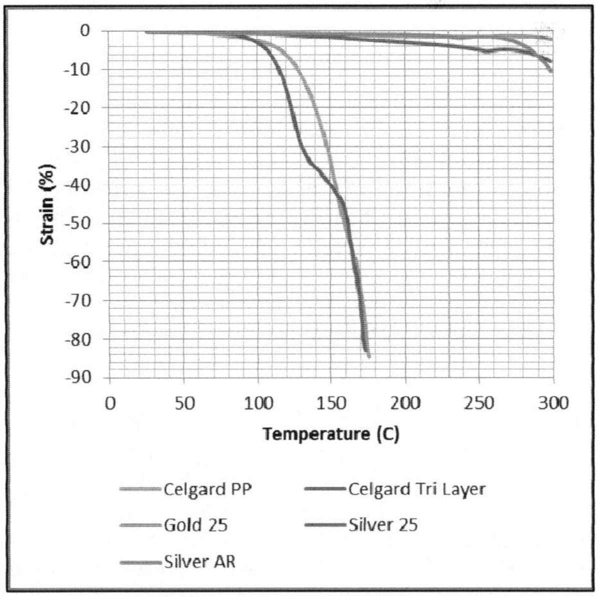

Figure 1: Machine direction TMA of five separators with expanded scale.

Results

TMA

The results are shown on the following pages. For TMA, there are dramatic differences in the behavior of the different separators above about 75 C, with the olefin materials shrinking sharply in the machine direction and undergoing catastrophic shrinkage above 100 C. The nonwoven materials shrink very little, less than 5%, up to 250 C, with the Dreamweaver Gold material showing only 2% shrinkage up to 300 C.

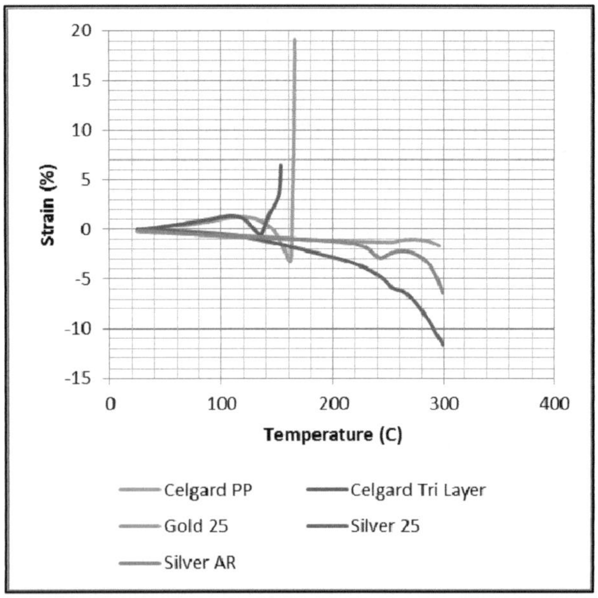

Figure 2: Cross direction TMA of five separators.

In the cross direction, the polyolefin separators have such low strength that when they begin to soften above 50 C, they stretch even with only 0.1 g/mm of force applied. At slightly higher temperatures, they begin to shrink, but then the softening causes the films to become too weak and they break under this tiny force. The Dreamweaver separators show almost isotropic shrinkage, with all values below 10% even up to 300 C, and the Dreamweaver Gold shrinking less than 2% up to 300 C in both directions.

DSC

The DSC runs show expected behavior. The dry-process PP separator shows only the melting peak centered near 165 C, while the tri-layer material shows two peaks, one near the polyethylene melt temperature of 130 C, and the other slightly lower than the normal PP melt temperature, centered around 158 C. The Dreamweaver separators show only a water elution peak centered around 100 C, and a melt peak for poly ethylene terephthalate, centered at 250 C. Note that the Dreamweaver separators were purposefully not dried so that the water evaporation could be discussed in a separate section, below.

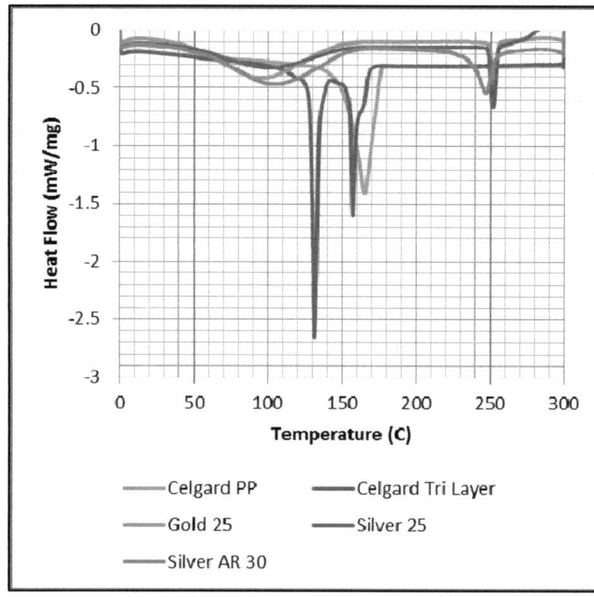

Figure 3: DSC of five separators.

TGA

All of the materials are stable under TGA up to 280 C. The olefin materials begin a sharp mass loss at 320 C, which goes to nearly 100% mass loss by 440 C, even in a nitrogen environment. In stark contrast, Dreamweaver Silver and Gold start to lose mass around 280 C, but then retain >25% mass even up to 500 C, and even higher for Silver. As is discussed below, this results in far different performance when exposed to a flame.

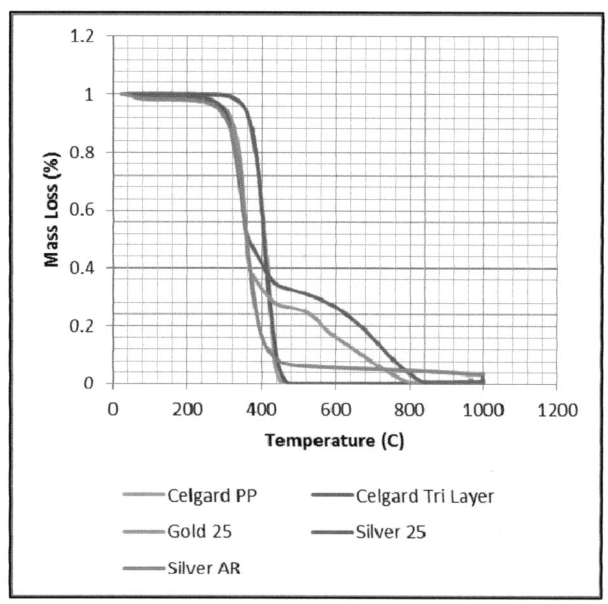

Figure 4: TGA of five separators.

Discussion

Water Evaporation

The polyolefin separators do not hold water, and so no evidence of water evaporation is present in any of the thermal studies. The Dreamweaver separators, all of which contain cellulose nanofibers, do show water evaporation with a peak that centers around 100 C, with all water having evaporated by 150 C when exposed to this thermal ramp of 10 C/min.

The three Dreamweaver materials, which were not prepared in any specific humidity environment but rather taken straight from the package, show water content that of 0.6% for Silver, 1.1% for Gold and 1.7% for Silver AR. Owing to the thermal stability of the materials, drying of the separator can be accomplished in reasonable time frames at temperatures ranging from 120 – 140 C, depending on the size of the roll that is to be dried.

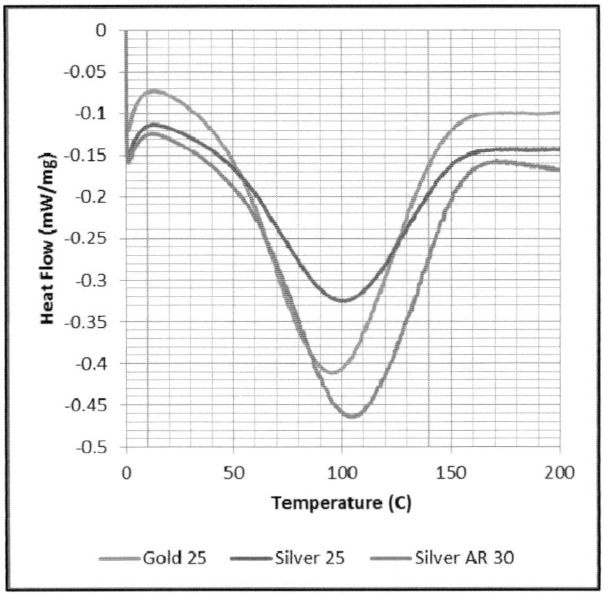

Figure 5: DSC of Dreamweaver separators highlighting the water evaporation peak.

Behavior on Exposure to Flame

Given the different thermal behavior shown and discussed above, and the fact that these separators perform their function while saturated in a mixture of flammable organic solvents, we thought a short study on how the separators may behave when exposed to flame would provide interesting results.

Three separators were tested—the polypropylene dry-process separator, Dreamweaver Silver and Dreamweaver Gold. All were saturated with lithium ion battery electrolyte and then placed on aluminum foil in an excess of electrolyte. The electrolyte was then lit, and all three separators were engulfed in flame as shown in the picture below.

After the flames self-extinguished, the Dreamweaver Silver and Dreamweaver Gold separators each retained their shape, showing some charring. The polypropylene dry-process separator began shrinking and melting immediately, and continued burning after the electrolyte had extinguished, finally being reduced to a few residual plastic balls and clumps. While this is not the same as a battery catching fire, the ability of a separator to retain its separation capability in the presence of burning electrolyte is likely to lead to better battery safety if the cell is engineered properly.

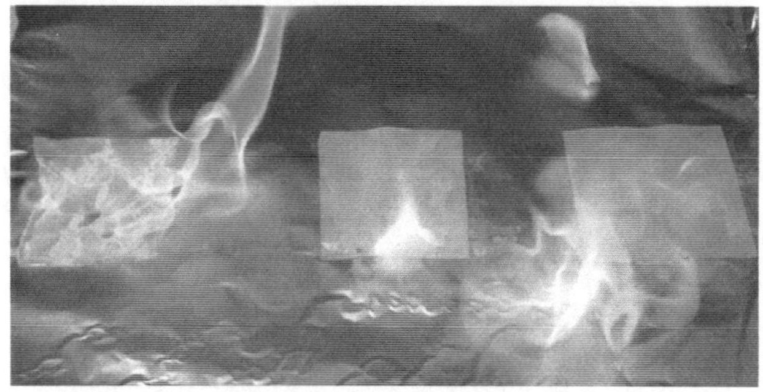

Figure 6: Photo of tri-layer, Dreamweaver Silver and Dreamweaver Gold separators that have been saturated in electrolyte and then lit on fire.

Figure 7: Photo of tri-layer, Dreamweaver Silver and Dreamweaver Gold separators after having been engulfed in flaming electrolyte.

Summary

In summary, five separators were tested for behavior at high temperature under TMA, DSC and TGA, and then also in a simulated flame test in the presence of lithium ion battery electrolyte. From these studies, the following conclusions can be drawn:

- Polypropylene and tri-layer separators shrink dramatically at temperatures above 100 C, and also soften at temperatures above 75 C.
- Dreamweaver nanofiber separators have <10% shrinkage up to 300 C, with Dreamweaver Gold having less than 2% shrinkage up to 300 C. The shrinkage behavior of Dreamweaver separators is roughly isotropic.

- Even under a tiny force of 0.1 g/mm, polypropylene and tri-layer separators extend toward a break in the cross direction at temperatures of 150 – 160 C.
- Mass loss in a Nitrogen atmosphere for polypropylene and tri-layer separators begins at 320 C and is nearly complete by 400 C.
- Mass loss in a nitrogen atmosphere for Dreamweaver separators begins around 280 C, but significant mass is retained up to over 600 C in the case of Dreamweaver Silver and Dreamweaver Gold.
- Dreamweaver separators need to be dried, and the water evaporates between 50 and 150 C when ramped at 10 C/min. Polypropylene and tri-layer separators show no evidence of water.
- When saturated with electrolyte and exposed to a flame, the polypropylene separator first shrinks catastrophically, then burns until long after the electrolyte has self-extinguished, finally stopping when the separator residue only covers a small portion of the original area.
- When saturated with electrolyte and exposed to a flame, Dreamweaver Silver and Dreamweaver Gold retain their shape while the electrolyte burns, and do show some charring but retain essentially the same shape and size as they did before the electrolyte was lit.

Acknowledgements

Sincere thanks to Kim Ivey at Clemson University Materials Science and Engineering Department for her assistance with testing materials for this document.

References

1. Huang, X. (2011). Separator technologies for lithium-ion batteries. Solid State Electrochem, 649-662.
2. Jianjun Zhang, Q. K. (2013). A highly safe and inflame retarding aramid lithium ion battery separator by a papermaking process. Solid State Ionics, 49-55.
3. Lara Jabbour, R. B. (2013). Cellulose-based Li-ion batteries: a review. Cellulose, 1523-1545.

Deep Discharge Characteristics of $LiMn_2O_{4-d}Cl_d$ Cathode Material

Terrill B. Atwater and Paula C. Latorre
US Army RDECOM
Communications, Electronics, Research, Development and Engineering Center
Aberdeen Proving Ground, MD 21005

Abstract: *A family of lithium manganese $AB_2O_{4-d}X_d$ materials was synthesized and evaluated as a cathode for lithium and lithium-ion electrochemical systems. The reversible region for the $Li//Li_xMn_2O_{4-d}Cl_d$ electrochemical couple was found to be on the order of $0.05 < x < 1.75$ in a two step thermodynamic charge-discharge profile. The high voltage twin plateau is centered on 3.95 volts and 4.35 volts and the low voltage plateau is centered on a potential of 2.85 volts. In comparison, $Li//Li_xMn_2O_4$ (non-doped lithium manganese-based AB_2O_4 spinel materials) needs to be maintained at $0.05 < x < 1.00$ and at a potential greater than 3.25 volts in order to maintain rechargeablity. Additionally, the ability to discharge the $Li//Li_xMn_2O_{4-d}Cl_d$ electrochemical system below 3.25 volts increases the capacity of the lithium spinel electrochemical couple nearly twofold.*

Keywords: $Li_xMn_2O_4$; Deep Discharge; Rechargeable Cells

Introduction

The benefits of lithium battery systems lie within their high energy density (Wh/L) and high specific energy (Wh/kg). Manganese dioxide (MnO_2) is an attractive active cathode material because of its high energy density and low material cost. MnO_2 is an intercalating compound for lithium that functions by solvating and desolvating lithium cations from the electrolyte in solid state. The lithium cations are deposited into the vacancies of the MnO_2 cathode crystal structure. The objective of this effort focuses on improving the cycle life of rechargeable lithium manganese-based electrochemical systems, specifically the capacity fading of the cathode. These two characteristics are still considered the major technology hurdles in rechargeable lithium battery technology.[1-4]

A family of lithium manganese $AB_2O_{4-d}X_d$ materials was synthesized and evaluated as a cathode for lithium and lithium-ion electrochemical systems. The general formula for the synthetic material is $Li_xMn_2O_{4-d}X_d$ where $x \approx 1$ and d ranges from 0.005 to 0.3. By introducing halogens into the starting material mixture and subsequently into the final product, the synthesis processing time of lithium manganese-based AB_2O_4 spinel materials is dramatically reduced. The material properties were verified with X-ray diffraction and X-ray fluorescence. Button cells were fabricated to evaluate thermodynamic and kinetic properties of the $Li//Li_xMn_2O_{4-d}X_d$ electrochemical systems. Results of these evaluations were reported previously and concentrated on the formulation processes and the 4.5 to 3.5 volt cycle window.[5-7]

During the development phase, $Li_xMn_2O_{4-d}X_d$ recovered electrochemically after deep discharge (a discharge to a 2.0 volt potential or lower). Deep discharges are routinely performed on developmental materials so that a complete electrochemical thermodynamic characterization can be established. It was discovered that deep discharges to 2.0 volts could be performed without any permanent damage to the electrochemical properties of the cell. It is this 3.5 to 2.0 volt region for the $Li//Li_xMn_2O_{4-d}X_d$ electrochemical systems that will be presented in this paper.

Background

Capacity fading is the loss of cycle capacity in a cell over the entire life of a battery system, limiting the practical number of cycles that may be used. In lithium battery systems, capacity loss is often attributed to the degradation of the active cathode material. This degradation is a result of both changes in composition and crystal structure of the active material that occurs during both charging and discharging of the cell. The crystal structure degradation is linked to the intercalation and deintercalation of lithium cations into the active material. Additionally, throughout the life of a cell, parasitic side reactions occur between the different chemical species of the cell. These include chemical dissolution and degradation of the active cathode material and oxidation-reduction of the electrolyte. Methods of reducing this effect include changing the crystal structure and composition of the active material or eliminating these parasitic mechanisms through other means. Capacity fading is currently a major setback for rechargeable lithium cells; therefore it is an active area of research.[2-12]

MnO_2 exists in different phase states or crystal structures. The common phases are referred to by the following prefixes: α, β, γ, and λ. α-MnO_2 is the most stable structure; it is a one-dimensional lattice containing both one-by-one and two-by-two channels for lithium insertion/extraction. γ-MnO_2 is a one-dimensional structure but has a one-by-two channel. λ-MnO_2 is created through the delithiation of Li-Mn-O type spinels ($Li_xMn_2O_4$). The crystal structure of the spinel is maintained through both delithiation and lithiation. The λ-MnO_2 crystal structure is a three-dimensional cubic array. This structure promotes mechanical stability and adequate pathways for lithium insertion/extraction. λ-MnO_2 is perhaps the most preferred rechargeable phase of MnO_2. Degradation of the λ-MnO_2 crystal structure forming α/γ-MnO_2 and other Mn_xO_y phases reduces the capacity of the cathode material. [13-20]

As lithium intercalates, the size and orientation of the crystal structures change. In $Li_xMn_2O_4$ spinel materials, the crystal structure is cubic (λ-MnO_2) when $0.05 < x < 1$. When $1 < x < 1.8$, the structure of $Li_xMn_2O_4$ (no longer an AB_2O_4 spinel) is tetragonal. Additionally, when $x < 0.05$, a phase transition to the more stable α, β, and γ MnO_2 occur. Over-discharge of the $Li_xMn_2O_4$ spinel increased lithium insertion into the cathode, promoting the transformation of λ-MnO_2 crystal structures to other cubic, tetragonal, and monoclinic phases. The preferred transition is λ-MnO_2 to other cubic phases since tetragonal and monoclinic crystal structures may become inactive, leading to the loss of active cathode material. Voltage control allows for control of the formation of unwanted crystal structures. [13-17] When the potential of the $Li//Li_xMn_2O_4$ electrochemical system is maintained between 3.0 and 4.25 volts, the λ-MnO_2 cubic phase is maintained. As the potential of the system drops below 3.0 volts, the $Li_xMn_2O_4$ cathode material undergoes a phase change from cubic to tetragonal.[13-20]

This effort focuses on the formulation, fabrication, and characterization of manganese-based metal oxide materials as a positive electrode for lithium electrochemical systems, with the goal of improving the overall performance characteristics of the system. The limited cycle life and limited rate capability are considered the major setbacks in rechargeable lithium battery technology and are the focus of the efforts described in the manuscript. A stable chlorine-modified lithium manganese based AB_2O_4 spinel material was formulated, fabricated, and characterized as a positive electrode for lithium batteries. The general formula for the fabricated material is $Li_xMn_2O_{4-y}Cl_z$ where $x \approx 1$, $y \approx z$, and $0.005 < z < 0.3$. The reversible region for the $Li//Li_xMn_2O_{4-y}Cl_z$ electrochemical couple is $0.05 < x < 1.75$.

The chlorine-modified $Li_xMn_2O_4$ cathode material allows for over-discharge protection. Reversibility in the material is maintained after cell potential excursions less than 2.0 volts are performed. When the chlorine-modified $Li_xMn_2O_4$ cathode material is coupled with a lithium anode, it successfully cycles between 5.0 and 2.0 volts without significant degradation. Conventional $Li_xMn_2O_4$ cathode materials tend to degrade as a result of stress/strain-induced material fracture and formation of Mn_2O_3 and Mn_3O_4. This is due to the cubic to tetragonal and cubic to monoclinic phase changes as a result of the Mn^{3+} valence state. Both of these conditions occur as the electrochemical cell potential transitions through 3.0 volts.

Experimental

Hydrothermal and solid state processes were used to fabricate the $Li_xMn_2O_{4-d}X_d$ material, where $x \approx 1$ and d ranges from 0.005 to 0.3 with MnO_2 or Mn_2O_3 and Li_2CO_3 or $LiOH$ as the principal starting materials. Halogens were introduced into the starting material mixture and subsequent final product using lithium and manganese halide salts. Mixtures were ground using a random orbit mixer mill and the subsequent material was then heated in air at 600°C for a time period no greater than 4 hours. The material was evaluated for its viability as a cathode material for rechargeable lithium batteries.

The material properties were verified with X-ray diffraction and X-ray fluorescence. Button and laboratory glass test cells with a lithium anode and an organic electrolyte were fabricated to evaluate the thermodynamic and kinetic properties of the $Li//Li_xMn_2O_{4-d}X_d$ electrochemical systems. The glass cell consisted of two machined pistons that are fitted into glass housings and secured with a threaded cap incorporating a pair of o-rings. The pistons, either aluminum, nickel, or stainless steel, had a surface area of 1.0 cm^2. The pistons served as electrode current collectors and are threaded, allowing for an inert captivating ring to be employed to maintain electrode alignment. The glass fixture allows for postmortem analysis of the cell components. Conventional button cells with a surface area of 2.85 cm^2 were also used.

The experimental cells were composed of a lithium anode separated from the cathode by a nonwoven glass separator. The $Li_xMn_2O_{4-d}X_d$ cathode was fabricated by mixing together the active material, carbon, and polytetrafluoroethylene with an 85:10:5 by weight ratio, respectively. The cathode mixture was rolled to 0.04 cm and dried in a vacuum oven. A 0.075 cm thick lithium foil was cut using a 12.7 mm or 19.0 mm diameter hole punch. The cathode was cut into 1.0 cm^2 and 2.85 cm^2 discs, resulting in a 0.05 g cathode for the glass cell and a 0.14 g cathode for the button cells. A 0.01 cm nonwoven glass separator was utilized for the separator and as a wick. The electrolyte used was 1 molar $LiPF_6$ in proportional mixtures of diethyl carbonate, dimethyl carbonate, and ethylene carbonate.

Cells were cycled with an ARBIN MSTAT4 battery cycler system controlled by MITS Pro software. The charge/discharge rates were maintained at 0.5 to 4.0 mA/cm^2, with the majority of electrochemical experiments cycled at 1.0 mA/cm^2. The cells were charged to a cut-off between 4.75 to 5.0 volts and discharged to a cut-off between 3.0 to 2.0 volts. A rest period of 15 minutes between charge and discharge cycles was used to allow for cells to achieve equilibrium on all experiments.

Results & Discussion

Figure 1 shows the molecular model of $Li_xMn_2O_{4-d}Cl_d$. The halogen element replaces an oxygen in the λ-MnO_2 structure. The impact of the halogen material on the entire structure is highly dependent on its concentration. For every chlorine atom inserted into the structure, it will influence the three adjacent manganese atoms and the twelve associated oxygen atoms. Once the concentration becomes too large where multiple chlorines are affecting the same central manganese atoms in a crystallite, the structure begins to reject the additional halogen. This was found to occur at $d = 0.3$

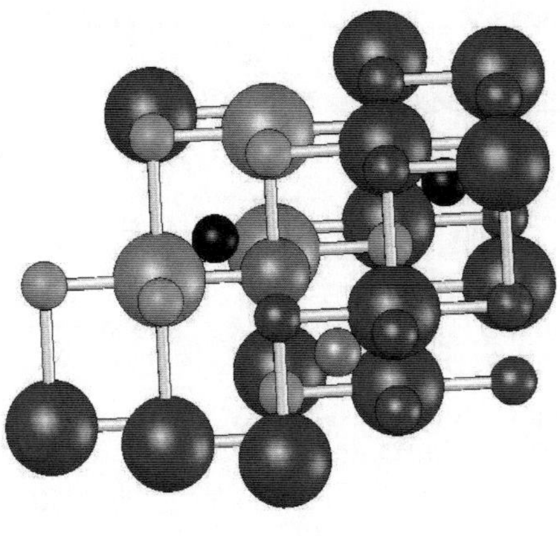

Figure 1. Molecular model of $Li_xMn_2O_{4-d}X_d$ with x being either Cl or F. The halogen element replaces an oxygen in the λ-MnO_2.

Figure 2 displays the results of a representative deep discharge experiment on a $Li//Li_xMn_2O_{4-y}Cl_z$ electrochemical cell where z is 0.05. For this experiment, a 125 uA/cm^2 charge/discharge cycle was interrupted every hour and the cell was allowed to rest for 15 minutes so that it could reach thermodynamic equilibrium. The data shows that the $Li//Li_xMn_2O_{4-y}Cl_z$ is fully reversible. This reversibility instigated further investigations into the behavior of the electrochemistry during cycles that routinely are cut off at 2.0 volts during discharge.

Figures 3 and 4 show the first three charge/discharge cycles of a representative $Li//Li_xMn_2O_{4-y}Cl_z$ electrochemical cell. Figure 3 displays the data as a potential verses time trace and Figure 4 displays the data as differential capacity. Figures 5 and 6 show data from the initial discharge/charge cycles of a representative $Li//Li_xMn_2O_{4-y}Cl_z$ electrochemical cell. Figure 5 displays the data as a potential verses time trace and Figure 6 displays the data as differential capacity. Comparison of data where charge verses discharge was used to initiate the formation cycle show significantly different behavior during the first cycle. Subsequent cycles, however, are comparable.

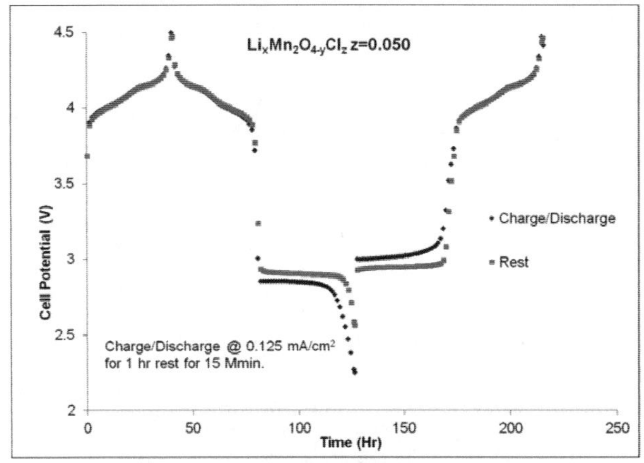

Figure 2. Cell potential data from an electrochemical thermodynamic experiment on a $Li//Li_xMn_2O_{4-y}Cl_z$ cell, where z is 0.05.

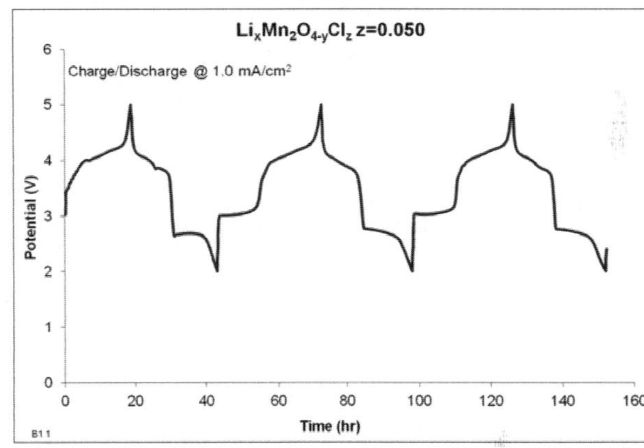

Figure 3. Cell potential data for a representative $Li//Li_xMn_2O_{4-y}Cl_z$ electrochemical cell during the forming, 2nd, and 3rd cycle.

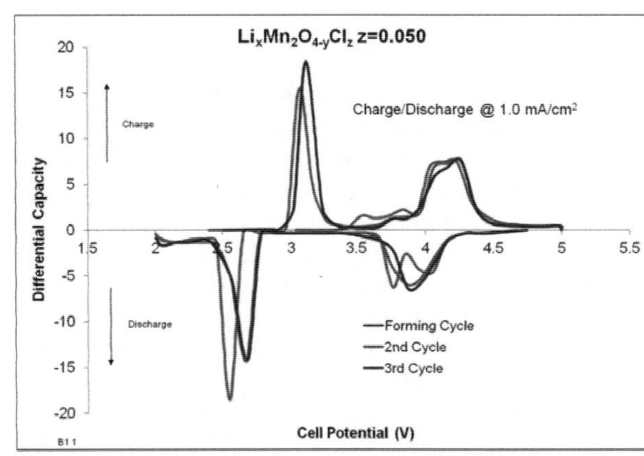

Figure 4. Differential capacity data for a representative $Li//Li_xMn_2O_{4-y}Cl_z$ electrochemical cell during the forming, 2nd, and 3rd cycle.

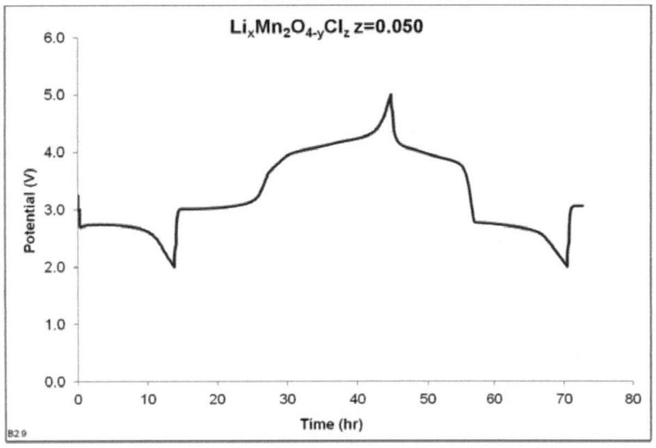

Figure 5. Cell potential data for a representative $Li//Li_xMn_2O_{4-y}Cl_z$ electrochemical cell where the initial cycles started with a discharge.

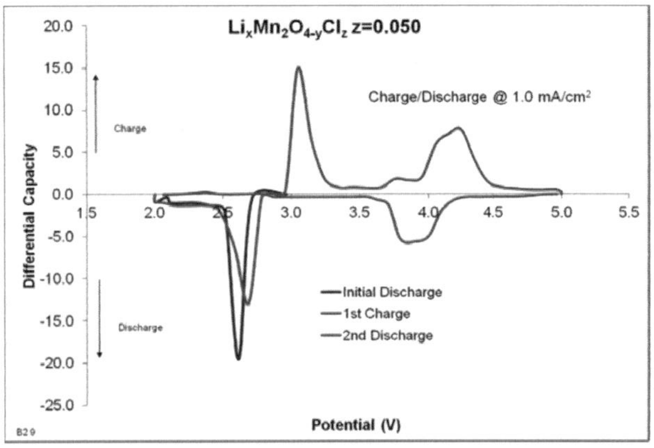

Figure 6. Differential capacity data for a representative $Li//Li_xMn_2O_{4-y}Cl_z$ electrochemical cell where the initial cycles started with a discharge.

Conclusion

A family of lithium manganese $AB_2O_{4-d}Cl_d$ materials was synthesized and evaluated as a cathode for lithium and lithium-ion electrochemical systems. The general formula for the material is $Li_xMn_2O_{4-d}Cl_d$ where $x \approx 1$ and d ranges from 0.005 to 0.3. By introducing halogens into the starting material mixture and subsequently into the final product, the synthesis process time of lithium manganese-based AB_2O_4 spinel materials is dramatically reduced. In addition to the reduction in formation time, the subsequent chlorine-modified material was evaluated for its viability as a cathode material for a rechargeable lithium battery. The reversible region for the $Li//Li_xMn_2O_{4-d}Cl_d$ electrochemical couple was found to be on the order of $0.25 < x < 1.75$ in a two-step thermodynamic charge-discharge profile. The high voltage twin plateau is centered on 3.95 volts and 4.35 volts and the low voltage plateau is centered on a potential of 2.85 volts.

The chlorine-modified $Li_xMn_2O_4$ cathode material allows for over-discharge protection. Reversibility in the material is maintained after cell potential excursions less than 2.0 volts are performed. When the chlorine-modified $Li_xMn_2O_4$ cathode material is coupled with a lithium anode, it successfully cycles between 5.0 and 2.0 volts without significant degradation. In comparison, $Li//Li_xMn_2O_4$ (non-doped lithium manganese-based AB_2O_4 spinel materials) needs to be maintained at $0.05 < x < 1.00$ and at a potential greater than 3.25 volts in order to maintain rechargeablity.

References

1. David Linden (Ed.); Handbook of Batteries 4th ed.; McGraw-Hill, 2011
2. Tarascon, JM, Guyomard D, *J. Electrochem Soc.*, Vol. 138, Oct. 1991, pg. 2864
3. Thackeray, MM, etal, *Mater Res. Bull.*, 1984, pg 179
4. Gabano, JP, Lithium Batteries; Academic Press; New York, NY; 1983
5. Atwater, TB and Tavares, P.C., *P. 45th Power Sources Conference*, 2012
6. Atwater, TB and Tavares, P.C., **US Patent No. 8,597,377**, December 3, 2013
7. Atwater, TB and Tavares, P.C., *SAE Int. J. Materials and Manufacturing*, 6(1):2013
8. Liu, W-R, et.al., *J. Power Sources*, 146 (2005) pg. 233-239
9. Kang, Y-J, et.al., *J. Power Sources*, 146 (2005) pg. 237-240
10. Kang, S-H, Goodenough JB, *J. Electrochem Soc.*, Vol. 147, No. 10, October 2000, pg. 3621-3627
11. Kang, S-H, Goodenough JB, *Electrochemical and Solid State Letters*, Vol. 3, No. 12, (2000), pg. 536-539
12. Sun, Y-K, et.al., *Electrochemical and Solid State Letters*, Vol. 3, No. 1, (2000), pg. 7-9
13. Inoue, T and Sano, M, *J. Electrochem Soc.*, Vol. 145, No. 11, November 1998, pg. 3704-3707
14. Larcher, D et.al.; *J. Electrochem Soc.*, Vol. 145, No. 10, October 1997, pg. 3392-3400
15. Wen, SJ et.al., *J. Electrochem Soc.*, Vol. 143, No. 6, June 1996, pg. L136-L138
16. Shao-Horn, Y et.al.; *J. Electrochem Soc.*, Vol. 144, No. 9, September 1997, pg. 3147-3153
17. Armstrong AR, et.al.; *J. Solid State Chem.*, Vol. 14, No.5 , 1999, pg. 549-556
18. Yang, XQ et.al., *Electrochemical and Solid State Letters*, Vol. 2, No. 4, (1999), pg. 157-160
19. Xia, Y and Yoshio, M, *J. Electrochem Soc.*, Vol. 143, No. 3, March 1996, pg. 825-833
20. Xia, Y et.al., *J. Electrochem Soc.*, Vol. 148, No. 7, July 2001, pg. A723-A729

The Cycling Performance and Surface Passivation Qualities of a Heterogeneous Amorphous Ni_xSiO_y/Polycrystalline $NiSi_2$ Core Shell Nanowire used as a Li-ion Battery Anode

Isaac N. Lund[1,2], Jae Ho Lee[1,2], Harry Efstathiadis[1], Pradeep Haldar[1], Robert Geer[1]
[1]College of Nanoscale Science and Engineering, SUNY Albany,
255 Fuller Rd, Albany, NY 12203
[2]Battery Energy Storage System -Technologies,
110 8th St, CII 8111, Troy, NY, 12180

Abstract: *Presented is the cycling performance and surface passivation qualities of a heterogeneous amorphous NixSiOy/polycrystalline NiSi2 core shell nanowire created through a silane chemical vapor deposition (CVD) process utilizing a pure Ni catalyst layer. The Ni catalyst layer is extinguished during the growth process to with continual deposition of amorphous silicon from silane that oxygen getters and is nickel doped from the inside nickel silicide inside core to create the core-shell architecture. The* $NiSi_2$ *core interacts with Li through intercalation retaining its rigid core even while Li charged, the dimensions of the structure reduce pulverization and the oxide doping in the amorphous shell creates a stable solid electrolyte interphase that is reduced through the inclusion of a conductive pathway through Ni doping. The nanowire morphology shows stable cycling and excellent charge rate capability having a stable capacity above 1700mAhr/g when cycled in a coin cell at 1/2C and retaining a capacity of 300mAhr/g when cycled at a 10C charge rate.*

Keywords: Li-ion battery; anode; heterogeneous nanowire; nickel silicide; silicon nanowire; SEI

Introduction:

The use of high capacity Si based anode for use in Li-ion batteries present three problems deriving from its phase transitions and volume swell when lithiated. The swelling occurs when Li alloys with Si through several phase changes to create a trigonal $Li_{22}Si_5$ phase that produces a volume change in Si of 400%. The volume expansion creates and propagates stress cracks eventually detaching active material from itself, pulverizing the anode. The second problem with Si is that it possesses an unstable passivating interface comprised of decomposition components of the electrolyte commonly called the solid electrolyte interphase (SEI). Due to the volume swell during charging new Si is brought to the interface and is passivated with SEI. During discharging the created SEI is insoluble in the electrolyte thus remaining solid even when detached from the Si anode during contraction. The SEI is composed of Li containing compounds that sequester Li away from transferring charge. The final problem is the electrical transition that Si goes through from semiconductor in Si phase to conductor when alloyed with Li in $Li_{22}Si_5$ phase. The transition happens at electrolyte electrode interface meaning if Li is pulled out too quickly the transition can happen at the interface trapping Li in the bulk of the structure creating large irreversibility.

Experimental:

Novel heterogeneous nanowires consisting of a multicrystalline $NiSi_2$ inner core and an amorphous $Ni_xSi_yO_z$ outside shell was grown by metal induced growth process directly onto a 304 stainless steel substrate with a 30nm Ni catalyst layer. The growth was performed by the catalytic decomposition of 1% diluted silane (SiH_4) precursor in Ar gas at a processing pressure of 150 torr and for a set time of 1 hour at 650^0C in a quartz horizontal tube furnace.
Chronopotentiometry is performed on half coin cells with a Li foil cathode, an electrolyte which is comprised of a 1M solution of lithium hexafluorophosphate ($LiPF_6$) in a 1:1 mixture of ethylene carbonate (EC):diethyl carbonate (DEC) and a 25um porous polyethylene (PE) separator from Celgard.

The morphology of the heterogeneous nanowires is investigated in a scanning electron microscope (SEM) with cross sectional morphology shown by high resolution transmission electron microscope (TEM). To determine the phases of the sample Raman spectroscopy were taken of the samples before and after lithium cycling with the post Li cycling samples in a completely discharged state. Energy electron loss spectroscopy (EELS) detector was connected to the TEM which allowed for compositional analysis of the amorphous shell. For compositional analysis of the nanowire and SEI X-ray photoemission spectroscopy (XPS) depth profile was taken of the samples in different states. Fourier transform infrared (FTIR) spectroscopy was taken by a Bruker Tensor 27. The TEM samples were made by sonicating a nanowire sample in an isopropyl alcohol (IPA) solution for a period of 5 minutes and then 5 drops of the solution were dropped onto a holy carbon film on a Cu TEM grid and let dry in air before placing into the TEM.

Results and discussion:

The SEM micrographs of the nanowire morphology through its different lithium charged conditions are shown Figure 1, a) being the as deposited nanowires, b) is the nanowires Li charged, c) is the nanowires after discharged, and d) is the nanowire sample after a quick rinse with diethyl carbonate a commonly used electrolyte solvent to rinse off any loosely adhered SEI components. The SEM micrographs in a) show a nanowires that are 80nm in diameter and 1um long, the nanowires in b) show a retention of their structure during charging due to NiSi2 core only reacting with Li through and intercalation reaction, in c) we observe that when discharged the nanowire retains its structure and obtains a rough surface coating compliant with SEI formation, and d) after the surface rinse we show the removal of the surface coating that is compliant with SEI production.

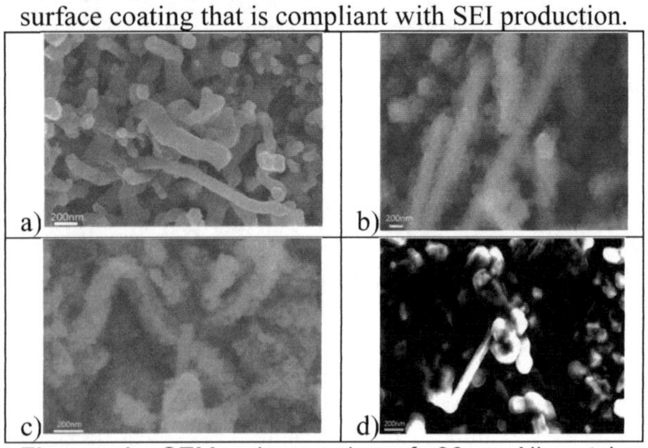

Figure 1: SEM micrographs of 30nm Ni catalyzed nanowires in a) as deposited, b) Li-charged, c) post Li cycled, and d) DEC surface rinsed.

TEM and EELS analysis were done on the as-deposited samples to the compositional constituents of the nanowires with results displayed in Figure 2. The TEM micrograph in a) shows a heterogeneous nanowire comprised of a polycrystalline core and an amorphous shell, b) shows the EELS mapped spectrum for Si showing Si signal from both the crystalline core and the amorphous shell, b) shows the EELS spectrum for Ni showing a large signal from the core and a smaller signal from the amorphous shell, and c) shows the EELS spectrum for O showing a large signal from the surface passivation and some signal from the amorphous shell. The Si spectrum is consistent with the metal induced growth process, with the continual deposition of Si from silane on the outside of the grown nanowire. The Ni in the core is compliant with the metal induced growth process with a lower signal coming from the shell due to the solid solubility of Ni in Si being 10%. The O signal in the amorphous shell is due to Si at higher tmeperatures oxygen gettering.

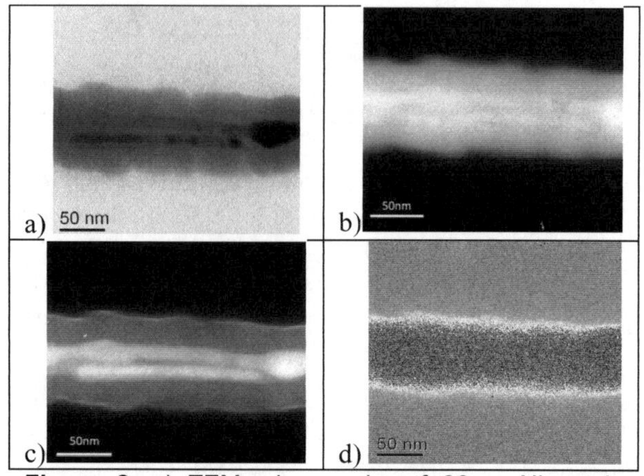

Figure 2: a) TEM micrographs of 30nm Ni catalyzed nanowires. EELS spectrum for b) Si, c) Ni, d) O.

To probe the phase of the nanowire, and to determine the phase transitions over charging states Raman spectroscopy was taken of the samples in the same states as shown in the SEM analysis. All of the samples are plotted on a single graph as shown in Figure 3 with the different spectrums artificially separated from one another. The spectrum for the as grown nanowire show a peak compliant with $NiSi_2$ at 371cm^{-1} from the core, Si at 520cm^{-1} from the amorphous shell and NiO at 1000cm^{-1}. The NiSi2 occurs due to the conservation of free Ni within the system when the Ni from the crystalline core diffuses into the amorphous shell doping it. The NiO signal shows that there is free Ni at the surface which needs to be passivated since NiO in the bulk would be reduced by any free Si. The Li charged nanowire sample shows the retention of the NiSi2 which is consistent with the intercalation reaction, while the crystalline Si peak becomes a broad amorphous Si peak due to the Si amorphization process during lithiation, and the disappearance of the NiO occurs due to NiO splitting into its atomic components during lithiation creating Li_2O and Ni. The Li_2O is an insulating compound commonly seen in the SEI components on graphite anodes and is beneficial for nanowire stability throughout its charging cycle. The post Li and surface rinsed spectrum show the reappearance of the original phases of the nanowires, which is consistent with that we see in the SEM analysis. The surface rinse sample shows a decrease in the NiO peak meaning some NiO species are not tightly bound to the nanowire surface.

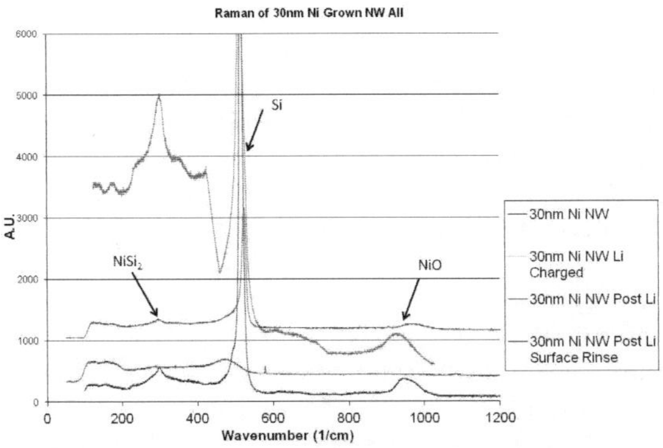

Figure 3: Raman spectroscopy of 30nm Ni catalyzed nanowires in different Li charged states.

FTIR is taken of the samples to determine the components of the SEI species. Since the NiO component reversibly produces Li_2O on the surface of the anode, we expect any other SEI constituents to be weakly bound to the surface. As has been previously shown the main constituents of Si anodes are carbonate decomposition products, lithium silicates, and Li-F components. This occurs since the Si-O end termination isreduced by the carbonate replaced solvents creating alkyl carbonate end terminations on Si, blocking future lithium charging reactions. The blocking of this decomposition pathway through the introduction of reaction displacement components on the surface of Si creates a reversible SEI interface. The FTIR analysis is shown in Figure 4 with the spectrum for the blank stainless steel substrate was shown for background elimination. The as deposited nanowire sample shows a FTIR signal shows a signal only compliant with Si-O as expected in the amorphous shell. The Post Li sample displays multiple peaks that are compliant with carbonate decomposition products along with peaks compliant with silicon alkyl carbonate products. The surface rinsed spectrum shows peaks compliant with Si-O showing that the silicon alkyl carbonate components are weakly bonded to the surface.

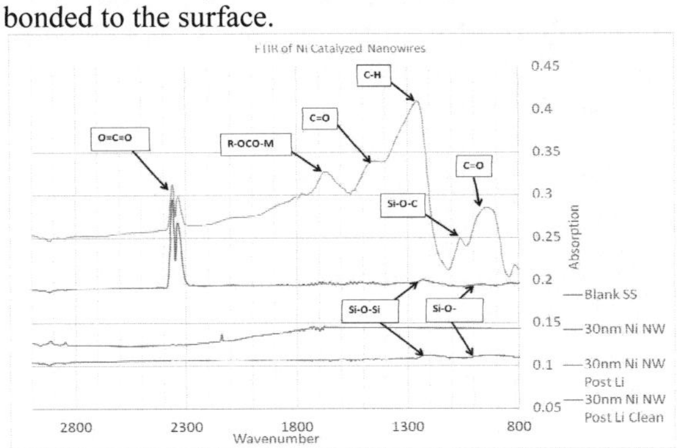

Figure 4: FTIR spectroscopy of 30nm Ni catalyzed nanowires in different Li charged states.

The FTIR spectrum shows that the silicon alkyl carbonate molecules are weakly bound to the nanowire surface leading to a mass loss decomposition pathway for silicon based anodes. However by incorporating a common reaction displacement anode surface (either Ni-O or Fe_2O_3) the silicon is shielded from the electrolyte and the alkyl carbonate end termination degradation pathway. To understand the amount of Ni doping in the surface of the nanowires and the constituents of the SEI XPS surface scan was run on the nanowire samples as deposited, post Li, and surface rinse with the results tabulated in Table 1. The as deposited shows a composition that is about 2:1 Si:O composition meaning all the deposited Si is now oxidized, and 10% Ni contribution which is the solid solubility limit of Ni in Si. The XPS analysis of the post Li cycled nanowires shows a large Li-F signal which is consistent with the Li-F constituents in the outside shell of the proposed Si SEI. The surface rinse sample showed a decrease in the Li-F compositional signal showing that it is weakly bound to the outside of the SEI shell. The C-O signal however increases due to the alkyl carbonate end terminations on Si. The NiO incorporated into the amorphous Si shell however provides a Li diffusion pathway to charge the whole structure instead of having the SEI Si alkyl carbonate components block the lithiation pathway.

	Composition						
Nanowire	Si	Ni	O	C	Li	F	P
30nm Ni NW	65	10	25	-	-	-	-
30nm Ni NW Post Li	3	6	17	19	25	28	2
30nm Ni NW Surface Rinse	3	0	48	20	3	8	3

Table 1: Composition of the as deposited nanowire, and the nanowire in different Li charged states.

To understand the gravimetric capacity as well as the cycling retention half cells were manufactured in a glovebox and tested in a coin cell on an Arbin galvanostat between 2.5-0.01V. After manufacturing the electrodes were allowed to sit for 3 hours to allow for complete electrode wetting before placing in chronopotentiometry testing. Figure 5 shows the chronopotentiometry testing of the nanowire anode when cycled at .5C for 350 cycles. We observe that the initial capacity is above 1800 mAhr/g which degrades in the first several cycles due to the setting up of the SEI layer as can be seen in the columbic efficiency mapped to the secondary y-axis. The capacity stabilizes at 1700mAhr/g for 150 cycles and then starts to slowly degrade hitting its 20% capacity retention mark after 300 cycles. The charge and discharge capacity track one another for a good columbic efficiency of 98-99% after the first several cycles making it a good anode for battery integration.

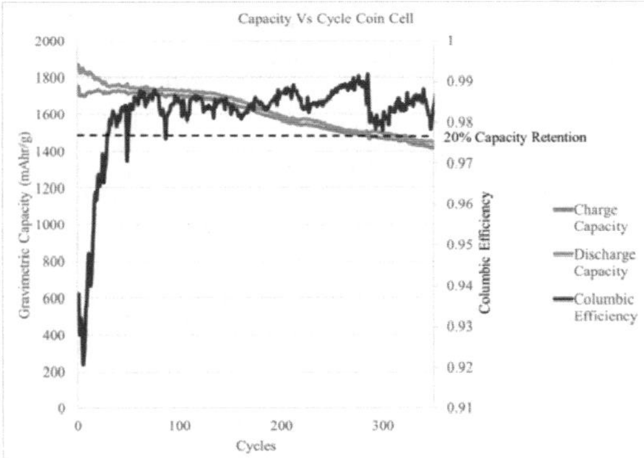

Figure 5: Cycling performance for half cell in a coin cycled at 0.5C rate for 350 cycles.

To understand how the highly surface nanostructured anode allows for higher charging rates the nanowire anode was placed into a coin cell and cycled at different charge rates between 0.1-10C and at a voltage range 2.5-0.01V, the results are shown in Figure 6. The charge rates step from .1C up to 10C and back to .1C to show capacity retention at higher charging rates. The .1C charge rate shows a capacity around 2000mAhr/g which is higher than the .5C charge rate due to Si based anodes being diffusion limited. The 1C cycle rate is lower than .5C by about 200mAhr/g. At higher C rates the capacity becomes less but still good with the gravimetric capacity of the nanowires at 10C having the same capacity as commonly used graphite anodes at .5C. The gravimetric capacity is shown to completely recover when the cycle rate is stepped back to .1C. The columbic efficiency is low during the first several cycles due to the setting up of the SEI layer but then sticks to around 100% with some variability due to noise in the instrument.

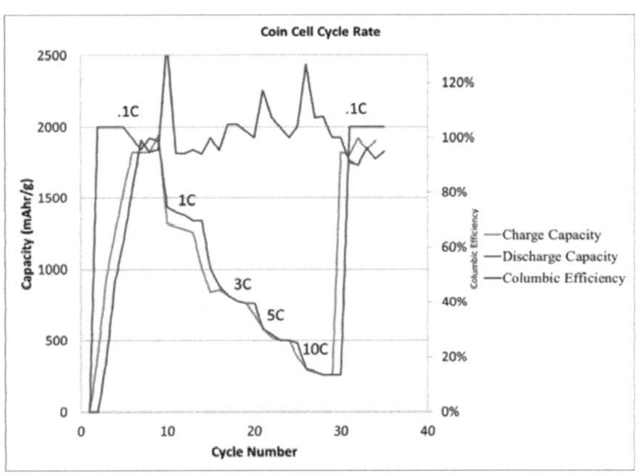

Figure 6: Cycle rate testing for a half cell in a coin cell cycled at rates between 0.1-10C

The good cycle rate performance of the nanowire anodes as shown in Figure 6 is due to the high surface area of the nanowire based anodes. Alloying based anodes such as Si based anodes are also less likely to degrade at higher cycle rates. This makes the nanowire based anode great for high power applications but also capable of higher energy applications as well, with a cycle stability that is capable of consumer electronics applications.

Conclusions

We have shown the production of a novel heterogeneous nanowire solution through the extinguishing of a Ni catalyst layer through a metal induced growth process. This nanowire has high capacity while retaining good SEI characteristics due to the integration of reaction displacement anode material (NiO) on the nanowire surface. The NiO passivates the surface during lithiation and insulates Si from degrading by becoming passivated by alkyl carbonate end terminations. The nanowire anode is shown to have a capacity that is 6X higher than graphite anodes and is stable for 300 cycles. The cycle rate shows that even at a high charge rate of 10C the nanowire anode still retains a capacity of 300mAhr/g which is the tested gravimetric capacity of graphite. The nanowire recovers when switched from a high to a low cycle rate showing no fast charging degradation mechanisms.

References

1. U. Kasavajjula, C. Wang, A. J. Appleby, "Nano- and bulk-silicon-based insertion anodes for lithium-ion secondary cells", *Journal of Power Sources* 163 (2007) 1003–1039
2. M. Nie, D. P. Abraham,Y. Chen, A. Bose, B. L. Lucht, "Silicon Solid Electrolyte Interphase (SEI) of Lithium Ion Battery Characterized by Microscopy and Spectroscopy", J. Phys. Chem. C 2013, 117, 13403−13412
3. W. Xu, PhD thesis, Lousiana State University, "SILICON NANOWIRE ANODE FOR LITHIUM ION BATTERIES: FABRICATION, CHARACTERIZATION, AND SOLID ELECTROLYTE INTERPHASE",
4. X. Ou, R. Kogler, A. Mucklich, W. Skorupa, W. Moller, X. Wang, J.W. Gurlach, B. Rauschenbach, "Efficient oxygen gettering of Si by coimplantation of hydrogen and helium", *App. Phys. Lett.* 93, 161907 (2008),

The Impact of Rechargeable Batteries on Soldier Missions

Shailesh Shah*, Tony Thampan, Steven Aviles, Deepal Shah, Clifford Cook
Power Division, Power Sources Branch, Fuel Cell Team
United States Army Communications – Electronics Research Development and Engineering Center
Aberdeen Proving Ground, MD 21005

Abstract: *Today's Warfighter is equipped with a myriad of situational awareness and communications capabilities. This has increased the need to provide new and better power sources in order to support these electronic devices. Batteries are the traditional power source used by the Soldier in order to support his power needs. Recently the Army has started promoting the use of rechargeable batteries in order to reduce cost and streamline the supply chain. The Small Unit Power (SUP) Capability Development Document (CDD) [1] released by the Maneuver Center of Excellence (MCoE) in 2013 has recommended the use of a centralized power source that is connected to all the peripheral devices on the soldier and serves to keep the individual batteries at the top of their state of charge. The conformal wearable battery (CWB) is a rechargeable battery that is being considered as a centralized power source. MCoE recommendations also include supporting equipment for battery recharging and energy management. These recommendations are based on a comprehensive Cost Benefit Analysis (C-BA) led by the Edgewood Chemical and Biological Center, Decision Analysis Team; conducted for various fielding options of the recommended equipment to support 72-hour mission durations in austere environments. This paper looks at the impact of substituting a Wearable Fuel Cell (WFC) for the CWB. We have compared the use of the WFC and its benefit on "cost", "soldier load", "convenience" and "logistics".*

Keywords: Soldier load, Cost, logistics, convenience, rechargeable batteries, primary batteries.

Background: Soldiers carry a significant amount of equipment (e.g., communication and locating devices) that are powered by multiple batteries and types, and are burdened by having to use/carry replacement batteries. The CECOM/MCoE Battery Analysis identified extensive battery requirements at all echelons:

- Eleven battery types and 1,418 batteries with a total weight of 400 pounds at the Platoon level (72 hour mission).
- Thirteen battery types and 4,733 batteries with a total weight of 1,413-1,557 pounds at the Company level (72 hour mission).

The preferred approach for providing power to small units in the field would be one that decreases Soldier load and logistical footprint, and allows them to self-sustain for up to 72 hours in an austere environment. However, a comprehensive analysis of the possible solutions must include other considerations in addition to load and logistical footprint. The Department of the Army, MCoE in Fort Benning, Georgia recently released a CDD [1] for SUP that has addressed the power gaps from all angles. The C-BA that resulted in the identification of the capability needs identified in the document is based on providing a "best balance" of quantifiable and non-quantifiable benefits, costs, risk, and second and third order effects. The fundamental premise of the document is that generating power and charging batteries forward in the operational environment will reduce the cumulative demand at higher echelons. The Army must reduce battery types and quantities carried by the Soldier and reduce the frequency of battery exchanges while exploring alternative power sources. The next section is a brief summary of the benefits assessment exercise for the various courses of action examined by MCoE for the development of the SUP CDD. Before the analysis for fuel cells is presented, the C-BA for rechargeable batteries examined by MCoE is reviewed below.

SUP Benefit Assessment (Rechargeable Batteries):
The SUP C-BA considered the following five courses of actions (COAs):

- **COA 1 - Status Quo Alternative**. Small Units carry rechargeable batteries (no recharge capability forward) with a planned resupply every 24 hours.
- **COA 2 - Full Fielding**. All 40 Infantry Brigade Combat Teams (IBCTs) receive their full basis of issue (BOI) of SUP systems. Full BOI includes Squad Power Manager (SPM), Integrated Soldier Power and Data System- Core (ISPDS-C), and Power Generation at the Platoon, Squad, and Individual level.
- **COA 3 - Limited Fielding**. All 40 IBCTs receive limited BOI of SUP systems. SUP quantities are only sufficient to support Company and below personnel with high energy demands. This COA provides the ISPDS-C at the Platoon, Squad, and Individual level, but at a reduced BOI.
- **COA 4 - Individual/Squad Focused Fielding**. All 40 IBCTs receive the same capabilities as COA 2, but does not include the Platoon level power source, (i.e., 900W generator).
- **COA 5 - Enhanced Full Fielding**. All 40 IBCTs receive their full BOI of SUP systems, with additional power generation capability at the team level provided by the Rucksack Enhanced Portable Power System.

The projected BOI of SUP equipment for a dismounted infantry platoon is shown in Table1 below:

Table 1: Power Generation/Supplying Systems per COA

Generation Capability Assumptions	COA 1	COA 2	COA 3	COA 4	COA 5
Platoon Power Generation (PPG)	0	1	1	0	1
Squad Power Generation (SqPG)	0	5	5	5	5
Soldier Power Generation (SoPG)	0	40	14	40	40
Team Power Generation (TPG)	0	0	0	0	8
ISPDS-C w/ 2 Conformal Batteries	0	40	14	40	40

The nominal power output and weight of the SUP equipment considered in Table 1 is given in Table 2 below:

Table 2: SUP Equipment Metrics

Generation Capability Assumptions	Nominal Power Output	Maximum Weight
Platoon Power Generator (PPG)	>900W	< 30 lbs
Squad Power Generation (SqPG)	>100 W	< 3 lbs
Soldier Power Generation (SoPG)	10 W	1 lb
Team Power Generation (TPG)	60 W	5.3
ISPDS-C w/ 2 Conformal Batteries	>10W	5.85

The various power consuming equipment and their associated battery particulars are given in Table 3 below:

Table 3: Infantry Platoon IBCT BOI – Systems Using Rch - Batteries

DEVICE	Battery Type	Batteries per System	Equip Run Time (hrs)	BCT System BOI
AN/PRC-154 (Rifleman Radio)	Rifleman Radio Battery	1	8	40
AN/PRC-148	MBITR Battery	1	12	6
AN/PRC-119F	BB-2590	1	33	2
AN/PSC-5 SATCOM	BB-2590	2	17	1

In order for the units to be self-sustained for 72 hours they must be equipped with the sum-total of the energy needed for the period. While COA1 assumes this energy need is met by the resupply of batteries every 24 hours, for COA's 2 thru 5 this energy need is met by carrying a limited amount of extra batteries and recharging batteries using the SUP equipment. The specific energy contribution assumed from each SUP equipment over the 72- hour period is shown in Table 4 below. Also shown in Table 4 is the carry weight imposed by the SUP equipment (note the carry weight of the PPG is assumed zero since it is assumed that that the PPG is not an item that will be carried by the Soldier, but rather transported to a location and stored for use during stops in a mission). Note also that the power generation equipment at all levels that provide the energy to charge batteries is assumed to operate at ~ 66% efficiency. Based on the specified hours of operation the net energy available from each piece of equipment over 72 hours is given in the last column of Table 4.

Table 4: Power Generation/Supplying Systems

Generation Capability Assumptions	Carry Wt	Power (W)	Hrs/ Day	Wh/ day	Wh/ 72 hr
Platoon Power Generation (PPG)	0	600	2	1200	3600
Squad Power Generation (SqPG)	6.5	66	3	198	594
Soldier Power Generation (SoPG)	1	6.6	3	19.8	59.4
Team Power Generation (TPG)	5.3	36.85	3	110.6	331.7
ISPDS-C w/ 2 Conformal Batteries	5.85	various	24	150	

The differences in the power generation equipment considered for each COA resulted in a different number of batteries that were required to be carried per 72 hour mission. This, results in a different total load burden for each COA considered as shown in Table 6.

The C-BA study team analyzed each COA based on the quantitative and qualitative factors shown in Table 5 below. Each factor was assigned a "weight" based on the relative importance of the factor.

Table 5: Evaluation Factors Considered and Weighting

Evaluation Factor	Nominal Power Output	Maximum Weight
PERFORMANCE		
Load – Weight/Bulk (Batteries Saved)	Soldier load with relation to battery weight	14
Energy Management	How effectively power can be managed.	17
Recharge Time	The amount of time required to recharge equipment.	11
Mission Interruptions/ Frequency	The amount of time between having to stop to replace batteries in systems.	20
Autonomy	Ability to charge independently at the lowest level.	10
Ergonomics/Ease of Use	Complexity of operating the system.	8
Environmental Flexibility	Impact of environmental conditions on capability.	6
LOGISTICS		
Training	The amount of training needed.	5
Logistics Footprint/Supply Chain	ILS requirements (i.e., temperature, space, humidity, disposal).	5
PROGRAMMATICS		
Producibility	Ability to manufacture the power system in required quantities.	4

The benefits assessment was based on Multi-Criteria Decision Making (MCDM). In MCDM, the COAs are scored relative to the benefit (non-cost) evaluation factors defined above. Decision analysis software (Logical Decisions Portfolio © (LDP)) was used to implement and document the assessment. Each COA was reviewed and scored against each benefit evaluation factor, using the performance scales. For the most part, the COAs were assessed on a relative basis, where the best COA for a particular factor received a 100 score, with the worst scoring 0, based on how the COAs compared to each other [2]. The assessment was based on available data and the knowledge and expertise of the SMEs. The total weight of equipment carried by the soldier for each COA and the final total weighted benefit score is given in Table 6:

Table 6: Total Weight and Weighted Benefit Score for each COA[1]

COA	Total Weight Carried in lbs	Weighted Benefit Score
1	359.2	39
2	387.7	79
3	331.6	65
4	434.2	52
5	414.5	73

1. Note that the total weight is just one of the factors that affects the weighted benefit score

Wearable Fuel Cells: As can be seen from Table 6 – COA 2 has the highest weighted benefit score – implying that all 40 Infantry Brigade Combat Teams (IBCTs) receive their full BOI of SUP systems including SPM, ISPDS-C, and Power Generation at the Platoon, Squad, and Individual level. While COA 2 is a reasonable approach, the SUP equipment adds to soldier burden and mission responsibility in terms of charging batteries. Each platoon is required to carry and maintain a 900 W generator, fuel (JP8) and three universal battery chargers to recharge the CWB's and other batteries in their inventory. On cloudy days the use of fueled generators may need to be increased beyond the proposed 2 hours/day (see Table 4), to make up for the energy that could not be tapped from the sun. **The biggest advantage of using the conformal rechargeable batteries and associated SUP equipment is that it theoretically places each soldier in a "netzero status". With the energy harvesting technologies provided to the soldier he can presumably go about his mission for significantly longer than the 72- hour requirement.**

The Army is developing wearable fuel cells in the same form factor as the CWB as a potential replacement for the CWB [3]. In this case, the energy need for the 72 hours is met by carrying additional cartridges of fuel. Since fuel cells are a "primary solution" this would eliminate the need to carry a platoon generator, universal battery chargers and fuel that would be required for charging conformal and 2590 batteries required for the 72- hour mission. This is a significant advantage, since it avoids the additional burden of carrying a bulky 30 lb generator and associated fuel, and saves the IBCT the trouble of charging 80 conformal batteries during the mission. Figure 1 shows an example of a WFC being developed by the Army and its associated metrics.

We have conducted a similar benefit analysis as was conducted for the conformal wearable batteries discussed above. The following three cases where fuel cells replaced the CWB as part of the suite of equipment provided to the soldier were analyzed:

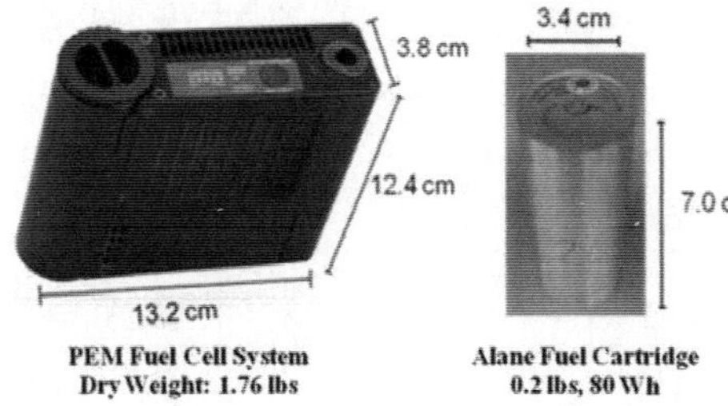

Figure 1: Wearable Alane Fuel Cell

- **COA 3'** Replace the 2 conformal batteries provided to each soldier with 2 WFC's and enough cartridges to make up for the energy that was originally planned for as coming from the rechargeable CWB and the platoon generator for the 72 hour mission
- **COA 4'** Same as COA-3' but without the soldier power generator –which is substituted with enough additional cartridges that make up for the energy that was planned from soldier power generation
- **COA 5'** Same as COA-4' but with additional cartridges that makes up for the energy that was relied upon as coming from the squad generator. This is the enhanced fielding option that provides additional primary energy from cartridges without eliminating the option of getting the same energy from squad power generator.

These three options were compared with the baseline option COA 1 and the full fielding option COA 2 that had the lowest and highest weighted benefit score respectively in the SUP analysis discussed above (Table 6). For the sake of completeness the inventory of different power equipment for the five options is given in Table 7.

Benefit assessment was conducted in the same manner as was done for the SUP equipment COA's and relative scores were assigned for each category. The weighting factors for each category were kept the same and a total score was established by multiplying the scores in each category by the weighting factor for that category. The relative scores for each category are shown in Table 8.

The total weighted score is shown in Table 9 along with the total energy available from each option for a 72 hour mission and the total weight of all power equipment including fuel needed for the 72 hour mission.

Comments on Wearable Fuel Cell Option: It can be seen from Table 9 that the weighted benefit score for the various WFC options are almost equal and nearly the same as the benefit score for the SUP equipment option COA 2.

Table 7: Power Equipment Inventory for Each COA

ITEM	COA 1	COA 2	COA 3'	COA 4'	COA 5'
Rifleman Radio Battery	360	60	60	60	60
MBITR Battery	36	12	12	12	12
BB-2590	6	4	4	4	4
BB-2590	10	4	4	4	4
Conformal Wearable Battery (CWB	0	80	0	0	0
Platoon Power Generator	0	1	0	0	0
Squad Power Generator	0	5	5	5	5
Soldier Power Generator	0	40	40	0	0
ISPDS-C	0	40	40	40	40
JP-8	0	1	0	0	0
Universal Battery Charger (MUBC)	0	3	0	0	0
Alane Fuel Cell	0	0	80	80	80
Alane Fuel Cartridges	0	0	195	250	328

Table 8: Relative Benefit Scores for Each Category

CATEGORY	Weight	COA 1	COA 2	COA 3'	COA 4'	COA 5'
Load	14%	100	0	70	100	80
Energy Management	17%	0	100	90	70	80
Recharge Time	11%	100	90	80	80	80
Mission Interruptions	20%	0	100	55	40	40
Autonomy	10%	0	100	80	70	90
Environmental Flexibility	8%	100	90	90	70	90
Ease of Use/Ergonomics	6%	0	100	50	100	50
Training	5%	100	60	60	70	80
Logistics Footprint/ Supply Chain	5%	0	100	80	75	65
Producibility	4%	100	75	75	80	80

Table 9:Total Weighted Benefit Score for Each COA

COA	Total Weight lbs	Total Energy Available in Option (Wh)	Weighted Benefit Score
1	359	28000[1]	42
2	455	32000	81
3'	391	32000	73
4'	361	32000	72
5'	377	39000	71

1. **Denotes energy needed for 72 hour mission**

The biggest difference in the weighted score is seen as arising from the individual scores in two main categories:

1. **Mission Interruptions:** The WFC options received a much lower score than COA 2 in this cartegory. This is likely due to the energy capacity of the fuel cell cartridge in the current design, which is only half of the energy capacity of the CWB. This increases the mission interruptions for the WFC case (to change cartridges) when compared to the CWB. It is the authors' opinion that this shortcoming can be rectified very easily by building a larger cartridge, thus minimizing the "mission interruptions" during operation.
2. **Load:** There is a significant reduction in total carried load for WFC options COA's 3'-5', when compared to COA 2 for the rechargeable CWB.

The NetZero Soldier: It is of utmost importance that any SUP option that is considered, allows the soldier the ability to operate in a NetZero mode. **It can be argued that the WFC option supports the goal of the "NetZero soldier" to the same extent as in the case of the use of CWB even though the capacity of the internal rechargeable battery in the WFCis only 20% of the capacity of the CWB. This is because, the recharge options based on solar (SqPG) and energy harvesting (SoPG) that allow the soldier to continue their mission in the "absence of resupply", have limited energy delivery capability. The amount of time the sun is shining and the soldier's ability to harvest energy dictates his ability to extend his missions and not the nominal capacity of the rechargeable battery that is carried by the soldier.**

Reliability and Other Considerations: Each WFC option considered in the analysis discussed in this paper includes a spare fuel cell as part of its BOI. This adds a dimension of reliability in the event that one WFC were to fail or get hit by a bullet etc. However, a number of questions/concerns regarding the WFC must be addressed before it can be deployed. These are:

- Environmental concerns regarding used/partially used cartridge disposal
- Safety/ignition characteristics upon bullet penetration
- Cost

CERDEC is working closely with contractors to answer the above questions and maturing the technology for wearable fuel cells.

Conclusions: The WFC is a strong option to consider for the SUP suite of equipment provided its cartridge capacity is increased to minimize mission interruptions.

References

1. Mr. Graham K, and Major Allen J., "Capability Development Document for Small Unit Power (SUP) Increment:1", Department of the Army, MCoE, Operational Energy Branch, Soldiers Division, Fort Benning, GA 31905-5000, 26 Sep, 2013.
2. Mr. Graham K, and Major Allen J., "Other Appendices for Capability Development Document for Small Unit Power (SUP) Increment:1", Department of the Army, MCoE, Operational Energy Branch, Soldiers Division, Fort Benning, GA 31905-5000, 26 Sep, 2013.
3. T. Thampan, D. Shah, C. Cook, J. Novoa, S. Shah, "Development and Evaluation of Portable and Wearable Fuel Cells for Military Use," *Journal of Power Sources*, vol. 259, pp. 276-281, August 2014.(to be published)

JP-8 to Liquefied Petroleum Gas Reformation

Michael K. Mayeda, Sungtak Kim, Erdem Sasmaz, Jochen Lauterbach
SAGE Energy Solutions, LLC
Columbia, SC 29208, USA

Abstract: *Exclusive use of military jet fuel (JP-8) in the battlefield hinders the use of commercial gas appliances and solid oxide fuel cells (SOFC). We report on a sulfur-tolerant catalyst capable of cracking JP-8 into a liquefied petroleum gas-like (LPG) mixture of hydrocarbons. The simple reaction operates at relatively low temperatures (300-500 °C) so as to avoid catalyst sintering. Furthermore, the reaction does not require additional inputs like steam, oxygen, or hydrogen. The product LPG is free of sulfur and is suitable for use in a SOFC. The condensed effluent can be recycled through the reactor to improve the efficiency from 20% to 35% (mass basis). Further improvements to 45-50% can be achieved by adjusting the recycling ratio. This technology will enable the use of a wide variety of devices in the battlefield.*

Keywords: JP-8; fuel conversion; liquefied petroleum gas; desulfurization; catalysis, reformer

Introduction

In the military battlefield, electric power is predominantly supplied by batteries and jet propellant (JP-8). The former is a mature technology that is convenient for portable applications such as communications, tracking, and illumination. The latter is an energy dense fuel that is useful for high-power applications such as vehicles, generators, and heaters. Because the military operates in desolate regions, soldiers and defense contractors necessarily spend longer periods "off the grid." Therefore, portable devices require numerous replacement batteries to endure lengthy operations. The added weight and heft of low energy density batteries is cumbersome for mobile operations. On the other hand, energy dense fuel cells can reduce weight by a factor of ten. However, the high sulfur content and average molecular mass of jet fuel precludes its use in fuel cells. Therefore, a system that converted available JP-8 supplies into a suitable fuel, such as LPG, would enable longer missions and more mobile soldiers.

JP-8 fuel reformation is typically accomplished using autothermal reformation (ATR), which is a mature reaction and efficiency hovers near 80% (energy basis).[1-2] Furthermore, ATR produces relatively high hydrogen concentrations using inexpensive catalysts. Despite the benefits of ATR, its widespread adoption is prevented by problems with sulfur poisoning, high temperature catalyst sintering, and coke formation.[1,3] The average sulfur concentration in JP-8 is 714 ppm, but specifications allow up to 3000 ppm.[1] Sulfur irreversibly binds to active sites on catalyst surfaces, which decreases efficiency and reactor lifetime. Also, high temperatures for ATR, above 750 °C, cause catalyst sintering. Sintering decreases catalytic efficiency by decreasing the active surface area and loss of active catalyst surface sites.[3-4] Finally, aromatic and olefin compounds within JP-8 contribute catalyst deactivation via coke formation.[5]

Therefore, a fuel processing approach that tolerates sulfur, operates at lower temperatures, and resists coking would enable energy-dense device use in the field. SAGE Energy Solutions' patented fuel cracking technology uses a novel catalyst to crack JP-8 down to a LPG mixture of hydrocarbons. The catalyst is sulfur tolerant, active at low temperatures, and easily regenerated from coking. Additionally, the LPG is sulfur-free and suitable for use in solid oxide fuel cells or commercial gas appliances. Finally, the LPG can be easily stored and transported, which means the process can be run continuously and transients are minimized. SAGE Energy Solutions' technology will add substantial versatility and mobility to military operations.

Methods

JP-8 was evaporated and passed over a fixed bed (350-500 °C); 150 mg of the proprietary catalyst was loaded into a 0.5-in quartz tube reactor. The effluent gas flowed through a condenser and the remaining gaseous product was analyzed by GC-MS. Liquid samples labeled "condensed" were collected from the condenser after a single pass through the reformer. Liquid samples labeled "recycled" were collected from the condenser after implementing a recycle system with a constant volumetric ratio of fresh JP-8 and recycled liquid; reactions with fresh JP-8 were allowed to run for 30 min to accumulate enough condensed liquid for recycling. In all cases, the catalyst was regenerated using ambient air while holding the reactor temperature constant for 1 h. Regenerations were performed every 10 h.

Gaseous products downstream of the condenser were characterized by a Shimadzu QP2010 Plus GC-MS equipped with a HaySep-D capillary column (0.53 mm ID × 30 m, Agilent), which was calibrated using gas standards. Helium was injected in the effluent gas after the reactor to carry the product through the GC-MS.

Condensed and recycled liquids were characterized by GC-MS and nuclear magnetic resonance spectroscopy (^{1}H NMR). ^{1}H NMR measurements were taken with a Bruker Avance III HD 300 using deuterated chloroform (7.26 ppm reference).

Results

Fuel reformation experiments were performed over a range of operating conditions. For our catalyst, we determined the optimum operating temperature to be within 350-500 °C, depending on the desired product distribution. All data reported here was for reactions performed at 450 °C. Figure 1 shows a typical deactivation and regeneration profile of a catalyst over a period of 80 h. Maximum achieved single-pass efficiency was 20% (mass basis).

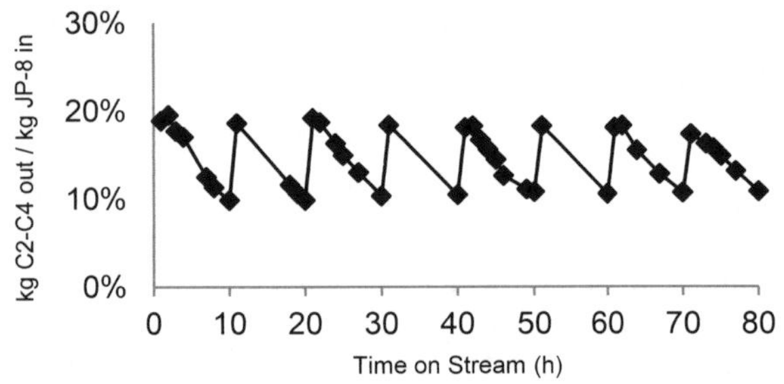

Figure 1. JP-8 to LPG reformation activity. The catalyst was regenerated in air every 10 h. Data points represent GC-MS injections.

Over 95% of the original catalytic activity was regenerated by flowing ambient air for 1 h. The catalyst underwent a noticeable color change from black to light gray during regeneration indicating complete coke removal.

The product distribution remained constant after regeneration. Product distributions associated with each regeneration step are shown in Figure 2.

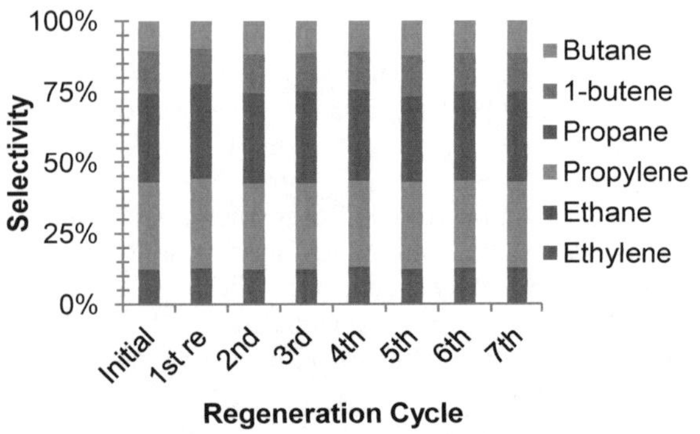

Figure 2. Gaseous product selectivity for C_2 through C_4 species. Data was taken immediately after regeneration steps. Composition was determined by GC-MS analysis.

A majority of the product is propane and propylene, both of which are suitable for use in fuel cells and commercial gas appliances. The distribution of product gases can be slightly altered towards smaller hydrocarbons by increasing the temperature.

It was previously known that paraffins were the primary source of LPG whereas aromatics and olefins contributed to catalyst coking. Because JP-8 is composed of approximately 70% paraffins and only 20% aromatics,[1] it was deduced that more LPG could be extracted from the JP-8 cracking. Therefore, condensed liquid was recycled through the converter. Recycling improved catalytic efficiency from 20% to 35%. ^{1}H NMR was used to characterize the quality of the JP-8 before and after cracking and during recycle experiments (Figure 3).

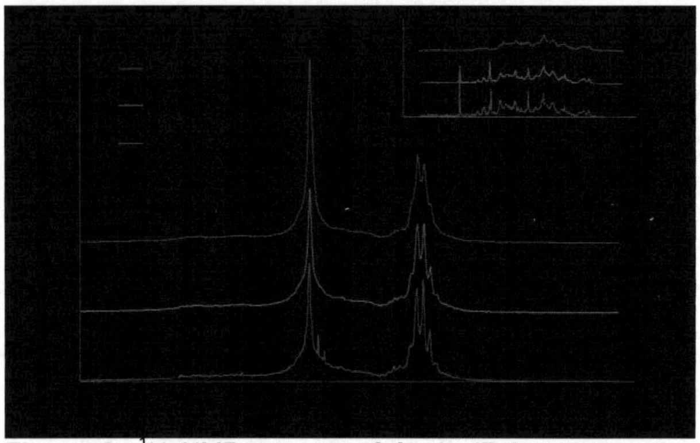

Figure 3. ^{1}H NMR spectra of fresh JP-8, post-reaction condensed liquid, and post-recycle reaction condensed liquid. Inset image shows the aromatic region. Spectra were vertically offset for comparison purposes. Intensity is measured in arbitrary units. The peak near 7.26 ppm is from the deuterated chloroform used in the measurement.

Spectra were normalized to the methyl proton peaks near 0.75 ppm. The peak near 1.2 ppm was attributed to aliphatic protons while peaks between 6.6 - 7.2 ppm represented aromatic compounds. Fresh JP-8 exhibited a large aliphatic peak due to the large amount of paraffins. After cracking and during recycling experiments, the aliphatic peak integrated area was decreased by 15%. The decrease in the aliphatic area suggested a decrease in the average carbon number after catalytic cracking. On the other hand, aromatic compounds remained relatively inert.

GC-MS spectra (Figure 4) show a dramatic decrease in paraffin components (C_{10} - C_{13}) when fresh JP-8 was cracked into LPG. This data corroborates ^{1}H NMR spectra and indicates that the linear hydrocarbons are the primary source of LPG during the fuel reformation.

Discussion

The reaction converts JP-8 into an LPG-like gas mixture and a condensable organic liquid. Figure 1 shows catalytic fuel cracking produced LPG with a 20 wt% efficiency ($LPG_{out}/JP\text{-}8_{in}$).[6] The catalyst exhibited a 50% activity reduction due to coking after 10 h. However, the catalyst was easily regenerated after 1 h of exposure to ambient air at reaction conditions. Regeneration steps increased the catalyst activity to greater than 95% of the original activity. The simple, but effective, regeneration steps indicated that the coke had a high hydrogen composition. The LPG product composition was self-consistent after each regeneration step (Figure 2).

Increasing the reaction temperature reduced the average LPG molecular weight. For the liquid phase, higher molecular weight compounds were condensed and recycled through the reactor to increase efficiency towards 35%.

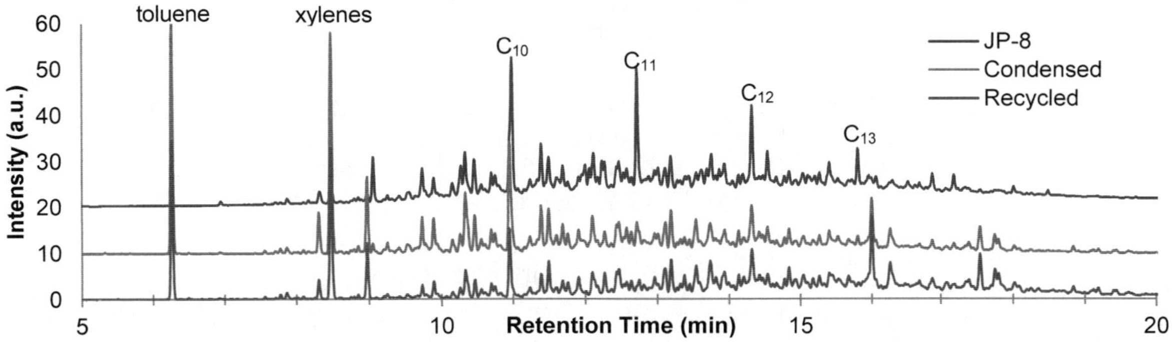

Figure 4. GC-MS spectra of JP-8, condensed liquid, and condensed liquid during recycling. Spectra were vertically offset for comparison purposes. C_x labels were used for decane, undecane, dodecane, and tridecane.

The boost in efficiency upon recycling indicated that LPG precursor compounds remained within the condensed liquid. Further adjustments to the recycling rate could improve the reformation efficiency to 45-50%. Indeed, ^1H NMR spectrum of the condensed liquid (Figure 3, green) showed a significant amount of remaining aliphatic protons. Compared to the JP-8 aliphatic proton peak, the condensed liquid aliphatic proton peak was decreased by 15%. The decrease corresponds well with the time-averaged efficiency of the catalytic cracking reaction (15%). It was initially assumed that paraffin compounds were the precursors to LPG.[7] However, an additional 15% efficiency improvement was made by recycling, despite a dramatic decrease in paraffin (C_{10}-C_{13}) compounds after only one cracking pass (Figure 4, green). Furthermore, the similarities in GC-MS spectra and ^1H NMR for condensed and recycled samples belie the increase in catalytic activity achieved by recycling. Therefore, in addition to paraffins, other hydrocarbon olefins, branched paraffins, and alkylated benzenes also must contribute to the LPG production.

When compared to commercially available propane, the LPG produced higher open circuit voltages when fed through a solid oxide fuel cell (not shown). The increase in open circuit voltage was due to a small amount of hydrogen in the LPG product. In addition to fuel cell performance, the gaseous product was successfully tested with a commercial propane lamp. The LPG product has proven to be an apt substitute for commercial grade propane in both cases.

One of the most important aspects of our fuel reformation technology is its sulfur tolerance. Despite, 556 ppm sulfur in the tested batch of JP-8, no sulfur was detected (LDL = 10 ppm) in the LPG product. In one test, a surrogate JP-8 was doped with 5,000 ppm dibenzothiophene; similar product distributions and activities and sulfur-free LPG were observed. The sulfur was believed to remain bound to aromatic species in the condensed liquid phase. Because sulfur primarily exists as aromatic thiophenes (e.g. benzothiophene, dibenzothiophene, etc.),[8] which are inert over our catalyst, our catalyst remains unperturbed by sulfur content. Low sulfur concentration is particularly important for solid oxide fuel cells. The nickel catalysts in SOFCs are poisoned by high sulfur concentrations (> 50 ppm). Undetectable sulfur concentrations in the product LPG make the reformation technology suitable for use with a SOFC system.

Conclusions

SAGE Energy Solutions has developed a fuel reformation unit that accepts sulfurized JP-8 and produces desulfurized LPG. The catalyst is sulfur tolerant, active at low temperatures, and easy to regenerate. A reformation efficiency of 20% was achieved and recycling improved the efficiency to 35%. Further adjustments to the recycling system could improve the reformation efficiency to 45-50%. It was determined that LPG was primarily produced from linear paraffins while aromatics passed inertly over the catalyst or contributed to coking. The catalyst was regenerated by oxidizing the coke in ambient air. LPG product distributions remained self-consistent after regeneration steps.

Acknowledgements

The authors acknowledge DARPA (BAA-10-55), Columbia Fuel Cell Collaborative, and University of South Carolina Proving Ground and SAGE Research Center for funding and facility use.

References

1. Xu, X. H.; Li, P. W.; Shen, Y. S., *Appl. Energy* **2013**, *108*, 202-217.
2. Brown, L. F., *Int. J. Hydrog. Energy* **2001**, *26* (4), 381-397.
3. Bartholomew, C. H., *Appl. Catal. A-Gen.* **2001**, *212* (1-2), 17-60.
4. Gudlavalleti, S.; Ros, T.; Lieftink, D., *Appl. Catal. B-Environ.* **2007**, *74* (3-4), 251-260.
5. Shamsi, A.; Baltrus, J. R.; Spivey, J. J., *Appl. Catal. A-Gen.* **2005**, *293*, 145-152.
6. Bedenbaugh, J. E.; Kim, S.; Sasmaz, E.; Lauterbach, J., *ACS Comb. Sci.* **2013**, *15* (9), 491-497.
7. Kubo, K.; Iida, H.; Namba, S.; Igarashi, A., *Microporous Mesoporous Mat.* **2012**, *149* (1), 126-133.
8. Lee, I. C.; Ubanyionwu, H. C., *Fuel* **2008**, *87* (3), 312-318.

Ceramic Fuel Cell Modules in Li-145 Form Factor

Simon S. Ang[1], Tom Cannon[2], Ryan Tian and Jingyi Chen
University of Arkansas, High Density Electronics Center (HiDEC)
700 W. Research Center Blvd., Fayetteville, Arkansas 72701
Siang@uark.edu [1] Tcannon@uark.edu [2] (479) 575-5031

Abstract: The Li-145 battery form factor fuel cell module has been developed based on microsystem-integration technology using a low-temperature co-fired ceramic (LTCC) technology. Three-dimensional interconnects and cavities, afforded by the LTCC technology, enable fuel cells to be completely integrated within a ceramic thin-slab to reduce footprint and to take advantage of the physical properties of LTCC. This leads to smaller cell size and faster response time, enables operation in extreme environments, and paves the way for integration of additional electrical power management devices or mechanical on-board functions. In each such module, many miniaturized fuel-cells can be integrated, connected in series or parallel configurations and controlled through the internal module interconnections. When connecting the modules to a central power bus, a "power pack" system is formed that can be scaled up or down, like playing Lego, in order to meet the customer's changing needs of current-outputs from 100s to 1,000s of amperes. LTCC gives us the flexibility of current collector cavity sizes from smaller than 0.5"x0.5" all the way through 8"x8". In this way the active area of the fuel cell can be tailored to a wide range of power source applications. For this LTCC-145 fuel cell design, three 24-cell LTCC modules are being used to form a power pack size that fits into the Li-145 battery form factor delivering similar energy density requirements with room for onboard fuel storage, super capacitors and control electronics. The expected power from the LTCC-145 is 25 Watts at an output voltage of 18.9V. While Nafion and platinum loaded carbon cloth are used as the membrane electrode assemblies (MEAs) for these ceramic fuel cell modules, nanostructured membranes and catalysts are being developed to improve the efficiency, life span and allow alternate fuel sources for these fuel cell modules.

Topic: Fuel Cells, Fuel Processing and Storage

Keywords: Ceramic fuel cell modules; miniaturized fuel cells; power pack; LTCC; Li-145 battery; nanostructures; nanostructured membranes; bimetallic catalysts; alternate fuel sources.

Introduction

Three dimensional interconnects and cavities afforded by low-temperature co-fired ceramic (LTCC) technology enable fuel cells to be completely integrated within a ceramic structure. This leads to smaller package size, enables operation in extreme environments, and paves the way for integration of additional electrical power management devices or mechanical on-board functions. A polymer electrolyte membrane fuel cell (PEM-FC) module in '3D Cube Form' was designed, fabricated and fully tested using the LTCC technology [1]. The membrane electrode assembly (MEA) functions to separate electrons at a conductive anode and to conduct the electrons to an external circuit. This must be done while allowing the hydrogen ion to pass through a gas barrier to the cathode so that it may recombine with electrons and ultimately balance the reaction. The structure of the LTCC-based MEA consists of gas channels and anode/cathode current collectors embedded in the LTCC structure. Two halves are mated to form the assembly that houses the gas diffusion layer and the gas barrier membrane. Many variables affect cell performance including gas channeling methods, diffusion layer construction, electrode-to-diffusion layer interface, and electrode conducting material [2].

Fuel Cell Construction

DuPont 951 Green Tape with a 10 mil thickness was used for fabrication of the cells. This tape is available in multiple thicknesses and is designed for use as an insulating layer [3]. As seen in Figure 1, both the anode and cathode plates have a similar build sequence. Each begins with a four-layer tape base. An AutoCAD software was used to design the artwork used for fabrication. The artwork was converted to run on an automatic tape-punching tool, where layers were then punched individually. Following this, the four layers were laminated together to form 40 mil-thick unfired end plates. The LTCC surfaces were then metallized by applying a paste mixture of silver and palladium. This conductive paste was used to form the current collectors and the conductors that connect to the outside of the cell. Following this step, extra layers of tape were laminated to the structure to form the MEA sealing lip.

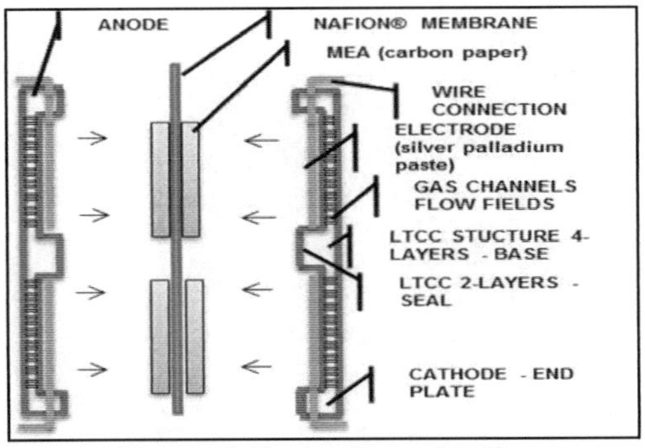

Figure 1. Fuel cell construction

The ceramic pieces were then fired in a furnace. Cell construction began with MEAs built using carbon cloth on carbon cloth doped with 0.5 mg/cm^2 of a platinum/ruthenium (Pt/Ru) in a 1:1 ratio. Fuel channel size was the first variable taken into consideration when designing the cells. It is already know that channel shape and size has a significant effect on output levels [4]. In order to establish a starting point, 20 mil round holes were selected using a 0.5 mm x 0.5 mm grid layout for the gas flow fields. A ceramic structure was designed that anchors four MEAs, channels the fuel, integrates the electrodes, and provides the necessary electrical interconnect for multiple cell configurations. Figure 2 shows the completed 4 x 4 fuel cell plates with fuel

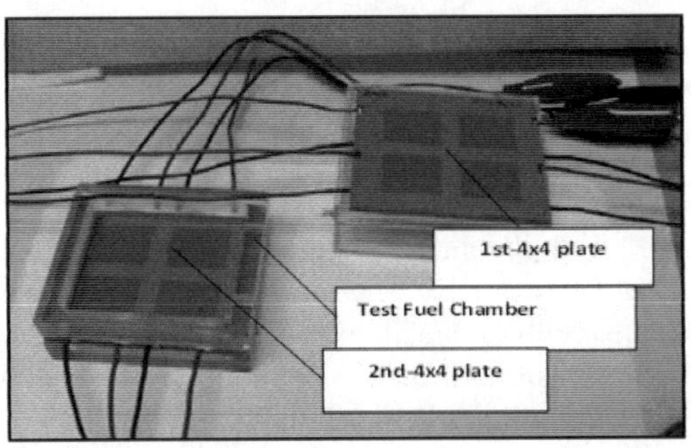

Figure 2. 8-cell fuel cell module with fuel storage.

storage to form the 8-cell fuel cell module.

The next step was to design a 12-cell plate and add the MEA's. A completed 12-cell place is shown in Figure 3. (45mm x 135mm x 1.5mm) A filter medium is used on the cathode of each of the three modules, to remove dust and particles and hold water vapor to help hydrate the fuel cell membranes. The fuel distribution chambers are designed with gas flow tubing to allow the fuel to flow in only one direction allowing full coverage of each of the 24 cells in the module as shown in Figure 4. The chambers also incorporate water collection capillaries to direct the water away from the anodes keeping the cells from becoming flooded. The output of water is redirected to the cathode air filters to hydrate the fuel cells. A sensor can be used to control the flushing of the chamber.

Adding the fuel chamber and a second 12-cell plate forms the 24-cell module. By connecting three 24-cell modules (45mm x 135mm x 8mm each) with fuel distribution chambers, the overall size will fit into the Li-145 form factor and still allow room for changeable fuel supply canister and controls, as seen in Figure 5-A & B.

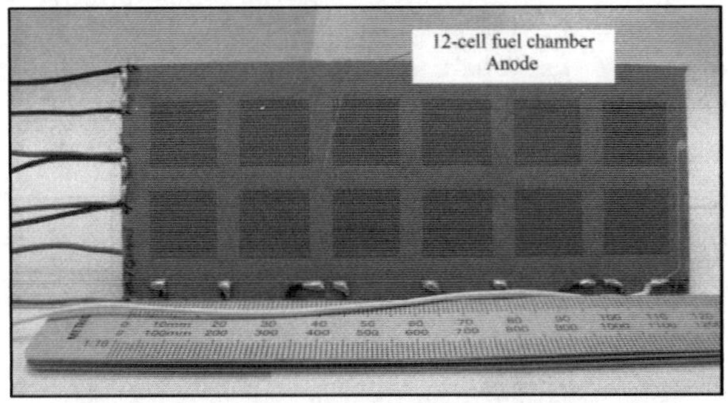

Figure 3. 12-cell Fuel Cell Plate

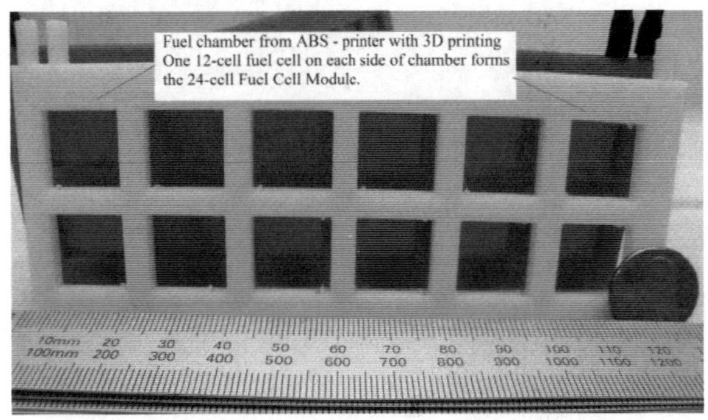

Figure 4. Fuel distribution chamber

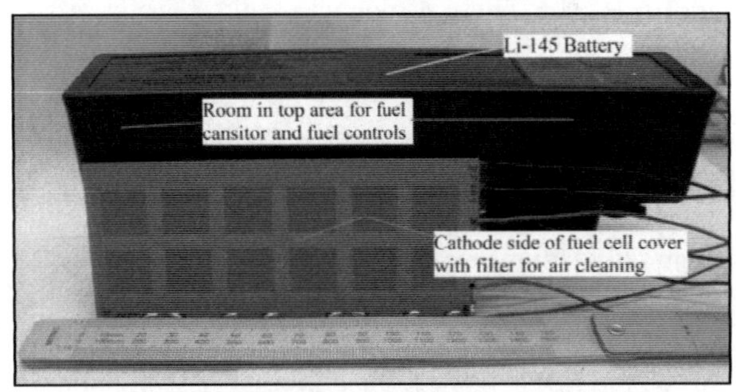

Figure 5A-B. LTCC 24-cell fuel cell with Li-145 battery – Depth and Thickness

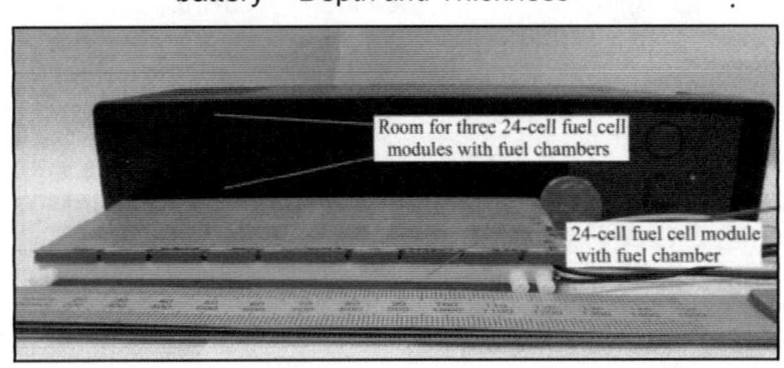

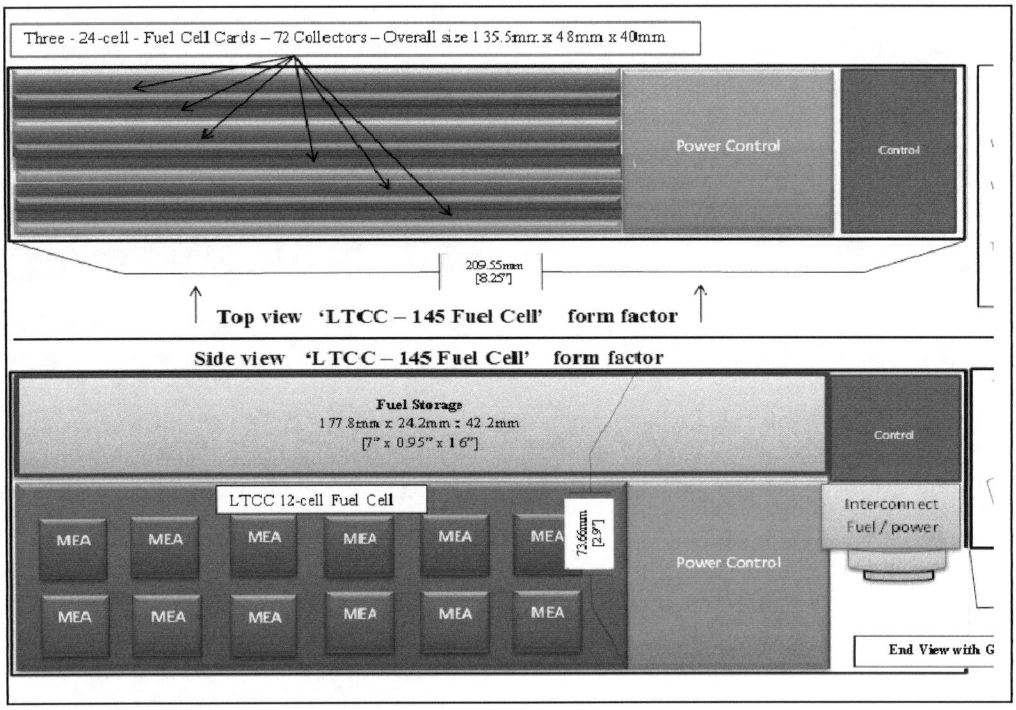

Figure 6. The LTCC-145 concept drawing

LTCC-145 Concept

This design of three 24-cell modules (45mm x 135mm x 8mm each) with fuel distribution chambers, has the overall size of 135mm x 45mm x 35mm, placed in the form factor of the Li-145 allows room for solid hydrogen fuel storage and electronic management, as seen in Figure 6. Since one liter of hydrogen will produce 2.89 Wh of work. (3.2–3.5 Wh per liter, deregulated due to temperature changes) [5], the canister volume size of 178mm x 24.2mm x 42.2mm that holds 60 liters of hydrogen in solid form can be expected to yield 173Wh (i.e., 2.89 x 60 = 173.4Wh). With an average power draw of 6.5W, the fuel cell is expected to run for over 26 hours before changing the fuel canister, this is based on a potential application with the Falcon AN/PRC-150 radio, with average operation times of 60%(I)30%(R)10%(T).

Testing

Current-voltage (I-V) performance data was collected by using a test circuit consisting of a two voltmeters. One voltmeter was set to measure the cell's output voltage, while the other was used to measure voltage across a 0.1 ohm precision current-sense resistor in series with a variable resistance. [6] Multiple current and voltage measurements were taken from open-circuit to short circuit condition using a purely resistive load. Before testing the performance of the 8-cells, we first characterized individual cells within each of the 4-cell plates. This was followed by the testing of various series and parallel cell combinations. Hydrogen was fed from a gas cylinder with back pressures of 1psi created by running the output gas port through a needle valve into a 500 ml beaker of water. The 8-cell module (45mm x 45mm x 8mm), with fuel storage and 0.5mg/cm² Pt loading, produces 2,448mV @ 1,042mA for 2.55Watts at 70% of Nernst Voltage as shown in Figure 7. On this basis, one 24-cell module (45mm x 135mm x 8mm), is three times that of the eight cell module, with the fuel storage and has a projected output power of 7.65Watts. When integrating 3 such 24-cell modules (i.e., 72 cells) to a central power bus, a compact FC "power pack" (45mm x 135mm x 35 mm) is formed that can produce an average output power of over 23Watts. At the time of this writing the 24-cell modules were undergoing testing for power, fuel consumption and cycle duration for 1,000 cycles.

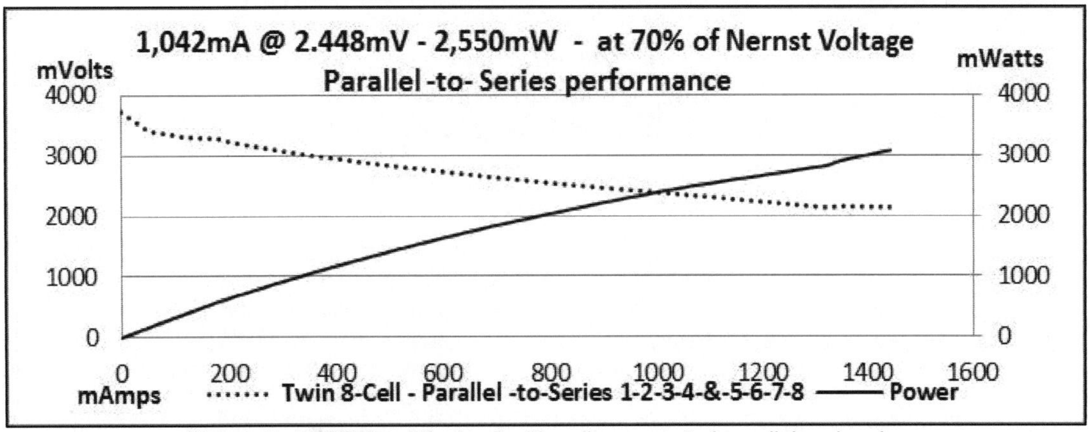

Figure 7. LTCC 8-cell fuel cell with cells connected parallel and series

Nanostructure Membranes and Catalysts

While Nafion and platinum loaded carbon cloth are used as the membrane electrode assemblies (MEAs) for these ceramic fuel cell modules, nanostructured membranes [7] and catalysts are being developed to improve the efficiency and life span of these fuel cell modules and to allow use of alternate fuels, like Natural Gas. [8] A high proton conductivity nanofiber with tunable pore structures and proton passage across the PEM is also being developed, for operations in hotter environments. [9]

Conclusion

A ceramic fuel cell module LTCC-145, in Li-145 form factor, has been fabricated for a direct replacement of the Li-145 battery.

References

[1] T. Cannon, S.S. Ang, M. Steger, K. Porter, E.V. Porter, and M Glover, "A Ceramic "Power Cube" Fuel Cell," 45th Power Sources Conference, Las Vegas (NV), June 11-14, 2012. Pg. 215-218.

[2] Colleen Spiegel, PEM Fuel Cell Modeling and Simulation, 84 Theobaid's Road London, Elsevier 2008 pp. 49-165.

[3] "LTCC Product Technical Information : DuPont Microcircuit Materials." [Online]. Available:http://www2.dupont.com/MCM/en_US/tech_info/products/ltcc.html#951.

[4] Uwe Partach, Adrian Goldberg, Michael Stelter, LTCC - Based Micro-Scale PEM Fuel Cell, IEEE Electronics System Integration Technology Conference, 1st Vol. 1, 2006 pp. 544-549

[5] Energy Density - facts and equations on hydrogen density and volumes. http://hypertextbook.com/facts/2005/MichelleFung.s www.siei.org/usefulequations.htm

[6] Shannon C. Page, Adnan H. Anbuky, Susan P. Krumdieck, and Jack Brouwer - Test Method and Equivalent Circuit Modeling of a PEM Fuel Cell in a Passive State, IEEE Transactions on Energy Conversion, Vol. 22, No. 3, September 2007 pp. 764-773.

[7] Novel Path to Nanocomposite Cathodes and Anodes Enabling High Power Li-ion and Next-Generation Batteries (Page 99) Daniel E. Morse, Hong-Li Zhang, Jon von Bulow, Lyle Kaplan-Reinig, Christie Reji, Nick Whelan, *LifeCel Technology Inc. & University of California, Santa Barbara,* 45th Power Sources Conference, June 2012

[8] J. Chen, B. Yao, C. Li, and G. Shi, "An improved Hummers method for eco-friendly synthesis of graphene oxide," Carbon, Volume 64, November 2013, pg. 225–229.

[9] W. Dong, Z. Shi, J. Ma, C. Hou, Q. Wan, S. Feng, A. Cogbill, Z.R. Tian, "One-pot redox syntheses of heteronanostructures of Ag nanoparticles on MoO_3 nanofibers," *J. Phys. Chem. B.* 2006, 110, 5845-5848.

Production of Liquid Fuels by Advanced Fischer Tropsch

Lyman J Frost
Joseph J Hartvigsen
S. Elango Elangovan
Ceramatec, Inc
Salt Lake City, UT 84119 USA

Abstract: *This paper discusses research conducted at Ceramatec related to small scale Fischer Tropsch. The system designed and tested by Ceramatec indicates the ability to produce a modular, road-transportable system for the same capital as large plants. Ceramatec has demonstrated the production of FT liquids from various feedstock options, including: natural gas, synthesis gas from co-electrolysis, biogas, and solid fuels.*

Keywords: Fischer Tropsch; Synthetic Fuels; GTL; CTL; BTL; modular synthetic fuel plants

Introduction

Ceramatec has been involved in research associated with synthetic fuels for a significant period of time. It has demonstrated the ability to produce Fischer Tropsch (FT) fuels from a variety of feedstock sources (e.g. co-electrolysis of steam and carbon dioxide, gas output by an anaerobic digester, natural gas, and heavier hydrocarbons). Ceramatec started not with a technology but with an objective to design a system that could eventually be built on a small scale for the same operating and capital cost that large, world-class FT plants are built. Since there are limited sites that can provide the volumes of natural gas needed for these larger plants, a solution to smaller volumes of hydrocarbons to liquids was needed.

The energy industry has developed a model for economies of scale of building very large, very efficient, and permanently sited synthetic fuels plants. In order to process the diverse, dispersed, and small field resources that are available, a different model is required. The Ceramatec vision is a mass-produced modular unit that is sized to be road transportable, constructed of normally available materials in a factory, and designed for minimum capital and operating cost. What is lost in plant size is made up for in number of plants produced, and by mass manufacturing of innovative designs developed using modeling tools and developed around advanced catalysts and supports. The economics simply don't work for one-of-a-kind designs, built on-site for a small and transient feedstock.

Ceramatec's reactor design philosophy attempts to reduce the costs and risks associated with reactor design, fabrication and operation by the following means:

- Using fixed bed reactors
- Limiting reactor train module size to 12"x12"x48" for over the road mobility
- Employing removable catalyst bed elements for off-site catalyst service
- Designing pressure boundary components fabricated from standard industrial piping and fittings
- Design for thermal management based on high activity catalysts
- Simplify the process scheme to minimize capital
- Achieve low thermal variation in reactor radial and axial profiles

Technical

Ceramatec successfully demonstrated a XTL reactor element at 43mm diameter and expanded this to a 100mm diameter reactor. Reactors are interoperable with a variety of structured reactor inserts and can be charged with highly active conventional or hybrid catalysts.

A Comsol Multi-physics model was used to maximize the total reactor production rate by varying seven parameters defining the profile geometry. The total catalyst volume productivity was maximized subject to a constraint on the limiting temperature within the domain. A Monte-Carlo technique was used to find starting points for subsequent Nelder-Mead optimization to converge on local optima. This approach yielded some non-intuitive reverse taper fin solutions where heat gathering surface area was more critical than heat (Figure 1).

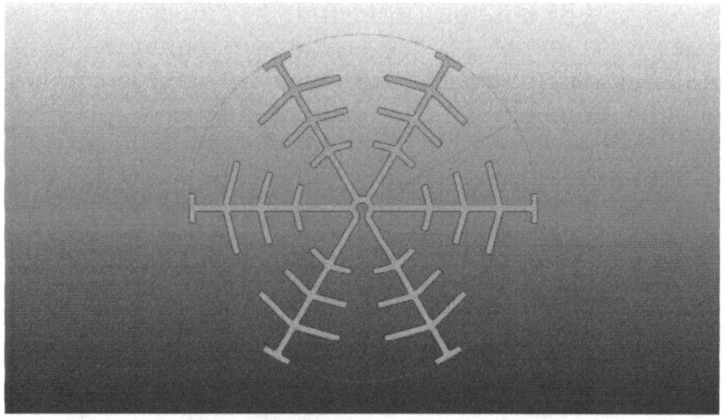

Figure 1: Internal reactor insert for thermal transfer

Ceramatec has an established synthetic fuels laboratory infrastructure with sufficient syngas generation and compression capacity to supply a 2 BPD reactor. The current laboratory implementation of this reactor is a ¼ length implementation of the 100mm reactor with a removable catalyst tube and a fixed cooling jacket. The cooling jacket features dual mode cooling with a forced convection pass on an annular zone in direct contact with the catalyst tube, surrounded by a boiling coolant outer shell. The forced convection pass coolant is held above the saturation pressure while the outer shell coolant is at saturation pressure. As the thermal stability of the 100mm diameter reactor is now proven, a 7-tube, ¼ length, 1 BPD reactor is in design to demonstrate a larger number of reactor tube elements.

The ¼ BPD GTL laboratory system is fed by a three (3) inch natural gas pipeline. After passing through a sulfur guard bed to remove any sulfur compounds, the synthesis gas is generated by a Ceramatec designed non-thermal plasma catalyzed reformer. This reformer is capable of processing up to 100 MSCF per day of high-BTU natural gas (i.e. enough for ~ 10 BPD of FT liquids). Figure 2 shows the reformer (~8' high; ~2' diameter).

Figure 2: 10 BPD Plasma Natural Gas Reformer

After production, the synthesis gas (CO and H_2) goes through several stages of compression. The first compression step uses a two-stage compressor with cooling to condense moisture after each stage (Figure 3). The synthesis gas exits the compressor at about 200 psig and is piped to an intermediate storage facility located external to the laboratory. When the intermediate storage in a 240 gallon 200 psig tank. When the tank is full, a second step of compression increases synthesis gas pressure to 800 psig and stores the material in two 500 gallon tanks (Figure 4). This serves as a buffer feedstock to the Fischer Tropsch reactor located within the laboratory.

Figure 3: Two-stage compression with cooling

Figure 4: Syngas storage (800 psig) and compressor

Each of the compression steps is sufficient to provide enough pressurized synthesis gas for ~ 2 BPD of FT liquids. The synthesis gas is then ready to be fed to the FT reactor. The reactor input is regulated to about 300 psig and is preheated prior to introduction into the FT reactor.

The FT reactor (Figure 5) operates at ~ 300 psig and ~225° C with internal heat transfer media to produce an even catalyst bed temperature in both axial and radial directions. The internal heat transfer structures have demonstrated the capability to maintain bed temperatures in a 4" reactor with a Co-Ru catalyst that varies by < 10° C.

Figure 5: FT reactor system (yellow skid)

The reactor has automated product collection for both light and heavy hydrocarbons (green skid in Figure 5). The system has a dual cooling system with integral cooling. A synthesis gas recycle system is also used to optimize utilization. The recycled synthesis gas is re-pressurized prior to mixing with the fresh feedstock. The cooling loop operates at atmospheric pressure by use of a synthetic coolant. At full production with a catalyst of appropriate activity the FT reactor (~5' high and 4" diameter) is capable of producing ~ ¼ BPD of FT liquids.

The carbon number distribution depends on the particular catalyst and the operating conditions of the reactor. Figure 6 shows the carbon distribution with two different catalysts. The distribution in blue is with a standard Ceramatec Co-Ru catalyst and the distribution in red is with a hybrid catalyst that is designed to terminate carbon polymerization. The hybrid has a special support structure.

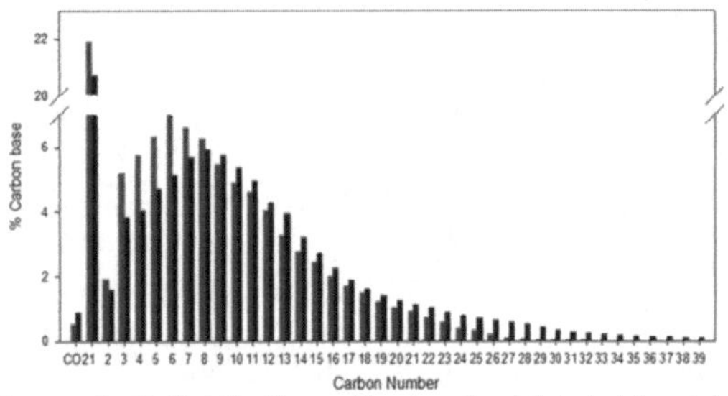

Figure 6: C distribution with standard & hybrid catalyst

The reactor has shown very stable operation and the catalyst used has demonstrated repeatable performance. The reactor was run for five hundred (500) hours and multiple product samples taken. The results tracked very well over time (Figure 7).

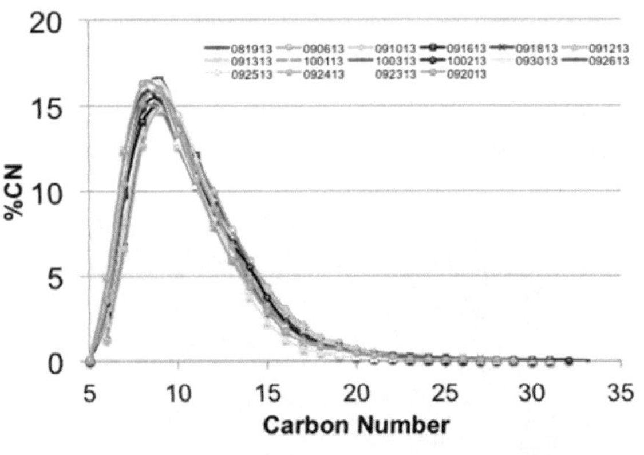

Figure 7: Plot of multiple samples from extended run

The stability of the reactor and catalyst has encouraged Ceramatec to design a 10 BPD pilot plant using the same components. The design was done in conjunction with an engineering and construction firm experienced in pilot plant construction. The 10 BPD pilot consists of three skids (skid 1 – 12'x12'x36'; skid 2 – 12'x12'x30'; skid 3 – 12'x12'x24') and a container for the synthesis gas compression. The plant is designed to operate on natural gas that has been largely cleaned of any sulfur compounds. The reformer operates in an autothermal mode using air and steam as oxidants. An artist's rendition of the facility is shown as Figure 8.

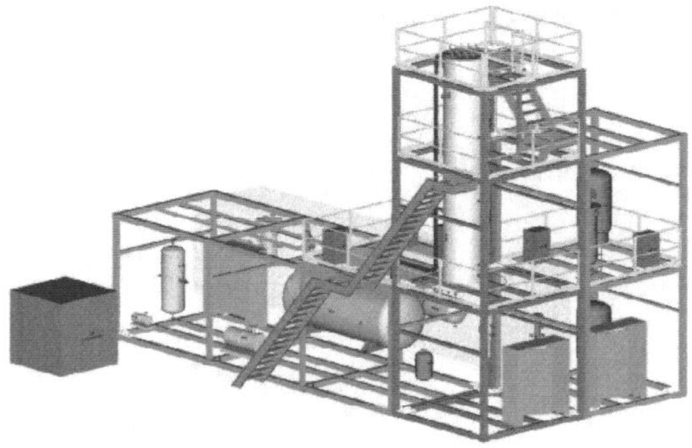

Figure 8: Proposed 10 BPD GTL facility

The compact size of the unit is made possible by the design of the FT reactor, operation of the reformer on air instead of oxygen, and the compact size of the reformer.

Ceramatec has also designed reactors that are capable of producing ~ 100 BPD of FT liquids but meet the standards for being transported by road without special requirements.

Summary

Ceramatec has been conducting research in the design of systems for the production of FT liquids. Most of the research has been done using natural gas as a convenient feedstock. Other feedstock options have been tried, including anaerobic digester gas, synthesis gas from the co-electrolysis of steam and carbon dioxide, and various reformed heavy hydrocarbons. The results demonstrate the ability to construct a modular, transportable system that is cost effective. Current laboratory data indicates that it is possible to build FT systems in this size range that will match the efficiency, capital cost per BPD capacity, and operating cost of larger FT plants. This provides the capability to utilize hydrocarbon sources that are not presently cost effective.

Acknowledgements

Portions of the FT reactor testing and catalyst design have been supported by the State of Wyoming and by the Office of Naval Research. A majority of the funding has come from private sources.

Deployment of Hydrogen Infrastructure to Support DoD Fleets in Hawaii

Stephen Szymanski
Proton Energy Systems, d/b/a Proton OnSite
10 Technology Drive, Wallingford, CT 06492

Abstract: *Proton OnSite is developing hydrogen infrastructure on the island of Oahu, Hawaii to support the deployment of a range of hydrogen ICE and fuel cell vehicles (FCVs) by the three DoD services. In this cooperative deployment program, the Army, Navy, and Air Force have formed the Hawaii Advanced Vehicle Working Group (HAVWG), with a focus on fuel cell vehicles, electric vehicles, and the associated infrastructure. In addition, the state of Hawaii in cooperation with the Air Force, has created a National Demonstration Center at Joint Base Pearl Harbor – Hickam to provide the test site for new vehicle and fueling technologies. Proton is currently providing the hydrogen fuel at that location, to support a fleet of GM vehicles, Ford Escape hydrogen ICE's, as well as several buses and a number of specialty flight line vehicles. In addition, Proton has a second station in operation at Schofield Barracks, which will allow for extended range of these vehicles on the island, and will provide both 350 bar and 700 bar fueling capability. The third station on Oahu will be located at the Kaneohe Bay Marine Corps base on the east end of Oahu, and will provide additional fueling capability at both 350 bar and 700 bar. An additional project of interest is a joint ONR/DOE demonstration on the Big Island, which will use a Proton electrolyzer to provide both hydrogen fuel for transit buses in Hilo, and to operate as a variable load to effect frequency regulation in a simulated grid. Proton's PEM electrolyzers act as a fast response variable load to correct both over-frequency and under-frequency events. The effectiveness of this approach has already been demonstrated at NREL using several Proton electrolyzers.*

Keywords: electrolysis; hydrogen; fuel cell; zero emission vehicles; renewable fuel

Introduction

DoD has taken a leadership role in the development and deployment of hydrogen technology in Hawaii. All three services have participated in the planning, design, implementation, and sponsorship of hydrogen fueling, hydrogen vehicle, and stationary fuel cell projects. With executive support from the U.S. Pacific Command (PACOM), and additional Federal and state policy development from DOE and Hawaii agency stakeholders, the hydrogen program efforts span several initiatives and working groups. In particular, the Hawaii Clean Energy Initiative (HCEI) is a Federal/state/private partnership which has developed a roadmap for achieving energy independence in Hawaii. HCEI also established working groups to address energy efficiency, renewable energy, biomass fuels, and transportation challenges toward the pursuit of 70% clean energy by 2030. DoD participates on these working groups and has its own set of progress metrics toward achieving that goal. For example, in the transportation sector alone, DoD has set aggressive goals for green fuel replacement between 2015 and 2020, as shown in the table below.[1]

SOURCE OF DEMAND	ESTIMATED TOTAL GREEN REPLACEMENT FUEL DEMAND (2020)
The HECO Companies	80 MGY renewable generation fuel (based off estimated RPS demand)
KIUC	TBD
The Department of Defense[9]	32 MGY renewable fuels
The Ground Transport Sector	50 MGY of renewable fuels

The HCEI green fuel replacement strategy includes the development of hydrogen infrastructure to support the deployment of hydrogen fuel cell vehicles. To complement the efforts of the HCEI transportation working group, DoD has established the tri-service Hawaii Advanced Vehicle Working Group (HAVWG), which has been working under the leadership of PACOM for coordination of activities. In addition, a Government/private partnership activity to deploy hydrogen fuel cell vehicles and infrastructure has formed under the Hawaii Hydrogen Initiative (H2I) banner. Again, DoD has actively participated in this collaboration effort as part of its top level commitment to achieving the goals of the HCEI roadmap.

With this backdrop, the intent of this paper will be to present an overview of hydrogen program activity in the Hawaiian islands, and how renewable electrolysis is playing a pivotal role in the deployment of hydrogen vehicle and stationary solutions in the state. In particular, Proton OnSite is the world leader in the commercialization of PEM electrolyzers, and has supplied equipment to all the major project sites in Hawaii. PEM electrolysis is the preferred technology for integration with renewable power sources, due to its fast response, high efficiency, and lower total cost of ownership. This paper will also provide an overview of advancements in the technology, and how they can benefit remote islands such as Hawaii, in terms of energy security and grid stability.

Hydrogen Fuel Cell Vehicle Deployments

As referenced previously, the DoD services have been a leader in the deployment of hydrogen fuel cell vehicles in Hawaii. Through coordinated activities of the HAVWG, PACOM, and the state of Hawaii, through its Hawaii Center for Advanced Transportation Technologies (HCATT), there are now 3 hydrogen fueling stations operating at 3 DoD sites on Oahu. The specific station configurations will be discussed later in this paper, but first it is important to discuss the vehicle portfolio being serviced by these stations. The table below summarizes the vehicles deployed on Oahu since 2004. Some of these vehicles have been taken out of service, including 6 of the GM Equinox FCV's.

Vehicle Description	Quantity Deployed	Fueling Pressure (bar)
GM Equinox FCV	16	350 or 700
Ford Escape HICE conversion	10	350
Class I fuel cell electric forklifts	20	350
Fuel cell crew bus	1	350
R12 refueling truck	1	350
C17 tug	1	350
Misc. flightline vehicles	4	350

The GM Equinox FCV represents a pre-production vehicle that has been demonstrated as a part of their Operation Driveway program. A total of 119 Equinox FCV's have been tested as part of that program, and have accumulated more than 3,000,000 vehicle miles, with a fleet leader at more than 100,000 miles.[2]

Figure 1. GM Equinox FCV

The 16 DoD Equinox FCV's were distributed between the three services in the HAVWG, with the Air Force operating 6, the Army with 6, and the Navy with 5. The unique technical feature of these vehicles is that they can take either a 350 bar (5,000 psi) fill, or a 700 bar (10,000 psi) fill. The advantage of the higher pressure is that you get a longer range from the vehicle (greater than 200 miles). So from a utility standpoint, there is a very big incentive to have 700 bar fueling capability available for these vehicles.

The Ford Escape hydrogen internal combustion engine (HICE) conversions were done by Quantum Technologies, and have been in service in Hawaii since 2008. The vehicles have provided extensive data on the viability of hydrogen as a fuel in combustion systems, and have also created a steady source of hydrogen fuel demand at the fueling station at Joint Base Pearl Harbor-Hickam (JBPHH) since their deployment. Funded and operated by TARDEC, these vehicles continue to provide excellent local utility, and are now primarily being fueled at the TARDEC sponsored station at Schofield Barracks.

Figure 2. Ford Escape HICE vehicle fueling at JBPHH

The class I fuel cell electric forklifts have been redeployed from the Defense Logistics Agency (DLA) Susquehanna depot site. These lift trucks were used in a 2 year demonstration at this distribution depot to provide operational data on how these vehicles compare to battery electric lifts. These vehicles have demonstrated excellent availability and operational efficiency, and will be well suited to continued operation at one of the DoD sites on Oahu. While these vehicles have yet to be put back in service, they should eventually provide good utility and create additional fueling demand for the home station they are attached to.

Figure 3. Fuel cell powered lift truck at DLA test site

The remaining vehicles in the table above have been developed and deployed by the Hawaii Center for Advanced Transportation Technology (HCATT). HCATT is part of the High Technology Development Center, a state agency commissioned to facilitate the development and growth of Hawaii's high technology industry. HCATT's mission is to develop and demonstrate advanced vehicle technologies for future military and commercial transportation systems. HCATT has been working with Air Force Research Laboratory (AFRL) to demonstrate a variety of alternative fuel and drivetrain systems at JBPHH. These vehicles have included a number of fuel cell utility vehicles designed for specific flightline applications at the base. These have included a special purpose step van, an aircraft tow vehicle, a flightline maintenance support vehicle, a flightline sweeper, and a mobile light tower. In addition, there have been various hydrogen fueled buses operating on the base, including both fuel cell and HICE configurations. HCATT has established a National Demonstration Center for Alternative Fuel Vehicles at JBPHH, in cooperation with AFRL, and continues to provide technology and policy leadership at the state level to promote hydrogen fueled transportation solutions.[3] It is also the primary operator of the hydrogen fueling station at JBPHH.

Figure 4. Fuel cell powered tug at JBPHH

Hydrogen Fueling Station Installations

There are currently three hydrogen fueling stations in operation on the island of Oahu, as depicted on the map below.

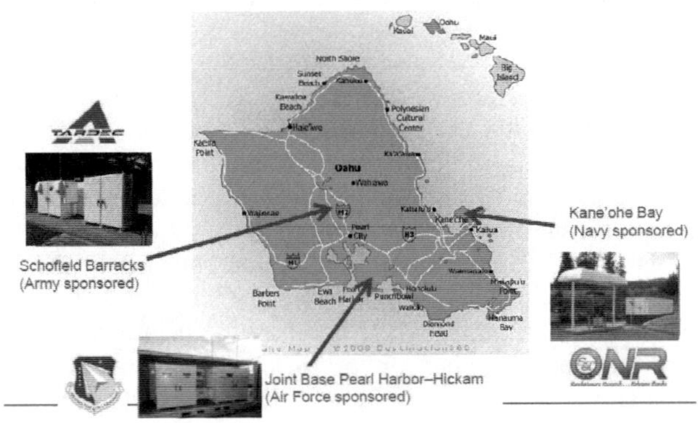

Figure 5. Location map of hydrogen stations on Oahu

The aforementioned station at JBPHH has been in operation since 2006, and is the first DoD fueling station to produce hydrogen from renewable power sources. The hydrogen dispensed at the station is produced by a PEM electrolyzer from Proton OnSite. The electrolyzer uses locally treated water and renewably generated electricity to produce high purity hydrogen. The hydrogen is compressed and stored in high pressure storage tubes for dispensing into the variety of vehicles that have access to the station. Vehicles that are rated for 350 bar hydrogen are filled with a simple "cascade" fill, with the stored gas flowing directly into the vehicle tank. For 700 bar fueling (specifically for the GM vehicles), there is a second boost compressor which increases the pressure of the stored hydrogen to the vehicle tank. The 700 bar dispensing is done through a second nozzle, which is specially designed not to fit on a 350 bar filling receptacle.

As mentioned previously, the station at JBPHH operates on locally produced renewable power, specifically solar and wind. The station has a 146 kW solar array, and 50 kW of vertical axis wind turbines that supplies most of the power for the site. The electrolyzer itself is nominally a 175 kW load in the system. When the wind turbine and PV output are not needed to produce hydrogen, the power is put onto the base grid and provides an offset to fossil fuel based power production. The solar array alone has provided about $40,000 per year in cost savings, above and beyond the value of the hydrogen produced.[4] The electrolyzer at the station is configured to operate in a "load following" mode, which allows for optimal performance in a variable demand system configuration.

Figure 6. Solar array and hydrogen station at JBPHH

The second hydrogen station to open on Oahu, is the TARDEC sponsored station at Schofield Barracks. The station at Schofield is primarily supporting the 10 Ford Escape HICE vehicles, as well as the Army's 6 Equinox FCV's. Proton OnSite was the prime contractor in building the station, and also supplied the same 175 kW electrolyzer installed at JBPHH. The 700 bar dispensing operation is somewhat different than at JBPHH however. At Schofield, there is 300 kg of primary hydrogen storage at about 425 bar (6,250 psi). For a 350 bar fill, the dispenser flows hydrogen directly from this storage to the vehicle tank. To accomplish the 700 bar fill, a second compressor is used to fill up a secondary bank of storage at about 850 bar (12,500 psi). This storage then flows into the vehicle in a direct cascade protocol. To provide a fast fill capability, there is a chiller that pre-cools the hydrogen to -20°C. This added process step allows for a 700 bar fill in a matter of minutes, without concerns for overheating the vehicle tanks. The fast fill capability is important for the adoption of commercial hydrogen vehicles, as the consumer has come to expect this kind of filling experience with today's commercial vehicles.

Figure 7. Hydrogen fueling station at Schofield Barracks, showing both the 350 bar nozzle (left) and the 700 bar nozzle (right)

The third station on Oahu is at Marine Corps Base Kane'ohe Bay. This station has been supporting the Navy Equinox FCV's, and has been using delivered hydrogen to date. An electrolyzer based system has been delivered to the base for installation in 2014. The Proton PEM electrolyzer to be installed is smaller than at JBPHH and Schofield (a 40 kW model), but it will be enough to support the Navy FCV's tied to it. This station is using a novel containerized design, integrated by Powertech Labs. This Vancouver based firm has successfully integrated Proton's electrolyzer with the compressor and storage in a site-ready container package. A second container will house the 700 bar compressor skid and ancillary components, to provide the same 700 bar fast fill capability available at Schofield. Once this station is fully operational, the DoD FCV's will be able to drive across the entire island without being stranded, as there will always be access to fuel within a reasonable driving distance.

Figure 8. Powertech containerized hydrogen fueling station

Stationary Hydrogen Projects

In addition to the vehicle/station projects discussed previously, there are two additional hydrogen projects of note currently ongoing. The first is a joint Department of Energy / Office of Naval Research project on the Big Island, being managed by the Hawaii Natural Energy Institute (HNEI) at the University of Hawaii-Manoa. In particular, this project will evaluate the value proposition of using utility-scale electrolyzers to both regulate the grid and use excess electricity from renewables to make hydrogen for various products. In the initial phase of the project, an electrolyzer will be installed at the Puna Geothermal Venture power plant on the Big Island. In this first phase, it will not be connected to the grid. The Proton supplied electrolyzer will be operated in a dynamic mode designed to simulate future operation as a grid-connected variable load that can be quickly ramped up and down to provide frequency regulation. Data will be collected to analyze the ability of the electrolyzer to ramp up and down, and to determine its durability and performance under dynamic operating conditions over a long duration. The hydrogen produced by the system will be used to fuel one hydrogen-fueled bus operated by the County of Hawaii MTA and two hydrogen buses operated at Hawaii Volcanoes National Park. A schematic of the project concept is shown in the figure below.[5]

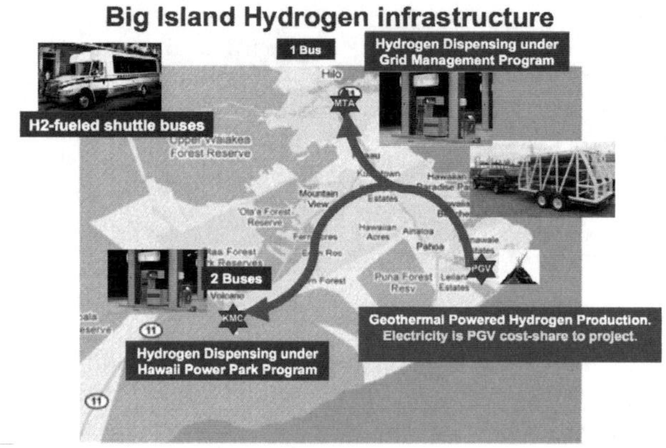

Figure 9. Hydrogen project concept on Big Island

The second project of note is a joint DOE/DOT (Maritime Administration) project in the port of Honolulu. In this project, a 100 kW fuel cell system will be installed at the port to provide refrigeration power for containers of perishable cargo. Sandia National Laboratories did the technical analysis for the project, and showed that the efficiency and emissions benefits will be substantial if diesel generators can be replaced with fuel cells for refrigeration in ports. The demonstration period will be 6 months, and the commercial partner for the project is Young Brothers, the primary shipper of goods into the Hawaiian Islands. The source of hydrogen for the fuel cell will be one of the hydrogen fueling stations already on Oahu, and it will be delivered by tube trailer to the port.

Acknowledgements

The author gratefully acknowledges the support and sponsorship from TARDEC, HCATT, HNEI, ONR, and DOE, in creating opportunities for hydrogen deployment in Hawaii.

References

1. Hawaii Clean Energy Initiative Roadmap, 2011 edition, p. 22.

2.http://media.gm.com/media/us/en/gm/company_info1.detail.html/content/Pages/news/us/en/2013/Oct/1022-fc-equinox.html

3. http://www.htdc.org/hcatt.html

4. HCATT presentation: "Renewable Hydrogen Production at Joint Base Pearl-Harbor Hickam", Asia Pacific Clean Energy Summit, 2010.

5. HNEI presentation: "Hydrogen Energy Systems as a Grid Management Tool", 2013 DOE Hydrogen and Fuel Cells Program Annual Merit Review.

Production of Hydrogen by Molten Salt Gasification of Various Carbon Feedstocks

Lyman Frost; Neil Camarta; Bruce Wilding; Terry Turner
Western Hydrogen Limited
1100 1st Street SE
Calgary, AB, Canada T2g 1B1

Abstract: Western Hydrogen Limited (WHL) is developing a new method for production of hydrogen from inputs of water and a carbon-bearing compound. The technology is licensed under an exclusive license from the Idaho National Laboratory and has been tested in the laboratory on such carbon compounds as asphalt, vacuum residual, pure carbon, natural gas, and glycerol. The laboratory results were used to design and fabricate a pilot facility capable of producing ~ 200 MSCF (thousand standard cubic foot) of hydrogen or synthesis gas per day. The hydrogen, or alternatively synthesis gas, is produced at pressures of up to 2000 psig. Results suggest the ability to produce the gas streams at a cost ~20% below the best current technology and with ~30% fewer GHG emissions.

Keywords: Hydrogen; synthesis gas; gasification; greenhouse gas reduction; low cost hydrogen; reforming; pilot plant

Introduction

The world is currently facing the dilemma of needing additional supplies of energy in highly concentrated forms and reducing the impact of greenhouse gas emissions. The continually growing world population demands energy to provide housing, environmental management, jobs, and food. Without energy the movement to a more sustainable and benign support for population cannot occur.

Much of the easily obtainable energy sources have been accessed. The new sources of hydrocarbons frequently involve heavy oils, bitumen from sources such as oil sand reserves, kerogen from oil shale, or other sources that cannot be easily distributed through current infrastructure. All of the heavy oils require the addition of hydrogen into their structures to allow the oils to be processed into forms that can be conveniently used by current technologies and distributed to meet the world's needs.

WHL is developing a new type of method for production of hydrogen called molten salt catalyzed gasification (MSG). The technology design results in the production of high-pressure hydrogen at ~2000 psig without the need for compression. This makes the process very efficient since the compression of hydrogen can require as much as 20% of the energy in the hydrogen. The MSG process uses a wide variety of low value (e.g. vacuum residuals, coke, asphaltenes, et al) or renewable (e.g. waste glycerol from biodiesel production) carbon-based feedstock to provide the energy that produces the hydrogen. The hydrogen comes from both the carbon feedstock (e.g. natural gas) and the input water. The very high thermal efficiency (i.e. theoretical 86%, expected 61%) of the process results in efficient use of resources and a low per unit cost for the hydrogen produced.

The aggressiveness of the MSG molten salt reaction will reform carbon-bearing materials into gaseous streams. The carbon in the waste is used to provide energy that reconstitutes the molten salts and thus the system requires little in the way of external energy. The process is in effect a chemical looping system that releases hydrogen.

Technical Discussion

The reactor can be operated at pressure by simple pressurization of the input water stream and the carbon feedstock. The first stage involves reacting sodium carbonate with water thus generating sodium hydroxide and carbon dioxide (Equation 1). The next step consists of reacting sodium hydroxide with carbon and water thus generating sodium carbonate and hydrogen (Equation 2). Experimental data indicates that the operating conditions, carbon / steam ratios, and molten salt ratios can be varied to generate either pressurized hydrogen and carbon dioxide, or synthesis gas (CO and hydrogen). The carbon sources that have been evaluated to date include methane, heavy residual oil, solid carbon (i.e. petroleum coke), and glycerol. The captured CO_2 is at pressure to directly allow sequestration or use in enhanced oil recovery. The net chemical reactions are shown below.

$$Na_2CO_3 + H_2O \rightarrow 2\ NaOH + CO_2 \qquad \textit{Equation 1}$$
$$2\ NaOH + C + H_2O \rightarrow Na_2CO_3 + 2\ H_2 \qquad \textit{Equation 2}$$

The equations shown as 1 and 2 are net equations and several intermediates are likely to be formed. For example, it is likely that sodium exists for brief time periods but since the reactor is operated with excess steam, the sodium will immediately combine at the elevated temperatures and pressures to form sodium hydroxide in accordance with Equation 3. If the input carbon compound also has hydrogen (e.g. methane) then additional hydrogen is generated from this content.

$$2\ Na + 2\ H_2O \rightarrow 2\ NaOH + H_2 \qquad \textit{Equation 3}$$

High pressure and the favourable chemical kinetics of the reactions allow the use of small reactors to generate large volumes in a continuous process. In the laboratory, hydrogen has been produced safely at 1450 psig and modeling has been done for higher-pressure systems. The advantage of the high pressure is the ability to directly produce a stream of pressurized hydrogen.

The MSG reactor process can be built from materials that are commonly available and that can be fabricated at most pressure vessel shops. Laboratory results indicate the ability to produce 2000 psig hydrogen from an Alberta based commercial scale MSG plant at a cost of ~$1.77 per kilogram using petroleum coke as feedstock.

Current projections are that the MSG process will consume less than 25 gpm (gallons per minute) of water for the 5 MMSCF (MMSCF) per day demonstration plant. Hydrocarbon contamination of the water does not affect the MSG process. In general, ultra-pure water as required for many gasification systems is not required in the MSG process. Based on laboratory results, a slight amount of hydrocarbon contamination in the input water does not affect the water reactions and actually has the beneficial effect of in-situ reconstitution of the sodium hydroxide – carbon reaction. Some of the produced water associated with hydrocarbon recovery and some of the water contaminated during refinery operations can be effectively used and actually increases the hydrogen yield from the process. Glycerol (i.e. a waste product from bio-diesel production) can also be blended with water in the sodium-water reaction. This increases the quantity of hydrogen produced in the water-sodium reaction and provides carbon for the reconstitution of the sodium. The presence of certain heavy metals and other compounds in the water would accumulate and deactivate the bed over time. Several methods have been developed for maintaining the bed activity while the system is operating on a continuous basis. These methods will be tested in the pilot plant.

The only greenhouse gas generated by the process when coke is used as the carbon source is carbon dioxide (CO_2). Assuming 100% of the carbon (using vacuum residual as carbon source) is processed and released as CO_2, the process generates under 8 metric tons/hour CO_2 for a 5 MMSCF per day demonstration plant (note: most of this will be in a separate pressurized stream that can be sequestered or used in EOR and only ~ 9000 tons per year will be emitted). The CO_2 is separated as a natural part of the MSG process and will be at pressure. Based on laboratory results, it is expected that the CO_2 will be of sufficient purity to be used for enhanced oil recovery and at sufficient pressure to be sequestered with little or no additional compression.

The feeds to the process will be water, a carbon bearing compound (e.g. heavy residual oil or coke), and sodium carbonate. There will be some small amounts of the sodium carbonate required for make-up to the process but laboratory results have shown that less than one (1) percent of the compounds are consumed in the process. The overall process flow is shown in Figure 1.

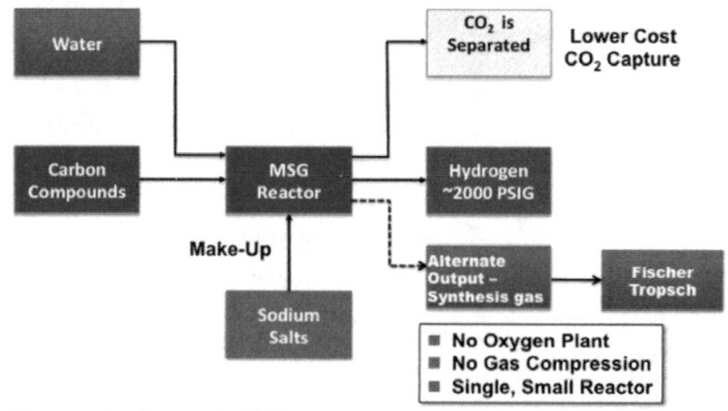

Figure 1: Overall MSG process flow

Depending on the desired output, the system operates in either an endothermic or near exothermic mode. The volume of steam used is the largest determinate of the energy requirement. An extensive amount of modeling was done in constructing the system. An example of the results of one modeling run is shown as Figure 2. This particular run was with 5300 kg of molten salts (NaOH, Na_2CO_3), varying stoichiometric amounts of water, a pressure of 2000 psig, and preset amounts of residual as the input carbon compound.

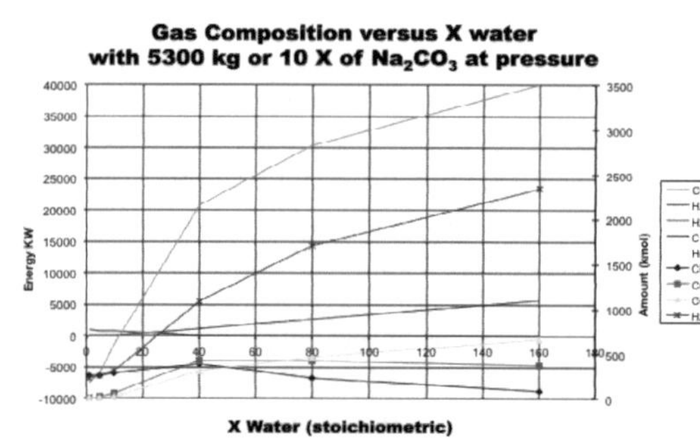

Figure 2: Modeling results from typical run

The run indicates that for low inputs of water, the reaction is actually exothermic. Unfortunately, the amount of hydrogen generated at the low input ratios of water (steam) the amount of hydrogen generated is also low.

The process is run at high temperature. Sodium hydroxide melts below 400° C but the sodium carbonate does not melt until about 850° C. To get the desired melt structure, the system is operated at about 900° C. Typically, the system is operated at a ratio of about two parts NaOH to one part Na2CO3. This is an aggressive chemical environment and must be considered in material selection. Laboratory tests were run to select the materials for the reactor and associated equipment. Conventional alloys, super metallic alloys, and ceramics were all tested in realistic conditions. At the high partial pressures of hydrogen generated by the MSG, conventional stainless material is a feasible selection for much of the system.

The gases generated by the system have been analyzed using a micro-channel gas chromatograph. Typical results operating on vacuum residual were: hydrogen – 65%, carbon monoxide – 5%, carbon dioxide – 25%, and methane – 5%. There were no measurable volumes of heavier hydrocarbons and only trace amounts of hydrogen sulfide. Based on laboratory results, it appears any sulfur in the input feedstock is captured by the sodium salts until a point of equilibrium is reached at which point hydrogen sulfide begins to be emitted. At high pressure, much of the hydrogen sulfide and carbon dioxide is captured in the excess water that is condensed. The mixture it treated before collection.

Facilities

The testing and results were generated using laboratory scale and pilot scale facilities. The laboratory scale system was originally installed at Idaho National Laboratory but has recently been moved to the pilot plant site in Alberta. The laboratory scale system consisted of a five inch (5") diameter reactor that operated on .1 - .2 kg per hour of vacuum residual. The laboratory system is shown in Figure 3.

Figure 3: Laboratory scale MSG system

The information gathered from the laboratory system provided sufficient data to allow design and construction of the WHL MSG pilot system. The pilot is located in an industrial area near Fort Saskatchewan, Alberta near a facility upgrading bitumen. The upgrading facility is a large user of hydrogen and a potential client for the MSG hydrogen. The exterior of the WHL facility is shown in Figure 4 and the pilot plant skid is shown in Figure 5. The key part of the pilot plant is the high pressure, high temperature MSG reactor which is shown in an artist's representation in Figure 6.

Figure 4: Exterior view of MSG pilot plant

From left to right, the tanks are for waste-water, residual storage, and fresh water. An air-cooled heat exchanger is shown adjacent to the building enclosing the pilot plant.

Figure 5: MSG pilot plant skid

The pilot plant skid is about12' high by 12' wide by 48' long. There are some pieces of equipment that extend above the 12' height. The facility includes a ten-ton crane (seen at top of picture), a control room, an electric enclosure, and associated infrastructure expected for a R&D facility.

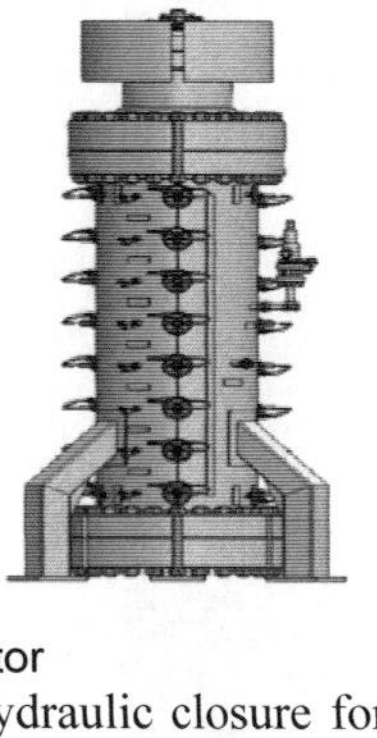

Figure 6: MSG reactor

The reactor has a hydraulic closure for easy access to the internals of the system. The reactor is about 4' in diameter and about 14' high with the closure in place.

Economics and GHG (greenhouse gases)

The best current available technologies for generation of hydrogen depend on the fuel available for use. If natural gas is available at a reasonable cost and in sufficient quantities, a steam methane reformer (SMR) is the technology of choice. The capital costs for a SMR is reasonable. Most of the hydrogen cost associated with an SMR is in the cost of the feedstock. The MSG system compares favorably with the capital and operating costs of the SMR. Further, since the SMR uses a good portion of its total consumption of natural gas to heat the catalyst beds that are part of the system, the SMR has higher GHG emissions compared to that of the MSG. Figure 7 accounts for both capital and operating cost in a graphical representation of the cost per Kg of H_2 for both a SMR and MSG.

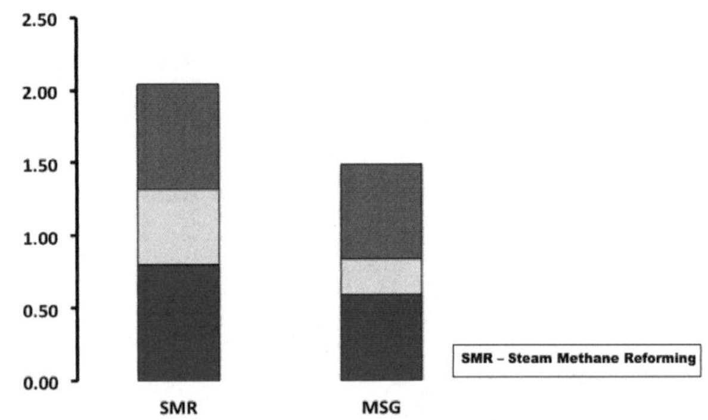

Figure 7: Cost per Kg of H2 for SMR and MSG

The red is the capital contribution, the yellow is the operating cost, and the blue is the cost of feedstock.

If heavier hydrocarbons are used as the feedstock, the technology selection is generally a gasification system. Most gasification systems include an oxygen system (i.e. an air separation unit). Oxygen plants are expensive in both capital and operating costs. The MSG system obtains all of the oxygen for the carbon oxidation from the input steam. This provides a significant financial advantage to the MSG system. The generation of hydrogen at high pressure also avoids the cost of pressurization of the output hydrogen, or synthesis gas.

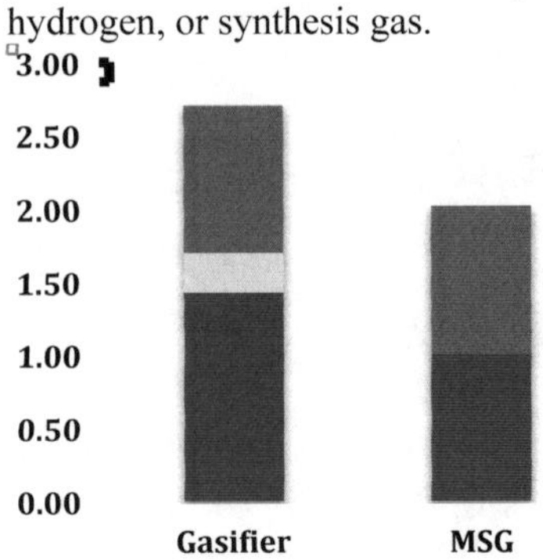

Figure 8: Cost per Kg of H2, gasification and MSG

The yellow is the cost of the oxygen plant. The blue is the feedstock cost. The red is the capital cost of the systems. Most of the cost associated with a gasification unit is in the initial capital cost.

In addition to the cost of the generated hydrogen, it is important in our current carbon constrained world to know the GHG emissions associated with the generated hydrogen. This is shown in Figure 9 for the MSG, a gasification unit, and for SMR. The MSG has lower GHG emissions compared to the SMR and gasification system.

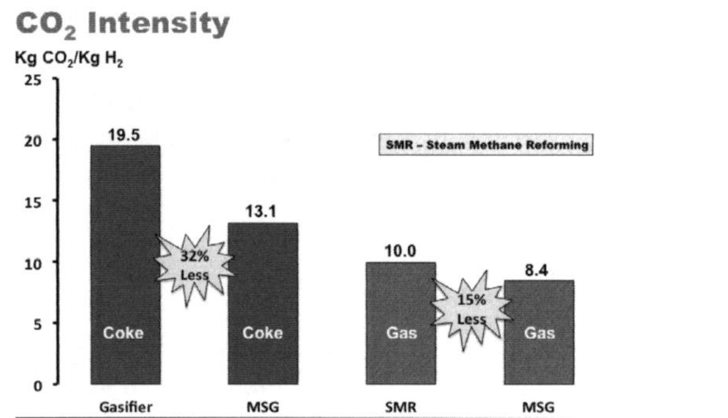

Figure 9: GHG emissions by technology

The data shown in Figure 9 was verified by two separate external organizations.

Summary

WHL is currently operating a pilot plant to prove a new technology for generation of hydrogen. The technology generates hydrogen at high pressure from inputs of any carbon-containing compound and water. The process uses chemical looping of sodium salt compounds to generate the hydrogen at attractive cost per kilogram of H_2 and at lower emissions of GHG per kilogram

Acknowledgements

A portion of the funding for the MSG project was provided by Sustainable Development Technology Canada (SDTC). SDTC is funded by the government of Canada but is not considered a government organization. SDTC funds projects that have the potential to improve the environment of Canada and its provinces. The large majority of funding has been provided for the MSG project by private sources.

Alternative Power Supply for Medium Caliber Fuzes

Harald Wich, Roland Hein and Sergio Moreno-Lechado
Diehl & Eagle Picher GmbH
Fischbachstr. 20, 90552 Roethenbach a.d. Pegnitz, Germany

Abstract: *The use of Constantan© and Chromel© was simulated und tested to fabricate a thermoelectric generator (TEG) for an electrical fuze. Opposite to the most research lines this TEG is characterized by its cylindrical and not parallel form. A heat pellet, which can achieve temperatures as high as 1400°C, was used as heat source. The simulation results show that the supplied energy after 5 seconds is higher than 1.3 J, sufficient for the small and medium caliber fuzes.*

Keywords: Electrical fuze; Thermoelectric Generator; Heat Pellet

Introduction

The use of some resistance alloys and thermoelectric alloys as thermocouples is well known due to their relatively high Seebeck effect response [1-2]. The Seebeck effect produces an electromotive force, which is modelled by equation 1, in response to a temperature difference across some materials.

$$U_{Seebeck} = N \cdot (\alpha_A - \alpha_B) \cdot (T_1 - T_2) \cdot 10^{-3} \quad (1)$$

Where $U_{Seebeck}$ is voltage of Seebeck (mV), N is the thermocouple number and α_A and α_B are the Seebeck coefficients (μV/K) of the materials A and B.

The properties of these materials [3] are optimal to fabricate Ultra High Temperature TEG (UHT-TEG). Table 1 shows some properties of the most common metals and alloys to fabricate thermocouples. As can be seen, a thermocouple of Constantan© and Chromel© has a thermoelectric power ($\alpha_A - \alpha_B$) of 63.2 μV/K. A thermocouple, which is a temperature sensor too, can be described like in figure 1: a voltage U is generated in a thermocouple due to a temperature gradient ΔT. Hence, when N thermocouples are connected electrically in series like in figure 2, a voltage N·U can be obtained.

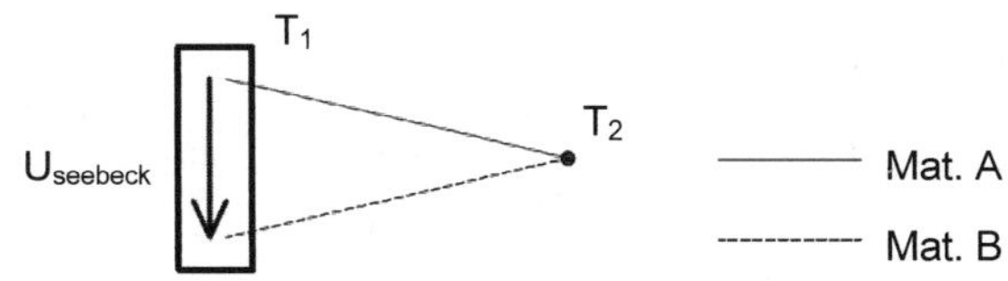

Figure 1. Model of a thermocouple

As shown in figure 2 the central junctions are hot junctions whereas the external junctions are cold junctions. The thermocouples are thermally connected in parallel but in a cylindrical form. Therefore, a cylindrical heat pellet can be used as energy source.

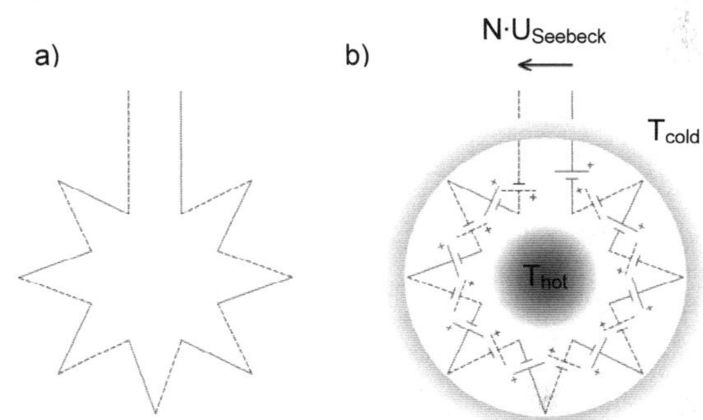

Figure 2. N thermocouples connected in serie

Heat pellets are used for manufacturing thermal batteries. These heat pellets are composed of iron and potassium perchlorate. Its pyrotechnic and exothermic reaction provides a huge amount of heat energy (Δh = 300 – 350 cal/g) which generates the necessary temperature gradient. The heat pellet chemical reaction is:

$$4Fe + KClO_4 \rightarrow 4FeO + KCl + \Delta H \quad (2)$$

Table 1. Properties of selected elements and commercial alloys with a significant thermoelectric power

Material	Specific heat Capacity C (J/kg·K)	Density ρ_d (kg/m³)	Thermal conductivity λ (W/m·K)	Electrical resistivity ρ_e (μΩ·cm)	Temperature coefficient of resistance (0-100°C) β (1/K)	Seebeck coefficient α (μV/K) 0-1000°C/mV	Melting range (°C)
Constantan (45Ni-55Cu)	397.5	8890	22.18	48.9	0.00002	-35.1	1270
Nickel	471	8902	90.7	6.84	0.00692	-14.8	1453
Platinum	133.9	21450	71.54	10.4	0.00393	0	1769
Copper	380	8941	392	1.74	0.0039	+7.5	1084
Nickel-chrome (80Ni-20Cr)	460	8300	15	109	0.00005	+11.4	1400
Iron	447	7874	80.2	9.71	0.00651	+19.8	1534
Chromel (90Ni-9Cr)	447.7	8730	19.25	70	0.00032	+28.1	1350

The properties of this pyrotechnic mixture are described in several books [4-5]. Benefits of the use of potassium perchlorate pellets are high heat density, fast activation and long shelf life. The heat pellets used have a diameter of 19 mm, a thickness of 0.4 mm and a total heat of approximately 100 cal. The burning rate is over 100 mm/s [6].

TEG Design

A fifteen thermocouples UHT-TEG is shown in figure 3. This small and fine geometry can be obtained by e.g. chemical etching of thin sheets.

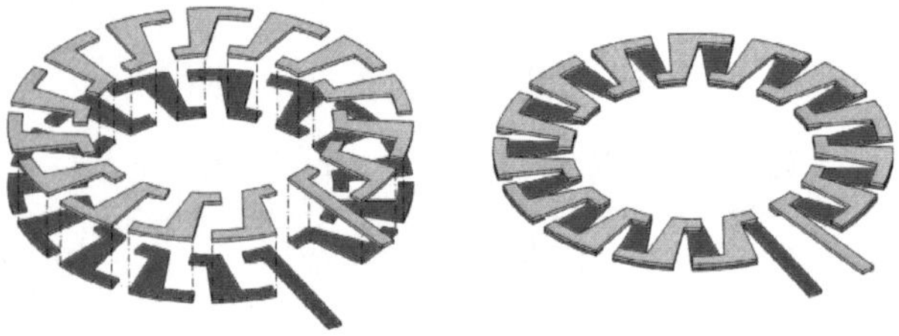

Figure 3. Structure of a UHT-TEG

As it was pointed out, a product of the heat pellet chemical reaction is iron oxide, which is an electric conductor. For this reason, an electrical insulator is necessary to be placed between the TEG and the heat pellet. A thermal sink, consisting of an aluminum cylinder, is used to keep a low temperature at the external points. A sketch of a power source based on a UHT-TEG is shown in figure 4.

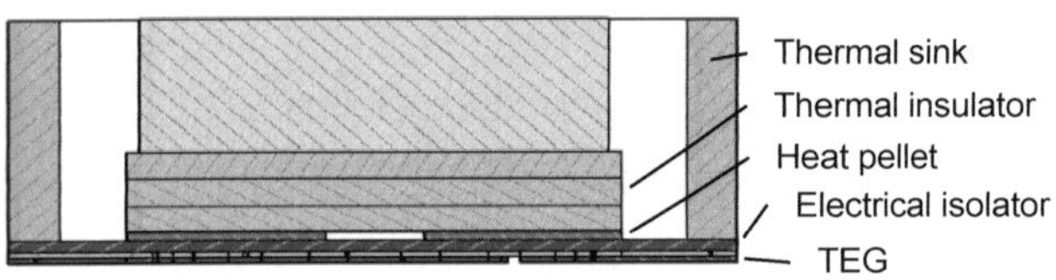

Figure 4. UHT-TEG power source

Electrical Model

The Seebeck Voltage was shown in equation 1. For this work it is assumed that its coefficients are constant and not dependent on the temperature. It is also considered that the electrical resistances and thermal conductivity are constant too. Actually, the temperature coefficient of resistance is not very significant for the selected materials.

Figure 5 illustrates the equivalent circuit of an electrical fuze connected to a TEG. The TEG is represented by an electromotive force and an internal resistance. The internal resistance R_{int} is calculated according to Ohm´s Law and depends on the electrical resistivity and the geometry of the legs. The resistance R_{equ} represents the electrical components of the fuze. Therefore, the consumed power of the equivalent resistance is given by:

$$P_{Max}^{R_{int}=R_{equ}}(t) = \frac{N^2 \cdot (\alpha_A - \alpha_B)^2 \cdot (T_{hot} - T_{cold})^2}{4 \cdot R_{int}} \quad (3)$$

$$P = U_{Load} \cdot I = U_{Seebeck}^2 \frac{R_{equ}}{\left(R_{int} + R_{equ}\right)^2} \quad (4)$$

Where T_{hot} and T_{cold}, which are not constant, are obtained in thermal simulations. Finally it is possible to calculate the electrical energy given by the TEG in a determined time (τ).

$$E = \int_0^\tau P(t)dt \quad (5)$$

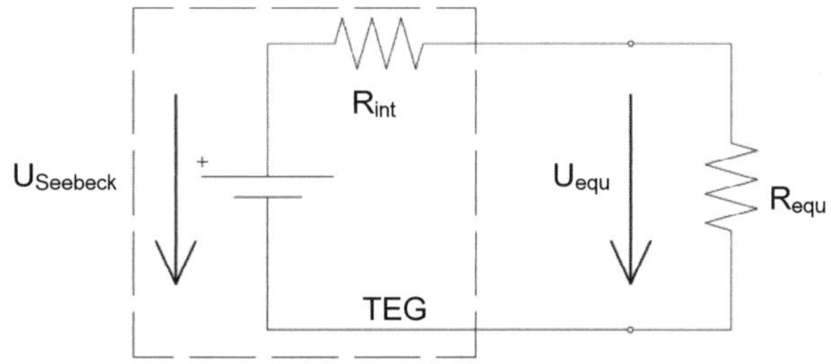

Figure 5. Equivalent circuit for TEG and electrical fuze

Thermal model and simulation

Simulation is a good tool to optimize the geometrical factors of the TEG due to the complexity of all the variables [7]. A commercial software based on finite elements method was used to simulate the thermal model of the power source. The thermal model used deserves some comments. The TEG is thermal simulated when its terminals are not connected, that means, an open-circuit. Under this condition, there is no electrical current. For this reason, the electrical and thermal models do not take into account the Joule effect nor Peltier nor Thomson effect. More simplifications were made. All the thermal properties are constant. It was assumed, that the exothermic pyrotechnic reaction of the heat pellet lasts only 0.1 s and is constant. The introduced power density is 38 W/mm³ approximately. Only five seconds were simulated to save file size because the trend is obvious.

Figures 6 and 7 illustrate the temperature distribution across the Chromel© legs one second after the heat pellet activation. The temperature references are taken at the most conservative contact point between the two legs.

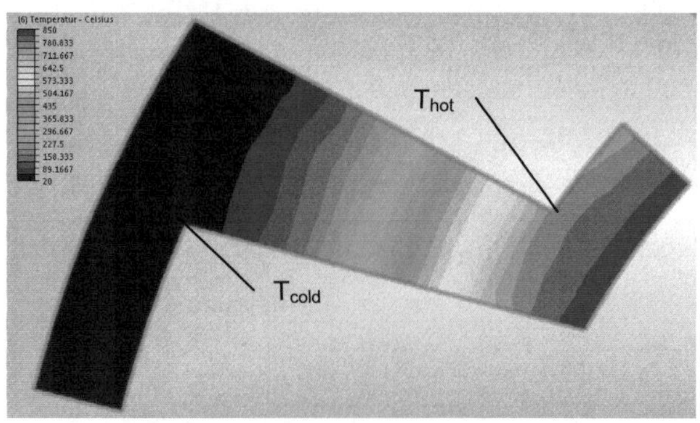

Figure 6. Leg temperature distribution

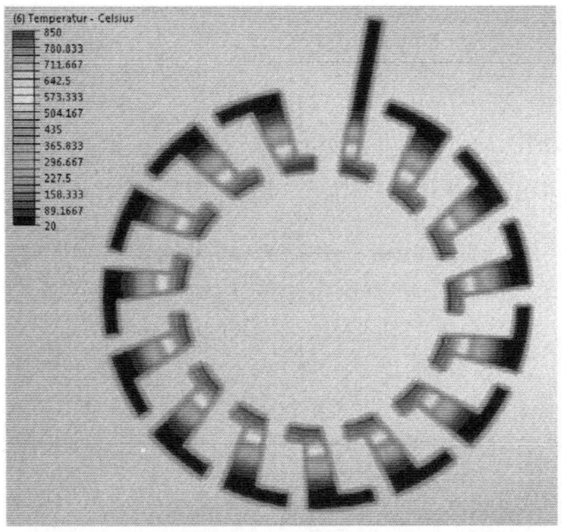

Figure 7. TEG temperature distribution

Figure 7 shows that the thermocouples are really thermally connected in parallel. The central junctions have a temperature above 800°C while the external junctions have 30°C. This temperature difference of 770°C generates a voltage of 48.7 mV per couple. The time dependence of the Seebeck voltage and the temperature for two different TEG geometries are shown in figure 8. Both TEGs have 15 couples but TEG_1 has a thickness of 0.25 mm and TEG_2 0.1 mm.

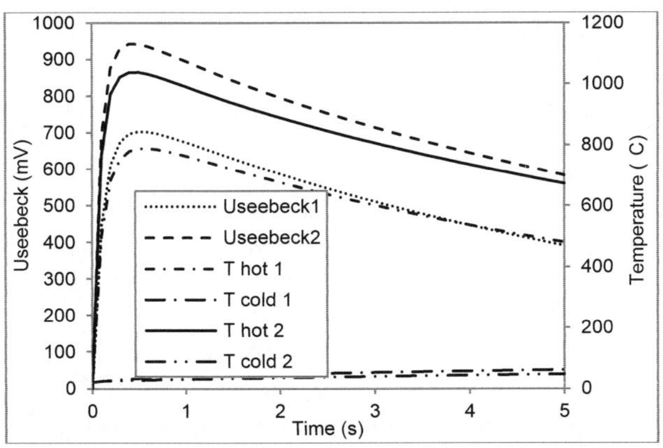

Figure 8. Temperature and $U_{Seebeck}$ of TEG_1 and TEG_2

As can be seen, both TEGs T_{hot} (and therefore the Seebeck voltage) achieves its maximal value in less than one second. Additionally, heat flows from the hot point to the cold point but the temperature of the cold point does not rise significantly because of the effect of the thermal sink. For TEG_2, T_{hot} is about 250°C warmer and the Seebeck voltage is 34% higher. This result is a consequence of the smaller mass of couples. However, the internal resistance R_{int} is 150% higher.

The electrical power and energy for TEG_1 are plotted in figure 9. Within five seconds 1.32 J are generated but the slope of the graph points out that much more energy can be obtained. The energy generated within five seconds for TEG_2 is 0.82 J, a 38% smaller. Therefore, it is demonstrated that thinner TEGs produce higher Seebeck voltage but due to the also higher R_{int}, less energy is generated.

The efficiency of TEG_1 at five seconds, given by equation 6, has a value of 0.16%. Obviously, this value is very low but the used energy source, heat pellets, have a sufficient high energy density, which makes them interesting for the use in UHT-TEG power sources.

$$\eta_E\ (5s) = \frac{E\ (5s)}{E_{Heat}} = \frac{E\ (5s)}{\Delta h_{Pellet} \cdot m_{Pellet}} \quad (6)$$

The maximum thermocouple efficiency for steady TEGs is calculated with equation 6 [8]:

$$\eta_{Max} = \frac{T_{hot} - T_{cold}}{T_{hot}} \cdot \frac{\sqrt{1 + Z_M \cdot \overline{T}} - 1}{\sqrt{1 + Z_M \cdot \overline{T}} + \frac{T_{cold}}{T_{hot}}} = \eta_{Carnot} \cdot \eta_r \quad (7)$$

Where η_r is the reduced efficiency. $\overline{T}$ and Z_M are defined by equations:

$$\overline{T}(K) = \frac{T_{hot} + T_{cold}}{2} \quad (8)$$

$$Z_M(K^{-1}) = \frac{(\alpha_A - \alpha_B)^2}{[(\lambda_A . \rho_A)^{0.5} + (\lambda_B . \rho_B)^{0.5}]} \quad (9)$$

The system is not steady, but analyzing these equations, it is easy to see that the higher is the temperature difference (T_{hot} - T_{cold}), the higher is the efficiency. UHT-TEG is made of materials which can support very high temperatures, generated by heat pellets. Therefore, it is assumed that the use of Constantan© and Chromel© has a relatively good efficiency when the temperature difference is very high.

Impedance matching

It is well known that the maximum power occurs when $R_{equ} = R_{int}$. Figure 9 shows the influence of the R_{equ} value for TEG_1. In this case [*], when R_{equ} is 100% higher, the maximal power is 88%.

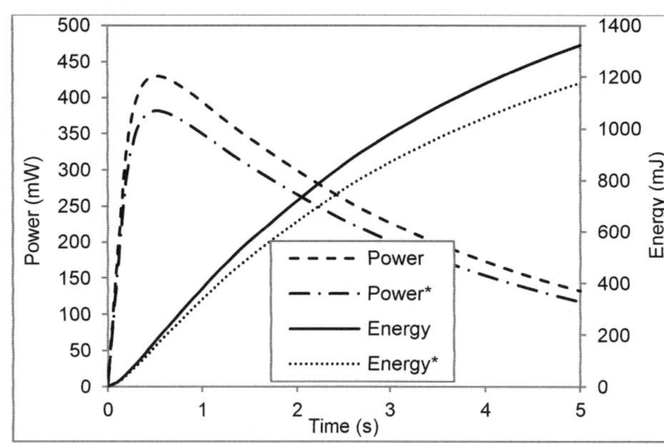

Figure 9. Influence of R_{equ} over energy and power for TEG_1

Experimental

The experimental data are shown and compared to the simulation results in figure 10. The voltage was measured by a LDS Dimension 4i.

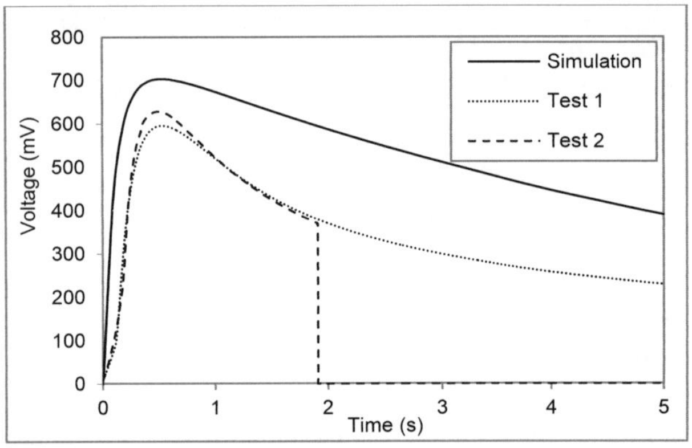

Figure 10. Comparison between experiment and simulation results

Test 2 had an unintended interruption but the trend is obvious. As can be seen, the measured voltage peak has a value 10 – 15% lower than the simulated voltage peak. However, the results confirm that the designed model is quite optimal. As it was pointed out, some simplifications were made in the model design. The thermal properties were considered as constant. This simplification is absolutely not correct but due to the ultra high temperature range of the TEG, it was not easy to find suitable references. The difference between the simulation and the test results can be justified by:

- The value of thermal conductivity of Chromel© and Constantan© increases at high temperatures
- The specific heat of these materials decreases at high temperatures
- The Seebeck coefficient decreases at high temperatures

Conclusions

The test results prove that Constantan© and Chromel© can be used to fabricate an UHT-TEG as power supply for medium caliber fuzes because the generated voltage and the time range are optimal for this use.

The use of these metallic alloys is interesting to fabricate a TEG when the temperature difference between the junction points is very high. It was possible to reach this temperature difference due to a high density energy source like the heat pellets produced at Diehl & Eagle Picher GmbH for the fabrication of thermal batteries.

A thermal model and an electrical model were designed and simulated. The experimental data show that the models are quite optimal for their purpose, the geometrical optimization of the TEG and the overall design.

References

1. Rowe, D., "CRC Handbook of Thermoelectric," London, CRC Pross 1996
2. Van Herwaarden, S., "Sensor applications of thermoelectric thin films," Proc. 16th Int. Conf on Thermoelectrics, 1997, pp. 47-55
3. Cardarelli, F., "Materials Handbook," 2008.
4. Linden, D., T. B. Reddy, "Handbook of Batteries," Mc-Graw Hill, 2001
5. Guidotti, R. A., "Development History of Fe/KClO4 Heat Powders at Sandia and Related Aging Issues for Thermal Batteries", 2001
6. Reed, J.W., R.R. Walters, R.A. Guidotti, A.K. Jacobson, "Burn-Rate Studies With Iron/Potassiun Perchlorate Heat Pellets," Power Sources Symposium, 1992, Page(s): 211 – 214
7. Markowski. P, A. Dziedzic, "Geometrical optimization of thermocuoples – theoretical background," 2009
8. Rowe, D. M., "Thermoelectrics handbook – macro to nano",Taylor & Francis, London, 2005, Chapter 1
9. Ioffe, A. F., "Semiconductor thermoelements and thermoelectric cooling", Infosearch, London, 1957

Novel Methods to Improve the Operation and Performance of Silver-Zinc Batteries

Dr. Bryan D. Hirschorn, Thomas T. Terjesen, Patrick V. Imhof
BST Systems, Inc.
78 Plainfield Pike Rd. Plainfield, CT, USA, 06374

Abstract: *BST Systems, Inc. has developed advanced, low-maintenance (sealed), safe 365 Ah silver-zinc cells featuring a proprietary composite catalyst for sealed operation, a negative electrode composition for enhanced cyclic capacity retention, and a non-cellulosic separator system for extended wet-life. The composite catalyst is formulated to consume hydrogen independently, and to recombine stoichiometric hydrogen and oxygen.*

Keywords: silver; zinc; safe; sealed; hydrogen; catalyst; rechargeable; maintenance; aerospace; underwater vehicles.

Introduction

Rechargeable silver-zinc batteries are a safe, high energy-dense power source used in a variety of Department of Defense and aerospace applications. Although they are one of the most energy and power dense batteries on the market, conventional silver-zinc batteries have limitations associated with cycle-life, wet-life, and gas release when cell relief valves open. Generally, limited cycle-life is associated with the instability of the zinc electrode (shape-change) and limited wet-life is associated with the degradation of the cellulosic separator in potassium hydroxide electrolyte. The hydrogen gas released during silver-zinc operation is generally managed, in enclosed underwater vehicles, through use of evacuation and backfill (with inert gas) procedures and, requires costly purging equipment and maintenance schedules. BST Systems, Inc. initiated an internal research and development effort that was followed by the award of a Phase I and Phase II SBIR contract (Contract # N00024-12-C-4119), with the objective of improving the operation and performance of silver-zinc batteries.

The objectives of the program are to provide silver-zinc cells capable of providing 10 or more cycles of sealed operation without catalyst replacement, substituting the conventional cellulosic separator system with a non-cellulosic separator system that is stable in alkaline electrolyte, and increasing the cyclic capacity retention of the negative electrode.

BST Systems, Inc. has delivered two (2) related 365 Ah cell sets utilizing technologies developed under this program. The first 365 Ah cell set is designed with a replaceable composite catalyst, an enhanced negative electrode, and a conventional cellulosic separator system. This cell set provides an improvement in cyclic capacity retention and 10 or more cycles of sealed operation before requiring catalyst replacement. The second 365 Ah cell set is designed with a replaceable composite catalyst, an enhanced negative electrode, and a completely non-cellulosic separator system. The second 365 Ah cell set provides 15 or more cycles of sealed operation before requiring catalyst replacement and potentially a longer wet-life than conventional silver-zinc cells with a trade-off of lower overall cyclic capacity retention.

Method

Screening tests were developed to evaluate catalyst materials for gas consumption, negative electrode additives for suppressed gassing, and conductivity and short-protection of non-cellulosic separators in potassium hydroxide electrolyte.

Composite Catalyst Development: Silver-zinc cells generate hydrogen gas in excess compared to oxygen gas during all stages of operation except the last stage of charge. Therefore, in the absence of oxygen, a recombination catalyst alone is insufficient for the purpose of sealing silver-zinc cells. A catalyst composite was developed that incorporated both a stoichiometric hydrogen/oxygen recombination catalyst and a material capable or consuming hydrogen gas independently at ambient pressure and temperature conditions [1-5].

Negative Electrode Additive: Negative electrode additives were incorporated into BST Systems' conventional negative electrode composition. The negative electrode additive candidates were evaluated in terms of their gassing rate in potassium hydroxide electrolyte.

Non-Cellulosic Separator System: Non-cellulosic separator candidates were screened for their conductivity in potassium hydroxide electrolyte, zinc penetration resistance, and silver penetration resistance.

Advanced Silver-Zinc 365 Ah Cell

The focus of the program is to improve BST Systems' conventional 365 Ah (MK89) cell currently used as the power source for the Seal Delivery Vehicle (SDV). The primary design constraint was that all new hardware had to remain below the terminals of the of the existing cell design.

Leading candidates from the screening tests were combined in 365 Ah cell prototypes and evaluated on the basis of sealed operation, initial capacity, and capacity retention. The best of these candidates became the basis for the design and fabrication of the 365 Ah cells, shown in Figure 1, which have a replaceable composite catalyst assembly, a pressure transducer, and a 30 psig safety valve.

Figure 1: BST Systems' sealed, 365 Ah cell product featuring a replaceable composite catalyst, a pressure transducer, and a safety relief valve.

Experimental

A cellulosic and a non-cellulosic version of the sealed, advanced 365 Ah cell have been developed. Both versions include the composite catalyst for sealed operation and an enhanced negative electrode.

The advanced 365 Ah cells were tested in a string of six (6) cells within a sealed battery vessel, shown in Figure 2, to simulate operation in an enclosed, underwater vehicle. The vessels included hydrogen, oxygen, and pressure sensors. The vessels were flushed with nitrogen and sealed prior to testing.

The sealed, advanced 365 Ah cells were cycled following a protocol similar to the Acceptance Test method for applications for this cell size. Individual discharges were performed at 60 A both timed and full discharge. Timed discharges to 400 Ah were performed on cycles 1 and 2, full discharges to 1.20 V were performed on cycles 5, 15, 25, 35, 45, 50. All other cycles were timed discharges to 300 Ah. Charges were performed at 10 A to a 2.02 V cut-off. Open-circuit periods were a minimum of 8 hours. The cycles timed to 400 Ah required at least 60 hours. The cycles timed to 300 Ah required at least 50 hours. The cycles with full discharges required up to 75 hours.

Figure 2: Sealed battery vessels equipped with internal hydrogen, oxygen, and pressure sensors capable of cycling a string of six (6) 365 Ah cells.

Results and Discussion

The cellulosic and non-cellulosic versions of the advanced 365 Ah cells were evaluated in terms of internal cell pressure, cyclic capacity retention, and period of sealed operation. The period of sealed operation is the number of cycles performed before the composite catalyst requires replacement, which is indicated by the cell pressure exceeding 25 psig. The catalyst assemblies, shown on the cell cover in Figure 1, have a hydrogen consumption capacity of approximately 12 l H_2 STP. The battery vessels were monitored for hydrogen content during cycling.

Advanced Cellulosic 365 Ah Pressure Performance: The internal cell pressure of one of the six sealed, 365 Ah cellulosic cells tested in the enclosed battery vessel as a function of cycle number is shown in Figure 3. Catalyst assemblies were replaced on cycles 10 and 27 when one of the six cells exhibited an increase in pressure to 25 psig, indicating an exhausted composite catalyst. The catalyst assemblies on all six cells were replaced during these maintenance intervals. As shown in Figure 3, the catalyst assemblies provided for a stable, low pressure between 0-10 psig for periods of 10 cycles initially, 17 cycles with the first replacement, and 20 cycles with the second replacement. The time period of sealed operation was 6, 6, and 12 weeks, respectively.

The hydrogen content within the enclosed battery vessel was monitored throughout cycling. As shown in Figure 4, the percentage of hydrogen within the vessel remained below 1% throughout cycling. A small increase in hydrogen percentage between cycles 39-47 was attributed to minor diffusional leaks from one or more of the cells. Nevertheless, the hydrogen content within the battery vessel remained well below the Lower Explosive Limit

(LEL) for hydrogen (4% in air). In addition, the battery vessel included a catalyst composite reactor designed to scrub residual hydrogen and maintain a low percentage in the event of minor diffusional leaks from the cells.

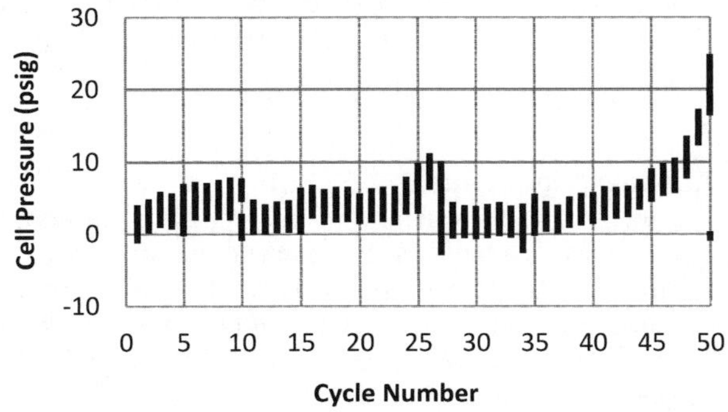

Figure 3: Internal cell pressure as a function of cycle number for one of the six sealed, 365 Ah cellulosic cells. The bars represent the pressure range over the complete cycle (charge/discharge/open-circuit). Catalyst assemblies were replaced on cycles 10 and 27.

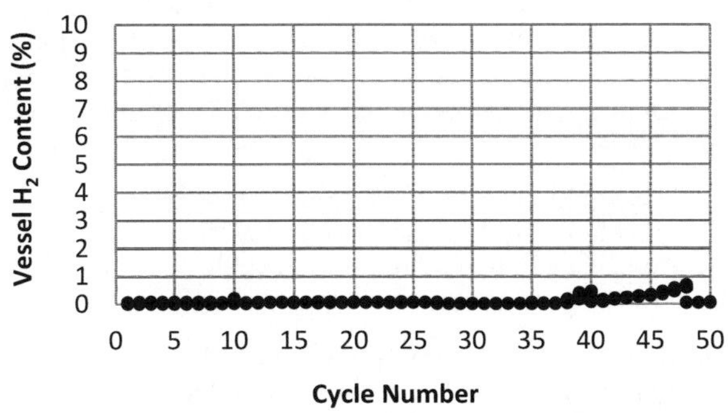

Figure 4: Percentage of hydrogen in battery vessel containing six (6) sealed, 365 Ah cellulosic cells (balance nitrogen).

Advanced Non-Cellulosic 365 Ah Pressure Performance: The internal cell pressure of one of the six sealed, 365 Ah non-cellulosic cells tested in the enclosed battery vessel as a function of cycle number is shown in Figure 5. Catalyst assemblies were replaced on cycles 17 and 34 when one of the six cells exhibited an increase in pressure to 25 psig, indicating an exhausted composite catalyst. The catalyst assemblies on all six cells were replaced during these maintenance intervals. As shown in Figure 5, the catalyst assemblies provided for a stable, low pressure between 0-20 psig for periods of 15 or more cycles. The time period of sealed operation was 7, 8, and 12 weeks, respectively.

The hydrogen content within the enclosed battery vessel was monitored throughout cycling. As shown in Figure 6, during initial cycling there was an increase in hydrogen content within the vessel. Analysis during maintenance showed that the cause of the leak was undersized o-rings, which were replaced on all the cells. As shown in Figure 6, the percentage of hydrogen within the vessel remained at zero throughout the remainder of the test.

Capacity Performance: The cyclic capacity retention of both the cellulosic and non-cellulosic versions of the sealed 365 Ah cells are shown in Figure 7. It is seen that the cellulosic version remained above 300 Ah for the duration of 50 cycles, which is a general requirement for this cell type. In addition, cyclic capacity retention exhibited an improvement over BST Systems' conventional 365Ah cell. This improvement was attributed to the enhanced negative electrode used in the design. The initial energy densities of the sealed, cellulosic 365 Ah cell were 175 Wh/kg and 395 Wh/l.

As shown in Figure 7, the non-cellulosic version exhibited a lower capacity and cyclic capacity retention compared to the cellulosic version and passed below 300 Ah on cycle 36. Nevertheless, the non-cellulosic version is expected to offer extended wet-life capabilities compared to the cellulosic version and may be advantageous for applications where longer wet-life is required more than a cycle life greater than 25 cycles. The initial energy densities of the sealed, non-cellulosic 365 Ah cell were 150 Wh/kg and 340 Wh/l.

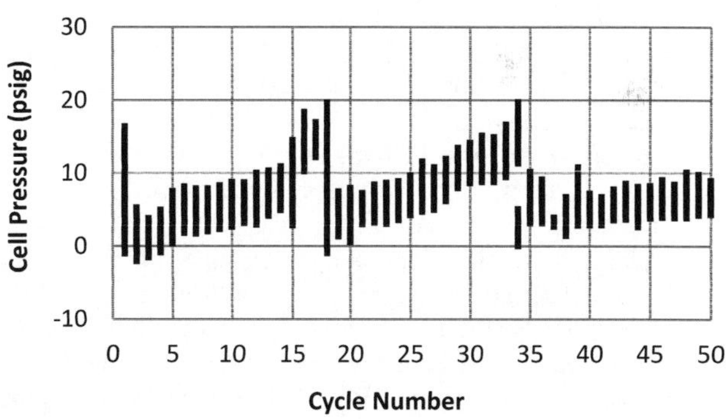

Figure 5: Internal cell pressure as a function of cycle number for one of the six sealed, 365 Ah non-cellulosic cells. The bars represent the pressure range over the complete cycle (charge/discharge/open-circuit). Catalyst assemblies were replaced on cycles 17 and 34.

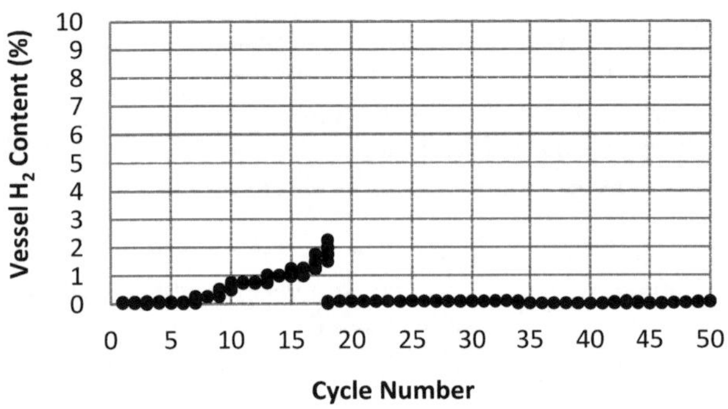

Figure 6: Percentage of hydrogen in battery vessel containing six (6) sealed, 365 Ah non-cellulosic cells (balance nitrogen).

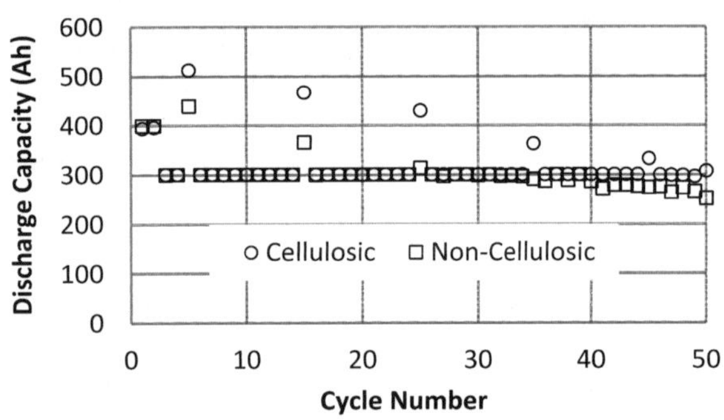

Figure 7: Average discharge capacity as a function of cycle number for the cellulosic and non-cellulosic versions of the advanced, sealed 365 Ah cells.

Conclusions and Future Work

BST Systems, Inc. has developed sealed, safe low-maintenance 365 Ah silver-zinc cells that feature a replaceable composite catalyst capable of recombining hydrogen and oxygen and consuming hydrogen independently. The catalyst assemblies allow for 10 or more sealed, maintenance-free cycles before catalyst replacement is required. Both cellulosic and non-cellulosic versions of the cells were developed, where the non-cellulosic version may provide extended wet-life capabilities at the sacrifice of lower overall capacity. Work is on-going to increase the capacity performance of the non-cellulosic version. BST Systems' advanced, sealed silver-zinc technology is ideal for applications that require safe, high energy-dense power sources, especially in enclosed environments found in underwater vehicles.

Acknowledgements

The authors wish to thank our government sponsors Mr. Aaron Pagnotti (Naval Sea Systems Command) and Mr. Philip R. Houle (Portsmouth Naval Shipyard) for their guidance and direction under this program. The authors also wish to acknowledge and thank the BST team for their support on this project.

References

1. Gaines, L., "Secondary Silver-Zinc Battery Technology," *Journal of the Electrochemical Society*, Vol. 13, No. 2, pp. 61C-67C, 1969.
2. Chung S.R., K.W. Wang, M.H. Teng, and T.P. Perng, "Electrochemical Hydrogenation of Nanocrystalline Face-Centered Cubic Co Powder," *International Journal of Hydrogen Energy*, Vol. 34, pp. 1383-1388, 2009.
3. Hu W. "Electrocatalytic Properties of New Electrocatalyst for Hydrogen Evolution in Alkaline Water Electrolysis," *International Journal of Hydrogen Energy*, Vol. 25, pp. 111-118, 2000.
4. Nakamori I., H. Nakamori, T. Hayano, and S. Kagawa, "The Thermal Decomposition and Reduction of Silver(I) Oxide," *Bulletin of the Chemical Society of Japan*, Vol. 47, No. 8, pp. 1827-1832, 1974.
5. Waterhouse G.I.N., G. A. Bowmaker, and J.B. Metson "The Thermal Decomposition of Silver(I, III) Oxide: A Combined XRD, FT-IR and Raman Spectroscopic Study," *Phys. Chem. Chem. Phys.*, Vol. 3, pp. 3838-3845, 1995.

Short-term Wind Power Prediction using Incremental Learning Based Artificial Neural Network

Arash Asrari[1] and Saeed Lotfifard[2]
Department of Electrical Engineering and Computer Science
University of Central Florida
Orlando, Florida, USA, 32816
[1]asrari@knights.ucf.edu and [2]s.lotfifard@ucf.edu

Abstract: *Wind energy is the most promising renewable energy source that expands rapidly throughout the world. An accurate wind power prediction enables efficient accommodation of wind power generation in the generation scheduling. In this paper, the concept of incremental learning is employed to train a multilayer perceptron neural network (MLPNN) in order to incrementally forecast wind power data. The idea of autocorrelation is utilized in this article to determine the input neurons of MLPNN. The hourly wind power data of PJM electricity market are used to demonstrate the performance of the presented forecasting model.*

Keywords: wind power forecasting; multi-layer perceptron neural network (MLPNN); backpropagation (BP); cyclical order incremental BP; random order incremental BP; Levenberg-Marquardt incremental BP; sample autocorrelation function.

Introduction

Because of the lower generation cost as well as global warming concerns, wind power is considered as an appealing alternative to fossil fuel power sources. The capacity of U.S. wind power market grew by %28 in 2012 and achieved the total capacity of 60,000 MW [1]. However, this rapid growth in wind generation brings about a number of undesirable consequences for power systems including power quality, reliability, stability and power dispatching. Due to its intermittent and uncertain nature, the output power of wind farms is too hard to control which makes it too complex to maintain the balance between generation and demand in power systems. Therefore, if wind power can be reliably predicted, the generation schedule will consider a reasonable combination of wind power and fossil fuel sources for each time period to guarantee the balance and stability of system. There are several forecasting techniques employed by researchers to estimate the wind speed/power as accurate as possible including numeric weather prediction (NWP) [2], neuro-fuzzy network [3], ARMA model [4], grey model [5], fuzzy logic [6], Wavelet Transform [7], Kalman filtering [8], Markov chain model [9], etc.

The family of artificial neural networks (ANNs) has been one of the most highly used strategies for the application of wind power/speed forecasting [10-12]. In this paper, multi-layer perceptron neural network (MLPNN) is used to incrementally estimate 168 hour-ahead (week-ahead) wind power data considering that the training samples are dynamically updated in each step. The concept of autocorrelation is suggested to determine the inputs of network. Moreover, the idea of incremental learning is utilized in this article to train MLPNN. This training technique is more commonly employed for dynamic networks, where new information are added to the data base as the forecasting algorithm proceeds. The efficiency of three incremental based training strategies is compared in this work through their application on the wind power data of PJM electricity market.

Overview of MLPNN and the Simulation Algorithm

Artificial neural networks (ANNs) are parallel distributed information processing algorithms utilizing the fundamentals of biological nervous systems in their structure. ANNs are considered as one of the best suited algorithms to deal with complex nonlinear problems and analyze the real world temporal data [13]. The most distinguishing features of ANNs are as follows [14]: (1) ANNs are data-driven self adaptive models. It means they learn all the required information from the available samples and they are capable of capturing the underlying relationships among the input and output data. (2) ANNs can generalize. It means they are able to perform accurate nonlinear modeling for the unseen data based on the learning knowledge of trained samples. (3) ANNs are universal functional estimator models. It has been proven that they can predict any continuous function to any desired accuracy as long as there is no limitation for the number of adopted neurons in the structure of network [15].

MLPNN is a feedforward ANN that is used as a universal function approximator to map input samples onto the desired output data. MLPNNs employ a hierarchical multi-layered structure to transfer the training samples through nonlinear functional nodes to capture the nonlinear relationship between input and output. Figure 1 illustrates the schematic of a typical MLPNN containing two nodes in the input layer, three nodes in the hidden layer and one node in the output layer. A unique coefficient value is assigned to each branch between each two nodes of the network. For instance, W_{jk} stands for the weight which transfers data from node *k* to node *j*. The duty of MLPNN is updating these weights while it learns the training samples during different epochs (i.e. iterations).

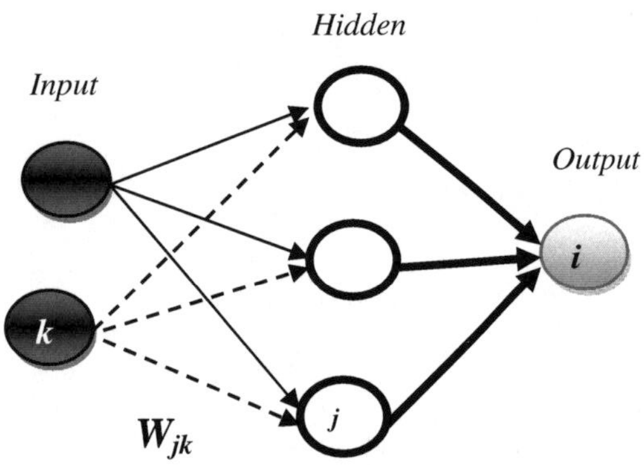

Figure 1. Schematic of MLPNN

The most commonly used technique in the literature to train MLPNN is backpropagation (BP) [16] which is a supervised training strategy propagating the received information backward in the network to update the corresponding weights. Batch learning and incremental learning are two different modes of BP. Batch mode is used for offline training when all the required training samples are available. On the other hand, incremental learning is suitable for the purpose of online training when the training information is continuously updated by new streaming samples over time. The main difference between Batch and incremental learning modes is that the first one updates the weights of the network after receiving all the training data at the end of each epoch; however, the latter modifies the weight values after the presentation of each training sample. That is the main reason explaining why the computation burden of Batch mode is noticeably less than that of incremental learning. However, Batch mode is not useful when dynamic or excessively sizeable training samples are aimed to be estimated. The procedure to implement MLPNN using incremental learning BP is as follows [17]:

Step 1) Initialize the weights; put epoch=1, and p=1.

Step 2) Present the *p*th input training sample (x(p)) and calculate the output of different nodes using Eqs. 1 and 2.

$$y_j^1(p) = g(net_j^1(p)) = g[\sum_{k=1}^{K} w_{jk}^1 . x_k(p)];\quad 1 \le j \le J \qquad (1)$$

$$y_i^2(p) = g(\text{net}_i^2(p)) = g[\sum_{j=1}^{J} w_{ij}^2 . \text{y}_j(p)];\quad 1 \le i \le I \qquad (2)$$

where, J and I represent the number of nodes in the hidden and output layers, respectively. And g is the adopted activation function for the network.

Step 3) If $y_i^2(p)$ equals $d_i(p)$, go to Step 5. Otherwise, calculate the error of each node using Eqs. 3 and 4.

$$\delta_i^2(p) = g'(\text{net}_i^2(p)).[d_i(p) - y_i^2(p)] \qquad 1 \le i \le I \quad (3)$$

$$\delta_j^1(p) = g'(\text{net}_i^2(p)).\sum_{i=1}^{I} w_{ij}^2 . \delta_i^2(p) \qquad 1 \le j \le J \quad (4)$$

Step 4) Update the weights of the network using Eqs. 5 and 6.

$$\Delta w_{ij}^2 = \eta . \delta_i^2(p). \text{y}_j^1(p) \qquad 1 \le i \le I,\ 1 \le j \le J \qquad (5)$$

$$\Delta w_{jk}^1 = \eta . \delta_j^1(p). \text{x}_k(p) \qquad 1 \le i \le I,\ 1 \le j \le J \qquad (6)$$

Step 5) If all the patterns are received, go to step 6. Otherwise, put p=p+1 and go to step 2.

Step 6) If the stopping criterion is satisfied, finish proceeding the algorithm and use the updated weights to forecast the unseen data. Otherwise, put epoch=opoch+1 and p=1 and go to Step 2.

The incremental learning BP can be implemented in different modes. Three incremental techniques are concentrated and compared in this work which are as follows: (1) Cyclical order incremental BP. In this mode, each vector is fed to the network in order with the updated weight and bias values. (2) Random order incremental BP. Applying this technique, all the training samples are presented in a different random order for each epoch. Weight and bias values are updated after the presentation of each data. (3) Levenberg-Marquardt BP. This strategy updates the weight and bias values according to Levenberg-Marquardt optimization. This method is capable of training any network as long as the weigh, net input and transfer functions are derivative. More details about these incremental learning methods can be found in [18].

Simulation Results

The presented incremental learning based MLPNN is developed in MALAB and the simulation process is done on a computer with the processor of Intel(R) Xeon(R) CPU E5-2603 0 @ 1.80 GHz. The performance of the elaborated forecasting method is verified in this article by its application on the historical hourly wind power data of PJM electricity market [19]. The purpose is incrementally estimating 168 hour-ahead wind power data. Therefore, the neural network is trained only one time. When the new sample is available in each hour, the weight and bias values of the forecasting network will be updated only for that sample. Implementing this incremental learning strategy, the old data will not be trained again that decreases the computation burden of the algorithm, significantly. The adopted training information in this work are the hourly wind power data in the RTO Company of PJM from 12:00 am on Jan 01, 2013 through 11:00 pm on Jan 11, 2013, containing 264 training samples, which are depicted in Figure 2.

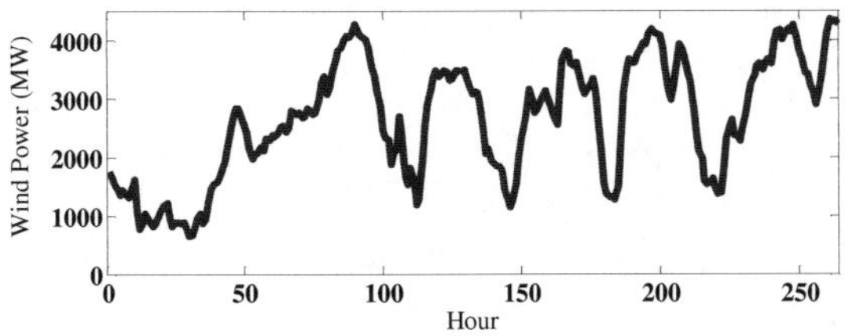

Figure 2. Training data

In order to determine the most relevant input values, the sample autocorrelation of training data is computed that is shown in Figure 3. As it can be gathered from this figure, the first three time lags (i.e. the first, second and third previous wind power data) have high autocorrelations with the current sample. As a result, three nodes are considered in the input layer of MLPNN.

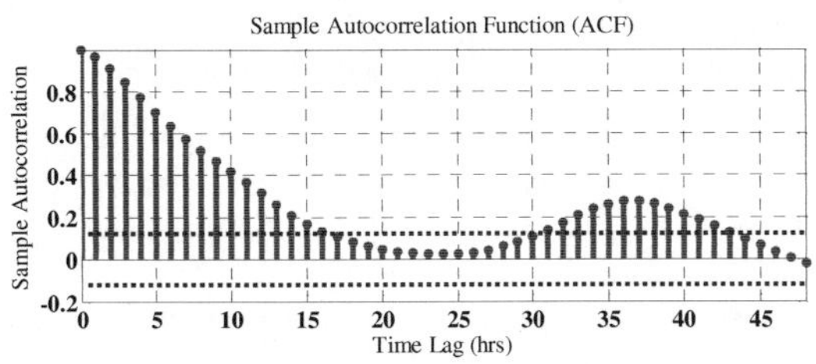

Figure 3. Sample autocorrelation function of training data

Accomplishing a trial and error procedure, eight nodes are adopted in the first layer (i.e. the hidden layer). The single node in the second layer is the output of MLPNN. The stopping criteria of the training process is reaching the 50th epoch or experiencing the training error of 1e-10, or less than that, for any sample in any iteration.

Implementing the developed MLPNN, the wind power value of the next hour will be predicted. Then algorithm waits for one hour until the actual value is known and recorded. Applying the new recorded data to the network, the weigh and bias values will be updated and the modified MLPNN will forecast the wind power of the next hour. This incrementally forecasting procedure is repeated until the wind power sample of the next week is estimated. The actual test data along with the wind power samples predicted by cyclical order incremental BP, random order incremental BP and Levenberg-Marquardt BP are illustrated in Figures 4-6.

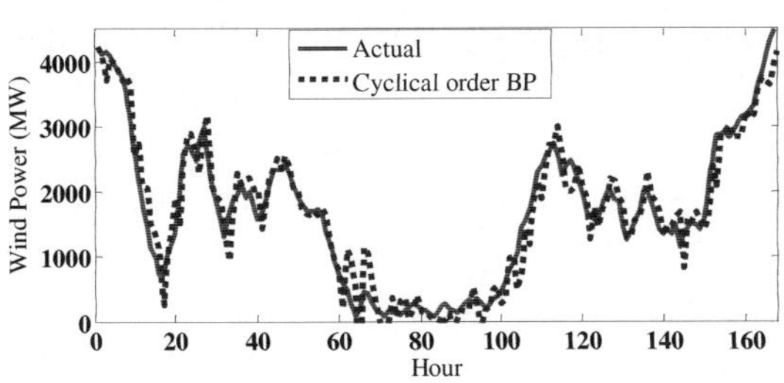

Figure 4. The forecasted test week data by cyclical order BP

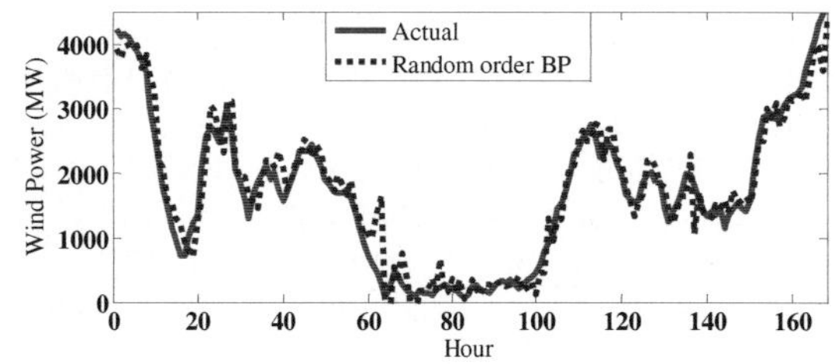

Figure 5. The forecasted test week data by random order BP

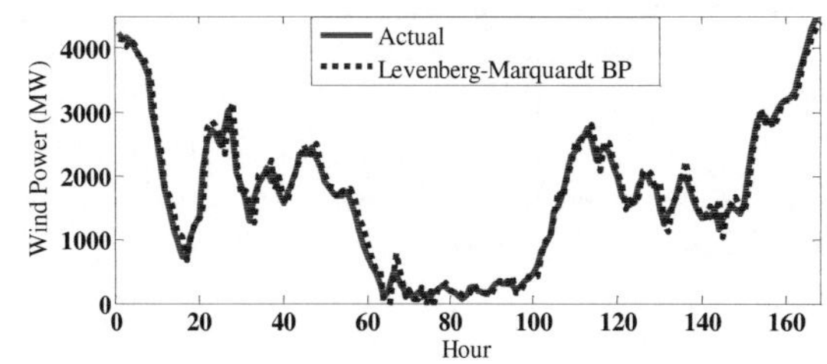

Figure 6. The forecasted test week data by Levenberg-Marquardt BP

A comparison among the efficiency of these forecasting methods is provided in Figure 7. As it can be realized, three significant points distinguish the superior performance of Levenberg-Marquardt BP that can be explained as follows: (1) The training time of this technique is only 1.236 sec which is considerably less than that of the two other training methods. (2) The MAPE (mean absolute percentage error) of this approach for the 168 test samples is only 12.44% which is noticeably less than the testing error of the two other strategies. (3) The difference between the training and testing errors is about 7% that is dramatically less than such a difference for the two other approaches. It means the Levenberg-Marquardt BP training technique has resulted in the most accurate generalization for the corresponding unseen wind power data.

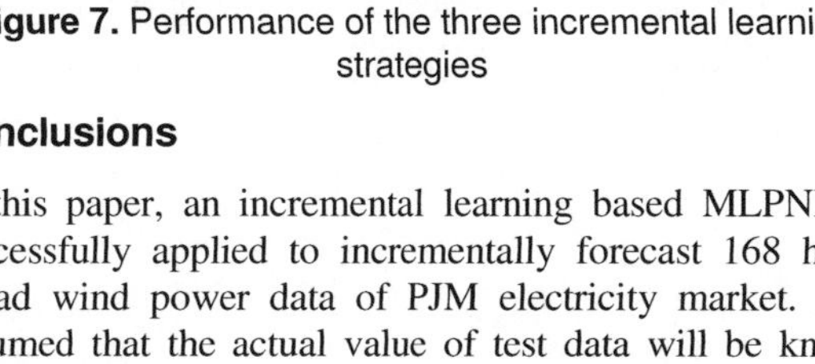

Figure 7. Performance of the three incremental learning strategies

Conclusions

In this paper, an incremental learning based MLPNN is successfully applied to incrementally forecast 168 hour-ahead wind power data of PJM electricity market. It is assumed that the actual value of test data will be known over time and after recording each new sample, the structure of MLPNN is incrementally updated.

Although the training time of cyclical order incremental BP is almost equal to that of random order incremental BP, the latter estimates the test data more accurately. It is also verified that the implementation of Levenberg-Marquardt BP will lead to a much faster training process and a more precise prediction results compared to the other two training techniques for the application of incrementally wind power forecasting.

References

1. 2012 Wind Technologies Market Report, available at: osti.gov/bridge
2. Landberg, L., "A Mathematical Look at a Physical Power Prediction Model," *Wind Energy*, Vol. 1, no. 1, pp. 23-28, September 1998.
3. Xia, J., P. Zhao, and Y. Dai, "Neuro-fuzzy Networks for Short-term Wind Power Forecasting," *2010 Int. Conf. Power System Technology (POWERCON)*, Hangzhou, China, pp. 1-5, October 2010.
4. Gao, S., Y. He, and H. Chen, "Wind Speed Forecast for Wind Farms based on ARMA-ARCH Model," *2009 Int. Conf. Sustainable Power Generation and Supply (SUPERGEN)*, Nanjing, China, pp. 1-4, April 2009.
5. El-Fouly T. H. M., E. F. El-Saadany, and M. M. A. Salama, "Grey Predictor for Wind Energy Conversion Systems Output Power Prediction," *IEEE TRANS. POWER SYS.*, Vol. 21, no. 3, pp. 1450-1452, August 2006.
6. Damousis, I. G., M. C. Alexiadis, J. B. Theocharis, and P. S. Dokopoulos, "A Fuzzy Model for Wind Speed Prediction and Power Generation in Wind Parks Using Spatial Correlation," *IEEE TRANS. Energy Conversion*, Vol. 19, no. 2, pp. 352-361, June 2004.
7. Khan, A. A. and M. Shahidehpour, "One Day Ahead Wind Speed Forecasting using Wavelets," *2009 Power Systems Conf. and Exposition (PSCE)*, Seattle, WA, pp. 1-5, March 2009.
8. Louka, P., G. Galanis, N. Siebert, G. Kariniotakis, P. Katsafados, I. Pytharoulis, G. Kallos, "Improvements in Wind Speed Forecasts for Wind Power Prediction Purposes using Kalman Filtering," *Journal of Wind Engineering and Industrial Aerodynamics*, Vol. 96, no. 12, pp. 2348-2362, December 2008.
9. Carpinone, A., R. Langella, A. Testa, M. Giorgio, "Very Short-term Probabilistic Wind Power Forecasting based on Markov Chain Models," *11th Int. Conf. Probabilistic Methods Applied to Power Systems (PMAPS)*, Singapore, pp. 107-112, June 2010.
10. Sideratos, G. and N. D. Hatziargyriou, "An Advanced Statistical Method for Wind Power Forecasting," *IEEE TRANS. POWER SYS.*, Vol. 22, no. 1, pp. 258-265, February 2007.
11. Zhao, P., J. Wang, J. Xia, Y. Dai, Y. Sheng, and J. Yue, "Performance Evaluation and Accuracy Enhancement of a Day-ahead Wind Power Forecasting System in China," *Renewable Energy*, Vol. 43, pp. 234-241, July 2012.
12. Monfared, M., H. Rastegar, and H. M. Kojabadi, "A New Strategy for Wind Speed Forecasting using Artificial Intelligent Methods," *Renewable Energy*, Vol. 34, no. 3, pp. 845-848, March 2009.
13. Yildirim, T. and H. K. Cigizoglu, "Comparison of Generalized Regression Neural Network and MLP Performances on Hydrologic Data Forecasting," *Proceedings of the 9th Int. Conf. Neural Information Processing (ICONIP)*, vol. 5, Singapore, pp. 18-22, November 2002.
14. Dragomir, O. E., F. Dragomir, L. Brezeanu, and E. Minca, "MLP Neural Network as Load Forecasting Tool on Short- term Horizon," *19th Mediterranean Conf. Control & Automation (MED)*, Corfu, Greece, pp. 20-23, June 2011.
15. Poggio, T. and F. Girosi, "Networks for Approximation and Learning," *Proceedings of the IEEE*, Vol. 78, no. 9, pp. 845-848, September 1990.
16. Rumelhart, D. E., G. E. Hinton, and R. J. Williams, "Learning Representations by Back-propagating Errors," *Nature*, Vol. 323, pp. 533-536, October 1986.
17. Christodoulou, C. and M. Georgiopoulos, "Applications of Neural Networks in Electromagnetics," First Chapter, January 2001.
18. Demuth, H. and M. Beale, "Neural Network Toolbox," Fourth Version, October 2004.
19. 2013 Hourly Wind Data of PJM Electricity Market, available at:

    http://www.pjm.com/Search%20Results.aspx?q=wind%20xls

Compressed Air for Non-Toxic Energy Storage for Energy Informed Operations

Nicholas Grossano, Thomas F. Podlesak and Mark L. Poppe
Power Division
U.S. Army Communications-Electronics Research, Development and Engineering Center
Aberdeen Proving Ground, MD 21005

Abstract:

Compressed air has been proposed as an energy storage medium on the utility scale. The methodology is to pump compressed air into large underground reservoirs, such as created by abandoned mines, and draw off high pressure air as needed to generate electrical power. This may be applied on a smaller scale to provide energy storage to fielded military units.

The literature reports that compressed air has the same energy density as conventional lead acid storage batteries. This assumes that the lead acid storage battery and the compressed air system are completely discharged. This is an improper comparison, in that discharging a lead acid battery to below seventy percent of capacity adversely affects the battery lifetime. There is no such restriction for compressed air. To make a more proper comparison, a battery bank capable of delivering the same energy as that of a comparable compressed air system would need to be three times as large. Otherwise stated, the compressed air system would be one third the size of the lead acid system.

Compressed air has the further advantage of not requiring hazardous chemicals, such as the lead compounds and sulfuric acid of a lead acid system. Further, its storage medium is ubiquitous. Safety, reduction in size and the ready availability of the medium make compressed air a very viable choice for energy storage for energy informed operations on the battlefield.

Energy Informed Operations seeks to improve the supply and utilization of energy on the battlefield. Closely paralleling technology being developed for Smart Grid, energy informed operations makes use of energy storage to capture for subsequent use excess energy generated by the overall power generation system, such as energy from renewable energy storage or energy from engine driven generators operating at peak efficiency but in excess of their current output demand requirement. Advanced battery systems have been proposed for this purpose, but are expensive, prompting a revisiting of highly efficient and low cost lead acid battery based systems. Compressed air promises to provide enhanced capability without hazardous, toxic chemicals.

Our proof of concept experiment consists of a large commercial air tank with a capacity of approximately 0.9 cubic meters and a maximum operating pressure of 600 psi (4.1 MPa) . It operates an air motor which turns, via a speed increaser, a 3 kW commercial generator. The entire apparatus occupies a 4 ft by 4 ft (1.2m by 1.2 m) footprint, chosen for ease of transport. The goal of the project is to generate 3 kW of electric power continuously for a period in excess of an hour. The limiting factor is to what pressure may the system be discharged to and still meet this criterion. Safety issues are also explored, not wishing to substitute the danger of high pressure for toxic substances. The experiment utilizes commercial components wherever possible. The air tank is cylindrical steel and is quite large and heavy. Compression and expansion functions are handled by separate components. A composite spherical tank should reduce the overall height of the system by half and allow for higher air pressures. Further volume reduction should be possible by combining the compression and expansion functions into one device. Twenty 4 ft by 4 ft by 4ft modules could then be fitted into a standard 20 ft container, and would provide 40 kW for over an hour in a field portable unit, at the current pressure

Keywords: energy storage, energy informed operations, non-toxic, renewables

Introduction

The Power Division of the U.S. Army Communications-Electronics Research Development and Engineering Center (CERDEC) has a major program entitled Energy Informed Operations (EIO) [1]. This effort seeks to establish optimal control over the provision of energy to fielded Army units via data networking between power sources and loads, utilizing principles being promoted for Smart Grid. This will enable energy demand to be most efficiently matched to energy supply and to prioritize loads. This will reduce the amount of fuel needed to be transported to the battlefield while assuring the sufficient fuel is available for mission support. Another way to reduce fuel required is to make use of renewable energy. Renewable energy is sporadic and requires effective methods of energy storage to provide energy when the renewables are incapable of supplying energy, such as solar systems at night. Energy storage may also be used to increase the effectiveness of conventional fuel generating systems by means of peak shaving and load leveling.

Power Division embarked on a program designated Hybrid Energy Storage Module (HESM) to improve energy storage. The principal author conducted an internal study to investigate various methods of energy storage for application to this task. In addition to conventional electrochemical systems (batteries), he also investigated some more advanced concepts of energy storage not based in electrochemistry.

The results of this investigation were rather disappointing. These advanced systems, in general, had major shortcomings that made them impractical for military applications of energy storage. Energy storing flywheels require magnetic bearings and need to operate in an evacuated containment vessel, to eliminate windage losses and to assure safety to surrounding equipment and personnel in event of a catastrophic failure, which they are prone to. Energy storing inductors need to be operated in cryogenic or, preferably, superconductive mode to reduce resistive losses. A particularly intriguing concept, pumped hydro storage, to take advantage of the ubiquitous nature of water in the battlefield, required enormous quantities of water, far more than practical to supply to the battlefield. This primarily due to water, being a liquid, is incompressible.

The fact that liquids are incompressible led to only one unconventional technology being investigated: compressed air. Air can be compressed to practically any degree, provided that there is a pressure vessel of sufficient strength to contain it.

Our concept is that compressed air could be used as replacements for lead acid batteries for battlefield energy storage applications. Lead acid batteries, though heavy, are extremely cheap and extremely efficient. Their volumetric and gravimetric energy densities are 0.08 kWh/l and 0.035 kWh/kg respectively. The energy densities of compressed air 0.042 kWh/l and 0.02 kWh/kg, which are comparable values. At first glance, lead acid batteries would appear to have an advantage over compressed air. However, lead acid batteries should only be discharged to 70% of charge [2]. Deeper discharge would result in shortened battery life. Compressed air does not suffer from this shortcoming. In terms of a practical system, a lead acid battery system to deliver an equal amount of energy as a comparable compressed air system would have to have three times the amount of batteries, causing the above energy density figures for lead acid batteries to be reduced by a factor of three. Lead acid batteries also require long charging times. Compressed air systems are restricted in charging time only by the power available to charge them. These values for compressed air, and lead acid and other batteries are summarized in Figure 1. Note that some parameters are weighted to show relevant importance.

Schoenung and Hassenzahl[3] and Janse van Rensberg [4] both have shown that not only is compressed air comparable with lead acid batteries with regard to energy density, but also with regard to overall cost. This is shown in Figure 2. Further, substituting compressed air for lead acid batteries not only eliminates the need for hazardous materials, but also uses a substance ubiquitous to the battlefield.

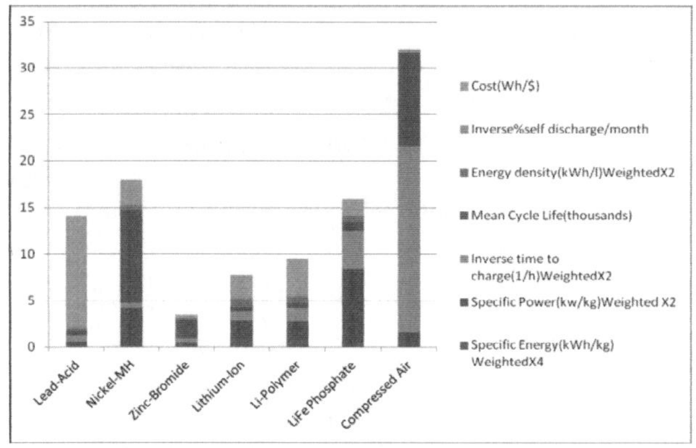

Figure 1. Comparison of system parameters for compressed air versus various battery chemistries. Note that certain parameters are weighted to indicate relative importance

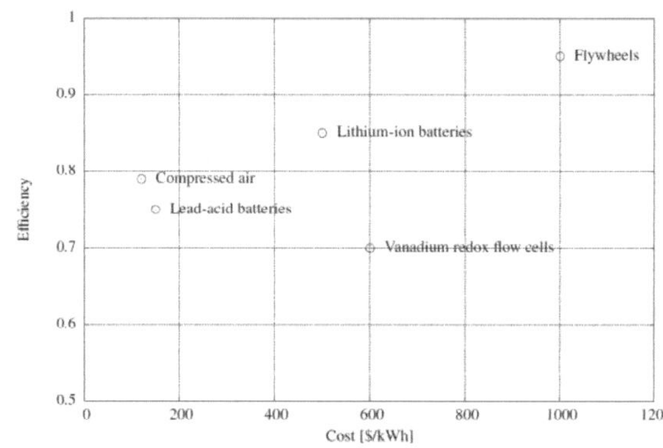

Figure 2. Efficiency versus cost for various energy storage media. Compressed air has the lowest cost and excellent efficiency. [3]

A study was instituted to measure the effectiveness of a compressed air energy storage system. A nominal value of 3 kW was selected, with the objective of being able to generate power at this level from stored energy for a time period in excess of an hour.

Experimental Apparatus

An experimental apparatus, shown in Figures 3 and 4 was constructed from largely commercially available parts, in an effort to minimize the time to procure and build such a system.

The most striking feature is the large 0.91 m^3 (240 gallon) air storage tank. The tank is rated at 4.1 MPA (600 psig) and is certified to the American Society of Mechanical Engineers Pressure vessel code. Compressed air is supplied via a shop air utility. The compressed air is supplied at only 680 kPA (100 psig). To reach the high

Figure 3. Compressed air energy storage experimental apparatus. The principal component is the large air tank rear. Air motor, generator and controls are in the foreground. An air pressure amplifier, for boosting facility shop air pressure to a useful level, is at the right.

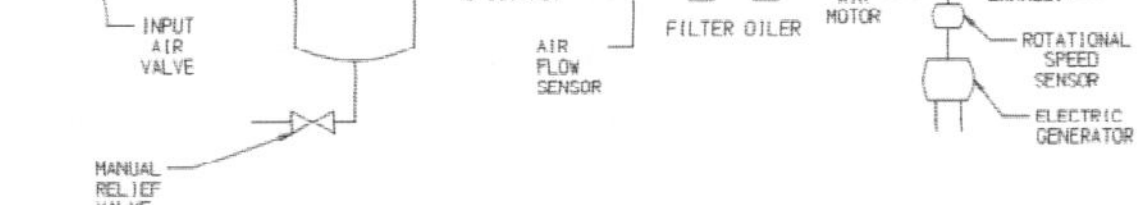

Figure 4. Schematic of compressed air experimental apparatus

pressures required for this study, a pressure amplifier, shown in Figure 5, was utilized. This device negated the

Figure 5. Pressure amplifier. Shop air enters via tubing in foreground, is compressed by air entering piston in center section, and exits at higher pressure via tubing at top background

need for an expensive high pressure compressor. The device consists of a coupled set of two pairs of opposed pistons. The first set generates reciprocating motion from the shop air supply. This motion drives a second set of opposed pistons that takes shop air and further compresses it to a higher pressure which is then conducted to the tank to raise the air stored in the tank to the desired pressure. A pneumatically controlled valve directs the stored air to a 3.7 kW (5 HP) air motor with a maximum speed of 2000 RPM. The motor is coupled to a 1:3 speed increaser to raise the rotational speed to a nominal 3600 RPM. This is the speed necessary to drive a 3 kW generator, which was originally from a commercial engine driven generator set.

The avoidance of hazardous materials does not make this system inherently safe. Stored energy in any form is potentially dangerous and compressed air at 4.1 MPA is no exception. The apparatus has redundant safety features. In addition to the aforementioned safety valve, the air tank has a remotely controlled relief valve which is controlled via a chain of emergency off functions. These include three emergency off push button switches, two on the apparatus itself and one on the control panel, three automatic shutoff functions based on operational parameters, i.e. tank over pressure, tank over temperature and generator over speed, and loss of control power and control air. In the case of the latter two, if there is a sudden loss in facility electrical power, the remote relief valve will open. This is implemented by a separate control air circuit, with its own storage tank, which keeps the relief valve in the closed position and will release the valve to the open position if electric power is lost or the control air is lost. A manual relief valve is also included. However, its main function is to prevent the air tank from being pressurized inadvertently, however remote that occurrence may be.

Control of the apparatus is via the control panel shown in Figure 6. Note the prominent red emergency off push button switch. The operator may shut the entire system off

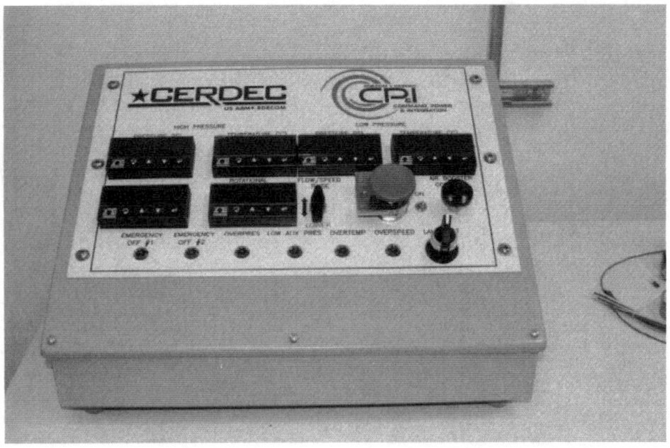

Figure 6. Apparatus operator's control panel. Control panel displays six system operational measurements, an emergency off switch, a control valve to control the main air control valve to the air motor, the enabling air for the pressure amplifier and indicator lights for the emergency off functions.

by simply activating that switch. The switch is capable of being locked out, as is the main air supply. Other features of the control panel are six digital panel meters measuring the following quantities

- Air tank air pressure
- Air tank air temperature
- Air motor air pressure
- Air motor air temperature
- Air motor air flow rate
- Generator rotational speed

The panel meters will normally display in green numerals. Where preset thresholds exist, parameters exceeding these values will display as red or, in the case of air tank pressure, yellow as it approaches limit, then red when attaining threshold. The control to open and close the main air control valve, a valve to enable the air amplifier and display lights to indicate which emergency off signal triggered the tank venting complete the control panel functions. The six digital panel meters are linked together via an RS-232 bus. They can be controlled by the air tank air temperature meter which has an Ethernet server integral to it and which can communicate via Ethernet to other devices on a data network. This capability was included as an afterthought to the original design, but has assumed new found importance as a means to validate the capability of energy storage to contribute to Energy Informed Operations.

The control panel is located in a room adjacent to the apparatus. All functions are controlled remotely via the control panel, so that the room in which apparatus is located will be unoccupied when the apparatus is operating.

Experimental Plan

Due to the hazards of operation delineated above, the system has yet to be certified for operation, so no experimental data is available at this time. The experimental plan is as follows:

- Validate claimed ability to produce 3 kW of electrical power from stored energy for over 1 hour
- Accurately measure both volumetric and gravimetric energy density and compare to values of lead acid batteries and other battery chemistries. Account for the impact of weight and volume due to ancillary equipment and less than ideal containment structure
- Determine lower pressure limit to which stored energy may be extracted
- Demonstrate remote operation of the system over a data network

The current system, assuming successful attainment of the abovementioned goals, still suffers a fundamental liability due to the nature of its largest component, the air tank. The current tank, chosen for ready availability, weighs over 500 kg (1200 lb_m). This is because the tank is steel and cylindrical. A spherical tank of similar volume would occupy one-half the volume of the current system and, if constructed from a high strength composite material, would weigh considerably less. Such as system would easily fit into cubical volume 1.22 m (4 ft) on edge. Twenty such systems could be fitted into a standard 20 ft trailer or container, and thus store twenty times the energy.

Another opportunity to reduce size and weight would be to replace the pressure amplifier and rotary air motor with linear motor-generator attached to compressor-expander, which could direct utilize atmospheric air.

References

1. DeJong, Marnie, "Energy Informed Operations," *Army Technology*, vol. 2, no. 1, pp. 8-9, January 2014
2. *Battery Handbook,* McGraw-Hill, p. 23.50, 2004
3. Schoenung, Susan M. and Hassenzahl, William V., "Long- vs. Short-Term Energy Storage Technologies A Life Cycle Cost Study A Study for the DOE Energy Storage Systems Program," Sandia National Laboratory Report SAND2003-2783, August 2003
4. Janse van Rensburg, Petrus J., "Energy Storage in Composite Flywheel Rotors," Master's Thesis, Stellenbosch University, South Africa, December 2011

Heuristic Diagnostics and Prognostics for Fielded Generators and ECUs to Support Energy Informed Operations

Warren Johnson[1], Chris Stimek[1] and Thomas F. Podlesak[2]

[1]WilliamsRDM Inc.
200 Greenleaf Street, Fort Worth, TX 76107

[2] Power Division
U.S. Army Communications-Electronics Research, Development and Engineering Center
5100 Magazine Road, Aberdeen Proving Ground, MD 21005

Abstract: *With approximately 100,000 tactical engine driven generators currently deployed to all three U.S. Armed Services, it is vital for effective military operations to maintain maximum availability of these resources. To not only quickly diagnose malfunctioning generators but also to anticipate imminent malfunctions and proactively intervene to prevent loss of capability is of utmost importance. This falls under the purview of Energy Informed Operations, which seeks to optimize provision of energy to the battlefield by not only assuring optimal delivery of fuel but also making certain that the capability to most effectively use such energy is made certain.*

To implement these diagnostic and prognostic functions, a project making use of heuristics is being implemented. The objective was to establish an innovative approach for and demonstrate methodology and modeling tools to provide prognostics and diagnostics for use on tactical electric power systems (5 kW - 200 kW) that complement Energy Informed Operation's goals to increase system reliability and reduce fuel consumption on the tactical battlefield.

This has been accomplished by implementing an architecture known as GenFIT. This system monitors the following generator set parameters:

- *Oil Pressure*
- *Coolant Temperature*
- *AC Output Voltage, Current and Frequency*
- *Air Intake Pressure (Intake Vacuum)*
- *Starter Current*
- *Engine Speed (RPM)*
- *Fuel Level*
- *Vibration*
- *Power Quality*
- *Battery Voltage and Current*
- *Alternator Charging Current*
- *Ambient Temperature*

The GenFIT architecture monitors these quantities and uses the calculated values to establish the normal operating mode for the generator with respect to ambient environmental and load conditions. It then continuously monitors the generator parameters and looks for deviations, in an attempt to detect deleterious events and alert support personnel to present or imminent malfunctions, allowing them to take corrective action. As part of Energy Informed Operations, these alerts will not only be made to personnel local to the system, but the data may also passed up the chain of command to initiate action at a higher level such as requests for refueling, provision of replacement parts, rotation of the affected system to depot for extensive repair or overhaul, and substitution of a replacement unit if necessary. Of all the above parameters, vibration analysis is the most significant and most useful. Wavelet analysis, a superior technique than the more conventional fast Fourier analysis, is used to make these evaluations.

We have implemented this system on a 10 kW Tactical Quiet Generator (TQG) and an 18 kW generator on a TMSS trailer. The latter system also has an environmental control unit (ECU) capable of 60,000 Btu/hr (17.5 kW) cooling or 9 or 18 kW heating collocated on the trailer. Since environmental control is the largest user of energy on the battlefield, the program is being expanded to include control of such devices

Keywords: heuristics, diagnostics, prognostics, power generation, energy informed operations, wavelet analysis, GenFIT.

Introduction

The Power Division of the U.S. Army Communications-Electronics Research Development and Engineering Center (CERDEC) has a major program entitled Energy Informed Operations (EIO) [1]. This effort seeks to establish optimal control over the provision of energy to fielded Army units via data networking between power sources and loads. In addition to optimizing fuel delivery and consumption, this will also increase power source availability and reliability by continuously monitoring power source status and not only detecting malfunctions but also anticipating them. Anticipating malfunctions will enable intervention before system failure, thus avoiding malfunctions and thereby increasing reliability, which in turn increases availability.

The increased operational tempo of the U.S. Military in harsh environments quickly wears out equipment, including the generators vital to providing electrical power to military units. Problems caused by wind-driven sand or rain often causes daily shutdowns to accommodate frequent preventive maintenance checks and services. Items such as air filters, battery cables, and engine oil should be checked daily, but even if done, visual inspections cannot detect all problems. These factors combine to reduced equipment availability and reliability on the battlefield. There is a need for an automated diagnostic/prognostic system installed on generators to provide real-time evaluation of the equipment while it is in use.

We have established the feasibility of the Generator Fault Investigation Technology (GenFIT) system architecture for heuristic prognosis and diagnosis of generators. The GenFIT architecture will provide real-time, measurement-based health status and fuel use rates of generators as a system. GenFIT simplifies the maintainers' work by automatically testing each major subsystem and providing advanced warning of impending failures due to either simple or complex faults. GenFIT provides measured fuel use rates to the user, allowing units to plan operations based on the actual needs of the equipment they have on the ground. These capabilities drastically improve the maintenance posture and energy awareness of units in the field. The basic software architecture of GenFIT is shown in Figure 1.

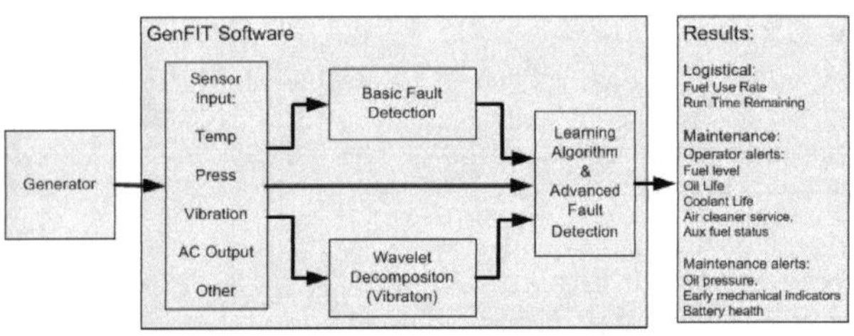

Figure 1. GenFIT architecture, showing input data sources arising from the generator (left), data processing (center) and resulting output data (right).

Of vital importance are the measurements of the key system parameters. There are two generators being utilized for this effort. The first is a 10 kW Tactical Quiet Generator, located at the WilliamsRDM Fort Worth facility. The second generator is an 18 kW generator mounted on a TMSS trailer and located at Aberdeen Proving Ground. The TMSS also includes a 5 ton Environmental Control Unit (ECU). Where possible, data from existing sensors are utilized. These are summarized in Table I. Supplementary data are necessary and obtained from additionally installed sensors. These are summarized in Table II. A major goal of the project is to develop a generic generator monitoring system capable of working with a wide range of generators. Adding sensors provides consistency across various generator makes and models. Where possible we add sensors in such a way as to preserve the original sensor allowing it to provide necessary information to the generator for proper operation of gauges and fault detection/protection systems.

The data obtained via these sensors is used to monitor current operational conditions as well as detect faults.

Table I. Existing sensors

Sending Unit	Subsystem	Measurement	Additional Information Gained
Engine Coolant	Engine cooling	Temperature	Thermostat operation, cooling system performance
Fuel Level	Fuel delivery	Gallons or %	Fuel use rate

Table II. Additional sensors required

Added Measurement	Subsystem	Measurement	Additional Information Gained
Vibration	Engine and Generator Mechanical	Acceleration	Mechanical integrity, accessory behavior
Intake Pressure/Vacuum	Engine air induction	Pressure or Vacuum	Air cleaner status
Oil Pressure	Engine Lubrication	Pressure	Lubrication System Performance
Battery Voltage and Current	Engine electrical	Hall Effect Sensor	Battery health, State of Charge, alternator status, charging current
AC Voltage and Current	AC generator	Ph A, B, C & N Voltage and Current	Output Frequency, Load Balance, Power Factor, Wet Stacking, Ground Fault, Output Power
Ambient Temperature	Operational Conditions	Temperature	Used to learn generator performance under ambient conditions

When first installed, the system learns characteristics of the data with respect to environmental and load conditions of the generator and provides indication of any deviation from these learned parameters to detect faults. Some common faults may be detected via a simple setting of operational points and thresholds, such as those listed in Table III.

Table III. Fault summary table

Fault	Fault Condition
Ground Fault	If the Expected Neutral Current and Actual Neutral Current Differ by More than 1.5A
Phase Imbalance Fault	If total power > 2000W and phase imbalance > 20%
Voltage Fault	If any phase is outside of the range 120V RMS +/- 10%
Frequency Fault	If phase A frequency is outside of the range 60Hz +/- 5%
Wet Stacking Warning	If generator output power < 55.5% of rated load (18kW) (Based on TMSS Generator Documentation)
Alternator Under Current Fault	If battery voltage < 28V and battery charging current < 1A
Alternator Over Current Fault	If battery voltage > 28.3V and battery charging current > 3A
Alternator Diode Fault	If the percent of time battery is discharging is > 20% when the average battery charging current is > 2A
Lightly Loaded Low Battery Fault	If battery voltage falls below 23.4V while supplying < 10A of current
Battery Charging Low Battery Fault	If the rate of change of battery charging current is less than 15mA/s (steady state), the engine is running and the charge current is > 8A
Degraded Battery Fault	If the engine has been running for 2 hours or more and the battery charging current is greater than 6A
Low Cranking Amps Fault	If battery voltage falls below 14V while supplying > 10A of current
High Oil Pressure	If the oil pressure rises above 85 PSI
Low Oil Pressure	If the oil pressure falls below 20 PSI
High Coolant Temperature	If the coolant temperature rises above 220 degrees Fahrenheit
Low Coolant Temperature	If the coolant temperature falls below 32 degrees Fahrenheit
High Intake Vacuum	If the intake vacuum is greater than 15 inH2O (Indicates clogged air filter)

The identification of other useful data is not as simple and straight forward. This would include data derived from such sources as the measurement of engine vibration. This program uniquely analyzes these data via wavelet analysis.

Wavelet Analysis

Wavelets provide a good compromise between time and frequency resolution. Instead of using a sinusoid of infinite duration like the Fourier transform, the wavelet transform uses a wavelet which can be thought of brief wave-like oscillation whose amplitude begins and ends at zero. One issue with the Fourier transform is that all time information is lost. So while we know the frequency content of the signal we do not know when an event with a particular frequency occurred. The Short Time Fourier Transform (STFT) attempts to resolve this issue by showing the frequency content of the signal over time.

One issue with using a STFT is that there is a tradeoff between frequency and time resolution [2]. The Wavelet transform provides a compromise between time and frequency resolution. To analyze a signal the wavelet scale is gradually increased while being slid across and correlated with the signal of interest. Locations within the signal with good correlation to the wavelet have a high value while places with low correlation have a low value. This approach is very powerful and allows a signal to be analyzed at the optimal detail at both large and small scales. [3,4]

Some of the applications of wavelets include:[5,6]

- Data and image compression (JPEG 2000)
- Signal de-noising
- Signal discontinuity detection
- Data Analysis

The selection of an appropriate wavelet is key to getting good results using the wavelet transform. There has been considerable debate as to how to select an appropriate wavelet since it is a complex topic. One approach is to assume that the wavelet characteristics should match the type of feature you are looking for. For example the Haar wavelet which resembles a step function is typically good at detecting discontinuities but doesn't do a very good job at filtering a signal due to its discontinuous property. In many applications a trial and error approach is taken to find a wavelet that shows the best performance.

There are two versions of the wavelet transform, the Continuous Wavelet Transform (CWT) and the Discrete Wavelet Transform (DWT). The CWT is typically used in scientific data analysis applications and uses a large number of wavelet scales to help visualize a signal's features. The DWT is used in more practical implementations because of its lower processing requirements. It uses a dyadic, power-of-two, method to break down the original signal into successively larger scales.

Since our vibration fault detection algorithm is implemented on a small resource constrained system we will focus our attention on using wavelets that can be used with the DWT. From our testing we found that we had better performance using wavelets with sinusoidal features such as the Daubechies (db20) which is somewhat asymmetric and the Dmey (dmey8) Wavelet which is highly symmetric. We ultimately selected the db20 wavelet for the GenFIT application because of its frequency bandwidth characteristics which have low pass-band ripple and attenuated stop bands.

Vibration Wavelet Analysis

Engine vibration, characterization and analysis is performed on the reconstructed low and high frequency vibration signals output from the wavelet filtering algorithm.

For the generator application we selected a sampling rate of 10,240 Hz which will properly position the DWT decomposition levels to allow us to analyze key signals of interest. Table IV shows the DWT decomposition frequency bands and their relevance to generator diagnostics.

Table IV. Wavelet Decomposition Level Bands

Level	Upper Frequency (Hz)	Lower Frequency (HZ)	Center Frequency	Relevance
(Approx. 8) a8	20	0	10	N/A
(Detail 8) d8	40	20	30	Engine Rotational Vibration (1800 RPM)
d7	80	40	60	Combustion Event Frequency
d6	160	80	120	N/A
d5	320	160	240	N/A
d4	640	320	480	N/A
d3	1280	640	960	Combustion Event Detail
d2	2560	1280	1920	Combustion Event Detail
d1	5120	2560	3840	Combustion Event Detail

The low frequency components in the d8 band come from the 30Hz unbalanced rotating mass of the engine operating at 1800 RPM. The d7 band is centered on 60 Hz that equates to the frequency of the combustion events of a 4 cylinder generator running at this RPM. The high frequency content in the d1, d2, and d3 levels comes from the various components of the engine cycle and includes the combustion event itself, valve train events as well as various resonances within the engine. From our analysis we found that the combustion event details have a fairly high bandwidth and span the d1, d2, and d3 bands. If only one or two of the bands are used then some detail is missed when the signal is reconstructed. For our analysis the low frequency signal is composed of the d7 wavelet coefficients comprising frequencies from 40-80Hz while the high frequency signal is composed of the d1, d2, and d3 wavelet coefficients and comprises frequencies from 1280Hz to 3840Hz. Figure 2 shows the low frequency waveform (red) overlaid on the high frequency waveform (blue). The low frequency signal is used as a timing reference to split the high frequency waveform into combustion events. The algorithm finds the negative slope zero crossing points in the low frequency waveform to effectively divide the high frequency waveform into combustion events.

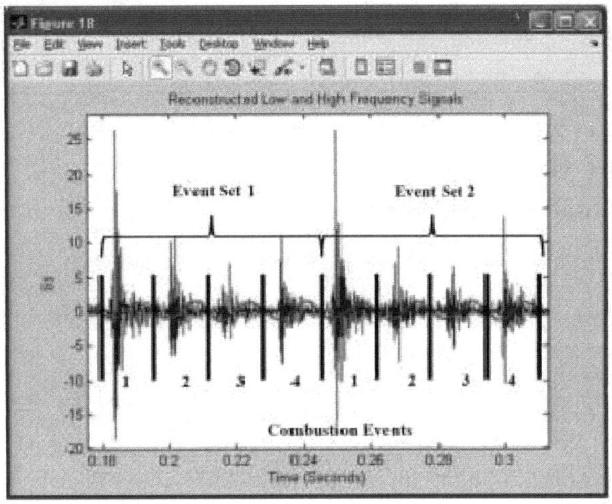

Figure 2: Event Set Example

Knowing the number of cylinders, four in this example, the algorithms divides each group of four cylinders into an event set. Since the diesel engine cycle consists of four strokes each event set consists of two crank shaft revolutions. Figure 2 shows how the vibration algorithm divides up the input waveform into combustion events and event sets. The event labels 1-4 in Figure 2 indicate the event within the set. They do not indicate which cylinder the event is associated with, that information is determined in a later step.

Once the data is divided into events and event sets the algorithm computes the Root Mean Square (RMS) of each combustion event as well as finds the peak of each event. Once this calculation is complete the algorithm averages all of the values for each event (e.g. event 1) in each set (e.g. sets 1 through N) together to measure the average value for that event. This results in an average RMS and average peak value for each event.

From experimentation we found that using the event peak values appears to provide a better indication of the combustion event intensity over the RMS of the event. Table V shows a comparison of the average values of the peak vs RMS for a loaded vs unloaded 10kW TQG. As you can see the RMS values for Cylinder 2 and Cylinder 3 are somewhat close together but the difference is more.

Table V. Peak vs Average Combustion Events

	No Load		10 kW Load	
	Peak (g)	RMS (g)	Peak (g)	RMS (g)
Cylinder 1	11.06	1.78	25.10	3.87
Cylinder 2	8.13	1.20	13.55	2.09
Cylinder 3	4.91	1.10	9.98	1.97
Cylinder 4	3.05	0.85	6.19	1.30

To detect faults using this data we evaluate the cylinder to cylinder intensity ratio, variance in combustion event pronounced in the peak data. As a result we primarily use the peak of the combustion event to determine event intensity intensity for a particular cylinder, and deviations from the learned baseline vibration data for a given operating condition. Additionally, the learning algorithm determines certain baseline information about the generator such as cylinder count, firing order and engine RPM.

These techniques, both simple thresholds and more sophisticated Wavelet analysis, are currently being implemented on both the 10 kW and 18 kW generators. Malfunctions are being simulated on the 10 kW, to allow the heuristic algorithms to apply what they have learned and to recognize imminent malfunctions and issue warnings to personnel, ideally in time to take not only corrective but preventative action.

References

1. DeJong, Marnie, “Energy Informed Operations,” *Army Technology*, vol. 2, no. 1, pp. 8-9, January 2014
2. Nijsen, Tamara M.E. et.al.,” Short Time Fourier and Wavelet Transform for Accelerometric Detection of Myoclonic Seizures,” *Proceedings of the IEEE/EMBS Benelux Symposium*, pp. 155-158, December 2006
3. Kumar, Praveen and Foufoula-Georgiou, Efi , “Wavelet Analysis for Geophysical Applications”, *Reviews of Geophysics* , Vol. 35, pp. 385-411, November 1997
4. Presentation on wavelet analysis; http://www.google.com/url?sa=t&rct=j&q=&esrc=s&source=web&cd=6&ved=0CFUQFjAF&url=http%3A%2F%2Ffaculty.kfupm.edu.sa%2Fee%2Fsamara%2FWT_lecture_1.ppt&ei=uEoqUrkcztTZBcmCgJAB&usg=AFQjCNFjOBR096KyVl9NmQqpM2kXBrBMtw&bvm=bv.51773540,d.b2I
5. Fengli Wang, Shulin Duan, Hongliang Yu “Fault Feature Extraction of Cylinder-Piston Wear in Diesel Engine with EMD”, *Advances in Intelligent and Soft Computing* Volume 169, 2012, pp 419-424
6. Parameswariah, Chethan , “Understanding Wavelet Analysis and Filters for Engineering Applications” Dissertation, Lousiana Tech University, May 2003

Development of Light Weight, Multi-Fuel, Generator Power Sources in the 0-1000 Watt Range

Clifford Cook, Tony Thampan, Shailesh Shah
US Army Communication-Electronics Research Development and Engineering Center (CERDEC)
Command, Power, & Integration (CP&I), Power Division
Aberdeen Proving Grounds, Maryland, US, 21005
Contact authors at www.cerdec.army.mil/contact/

Abstract: *The US Army Communication-Electronics Research Development and Engineering Center (CERDEC) is seeking to address the emerging need for power generation at the platoon level. Devices are sought that can generate 900-1000 W to help fulfill this requirement. Reported here will be the development of a light weight, multi-fueled, 1 kW generator. Exhaust gas analysis on JP-8 will be shown. Carbon monoxide (CO) readings taken at the exhaust port have indicated as high as 126,700 ppm, averaged over 1 minute (OSHA permissible exposure limit is 50 ppm / 8 hours). The analysis includes modeling the dispersion of these potentially harmful gases within the immediate area. Also included in this report are physical characteristics, fuel consumption/efficiency, and endurance testing of the systems.*

Keywords: multi-fuel; JP-8, JP8, generator; multi-fuel; platoon level requirements; 1000 W; CO; carbon monoxide; NOX; fuel efficiency; fuel consumption; exhaust; emissions; OSHA; EPA.

Introduction

In order to provide an operational edge, the US Army equips soldiers with a range of power and energy hungry technologies. This has created a situation where soldiers are required to carry numerous batteries on even short duration missions decreasing mobility and increasing risk of musculoskeletal injuries. [1] One possible solution is in rechargeable batteries, which would require a recharging solution in a forward operational environment. As such, the US Army is seeking to address the need for power generation devices at the platoon and squad level in these environments. A recent Army capability development document (CDD) addressing small unit power [2] addresses these requirements, see Table 1. One area that has seen a recent spike in development are the small, light weight generators/inverters, sub 1 kW. Many of these systems have come about due to the advances in aluminum and aluminum alloy based motors giving rise to light weight powerful engines. Two particular manufactures, Yamaha and Honda, have produced portable 1 kW generators. These commercial off the shelf (COTS) systems are spark-ignition gasoline generators that satisfy many of the requirements shown in table 1. However, the COTS systems fall short in the utilization of standard military fuel, jet-propellant #8 (JP-8).

Table 1. US Army requirements for power generation devices at the platoon level.

Requirement	Threshold	Objective
Power	900 W	1000 W
Fuel	JP-8	Multi-fuel
Weight	13.6 kg (30 lbs.)	6.8 kg (15 lbs.)
Volume	49.2 L (3000 in^3)	24.6 L (1500 in^3)
Voltage	120 VAC, 24 VDC	120 VAC, 24 VDC

JP-8 is kerosene based heavy distillate fuel with low octane rating (high cetane rating) that would be suitable for use in diesel engines. However, in a gasoline based spark ignition engine a number of challenges arise. JP-8 has a flash point of 38 °C (100 °F), too high for cold start in ambient conditions. [3] A minimum concentration of fuel in the vapor phase is required for the proper fuel to air mixture for ignition. In addition, heavy distillate fuels require a longer duration combustion cycle for complete firing of the fuel. Failure to completely burn results in a loss of power and fuel economy as well as gum and carbon deposits within engine cylinders. Additionally, in a 4-stroke motor pre-detonation or knocking can occur during the compression stroke if the mixtures auto-ignition temperature is reached prior to spark ignition.

This challenge has given rise to a number of research and development efforts focused on the modification of the COTS systems. Two approaches have been taken to modify these systems to run on JP-8, a direct and indirect approach. Although specifics may not be given for proprietary reasons the general ideas are presented.

Direct approach: The direct approach tackles the issues discussed above, high flash point, incomplete combustion, and pre-detonation, which are associated with using a heavy distillate fuel, specifically JP-8, in a gasoline based spark ignition engine. Modifications are made to the fuel handling procedures as well as the engine itself.

Indirect approach: The indirect approach avoids the problems with using a heavy distillate fuel by the installation of a fuel reforming kit replacing the carburetor or fuel injection systems. The heavy distillate fuel is reformed into a higher octane fuel similar to gasoline and injected into the combustion chamber; thereby avoiding the need for modifications to the engine.

In this study a multi-fuel generator has been tested and exhaust emissions analyzed. The results are given here.

Experimental

System Description: The 1 kW multi-fuel generators used in this experiment were converted, via the direct approach discussed above, from a Yamaha EF 1000iS gasoline spark-ignited generator to operate on multiple fuels including: gasoline, JP-8, heavy fuels (up to diesel #2), alcohols, natural gas, propane gas, and others. The generator is equipped with a 50 cc, overhead valve (OHV), air-cooled, single cylinder, 4-stroke engine. A DC/AC inverter with standard 120 VAC, 60 Hz rated for 600 W nominal output and 1000 W peak output (fuel dependent). Additionally, a DC/DC converter gives an auxiliary 12 VDC rated for 8 A or 96 W output. The system dry weight is approximately 14.5 kg (32.0 lbs), wet weight (includes full fuel tank, 2.5 L of JP-8 and 0.3 L oil) 16.3 kg (35.9 lbs). The system dimensions are 45.4 cm (17.9 in) X 30.5 cm (12.0 in) X 37.5 cm (14.7 in), which includes any protrusions from the main body. The system may be run in either normal or economy mode. Economy mode increases fuel economy by lowering the idle speed and overall engine speed up to a power demand specified as ~600 W. The generator is equipped with a pull start mechanism, choke, and starting fluid for start-up.

Voltage/Current: Power was calculated with voltage and current readings taken on the Agilent data acquisition unit (model # 39470A). Voltage is monitored directly; current was monitored with Dent Instruments current transducer (CT) (Model # CT-SC-S-0050) accurate within +/- 1%.

Load: A 1200 W resistive AC load was used. Output was varied with Automation Technology variac (model # TDGC-3KM).

Fuel Consumption/Efficiency: Fuel consumptions was tested using an external fuel tank and Ohaus Adventure Pro series scale (model # AV8101), accurate within +/- 0.2 g, with most recent calibration in Aug 2013. The experiment was automated with a National Instruments Lab View program designed to record fuel weight approximately every 5 minutes.

Exhaust Analysis: Engine exhaust was collected at the tail pipe using a Dyne Systems Gas Analyzer (Model # XM2000). Gases collected were hydrocarbons (HC) (n-hexane) accurate within +/- 4 ppm, carbon monoxide (CO) accurate within +/- 0.02%, carbon dioxide (CO_2) accurate within +/- 0.3%, nitrogen oxides (NO_x) accurate within +/- 25 ppm, and oxygen (O_2) accurate within +/- 0.1%. Modeling was done using Ansys CFX software using the computational fluid dynamics (CFD) tool.

Results and Discussion

Fuel consumption was run initially upon receipt of the system and every 100 hours subsequent. The fuel consumption was run in both normal and economy mode.

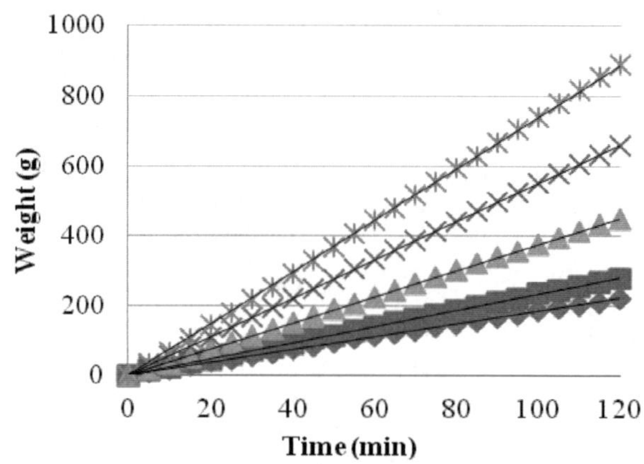

Figure 1. Average fuel consumption at 200 hours of lifetime in economy mode at no load (blue ◆), 200 W (red ■), 400 W (green ▲), 600 W (purple ×), and 800 W (light blue ✳). The slope of the trend line gives the fuel consumption in g/min.

Displayed in Figure 1 is the average fuel consumption at 200 hours lifetime in economy mode at no load, 200 W, 400 W, 600 W, and 800 W. The fuel consumption is taken as the slope of the trend line fit to the data. Fuel consumption data is as expected where the least amount of fuel is consumed at no load, and the most amount of fuel is consumed at 800 W.Fuel efficiency is calculated with the fuel consumption using the following equations:

$$\eta_{\text{fuel}} = W_{out} / W_{in}$$

$$W_{in} = \text{FC} * \text{LHV}_{\text{JP-8}}$$

Where η_{fuel} is fuel efficiency, W_{out} is the output power, W_{in} is the theoretical input power. FC is the fuel consumption in kg/hr, $\text{LHV}_{\text{JP-8}}$ is the lower heating value of JP-8 equal to 12017 Whr/kg. The average fuel efficiency vs. power output at 200 hours lifetime in both normal and economy mode are displayed in Figure 2.

The economy mode shows better fuel efficiency at and below 600 W. The system electronically regulates the fuel consumption by decreasing idle speed and thereby overall engine speed up to ~600 W. While this does increase fuel efficiency it is done at the expense of stability. For example, if a large load is instantaneously introduced while the system is in economy mode stabilization becomes difficult and often results a system stall or the throttle control revolving between high and low engine speed for an extended period of time. At greater loads the fuel efficiencies should be approximately equal as the power demand becomes sufficiently large however this does not seem to be the case. The discrepancies are likely due to the instability.

The fuel efficiency at 600 W was used to determine the performance of the system over its lifetime. Lifetime hours were accumulated by running in normal mode at nominal output, 600 W, on JP-8. Figure 3 shows the average fuel efficiency at 600 W, normal and economy mode, at receipt of systems, 100, 200, and 300 hours lifetime.

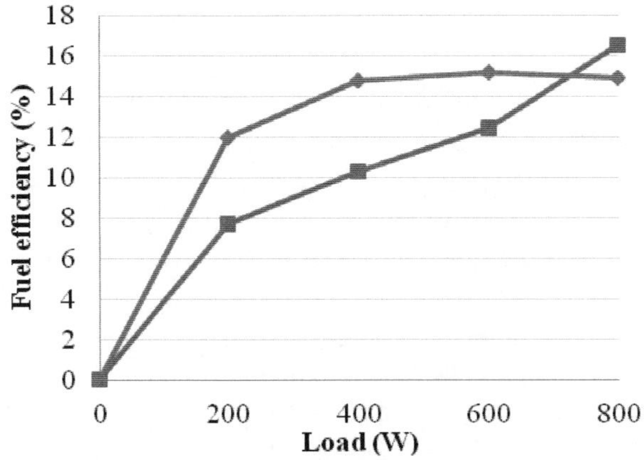

Figure 2. Average fuel efficiency vs load at 200 hours of lifetime in both normal (red ■) and economy (blue ◆) mode.

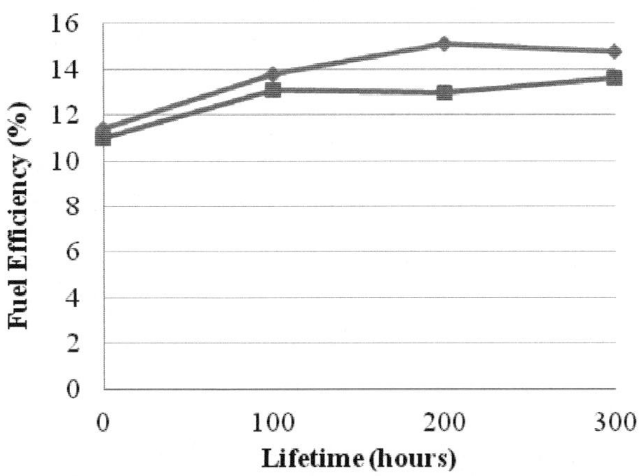

Figure 3. Average fuel efficiency (%) at 600 W vs. lifetime in both normal (red ■) and economy (blue ◆) mode.

The fuel efficiency is trending slightly up over the lifetime suggesting a "breaking-in" period. As testing continues it is expected to level off before eventually tapering into a downward trend. Additional work is needed for a more complete picture of the systems lifetime performance.

Emissions data was collected at 220 hours lifetime in both normal and economy modes for multiple fuels: JP-8, diesel, propane, and isopropyl alcohol; at multiple loads: no load, 200 W, 400 W, 600 W, and 800 W; and for multiple gases: hydrocarbons (HC, n-hexane), nitrogen oxides (NO_x), carbon monoxide (CO), carbon dioxide (CO_2) and oxygen (O_2). The discussion will be limited to JP-8, however, a complete summary of all fuels can be given with correspondence with the author. Figure 4 and 5 are graphical representation of the emissions profile of JP-8 in normal and economy mode respectively.

From figure 4 and 5 it can be seen that as the load increases the CO levels increase and CO_2 levels decrease, O_2 levels remain relatively low, largely less than 1%. This is an indication that combustion efficiency decreases with load

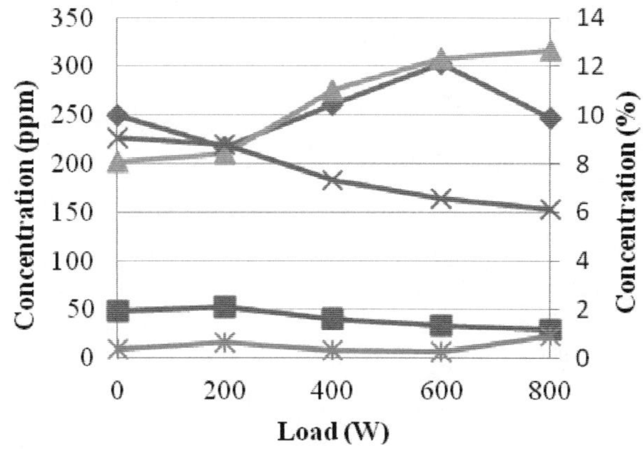

Figure 4. Emissions profile of JP-8 in normal mode. Gases are represented by HC (blue ◆, left hand axis, ppm), NO_x (red ■, left hand axis, ppm), CO (green ▲, right hand axis, %), CO_2 (purple ×, right hand axis, %), and O_2 (light blue ✳, right hand axis, %)

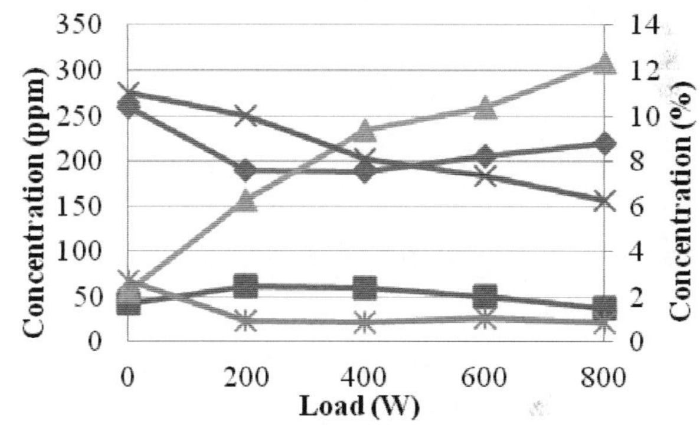

Figure 5. Emissions profile of JP-8 in economy mode. Gases are represented by HC (blue ◆, left hand axis, ppm), NO_x (red ■, left hand axis, ppm), CO (green ▲, right hand axis, %), CO_2 (purple ×, right hand axis, %), and O_2 (light blue ✳, right hand axis, %)

demand and the system is likely burning fuel rich. The combustion efficiency is calculated using the following equations:

$$\eta_{comb} = 100\% - (LHV_{out} / LHV_{in}) * 100\%$$
$$LHV_{out} = \dot{m}_{CO}(LHV_{CO}) + \dot{m}_{HC}(LHV_{HC})$$
$$LHV_{in} = \dot{m}_{JP\text{-}8}(LHV_{JP\text{-}8})$$

Where η_{comb} is combustion efficiency, LHV_{out} is the total mass loses of unconverted hydrocarbons or CO in kW, LHV_{in} is the fuel heating value in kW. $\dot{m}_{CO}$ is the mass flow rate of CO in kg/sec, LHV_{CO} is the lower heating value of CO at 10112 kJ/kg, $\dot{m}_{HC}$ is the mass flow rate of hydrocarbons in kg/sec, LHV_{HC} is the lower heating value of hexane at 45101 kJ/kg, $\dot{m}_{JP\text{-}8}$ is the mass flow rate of JP-8 in kg/sec, and $LHV_{JP\text{-}8}$ is the lower heating value of JP-8 at 42,900 kJ/kg. Figure 5 shows the combustion efficiency of both normal and economy modes. As the load demand increases the throttle control allows for more fuel in enter

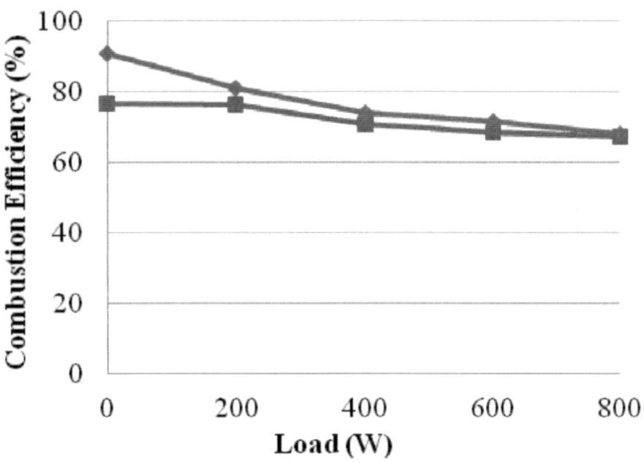

Figure 6. Average combustion efficiency vs. load in both normal (red ■) and economy (blue ◆) mode.

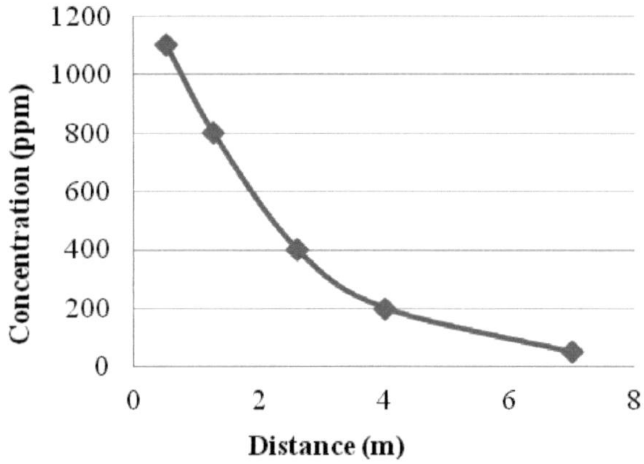

Figure 7. CO dispersion distance vs. concentration with the exhaust port as the origin. The line between data points is to guide the eye and does not represent data.

the combustion chamber. This increase in fuel consumption causes the inefficiencies to become more pronounced.

Emissions data is of interest for several reasons. Of primary importance is safety of the soldiers in the surrounding area. As a guideline one can look to the Occupational Safety & Health Administration (OSHA) permissible exposure limits (PEL) for air contaminants over an 8-hour period. The PEL for CO is 50 ppm. [4] By comparison Figure 4 for JP-8 at 600 W shows a value of 123,200 ppm, CO, at the exhaust port. Given the initial concentration of CO, exhaust flow (7.5 slpm CO), exhaust temperature (recorded experimentally) 220 °C (428 °F), and a slight wind speed (0.5 m/s) in the direction of the exhaust plume a model was developed and exploited to generate Figure 7. Figure 7 shows the approximate concentration at a given distance directly behind the tailpipe. It should be noted that the model has not been confirmed and requires some

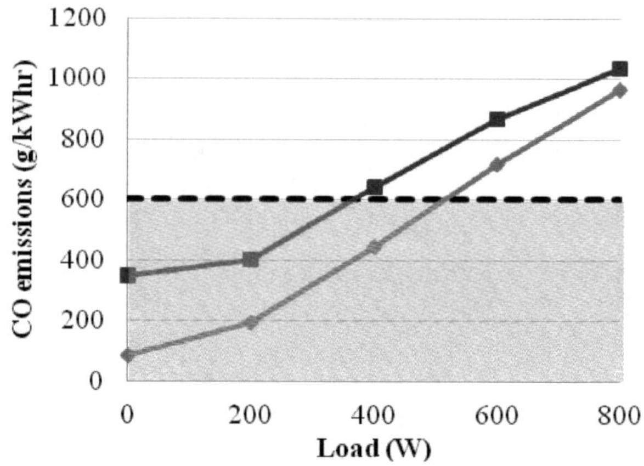

Figure 8. CO emissions of JP-8 vs load in both normal (red ■) and economy (blue ◆) mode. The dotted demarcation line represents the EPA limit of CO, 603 g/kWhr. The green box is within spec.

experimentation to confirm the results. With this data a "safe" distance directly behind the tailpipe can be estimated. At approximately 7 m (22 ft.), the CO concentration has dissipated to 50 ppm.

Environmental concerns may also be of interest. As a guideline the Environmental Protection Agency (EPA) standard for air contaminants of a 50 cc engine for CO is 603 g/kWhr. [5] Figure 8 shows CO emission at a given load in both normal and economy mode. Some additional work will be needed in order to bring the system within EPA specification.

Conclusions

While this system will require some additional work it does meet many of the requirements put forth by the US Army and shows great promise for future efforts.

References

1. K. E. Yancosek, T. Roy, M. Erickson, "Rehabilitation programs for musculoskeletal injuries in military personnel" *Current Opinion in Rheumatology*, vol. 24, no. 2, pp. 232-236, 2012.
2. K Graham, J. Allen, "Capability Development Document for Small Unit Power" Vol. 1, pp. 15-16, 26 September 2013.
3. "Detailed Specification of Turbine Fuel, Aviation, Kerosene types, Nato F-34 (JP-8), NATO F-35, and JP-8+100" *MIL-DTL-83133*, Jan. 29, 1992.
4. Occupational Safety & Health Administration, 29*CFR* 1910.1000 Table Z-1.
5. Environmental Protection Agency, 40 *CFR* 1054.103Table 1, April 2014.

Locational Marginal Pricing for Optimization of Energy Informed Operations

Thomas F. Podlesak and Darren Z. Stephens
Power Division
U.S. Army Communications-Electronics Research, Development and Engineering Center
5100 Magazine Road, Aberdeen Proving Ground, MD 21005

Abstract: *Energy Informed Operations seeks to optimize the utilization and provision of energy on the battlefield. Using principles similar to the civilian Smart Grid, it provides energy for military operation in the most effective manner.*

It does this by use of renewable energy, energy storage and the economical provision of more conventional resources such as fuel and replacement batteries.

To deliver fuel most efficiently, it is possible to use a variation of the technique used for electric power transmission known as locational marginal pricing. In the wholesale electrical market, generated energy is offered to consuming utilities at a locational marginal price, in units of dollars per megawatt-hour. This energy is offered at the point of generation and is placed on the complex electrical network as a fungible quantity, with no initial reference to the point of use except as a financial transaction. Its flow is governed solely by the parameters of the entire network. The price consists not only of the cost of the energy with overhead (depreciation of generation assets, maintenance of plant, etc.) but with a cost of congestion. Injection of energy at a given point that would result in the overloading of a transmission line would cause a high price, while injection at a point where the result would be an even sharing of the transmission assets would result in a lower price. The consuming utility inevitably chooses the least expensive energy. The system is interactive and once the particular transaction is made, then and only then is the consuming utility's removal of energy factored into the operation of the transmission network, thus altering the next set of locational marginal priced energy to be offered.

Renewables have a most unusual impact on these activities, often offering energy at negative price-in other words paying the utility to take the power-to satisfy minimum annual power generation requirements necessary to gain tax advantage.

These principles may be applied to the distribution of fuel to and on the battlefield. A price may be set for a given amount of fuel based on two factors. The first is the fundamental cost of the fuel. This includes not only the base cost of a unit of fuel but also the amount of fuel necessary to bring the fuel to the point of consumption.

Transport of fuel by air, as opposed to ground, may result in a large quantity of fuel being used to transport the given amount of fuel. For example, 25 gallons of fuel may be needed to transport just one gallon of fuel. This is the source of the often misquoted prices of hundreds of dollars per gallon fuel delivered on the battlefield. The other factor is the time necessary to transport a unit of fuel. For example, what may take twenty hours to transport via ground may take only four via air, thus negating the high initial unit cost of air transport. An additional factor is the probability of successful delivery, where the danger of attack on a ground based fuel convoy results in a lower probability of success than that of air delivery. These two quantities can be added to yield a local marginal fuel price, expressed in pseudo dollars, since the former quantity may be truly expressed in monetary units, but the latter cannot, yet is of similar magnitude and thus the analogy is reasonable. As in the case of civilian power transmission, renewables can play a substantial role in the reduction of fuel needed with a commiserate reduction in cost of delivery, including the cost to transport a renewable system to point of use as opposed to continuous transport of fuel to supply generators dedicated to a military unit.

We have devised a simple Excel spreadsheet model that calculates these local marginal prices using this methodology. It accounts for delivery of fungible fuel into the theatre of operations and particular routing over multiple paths to minimize congestion and assure timely delivery. It will account for renewables, as well as energy storage, for fuel transport cost avoidance and may be expanded to account for delivery of other commodities, such as batteries.

Keywords: locational marginal pricing; power generation, energy informed operations, renewables.

Introduction

The Power Division of the U.S. Army Communications-Electronics Research Development and Engineering Center (CERDEC) has a major program entitled Energy Informed Operations (EIO) [1]. This effort seeks to establish optimal control over the provision of energy to fielded Army units via data networking between power sources and loads. This will enable energy demand to be most efficiently matched to energy supply and to prioritize loads. This will reduce the amount of fuel needed to be transported to the battlespace while assuring the sufficient fuel is available for mission support.

EIO makes use of the technologies and techniques being developed for Smart Grids [2] and microgrids [3]. One particularly useful technique is known as Locational Marginal Pricing.

Locational Marginal Pricing [4] is used by the commercial electric utility industry to regulate the transmission of electrical power. The transmission of electric power is controlled by Independent System Operators (ISOs), which are not for profit entities owned by the electric utilities in a large specified area. These entities typically cover several states and hundreds, if not thousands, of miles of high tension electrical transmission lines. Energy is offered at a particular price at the point of generation, and the member utilities may make offers to buy energy at that price. The price is composed of not only the raw price of the energy and any associated overhead costs, but is also structured to encourage efficient transmission of the electrical energy.

The transmission line network is a complex electrical network with sources and users of energy. Power generators inject power into the network and power users withdraw energy from the network. This places the network in a constant state of flux. Depending on where energy is being injected or withdrawn, electrical power flows in an essentially uncontrolled manner and would, if not properly governed, do so extremely inefficiently, with excessive amounts of electrical current flowing down certain transmission lines and nearly none down others.

To mitigate this situation, Locational Marginal Pricing is used. The electrical transmission network is solved for given amounts of energy injection and withdrawal. Through sophisticated computer based real time analysis using calculus of variations and solving for Lagrange multipliers, an optimal configuration is determined. These Lagrange multipliers are assigned to each node of injection, with the most optimal solutions resulting in the lowest values of the Lagrange multipliers. These Lagrange multipliers are designated as the Locational Marginal Prices, and are commonly expressed in terms of dollars per megawatt-hours of electrical energy. Utilities seeking to buy energy would naturally gravitate to the source offering the lowest price. The buying utility would offer to buy energy at the stated price, the energy producer would agree to sell at that given price, the producer would inject that energy into the transmission line network and the utility would begin to draw the agreed upon amount of energy from the network. This of course, alters the operation of the network, so a new set of Locational Marginal Prices is then calculated, in anticipation for the next energy transaction. This effort is done in real time, at intervals of a few minutes, 24 hours a day, 365 days a year.

It is our intent to use a similar method of energy offering to provide energy to fielded military units. Instead of megawatt-hours, the energy will be measured in gallons of JP-8 military fuel, and instead of high tension electrical transmission lines, the method of transportation will be military vehicles.

A comprehensive study of supply of fuel to the battlespace has been performed by the Institute for Defense Analysis [5]. Their study examined the supply of fuel to a humanitarian aid mission in Africa. Fuel was introduced into theatre by sea to a Sea Port of Debarkation, transported to an Air Port of Debarkation, then transported to a Forward Operating Base (FOB) and then to a series of combat outposts (COs). Fuel was to be transported by the following vehicles

- 5000 gallon tanker trucks
- UH-60 Blackhawk helicopters
- CH-47 Chinook helicopters
- C-130 Hercules fixed wing aircraft
- C-17 Globemaster fixed wing aircraft

This study accounted for all users of fuel, including power generation, and fuel for ground and air vehicles. CERDEC Power Division's mission is restricted to power generation and so our model did not consider fuel for vehicles. The largest consumer of fuel in wartime is not vehicular, but power generation [6], so restricting our study to this one aspect is most relevant

The amount of fuel used by a particular installation is normally very difficult to quantify. The prior study solved this problem by expressing daily fuel consumption as a function of the number of personnel at each installation, specifically 2.55 gallons of fuel per day per person. In our study, we also use this metric. In a similar vein, the Corps of Engineers has determined that each person at one of these installations requires 700 W of power generation capability; thus an installation with 100 people would require 70 kW power generation capability [7].

The key parameters for the vehicles, which will determine the amount of fuel necessary to deliver a given amount of fuel are summarized in Table I.

Table I. Key parameters of fuel delivery vehicles

Vehicle	Capacity (gal.)	Speed (km/hr)	Mileage (km/gal)
5000 gallon truck	5000	50	10
UH-60	1142	240	2
CH-47	3571	240	0.7
C-130	6428	540	0.63
C-17	24300	833	0.38

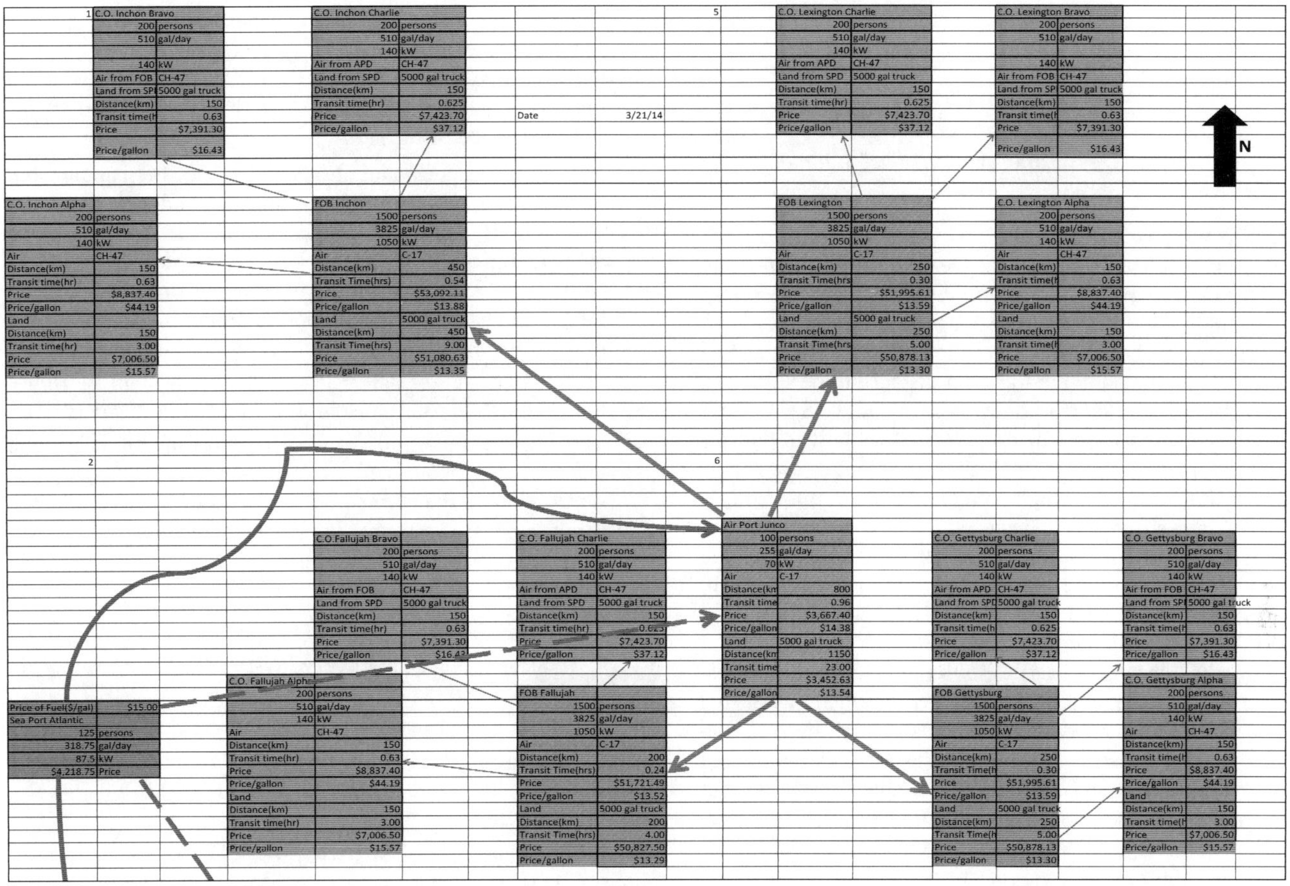

Figure 1. Northwest quadrant of the Large Fuel Model, showing Sea Port of Debarkation(extreme left-turquoise blue), Air Port of Debarkation (center-darker blue), four Forward Operating Bases (green) and twelve Combat Outposts (orange). Land routes from Sea Port to Air Port are shown solid, air routes dashed. Lines emanating from the bottom of the Sea Port are to the southwest quadrant..

The Large Fuel Model

A quadrant of the Large Fuel Model is shown in Figure 1. The operative word here is large, so only one quarter of the entire model is shown in the illustration. Full size, the printed (analogous to a map) model measures approximately 685 mm x 915 mm (27 by 36 inches). Using a scale of 100 km per inch, the area covered by the model is approximately 2700 x 3600 km (1700 x 2200 miles), a large area approximately the size of the United States. The large size was chosen to provide significant distances between installations. The model is an Excel spreadsheet, selected for ubiquitous familiarity, ease of use and inherent openness of the software. It is the intent that this software be made widely available for general use which predicates the use of a somewhat simple but highly accepted software package. The model shows the interaction between two Sea Port of Debarkation, designated Atlantic and Pacific. The Sea Ports each service two Air Ports of Debarkation, for a total of four, each designated by species of birds (Eagle, Osprey, etc.). Each Air Port services four Forward Operating bases, for a total of sixteen, each designated by a famous battle (Gettysburg, Yorktown, etc.). Each FOB services three Combat Outposts, for a total of forty-eight, designated by name of the associated FOB and the designation Alpha, Bravo or Charlie (Gettysburg Alpha, Yorktown Charlie, etc.) Each of the blocks corresponding to any of the basing entity shows the number of personnel, and the corresponding power generation requirement and daily fuel consumption, the distance to the supplying entity, a selection box for designating the air and land vehicles proposed to deliver the fuel, and calculations of the total delivered price and price per gallon for each method of delivery.

Fuel Pricing was calculated by the following formula. Note the mix of units (e.g. gallons and kilometers). This reflects common usage.

$$P = C(1+D/cM) \quad \text{where} \qquad (1)$$

P=total cost per gallon, $

C=cost per gallon delivered to Sea Port

D=distance transported, km

c=capacity of transport vehicle, gallons

M=mileage of transport vehicle, kilometers per gallon

Preliminary Results

The first results of this analysis were somewhat surprising, in that there was very little difference between the prices per gallon of fuel delivered by air versus by land. Assuming the base price per gallon delivered to the Sea Port is $15/gallon and the transport distance to be 1000 km, the price per gallon for delivery by land is $15.60 per gallon and, worst case scenario, the price to deliver via UH-60 helicopter is $28.50 per gallon. In both cases, it is assumed that each vehicle returns to its origin empty. These values may be explained by the relatively low amount of fuel to transport a gallon of fuel, in this case 0.04 per gallon via land and only 0.87 per gallon via the UH-60 helicopter. We assume, due to the large quantities of fuel needed to be supplied (a 5000 gallon truck would not supply the needs of a FOB for two days) that each vehicle is carrying a full fuel load. In this case, 200 gallons of fuel are required to transport 5000 gallons of fuel via land and 1000 gallons of fuel is required to transport 1147 gallons of fuel by air- doubling of the price of the delivered fuel, but much less than the widely reported hundreds of dollars per gallon fuel cost. This figure is only plausible if, for example, 1000 gallons of fuel were used to transport 40 gallons of fuel, which at $15/gallon would result in $390/gallon fuel.

Turning now to the best case scenario, transporting fuel via a C-17 tanker aircraft results in a delivered charge of $18/gallon, which is almost as economical as transporting the fuel by truck. This is because of the increased capacity of the aircraft (24300 gallons versus 5000), even though the aircraft travels only 0.38 kilometers per gallon versus the 10 for the truck.

It would seem reasonable to transport fuel, whenever possible via air as opposed to land. This was the conclusion of the prior study and we concur, based on the above analysis. Two more factors enhance the argument.

The first is the notion of locational marginal price, which accounts for raw cost plus minimizing the cost due to congestion. In the case of the electrical transmission network, this is a complex calculation. In this case, the key quantity is much simpler: the product of the initial cost by the delivery time. Lower initial cost, lower price. Shorter transport time, lower price. Obtaining a locational marginal price based on these criteria should have a significant impact, taking the above example of a 1000 km distance, requiring 20 hours by truck and an hour and 15 minutes by C-17. Another factor to be considered is the availability of transport, in that a more expensive form of transport may be used if a cheaper form is unavailable. This would extend to alternative sources of fuel, in that transport may be available at an alternate source site and it may have a lower marginal price than that of waiting for transport at the prime site.

The second factor is the often cited loss of life encountered by road convoys in recent conflicts. Prado et.al. [8] has analyzed data from Afghanistan and has determined an average figure of 90 deaths per 250 million gallons fuel delivered. Using the common estimate of the value of a human life as $6 million, this adds approximately $2 to the price of gallon of fuel delivered via ground. This extra cost further reduces the gap between air and ground transport, not even considering the intangible cost of human lives..

This will be applied to future versions of the model. Other areas of expansion will be the inclusion of renewables, which, like wind farms on transmission networks, will result in negative pricing due to fuel avoidance. These will be augmented by energy storage, again reducing fuel supply needs.

References

1. DeJong, Marnie, "Energy Informed Operations," *Army Technology*, vol. 2, no. 1, pp. 8-9, January 2014
2. Schweppe, Fred C.et.al , "Homeostatic Utility Control," *IEEE Transactions on Power Apparatus and Systems,* Vol. PAS-99, no. 3, pp. 1151-1163, May/June 1980
3. Lasseter, Robert H., "Microgrids and Distributed Generation," *Journal of Energy Engineering*, Vol. 133, pp. 144-149, September 2007
4. Cheverez-Gonzalez, Daniel, and DeMarco, Christopher L., "Laplacian Structure in Power Network Constraints and Inherent Zonal Price Regions," *Proceedings of 38th North American Power Symposium*, Carbondale, IL, pp. 303-309, 2006
5. Hurley, William J. et. al, "The Operational Value of Reductions in Fuel Demand in a Contingency Basing Operation," Institute for Defense Analysis Paper P-5044, Alexandria, VA April 2013 .
6. Report of the Defense Science Board Task Force on DoD Energy Strategy, "More Fight-Less Fuel", p. 44, February 2008.
7. Vavrin, John, "Power and Energy Considerations at Forward Operating Bases," e2s2.ndia.org/pastmeetings/2010/tracks/Documents/9874.pdf, June 16, 2010
8. Prado, Valentina et.al., "A Systematic Thermodynamic analysis of Fuel Consumption at Forward Operating Bases", *Proceedings of the 2011 IEEE International Symposium on Sustainable Systems and Technology*

Evaluation of Alane as a Hydrogen Storage Material for Wearable Power Applications

Kyle N. Grew[1], Zachary B. Brownlee[2], Kailash C. Shukla[3], & Deryn Chu[1]

[1] Sensors & Electron Devices Directorate
U.S. Army Research Laboratory
Adelphi, MD, USA 20783

[2]Dept. of Civil & Mechanical Engineering
U.S. Military Academy at West Point
West Point, NY, USA

[3]U.S. Army Natick Soldier Research Development & Engineering Center
U.S. Army Natick Soldier Systems Center
Natick, MA, USA 01760

Corresponding Author Email: kyle.n.grew.civ@mail.mil

Abstract: *Fuel cell systems can provide a large gravimetric energy density, which makes them attractive for soldier wearable power sources. Such a system also needs to be small, light, rugged, safe, and come at a reasonable cost. The choice of fuel and how it is stored and managed goes a long way often goes a long way to determine how these issues are met. Hydrogen (H_2) fuel offers the largest specific energy and is the easiest to electrochemically oxidize; however, it is not easy to store and transport. Aluminum hydride (AlH_3), commonly known as Alane, has been proposed as a solid state hydrogen storage material offering storage capacities (10 %wt hydrogen); much greater than standard chemical- and metals-hydrides. Alane offers a mildly endothermic dehydrogenation, meaning that hydrogen release is thermally controlled. While these are attractive material properties, the practical requirements for the use of Alane as a hydrogen storage material for wearable fuel cell systems needs to be explored. This paper examines the thermally activated dehydrogenation process for Alane for a wearable power source. This proceeding focuses on potential hydrogen and energy losses which could occur during cycling.*

Keywords: Wearable power; Alane; hydrogen storage; fuel cell system.

Introduction

One of the burdens placed on our soldiers is the weight they carry in the field. Among the more significant contributors is that which is attributed to the energy (and any associated conversion device) they must carry with them to sustain their operations. Integrating power sources with increased energy densities, such as fuel cell technologies, can provide a means to lighten the load carried by our soldiers.

There are a limited number of practical types of fuels and fuel cells which can be used for a wearable/portable fuel cell of relatively low power (e.g., 25 W). Direct methanol fuel cell (DMFC) and the reformed methanol fuel cell (RMFC) utilize the large specific energy and ease of storage/use of liquid methanol fuel to provide exceptional energy densities; cost and size of balance of plant are ongoing challenges. These fuel cell systems typically use acidic proton exchange membranes (PEMs); however, there are recent efforts to integrate alkaline anion exchange membranes (AEMs) to address present limitations. Alternatively, PEM and AEM based fuel cells have also been considered with a H_2 fuel; stored as a chemical- or metal-hydride. Hydrides typically have issues with complete H_2 utilization and low storage capacity, which have limited their adoption.

In this study, we explore Alane as a solid hydrogen storage material. Alane undergoes an endothermic dehydrogenation process when heated, decomposing to H_2 and aluminum (Al). It has a reasonable volumetric hydrogen capacity with a density of $\rho_{AlH_3}\left(= 1480\,\frac{kg}{m^3}\right)$ and a gravimetric H_2 capacity of greater than 10 %wt, which exceeds typical chemical- and metal-hydrides [1]. For the purposes of this work, we explore the use and integration of an Alane hydrogen storage media with a proton exchange membrane fuel cell (PEMFC) stack.

In a previous study, we showed that Alane served as an effective H_2 storage media for portable power applications [2]. It was shown that a fuel cell with a large energy density could be achieved. However, several risks associated with H_2 pressure buildup were also noted. Pressure buildup could occur if (i) fuel utilization of the fuel cell stack were to drop, and/or (ii) insufficient heat is able to be removed from system during steady state operation or during a cool down to manage the dehydrogenation (i.e., due to a non-linearity in the dehydrogenation rates) [2]. It was additionally noted that Alane is metastable and quite energetic at standard temperature and pressure; this means a significant perturbation (e.g., a projectile) could result in a catastrophic failure. Such a situation would need independent evaluation to assess associated risks. In this study, we provide additional results pertaining H_2 and energy loss during a cycle of the fuel cell system.

Fuel Cell System & Alane

We restrict ourselves to a conceptual 30 W fuel cell system for this study, which assumes 20 to 25 W of electrical power for the user with an additional 5 to 10 W of power for the balance of plant and recharging of a hybrid battery. The fuel cell stack is assumed to operate at 0.7 V/cell, which is typical of modern DuPont Nafion based H_2/air PEMFC. The balance of plant requires the addition of a heater to support the thermal dehydrogenation of Alane and integration of a hybrid rechargeable battery. Configurations with and without an integral pressure vessel for storing the released H_2 gas are considered.

The mass of Alane used as a H_2 source can be size according to its hydrogen content. The capacity for the ideal two-electron electrochemical H_2 oxidation is $C_{H_2}^{ideal} = 2F/MW_{H_2}\left(= 26.8\, A\cdot hr\cdot g_{H_2}{}^{-1}\right)$. H_2 occupies 10 %wt of the Alane, meaning the mass of the H_2 content is $m_{H_2} = 0.10\cdot m_{AlH_3}$. Assuming all of the Alane's H_2 can be dehydrogenated, the mass of Alane needed to operate the fuel cell for a specified period of time t can be determined.

$$m_{AlH_3} = \frac{P_e\cdot t}{0.1\cdot C_{H_2}^{ideal}\cdot V_e\cdot \eta_{FU}} \quad (1)$$

At 100% fuel utilization $\boldsymbol{\eta_{FU}}(=\mathbf{100\%})$, approximately $\boldsymbol{m_{AlH_3}}(=\mathbf{16\ g})$ of Alane are required per hour of operation for a fuel cell producing $\boldsymbol{P_e}(=\mathbf{30\ W})$ of power at $\boldsymbol{V_e}(=\mathbf{0.7\ V/cell})$. Therefore, 0.4 kg of Alane can provide up to 25 h of operation while occupying a volume of 0.27 L. For this study, we assume 0.4 kg cartidges of Alane are used as fuel. The Alane is assumed to be cylindrically shaped with a hollow core for a cartridge heater. Inner and outer radii of R_i(=0.01 m) and R_o(=0.03 m) are assumed, yielding a height of L_{an}(=0.108 m).

Graetz and Reilly have examined isothermal dehydrogenation of the α-, β-, and γ- polymorphs using a reactor chamber, arriving at an exponential rate equation for the dehydrogenation process [3].

$$\alpha = 1 - exp\{-(At)^b\}\ ;\ A = A_o exp\left\{-\tfrac{E_A}{RT(t)}\right\} \quad (2)$$

Equation 2 provides the extent of the dehydrogenation α as a function of time. The power $b(=2)$ indicates the type of growth during dehydrogenation [3]. An Arrhenius rate expression using an initial rate constants A_o and activation energy E_A are used.

The dehydrogenation rate $d\alpha/dt$ is an equally important property. The time and temperature are implicitly linked in Eq. 2, so the rate change in temperature dT/dt also influences the dehydrogenation process.

$$\frac{d\alpha}{dt} = exp\{-(At)^b\}b[At]^{(b-1)}A\left[\frac{tE_A}{RT^2}\frac{dT}{dt}+1\right] \quad (3)$$

In Eq. 3, the dehydrogenation rate is a function of heating rate dT/dt, temperature T, and time t. This rate is used extensively in this study as it is directly proportional to the molar rate of H_2 production $\dot{n}_{H_2}^{prod.}$.

$$\dot{n}_{H_2}^{prod.} = m\gamma_o\frac{d\alpha}{dt} = m\gamma_o\frac{d\alpha}{dT}\frac{dT}{dt} \quad (4)$$

In Eq. 4, the molar ratio $\gamma_o\left(= 0.05\ mol\,H_2/g_{AlH_3}\right)$ is used to identify the molar rate of H_2 being released from the Alane. Likewise, the pressure-volume energy accumulating in a fuel cell with a dead headed fuel supply (or internal reservoir) the reservoir PV_{H_2} is a cumulative function of time. It can increase or decrease depending upon the rates of H_2 production and consumption. Implementing the ideal gas law, the difference between the molar rates of H_2 produced from the Alane and that which was consumed by the fuel cell $\dot{n}_{H_2}^{req.} = P_e/(2FV_e)$ can be integrated to calculate the energy attributed to the pressure-volume term.

$$\begin{aligned} PV_{H_2} &= RT\int_0^t\left(\dot{n}_{H_2}^{prod.} - \dot{n}_{H_2}^{req.}\right)dt \\ &= RT\int_0^t\left(m\gamma_o\frac{d\alpha}{dT}\frac{dT}{dt} - \frac{P_e}{2FV_e}\right)dt \end{aligned} \quad (5)$$

Numeric Model

Thermal dehydrogenation of the Alane can be examined using the energy equation.

$$\rho C_p\left(\frac{\partial T}{\partial t} + \vec{v}\cdot\nabla T\right) = \nabla\cdot(k\nabla T) + \frac{1}{V}\sum\dot{E}_\iota \quad (6)$$

Alane is a fixed solid mass so internal convection is neglected. Isothermal conditions are assumed within the Alane here, so Eq. 6 simplifies to a balance between the stored thermal energy and that of the sources and sinks.

$$\rho VC^p\frac{\partial T}{\partial t} = \dot{E}_S + \dot{E}_L + \dot{E}_R \quad (7)$$

The thermal energy stored in the Alane of density ρ, volume V, and specific heat C^p is proportional to source terms $\dot{E}_\iota$. The mass may be used in place of ρV.

Equation 7 uses three source terms. The first is the heat supplied to the Alane via a cartridge heater $\dot{E}_S$ that drives thermal dehydrogenation process. Second, the convection of heat to the surroundings occurs at an effective rate of $\dot{E}_L = R_{insu}^{eff\ -1}[T - T_\infty]$ based on an effective insulation resistance R_{insu}^{eff} and ambient temperature T_∞. Third, the endothermic reaction consumes heat at a rate $\dot{E}_R = m\gamma_o\Delta H_R(d\alpha/dT)(dT/dt)$, which is a function of the heat of reaction ΔH_R and the rate of thermal dehydrogenation of the Alane $m\gamma_o(d\alpha/dT)(dT/dt)$. Rearranging Eq. 7 accordingly, the rate change in the temperature is derived.

$$\frac{dT}{dt} = \frac{\left[\dot{E}_S - \frac{(T-T_\infty)}{R_{ins}} - m\gamma_o \Delta H_R b A^b t^{b-1} e^{\{-(At)^b\}}\right]}{\left[mC_p RT^2 + m\gamma_o \Delta H_R E_a b (At)^b e^{\{-(At)^b\}}\right]} RT^2 \qquad (8)$$

Equation 8 is a nonlinear, ordinary differential equation (ODE), subject to the initial condition of the initial temperature of the Alane T_o. Solving Eq. 8 numerically, the dehydrogenation rate (Eq. 3) and molar rate of H_2 production (Eq. 4) can be determined. Pertinent properties of the Alane and model system are provided in Table 1.

Table 1. Key Alane material and model properties.

Variable	Value	Note	Reference
A_o	$1.2x10^{10}\ s^{-1}$	α-polymorph	[3]
E_A	$102.2\ kJ \cdot mol^{-1}$	α-polymorph	[3]
b	*2*	2D growth	[3]
m_{AlH_3}	*0.4 kg*	Assumed for 30 W @ 1 day	[2]
$C^p_{AlH_3}$ C^p_{Al}	$1333\ J \cdot kg^{-1} \cdot K^{-1}$ $903\ J \cdot kg^{-1} \cdot K^{-1}$	Linear dependence	[4, 5]
ΔH_R	$6.6 \pm 0.4\ kJ \cdot mol_{H_2}^{-1}$	α-AlH_3 → Al + H_2	[6, 7]
R^{eff}_{insu}	$53.7\ K \cdot W^{-1}$	Effective thermal resistance of air, H_2, and packaging	[2]
V_{H_2}	*0.3 L*	Volume available for H_2	[2]

Results & Discussion

Cycling is an important issue which should be considered with the use of Alane as a H_2 storage material for a fuel cell power sources. Several facets need to be considered: (i) H_2 loss due to sustained dehydrogenation while the process is quenched via the endothermic heat of reaction and natural convection processes, (ii) thermal energy which is lost and must be supplied back to the Alane to initiate the dehydrogenation reaction, and (iii) the electrical energy which must made available by a hybrid battery to provide the user power and heat to the cartridge heater during start-up. We address these issues in this order.

Because the dehydrogenation process is nonlinear, the H_2 lost from the Alane while the reaction is quenched is a function of the temperature and fractional extent of the dehydrogenation α_o at the onset of the cool down. This is used to calculate the energy of the H_2 that is released from the Alane while it cools. The cooling process occurs both as a result of the propagation of the endothermic reaction and through natural heat transfer modes. The energy of the H_2 that is liberated while the Alane cools is provided in Figure 1, which is based on $C^{ideal}_{H_2}$ and a PEM fuel cell stack producing 30 W (total electrical) at 0.7 V/cell. This may alternatively be shown in Figure 2 as the equivalent H_2 gas pressure for a 0.3 L volume (i.e., dead-headed anode feed and/or intermediate H_2 reservoir).

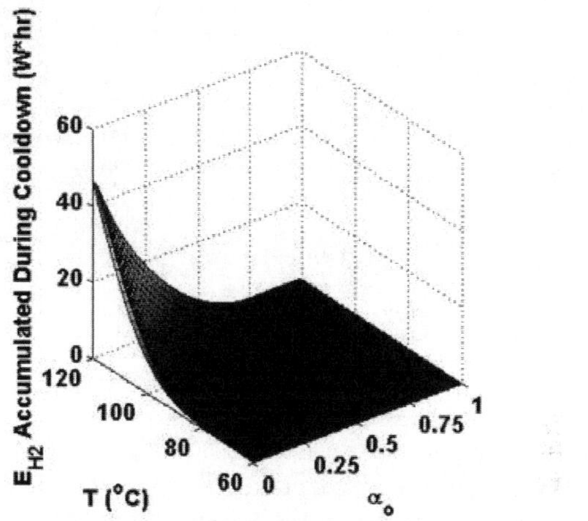

Figure 1. H_2 Energy lost during a fuel cell power cycle. H_2 lost due to dehydrogenation during cool down as a function of temperature and fractional dehydrogenation at onset of cool down.

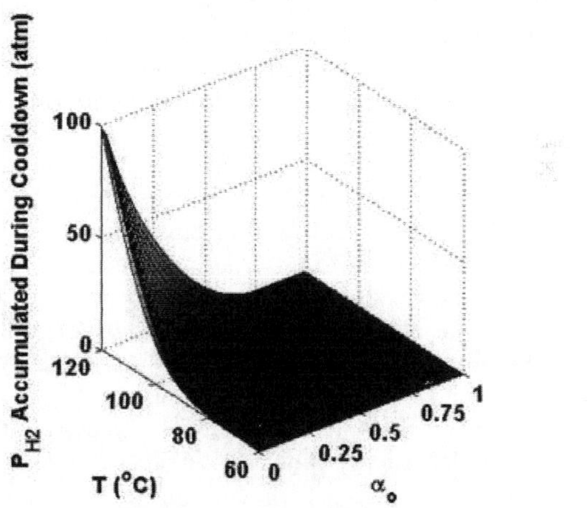

Figure 2. H_2 pressure accumulation in a sealed volume during a fuel cell power cycle as a function of temperature and fractional dehydrogenation at onset of cool down.

In examining Figures 1 and 2, several points can be made. First, especially at higher temperatures and low fractional extent of the dehydrogenation values, considerable energy loss can occur via the propagation of the dehydrogenation of the Alane during cooling. This energy lost is much more modest at lower temperatures and higher fractional extent of the dehydrogenation values (i.e., when the Alane is nearly exhausted). Second, if an internal reservoir is being used or the cell is operated such that the hydrogen feed is dead-headed to the fuel cell stack, considerable H_2

pressures could build-up and present an over-pressurization risk. Again, this is primarily a concern at elevated temperatures and low degrees of dehydrogenation. If the configuration was such that the excess H_2 is allowed to vent from the system, additional consideration should be given prior to use in confined spaces (e.g., vehicles, indoors, etc.).

The second consideration for such an analysis is the thermal energy which is lost from the Alane during such a cycle. Because R_{ins}^{eff} is large, we can do a simple calculation by neglecting convective while estimating the power P_s^{req} and energy E_s^{req} requirement to heat a 0.4 kg Alane sample. This would be energy from a hybrid battery which is supplied to a cartridge heater to initiate dehydrogenation.

$$P_s^{req} = \rho V C^p \frac{dT}{dt} + \Delta H_R \cdot \frac{\dot{n}_{req}}{\eta_{F.U.}} \quad (9)$$

$$E_s^{req} = \int_{t_o}^{t_{start}} P_s^{req} \cdot dt \quad (10)$$

Equation 9 has two components, the first is the power required to increase the temperature of the Alane from an initial temperature, taken here as $T_o (= 20\ °C)$, to the dehydrogenation temperature T_d, approximated as $T_d (= 100\ °C)$. Rather than explicitly defining the heat consumed by the dehydrogenation process, it is estimated using $\dot{n}_{req}$. The fuel utilization in Eq. 9 is taken to be 100% for a dead-headed anode.

Based on this rather simple analysis, 12.6 Whr of thermal energy are needed to raise 0.4 kg of Alane the 80 °C referenced above over a 30 minute period. These values were selected based on the nominal Alane dehydrogenation temperature and power ratings typical of a cartridge heater of this size. If 25 W of user power were also needed during this period, this would amount to an additional 12.5 Whr of power. This means 25.1 Whr of power would need to be supplied to initiate a 0.4 kg Alane fuel cartridge. Practically speaking, addition thermal energy will be needed to negate convective losses. The fuel cell should also be able to produce some power while the hydrogen pressure builds within the system; however, that is a power integration issue as our calculations assume 100% fuel utilization (i.e., energy content of that fuel was not lost).

Conclusions

This work examined Alane for use in wearable power sources. It was an extension of our previous efforts which explored issues related to the safe and practical use of Alane as a hydrogen storage material [2]. A 0.4 kg cartridge of Alane was used as a baseline for this study, which should be sufficient to enable a fuel cell to produce 30 W of total electrical power for just over one day. Aspects of energy and hydrogen loss during the cycling of a fuel cell were examined in this work.

The 0.4 kg Alane cartridges considered in this study contain enough hydrogen to produce about 750 Whr worth of energy at the specified fuel cell operating conditions (30 W total, 0.7 V per cell). Based on the calculations performed, there is more than a 3.3% penalty in energy loss attributed to the thermal and user power while initiating the dehydrogenation process. This is irrespective of if it is a new Alane cartridge or the re-initiation of a partially used one. Up to another 5% of available hydrogen energy can be lost due to continued release of H_2 during cool down (i.e., after power-down), which assumes excess is used or vented. If the excess H_2 is not released or vented during this process, there is significant risk of over-pressurization and corresponding failures. The tradeoffs of using different masses of Alane as pertains cycling require further study.

Acknowledgements

The authors gratefully acknowledge support from the U.S. Department of the Army. ZBB's contributions to this work were performed through the U.S. Military Academy's Advanced Individual Advanced Development program, carried out at the U.S. Army Research Laboratory. Discussions with Dr. Tony Thampan, U.S. Army Communications-Electronics Research, Development and Engineering Center (CERDEC), are gratefully acknowledged. The views and conclusions are those of the authors and should not be interpreted as representing official policies, either expressed or implied, of the U.S. Army Research Laboratory, U.S. Military Academy, U.S. Army Natick Soldier Research Development & Engineering Center, or the U.S. Government.

References

[1.] J. Graetz, J. J. Reilly, V. A. Yartys, J. P. Maehlen, B. M. Bulychev, V. E. Antonov, B. P. Tarasov and I. E. Gabis, "Aluminum hydride as a hydrogen and energy storage material: Past, present and future," *J Alloy Compd,* vol. 509, pp. S517-S528, 2011.

[2.] K. N. Grew, Z.B. Brownlee, K.C. Shukla and D. Chu, "Assesment of Alane as a hydrogen storage media for portable fuel cells," *J Power Sources,* vol. 217, pp. 417-130, 2012.

[3.] J. Graetz and J. J. Reilly, "Decomposition kinetics of the AlH3 polymorphs," *J Phys Chem B,* vol. 109, pp. 22181-22185, 2005.

[4.] V. E. Antonov, A. I. Kolesnikov, Y. E. Markushkin, A. V. Palnichenko, Y. Ren and M. K. Sakharov, "Heat capacity of alpha-AlH(3) and alpha-AlD(3) at temperatures up to 1000 K," *J Phys-Condens Mat, vol.* 20, 2008.

[5.] F. P. Incropera and D. P. DeWitt, *Fundamentals of heat and mass transfer*, 5th ed. (Wiley, New York), 2002.

[6.] J. Graetz and J. J. Reilly, "Thermodynamics of the alpha, beta and gamma polymorphs of AlH3," *J Alloy Compd, vol.* 424, pp. 262-265, 2006.

[7.] J. Graetz, J. J. Reilly, J. G. Kulleck and R. C. Bowman, "Kinetics and thermodynamics of the aluminum hydride polymorphs," *J Alloy Compd, vol.* 446, pp. 271-275, 2007.

Air Independent Fuel Cell System for an Autonomous Underwater Vehicle

Martin Gilljam, Torleif Lian, Helge Weydahl, Tom Cato Johannessen, Øistein Hasvold
Norwegian Defence Research Establishment (FFI)
Instituttveien 20, NO-2027 Kjeller, Norway

Abstract: *The Norwegian Defence Research Establishment (FFI) is currently developing an air independent fuel cell system for an autonomous underwater vehicle (AUV). The power supply system is based on a water cooled proton exchange membrane (PEM) fuel cell stack from Ballard. Tests in a semi-closed compartment have showed stable and reliable performance for eight hours. This included production of oxygen from hydrogen peroxide on demand and the system was operated with automated control and needed no external intervention. Container temperature and relative humidity were kept well within acceptable boundaries during tests and there was no build-up of hydrogen in the container.*

The size and shape of the fuel cell power system are designed to fit a commercial AUV from Kongsberg Maritime. If tests of the submersed power system go well and FFI succeed in developing a suitable hydrogen storage system, a sea trial is a possibility within the next project.

Keywords: Fuel cell; Hydrogen peroxide; AUV; UUV

Introduction

The Norwegian Defence Research Establishment (FFI) has been working with power sources for autonomous underwater vehicles (AUVs) for more than two decades. In cooperation with Kongsberg Maritime (KM), Statoil and Norwegian Underwater Intervention, FFI developed the HUGIN AUV, which is dominating the market for subsea survey AUVs [1]. Kongsberg Maritime is the commercial producer of the HUGIN AUV [2], which is one of several classes in the KM AUV family that also include portable systems and gliders.

FFI has developed several power sources for AUV, including sea water batteries [3], aluminum/hydrogen peroxide (Al/HP) semi fuel cells [4] and pressure tolerant Li-ion batteries. To facilitate an extended operating range, FFI is currently developing an air independent fuel cell system (see picture in Figure 1).

Calculations at FFI show that KM's commercial AUV has the potential to double its endurance by switching from Li-ion ion batteries to a fuel cell system. Different assumptions may change the outcome from these calculations in both directions. The benefit of fuel cells in AUVs is highly dependent on size, depth rating and power consumption. Optimizing AUV fuel cell systems for different choices of scenarios will result in different fuel cell types, fuel and oxidant – and will not necessary be beneficial to an AUV.

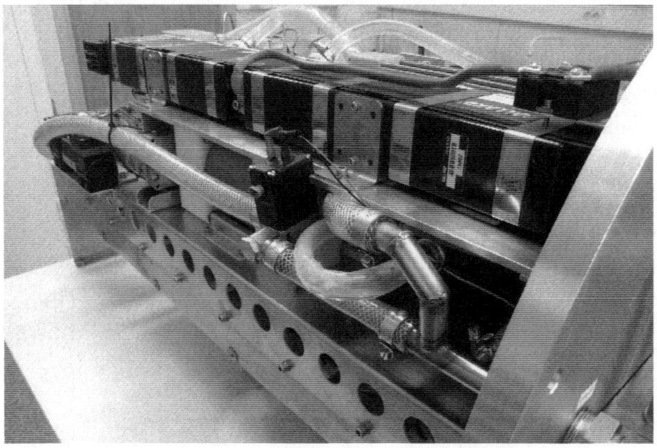

Figure 1. Picture of FFI's fuel cell system for AUV

Fuel cell powered AUVs have been demonstrated before [5, 6], but is still not commercialized. Further development, especially on storage of oxidizer and fuel, is needed before fuel cells can outperform batteries or Al/HP semi fuel cells.

Challenges for fuel cell systems on AUVs

A fuel cell system roughly consists of four sub systems: *fuel cell* with balance of plant, *electronics* (including buffer battery and DC/DC converter), *fuel* and *oxidizer*. Compared to most "normal" open air systems, only the electronics stay unchanged when entering the ocean onboard an AUV.

The most obvious constraint for an AUV fuel cell system is the *absence of air*, which means the energy system needs to include an oxidizer in addition to the fuel. This will lower the energy density compared with ground systems and gives batteries an edge over fuel cell systems. To be competitive, both oxidizer and fuel storage (and potentially conversion) system need to be compact. There are several possible solutions [7], where all have their pros and cons – much dependent on the intended use.

Fuel and oxidizer can be stored as gas in high pressure cylinders, cooled as liquid, bonded as a chemical substance or produced on demand from a chemical reaction. The aim when selecting storage and generation method is to obtain the highest volumetric and gravimetric energy density, while retaining neutral buoyancy for the AUV as a whole. Pressure cylinders ensure a simple system and are great for obtaining buoyancy, but are bulky. Liquid oxygen (LOX) has by far the highest gravimetric and volumetric oxygen density of possible oxidizers, but is complex and less favorable for small AUVs designed for deep diving. Chemically bonded oxidizers and fuel can be stored very compact. Depending on the method, they could both need a conversion system and give by-products that must be discharged.

The AUV fuel cell system must be operated in a pressure hull. Product water from the fuel cell and by-products from any oxidant or fuel conversion must be removed to minimize the needed pressure hull volume. This demands systems that will add weight and complexity. The gaseous impurities should be held at a minimum when working in a pressure hull, as they are not easily removed.

The list of challenges also includes safety issues, change in ballast and trim, controlling relative humidity and temperature in the pressure hull, and more. In addition, the fuel cell system must work autonomously for days and handle unforeseen incidents.

Description of the power supply system

The power supply system is based on a PEM fuel cell stack from Ballard (9SSL V4). This stack not designed to operate on pure oxygen, which is defining our principal approach. Figure 2 shows a schematic of the system, built into an AUV. The vessel hull protects the interior of the AUV against mechanical damage and reduces drag, but is open to the ambient sea water. All sensitive equipment, including the fuel cell, oxygen generator and electronics, must be placed inside a sealed pressure hull to protect it from the ambient sea water and pressure.

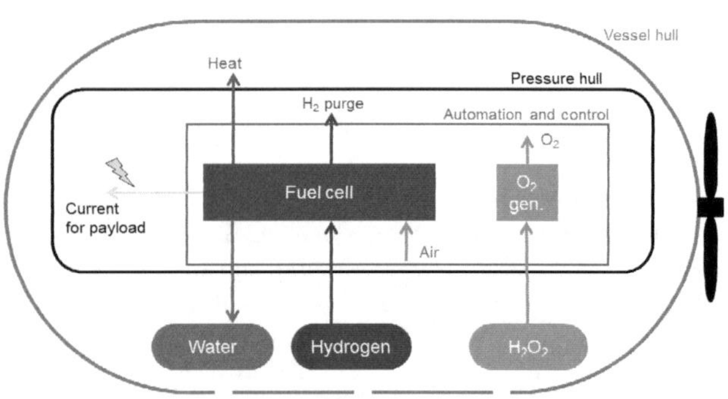

Figure 2. Schematic lay-out of the power supply system

Hydrogen is supplied from a pressure tank outside the pressure hull. Alternative storage concepts, such as methanol reforming or metal-water reactions, are also considered. The hydrogen feed is regulated to maintain the anode pressure, and a recirculation pump ensures constant flow of hydrogen through the anode. To avoid cell voltage drop, about 1 % hydrogen is purged into a hydrogen processing unit where it is combined with oxygen before fed to the internal atmosphere of the pressure hull.

Oxygen is produced on demand and fed to the internal atmosphere of the pressure hull. While air from the pressure hull is supplied to the fuel cell, this maintains a constant oxygen concentration. Oxygen is produced by catalytic decomposition of industrial grade hydrogen peroxide (HP) in an oxygen generator. HP is a liquid and can be stored outside the pressure hull in a flexible plastic container. It is pumped into the reactor where it is converted to oxygen and water. A filter removes impurities that are associated with industrial HP before oxygen is separated from water in a 0.4 MPa buffer tank. Oxygen is then mixed with the cathode outlet stream and fed to the container.

Product water, both from the fuel cell reaction and the oxygen generator, is collected in a rigid water container outside the pressure hull. A part of this water must be pumped to the ambient in order to maintain neutral buoyancy as hydrogen and HP is being consumed.

Cooling water is supplied to three heat exchangers: cooling fan in the container, oxygen cooler, exhaust air cooler and stack cooler. The stack is cooled by deionized water in a separate cooling loop.

The fuel cell stack current is controlled by an electronic load. The system is controlled and fully automated using National Instruments LabView™ and Compact FieldPoint. The system starts automatically and is self-regulating according to the set current draw.

The fuel cell system is mounted on a rack. In one end it has an end-plate with subsea connectors for gases, liquids, power and signals (see picture in Figure 3). The assembly is equipped with wheels and can slide into the pressure hull.

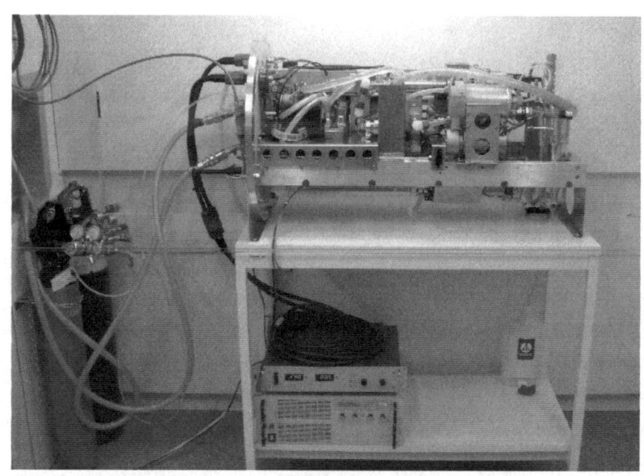

Figure 3. View of fuel cell test bench.

Without using the pressure hull, the layout also makes it easy to emulate a closed container by simply covering the rack with a plastic sheet, thus forming a semi-closed compartment. This has enabled us to study the system's ability to control hydrogen leakage, oxygen concentration, humidity and temperature, as well as circulation of gases in the container. However, pressure changes, build-up of inert gases and the thermal interface is not representative.

Test results

Results presented in this paper are from one of numeral tests conducted in a *semi-closed container*. At the time of writing, one under-water test in a *sealed container* has been performed, but results will not be presented here. Tests have mostly been carried out with the same routine: Start-up to 15 A, increase to 60 A, run at 60 A for up to 8 hours before shutdown.

The system has shown stable and reliable performance. Figure 4 shows the stack voltage during a 4 hour test in a semi-closed compartment using bottled hydrogen and industrial HP as reactants. The results show a small voltage decrease throughout the test. The same trend also appears with bottled oxygen. The loss is largely recoverable, and the cell voltage is close to the last start value in the next run.

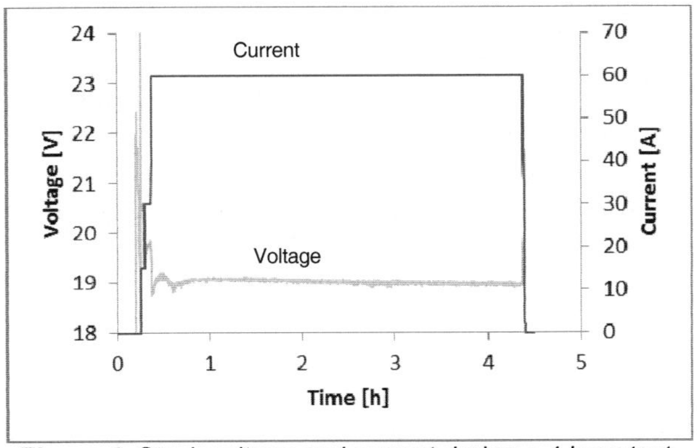

Figure 4. Stack voltage and current during a 4 hour test.

Figure 5 shows the *container conditions* during the same test. The container temperature and relative humidity reach level within acceptable limits.

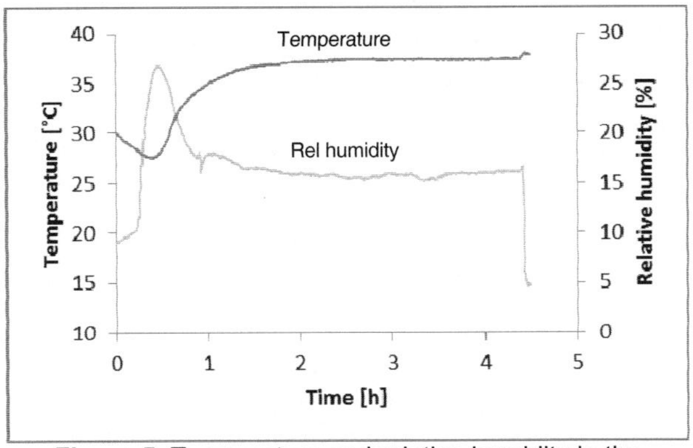

Figure 5. Temperature and relative humidity in the container during a 4 hour test.

Figure 6 shows the oxygen and hydrogen concentration in the container. The hydrogen processing unit manages to keep the hydrogen concentration practically at zero, also during the startup routine. The oxygen concentration is kept at 21% within 0.1% points.

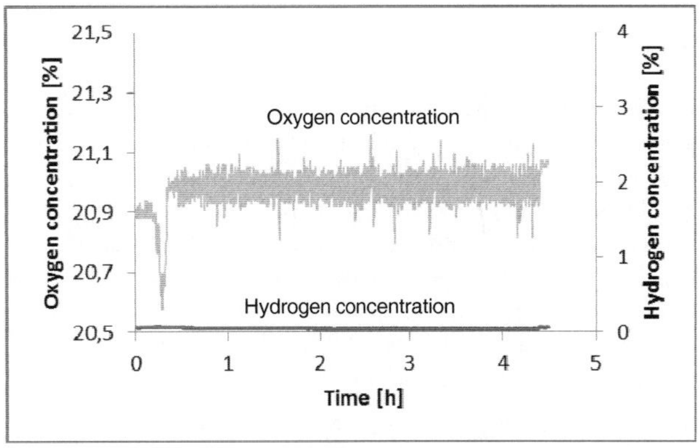

Figure 6. Oxygen and hydrogen concentration in the container during a 4 hour test.

Future work

The target for the next project will be to operate the fuel cell system in a diving AUV for several days. The AUV must operate autonomously at several hundred meters depth and include a selection of commercial sensors.

Although there is a potential for further weight and volume reduction of the fuel cell system, the size and functionality is already at target for a demonstration, so major improvements will not be prioritized at the present stage. The main focus the next few years will be to develop a safe and compact hydrogen source, build a system for ballast and trim adjustments, and a system for removal of product water against external pressure. In addition, much work will be put into construction, building and testing of the AUV fuel cell demo vehicle.

Figure 7. Power supply system in the water basin.

The first step towards a sea trial is to demonstrate the fuel cell system in a pressure hull under water for 24 hours, without any interaction from the user. The first "dive" was conducted in a water basin the same week as the submission of this paper. Figure 7 shows the pressure hull, containing the power system, immersed.

Conclusion

FFI is currently developing an air independent fuel cell system, based on a water cooled PEM fuel cell stack from Ballard. Tests in a semi-closed compartment have showed stable and reliable performance for eight hours, without intervention from an operator. This includes production of oxygen from hydrogen peroxide on demand. Container temperature and relative humidity were kept well within acceptable boundaries during tests and there was no build-up of hydrogen in the container.

The size and shape of the fuel cell power system are designed to fit a commercial AUV from Kongsberg Maritime. If tests of the submersed power system go well and FFI succeed in developing a suitable hydrogen storage system, a sea trial is a possibility within the next project.

References

1. Hasvold, Ø., N. Størkersen, "Electrochemical power sources for unmanned underwater vehicles used in deep sea survey operations", *Journal of Power Sources* no. 96, pp. 252–258, 2001.
2. www.km.kongsberg.com.
3. Hasvold, Ø., T. Lian, E. Haakaas, N. Størkersen, O. Perelman, S. Cordier, "CLIPPER: a long-range, autonomous underwater vehicle using magnesium fuel and oxygen from the sea," *Journal of Power Sources* no. 136, pp. 232–239, 2004.
4. Hasvold, Ø., K. H. Johansen, O. Mollestad, S. Forseth, N. Størkersen, "The alkaline aluminium/hydrogen peroxide power source in the Hugin II unmanned underwater vehicle", *Journal of Power Sources* no. 80, pp. 254–260, 1999.
5. Maeda, T., S. Ishiguro, K. Yokoyama, K. Hirokawa, A. Hashimoto, Y. Okuda, T. Tani, "Development of Fuel Cell AUV URASHIMA" *Mitsubishi Heavy Industries, Ltd. Technical Review*, Vol. 41, no. 6, December 2004.
6. Raugel, E., V. Rigaud, C. Lakeman, "Sea experiment of a survey AUV powered by a fuel cell system", http://archimer.ifremer.fr/doc/00122/23312/21138.pdf
7. RTO-TR-AVT-103 - Fuel Cells for Land, Sea and Air Vehicles.

Development of Soldier Wearable Fuel Cells

Deepal J. Shah, Tony Thampan, Clifford Cook, Shailesh Shah
US Army – RDECOM – CERDEC – CP&I – Power Division
5100 Magazine Road, Aberdeen Proving Ground, MD 21005

Abstract: *Communications-Electronics Research, Development, and Engineering Center (CERDEC) is developing wearable fuel cell power sources for dismounted soldier applications in the US military. These systems are based on low temperature PEM technology and utilize H_2 fuel stored as a chemical hydride. The tested systems have a high power density (28 W/kg) and a high energy density (636 Wh/kg for a 72 hr/20 W mission) and therefore can aid in minimizing the soldier's load burden [1]. Together with industrial partners, CERDEC has developed a wearable system based on AlH_3 which has been evaluated with soldiers in an operationally relevant environment. Testing was conducted at CERDEC to evaluate the performance of an aluminum hydride fuel cell prototype and determine if this fuel cell could be a viable source for wearable power. The development, test and evaluation results as well as future designs for a wearable fuel cell system are presented.*

Keywords: fuel cell; wearable; chemical hydride; alane; aluminum hydride; high power density; high energy density

Introduction

Power and energy are critical to assure communications and situational awareness capabilities for soldiers. The widespread use of communication networks such as the Tactical Warfighter Information Network (WIN-T) and the deployment of network devices such as the Joint Tactical Radio System (JTRS) and the Nett Warrior system by the US Army, increasingly allow the dismounted soldier continuous access to a secure mobile network without the need for fixed-site infrastructure. The additional information sharing capabilities lead to increased situational awareness, potentially resulting in improved mission execution. These capabilities are particularly valuable for use in an austere environment where there is limited access to resupply, vehicular transportation, and a reliable source of electricity.

However, to fully realize the aforementioned capabilities on the dismounted soldier, the soldier's total gear weight cannot increase. The average soldier carries 10-15 pounds of batteries for their electronic gear in addition to all other required equipment for a 72 hour mission. This high weight leads to lower mobility and higher risks of musculoskeletal injuries [2]. Since fuel cell systems have high gravimetric energy density, the US Army sees wearable fuel cells as a potential solution. Although all system components require miniaturization, a constant challenge has been the reduction in the volume and weight of the power devices [3]. As a result, the US Army is supporting fuel cell development in conjunction with other government agencies [4] and industrial partners. The application, performance, feedback, and future efforts of a wearable fuel cell system are discussed in this article.

Description of Wearable Fuel Cell: A wearable fuel cell can be worn on the soldier and provide power to peripheral devices that are attached to it. Examples of peripherals that would be worn on the soldier are tactical radios, Global Positioning System (GPS) receivers, and End User Devices (EUD). The fuel cell can be integrated with devices via an Integrated Soldier Power and Data System (ISPDS) or a power manager so that power can be transferred from the fuel cell to multiple peripherals simultaneously. This set up would also allow the soldier to manage the energy consumption of the peripherals and monitor the remaining energy in the fuel cell system. As part of the Lightweight Portable & Soldier Power Sources program, CP&I launched a Wearable Fuel Cell effort. As a result of the effort, a wearable fuel cell system was developed. This system contains a 60 Wh AlH_3 (Alane) fuel cartridge, a H_2 control system integrated with a low temperature PEM stack, and a 30 Wh internal battery pack. The fuel cartridge is inserted in an insulated chamber where H_2 is produced through heating.

CERDEC Testing and Evaluation of an AlH_3 Wearable Fuel Cell

CERDEC performed a series of tests on the Alane wearable fuel cell shown in Figure 1 to evaluate its performance.

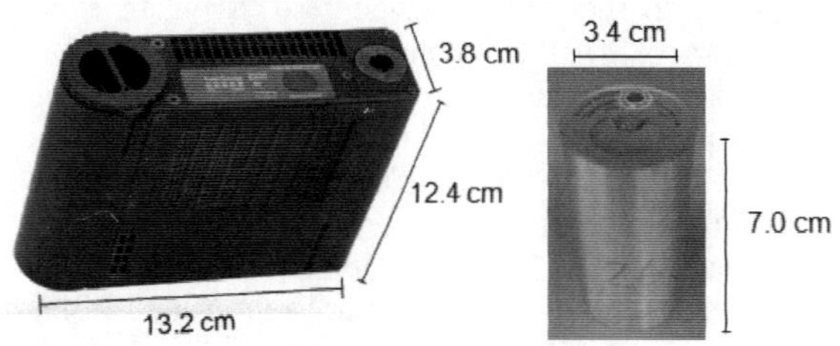

Figure 1. Alane fuel cell system shown on the left, and the cartridge on the right

The tests that were conducted were constant load, peak power, cycle, orientation, test in Molle pouch, high temperature test, and power manager test. During each of these experiments, the surface temperature of the system was measured with thermocouples and the efficiency was calculated. The threshold and objective specifications are shown in Table 1 along with the actual test results of the measured parameters.

Table 1. Comparison of Wearable Fuel Cell Specifications and Results

Parameter	Threshold	Objective	State of the Art
Power (W)	≥ 15	≥ 20	20
Peak Power and Duration	25 W for 5 min	35 W for 10 min	35 W for 10 min
Energy Density Targets for 24 hr mission	300 Wh/kg	400 Wh/kg	385 Wh/kg
Dry Weight Target (kg)	≤ 0.7	≤ 0.5	0.698
Volume Target (ml)	≤ 650	≤ 650	622
Form Factor	Thickness not to exceed 3.8 cm / 1.5 in	Thickness not to exceed 1.8 cm / 0.7 in	Thickness of 3.8 cm
Environmental Operating Temperature Range	-20°C to +50°C	-20°C to +55°C	Up to 45°C
Orientation	Transport: any orientation, Operation: any orientation		Operation: any orientation

System Measurements: The weight and volume of the system and cartridge were measured with a mass balance and caliper. The system weight and volume are 0.698 kg and 622 ml, while the cartridge weight and volume are 0.068 kg and 64 ml.

Constant Load Test: The performance of the system was monitored for 10 hours, replacing the cartridge every time the LED indicated the cartridge was depleted, for a total of three cartridge change outs. A constant current of 1.33 A was applied to the system which resulted in an average power drawn of 20.1 W and an average voltage of 15.2 V. For each cartridge that was used, the energy was measured based on power and time as shown in Table 2. Energy varied for each cartridge sample from 61 Wh to 66 Wh. Based on the best case cartridge energy density, the energy density for a 20 W/24 hr mission is calculated as 385 Wh/kg and the energy density for a 20 W/72 hr mission is calculated as 636 Wh/kg. Also shown in Table 2 is the cartridge weight loss due to H_2 production, which varies from 5 to 6 g. The percent of H_2 yield by the cartridge was calculated based on the measured weight change, the design specification for Alane material (60 g) in the cartridge and the theoretical amount of H_2 (10.1%) in Alane, as shown in Eq. 1. This percent of H_2 yielded for all the cartridges varied from 81% to 104%. The latter value is due to experimental error.

$$\%\,H2\,Yield = \frac{Weight\_Change_{Measured}}{Alane\_Packed_{Design\_Spec} \cdot Wt\%_{H2inALANE}} \qquad \text{EQ. 1}$$

Utilizing the mass loss data and the LHV of H_2 (33611 Wh/kg), the total energy from the H_2 produced can be estimated and varies from 164 Wh to 215 Wh. The battery SOC is also shown in Table 2; cartridge #23 had a data acquisition error and the EOT SOC could not be obtained. Based on the calculated total H_2 energy and the measured energy produced, excluding the contribution from the battery, a system efficiency can be calculated as shown in Eq. 2, and varies from 31% to 33%.

$$\eta = \frac{Wh_{meas} - Wh_{Battery}}{Weight\ Change_{H2} \cdot LHV_{H2}} \qquad \text{EQ. 2}$$

Peak Power Test: To determine if the system met the specified peak power, a current of 2.7 A was applied for ten minutes while the voltage and response time were monitored. As shown in Figure 2 below, the load was initially brought to 20 W and within one minute, the system power increased to 38 W. The fuel cell stack power production begins when the battery SOC is drawn down to the minimum control value. As indicated by the battery SOC, at peak power both the fuel cell stack and the internal battery provide power to meet peak demand. When the load returns to nominal power, only the fuel cell is required.

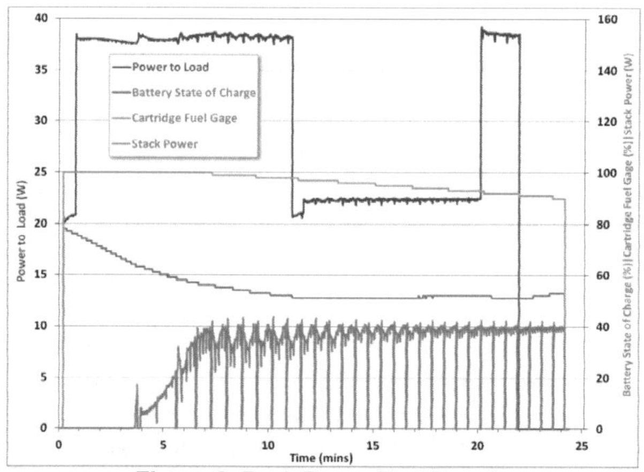

Figure 2. Peak Power Test Results

Table 2. Measured and Calculated Cartridge Parameters from Constant Load Test

Cartridge #	Meas. Energy Ex. Batt. Energy (Wh)	BOT Mass (g)	EOT Mass (g)	Weight Change	% H2 Yield	Total H2 LHV (Wh)	Eff.	BOT SOC	EOT SOC
20	61	73.1	67.6	5.5	91%	185	33%	98%	70%
23	65	72.9	68.0	4.9	81%	164	NA	67%	error
26	66	73.7	67.3	6.4	104%	215	31%	71%	75%

BOT: Beginning of Test EOT: End of Test LHV: Lower Heating Value of H2 SOC: Battery State of Charge

Cycle Test: The current applied varied from 1.5 A to 0.3 A with a 10/90 time split (23 W/6 sec and 5 W/54 sec) until the system ran out of fuel after 7.5 hours; this cycle is based on the Rifleman radio cycle. The system was able to successfully cycle power output from 5 W to 23 W indicating that the system can load follow while maintaining system control, specifically H_2 production and consumption. The calculated efficiency was 20%, significantly lower than the constant load test (30%). It is hypothesized at the lower power level (6.6 W average), the stack power output decreases but the parasitic balance of plant energy consumption remains constant.

Orientation Test: The system was tested in six orientations as depicted in Figure 3 below with a 1.25 A current for a total of three hours. The calculated efficiency was 30%, which is comparable to the measurements obtained from the constant load test. This indicates that there was no additional efficiency loss due to orientation. The maximum surface temperature measured was 48°C at the cartridge/lid interface as shown in Figure 4.

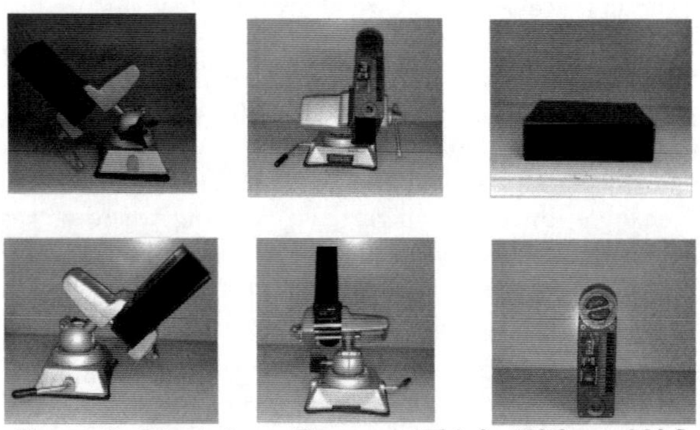

Figure 3. Orientations: Top row: 45° left, 45° front, 90° flat horizontal. Bottom row: 45° right, 45° back, 90° flat vertical.

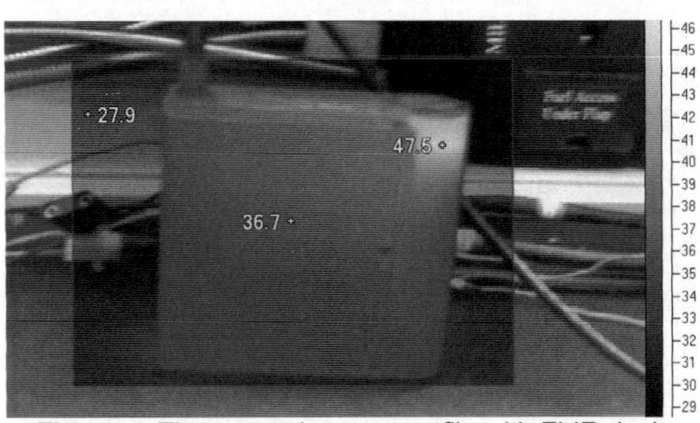

Figure 4. The system's temp. profile with FLIR device

Molle Pouch Test: A current of 1.3 A was applied to the system when it was placed in a Molle Pouch (Battery Pocket Mesh, F206131, Specialty Defense System/Specialty Plastic Product PA USA) until the system ran out of fuel in 4.8 hours. Thermocouples were placed both on the surface of the test unit as well as outside of the mesh on a potential interface with the user. The calculated efficiency was 32%, indicating that there were no efficiency losses due to Molle Pouch operation. The maximum operating temperature reached by the thermocouple in the pouch was 50°C, while the maximum temperature outside the pouch was 30°C. This test indicates that the system can be operated in a Molle Pouch and utilized for a wearable application.

High Temperature Test: To determine the baseline performance, the unit was operated in an environmental chamber at 20°C for half an hour with a constant 1.3 A load. The environmental chamber was brought up to 45°C and the fuel cell was stored at this condition for four hours. At the end of the storage period, a load of 1.3 A was applied, but the fuel cell stack did not produce power. The system went into an error state, and it is hypothesized that the stack's electrolyte looses water at high temperature resulting in low conductivity stack. The unit did not pass the threshold specification for operation at 50°C and further developmental work is required.

Power Manager Test: Since this fuel cell system is meant to be worn on the soldier, it can be used in conjunction with a power management device to provide power to multiple peripherals. The power management device intelligently distributes power from a power source to peripherals with various voltage requirements. In this experiment, the power management device was connected to the fuel cell and an Li-80 battery. Initially, due to the demand of the Li-80, about 5 A were drawn from the fuel cell which resulted in overloading the load circuitry and the system was shut down. The cable from the fuel cell to the power manager was then reprogrammed to limit the current from the fuel cell to 1.2 A. This avoided overload conditions and the fuel cell was then able to operate for 3.3 hours before it ran out of fuel and charged the Li-80 from 34% to 89% SOC via the power manager. A fuse has since been developed for overload protection.

Other Observations: General observations that were identified during the laboratory evaluation of the prototypes are:

- The control system should allow for at least 3 restarts before requiring external power. The initial system that was tested continued to operate after the fuel cartridge was depleted, utilizing power supplied from the internal battery until it was fully discharged. While this provides a longer run time, it prevents subsequent restarts with a new cartridge without first charging the battery externally. This issue has since been rectified to allow for subsequent restarts.
- In storage, the unit must be placed in storage mode to avoid trickle discharge of the battery. This can be done by switching the toggle to disable mode.
- Errors were observed on the accuracy of the fuel cartridge indicator, providing misleading remaining cartridge runtime.
- While the system passed several of the specifications, it failed to meet the high temperature specification.

- Safety: The cartridge is heated to ~180°C to release H_2 when the fuel cell is operating; however the insulation ensures the unit is safe to touch except when hot swapping a cartridge. For hot swapping a cartridge, protective gloves rated for temperatures over 100°C should be worn in case of accidental contact with the released cartridge. Once exposed to ambient air, a hot cartridge rapidly cools (< 5 minutes).

Soldier Evaluation of Wearable Fuel Cell

Soldiers had a chance to use the wearable fuel cell during the NetMod event in July 2013 and provide their feedback. The system was used to power a Rifleman Radio, Soldier PDA, and Soldier Power Manager.

Two soldiers ran the systems for a total of 27 hours in environmental conditions including high temperatures (90-100°F), high humidity, and dust. The soldiers wore the systems in various orientations, and had no issues with operation. The soldiers provided positive feedback including liking that the system was small and lightweight. They also did not notice any heat generated by the system and liked the size and weight of the cartridges. Although they did notice the purge and fan noise, they said it faded into the background and would not bring any attention to the soldier.

The soldiers also provided some constructive feedback indicating that the screw lid to change cartridges was relatively hard to open and close. Successful participation in the NetMod exercise allows the system to be classified at a TRL 6.

Figure 5. Soldiers with wearable fuel cell system mounted on the vests in Molle Pouches

Other feedback: Numerous meetings were held with Project Manager Soldier Warrior (PM SWAR) to obtain their input and feedback on the system. The main feedback that was received was a desire for the system to be thinner and conform to a Small Arms Protective Insert (SAPI) plate, increased cartridge runtime, and reduced price for the fuel cartridges.

Future Design Direction

The next system iteration will have improved cooling mechanisms so the system can operate at higher temperatures.

Additionally, the next system iteration will be designed to meet key ruggedization objectives. Preliminary ruggedization testing has been conducted for noise, solar, vibration, rain, dust, and drop and the results appear promising [5].

Taking into consideration the feedback from the Soldiers and PM SWAR, a new iteration of the system is in development. The new prototype will have an 80 Wh cartridge, and its dimensions will mimic that of a SAPI plate (17.8 x 20.3 x 2.0 cm). The cartridge lid will be easier to open and close.

A significant concern for any system is affordability. A major cost driver for this chemeical hydride system is the Alane fuel cost and efforts are being investigated to lower the Alane production cost.

Conclusion

The Alane wearable fuel cell system passed the objective targets for the nominal power test, peak power test, and start up time. The system passed the threshold requirements for weight, volume, thickness, and energy density. The system was also orientation independent and was able to operate in a Molle pouch with an external temperature that is safe for a wearable application. A key concern addressed through the cycle power test was the ability to control the H_2 production/consumption process. The system is able to load follow while maintaining H_2 fuel control. System efficiency for all the tests conducted at CERDEC was 30-33% except for the low/high power cycling where it was 20% due to the lower efficiency at lower stack power.

Through laboratory testing and limited soldier demonstrations, the system has already demonstrated that it can decrease the carried battery weight and volume by more than 50% for a 20 W/72 hr mission.

Significant improvements have been made to the system since it was tested at CERDEC. This technology seems to be promising in meeting the power demands of capabilities on dismounted soldiers.

References

1. T. Thampan, D. Shah, C. Cook, J. Novoa, S. Shah, "Development and Evaluation of Portable and Wearable Fuel Cells for Military Use," *Journal of Power Sources,* vol. 259, pp. 276-281, to be published August 2014.
2. E. Beidel, "Army Shifts Focus to Dismounted Soldiers," *National Defense Magazine*, April 2011.
3. Y. Tradjdeh, "Researchers Tackle Troops' Physical, Cognitive Challenges," *National Defense Magazine*, April 2013.
4. K N. Grew, Z B. Brownlee, K. C. Shukla, D Chu, *J. Power Sources*, vol. 217, pp. 417-430, 2012.
5. Phase I Mid and Final Project Report, CERDEC WFC20 – Wearable Fuel Cell, Ardica Technologies, September 2013.

Development and Validation of MW Scale PEM Electrolysis for Renewable Energy Storage

Stephen Szymanski, Everett Anderson, Katherine Ayers
Proton Energy Systems, d/b/a Proton OnSite
10 Technology Drive
Wallingford, CT 06492

Abstract: *With the ever-increasing addition of wind and solar renewable energy to the traditional electric grid, the need for energy storage also grows. A recent study projects the value of energy storage for wind and solar integration worldwide to exceed $30 Billion by 2023 [1]. Hydrogen from electrolysis is a promising technology for renewable energy capture as it has the capability to store massive amounts of energy in a relatively small volume. In addition, electrolysis can also provide ancillary services to the grid such as frequency regulation and load shifting resulting in multiple value streams. The hydrogen produced can alternatively be injected into the natural gas pipeline (thus making that energy carrier more green), in the production of high value chemicals such as ammonia, in upgrading of methanization-produced biogas, or used as a transportation fuel.*

Europe in particular has been committed to these pathways and making heavy investment in both materials research and system design and development as well as technology demonstration. In Germany, hydrogen is looked upon as a key part of the energy storage solution under "Energiewende," their national sustainable energy transition plan. Hydrogen provides a unique link between the electric and gas grid infrastructures (often referred to as "Power-to-Gas"). Germany is also considered the global leader in biogas energy generation, with 18,244 GWh of generation in 2012 forecasted to grow to 28,265 GWh by 2025 [2].

Water electrolysis has benefits over other hydrogen generation technologies due to the lack of carbon footprint when integrated with a renewable source of energy. Specifically, proton exchange membrane (PEM) electrolysis is a promising technology for hydrogen generation applications because of the lack of corrosive electrolytes, small footprint, and ability to generate at high pressure, requiring only water and an energy source. Several companies have already announced plans to develop megawatt (MW) commercial scale PEM electrolysis units in the 2014-2015 timeframe for these applications. There have also been recent announcements of large scale renewable energy storage project based on electrolysis.

Keywords: electrolysis; proton exchange membrane; hydrogen; energy storage; renewable energy; ancillary services; power to gas.

Introduction

Proton OnSite, the leader in PEM-based water electrolysis, is developing a MW-scale electrolyzer product in response to this emerging market demand. Proton's industrial hydrogen generators have a proven track record with more than 2000 units in customer hands in over 75 countries representing an installed base of over 10 MW. This unique product experience is invaluable in developing the larger scale product. This summary will provide an overview of Proton's current plans for introduction of a MW-scale product for the renewable energy storage market.

Electrolysis System Scale-up

As the world leader in proton exchange membrane-based electrolysis systems, Proton OnSite has a wealth of experience in developing commercial PEM systems and continued scale up in capacity. Proton has developed systems at a variety of output capacities ranging from <100 mL/min up to 10's of Nm^3/hr (Figure 1, smallest products not shown). This increase in capacity has been accomplished through a combination of increases in cell stack active area, stack height, and number of stacks/system. The impact of scale on capital cost is also illustrated in Figure 1. Increasing system output by an order of magnitude has resulted in the realization of more than 70% reduction in $/kW for Proton's current commercial product line. This cost reduction can be attributed to several factors including impact of larger electrolysis cell stack architectures and the non-linear scaling of the system balance-of-plant cost.

	HOGEN S-Series	HOGEN H-Series	HOGEN C-Series
Product Type			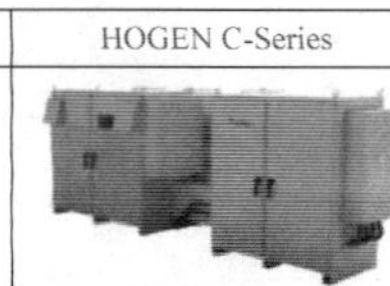
Product Launch	2000	2003	2011
Cells/stack	10-20	34	65
Stacks/system	1	1-3	1-3
H_2 Output (Nm^3/hr)	0.5-1.05	2-6	10-30
$/kW vs. S-series	100%	43%	28%

Figure 1. Electrolyzer scale-up progression

Cost modeling for the MW product indicates a similar cost trajectory is required to meet the energy storage market price points (Figure 2). Proton's analysis indicates that these levels of cost reduction at the MW-scale are achievable. Furthermore, development work at Proton has already been completed to de-risk the major technology elements required to realize these reduced costs. Proton believes that the cost reduction trajectory can now be achieved through straight-forward engineering scale-up and those activities are well underway at this time.

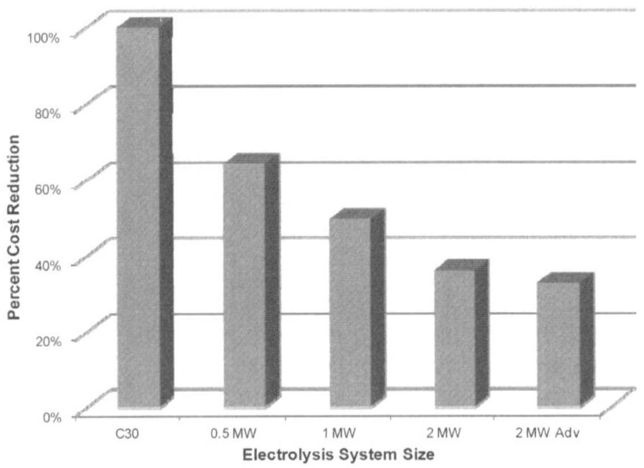

Figure 2. Electrolyzer cost reduction as a function of size

MW Scale Product Development

Proton's MW product is being designed based upon input energy capture. The multi-MW design uses a 1 MW electrolysis module. Power supplies, controls and ancillary modules will be sized at the multi-MW size. The initial product offering will be a 2 MW unit with a 1 MW version also available. Similar to Proton's other products, the MW product is based on a multi-stack system that utilizes a new large active area stack platform. The MW system is an open frame skid modular design made for either indoor or outdoor installation. The outdoor version will utilize separate containers for the electrolysis subsystem and the power electronics and controls (Figure 3).

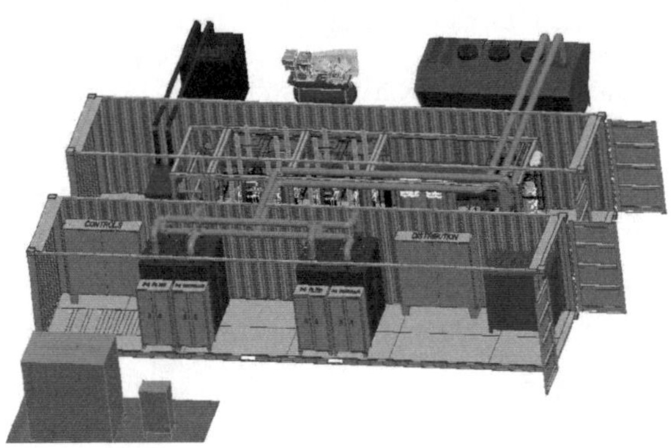

Figure 3: Containerized MW Product

All of Proton's product development efforts have led with development of the cell stack configuration. For the MW platform, the basic cell design is already well into the validation process. The cell stack active area is approximately a three-fold increase vs. the HOGEN® C-series stack (currently Proton's largest commercially available PEM cell stack). Proton originally began development of a larger active area cell stack design in 2008 and has already proven component manufacturing capability of relevant size. Multi-cell prototype stack hardware has been fabricated and validated for over 20,000 hours of operation (Figure 4). This design is now in its second iteration, including significant cost reduction of the bipolar assembly. In Figure 5 a comparison of the first and second generation cell stacks is presented. The active area of the second generation cell stack (Gen 2) has been increased by 15% while significantly reducing the overall footprint. More importantly, this Gen 2 cell stack is 40% lower cost than the first generation (Gen 1) counterpart.

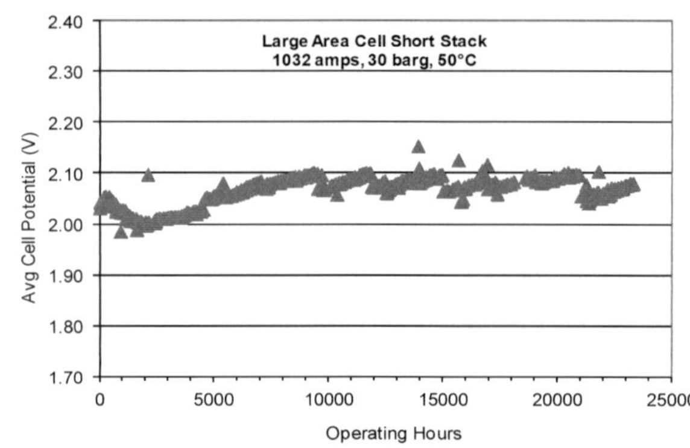

Figure 4. Operation of large active area stack

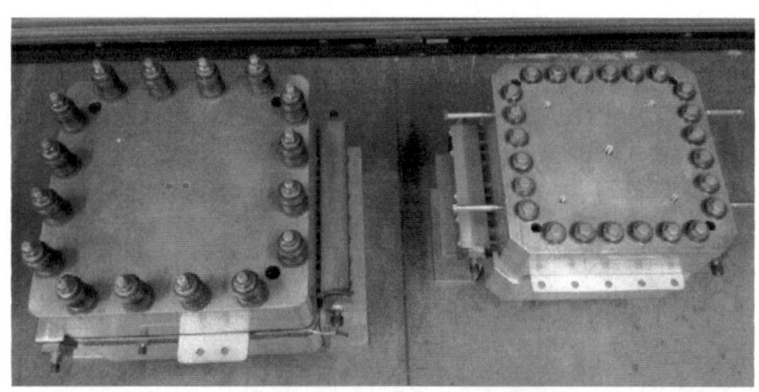

Figure 5. First generation (left) and second generation (right) MW stack platforms. Second generation stack has a 15% larger active area at 40% less cost.

Rigorous testing of the Gen 2 cell stack is now well underway. This testing includes dynamic load and overcapacity (i.e. overload) testing to simulate integration with a variable renewable energy source As shown in Figure 6, the cell stack responds very rapidly and repeatedly to variable loads at overcapacities nearing 200%. Operation at near zero output is achievable repeatedly without any significant build up of hydrogen in the oxygen vent stream. The overall functionality demonstrated with this testing is critical to the success of the MW electrolyzer for energy storage applications.

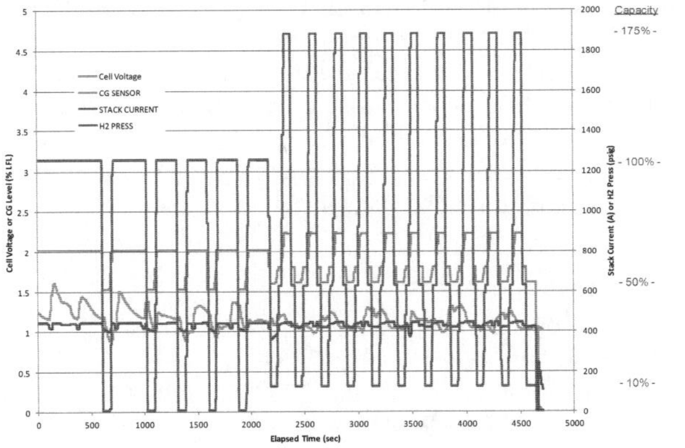

Figure 6. Load cycle testing of Gen 2 MW Electrolysis Cell Stack

Future Technology Development

Development of PEM electrolysis technology does not stop with the introduction of Proton's MW product. Continued efforts are needed in the areas of cost reduction and efficiency improvement to ensure success in the future energy storage market. To support these efforts, Proton has developed a detailed technology roadmap. A balanced portfolio of projects, addressing both cost and efficiency, is required to meet these long term market needs. Efficiency in the cell stack is limited by the membrane thickness and the oxygen reaction overpotential. At the typical operating current densities of 1.5 – 2 A/cm^2, each of these factors can contribute around 250-300 mV to the cell voltage. For cost, the highest factors are the bipolar assembly and the membrane electrode assembly (MEA), representing nearly 75% of the stack cost combined, or up to 35-40% of the system cost. The Gen 2 MW cell stack has already taken significant cost out of the bipolar assembly, leaving current work focused on advancing the cost and performance of the MEA. Proton's advances in these areas as described in the following sections.

Membrane Efficiency. Typical commercial electrolysis membranes range from 175-250 microns in thickness vs. standard fuel cell membranes of 25-50 microns, due to the higher operating pressures in the electrolyzer cell. In order to maintain integrity in the seal area under the high mechanical loads required for sealing to high pressure, new strategies such as membrane reinforcement or changes in polymer chemistry to reduce the creep characteristics of standard Nafion are needed to enable thin membranes. The durability requirements of the electrolyzer cell also make qualification of new materials challenging. Proton has examined new, stronger membranes from multiple suppliers ranging from 50-100 microns in thickness which also pass accelerated stress testing. Performance curves are shown in Figure 7 for 60 and 90 micron samples from W. L. Gore. These samples were also operated at 80°C for 1000 hours without failure. The new membrane types enable approximately double the hydrogen output for the same cell voltage, or can decrease the cell overpotential by over 250 mV for the same current.

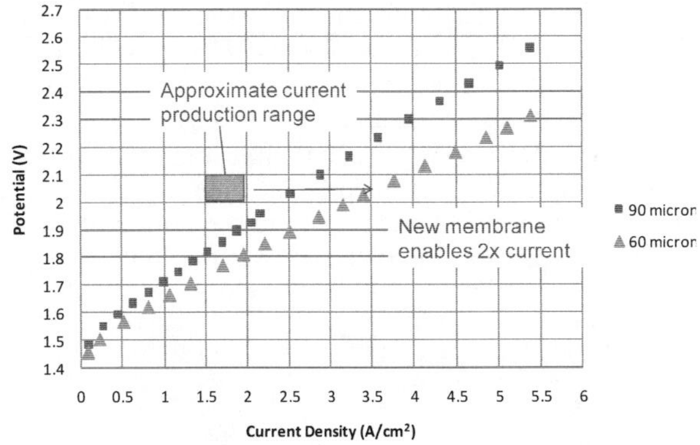

Figure 7. Polarization data for cells using reinforced membrane

Catalyst Efficiency. Proton has demonstrated improvements vs. current catalyst performance with mixed metal oxides designed with a high activity component as well as a structural component for stabilization. The estimated impact on activity is a 20-fold improvement based on the current-voltage polarization curves [4].

The combination of the catalyst enhancements with the membrane work above is shown in Figure 8. The polarization curves below are all measured at 435 psi hydrogen generation pressure in commercial hardware, and have been validated for stable performance over at least 1000 hours. This progression contradicts the general perception that because few improvements had been made in electrolysis efficiency over the last few decades, the technology had reached its peak. Clearly there is substantial promise to bring PEM electrolysis technology to practical energy efficiencies, through leveraging of materials developments in other fields including fuel cells.

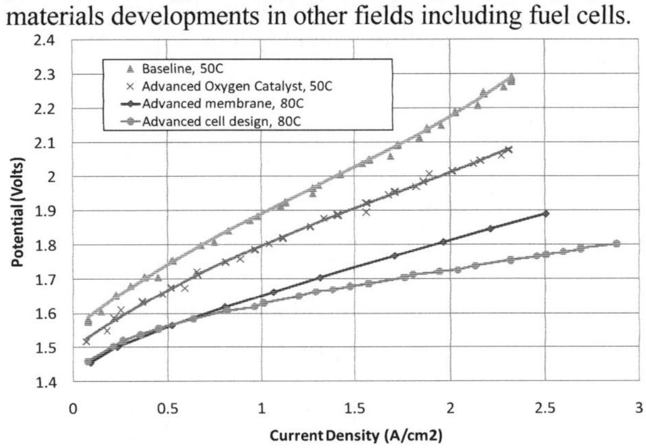

Figure 8. Efficiency improvements based on recent electrolysis materials research

Impact on Cost of Hydrogen and Conclusions. The overall lifecycle cost of hydrogen production from electrolysis is calculated using the U.S. Department of Energy's (DOE) H2A model. This model includes capital cost of the system, maintenance costs, cost of electricity, taxes, depreciation, utilization factor, and other factors. The baseline electricity cost assumed by DOE is \$0.05/kWh, for equal comparison across technologies. Proton also has an electrochemical model interface to the H2A model, which enables input of the polarization curve for a given stack design and system configuration. The impact of the system scale up from the 22 kg/day stack to the 50 kg/day stack platform is shown in Figure 9, relative to the DOE targets.

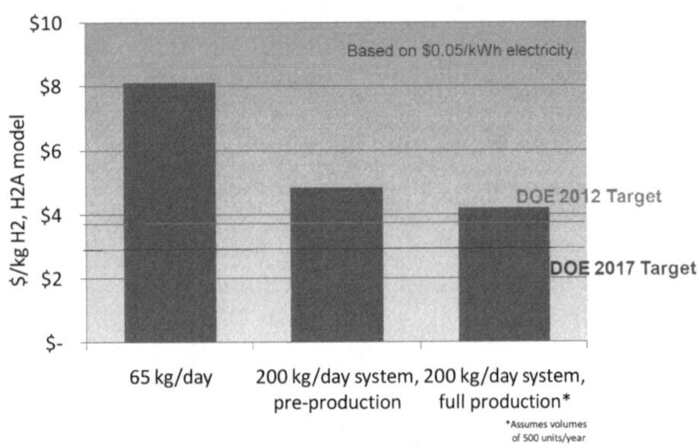

Figure 9. Hydrogen production cost projections based on current stack efficiencies

Summary

Hydrogen from electrolysis is a promising technology for renewable energy capture as it has the capability to store massive amounts of energy in a relatively small volume. Proton's MW product development program was initiated in early 2013 to address this market and is currently in the prototype development. A functional MW-scale unit is anticipated to be under test later this year with full production release of a commercial MW-scale product by the middle of 2015. Proton has already shown rapid improvements in the capabilities of our systems, including larger capacity, higher pressure, and increased efficiency. Continuing advancements can be achieved through leveraging of existing science into the field of electrolysis, rather than requiring completely new invention.

Acknowledgements

The authors would like to acknowledge the U.S. Department of Energy, Department of Defense, and the National Science Foundation for their support in funding portions of this development effort.

References

1. http://www.navigantresearch.com/blog/matching-renewable-power-worth-billions-to-load

2. Gas World Magazine, 95, April 2013, p22.

3. "Renewable Electrolysis Integrated Systems Development and Testing," K. Harrison, C. Ainscough, and M. Peters, Excerpt from the Department of Energy's Annual Progress Report, (December 2012).

4. "Efficient Generation of High Energy Density Fuel from Water", Katherine E. Ayers, Luke T. Dalton, and Everett B. Anderson, ECS Trans. 41 (33), 27-38 (2012)

Safe Energy System that Allows Enhanced UUV Missions

Jonathan Reeh, Mark Nelson, Christopher Rhodes, Brian Hennings*
Lynntech, Inc.
2501 Earl Rudder Fwy S, College Station, TX, USA, 77845, www.lynntech.com
*Corresponding Author: Email: Brian.Hennings@Lynntech.com

Abstract: *Unmanned underwater vehicles (UUV) are seeing an increased role within the Navy for high-priority missions. These UUVs are currently battery powered and have limited energy density, which limits mission endurance and capability. Lynntech is developing innovative hybrid energy systems that are flexible, modular, and consist of a low temperature fuel cell, a battery, and advanced power management system architecture. This technology has been demonstrated to produce the desired power that follows the load profile at various power levels, utilizing various chemical hydride based fuel and peroxide based oxidizer reactants. The fuel and oxidizer are both stored in liquid form, are inexpensive, and are safe to transport and handle. Refueling simply requires replenishing the two liquids with no waste to be disposed and no extended delays for battery recharging.*

Enabling these enhanced missions will greatly increase the flexibility and utility of the UUV platform. The additional energy can be used to extend mission duration or to employ new or additional payloads.

Keywords: Hybrid Energy System; Fuel Cell; Chemical Hydride; Hydrogen Peroxide; UUV Energy System, Air-independent Energy System.

Introduction

Unmanned underwater vehicles (UUV) are seeing an increased role within the Navy for high-priority missions such as fleet protection, inspection/identification, oceanography, communication and navigation, payload delivery, information operations and time critical strike operations. The Navy is actively pursuing the development of four UUV classes that range in size from 9" to 48" (outer diameter). These UUVs are currently battery powered and have limited energy density, which limits mission endurance and capability.

Aside from military applications, several civilian uses exist for small autonomous, long endurance UUVs. Past uses include searching for wreckage and sunken debris, gas/oil pipeline inspection, aqueduct tunnel inspection, general marine research (shark tracking), and seafloor topographical mapping (bathymetry) [1].

For each application endurance is usually a limiting factor with current durations limited to <24 hours depending on UUV size and operational conditions. These durations are defined by current battery energy density and specific energy limitations. Another critical mission limitation is the recharging time. The size and compactness of the batteries require a recharging time of ~8 hours. Lynntech is currently developing emerging technologies which addresses the shortfalls of the current energy systems.

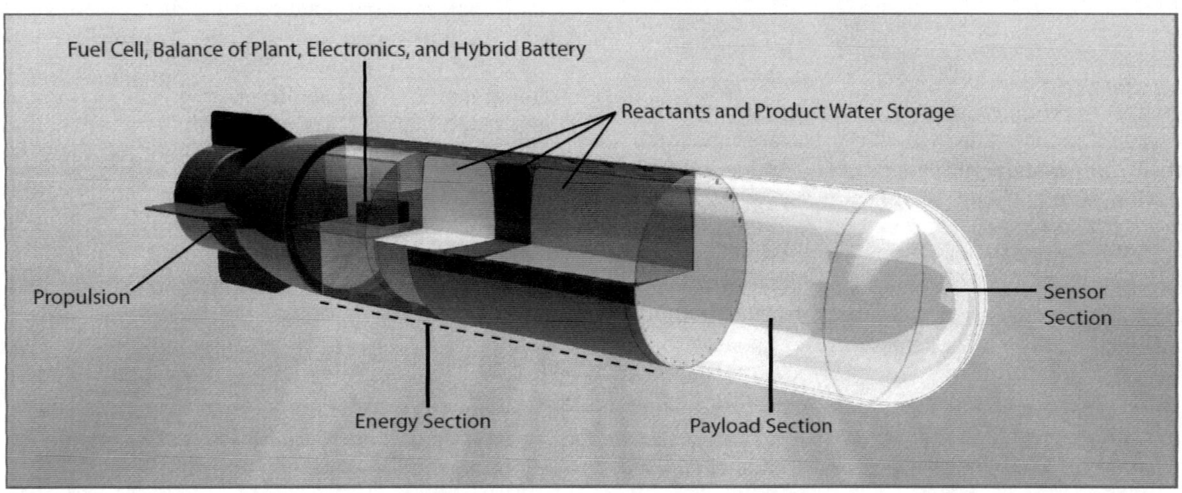

Figure 1. CAD rendering of envisioned hybrid energy system integrated into a generic UUV.

Lynntech's Hybrid Energy System Architecture

Lynntech is developing innovative hybrid energy systems that are flexible, modular, and can meet the varied power requirements as dictated by the mission while significantly increasing duration and reducing the re-deployment time (Figure 1).

One challenge in the development of a fuel cell based UUV energy system are the large transient loads. The fuel cell is not well suited to deal with these rapid, high amplitude power demands. Therefore Lynntech has developed a hybrid power system architecture which incorporates a secondary battery. The high power density battery handles the short term high power requirements of the load profile, while the high energy density fuel cell provides power at a stable rate for the base load and recharges the small battery during low power intervals.

Another challenge associated with any high energy density PEM Fuel Cell system is the safe, compact and lightweight storage of the hydrogen fuel required. To address this Lynntech has investigated several chemical hydride based fuels. By focusing on liquid based fuels, Lynntech avoids the complex and problematic processing of solids. These liquid fuels are safe to store, have high energy densities, high specific energies and can be effectively pumped into and out of the energy system for quick refueling.

When hydrogen is needed, the liquid fuel is pumped into specially design reactors to produce high purity, pressurized hydrogen gas on demand. These reactors have been specifically designed to meet the transient loads of the UUV and can produce full scale hydrogen production in less than 10 seconds.

Since UUVs are submerged during operation, an air-independent energy system is required. Therefore, the oxidant required must also be stored onboard the UUV. Lynntech has internally developed the use of liquid peroxides to produce high purity oxygen on demand for the fuel cell. The Navy has been using peroxides as a propellant for over 50 years. However, Lynntech pumps the high gravimetric/volumetric oxygen content peroxide solution into a special reactor where the peroxide produces pure oxygen. Similar to the fuel reactor discussed previously, the peroxide reactor is capable of producing full oxygen flow within 10 seconds to meet the transit loads. Both the fuel and oxidizer are stored onboard the UUV in specially designed bladders.

Many systems aboard the UUV produce waste heat during operation including the sensors, electronics, fuel cell, fuel and oxidant generation systems. Lynntech effectively removes this waste heat with an integrated coolant loop and heat exchanger. Heat is actively rejected to the sea water to maintain safe temperatures for all of the internal components.

Buoyancy control is critical to any under-sea vehicle, reducing power and increasing stability and control. The vehicle remains neutrally buoyant throughout the mission with the use of an onboard active ballast system. If need be, the sea water can be expelled, increasing the UUVs buoyancy and allowing it to efficiently rise to the surface for retrieval and refueling.

Quick, safe refueling of the system is accomplished in less than an hour by simply topping off the fuel and oxidant bladders. Refueling simply requires replenishing the two liquids with no waste to be disposed and no extended delays for battery recharging.

This approach has been demonstrated to produce the desired power that follows the load profile at various power levels while significantly increasing the endurance and reducing the re-deployment time.

Comparison to Current Batteries

Multiple advantages are realized over rechargeable batteries by Lynntech's hybrid energy system. Primarily the energy system scales up favorably over batteries. Since batteries have a fixed energy density and specific energy, they scale linearly in mass and volume to additional energy needs. However, after the fuel cell and BOP components are accounted for, only additional fuel and oxidant are needed to increase the energy of Lynntech's hybrid system. Figure 2 illustrates the scaling advantages of Lynntech's hybrid energy system. Assuming a UUV outer diameter of 12.75", the energy section length in increased to offer additional mission duration and energy storage. When compared to secondary batteries, Lynntech's system is projected to significantly increase the energy storage after a hull length of 30". The increased effective energy density and specific energy are also shown as a function of hull length. These projections are based on UUV energy sections with neutral buoyancy for an equivalent comparison.

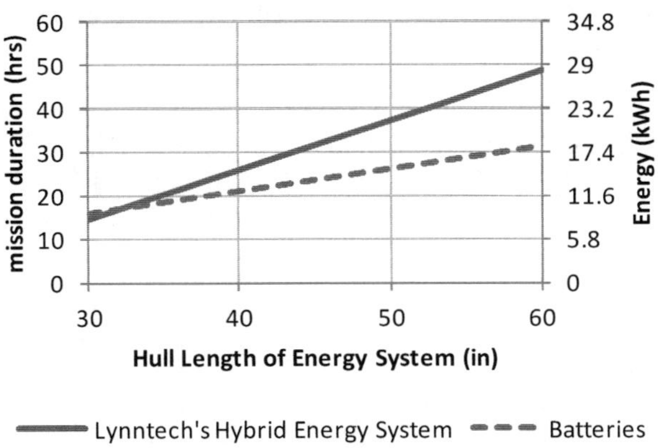

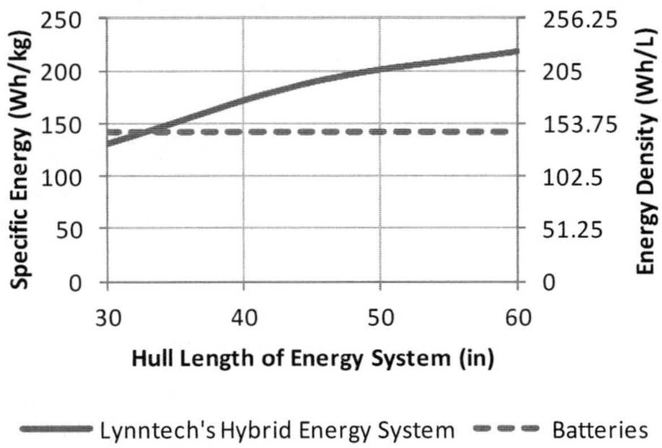

Figure 2. Comparison of Lynntech's Hybrid Energy System to batteries vs. section length.

Experimental Results

The previously discussed UUV hybrid energy system has been internally developed for a 12.75" UUV platform. Lynntech has demonstrated in the lab that the breadboard system meets or exceeds the power profile and total stored energy requirements for the enhanced mission while delivering ~1 kW of power.

The developed system is highly scalable and the form factor can be adapted to be applicable to most UUV sizes. Current efforts are focused on developing a packaged prototype system that can be integrated into the UUV for field testing. Enabling these enhanced missions will greatly increase the flexibility and utility of the UUV platform. The additional energy can be used to extend mission duration or to employ new or additional payloads.

Future Work

Future work includes transitioning to a brass board system and integrating and packaging this hybrid energy section into a 12.75" UUV hull section. This work is expected to begin in the second quarter of 2014. Developmental testing will be first performed in a controlled aquatic environment. Subsequent developmental testing followed by operational testing will be performed in the open ocean to verify mission performance.

Conclusions

Lynntech's air independent, hybrid energy system offers distinct advantages over batteries in subsea environments. Advantages include increased energy density/specific energy, better scaling characteristics, safer energy storage and faster turnaround time (refueling).

Other potential applications of Lynntech's hybrid energy system include stationery underwater power sources for sensors networks and UUV recharging, man portable power supplies for primary power and battery charging, as well as powering other unmanned vehicles such as Unmanned Ground Vehicles (UGVs), Unmanned Aerial Vehicles (UAVs), and Unmanned Surface Vehicles (USVs).

Acknowledgements

The Authors would like to especially acknowledge the support of this work from Navy Funding (NSWC contract N00167-11-C-0004, COTR: Dr. Julie Banner. Miscellaneous NASA and DOD (Army, Navy, Air Force, Marines) entities are also acknowledged for previous funding of founding technologies used here within.

Reference

1. Woods Hole Oceanographic Systems Laboratory website. www.whoi.edu/osl/remus-auv.

High-efficiency, Flexible, Impact Tolerant Photovoltaic Panels made Possible by a Novel Mesh-based Metallization Approach

Bob Brainard[1], Steve Babayan[2], Arvind Chari[1], Alejandro De La Fuente[1], Venkatesan Murali[1], Gopal Prabhu[1], Arthur Rudin[1], Ven Subbaraman[1], David Tanner[1], Michael Vyvoda[1], Dong Xu[1]

[1]GT Advanced Technologies, Inc.
2526 Qume Drive Unit 23, San Jose, CA 95131
[2]Applied Materials, Inc.
974 E. Arques Ave., Sunnyvale, CA 94085
Corresponding author email: Michael.vyvoda@gtat.com

Abstract: *Terrestrial photovoltaic power generation technology has historically been segmented into two distinct groups: relatively high light conversion efficiency (~16-22%) panels built with crystalline Si technology, and lower-efficiency (<~11%) "thin-film" based panels. The former tended to be rigid and heavy in order to maintain the integrity of the fragile Si solar cells and interconnects, and the latter, while inherently more flexible and mechanically forgiving, required much larger surface area for a given level of desired power output. Installers of both types of panels, including the US military, have traditionally had to choose between high efficiency (and therefore low cost/Watt generated), and flexibility.*

We have developed what we believe is the first high-efficiency, crystalline Si based photovoltaic panel technology that provides the best of both words: high power output per unit area, low cost, as well as flexibility and a mechanically forgiving nature. This has been accomplished by the development of a novel intra- and inter-cell metallization technology, applied to standard crystalline Si solar cells. In this paper, we will outline the details of this approach as well as its benefits, with a focus on its suitability for military applications of photovoltaic power generation.

Keywords: photovoltaics; PV; renewable energy; solar energy; crystalline silicon.

Introduction

The Defense Department pledge to obtain 25% of its energy from renewable sources by 2025 is on-track and PV is a large component of that effort. The transition to renewable energy sources on fixed platforms is based on both ownership of hardware and on PPAs with energy suppliers. Although National Security policy regarding greenhouse gas emissions and energy independence is the principal driver behind the pledge, cost of energy cannot be ignored. Since 50% of the cost of a PV installation is in the installation and packaging of the PV panels, any cost savings in packaging translates directly into a lower cost of energy, whether supplied in a PPA or through ownership of the system. In the case of deployable power for the Warfighter, the motivation for renewable energy sources is the reduced logistics requirement and reduced casualty count. PVs used in the field are required to have high efficiency, be lightweight, and in addition, they must be highly resilient. This often translates into being highly flexible.

Photovoltaic power generation technology has historically been segmented into two distinct groups: relatively high light conversion efficiency (~16-22%) panels built with crystalline Si technology, and lower-efficiency (<~11%) "thin-film" based panels. The former tend to be rigid and heavy in order to maintain the integrity of the fragile Si solar cells and interconnects, and the latter, while inherently more flexible and mechanically forgiving, require much larger surface area for a given level of desired power output.

This paper discusses novel packaging of standard crystalline silicon PV cell technology. It provides advantages for both fixed platforms and for the Warfighter. This dual use capability incorporates reduced panel weight, improved overall efficiency, is highly flexible and reduces overall cost.

Approach

Figure 1 below shows the fundamental structure of our novel metallization scheme. As can be seen, traditional silver busbars and ribbons are replaced by frontside and backside grids, primarily composed of copper and therefore low cost. Cell-to-cell interconnection is simple, with the frontside grid of cell N in the module string connecting directly to the backside grid of cell N+1.

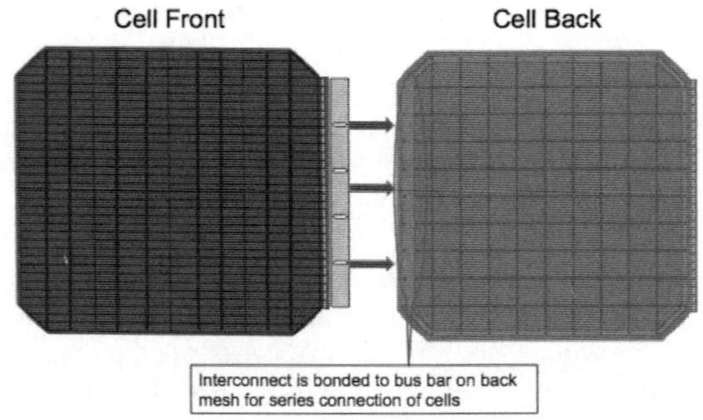

Figure 1. Schematic illustration of the grid-based metallization design, showing frontside and backside grids as well as cell – cell interconnecting tab

Modules built using this approach do not require traditional tabbing and stringing, as this front-to-back layup method can be easily used to string together the entire module: cells with pre-attached grids are "tiled" and connected to form strings, completely eliminating bussing ribbons. Right-angle turns are made simply by turning cells 90 degrees as there is no directional dependence to this cell – cell attachment method.

Selected Results

The large current-carrying copper volume provided by the new grid approach is effective in reducing resistive "cell-to-module" losses. Figure 2 below shows a routinely-measured IV curve for traditional versus grid-based cells. Base cells used in this study were identical, with only the finger – busbar – ribbon versus grid metallization scheme differing. Tester contacting in the study was properly adjusted to ensure that comparisons are meaningful.

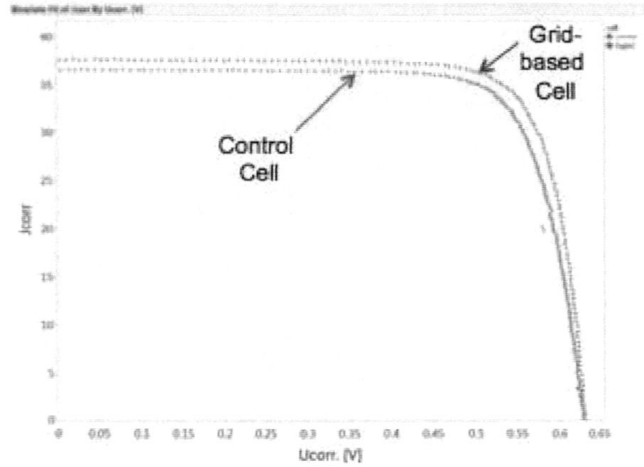

Figure 2. Comparison between traditional IV measurements of a standard mono-crystalline Si cell (busbar/ribbon) versus a grid-based cell. Contacting scheme is adjusted to ensure proper comparison.

Numerically, we measure a 0.7% absolute light conversion efficiency improvement at the interconnected cell level, which is due to a combination of higher fill factor from the reduced series resistance and higher current from reduced cell shading; this is a significant increase particularly in light of the attendant cost reduction due to the decrease in silver use. The practical consequence of this result would be an increase in module power even though exactly the same base cell is used, at lower cost. The metallization scheme is equally applicable to both mono and multi crystalline silicon cells.

The benefits of the new scheme are as summarized as follows:

- Silver content reduction as high as 80% by complete elimination of busbars along with reduction in silver paste volume in the screen printed fingers.
- Reduced dependence on high-aspect ratio Ag finger printing to reduce finger series resistance. This would enable manufacturers to relax printing aspect ratio requirements and minimize shading-related current losses.
- Low resistance copper metallization without the necessity of copper wafer plating.
- Improved light trapping performance in the module driven by specific architectural benefits of the grid topography.
- Increased cell flexibility and breakage resistance, resulting from the inherently supportive structure of the attached grid.
- Large improvement in cell – cell and module flex tolerances, as a result of thickness reduction in the cell – cell interconnecting tab relative to traditional ribbons (while increasing total current-carrying volume).
- Installed cost reduction, due to the combined benefits of silver reduction, simplification of balance of system (BOS) components, and weight reduction made possible by the more flexible, resilient cells described above.
- Technology risk mitigation: no new or untested materials, with mature technology elements and proven reliability characteristics, along with ease of insertion into current module manufacturing lines.

Furthermore, many of these benefits that apply to fixed panels apply to both forward-deployed panels that are shipped to conflict areas, as well photovoltaics designed specifically for squad-level or personal warfighter deployment. This is detailed in the next section of this paper

Light Weight and Flexible

Military applications of this novel photovoltaic technology are threefold:

1. Static panels deployed at US-based military installations, many of which have active programs in place to increase their use of photovoltaics over the coming decade.
2. Static panels deployed to forward operating bases.
3. Highly mobile power units that are either worn by the Warfighter, or used at the squad level for battery charging or other applications.

For item 1., our approach for building photovoltaic panels is attractive for cost reasons, as well as for the added energy security provided by panels made with our technology. By reducing silver content compared to a traditional panel, along with additional balance of systems benefits, we calculate at least 10% fully-installed cost reduction as compared to a traditional installation. That figure is a substantial savings as most economies of scale are already factored in to today's pricing of traditional systems, and additional price reduction means are not obvious.

Equally important is the security that photovoltaics in general, and our novel technology in particular, brings compared to fossil fuels. Figure 4 below shows the impact tolerance of our technology compared to traditional panels. In the event of cell breakage that might occur in a conflict, panels made with our grid metallization approach are significantly more breakage tolerant, retaining a high fraction of specified power output. This is a direct result of our grid metallization acting as an "exoskeleton" surrounding the solar cell, effectively holding the cell together in the event of breakage and preserving its current collecting capabilities.

For item 2. (static panels deployed to forward operating bases), the weight reduction potential of our novel photovoltaic panels, as compared to traditional panels, could prove to be highly beneficial. The primary motivation for installing photovoltaics at forward operating bases is to reduce the need for fuel delivery, which is both expensive and highly dangerous when such forward operating bases are within hostile territory. As a result, there has been strong interest in shipping photovoltaic panels to such bases. However, the weight-to-power output ratio of traditional photovoltaic panels is not favorable: a typical 250 Watt panel (peak rating; tested at standard conditions), weighs approximately 50 lbs. With our novel metallization approach, panels can be made almost 50% lighter, better than halving the weight-to-power ratio. This reduces shipping costs and burden substantially, since twice the wattage can be delivered for the same payload limit.

For item 3. (mobile power units), the combination of flexibility and weight reduction (for a specified power produced), are strong drivers for the use of this technology in squad-level power generation as well as wearable devices.

Figure 4 below shows what is commonly known as a Squad Power Unit, typically specified to generate >100W with a device surface area <15 ft^2. Historically, this type of device has been constructed using so-called "thin film" solar technology, mainly using amorphous Si cells. Using our flexible cell and interconnection technology, we can construct such a device having a surface area 50% smaller than specified (or, equivalently, twice the power generated for the same area). This is done at the low cost levels inherent to this crystalline Si technology.

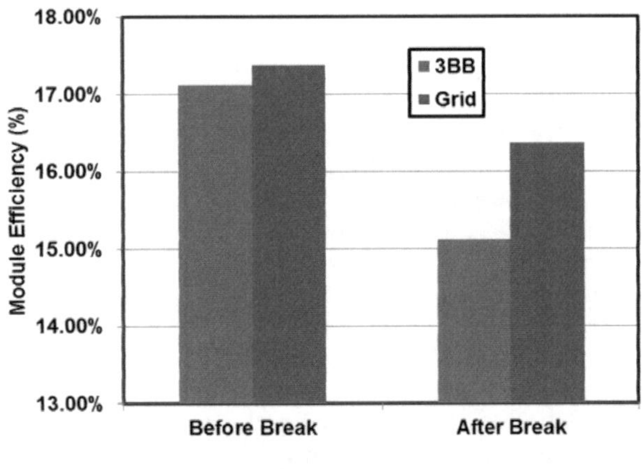

Figure 3. Photovoltaic module light conversion efficiency for traditional ("3BB") versus our grid-based metallization approach. After cell cracking in the module package, significantly higher efficiency is retained with the grid approach

Figure 4. Squad Power Unit constructed using the GT Advanced Technologies metallization approach. Devices built with this technology have twice the power output for a given surface area, compared to thin-film based products

Summary

We have developed a new intra- and inter-cell metallization scheme, and resulting module construction approach, that complements the dramatic improvements in cell efficiency gains made over the past several years. The nature of the grid approach overcomes many of the shortcomings of traditional module construction schemes, including compromised module power output as a result of high resistive losses, high silver cost and inherently heavy and rigid module designs. Because of the resulting cost reduction, breakage tolerance and flex capability of the grid-based cells and modules, these developments should usher in a new phase of lighter, more easy to install, and less expensive PV modules, accelerating our progress towards grid parity. Furthermore, the many benefits of this approach have direct, positive implications for military deployment: low cost and weight-to-power ratios for static modules, breakage tolerance, as well as very high power-to-surface area ratios for squad-level and wearable devices.

Value Proposition of Lithium Ion versus Pb-Acid for Military Vehicles

Jeff Helm
Defense Sales Manager
Saft America, Space and Defense Division
107 Beaver Court
Cockeysville, MD 21030

Abstract: *28VDC batteries are commonly used on various military ground vehicle and aeronautical platforms. On ground vehicles, these 28VDC systems are often comprised of two 12VDC lead-acid (Pb-acid)batteries strung in series. The batteries were originally used for just starting, lighting and ignition (SLI) loads, but as the complexity of vehicle integrated systems increases, along with the need for vehicles to operate in silent watch, the vehicle batteries are now called upon to provide higher power loads and be cycled at up to 80% depth of discharge in addition to providing SLI power.*

The NATO 6T battery format is the most common battery used in military vehicles around the world. These batteries are also commonly used in renewable power systems and other systems such as DoD firing range targets. Advances in lithium-ion (Li-ion) battery solutions have demonstrated their ability to provide higher power, operate for significantly more depth of discharge cycles and have the potential of demonstrating a lower life cycle cost compared to lead-acid batteries

This paper will focus on understanding the value proposition associated with utilizing advanced lithium-ion 6T solutions versus legacy Pb-acid 6Ts for military ground vehicles. The value proposition will include an analysis of the benefits associated with lithium-ion 6T batteries and reduction in life cycle cost (LCC). The analysis of benefits will include comparative discharge curves at various rates and temperatures, discuss enhancements features such as an integrated battery management system that provides real-time battery diagnostics via CANBus J1939 protocol, increased power/energy density, reduced charge time and increased cycle life. The LCC analysis will investigate acquisition cost comparison, replacement rates, and reduced installation & transportation costs. The LCC analysis concludes with a detailed review of how the lithium-ion 6T solution can drastically reduce the operation and maintenance (O&M) cost of the Joint Light Tactical Vehicle (JLTV) over its 20 year life..

Keywords: Batteries; 6T; Lithium-ion; Battery Management System; Military Vehicles, Silent Watch; Total cost of ownership, MIL-PRF-32143B, life-cycle cost;

Introduction

In the past, military support vehicles have had relatively modest power requirements with onboard electric loads seldom exceeding that required to support radio systems. Not so long ago, vehicle electronic systems could be operated for short periods of time without starting the vehicle's engine.

Figure 1. Sample of Electronic Loads on base HMMWV

As modern military operations have shifted away from historical modes of conflict where force-on-force combat occurred on a "front line," the distinction between combat and logistical vehicles has become blurred. In today's threat environment, logistics and other noncombat vehicles commonly encounter the same range of threats as combat vehicles. As a result, the ability to generate significant amounts of electrical power has become increasingly critical for the full spectrum of military vehicles. Non-combat vehicles are increasingly designed to accommodate combat-grade vehicle electronic systems, or what the military calls "vectronics," including sensors, jammers, communication and control equipment. The ability to support the electric power needed to operate these systems has become a critical issue.

The need to power the plethora of emerging sensors and communication systems installed in military vehicles is putting a significant strain on current vehicle power systems, specifically legacy Pb-acid 6T batteries.

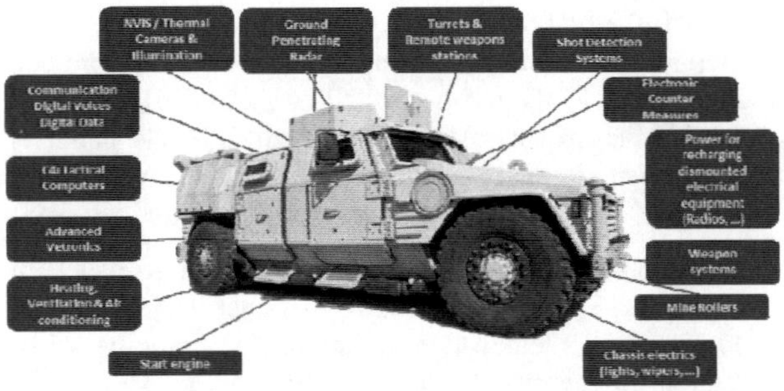

Figure 2. Sample of Electronic Loads on JLTV

The strain placed on legacy Pb-acid 6T batteries, in turn causes issues such as premature failure by excessive discharge, improper charging and extreme internal temperatures. The consequence for these actions are frequent replacements, which requires high levels of spare stock, and limited trust by Warfighters for use in deep-cycle applications. Another shortfall of legacy Pb-acid 6T batteries is that State of Charge (SOC) / State of Health (SOH) is difficult to detect, whichcould cause unexpected loss of power. This unexpected loss of power can lead to engine start failures, and inability to complete missions, and has the potential to put the Warfighter in harm's way.

Performance Comparison Lithium-ion vs. Pb-acid:

The performance comparison section of this paper will focus on effects of discharge rates, energy/power densities, benefits of an integrated battery management system and cycle life.

All Capacities are not equal, normally a "120Ah" Pb-acid battery gives an implication that, it could give 1A for 120 hours, or 120 A for 1 hour, or 20A for 6 hours or whatever combination of that which gives 120AH as the multiplication output.

In reality this is not the case. Faster discharging reduces the available capacity of the battery drastically. Available capacity of a battery could be computed using an empirical

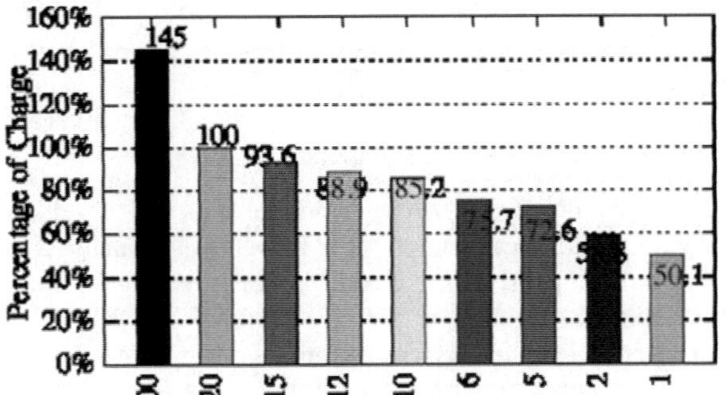

Figure 3. Pb-acid available capacity as a function of discharge time

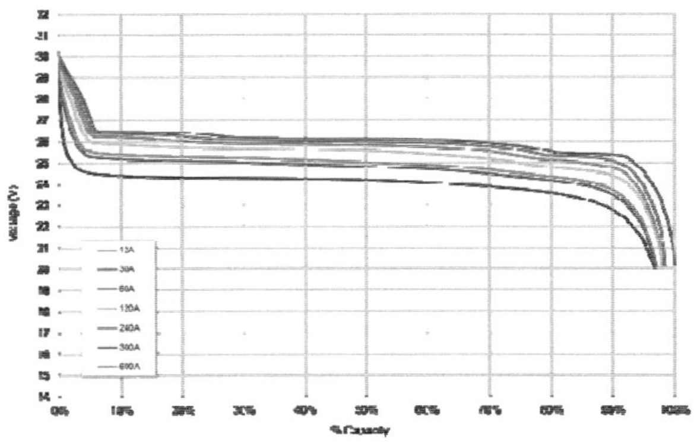

Figure 4. Saft Li-ion 6T available capacity as a function of discharge time

law named "Peukert's law." Figure 3 displays the available capacity of a typical lead-acid battery against discharge time. 100% capacity is stated for 20 hours.

In comparison, the peukert effect is not as severe for lithium-on batteries. Figure 4, is a graphical representation of Saft's Super-Phosphate™ 6T lithium-ion battery discharged at various rates. The rate of discharge shown varies between C/5 to 10 C-rate, and the resulting capacities vary only 4% of sticker label capacity.

Consistent capacity over various discharge rates is related to increases in energy density of lithium-ion batteries when compared to legacy Pb-acid. Take the HMMWV as an example; today the vehicle is outfitted with two (2) Pb-acid 6T batteries that weigh 88lbs each. Purely looking at sticker label energy, the two (2) batteries equate to a 2.88 kWh. However, if the HMMWV is equipped with surveillance and reconnaissance mission equipment, it may require the batteries to provide up to 120 amp discharge rate (or 1C-rate) during silent watch. Due to the peukert effect, the actual capacity would be 50% of the sticker label, or 60 AHs, resulting in actual energy of 1.44 kWh. Today, lithium-ion battery manufacturers have developed 24V 6T lithium-ion equivalents that weigh 50lbs each and contain at minimum 1.44 kWh of energy at C-rate discharge. This results in a 72% decrease in weight and a "two-for-one" replacement in volume per system (or 50% reduction).

In addition to energy density, it is also important to compare power density between the two electro-chemistries. The Pb-acid 6T battery is required to provide 1,100 amps for 30 seconds at -18C°, and 400 amps for 30 seconds at -40 C°. Lithium-ion battery manufacturers have developed 24V 6T lithium-ion equivalents that deliver the same power capability. Figure 5, displays Saft's lithium-ion 6T voltage profile while delivering 1,100 amps for 30 seconds at -18C.

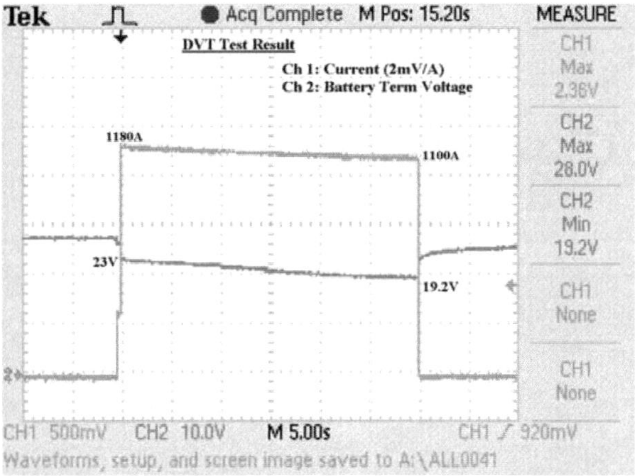

Figure 5. Saft Li-ion 6T 1,100 amp discharge pulse at -18C

All lithium-ion batteries are required to have some form of battery management system. For lithium-ion batteries to operate safely and provide a long lifetime, they must be constrained to an operational envelope that prevents over current, over temperature, low temperature charging, and most significantly, overcharge and over discharge of each individual cell, and cell balancing.

Initially, you may consider it a burden to have a battery management system within lithium-ion batteries as it increases the amount of electronics and cost. However, when analyzing failure modes of Pb-acid batteries in military operation, the number one failure mode was improper charging of the battery. BMS's within lithium-ion batteries often prevent improper charging, therefore removing or drastically reducing this failure mode for the Warfighter.

The inclusion of a BMS in a lithium-ion battery provides the opportunity for the battery to communicate information externally to logisticians, Warfighter, OEMs and other vehicle systems. This provides the user(s) with real-time diagnostic information on the battery; e.g. battery voltage, cell string voltages, State of Charge (SOC), State of Health (SOH) and diagnostics/maintenance messages. These battery management systems provide the warfighter with accurate information about the battery state of charge in real time so it can be used with confidence, and ensure there is enough power remaining for an engine crank at the end of a silent watch mission.

Life Cycle Cost Comparison:

The life cycle cost section of this paper will focus on cycle life comparisons of Pb-acid versus lithium-ion batteries, and the cost savings associated with transportation and installation as a result of increased cycle life.

The Pb-acid batteries are qualified today to provide (at a minimum) a cycle life of 360 shallow cycles (40% depth of discharge) and 120 deep cycles (70% depth of discharge) per MIL-PRF-21143B. As discussed earlier, military vehicle batteries nowadays are called upon to provide higher power loads and be cycled at up to 80% depth-of-discharge. This change in use of legacy Pb-acid batteries has led to shortened operational life, resulting in increased numbers of spares and field replacements required.

Lithium-ion batteries typically provide a longer cycle life than lead-acid batteries, meaning that each battery can be used for more silent watch and/or engine cranking when using this chemistry. This longer battery life provides a life cycle cost advantage and reduces required maintenance. Lithium-ion industry standards, at a minimum, require 1,000 100% depth-of-discharge cycle life. Saft's Super-Phosphate™ VL30PFe cell has proven cycle life of 3,000 cycles, at 100 % full depth-of-discharge, and 5,000 cycles at 40% depth-of-discharge at 25°C. In comparing Saft's cycle life versus the Pb-acid, you can potentially achieve a 25X increase in full depth-of-discharge and a 14X increase in shallow discharge capability. This translates to less battery replacements, which in-turn results in reduced shipments and volumes of stored batteries. Based on the study conducted by US Army Materiel Systems Analysis Activity in May of 2011, it costs the Government $125 to transport and $105 to install one (1) 6T Pb-acid battery. Historically, averaged over the past 10 years, the US Army Department Logistics Agency (DLA) has purchased about 500,000 6T Pb-acid batteries per year, with a maximum of 700,000 per year during this timeframe. Taking into consideration the average, this translates into a $115M dollars of transportation and installation cost per year, excluding acquisition cost. If you evaluate the number of military vehicles, and corresponding numbers of 6T Pb-acid batteries per vehicle, at any one time the service is utilizing 700,000 batteries. Based on this information the government is getting an average of 1-1.4 year service life from the Pb-acid 6T battery.

Currently, the DLA purchases Pb-acid 6Ts at about $.40 per watt-hour versus li-ion 6Ts targeting $1.25 per watt-hour. The $.40 per watt-hour figure is comprised of two (2) 12V Pb-acid in series to power a military vehicles 28V electrical buss. Cost to manufacture lithium-ion cells is reducing, but it will be sometime before the acquisition costs of the batteries are equivalent.

It is becoming increasingly important on new vehicle programs for the government to conduct a LCC analysis of systems during the procurement phase. In order to reduce the vehicles' LCC, it is imperative to have subsystems that can meet a high Mean Miles between Failure (MMBF) and Mean Miles between Hardware Mission Failure (MMBHMF). Beyond just cell cycle life testing as discussed earlier, Saft has conducted analysis of projected lithium-ion battery life based upon the actual missions, roles, and environments over the life of the JLTV vehicle. Results of this analysis determined, at minimum, Saft's lithium-ion 6T battery would last 7 years. Figure 5, shows the resulting comparison when analyzing acquisition cost in \$/Wh and the expected replacement rates of the two electro-chemistry systems over the 20 year life of the JLTV program.

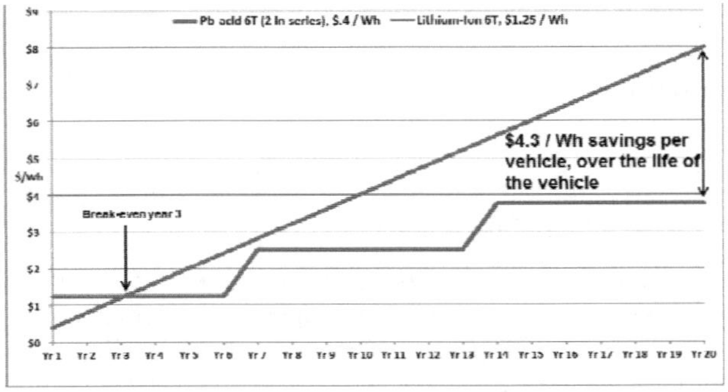

Figure 6. LCC Comparison of Pb-acid and lithium-ion

The breakeven point for the increased acquisition cost of the lithium-ion 6T is reached at year 3. The \$4.3/Wh savings per vehicle, translates to a savings of \$9,936 per vehicle. Similar to reduced transportation and installation costs discussed earlier, when you multiply the \$9,936 per vehicle savings, by the expected JLTV fleet sizeof 20,000 vehicles, you experience a \$200 million life cycle cost savings for the program!

Summary:

Lead acid batteries have been the energy storage backbone of the US military's fleet for a number of years. As DoD varies their operational tempo and fighting style, so does the way they use energy in peacetime and during deployments. Lead acid batteries will always have their place on today's battlefield for legacy systems and for applications where very high power and energy density are not critical. However, as the power and energy demands on vehicles increase, so does the need for advanced chemistry batteries, such as lithium ion.

With the leadership of TARDEC's Energy Storage Team the realization of lithium-ion 6T as a drop-in replacement to legacy PB-acid batteries is not far away. Additionally, vehicle acquisition programs, for example the Joint Light Tactical Vehicle (JLTV) have expressed interest in lithium-ion 6T batteries as a way to help meet the weight target and reduce the vehicle's lifecycle cost. Saft has already delivered lithium-ion 6T batteries to the JLTV Engineering Manufacturing Development (EMD) phase of the program, and is currently installed in vehicles under government test. This battery has also been evaluated in other vehicle platforms such as the High Mobility Mulit-Purpose Wheeled Vehicle (HMMWV) and a Mine Resistant Ambush Protected vehicle (MRAP).

Due to the dependence on the batteries for soldier protection and because lead acid battery cycle life and weight are a significant logistics burden, a new, improved battery (i.e lithium -on battery) that fulfills this need is required to fight on today's battlefield. There are many benefits of using Li-ion batteries over Pb-acid for most military vehicles. These advantages include longer cycle and calendar life, consistent power over batteries' State of Charge (SOC), re-charge at higher C rates, and the ability to perform full depth of discharge without degrading life or performance of the battery. As today's battlefield changes…so does the way we transport and use energy.

Acknowledgements

Saft would like to acknowledge TARDEC, particularly Larry Toomey, Sonya Zanardelli, Dave Skalny and, James Mainero for their continued support of DOD's lithium-ion 6T battery research and initiative.

References

1. MIL-PRF-32143B 6T Lead acid Specification
2. US Army Materiel Systems Analysis Activity (AMSAA) Field Studies Branch Hawker Batteries, May 2011
3. Challenges with Specification Development of Lead Acid Replacement Batteries, GVSETS, A123 Systems, Livonia, MI August 2012
4. Hawker Data Sheet Supplement, 12V, 120Ah C20, ABSORBED GLASS MAT (AGM)

About the Company

Saft (Euronext: Saft) is a world leading designer and manufacturer of advanced technology batteries for industry. The Group is the world's leading manufacturer of nickel batteries and primary lithium batteries for the industrial infrastructure and processes, transportation, civil and military electronics' markets. Saft is the world leader in space and defense batteries with its Li-ion technologies which are also deployed in the energy storage, transportation and telecommunication network markets. More than 3,800 employees in 18 countries, 14 manufacturing sites and an extensive sales network all contribute to accelerating the Group's growth for the future.

Saft batteries. Designed for industry.
www.saftbatteries.com.

SG270-BV-SAF-010 Revision A Highlights

Dan Kieffner
Energy, Power, and Interconnect Technologies Division
Naval Surface Warfare Center – Crane Division
Crane, Indiana, U.S.A., 47522
E-mail: dan.kieffner@navy.mil

Abstract: *The previous version of the subject document described processes necessary to characterize the safety hazards and risks associated with integration and use of large lithium batteries aboard Navy platforms, as well as the processes by which these hazards and risks are evaluated and adjudicated. The subject document expands the technology scope to include fuel cell systems. The paper includes a description of Navy shipboard considerations appropriate for all electrochemical energy storage systems, issues associated with lithium battery systems and fuel cell systems, and decision processes for allowing large electrochemical energy storage systems on Navy vessels.*

Keywords: systems; safety; Navy; battery; fuel cell; lithium-ion.

Introduction

In response to failures associated with high energy systems, the predecessor of the subject document [1] was introduced in 2011. At the time of publication, because other large electrochemical systems were not under consideration for deployment, the initial focus was ship integration hazards of large lithium battery systems. Battery systems included within the scope of [1] contain total stored electrical energy greater than 1.0 kilowatt hour (kWh) per battery pack or 2.0 kWh per total battery system.

As illustrated in recent publications, fuel cell technology has advanced to the point of advanced demonstrations in the laboratory and in military applications. Ellsworth, Rottmayer, and Miller [2] found that a hybrid lithium ion battery - sodium borohydride fuel cell system could deliver favorable results in an unmanned air vehicle application. Dalton, Ebner, Anderson, and Ayers [3] reported that a large fuel cell operating from compressed gases delivers useful energy in an air-independent environment. Novoa, Dominick, Shah, and Thampan [4] described the functionality of propane-fueled solid oxide fuel cells and reformed methanol fuel cells for remote battery charging applications.

After publication, the initial document [1] required an update. Advances in fuel cell system technology maturity have combined with demands for increased energy density to compel development of preliminary fuel cell platform integration process guidelines. Approval process exceptions have been requested for rare and temporary need situations. Several terminology changes were required for clarification.

Due to recent project scope changes, the subject document is in the review and revision stage. The scope of the revision has expanded to include an example of shipboard design integration guidance. A key systems safety document [5] has been updated, and those updates will be propagated to maintain consistency.

Ship Integration Considerations for Electrochemical Energy Storage Systems (EESS) Implementation

Multiple types of hazards could exist due to the presence of an EESS. A large EESS contains at least 1.0 kWh of stored electrochemical energy per package or at least 2.0 kWh of total stored electrochemical energy throughout the system. Depending upon the nature of the EESS, the hazard could be a rapid release of pressure, kinetic energy, heat, caustic chemicals, or other energy releases. The integrator of an EESS used on a ship, known as a ship design manager (SDM), should anticipate and design an EESS – ship interface to accommodate credible energy release events and other hazards.

Safety Certification Process: If a large EESS is expected to be temporarily or permanently deployed aboard a ship or submarine platform, then a SDM will need to generate data to support a risk assessment. Depending upon the system design and maturity, the necessary data may include a Preliminary Hazards List, Preliminary Hazard Analysis, Failure Modes and Effects Analysis, Test Plan, Hazard Log Record, and Software Hazards. As the design matures and as mitigations are developed to reduce risk to the platform, Naval Sea Systems Command (NAVSEA) technical experts will provide reviews and comments concerning the residual risk. The EESS designer contributions to this process are in assisting with identification and assessment of hazards associated with deployment of an EESS and in development of test data to support hazard quantification.

Design: An EESS should be designed to survive transportation environments and provide electrical utility in its intended deployment environment. EESS designs must include appropriate safety devices. A large EESS must include an energy storage management system (ESMS). Any ESMS should be capable of reducing risk commensurate with the hazards created by the EESS; for a fuel cell, this could include monitoring and reporting of environment combustibility characteristics. Upon detection of an anomalous condition, the ESMS shall be capable of deactivating or disconnecting the EESS. Finally, ESMS control software shall be designed and tested by an approved Government agent, and safety-critical software shall be approved by NAVSEA.

Testing and Analyses: Based upon hazards identified by the safety certification process, the SDM and EESS developer will establish a test sequence to confirm adequacy of platform mitigations. Any other applicable guidance, such as [6], should be combined with the hazard analysis results to minimize the tests required. Figure 1 depicts a notional phasing of various tests including EESS casualty characterization tests (ECCT).

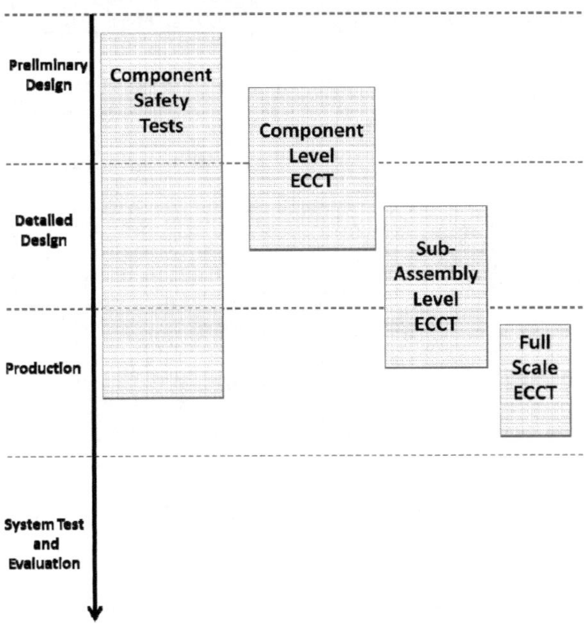

Figure 1. Example of phasing and coordination of tests between a component safety technical manual and NAVSEA TM SG270-BV-SAF-010.

The ultimate purpose of testing is to determine the impact to a platform of a worst credible event (WCE) caused by an EESS malfunction. The tests will be selected based upon the unique circumstances of the EESS hazard analyses, characteristics, and potential impacts on the platform. Aggravating circumstances, such as unintentional EESS drops or accidental crushing, will be considered for test plan inclusion. If not sufficiently verified at lower subassembly levels, tests of a full EESS are required to confirm platform survivability and recoverability.

Software Hazard Assessment: For software modules deployed within an EESS, and with the EESS developer, the SDM shall conduct a software hazard criticality assessment. Figure 2 provides guidance for generation of a software hazard criticality matrix (SHCM) for each software module. The SHCM guides the level of risk and the corresponding level of mitigation that will likely be required by an approval authority at NAVSEA.

			Hazard Category			
			I	II	III	IV
			Catastrophic	Critical	Marginal	Negligible
Software Control Category	I	Autonomous	1	1	3	5
	II a	Semiautonomous (Control)	1	2	4	5
	II b	Semiautonomous (Data/Display)	1	2	4	5
	III a	Permissive (Control)	2	3	5	5
	III b	Permissive (Data/Display)	2	3	5	5
	IV	No Control	3	4	5	5

SHCM Index	Description
1	**High Risk** - Detailed requirements and structured design to Software Standard IEEE 12207, Low Cyclomatic complexity. Significant analysis and testing required, including 100% Basis Path.
2	**Medium Risk** - Detailed requirements, design, and code analysis required, with sufficient testing to ensure safety implementation
3-4	**Moderate Risk** - High-level requirements, design, and code analysis and testing as needed.
5	**Low Risk** - Acceptable

Figure 2. Software Hazard Criticality Matrix example.

Ship Integration Considerations for Fuel Cells

Due to technology maturity, several fuel – oxidant pairs are of near-term interest to the Navy for fuel cell deployment. Fuel cells employing other reactants may be considered; however, it is possible that reviews will require additional time and cost. Fuel cells with compressed gas reactants applications less than 5000 psi will typically use oxygen and hydrogen. Liquid reactant fuel cells may use hydrogen peroxide and JP-5, JP-8, or JP-10. Cryogenic reactant fuel cells will typically use liquid oxygen and liquid hydrogen. Each set of the reactants has unique hazards that require mitigation before deployment in a maritime environment.

In addition to general considerations for an EESS, a fuel cell system will require a determination of a Net Explosive Weight (NEW) equivalent by the SDM, EESS developer, NAVSEA, and possibly the Naval Ordnance Safety and Security Activity (NOSSA) or another organization. The NEW rating will drive the WCE determination and overall EESS hazard rating. Figure 3 provides a summary depiction of the risk determination and acceptance process.

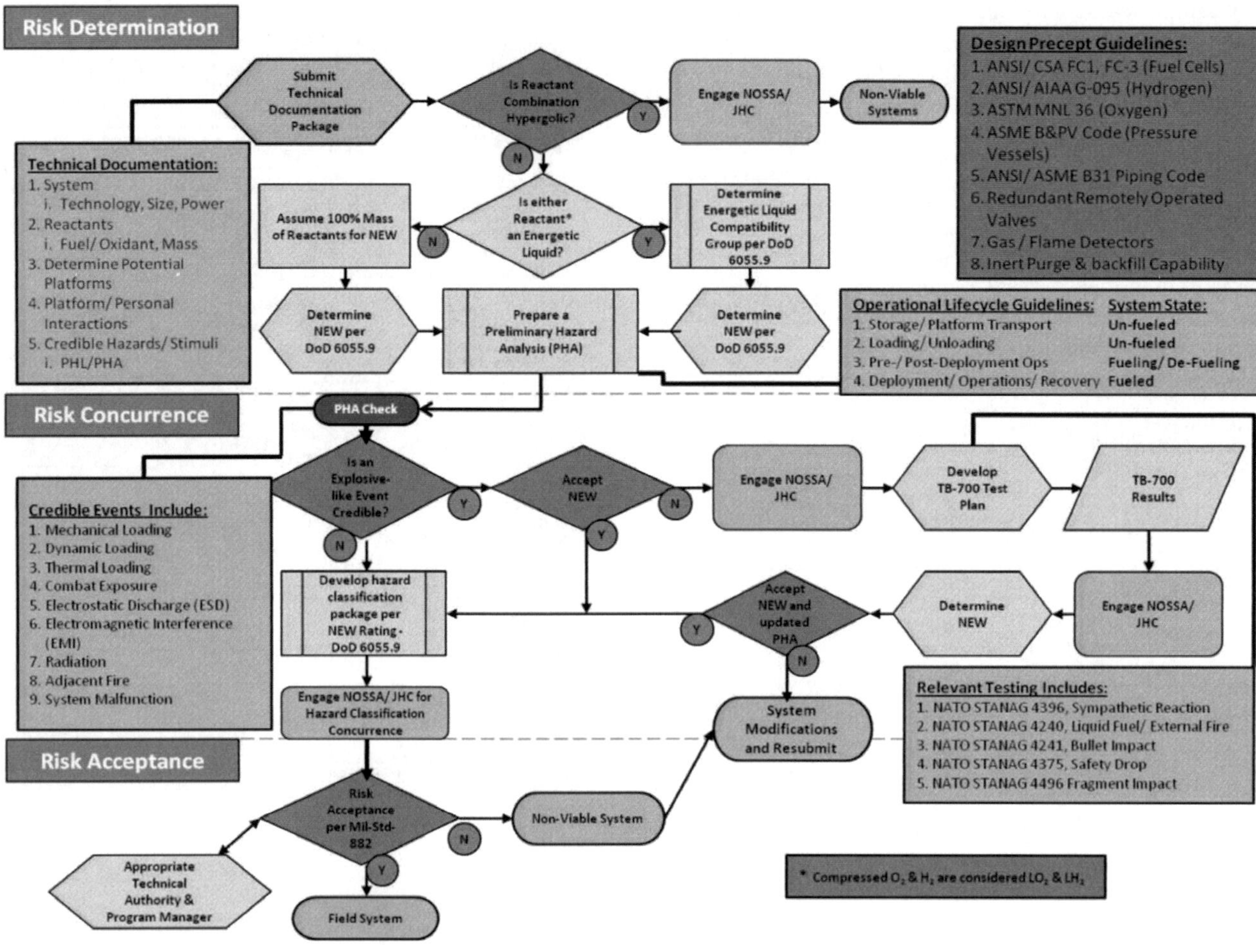

Figure 3. Proposed risk determination and acceptance process for fuel cell systems.

The technical documentation package generated by the SDM should address requirements of related industry and government standards for fuels, gases, fuel cells, pressure vessels, and process piping as appropriate. The package should consider possible hazard types such as mechanical, thermal, electromagnetic, electrostatic, or radiation exposure as well as bullet impact and subsystem malfunctions or defects. After development and execution of any tests of mitigation approaches, NAVSEA will work with the SDM and NOSSA to determine acceptance of residual risk as guided by [5].

Currently, little information is widely available to support fuel cell system component failure probability. The EESS developer should be able to provide or produce objective evidence to assist in probability calculation. Conservative or worst case values shall be used for every fuel cell component to ensure a conservative overall failure figure. Materials fatigue over the life of the fuel cell system shall be considered. Fault tree elements informing the reliability calculation include fuel cell design, software design and complexity, manufacturing processes and quality control, user error, support equipment failure, and environmental stresses.

Other Changes to Ship Integration Considerations

Although most of the original lithium battery content has not changed, the EESS considerations unique to lithium batteries are identified in an appendix to the subject manual. An EESS approval process for a temporary urgent and critical deployment is now included. The WCE consideration superseded references to maximum credible events.

Future Efforts

As EESS technologies mature, it is likely that the content and processes associated with the subject manual will require updates. Further experience with the fuel cell review and release process will result in process refinements. Developer and user comments are welcome and encouraged.

Acknowledgements

The author wishes to thank Gary Bayles, David Cherry, David Delafuente, Keith DeVries, Joseph Fontaine, Paul Jawlik, Christian Schumacher, John Timler, David Voshol, and Clint Winchester for feedback on the content of the SG270-BV-SAF-010 Revision A drafts produced to date.

References

1. Naval Sea Systems Command. (2011). *High Energy Storage System Safety Manual, SG270-BV-SAF-010.* Retrieved from https://www.fbo.gov/index?s=opportunity&mode=form&id=4a4ef5f3e26e78711f743e2ec348d2ea&tab=core&_cview=0
2. Ellsworth, N., Rottmayer, M., & Miller, R. (2012). Group I SUAS power system analysis. *Proceedings of the 45th Power Sources Conference*, 491-494.
3. Dalton, L., Ebner, C., Anderson, E., & Ayers, K. (2012). Advancements in closed loop regenerative fuel cell systems for air independent applications. *Proceedings of the 45th Power Sources Conference,* 413-416.
4. Novoa, J., Dominick, M., Shah, S., & Thampan, T. (2012). Portable 300-W fuel cells as a tactical power source. *Proceedings of the 45th Power Sources Conference,* 263-266.
5. Department of Defense (2012). *Department of Defense Standard Practice –System Safety, MIL-STD-882E.* Retrieved from http://www.system-safety.org/Documents/MIL-STD-882E.pdf
6. Naval Sea Systems Command. (2010). *Technical Manual for Navy Lithium Battery Safety Program Responsibilities and Procedures, S9310-AQ-SAF-010.* Retrieved from http://www.everyspec.com/USN/NAVSEA/NAVSEA_S9310-AQ-SAF-010_4137/

Development of a Fuel Cell Power System for Unmanned, Undersea Vehicles (UUV)

Eric A. Nelson and Robert J. Roy
Hamilton Sundstrand Corporation
A UTC Aerospace Systems Company
Windsor Locks, CT 06096
Contact author email: robert.j.roy@utas.utc.com

Abstract: *Unmanned, undersea vehicles (UUV) provide the U.S. Navy and commercial companies with a wide range of capabilities, including mine countermeasures, Intelligence, Surveillance, Reconnaissance (ISR), fleet protection, undersea survey missions and inspection of oil and gas platforms. Current and anticipated energy storage systems based solely on high-energy density batteries will not provide the range or endurance required to meet expanding mission goals. Advanced power and energy storage systems with increased specific energy of 500 W-hr/kg and greater are necessary.*

A proton exchange membrane (PEM) fuel cell system operating on hydrogen and oxygen can facilitate extended range and higher power missions compared to conventional battery energy-storage systems. Both the cell stack assembly and the reactant storage system can be adapted and integrated to fit into a variety of platforms to provide power and energy storage, and can be shipped in a non-hazardous state.

Through a contract with the Office of Naval Research (ONR), Hamilton Sundstrand is developing an energy-dense, air-independent energy system for long-endurance, undersea vehicle propulsion (LEUVP). The system is being designed to safely deliver 68 kW-hr of energy over a defined power profile within a 30-inch segment of a 21-inch diameter UUV. The design of the PEM fuel cell for this application utilizes cell and cell stack advances made during the development of a 300-kW PEM fuel cell power module recently qualified for use on-board an air-independent propulsion (AIP) submarine, where key issues such as reactant leakage through stack edge surfaces, extended life, shock and vibration tolerance, and fluid handling during pitch and roll maneuvers were successfully mitigated. The energy storage system features cryogenic oxygen and hydrogen storage tanks specifically designed by Ball Aerospace & Technologies Corporation (BATC) to achieve ONR's energy storage metrics within the physical constraints of the vehicle. Hamilton Sundstrand leads the integration of the PEM fuel cell with a cryogenic storage system, including the design of the thermal and fluid control systems to ensure gaseous reactants are fed to the cell stack assembly at the correct pressure, temperature and flow rate while ensuring the safety of the vehicle and crew or personnel servicing the vehicle.

In parallel with the ONR program, Hamilton Sundstrand is making internal investments in energy storage systems by advancing key balance-of-plant system components, defining interface requirements between working UUVs and advanced energy storage systems, and investigating servicing and refueling requirements for a fully-deployed vehicle. This paper provides an overall status of the effort to develop an energy-dense solution to meet future energy needs of UUVs.

Keywords: undersea power; undersea propulsion; energy storage; fuel cell; proton exchange membrane; cryogenic energy storage.

Introduction

The U.S. Navy has identified a need for advanced power and energy storage systems for unmanned, undersea vehicles (UUVs) that would permit higher power payloads and increased endurance to address a variety of missions. In response, the Office of Naval Research (ONR) issued a Broad Agency Announcement in 2011 soliciting proposals for an energy-dense, air-independent propulsion and power system for long-duration undersea vehicles that are safe, refuelable/rechargeable and scalable, making them applicable for a number of different vehicles and platforms. ONR planned three phases for the program; key tasks are defined:

- Phase I Base program, where the key elements of the power and energy storage system are demonstrated in an integrated test program to a Technology Readiness Level-4 (TRL-4). Additionally, the design of a TRL-6 system is advanced to the Preliminary Design Review (PDR) phase, including a preliminary safety assessment and hazards analysis of the proposed solution. The TRL-6 system is designed to fit within a vehicle hull having an inside diameter of 18.5" and an overall length of 30".
- Phase I Option program, where the TRL-6 system design from PDR is advanced to the Critical Design Review (CDR) phase.
- Phase II program, where the TRL-6 system is assembled and tested within a government-furnished equipment (GFE) hull.

Under contract to the ONR, Hamilton Sundstrand completed Phase I of the program in the first quarter of 2014 and was recently awarded the Phase I Option program. The results from the Phase I program are presented in this paper. Additionally, similar to the fact a battery system needs a recharger, Hamilton Sundstrand has also begun investigating safe refueling of energy-dense power systems for UUVs through an independent research & development program.

Energy System Requirements

Performance specifications and characteristics of the LEUVP power and energy storage system are defined at two different levels: Threshold and Objective; these are summarized in Table 1. During the Phase I Base program, Threshold performance must be demonstrated, with a pathway for the TRL-6 system design to meet Objective metric requirements defined.

Table 1. Threshold and Metric Objectives [1]

Characteristic	Threshold	Objective
Nominal Power Density (Watts/Liter)	10.6	17.2
Energy Section Length	30" (76.2 cm)	30" (76.2 cm)
Energy Volume (Liters)	132	132
Energy Mass (kg) without hull & bulkhead	132 (neutrally buoyant)	132 (neutrally buoyant)
Energy (kW-hr)	42	68
Duration (hr)	$\geq$30	$\geq$30
Energy Density (W-hr/L)	318 – 515, neutrally buoyant	
Stop / Start Cycles	3 – 5	
Power Profile	Figure 1	Figure 2
Refueling Time (hr)	$\leq$2	$\leq$1
Vehicle Bus Voltage (Vdc)	24 - 48	

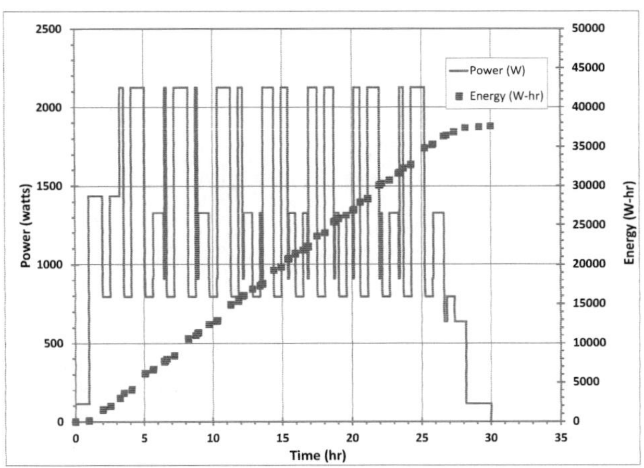

Figure 1. 42 kW-hr Threshold Power and Energy Profile

Technical Approach

Hamilton Sundstrand's approach for solving the energy problem for UUVs is depicted in Figure 3. The power and energy system features a proton exchange membrane (PEM) fuel cell developed for an air-independent propulsion (AIP) submarine, adopted for use on pure

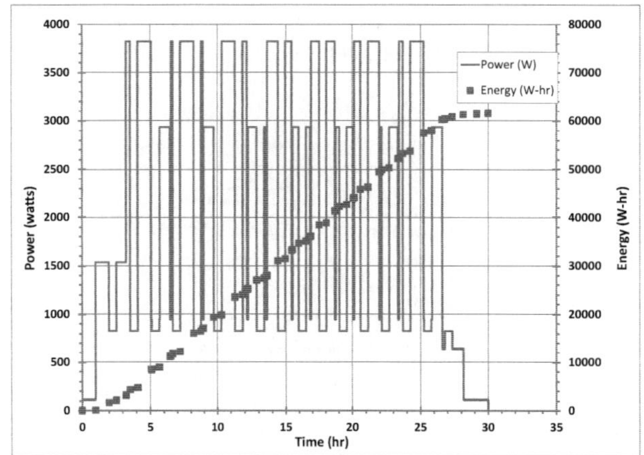

Figure 2. 68 kW-hr Objective Power and Energy Profile

oxygen and hydrogen for the UUV. The PEM fuel cell incorporates passive water transport within each cell, meaning no external humidification of reactants or external blowers to provide motive force to remove the byproduct water from the fuel cell are required. A new ultra-low leakage seal design has also been developed for closed environments to minimize emissions of potentially hazardous gases to ambient. A photograph of 50-kW PEM fuel cell stacks in production for AIP submarines is included in Figure 4; a photograph of the 20-cell stack assembly used for the TRL-4 demonstration program is included in Figure 5.

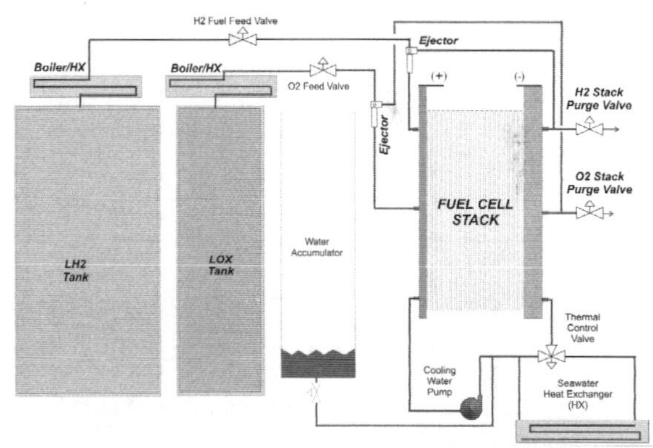

Figure 3. Power and Energy Storage System for UUVs

Figure 4. 50-kW PEM Fuel Cell Stacks for AIP Submarine

Figure 5. 20-cell PEM Fuel Cell Stack for the TRL-4 Demonstration Test Program

The energy storage solution selected for the UUV is cryogenic hydrogen and oxygen due to their high volumetric and gravimetric density. In comparison compressed gas storage, reversible metal hydrides as well as non-regenerable chemical systems for generating hydrogen and oxygen have lower energy density. Reformation of hydrocarbon fuels as a source of hydrogen was not considered due to the complexity of the balance of plant design. The design of the Dewar, developed by Ball Aerospace & Technologies Corporation (BATC), features cryogenic hydrogen and oxygen tanks packaged within a single vacuum shell to minimize weight and volume. A photograph of this unique Dewar design is provided in Figure 6. The remaining balance of plant is greatly simplified by the passive fuel cell design – the only moving parts are the cooling pump, storage water pump and solenoid valves. The design maintains neutral buoyancy by storing the byproduct water in accumulators within the vehicle energy section hull.

Figure 6. BATC Land-based Prototype Dewar Assembly for Storage of Cryogenic Hydrogen and Oxygen

TRL-4 Demonstration Test

The TRL-4 Demonstration Test Program was designed to separately evaluate the performance of the fuel cell system and the cryogenic fluid storage and delivery system prior to integration and testing of the complete prototype system. Seven test objectives were defined for the demonstration test program, with each objective designed to minimize risk to the test system hardware as well as to minimize jeopardy to the program schedule while gaining confidence in the overall system approach. Test objectives 1-4 were completed with reactants provided from compressed gas cylinders; while test objectives 5-7 were completed using reactants derived from the BATC cryogenic storage and delivery system. A summary of the test objectives is included as Table 2. As is apparent from a review of Table 2, the test approach incrementally advanced the technology readiness of the fuel cell power and energy storage system as each objective was successfully demonstrated.

Table 2. TRL-4 Demonstration Test – Test Objectives

TEST OBJECTIVE	PURPOSE
1	Establish a performance baseline of the PEM fuel cell system using reactants supplied from a compressed gas farm.
2	Operate the PEM fuel cell system against the 30-hr Threshold power profile • Measure the mass flow rate to support each power level defined within the profile • Measure the total mass of reactants required to support 42 kW-hr of energy storage against that profile for the TRL-6 system
3	Operate the PEM fuel cell system against the 30-hr Objective power profile • Measure the mass flow rate to support each power level defined within the profile • Measure the total mass of reactants required to support 68 kW-hr of energy storage against that profile for the TRL-6 system
4	Demonstrate stop/start cycles of the PEM fuel cell system using the approach defined for the TRL-6 system
5	Conduct check-out testing of the cryogenic storage and delivery system • Establish a performance baseline for the Dewar assembly, control valves and heaters • Measure the Dewar assembly heat leak and correlate with model predictions for TRL-6 system design
6	Repeat Test Objective #1, but with reactants derived from the cryogenic storage and delivery system
7	Operate the integrated cryogenic storage and delivery system and the PEM fuel cell system against the 30-hr Threshold power profile • Demonstrate safe storage of hydrogen at supercritical conditions to achieve the density target for the TRL-6 system design • Demonstrate the performance of the reactant management system through the Threshold power profile: o Pressure control performance, from the cryogenic fluid tanks to the inlet of the cell stack assembly o Vaporizer performance through the full power profile range • Demonstrate safe management of cryogenic fluids through the mission profile, including stop/start cycles • At the conclusion of the 30-hr test, operate the integrated system at the maximum net power defined for the Objective metric to demonstrate proper performance of the key system elements defined above

All objectives for the test program were satisfactorily completed, including efficient operation of the fuel cell system through the Threshold and Objective power profiles defined in Figure 1 and Figure 2, respectively, as well as the safe management of cryogenic hydrogen and oxygen through all aspects of operation (charging; fuel cell operation; stop/start; tank safing). The test results from Test Objective #7 are provided in Figure 7; sustained stop cycles near the end of the test program were the result of test facility power faults and were not the result of the test hardware itself. Operation at the peak power level of 3825 watts, net, was successfully completed at the conclusion of the 30-hr test run as can be seen in Figure 7.

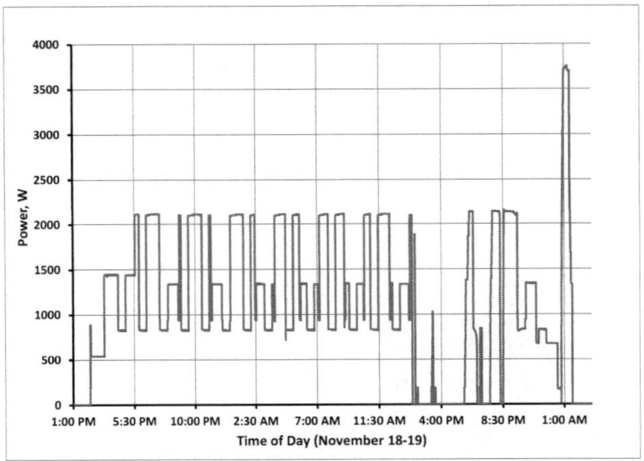

Figure 7. Results of Integrated Cryogenic Storage and Fuel Cell System – 30-hr Threshold Test

TRL-6 System Design

During the Phase I Base program Hamilton Sundstrand and BATC developed the design of a TRL-6 power and energy storage system against the Threshold metric requirements. The primary objective for this work element was development of a 3-D solid model of the power and energy storage system that meets, as a minimum, the Threshold metric requirements defined in Table 1. The TRL-6 package features:

- A 30-cell PEM fuel cell stack assembly with an advanced stack retention system that reduces installed weight and volume while meeting all performance requirements for both Threshold and Objective metrics
- Cryogenic hydrogen and oxygen tanks within a common vacuum annulus to achieve high-energy density storage with minimum Dewar weight and volume
- Compact, manifold-mounted balance-of-plant components that minimize system volume and weight while facilitating assembly
- A zero-emission, zero-observable, neutrally-buoyant system that is fully-scalable to meet varying UUV mission power and energy storage profiles

The design activity was supported by a number of contract deliverable items, including a Preliminary System Safety and Hazards Analysis. The proposed solution, while highly-energetic in nature due to the packaging density requirements, did not identify any hazards that could not be successfully mitigated through either engineering controls or vehicle ConOps (concept of operations). A solid model of the TRL-6 system design is included as Figure 8.

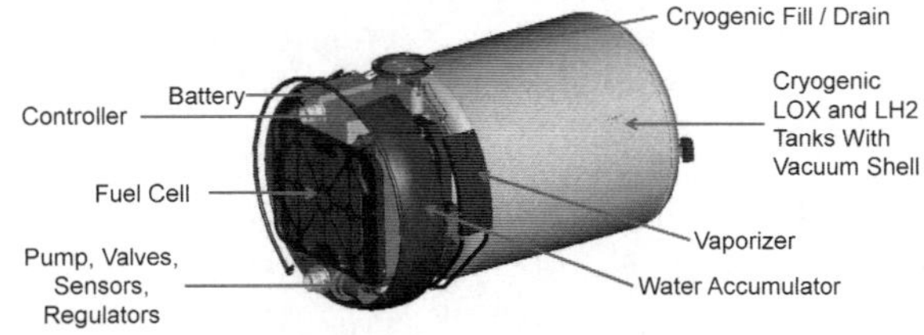

Figure 8. TRL-6 System Package Design – 3-D Solid Model

Internal Investment

Hamilton Sundstrand is making internal investments to more closely examine refueling approaches that considers logistics, supply chain and crew safety. A concept for a Refueling and Servicing Package (RASP) has been developed that only requires water and electricity to safely produce, store and dispense cryogenic reactants to refuel UUVs utilizing a PEM fuel cell power plant. The RASP also incorporates other features to essentially allow hands-off maintenance of the vehicle through all aspects of operation pre- and post-mission.

Conclusions

The ONR Phase I Base program recently completed by Hamilton Sundstrand included a safe demonstration of a TRL-4 system that showed the viability of an integrated cryogenic storage and fuel cell system to provide energy for a UUV. Through a preliminary design activity that resulted in a 3-D solid model of a TRL-6 system, a scalable system solution has demonstrated that high specific energy can be attained within a UUV hull. Future effort on this program only requires sound engineering – no invention is required to bring this solution forward to the Navy's fleet of UUVs.

Acknowledgements

The authors would like to extend our most sincere thanks and appreciation to Maria Medeiros, Program Officer at the Office of Naval Research, and her entire undersea energy and propulsion team for their support of our Phase I Base effort to advance power and energy system technology for unmanned, undersea vehicles.

Reference

1. ONR BAA Announcement #11-016, Long Endurance Undersea Vehicle Propulsion, dated 31-March-2011

Novel Air-independent Power Sources for Unmanned Underwater Vehicles

Robert Reeve and Darren Browning
Physical Sciences Department, Defence Science and Technology Laboratory
Porton Down, Salisbury, Wiltshire, UK, SP4 0JQ

Abstract: *This paper presents the results of research into electrochemical power sources using a unique type of polymer electrolyte membrane, namely a bipolar membrane. Batteries and a fuel cell option using such membranes were investigated and their performance in terms of power density and coulombic efficiency is presented. In each case the cathode reaction utilised hydrogen peroxide as the oxidant for air-independent operation. In this configuration, the bipolar membrane offered a unique advantage; the ability to decouple the pH of the anode and cathode reactions. This allowed a range of alkaline stabilised fuels (e.g. high energy metals and sodium borohydride solutions) to be operated in conjunction with acidified hydrogen peroxide. The advantage here being greater stability and coulombic efficiency for both anode and cathode reactions. Early indications suggest that power systems based on this concept could compete favourably with lithium-ion batteries, especially for long endurance applications.*

Keywords: UUV; bipolar membrane; battery; fuel cell; sodium borohydride; hydrogen peroxide; aluminium; zinc, magnesium.

Introduction

Air-independent power is a subject of much research due to its relevance to undersea platforms such as unmanned underwater vehicles (UUVs). The capability offered by such platforms can be limited by their range and endurance which is dictated by the energy content of their batteries (typically silver zinc or lithium-ion). Recent work at Dstl have investigated novel power sources for such applications including batteries using high energy metal anodes and fuel cells using alkaline sodium borohydide fuel solutions. These fuels were discharged in a cell configuration utilising hydrogen peroxide as the oxidant, thus allowing for air-independent operation. Specifically, the peroxide solution was reduced directly in the cell (i.e. electrochemically) as opposed to its indirect use as a source of oxygen. A key innovation in the research was the use of an electrolyte separator known as a Bipolar Membrane (BPM). The advantage of this membrane is its ability to regulate the pH in the cell such that one side of the cell operates in alkaline media while the other side operates in acidic media. In this way alkaline stabilised fuels can be discharged opposite acid stabilised hydrogen peroxide with bestowed advantages of greater chemical stability and improved coulombic efficiency.

Conduction in BPMs: A BPM is essentially a layered combination of a Cation Exchange Membrane (CEM) and an Anion Exchange Membrane (AEM). In some cases, the interface region is functionalised with an additional catalyst layer. The conduction process in a BPM is summarised in Figure 1. In brief, water molecules diffuse to the interface region of BPM where they dissociate into protons and hydroxyl ions which then conduct away from the interface through their membranes. The energy associated with the water splitting process results in voltage drop across the BPM of approximately 0.83 V, although this is compensated by a comparable increment in the cell EMF afforded by the pH gradient across the cell.

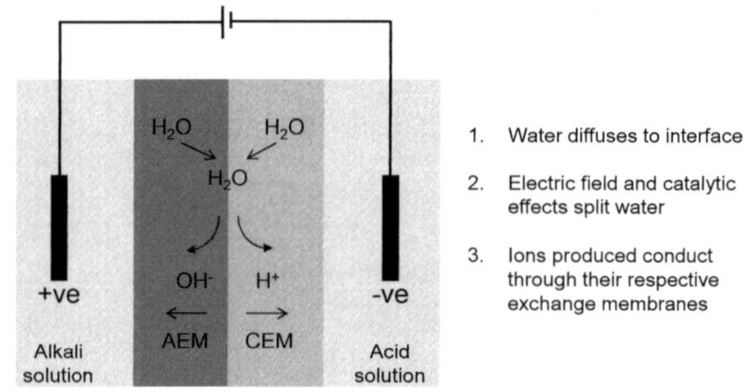

Figure 1. Ionic conduction process in a BPM

Application of BPMs to Power Sources: Dstl have investigated fuel cell and battery options using BPMs. The theoretical specific energy (i.e. reagent basis) of these power sources is shown in Table 1 and highlights the high energy content associated these reagents. In the case of the fuel cell, this used alkaline sodium borohydride solution and is reported in a previous paper [1]. The work presented in here builds on this previous research to include battery options using the metal anodes in Table 1.

Table 1. Theoretical specific energies for a selection of BPM – hydrogen peroxide power sources (reagent based values, excluding hardware)

Anode	Voltage/ V	Specific Energy/ Wh·kg^{-1}	
		100% H_2O_2	60% H_2O_2
Mg	3.64	3,339	2,405
Al	2.61	2,687	1,871
Zn	1.71	920	749
$NaBH_{4\ (s)}$	2.19	2,686	1,772
30 w/o $NaBH_{4\ (l)}$	2.19	1,778	1,329
Li-ion	3.6	<1,000 (250 practical)	

Experimental

Electrochemical cells were produced and tested in a small test cell adapted from a commercial fuel cell (e.g. Electrochem Inc., EFC-05-02-ref, Figure 2). In this case graphite gaskets were used to accommodate the metal fuel plates and allow electrolyte to flow over them.

Figure 2. Electrochemical test cell for evaluation of the metal – hydrogen peroxide batteries

A schematic of the accompanying test equipment for evaluation of the batteries is shown in Figure 3.

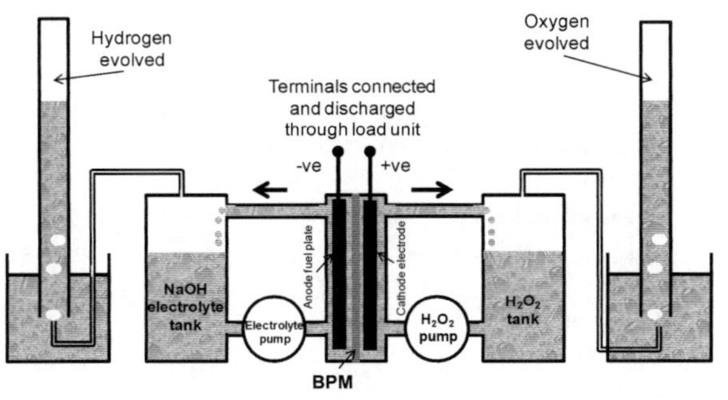

Figure 3. Schematic of the test station for evaluation of the metal - hydrogen peroxide batteries

Electrolyte (typically 6 M NaOH) was circulated between the metal fuel plates and the BPM using a peristaltic pump. Any hydrogen gas produced from the corrosion of the fuel plate was measured by displacing water from an upturned burette.

The cathode used in each cell was a platinum/carbon gas diffusion electrode (Johnson Matthey Fuel cells, ELE0079). The oxidant was 3% hydrogen peroxide mixed with one molar sulphuric acid supplied to the cell using a second peristaltic pump. Any oxygen produced by the decomposition of hydrogen peroxide on the cathode catalyst was again measured by displacement of water.

The BPM used to separate the two halves of the cell was supplied by Fumatech GmbH (Fumasep FBM).

Cell polarisation was measured under galvanostatic conditions using a load unit in conjunction with a power supply. Each measurement was taken after an applied load of five minutes in order to obtain steady state results. The cell operating temperature was monitored using a type K thermocouple embedded in the cell flow plates.

Results and Discussion

Aluminium/ BPM /hydrogen peroxide battery development: A schematic representation of the reaction sequence for this battery is shown in Figure 4.

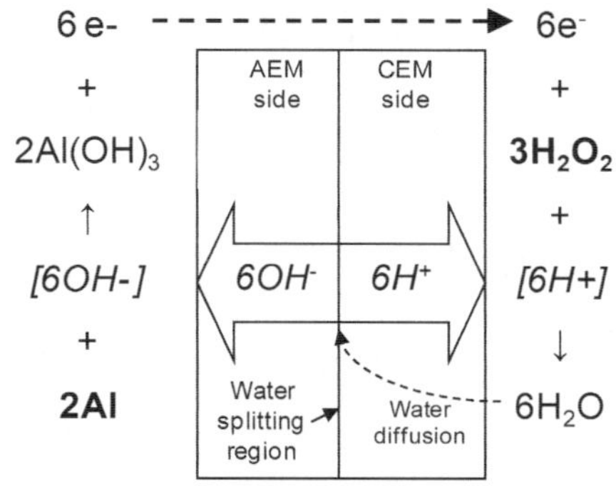

Figure 4. Schematic reaction sequence for an aluminium – hydrogen peroxide battery using a bipolar membrane

The polarisation and power characteristics for the battery are presented in Figure 5. This cell used a specialist alloy (i.e. Al 98.30, Mg 0.39, Sn 0.10, Ga 0.05) developed previously for aluminium air batteries and produced an impressive peak power of 66 mW·cm^{-2}.

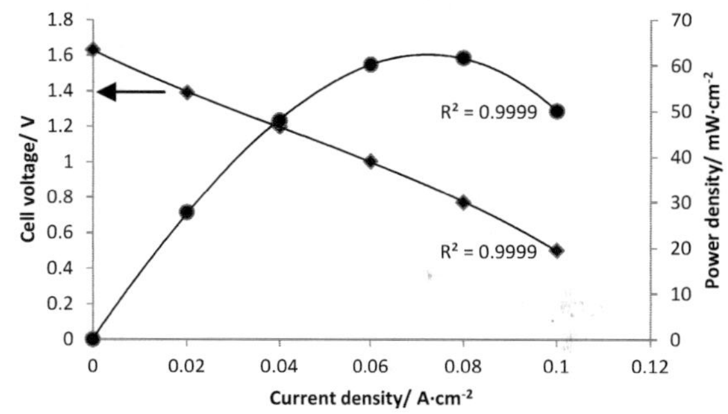

Figure 5. Polarisation and power characteristics of an aluminium - hydrogen peroxide battery using a BPM separator at 20°C

Despite the promising power density, the performance of the cell was observed to deteriorate if left off load for any appreciable time (e.g. three hours or so). This effect became more severe throughout the life of the cell and eventually it was necessary to remove the aluminium plate from the cell and physically remove surface layers from the plate in order to obtain adequate performance. Alternatively, if the cell was operated on constant load, the performance remained highly stable.

The observations would suggest passivation of the anode surface with $Al(OH)_3$. In addition to aluminium oxidation, passivation can also occur by corrosion of aluminium i.e.

$$Al + 3H_2O \rightarrow Al(OH)_3 + 3/2H_2$$

Visual inspection of the gassing rate from the anode indicated that this was more prevalent at open circuit.

The coulombic efficiency of the anode reaction was determined to quantify the degree of corrosion in the cell and how this related to the cell operating conditions. The results are shown in Figure 6 and show a maximum efficiency of 95% at the 0.1 A·cm^{-2}. Operating the cell at lower loads (and open circuit) incurred a greater corrosion and hydrogen release rate. In view of these results, the performance degradation under these conditions may be attributed to greater passivation resulting from corrosion.

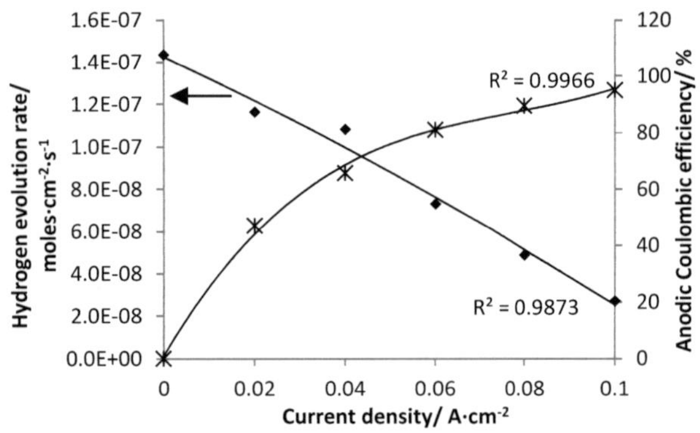

Figure 6. Coulombic efficiency for the anode of the aluminium - hydrogen peroxide battery shown in Figure 5

Several attempts were made to increase the efficiency and power stability of the anode reaction, including the following strategies:

1 Use of pure aluminium and different anode alloys;

2 Use of electrolyte additives (e.g. sodium tin (IV) oxide trihydrate);

3 The use of $Al(OH)_3$ seeding agents. Ideally, $Al(OH)_3$ produced at the anode (either by corrosion or by oxidation) is solublised by reaction with the electrolyte i.e.

$$Al(OH)_3 + OH^- = Al(OH)_4^-$$

If, however, the $Al(OH)_4^-$ concentration at the electrode surface reaches its solubility limit, solid $Al(OH)_3$ can precipitate. Seeding agents can be used to preferentially precipitate $Al(OH)_3$ away from the electrode surface (e.g. in a separate waste tank) to avoid passivation.

In brief, the approaches described above did not fully resolve the stability issues observed at low loads, although the current study did not examine all possible formulations. Studies on aluminium – air batteries would suggest this issue should not be unsurmountable [2,3].

In addition to the anode efficiency, hydrogen peroxide can also decompose on the cathode catalyst to produce oxygen. Again, this decreases the efficiency. The observed trend in the cathode efficiency is shown in Figure 7 and shows the efficiency to increase as load is placed on the cell. At the optimum power output of the cell the hydrogen peroxide efficiency was 100%.

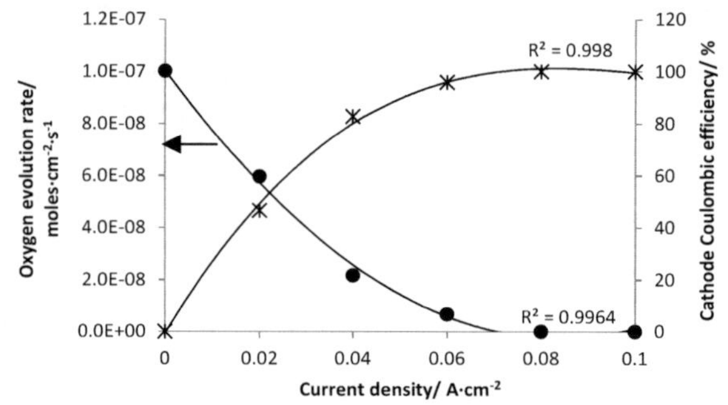

Figure 7. Coulombic efficiency for the cathode of the aluminium - hydrogen peroxide battery shown in Figure 5

Calculations were undertaken to gauge the potential of the aluminium/ BPM/ hydrogen peroxide system in terms of a system level specific energy. Clearly, such calculations are subject to many assumptions and a sucessful outcome of the development work required to achieve stable long term discharge of aluminum. The results are shown in Figure 8 for a hypothetical 2.5 kW power system and suggest specific energies in excess of 250 Wh·kg^{-1} could be realised. This equates to about twice that of a large format lithium-ion battery system (i.e > 20 kWh). Examination of Figure 8 shows the benefits of the system are only realised if the system is configured for moderate to long term discharge (i.e. 15 hour or greater). If configured for shorter durations the system offers a diminished and a non competative performance due to the overriding parasitic weight of the battery hardware.

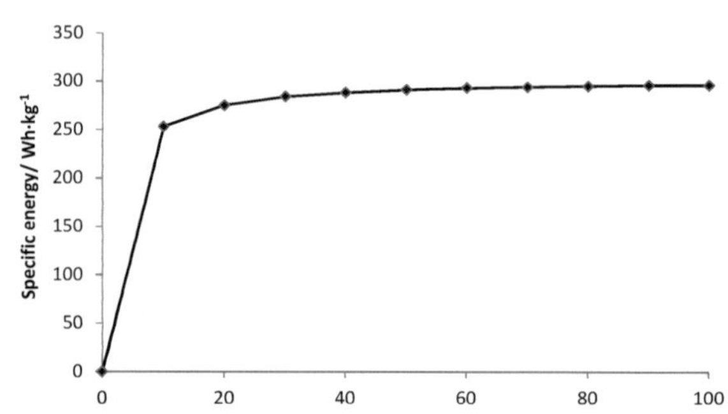

Figure 8. Estimated system level specific energy for aluminium - hydrogen peroxide battery

The values presented in Figure 8 are based on the assumptions provided in Table 2 and assume the system operates at a constant power output with no degradation in cell power density or efficiency. It is clear that the operation of the aluminium system (especially at high depths of discharge) is complex and will require further work to de-risk these aspects. This is identified here as a priority area of work.

Table 2. Assumptions used in the system model for the aluminium/hydrogen peroxide battery

Anode Coulombic efficiency	81%
Anode depth of discharge	75%
Hydrogen peroxide concentration	60%
Cathode Coulombic efficiency	96%
Cathode depth of discharge	95%
Cell voltage	1.003 V
Cell current density	0.06 A·cm^{-2}
Parasitic power	10%
Battery hardware make up (adapted from reference 4)	31w/o aluminium and 69 w/o peripherals (i.e. module housing, cathode, seeding agent, crystalliser, cooling, KOH and water)
Oxidant pump/ kg	5
Power management/ kg	10

Zinc/ BPM/ hydrogen peroxide battery development: Metallic zinc, either in plate or particulate form, has been used extensively in zinc-air batteries with applications ranging for hearing aids to military communications. As such, the adaptation of zinc into a hydrogen peroxide variant of the battery would appear to be a nearer term proposition than the aluminium battery described above.

A zinc/ BPM/ hydrogen peroxide battery was constructed and evaluated according to the same test conditions described previously. The polarisation and efficiency results are presented in Figure 9. A notable feature of this cell was the lack of corrosion observed previously with aluminium.

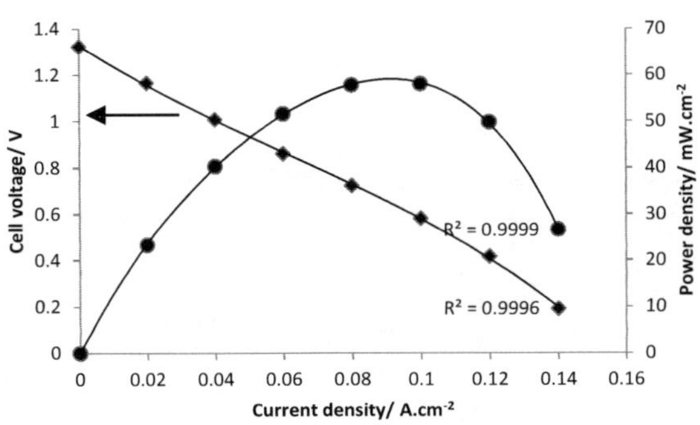

Figure 9. Polarisation and power characteristics of a zinc – hydrogen peroxide battery

Despite the favourable properties described above, zinc has a considerably lower capacity than aluminium and so the energy offered by this battery is somewhat limited. Using the performance data in Figure 9, it is estimated that a battery system would contain about half the energy of that with aluminium. As such this battery offers only an incremental improvement over conventional batteries, albeit at lower technical risk.

Magnesium/ BPM/ hydrogen peroxide battery development: This battery offers the greatest theoretical capacity of the metal options investigated. Batteries were constructed and evaluated using two different anodes:

1 Pure magnesium (neutral electrolyte battery anode)

2 Magnesium (96%), aluminium, zinc alloy

Despite much effort, the cells failed to deliver useful levels of power due to passivation of magnesium in the alkaline environment. Although some academic literature sources refer to magnesium alloys with passive films that can breakdown during the passage of current [5], it appears that this battery option is a long term, high risk option. Additional strategies could include electrolyte additives to break down the passive film.

Fuel cell research: Fuel cell research focussed on the use of sodium borohydride as the fuel. Details of this fuel cell are detailed elsewhere [1] and typical performance data is provided in Table 3. The fuel cell provided lower power than the metal batteries described above due to a lower nominal voltage. A priority research area for this fuel cell is managing the separation of the sodium borate reaction product for the fuel during long term discharge.

Table 3. Performance data for a sodium borohydride/ hydrogen peroxide battery using a BPM at 30°C. Fuel: 0.25 M $NaBH_4$ in 6 M NaOH. Oxidant – as previous

Fuel reaction	$NaBH_4 + 8OH^- \rightarrow NaBO_2 + 6H_2O + 8e^-$
Cathode reaction	$4H_2O_2 + 8H^+ + 8e^- \rightarrow 12OH^-$
Cell output	0.89 V open circuit. 0.47V at 0.1A·cm^{-2} (maximum power)
Anode efficiency (Pt/C, ELE0079)	91% at maximum power point (0.1 A·cm^{-2})
Cathode efficiency (Pt/C ELE0079)	91% at maximum power point (0.1 A·cm^{-2})

Acknowledgements

The authors would like to thank Dstl for funding this work under the Dstl associate scholarship scheme.

References

1. Reeve, R. W, *ECS Transactions*, 42 (1) 117-129 (2012).
2. Hunter et al. US patent number 5,004,654 (1991).
3. O' Callagham, B. W. Patent application WO1992004739A1 (1993).
4. Yang, S and Knickle, H, *Journal of Power Sources*, 12, 162-173 (2002).
5. Zongping, G et al, *International Journal of Hydrogen Energy*, 34, 467-472 (2009).

Modeling of a Hybrid Electric Energy Source based on Fuel Cells and Secondary Lithium-ion Batteries

Grzegorz Grzeczka[1], Adam Polak[2]
Faculty of Mechanical and Electrical Engineering, Institute of Electrical Engineering and Automatics
Polish Naval Academy
69 Smidowicza St., 81-103 Gdynia, Poland
[1] g.grzeczka@amw.gdynia.pl, [2] a.polak@amw.gdynia.pl

Abstract. *The paper presents an attempt to model the hybrid electric energy source that powers dismounted soldier systems. The hybrid power source consists of a proton exchange membrane fuel cells system (PEM FCS) and a high energy density lithium-ion rechargeable battery pack. The model of the hybrid electric energy source was designed such that the requirements defined in STANAG 4695 for the electric energy source, powering the NATO dismounted soldier, are fulfilled. The model was created to investigate how the fuel cells and rechargeable batteries will cooperate with each other. Moreover, due to the possibility of changing the parameters of the model, which concern the fuel cells stack, the battery pack and the electrical load, the created model was used to determine the proper capacity of the battery pack that is needed to provide supply of electric energy for the dismounted soldier for 72 hours in different operating scenarios. The results obtained from the simulations are presented and discussed in the paper.*

Keywords: fuel cells; lithium-ion batteries; hybrid energy source.

Introduction

The fuel cells technology, and especially the Proton Exchange Membrane Fuel Cell (PEM FC) technology, is currently one of the most promising technologies of the electric energy generation, and therefore, research and science institutions all over the world have been developing it intensively. It is caused by various advantages of fuel cells that emerge while being compared with other electric energy sources. But, despite many years of research, there are still some limitations and unresolved problems concerning FC. Most of these disadvantages, however, can be eliminated or significantly reduced by using them in a hybrid power source with other electric energy sources, for instance, different kinds of rechargeable batteries or ultra capacitors [1, 2, 3, 4, 5].

Plenty of published papers focus on theoretical description and strategies of the cooperation of different electric energy sources, however; too few of them describe methods of sizing each separate electric energy source in relation to a different load profile [6, 7, 8]. In this paper, we describe a simulation model of the hybrid electric energy source, composed of lithium-ion rechargeable batteries and PEM FC, whose task is to help in assessment whether the proposed base elements of the system were selected properly for the demanded load profile. The paper also presents the results of the simulations performed on the presented model.

Elements of the modeled system

The hybrid electric energy source consists of two base components, i.e. a PEM FCS and a lithium-ion battery pack. The PEM FC and the Li-ion batteries have different operational characteristics, and thus the hybrid power source requires to be equipped with the Power Management System (PMS), whose main task is to control the energy flow between the components of the system, protect the cells against failures of system (short circuit, overcharge, overdischarge) and stabilize output voltage. The electric load consists of devices that are powered by the hybrid energy source which in case of use for a dismounted soldier are named Dismounted Soldier Systems (DSS). The diagram of the 20W mobile power system is presented in the Fig. 1.

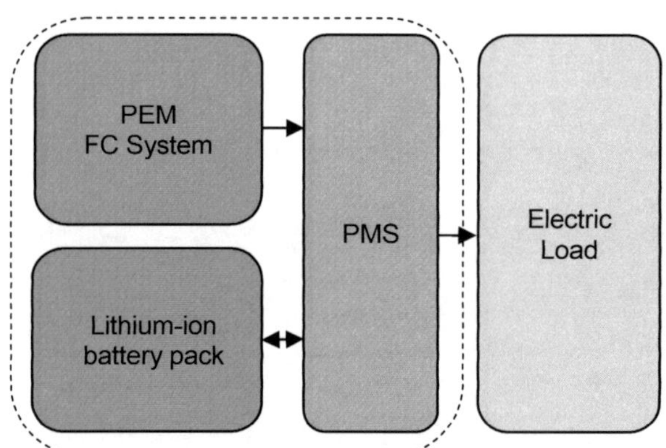

Figure 1. Diagram of the hybrid power source with PEM FCs stack and Li-ion battery pack

Electric load. The parameters of the electric load of the hybrid energy source are defined by the STANAG 4695 [9] in the section describing the requirements for a DSS power source. It assumes that DSS total power consumption cannot exceed the value of 50 W and 5 A. Additionally, it was assumed that the average required power equals 20 W and the maximal duration of the mission equals 72 hours.

PEM FC system. The selected for the hybrid power system PEM FC stack is composed of 13 cells. Its main parameters are as follows:

- open circuit voltage: 12 [V]
- nominal Power: 20 [W]
- nominal voltage: 7,8 [V]
- nominal current: 2,6 [A]
- reactants: hydrogen and air
- maximal temperature: 55[°C]
- nominal efficiency: ~40 %.

The PEM FC system was selected to provide continuous power supply on an average power level required by DSS.

Li-ion battery pack. As a second energy source in the hybrid power source a lithium-ion technology was selected, which currently offers the best coefficients of gravimetric and volumetric energy density of the secondary galvanic cells. The parameters of the selected cells in laboratory conditions were as follows:

- capacity – 3150 [mAh]
- nominal voltage – 3,6 [V]
- charging voltage – 4,2 [V]
- charging current 1625 [mA]
- Volumetric Energy Density 676 [Wh/l]
- Gravimetric Energy Density 243 [Wh/kg].

Power Management System. The Power Management System was built based on two power electronic DC/DC converters controlled by the embedded CPU. The first DC/DC converter is responsible for proper adjustment of the output voltage of the PEM FC stack to the actual operating point of the Li-ion battery pack in the way enabling continuous operation of the fuel cells stack with its nominal power. The second converter maintains the output voltage of the hybrid power source at the desired level. It was determined that the PMS operates with efficiency equal to 90 % (at a nominal point of work). However, during the idle operation of the system, power losses equal to 2 W.

Simulation model

Simulation studies of the hybrid power source, composed of the PEM FC stack and the lithium-ion battery pack, were performed in Matlab/SIMULINK environment. The model of the hybrid electric energy source consists of four subsystems, i.e. the Li-ion battery pack, the fuel cells stack, the DC/DC converter and the electrical load. The Li-ion battery pack and the PEM fuel cells stack were modeled with help of available in Matlab/Simulink libraries predefined blocks, which were previously tuned up with the parameters of real elements. The simulation model also contains the model of the PMS, programmed to reflect the behavior (especially in terms of efficiency) of the real PMS described in the previous section. The model of the electric load was built with help of the models of a resistance branch and an ideal switch, programmed to behave in a desired way. Fig. 2 presents the diagram of the simulation program.

Simulation assumptions

Simulations were performed according to the following assumptions:

a) continuous operation of the hybrid power system lasts for 72 h with average power equal to 20W and peak power equal to 50W,

b) electric load is supplied through the PMS,

c) PEM FC stack operates 72 hours with its nominal power (20W) supplying through PMS an external electric load or charging the battery pack,

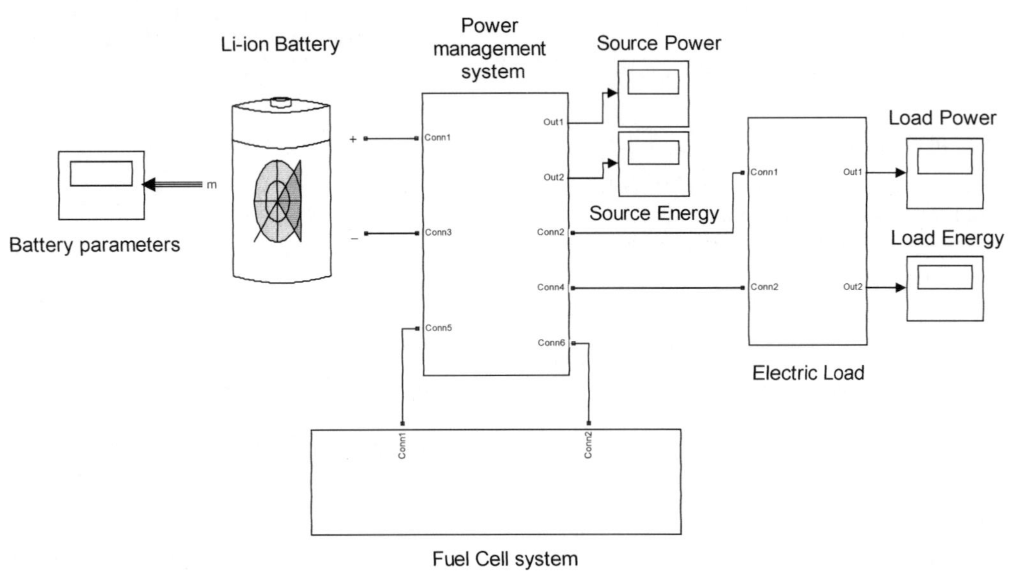

Figure 2. Simulation model of the portable hybrid power source with 20 W PEM FC stack and the lithium-ion battery pack developed in Matlb/Simulink environment

d) nominal PMS efficiency equals 90% and the idle power loss equals to 2W,

e) PMS stabilizes the output voltage of the hybrid system and assures operation of the PEM FC at its nominal power.

Simulations were performed for three different load profiles that meet the assumed levels of average and peak power. Two of them are simple profiles, with periodically changing load from zero to peak power, which differ from each other in the length of their period (see Fig. 3). The first one has a period length equal to 0,5 h and the second one has the period equal to 12 h. The third load profile is a random load in ranging from 0 to 50 W, with average power for 72 hours equal to 20W (see Fig. 4).

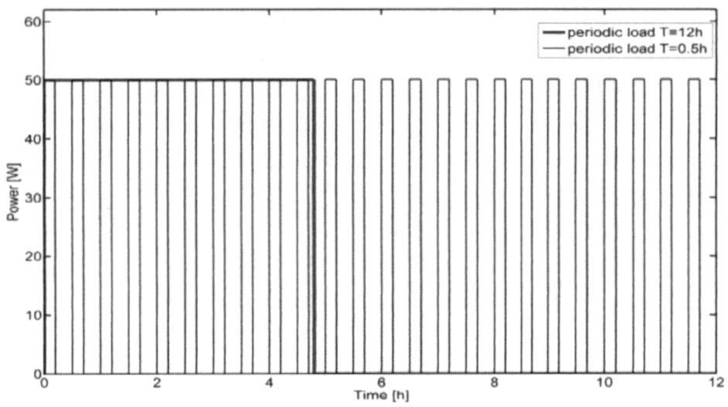

Figure 3. Periodic load profile (T1=30min, T2=12h, P_{max}=50W, P_{min}=0W, P_{av}=20W)

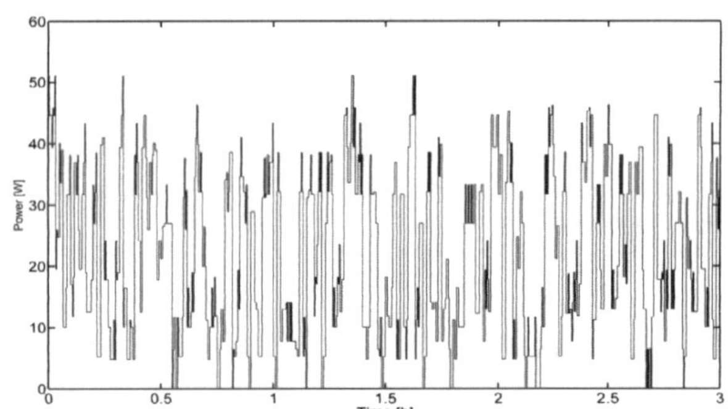

Figure 4. Random load profile (P_{max}=50W, $P_{av,72h}$=20W)

The simulations were performed for several different Li-ion battery packs. Simulated battery packs are multiples of the basic package, consisting of five cells connected in series. This combination enabled obtaining battery packs of nominal voltage equal to 18 V and the charging voltage equal to 21 V. The parallel combination of such packages enabled obtaining the following capacity of the Li-ion battery packs:

$Q_{Li,1} = 57.6Wh$ (5x1 cells), $Q_{Li,2} = 115.2Wh$ (5x2 cells), $Q_{Li,3} = 172.8Wh$ (5x3 cells), $Q_{Li,4} = 230.4Wh$ (5x4 cells), $Q_{Li,5} = 288Wh$ (5x5 cells), $Q_{Li,6} = 345.6Wh$ (5x6 cells), $Q_{Li,7} = 403.2Wh$ (5x7 cells).

Simulation results

The simulations were carried out according to the program which takes into account all combinations of lithium-ion battery packs and load profiles presented in the previous sections. A fragment of the series of simulations that correspond to increasing the number of lithium-ion cells at the same load profiles are presented in the Fig. 5, Fig. 6, Fig. 7 and Fig. 8.

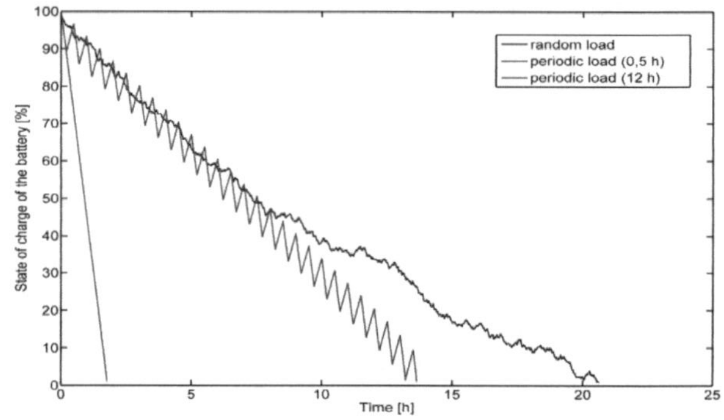

Figure 5. Change of the state of charge of the Li-ion battery pack (5x1) during powering the electric load

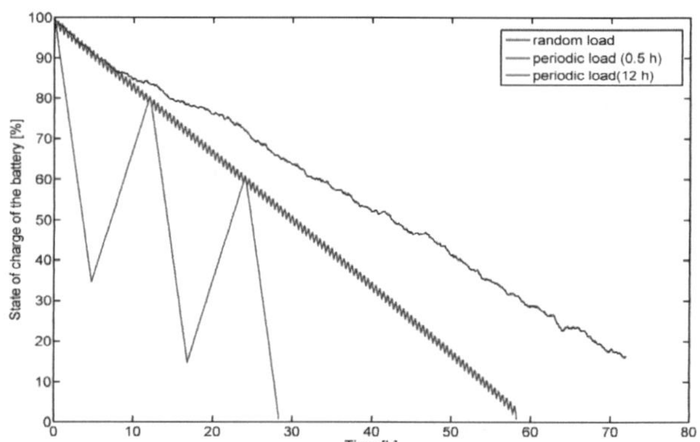

Figure 6. Change of the state of charge of the Li-ion battery pack (5x4) during powering the electric load

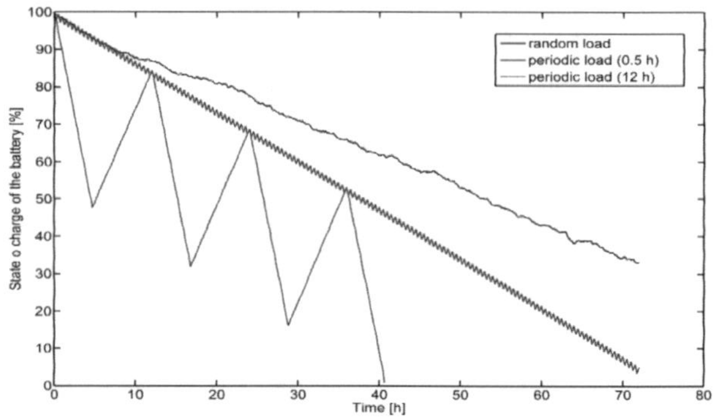

Figure 7. Change of the state of charge of the Li-ion battery pack (5x5) during powering the electric load

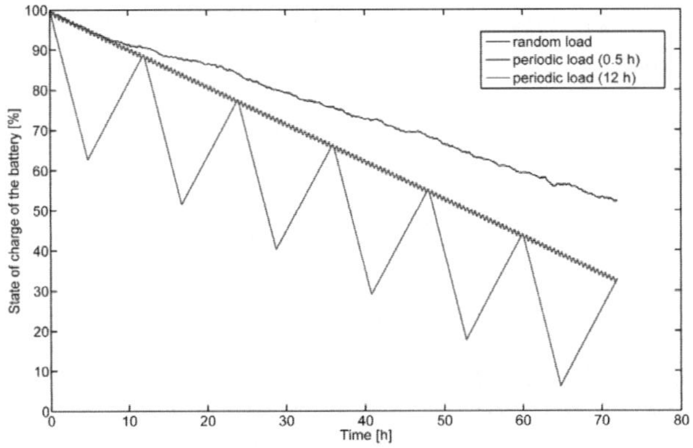

Figure 8. Change of the state of charge of the Li-ion battery pack (5x7) during powering the electric load

Figures 5-8 present changes of the state of charge of the battery pack during supplying the electric load from the hybrid power source. In each figure there are three plots that correspond to the assumed load profiles – two periodic load profiles and one random load profile.

From the presented results it may be concluded that for the assumed system parameters, for each load profile, after a certain operation time, the battery pack will be completely discharged. It is caused by the power losses inside the PMS and the selection of the PEM FC stack whose nominal power equals to the average power required by the electric load (DSS).

It also can be concluded that the knowledge about the values of average and peak power of the electric load is insufficient for proper selection of the components of the hybrid power source. The load profile plays a significant role in proper sizing of the energy source. In the Fig. 5-8 the influence of the load profile is presented. For example, for the random load profile the suitable battery pack will consist of 5x4 Li-ion rechargeable cells that stores 230.4 Wh, while for supplying the electric load that has a periodic work profile with period time equal to 12 hours, the demanded battery pack should consist of 5x7 Li-ion rechargeable cells that can store up to 403.2 Wh.

It is also necessary to note that the efficiency of the PMS system also influences the size of the battery pack. For each Watt of average power loss inside the PMS the energy source must provide 72Wh per 72 hour of operation. In other words, if the average power losses inside PMS would be reduced by 1 Watt, the battery pack for each load profile could be smaller for about one basic battery package (five cells in series).

Conclusion

The presented results of the simulation studies are part of the larger research program aimed at developing a hybrid power supply system for soldiers, funded by the National Centre for Research and Development in Poland. The conclusions derived from the simulation studies, after verification with help of the physical model will allow the optimization of the proposed hybrid power system, and thus minimization of the weight and dimensions of the energy supply source of a dismounted soldier. The presented results demonstrate the influence of the load profile on the total size of the hybrid power system. Therefore, in addition to the work on optimizing the power sources, there should be done also the optimization of the work characteristic of the electric load.

References

1. A. Folkesson, C. Andersson, P. Alvfors, M. Alakula, L. Overgaard, "Real life testing of a Hybrid PEM Fuel Cell Bus", *Journal of Power Sources*, vol. 118, pp. 349-357, 2003.
2. A. Jossen, J. Garche, H. Doering, M. Goetz, W. Knaupp, L. Joerissen, "Hybrid systems with lead-acid battery and proton-exchange membrane fuel cell", *Journal of Power Sources*, vol. 144, pp. 395-401, 2005.
3. Q. Li, W. Chen, Y. Li, S. Liu, J. Huang, "Energy management strategy for fuel cell/battery/ultracapacitor hybrid vehicle based on fuzzy logic", *Electrical Power and Energy Systems*, vol. 43, pp. 514–525, 2012.
4. J. J. Hwang, W. R. Chang, "Characteristic study on fuel cell/battery hybrid power system on a light electric vehicle", *Journal of Power Sources, vol.* 207, pp. 111– 119, 2012.
5. A. Polak, "Experimental Studies of Direct Cooperation of PEM Fuel Cells and Secondary Batteries", *Solid State Phenomena*, vol. 210, pp. 87-96, 2014.
6. Q. Cai, D.J.L. Brett, D. Browning, N.P. Brandon, "A sizing-design methodology for hybrid fuel cell power systems and its application to an unmanned underwater vehicle", *Journal of Power Sources, vol.* 195, pp 6559–6569, 2010.
7. M. J. Vasallo, J. M. Bravo, J. M. Andujar, "Optimal sizing for UPS systems based on batteries and/or fuel cell", *Applied Energy,* vol. 105, pp. 170–181, 2013.
8. L. Xu, M. Ouyang, J. Li, F. Yang, L. Lu, J. Hua, "Optimal sizing of plug-in fuel cell electric vehicles using models of vehicle performance and system cost", *Applied Energy,* vol. 103, pp. 477–487, 2013.
9. NATO Army Armaments Group, STANAG 4695 – Electrical Interface Specifications for Dismounted Soldier Systems (DSS) Level 2 Power Interoperability, 2013.

Evaluation and Implementation Guide Development of Betavoltaic Hybrid Power Sources for Milliwatt to Microwatt Applications

Marcus Spiker[1]* (marcus.spiker.ctr@navy.mil, 812-854-2117)
Tom Adams[1, 2] (adams30@purdue.edu, 440-897-6801)
Shripad Revankar, PhD[2] (shripad@purdue.edu, 765-496-1782)
Steve Chapple[3] (schapple@cymbet.com, 763-633-1780)
Peter Cabauy,PhD[4] (peter.cabauy@citylabs.net, 305-909-7593)
Bret J. Elkind,PhD[4] (bret.elkind@citylabs.net, 305-909-7593)
Jesse Grant[4] (jesse.grant@citylabs.net, 305-909-7593)

1. Naval Surface Warfare Center, Crane Division, 300 Highway 361, Crane, IN, 47522
2. Purdue University, 400 Central Drive, West Lafayette, IN, 47907
3. Cymbet Corporation 18326 Joplin St NW, Elk River, MN, 55330
4. City Labs, Inc., 301 Civic Court, Homestead, FL, 33030

Abstract
The Naval Surface Warfare Center, Crane Division (NSWC Crane) is testing and evaluating betavoltaics and hybrid designs using lithium solid-state rechargeable (Li-SS) batteries for insertion into military and other government agency platforms. Unlike electrochemical batteries, betavoltaics have been demonstrated to operate continuously over decadal time-periods in extreme temperatures (-50°C to 150°C) without affecting performance. Solid-state batteries operate in a smaller temperature range (-20°C to 70°C) but offer long operating and cycle lives, and low degradation due to the solid electrolyte; they can be stored under exposure to a temperature range of -40°C to 125°C and intermittently operated up to 80°C. It should be noted, that the combination of a betavoltaic trickle charging a Li-SS battery significantly extends the capacity of the hybrid system. NSWC Crane has procured betavoltaics (Model P100a NanoTritium™) from City Labs, Inc. and lithium solid-state rechargeable batteries (EnerChip™) from Cymbet Corporation. The betavoltaics and batteries will be evaluated separately first to assess individual performance under temperature, and then evaluated together in a hybrid design at temperatures ranging from -40°C to 80°C. A betavoltaic / Li-SS battery hybrid can provide continuous, uninterrupted power in the microwatt range with burst power in the milliwatt range. Applications intended for insertion of the betavoltaic-battery hybrid design include autonomous wireless sensors, continuous health monitoring of missile platforms, miniature bio-implant sensors, and anti-tamper sensors for weapons platforms. The results for the individual and hybrid evaluations will be discussed along with an overview of the betavoltaic and Li-SS battery technologies; a roadmap will be presented for insertion pathways for betavoltaic hybrid designs in applications. In addition, a preliminary outline of a betavoltaic implementation guide for DoD program managers, and validation and verification community will be highlighted. The implementation guide will serve as a manual for application insertion, specification in application, performance measurement, handling, and disposal for betavoltaic based power sources.

Keywords Betavoltaic; Lithium-solid state; Trickle-charging, Hybrid

Introduction
In June 2010, City Labs Inc. was awarded an Air Force Research Laboratory (AFRL) contract [1] to produce a betavoltaic power solution for DoD applications. A pair of betavoltaic batteries were successfully produced and subsequently transferred to Purdue University for testing in compliance with said contract under the auspices of NSWC Crane. During this same period, the Air Force and Navy mutually agreed to expand the boundaries of radioisotope electrical power research by agreeing to fund a larger population of similar betavoltaic devices to facilitate a more robust evaluation. In November of 2013, AFRL issued a data call that outlined eleven specific mission parameters for innovative low power solutions. That request (Table 1) expressed the thresholds and future objectives for low power DoD applications.

Concomitant with this request, NSWC Crane and Purdue University compiled a corresponding list of leading commercial Original Equipment Manufacturers (OEMs) actively engaged in the pursuit of low-power technologies in order to pursue a potential *hybrid* low-power system. Some OEMs emerged from a list of 10 qualifying providers, who specifically met most of the AFRL requirements. City Labs, in particular, met said requirements and is a generally licensed betavoltaic OEM. The choice for commercial secondary battery systems fell to Cymbet Corp, given their small form factor (thin film), low discharge rate, and mechanically robust LI-PON solid state rechargeable batteries; both City Labs and Cymbet presented with a relatively broad temperature range of operation in their respective power source classifications and seemed compatible from a hybrid system perspective. Therefore, the idea of merging these top two technologies

Req ID	Requirements		
	Parameter	Threshold	Objective
R1	Temperature	-40°C to 80°C	-55°C to 125°C
R2	Vibration and shock	DOT shipping and handling	MIL-STD-810G, application specific
R3	Voltage	3.0 V	Objective: >3.5 V
R4	Consistent Current	10 μA	>50 μA
R5	Surge Current	1 mA for 1 second	>1 mA
R6	Operating Life	15 years	20 years with 5-year shelf life
R7	Size	< 2" x 2" x 0.5" (5.1cm x 5.1cm x 1.3cm)	< 0.25" x 0.25" x 0.5" (0.64cm x 0.64cm x 0.32cm)
R8	Weight	4 ounces (113.4 grams)	< 4 ounces (113.4 grams)
R9	Low Pressure (Altitude)	8000 ft. to 40,000 ft. (0.74 atm to 0.18 atm)	Vacuum (Space)
R10	NRC regulatory driven handling and storage	General license	Exempt
R11	Hazardous	No caustic materials	Inert

Table 1 – AFRL Mission Requirements

together into a hybrid configuration provides a potentially viable solution for long-life operation in extreme temperature conditions.

Pursuant to the AFRL data call, the Air Force (via NSWC Crane) funded a purchase order for 24 additional betavoltaic devices (P100a NanoTritium™) from City Labs and a complement of 6 Li-SS rechargeable evaluation kits from Cymbet Corporation (Cymbet). The intent behind this acquisition serves a two-fold purpose; initially, the study intends to produce an independent performance & characterization evaluation of each type of power device. Thereafter, a subsequent effort seeks to merge both power technologies into a viable hybrid power system in order to explore the opportunity of developing an exceedingly long-term, temperature insensitive power system as a solution for diminutive low-power applications.

Test & Evaluation (Purdue University)

Test Bed Configuration:

Figure 1 provides a definitive schematic representation of the proposed test bed used at Purdue to thermally cycle, electrically test, and monitor both betavoltaic and Li-SS batteries individually and eventually in a hybrid battery configuration.

Test System Functionality: The test system is designed to be controlled and monitored using LabVIEW™ (2013). I-V data sweeps are performed multiple times daily using a PC tied to a Keithley 2701 DMM and Keithley 7702 Multiplexer. Thermal Chamber command and control is correspondingly accomplished via PC using LabVIEW™.

Equipment Required: Listed herein below and shown in Figure 2 are the principal components of electronic/thermal testing and measurement equipment (T&ME) that are required to conduct the aforementioned assessments:

1. Thermal Chamber (Test Equity Model 107) GPIB/RS232 – TC-PC Ethernet interface

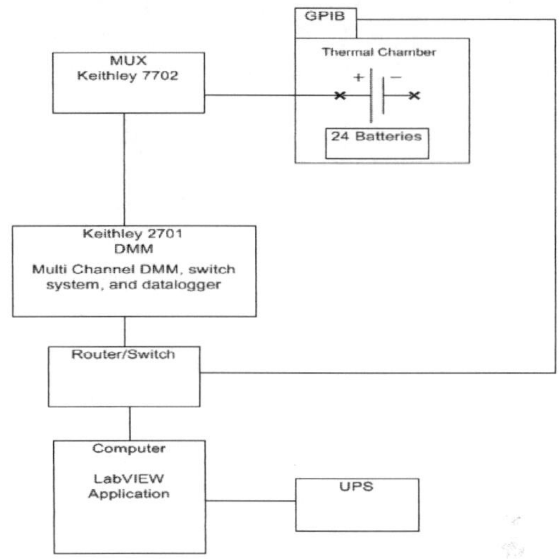

Figure 1-Test Bed Configuration

2. Multiplexer (Keithley Model 7702, 40-Ch, Diff Mux Module)
3. DMM (Keithley Model 2701, DMM/DAQ system)
4. DCHP Switch
5. PC
6. UPS (Back-up power)

Software Required:

1. LabVIEW™ 2013 - Data Acquisition (DAQ) VI to support hourly IV sweeps.
2. MS Excel - mathematical computation, graphical analysis.

Additional Materials Required:

Approximately two (2) meters of AWG28-10/F/300 shielded ribbon cable used for PCB/MUX connectivity (or suitable substitute).

Printed Circuit Boards:

Six (6) custom-designed printed circuit boards (PCB) and Six (6) Cymbet Li-SS battery evaluation kits are required to perform this seminal study. Figure 4 depicts a top-down representation of the final betavoltaic board design with associated DIP ZIF connectors for battery insertion (6 per board).

Betavoltaic PCB Fabrication Specification:

IPC Class: 2
Material Type: Standard FR4
Layer Count: 3
Overall Thickness: .062" (or default standard)
Matched Impedance: No
Copper weight: 0.5oz (or 1oz if default)
Finish: Tin/Lead

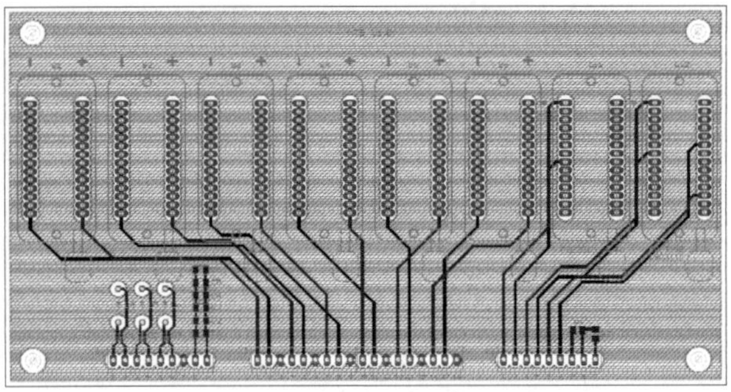

Figure 2 – Full 3 layer PCB (Topside +)

Each Betavoltaic PCB is populated with the following components (Table 2).

Distributer	Description	Purchase Qty
Digikey	CONN TERM BLOCK T/H 9POS 3.5MM	6
Digikey	TVS DIODE 7VWM 22.7VC SOD523	10
Digikey	DIODE SCHOTTKY 0.7V DROP 40V REV 0.25A SOD523	10
Digikey	CAP CER 0.1UF 50V 10% X7R 1206	10
Digikey	RES 806K OHM 1/4W 1% 1206 SMD	10
Digikey	RES 220K OHM 1/4W 1% 1206 SMD	10

Table 2 – PCB Component List

Figure 3 illustrates the electrical schematic and discrete component arrangement for each PCB. The board design reduces noise susceptibility in order to allow a variety of test configurations to be performed. It utilizes an array of screw terminal blocks that provide the user with toolset selectability for a variety of components including: voltage reduction diodes, a transient voltage suppressor to control electrostatic discharge, capacitor bank for noise reduction / control, shunt resistors to govern the charge of a lithium cell, three(3) lithium ion test cells, and six (6) betavoltaic batteries.

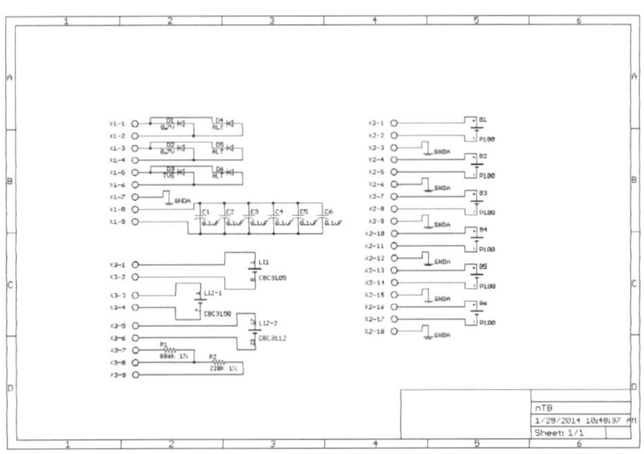

Figure 3 – PCB Electrical Schematic

Battery Performance Study

The Purdue University battery performance study is comprised of three (3) separate test objectives to be conducted in the following order: 1) Li-SS testing, 2) Betavoltaic testing, and 3) Hybrid system evaluation.

Test data results (I-V sweeps, energy, and power densities) that speak to individual and hybrid evaluations will be parametrically analyzed and presented along with a technical overview of both Li-SS and betavoltaic battery technologies.

LiPON Solid-State (Technical Overview)

With the advent of semiconductor fabrication processes, discrete form-factor thin film Li-SS rechargeable storage devices began being produced. Of all lithium battery types, LI-PON proved to be the best. Conceptually, the merging of these two technologies together in a hybrid configuration may provide the best solution for long-life operation in extreme temperature conditions. Cymbet's Enerchip™ was selected for its demonstrated low self-discharge, wide temperature operation, low ampere-hour capacity, small footprint and demonstrated reliability. Li-SS batteries operate in a narrower temperature range (-20°C to 70°C) but offer long cycle lives, with low degradation due to the solid electrolyte; storage temperatures typically range from -40°C to 125°C with intermittent operation up to 80°C.

Betavoltaics (Technical Overview)

Photovoltaic devices derive electrical power from visible spectrum photons (sunlight or other light sources) that interact with a p-n junction (diode). Photon energies in the visible EM spectrum generate approximately 1eV – 4eV and, therefore, produce approximately 1-3 electron-hole pairs (EHP) per photon, equating to power densities ranging from approximately 0.012 W/cm^3 – 0.106 W/cm^3. Analogous to Photovoltaics, Betavoltaic systems invoke electrons (beta particles) instead of photons; these beta particles, derived from radioactive decay processes, also induce hole–pair generation but possess considerably higher energies, e.g. 10's – 100's keV (compared to visible light photons) and can produce hundreds or thousands of electron-hole pairs in a p-n junction. The primary strength of photovoltaics lies within the large radiant flux of photons that actually participate in the hole-pair generation process, whereas its weakness is defined by the availability of visible light, which can be easily inhibited by weather, time-of-day, or mechanical obstructions associated with line-of-sight to a light source. Betavoltaic processes, while capable of generating large quantities of hole-pair events from a single beta particle, are typically limited by the number radioactive decay events themselves; subsequently, betavoltaics can tend to produce power densities of approximately 100μW/cm^3 – 0.1 W/cm^3 using source films < 1 μm. While this range of power output seems low, power generation can continue unabated over decadal time-periods depending upon the choice of radioisotope, e.g. tritium half-life:12.3 yrs. Numerous device applications are now in existence that can effectively utilize long-term, uninterrupted power derived from betavoltaics' continuous diminutive power outputs, and therein resides one of its primary advantages for low-power applications. Unlike conventional electrochemical batteries, betavoltaics operate continuously over decadal time periods in extreme temperatures (-50°C to 150°C). The fundamental operational model for betavoltaic power sources is illustrated in Figure 4.

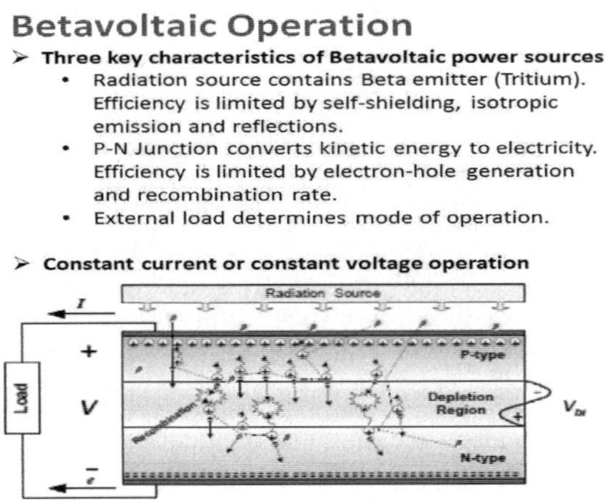

Figure 4 – Betavoltaic Operation

Development of Hybrid Power Source (Technical Overview)

In April 2013, City Labs successfully conducted a partial trickle-charging of a depleted Cymbet EnerChip™ secondary power source (12 μAhr) [2], utilizing four (4) of its NanoTritium™ P100 devices. While these results represent both a first within the betavoltaic industry and a clear proof-of-concept for the potential of developing betavoltaic/Li-SS hybrid systems, a complete charging was not accomplished as the Li-SS battery voltage was below the minimum 3.0V threshold where permanent capacity loss can result. Despite these encouraging results, there is a profound dearth of data relating to the betavoltaic /Li-SS hybrid system concept from which to draw upon; therefore, both the rationale and impetus for this study is to extend and deepen the understanding of betavoltaic/Li-SS hybrid systems at this very early stage of development within the betavoltaic industry. By definition, a theoretical hybrid power system (Figure 5) is interdependent upon one source feeding the other. It is hoped that by merging both betavoltaic and Li-SS power technologies together that the combination will create a single hybrid power system designed to extend a diminutive-power platform's lifetime to decadal time periods with a superior resistance to a broad range of operational temperatures.

Evaluation Methods

It is proposed that each battery type undergo a regimen of differing temperature cycle ranges, as well as load conditions under varied ramp and soak times for several weeks. Strict temperature observance over Li-SS is required (-20°C to 70°C) with increases to 80°C for brief periods to observe changes in electrical characteristics. Betavoltaics will be subjected to a slightly wider temperature range (-40°C to 125°C) to determine similar electrical characteristics. Testing will culminate with the exposure of a Hybrid–Betavoltaic configuration to the same conditions described above and over a temperature range of -40°C to 80°C.

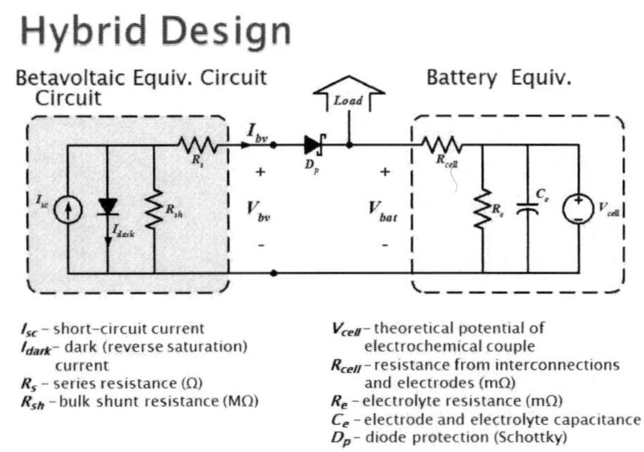

Figure 5 – Theoretical Hybrid Design Model

Implementation Guide

As an essential component and deliverable of this study, a preliminary outline of a betavoltaic implementation guide for DoD program managers and the V&V community will be produced. The implementation guide will serve as a manual supporting the application, insertion, specification in application, performance measurement, handling, and disposal for hybrid and betavoltaic-based power sources.

Conclusions

Testing is currently underway, and final conclusions will be provided at a later date and upon request.

Acknowledgements

Alexander Soles – Electronic Hardware Development

References

1. AFRL BAA Contract No. FA8650-10-C-1874
2. City Labs' NanoTritium™ Betavoltaic Trickle Charges Cymbet LiPON Thin Film-Battery (09April 2013)

JP-8 Fueled, Single-Soldier Portable Gensets

Subir Roychoudhury*, David Spence, Curtis Morgan, Richard Mastanduno, Francesco Macri, Christian Junaedi, and **Brian Freeman
Precision Combustion, Inc.
410 Sackett Point Road, North Haven, CT 06473
*contact author: sroychoudhury@precision-combustion.com
(** Affiliated with Hyperion Technology Group, Inc.)

Abstract: *Precision Combustion, Inc. (PCI) has recently developed a tactical soldier portable power generator via implementation of a JP-8 conversion kit. The kit can be adapted to lightweight gasoline engines. It is applicable for a range of military power generation systems and has been demonstrated at 350 W to 2 kW variants. The primary advantage of PCI's solution over other fuel conversion approaches is fuel-conditioning that enables fuel properties suitable for reliable operation of spark ignited engines. Operation of the conversion kit with JP-8 containing up to 3000 ppm$_w$ sulfur has been demonstrated. The solution is being scaled to other engines of various sizes.*

Military applications of interest include power generation for battery chargers, tactical gensets, UGVs and UAVs. The compact size of the fuel conversion kit permits commercial off-the-shelf, lightweight generators to operate on military fuels in a lightweight package. This paper highlights data obtained from prototypes at various power levels and their suitability for STEP (Small Tactical Electrical Power). The prototype is hybridized with a rechargeable battery and is currently at TRL-6. Size and weight specifications along with MIL SPEC compliant electrical and environmental performance data are presented. A description of the operational hardware and prototype units that meet viable cost/performance targets for military use is included. This new generation of portable power generators will enhance frontline capability for the warfighter.

Keywords: JP-8; diesel; generator; lightweight; engines; conversion; prototypes.

Introduction

JP8-fueled military compression ignition engines are heavy and not readily available at small displacements and low power levels. Lightweight, portable 1 kW gasoline gensets are ubiquitous. However, these gensets operate only on gasoline. Adapting them to operate on JP-8 would significantly alter the frontline soldier-power availability. Gasoline gensets are spark ignited (SI) and operate satisfactorily with high octane fuels. Operating these engines with JP-8, with octane number ranging between 15 and 25, is a challenge.

PCI has developed an extremely compact "Fuel Conditioner Kit" that enables operation of these gasoline engines on JP-8. The simplicity of the approach makes it readily adaptable to engines from different manufacturers. JP-8 fueled 0.35, 1 and 1.5 kW$_e$ prototypes have been developed and demonstrated with CERDEC support. High TRL 1-kW$_e$ prototypes, weighing ~39 lbs, are being matured for Army expeditionary field operations. An open architecture approach capable of operating with SI engines from various manufacturers and different displacements has been examined. The fuel conditioning kit includes all balance of plant components, including controls, required for operating the genset as a standalone device.

Installation of the system required relatively non-invasive modifications to the engine/generator. The integration kit consists of modifying the engine's fuel intake, plugging into the control hardware, and mounting the accessory kit. A complete generator is shown in Figure 1.

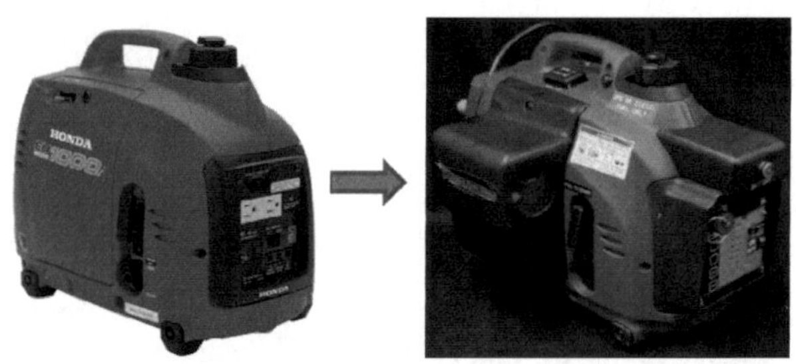

Figure 1: Photo of a COTS 1 kW generator (left) converted by PCI to operate on JP-8 (right). The conversion kit (bumpout) with all BOP components for fueling the genset. Control board and start battery located in the front pod.

JP-8 was obtained from Wright-Patterson Air Force Base containing 620 ppm sulfur. On road diesel (DF-2) was obtained from a local supplier. The fueling rate was varied based upon load. Mapping of engine operation at various loads was conducted to develop algorithms for transients (starting, shut down) and steady state operation. Start-up was achieved in 3 pulls or less of the starting cord. Steady state was reached in ~1 minute and peak power was available in ~2 minutes. Load transients were near instantaneous (<<1 second).

The genset was alternately operated on gasoline, DF-2, and JP-8. The fuel conditioning kit was used for JP-8 and DF-2 and the OEM carburetor was used for gasoline. The efficiencies at various power output showed minimal difference with the different fuels.

Operation of the genset on high sulfur fuels was also completed. Stable operation was confirmed with 3000 ppm S JP-8 at various power levels (Figure 2) indicating that the approach could be successfully applied to the full range of JP-8 fuels. Long duration generator performance confirmation over multiple 100 hours was also tested.

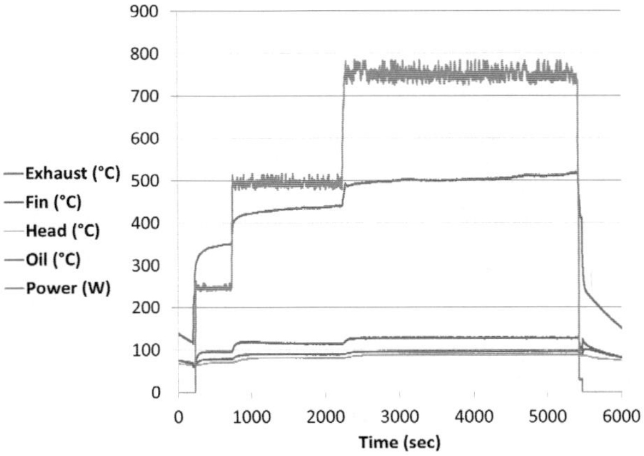

Figure 2: Stable generator operation at various loads on 3000 ppm sulfur JP-8.

Scalability and durability of the approach was examined by applying the concept to another generator set and operated for 120 hours at various loads, with multiple start/stops (Figure 3). This demonstrated the flexibility of the open architecture design approach. The power output was limited to 1.1 kW_e via fuel control. The engine was operated on JP-8 and DF-2 during the test.

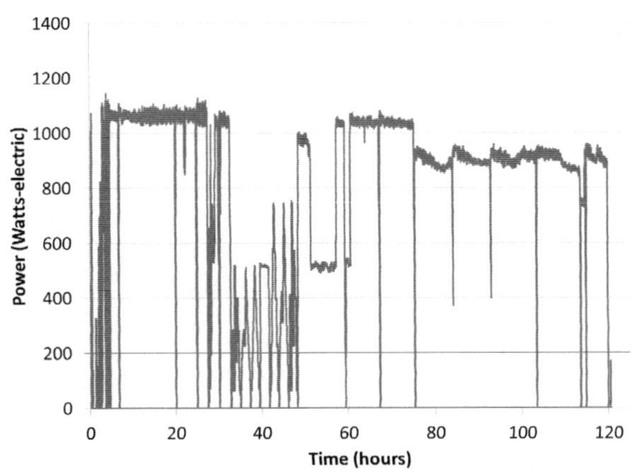

Figure 3: Operation of genset for 120 hours on JP-8 w. multiple start/stops and loads.

Engine Selection

Several high output engine options (2-stroke, 4-stroke, Rotary or Microturbine) and generator combinations (Custom matched or Pre Integrated COTS) were identified that could meet the 1 – 1.5 kW Power Target. Twelve possible combinations of features were then analyzed on the basis of six metrics and a weighting factor totaling 100% (Table 1). A probability of success was assigned to each genset configuration for meeting the given performance metric at both the threshold and objective values, by applying the weighting factors. All 12 options were examined to determine the hardware configuration to be developed in the program. Based on this sensitivity analysis a COTS, 4-stroke, 1 kW, system was identified as the optimum choice.

Table 1: Weighting Factors in genset evaluation.

Metric	Metric Weighting (%)
Weight	15%
Life	10%
Fuel Consumption	10%
Noise	10%
Power	30%
Integratability	25%

Engine Oil and Temperatures:

To ensure that the modifications would not limit the life of the generator, it was instrumented with thermocouples in key locations. Engine oil, block, head and exhaust temperatures at various operating conditions and fuels were monitored (Table 2). The results did not show any significant life limiting issues.

Table 2: Typical engine temperatures (°C) on various fuels (gasoline/JP-8/Diesel) and power levels

	Gas 1000W	Gas, 750W	JP-8, 750W	JP-8, 3000ppm, 750W	JP-8, 1000W
Exhaust	578	548	526	513	561
Fin	105	100	97	95	97
Head	100	94	91	88	85
Oil	147	138	131	127	136

The prototypes were operated with gasoline, diesel and JP-8. Data comparing oil properties (viscosity, fuel content in oil and oil additive content) change are plotted in Figures 4, 5 and 6 respectively.

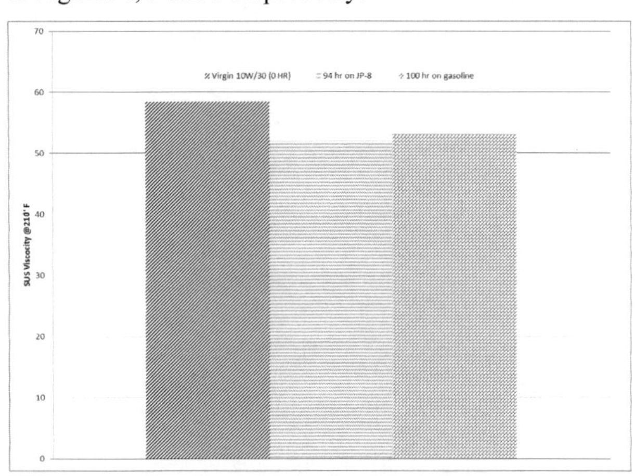

Figure 4: No significant oil viscosity change after long duration testing on JP-8 and gasoline.

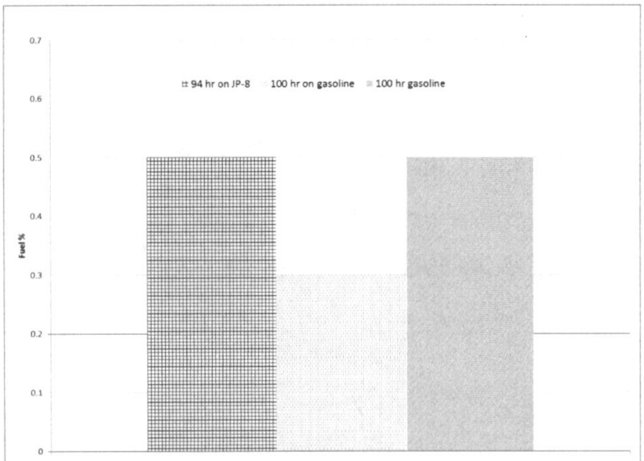

Figure 5: No significant change in fuel content in oil after long duration testing on JP-8 and gasoline.

The external controls were mated and matched with the OEM controls. Fuel flow could be readily varied to follow load changes. The external controls provide enhanced capabilities not found of the OEM gensets. These resemble many of the features of modern fuel injection such as altitude compensation, mixture control, data logging, and health monitoring.

Conclusions

The feasibility of operating a lightweight gasoline engine on distillate fuels (i.e. diesel and JP-8), in addition to gasoline was clearly illustrated. Two engines were experimentally validated to meet rated output

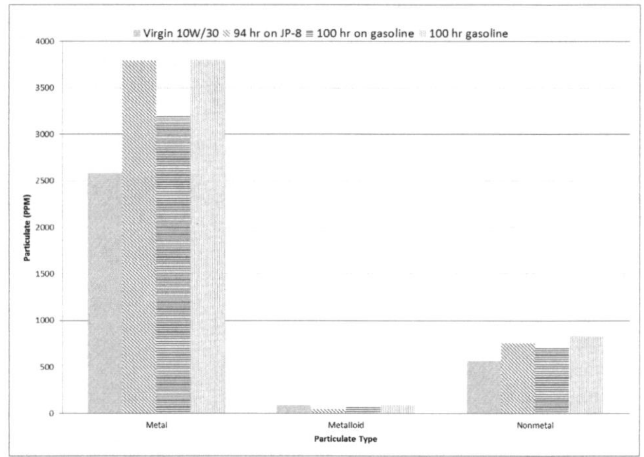

Figure 6: No significant change in oil property after long duration testing on JP-8 and gasoline.

Acknowledgements

The authors acknowledge the support of the DoD (CERDEC, WPAFB). Any opinions, findings, and conclusions or recommendations expressed in this paper are those of the authors and do not necessarily reflect the views of the DoD.

Wireless Power Transfer Using Microwave and Infrared Radiation

Edward B. Dawidowicz, Thomas F. Podlesak, Fee C. Leung
Power Division
U.S. Army Communications-Electronics Research, Development and Engineering Center,
5100 Magazine Road, Aberdeen Proving Ground, MD 21005

Abstract *The purpose of this paper is to explore both microwave and laser technologies in applications to power transmission over relatively large distances without the use of wires. The optimal selection and design of components for such wireless power transmission (WPT) systems requires careful consideration of the application requirements of their components. To help in the development of an optimal design for a particular system their components performance parameters will be discussed.*

Keywords: wireless power transmission; laser; microwave; rectenna; pencil beam antenna; reflectarray; thermophotovoltaic; phased array; thermoelectric generator; metamaterials.

Introduction

The WPT allows energy transfer to take place between a transmitting source and a receiving load without the use of wires. Eliminating conductors and contacts improves reliability of a system while reduces costs of wiring and setup time. A wireless connection can allow land and aerial vehicles to recharge while in motion, alleviating the need to stop or land, thereby significantly extending their operational time. Aerial vehicle are mostly prone to damage during landing and recharging them in flight could extend their mean time between failures.

WPT over long distances is best accomplished by using electromagnetic waves. The frequency range of potential candidates spans from microwave to light spectrum. Particularly from low GHz to upper THz encompassing frequency spectrum from 300MHz – 300GHz for microwave and from 300GHz to 430THz for infrared.

The selection of system's type is not straight forward since each of them has their strengths and weaknesses and the optimal design of an effective system depends on system cost, distance of transmission and technological limitations of available components. Focusing on optimum system design the consideration of performance parameters of both transmitter and receiver and safety aspects associated with system use and maintenance must be explored.

Generalized WPT System

In general, all WPT systems share a similar structure as shown in Figure 1. A signal of particular frequency is amplified and fed into impedance matched energy emitter. An energy emitter or a transmitter is designed to transmit energy across a medium. In our case it is a beam of

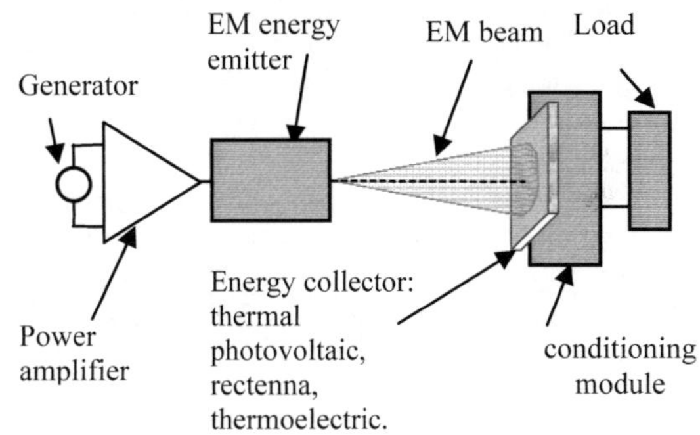

Figure 1. Generalized EM wave WPT system

electromagnetic (EM) radiation transmitted across airspace. A beam of small divergence is desired to maintain a high power density on the energy collector module some distance away. Depending on the properties of the collector a power conditioning module is used to efficiently transfer power from the energy collector to the load.

Microwave System

In microwave WPT system the energy of the source is radiated by an antenna across the free space and is transmitted by antenna in a direction towards the desired target by narrowest possible beam to maximize energy transfer. The target is equipped with a receiving antenna to convert incoming radiation to direct current. This is schematically shown in Figure 2.

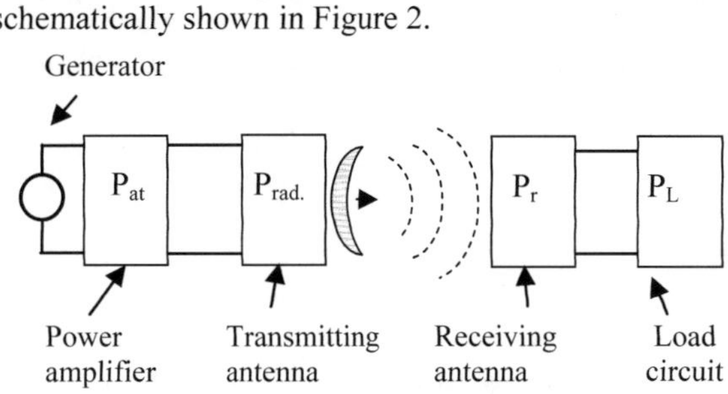

Figure 2. Microwave energy transfer system.

The transfer of power between power source P_g and the load P_L can be formulated by employing coefficients of transfer between generator and transmission line $\eta_{at} = P_{at}/P_g$, radiated and power delivered to the antenna $\eta_{rad} = P_{rad}/P_{at}$, power radiated and power received by receiving antenna $\eta_r = P_{rad}/P_r$ and finally the power received by antenna and converted to electric power delivered to the load $\eta_L = P_L / P_r$

$$P_L = \eta_{at}\, \eta_{rad}\, \eta_r\, \eta_L\, P_g \quad (1)$$

This antenna is an array of elements, with each element incorporating an ultra fast Schottky diode, is called rectenna. The term rectenna was coined by William C. Brown [1,2] who successfully demonstrated electrical energy transfer, by employing microwaves, from the ground to the tethered helicopter some short distance away. A rectenna is still is the most efficient way to convert EM energy to electricity for low to mid microwave frequencies [3].

Antennas

There are no shortages on types and configuration of radiating antennas available for consideration. Fortunately only these that provide direct and narrow beams of high gain are of interest. The parabolic dish, antenna array and reflectarray are potentially good candidates for selection.

The gain of an antenna G is the ratio of power projected in a particular direction to the power emitted by an isotropic source emanating in all direction. The power gain relative to an isotropic radiator is expressed in dBi unit is as:

$$G(dBi) = 10\log(G) \quad (2)$$

A gain of an antenna, as an ideal case, is expressed in terms of its effective area A_{eff} [1] and wavelength λ as [4, 5, 6, 7]:

$$\text{Gain } G = 4\pi A_{eff}/\lambda^2 \quad (3)$$

There is a relationship between the effective and physical area an antenna however it is not straight forward. A wire antenna would have an elliptical A_{eff} with major axis about equal to its length however have a negligibly small $A_{physical}$. Dish, horn and array antennas have a physical area closely related to the effective area. For these cases the ratio between their areas is define as aperture efficiency:

$$e_{ae} = A_{eff}/A_{physical} \quad (4).$$

[1] An effective area of an antenna or the effective aperture A_{eff} is related to the power available to the antenna.

Aperture efficiency ranges from 0.35-0.55 for simple designed to 0.65-0.75 well designed reflectors.

Since we are looking to direct the power at a particularly small target antenna of a small area we have to shape the beam to the smallest possible angle. The power W_o, is a function of distance R from the transmitter to the receiver, isotropically radiated away from a transmitting antenna emitting a signal of power P_{rad} can be expressed as [8 p92,93] :

$$W_o = P_{rad}/4\pi R^2 \quad (5)$$

By employing directivity D the radiation is no longer radiated in all directions and is focused in a particular path towards a particular target area. The desirable radiation pattern is shown in figure 3. The power density

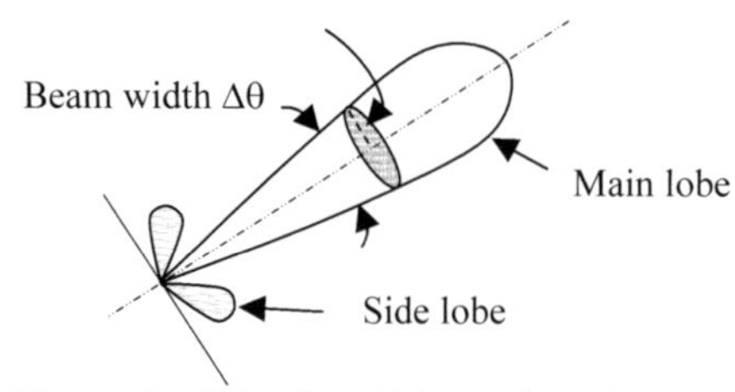

Figure 3. Directional high gain antenna radiating pattern

W_t projected on that target area is:

$$W_t = W_o D = P_{rad} D/4\pi R^2 \quad (6)$$

The directivity of an antenna D is related to gain G by is radiation efficiency of the antenna e_r:

$$G = e_r D \quad (7)$$

Where e_r is the efficiency of the antenna. Equation (3) shows that the effective area A_{eff} of the antenna is proportional to the gain G and inversely proportional to the square of the wavelength λ. Intuitively higher gain allows for narrow beam angle and therefore projects higher power densities at larger distances. The relationships between main beams solid angle $\Delta\Omega$ and directivity is given [6 p697] as

$$D_{max} = 4\pi/\Delta\Omega \quad (8)$$

Then employing equation (3) the power density at the receiver at a distance R is:

$$W = P_{rad} D/ \Delta\Omega R^2 \quad (9)$$

Consider an example where a 500W of power delivered to the load over 500m by using dish antenna of aperture efficiency $e_{ae} = 0.5$, antenna efficiency $e_r = 0.9$and gain 35dB, amplifier efficiency $\eta_{at} = 0.75$, transmitting efficiency $\eta_{rad} = 0.8$ at frequency f = 4GHz. (λ=75mm) Total efficiency from electricity to radiated power is therefore 0.54. The receiving antenna converts incoming power $\eta_r = 0.8$ and efficiency of power transfer to the load $\eta_L = 0.85$.

The effective area of the antenna can be calculated using equation (3) as:

$$A_{eff} = G\,\lambda^2/4\pi = G\,(c/f)^2/4\pi = 10^{35/10}\,(3x10^8 / 4x10^9)^2 / 4\pi = 1.41\ m^2$$

The physical area of the transmitting antenna is computed, using equation (4), to be:

$A_{physical} = A_{eff} / e_r = 1.09 / 0.5 = 2.83\ m^2$ or a dish of about 1.9m in diameter.`

The power required to produce 500W at the load require 735W to be incident upon rectenna:

$P_r = P_L / \eta_r\,\eta_L = 500/(0.8 \times 0.85) = 735W$

For a receiving antenna of e_{ae}=0.5 and effective area of $1m^2$ (physical area $2m^2$) the power density is $W_t = P_r / A_{eff} = 735W/\ m^2$

At the gain of 25dB the power radiated to 500m away from the receiver can be computed using equations (6) and (7)

$P_{rad} = W_t\ (4\pi R^2\ e_r)/G = 735\ (4\pi \times (500)^2\ 0.9)/10^{3.5} = 657kW$

Finally the power required to be produced by the generator to transfer 500w to the load 500 m away having and amplifier efficiency of 0.75 and antenna transmission efficiency 0.8 is:

$$Pg = P_{rad}/\eta_{at}\eta_{rad} = 657kW / (0.75 \times 0.8) = 1095\ kW$$

The overall efficiency of this system at 500 meter is:

$$\eta_{500} = 100\%\ (P_L/P_g) = 0.045\%$$

however at 100m the efficiency becomes:

$\eta_{100} = 1.1\%$

One can observe a strong influence of the distance on efficiency of power transfer. The efficiency can be increased by increasing the gain, equation (3) which can be accomplished by going to a shorter wavelength or higher frequency. Increasing the physical size of the antenna will improve the gain however for mobile applications is not desirable.

Laser Systems

By revisiting equations (3) the gain of a transmitting antenna is inversely proportional to the square of the wavelength. Higher frequencies suggest higher gains and therefore higher power densities delivered to the target then by using equations (6, 7) we have.

$$W_t = P_{rad}\ A_{eff} / (e_r\ R^2\ \lambda^2). \tag{10}$$

Evidently from equation (10) since lasers operate on even shorter wave length will deliver a greater power density at a larger distance [9]. There is no shortage of variations of available lasers [10,11,12,13] however only these that are efficient in conversion of electric power to light and systems capable of producing low divergence beams are of particular interest to WPT applications. The most efficient DC-to-laser converters are solid-state laser diodes commercially used in applications ranging from fiber optic communications to welding. While the power conversion electrical-to-optical or wall-plug efficiency was claimed to exceed 30% and propagations of 90% over 1.5 km [11] this performance of 27% has room for improvement.

The wall-plug efficiency is only a part of the overall transfer performance. Capture of optical energy poses even a greater a challenge. There are potentially several ways to capture energy emitted by a laser system: infrared rectenna, thermal photovoltaic (PV), visible spectrum PV and using thermo electric generators.

Infrared rectennas prove to be a challenge in near infrared range [14,15] and so far their efficiency is in a fraction of a percent range. However the seeming simplicity of their construction makes them a particularly engaging area of further research. The thermal PV in conjunction with TEG in conjunction with a good temperature gradient could potentially provide a reasonable efficiency in capturing and converting light into electrical energy. The efficiency of transferring optical to electrical energy is about estimated to be 10-15%.

Conclusion

Accomplishing WPT by both laser and microwave appear to be practical for particular applications. Microwave, using our example, is 54% efficient and is a conservative number. However the microwave signal is subject to the inverse square law and today we can potentially transmit power over several kilometers with 27% wall-plug efficiency across 1500 m [11]. Based on these numbers the laser system seems to transmit at about half the efficiency at three times the distance. However it suffers at the receiving end with optical to electricity energy conversion at about 15%. This brings overall performance to 4%

The microwave system is however a subject to the inverse square law of the distance across which the power is being transferred. From our example we required a power plant of just over 1MW to deliver 500W over 500m with 0.04% overall efficiency.

The efficiency of the laser systems appears to show continuous improvement. In this example the overall efficiency of 4% is 100 times better than the microwave system at three times the distance.

The applications of WPT over distances of several hundred meters to several kilometers is specifically resonant with recharging of energy efficient ground sensors, unmanned aerial vehicles and small unmanned ground vehicles. This will alleviate the need to recharge the sensor in combat zones by people and avoid placing them at risk. The aerial vehicles ability to recharge in flight without the need to land will extend extending their airborne time.

References

1. Brown W.C., Experiments Involving a Microwave Beam to Power and Position a Helicopter", Aerospace and Electronic Systems, IEEE Transactions on (Volume:AES-5,Issue: 5), Sept. 1969
2. Brown W. C., "A Microwaver Powered, Long Duration, High Altitude Platform", Microwave Symposium Digest, 1986 IEEE MTT-S International, 2-4 June 1986
3. J. O. McSpadden, "Design and Experiments of a High-Conversion-Efficiency 5.8-GHz Rectenna" , IEEE TRANSACTIONS ON MICROWAVE THEORY AND TECHNIQUES, VOL. 46, NO. 12, DECEMBER 1998
4. Silver S., Microwave Antenna Theory and Design, 1949 (Volume 12 of Radiation Laboratory 1984)
5. S. V. Hum and J. Perruisseau-Carrier, "Reconfigurable Reflectarrays and Array Lenses for Dynamic Antenna Beam Control: A Review", IEEE Transactions on Antennas and Propagation, Vol. XX, 2013
6. S.J. Orfanidis, Electromagnetic Waves and Antennas Rutgers University 2002 ISBN: 0130938556
7. Wheeler H. A., "Fundamental Limits of Small Antennas," Proceedings of The I.R.E. (IEEE), December 1947, pg. 1479-1484
8. C.A. Balanis, Antenna Theory: Analysis and Design 3nd ed. Wiley, 2005
9. L. Summerer, O. Purcell, "Concepts for wireless energy transmission via laser", http://www.esa.int/gsp/ACT/doc/POW/ACT-RPR-NRG-2009-SPS-ICSOS-concepts-for-laser-WPT.pdf
10. Milonni P. W., Eberly J H., Laser Physics, John Wiley & Sons, 2010
11. P. Sprangle et al., "High-Power Fiber Lasers for Directed-Energy Applications", 2008 NRL REVIEW.
12. Gary B. Hughes et al., "DE-STAR: Phased-Array Laser Technology for Planetary Defense and Other Scientific Purposes" , Nanophotonics and Macrophotonics for Space Environments VII Proceedings: San Diego, CA, August 25, 2013.
13. M. A. Vorontsov,., et al. "Adaptive array of phase-locked fiber collimators: analysis and experimental demonstration." Selected Topics in Quantum Electronics, IEEE Journal of 15.2 (2009): 269-280.
14. M. Dagenais, et al., "Solar Spectrum Rectification Using Nano-Antennas and Tunneling Diodes" , Optoelectronic Integrated Circuits XII. Edited by Eldada, Louay A.; Lee, El-Hang. Proceedings of the SPIE, Volume 7605, pp. 76050E-76050E-12 (2010).
15. N. G. Dhere. "Polycrystalline-Thin-Film Thermo photovoltaic Cells", American Institute of Physics, 1996

Development of Man-Packable JP-8 Power Source

Tony Thampan, Terry DuBois, Deepal Shah, Clifford Cook, Shailesh Shah
U.S. Army RDECOM CERDEC CP&I
5100 Magazine Rd.
Aberdeen Proving Ground, MD 21005

Abstract: *Communications-Electronics Research, Development, and Engineering Center (CERDEC) together with industrial partners, is developing man-packable JP-8 power sources for dismounted soldier applications. These power sources will provide an on the move battery charging capability in a smaller form factor than portable generators and previously developed portable methanol /propane fuel cell systems. The technical issues as well as modeling and test results necessary for the design and development of JP-8 fuel cell system will be discussed.*

Keywords: fuel cells, JP-8 fuel, ATR, HT PEM, system

Introduction

The use of rechargeable batteries in the field coupled with the single fuel forward policy of the US ARMY has resulted in the requirement for JP-8 fueled power sources [1]. Although combustion based engines offer very high power densities [2], the existing generator solutions have undesirable gas and noise emissions [3] requiring improved solutions including fuel cell based power systems.

This paper describes the technical issues on the design of JP-8 fuel cell systems including test and modeling results necessary for the design of a man-packable 50W JP-8 system.

Previous Work Although a significant amount of work has been done on JP-8 fuel cell systems [4, 5, 6, 7], less work has been done on JP-8, man-packable fuel cell systems. Small JP-8 systems previously tested by CERDEC [8] have resulted in a 50 W system weighing 10 kg with a fuel to electric efficiency of 12%. The large weight and poor reliability of previous systems has prevented them from being transitioned for fielding.

System Design

The critical components of a JP-8 fuel cell system are the fuel cell stack, reformer and balance of plant components. These components are described below.

Fuel Cell Stack

The fuel cell stack is critical to system design as it converts the fuel feed to electricity and heat. There are different stacks available including solid oxide fuel cells (SOFC), high temperature polymer electrolyte fuel cells (HT PEM) and low temperature polymer electrolyte fuel cells (LT PEM). The availability of stacks for integration at a high technological readiness level [9] was investigated together with industry.

SOFC Although there are a large number of SOFCs systems available, the smallest high TRL system available, was a 300 W stack that weighs 6 kg, which is large for a man-packable application. The system specifications are shown in Table 1. This system can tolerate < 1 ppm S, and no performance loss has been observed with up to 16% CO in the fuel. The system's performance is significantly derated beyond 1000 start stop cycles, especially if high power density systems are desired. This is a significant barrier for use as a man-packable system as it be expected to be utilized for intermittent load demands. Conventionally the use of SOFC stacks has been pursued for integration with JP-8 systems due to system's tolerance of high levels of CO. However, the lifetime limitations and the present unavailability of small stacks are significant disadvantages for a man-packable JP-8 system.

Table I Specifications of high TRL fuel cell stacks

Stack Technology	Smallest COTS Stack Size Available (W)	Sulfur Tolerance	CO tolerance	Estimated Lifetime/ start stop cycles	Power Density (W/kg)
SOFC	300	< 1 ppm	no derating obs.	< 1000	98
HTPEM	55	< 1 ppm	< 3%	> 1000	84-170
LT PEM	25	~ppb	ppm	> 2000	255

LT PEM systems are available in small sizes suitable for a man-packable system while offering very high power densities. However the low tolerance of these systems to CO [10] and S [11] results in a large fuel processor unsuitable for a man-packable JP-8 system.

HT PEM systems have been utilized for man-packable reformed methanol systems and are at a high technology maturity level [2, 12]. Although CO tolerance is not as high as an SOFC system, operation with 3% CO has been demonstrated. [13, 14]. Higher S tolerance is achievable as long as CO partial pressure is low [14]. As shown in Table 1, the HT PEM stack power density ranges from 84 W/kg to 170 W/kg, the higher power density systems result if shorter lifetime / higher cost systems are acceptable. It is also noted that SOFC systems show high power densities if cost and shorter lifetimes are acceptable. Considering the attributes of a HT PEM system, it was selected as the stack for the initial JP-8 man-packable design.

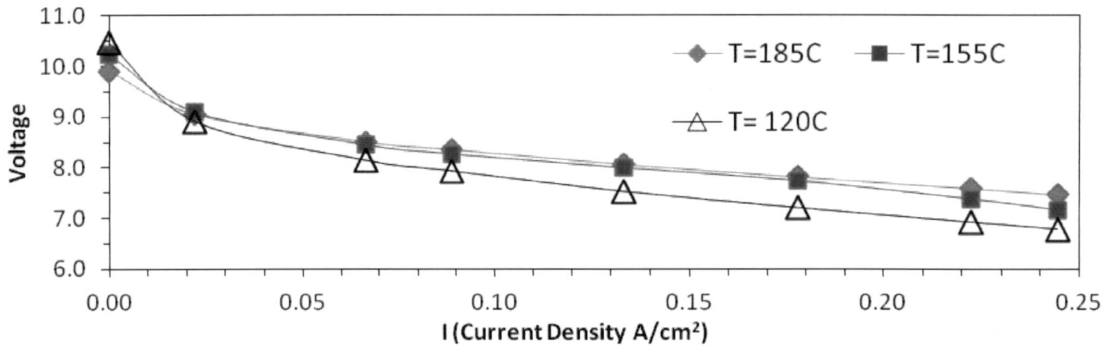

Figure 1 Performance of a 50W HT PEM stack. The system is able to produce power over a wide operating temperature range . This allows quick start of the unit and provides a method to mitigate CO poisoning.

HT PEM Testing A high TRL 55W stack made up of Polybenzimidazole based membranes was obtained for testing. Figure 1 shows the stack performance in a H_2 stream at 120°C, 155°C and 185°C. It can be seen that with a H_2 feed, the stack produces power at lower temperatures. The operating temperature is limited to avoid water condensation in the stack to minimize H_3PO_4 removal. The low temperature operation provides a method for rapid system start up, while the higher temperature operation (185°C) provides an operating point to mitigate CO content in the feed stream [13]. Figure 2 shows the stoichiometry corrected efficiency of the stack at 155°C as well as the power characteristics. It can be seen that the efficiency ranges from 50% to 60% based on the fuel (LHV of H_2) to electric conversion. The efficiency is very high compared to other portable power sources [3, 15].

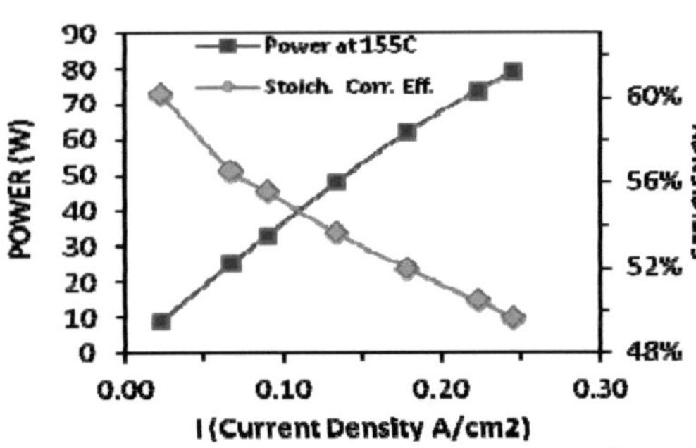

Figure 2: Efficiency of a 50W stack with H_2 / Air

Additionally, with the use of the appropriate control system and rechargeable battery, the system can be designed to operate the stack at the highest efficiency point.

Fuel Processor

The design of the fuel processor sub system is described including the fuel conversion (reformer, shift reactors) and sulfur clean up, in the following section.

Reformer The reformer is the reactor unit that converts the JP-8 fuel to a H_2, CO stream (synthesis gas). Based on a survey of reformer development [16], steam reforming and autothermal reforming appear appropriate for a JP-8 man-packable system, and are described below.

Steam Reforming is a proven industrial process to produce H_2 and occurs as shown below in a general form [16]:

$$C_aH_b + aH_2O \rightarrow aCO + \left(a + \frac{1}{2}b\right)H_2$$

Large amount of CO_2 are also formed as a result of the water gas shift reaction described later. The issues described below occur with JP-8 steam reforming, resulting in a challenging man-packable implementation.

1. Steam reforming is an endothermic reaction requiring a large amount of heat transfer at high temperatures, requiring the use of micro-channel reactors with high activity, precious metal catalyst [16,17].
2. To avoid carbon formation (coking), large amounts of steam are required, usually > 2.5 S/C [16]. However as shown in the equilibrium calculations in Figure 3, the S/C increase beyond 2.0, is not necessary for fuel conversion. The additional steam increases the water recovery requirements resulting in high parasitic power requirements.

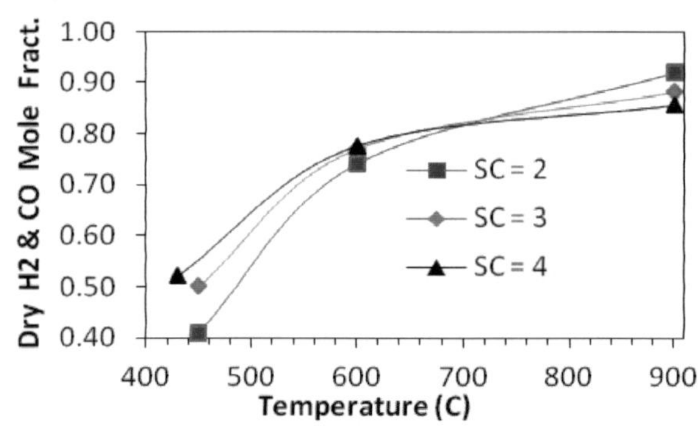

Figure 3: Equilibrium calculations on the effect of S/C ratio and temperature for JP-8 steam reforming.

The equilibrium calculations at constant temperature and pressure were based on Gibbs free energy minimization, utilizing a 79.2 mol. % n-dodecane and 20.8 mol. % 2,6-dimethylnaphtalene mixture to simulate JP-8.

Autothermal Reforming [5,7,18,19,20] is similar to steam reforming except that it includes the addition of oxygen, as shown in the generalized form. CO_2 formed due to the water gas shift reaction is described later.

$$C_aH_b + \frac{1}{2}aH_2O + \frac{1}{4}aO_2 \leftrightarrow aCO + \frac{1}{2}(a+b)H_2$$

The partial oxidation reaction provides the heat required for the steam reforming reaction resulting in a net energy neutral system with no heat transfer limitations.

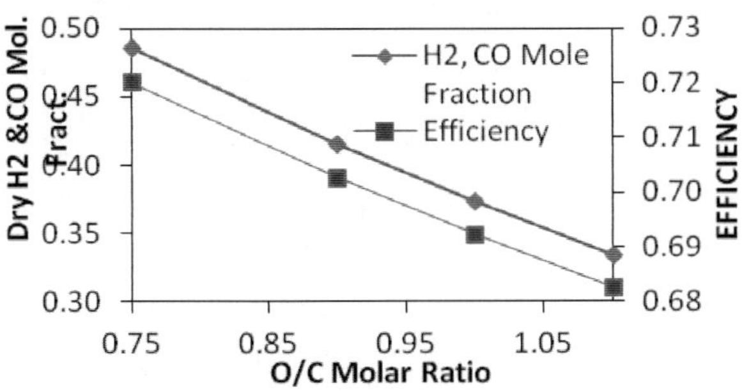

Figure 4 Equilibrium calculations on the effect of O/C molar ratio on composition and conversion efficiency

For a man-packable system, the O_2 is provided by the addition of air resulting in the dilution of the H_2 stream. The equilibrium compositions as well as the estimated efficiencies as a function of the O/C molar ratio are shown in Figure 4. The efficiency decreases with increasing air addition as more fuel is being oxidized to provide the heat input for the reforming reaction. These efficiencies have been experimentally validated [6] and provide a promising fuel processor option for a man-packable system.

Water Gas Shift reaction is utilized to covert CO to H_2 via an exothermic reaction:

$$CO + H_2O \leftrightarrow CO_2 + H_2$$

As shown in Figure 5, by controlling the reactor temperature and selection of the appropriate catalyst [21], the CO concentration can be limited to maintain optimum fuel cell performance. However the lower the temperature, the higher the cooling requirements and catalyst sensitivity to fuel contaminants (e.g. Cl, S).

Sulfur Removal is necessary as all the high TRL fuel cell stacks available are poisoned by sulfur containing compounds. There are two options to remove the sulfur, fuel desulfurization or synthesis gas desulfurization.

Fuel desulfurization [22, 23] involves treating the JP-8 fuel to produce a fuel with S levels meeting fuel cell specifications. These systems utilize a dual adsorbent bed system to allow for adsorbent regeneration without interrupting fuel desulfurization. Regeneration is accomplished by adsorbent bed oxidation in air. As it is possible to produce a desulfurized liquid fuel, the desulfurization unit can be separate from the man-packable system, resulting in a smaller system.

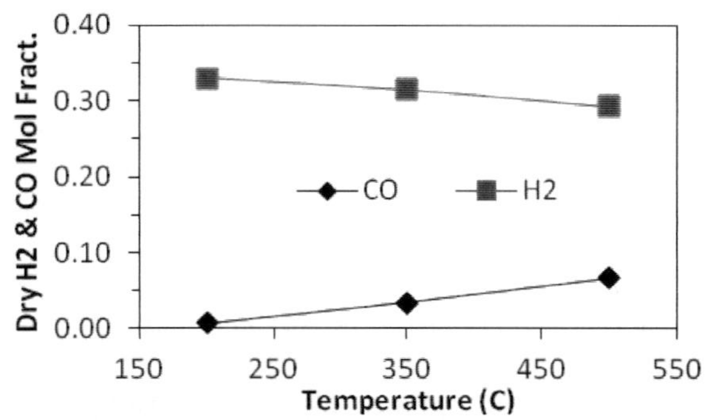

Figure 5 Equilibrium calculations on the effect of reactor temperature on composition

However this separate desulfurization unit increases the logistics as a desulfurized fuel will have to stored and transported separate from the standard fuel. Additionally operators will have to be trained to operate the sulfur removal unit as well as only utilize S free fuel in the man-packable system.

Synthesis gas desulphurization involves the use of S tolerant reformer and shift catalysts [24]. To minimize weight, a man-packable system will utilize non–regenerative desulfurization units, requiring the change out of the adsorbant cartridge during maintenance. Based on a 1000 h maintenance cycle, assuming a 50 W power draw and a 30 *wt.* % H_2S adsorption capacity [25], the mass of sulfur adsorbent requiring replacement is 155 g.

System Integration

Figure 6 shows a potential integration of a JP-8 system. The fuel, water and air are fed to an ATR to produce syngas. This sygas stream is cooled prior to introduction to the sulfur removal reactor and the shift reactor. A large amount of excess water is required for JP-8 reforming, requiring water recovery from the fuel cell effluent and product stream. This water is converted to super heated steam via the syngas cooler. Water is also condensed from the fuel cell feed to avoid condensation in the HT PEM stack which would destroy the electrolyte.

Other components in the system include: a burner for combusting unutilized fuel and providing additional heat for steam production; and a battery to provide load following capability as well as start up power. System start up requires water to be stored in the system or development of a reformer capable of operation without water addition i.e. in a partial oxidation mode.

Conclusion

Based on the performance estimates of the stack and reformer, it is expected that a man-packable JP-8 system will have a 30 -35% efficiency before any parasitic power draws are included, significantly higher than other portable JP-8 systems [3]. CERDEC together with industrial partners are developing prototype systems ranging from 50W to 300W to demonstrate the potential.

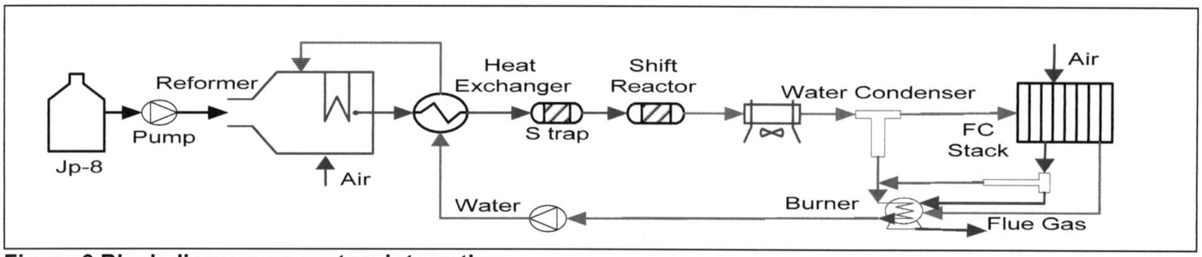

Figure 6 Block diagram on system integration

References

1. Capability Development Document For (U) Small Unit Power (SUP) Increment: , US Army, HQDA G3, 26 SEP 13, Maneuver Center of Excellence, Operational Energy Branch, Soldiers Division, Fort Benning, GA
2. T. Thampan, D. Shah, C. Cook, J. Novoa, S. Shah, "Development and Evaluation of Portable and Wearable Fuel Cells for Soldier Use" J Power Sources 259 (2014) 276.
3. C. Cook, T. Thampan, S. Shah, "Development of Light Weight, Multi-Fuel, Generator Power Sources in the 0-1000 Watt Range" 2014 Power Sources Conference, Orlando, FL, June 9-12, 2014
4. T. DuBois, S. Nieh, "Design and Performance of an Experimental 3 kW Autothermal Reformer Test Bed for Heavy Hydrocarbon Fuels," 43rd Power Sources Conference, pp. 133-136, Philadelphia, July 7–10, 2008.
5. S. Roychoudhury, D.Walsh, D. Chu, E. Kallio "Performance of a Diesel, JP-8 Reformer", Proc. of the 25th Army Science Conf., Orlando, FL, November 27-30, 2006
6. D. Maslach, M. Rottmayer, "JP-8 Fuel Reforming APU for Military Vehicles", 2011 Fuel Cell Seminar, Orlando, FL
7. S. Roychoudhury, C. Junaedi, S. A. Vilekar, C. Morgan, D. Walsh, and R. Mastanduno, "Fuel-Flexible Reforming Systems for Efficient Fuel Cell Power Generators", 2013 Fuel Cell Seminar & Energy Exposition, Columbus, OH
8. P. K. Cheekatamarla, C. M. Finnerty, C. R. Robinson, S. M. Andrews, J. A. Brodie, Y. Lu, P. G. DeWald, "Design, integration and demonstration of a 50WJP8/kerosene fueled portable SOFC power generator", J Power Sources 193 (2009) 797.
9. DOD Technology Readiness Assessment (TRA) Guidance , ASD(R&E), 13 May 2011
10. J. Zhang, T. Thampan, R. Datta, "Influence of Anode Flow Rate and Cathode Oxygen Pressure on CO Poisoning of Proton Exchange Membrane Fuel Cells", J. Electrochem. Soc., 149 ~6, A765 (2002)
11. V. A. Sethuraman, J.W. Weidner, "Analysis of Sulfur Poisoning on a PEM Fuel Cell Electrode", Electrochimica Acta, 55(20), 5683 (2010)
12. T. Thampan, M. Govoni, J. T. Clark, "Fuel Cell Systems as Power Sources for Sensor Applications" J. Fuel Cell Sci. Technol. 10, 044501 (2013)
13. D. C. Seel, B. C. Benicewicz, L. Xiao and T. J. Schmidt, "High-temperature polybenzimidazole-based membranes", *Handbook of Fuel Cells – Fundamentals, Technology and Applications*. Eds: W. Vielstich, H. Yokokawa, H. A. Gasteiger. Vol. 5: *Advances in Electocatalysis, Materials, Diagnostics and Durability*. John Wiley & Sons, Ltd. (2009)
14. T. J. Schmidt and J. Baurmeister, "Durability and Reliability in High-Temperature Reformed H2 PEFCs", *ECS Transactions*, 3 (1) (2006) 861-869
15. A. Gomez, J. J. Berry, S.Roychoudhury, B. Coriton a, J. Huth, "From jet fuel to electric power using a mesoscale, efficient Stirling cycle", Proc. Combust. Inst. 31 (2007) 3251
16. J. D. Holladay, Y. Wang, E. Jones, "Review of Developments in Portable Hydrogen Production Using Microreactor Technology", Chem. Rev. 104 (2004) 4767
17. Q. Ming, P. Irving, J. Berry, A. Reis, "Diesel reformer- a key component for a truck fuel cell APU", Fuel Cells Bulletin 1 (2010), 12
18. M Krumpelt, T.R Krause, J.D Carter, J.P Kopasz, S Ahmed, "Fuel processing for fuel cell systems in transportation and portable power applications" Catal. Today 77 (2002), 3
19. F. Barrai and M. J. Castaldi, "Experimental Investigation of a JP8 Fuel Processor: Autothermal Reformer and CO-Cleanup Train", F. Barrai, M. J. Castaldi, Ind. Eng. Chem. Res. 49, (2010), 1577
20. P K. Cheekatamarla, A. M. Lane, "Catalytic autothermal reforming of diesel fuel for hydrogen generation in fuel cells I. Activity tests and sulfur poisoning", J Power Sources 152 (2005) 256
21. B. Smith R J, M. Loganathany, M. S.r Shanthaz, "A Review of the Water Gas Shift Reaction Kinetics" Intl. J Chem. Reactor Eng. 8 (2010) R4 1
22. Z. Li, D. Fokema, W. Rhine, "Hydrocarbon Fuel Processing For H2 Generation", US Patent # 7,332,003 B1 2/19/2008
23. G Alptekin, A. Jayaraman, M. Dubovik, M. Schaefer, and J. Monroe, "Novel Oxidative Fuel Desulfurization System", 11th Intl. Symposium on Solid Oxide Fuel Cells, 216th ECS Meeting, Vienna, Austria, 10/4, 2009
24. C. Hulteberg, "Sulphur-tolerant catalysts in small-scale hydrogen production, a review" Int J Hydrog Energ 37 (2012) 3978 -
25. TSR-121E Unicat Catalyst – Product data accessed on 4/1/2013 at http://www.unicatcatalyst.com/sulfur-removal.html

Sulfur Tolerant, Compact Fuel Processors

Subir Roychoudhury, Saurabh A. Vilekar, Christian Junaedi, Dennis Walsh, and Richard Mastanduno

Precision Combustion, Inc.,
410 Sackett Point Rd., North Haven, CT 06473
sroychoudhury@precision-combustion.com

Abstract: *Some of the challenges affecting widespread deployment of fuel cell power generation solutions are sulfur poisoning, coke formation, and water recovery. Sulfur tolerant fuel processors operating under water neutral conditions combined with downstream gas phase sulfur removal system provide a significant improvement over fuel processors relying on upstream liquid fuel desulfurizer units. PCI has developed fuel-flexible, sulfur-tolerant reforming solutions which have been integrated with multiple stack technologies. These reformers utilize an ultra-short channel length substrate structure, trademarked Microlith®, that is combined with advanced catalyst coatings, offering significant performance and durability advantages over conventional reactors. Application of Microlith technology allows process intensification by close coupling steam generation, sulfur cleanup, and reforming catalyst in an ultra-compact, lightweight package. These fuel processors also lend themselves to being scaled-up to higher throughputs. This paper will report reformer data obtained from 1-2 kWe fuel processors operating with JP-8 containing up to 3000 ppm_w sulfur and sulfur cleanup to <1 ppm_v, along with water-neutral system design and integration with fuel cell stacks for various military and commercial applications.*

Keywords: Fuel Processor, Fuel Reformer, Sulfur Tolerant, JP-8, Logistic Fuels, Microlith, Lightweight, Compact, Fuel Cells

Introduction

It is desirable to use military logistic fuels like JP-8 and JP-5 in battlefield fuel cell-based power generation units. Robust logistic fuel reformers that can operate for thousands of hours are required to realize this goal. An obstacle to this application, however, is the sulfur-sensitivity of reforming catalysts, hydrogen separators, and electrocatalysts used in such units. Effectively removing sulfur from JP-8 has been a persistent hurdle for military use of fuel cells. A variety of approaches such as liquid fuel sorbents, membranes, fractionators, and hydro-desulfurization, have proved to be inefficient and complex for compact, simple systems. Precision Combustion, Inc. (PCI) has developed a simple breakthrough process for reforming high sulfur containing fuels. This allows development of compact and economical fuel processors that are capable of operating with high selectivity and low C2+ hydrocarbons slip while being resistant to coke formation, sintering (temperature spikes), and sulfur poisoning. This paper highlights the state of progress of these fuel processors. We report results, including experimental data on sulfur tolerance and durability for 1-2 kWe fuel processors along with a brief description of large scale prototypes.

Overview of Microlith® Technology: The compact, lightweight, and modular catalytic fuel reformers discussed here are based on PCI's patented Microlith® substrates and catalyst technology (1). The Microlith technology consists of a series of catalytically coated, microfabricated metal meshes. The meshes each have ultra-short channel lengths, high cell density, and low thermal mass. The resulting reactor is very compact, has rapid transient response, and only requires small amounts of precious metal catalysts due to the high catalytic activity. The benefits of this design are results from the reduction in mass transfer limitations as compared to conventional monoliths having relatively thick boundary layers. The Microlith substrate also provides about three times higher geometric surface area over conventional reactors (e.g., monoliths) with equivalent volume and open frontal area. Additionally, it packs more active surface area into a small volume, and thus provides more effective fuel conversion for a given pressure drop as well as a higher catalyst utilization. The effectiveness of the Microlith technology and long-term durability of PCI's proprietary catalyst coatings have been systematically demonstrated in different applications, including exhaust aftertreatment, catalytic combustion, partial oxidation of methane, (2,3) as well as liquid fuel reforming and water gas shift reactors in fuel processors (4,5,6,7).

Sulfur Tolerant Fuel Processor

PCI's auto thermal reforming (ATR) reactor consists of a Microlith catalyst core integrated with steam generation heat exchanger and downstream sulfur cleanup (i.e., gas phase H_2S removal). Fuel injection, mixing, vaporization, and reforming are all performed within the coiled catalytic reactor. Our first generation conventional ATR reactor has been demonstrated to be sulfur tolerant up to 400 ppm_w sulfur with JP-8, while producing fuel cell quality reformate (8). The reformer design allows operation at low steam-to-carbon (H_2O/C) ratio of ~0.9-1.2 with a corresponding oxygen-to-carbon (O/C) ratio of ~1. This allowed the reformer to maintain complete fuel conversion and ≥80% reforming efficiency with minimal degradation/catalyst deactivation over 1000 hours. In an effort to further improve the sulfur tolerance, PCI recently developed a modified ATR process. The second generation ATR reactor is configured with a unique, sulfur-tolerant, catalyst that converts the myriad sulfur compounds in Jet Fuels to H_2S. This is possible under a unique set of operating conditions discovered recently at PCI. The reforming catalyst is relatively unaffected by the H_2S. The reformate stream is heat exchanged with the recycled exhaust water to create steam for the reformer. This lowers the reformate temperature to a level suitable for subsequent efficient H_2S removal in a high capacity sorption bed. Nano ZnO supported on high surface area meshes is used as the sulfur sorbent bed. Consequently, fuel cell quality reformate with adequate sulfur cleanup is produced from Jet Fuels for fueling the fuel cell stacks. A photo of the 1 kWe modified ATR reactor including steam generator, mixer and sulfur cleanup bed is shown in Figure 1.

Figure 1. Photo of 1 kWe modified ATR reformer capable of reforming up to 3000 ppm_w sulfur containing logistic fuels.

PCI's modified ATR has been tested with up to 3000 ppm_w sulfur JP-8. Figure 2 shows stable reformer performance during the 1000 hour durability testing with 1000 ppm_w sulfur JP-8 (620 ppm_w naturally occurring sulfur JP-8 from Wright-Patterson AFB was doped with dibenzothiophene). No C3s (i.e., propane and propylene) were observed over the 1000 hour testing, while only trace amounts of C2s (i.e., ethane and ethylene) were detected. The sulfur level in the reformate stream was monitored using a GC/FPD and showed near complete sulfur balance. All the fuel bound sulfur was converted predominantly to H_2S with trace amounts of COS. The modified ATR was also capable of achieving complete fuel conversion with 3000 ppm_w sulfur JP-8. Operating the reformer at low H_2O/C ratios allows downstream gas phase desulfurization to produce a reformate stream with less than 1 ppm_v sulfur (suitable for fuel cells) using a sulfur trap to achieve the desired sulfur removal. This makes for a very simple reforming system, avoiding any upstream liquid fuel desulfurization. Current efforts are ongoing for design optimization to maximize the reforming efficiency. Note that the reforming efficiency is calculated as the ratio of the lower heating value (LHV) of H_2 and CO in the reformate stream to the LHV of the fuel fed to the reformer.

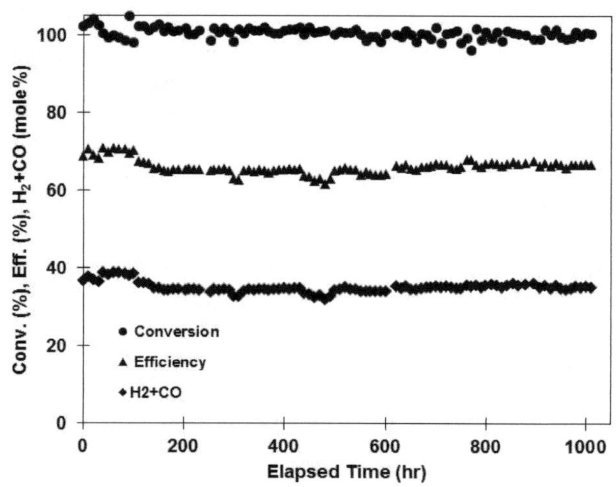

Figure 2. Fuel conversion, reforming efficiency (LHV-based) and H_2+CO concentration (mole %, dry basis) from the 1000-hr test with 1000 ppm_w sulfur JP-8.

The modified ATR demonstrated unique fuel flexibility and has been tested with multiple fuels (e.g., diesel, S-8, biofuels, military logistics fuels including JP-8) providing stable, equilibrium-limited reformate composition.

Compact Efficient Sulfur Clean-up

Development of an efficient, compact downstream sulfur trap is critical for removing the gas phase sulfur (in the form of H_2S) that is present in the reformate stream of the modified ATR approach described above, before feeding it to the fuel cell. Conventional wisdom says that a ZnO-based sorption bed, downstream of the reforming reactor, would require frequent replacement due to the moisture in the reformate stream. PCI has circumvented this concern by efficiently operating the reformers at low H_2O/C ratios with complete fuel conversion and without coking. We have developed a formulation and an application method for coating the ZnO nano-powder on Microlith metal meshes. Microlith substrate can pack more active surface area (high dispersion) into a small volume, thereby increasing the sorption capacity for a given pressure drop. H_2S sorption tests were performed on the traditional ZnO pellets and the ZnO-coated Microlith substrate using a surrogate gas mixture consisting of 115 ppm_v of H_2S to evaluate and compare sulfur sorption capacity. Note that due to dilution upon mixing with the other feed components and molar expansion upon reaction in the ATR, 115 ppm_v of H_2S in the reformate stream corresponds to ~1200 ppm_w of sulfur in the fuel. The test results showed that ZnO-coated Microlith bed gave a H_2S sorption capacity of ~33-34 wt.% based on the ZnO coating (i.e., 0.33-0.34 gram of H_2S uptake per gram of ZnO coating). Figure 3 shows the H_2S

breakthrough profiles from both tests. The H_2S sorption test on the ZnO pellet bed using the same operating conditions as in the tests on the ZnO/Microlith beds indicated a breakthrough after only 146 hours of continuous exposure to 115 ppm_v H_2S, which was much lower than the breakthrough time observed with the ZnO/Microlith beds (~230 hours).

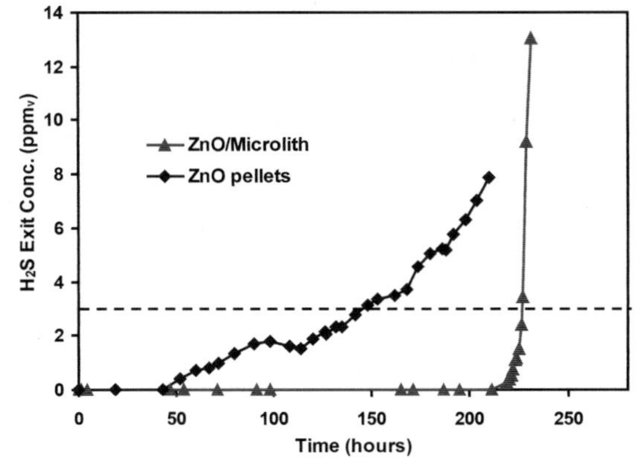

Figure 3. H_2S exit concentration vs. time obtained from H_2S sorption tests on the ZnO/Microlith bed and ZnO pellets. The H_2S breakthrough is indicated by a dashed line.

The test with ZnO pellets showed H_2S sorption capacity of only 6.95 wt.% based on the ZnO pellets (i.e., 0.0695 gram of H_2S uptake per gram of ZnO pellets). Thus a five-fold higher capacity (weight basis) was observed on ZnO/Microlith beds as compared to the ZnO pellets at the same operating conditions. The results from the sulfur sorption tests showed that the ZnO-coated Microlith metal meshes were able to reach nearly full ZnO capacity, at ~33-34 wt.% based on the ZnO coating, with high bed utilization. Finally, the volumetric sorption capacity for the ZnO/Microlith system based on the bed volume was 0.145 gram H_2S uptake/cm^3, which was higher than the volumetric sorption capacity for ZnO pellets systems despite the presence of inert Microlith substrate. This approach reduces the size and weight of the downstream sulfur clean-up unit for the portable applications, resulting in fuel cell systems with higher power densities. The desulfurizer bed was also successfully tested directly downstream of a JP-8 reformer. For a 5 kW_{th} system, an adsorber bed volume of ~0.3 L was used with 400 ppm_w sulfur JP-8. The desulfurizer bed lifetime will depend on the fuel-sulfur content. For example, a 5 L bed could last for over 1000 hours providing <1 ppm_v sulfur in the reformate stream with 1500 ppm_w fuel-sulfur. Moreover, the adsorber can be readily scaled for a desired throughput.

Fuel Processor Scale-up

The flexible architecture of the Microlith substrates results in a highly modular and scalable reformer design ranging in size from D-cell batteries for 1 kWe fuel cells to "1 gallon-size" for 250 kWe fuel cells. One such hardware example is shown in Figure 4 of an 800 kW_{th} fuel processing system consisting of fuel/air/steam injector, ATR, steam generator HEX, and downstream sulfur cleanup. This fuel processor has been tested for multiple hours with ULSD showing uniform flow distribution, no local hot spots, good temperature control, complete fuel conversion, equilibrium limited product distribution, 7:1 turndown and >80% reforming efficiency.

Figure 4. 800 kW_{th} skid-mounted integrated fuel processor with BOP.

Conclusions

PCI has designed and developed novel Microlith-based sulfur tolerant fuel processor that can be combined with downstream high-capacity sulfur cleanup to achieve fuel cell quality reformate. This approach shows several advantages over fuel processors relying on upstream liquid fuel desulfurizers, including simple process design and operation, ease of scalability, and high power density. Application of Microlith technology allows process intensification by close coupling steam generation, sulfur cleanup, and reforming catalyst in an ultra-compact, lightweight package.

Acknowledgement

We acknowledge the support of the DoD (ONR, TARDEC, ARL, CERDEC, NAVAIR, and WPAFB) and the DOE (Morgantown). Any opinions, findings, and conclusions or recommendations expressed in this paper are those of the authors and do not necessarily reflect the views of the DoD and DOE.

References

(1) Pfefferle, W. C., Microlith Catalytic Reaction System. *U.S. Patent 5,051,241*, Sep 24, 1991.

(2) Lyubovsky, M.; Karim, H.; Menacherry, P.; Boorse, S.; LaPierre, R.; Pfefferle, W. C.; Roychoudhury, S., *Catal. Today*, Vol. 83, pp. 183, 2003.
(3) Lyubovsky, M.; Roychoudhury, S.; LaPierre, R., *Catal. Lett.*, Vol. 99, pp. 113, 2005.
(4) Roychoudhury, S.; Castaldi, M. J.; Lyubovsky, M.; LaPierre, R.; Ahmed, S., *J. Power Sources*, Vol. 152, pp. 75, 2005.
(5) Castaldi, M. J.; LaPierre, R.; Lyubovski, M.; Pfefferle, W. C.; Roychoudhury, S., *Catal. Today*, Vol. 99, pp. 339, 2005
(6) Roychoudhury, S.; Junaedi, C.; Walsh, D.; Morgan, C.; Mastanduno, R., *Prepr. Pap. - Am. Chem. Soc., Div. Fuel Chem.*, Vol. 54 (2), pp. 417, 2009.
(7) Junaedi, C.; Vilekar, S. A.; Walsh, D.; Mastanduno, R.; Morgan, C.; Roychoudhury, S., *Int. J. Hyd. Energy*, http://dx.doi.org/10.1016/j.ijhydene.2012.01.123, 2012.
(8) Junaedi, C.; Vilekar, S.; Morgan, C.; Walsh, D.; Mastanduno, R.; Roychoudhury, S., *Proceeding of the 44th Power Sources Conference*, Las Vegas, NV, June 14-17, 2010, Paper 22.5, pp. 509.

Dual Firing of Hydrogen and JP-8 for External Combustion Based Power Sources

Michael Seibert, Terry DuBois
Command, Power & Integration Directorate
US Army RDECOM, CERDEC
5100 Magazine Road
Aberdeen Proving Ground, MD 21005

Sen Nieh
Professor and Chair
Department of Mechanical Engineering
The Catholic University of America
620 Michigan Ave, N.E.
Washington, DC 20064
nieh@cua.edu

Abstract: *Flame control, particularly at lean conditions, is a critical requirement for external combustion based power sources such as thermoelectric and thermophotovoltaic generators. This research investigates the use of hydrogen co-fired with heavy hydrocarbons for improved fuel efficiency, operational characteristics, and environmental protection. The availability of in-situ produced hydrogen from JP-8 fuel reforming allows dual firing of hydrogen and JP-8 to be a feasible approach for small power applications, such as the battlefield. Previous numerical simulations indicate that hydrogen reformate can provide improved fuel conversion, better flame stability and higher fuel burnout. In the present research, experiments are conducted on the impact of hydrogen on a 9 kW_{th} JP-8 combustion test stand. Temperature profiles and emissions are studied. In the open diffusion flame, hydrogen addition increases flame temperature and reduces hydrocarbon and carbon monoxide emissions. NO_x emissions are generally increased due to the increased temperatures. The reduction in hydrocarbon emissions is especially evident with coaxially introduced secondary air. Hydrogen provides higher temperatures throughout the flame, which contribute to complete combustion. Complete combustion is important for fuel efficiency, operational reliability and emissions control. The benefits of hydrogen addition are observed with hydrogen providing only 5-10% of the energy content which is important for implementing this technique in practical power sources.*

Keywords: hydrogen; fuel reforming; external combustion; jet fuel.

Introduction

To simplify logistics, the US Military has mandated that only one fuel be taken to the battlefield since 1988. The chosen fuel, JP-8, is a middle distillate kerosene fuel similar to civilian Jet A. Like diesel fuel, it has a low octane rating and cannot be used in unmodified spark ignition engines. Compression ignition engines do not work well at small scales because the high pressure required results in high weight (reduced power density). As a result, there is a lower limit to the power sources that can be supplied by battlefield fuels. For example, the military does not currently field any diesel or JP-8 fueled electric power sources smaller than 2 kW. This leaves a power gap between portable batteries and 2000 W. This power range includes loads such as laptop computers, radios, power tools, battery chargers, etc.

This need presents an opportunity for Stirling engines, thermionic generators, thermoelectric generators, and thermophotovoltaic generators which would not be able to compete directly with internal combustion engines at higher power levels. These power sources can all produce power up to 2000 W, and all use an external combustion heat source. Techniques improving the combustion of JP-8, to provide energy to these systems would fill this power gap.

A viable external combustion power source requires complete combustion over a wide range of operating conditions. Complete combustion is necessary both to fully utilize the energy available in the fuel and to limit harmful emissions.

Previous work in small combustors examined the effect of oxygen enriched air on the combustion of JP-8 [1]. This work showed increased burner capacity and temperature at increased levels of oxygen enrichment.

Recent advances in fuel reforming for fuel cell applications allow the generation of hydrogen on the battlefield from JP-8 [2]. Due to this availability of hydrogen, the possibility of dual firing hydrogen and JP-8 was investigated.

Previous work in hydrogen enriched combustion has shown success in other areas. Schefer at Sandia National Labs added hydrogen to methane-air flames and found that it improved lean flame stability and reduced NO_x emissions [3]. Kumar and Mishra added hydrogen to liquefied petroleum gas (LPG) flames which lowered NO_x emissions while increasing CO [4]. Several researchers have used hydrogen as a supplementary fuel for diesel engines with mixed results [5,6]. Most researchers have reported reduced specific fuel consumption but the impact on NO_x emissions is mixed.

Research in hydrogen enriched combustion for aircraft engines with kerosene (similar to JP-8) has shown improvements in flame stability, including the ability to extend the lean burning limit, reducing NOx without increasing CO [7-9].

Simulations of a closed combustor showed that both hydrogen and reformate can increase JP-8 combustion efficiency and extend the lean blow out limit [10].

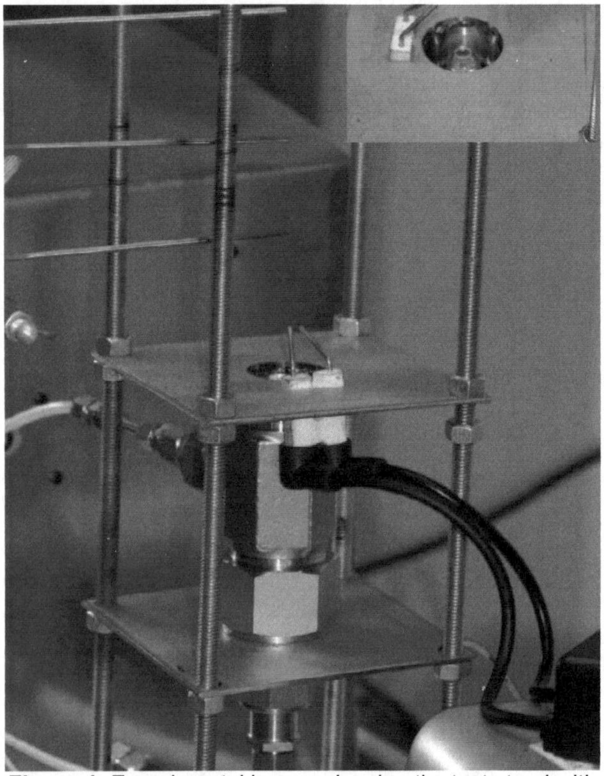

Figure 1. Experimental burner showing the test stand with thermocouples and fuel supply line (left side). The nozzle and igniter are shown in the inset.

Experimental Set-up

Experiments were conducted using an open flame. JP-8 is sprayed upwards through an air siphon nozzle (Delevan 30609-2) and ignited with an arcing electrode as shown in Figure 1. A constant level oiler maintains the fuel lift height at a constant 20 cm below the nozzle. The constant level oiler is placed on a platform scale with fuel flow rate being determined by the change in weight over time. Secondary air is introduced through a 1.5" tube mounted concentrically around the fuel nozzle. Hydrogen is introduced by mixing with the nozzle air supply. Exhaust gas composition is measured with an XM-2000 Gas Analyzer with the sample probe placed approximately 20 cm above the nozzle. Gas flow rates are measured and controlled using pressure based mass flow controllers: 0-20 slpm for hydrogen, 0-50 slpm for the nozzle air and 0-1000 slpm for the secondary air. Flame temperature is measured using one 1/16" K-type thermocouple mounted to a linear slide, allowing a detailed axial temperature profile.

Fuel flow rate is controlled by the air flow through the nozzle. This air supplies approximately 10% of the air necessary for full combustion. To test combustion performance at approximately constant fuel energy input, air flow was reduced as hydrogen was added. This reduction accounted for both the energy input from hydrogen and the increased liquid fuel pulled by the additional gas flow (See Table 1). Total fuel energy input to the burner was maintained at approximately 9 kW. Secondary air was added concentrically through the tube around the nozzle starting at 100 slpm and increasing in 20 slpm increments until blowout. Each condition is maintained for 5-10 minutes to collect data and to allow the flame to stabilize.

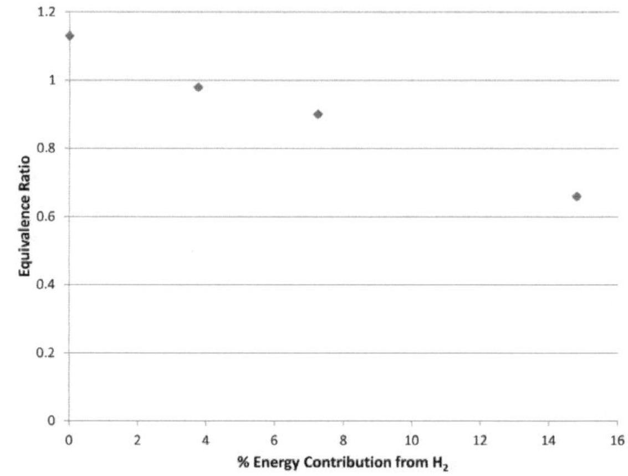

Figure 2. Lean blow out reduction with hydrogen addition. Note that the measured lean blow out does not account for air entrained from the surroundings.

Table 1. Nominal nozzle gas and fuel flow rates

Air (slpm)	H_2 (slpm)	H_2 (kW)	JP-8 (g/min)	JP-8 (kW)	% energy from H_2	Total kW
15	0	0.0	12.1	8.6	0.0	8.6
13	2	0.3	11.6	8.3	3.8	8.6
12	4	0.7	11.8	8.4	7.2	9.1
9	8	1.3	10.8	7.7	14.5	9.0

Results

Figure 2 shows the effect of hydrogen on lean blow out limit. The blow out equivalence ratio is calculated on the basis of air supplied through the nozzle and secondary air tube. It should be noted that the actual equivalence ratio would be lower due to additional air entrained to the open flame. With no hydrogen, the leanest sustainable flame is at 120 slpm secondary air. When 2 and 4 slpm hydrogen are added through the nozzle, flames are sustained at 140 and 160 slpm secondary air respectively. Adding 8 slpm hydrogen substantially extends the lean burning limit, supporting a sustained flame with 220 slpm secondary air. It is clear that hydrogen provides enhanced flame stability. This expanded range of flammable conditions is important for developing a robust power system.

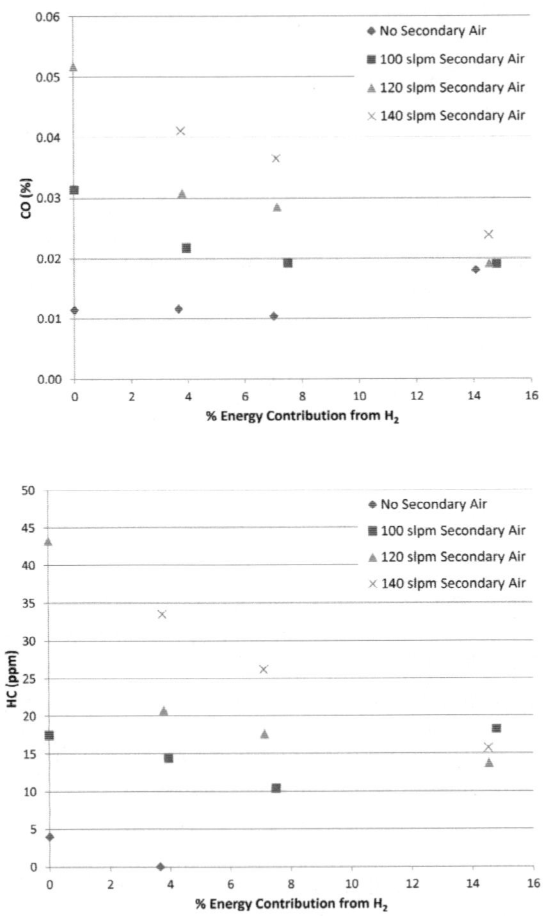

Figure 3. Carbon monoxide (top) and unburned hydrocarbon (bottom) concentrations in exhaust gas.

Combustion completeness is analyzed by emissions measurements as seen in Figure 3. Carbon monoxide and hydrocarbons are signs of incomplete combustion. They represent energy from the fuel that is lost and also present a hazard to the user. Figure 3a shows the amount of carbon monoxide in the exhaust decreasing substantially as hydrogen is added. The most significant decrease is between no hydrogen and 2 slpm hydrogen with 120 slpm secondary air. As shown in Figure 2, this is near the lean blow out limit for the JP-8/air only case. This is consistent with hydrogen improving flame stability and combustion in lean conditions, and extending the lean blow out limit. Figure 3b shows a similar effect with unburned hydrocarbons. Again, hydrogen improves stability, especially near lean blow out conditions. Without secondary air, the JP-8 and hydrogen burn in a condition that more closely approximates a fuel-rich diffusion flame since the air must be entrained from the ambient environment. This results in slower gas velocities, allowing more time for complete combustion and allowing the gas mixture to reach higher temperatures.

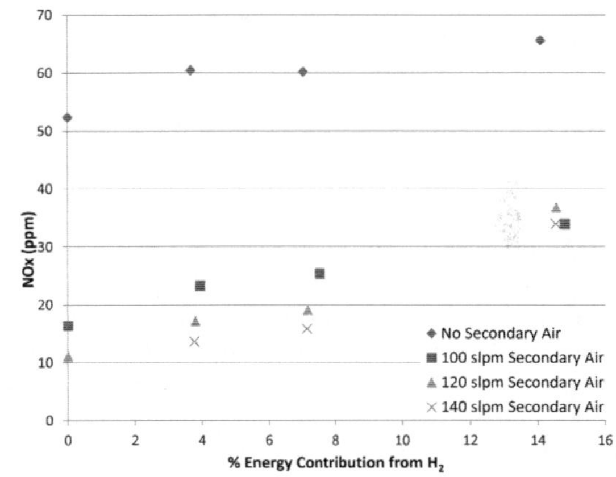

Figure 4. NO_x concentrations in exhaust gas.

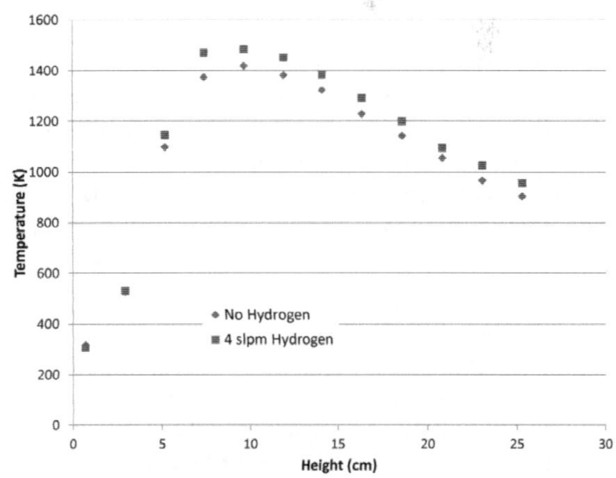

Figure 5. Temperature profiles for flames with 100 slpm secondary air, with and without hydrogen addition.

The trade off that must be considered in dual firing hydrogen and JP-8 is the effect of hydrogen on NO_x formation. Figure 4 shows NO_x concentrations with hydrogen addition. With other conditions constant, hydrogen results in higher NO_x concentrations. This is consistent with hydrogen providing more complete combustion and higher temperatures. It is encouraging to note that the increase in NO_x with 2 slpm hydrogen is modest, especially when compared to the significant decreases in CO and hydrocarbons with 2 slpm hydrogen. It should also be noted that secondary air flow (lean combustion) reduces NO_x concentration. If hydrogen enhances flame stability to allow a lean enough burn, it could reduce NO_x emissions as well.

Temperature profiles of two flames with 14 slpm primary nozzle air and 100 slpm secondary air are shown in Figure 5. One flame is only JP-8 and air, the other is JP-8 with 4 slpm hydrogen (~7% of the fuel energy). In the early preheat, droplet vaporization section of the flame, hydrogen has no visible impact on temperature. Above 5 cm, the effect of hydrogen becomes more significant with temperatures roughly 50-100K higher than the JP-8 only flame. The higher temperatures contribute to the more complete combustion (reduced CO and HC) and greater flame stability observed above. These higher temperatures are also consistent with the increased NO_x observed in Figure 4.

Discussion

Previous computational work in closed combustors showed a greater benefit to dual firing with hydrogen at lean conditions than at stoichiometric or fuel rich conditions [10]. This is consistent with the present experimental results in which the open JP-8 flame without secondary air had minimal differences when hydrogen was added. Without secondary air, reactant and product gases move more slowly, allowing time for reactions to complete and temperature to increase forming a hot stable flame. When secondary air is added, the gas stream moves quickly through the reaction zone reducing temperature and the time available for combustion completion. Hydrogen is a fast burning fuel which provides additional thermal energy to maintain flame stability and complete combustion. The increased temperature is present throughout the flame as seen in Figure 5.

Summary

The experiments in this study demonstrate the benefits of using hydrogen as a supplement to JP-8 in an external combustion based power application. Small amounts of hydrogen were shown to improve combustion stability and reduce the emission of incomplete combustion products. The enhanced combustion is due to the higher reactivity of hydrogen, improving the thermal environment and increasing radical concentrations. The improved stability allows more flexible flame control for better power system performance and operational flexibility. Further investigation is warranted to optimize the dual fuel performance with the weight and cost of a fuel reformer.

Acknowledgement

The authors gratefully acknowledge the US Army Communications-Electronics Research Development and Engineering Center's support in the form of an In-House Laboratory Independent Research project that funded much of this work.

References

1. Coombe HS, Nieh S, Polymer membrane air separation performance for portable oxygen enriched combustion applications, *Energy Conversion and Management* (2007)Volume 48, Issue 5, Pages 1499-1505
2. DuBois TG, Nieh S, Selection and performance comparison of jet fuel surrogates for autothermal reforming, *Fuel* (2011) vol 90 1439-1448
3. Schefer, R. W. "Combustion of Hydrogen-Enriched Methane in a Lean Premixed Swirl Burner." *Proceedings of the 2001 Department of Energy Hydrogen Program Review*
4. Kumar, P. and Mishra, D.P. "Experimental investigation of laminar LPG-H_2 jet diffusion flame." *International Journal of Hydrogen Energy* 33 (2008) 225-231.
5. Abu-Jrai, A., Tsolakis, A., Megaritis, A. "The influence of H_2 and CO on diesel engine combustion characteristics, exhaust gas emissions, and after treatment selective catalytic NO_x reduction." *International Journal of Hydrogen Energy* 32 (2007) 3565-3571
6. Kumar, S, M. Ramesh, A., Nagalingam, B. "Use of hydrogen to enhance the performance of a vegetable oil fueled compression ignition engine." *International Journal of Hydrogen Energy* 28 (2003) 1143-1154
7. Frenillot, J.P., Cabot, G., Cazalens, M., Renou, B., Boukhalfa, A.M. "Impact of H2 addition on flame stability and pollutant emissions for an atmospheric kerosene/air swirled flame of laboratory scaled gas turbine" *International Journal of Hydrogen Energy* 34 (2009) 3930-3944
8. Burguburu, J., Cabot, G., Renou, B., Boukhalfa, A.M., Cazalens, M., "Effects of H2 enrichment on flame stability and pollutant emissions for a kerosene/air swirled flame with an aeronautical injector" *Proceedings of the Combustion Institute* 33 (2011) 2927-2935
9. Burguburu, J., Cabot, G., Renou, B., Boukhalfa, A.M., Cazalens, M., "Comparisons of the impact of reformer gas and hydrogen enrichment on flame stability and pollutant emissions for a kerosene/air swirled flame with an aeronautical fuel injector" *International Journal of Hydrogen Energy* 36 (2011) 6925-6936
10. Seibert, M., Nieh, S., "Simulation of Dual Firing of Hydrogen-Rich Reformate and JP-8 Surrogate in a Swirling Combustor," *International Journal of Hydrogen Energy* 38 (2013) 5911-5917

Chemical Modeling of Thermal Partial Oxidation of a JP8/Jet A Surrogate

Richard Scenna[a], Terry Dubois[b], Ashwani K. Gupta[c]
[a] US Army Research, Development and Engineering Command, CERDEC, CPI
[b] US Army Research, Development and Engineering Command, CERDEC, CPI
[c] University of Maryland, Department of Mechanical Engineering, College park, MD 20742
E-mail: akgupta@umd.edu

Abstract: *Multiple JP8/Jet A surrogates have been proposed to replicate various aspects of combustion in the literature that range from flame speed, thermal stability, ignition delay, and other reaction and rheological parameters. However, only limited data on surrogates have been validated experimentally under reforming conditions (Φ~3.0). Chemical modeling of a single, binary, and tertiary JP8 and Jet A surrogate were evaluated at several equivalence ratios in the range of 1.5< Φ <3.0. It was found that under reforming condition (Φ~3.0), the tertiary surrogate (consisting of iso and normal alkanes content with dodecane (70%vol), cyclo-alkanes content with decalin (10%vol) and mono-aromatics content with toluene (20%vol)) was best able to predict both hydrogen formation (experimental =15.0%, modeling = 15.03%) and carbon monoxide formation (experimental =19.0%, modeling = 18.87%). This work examines the improved chemical modeling of thermal partial oxidation of JP8/Jet A fuels based on the work on catalytic reforming of JP8/Jet A surrogates.*

Keywords: Fuel Reforming, Fuel Processing, Thermal Partial Oxidation, Modeling the Reforming of JP8 and Jet A Surrogate

Introduction

JP8 and Jet A are kerosene based middle distillate fuels composed of hundreds of hydrocarbons compounds. JP8 is chemically very similar to Jet A except for three additional additives; corrosion inhibitor, lubricity promoter, icing inhibitor, and a static dissipater[1]. The average chemical composition of JP8 on a volume basis is: iso and normal alkanes (50-65%), cyclo-alkanes (10-20%), mono-aromatics (15-20%) and poly-aromatics (1-3%). JP8 has an average molar hydrogen to carbon ratio (H/C) of ~ 1.9 and an average molecular formula was chosen for this work of $C_{11}H_{21}$. Dagaut reported that the average molecular formula of JP8 vary between $C_{10.9}H_{20.9}$ to $C_{12}H_{23}$[2]. The average molecular weight of JP8 is 153.28 g/mol and a lower heating value range between 42.48-43.22 MJ/kg.

The first surrogate evaluated represented iso and normal alkanes that represent the primary component of JP8, with dodecane. This single component surrogate has H/C=2.16 and a molecular formula $C_{12}H_{26}$. The surrogate has a molecular weight of 170.33 g/mol and a lower heating value of 44.11 MJ/kg. A binary surrogated proposed by Gould [5] was also evaluated which represents iso and normal alkanes content with dodecane (62.51%$_{vol}$) and aromatic content with tetralin (37.49%$_{vol}$)[3]. This surrogate has a molecular weight of 151.27g/mol and a lower heating value of 42.75 MJ/kg. This results in an H/C ratio = 1.73 and average molecular formula of $C_{11}H_{19}$. A tertiary surrogate was proposed by Dubois, which represent the iso and normal alkanes content with dodecane (70%$_{vol}$), the cyclo-alkanes content with decalin (10%$_{vol}$) and mono-aromatics content with toluene (20%$_{vol}$)[4]. This results in an H/C =1.89 and an average molecular formula of $C_{10.1}H_{19.0}$. This surrogate has an average molecular weight of 140.4 g/mol and a lower heating value of 43.12 KJ/kg.

	JP8	Single	Binary	Tertiary
Molecular Formula	$C_{11}H_{21}$	$C_{12}H_{26}$	$C_{11}H_{19}$	$C_{10.1}H_{19.0}$
Molar H/C Ratio	~1.9	2.16	1.73	1.89
LHV(MJ/kg)	42.48-43.22	44.11	42.75	43.12
MW(g/mol)	153.28	170.33	156.05g	140.4
Density(g/L)	0.775-0.840	0.749	0.832	0.788
Dodecane(%$_{vol}$)	-	100%	62.51%	70%
Decalin(%$_{vol}$)	-	0%	0%	10%
Toluene(%$_{vol}$)	-	0%	0%	20%
Tetralin (%$_{vol}$)	-	0%	37.49%	0%

Table 1. Surrogate Fuel Properties and Composition

Kinetic Modeling

The kinetic model used in this work contains the detailed kinetic data for alkanes with carbon number in the range of C8 to C16 and this also includes soot formation reactions[5]. The model was originally validated for pyrolysis and combustion conditions over a range of equivalence ratios from 0.2 to 2.0, pressures ranging from 0.08 atm to 50 atm and temperatures from 550 to 2000°K. The model is composed of 13,532 reactions.

Chemical modeling was conducted using Chemkin Pro and compared against experimental data for Jet A under equivalence ratios 1.5< Φ <3.0[6][7].

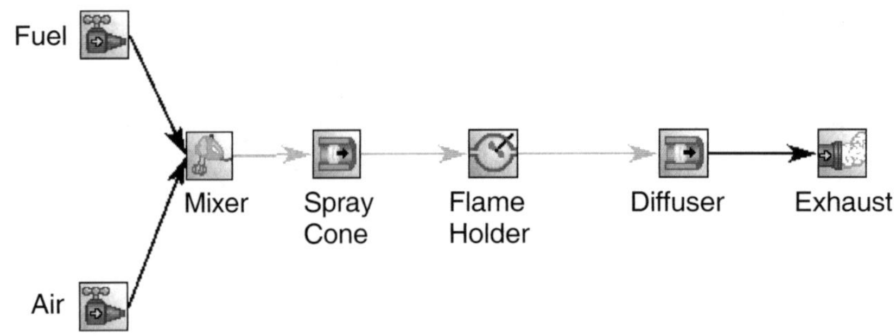

Figure 1. Schematic of the Reactor Network.

Figure 1 shows a schematic of the reactor network. The network was comprised of three sections, the spray cone, flame holder and diffuser. A similar approach was used by Vourliotakis[8] to model thermal partial oxidation of methane in a porous media.

The spray cone developed from the nozzle consisting of fuel and air mixture was modeled as an adiabatic plug flow reactor with a variable cross-sectional area. The diameter was varied linearly from 1 mm (inlet size) to 70 mm at a distance of 100 mm. The second section of the model was the fine bead layer, which acted as a flame holder. In the experiment, the flame holder consisted of a layer of alumina beads with diameter in the range of 2 to 4 mm and had a spark plug. The flame holder and spark plug were modeled as a continuously stirred transient reactor (CSTR) with a void space of the flame holder of 74.92 cm^3. The third section of the reactor was comprised of porous media in the quartz tube that acted as a diffuser. The porous media consisted of zirconia oxide foam obtained from Linik (VukoporHT). The reactor dimensions were 70 mm diameter and 150 mm long. In Chemkin the diffuser was modeled as an adiabatic plug flow reactor (PFR) with diameter of 70mm and a length of 135mm.

Comparison of Surrogates

Under ideal reforming conditions (Φ~3.0), the experimental data was best predicted by the tertiary surrogate as shown in figures 2-3. The single component surrogate over predicted hydrogen formation (experimental =15.0%, model= 15.28%) and under predicted both carbon monoxide (experimental =19.0%, model=17.29%) and carbon dioxide (experimental= 3.0%, model=2.7%) formation. This was partially attributed to the single component surrogate (H/C=2.16) having a higher hydrogen to carbon ratio than JP8 (H/C=1.9). In addition surrogate only represent a single component of JP8. The single component surrogate accurately predicted methane formation at Φ~3.0 (experimental= 2.90%, model =2.94%) but under predicted methane formation at lower equivalence ratios. Acetylene formation was significantly over predicted (experimental=0.10%, model=1.69%).

The binary surrogate under predicted both hydrogen formation (experimental=15.0%, model= 14.67%) and over predicted the carbon monoxide formation (experimental=19.0%, model =19.78%). This was also partially attributed to the binary surrogate (H/C=1.73) having a lower hydrogen to carbon ratio than JP8 (H/C=1.9).

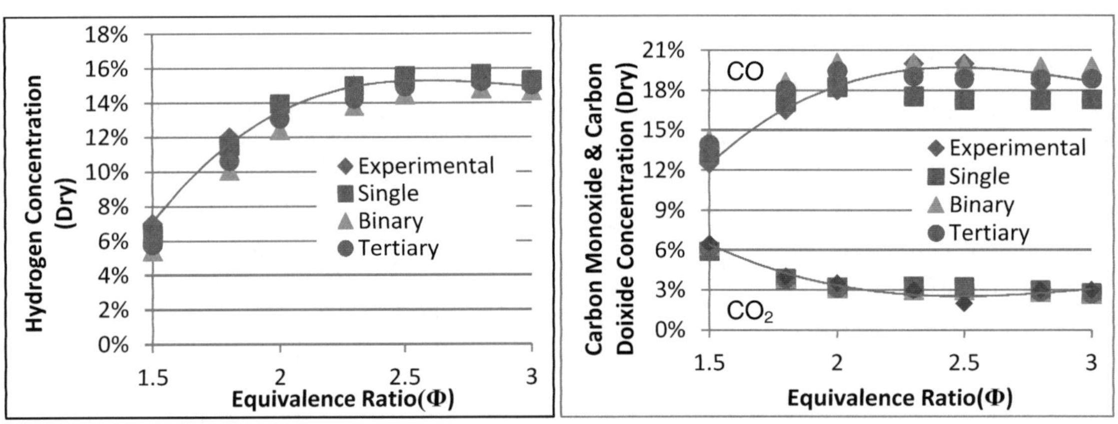

Figure 2. Hydrogen and Carbon Formation at Different Equivalence Ratios

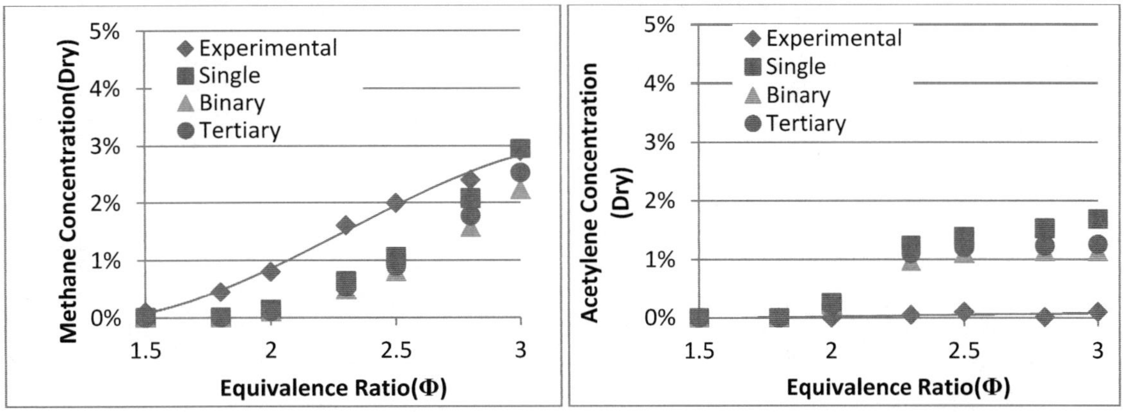

Figure 3. Methane and Acetylene Formation at Different Equivalence Ratios

The binary surrogate under predicted carbon dioxide formation (experimental=3.0%, model =2.66%). The binary surrogate slightly under predicted methane formation (experimental= 2.90%, model = 2.23%) but over predicted acetylene formation (experimental=0.10%, model= 1.13%). While the average molecular formula of binary surrogate is comparable to JP8, the aromatic content of the binary surrogate (37.4$\%_{vol}$) is significantly higher than that of typical JP8 fuel (20$\%_{vol}$).

The tertiary surrogate accurately predicted both hydrogen formation (experimental =15.0%, model = 15.03%) and the carbon monoxide formation (experimental=19.0%, model= 18.87%) but under predicted carbon dioxide formation (experimental =3.0%, model =2.72%). This surrogate represents the major classes of the hydrocarbon and has hydrogen to carbon ratio similar to that of JP8. The tertiary surrogate slightly under predicted methane formation (experimental= 2.90%, model =2.53%) but over predicted acetylene formation (experimental =0.10%, model = 1.25%).

Conclusions

Chemical modeling of JP8/jet A surrogate in the form of single, binary, and tertiary fuel showed suitable surrogates for JP8 under thermal partial oxidation reforming conditions. Amongst the primary, secondary and tertiary fuels, the tertiary surrogate (dodecane 70$\%_{vol}$, decalin 10$\%_{vol}$, toluene 20$\%_{vol}$) provided most favorable prediction on reformate composition. Specifically, the hydrogen formation (experimental =15.0%, tertiary model= 15.03%) and carbon monoxide (experimental =19.0%, tertiary model= 18.87%) formation provided good agreement between the experimental and modeling results. All surrogate showed some level of difficulty in predicting the formation of lower hydrocarbons. The better performance with the tertiary surrogate is attributed to hydrocarbons representing the iso and normal alkanes, cyclic-alkanes and mono aromatics and hydrogen to carbon ratio very close to JP8(Tertiary H/C =1.89 & JP8 H/C=1.9). The results showed that a closer representation of true hydrocarbons present in JP8/Jet A can result in good favorable representation of thermal partial oxidation under reforming conditions.

Acknowledgments

The author acknowledge the support of the US Army ILIR Program and the support of University of Maryland Department of Mechanical Engineering.

References

[1] LePera M., 1999, JET A1 vs. JP-8 Differences and Effects on Long Term Use.

[2] Dagaut P., and Cathonnet M., 2006, "The ignition, oxidation, and combustion of kerosene: A review of experimental and kinetic modeling," Prog. energy Combust. Sci., **32**, pp. 48–92.

[3] Gould B. D., Tadd A. R., and Schwank J. W., 2007, "Nickel-catalyzed autothermal reforming of jet fuel surrogates: n-Dodecane, tetralin, and their mixture," J. Power Sources, **164**(1), pp. 344–350.

[4] DuBois T. G., and Nieh S., 2011, "Selection and performance comparison of jet fuel surrogates for autothermal reforming," Fuel, **90**(4), pp. 1439–1448.

[5] Ranzi E., Frassoldati A., Grana R., Cuoci A., Faravelli T., Kelley a. P., and Law C. K., 2012, "Hierarchical and comparative kinetic modeling of laminar flame speeds of hydrocarbon and oxygenated fuels," Prog. Energy and Combustion Science, **38**(4), pp. 468–501.

[6] Pastore A., 2010, "Syngas production from heavy liquid fuel reforming in inert porous media," Cambridge.

[7] "Chemkin", www.ReactionDesign.com

[8] Vourliotakis G., Skevis G., Founti M., Alhamamre Z., and Trimis D., 2008, "Detailed kinetic modelling of the T-POX reforming process using a reactor network approach," Int. J. Hydrogen Energy, **33**(11), pp. 2816–2825.

Optimization of Wearable Kinetic Energy Harvesting Device Test Protocol

Julianne S. Douglas, Sabrina L. Rawlings, & Terrill B. Atwater
US Army RDECOM, CERDEC, Power Division
5100 Magazine Rd, Aberdeen P.G., MD 21005

José Collazo
Oak Ridge Institute for Science and Education
4692 Millennium Drive Suite 101
Belcamp, MD 21017

Abstract: *Within recent years, the Army has placed a renewed emphasis on decreasing soldier-borne load through the incorporation of kinetic energy harvesting devices. The importance of kinetic energy harvesters (KEHs) stems from their ability to take natural human motion and convert it into electrical energy for operating equipment or recharging a central battery, thereby reducing the quantity of batteries that would be needed for extended missions. Successful implementation of KEHs could lead to energy independence for the Soldier on dismounted missions.*

Military test protocols and standards will be needed to evaluate the efficiency and applicability of KEHs for military use and fielding. Military test standards and protocols already exist for traditional power sources to enable quantifiable comparisons across different devices. The goal of this effort is to establish and optimize a laboratory test protocol for induction-based, wearable, kinetic energy harvesting devices. The project end goal is to modify the test protocol and verify that the performance data applies consistently and fairly for all relevant device implementations (i.e., placement and method of human integration). The project will eventually adapt the protocol for varying KEHs. This paper discusses modeling, test apparatus techniques, and experimental validation.

Keywords: energy harvesting; kinetic; wearable; induction; test protocol; test standards

Introduction

The U.S Army has identified a need for lightweight energy harvesting devices to provide the individual Soldier with energy independence during extended dismounted missions. For missions of less than 48 hours, existing battery chemistries provide excellent portable power sources. For extended duration missions or in the event of contingency operations, KEHs can provide the Soldier with energy independence, the ability to conduct the mission in the absence of energy (battery or fuel) resupply, and even offer weight savings to the Soldier.

The baseline requirement for a renewable source has been cited as 3.5-10 watts continuous for the dismounted Soldier. This energy output is the goal for the energy harvesting device developments currently being conducted within the U.S. Army Research, Development, and Engineering Command (RDECOM) community. The U.S. Army has investigated several areas of kinetic energy harvesting including heel-strike, knee-brace, and suspended-mass induction technologies. The research and development efforts have brought about the need for test protocols to allow for consistent and quantifiable evaluation. Eventually, standardized comparisons between different devices and implementations of KEHs will need to be made in order to inform future requirements and applications of the energy harvesting technology.

This study focuses primarily on a linear inductive kinetic energy harvester and the issues of analyzing its raw power output and comparing results across tests varying resistance and simulated human stride frequency.

Background

Energy harvesting is the process of transforming surrounding energy into useful energy. Surrounding energy could include the kinetic energy of a moving body, the energy of sunlight, or the human thermal energy emitted as waste. An energy harvesting device collects the energy that would otherwise be wasted from the environment while minimally altering the characteristics of its host structure or its surroundings [1]. Energy harvesting technology has been growing in relevance as small devices with lower power demand keep increasing in popularity [2]. Energy harvesters are being used in a variety of applications such as rechargeable batteries, air pressure sensors in automobile tires, unmanned autonomous vehicles, embedded and implanted medical sensors, and structural health monitoring [3].

There are several energy harvesting methods that convert mechanical energy into electrical energy. Electromagnetic energy harvesters (also called induction energy harvesters) utilize the motion of a permanent magnet to induce a voltage across the terminals of a coil of wire. This voltage is used to energize an electrical circuit [1].

The Maxwell equations help describe the interaction between magnetic and electric fields. Faraday's law of induction describes how a time-varying (t) magnetic flux (Φ_B) will induce an electric potential or voltage (V) in a coil. The voltage is proportional to the number of turns of the coil (N). The direction (or sign) of the electromotive force is determined by Lenz's Law.

$$V = -N\frac{d\Phi_B}{dt}$$

Thus, a permanent magnet moving relative to a conductive coil of wire will induce an electric potential (i.e., a voltage) across the terminals of the coil.

Inductive energy harvesters can be categorized by how they achieve a relative velocity between the coil and the magnet. This project focuses on linear harvesters, as they feature the magnet moving along a straight line relative to the coil. This model effectively simulates wearable kinetic energy harvesting as the vertical motion is used to oscillate the magnet through a coil.

The amount of energy that can be harvested from the human body can be calculated theoretically from the work done from a center of mass perspective. Assuming no exchange of kinetic and potential energy, the following equation described by Reimer [4] can be used to estimate the amount of energy input into the device during one gait cycle: $E_{in} = 2mgh$, where E_{in} is energy, m is mass, g is gravitational acceleration and h is height. A vertical displacement of 2.5 cm is used for the height based on device stroke. By applying this equation for the work done by a 60 kg body's center of mass motion, there is a potential 30 J to be harvested per gait cycle, assuming two steps (one gait cycle) per second.

The energy that a vertical induction device can harvest from this process can be calculated with the following equation and by applying Ohm's law ($V = IR$) and Faraday's law (described above):

$$E_{in} = Power \cdot time = \left(\frac{V^2}{R}\right) \cdot t$$

where V is the raw sinusoidal output voltage, R is the load resistance and t is the time. Assuming the induction device produces 5 V and using a resistance of 350 Ω in the time interval of 1s, it would generate 0.07 J (E_{out}). Calculating the theoretical efficiency of the device from energy harvested over potential energy input from walking two steps per second gives:

$$\eta_{th} = \frac{E_{out}}{E_{in}} \times 100 = \frac{0.07J}{30J} \times 100 = 0.23\%$$

This low efficiency supports the importance of further optimization of device design and the experimentation process. Some potential design improvements are increasing stroke, frequency, and mass; optimizing coil geometry; and maximizing magnet strength. Since the kinetic energy ($½mv^2$) input relies on mass and velocity (stroke times frequency), increasing the stroke length, frequency, and mass directly impacts the energy available to be harvested. For this implementation of the linear inductive KEH, the stroke size is limited to 5 cm [5], and frequency and mass are limited by human capabilities (i.e., gait speed and Soldier burden). Coil geometry improvements would also be of benefit to the efficiency; for instance, the number of turns in the coil is proportional to the voltage. Magnet strength also directly affects the magnetic field necessary to induce a current in the coil. Greater insight into each parameter's effect on device performance, and therefore efficiency, can be achieved by standardizing the experimental design and analysis protocol.

Experimental Design

In these experiments, the linear inductive component of a commercial-off-the-shelf device was tested. A simple test-bed was developed in-house by the Army and used to simulate different speeds of human walking gaits and apply a wide spectrum of resistive electrical loads (representing equivalent series resistance) to the device. A simple circuit harnesses the energy of the passing magnet consisting of the AC voltage source (coil), the coil inductance, and the resistive load in series.

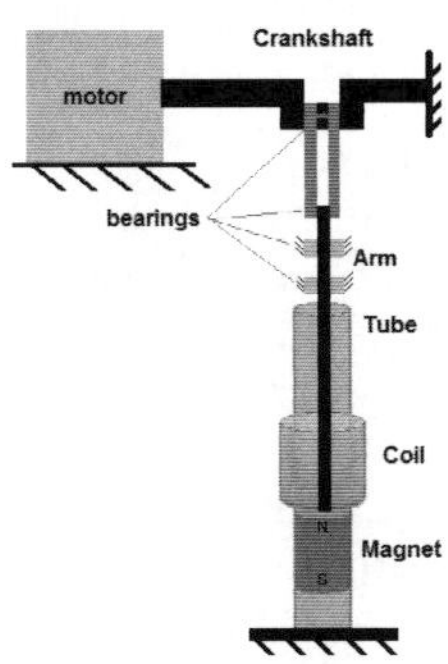

Figure 1: Test apparatus concept

The tests were conducted with input stride frequencies (i.e., right foot toe-off to left foot toe-off, which is equivalent to half a gait cycle) of approximately 1, 2, 3, and 4 Hz or steps per second and at each resistive load between 200 to 1000 Ω at intervals of 100 Ω and, near the optimal power output load range, resolution was doubled to 50 Ω to experimentally find the circuit's best equivalent load.

Results

Linear inductive-based kinetic energy harvesting performance can be broken down into the input energy, both kinetic ($mv^2/2$) and potential (mgh), and electrical output, which is based on the law of induction (Faraday and Lenz) and Ohm's Law. One way to quantify the input energy is determining the mass and stroke of a system and measuring the proof mass's displacement over time. Rough approximations of the energy output and measurements are fairly simple. However, precise calculations for in depth analysis can be more difficult and this study benefited from the use of precision analysis software. Some of the issues faced while trying to compare test results of various loads and frequencies to one another are described below.

First, in order to compare output at one stride versus another at different frequencies, the output at each step needs to be broken out by curve, the zeros interpolated, and the step cycle boundaries established. For the purposes of these tests, a relationship between voltage output and vertical magnet motion input during one step (right foot toe-off at 0.09 s to left foot toe-off at 0.57 s) is shown by the following diagram.

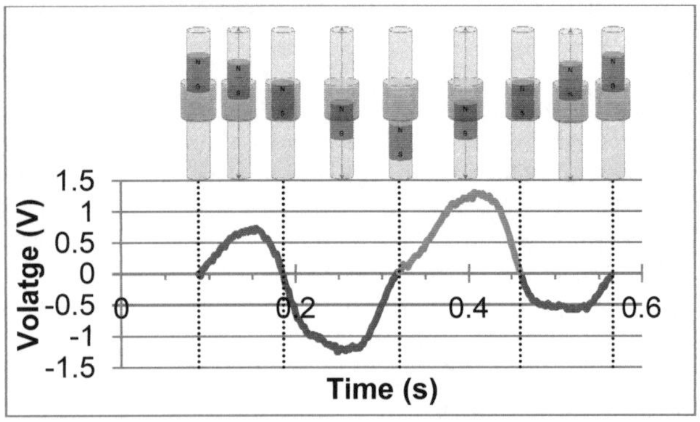

Figure 2: Relationship between physical input (magnet motion) and electrical (voltage) output

Figure 2 illustrates the relationship between physical input and electrical output of the linear inductive device. It is important to note that once again the device's stroke plays an important role in output voltage curve shape (especially for magnet centering within coil / magnet clearance of coil such as in cases where magnet position depends on fatiguing / elongating springs). This study used a slightly off-center magnet stroke, where the south pole of the magnet never completely exits the coil at toe-off (0.9 s and 0.57 s), which means that the south pole has a shorter active coil distance and time, and thus a smaller rate of change of magnetic flux over time results in a smaller output voltage curve. However, the north pole completely exits the coil before toe-off as well as during heel-strike (at 0.33 s), resulting in large voltages as seen in the middle sections of Figure 2.

A linear interpolation algorithm was devised to find the true, singular zero crossing points of each curve and find the step boundaries in order to compare step cycles from different tests. Due to the complex shape of the output voltage data, standard midlevel crossing algorithms do not correctly find the curve or step boundaries, since it is not a bi-level waveform. Analysis using MATLAB® Curve Fit Toolbox™ indicates that the voltage data can be best modeled by the two-term Fourier series equation described below.

$$V(t) = a_0 + a_1\cos(\omega t) + b_1\sin(\omega t) + a_2\cos(2\omega t) + b_2\sin(2\omega t)$$

where V is raw voltage, t is time, ω is frequency, a_0 is the mid-level crossing, and a_1, a_2, b_1, and b_2 are each amplitude coefficients for voltage height. Expanded Fourier series typically indicate harmonics in power systems, such as harmful vibrations or torsion. Further harmonics and eye-patterns of unknown significance were found during longer test while using an oscilloscope. Future work could involve investigating the source of these harmonics and determining if the pattern comes from the test apparatus or if it is a natural device response and what effect, if any, it has on useable energy output.

Power calculations were completed using the voltage across the resistive load (which was assumed equal to the source voltage) squared divided by the load resistance as described in the Background, and the circuit description in the Experimental Design section above. The average power output versus load by step frequency is shown in Figure 3.

Energy output, area under the power versus time curve, was calculated using trapezoidal integration of each power curve and step over their respective time intervals. Trapezoidal integration was necessary due to the appearance of multiple peaks per curve, or doublets, and noise as illustrated by each of the frequencies in Figure 5.

Discussion

A graph of the average power output per step over a representative range of stride frequencies from slow to walking (1.8 Hz according to Winter [5]) to running (approximately 3.8 Hz at maximum muscle power output according to Cavagna [6]) speeds versus resistive load is shown in Figure 3 below.

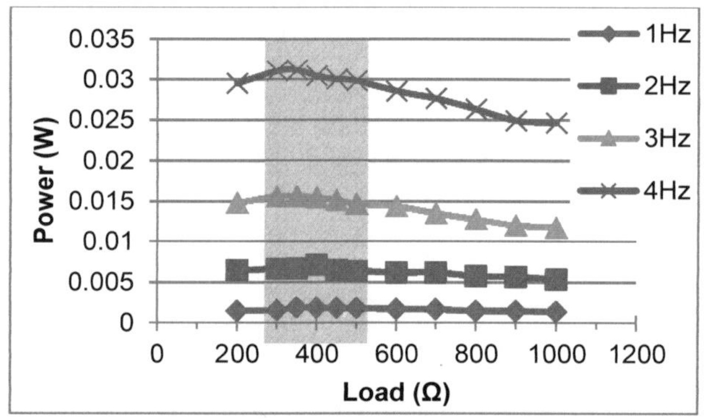

Figure 3: Average power output versus load by step frequency

As expected, the average power output increases proportionally with frequency as described by Faraday's Law and Ohm's Law, which coincides with the increase in velocity and thus kinetic energy ($mv^2/2$) input to the device. Notice that the optimal output range is shaded between 300 and 450 Ω and the optimal load varies within this range for each frequency. For example, at 4 Hz, the average power curve peaks at 350 Ω, indicating the maximal power output occurs when a 350 Ω equivalent circuit is used to match the impedance of the energy harvester's coil. This poses an efficiency issue, since a wearable KEH's purpose is recharging the central battery and the equivalent resistance of the battery varies with its state of charge. Adding advanced circuitry may be one way around this issue. Additionally, the Army is investigating the electrochemical storage aspect of KEH output power pulses. The goal is to maximize energy harvested to energy delivered to an end item [7].

The voltage versus time by load at 4 Hz step frequency results shown in Figure 4 indicate that the voltage increases proportionally with load as expected due to Ohm's law (V=IR). Also, the area under the voltage curve increases (width and height) with increasing load. However, the energy (area under the power curve) results do not always increase with load, but instead form more of a Gaussian curve peaking at 350 Ω, similar to Figure 3 power curves.

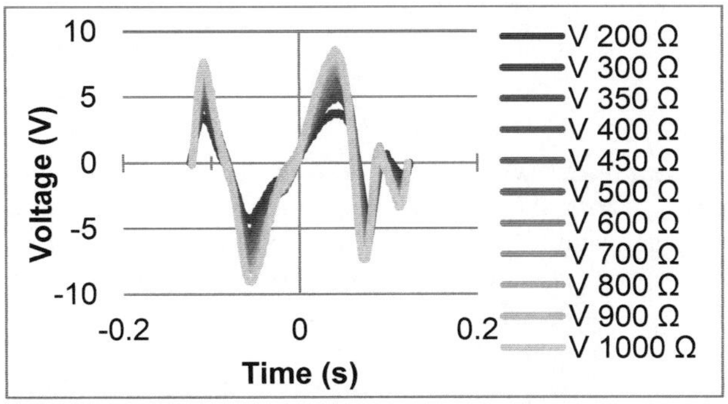

Figure 4: Output voltage versus time by load at 4 Hz step frequency

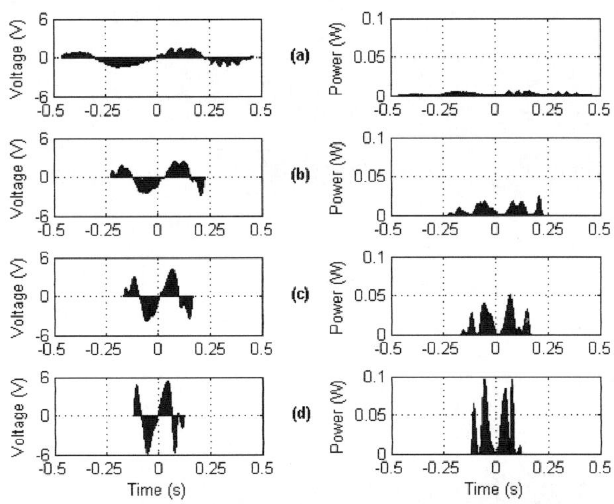

Figure 5: Single step voltage (left) & power (right) versus time at a 350 Ω load at (a) 1 Hz, (b) 2 Hz, (c) 3 Hz, and (d) 4 Hz step frequency

Figure 5 shows four graphs each of voltage versus time (left) and power versus time (right) at a 350 Ω load to illustrate the effect increasing frequency has on device output. As frequency increases, the step cycles become compressed and output curve peaks increase. However, the peaks grow faster than they can be compressed. Thus, the area under the voltage curve increases slightly with frequency, whereas the area under the power curve increases significantly due to Ohm's law. This signifies that as the kinetic energy input to the device increases, the available energy output also increases proportionally with efficiency due to conservation of energy. A real-time position versus time sensor could be used in future tests to calculate energy input, obtain device efficiency, and determine its optimum operating frequency.

Conclusion

These results prove that test standards for linear inductive-based kinetic energy harvesting systems need to include frequency and load testing with position sensors or metabolic input to get a reliable baseline performance characterization.

Further work is in progress on designing and testing linear and rotary inductive-based kinetic energy harvesting systems to inform future test protocol and device improvements. Human integration factors such as metabolic cost, coefficient of harvesting, and more comprehensive cost-benefit trade studies will need to be considered in the Army's search for energy independence.

Debates will continue over the advantages and disadvantages of utilizing KEHs. Meanwhile, the RDECOM community strives to advance the KEH technologies and develop standardized testing approaches.

Acknowledgments

This research was supported in part by an appointment to the Postgraduate Research Participation Program at the U.S. Army Communications-Electronics Research, Development and Engineering Center, administered by the Oak Ridge Institute for Science and Education through an interagency agreement between the U.S. Department of Energy and CERDEC.

References

1. Joyce, B.S., "Development of an Electromagnetic Energy Harvester for Monitoring Wind Turbine Blades (thesis)," Virginia Polytechnic Institute and State University, December 2011.
2. R. Amirtharajah and A. P. Chandrakasan, "Self-powered signal processing using vibration-based power generation," *IEEE Journal of Solid-state Circuits*, vol. 33, no. 5, pp. 687-695, 1998.
3. D. J. Inman and P. S., "Energy Harvesting Technologies", New York, NY: Springer, 2009.
4. Reimer, R. and Shapiro, A. "Biomechanical energy harvesting from human motion: theory, stated of the art, design guidelines, and future directions," *J. Neuroengineering and Rehabilitation*, vol. 8, no. 22, 2011.
5. Winter, D.A., "Biomechanics and motor control of human movement," Vol. 3, Hoboken, NJ: John Wiley and Sons, 2005.
6. G. A. Cavagna, et.al., "The Two Power Limits Conditioning Step Frequency In Human Running," *J. Physiology*, 437, pp. 95-108, June 1991.
7. Yakira J Kirzner and Terrill B. Atwater, "Potassium-Doped Lithium Manganese Spinel Cells for Use in Energy Harvesting Applications," *P. 46th Power Sources Symposium*, 2014.

Remote Auxiliary Power Deployment System for Battlefield Power and Energy

Nate Hobbs
New Product Development
EaglePicher Technologies, LLC.
P.O. Box 40, Joplin, MO 64801
www.eaglepicher.com
nate.hobbs@eaglepicher.com

Abstract: *Energy is playing an ever increasing role in today's combat zones. The Remote Auxiliary Power Deployment System (RAPiD System) is EaglePicher's newest addition to its portable power portfolio. Combining renewable energy sources with traditional heavy fuel energy generation and battery storage, the RAPiD System reduces Forward Operating Base (FOB) manpower and fuel requirements. Power reliability is increased with deployment of the RAPiD System as generator wear is reduced; Soldier exposure is reduced as fuel related exercises are minimized, and mission capabilities are extended as fuel lasts longer.*

Keywords: Battlefield Power; Battlefield Energy; Mobile Power; Portable Power; Tactical Power Source; Alternative Energy; Renewable Energy; Solar Energy.

Introduction:

The RAPiD System is EaglePicher's portable hybrid power solution to the military's energy needs. In 2013 the Marine Corp was interested enough in hybrid power systems to focus Experimental Forward-Operating-Base (ExFOB) 2013-1 on hybrid power systems, [1]. The power systems it called for were divided into four categories based on power demand, attributes, and transport requirements, [1] [2]. The four categories are Mobile Electric Hybrid Power Sources (MEHPS) Lightweight, MEHPS Medium, MEHPS Micro-Grid Medium, and Micro-Grid Heavy. In addition to the ExFOB there were also several solicitations relating to portable power for military applications, [3]. Using these calls as a technology direction EaglePicher began development of the RAPiD System.

System Sizing: With a 5.0 kW peak power capability the RAPiD System falls between the MEHPS Lightweight and the MEHPS Medium. The specification for the MEHPS Lightweight states that the system should be capable of 3.0 kW peak power, and should include energy storage, energy harvesting from renewables, and auto-control of a single generator. The MEHPS Medium has identical specifications with the exception that the peak power requirement is 10.0 kW.

RAPiD System Status: Currently EaglePicher has completed two fully functional prototypes of the RAPiD System one of which can be seen in Figure 1 The systems include both solar and conventional energy generation as well as a significant amount of energy storage.

Figure 1: RAPiD System Prototype 001

System Architecture & Design:

A hybrid power system by definition requires multiple power sources, and in the case of the RAPiD System also requires energy storage. The basic architecture of the system is shown in Figure 2.

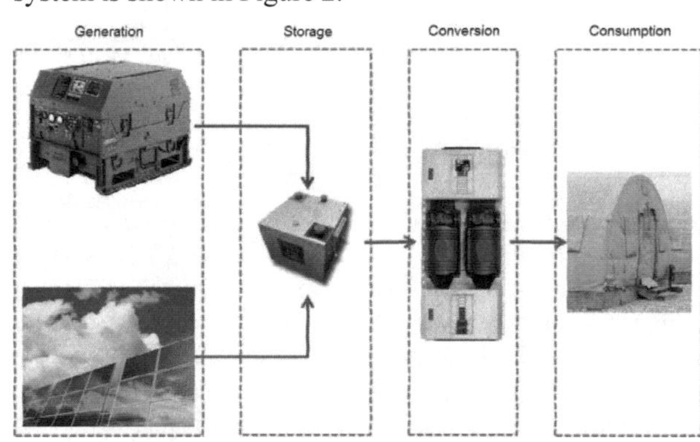

Figure 2: RAPiD System Architecture

The architecture is simple. Energy generation whether it is solar, conventional fuel, or another alternative energy source charges the batteries that comprise the energy storage. This energy is then converted into standard single phase AC power which is compatible with the existing AC distribution network.

Energy Generation Specifications – Generator: The generator used on the RAPiD System is the standard 3.0 kW Tactical Quiet Generator (TQG). The energy storage portion of the system allows for the generator to be sized smaller than the peak power requirement of the system. Though the generator is only 3.0 kW, the power conversion stage that handles charging of the batteries is sized to accommodate a 5.0 kW generator.

Energy Generation Specifications – Solar: The system utilizes solar panels and cases that have already been qualified by the Marine Corp. These panels are controlled by a standard Max Power Point Tracking (MPPT) solar controller to optimize their generation. The RAPiD System can support up to 3.6 kW of solar power. With both generation sources combine the system is capable of storing 6.6 kW of power at a given time.

Energy Storage Specifications: For the prototype systems a lead acid pack was utilized. This lead acid pack is comprised of standard 6T form factor batteries configured to provide 35 kWh of energy storage. However, the system controller is independent of battery chemistry, and the pack can be tailored to meet custom mission requirements. Future models will the lead acid batteries with EaglePicher's newly developed 6T format Lithium Ion battery. This replacement is expected to reduce the weight of the battery pack by 50% or increase the energy storage of the pack to 200% of current value. The Lithium-Ion battery will also increase the life of the RAPiD System by increasing the number cycles available before replacement is needed. This is especially critical in the harsh environments in which the system is expected to operate.

Power Distribution Specifications: Power distribution in the FOB is comprised of a network of single and three phase power. The initial RAPiD System was configured to supply 120VAC split or single phase. Higher power models will be available in single or three phase versions.

Mechanical Platform Specifications: The RAPiD System housing was built on a Light Tactical Trailer (LTT). This is a standard issue trailer. The battery system is mounted on a sliding rack which extends out of the housing allowing full access and hot swapping of batteries.

Applications and Operations

Currently, in and near to active combat zones power generation is rather an afterthought. A number of generators are placed in a row and started. The number of generators depends on the peak loads which may only occur for an hour or two a day. For that hour or two the generators are operating near their designed loading point. The rest of the day the generators may only be operating at 10-20% loading. Not only is this extremely inefficient from a fuel usage standpoint, it also causes wet stacking of the generators. This condition occurs only at light loads and leads to significant mechanical problems if it occurs routinely.

Forward Operating Bases (FOB): Based on preceding operating scenario, the most obvious application of the RAPiD System is to replace some of generators at a FOB. By replacing a generator with a RAPiD System all the power of the generator is still available, but rather than having to be produced when required, the system allows it to be produced under convenient and ideal operating conditions.

In this application fuel usage and mechanical maintenance intervals are the most obvious benefits. However, they are not the most significant benefits when the logistics and supply chain are taken into account. When manpower needed to transport and protect fuel to FOBS is taken into account, the savings are enormous and cannot be assigned a dollar value. Fewer convoys result in fewer casualties due to convoy attacks. Fewer convoys and fewer convoy protection missions mean more men are available to perform missions critical to the goals of the conflict. If a RAPiD System requires 50% less fuel than traditional power generation techniques, this means that there are also 50% less manpower requirements to keep power generation running.

Remote Surveillance Outpost: These outposts may have very limited power requirements and be extremely difficult to access. The load may be as small as only running a radio. A RAPiD System can supply this load much more effectively than running a generator.

Remote Unmanned Stations: Another excellent application for the RAPiD System is an unmanned station. These may be communication towers or remote sensor networks. The RAPiD System could allow these stations to run for days or weeks between onsite maintenance and refueling visits.

Expected Loads and Results

Predicting electrical loads for any type of system is never easy, especially when considering the wide range of applications mentioned in the previous section. Loads can vary from just a few watts to the kilowatt range. This paper will not address all possible load profiles but will just focus on one.

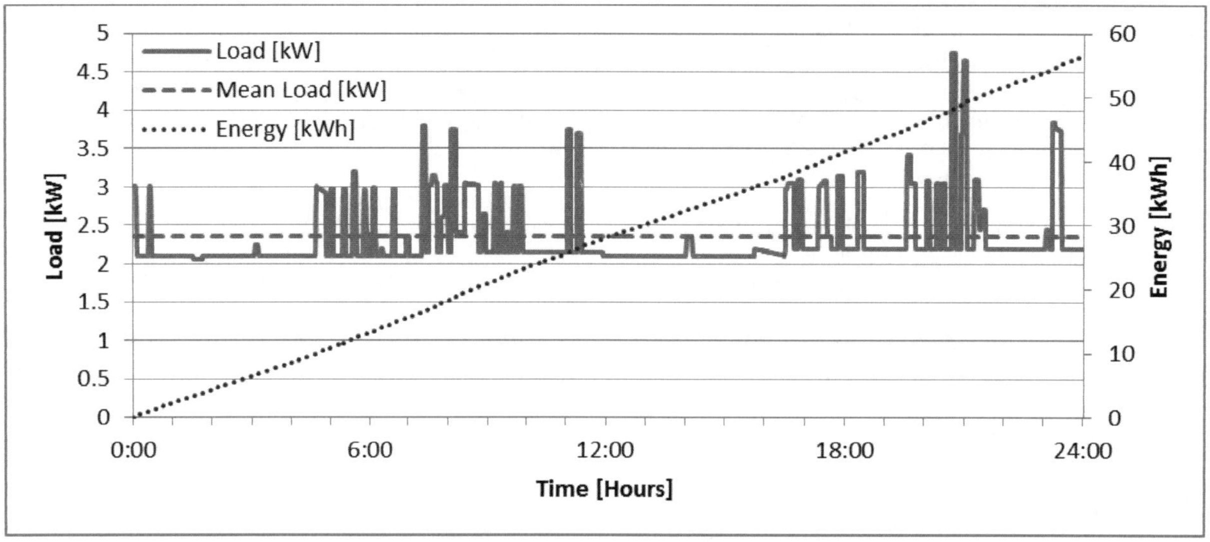

Figure 3: MEHPS Medium (5kW) Concept Profile

Example load profiles were provided for each of the four categories listed in the introduction. Figure 3 shows the profile for the MEHPS Medium and is representative of a load which the RAPiD System would experience.

Testing Results: The results of testing a solar system are tightly coupled with weather. All testing on the RAPiD System has been completed on sunny days to show the systems performance. Based on initial testing using the RAPiD System with the profile shown in Figure 3 would result in a greater than 48 % fuel savings. The profile requires 56 kWh of energy over a 24 hour period of which only about 12 hours will produce any significant solar energy. Over the course of the day 27.3 kWh of solar energy was produced. The generator was required to produce the other 29 kWh of energy. The generator will run for approximately ten hours to recharge the batteries. At the end of the 24 hour cycle the RAPiD System will be storing the same amount of energy as was stored at the beginning of the cycle. If required by the operational scenario, the RAPiD System could supply the whole cycle and never start the generator. This, however, would be extremely detrimental to batteries as only 15% state of charge would be remaining at the end of the cycle.

Future Improvements

There are a number of future planned improvements to the system to improve it for both the defense industry and for the commercial industry.

System Autonomy: Though the system operates completely autonomously as it is currently configured, it still requires occasional supervision to check fuel levels, run times, and maintenance requirements. By implementing remote communication to and from the system, the operator can be notified when maintenance is required or be able to remotely view the operational variables of the system.

Alternative Chemistry: The first battery pack used was based on a lead acid chemistry. Future models will utilize Lithium-Ion chemistry. This will decrease the weight, increase the storage capacity, or an optimized trade-off of the two. This will also increase the life of the system as lithium chemistries have better cycle life performance.

Alternative Sizes: The architecture of the RAPiD System lends itself easily to being scaled up or down. EaglePicher currently has plans to scale the system to the following sizes: 1.0 kW, 10.0 kW, and 25.0 kW.

Commercial System: These first prototypes were built with the defense industry in mind. However, there are many other applications in which the commercial sector could benefit. This system with a few modifications could be used commercially for disaster relief after tornados and other natural disasters. In these applications powering communications to the outside world will be key, as often the support infrastructure has been damaged in the event.

Conclusion

The Remote Auxiliary Power Deployment System was designed to save the warfighter from exposure to potential threats. This hybrid power solution, though it can never replace traditional generation, complements traditional generation and provides not only fuel savings, but also the intangible benefits of the lives that are no longer put in harm's way to when supporting the generation of power and energy.

Acknowledgements
The author would like to acknowledge the engineers and technicians involved in this project for their invaluable support, design ideas, and construction of the prototypes.

References
1. Brief to Industry Mobile Electric Hybrid Power Sources(MEHPS)
   http://www.hqmc.marines.mil/Portals/160/FINAL%20 MEHPS%20Brief%20to%20Industry_0201.pdf
2. Hybrid Power Systems ExFOB 2013-1
   https://www.fbo.gov/?s=opportunity&mode=form&id =aa80c12274093afeaba02966f0a7aa07&tab=core&_ cview=0
3. Medium Hybrid Expeditionary Energy Systems (MHEES)
   https://www.fbo.gov/?s=opportunity&mode=form&id =b596d439561ced85fc3030689c8f63dd&tab=core&_ cview=0

Development of a Man-portable Gas Turbine Generator

Kousuke Isomura
IHI Corporation
3975-18 Haijima-cho, Akishima-shi
Tokyo 196-8686, Japan

Abstract: *A 1.5kW portable gas turbine generator is under development. The engine is already running and generating over 1.5kW of power has been test proven. The test results suggest that a thermal efficiency of this engine is higher than that of portable power generators currently in market. This gas turbine generator is the only portable generator that can satisfy the requirements of both power density and energy density for robots shown in DARPA's Palm Power Project.*

Keywords: Micro-turbine; oil free; gas turbine; generator.

Introduction

Modern soldiers have come to require more and more electric power and the weight of the batteries is already at a limit that a soldier can carry. Also, varieties of autonomous robots have been developed, but the low energy density of the battery power source is limiting the application to short mission time works.

In general, batteries have very high power density with very fast response time, but their energy density is very low that the duration time is limited. The energy density of the latest Lithium-Ion secondary batteries is only about 250Wh/kg. One of the alternative power sources that can provide high energy density is fuel cells. However, fuel cells have very poor power density and also, their efficiency and the life rapidly drop when large current flows through the cells. Hence, fuel cells will be good for minimum amount of wearable electric equipments for the soldiers, but not for robots which a lot of servo motors require large current. A type of power sources that can provide both high power density and high energy density is combustion engine. Kerosene fuel contains as high as 12700Wh/kg (or 10200Wh/Litre) of energy and the combustion process release this large energy in very short time period at very high efficiency.

However, the power range that soldier power and robots require is more than an order smaller than those typical combustion engines provide. Hence, very small combustion engines are required. When the engine becomes small, its thermal efficiency drops mainly due to the heat loss and the friction loss. Heat dissipation is proportional to the surface

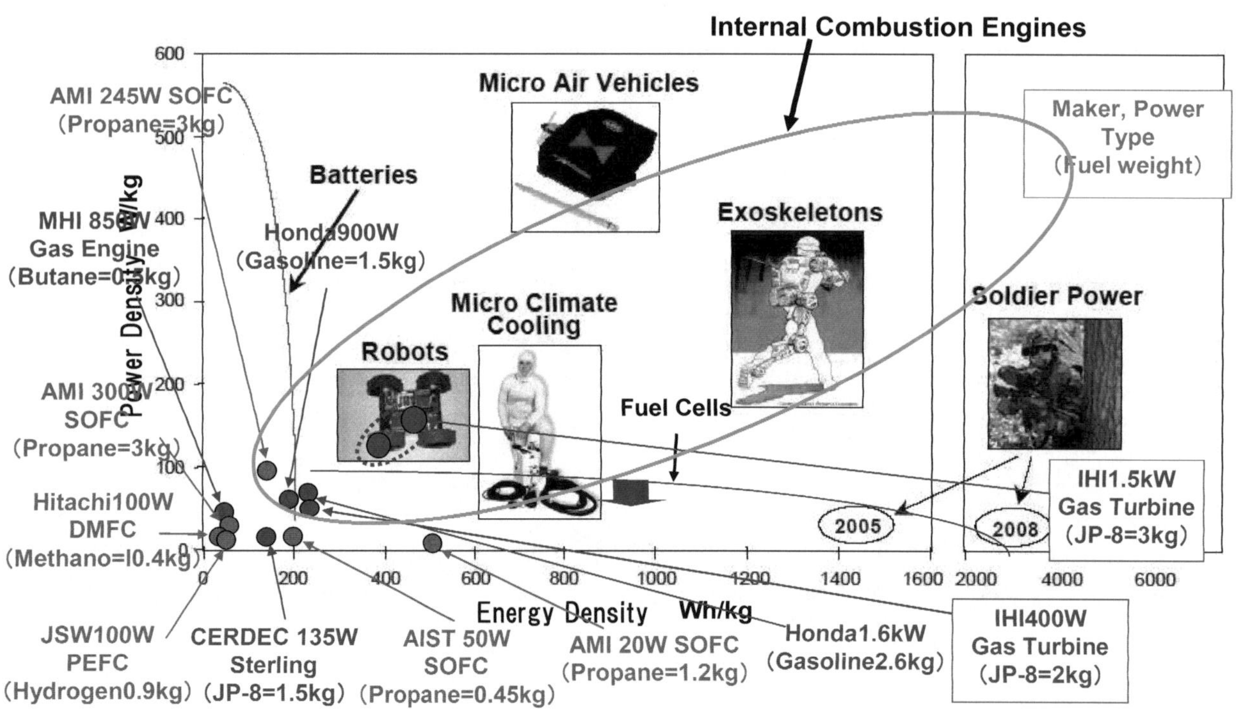

Figure 1. Energy densities and power densities of various portable power sources

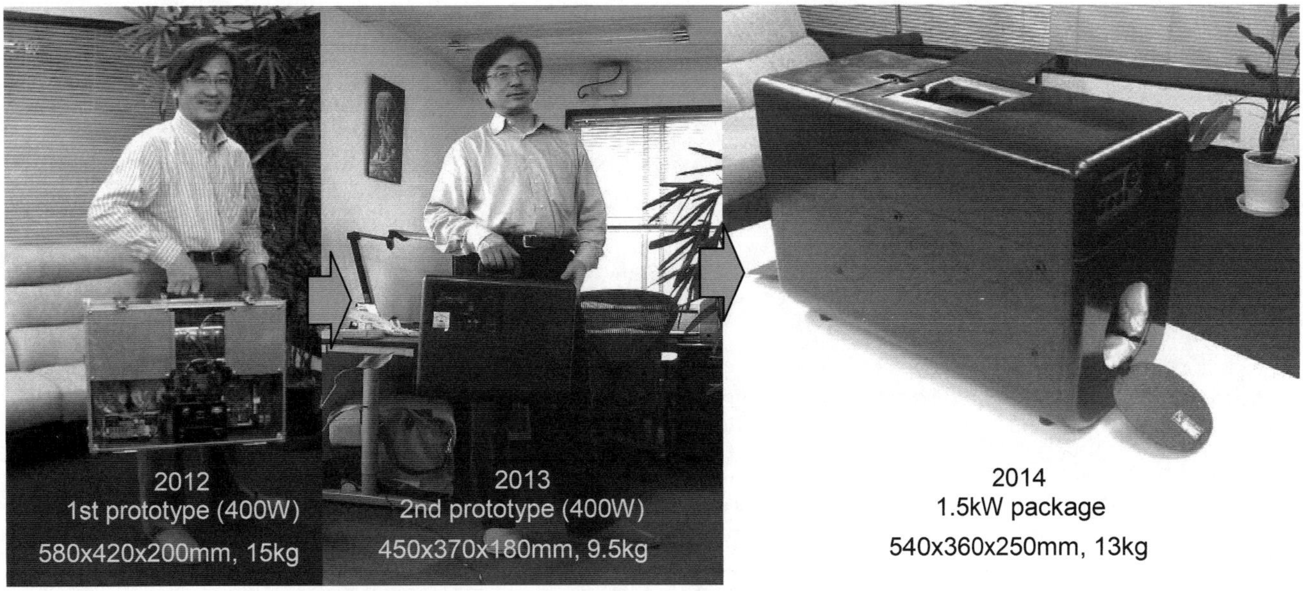

Figure 2. Evolution of IHI meso-scale gas turbine generators

area $[L^2]$, and the heat generation is proportional to the combustion chamber volume $[L^3]$. Hence, the relative heat loss which is the heat dissipation divided by the heat generation is $[L^2]/[L^3] = [1/L]$, and it increases when the length scale L decreases. When heat loss increases, the combustion efficiency decreases. Also, the friction loss relative to the generated power increases because the friction loss is proportional to the surface roughness which is partly a property of the material and hence the loss cannot be reduced proportional to the power.

Under such conditions, the best type of combustion engine would be gas turbine engine, because the combustion is continuous and the friction occurs only at the bearings. Reciprocating engine will suffer in propagating the combustion flame to the end of the chamber due to the large heat dissipation at the wall, and the friction loss between the piston and the cylinder is large. Moreover, gas turbine is known to be the lightest among all the combustion engines, so it has an advantage for portable use. The energy density and the power density of various portable power generators under 2kW are compared in Figure.1. The various applications in the figure are taken from DARPA Palm Power Project (Ref.1). The gas turbine generator clearly shows the best capability and is the only power source that can meet both the required energy density and the power density for robots.

In IHI Corporation, we have continued developing a meso-scale gas turbine generator for many years. In February 2012, we press-released a successful demonstration run of the first prototype of a 400W class gas turbine generator, and in 2013, we improved it to smaller and lighter package. However, by showing the prototype generator to many potential customers, we recognized that the needs are in larger power class, and hence, we have started developing a 1.5kW gas turbine generator from April 2013 and the first engine has successfully started running in March 2014. These generators are shown in Figure 2.

The features of the engine and the package

The basic cycle of the engine is recuperated Brayton cycle. The rotor shaft consists a single stage centrifugal compressor and a single stage centrifugal turbine connected by a shaft holding a generator in the mid. The bare engine containing generator is shown in Figure 3 and the major specifications of the generator package are shown in Table 1. The most significant features of this engine generator are its light weight and high operability. Both energy density and power density are very high and it starts generating the rated electric power within a minute from pushing the start button. Stopping is as easy as just pushing a stop button and the engine stops after automatic cooling sequence for a couple of minutes.

The adiabatic efficiency of the compressor and the turbine is kept as high as 80%. In most of the gas turbine generator, the generator is connected to the gas turbine by a shaft extending out from the compressor. In such layout, the compressor efficiency is known to be dropped significantly by sucking the hot air generated by the generator into the compressor (Ref.2,3). In current engine, a clean compressor inlet is realized by locating the generator in between the compressor and the turbine.

For meso-scale gas turbines, the largest technical difficulty lies in ultra high-speed rotation beyond the speed that can be realized by ball bearings. Since the rotor tip speed is the

Figure 3. The 1.5kW meso-scale gas turbine engine

Table 1. Specifications of the family of IHI meso-scale gas turbine generator packages

	1st Prototype	2nd Prototype	Current	Future
Rated Power	400W		1.5kW	
Weight	15kg	9.5kg	13kg	10kg
Power Density	27W/kg	42W/kg	115W/kg	150W/kg
Energy Density	40Wh/kg	222Wh/kg	358Wh/kg	441Wh/kg
Fuel	Gas: Propane, Propane/Butane, Liquid: JP-8/Kerosene, Diesel			
Efficiency	5% (Simple cycle)	10% (Recuperated)	15% (Recuperated)	
Fuel weight	1kg (gas)	2kg (liquid)	3kg (liquid)	
Duration time	1.6 hours	6.4 hours	4.6 hours	
Emission	Gas: CO=50ppm, NOx=15ppm Kerosene:CO=90ppm, NOx=30ppm			
Noise	44dB@7m side			
Exhaust gas temp	73degC@15cm downstream (@amb=21degC)			

controlling parameter of the compressor pressure ratio, small compressor has to rotate faster to get the same pressure ratio as a large compressor. If a 10kW engine has been designed to run at 100,000rpm, the scaled 1.6kW and 400W engines have to run at 250,000rpm and 500,000rpm, respectively to achieve the same compressor pressure ratio. A new kind of hydrodynamic gas bearings called foil bearings are used in current engine, and the engine runs completely oil free. This also gives big advantages to the generator package for its light weight, operability at very low temperature and the clean emission. In engines with ball bearings, the oil pump and cooling system cause a big weight increase, the oil cause difficulty in starting the engine at very low temperature due to its high viscosity, and for very small gas turbine the carbon particle emission is high because it is hard to completely isolate the lubrication oil from hot sections that burns the oil.

The specifications of the 1.5kW generator under development and its ancestors are tabulated in Table.1. The generator for both gas fuel and liquid fuel exist. The type of the fuel can easily be changed by changing the combustor module and fuel supply units. The engine has a module structure that only the combustor can be changed. If required, a combustor to handle both type of fuel can be developed. The significant feature to be noted is that the engine for gas fuel can be operated indoor due to the very clean emission. This probably is the only combustion type generator that can be run indoor.

Another significant feature is its quietness. The main noise source of a high speed rotating machine is harmonics of the rotational speed. Higher order harmonics go easily beyond the human audible limit and even if it is within the audible frequencies, high frequency pure tone nois is easy to attenuate by light acoustic lining. As a results, the noise measured by the 400W class prototype engine was only 44dB at 7m side which was similar to the cooling fan noise of server computers.

The exhaust gas temperature can be controlled. The exhaust gas from the engine is mixed with a cold air to be exhausted out from the generator package. By increasing the flow capacity of the electric fan to feed more cold air, the exhaust gas temperature from the package can be made under 70degC.

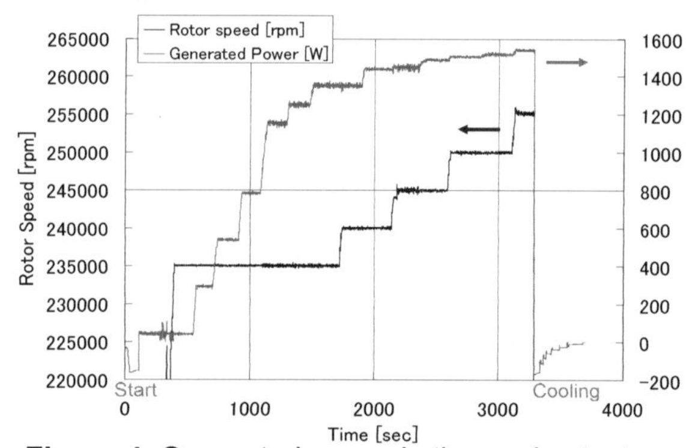

Figure 4. Generated power in the engine test

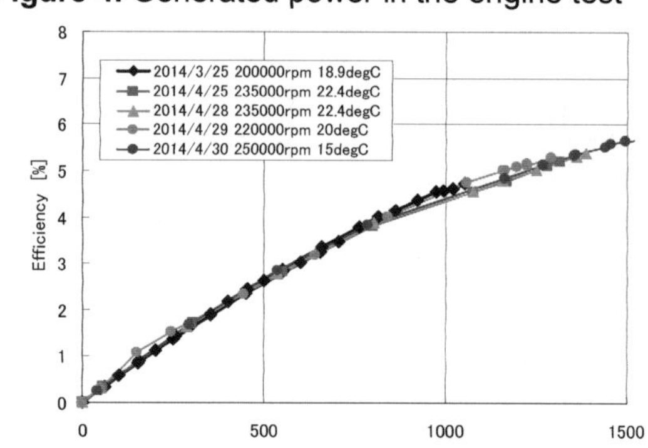

Figure 5. Measured efficiency in the simple cycle engine test

Test Results

The first prototype of 1.5kW engine has started running in March 2014. The gas turbine used at this time was of a simple cycle configuration. At the end of April, the engine recorded over 1500W of power generation at 250,000rpm which is the design speed (Fig.4). The fuel to electric efficiency at this condition was 5.7% (Fig.5). By installing the recuperator which is under development, the efficiency is expected to increase to at least 15%. The recuperator is designed to have the temperature efficiency 80%. This fuel-to-electric conversion efficiency of 15% is higher than those of small generators under 5kW in market using gasoline or diesel engines, which is about 13%. The weight of the package is about 13kg without fuel. The weight of the engine and the recuperator are not optimized, yet. Hence there is still a room for further weight reduction.

Future Plan

Engine tests with recuperator will be conducted to confirm the maximum efficiency of the generator package. Then the endurance tests and the environmental operability tests (high & low temperature, high altitude) will be conducted to confirm the operational envelop. These tests will be repeated for both gas and liquid fuels. Also, foreseeing the possible application for the power sources for robots, the tests of durability against the motion of the engine attitude will be conducted to check limit of the operability on mobile machines. The gyro moment of the high speed rotating machine may limit the motion of the robots, due to the smaller load capacity of air bearings than that of ball bearings. Also, in the case of the recuperated engine, the long shut down cooling time may cause a practical operability problem, and a flow bypass mechanism will be developed to shorten the system shut down time. In parallel to these activities, the weight reduction of the engine and the recuperator, and manufacturing cost reduction study will be continued. The cost reduction by developing high precision mass production methods may be a key to the commercial success of this generator. The priority of all these activities depends on the application and the requirements of the launch customer, whom we are now looking for.

Summary

A 1.5kW class gas turbine generator has been developed. It will provide both higher energy density and higher power density than any other existing portable power sources using combustion engines. The first engine has successfully generated over 1.5kW of electric power during the first round tests. The recuperator is also under development. From the test data, the recuperated engine is expected to achieve 1,5kW of power output with over 15% of the fuel to electric efficiency. We are now looking for a launch customer for this generator to start the development based on the customer specification.

References

1. DoD End User Perspective and DARPA Palm Power Program http://www1.eere.energy.gov/hydrogenandfuelcells/pdfs/129.pdf.
2. Isomura K. *et al*, "Micromachine Gas Turbine for Palm Top Power Generation" ASME GT2004-54427, June 2004.
3. Monroe M.A., Epstein A.H. *et al*, "Component Integration and Loss Sources in 3-5 kW Gas Turbines" ASME GT2005-68715, June 2005.

Bio-Battery: Alternative Power Source for Extracting Energy from JP-8 without Fuel Processing

Sameer Singhal[1], Jenny Ulyanova[1], Ulf Lindstrom[1], Erica Pinchon[1], and Shelley Minteer[2]

[1]CFD Research Corporation
701 McMillian Way, Huntsville, AL, USA, 35806
ss2@cfdrc.com, http://www.cfdrc.com/biobattery

[2]Univerity of Utah
Department of Chemistry and Materials Science
Salt Lake City, Utah 84112

Abstract: *CFDRC has demonstrated a Bio-Battery (enzymatic fuel cell) which converts readily-available fuels such as sugar and alcohol directly into electrical energy. The main advantages of the technology are: high energy density, fuel flexibility, and renewable bio-catalysts. CFDRC's Bio-Battery is a platform technology which has been developed over the last several years in collaboration with DoD. Recent developments have allowed us to further adapt and demonstrate the Bio-Battery by implementing a cascade of enzymes capable of electrochemically converting JP-8 directly into electrical energy. This technology has significant advantages over existing generators used to convert JP-8 into energy. Namely the energy generation process is silent and occurs under ambient conditions while producing >2X the efficiency. The Bio-Battery also has advantages over traditional fuel cell technologies which use metal catalysts that are susceptible to sulfur poisoning and thus require the JP-8 to be reformed prior to use. The enzyme catalysts reported here are naturally sulfur tolerant, allowing the use of JP-8 in its native form.*

Keywords: Bio-Battery; enzymatic fuel cell; JP-8; Silent Watch; energy harvesting

Introduction

JP-8 is the dominant fuel used in military supply chains. It has been designed to operate in all relevant environments (freezing temperatures) as well as desert conditions and with high degree of safety (non-flammable). However, the current methods for JP-8 conversion are insufficient. The dominant mechanism for decomposing JP-8 is through a standard internal combustion engine or tactical quiet generator (TQG). There are numerous issues with this method including low efficiency (<30% at peak load and significantly lower at non-optimal loads) and large signature (both thermal and acoustic). Based on these shortcomings a solution for electrochemical decomposition of JP-8 is highly desirable. There has been significant research into the use of solid oxide fuel cells (SOFCs) for conversion of JP-8 into energy. However, the rare-earth metal catalysts in a traditional SOFC are poisoned by the sulfur inherent in JP-8 which can vary from 400 to 1600ppm [1-2]. In order to use the SOFCs a reformer needs to be placed in front of the fuel cell adding complexity and weight to the overall solution. The SOFC catalysts also require very high temperatures (>500°C) [1]. CFDRC has previously reported on its Bio-Battery (enzymatic fuel cell) technology which uses biological catalysts to convert readily-available and non-toxic fuels such as sugar and alcohol into energy [3-5]. In this work we report on the further advancement of the technology to convert JP-8 into energy. Figure 1 below shows a snapshot of the value proposition which is further expanded upon in this paper.

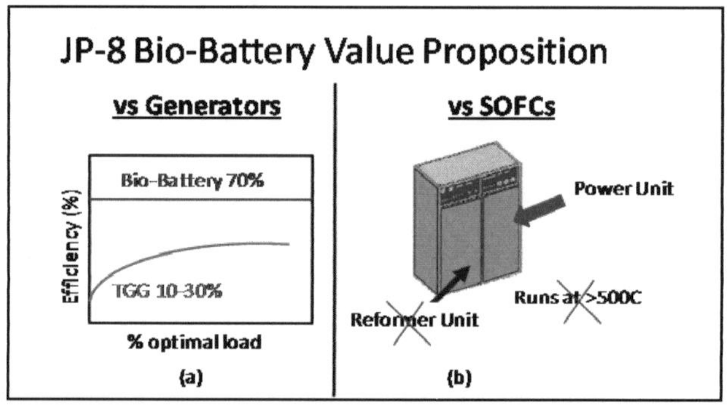

Figure 1. Advantages of Bio-Battery over (a) TQGs with efficiency >2X higher across all loads and (b) SOFCs where the Bio-Battery is able to operate without a reformer and at room temperature

Background

CFDRC has developed a Bio-Battery device for the U.S. Army's warfighter program, and was ***awarded the "2008 SBIR Achievement Award" for the Bio-Battery Phase II work***. The fundamental technology component of the Bio-Battery is the enzyme based nanocomposite anode. The anode is comprised of CFDRC's patented carbon nanotube (CNT)-based ink process. The ink consists of CNTs, binding polymers, cross linking agents, and the enzymatic catalysts. The enzymatic catalysts can be varied depending on the substrate (fuel) to be oxidized. The majority of effort has been placed of the glucose based system and the working principle for this version of the Bio-Battery is shown in Figure 2. The enzyme, glucose oxidase, is immobilized on the nanocomposite anode and biooxidizes glucose based fuel. In the mediated glucose biooxidation two electrons are produced from one glucose molecule.

The cathode reduces oxygen with hydrogen protons generated by the anode [3-5].

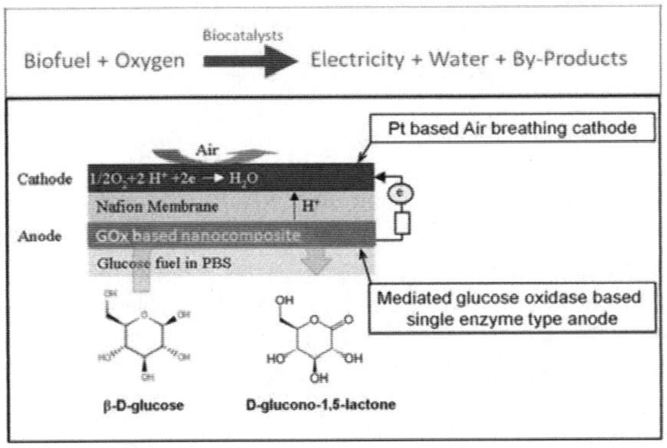

Figure 2. Working Principle for Bio-Battery

In this case work we have extended these results to JP-8 (or more generally diesel based fuels) by utilizing a proprietary enzyme to convert the hydrocarbons in JP-8 into long chain alcohols. These alcohols can then be converted into energy using electro-oxidizing enzymes such as Alcohol Dehydrogenase or Alcohol Oxidase.

Results from JP-8 Bio-Battery

JP-8 is a kerosene based fuel made of a series of hydrocarbons between C6 and C16. In order to prove that the enzyme was capable of converting hydrocarbons into alcohol we used Octane as a surrogate for JP-8 and a spectroscopic technique known as UV-Vis to show conversion of fuel. Figure 3 shows response for a control (non enzymatic system) and for a system with the proprietary enzyme. Furthermore samples spiked with 1,000 and 2,000 ppm sulfur were also tested. There was no degradation in performance seen with the sulfur addition, validating the ability to use native JP-8 with no fuel pre-processing.

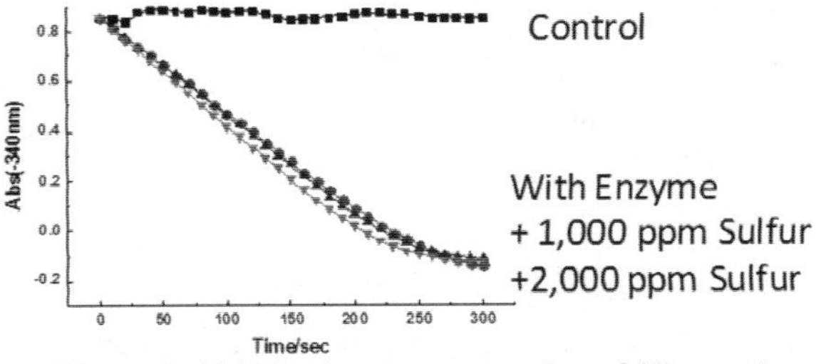

Figure 3. UV-Vis showing conversion of Alkanes to Alcohols; No conversion for control, Complete conversion with enzyme, No inhibition with up to 2,000ppm sulfur

Based on these positive results we built a multi-enzymatic anode and combined it with existing cathode to perform a full Fuel Cell test. The test used JP-8 from a military motor pool as a fuel source. The JP-8 was mixed with a buffer solution to increase its ionic conductivity but otherwise unmodified from its native form. Results shown in Figure 4 include power density of $3mW/cm^2$ with associated current density of $15mA/cm^2$ at a voltage of 0.35V. The device is able to run as long as JP-8 fuel is available and the power generation has no thermal or noise signature associated with it.

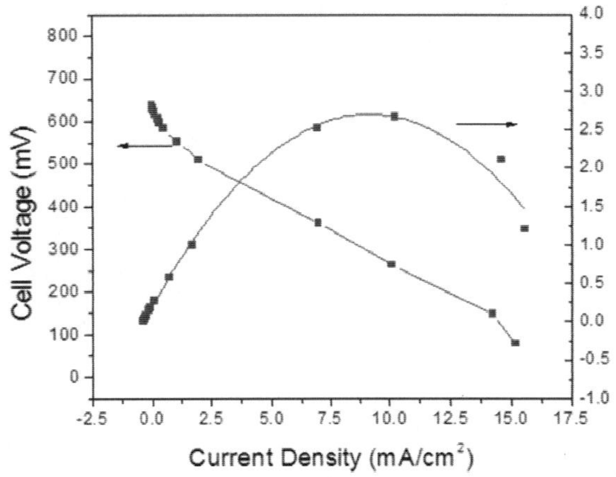

Figure 4. Performance of CFDRC Bio-Battery with JP-8 fuel showing $3mW/cm^2$ at $15mA/cm^2$ and 0.35V

Prototype Scale-Up

In order to meet real application demands the technology was scaled up to 5V/5W prototype capable of re-charging portable electronic devices (smart phones, etc). The design consisted of a bipolar stack with $85cm^2$ of electrode area to generate ~1A of current and 15 cells stacked in series to generate ~5V at operating condition. A picture of an individual plate as well as an exploded view of the prototype is shown in Figure 5.

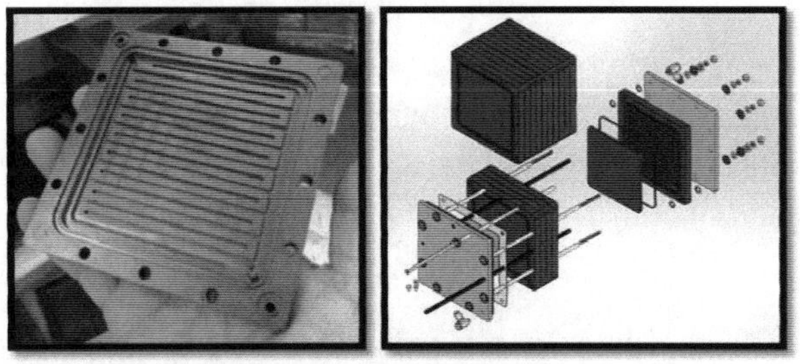

Figure 5. Photograph of single plate (left) and CAD drawing of 15 cell stack (right)

In order to test the prototype the previously developed sugar based system was employed. The results in Figure 6 show an open circuit voltage of ~10V and at the operating condition of 5V the current is just below 1A and the power is ~4.5W [5]. The system was outfitted with a USB connector and used to recharge a standard smart phone as shown in Figure 7.

The JP-8 technology described here is currently being combined with this scaled-up 5V/5W prototype to create a signature free way to recharge electronic devices with 24/7 operation using logistically favorable JP-8 fuels with no reforming and high efficiency independent of load. A conceptual drawing of such a unit is shown in Figure 8. This device would be capable of recharging a smart phone 20 times with 1L of JP-8 fuel using today's technology and further improvements to the fuel utilization (addition of enzymes for deeper oxidation of fuel) could lead to 200 recharges from the same 1L of JP-8.

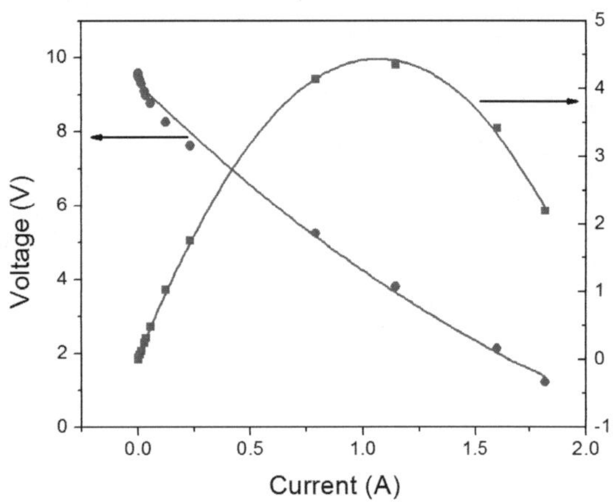

Figure 6. Performance of scaled-up Bio-Battery with sugar as fuel showing 4.5W power with current of 0.9A at 5.0V

Figure 7. Photograph of scaled-up Bio-Battery recharging a standard smart phone

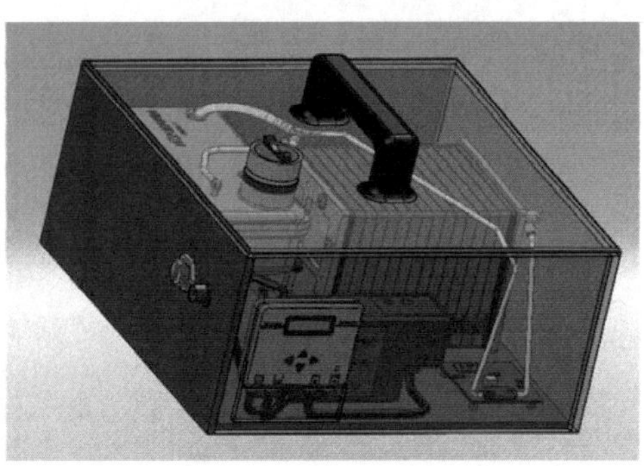

Figure 8. Conceptual drawing of a system with Bio-Battery, Power Manager, Buffer Battery, and Fuel Tank

Application Examples

Using the data from the 5W prototype described above we performed application studies to look at the advantages of the Bio-Battery technology in both dismounted soldier applications and larger "silent watch" applications.

Power for Dismounted Soldier

The dismounted soldier utilizes an increasing number of electronic devices to increase his situational awareness, ability to communicate, and overall operational effectiveness. However, battery technologies are not keeping pace with the proliferation of portable power devices. On a typical 100hr mission a soldier will need ~3,000Wh of energy for devices such as his radio, GPS, night vision, etc. For the analysis below we consider the standard BB2590 battery which weighs 1.4kg and contains 200Wh of energy. As the soldier needs more energy he needs to add another BB2590 to his load (the red line in Figure 9). Therefore at 3,000Wh the soldier is carrying 15 batteries or 21 kg (33.6 lbs) weight. By contrast with the Bio-Battery technology the soldier can carry a fixed weight (4kg) of the Bio-Battery prototype and then enough fuel to meet his mission needs. The blue line represents the performance of the currently available Bio-Battery technology, showing that at mission requirements of >1,000 Wh there begins to be a weight advantage for the Bio-Battery technology. The green line shows the projected performance of future generations of the Bio-Battery with more efficient fuel utilization (by adding additional enzymes to the system). At the described 3,000Wh requirement our analysis shows a 6.5kg (33%) savings with today's technology and a 15kg (75%) savings with the future technology.

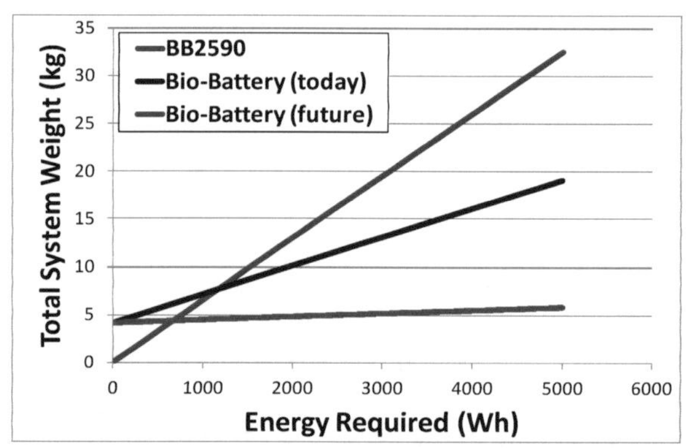

Figure 9. Bio-Battery prototype versus traditional batteries in soldier application. At 3000Wh (typical 100 hour mission), today's Bio-Battery technology saves 33% weight, future technology could save 75% weight

Power for "Silent Watch"

Another compelling example for this technology application is its use in ground combat systems as an auxiliary power unit that can enhance "silent watch" operations by augmenting power to significantly reduce the requirement to start the platform engine in order to recharge the vehicles batteries. Combat vehicles rely upon the platform's batteries to run the vehicles communications, sensor/optics, and fire control systems. This creates a need to restart the vehicle about every 30 minutes to ensure the batteries remain charged. Starting the vehicle consumes more JP-8 and increases the risks of being located and identified. As the Bio-Battery has no thermal or acoustic signature it is ideal for these applications where the vehicle needs to remain stealthy. There are other cases where tactical quiet generators (TQGs) or "Little Joe" generators are used to augment a vehicles battery system. Typically, TQG's run at maximum efficiencies of 30% with the efficiency being load dependent and dropping down to single digits at non-optimal loads. By contrast the Bio-Battery is projected to perform with 70% efficiency and is load independent as shown in the Figure 1.

Figure 10 below shows a comparison for 2kW TQG versus the Bio-Battery technology for missions from 1 day up to 100 days. For the analysis below we consider a standard TQG operating at 20% efficiency. The generator has a fixed weight of 81kg. The total required weight includes the weight of the system and the weight of the fuel needed for the mission duration (red line in Figure 10). For a 60 day mission the total weight would equal 1,500 kg. The blue line shows where the Bio-Battery technology currently available today would perform and at mission requirements of >30 days there begins to be an advantage to the Bio-Battery technology in terms of weight savings. Of course the advantage in terms of signature free operation is also present from Day 1. The green line shows the projected performance of future generations of the Bio-Battery with more efficient fuel utilization. In just 10 days of mission time the platoon will realize a total weight savings (device + fuel) of >150kg or in terms of consumables a reduction of diesel fuel needed of 250L (~80%).

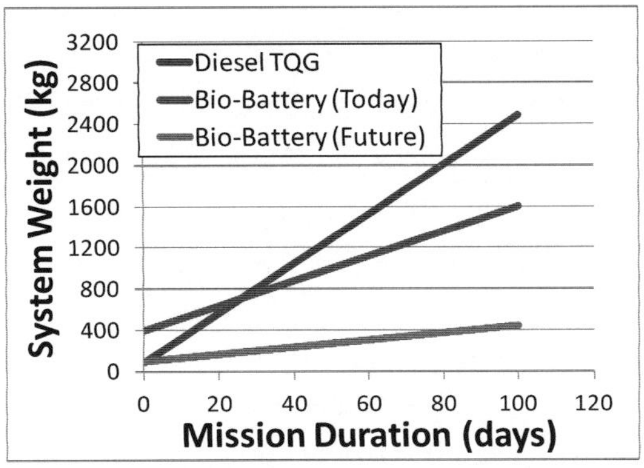

Figure 10. Bio-Battery prototype versus traditional 2kW tactical quiet generator showing potential for ~80% in fuel savings

Conclusions

CFDRC has previously developed a Bio-Battery with advantages including:high energy density, fuel flexibility, and renewable bio-catalysts. In this work we have shown the adaptation of the Bio-Battery to handle JP-8 fuel with no reforming. The system was shown to work with sulfur levels up to 2,000ppm. Electrochemical testing showed results of $3mW/cm^2$ from a single cell running on JP-8. Additionally the Bio-Battery was scaled-up to a 5V/5W system and demonstrated with sugar-based fuels to recharge a smart phone. The combination of JP-8 enzymatic technology with the scaled-up prototype will create a signature free method for recharging electronic devices with 24/7 operation using logistically favorable JP-8 fuels with no reforming and high efficiency independent of load. This will be a compelling solution for the dismounted soldier where there is a potential for 75% weight savings over the course of a 100hr mission and also for replacement of TQGs where a fuel savings of 80% is possible. Furthermore the enzymatic catalysts are selective enabling fuel flexibility, whereby the same Bio-Battery can process a variety of readily-available fuels including: sugars, alcohols, and diesel.

Acknowledgements

The core Bio-Battery technology has been developed through SBIR programs from the Army and Air Force. The adaptation for JP-8 described in this paper was supported by Northrop Grumman Corporation.

References

1. Ma, X., Velu, S., Sun, L., Song, C., "Adsorptive Desulphurization of JP-8 Jet Fuel and its light fraction over nickel-based adsorpents for fuel cell applications," *Prepr. Pap.-Am. Chem. Soc., Div. Fuel Chem.*, 48(2), 689, 2003
2. Muzzell, P., et al., "Properties of Real and "Virtual" Blends of FT IPK and JP-8," *TARDEC CFFS 2007 Annual Technical Review Meeting*, July 30, 2007.
3. Singhal, S., Svoboda, V., Wei, J.J., Northcutt, S., "Bio-Battery Platform for Soldier Portable Power Sources", *44th Power Sources Conference*, Las Vegas, NV., 2010
4. Ulyanova, Y., Svoboda, V., Wei, J.J., Northcutt, S., Singhal, S., "Bio-Battery Platform for Soldier Portable Power Sources", *45th Power Sources Conference*, Las Vegas, NV, 2012
5. Ulyanova, Y., Pinchon, E., Lindstrom, U., Singhal, S., "Bio-Battery: A MicroPower Source for Portable Electronics" Battery Power 2013, Denver, CO, 2013

Performance Testing and System Efficiency Analysis of Small Hybrid Power Systems

Eric B. Shields, Evan T. Rule
Naval Surface Warfare Center, Carderock Division
9500 MacArthur Blvd West Bethesda, MD 20817
Office: 301-227-4777 | Fax: 301-227- 5436 | Email: eric.b.shields@navy.mil

The recent conflicts in Iraq and Afghanistan highlighted vulnerability in US military operations associated with the need to provide a continuous supply of logistics fuel to forward deployed locations. This vulnerability has been the impetus for a significant amount of investment in the area of renewable energy, hybrid power systems, microgrids, and energy efficient technologies by each of the Services. In the most austere locations where power demand is often very low, fuel deliveries can be most challenging. The Army and Marine Corps have made many investments in small hybrid power systems to improve system efficiencies and reduce fuel consumption in such remote areas, though the performance improvements each system provides are heavily dependent on use conditions.

This work will compare the performance of a standalone 3kW diesel generator with that of multiple 3kW hybrid power systems which consist of an energy storage component, a bi-directional inverter, a diesel generator, and a small photovoltaic array. Due to the complex nature, and response of these components to changes in load, solar incidence, and system set points, each hybrid system configuration yields advantages over diesel generators in different regions of the performance range. When fuel savings advantages and periods of silent operation under these different use scenarios are compared with impacts to the cycle life of the energy storage system, weight, maintenance requirements, and cost, a complete understanding of the benefits of hybrid power systems can be defined. These tradeoffs and the impacts of the efficiencies of individual system components will be presented in detail.

For Submission to Hybrid Power Systems

Load Estimation for Electric Power Distribution Networks

Chiebuka Eyisi, Saeed Lotfifard
Department of Electrical Engineering and Computer Science
University of Central Florida
Orlando, U.S.A

Abstract: *Distribution Load Estimation (DLE) is a key function of Distribution Management System (DMS). In this paper a novel method for presenting historical load data in the form of Representative Load Curves (RLC) is presented. Adaptive Neuro-Fuzzy Inference Systems (ANFIS) is used in this regard to estimate the RLC. Accurate RLCs provide better pseudo-measurements for real-time load estimation in distribution networks. The performance of the proposed method is demonstrated on an 11kV radial distribution network with the aid of the MATLAB software. The mean absolute percent error (MAPE) criterion is used to quantify the accuracy of the estimated RLC.*

Keywords: ANFIS; Load Estimation; Radial Distribution Networks; Representative Load Curves.

Introduction

In the electricity industry, the major determinant in electricity supply strategy is the quantity of demand. Direct measurements and historical measured data are two reliable sources of data commonly utilized in several distribution load estimation (DLE) techniques. Distribution substations, transformers, and some important loads are usually the only sources of direct measurements. With the aid of historical data, one can generate more accurate pseudo-measurements in the form of estimate representative load curves (RLC) to help augment unavailable measurements in a given DLE process. An RLC is a curve representing load's aggregate behavior over a particular period or specified time span. They are usually built in the set of similar load curves.

For efficient operation and control of power distribution networks, updated nodal load information is needed to represent customers accurately. How electric energy is used at various times and the aggregated customers' share of the utility's total load is of major emphasis to Distribution System Operators (DSO). Load estimates are needed in advanced functions of Distribution Automation (DA). Historical data is usually mined for the abstraction of load information from billing cycle customer kWh consumption and major distribution substations and equipment installations and used to augment unavailable measurements. Estimate RLCs are obtained from this data as presented in this paper.

Related Work

An overview of DLE is presented in [1]. In [2], [3], load estimates were attained by scaling measurements according to transformer's peak load analysis. In [4], actual load curves were used to scale measurements to obtain load estimates. In [5], [6], the idea using distribution state estimation (DSE) techniques for DLE is proposed. In [7], a two-step procedure combining load allocation with DSE techniques is proposed. A statistical load modeling method to express the variation of active power demand in radial networks is proposed in [8]. In [9], fuzzy regression is utilized in radial networks to express the correlation between substation peak active loads and supplied customer active loads. In [10], expert knowledge and operator experience are utilized, where fuzzy variables were used to represent linguistic descriptions for the size of loads. In [11], a Weighted Least Absolute Value (WLAV) approach is proposed to reduce the effect of gross errors in measurements. In [12], neural and fuzzy set techniques are used to obtain load curves for customers' classes based on their monthly energy consumption and a large set load curves' data obtained from measurements. A zonal load estimation that divides radial distribution networks into several zones is proposed in [1], [13], [14]. In [15], a Weighted Least Squares (WLS) method is proposed for DLE.

A Case-Based-Reasoning (CBR) method is presented for distribution network nodal load estimation in [16]. A DLE method using clustering techniques is presented in [17] in which k-means clustering is used as part of the estimation process to obtain coarse estimates and these estimates are further refined to obtain the estimated load. In [18] Fuzzy Inference Systems (FIS) are utilized to estimate substation load by aggregating individual FIS of Takagi-Sugeno type. Pseudo-measurements play a significant role in the accuracy of the load estimates. Some choices include; average daily customer demand and/or classified typical load curves. RLCs are customer/node dependent and are obtained from historical data.

Highly accurate Representative Load Curves can be used to describe electricity demand. In [19], Multiple Discriminant Analysis (MDA) is used to cluster daily load curves into a set of RLCs. It's important that RLCs capture the dynamics of demand variations. An order-specific clustering algorithm for the determination of representative load curves is proposed in [20]. In [21], RLCs were built on the basis of their electricity behavior utilizing Fuzzy K-Means (FKM). In [22], FKM was also applied to determine typical load profiles of consumers. An algorithm utilizing FKM and hierarchical clustering for determining RLCs is also presented in [23]. In this paper, a method utilizing ANFIS is proposed to estimate RLCs from historical measured data.

Anfis

ANFIS integrates the best features of Fuzzy Systems (FS) and Artificial Neural Networks (ANN) and involves utilizing linguistic information from the FS as well as the learning capability of an ANN for automatic fuzzy IF-THEN rule generation and parameter optimization [24]. ANFIS comes into play when one can't ascertain what membership functions look like simply from looking at data. With

ANFIS, one can construct a FIS whose membership function parameters are tailored using a *hybrid algorithm* (back-propagation and least-squares), on a well-represented input/output dataset in order to account for variations in the data values. The ANFIS architecture consisting of two fuzzy IF-THEN rules based on Takagi and Sugeno's type is as follows [25].

Rule 1: if x is A_1 and y is B_1, then $f_1 = p_1x + q_1y + r_1$.
Rule 2: if x is A_2 and y is B_2, then $f_2 = p_2x + q_2y + r_2$.

Each layer contains nodes (neurons) described by the same function. In summary, when the values of the premise parameters are learned, the overall output can be expressed as a linear combination of consequent parameters [24].

Methodology

A *Time Series Estimation* was attempted heuristically on the input/target dataset to estimate RLCs. Both sets of data must be within the load profile. Various adaptations for the input dataset could include: present load (t), previous 24 hour load (t – 24), previous week same hour load (t – 168), weekly model factor (WMF), daily model factor (DMF). The model factors are computed using historical substation or nodal data by dividing the average load in its specific week or day by the maximum load in that same select week or day. These adaptations are chosen heuristically for different cases with the sole objective of seeking a model that generates the least Minimum Absolute Percent Error (MAPE). 4 weeks in each month are heuristically selected to be used to determine some sort of Weekly and Daily RLCs for each month with regards to the overall system load (RTD) or nodal demand. This was attained with the aid of the MATLAB software [26] as somewhat of a data-fitting process. A daily and/or weekly RLC was chosen on one basic criterion:

The Mean Absolute Percent Error (MAPE) between the corresponding sections/windows (between the selected estimated RLC and the target vector) must be the least.

For instance, the utilized historical load data in this paper is for a 2-year period. In March, only 8 weeks are to be used in this analysis (first 4 weeks in 2009 & 2010). In selecting the weekly RLC, from the estimated RLC (fitted ANFIS output), the estimated RLC and the corresponding target vector are divided into eight sections/windows to represent the selected eight weeks (1344 hours' samples of data). Hence there are two sets of data broken into 168 samples. That's eight sections/parts with 168 hours' samples each.

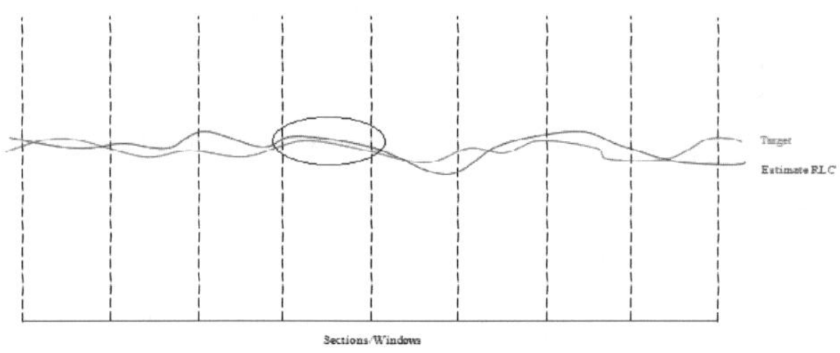

Figure 1. Selected Estimate RLC Description

Comparing each section, the method selects the section of the estimated RLC that has the least MAPE when compared with the corresponding target data. This selection of the fitted ANFIS output then represents the weekly RLC. A pictorial description is shown in fig. 1. In this case the encircled fourth window is therefore selected. Same analogy can be applied in selecting the daily RLC using the same 8 weeks in this case. Corresponding days (Mondays, Tuesdays, etc) of the target vector are grouped together and the daily RLC is selected again upon the basic MAPE criterion. Heuristically, after trying different adaptations of the respective target output, the models summarized below achieved the least overall MAPE when estimating weekly/daily RLCs to represent monthly historical data for the overall system load and/or select node; whatever the case may be. For instance, Y(t) would represent the present load in the load profile used in our case study and is one of the inputs to the ANFIS as described below. This input/target pair must be within the specified load profile. The input/target pair to the ANFIS are as follows:

Weekly/Daily RLC for Overall System Load:
Inputs (X): WSMF/DSMF, Y(t – 168), (Y(t – 24)), Y(t). Target (T): Y(t + 24). WSMF/DSMF represent weekly system model factor and daily system model factor respectively.

Weekly/Daily RLC for Select Node:
Inputs (X): WNMF/DNMF, Y(t – 168), Y(t – 24), Y(t). Target (T): Y(t + 24). WNMF/DNMF represent weekly nodal model factor and daily nodal model factor respectively.

The summarized modeling criterion used for both cases in the MATLAB software is shown in table I. In both cases, the input/target dataset is split into two (training and checking). Then an initial FIS is generated with the training dataset and validated with the checking dataset. Also, because the previous week's data is needed as one of our selected inputs, the estimate RLCs obtained from the ANFIS fit excluded the 1st week's data (168 samples) in the estimation/data-fitting process. This entry is replaced with NaN.

TABLE 1
MODELING CRITERION FOR ESTIMATING RLCS

S/N	*Custom ANFIS*	*Variables*
1	Number of Inputs	Four
2	Membership Function Type	Generalized Bell
3	Number of Membership Functions	Varied from 2 to 3
4	Learning Algorithm	Hybrid Learning Algorithm
5	Epoch Size	Varied from 50 to 100
6	Data Size	Data per Hour (17520 Samples)
7	Sugeno-Type System	First Order
8	Output Type	Linear
9	Initial Step Increase/Decrease Size	1.1/0.9
10	Number of Linear Parameters	80
11	Number of Nonlinear Parameters	24
12	Number of Nodes	55
13	Number of Fuzzy Rules	16
14	Data/Parameter Ratio	≈ 84

The discussed method is summarized using the following steps:

1) Heuristically organize input/output dataset.
2) Initialize the fuzzy system using pre-defined MATLAB functions.
3) Give other parameters for ANFIS learning: Error (Tolerance), Number of Epochs.
4) Begin ANFIS learning using MATLAB *anfis* command. Stop when the number of epochs is reached or tolerance is obtained.
5) Validate with independent data adressing any over-fitting concerns.
6) Use defined MAPE criterion to obtain estimate RLC if step 5 above is confirmed. Else go to step 1 and repeat process.

Case Study and Results

The proposed method for estimating RLCs is implemented on a sample 11kV radial distribution feeder employed from [28]. System loads are considered as constant (PQ) power or spot loads. The load data used was mined and extracted data from [29] and was adapted to suit the test network. This dataset comprised two years of historical hourly measured data (Jan 1st 2009 – Dec 31st 2010).

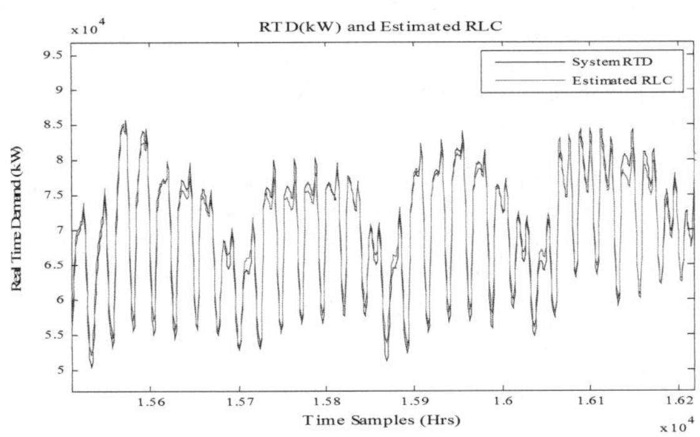

Figure 2. Magnified Estimate RLC & System RTD (for Weekly RLC)

The ANFIS structure follows the modeling criterion in table 1 for both cases explained in the methodology. The results upon training/testing the ANFIS of the estimated RLC and system RTD, intended for weekly estimate RLC are further shown in fig. 2 with overall MAPE of 2.5071% and root mean square error, RMSE of 6.2790 $\times$ 10^3 kW. Similar results can be obtained for a selected node with similar adaptations. The initial and adjusted input membership functions for this estimation are shown in the figs. 3 and 4 respectively.

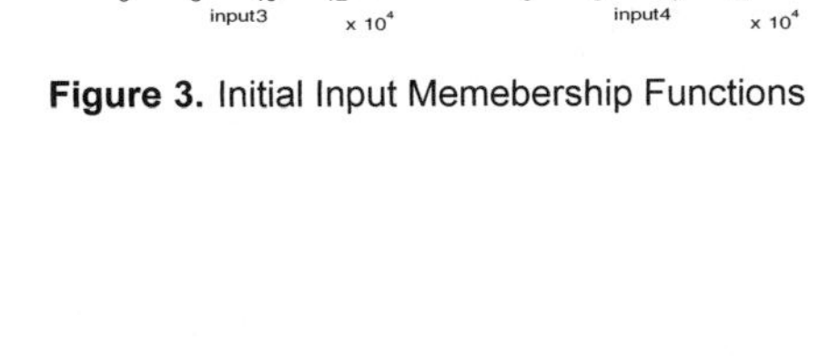

Figure 3. Initial Input Memebership Functions

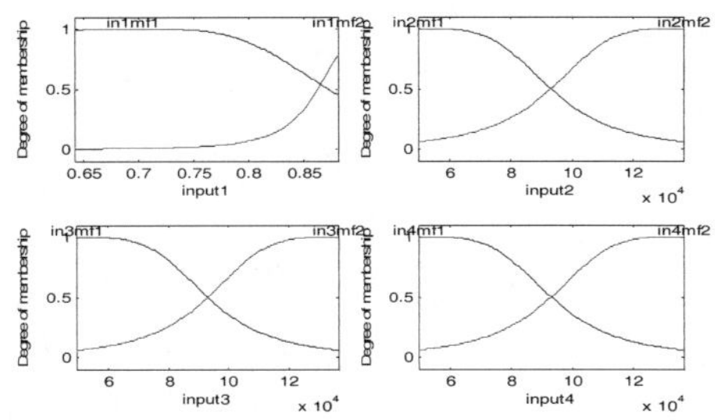

Figure 4. Adjusted Input Membership Functions

The error between system load and estimate RLC (intended for weekly RLC) in kW is shown in fig. 5.

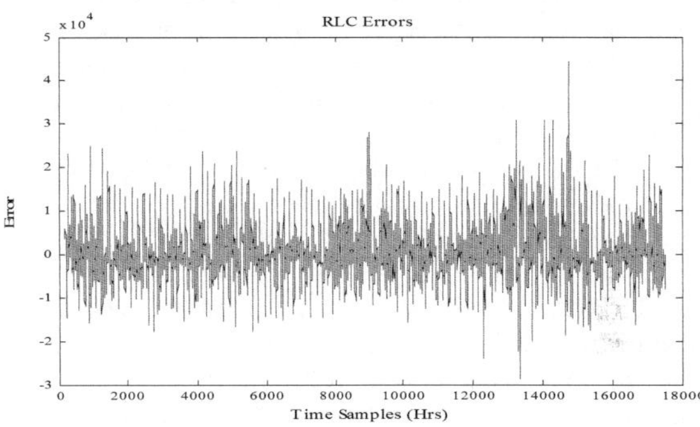

Figure 5. Error between System Load & Estimate RLC (for Weekly RLC)

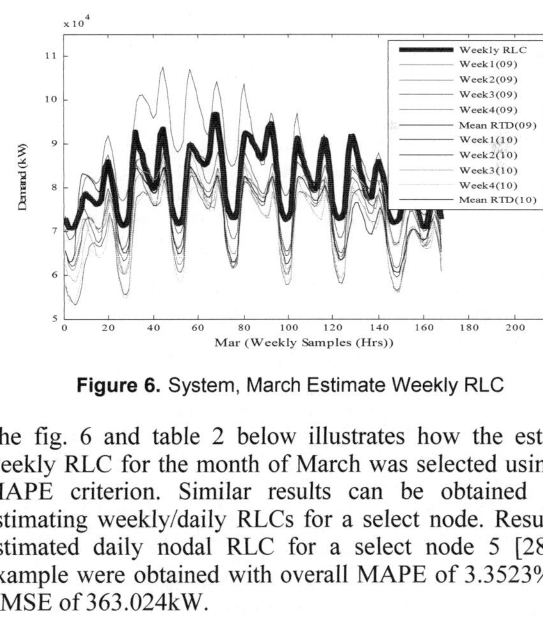

Figure 6. System, March Estimate Weekly RLC

The fig. 6 and table 2 below illustrates how the estimate weekly RLC for the month of March was selected using the MAPE criterion. Similar results can be obtained when estimating weekly/daily RLCs for a select node. Results of estimated daily nodal RLC for a select node 5 [28] for example were obtained with overall MAPE of 3.3523% and RMSE of 363.024kW.

TABLE 2
TABULAR MAPE SHOWING WEEKLY COMPARISONS

	Year 2009				*Year 2010*			
	January							
Window/ Week	1	2	3	4	1	2	3	4
Estimate RLC MAPE	NaN	3.0439	3.6580	2.0672	3.5247	4.2699	**1.9837**	3.4545

	Year 2009				Year 2010			
	February							
Window/ Week	1	2	3	4	1	2	3	4
Estimate RLC MAPE	2.98 59	2.18 57	**1.25 55**	1.82 72	3.55 04	2.44 85	3.56 48	1.90 84
	March							
Window/ Week	1	2	3	4	1	2	3	4
Estimate RLC MAPE	2.77 75	2.94 44	1.45 36	1.91 65	**1.20 02**	2.77 85	1.96 62	2.55 29

Conclusions

A systematic approach using ANFIS is developed to construct a Representative Load Curve from historical data. The present load, previous 24 hour load, previous week same hour load and weekly system model factors or daily system model factors are used as inputs to obtain the best representative curves for a select week or day as the case may be. Least Minimum Absolute Percent Error (MAPE) is defined as a criteria to quantify the accuracy of the estimates. The proposed algorithm was implemented on an 11kV network and it is demonstrated that the accuracy of the estimates were within 2-4%. Although the proposed algorithm was demonstrated for substation data, it can be applied to nodal load data as well. The constructed RLC can be utilized for real-time distribution load estimation.

References

[1] Jie Wan, "Nodal load estimation for electric power distribution systems", *Ph.D. Dissertation*, Drexel University, 2003.

[2] V. Borozan and N. Rajakovic, "Load estimation for distribution systems with minimum information," *Euro. Trans. On Electr. Power*, iss. 14, pp. 331-345, Aug. 2004.

[3] V. Borozan and N. Rajakovic, "Minimum loss distribution network configuration: analyses and management," Electricity Distribution. Part 1: Contributions. CIRED. *14th International Conference and Exhibition on IEE Conference*, no. 438, vol. 6, 1997, pp. 18/1 - 18/5.

[4] R. P. Broadwater, A.H. Khan, H. E. Shaalan and R. E. Lee, "Time varying load analysis to reduce distribution losses through reconfiguration," *IEEE Trans. Power Delivery*, vol. 8, no. 1, pp. 294-300, Jan. 1993.

[5] M. E. Baran and A. W. Kelley, "State estimation for real-time monitoring of distribution systems," *IEEE Trans. Power Syst.*, vol. 9, no. 3, pp. 1601-1609, Aug. 1994.

[6] M. E. Baran, "Load estimation for distribution system analysis," Panel Summary, *Proceedings of the 2001 IEEE Power Engineering Society Summer Meeting*, Vancouver, Canada.

[7] T. Wang and M. Fan, "A novel load estimation method in distribution networks", in *Proc. Power Systems Technology*, vol. 1.1, 1998, pp. 567-571.

[8] A. K. Ghosh, S. L. Lubkeman and R. H. Jones, "Load modeling for distribution circuit state estimation," *IEEE Trans. Power Delivery*, vol. 12, no. 2, pp. 999-1005, Apr. 1996.

[9] J. Nazarko and W. Zalewski, "The fuzzy regression approach to peak load estimation in power distribution systems", *IEEE Trans. on Power Systems*, vol. 14, no.3, pp. 809-814, Aug. 1999.

[10] H. Kuo and Y. Hsu, "Distribution system load estimation and service restoration using a fuzzy approach", *IEEE Trans. On Power Delivery*. vol. 8, no. 4, Oct. 1993.

[11] M.R. Irving and C.N. Macqueen, "Robust algorithm for load estimation in distribution networks", IEE Proc.-Gener. Transm. Distri., vol. 145, no. 5, pp. 499-504, Sept. 1998.

[12] D. M. Falcao and H. O. Henriques, "Load estimation in radial distribution systems using neural networks and fuzzy set techniques," Panel Summary, *Proceedings of the 2001 IEEE Power Engineering Society Summer Meeting*, Vancouver, Canada.

[13] J. Wan, K.N. Miu, "A zonal-load estimation method for unbalanced radial distribution networks", *IEEE Trans. on Power Delivery*, vol. 17, no. 4, pp. 1106-1112, Oct. 2002.

[14] J. Wan, K.N. Miu, "Load estimation in radial electric power distribution networks using limited measurements", in *Proc. IEEE International Symposium on Circuits and Systems*, vol.2, Geneva, Switzerland, 2000, pp. 517-520.

[15] J. Wan, K.N. Miu, "A WLS Method for load estimation in unbalanced distribution networks", *IEEE Power Engineering Society Winter Meeting*, vol. 2, pp. 969-974, Jan. 2002.

[16] J. Wu, Y. Yu, "CBR-based load Estimation for distribution networks", in *Proc. IEEE Electrotechnical Conference*, MELECON, Malaga, Spain, May 2006, pp. 952-955.

[17] G. Grigoraş, F. Scarlatache and G. Cârţină, "Load estimation for distribution systems using clustering techniques", *Optimization of Electrical and Electronic Equipment (OPTIM), 2012 13th International Conference*, pp. 301 – 306, May 2012.

[18] T. Konjic, V. Miranda and I. Kapetanovic, "Fuzzy inference systems applied to LV substation load estimation", *IEEE. Trans. On Power Sys.*, vol. 20, no. 2, pp. 742-749, May 2005.

[19] P. Balachandra and V. Chandru, "Modelling electricity demand with representative load curves", Elsevier Energy, vol. 24, iss. 3, pp. 219-230, Mar. 1999.

[20] C.H. Marton, A. Elkanel, T.A. Duever, "An order-specific clustering algorithm for the determination of representative demand curves", Elsevier Computer and Chemical Engineering, vol. 32, pp. 1365-1372, Jun. 2007.

[21] P.T.T. Binh, N.H. Ha, T.C. Tuan and L.D.Khoa, "Determination of representative load curve based on Fuzzy K-Means" in *Proc. 4th Intl. Power Engineering and Optimization Conf (PEOCO2010)*, Malaysia, pp. 281-286, Jun. 2010.

[22] J. Hossain, A.N.M. Enamul Kabir, M. Rahman, B. Kabir and R. Islam, "Determination of typical load profile of consumers using Fuzzy C-Means clustering algorithm", *International Journal of Soft Computing and Engineering (IJSCE)*, vol. 1, iss. 5, pp. 169-173, Nov. 2011.

[23] D. Gerbec, S. Gasperic, I. Simon and F. Gubina, "Consumer's load profile determination based on different classification methods", in *Proc. Power Engineering Society General Meeting*, vol. 2, pp. 900-905, Jul. 2003.

[24] J.S. Jang, "ANFIS: adaptive-network-based fuzzy inference systems", *IEEE Trans. Sys. Man. Cybern.*, vol. 23, Iss. 3, pp. 665-685, May/Jun 1993.

[25] T. Takagi and M. Sugeno, "Derivation of fuzzy control rules from human operator's control actions", in *Proc. IFAC Symp Fuzzy Inform, Knowledge Representation and Decision Analysis*, pp. 55-60.

[26] Fuzzy Logic Toolbox™ User's Guide. www.mathworks.com Available [Online].

[27] J.-S. R. Jang, "Input selection for ANFIS learning", *in Proc. 5th IEEE Intl. Conf. on Fuzzy Systems*, vol. 2, pp.1493-1499, Sep. 1996.

[28] D. Das, D.P. Kothari and A. Kalam, "Simple and efficient method for load flow solution of radial distribution networks", Elsevier Electric Power and Energy Systems, vol. 17, no. 5, pp. 335-346, 1995.

[29] Historical Metered Load. www.pjm.com/markets-and-operations/ops-analysis/historical-load-data.aspx Available [Online].

[30] W.H. Kersting, *Distribution System Modeling and Analysis*, CRC Press Inc, New Mexico, 2002.

[31] J.M. Zurada, Introduction to Artificial Neural Systems, West Publishing Company, Minnesota, 1992

[32] A. Kandel, *Fuzzy Expert Systems*, CRC Press Inc, Boca Raton, Florida, 1992.

Role of Aliphatic and Aromatic Hydrocarbon Compounds on Carbon Formation in Fuel Reformers

Terry G. DuBois, Richard Scenna
Command, Power and Integration Directorate
US Army Research, Development
and Engineering Command
5100 Magazine Road
Aberdeen Proving Ground, MD 21005

Sen Nieh, James Kimmel
The Catholic University of America
620 Michigan Avenue, NE
Department of Mechanical Engineering
Washington, D.C. 20064

Abstract: *A major challenge with reforming of liquid hydrocarbon fuels is avoiding operating conditions that can result in carbon formation. The propensity for forming solid carbon particles within an oxidative reformer increases with increasing fuel carbon number and the presence of aromatic compounds. In addition, the desire to maximize reformer efficiency by minimizing the steam-to-carbon molar ratio and oxygen-to-carbon molar ratio, also increases the likelihood that carbon will form. To gain a better understanding of carbon formation resulting from JP-8 reforming in an adiabatic autothermal reactor, a series of experiments involving aliphatic (n-pentane, n-octane, n-decane, n-dodecane,) and aromatic (methylbenzene, naphthalene) components found in JP-8 were investigated. These hydrocarbon components were evaluated as pure compounds and as blends. All hydrocarbon compounds and blends were reacted in an atmospheric pressure autothermal reformer with supported Pt/Rh based noble metal catalysts (catalysts loading of 0.12 g/cm^3) deposited on a 600 cpsi cordierite monolith under steam-to-carbon ratios of 2, fuel equivalency energy flow of 3.3 kW thermal (5.9 ml/min.), space velocities of 25,000 hr^{-1} to 45,000 hr^{-1} and variable oxygen-to-carbon ratios of 0.8 to 1.2.*

Results show that carbon formation tendency, as measured by olefins concentration in the reformate stream, are more likely in the order of polyaromatics>> normal paraffins>mono-aromatics. For paraffinic components, carbon formation tendency increases with increasing carbon number. The onset of carbon formation is also accompanied by reduced fuel conversion and a decrease in endothermic steam reforming reactions, all of which reduce hydrogen yield and reactor thermal efficiency. In fuel blend experiments, the addition of relatively small quantities (0.8 wt% max) of naphthalene (1-methylnaphthalene) has a strong negative effect on olefin concentration. Results provide insight into how hydrocarbons components present in JP-8 contribute to carbon formation within ATR reactors and how operating conditions can be altered to minimize this effect.

Keywords: carbon formation; autothermal reforming; jet fuel; paraffin hydrocarbons, aromatic hydrocarbons; poly aromatic hydrocarbons

Introduction

The reforming of readily available liquid hydrocarbon fuels, such as middle distillate fuels (kerosene, diesel, jet fuel, etc.), is seen as a near-term viable path for hydrogen generation for fuel cell power applications. These fuels consist primarily of long chain paraffins and aromatics. The largest hydrocarbon class found in jet fuels are paraffins with normal-paraffins and iso-parafins each representing approximately one-third of the fuel components and naphthenes (cycloparaffins) ranging from ten to twenty percent. Aromatics are another major component of jet fuels consisting of mono-aromatics (15% to 20%) and polyaromatics (1% to 3%).

Carbon formation within catalytic reactors is an insidious problem that can impair catalytic performance/activity and can ultimately lead to catalysts deactivation and reactor plugging. Reactions associated with carbon formation are given below:

$$2CO \rightarrow C + CO_2 \tag{1}$$

$$CO + H_2 \rightarrow C + H_2O \tag{2}$$

$$C_nH_{2m} \rightarrow nC + mH_2 \tag{3}$$

$$C_nH_{2n} \rightarrow nC + nH_2 \tag{4}$$

Under certain operating conditions, carbon formation is thermodynamically favored. Equations (1) and (2) are thermodynamic or Boudouard carbon formation reactions. Carbon can also be formed though the cracking or pyrolysis of hydrocarbons compounds as shown in equation (3). The dehydrogenation of olefinic compounds, shown in equation (4), is also very common and can occur rapidly in reformers. There are many different mechanisms and types of carbon that can be formed in catalytic reactors: carbon can be chemisorbed or physically absorbed blocking metal sites from reactants and reducing catalysts activity, carbon can completely encapsulate catalysts sites resulting in deactivation, carbon can obstruct or block meso and micropores denying access to reactants, and carbon can buildup and grow within pores until the catalysts support is fractured resulting in deactivation [1]. For high temperature (> 600°C) noble metal catalytic ATR operation on heavy hydrocarbon fuels, such as jet fuel, the primary type of carbon formed is pyrolytic carbon. Pyrolytic carbon can lead to catalysts deactivation via catalysts encapsulation [2]. The presence of olefins in the reformate (primarily ethylene) is a strong precursor to carbon formation. Pyrolytic carbon formation is thought to proceed along the following reaction path (Eqn. 5):

$$C_nH_m \rightarrow olefins \rightarrow coke \rightarrow \text{graphitic carbon} \quad (5)$$

The production of olefins is generally attributed to homogeneous hydrocarbon reactions in regions which are deficient in oxygen. Once olefins are formed, the progression to coke formation can be very rapid [3]. Because the formation of olefins are strong precursors for carbon formation and are easily measured, this paper focuses on these components to indicate carbon formation within a catalytic reactor.

This paper presents experimental results of autothermal reforming of normal paraffins (n-dodecane, n-decane, n-octane, and n-pentane) and aromatics (methylcyclohexane, 1-methylnaphthalene). These components represent major hydrocarbons classes present in jet fuels and should provide insight into challenges and operating consideration with JP-8 reforming.

Experimental Apparatus

A more detailed discussion of the experimental apparatus and its operation has been described elsewhere [4]. Figure 1 shows a schematic diagram of the experimental setup. In general, water and fuel were pumped via two, high performance liquid chromatographic pumps, where the mass flow was determined through scale measurements. Water was vaporized through a two stage vaporizer/superheater consisting of annualar flow of water around heating elements. The fuel was vaporized in a tube furnace and then mixed with the superheated water. Air was supplied from a typical air compressor and controlled through a Brook mass flow controller and heated by an in-line heater. At approximately, 25 cm before the reactor's entrance the steam and vaporized fuel were combined with the heated air. The temperature of the reactants was controlled to 425 °C ± 10 °C for all experiments. The reactants then passed through a stainless steel, static mixer and a then through a porous metal foam material (2.5 cm in length) adjacent to the reactor. The reactor volume is 87 cm^3 (1.9 cm diameter and 30.5 cm in length). All hydrocarbon compounds and blends were reacted in an atmospheric pressure autothermal reformer with supported Pt/Rh based noble metal catalysts (catalysts loading of 0.12 g/cm^3) deposited on a 600 cpsi cordierite monolith. Reformate exiting the reactor passes through a condenser where liquids were removed and measured via a scale. A slip stream of reformate was obtained at the reactor exit, passed through a dryer to remove moisture and then sent to an on-line gas chromatograph for analysis.

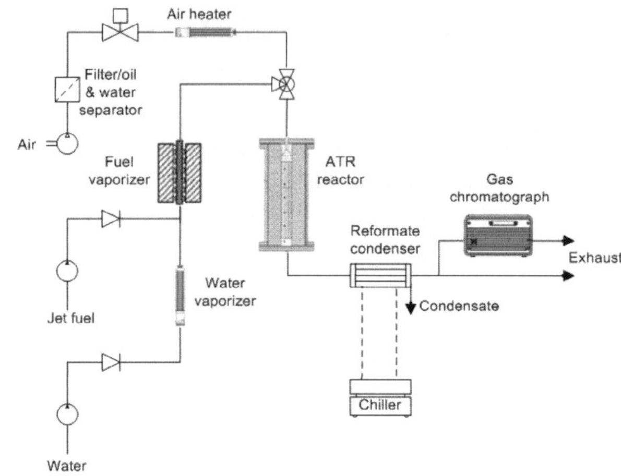

Figure 1. Experimental instrumentation and process flow diagram of the reformer test bed.

Analysis

Fuels were obtained from a commercial supplier with n-dodecane (99+%), n-decane (99%), n-octane (97%), n-pentane (99%), methylcyclohexane (99%), and 1-methylnaphthalene (97%). The gaseous reformate stream was analyzed by an on-line gas chromatograph (Agilent Technologies, Micro GC 3000) with four columns using thermal conductivity detectors: (i) molecular sieve column (10 m x 0.32 mm), (ii) Plot U column (8 m x 0.32 mm), (iii) alumina column (10 m x 0.32 mm), and (iv) OV1 column (10 m x 0.15 mm x 2.0 μm). Multiple level calibration curves were used for all compounds with the calibration gases at 0.02% analytical tolerance.

For the data presented, fuel conversion is defined as:

$$\text{Fuel conversion to } CO_x\ (\%) = \frac{CO + CO_2}{m \cdot (\text{hydrocarbon fuel})_{in}} \cdot 100\%$$

where, m is the number of carbons in the hydrocarbon fuel fed to the reactor. Under conditions where complete fuel conversion are anticipated, O/C $\geq$ 1.0, the carbon balance were in the range of 100% ± 5%. Over the conditions tested the GHSV ranged from 24,000 hr^{-1} to 45,000 hr^{-1}.

Discussion and Results

A series of single component paraffins and aromatic blends were reacted in a ceramic monolith reactor over a noble metal based catalysts to observe the propensity for carbon formation. The fuel flow rate for all experiments was set at a thermal energy rate of 3.3 kW_{th} (5.9 ml/min.). In order to minimize potential deleterious effects from carbon formation, the steam-to-carbon ratio was held at 2.0 and the minimum molar oxygen-to-carbon ratio (O/C) was generally kept at around 0.70. Over all testing conditions, no change in reactor pressure drop was observed indicating that no significant carbon disposition occurred.

n-Paraffin Reforming: A comparison of fuel conversion and reformate olefin concentration for single component paraffins is shown in Figures 2 and 3. All single component fuels achieved full fuel conversion. For paraffinic fuels, full fuel conversion occurred at lower O/C ratios as an inverse relationship to carbon number. This is indicative of higher reactivity, but is likely a function of higher reactor operating temperatures. Olefin production of normal paraffins, shown in Fig. 3, is highest at lower O/C ratios (corresponding to lower reactor operating temperature) and is reduced to undetectable levels (< 10 ppm) at higher O/C levels. Olefin composition follows carbon number with higher carbon number resulting in higher olefin yields. A significant change is seen comparing n-pentane (C5) to n-octane (C8); where the olefin production is greatly reduced and nondetectable levels of olefin are reached at a lower O/C ration (O/C ~1.0).

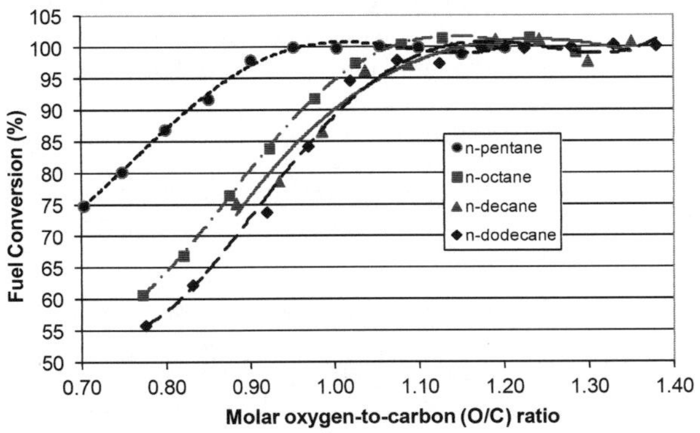

Figure 2. Fuel conversion to CO_x for n-dodecane ($C_{12}H_{26}$), n-decane ($C_{10}H_{22}$), n-octane (C_8H_{18}), and n-pentane (C_5H_{12}) with H_2O/C = 2.0.

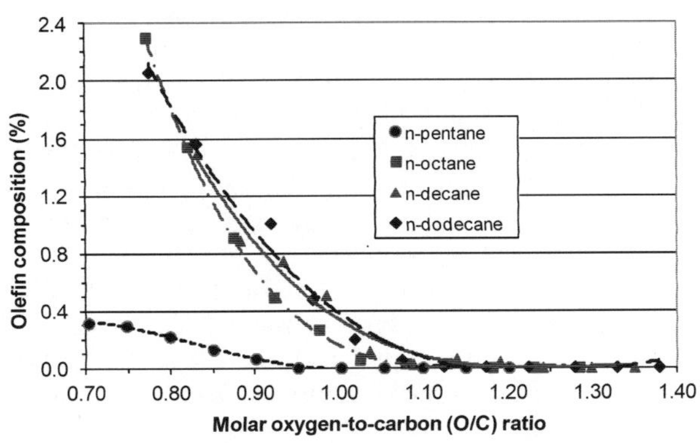

Figure 3. Olefin concentration for n-dodecane ($C_{12}H_{26}$), n-decane ($C_{10}H_{22}$), n-octane (C_8H_{18}), and n-pentane (C_5H_{12}) with H_2O/C = 2.0

Reforming mono-aromatic and mono-aromatic/paraffin blend: A comparison of fuel conversion is shown in Fig. 4 for n-dodecane, toluene and a blends (volume percent) of the two. All four fuels achieved full fuel conversion with toluene having significantly better reactivity than n-dodecane, reaching full fuel conversion at an O/C ratio of 0.96. The binary blend (50/50) produced results almost identical to toluene showing little influence from the paraffinic component. This is an interesting result as aromatic hydrocarbons are generally considered very stable having higher activation energies than paraffins which might imply that fuel conversion would lag conversion of parafins. Similar results were observed by Gould, et. al. [5] when conducting ATR reforming of n-dodecane, tetralin and an equimolar binary combination of the two. Model fuels that appear more reactive are accompanied by higher reactor operating temperatures which can account for achieving full fuel conversion at lower O/C ratios. The 80/20 blend does show the influence of n-dodecane on fuel conversion. Olefin composition is shown in Fig. 5. Olefin composition was low (≤ 0.1%) for toluene (comparaed to paraffins) increasing with decreasing O/C ratios. The binary blend of toluene and n-dodecane produced higher levels of olefins (at O/C < 1.0), but still substantially less than n-dodecane (e.g. at an O/C = 0.8; toluene = 0.04%, binary mixture = 0.13%, 80/20 blend = 0.92%, and n-dodecane = 1.98%). Results show that normal paraffins have a higher propensity for carbon formation than mono-aromatics.

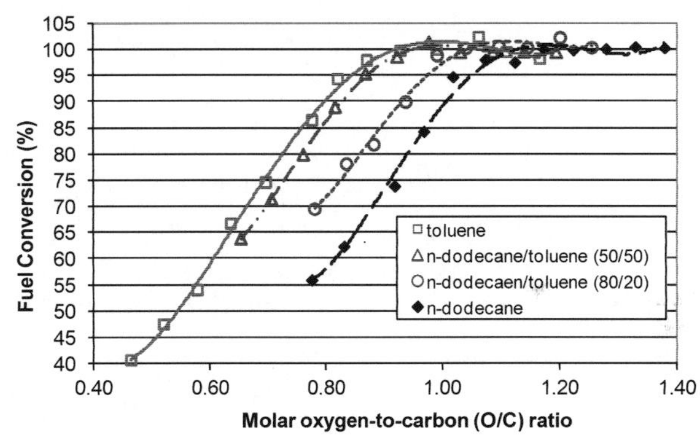

Figure 4. Fuel conversion to CO_x for n-dodecane ($C_{12}H_{26}$), toluene (C_7H_8) and blends ($C_{12}H_{26}$ + C_7H_8) with H_2O/C = 2.0

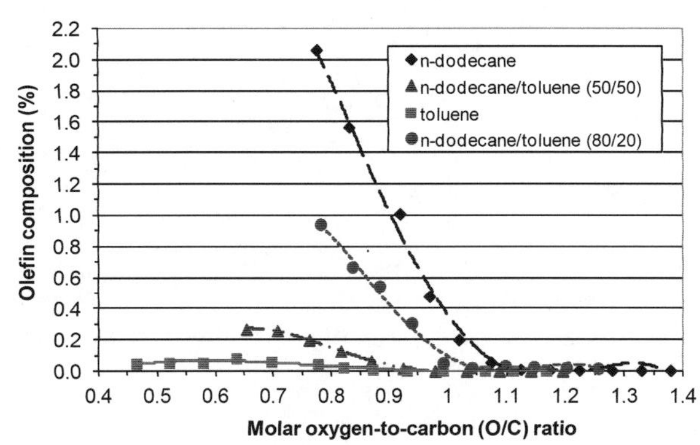

Figure 5. Olefin concentration for n-dodecane ($C_{12}H_{26}$), toluene (C_7H_8) and blends ($C_{12}H_{26}$ + C_7H_8) with H_2O/C = 2.0.

Reforming of polyaromatic and synthetic paraffinic kerosene (SPK) blends: Fuel conversion and olefin concentration is shown in Figures 6 and 7 for synthetic paraffinic kerosene with 1-methlynaphthalene (naphthalene) blends. Because 1-methylnaphthlene has been associated with irreversible catalysts deactivation [6], we chose to evaluate this polyaromatic compounds in a diluted form with an SPK fuel. For low concentrations of naphthalene (≤ 0.2 wt%) fuel conversion in excess of 99% can be achieved. At higher naphthalene levels, fuel conversion declined with increasing polyaromatic levels (97.4% at 0.2 wt%, 94.5% at 0.4 wt%). As the polyaromatic content increased, the point of maximum fuel conversion occurred at progressively lower O/C levels. Olefin concentration, Fig. 7, increased with increasing polyaromatic content and could not be entirely eliminated under any O/C ratio observed.

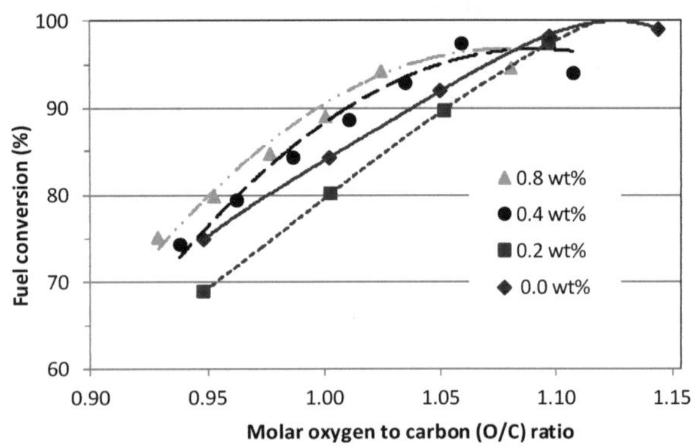

Figure 6. Fuel conversion of 1-methylnaphthalene blends with synthetic paraffinic kerosene. Weight percentages shown are of 1-methylnaphthalene. With $H_2O/C = 1.3$.

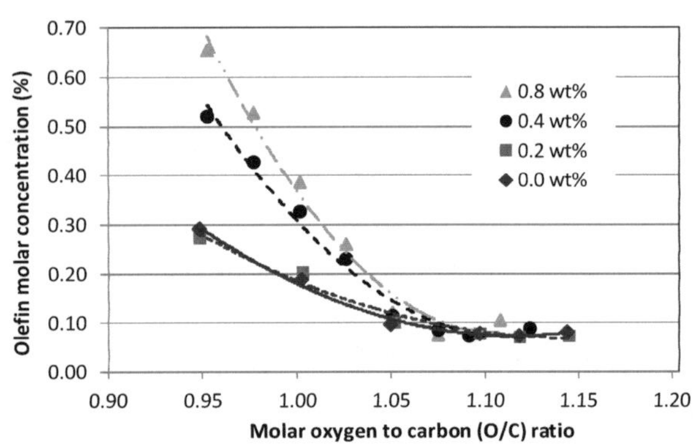

Figure 7. Fuel conversion of 1-methylnaphthalene blends with synthetic paraffinic kerosene. Weight percentages shown are of 1-methylnaphthalene. With $H_2O/C = 1.3$.

Summary

A series of ATR experiments were performed on paraffins, mono-aromatics, and polyaromatic blends to observe the propensity for carbon formation as indicated by olefin production. There is a clear relationship between fuel carbon number and carbon formation for normal paraffins; with carbon formation tendency increasing with fuel carbon number. Also, of note is that there is a large reduction in carbon formation tendency for paraffins between C8 and C5 fuels. The mono-aromatic fuel (methylbenzene) showed a low propensity for carbon formation. Polyaromatics, even in relatively low concentrations, did show a strong carbon formation tendency and reduced fuel conversion. Others have postulated that aromatics, particularly polyaromatics, can be strongly absorbed on the metal sites resulting in reduced catalytic activity [7]. A reduction in active catalysts sites increases homogeneous reactions which are associated with ethylene production which can, through consecutive dehydrogenation reactions, result in carbon/coke formation [8].

Additional experimental work is needed to investigate other hydrocarbon functional groups within JP-8 and within each functional group further experimental work is needed in looking at molecular size and other physical characteristics that might impact carbon formation with catalyst autothermal reforming.

Acknowledgements

The authors gratefully acknowledge the *US Army Communications-Electronics RDE Center's* support.

References

1. Rostrup-Nielsen JR, Christensen TS, Dybkjaer I. Steam reforming of liquid hydrocarbons. *Stud Surf Sci Catal*, vol. 113, pp. 81-95, 1998.
2. Rostrup-Nielsen JR. *Catalytic Steam Reforming*; editors J. Anderson and M. Boudart, *Catalysis: Science and Technology*, 1984, Springer.
3. Bartholomew, CH. Mechanisms of catalysts deactivation. *Appl. Cat. A: Gen.*, vol. 212, pp. 17-60.
4. DuBois TG, Nieh S. Design and performance of an experimental 3 kW_{th} autothermal reformer test bed for heavy hydrocarbon fuels. 43rd Power Sources Conference, July 7-11, 2008, pp. 133-136.
5. Gould BD, Tadd AR, Schwank W. Nickel-catalyzed autothermal reforming of jet fuel surrogates: n-dodecane, tetralin, and their mixture. *J Power Sourc*, vol. 164, pp. 344-350, 2007.
6. Shekawat, Gardner, Berry, Salazar, Haynes, Spivey. Catalytic partial oxidation of n-tetradecane in the presence of sulfur or polynuclear aromatics: Effect of support metals. Appl Catalysis A: Gen, vol. 311, pp. 8-16, 2006.
7. Yoon S, Kang I, Bae J. suppression of ethylene-induced carbon deposition in diesel autothermal reforming. *Int J. Hydrogen Energy*, vol. 34, pp1844-1851, 2009.
8. Hartmann M, Kaltschmitt T, Deutschmann O. Catalytic partial oxidation of higher hydrocarbon fuel components on Rh/Al_2O_3 coated honeycomb monoliths. Catalyst Today, vol. 1475, pp. S204-S209, 2009.

Fuel Agnostic Power Sources for Tactical Power and Un-manned Systems

Hiep Nguyen, Ru Chen, and Ian Kaye
UltraCell LLC
399 Lindbergh Avenue
Livermore, CA 94551

Abstract: *UltraCell's high temperature PEM fuel cell can be used with a variety of hydrocarbon based fuel sources due to its high tolerance of carbon monoxide in the reformate stream. UltraCell has developed and matured several reformed methanol fuel cell systems based on steam reforming technology that can provide extended runtime to various classes of tactical power systems. UltraCell high temperature PEM fuel cell stack can also be integrated with an autothermal reformer that is powered by high energy density fuels such as JP-8 to provide long runtime to unmanned systems such as unmanned aerial vehicle (UAV) or ground-based vehicles.*

Keywords: Reformed methanol fuel cell; Proton exchange membrane (PEM); Membrane electrode assembly (MEA); Fuel processor; Steam reforming; Autothermal reforming; Reformate; Hydrogen; Methanol; propane; JP-8.

Introduction

A fuel cell is an electrochemical device that converts fuel into electricity. One of the most common types of fuel cells is the hydrogen proton exchange membrane fuel cell (PEMFC). Hydrogen is fed to one side of the cell (anode) while air is fed to the opposite side (cathode). Hydrogen reacts in the presence of catalysts to generate electrons and protons. The protons are able to pass through the membrane, but the electrons cannot – they are forced around the fuel cell in an external electrical circuit. The flow of electrons produces the electrical current needed to power electronic devices. The electrons and protons are then united at the cathode, reacting with oxygen in the air stream in the presence of catalysts to form water. In order to achieve higher voltage and power, individual cells are assembled together in what's called the fuel cell stack.[1] It is the core engine of any fuel cell system.

Technologies

Although pure hydrogen is an ideal fuel source for PEM fuel cell, the fact that it is difficult to obtain and store makes it logistically undesirable. UltraCell has utilized several fuel reforming technologies in which hydrogen can be generated on-the-fly from several high energy density hydrocarbon fuel sources. First is the reformed methanol fuel cell in which methanol acted as a fuel source for hydrogen generation via the steam reforming process [2] as shown in Figure 1. Methanol-water fuel mixture is fed to the reformer operating at 280 ºC where it is converted into hydrogen and carbon dioxide (CO_2). The reformed products, dubbed reformate, is then fed to the fuel cell stack and power is generated. The system only emits water, carbon dioxide and unconsumed air.

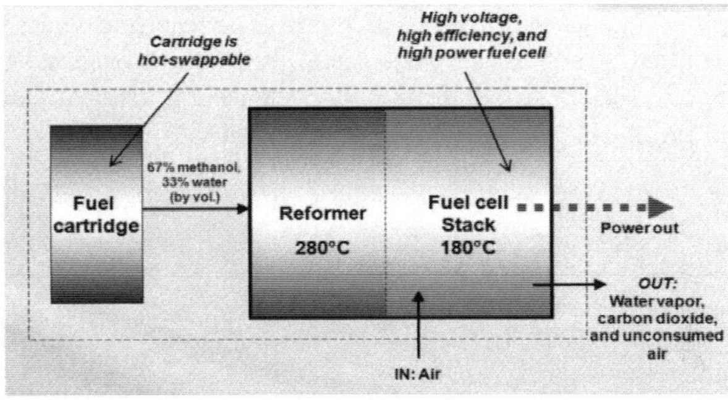

Figure 1. Schematic of UltraCell reformed methanol fuel cell technology. Hydrogen is produced in the reformer and fed to the stack for power generation

UltraCell utilizes high temperature PEM fuel cell stack technology that can operate up to 200 ºC. This technology allows the reformate stream to contain high percentage of carbon dioxide (CO) without experiencing a large performance penalty as often observed in low temperature PEM fuel cell.[3] This characteristic allows the stack to operate from a wide range of reformate products with high CO concentration.

Autothermal reforming (ATR) can also be used to process other hydrocarbon fuels such as propane and jet propellant JP-8[4]. Figure 2 shows the top level schematic of UltraCell fuel cell system with ATR fuel processor. The advantage of the ATR process compared to steam reforming is simpler fuel processor and faster startup time. The quality of the reformate products is adequate to operate UltraCell high temperature fuel cell stack.

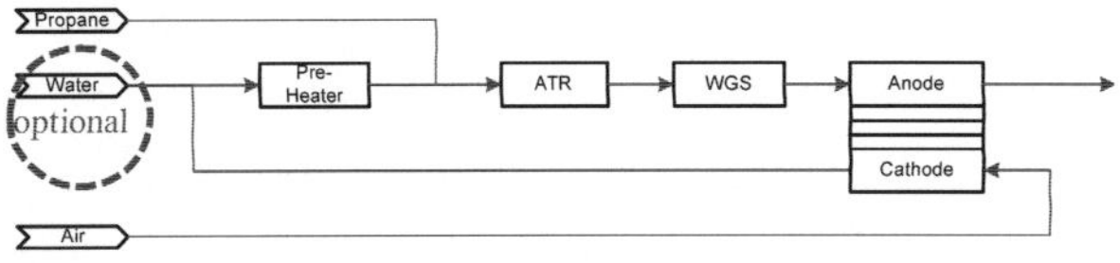

Figure 2. UltraCell ATR based fuel cell system schematic. The system fuel source can be propane or JP-8

Experimental Results

UltraCell high temperature fuel cell stack and single cell were tested with various reformate compositions for performance characterization. Figure 3 shows the single cell performance as function of current density for 165 cm^2 active area membrane electrode assembly (MEA) that can be easily replicated at the stack level under pure hydrogen (R1), 71% hydrogen stream (R2), and 25% hydrogen stream (R3). The cell operated at 170 °C cathode outlet temperature for CO concentration equal or less that 2.1% and steadily increased operating temperature as the CO concentration increased. The cell performances at 0.21 A/cm^2 (35A) under hydrogen R1, R2, and R3 were 630 mV, 600, and 580 mV, respectively. The results indicated that the fuel cell can produce power from various reformate sources with different hydrogen concentration without suffering a large performance penalty.

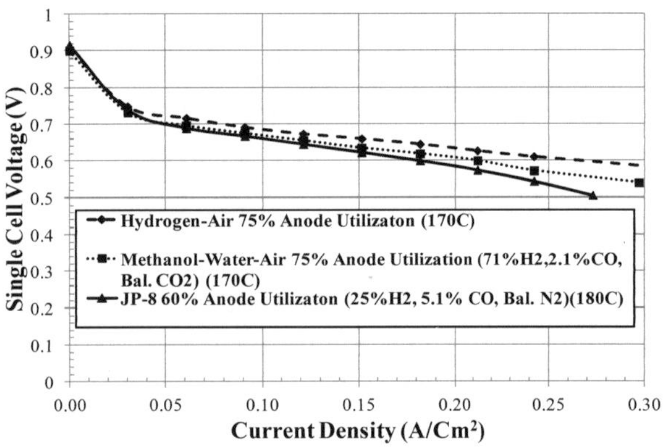

Figure 3. UltraCell high temperature single cell voltage as function of cell current density under hydrogen, 71% hydrogen reformate, and 25% hydrogen reformate. Cathode gas is air

An UltraCell 8-cells high temperature stack based on 45 cm^2 active area MEA was life tested to characterize its performance as a function of runtime. Figure 4 shows the stack's average cell voltage as function of runtime at 10A (0.22 A/cm^2 current density) under reformate with 71% hydrogen at 165 °C cathode outlet temperature. The stack ran over 4000 hours before falling below 80% of its initial voltage. The results showed that UltraCell high temperature stack is reliable and can be used with confidence.

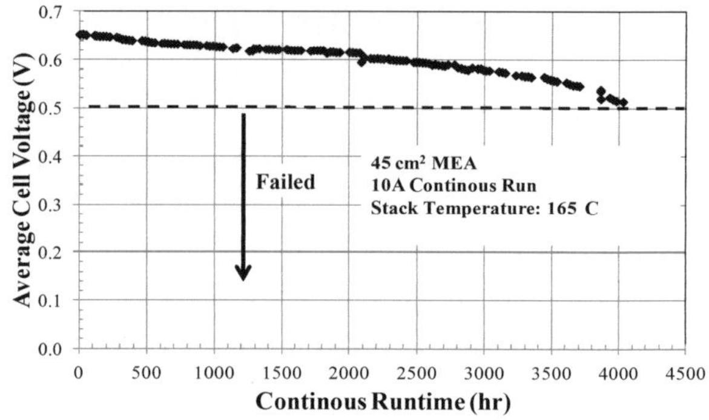

Figure 4. UltraCell 45 cm^2 MEA 8-cell stack average cell voltage as a function of runtime using 71% H_2 concentration reformate. Cell current is 10A. Anode and cathode utilizations are 75% and 45%, respectively. Cathode gas is air.

Products and Applications

UltraCell has developed several methanol based fuel cell systems that are currently in production. These systems are quiet and can operate from -20 °C to +50 °C ambient temperature without requiring any special heating kits or cooling schemes due to low freezing temperature of the methanol-water fuel mixture and high operating temperature of the fuel cell stack. Figure 5 shows UltraCell XX55™ and Blade fuel cell systems with a removable fuel cartridge. The fuel cells meet OSHA emission standard and can be operated indoor or outdoor.

The advantage of using UltraCell fuel cell over battery is that it can reduce the user weight burden over long runtime duration. The XX55™ has a dry weight of 3.0 kg and has a runtime of 11 hours at 40W using an UltraCell standard 550cc cartridge and can run continuously up to 13 days at 40W net output using UltraCell XRT-1000 12,500 Whr extended runtime cartridge.

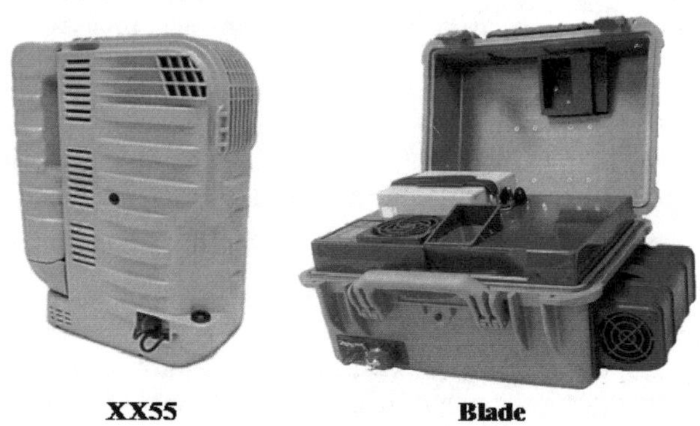

Figure 5. UltraCell XX55 fuel cell (left) and Blade fuel cell that can deliver continuously 50W and 165W net power output, respectively

UltraCell has developed several men wearable fuel cell products aimed to reduce soldier energy source weight burden. First is the XX25™ fuel cell that has a dry weight of 1.0 kg that is capable of outputting 25W continuously. Second is the XX55™ fuel cell that is capable of outputting 50W continuously as shown in Figure 6. These units are powered by methanol-water fuel mixture that can significantly reduce soldier energy weight burden on long missions. The fuel cells can be used to run an electronic load directly, hybrid with a battery, or charge battery. The systems have been tested under Military Standard 810.

Figure 6. UltraCell XX55™ fuel cell wore by a soldier

Fuel cells are excellent energy sources for remote and long runtime applications such as radio and satellite communications, laptops, and surveillance systems. The unit can be buried under ground via a snorkel system that hides the fuel cell from plain sight. Figure 7 shows UltraCell Blade fuel cell with the attached snorkel system. Air is drawn into the fuel cell system via the bellows from the left to drive the fuel cell system. The exhausted fuel cell product is discarded to the environment via the bellows on the right, leaving the fuel cell core fully buried. The snorkel fuel cell system operation is autonomous, quiet, and rugged.

Figure 7. UltraCell Blade fuel cell buried underground via a propriety snorkel system

Fuel cell powered UAV offers long loiter through the use of high energy density hydrocarbon based fuel such as JP-8 and the dash capability can be achieved through state of the art aerospace Li-ion batteries. The UAV energy source can be refilled quickly compared to batteries based system allowed for faster reemployment. The fuel cell is integrated directly into the air plane airframe from the get-go and power distribution to the payload, propulsion, batteries, auto pilot, digital data link (DDL) and control surfaces. Figure 8 shows a UAV concept that is currently being developed at UltraCell powered by JP-8 fuel. JP8 fuel is pumped into the reformer in which hydrogen is generated and fed to the fuel cell stack for power generation to drive onboard electronics. A high energy density lithium-ion battery is used to dash the plane during take-off.

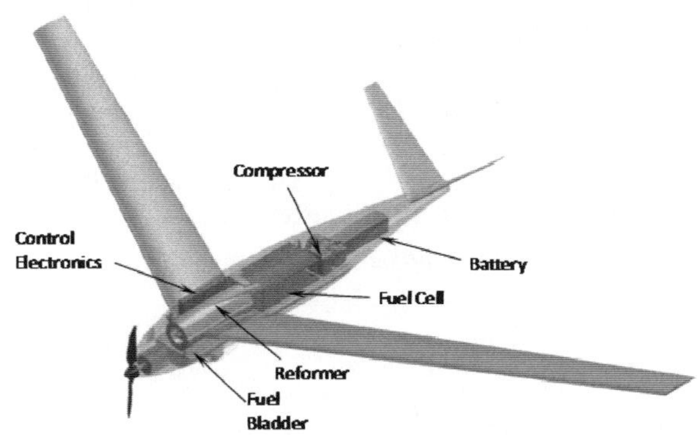

Figure 8. Unmanned aerial vehicle (UAV) powered by UltraCell fuel cell in which the fuel source is JP8

The UAV and its power system were designed for high speed dash and loiter. Table 1 summarizes the UAV design parameters and the associated performance metrics. The UAV is designed for 150 MPH dash speed in which the surge energy is supplied by an onboard high energy density lithium-ion battery pack that is capable of outputting peak power of more than 5 kW. The plane is designed for a loiter speed of 55 MPH in which the energy is supplied directly from the fuel cell. At a gross-take-off weight of 30 lbs, the plane has a flight endurance of 15 hours and an average cruising power of 600W.

Table 1: UltraCell UAV design parameters

Parameter	Rating
Speed	55 MPH Loiter, 150MPH Dash
Fuel	JP-8
Gross Take-off Weight	30 lbs
Average Cruise Power	600 W
Flight Duration	15 hours

Conclusion

Fuel cell technology has been proven to be a reliable and a clean energy source. Although pure hydrogen is an ideal fuel source for proton exchange membrane fuel cell, the fact that it is difficult to obtain and store makes it logistically undesirable. Hydrogen, however, can be obtained directly from existing hydrocarbon fuel sources such as methanol or JP-8 via steam and autothermal reforming, respectively. These reforming processes also generate production gases other than hydrogen such as carbon monoxide (CO) that can significantly reduce the performance of low temperature PEM. UltraCell high temperature PEMFC solves these problems. The XX55 and Blade fuel cell systems utilizes the methanol-water fuel mixture to generate hydrogen-rich reformate stream on-the-fly where it is fed to the fuel cell stack for power generation. A similar fuel cell system is designed in which hydrogen is generated from propane or JP-8 fuel via the autothermal reforming process. UltraCell fuel cell has a wide range of applications including remote communication and unmanned aerial vehicle (UAV). The system can be deeply buried underground for quiet and long duration operation. UltraCell technology allows long UAV flight duration via the JP-8 fuel source.

Acknowledgement

The authors wish to thank the U.S Army and U.S Air Force for their supports in developing the fuel cell systems.

References

1. Larminie, J. and A. Dicks, “Fuel Cell Systems Explained,” John Wiley & Sons: Chichester, England (2000).
2. Peppley, B.A., J. C. Amphlett and R. F. Mann, in “Handbook of Fuel Cells – Fundamentals, Technology and Applications,” Vol. 3, W. Vielstich, H. A. Gasteiger, A. Lamm, Editors, Chapter 11, John Wiley & Sons (2003).
3. Seel, D.C., B.C. Benicewicz, L. Xiao, T.J. Schmidt, in “Handbook of Fuel Cells-Fundamentals, Technology and Applications”, Vol 5. W. Vielstich, H. Yokokawa, H.A. Gasteiger Editors, Chapter 19, John Wiley & Sons (2010).
4. Baumann, F., W. Wieland, M. Himmen, D.W. Agar, in “Handbook of Fuel Cells – Fundamentals, Technology and Applications,” Vol. 3, W. Vielstich, H. A. Gasteiger, A. Lamm, Editors, Chapter 19, John Wiley & Sons (2003).

Synthesis of ZnO-Based Materials for H_2S Desulfurization

Dat T. Tran and Charles Rong
U.S. Army Research Laboratory, Sensor & Electron Devices Directorate
2800 Powder Mill Road
Adelphi, MD 20783
dat.t.tran4.civ@mail.mil; charles.c.rong.civ@mail.mil

Abstract: *Pure and transition metal-doped ZnO materials are synthesized by hydrogel method. The structure and morphology of the as-synthesized ZnO materials are characterized by X-ray diffraction (XRD), Scanning Electron Microscope (SEM) and BET surface area measurements. The performance of H_2S desulfurization of these metal oxide materials versus commercial ZnO in a simulated fuel processing gas mixture is studied at 430°C with the initial H_2S concentration slightly above 400 ppmv. The results show that the as-synthesized materials perform much better than the commercial ZnO. The characteristics of H_2S adsorption capacity of these materials will be discussed.*

Keywords: Hydrogel; ZnO; H_2S, desulfurization; metal oxide.

Introduction

One of the challenges of making pure hydrogen for Army fuel cell applications from military jet fuels through logistic fuel reformation is gas phase H_2S desulfurization. Gas phase removal of H_2S is an essential step for proper fuel processing and fuel cell operations. The H_2S gas is not only harmful to the environment but also to the reformer and fuel cell catalysts. Therefore, development of effective sorbent materials for removal of H_2S is a key aspect for this technology to advance.

In the past years, researchers have explored lanthanum oxide-based H_2S sorbents for high temperature fuel cell applications such as molten carbonate fuel cell (MCFC) and solid oxide fuel cell (SOFC) systems [1-2]. Recently, a review reported by Jung et al. focused on a study of Zn-based sorbent materials for H_2S removal in the Integrated Gasification Combined Cycle (IGCC) at a wide range of temperatures from 400 – 700°C [3]. This technology presents benefits of both lower cost power generation and lower emissions than conventional power plants with fuel gas desulfurization process. Other studies on the removal of H_2S were performed by using three-dimensionally ordered macroporous iron oxide at 300 – 350°C [4], as well as those focused on the removal of H_2S from biogas [5-8].

In a previous study, we developed silica-based materials for liquid phase JP-8 fuel desulfurization of organic sulfur compounds [9]. In this paper, we report our current approach using hydrogel as a template to prepare 3D network and porous zinc oxide-based sorbents for the removal of H_2S. The synthesis, characterization, and preliminary study of H_2S removal with these sorbents will be discussed.

Experimental

All chemicals were used as received from Sigma-Aldrich. Pure form of ZnO and Ni-doped ZnO were synthesized using hydrogel as a template. A solution of 0.045M $Zn(NO_3)_2{\cdot}6H_2O$ with hydrogel (2%) was prepared by dissolving zinc nitrate in deionized water followed by addition of hydrogel. The solution was slowly heated to boiling. After the solution became clear, it was transferred to a Petri dish and allowed to cool down to room temperature overnight forming a gel. The solid gel was cut into many small pieces and placed in a crucible for calcination. It was heated to 600°C at a ramp rate of 0.4°C/min and held at 600°C for 5h in the presence of air.

Sorbent sulfidation tests were carried out at 430°C in a down flow packed-bed quartz-tube reactor (inner diameter of 1.0 cm) with a total amount of 0.10g sorbent under the pressure slightly higher than atmospheric pressure. All gases used in the experiment (to simulate processed fuel steam composition) were from Airgas with analytical grade. The incoming gas mixture stream composed of 51% H_2, 30% He, 10% water, 8% CO_2, and 8% H_2S containing gas cylinder (a mixture of 0.05% H_2S balanced with 99.5% He) at the rate of 100 ml/min. The H_2S level in the exit from sorbent column was recorded by sulfur analyzer continuously in real time. Water was removed by a condenser before the analyzer.

Phase(s) of samples determined by powder x-ray diffraction (PXRD) were obtained from a Rigaku Ultima III instrument with CuKα radiation (λ = 1.5418 Å) using a Bragg-Brentano Configuration. The measurements were conducted with scan rate of 1.0 degree (2θ) per minute and each diffraction data point was collected at the interval of 0.02 degree (2θ) for the total spectrum range of 20 to 80 degree (2θ). The morphology of the sorbent materials was examined using a FEI QUANTA 200 F scanning electron microscope (SEM). The Brunauer, Emmett and Teller (BET) surface areas of the sorbent samples were measured with a Micromeritics TriStar II (TriStar II 3020 V1.03) Analyzer using N_2 gas as the adsorbate at 77.3°K. Adsorption/desorption isotherm measurements were collected in the relative pressure range P/Po from 0.05 to 1.0. The samples were de-gassed at 200°C prior to the adsorption analysis.

Results and Discussion

A pure ZnO sorbent was synthesized using hydrogel as a template. As shown in Figure 1, the PXRD pattern of commercial ZnO (blue) and ZnO as-synthesized are exactly the same as pure phase of ZnO (PDF # 01-089-0510). The broadened line width of as-synthesized ZnO in the PXRD patterns also indicates that the crystallite size should be smaller, which is confirmed by SEM below. Additionally, we found that when 4 wt% of Ni was doped in ZnO (green), the structure of ZnO is still predominant, except for very small NiO peaks that are indexed at around $2\theta = 37°$ and 43° (PDF # 01-089-7390), indicating NiO as identifiable entity that may well be dispersed within the ZnO structure.

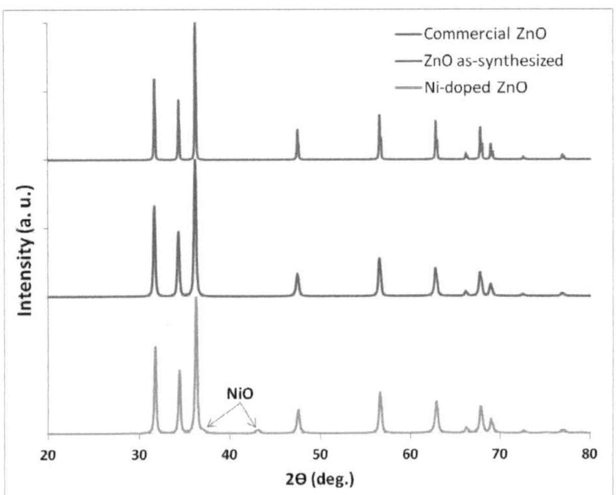

Figure 1. The PXRD patterns of commercial ZnO (blue), ZnO as-synthesized (red), and ZnO doped with 4% wt. Ni (green).

Figure 2 shows the SEM images of commercial ZnO (top) and ZnO as-synthesized (bottom). The former has a plate-like morphology, whereas the latter consists of a 3D network with a highly porous structure. The morphology of ZnO doped with Ni has the same porous structure as the bottom image of ZnO as-synthesized (data will be published elsewhere after further investigation).

Surface areas of these sorbent materials were also examined by BET measurement. The commercial ZnO has a low surface area of 1.5 m^2/g, while the pure ZnO as-synthesized has a much higher surface area of 10.2 m^2/g. The higher surface area of this sorbent material can be attributed to its high degree of porosity through the entire structure. When ZnO was doped with Ni, the surface area was reduced to 6.8 m^2/g, but still retains high porosity and porous morphology.

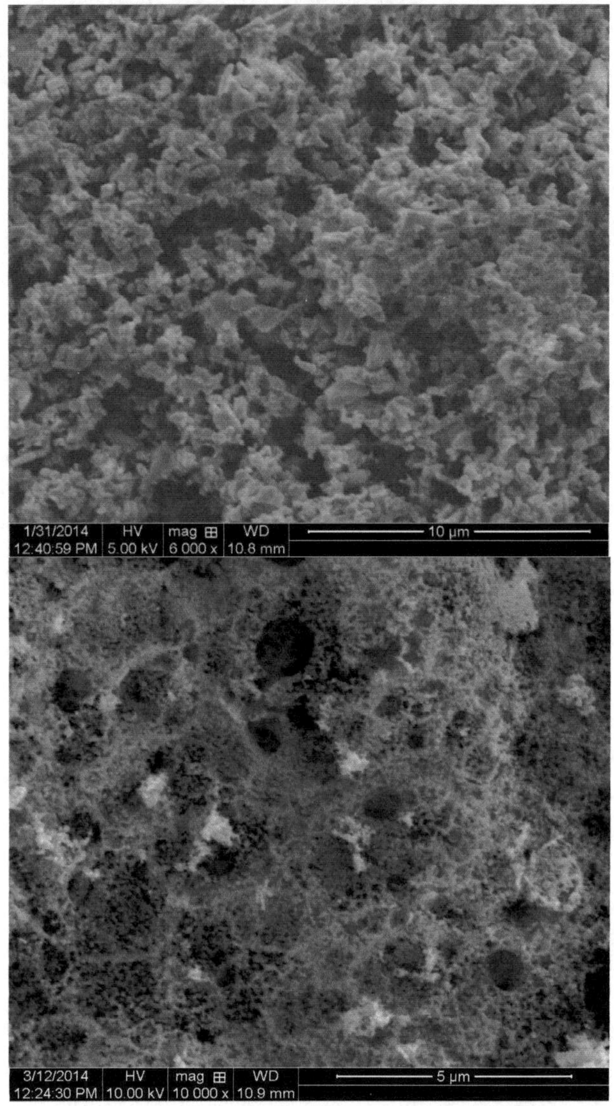

Figure 2. The SEM images of commercial ZnO (top) and porous ZnO as-synthesized (bottom).

The sulfidation capacity of the samples is defined as the milligrams of sulfur absorbed per gram of adsorbent as (mgS/g). Figure 3 shows the experimental sulfur removal results obtained by 0.1g of adsorbents at 430°C with incoming H_2S concentration of 400ppm as one of the simulated reformate gas conditions (water, H_2S, H_2, He, and CO_2). From the experimental data, it was possible to determine the sulfur capacity by integrating under the curve of sulfur removal data and normalizing per unit mass. The results show that commercial ZnO has a low sulfur removal capacity of 245.2 mgS/g; whereas ZnO as-synthesized has much higher sulfur uptake capacity of 457.3 mgS/g. Moreover, when ZnO was doped with Ni, the sulfur uptake capacity of this sample was even further improved with a capacity at least at 592.0 mgS/g level. This improvement can be attributed to the addition of a small amount of Ni (4 wt%) doped in the ZnO structure. We also noted that when ZnO was doped with more than 4 wt% of Ni, the sulfur removal capacity was decreased to about 300 mgS/g. Further investigation on the doping effect is underway.

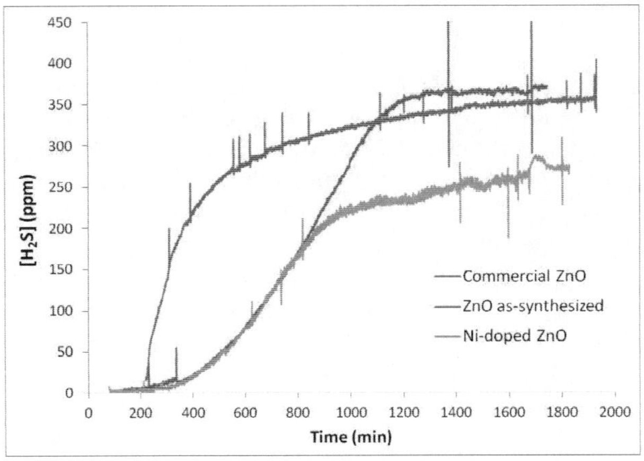

Figure 3. Plot of H_2S concentration outlet as a function of time for commercial ZnO (Blue), ZnO as-synthesized (red), and 4% weight of Ni doped in ZnO (green).

The samples after sulfur adsorption were examined with PXRD and found that pure ZnO reacted with H_2S yielding ZnS ($ZnO + H_2S = ZnS + H_2O$), whereas a mixture of products of ZnS and NiS was formed with Ni doped ZnO sample.

Conclusion

Pure phase of ZnO was synthesized by using hydrogel as a template. This approach enables us to create a 3D networked and highly porous sorbent materials. The results show that the sulfur removal capacity of ZnO as-synthesized is almost doubled compared to commercial ZnO. Moreover, when ZnO was doped with 4 wt% of Ni, the sulfur removal capacity was increased further.

References

1. Valsamakis, I.; Si, R.; Flytzani-Stephanopoulos, M., *J. Power Sources*, **2010**, *195*, 2815-2822.
2. Rong, C.; Jiang, R.; Chu, D., U.S. Pat., No. 8,465,712 B2, **2013**.
3. Jung, S.Y.; Lee, S.C; Jun, H. K., *Catal. Surv. Asia*, **2013**, *17*, 85-102.
4. Fan, H.L.; Sun, T.; Zhao, Y.P.; Shangguan, J.; Lin, J.Y., *Environ. Sci. Technol.*, **2013**, *47*, 4859-4865.
5. Monteleone, G.; Francesco, M.D.; Galli, S.; Marchetti, M.; Naticchioni, V., *Chemical Engineering J.*, **2011**, *173*, 407-414.
6. Hussain, M.; Abbas, N.; Fino, D.; Russo, N., *Chemical Engineering J.*, **2012**, *188*, 222-232.
7. Ramos, I.; Perez, R.; Fdz-Polanco, M., *Bioresource Technology*, **2013**, *142*, 633-640.
8. Micoli, L.; Bagnasco, G.; Turco, M., Langmuir, *Int. J. Hydrogen Energy*, **2014**, *39*, 1783-1787.
9. Tran, D.T.; Dunbar, Z.W.; Chu, D., *Int. J. Hydrogen Energy*, **2012**, *37*, 10430-10434.

An Electrochemical Model and Experimental Analysis of Alkaline Water Electrolysis

Md Opu and Po-Ya Abel Chuang
School of Engineering Technology
Purdue University
West Lafayette, Indiana, USA, 47907

Abstract: *This work aims to develop experimental method and analytical model of alkaline water electrolysis. The 1-D water electrolysis model captures fundamental mechanisms inside a water electrolyzer to predict experimental data. The model includes components that cover thermodynamics, kinetics, ohmic and mass transfer calculations. The ohmic and kinetics parameters are estimated from the experimental data fitting. Experimental results will be presented and compared with the model prediction. The experimental data fitting will provide the estimated values of some important process parameters and their trend at different electrolyte concentrations. The methods to estimate Tafel slope, exchange current density and reaction order of HER and OER separately will be developed and presented during oral presentation.*

Keywords: Electrochemical model; experimental analysis; alkaline water electrolysis; kinetic parameters;

Introduction

Hydrogen is an important energy source for sustainable development and is believed as safe for commonly used fuels [1]. Hydrogen can be produced from water via different existing technology like photo-catalysis, thermochemical cycles, and water electrolysis [2]. These methods offer renewable and clean production of hydrogen fuel and, therefore, have attracted increasing research interests in recent years. Among these technologies, water electrolysis is the most promising technology for large-scale hydrogen production. However, a significant challenge exists for water electrolysis, which is to improve its efficiency, which in turn reduces energy consumption at high hydrogen production rate.

The driving force of chemical reactions in water electrolysis is electrical energy. By passing a current through electrodes in a solution of water and electrolytes, water molecules (H_2O) decompose to hydrogen (H_2) and oxygen (O_2) gas through an electrochemical reaction. There have been various attempts to improve efficiency and reduce energy consumption of water electrolysis process, such as development of new cell geometry, electrocatalytic materials for electrodes, etc [3]. In contrast, a more popular way of improving electrolysis efficiency is increasing the process temperature, which lowers the voltage required to electrolyze the water.

The objective of this research is to develop a reliable water electrolysis experimental method, show the theoretical model, which has been developed to understand the experimental polarization curve, and to fit the experimental data to estimated the kinetics, ohmic parameters. LeRoy et al [4] developed a water electrolysis model, which allows estimation of the different contributions to cell voltage of the reversible potential, of electrode and ionic ohmic resistance and of the electrode overvoltage. Very few papers have been published to investigate the bubble phenomena, which contributes very significant amount of voltage losses at high current density. Mandin et al presented the work of modeling and the numerical simulation of the local gas production at an industrial scale vertical electrode. According their findings, bubbles modify electricity, species and heat transport and there is strong connection between all these phenomena. One of our efforts will be to find experimental fitting parameters that can estimate the mass transfer effect due to bubble disturbance.

Experimental Setup

Water electrolysis is the decomposition of water into oxygen and hydrogen gas due to an electric current being passed through the water between two electrodes separated by an aqueous electrolyte with good ionic conductivity. For electrolysis process, two electrochemical reactions are occurring simultaneously as listed below for acid electrolyzer (1) and Alkaline electrolyzer (2):

$$\text{Anode: } H_2O \rightarrow 2H^+ + 2e^- + \tfrac{1}{2}O_2; \quad \text{Cathode: } 2H^+ + 2e^- \rightarrow H_2 \tag{1}$$

$$\text{Anode: } 2OH^- \rightarrow H_2O + \tfrac{1}{2}O_2 + 2e^-; \quad \text{Cathode: } 2H_2O + 2e^- \rightarrow H_2 + 2OH^- \tag{2}$$

Based on this principle of water electrolysis, our experimental alkaline water electrolyzer was constructed for baseline experiment with 200 ml, 0.4 M potassium hydroxide (KOH) electrolyte. Each electrode was made up of a 5 cm long, 0.5 mm diameter straight platinum wire, with a 2 cm length submerged in KOH solution. The two electrodes were kept 1 cm apart. The electrodes were connected to a DC power supply (BK Precision Model 9130). The geometric surface area of electrode in electrolyte was calculated to be about 0.316 cm^2. A mercury thermometer was used to monitor the temperature of the electrolyte during testing. A hotplate stirrer is used in purpose of homogeneous distribution of reactant to the catalyst surface sites for faster reaction kinetics during experiments. Figure 1 illustrates the experimental setup for water electrolysis including electrolyte, battery (power supply) and electrodes (cathode and anode).

Our first experimental design approach was to optimize the parameters that contribute the performance discrepancy. After optimizing all the parameters and getting reproducible data we constructed a well-established baseline or control experiment. Figure 2 represents the baseline experimental set-up.

Experimental Results and Discussion

Parametric studies were conducted to investigate the key parameters effect on cell performance. We used only platinum throughout our experiments and it is considered to have the fastest kinetics for hydrogen evolution reaction rate. We used data at 60, 80 and 100 sec and average the data for any specific current density. The experimental condition for the baseline experiments is atmospheric pressure and room temperature with stir-bar rotation setting of 3. It consists with simple straight design of two platinum wires as anode and cathode apart from each other precisely 1 cm and submerged approximately 2 cm in the center of the biker containing 200 ml of 0.4 M KOH solution. To investigate the key parametric effect, the controllable parameters and their effect on reversible voltage, kinetic, ohmic and mass transport losses of water electrolysis performance are shown in Table 1.

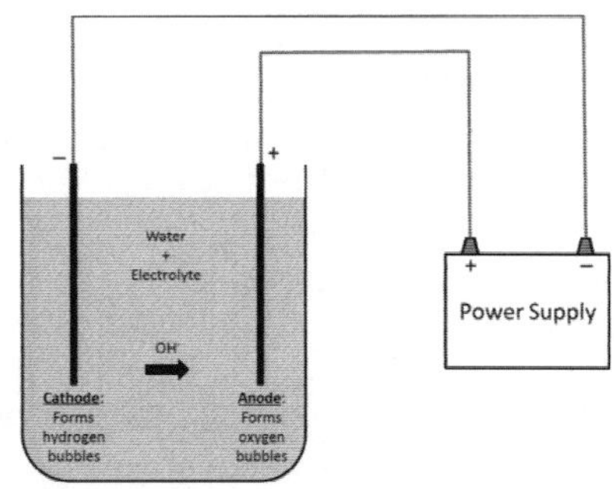

Figure 1. Illustration of water electrolysis setup

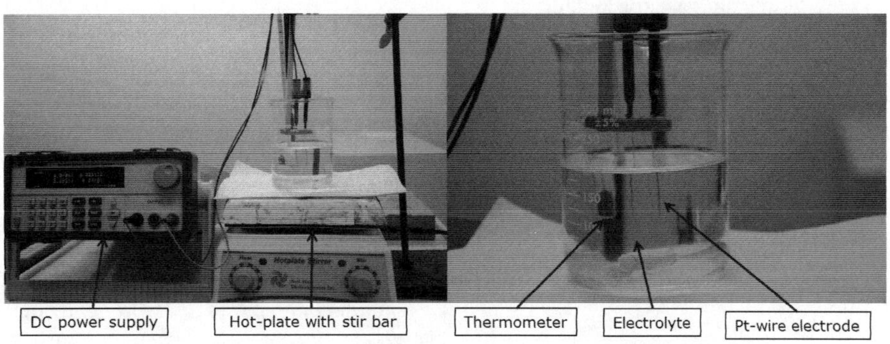

Figure 2. Design of experimental setup for baseline experiment.

Table 1. Controllable parameters and their effect in electrolysis performances.

Parameters	Reversible Voltage	Kinetic Loss	Ion Transport Loss	Mass Transport Loss
1. Stir-bar rotation		×	×	×
2. Electrode location in beaker			×	
3. Electrolyte volume			×	
4. Electrode submerged length		×		
5. Electrode distance			×	×
6. Electrolyte concentration			×	
7. Operating T	×	×	×	

Figure 3 shows the results of 6 baseline tests and the data are relatively repeatable. Based on experimental design represented in Table 1, several experiments were conducted to know the parametric effects on cell performance. Data shows that no detectable differences can be observed at different stir-bar setting, electrode placement inside the biker, electrolyte volume and electrode submerged length inside electrolyte.

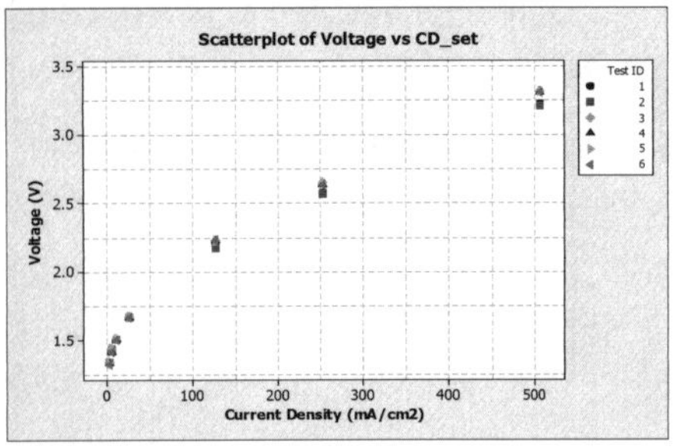

Figure 3. Results of test reproducibity from 6 baseline data set

Distance between anode and cathode electrode affects the electrolyte resistance. The longer the distance between the electrodes, the tougher the situation should be for OH- ions to move from one electrode to another and releases its electron. When the space between the pair of electrodes decreases, the performance of the cell increases due to the resulting decreases in electrical resistance between the electrodes that in turn leads to an increase in the electrical current. Figure 4 shows the results and as expected, the ion transport resistance increases with electrode distance.

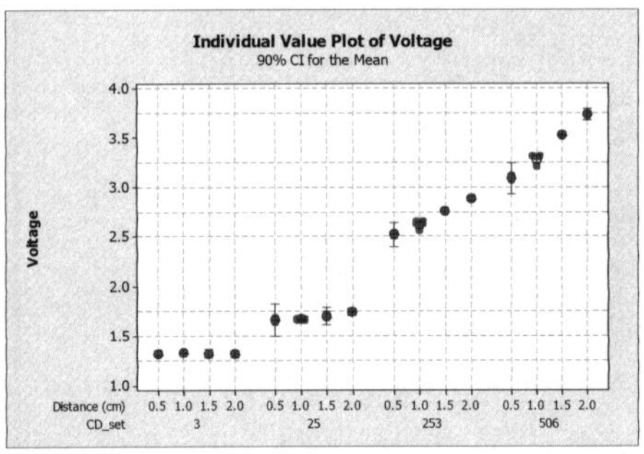

Figure 4. Effect of distance between electrodes.

The ohmic performance of water electrolysis is expected to be strongly dependent on concentration of the electrolyte solution. The higher concentration means that higher number of available reactants at the electrode surface for reaction at the same power input which leads to increase in hydrogen production efficiency. Electrolyte concentrations were studied at 0.1, 0.2 and 0.4 M. Figure 5 shows the result and confirms as expected, the ion conductivity increases with electrolyte concentration. This behavior is attributed to the increase in the electrical conductivity of the solution due to the increase in the concentration of the potassium hydroxide. Increasing the electrical conductivity leads to an increase in the electrical current passing through the solution and consequently to a decrease of requirement of less voltage at same current density operation.

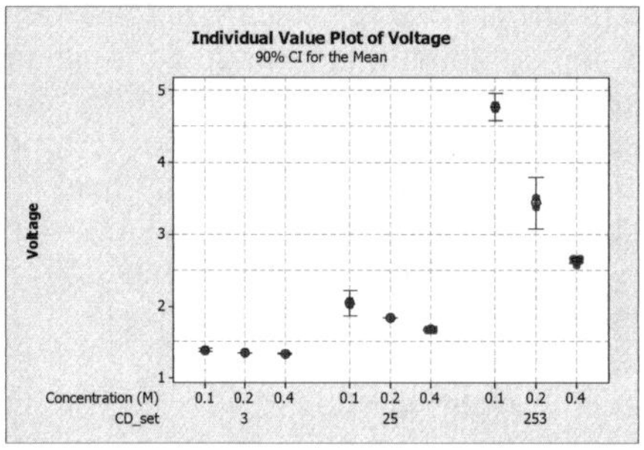

Figure 5. Impact of electrolyte concentration on cell performance.

Analytical model description

The development of a 1-D analytical model was initiated. It is built on an Excel platform. The performance of electrolysis cells are typically compared by plotting their polarization curves, which is obtained by plotting the cell voltage against the current density. The primary sources of increased voltage over reversible potential, which corresponds to a zero reaction rate, may include ohmic loss of electrolyte, overvoltage associated with oxygen and hydrogen evolution reactions, and voltage losses due to mass transfer resistance resulting from bubble interaction formed by O_2 and H_2 gas in anode and cathode surfaces respectively. Both overvoltage and ohmic loss increase with the increasing current density.

The enthalpy energy required for this endothermic reaction is: $\Delta H_r^o = 286.03$ kJ/mol. Since the Gibbs free energy, ΔG^o, is the key to the work potential of a reaction, it is necessary to determine ΔG^o:

$$\Delta G^o = \Delta H_r^o - T\Delta S^o \qquad (3)$$

where ΔS^o is the change of entropy and T is the temperature in Kelvin. In other words, the total reaction enthalpy energy required comprises of work potential (ΔG^o) and thermal energy ($T\Delta S^o$). The minimum necessary cell voltage to start water electrolysis is the reversible potential, which can be calculated by Gibbs free energy and it is 1.23V at 25°C. The reversible potential termed as OCV (open circuit potential) is temperature and pressure dependent and can be simplified by the equation (4) at below. The cell potential (E_{cell}) for the electrolysis of water expressed by equation (5) is calculated considering reversible potential (E_{rev}), potential gain due to hydrogen evolution reaction (η_{HER}) and oxygen evolution reaction (η_{OER}), electron conduction resistance (R_e-), hydroxyl ion conduction resistance ($R_{OH}-$), and mass transfer resistance (η_{mx})

$$E_{rev} = E_{rev}^0 + \frac{\Delta S}{nF}(T - T_0) + \frac{RT}{nF} ln\left(\frac{a_{H_2}a_{O_2}^{0.5}}{a_w}\right) \qquad (4)$$

$$E_{cell} = E_{rev} + \eta_{OER} + |\eta_{HER}| + i\times(R_e- + R_{OH}-) + \eta_{mx} \qquad (5)$$

Using Tafel approximation the cathode overpotential caused by hydrogen evolution reaction can be calculated by cathodic Tafel slope (b_c), current density (i), exchange current density ($i_{o,\mathrm{HER}}$). Similarly, the anode overpotential caused by oxygen evolution reaction can be calculated by anodic Tafel slope (b_a), current density (i), exchange current density ($i_{o,\mathrm{OER}}$)

$$|\eta_{HER}| = b_c\, log_{10}\left(\frac{i}{i_{o,HER}}\right) \quad (6)$$

$$\eta_{OER} = b_a\, log_{10}\left(\frac{i}{i_{o,OER}}\right) \quad (7)$$

The resistance from OH^- conduction depends on electrode distance, electrolyte concentration: and can be calculated as:

$$R_{OH^-} = \frac{d}{k_{OH^-}} \quad (8)$$

Where $k_{OH^-}$is hydroxyl conductivity (S/cm) in electrolyte solution, which depends strongly on type of electrolyte and electrolyte concentration; d is the distance between two electrodes.

The mass transfer losses might happen due to hydrogen and oxygen bubble formation, which block the available electrode reaction surface and add the resistance for hydroxyl ions transport from bulk electrolyte to electrode surface. Hydrogen and oxygen gas bubbles are continuously formed during electrolysis process on the anode and cathode electrode surfaces respectively and removed from the surfaces when they grow big enough. The increased number of gas bubbles can adversely hinder the contact between electrolyte and electrode, which ultimately pose the mass transfer limitation. The presence of bubbles electrode surfaces adds extra resistance to electrode surface electrochemical reaction. These phenomena increase with increasing cell current. Mass transfer limitation due to bubble coverage on electrode surface needs to consider quantitatively though measurement is extremely difficult.

O_2 and H_2 bubbles due to OER and HER reduce the available geometric reaction surface of anode and cathode electrode respectively which leads to increase in current density. This effective current density due to surface coverage by bubble increases the activation overpotential, which ultimately results in increase of cell potential. Mass transfer voltage losses can be expresses as:

$$\eta_{mx} = -b_a log\left(\frac{A_{eff-OER}}{A_{std}}\right) - b_c log\left(\frac{A_{eff-HER}}{A_{std}}\right) \quad (9)$$

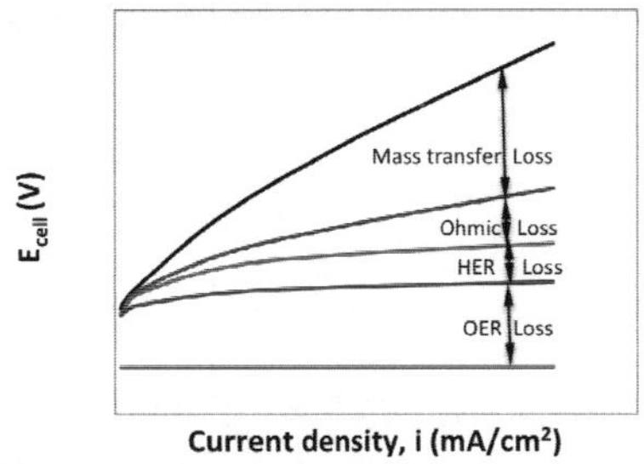

Figure 6. cell voltage distribution from reversible cell potential to various losses of kinetic, ohmic and mass transfer

Discussion

Figure 6 shows a typical experimental cell voltage analyses and voltage losses due to kinetic, ohmic and mass transfer resistances. The methods will be developed to estimate the kinetic parameters Tafel slopes and exchange current density and ohmic parameter electrolyte conductivity from the experimental data fitting. Our expectation is that the developed model based on these parameters will be able to predict the experimental cell voltage distribution as represented by Figure 6.

Acknowledgements

The authors wish to thank ALDI far-IR products for their financial support to carry this project.

References

1. Gardner D. Hydrogen production from renewables. Renewable Energy Focus. 2009;9:34-7.
2. Schulte I, Hart D, Van der Vorst R. Issues affecting the acceptance of hydrogen fuel. International Journal of Hydrogen Energy. 2004;29:677-85.
3. Zoulias E, Varkaraki E, Lymberopoulos N, Christodoulou CN, Karagiorgis GN. A review on water electrolysis. TCJST. 2004;4:41-71.
4. LeRoy R, Janjua M, Renaud R, Leuenberger U. Analysis of Time-Variation Effects in Water Electrolyzers. Journal of The Electrochemical Society.
5. Mandin P, Aissa AA, Roustan H, Hamburger J, Picard G. Two-phase electrolysis process: From the bubble to the electrochemical cell properties. Chemical Engineering and Processing: Process Intensification. 2008;47:1926-

Development of Low-temperature and High-rate Lithium-ion Cells for LMAMS Munition*

Zhiqiang Xu*, Zhiwei Zhang and Chul Chai
SKC Powertehc, Inc.
Mt. Olive, New Jersey

William J. McMahan, Spencer L Hudson, Steven B. Andrews and Steven E. Horn
U.S. Army, Aviation and Missile Research, Development, and Engineering Center (AMRDEC)
Redstone Arsenal, AL

Abstract: *This work was performed under a contract supported by U.S. Army, Aviation and Missile Research, Development, and Engineering Center (AMRDEC) to develop low-temperature high rate lithium-ion polymer batteries for LMAMS munitions (small UAV). Existing batteries are bulky and heavy, particularly do not work at low temperatures, e.g. below 0℃. Through extensive research work on electrode (both cathode and anode), separator, electrolyte and new cell design technology under this contract, we have produced prototype cells which delivered dramatically higher power at both low and high temperatures. Moreover, these cells also have an energy density as high as ~210Wh/kg, which is 17~20% higher than the existing cells.*

Keywords: High power; high energy; Li-ion cell; low-temperature operation; LMAMS munitions; UAV.

Introduction

The Army's Lethal Miniature Aerial Munitions System (LMAMS) is a type of small UAV. The power system for such a UAV needs a battery to ensure necessary duration and peak power capabilities over a wide operating temperature range. Existing batteries are bulky and heavy, which severely limits the payload and maneuverability of small UAVs. In particular, their lack of high power capabilities after low temperature soaking has limited their use in training and/or combat missions, causing field use issues. The objective of this work is to develop and produce prototype cells for such UVA being capable of high-rate discharge from cold soak and continual discharge at lower rates without dropping below the minimum voltage requirement during the operation.

The objectives of this program were to identify the limiting factors of high rate (fast discharge) at a wide temperature range for the polymer Li-ion pouch cells, and to develop electrodes, electrolytes, new design and processes to maximize power performance at low temperatures.

The power system for such systems and munitions needs a battery to ensure necessary duration and peak power capabilities over a wide operating temperature range. Specifically, cells for such UAV systems should deliver at least 1.9Ah (0.2C) and should be able to discharge at 12C (pulse current) with 3.0V cut-off at low temperature (down to -32°C) to 60°C. Most critically the cells require a Gravimetric Energy Density as high as 190Wh/Kg and a Volumetric Energy Density as high as 380 Wh/L.

Experimental

$LiCoO_2$ and/or $LiMn_2O_4$ were used as cathode materials. Modified graphite and/or graphene nano-platelets were served as anode materials. Electrode fabrication utilized slurry-coating technology with either polyvinylidene fluoride (PVDF) or Styrene Butadiene Rubber (SBR) as binder. Electrolyte solutions used in this work generally consisted of one or two Lithium salts dissolved in two to four solvents. Additive Lithium salts were made in-house. Solutions were prepared in a dry room (<1% humidity) and transferred to a glove box, inside which the salt and polymer gelling agents were added before use. All the separators used in this project were either polyethylene (PE) or polypropylene (PP) with a thickness of 7um~16um and porosity 40~50%, which were obtained from various vendors including SKC Co. Ltd.

Cells had a format of 6.0mm x 50mm x60mm (TxWxH) based on SKCP's pouch type design. The existing design employed a stacking process, in which electrodes were sandwiched in a Z-folded one-piece separator. Electrodes were vacuum-dried for at least 5 hours at 65°C-85°C prior to and after the assembly. Inside the glove box, electrolyte was injected into the pouch to activate the cells. After allowing enough time to have electrodes and separator fully wetted, the cells were gelled at elevated temperatures, pre-charged, degassed, formed and aged. All cells were formed and tested on either Maccor 4000 or Arbin BT-2000.

---

* DISTRIBUTION A - Approved for public release; distribution unlimited. Review completed by the AMRDEC Public Affairs Office (9APR2014, Control No. PR0904)

Results and Discussion

Table 1 lists some UAV cell specifications. In particular, cells for such UAV systems shall deliver at least 1.9Ah (0.2C) and shall be able to discharge following a Discharging Protocol: pulse current 23A (12C) for 10 seconds then mission in 27W (>4C) with 3.0V cut-off at low temperatures (down to -32°C) to 60°C. The cells require 40g in weight and 6.0mm(T) x 50mm(W) x 60mm(H) (605060) in dimension, corresponding to a Gravimetric Energy Density as high as 190Wh/Kg and a Volumetric Energy Density as high as 380 Wh/L. One of the critical requirements is that the discharge cut-off shall be 3.0V even at low temperatures with high power operation.

Table 1. Requirement of UAV Cell Specifications

Item	Specification
Cell Dimensions	Thickness: 6.0mm max after initial full charge
	Width: 50.0 +/- 0.3 mm
	Height: 60.0 +1.5/-0.0 mm
Nominal Capacity	1900 mAh minimum @ 0.2C discharge rate
Charging Voltage	4.2V
Nominal Voltage	3.7V
Discharge Cut-off Voltage	3.0V
Cell Weight	40 g max

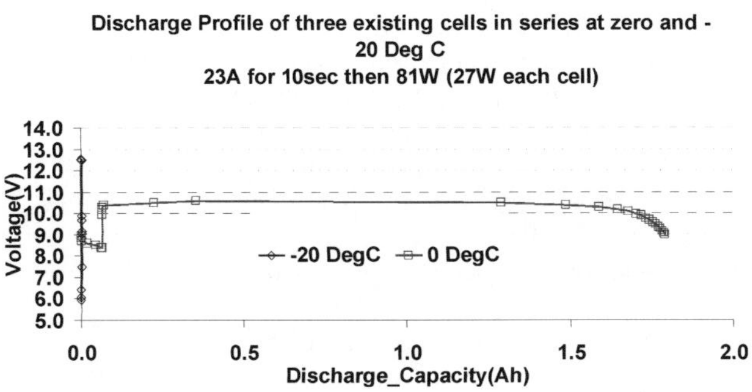

Figure 1. Discharging profile of 3-existing cells in series at 0 and -20°C, 23A pulse discharge for 10 seconds (7.5V cut-off) then constant power (81W, 27W each cell) discharge to 9V

The existing cell delivered 1.84Ah (C/4) at room-temperature, which is close to the required capacity. However, the cell did not work based on the discharging protocol when temperature goes to below 0°C (**Figure 1.**)

Table 2. UAV cell basic parameters and performance comparison

Cell Type (605060)	Existing cell	SKCP Cells		
		Baseline	Regularly-designed	Newly-designed
Thickness(mm)	6.14	6.45	6.35	5.85
Weight(g)	>37.0	37.9	40.4	39.7
Capacity(Ah) at C/4	1.840	1.952	1.976	2.156
Energy (Whr)	7.021	7.455	7.566	8.283
Gravimetric Energy Density(Wh/Kg)	189.8	196.7	187.3	208.6
Volumetric Energy Density(Wh/L)	381.2	385.3	397.2	472.0

Before this project, we have demonstrated high power capabilities in smaller cells (0.2-0.5Ahs/cell), which cold be discharged at rates up to 30C. These cells exhibited high power densities of 4200W/kg and 6600W/L when discharged at 30C-rate continuously, but with reduced performance at lower temperatures. We also have developed new salts and corresponding low temperature electrolytes. These novel electrolytes can significantly increase the power capability at low temperatures as demonstrated in the discharge of a 100wh section of BB2590 battery at 75W, 200W and 300W. It showed that at 2C (200W) and -32°C soaking, the battery could be discharged without cut-off (2.2V/cell). Combined those hands-on technologies, we have made SKCP baseline UAV cells (**Table** 2). Compared to existing cells, the baseline cells showed much better power performance especially at low-temperatures (**Figure 3** and **5**). However, like the existing cells, those baseline cells are far from meeting the requirements for the UAV application in terms of their thickness and low-temperature performance.

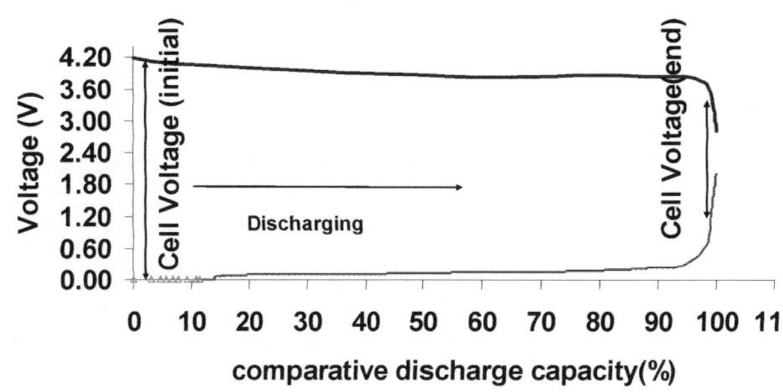

Figure 2. Schematic view of new design concept for SKCP UAV cells. Anode is a composite of carbon (graphite) and Li metal (10~15%) to elevate the initial discharge voltage plateau

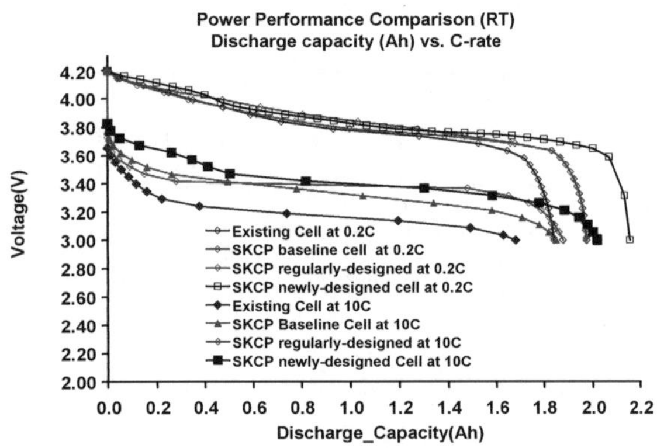

Figure 3. Power performance comparison

To solve the issue, we have identified the limiting factors of high rate (fast discharge) at a wide temperature range for the polymer Li-ion pouch cells and developed cell components including electrodes, separators, electrolytes, and processes to maximize power performance at low temperatures. The cells with the new components (called regularly-designed cell in **Table 2**) showed similar specification parameters, e.g. capacity and thickness **(Table 2)** but much improved power performance at both room-temperature and low-temperature indicated by higher discharge voltage plateau at high C-rates, e.g. 10C (**Figure 3**) and much higher initial discharge voltage plateau at low-temperatures(**Figure 5**)

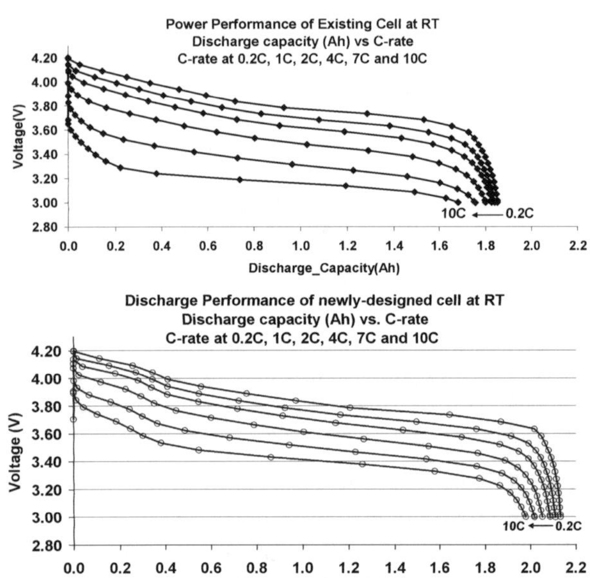

Figure 4. Discharging profiles of existing cell (top) and SKCP newly-designed cell (bottom), Capacity vs. C-rates

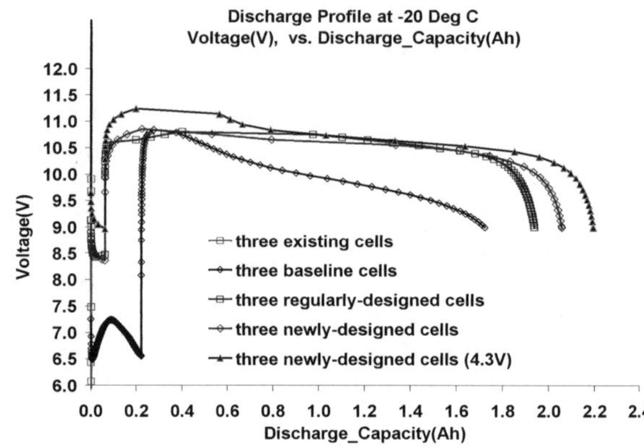

Figure 5. Comparison of discharging profile of three cells in series at -20°C, 23A pulse discharge for 10 seconds (7.5V cut-off) then constant power (81W, 27W each cell) discharge to 9V

The regularly-designed UAV cells have showed very encouraging low-temperature power performance. However, thickness or the volumetric energy density is still did not meet the requirement.

These baseline and regularly-designed cells were designed normally in terms of cathode/anode balancing. It is clear that the key for this project is to dramatically bring the energy density up while keep the power performance the same or better. One way is to use high capacity anode such as carbon composite with Li, Si, Sn et al. Both Si and Sn or other metals will lower cell voltage plateau if using as anodes, therefore they are not the choices. However, cells with Li metal as anode have the highest voltage plateau because Li metal anode has lowest de-lithiating potential over any other anode materials, e.g. Carbon, Sn, Si et al. In other words, lithium metal serving as anodes may be the answer. It is well-known that a lithium metal rechargeable cell shows a higher energy density, but possesses safety issues. Besides, such cells with Li metal anode have inferior power capability compared to cells using graphite anodes.

During this work, we took the advantages from both graphite (high power) and Li metal (high capacity and high voltage plateau), by which these newly-designed UAV cells used composite graphite/Li (optimized Li metal). We achieved this either by using lithiated graphite anode or reverse balancing design. In reverse balancing design, the graphite anodes in the new cells will be over-lithiated when cells are fully charged (i.e. 4.2V). A cell by such a design could show higher initial voltage and remain the same high power capability. **Figure 2** schematically showed the new design.

Based on this concept, the newly-designed cells have been assembled and tested. **Table 2** lists their specifications, which shows that their gravimetric and volumetric energy densities have been significantly increased. By such a design, the new cells delivered ~9% more capacity than the regularly-designed cells. Compared to the existing cells the new cells deliver 17% more capacity, and 18% more energy. Most importantly, the new cells have met the thickness requirement.

Figure 4 and **5** show that the newly-designed UAV cells possessed better power performance than regularly-designed cells demonstrated by higher discharging voltage plateau over entire high C-rate ranges. This result also indicated that the small amount lithium in the graphite anode could dramatically increase the cell energy density while keeps the cell power performance the same (or better since the cell thickness cab be reduced).

If operated at higher charge volt e.g. 4.3V, newly-designed UAV cells could deliver significantly more energy at -20°C (**Figure 5**)

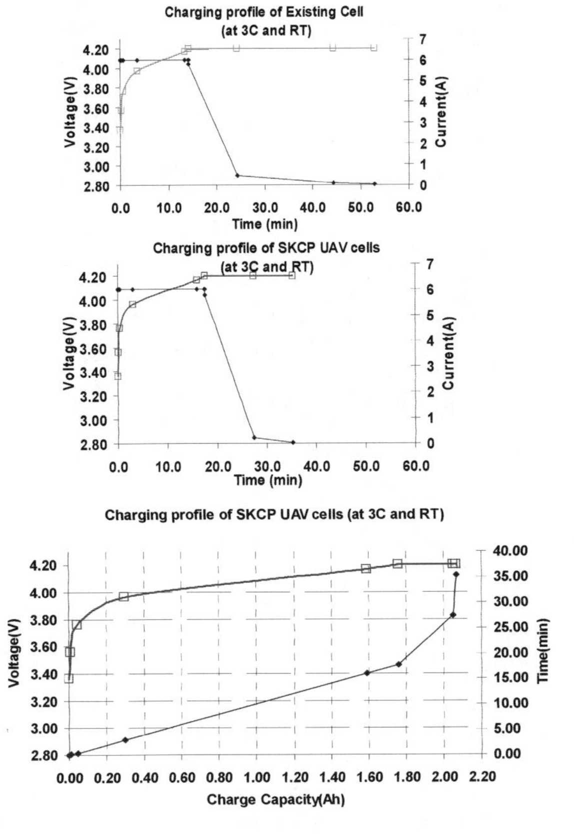

Figure 6. Fast charge profiles of the existing cell (top) and SKCP newly-designed cell (middle and bottom), 6A (3C) at room temperature

SKCP UAV cells also exhibited 3C charge capability. **Figure 6** shows that the existing cells only reached ~75% charge while the SKCP cells were 86% charged with 3C-rate (6A) to 4.2V. SKCP UAV cells could be fully charged within 30~35 min, while it would take 55 min to 1hr for the existing cells to be fully charged.

Conclusions

Through extensive developmental work on cell components and cell design optimization, especially with new cell design—reverse cathode/anode active material balancing, SKCP has developed LPCS 605060 cells with 2.15Ah (0.2C) and over 93% capacity at 10C (RT). The cells met the contract required dimension and weight requirement (39.7g and 5.9mm(T)x50mm(W)x60mm(H)). SKCP cells have demonstrated much improved low-temp power performance compared to existing cells. Based on testing on 3-cell in series, SKCP cells could be discharged following the above Discharging Protocol even though down to -20°C.

Further improvement on the low-temp power performance can be achieved with more advanced cell components, e.g. cathode active materials and additives, anode active materials and additives, electrolyte and additives, et al.

References

1. Zhiqiang Xu, Chi Kyun Park, Zhiwei Zhang, Chul Chai, "Organic Lithium Salt Electrolytes Having Enhanced Safety for Rechargeable Batteries and Methods of Making the Same", *US Patent 20060068295.*

2. "High-Rate Rechargeable Lithium-Ion Battery", *SKC Powertech/US Army Communications-Electronics Command Contract W15P7T-04-C-P016*

3. "High Energy and High-Rate Rechargeable Lithium-Ion Battery", *SKC Powertech/US Army Communications-Electronics Command Contract W15P7T-05-C-R009*

4. "The Development of Novel Electrolytes for Polymer Li-ion cells with wider operating temperature ranges"*SKC Powertech/US Army Communications-Electronics Command Contract W15P7T-06-D-A402*

5. Chi Kyun Park, Zhiwei Zhang, Luying Sun, Chul Chai, "High ionic conductivity gel polymer electrolyte for rechargeable polymer batteries", *US Patent 6,841,303*

Acknowledgement

The authors gratefully acknowledge U.S. Army AMRDEC for funding this work under the contract W911NF-11-D-0001 DO# 0143

Development of 12V/24V, 6T Lithium-Ion Batteries

Jeff Dermott[1], John Pugsley[1], Rick Heilbrun[1], Ted Bloch-Rubin[2], Jasna Tomic[2], Jean-Baptiste Gallo[2], and Laurence Toomey[3]

[1]EaglePicher Technologies, LLC
Joplin, MO, USA
Jeff.Dermott@eaglepicher.com
John.Pugsley@eaglepicher.com
Richard.Heilbrun@eaglepicher.com

[2]CALSTART
Pasadena, CA, USA
tbloch-rubin@calstart.org
jtomic@calstart.org
jgallo@calstart.org

[3]TARDEC
Warren, MI, USA
laurence.toomey2.civ@mail.mil

Abstract: The purpose of this paper is to document the development and initial performance testing of Lithium-ion based 12V and 24V batteries built to meet the physical dimension requirements of the 6T form factor per MIL-PRF-32143. By using Lithium-ion cells as the basis for the battery designs, EaglePicher can now offer a 6T battery with improved power density, energy density and cycle life over existing lead acid alternatives. This effort focused on packaging currently available commercial Lithium-Ion cell technology into a Gen 1 battery design for evaluations by commercial trucking fleets and the military for performance testing and field data collection.

Keywords: 6T, Lithium-ion, 12V, 24V

Introduction: EaglePicher was awarded a contract by CALSTART, a non-profit organization dedicated to advanced transportation technologies, to develop and deliver 12V and 24V Lithium-ion batteries in the 6T form factor. The approach used by EaglePicher was to select commercially available cells and integrate them with the appropriate electronics to provide a safe and reliable battery assembly. Integrated with each cell stack is a Battery Management System (BMS) that provides protection from over-temperature, under-temperature, over-current, over-voltage and under-voltage. The BMS will also disconnect all loads from the cell stack if communications are lost with any cell. Additionally the BMS will operate internal heaters to facilitate cold weather charging and discharging.

The 12V batteries were installed in two separate commercial delivery vehicles to provide field testing in warm and cold weather climates. The 24V batteries have been delivered to the TARDEC military test facility in Warren, Michigan to undergo performance characterization and life cycle testing. The design of each system and initial test results for the 12V batteries, both in the field and the test lab will be presented in this paper.

12V Battery: EaglePicher's 6T, 12V battery assembly (shown in Figure 1) consists of a plurality of 196 lithium ion 26650 format cylindrical cells in a 49 parallel, 4 series (49P, 4S) electrical configuration. EaglePicher has selected 26650 format Lithium-ion cells due to commonality with commercial applications. These cells employ a Lithium-Iron Phosphate electrochemistry for improved cycle life and added safety margin over other conventional Lithium-ion batteries.

The 12V battery has a nominal working voltage of approximately 13.2 Volts and will deliver in excess of 120 ampere hours when discharged at a C-rate and in an ambient air environment of twenty-five degrees Celsius.

Figure 1. EaglePicher 12V, 6T Battery

Properties of the 12V, 6T Battery	
Nominal weight:	56 lbs/25.5 kg
Nominal Capacity:	120 AH
Height:	10.00 inches
Width:	10.00 inches
Length:	10.51 inches

24V Battery: The 24V battery assembly consists of a plurality of 192 Lithium-ion 26650 format cylindrical cells in a 24 parallel, 8 series (24P, 8S) electrical configuration. The 24V battery has a nominal working voltage of approximately 26.4 Volts and will deliver in excess of 60 ampere hours when discharged at a C-rate and in an ambient air environment of twenty five degrees Celsius. The battery is packaged in the same container as the 12V system and thus has the same footprint and approximately the same weight.

Battery Management System: Each battery contains a Battery Management System (BMS) to protect cells and control the battery operation. A block diagram of the 24V system is shown in Figure 2. The 12V system is shown in Figure 3.

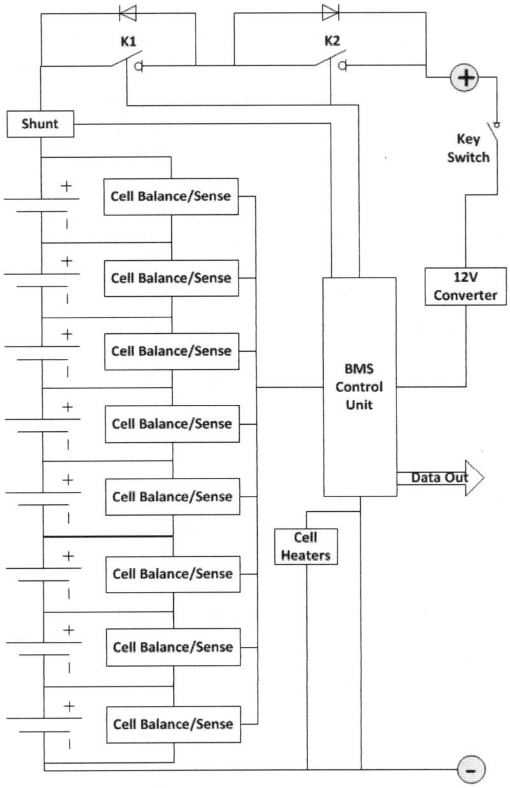

Figure 2. 24V, 6T BMS

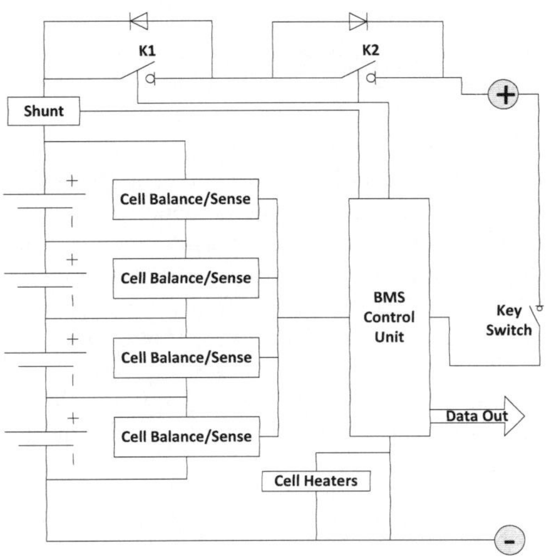

Figure 3. 12V, 6T BMS

The BMS consist of the following primary components:

- BMS Control Unit
- K1 (normally closed contactor)
- K2 (normally open contactor)
- Cell Balance and Sense Boards
- Cell Module Heaters
- Current Shunt

The Control Unit is the focal point of the protection system. It can receive information from external sources, such as a key switch and can also send J1939 CAN data to an external data collection system. The Control Unit is responsible for operating the individual Cell Balance Boards, the Cell Heaters and the Charge/Discharge Contactors. It will also monitor for the following fault conditions.

- Over Temperature
- Under Temperature
- Over Current
- Over Voltage
- Under Voltage
- Cell Communications

The Charge and Discharge contactors (K2 and K1) are used to control the inflow and out flow of bulk currents to and from the cells. K1 is a normally closed contactor and will only open if a fault condition is detected.

When the battery is installed in the end application if there is no +12V or +24V key switch signal present at the J2 connector (vehicle key is off) K1 will be closed and K2 will be open. This will allow the battery to be discharged through K1 and the protection diodes in parallel with K2. When the BMS receives a +12V or +24V signal (key switch on) via the J2 connector and the cell temperatures are $\geq$ +5°C the BMS will close K2 which bypasses the protection diodes in parallel K2. This will allow the battery to charge and discharge through a low impedance path.

If the BMS has a key switch signal but the cell temperatures are < +5°C then K2 will remain open and battery can be discharged but not charged. This mode of operation is in place to prevent Lithium plating which can occur if the cells are bulk charged at cold temperatures.

The battery employs cell module heaters that activate when the cell temperatures are too low for safe charging. Once the cells warm to the proper charging temperature K2 will close and the cell modules will be allowed to charge. The heaters can also be used in cold weather start situations to self-heat the cells and boost the discharge voltage during a start attempt.

During bulk charging the Cell Balance and Sense Boards shunt variable amounts of current away from the higher voltage cells to achieve uniformly charged cell modules.

12V Battery Test Data: The 12V units were the first batteries developed by EaglePicher in the 6T configuration. As of the writing of this paper these units have been deployed and completed their field service as starter batteries in Class 8 commercial delivery trucks. This provides a unique opportunity to characterize the performance change in the batteries after several months of real world usage.

Three 12V battery packs were installed in parallel in a fleet delivery vehicle in San Bernardino, CA in August of 2013. These batteries replaced four lead acid batteries normally used as starter batteries. The vehicle ran a delivery route in the southwest United States that included cities such as Phoenix, Tucson, Las Vegas and the greater Los Angeles area. In this particular application, the combination of warm ambient temperatures and anti-idling laws provided a very challenging environment for the batteries. The batteries remained in the vehicle until February 2014 at which time they were removed and returned to EaglePicher for evaluation. A summary of the batteries' activity while in service are given in Tables 1-4 below, where each table includes data on the particular battery pack.

Table 1. Battery Activity Data

Recorded Days	Start Events	Total Miles	Min. Amb. Temp.	Max. Amb. Temp.
96	2,525 (26/day)	17,775	-16.3°C	+45.6°C

Table 2. Battery Pack 1 Data

Avg. SOC	SOC Range	Min. / Max. Cell Volt.	Avg. Bat. Volt.	Min. Cell Temp.	Max. Cell Temp.
81%	min 62% max 88%	3.32V / 3.65V	14.04V	+5°C	+51°C

Table 3. Battery Pack 2 Data

Avg. SOC	SOC Range	Min. / Max. Cell Volt.	Avg. Bat. Volt.	Min. Cell Temp.	Max. Cell Temp.
81%	min 63% max 88%	3.30V / 3.67V	14.01V	+7°C	+53°C

Table 4. Battery Pack 3 Data

Avg. SOC	SOC Range	Min. / Max. Cell Volt.	Avg. Bat. Volt.	Min. Cell Temp.	Max. Cell Temp.
81%	min 63% max 89%	3.32V / 3.67V	14.03V	+7°C	+51°C

Prior to shipment from EaglePicher the battery packs were subjected to capacity and voltage characterization testing. After they were returned in February 2014 some of these tests were repeated to understand if any significant degradation had occurred as a result of the operation in the field.

In this particular application the delivery fleet and anti-idling laws require that drivers turn the vehicle off frequently and thus the batteries must perform many start sequences each day; 26 per day on average. During acceptance testing at EaglePicher the start sequence was simulated by applying a 1000A load to three battery packs tied in parallel. The requirement followed by EaglePicher for this test was to remain above 7.2V during the 30 second, 1000A load. This test was also repeated after the batteries were returned to EaglePicher. The voltage curves for initial Beginning-of-Life (BOL) test and the repeat test, after 4 months of field service, are shown in Figure 4. The End of Discharge Voltage (EODV) degraded from 12.21V to 11.90V after the 4 month service period. Assuming a linear degradation over the life of the batteries implies they would last more than 5 years before falling below the 7.2V requirement at room temperature.

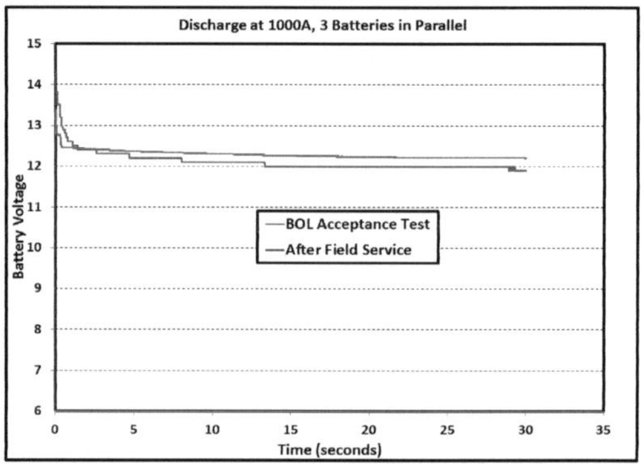

Figure 4. Battery Voltage Comparison

At cold temperatures, typically below 0°C, it will be necessary to self-heat the battery prior to attempting to support a high rate starter load, thus capacity degradation must also be considered a life limiting characteristic. EaglePicher performed a room temperature capacity cycle on the batteries after their 4 months of field service and they delivered an average of 110 AH. This same cycle delivered 117 AH during the BOL acceptance testing. This gives us a capacity degradation of 1.77 AH per month. Using this capacity degradation rate, the heater power consumption, the associated self-heating rate, and assuming that we would need to heat to 20°C at End of Life (EOL) to support a start attempt, a projected battery life can be calculated at various temperatures. These life projections are summarized in Table 5. These data indicate capacity degradation would limit the battery life to 4-5 years for this application under cold temperatures.

Table 5. Battery Life Projections

Batt Temp C	Temp Rise C	Rise Time (hr)	Self Heating AH	Start AH	Life (years)
-40	60	0.40	32.00	2.78	3.86
-30	50	0.33	26.67	2.78	4.11
-20	40	0.27	21.33	2.78	4.36
-10	30	0.20	16.00	2.78	4.61
0	20	0.13	10.67	2.78	4.86
10	10	0.07	5.33	2.78	5.11
20	0	0.00	0.00	2.78	5.36

Vibration testing per MIL-STD-810G, Method 514.6, Annex C, Category 4 was conducted on one of the batteries prior to shipping. These levels are shown in Figure 5 below. During testing, the battery was discharged at a rate of 15 +/- 0.1A from a 100% SOC. Battery voltage and current were monitored and recorded during the discharge. The test was performed at room temperature. The battery survived the test with no physical damage or electrical discontinuities noted. Likewise, the battery packs that were returned to EaglePicher after their 4 months of field service displayed no physical damage or degradation.

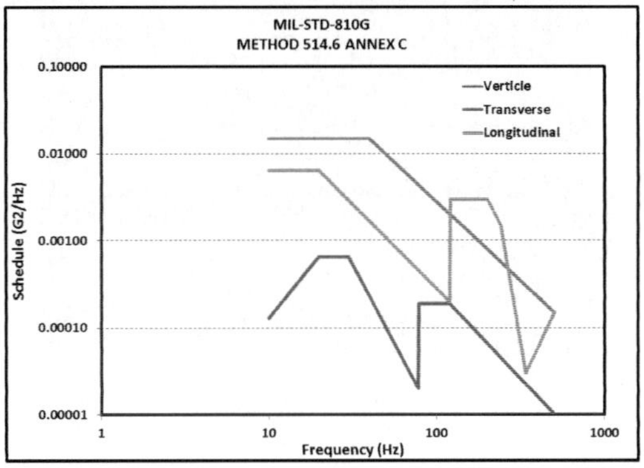

Figure 5. Battery Vibration Test Levels

Summary: In summary, EaglePicher has designed and tested Lithium -ion batteries in both 12V and 24V, 6T configurations. These batteries include a Battery Management System to protect and maintain the health of the Lithium-ion cells. The 12V batteries have also undergone 4 months of in-field service with minimal electrical performance degradation. Voltage and capacity testing after the field service indicate the batteries could be expected to last at least 4-5 years in the warm temperature climate where they were used.

Acknowledgments: The authors wish to acknowledge the support of CALSTART and TARDEC, who provided funding for this project. The authors would also like to acknowledge the efforts of the EaglePicher personnel who participated in the research, development and installation of the batteries.

24V Lithium-Ion 6T Battery Cell Chemistry Development

Chris Silkowski[1], Mike Wixom[1], Hongxia (Jane) Zhou[1], Pu Zhang[1], Pat Hagans[1], Brian Glomski[1], Tony Knakal[1], Laurence Toomey[2]

[1]Navitas Advanced Solutions Group
4880 Venture Drive
Ann Arbor, MI 48108

[2]US Army RDECOM-TARDEC
6501 E. 11 Mile Road
Warren, MI 48397

Corresponding Author Contact: csilkowski@navitassys.com

Abstract: *The lithium-ion cell chemistry that will serve as the basis of Navitas Advanced Solutions Group's second generation 24V lithium-ion 6T vehicle start battery was developed. The major technical challenge was to increase the capacity of Navitas' first generation lithium-ion 24V 6T battery from 60 to >100 Ah, with a desire to increase cold crank performance from 1,100A to 1,400A. The challenge was addressed by developing an optimized cell chemistry and electrode design, as well as a custom-size metal prismatic cell can optimized for integration within the 6T battery volume. At the completion of this program, the second generation 24V battery is projected to deliver 96 Ah and 1,300+ cold crank amps.*

Keywords: Navitas, 6T battery, starter battery, lithium-ion, cold crank, silent watch

Introduction

The U.S. Army desires to phase out current 12V, 120Ah lead-acid 6T ground vehicle starter batteries, and replace them with 24V, 120Ah lithium-ion 6T batteries of otherwise equal or advanced performance in certain applications. This will allow a vehicle to halve the number of batteries it currently carries, or effectively double up the number of batteries it carries in the same space, greatly enhancing silent watch run time. Lithium-ion batteries also feature lighter weight, longer shelf life, and longer (2-3x) operational life vs. lead-acid batteries, reducing logistical and maintenance burdens. Navitas Advanced Solutions Group (ASG) has developed a Gen 1 li-ion 6T product, and Gen 2, featuring an application-optimized chemistry and cell design, is under development. Gen 2 cell chemistry performance data and projected performance of the Gen 2 battery will be presented.

Navitas Lithium-Ion 6T Battery Overview

Navitas ASG currently produces two Generation 1 lithium-ion 6T batteries, a 12V, 120 Ah model and a 24V, 60 Ah model. These devices are based on automotive-class 3.3V, 20Ah lithium iron phosphate (LFP) pouch cells. Figure 1 shows the Navitas 6T battery. The Generation 2 goal, ideally a 24V, 120Ah high power device, is a challenging one—perhaps beyond the capabilities of current practical state of the art lithium-ion battery technology. To approach Gen 2 battery goals, a battery designer must address and optimize the cell chemistry, the electrode and core cell design, and the mechanical design of the component cell.

Navitas has developed an optimized Gen 2 cell chemistry based on graphite/NMC materials. NMC enables a higher energy density and a higher operating voltage, beneficial for cold crank. Table 1 shows the Gen 2 6T battery performance goals and performance of the Navitas Gen 1 and projected Gen 2 24V batteries. Due to the high power design needed to support 1,100A+ cold crank at -18°C, the projected battery does not meet Gen 2 capacity and energy targets, but does boost capacity and energy density by 60% over Gen 1, boosts cold crank to 1,300A, delivers 1000+ deep cycles, and weighs 40% less than a lead acid 6T battery.

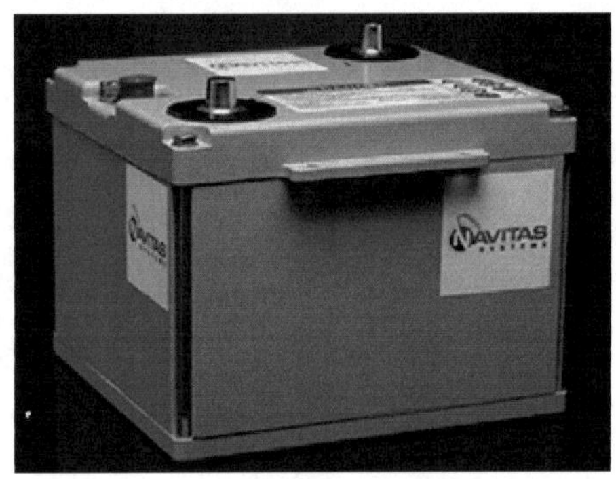

Figure 1. Navitas lithium-ion 6T battery.

Table 1. Gen 2 lithium-ion 24V 6T battery goals and Navitas battery performance.

Parameter	Lead Acid 6T	Navitas Gen 1 6T	Navitas Gen 2 6T (projection)	Gen 2 6T Target
Capacity (Ah)	120 at 12V	60 at 24V	96 at 24V	120 at 24V
Energy Density (Wh/L)	102	110	180	220
Cold Crank, 30s (A at -18°C)	1,225	1,100	1,300	1,400
Power Density (W/L)	TBD	2,200	>4,000	>2,000
Operating Temperature	-46 to +71°C	-46 to +71°C	-46 to +71°C	-46 to +71°C
Cycle Life (cycles at 80% DOD)	360	1,000++	1,000+	1,000+
Mass (kg)	40	22	25	---

Navitas Gen 2 6T Cell Test Data

The Gen 2 chemistry was developed and validated in 9 Ah pouch cell test vehicles. A larger footprint, 6 x 113 x 174 mm, was selected to simulate the chemistry's performance in the future large format metal can prismatic cell. The 9 Ah, 255 g cell is pictured in Figure 2. The cell chemistry features graphite anode, NMC cathode, polyolefin separator, and proprietary carbonate electrolyte blend optimized for low temperature operation and cold crank. The cell operates between 3.0–4.2V, with 3.7V nominal voltage.

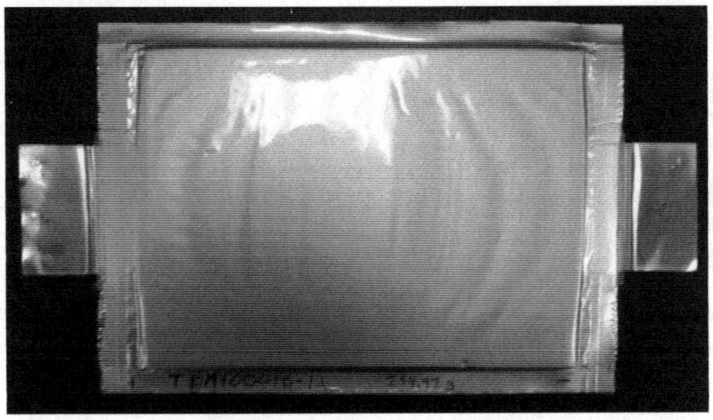

Figure 2. Navitas 9 Ah Gen 2 cell chemistry test cell.

Test Hardware: Electrical testing was conducted with a Maccor, Inc. Series 4000 Automated Test System outfitted with auxiliary temperature (thermocouple) sensors for synchronized data acquisition. Temperature control was provided with a Tenney TUJR environmental chamber. Short Circuit was performed with a Filnor knife switch, connected to the cell via OOOO cable. Nail Penetration was conducted with a Navitas-made manual test device. Penetration was performed with a 3mm OD blunted steel nail.

Rate Capability Testing: The 9 Ah cell's discharge rate capability was measured at 23, -20, and -46°C. Cells were charged at room temperature, then stabilized at temperature and soaked for at least 4 hours before discharging. The Gen 2 chemistry is capable of 20C rate discharge. High discharge capacity was retained at -20°C, and low rate operation was verified at -46°C. Figure 3 shows rate capability.

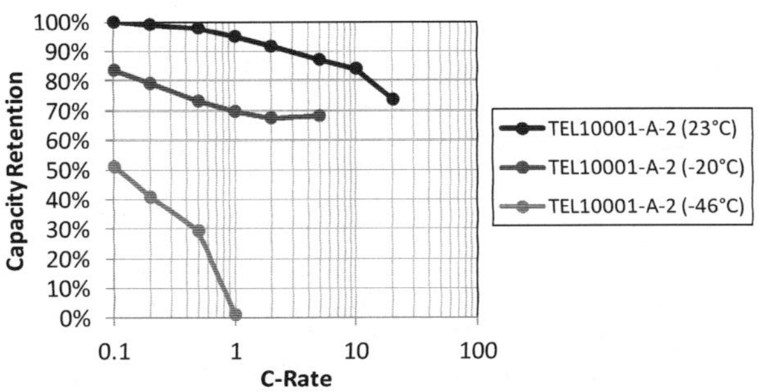

Figure 3. Navitas 9 Ah Gen 2 cell discharge rate capability performance [4.2-3.0V (23°C), 4.2-2.5V (Low T)].

Power Capability Testing: The US Freedom Car HPPC (Hybrid Pulse Power Capability) protocol[1] was used to determine the discharge power delivery capability. The cell was thermally equilibrated at room temperature or in an environmental chamber at 0 or -20°C, and then subjected to a series of 10 s long, constant-current discharge pulses at nominal 90%, 80%...10% SOC setpoints. DC Resistance values are calculated at the end of each 10 s pulse. From the resistance values, device power capabilities can be calculated at each SOC setpoint. Parameters used to determine the power data presented herein: -100A pulse current (RT), -50A pulse current (Low T), V_{min} = 2.4V. Power was then projected up to 6T battery level. The Gen 2 chemistry is capable of high power delivery at RT, 2-7 kW/L between 20-100% SOC. The cell can deliver >2,000 W/L, meeting the Gen 2 battery goal down to 0°C. The battery is capable of delivering pulse power at -20C, 1 kW/L at full charge. Figure 4 shows power capability.

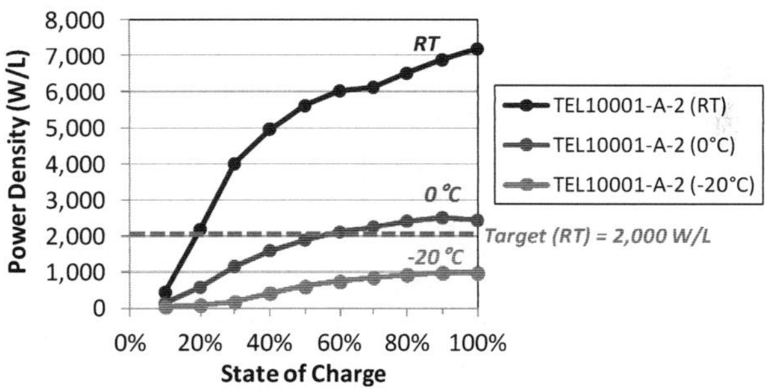

Figure 4. Navitas Gen 2 battery power capability, projected from cell test data.

Cold Crank Testing: The 9 Ah cell's cold crank performance was measured at 100% SOC. Cells were charged at room temperature, then stabilized at -18°C and soaked for at least 4 hours before the 30 s cold crank test was performed. Discharge current was 15C rate, equivalent to a 100 Ah battery cranking at 1,500 CCA level. At Beginning of Life (BOL), the Gen 2 chemistry successfully delivers 15C rate current (150A) for 30+ sec at -18°C. Figure 5 shows cold crank at BOL.

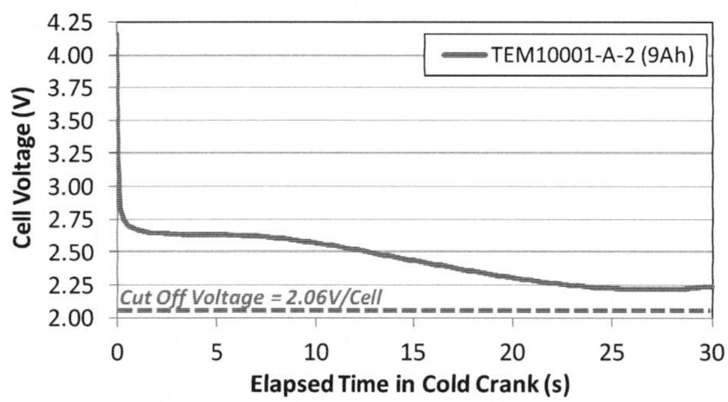

Figure 5. Navitas Gen 2 cell cold crank performance at BOL, outputting 15C rate current (equivalent to 1,500 CCA at 6T battery level) at -18°C.

A cycling cell was subjected to cold crank tests after every 100-200 deep cycles. This cell was subjected to 12C rate cold crank discharge current, equivalent to a 100Ah battery cranking at 1,200 CCA. The cell successfully delivered 12C rate current for 30+ sec at -18°C over the full 1000 cycles. Figure 6 shows cold crank performance between cycles 0-1000. At cycle 1000, the cell just delivers 12C rate without sagging below the cut-off voltage of 2.06V/cell.

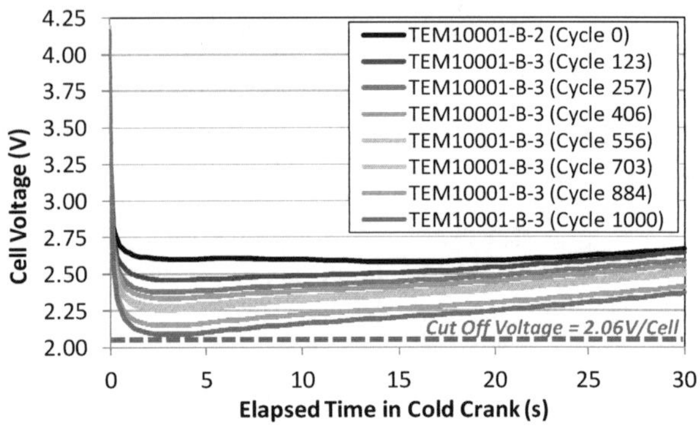

Figure 6. Navitas Gen 2 cell cold crank performance between cycles 0-1000 outputting 12C rate current (equivalent to 1,200 CCA at 6T battery level) at -18°C.

Cycle Life Testing (80% DOD): 9 Ah cells were cycled at 80% Depth of Discharge at Room Temperature. Cells were fully charged at 1C rate, and then discharged by 80% of BOL 1C discharge capacity (80% of 8.6 Ah) at 2C rate (18A). The Gen 2 chemistry successfully delivers 1000+ cycles at 80% DOD. Figure 7 shows the End of Discharge Voltage (EODV) as a function of cycle number, i.e., the voltage level the cell ends at after discharging by 80% DOD. As cell capacity fades, the EODV will move lower. As long as EODV remains above 3.0V, the cell is delivering 80% DOD.

Elevated Temperature Storage Testing: 9 Ah cells were fully charged, then stored at 45, 60, and 71°C for 28 days. Following the elevated temperature exposure, cells were allowed to cool to room temperature before retained capacity (the amount of charge remaining in the cell) and recovered capacity (cell discharge capacity following a full charge) was measured at 1C rate. Appearance before and after storage was also noted. 45°C exposure was minimally degrading to this chemistry—cells lost only ~2% of BOL capacity, and retained a "tight" appearance (i.e., no looseness or swelling from evolved gas). After 60°C exposure, cells lost ~10% of BOL capacity, and showed signs of minor gas evolution. 71°C exposure was substantially more damaging; cells lost ~25% of BOL capacity and swelled with gas. Though swollen, the seals remained intact; the cell did not vent. A Gen 2 6T battery will continue to operate following extended 71°C exposure, though its performance will be degraded. Table 2 shows the storage performance.

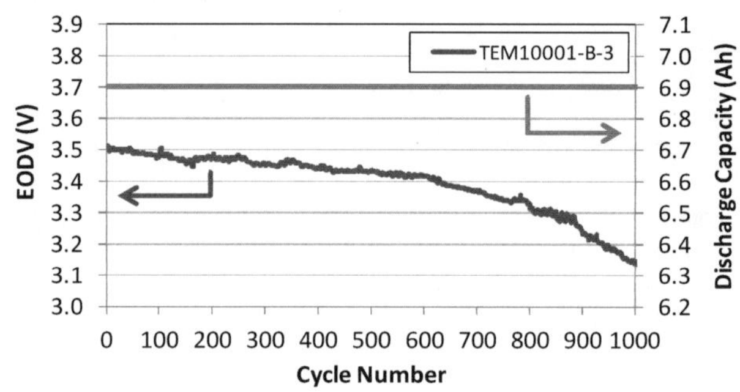

Figure 7. 1C/-2C/RT cycling of Navitas 9 Ah cell at 80% Depth of Discharge.

Overcharge Testing: 9 Ah cells were overcharged using methods consistent with MIL-PRF-32383. Cells were fixtured between fiberglass plates (to simulate a pack environment), charged to 4.2V, then overcharged to failure at C/2 rate (12V max, 8h run time). Cells vented (gas, not smoke) after reaching approximately 7.5V, and reached a maximum recorded surface temperature of 76°C. No thermal runaway events were observed.

Short Circuit Testing: Charged 9 Ah cells were fixtured between fiberglass plates, connected to a Filnor knife switch, and short circuited until surface temperature returned to room temperature. Shortly after the cells were shorted, they swelled with gas and vented (gas, not smoke). Maximum recorded surface temperature was 102°C. No thermal runaway events were observed.

Table 2. Elevated temperature storage performance of Gen 2 6T cell chemistry.

		Initial Measurements		After 28 Days of Storage at T				
Storage T (°C)	Cell	D. Capacity (Ah)	Appearance	D1 Capacity (Ah)	D2 Capacity (Ah)	Retained Capacity	Recovered Capacity	Appearance
45°C	TEM10001-B-5	9.03	Tight	8.07	8.71	89.3%	96.4%	Tight / slightly loose
	TEM10001-C-4	8.63	Tight	8.06	8.57	93.3%	99.2%	Tight
	Average					*91.3%*	*97.8%*	
60°C	TEM10001-B-6	9.28	Tight	7.11	8.07	76.6%	86.9%	Loose; some gas present
	TEM10001-C-6	8.60	Tight	6.17	7.90	71.7%	91.8%	Tight / slightly loose
	Average					*74.2%*	*89.4%*	
71°C	TEM10001-B-7	9.06	Tight	5.45	6.57	60.2%	72.5%	Swollen; loose
	TEM10001-C-5	8.65	Tight	5.57	6.71	64.4%	77.6%	Swollen; loose
	Average					*62.3%*	*75.0%*	

Heat Exposure Testing: Charged 9Ah cells were ramped to 130°C and held for 35 min, essentially consistent with UL1642. The 35 min hold allowed the cells to equilibrate to 130°C. The cells vented during this test (gas, not smoke) but did not thermally run away.

Nail Penetration Testing: 9 Ah cells were charged to various states of charge between 58-100% SOC and penetrated through with a blunt steel nail. Responses varied between from "vent with white smoke" at 58% SOC to "vent with black smoke" at 100% SOC. No thermal runaway events were observed. Table 3 summarizes the results. Figure 8 shows post-test condition of cells; cells penetrated at high SOC are heat-affected but remain intact.

Table 3. Nail penetration test results on 9Ah cells

State of Charge	Max. Surface T	Result
58%	77°C	Leaked white smokes at penetration point.
68%	96°C	Vented white smoke.
79%	*	Vented white smoke.
90%	236°C	Vented white smoke.
90%	140°C	Cell was fixtured between plates in this test. Cell vented white smoke with brief (<1 sec) initial flame.
100%	144°C	Vents black smoke.

*Thermocouple malfunctioned during test

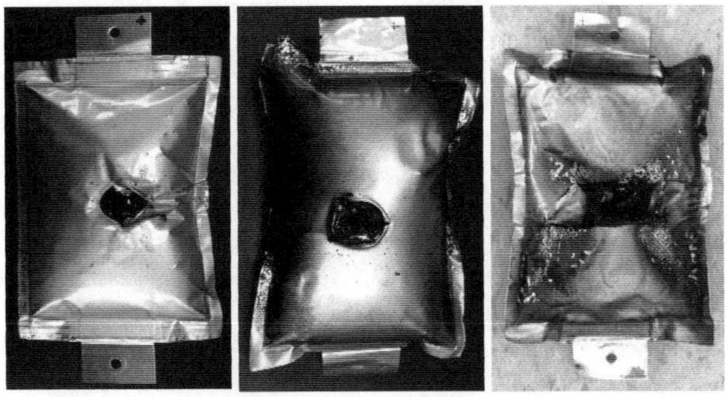

Figure 8. Navitas 9 Ah cells following nail penetration testing (68%, 90%, 100% SOC).

Gen 2 Prismatic Metal Can: Navitas ASG is presently at work on the mechanical design and prototype development of the Gen 2 cell. Figure 9 shows the current Gen 1 battery mechanical design, featuring a module based on twenty-four 20Ah LFP pouch cells. Not shown explicitly in this drawing are the aluminum heat sink plates and compliant pads that are interleaved between the pouch cells; these supporting components consume space and reduce the quantity of energy that can be carried by the battery. Figure 10 shows a conceptual mechanical design of the Gen 2 battery, based on fourteen 48 Ah Gen 2 metal can prismatic cells. The Gen 2 design removes intra-cell compliant pads and the metal cell packaging acts as intrinsic heat sinks. As such, volume utilization is maximized.

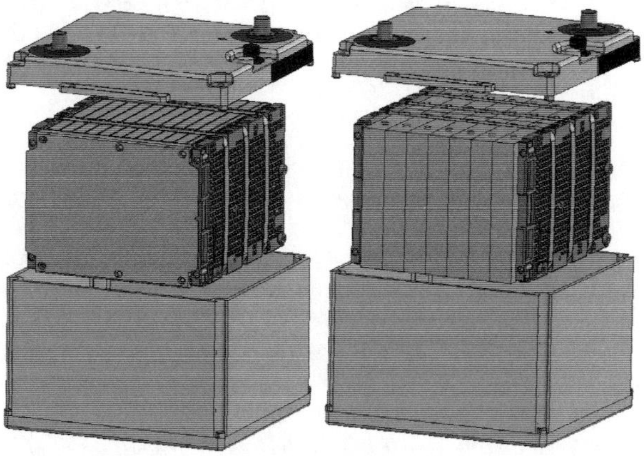

Figure 9 (Left). Mechanical drawing of Navitas Gen 1 lithium-ion 6T battery, featuring 24 pouch cells.
Figure 10 (Right). Conceptual drawing of Navitas Gen 2 lithium-ion 6T battery, featuring 14 prismatic can cells.

Conclusions

Navitas Advanced Solutions Group's Gen 2 6T lithium-ion ground vehicle battery is projected to offer a significant boost to 24V lithium-ion 6T battery performance with Gen 2 cell chemistry packaged into a prismatic metal can cell. Capacity, energy, cold crank, low temperature operation, and power will all be enhanced. 1000+ cycles at 80% DOD are possible with the Gen 2 cell chemistry. The cell chemistry shows high abuse tolerance, resisting thermal runaway and energetic failure modes in overcharge, short circuit, heat exposure, and nail penetration testing, promoting warfighter safety while moving to a more energetic battery. With this performance level, battery logistics and maintenance burdens will be reduced, while enabling vehicles to carry significantly greater energy to service silent watch needs.

Acknowledgements

Navitas wishes to thank Alion Science and Technology and the U.S. Army RDECOM Tank Automotive Research, Development and Engineering Center (TARDEC) Energy Storage Team for their partnership and funding of this work.

References

1. US Department of Energy, "FreedomCAR Battery Test Manual For Power-Assist Hybrid Electric Vehicles," October 2003, www.uscar.org/commands/files_download.php?files_id=58.

An Unsupported Metal/Non-metal Compound Pd-Ni-P for Catalytic Ethanol Oxidation Reaction in Alkaline Electrolyte

Rongzhong Jiang, Dat T. Tran, Joshua McClure, and Deryn Chu
Sensors and Electron Devices Directorate, U.S. Army Research Laboratory
2800 Powder Mill Road, Adelphi, MD 20783-1197

Abstract: *An unsupported Pd-Ni-P compound containing metals Pd-Ni and non-metal phosphorus (P) elements is synthesized for catalytic ethanol oxidation reaction (EOR) in alkaline media. As characterized with X-ray diffraction (XRD), BET-surface area, and transmission electron microscopy (TEM), the Pd-Ni-P has more amorphous structure, higher BET surface area, and smaller particle size than the Pd-Ni and Pd nano-materials without doping phosphorus. The catalytic activity of EOR at the catalyst coated electrode in 0.1M KOH was investigated. The catalytic wave of the Pd-Ni-P coated electrode in 0.1M KOH containing 1 M ethanol extends a wide potential range from -0.9V to +0.4V (vs. SCE) with a peak potential (Ep) at -0.27V, which is 50 mV more negative than that of EOR at Pd-Ni catalyst coated electrode (Ep = -0.23V), and 110 mV more negative than that of EOR at Pd black coated electrode (Ep =-0.16V). The Pd-Ni-P coated electrode also shows the highest catalytic peak current for EOR. The KOH concentration substantially affects the catalytic activity of Pd-Ni-P. When KOH concentration changes from 0.1 M to 2.0 M, the catalytic current at the Pd-Ni-P coated electrode is increased from 19 mA/cm^2 to 350 mA/cm^2 with 1 M ethanol. The catalytic process of EOR at Pd-Ni-P catalyst belongs to 4-electron oxidation to produce acetate in the alkaline media.*

Keywords: Direct ethanol fuel cell, EOR, Electrocatalysts, Alkaline electrolyte, Phosphorus-doped metal alloy.

Introduction

Alkaline electrolyte membrane (AEM) fuel cells have received much attention [1] since non-Pt and non-noble metal electrocatalysts are more stable in high pH condition. Many reports have shown that Pd-based alloys are candidates for catalytic alcohol and formic acid oxidation reactions [2-4]. Furthermore, these reports attempt to modify the electrocatalytic properties of Pd by alloying with other transition metals to create binary, ternary or quaternary metal/metal alloys, as well as incorporation of a broad range of dopants. For example, Pd-based catalysts composed of metals, alloys and non-metal dopants studied include the following: Pd-P [5-6], Pd-B [7], Pd-Ni-P [8], Pt-Ni-P [9], Pt-Sn-P [10] and Pd-Ni-Cu-P [11]. These Pd-based electrocatalysts are different from previously studied electrocatalysts in composition, electronic structure and electrochemical performance. The various binary, ternary and quaternary Pd electrocatalysts are essentially a new class of electrocatalysts that may be able to electrocatalytically oxidize ethanol more efficiently. Ethanol is an eco-friendly fuel, possesses a high theoretical energy density of 8030 Wh/kg, and is easily contained for transportation and delivery. Moreover, ethanol is also the second most extensively studied alcohol other than methanol for both acidic and alkaline electrolytes [12-13]. However, the ethanol molecule contains a carbon-carbon (C-C) bond that makes the complete oxidation a challenge. The payoff for being able to break the C-C bond for direct ethanol fuel cell (DEFC) would have a profound impact on the fuel cell area. This article focuses on synthesis, characterization and the electrochemical performance of a ternary Pd-Ni-P electrocatalyst for the ethanol oxidation reaction (EOR) in alkaline media.

Experimental

Pd-Ni alloy nano-particles were synthesized using an in-house developed wet chemical method. In a typical synthesis, 1.0 g palladium chloride ($PdCl_2$), 5 ml hydrochloride acid (HCl) and 100 ml water were added into a 500 ml flask and stirred until fully dissolved. Next, another 100 ml water and 0.68 g nickel chloride hexahydrate ($NiCl_2{\cdot}6H_2O$) were added in the flask while stirring. The reducing agent, 5 ml hydrazine monohydrate, was slowly dropped into the reactor, which resulted in forming dark precipitate as a result of the production of nano-sized Pd-Ni alloy. The precipitate was separated from the liquid via centrifugation, and washed with water and alcohol repeatedly up to five times. After drying at ~40-50 °C under vacuum overnight ~0.7 g product was obtained. The Pd-Ni-P samples were synthesized similar to the aforementioned procedure for the Pd-Ni synthesis except 0.6 g sodium hypophosphite hydrate ($NaH_2PO_2{\cdot}H_2O$) was added to the reaction solution prior to the addition of hydrazine monohydrate. The final Pd-Ni-P dry product obtained was ~0.6 – 0.7 g. All synthetic experiments were carried out at room temperature.

Transmission electron microscope (TEM) images were obtained with a high-resolution JEOL 2100 FE TEM equipped with an EDAX X-ray detector. Before imaging, a solution was prepared by adding 5 mg of the catalyst into 5 mL of 1-propanol followed by a short ultrasonic bath (Branson 3510) treatment. An aliquot of ink was loaded onto the CF400-Cu Carbon film (Electron Microscopy Science) with a micro-pipette, and the sample was dried overnight at room temperature. Energy-dispersive X-ray spectroscopy (EDS) analysis was also obtained during the TEM measurements.

X-Ray Diffraction Analysis (XRD) results were obtained from a Rigaku Ultima III instrument with Cu Kα radiation (λ = 1.5418 Å) using a Bragg-Brentano Configuration. The measurements were conducted with scan rate of 1.0 degree (2θ) per minute and each diffraction data point was collected at the interval of 0.02 degree (2θ).

The Brunauer, Emmett and Teller (BET) surface areas of the catalyst samples were measured with a Micromeritics TriStar II (TriStar II 3020 V1.03) using N_2 gas as the adsorbate at 77.3 K. Adsorption/desorption isotherm measurements were collected in the relative pressure range P/Po from 0.05 to 1.0. The samples were pre-treated in an oven at 80°C for 2 hr and then de-gassed at 110°C prior to the adsorption analysis.

A Pine Bipotentiostat RDE4 was used for electrochemically analyzing the synthesized catalysts by depositing catalyst samples from ink mixtures onto a glassy carbon (GC) disk electrode. The catalyst ink contained 4 mg of total sample (Pd black, or Pd-Ni alloy, or Pd-Ni-P) per milliliter of solution (1:1 water/1-propanol + 5% Nafion solution). The ink was ultrasonically treated with a Branson Sonifier 450 at a duty 30 and output 8 for 10 minutes. Next, 10 μl of catalyst ink was coated on GC disk working electrode (0.196 cm^2), and dried at 30°C under vacuum for ~30-40 minutes. The final coating on the GC disk electrode contained 95% total catalyst and 5% Nafion with an electrocatalyst loading of 0.2 mg/cm^2. All voltammetry experiments were performed in Argon (Ar) saturated potassium hydroxide (KOH) solution at room temperature (20 ± 1°C) with and without adding ethanol. A platinum wire counter electrode, and a saturated calomel reference electrode (SCE) were used for all studies. The current density reported in this article is based on the geometrical area of the GC disk electrode (mA cm^{-2}), which can be changed to (mA mg^{-1}) by simply multiplying a factor of 5 according to the mass of the catalyst loading.

Results and discussion

Charge Transfer between the atoms within Pd-Ni-P Crystals

In order to understand the relevance between crystal structure and catalytic activity of the Pd-Ni-P compounds, we performed a qualitative analysis of the electronic charge transfer between the atoms within Pd-Ni-P crystals. Figure 1A shows crystal structures of a substitutional alloy Pd-Ni and an interstitial alloy Pd-Ni-P obtained by doping phosphorus into Pd-Ni. Figure 1B shows the atom arrangement and electronic charge transfer analysis for 4 adjacent unit cells of the relevant face centered cubic (fcc) crystal structures. When lattice points occupied by the Pd-atoms are replaced by Ni-atoms, a substitutional alloy is formed since Pd and Ni both have a similar crystal structures (fcc) and atomic sizes. The Pd-atoms become negatively charged in the Pd-Ni alloy since the ionization energy of Pd is higher than that of Ni [3], which results in electronic charge transfer from the Ni atoms to the Pd atoms. In the Pd-Ni-P compound, P atoms enter the interstitial spaces, and forms a mix of substitutional and interstitial alloying. The arrows in Figure 1B mark the electronic charge transfer directions, and the symbol "δ^-" denotes the negative charge state of the atoms. Phosphorus is able to form an interstitial alloy with Pd or Ni metals since it is part of the triclinic crystal system with a small atomic size. The Pd atoms in Pd-Ni-P compound are further negatively charged by both Ni atoms and P atoms. As expected, the negatively charged Pd is more efficient for the catalytic ethanol oxidation reaction since it facilitates the removal of intermediate products that have negative charges [5], such as $(CH_3COO^-)_{ads}$ and $(CO^-)_{ads}$ and simultaneously prohibits the build-up of $(CO^-)_{ads}$ on the catalyst surface. The removal of the intermediate species and simultaneously mitigation of the build-up may lead to the desirable complete oxidation of ethanol (i.e. breakage of the C-C bond) [3].

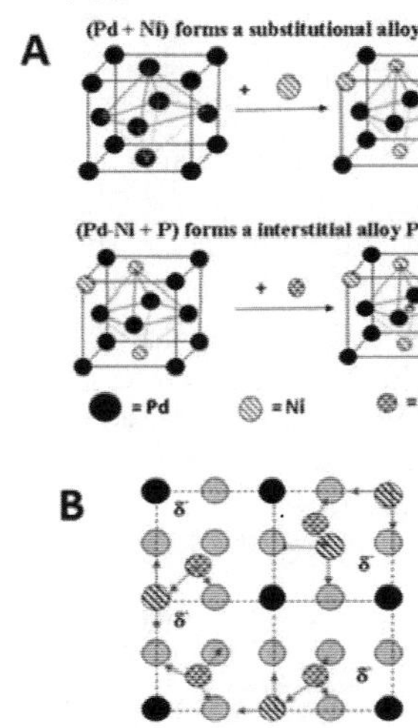

Figure 1. (A) crystal structures of a substitutional alloy Pd-Ni and an interstitial alloy Pd-Ni-P obtained by doping phosphorus into Pd-Ni; (B) Electronic charge transfer within Pd-Ni-P.

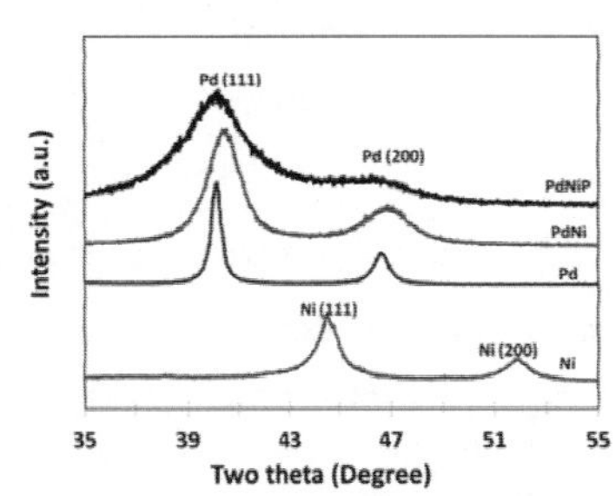

Figure 2. X-ray diffraction (XRD) patter of Pd-Ni-P, Pd-Ni, Pd-black, and Ni-powder samples.

Physical Characterization

The Pd-Ni-P and Pd-Ni catalysts were analyzed with EDS, TEM, SAED and BET. The relative compositions of the

Pd-Ni-P and Pd-Ni samples yield the following compositions: $Pd_{0.8}Ni_{0.1}P_{0.1}$ and $Pd_{0.7}Ni_{0.3}$, respectively. Figure 2 shows X-ray diffraction (XRD) patter of Pd-Ni-P, Pd-Ni, Pd-black, and Ni-powder samples. The peak for the (111) plane broadens when Ni and/or P are added to Pd. The broadening increase is in the following order with Pd < Pd-Ni < Pd-Ni-P. The broadening suggests that the resulting catalytic material develops a more amorphous structure after alloying with Ni and/or doping with phosphorus. Comparing the XRD patterns of the Pd-Ni-P and Pd-Ni samples to that of pure Ni we have noticed three peaks at 2θ of ~44.5° and ~51.9° for pure Ni, which are not seen for the Pd-Ni-P and Pd-Ni diffractograms. The disappearance of the Ni peaks for the Pd-Ni-P and Pd-Ni diffractograms demonstrates that the alloying process is complete and no unalloyed nickel metal exists. Table 1 shows peak position (2θ), d-spacing (in nm), particle size and BET surface area obtained from XRD, TEM and BET results. The surface area increases in the following order for Pd < Pd-Ni < Pd-Ni-P, however the particle size decreases with the opposite trend with Pd-Ni > Pd-Ni-P. The d-spacing and peak positions obtained from the XRD data of Pd-Ni-P, Pd-Ni and Pd catalysts. For the Pd-Ni sample, the 2θ peak position for plane (111) is larger with a smaller d-spacing compared to the Pd sample, which implies that the Pd lattice structure shrinks after alloying with Ni. However, from the Pd-Ni to Pd-Ni-P samples, the 2θ value decreases, and the d-spacing increases, which indicates that the Pd-Ni lattice structure expands after doping with P atoms. In what follows, the variations in structure, composition, and morphology of each of the catalysts studied are correlated to the electrochemical performance for the catalytic ethanol electro-oxidation.

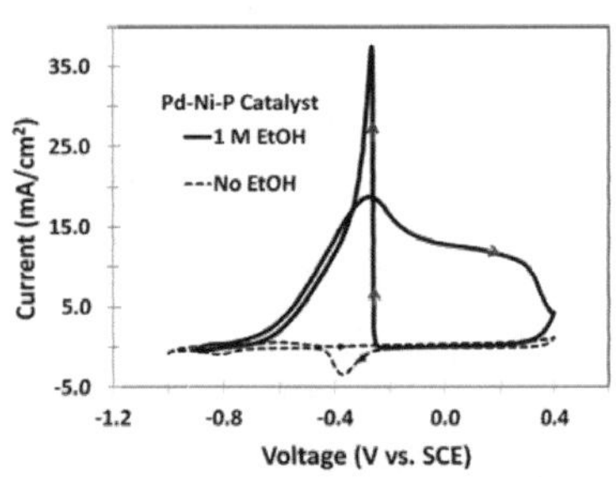

Figure 3. Cyclic voltammograms of Pd-Ni-P coated GC electrodes in 0.1M KOH in the presence and absence of 1M ethanol. Catalyst loading 0.2 mg/cm^2. Scan rate: 10 mV/s.

Electrocatalytic Activity of EOR

The electrocatalytic activity of the Pd-Ni-P for EOR was examined by coating the catalyst on a GC disk electrode, and tested in argon saturated alkaline media. Figure 3 shows cyclic voltammograms of Pd-Ni-P coated GC electrodes in 0.1M KOH in the presence and absence of 1M ethanol. In the absence of ethanol, a small cathodic peak is seen at -0.37 V. While 1 M ethanol is added in the electrolyte, a large anodic wave appears across a wide potential range from -0.9 V to +0.4 V. By reverse scanning from +0.4 V to -0.9 V, the small cathodic peak disappears; and a current ramp is created with a subsequent "sharp peak" at approximately -0.3 V. The current ramp is attributed to ethanol oxidation at the freshly exposed catalyst surface on the electrode, since the oxide layer that is formed during anodic scanning is rapidly removed at more negative potentials. The electrochemical parameters of catalytic ethanol oxidation at different catalysts are compared in Table 2. In the presence of 1 M ethanol in 0.1M KOH, the Pd-Ni-P catalyst has the lowest onset potential (i.e. E_{onset} is 50 mV lower for Pd-Ni and Pd-blk catalysts), the most negative peak potential (i.e. E_p is 40 mV lower than that of Pd-Ni catalysts and 110 mV lower than that of Pd-blk catalyst), and the highest peak current (i_p) for EOR. While in the absence of ethanol, the Pd-Ni-P catalyst coated GC electrode has the highest cathodic peak current, which implies that the Pd-Ni-P catalyst has the highest electroactive surface area to enable the highest electrochemical activity.

Table 1. Peak position (2θ), d-spacing (in nm), particle size and BET surface area obtained from XRD, TEM and BET results

Materials	Plane-111 2θ & (d-value) (XRD)	Plane-200 2θ & (d-value) (XRD)	Particle Size (TEM)	Surface Area (BET)
Pd	40.04 (0.2246 nm)	46.60 (0.1948 nm)	N/A	12.2 m^2/g
Pd-Ni	40.36 (0.2230 nm)	46.74 (0.1936 nm)	6 – 8 nm	15.4 m^2/g
Pd-Ni-P	40.12 (0.2246 nm)	46.22 (0.1945 nm)	4 – 6 nm	32.5 m^2/g

Table 2. Electrochemical parameters obtained from the CVs at the different catalyst-coated electrodes in 0.1 M KOH in the presence and absence of 1 M ethanol. Scan rate: 10 mV/s.

Catalyst sample	E_{onset} (V) 1 M EtOH	E_p (V) 1 M EtOH	I_p (mA/cm^2) 1 M EtOH	E_p (V) No EtOH	I_p (mA/cm^2) No EtOH
Pd-Ni-P	-0.88	-0.27	18.75	-0.37	-3.40
Pd-Ni	-0.83	-0.23	16.02	-0.38	-1.89
Pd	-0.83	-0.16	17.01	-0.34	-1.18

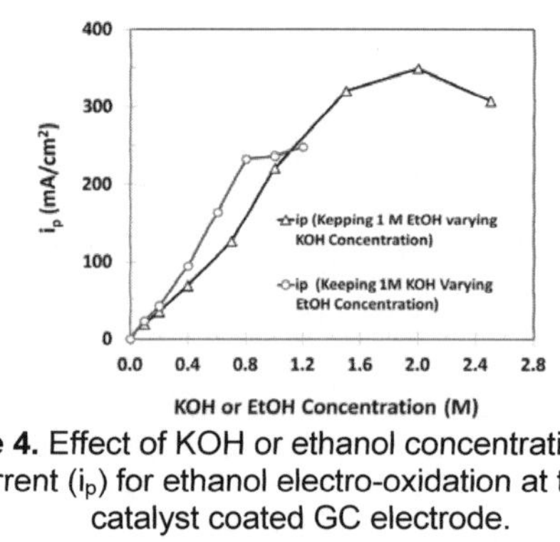

Figure 4. Effect of KOH or ethanol concentration on the peak current (i_p) for ethanol electro-oxidation at the Pd-Ni-P catalyst coated GC electrode.

The catalytic current of EOR at Pd-Ni-P catalyst coated electrode is further investigated by varying KOH and ethanol concentrations. Figure 4 shows Effect of KOH or ethanol concentration on the peak current for ethanol electrooxidation at the Pd-Ni-P catalyst coated GC electrode. The catalytic current of EOR is very sensitive to KOH concentration. The peak current (ip) is increased from 19 mA/cm^2 to 350 mA/cm^2 when KOH concentration is changed from 0.1 M to 2.0 M. If the KOH concentration is more than 2.0 M, the peak current begins to drop because a thicker oxide layer is formed at more positive potential. By keeping KOH concentration as 1 M and varying ethanol concentration, the peak current increases with increasing ethanol concentration until reaching 0.8 M. No further peak current increases by adding more ethanol in the solution except to increase the KOH concentration. It is apparent that the solution pH plays an important role in the process of EOR at the catalyst coated electrode.

The electrocatalytic oxidation of ethanol is complex and may result in various final products, including an undesirable acetaldehyde (CH_3CHO) product, an undesirable acetic acid (CH_3COOH) product and/or a desirable carbon dioxide (CO_2) product. In alkaline solution, the possible ethanol electroreactions are:

$$CH_3CH_2OH + 2OH^- \rightarrow CH_3CHO + 2H_2O + 2e^- \quad (1)$$

$$CH_3CH_2OH + 5OH^- \rightarrow CH_3COO^- + 4H_2O + 4e^- \quad (2)$$

$$CH_3CH_2OH + 16OH^- \rightarrow 2CO_3{}^{2-} + 11H_2O + 12e^- \quad (3)$$

Liang and Zhao et al [14] studied the various products of ethanol electrooxidation. Their experiments confirmed that acetaldehyde is oxidized at Pd-black coated electrode in alkaline media, resulting in a high catalytic current; however, no catalytic current for acetic acid electrooxidation was observed at the same Pd-coated electrode. Here, we have used the same method to determine the electron number of catalytic ethanol oxidation at Pd-Ni-P catalyst coated electrode. We repeated the experiment shown in Figure 3 but using 1 M potassium acetate to replace 1 M ethanol in 0.1 M KOH solution. No anodic current was observed at the Pd-Ni-P catalyst coated electrode. This experiment leads us to believe that the Pd-Ni-P electrode catalyzes the ethanol oxidation via a 4-electron process to acetate.

Conclusions

The phosphorus doped transition metal or alloy, such as Pd-Ni-P, is a new class of metal/non-metal electrocatalysts. The Pd-Ni-P compound contains Ni and P atoms that modify the crystal structure and charge transfer to the nearby Pd atoms proved to be relevant for the EOR catalytic activity in alkaline media. For comparison, unsupported Pd-Ni-P and Pd-Ni catalysts were synthesized with $Pd_{0.8}Ni_{0.1}P_{0.1}$ and $Pd_{0.7}Ni_{0.3}$ (a.u.) compositions, respectively. The Pd-Ni-P catalyst structure was more amorphous with smaller particle sizes than the Pd-Ni and Pd-blk samples as determined by XRD, TEM, and BET surface area analyses. For EOR in 0.1 M KOH, the Pd-Ni-P catalyst was proved to have the lowest onset potential, the most negative peak potential and the highest catalytic current. Also, there was a 110 mV reduction of overpotential in comparison with Pd-blk catalyst for catalytic ethanol oxidation in alkaline media. Alkaline media plays an important role in the process of EOR at the Pd-Ni-P catalyst; and higher KOH concentration results in higher catalytic current. The electrooxidation of ethanol at Pd-Ni-P catalyst reveals a 4-electron oxidation to acetate.

Acknowledgments

The authors would like to thank Dr. Panju Shang at University of Maryland for assisting TEM analysis. Thanks to Dr. Cynthia Lundgren for helpful discussions. Finally, thanks to the U.S. Department of the Army and U.S. Army Materiel Command for supporting this work.

References

1. Merle, G.; Wessling, M.; Nijmeijer, K. . Membrane Science 377 (2011) 1– 35.
2. Qi, Z.; Geng, H. R.; Wang, X. G.; Zhao, C. C.; Ji, H.; Zhang, C.; Xu, J. L.; Zhang, Z. H. J. Power Sources 2011, 196, 5823–5828.
3. Dutta, A.; Datta, J. J. Phys. Chem. C 2012, 116, 25677–25688.
4. Shen, S. Y.; Zhao, T. S.; Xu, J. B.; Li, Y. S. J. Power Sources 2010, 195, 1001–1006.
5. Yang, G. X.; Chen, Y.; Zhou, Y. M.; Tang, Y. W.; Lu, T. H. Electrochemistry Communications 2010, 12, 492–495.
6. Zhang, L. L.; Tang, Y. W.; Bao, J. C.; Lua, T. H.; Li, C. Journal of Power Sources 2006, 162, 177–179.
7. Wang, J. Y.; Kang, Y. Y.; Yang, H.; Cai, W. B. J. Phys. Chem. C 2009, 113, 8366–8372.
8. Wang, Y.; Shi, F. F.; Yang, Y. Y.; Cai, W. B. Journal of Power Sources 2013, 243, 369-373.
9. Ding, L. X.; Wang, A. L.; Li, G. R.; Liu, Z. Q.; Zhao, W. X.; Su, C. Y.; Tong, Y. X. J. Am. Chem. Soc. 2012, 134, 5730−5733.
10. Xue, X. Z.; Ge, J. J.; Tian, T.; Liu, C. P.; Xing, W.; Lu, T. H. Journal of Power Sources 2007, 172, 560–569.
11. Sekol, R. C.; Carmo, M.; Kumar, G.; Gittleson, F.; Doubek, G.; Sun, K.; Schroers, J.; Taylor, A. D. International Journal of hydrogen energy 2013, 38, 11248-11255.
12. Yu, E. H.; Krewer, U. Scott, K. Energies 2010, 3, 1499-1528.
13. Liu, J. P.; Zhou, H. H.; Wang, Q. Q.; Zeng, F. Y.; Kuang, Y. F. J. Mater. Sci. 2012, 47, 2188-2194.
14. Liang, Z. X.; Zhao, T. S.; Xu, J. B.; Zhu, L. D. Electrochimica Acta 2009, 54, 2203–2208.

A Comparison of Metal-Containing (Fe, Co, Ni or Zr) Anion-Exchange Membranes for Alkaline Fuel Cells

Joshua P. McClure, Kyle N. Grew and Deryn Chu
Sensors and Electron Devices Directorate, U.S. Army Research Laboratory
2800 Powder Mill Road, Adelphi, MD 20783-1197

Abstract: *Anion-exchange polymer membranes (AEMs) have received considerable attention for use in alkaline fuel cells. Incorporating metal-cations into a polymeric matrix may provide a route to circumvent the traditional concerns with organic AEMs. In this study, metal-containing fibrous frameworks embedded in a polymer filler matrix are prepared by co-electrospinning. A series of metal-containing (Fe, Co, Ni or Zr) fibrous frameworks are considered, and have potential for inclusion of OH^- mobile ion carriers. The high-aspect ratio metal-containing fibrous frameworks and subsequent composites (i.e. filler + metal-containing frameworks) are subjected to various chemical and thermal treatments. The isolated and the composite electrospun mats are analyzed with a variety of different physical characterizations. Future studies will address the experimental ion-transport properties. Structural considerations for the metal-containing frameworks will be considered using a combined experimental/computational effort.*

Keywords: Alkaline fuel cell, Electrospinning, Metal-organic framework

Introduction

A considerable amount of literature is dedicated to exploring proton-exchange membranes (PEMs) for low pH fuel cells. However, low pH environments and high temperature operating conditions in PEM fuel cells create a need for noble metal electrocatalysts. Electrocatalyst materials comprised of platinum-group metals (PGMs) are primarily considered for the anodic and cathodic reactions in PEM fuel cells but are costly. Alternatively, one may consider shifting from PGMs to non-PGMs by increasing the pH of the fuel cell operating environment. Non-PGM electrocatalysts mitigate fuel cell costs, thereby making high pH fuel cells such as anion-exchange membrane (AEM) fuel cells a potentially affordable option.[1]

Despite the promising advancements of non-PGM electrocatalysts for alkaline fuel cells, anion-exchange organic membranes have yet to demonstrate considerable advancements. A large number of organic AEMs exhibit low chemical stabilities and low ionic conductivities (OH^-, CO_3^{2-} or mixed ion form) under prolonged exposure to high pH media and temperatures > 60°C.[2] In addition, two problems are encountered when studying AEMs. First, the OH^- ion mobility for AEMs is intrinsically lower than the H^+ ion mobility for PEMs. Novel chemistries and membrane morphologies are being explored to better facilitate OH^- transport in AEMs.[3] Second, the lower OH^- mobility usually requires increasing the ion-exchange capacity (IEC) of the AEM. An increase in IEC is generally accompanied by a concomitant increase in membrane swelling.[4] Therefore, steps must be taken to balance the membrane swelling with the ionic conductivity to create an efficient charge-carrying AEM.

Alternatively, incorporating metal-cations into a polymeric matrix may provide a route to circumvent traditional concerns with organic AEMs. The use of metal-cation exchange groups may overcome the chemical instabilities and degradation mechanisms (e.g. Hoffman degradation and nucleophilic OH^- attack) commonly reported for organic AEMs.[5] Moreover, the inclusion of metals may affect an increase in the density and number of anions per metal cation sites.[6] For example, a stable OH^--conducting zeolitic imidazolate framework (ZIF-8), i.e a well-studied metal organic framework (MOF), was prepared by salt-inclusion.[7] The authors reported four orders of magnitude increase in the OH^- conductivity compared to the ZIF-8 without the treatment. The OH^- conducting MOF is an attractive alternative for AEM materials since the MOF provides a potential route for creating thermally stable materials with pore structures designed for OH^- transport.

In this study, we prepared nanofibrous membranes by co-electrospinning. The nanofibrous anion-exchange membranes were prepared with and without the addition of metal-containing precursors. The electrospinning method provides a means for combining polymeric materials that contain various desired physical and chemical properties. Park et al.[8] prepared electrospun organic AEMs by embedding chloromethylated polysulfone (CMPSF) into an inert matrix of polyphenylsulfone (PPSU) followed by a series of chemical treatments to create a hydroxide-exchange membrane. The co-electrospinning process allows multi-dimensional control to tailor the AEM properties such as swelling, IEC, etc. We use the electrospinning method and create metal-containing fibrous frameworks embedded within a filler polymer matrix. The subsequent electrospun fiber composite mats are subjected to various chemical and thermal treatments followed by different physical and ion-transport measurements.

Experimental

Co-Electrospinning - Electrospun fibers were created by pumping solutions/mixtures (i.e at variable flow-rates)

through a 10-mL syringe fitted with a 22-gauge needle. The distance between the rotating collector roll and needle was fixed anywhere from ~10-15 cm. A range of applied voltages (~8-20 ± 0.2 kV) was investigated for the metal-containing polymer mixtures and filler polymers. The filler polymers were polysulfone (PSF), polyphenylsulfone (PPSU) and chloromethylated PSF (CMPSF). Metal-containing (Fe, Co, Ni or Zr) polymer mixtures were created by mixing a certain polymer with the appropriate metal precursors. Electrospinning was performed at various times (~2-4 hr) under ambient conditions.

X-Ray Diffraction - X-Ray Diffraction Analysis (XRD) results were obtained from a Rigaku Ultima III instrument with Cu Kα radiation (λ = 1.5418 Å) using a Bragg-Brentano Configuration. The measurements were conducted with scan rate of 4.0 degree (2θ) per minute and each diffraction data point was collected at the interval of 0.02 degree (2θ).

Nuclear Magnetic Resonance – ^{1}H NMR spectroscopy were performed with a Bruker NMR. Spectra were collected for synthesized chloromethylated polysulfone (CMPSF) by dissolving in $CDCl_3$ solvent. The spectra were collected at 296 K with a spectrometer frequency of 500.13 MHz.

Results and discussion

Co-electrospinning Fabrication of AEM

An in-house co-electrospinning unit was developed for preparing the metal-containing polymer fibrous framework coupled with a separate station dedicated to the filler polymer material. Figure 1 shows a schematic of the electrospinning unit considered in this study, whereby a number of polymeric materials may be electrospun simultaneously. Furthermore, the process is designed to create uniform mixing of the various polymer fibers with multi-dimensional control of the membrane architecture.

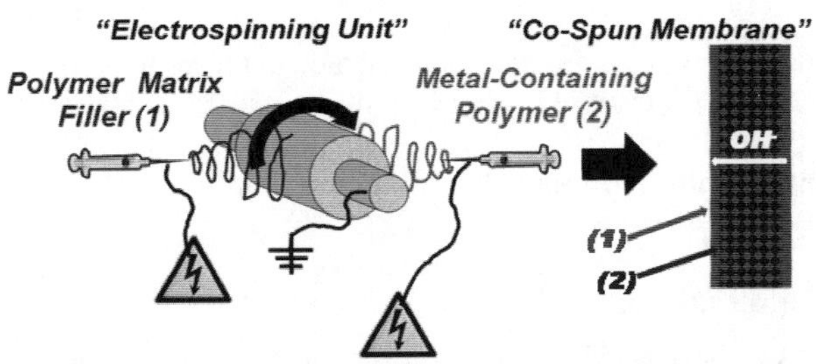

Figure 1. Co-Electrospinning apparatus for fabricating metal-containing electrospun polymer fibers embedded in different polymer matrix fillers. The process allows for mid-to-long range fabrication ordering.

Physical Characterizations

The polymeric fillers considered in this study are polysulfone (PSF), polyphenylsulfone (PPSU) and chloromethylated polysulfone (CMPSF). CMPSF was synthesized using a modified previously described procedure.[9] Figure 2 shows the ^{1}H-NMR spectra for CMPSF. A shift is observed around ~4.5 ppm and is assigned to the $-CH_2Cl$ group (circled in red). The $-CH_2Cl$ group provides a versatile functional group and chemistry for subsequent post-membrane modifications. The different polymer fillers are considered to better understand the affect of the filler matrix (i.e. hydrophobic/hydrophilic) properties on the overall membrane performance in combination with the metal-containing fibrous polymer framework.

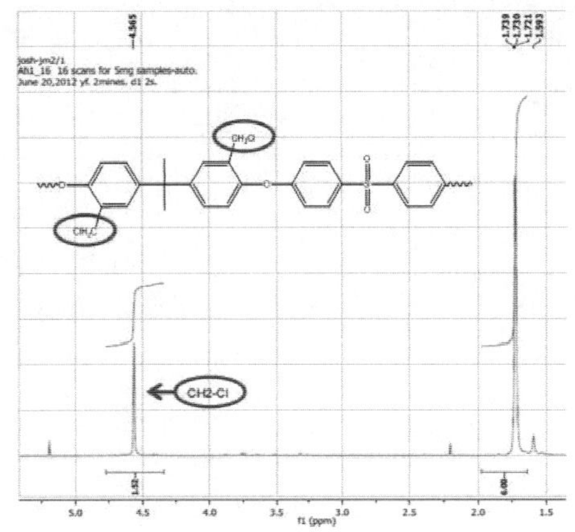

Figure 2. ^{1}H NMR spectra of chloromethylated polysulfone (CMPSF).

The PSF, PPSU and CMPSF filler polymers were dissolved in an appropriate solvent with varying concentrations (~10-25 wt% polymer). The polymer solutions were electrospun using the co-electrospinnnig apparatus shown in Figure 1. Figure 3b shows a representative SEM image of electrospun fibers from CMPSF. The as-spun CMPSF fibers had diameters of ~200-350 nm. The metal-containing polymeric fibers were created by adding a certain quantity of Fe, Co, Ni or Zr additive (i.e. varying wt. ratio of metal precursor to polymer) to the polymer solution followed by electrospinning. Figure 3a shows polymer fibers for the base polymer without metal addition, whereas Figure 3c shows a representative Co-containing polymer fiber framework. The fiber diameters for the native and metal-containing polymers are ~350 nm. Figure 3d shows a representative electrospun mat. The mat in Figure 3d is a composite mat with Fe-containing fibers embedded in a PSF filler matrix.

Electrospun PSF and PPSU fibers were also prepared (Note: images not shown). The attenuated reflection infrared (ATR-IR) spectra for the PSF, PPSU and CMPSF electrospun fiber mats are shown in Figure 4. Two additional spectra are shown for the PSF electrospun mats with different thermal treatments post-membrane fabrication (denoted PSF_1 and PSF_2 for different thermal treatments).

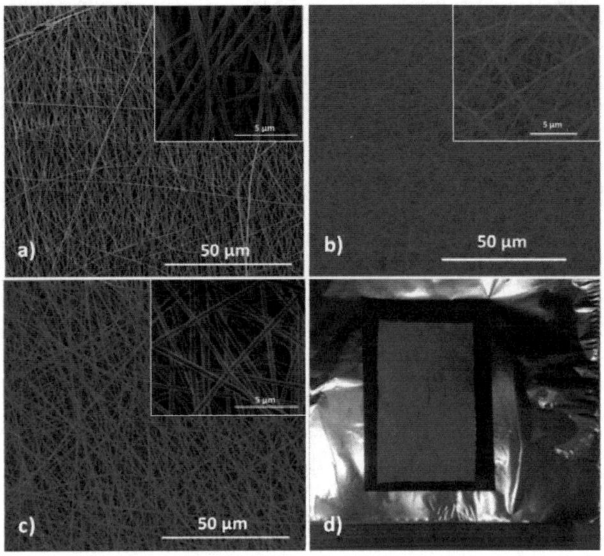

Figure 3.SEM images of as-electrospun fiber mats a) without metal precursor b) CMPSF c) containing Co precursor. A representative electrospun mat is shown in d) for and Fe-containing mat.

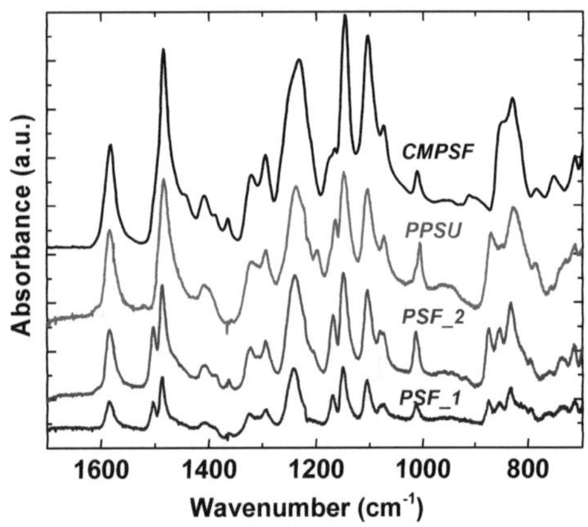

Figure 4. ATR-IR spectra for electrospun fiber mats containing CMPSF, PPSU, PSF_2 or PSF_1. (Note: the 1 and 2 after PSF denotes different fabrication conditions)

X-ray diffraction measurements were performed on the different metal-containing electrospun fiber mats. Figure 5 shows the XRD patterns for a number of metal-containing polymer mats without the polymer filler matrix. XRD patterns were also obtained for the composite mats (Note: patterns not shown). The XRD patterns show a broad amorphous peak centered ~25° 2θ for samples Figure 5a-i. Depending on the synthesis conditions a more intense peak appears ~17° 2θ and indicates additional ordering for structures in Figure 5a-g. The amorphous/semi-crystalline nature of the metal-containing fibrous framework has received recent interest for tailoring the mechanical properties and chemical linkages of MOFs.[10]

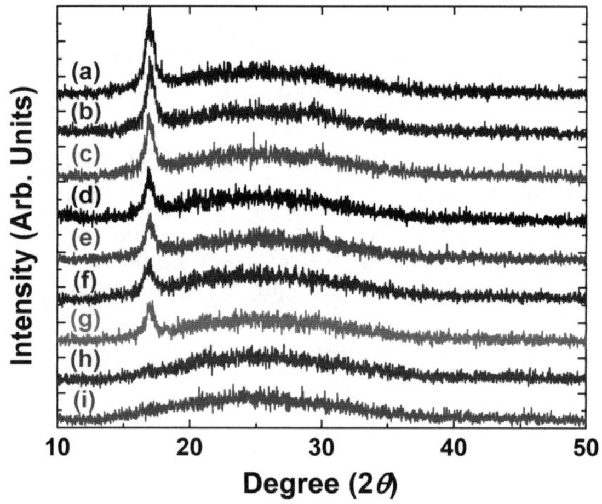

Figure 5. X-ray diffraction patterns of electrospun fiber frameworks. Patterns shown for electrospun composite fiber mats containing a) Fe 1:3 b) Co 1:2 c) Co 1:3 d) Fe 1:3 e) Ni 1:2 f) No metal_HT1 g) Co 1:1 h) No metal_HT2 i) Co 1:1. (Note: HT1 and HT2 denote heat-treatment 1 and a different heat-treatment 2 condition, respectively)

Future and ongoing studies will focus on optimizing and understanding the metal-containing fibrous frameworks. In addition, OH^--transport properties will be measured to compliment the structural analysis. The filler-to-metal-containing polymer composite will be optimized by altering the filler polymer material (PSF, PPSU and CMPSF), as well as the quantity of metal-containing matrix to filler polymer quantities. In addition, Zr-containing membranes will be explored and discussed. Various voltammetry experiments will be employed to measure the redox behavior of each metal-containing membrane. Additionally, a detailed investigation of the ionic conductivity (σ), water uptake (WU) and dimensional changes will be presented. Lastly, the experimental measurements will be complimented with computational work to provide additional insight for the structural nature of the fibrous metal-containing framework, as well as information concerning hydroxide transport.

Conclusions

We performed various characterizations on a series of metal-containing (Fe, Co or Ni) electrospun polymer fiber frameworks in isolated and composite form. The AEM membranes developed contain a metal-containing polymer framework embedded in a filler polymer material.

Electrospun fibers were developed for the filler polymer materials (PPSU, PSF and CMPSF). The CMPSF polymer filler was successfully synthesized and chloromethyl attachments were verified by H^1-NMR. SEM images revealed that additional electrospinning optimization is needed for the CMPSF polymer filler. SEM images revealed uniform metal-containing fibers formed during the electrospinning process for the metal-containing polymers. Moreover, the metal-containing fibers revealed semi-crystalline to amorphous behavior dependent on the preparation conditions. Also, co-electrospun metal-containing and filler polymer composites were successfully prepared, although optimization of the quantities of each are in progess. XRD patterns showed that the chemical and heat treatments affect a change in the amorphous/crystalline nature of the isolated and composite fiber mats. The non-crystalline metal-containing mats may provide a framework in combination with the filler polymer for affective OH^--transport.

ACKNOWLEDGMENTS

Thanks to the fuel cell group for support and collaboration. Thanks to the U.S. Department of the Army and U.S. Army Materiel Command for supporting this work.

References

[1] M.K. Debe, Nature 486 (2012) 43.
[2] Y.-J. Wang, J. Qiao, R. Baker, J. Zhang, Chemical Society Reviews 42 (2013) 5768.
[3] J. Pan, C. Chen, Y. Li, L. Wang, L. Tan, G. Li, X. Tang, L. Xiao, J. Lu, L. Zhuang, Energy & Environmental Science 7 (2014) 354.
[4] C.G. Arges, V. Ramani, P.N. Pintauro, Electrochemical Society Interface (2010) 31.
[5] H. Long, K. Kim, B.S. Pivovar, The Journal of Physical Chemistry C 116 (2012) 9419.
[6] Y. Zha, M.L. Disabb-Miller, Z.D. Johnson, M.A. Hickner, G.N. Tew, Journal of the American Chemical Society 134 (2012) 4493.
[7] M. Sadakiyo, H. Kasai, K. Kato, M. Takata, M. Yamauchi, Journal of the American Chemical Society 136 (2014) 1702.
[8] A.M. Park, P.N. Pintauro, Electrochemical and SolidState Letters 15 (2011) B27.
[9] E. Avram, E. Butuc, C. Luca, I. Druta, Journal of Macromolecular Science, Part A 34 (1997) 1701.
[10] T.D. Bennett, A.K. Cheetham, Accounts of Chemical Research (2014) 140407143228008.

Electro-catalysts for Alkaline Direct Alcohol Fuel Cells for Future Soldier Power

Carsten Cremers[1*], Tilman Jurzinsky[1], Florina Jung[1], Alexey Serov[2], Plamen Atanassov[2], Karsten Pinkwart[1], Jens Tübke[1]

[1]Fraunhofer Institute for Chemical Technology ICT, Department for Applied Electrochemistry
Joseph-von-Fraunhofer-Str. 7, 76327 Pfinztal, Germany
[2]University of New Mexico, School of Engineering
Albuquerque, NM 8731-0001, USA
*email: carsten.cremers@ict.fraunhofer.de; phone: +49-721-4640-665, fax: +49-721-4640-800665

Abstract: *In this contribution the development of palladium based anode materials with non-platinum group metals is presented. It is shown that the performance of the alcohol electrooxidation can be significantly enhanced by alloying palladium with silver or nickel. The best performance in electrochemical measurement and in alkaline direct ethylene glycol fuel cell testing was observed for Pd_3Ag/C catalyst. Using differential electrochemical mass spectrometry also the product composition is determined. It is shown that structured PdCu black catalyst synthesised by the University of New Mexico (UNM) yielded a high CO_2 current efficiency in the ethylene glycol oxidation. In addition to the anode catalyst development results on noble metal free cathode catalysts of the MnO_2 type, are reported regarding to their catalytic activity towards oxygen reduction reaction while alcohol is present.*

Keywords: electro-catalyst; alkaline direct alcohol fuel cell; ethylene glycol; alcohol oxidation reaction; oxygen reduction reaction; anion-exchange membrane.

Introduction

Direct Alcohol Fuel Cells (DAFCs) have attracted enormous attention as potential power sources for dismounted soldiers due to higher volumetric energy density than gaseous fuels such as hydrogen.[1] The most common DAFC is the Direct Methanol Fuel Cell (DMFC), which at the moment is the closest to commercialization.[2] Also other alcohols like ethanol (EtOH), ethylene glycol (EG), etc. are of interest for DAFC applications. However, the issues like slow electro-kinetics of alcohol oxidation in acidic media, costs of membranes and catalysts as well as alcohol crossover are hindering the commercialization of DAFCs.[2] Recent studies could show that the electrocatalytic activity of alcohols oxidation in alkaline media is much higher than that in acidic media.

The oxidation of EG in alkaline media has shown higher current densities and smaller overpotentials compared to those in acidic media.[3] Besides the improved kinetic of anodic alcohol oxidation reaction (AOR) the cathodic oxygen reduction reaction's (ORR's) kinetic is also enhanced in alkaline media.[4] Another advantage of Alkaline Direct Alcohol Fuel Cells (ADAFCs) is the possible usage of cheaper and more efficient catalysts for AOR and ORR than platinum (Pt).[5-7] In addition, the ORR catalysts are also tolerant to alcohol crossover, because they are active for ORR but almost inactive for AOR in alkaline media.[4,7]

A disadvantage of ADAFCs is the carbonation of the solution by CO_2 from the air feed or even from the AOR itself. This process reduces the pH, which results in loss of reactivity for AOR.[8] Matsuoka et al. investigated the AOR of different alcohols in KOH and K_2CO_3 solutions using platinum electrodes and showed that EG has the highest reactivity in both solutions.[9,10] Therefore, ethylene glycol has a potential to lower or even overcome the parasitic losses of reactivity via carbonation. Besides this EG is less toxic then methanol and not aggressive towards most metals and plastics making it easy to transport and handle. Due to its usage as anti-freeze agent and raw material for polyester fiber manufacturing the worldwide capacity for EG production is estimated to be $7x10^6 t\ a^{-1}$.[11] Therefore EG already has a worldwide production and logistic infrastructure making it a promising fuel for ADAFC applications.

Palladium has proved to be a good electrocatalyst for AOR in alkaline medium, showing higher activity and better steady-state behavior than Pt.[12-14] In order to improve the activity and stability towards AOR, Pd-based catalysts including Pd-oxide composite, Pd-based binary and Pd-based ternary catalysts have been investigated by several research groups.

With respect to the cathode side the kinetic of the oxygen reduction reaction (ORR) is much enhanced in the alkaline environment. This allows the usage of alternative catalysts. The classic alkaline fuel cell often uses silver as cathode catalyst. For the use in anion exchange membrane fuel cells also manganese oxides and iron or copper porphyrins are discussed.

In a former study it could be shown that Ni or Ag containing bimetallic Pd-based catalysts are suitable for MeOH and EtOH electrooxidation.[15] PdCu black catalyst was evaluated for 2-propanol electrooxidation by Serov et al. in a former study.[16] In this work the preparation and electrochemical evaluation of carbon supported bimetallic PdNi and PdAg catalysts with different Pd to metal ratios for ethylene glycol oxidation in alkaline media is shown. Interesting alcohol electrooxidation results are obtained and compared to that of Pd/C electrocatalyst. Besides this the CO_2 current efficiency of the ethylene glycol oxidation is evaluated via differential electrochemical mass spectrometry for PdCu black catalysts prepared at the University of New Mexico (UNM). In addition results of the oxygen reduction at MnO_2 catalyst is presented.

Experimental and procedures

PdM/C (M=Ni orAg) and PdCu black catalyst preparation

Unsupported (black) PdCu catalyst was prepared by modified Sacrificial Support Method (SSM) developed at UNM. Palladium and copper were reduced on the surface of silica with sodium borohydrate followed by removal of SiO_2 with 7M KOH.[16]

PdM/C (M=Ni or Ag) catalysts were synthesized by co-reduction with sodium borohydrate in presence of Vulcan XC72R as support; details are given elsewhere.[15]

AOR electrocatalyst testing

Chronoamperometry (CA) and cyclic voltammetry (CV) experiments were conducted to study the electrocatalytic behavior of the anode catalyst by using a three-electrode cell assembly with a Pt foil and a Hg/HgO electrode (MMO) as the counter and reference electrode, respectively. The working electrode was a glassy carbon disc (5mm in diameter with an area of 0.196cm²) covered with a thin layer of catalyst. To get a catalyst layer 2µl of catalyst ink (solvent: ethanol; binder: PTFE) was pipetted on top of the glassy carbon disc. CA tests were carried out at -0.25V (vs. MMO) for 1000s. CV tests were carried out at 25mV s^{-1} from -0.8 to 0.3V. CV and CA tests were done in Ar-saturated solution of 1M KOH + 1M EG with a PGSTAT128N (Eco Chemie B.V., Netherlands) potentiostat at room temperature.

Loading on carbon was measured by thermogravimetric analysis (TGA, TGA 2950, TA instruments, temperature range: 30-700°C, heating rate: 10°C min^{-1}, in air atmosphere). X-ray diffraction (XRD) patterns were measured using Cu Kα radiation in the 2θ range from 10 to 85° (scan rate: 0.014° s^{-1}). The tube current was 20mA with a tube voltage of 40kV. The average crytallite size d of the catalyst was calculated by using Pd(220) peak datas in Scherrer equation.

Samples of the PdCu (UNM) and Acta Hypermec® catalysts were analyzed using a flow-through DEMS cell as described elsewhere.[17] CO stripping experiments were used to calibrate the set-up for CO_2 current efficiency measurements. Cyclic voltammetric and chronoamperometric measurements were performed with sprayed electrodes of PdCu or Acta catalyst or sputtered palladium, respectively, in 1mM ethylene glycol, 0.1M KOH solution at ambient temperature. During these measurements mass spectrometer signals for m/z = 15, 22 and 44 were monitored to monitor the evolution of CO_2 (m/z = 22 and 44), acetaldehyde (m/z = 15 and 44) or other volatile organic compounds (m/z 15 only).

ORR electrocatalyst testing

ORR measurements were performed at a rotating ring disk electrode consisting of an electrode tip with glassy carbon disc, Pt ring, rotator shaft (AFE6M) and rotator (AFMSRCE, all Pine Instruments). A reversible hydrogen electrode (Hydroflex, Gaskatel) was used as reference, connected via a capillary. As counter electrode a platinum foil was used. The working electrode was prepared by dispersing appropriate amounts of the MnO_2 catalyst and Nafion® dispersion (Sigma-Aldrich) by ultrasonication and applying an aliquot of the dispersion onto the disk of the tip. The electrode was then let drying in air at ambient temperature. Tests were performed in 0.1 M KOH solution bubbled with oxygen till saturated. For the test of the alcohol tolerance a defined amount of EG was added prior to the test.

Results

XRD and TGA data of PdNi/C and PdAg/C catalysts is summarized in Table 1. Electrocatalysts were synthesized with a theoretical loading of 20wt% metal on carbon support and a varying ratio of Pd and Ag or Ni. The values of calculated and actual loading show a slight variation, but in general the predicted and measured loading values are roughly the same. XRD data shows an average metal particle size from 3.1 for Pd_3Ni/C up to 3.7nm for Pd_5Ag/C.

Table 1. Summary of obtained electrocatalysts and data derived from TGA and XRD.

Catalyst	Particle size, d [nm]	Measured loading [wt%]
Pd/C	3.6	21.0
Pd_3Ni/C	3.1	19.6
Pd_5Ni/C	3.3	20.0
Pd_3Ag/C	3.5	20.3
Pd_5Ag/C	3.7	20.7

To investigate the activity of the PdNi/C and PdAg/C catalysts for ethylene glycol oxidation in alkaline media, CV and CA tests were done in 1M KOH + 1M EG solution.

The CVs of EG electrooxidation on Pd/C and the bimetallic catalysts are presented in Fig. 1. The onset potential for EG oxidation on the Pd_3Ag/C catalyst is obviously more negative than those of PdNi/C catalysts, Pd_5Ag/C and Pd/C. Furthermore the mass current densities of Pd_3Ag/C catalysts are higher than those of the other samples.

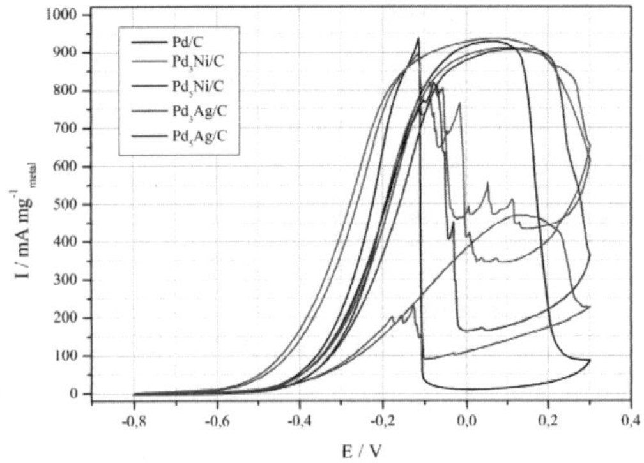

Figure 1. CV plots in 1M EG + 1M KOH solution for Pd/C, Pd_3Ni/C, Pd_5Ni/C, Pd_3Ag/C and Pd_5Ag/C from -0.8 to 0.3V (vs. MMO) at 25mV s^{-1}.

Besides CV, more representative information on the relative activities and stabilities of electrocatalysts is obtained by chronoamperometric measurements. CA plots for EG oxidation at a potential of -0.25V (vs. MMO) are shown in Fig. 2. The initial high currents are due to the double layer charging. A gradual decrease in the oxidation mass current density with time is observed indicating the poisoning of catalyst. The current for EG oxidation on Pd_3Ag/C is nearly 2 times larger than that of Pd/C. But the current decays continuously over time and there is no steady-state during the whole measurement indicating poisoning is still going on. Still, these results indicate a remarkable activity of the Pd_3Ag/C catalysts for EG. Nickel doesn't seem to promote catalytic behavior of Pd in the case of EG as well as the Pd_5Ag/C catalyst.

Table 2 summarizes CV and CA data for EG electrooxidation.

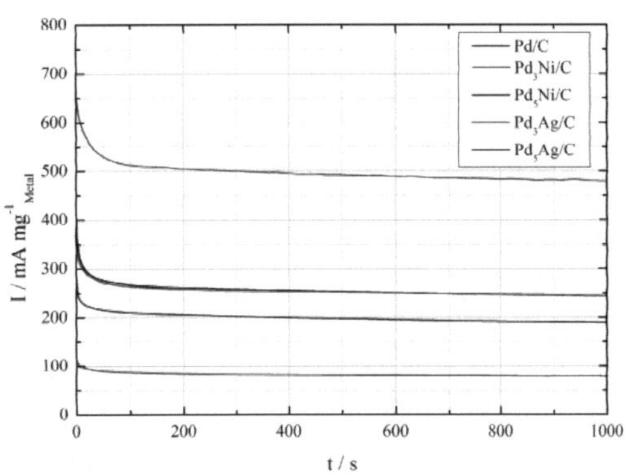

Figure 2. CA plots in 1M EG + 1M KOH solution for Pd/C, Pd_3Ni/C, Pd_5Ni/C, Pd_3Ag/C and Pd_5Ag/C at -0.25V (vs. MMO) for 1000s.

Table 2. Summary of CV and CA data for EG electro-oxidation.

Catalyst	Onset potential [V] (vs. MMO)	Peak current [mA mg^{-1}_{metal}]	Current after 1000s [mA mg^{-1}_{metal}]
Pd/C	-0.472	928.6	244.4
Pd_3Ni/C	-0.474	910.1	244.5
Pd_5Ni/C	-0.462	908.0	189.2
Pd_3Ag/C	-0.581	936.3	479.4
Pd_5Ag/C	-0.464	470.8	78.2

Under potentiodynamic conditions the PdCu catalyst achieved an integral CO_2 current efficiency of 86% for the positive half sweep of the CV (Fig. 3).

As summarized in Table 3 under potentiostatic conditions the CO_2 current efficiency of the PdCu catalyst was determined with 36% which is significantly higher than for the other palladium catalyst.

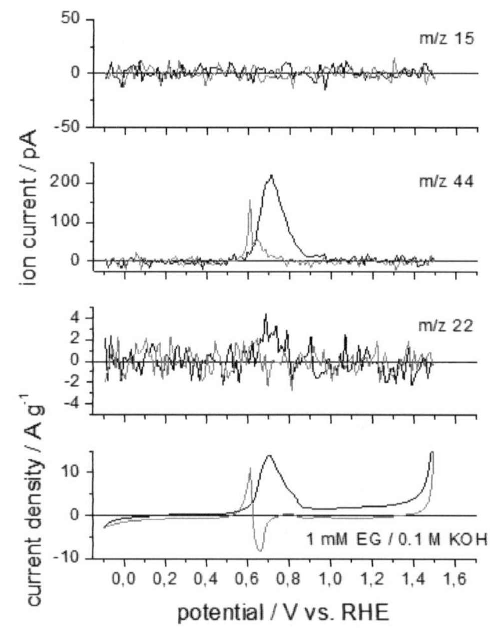

Figure 3. Oxidation of 1mM EG + 0.1M KOH in CV. Scan rate 10mV s^{-1}; 3rd cycle and corresponding signals for m/z 15, 44 and 22 are displayed.

Table 3. Summary of potentiostatic DEMS data for EG electro-oxidation.

Catalyst	CO2 current efficiency at 0.7V vs. RHE [%]
Sputtered Pd	24.2
Acta Hypermec	10.2
PdCu black (UNM)	35.9

MnO_2 was tested as ORR catalyst (Fig. 4). In order to raise the electronic conductivity to a useable level the MnO_2 was mixed with Vulcan XC72R carbon black. In pure oxygen saturated KOH solution the electrode showed promising activity for the ORR. The tolerance of the MnO_2 electrode for alcohol was tested using EG. Here it was found that an EG concentration of 10mM l^{-1} caused no significant decrease of the ORR activity even if the electrode was aged for a day.

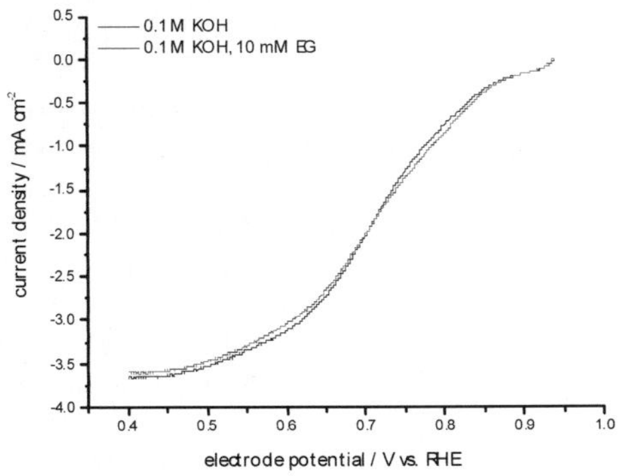

Figure 4. Linear sweep voltammogram of a MnO_2+C electrode in 0.1M KOH saturated with oxygen at 1600 rpm in absence and in presence of ethylene glycol.

Conclusion

In this study it could be shown that it is possible to enhance the activity and efficiency of the ethylene glycol electrooxidation by mixing transition metals like Ni, Ag or Cu to Pd. Besides this it was shown that MnO_2 is a highly active and ethylene glycol tolerant cathode catalyst. These anode and cathode catalysts being cheaper than Pt are promising candidates for the use in ADAFC applications. Further tests including single cell testing are ongoing and will determine if a usage of these catalysts is suitable for ADAFCs.

References

1. Lamy, C.; Belgsir, E. M.; Leger, J.-M. *Journal of Applied Electrochemistry* **2001,** *31* (7), 799-809.
2. Apanel, G.; Johnson, E. *Fuel Cells Bulletin* **2004,** *2004* (11), 12-17.
3. Demarconnay, L.; Brimaud, S.; Coutanceau, C.; Leger, J.-M. *Journal of Electroanalytical Chemistry* **2007**, 601 (1-2), 169-180.
4. Kinoshita, K. *Electrochemical Oxygen Technology;* John Wiley & Sons Inc.: **1992**.
5. McLean, G. F.; Niet, T.; Prince-Richard, S.; Djilali, N. *International Journal of Hydrogen Energy* **2002**, 27 (5), 507-526.
6. Ma, L.; Chu, D.; Chen, R. *International Journal of Hydrogen Energy* **2012**, 37 (15), 11185-11194.
7. Spendelow, J. S.; Wieckowski, A. *Physical Chemistry Chemical Physics* **2007**, 9, 1654-2675.
8. Parsons, R.; VanderNoot, T. *Journal of Electroanalytical Chemistry and Interfacial Electrochemistry* **1988,** *257* (1-2), 9-45.
9. Matsuoka, K.; Inaba, M.; Iriyama, Y.; Abe, T.; Ogumi, Z.; Matsuoka, M. *Fuel Cells* **2002,** *2* (1), 35-39.
10. Matsuoka, K.; Iriyama, Y.; Abe, T.; Matsuoka, M.; Ogumi, Z. *Electrochimica Acta* **2005,** *51* (6), 1085-1090.
11. Rebsdat, S.; Mayer, D. *Ullmann's Encyclopedia of Industrial Chemistry,* Wiley-VCH Verlag GmbH & Co. KGaA: 2000.
12. Xu, C.; Shen, P. K.; Liu, Y. *Journal of Power Sources* **2007,** *164* (2), 527-531.
13. Wang, D.; Liu, J.; Wu, Z.; Zhang, J.; Su, Y.; Liu, Z.; Xu, C. *International Journal of Electrochemical Science* **2009,** *4* (12), 1672-1678.
14. Xu, C.; Cheng, L.; Shen, P.; Liu, Y. *Electrochemistry Communications* **2007,** *9* (5), 997-1001.
15. Jurzinsky, T.; Cremers, C.; Pinkwart, K.; Tübke, J. *ECS Transactions* **2013,** *58* (1), 633-636.
16. Serov, A.; Martinez, U.; Falase, A.; Atanassov, P. *Electrochemistry Communications* **2012**, 22, 193-196.
17. Bayer, D.; Cremers, C.; Baltruschat, H.; Tübke, J. *ECS Transactions* **2010**, 25 (13), 85-93.

Developing Non-precious Metal Catalysts for Alkaline Anion Exchange Membrane Fuel Cells

Xiaoming Ren and Deryn Chu
U.S. Army Research Laboratory
2800 Powder Mill Rd. RDRL-SED-C, Adelphi, MD 20783, USA

Abstract: *In this presentation, we report our efforts in developing non-precious metal catalysts for anion exchange membrane fuel cells (AEMFCs) at Army Research Laboratory. Instead of using the expensive transition metal macrocycle compounds as the precursors, the current method uses in-situ synthesized nitrogen containing polymers on carbon support mixed with transition metal salts as the precursors, which was then subjected to a high temperature heat treatment under nitrogen to form the catalysts. The roles of carbon, transition metal, nitrogen center played in the catalysts towards the oxygen reduction reaction (ORR) were examined in a comparison study on various catalysts thus synthesized containing single and multiple components. With the optimized catalyst composition and synthesis procedure, the best performing non-precious metal catalyst demonstrated comparable ORR performance to that of commercial fuel cell grade 40 wt.% Pt/C catalyst in alkaline medium, and good performance stability in potential cycling and acid treatment tests.*

Keywords: oxygen reduction reaction (ORR); non-precious metal catalysts; transition metal centers; nitrogen centers; alkaline anion exchange membrane fuel cell;

Introduction

To achieve sustainable development with limited natural resources and environmental concerns, fuel cells are expected to play an important role in providing clean power at high efficiency. After past decades of intensive development, the proton conducting polymer electrolyte membrane fuel cells (PEMFCs) have made substantial advancements in cost, performance and durability. As the results, some viable commercial applications have been demonstrated around the world, such as in combined heat and power generations, vehicle powers, stationary backup powers, and portable powers.[1] Still, the high cost and scarceness of platinum based catalysts and their performance stability in the strong acid environment under dynamic fuel cell operation conditions remain as the major challenges for the PEMFCs to reach widespread mass applications. To address these difficulties, alternative approach in developing alkaline anion exchanging membrane fuel cells (AEMFCs) has recently gained momentum.[2] In this presentation, we report our efforts in developing the non-precious metal catalysts for AEMFCs at Army Research Laboratory. We intend to produce high performance catalysts for oxygen reduction reaction (ORR) at low cost by using nitrogen containing polymers[3-5] incorporating transition metals on carbon support as the precursors, instead of the expensive transition metal macrocycle compounds.[6] Catalysts were prepared from these low cost precursors after high temperature heat treatment, and were examined for their ORR activity using a rotating ring disc electrode in 0.1 M KOH saturated with oxygen. To optimize the catalyst performance, several important variables involved for the catalyst synthesis were examined, which include the types of nitrogen containing polymers, loading of polymer on C, types of transition metal, loading of transition metal on polymer coated carbon, and heat treatment conditions. With the optimized catalyst composition and synthesis procedure, the best performing non-precious metal catalyst demonstrated comparable performance for ORR to that of a commercial fuel cell grade 40 wt.% Pt/C (JM) catalyst in alkaline medium.

Experimental

Catalyst synthesis: Fig. 1 shows the schematic diagram of catalyst synthesis from carbon black (C), to intermediate precursors, and then to the final catalysts. The nitrogen containing polymer (P) was in-situ chemically polymerized from m-phenylenediamine using ammonium persulfate as oxidant at 5°C on Ketjen black carbon (EC-600 JD, Akzo Nobel). Uniform deposition of the polymer on the carbon surface was evidenced from the SEM micrographs shown in Fig. 2 for no obvious change in morphology between the carbon and the polymer coated carbon even at 1:1 carbon:polymer weight ratio. Ammonium ferrocyanide and cobalt chloride were refluxed with the polymer coated carbon at 100°C for 48 hs and then dried using a rotavapor to produce the precursors.

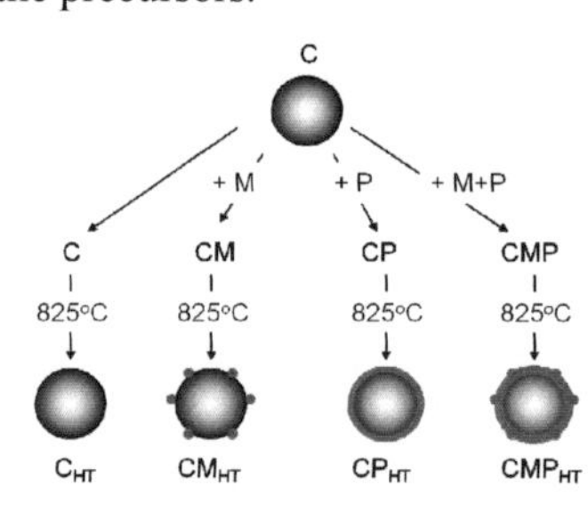

Figure 1. Catalyst synthesis procedures from carbon black (C), transition metal (M) and nitrogen containing polymer (P) to form precursors, followed by heat treatment at 825°C for 4 hours under N_2 gas to form the catalysts.

Figure 2. SEM micrographs: (A) --carbon black C; (B) precursor CMP; and (C) Catalyst CMPHT.

Results and Discussions

Using rotating ring disk electrode method, a thin catalyst film is placed on the rotating disk electrode to conveniently evaluate its catalytic activity, with a ring electrode to provide information on the byproduct formation. ORR in alkaline medium can proceed in either the 4-electron process to produce water or the 2-electron process to produce the undesirable H_2O_2, shown in Eqs. (1) and (2), respectively. The electro-oxidation of H_2O_2 on the Pt-ring electrode held at 1.20 V vs RHE proceeds according to Eq. (3).

$$O_2 + 4\,e^- \rightarrow 2\,H_2O + 4\,OH^- \quad (1)$$

$$O_2 + 2\,e^- \rightarrow H_2O_2 + 2\,OH^- \quad (2)$$

$$H_2O_2 + 2\,e^- \rightarrow 2\,H_2O + 2\,OH^- \quad (3)$$

Yield (molar fraction of the reaction products) of H_2O_2 measures the selectivity of the 2-electron process, and is calculated by the disk current (I_{disk}) and ring current (I_{ring}), adjusted by the ring electrode current collection efficiency (n), according to Eq. (4).

$$S_{H2O2} = \frac{2\,I_{Ring}/n}{I_{Disk} + I_{Ring}/n} \quad (4)$$

Fig.3 compares the ORR catalytic activities of the four catalysts examined using a rotating ring disk electrode in 0.1 M KOH saturated with O_2. ORR on the carbon surface has the lowest onset potential (defined as the potential to generate 0.1 mA cm^{-1} ORR current density, 0.81 V vs RHE), and poor 4-electron O_2 reduction selectivity with a generation of nearly 60% H_2O_2. By incorporating transition metals on the carbon surface, CMHT showed improved ORR onset potential (0.85 V) and a lower yield of H_2O_2 formation. With the incorporation of nitrogen centers on the carbon surface, CPHT demonstrated further improvements in both higher onset potential (0.91 V) and lower yield of H_2O_2. However, the best performance was achieved by incorporating both transition metals and nitrogen centers in CMPHT, which has a high onset potential (0.96 V) and 4-electron process selectivity.

N 1s X-ray photoelectron spectrostroscopies (XPS) of the catalyst samples, shown in Fig. 4, were obtained using a Physical Electronics PHI 5800 ESCA systems with a Mg Ka (1253.6 eV) X-ray source operated at 15 KV and 27 mA. Each catalyst powder sample was evenly dusted on a conductive carbon tape and analyzed at an electron take-off angle at 70°, measured with respect to the catalyst surface plane. The in-situ produced polymer (P) form the chemical oxidation reaction of m-phenylenediamine contains –N= (the quionoid imine, at 399.2 eV) and –NH- (the benzenoid amine, at 400.2 eV) nitrogen units. The polymer structures approach that of graphene with a high density uniformly distributed nitrogen units.[7] After high temperature treatment, the nitrogen units in the polymer change to pyridinic-N (398.5 eV), pyrrolic-N (400.5 eV) and graphitic-N (401.1 eV) units. It is believed that the graphitic-N is the most stable and active for ORR reaction. The fact that CMPHT is the most active catalyst with the highest 4-electron reduction selectivity indicates the synergistic effects for the ORR reaction when both transition metal and nitrogen centers exist. With the optimized catalyst composition and synthesis procedure, the best performing non-precious metal catalyst demonstrated comparable ORR performance to that of commercial fuel cell grade 40 wt.% Pt/C catalyst (JM) in alkaline medium, as shown in Fig. 5 for the polarization curves, and in Fig. 6 for the Tafel plots of ORR kinetic current density.

The Tafel slopes of Pt/C and CMPHT at low loadings are similar at 75 mV/dec. However, for the CMPHT at a high loading, the Tafel slope is higher, which could be caused by the increased internal resistance and unaccounted transport limitation for a thick catalyst layer.[8]

Table 1 lists the catalytical mass activity for ORR evaluated as 0.9 V vs RHE from the RDE measurements for both Pt/C and CMPHT catalysts. Even on the mass basis, the catalytical activity of CMPHT is approaching that of 40 wt.% Pt/C catalyst.

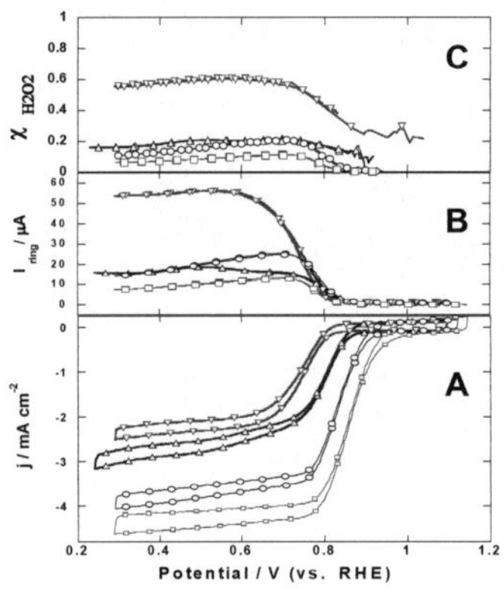

Figure 3. (A) Polarization curves of catalysts (symbols: ∇--CHT; Δ--CMHT; O-- CPHT, and □-- CMPHT) in O_2 saturated 0.1 M KOH at 10mV s^{-1} at 900 rpm. Catalyst loading:72 ug cm^{-2} geo placed on glassy carbon disk electrode; (B) H_2O_2 oxidation current detected on the Pt ring electrode held at 1.25 V vs RHE ; and (C) H_2O_2 yield.

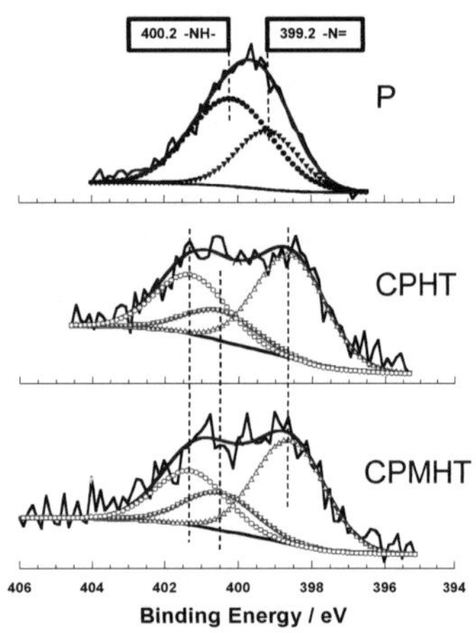

Figure 4. XPS spectra of the N1s region for P, CPHT and CPMHT.

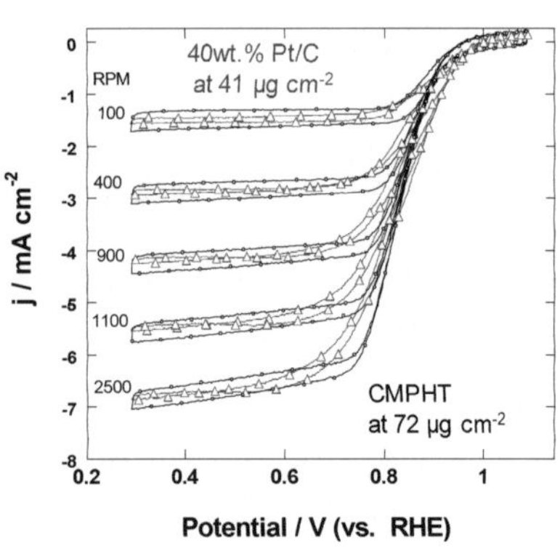

Figure 5. Polarization curves of CMPHT and 40%Pt/C in O_2 saturated 0.1 M KOH at 10mV s^{-1} at 400, 900, 1600 and 2500 rpm.

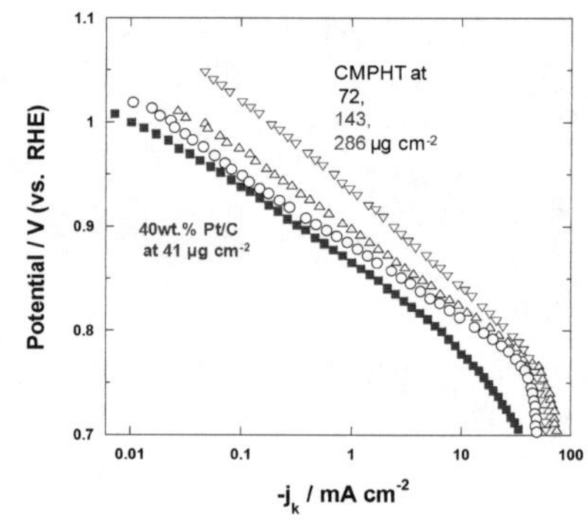

Figure 6. Tafel plots of ORR for 40 wt.% Pt/C and CMPHT at different loadings in O_2 saturated 0.1 M KOH.

Table 1. Catalytical mass activity for ORR evaluated at 0.9 V vs RHE from RDE measurements.

Catalysts	Mass Activity at 0.9 V	
	A g_{cat}^{-1}	A $g_{Pt\ or\ N}^{-1}$
40 wt.% Pt/C	8.59	21.46
CMPHT	6.9	69.04

A high stability of the catalytical activity is essential for any practical appliations. Catalyst stability were evaluated in both potneial cycling and acid treatment tests. As shown in Fig. 7, CMPHT demonstrated remarkable stability when cycled between 0.6 and 1.2 V vs RHE in 0.1 M KOH.

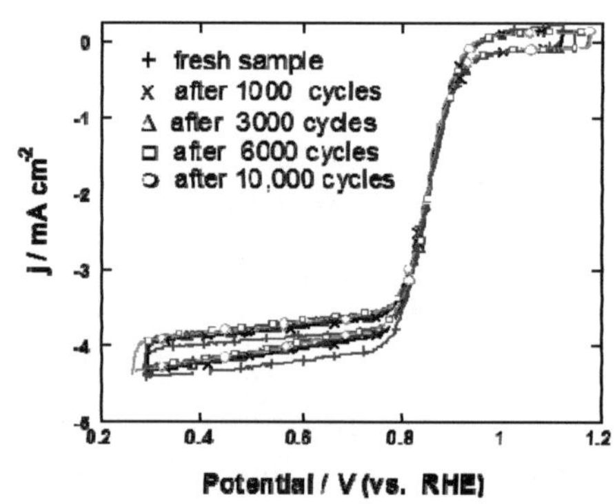

Figure 7. Stability of CMPHT Catalyst subjected to potential cycling between 0.6 and 1.2 V vs RHE at 10 mV s^{-1} in 0.1 M KOH.

To subject the CMPHT catalyst to much more aggressive environmental conditions than those encountered in AEMFCs, the catalyst was immersed in sulfuric acid and nitric acid at 80°C for 4 hours. As shown in Fig. 8, the treated CMPHT catalysts maintain essentially the same ORR activity as the untreated sample.

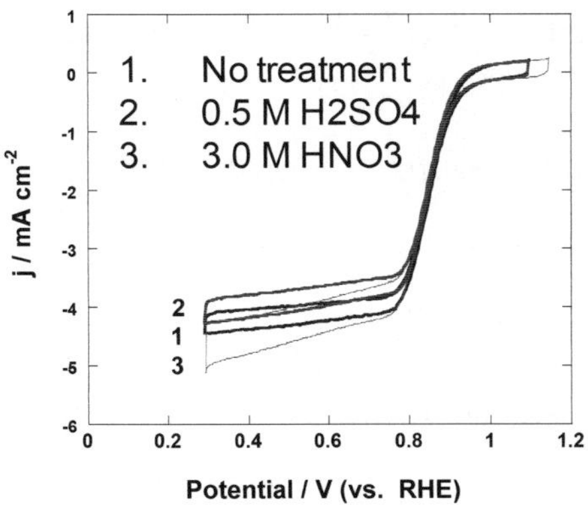

Figure 8. Polarization curves of CMPHT with and without acid treatments in O_2 saturated 0.1 M KOH at 10mV s^{-1} at 900 rpm.

Table 2 lists the elemental analysis of the acid treated and untreated CMPHT catalysts. Acid treatments cause a decrease in metal contents, especially with nitric acid. Table 3 lists the Brunauer Emmett Teller (BET) surface areas using N_2 gas adsorption at 77K for these catalysts. It shows that there are no significant changes in catalsyt surface areas before and after the acid treatments.

Table 2. Elemental analysis of CMPHT catalysts with and without acid treatments

Samples	Fe %	Co %	C %	H %	N %	Others %
No treatment	4.42	2.04	68.14	0.83	10.23	14.3
0.5 M H2SO4	3.22	1.58	64.19	1.03	9.39	20.6
4.0 M H2SO4	3.10	1.54	57.88	0.96	8.57	28.0
3.0 M HNO3	0.966	0.675	65.5	1.59	9.64	21.6

Table 3. BET surface area measurements on CMPHT catalysts with and without acid treatments

Samples	BET / m^2 g^{-1}
No treatment	727
0.5 M H2SO4	770
4.0 M H2SO4	734
3.0 M HNO3	674

Tests of CMPHT incorporated in the cathode of an AEMFC are currently in progress in our laboratory.

Conclusions

Carbon black has been widely used as the support material of electrochemical catalysts to provide excellent electronic conductivity and a large supporting surface area. However, as shown by this study and other studies, carbon surface alone has poor ORR catalytic activity and poor 4-electron process selectivity, with H_2O_2 generated from the ORR as the major reaction product. By incorporating transition metal centers on carbon surface, ORR catalytic activity improves as shown by the increase in the onset potential and the decrease in H_2O_2 formation. Incorporating N-centers from the polymer precursor on the carbon surface has much better improvement than incorporating the metal centers does. By incorporating both metal and nitrogen centers on the carbon surface, the most active ORR catalyst, CPMHT, was obtained. Since the improvement observed in CPMHT is significantly higher than the mere addition of the activities of CPHT and CMHT, in addition to the highest 4-electron process selectivity, it indicates the synergistic effects for the ORR catalytic activity when both transition metal and nitrogen centers exist.

With the optimized catalyst composition and synthesis procedure, the best performing CMPHT catalyst demonstrated comparable ORR performance to that of commercial fuel cell grade 40 wt.% Pt/C catalyst (JM) in alkaline medium.

CMPHT also demonstrated remarkable catalytical stability when cycled between 0.6 and 1.2 V vs RHE in 0.1 M KOH and when subjected to strong acid treatments.

Acknowledgements

Supports of this work by US Army Research Laboratory are gratefully acknowledged.

References

1. Wang, Y.; Chen, K. S.; Mishler, J.; Cho, S. C.; Adroher, X. C. Applied Energy 2011, 88, 981.
2. Arges, C. G.; Ramani, V.; Pintauro, P. N. Electrochemical Society Interface 2010, 19.
3. Olson, T. S.; Pylypenko, S.; Atanassov, P.; Asazawa, K.; Yamada, K.; Tanaka, H. Journal of Physical Chemistry C 2010, 114, 5049.
4. Wu, G.; More, K. L.; Johnston, C. M.; Zelenay, P. Science 2011, 332, 443.
5. Liu, G.; Li, X. G.; Ganesan, P.; Popov, B. N. Applied Catalysis B-Environmental 2009, 93, 156.
6. Feng, Y. J.; Alonso-Vante, N. Physica Status Solidi B-Basic Solid State Physics 2008, 245, 1792.
7. Zhang, L. Y.; Chai, L. Y.; Liu, J.; Wang, H. Y.; Yu, W. T.; Sang, P. L. Langmuir 2011, 27, 13729.
8. Shih, Y. H.; Sagar, G. V.; Lin, S. D. Journal of Physical Chemistry C 2008, 112, 123.

Predicting Carbonate/Bicarbonate Formation in Anion Exchange Membranes in the Presence of Carbon Dioxide

Timothy D. Myles[1], Kyle N. Grew[2], Aldo A. Peracchio[1], and Wilson K. S. Chiu[1,*]

[1]Department of Mechanical Engineering
University of Connecticut
Storrs, CT, USA, 06269-3139

[2]Sensors and Electron Devices Directorate
U. S. Army Research Laboratory
Adelphi, MD, USA, 20783

*Corresponding author: wchiu@engr.uconn.edu

Abstract: *A commonly cited issue with anion exchange membranes is the ion exchange which takes place when the membranes are exposed to carbon dioxide. Even in small amounts, carbon dioxide converts these membranes from a hydroxide form to a carbonate/bicarbonate form which has reduced conductivity. In this work a model is presented which examines the transient process. Titration data available in the literature for two commonly investigated membranes is used for validation.*

Keywords: Anion exchange membranes, carbonate, bicarbonate, carbon dioxide, transient

Introduction

Anion exchange membrane fuel cells have received attention recently due to their potential as portable power sources. These membranes offer several advantages over competing proton exchange membrane technology due to the potential use of non-precious catalyst materials, the alkaline environment supporting the use of less expensive packaging materials, as well as opportunities for a simplified balance of plant [1-5]. One standing issue with these membranes involves exposure to carbon dioxide, which causes a conversion of the membrane from a hydroxide form to a carbonate/bicarbonate form. When this occurs the membrane suffers from lower ionic conductivity due to the larger, less mobile anionic species being conducted and, if the membrane is in certain fuel cell configurations, a pH imbalance between electrodes can lead to further thermodynamic losses. Experimental measurements for the transient ion exchange are available in the literature for Tokuyama A201 membranes and Varcoe and associates radiation grafted ETFE membranes [6,7]. In both those cases, membranes initially in a pure hydroxide form and fully hydrated, were exposed to the carbon dioxide levels found in air and the concentrations of the individual anions (OH^-, HCO_3^-, and CO_3^{2-}) were measured using Warder's titration method. The focus of the work presented here is on modeling carbonate/bicarbonate formation in anion exchange membranes exposed to carbon dioxide in an attempt to elucidate the important mechanisms in the process. A firm understanding of the ion conversion is a necessary step for developing mitigation strategies in the future. The ion exchange process will be described using diffusion-reaction equations where the kinetics are assumed to mimic the formation of carbonates and bicarbonates in pure water.

Theory

To describe the ion exchange process during exposure to carbon dioxide, it is assumed that the carbonate and bicarbonate formation in the membrane environment mimics pure water. This assumption was utilized by Grew et al. [8]. Eq. 1-3 provide the associated reaction kinetics occurring in the dissociated ionic solution while eq. 3-6 provide the dissociation chemistry between the benzyltrimethylammonium functional groups.

$$CO_{2(aq)} + OH^- \leftrightarrow HCO_3^- \tag{1}$$

$$HCO_3^- + OH^- \leftrightarrow CO_3^{2-} + H_2O \tag{2}$$

$$H_2O_{(l)} \leftrightarrow H^+ + OH^- \tag{3}$$

$$(TMA)OH \leftrightarrow (TMA)^+ + OH^- \tag{4}$$

$$(TMA)HCO_3 \leftrightarrow (TMA)^+ + HCO_3^- \tag{5}$$

$$(TMA)_2CO_3 \leftrightarrow 2(TMA)^+ + CO_3^{2-} \tag{6}$$

If advection is assumed to be negligible, the time rate of change for each species within the membrane can be written as a diffusion-reaction equation.

$$\frac{\partial C_i}{\partial t} = \frac{\partial}{\partial x}\left(D_i^{eff} \frac{\partial C_i}{\partial x} \right) + \dot{R}_i \tag{7}$$

The effective diffusivity in eq. 7 is calculated based on Bruggeman's unsymmetrical formula where all TMA based species are assumed immobile ($D_i^{eff} = 0$). The kinetic source term, R_i, is derived for each species using eq 1-6 and assuming elementary reactions. Equilibrium constants and kinetic rate constants for the first three reactions are available in the literature [9,10]. Equilibrium constants for eq. 4-6 have been previously fitted and the rate constants are treated as fitted parameters here.

Boundary conditions can be set for the membrane at the membrane-air interface and the centerline as given by eq. 8.

$$\begin{aligned} &J_{CO_{2(aq)}}(0,t) = k_{abs}\left(P_{CO_2} k_H - C_{CO_{2(aq)}}\right) \\ &J_i(0,t) = 0; \quad i \neq CO_{2(aq)} \\ &J_i(L/2,t) = 0 \end{aligned} \tag{8}$$

In eq. 8 the only flux through the membrane-air interface is of carbon dioxide where the convective mass transport coefficient, k, is a fitted parameter and the equilibrium behavior is assumed to follow Henry's law where the equilibrium aqueous concentration is the product of the partial pressure of carbon dioxide, P_{CO2}, and Henry's constant, k_H. The flux at the membrane centerline of all species is equal to zero due to symmetry (both surfaces of the membrane are exposed to carbon dioxide). Initial conditions for the system are given by eq. 9.

$$\begin{aligned} &C_{OH^-}(x,0) = \alpha C_0 \\ &C_{(TMA)OH}(x,0) = (1-\alpha)C_0 \\ &C_{H_2O_{(l)}}(x,0) = \frac{\rho_{H_2O_{(l)}}}{M_{H_2O_{(l)}}} \\ &C_i(x,0) = 0 \end{aligned} \tag{9}$$

The initial conditions given by eq. 9 specify that the membrane starts in a pure hydroxide form where the dissociated concentration of hydroxide is the product of the degree of dissociation, α, and the fixed charge concentration, C_0. The associated hydroxide concentration is just the remaining proportion of the hydroxide in the membrane, 1-α. The water concentration is assumed to be that of pure water and all other ion concentrations are assumed to be zero initially.

To solve the system there are 10 species which require consideration: $CO_{2(aq)}$, $H_2O_{(l)}$, H^+, $(TMA)^+$, OH^-, HCO_3^-, CO_3^{2-}, (TMA)OH, $(TMA)HCO_3$, and $(TMA)_2CO_3$. To solve this system the partial differential equation (PDE) in eq. 7 is specified for CO_2, H_2O, OH^-, HCO_3^-, CO_3^{2-}, (TMA)OH, and $(TMA)HCO_3$. Of the remaining species, H^+ is assumed to equilibrate instantaneously and can be calculated with the water dissociation equilibrium constant, $(TMA)^+$ concentration is determined via the electroneutrality condition, and $(TMA)_2CO_3$ is determined by a species balance. Physical properties are available in the literature for both A201 [7,8,11] and the radiation-grafted ETFE [6,12] membranes. In solving the equations it is assumed that the temperature is 20 °C, the membranes are fully hydrated, and the carbon dioxide levels surrounding the membranes is 385 ppm.

Results and Discussion:

Table 1 shows the comparison between the experimental data taken from the literature and the modeling results. It is assumed in this case that the appropriate comparison to make to the experimental values is the sum of both the dissociated and associated concentrations of a given anion species because the titration method should displace all the anions in the membrane.

Table 1. Comparison between numeric and experimental data available in the literature in terms of anion contributions to overall IEC

Time (min)	Experimental IEC (mmol/g) OH, HCO3, CO3	Numeric IEC (mmol/g) OH, HCO3, CO3
	A201	
0	1.48, 0.00, 0.00	1.58*, 0.00, 0.00
5	0.50, 0.00, 0.50	1.07, 0.00, 0.26
10	0.20, 0.00, 0.69	0.76, 0.00, 0.41
30	0.00, 0.14, 0.69	0.00, 0.00, 0.79
60	0.00, 0.38, 0.57	0.00, 0.12, 0.73
120	0.00, 0.62, 0.46	0.00, 0.24, 0.67
∞	-	0.00, 0.37, 0.61
	ETFE	
0	1.45, 0.00, 0.00	1.52*, 0.00, 0.00
30	0.19, 0.00, 0.67	0.36, 0.00, 0.58
60	0.00, 0.02, 0.77	0.00, 0.02, 0.75
120	0.00, 0.36, 0.61	0.00, 0.14, 0.69
240	0.00, 0.39, 0.51	0.00, 0.26, 0.63
∞	-	0.00, 0.39, 0.57

*Total IEC values taken to be the average of the total equivalent of experimental titration data.

When comparing the experimental data from the literature to the model it is apparent that the model does capture the trend of the data. However, there are discrepancies between the two that are significant in some cases, particularly in the case of the A201 membrane. It is worth noting that uncertainty analysis was not provided with the A201 membrane data. Uncertainty analysis provided with the ETFE data in the literature expresses error bars with a somewhat large spread for one standard deviation. The simulation efforts reported here assumed a standard carbon dioxide concentration of 385 ppm in the surrounding atmosphere which is subject to variation depending on when and where the experiments were performed. The fact that trends are well captured points to the validity of the model.

As mentioned earlier the kinetic rate constants and the convective mass transport coefficient were treated as fitting parameters in this study. In fitting these values it was found that the best comparison to experimental data is obtained when these parameters are set very large such that they do not contribute to the overall rate of the conversion. Table 1 shows that the model tends to predict a slower ionic conversion then the experimental data even in this limit. Possible reasons for the discrepancy are discussed above.

The trend of both the model and the experimental data involves a sharp drop off in the amount of hydroxide in the membrane when it is initially exposed to carbon dioxide until none remains. Initially, as the hydroxide is being depleted, it is solely replaced with carbonate. After the carbonate concentration peaks, and the hydroxide concentration is approximately zero, bicarbonate begins to accumulate within the membrane. This behavior can be explained by considering the kinetics of the reactions occurring within the membrane. Eq. 1 and 2 have equilibrium constants defined by eq. 10 and 11.

$$K_1 = \frac{C_{HCO_3^-}}{C_{CO_2^{(aq)}} C_{OH^-}} \tag{10}$$

$$K_2 = \frac{C_{CO_3^{2-}} C_{H_2O}}{C_{HCO_3^-} C_{OH^-}} \tag{11}$$

K1 >> K2 >> 1 for the definitions given by eq. 10 and 11. This indicates a strong propensity for the reactions given by eq. 1 and 2 to proceed in the forward direction when there is an abundance of hydroxide and carbon dioxide is available. Due to the large value of K_2 and the fact that reaction 1 is the rate limiting reaction, the system only produces carbonate initially. Once the hydroxide levels are depleted, reaction 2 begins to proceed in the reverse direction, producing bicarbonate, while reaction 1 continues in the forward direction, producing some additional bicarbonate while preventing the accumulation of any hydroxide produced by the reverse reaction 2. Eventually the system reaches an equilibrium which consists of a mixture of carbonate and bicarbonate without hydroxide existing in any substantial amount.

In comparing the two membrane types, it seems the ETFE membrane requires a much longer time to convert than the A201. This behavior can be potentially explained by the large thickness discrepancy between the membranes. The ETFE membranes have a thickness of 80 μm while the A201 membranes are only 28 μm, resulting in greater diffusion time for carbon dioxide entering the system in the case of the ETFE membrane.

Conclusions

The work presented here describes the transient ion exchange of an anion exchange membrane. The membrane is initially in a hydroxide form, but converts to a carbonate/bicarbonate form when exposed to air. This work attempts to elucidate the important mechanisms during this ion exchange process. It was assumed that the system follows the behavior of the diffusion-reaction equation and that the forming of carbonates and bicarbonates in the membrane mimics their formation in pure water. The results were compared with data published in the literature for the Tokuyama A201 membrane and Varcoe et al.'s ETFE membrane. While there were some discrepancies in the values of the anion concentrations in the membrane, it was found that the overall trend agreed. Several conclusions could be drawn from the work: the absorption of carbon dioxide is fast compared to the diffusion and kinetics, the dissociation chemistry of the membrane occurs very rapidly, and the diffusion process is important due to the large time discrepancy in conversion between the two membranes studied which was explained by their different thicknesses.

Acknowledgements

T.D.M. gratefully acknowledges a 2013 summer internship at the U. S. Army Research Laboratory made possible through the Science and Engineering Apprenticeship Program – College Qualified Leaders (SEAP-CQL). T.D.M. and W.K.S.C. acknowledge financial support from the Army Research Office (award number W911NF-12-1-0148). K.N.G. gratefully acknowledges support from the U.S. Department of the Army and U.S. Army Materiel Command. The authors would also like to acknowledge the support of and discussions with Dr. Cynthia Lundgren and Dr. Deryn Chu of the U.S. Army Research Laboratory.

References

1. Varcoe J. R and R. C. T. Slade "Prospects for Alkaline Anion-Exchange Membranes in Low Temperature Fuel Cells," *Fuel Cells*, vol. 5, no. 2, pp. 187-200, 2005.
2. Yu E. H., Krewer U., and K. Scott, "Principles and Materials Aspects of Direct Alkaline Alcohol Fuel Cells," *Energies*, vol. 3, no. 8, pp. 1499-1528, 2010.
3. Spendelow J. S. and A. Wieckowski, "Electrocatalysis of Oxygen Reduction and Small Alcohol Oxidation in Alkaline Media," *Phys Chem Chem Phys,* vol. 9, pp. 2654-2675, 2007.
4. Antolini E. and E. R. Gonzalez, "Alkaline Direct Alcohol Fuel Cells," *J. Power Sources*, vol. 195, no. 11, pp. 3431-3450, 2010.
5. McLean G., Niet T., Prince-Richard S., and N. Djilali, "An Assessment of Alkaline Fuel Cell Technology," *Int. J. Hydrogen Energy*, vol. 27, no. 5, pp. 507-526 , 2002.

6. Kizewski J. P., Mudri N. H., Zeng R., Poynton S. D., Slade R. C. T., and J. R. Varcoe, "Alkaline Electrolytes and Reference Electrodes for Alkaline Polymer Electrolyte Membrane Fuel Cells," *ECS Transactions*, vol. 33, no. 1, pp. 27-35, 2010.

7. Yanagi H. and K. Fukuta, "Anion Exchange Membrane and Ionomer for Alkaline Membrane Fuel Cells (AMFCs)," *ECS Transactions*, vol. 16, no. 2, pp. 257-262, 2008.

8. Grew K. N., Ren X., and D. Chu, "Effects of Temperature and Carbon Dioxide on Anion Exchange Membrane Conductivity," *Electrochem. Solid St.*, vol. 14, no. 12, pp. B127-B131, 2011.

9. Wang X., Conway W., Burns R., McCann N., and M. Maeder, "Comprehensive Study of the Hydration and Dehydration Reactions of Carbon Dioxide in Aqueous Solution," *J. Phys. Chem. A*, vol. 114, no. 4 pp. 1734-1740, 2010.

10. Nikonenko V., Lebedev K., Manzanares J. A., and G. Pourcelly, "Modelling the Transport of Carbonic Acid Anions through Anion-exchange Membranes," *Electrochim. Acta*, vol. 48, no. 24, pp. 3639-3650, 2003.

11. Li Y. S., Zhao T. S., and W. W. Yang, "Measurements of Water Uptake and Transport Properties in Anion-exchange Membranes," *Int. J. Hydrogen Energy*, vol. 35, no. 11, pp. 5656-5665, 2010.

12. Varcoe J. R., "Investigations of the Ex Situ Ionic Conductivities at 30 °C of Metal-cation-free Quaternary Ammonium Alkaline Anion-exchange Membranes in Static Atmospheres of Different Relative Humidities," *Phys. Chem. Chem. Phys.*, vol. 9, pp. 1479-1486, 2007.

Dual-graphite Batteries for Energy Storage

Jeffrey Read,* Arthur v. Cresce, Matthew H. Ervin, and Kang Xu
U.S. Army Research Laboratory
RDRL-SED-C
2800 Powder Mill Road
Adelphi, MD 20783-1197

Abstract: *Electrochemical cells utilizing graphite intercalation compounds at both electrodes have been proposed as an energy storage technology where the electrolyte salt is stored in the electrodes on charge and reformed on discharge. Anion intercalation of graphite has been studied by a number of investigators and typically occurs in the voltage range from 4.5V to 5.5V, above the stability limit of most organic electrolytes. Several non-aqueous electrolytes have shown good stability against oxidation at these high potentials but have not proven to be suitable for intercalation of lithium at graphite anodes. This paper shows some recent work on an electrolyte system capable of supporting both anion and cation intercalation in graphite and discusses the possible benefits of a dual-graphite grid storage battery from the perspective of cost and safety.*

Keywords: graphite-graphite cells; dual graphite cells; fluorinated electrolyte; high voltage electrolyte

Introduction

The need for robust energy storage for Army microgrid applications arises from the high cost of transporting fuel in difficult environments as well as the prevalence of distributed power systems at many forward operating bases. One technology that is potentially low cost and safe for this application is the dual-graphite intercalation chemistry. Electrochemical cells that utilize a graphite intercalation compound as cathode have been demonstrated by a number of researchers.[1-11] Anions that can be electrochemically intercalated into graphite include among others ClO_4^-, BF_4^-, PF_6^-, $AlCl_4^-$, $CF_3SO_3^-$, $(CF_3SO_2)_2N^-$, as well as the fluoride-anion acceptor complexes[1-5]. The dual-carbon cell with non-aqueous electrolyte was first proposed as a rechargeable battery in patents by McCullough et al.[12-15] In a dual-carbon cell, the lithium salt is electrolyzed on charge with the Li^+ being stored in the anode and the anion intercalating into the cathode. The salt is depleted from the electrolyte on charge and replenished upon discharge with the energy capable of being stored in practical cells depending largely on both the solubility limit of the electrolyte salt[16]and the anion storage capacity of the graphite cathode.

Anion intercalation into graphite occurs at potentials above 4.5V where the oxidation of both electrolyte solvents and salt is of major concern. The electrolyte solvents that have been investigated previously for high oxidation stability include propylene carbonate (PC), dimethyl sulfoxide (DMSO), dimethyl formamide (DMF), ethyl methyl sulfone (EMS), ethylene carbonate (EC), diethyl carbonate (DEC), dimethyl carbonate (DMC) and the ionic liquid Pyr_{14}TFSI. These solvents show varying degrees of stability at high potential, with stability of the electrolyte being cited as the major reason for cycling efficiencies of less than 100% and the poor storage performance of the anion intercalated graphite.[8]

Table 1 summarizes a number of studies that utilized graphites or hard carbon cathodes for anion intercalation as reported in the literature. The cell chemistry used in the McCullough patents[12-15] is based on $LiClO_4$ or $LiPF_6$ salts in propylene carbonate (PC) solvent and binderless pyrolyzed polyacrylonitrile (PAN) electrodes. The McCullough patents that contain discharge data[12,13] show that for the $LiClO_4$ based electrolyte, the cycling efficiency approaches 85% and for the $LiPF_6$ containing electrolyte, the efficiency is reported as 90% at a capacity of 69 mAh/g at a C/3 cycling rate. Several patents filed later[14,15] claimed higher capacities and efficiencies, although no discharge curves were provided. Separate studies on natural graphite electrodes utilizing $LiClO_4$ in PC demonstrated cycling efficiencies of 84% for Li^+ and 79% for ClO_4^- intercalation in graphite using the area integrated from CV scans.[2]

Electrochemical intercalation of PF_6^- anion in Fluka graphite was studied by Seel and Dahn[4] with 1M and 3M $LiPF_6$ in EC/DEC (33:67) and 2 M $LiPF_6$ in EMS. At low rate, the EC/DEC electrolyte could not be charged above 5.2V and gave low discharge capacities and poor efficiencies while the EMS electrolyte could be charged up to 5.6V giving consistently higher capacities and better cycling efficiencies. However, EMS could not be used on graphite anodes as exfoliation occurs, and therefore full dual-graphite cells could not be evaluated.

1M LiTFSI in Pyr_{14}TFSI electrolyte was evaluated with KS-6 graphite by Winter[8] in lithium half cells. Improved cycling efficiencies of 96% were observed when using a 5.2V upper charge voltage and 1 C rate. The cycling efficiency is lower than that in a typical 4V lithium-ion system although no organic electrolyte was present. The authors suggest that decomposition of the anion intercalate is the source of this inefficiency. The $Pyr_{14}TFSI$ electrolyte does not support lithium intercalation in graphite but does support intercalation in lithium titianium oxide (LTO) anodes. Graphite-LTO cell were built and cycled and demonstrated 98% efficiency at a C rate.

The literature indicates that cycling efficiency is a significant issue with the dual graphite cell and that in order to make this energy storage system feasible, an electrolyte system capable of high efficiencies on both the anode and cathode needs to be developed. The electrolyte solvents PC, DMSO, DMF, EMS, and $Pyr_{14}TFSI$ are poor solvents for intercalation of Li-ion into graphite, causing exfoliation and destruction of the graphite lattice. The electrolyte systems based on carbonate solvents alone allow for intercalation of Li-ion into graphite but do not give the high cycling efficiencies needed at voltages over 5.0V and degrade rapidly with cycling. We have recently reported work on a monofluoroethylene carbonate (FEC) based electrolyte system that demonstrates improved stability on graphite cathodes at 5.0-5.2V and excellent stability on graphite anodes.[18] The electrolyte has allowed us to build and cycle full dual-graphite cells out to 50 cycles at 70% initial capacity. That work also demonstrates that a soluble species is forming on the graphite cathode above 4.5V and that this species could be responsible for the poor cycling efficiencies observed in these anion intercalation systems.

Experimental

SFG-44 graphite from Timcal was used for the cathode graphite. Cathodes were prepared by mixing graphite, carbon black (Super P, M.M.M. Carbon), and vinylidene fluoride copolymer (Kynar 2801, Arkema) at weight ratios of 88:3:9 with N-Methyl-2-pyrrolidone in a Spex mill for 5 minutes. The resulting slurry was cast on carbon coated Aluminum foil and dried in air at 100°C. The films were dried under vacuum at 105°C for 1 hour before cell assembly. Cells were constructed in a dryroom using 2035 coin cell hardware (Hoshen). Aluminum clad cathode cans and stainless steel anode cans were used for half cells. The aluminum clad cathode cans were prepared for high voltage cycling by coating the inside of the can with a Super P/ polyethylene acrylic acid based primer (MICA D-709) in a 1:1 by weight ratio. The carbon black coating or Pt foil reduced the buildup of contact resistance that would result in random cell failure after 40-60 cycles in 2035 coin cells. Cells were assembled using 0.020" lithium foil, 2 layers of Celgard 3401 separator, one on either side of a non-woven polypropylene separator, and excess electrolyte. Cell impedance and OCV were measured for each cell before being placed on test. All cells were cycled on a Maccor Series 4000 cycler. Electrolytes were prepared in a drybox at < 1 ppm moisture using monofluoroethylene carbonate (FEC) from Solvay, ethylmethylcarbonate (EMC) from Ferro, and $LiPF_6$ from Stella.

Table 1. Summary of Anion intercalation systems

Salt	Solvent	Cathode Carbon	Capacity (mAh/g)	Cycle #	Rate	Voltage	Efficiency	Ref
1.6m $LiClO_4$	PC	pyrolyzed PAN	69	Unknown	Unknown	5.00	85%	12
1.6m $LiClO_4$	PC	pyrolyzed PAN	69	2800	C/3	5.30	90%	13
1.2m $LiPF_6$	PC	pyrolyzed PAN	55-84	Unknown	Unknown	5.00	98%	15
1.6m $LiPF_6$	PC	pyrolyzed PAN/VC/MA	84-97	Unknown	Unknown	5.50	99%	14
1M $LiClO_4$	PC	Natural Graphite Flake	"---------"	Unknown	Unknown	5.80	79%	2
2M $LiPF_6$	EMS	Fluka Graphite	95	1	C/7	5.45	82%	4
2M $LiPF_6$	EMS	Fluka Graphite	90	2	C/7	5.45	92%	4
2M $LiPF_6$	EMS	Fluka Graphite	91	10	C/7	5.45	91%	4
2M $LiPF_6$	EMS	Fluka Graphite	90	1	C/40	5.30	67%	17
1M $LiPF_6$	EC:DEC	Fluka Graphite	36	1	C/40	5.10	58%	17
3M $LiPF_6$	EC:DEC	Fluka Graphite	40	1	C/40	5.00	53%	17
1.8M AR	PC	Alfa Aesar Graphite	50	1	C	5.50	67%	5
1.8M AR	PC	Alfa Aesar Graphite	58	10	C	5.50	87%	5
1M $LiPF_6$	EC:DMC (1:2)	KS-6 TIMREX	81	1	C	5.50	70%	7
1M $LiPF_6$	EC:DMC (1:2)	KS-6 TIMREX	74	10	C	5.50	95%	7
1M $LiPF_6$	EC:DMC (1:2)	Petca FM-14	85	1	Unknown	5.50	65%	6
1M LiTFSI	$Pyr_{14}TFSI$	KS-6 TIMREX	85	50	C	5.20	96%	8
1M LiTFSI	$Pyr_{14}TFSI$	KS-6 TIMREX	85	50	C	5.30	90%	8

Discussion

The basis for pursuing a dual-graphite energy storage cell is predicated on the ideas that the cost will be lower than conventional Li-ion chemistries, due to the fact that a transition metal cathode will not be used in the battery, and that the system will be safer than other grid storage batteries due to the fact that overcharge can be controlled by limiting the salt concentration in the electrolyte. The main drawback of the dual-graphite chemistry is that the specific energy and energy density is limited both by the anion intercalation capacity of the graphite, and the amount of salt that can be dissolved in the electrolyte. Table 1 shows that the upper limit on the specific capacity for anion intercalation in graphite falls in the range of 90-95 mAh/g for the best electrolyte systems. These values are consistent with our data shown in Figure 1 for SFG-44 graphite half-cells that have undergone storage testing and post storage cycling. The maximum solubility of $LiPF_6$ salt in carbonate based solvents is typically in the range of 1.5 to 3M. For the electrolyte system we investigated, the maximum electrolyte concentration prepared was 2.0M.

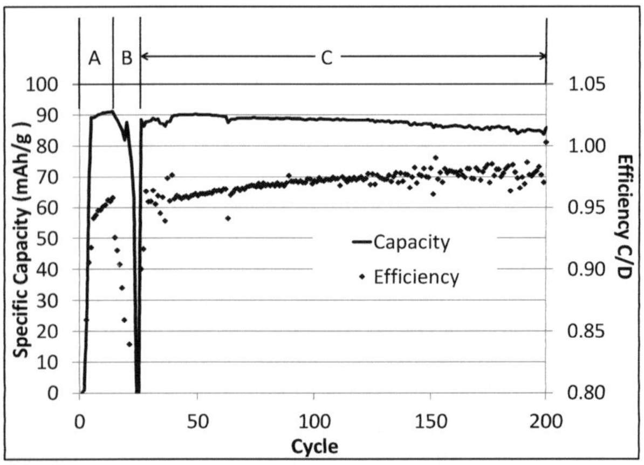

Figure 1. (A) Initial cycling (B) Storage and (C) post storage cycling on SFG-44 graphite cathode in 2M $LiPF_6$ FEC:EMC electrolyte between 5.2 and 4V vs. Li/Li^+.

To calculate the energy density and specific energy for this dual-graphite cell, we use equations 1 and 2 developed by Dahn and Seel.[16] The anode capacity (q_a), cathode capacity (q_c), salt molarity in the charged (M_c) and discharged states (M_d), electrolyte density (ρ_e), graphite density (ρ), cell voltage (V) and the charge stored per liter of 1M electrolyte solution (R) are all given in Table 2 for the system we studied. Based on these parameters, we calculate an energy density of 149 Wh/l and a specific energy of 95 Wh/kg for the dual-graphite cell. With a 20% de-rating for inert materials such as cell case, collectors, separator and tabs, these values become 119 Wh/l and 76 Wh/kg. These values are low when compared to conventional Li-ion where these values are 600 Wh/l and 230 Wh/kg at the cell level.

For grid storage applications, the most important driver is cost per energy stored amortized over the lifetime of the system ($/kW-yr), not specific energy or energy density.[19]

$$Energy\ Density = \frac{Vq_a\rho}{\left(1+\frac{q_a}{q_c}\right)+\frac{q_a\rho}{(M_d-M_c)R}} \qquad \text{Eq.1}$$

$$Specific\ Energy = \frac{Vq_a}{\left(1+\frac{q_a}{q_c}\right)+\frac{q_a\rho_e}{(M_d-M_c)R}} \qquad \text{Eq.2}$$

Table 2. Parameters for use in Eq.1 and Eq. 2.

Parameter	Value
Anode capacity, (q_a)	340 mAh/g
Cathode capacity, (q_c)	85 mAh/g
Molarity when charged, (M_c)	0.5M
Molarity when discharged, (M_d)	2.0M
Average cell voltage (V)	4.7V
Graphite density, (ρ)	$2.2g/cm^3$
Electrolyte density (ρ_e)	$1.4\ g/cm^3$
charge stored per liter of 1 M electrolyte solution (R)	26.8 Ah l/M

The most widely employed energy storage technology, capturing over 95% of the market, is pumped hydro. It is also a very low energy density storage technology but low cost due to a 60 year lifetime. For commercial and residential energy storage applications, electrochemical energy storage is preferred due to the higher energy density. The battery lifetimes are shorter and therefore the installed cost and amortized cost are both important. For Li-ion batteries in residential and commercial applications in the range of 10-500kWh, the amortized cost ranges from $600-$2500/kW-yr, with the higher cost for lower sized applications. The lifetime is specified as 5 years before replacement. The battery cost alone for these applications can range from $550 to $1500/kWh, with additional costs for installation and connection to the grid.[20] These high costs result in slow adoption of the technology, although Li-ion is still the fastest growing segment of the commercial and residential scale market. Replacing Li-ion with a similar, lower cost technology would speed the implementation of this scale of energy storage.

The typical cathode materials cost for a large Li-ion storage battery is in the range of 20-40% of the total material costs depending on cathode material. Lithium manganese spinel ($LiMn_2O_4$) is the lowest cost cathode material at \$10-\$12/kg, while lithium iron phosphate is \$20/kg. The oxide cathode materials containing Nickel and Cobalt fluctuate in price depending on metals prices with the $LiNi_{0.80}Co_{0.15}Al_{0.05}O_2$, and $Li_{1.05}(Ni_{1/3}Mn_{1/3}Co_{1/3})_{0.95}O_2$ roughly \$30/kg.[21] In order for graphite to replace these materials, the cost must be lower than \$10/kg. Current natural graphite prices are \$10/kg while synthetic graphite prices are twice that at \$20/kg. Given these prices, it is difficult to see that replacing a cathode material such as $LiMn_2O_4$ with graphite would result in any decrease in cost for cell manufacture.

The safety of dual-graphite systems has not been evaluated and therefore the proposal that safety will be better in these systems is based on several assumptions. The assumptions are that the intercalated anion is less reactive than de-lithiated metal oxide and will not decompose releasing oxygen. This has not been demonstrated in the literature. The other assumption is that the concentration of the salt can be controlled to prevent overcharge at the anode and cathode. Overcharge at the cathode would likely not be an issue as the anion intercalation proceeds to a capacity of ~90mAh/g and then the voltage at the cathode simply rises. Overcharge of the anode could be prevented simply by a choice of salt concentration and this may be beneficial to a large scale energy storage system.

Conclusions

Full dual-graphite cells utilizing FEC based electrolytes can now be built and show a cycling behavior of 70% at 50 cycles. Half-cell cycling on SFG-44 cathodes demonstrates an anion intercalation capacity of 90mAh/g out to several hundred cycles, consistent with most literature. The energy density and specific energy of dual-graphite cells is lower than conventional Li-ion, although for grid storage applications, cost, service life, and safety are the most important factors. From a simple cost analysis, it appears that the benefits of a dual-graphite grid storage battery are not significant, especially when compared to $LiMn_2O_4$ based cells. Safety needs to be explored for these dual-graphite systems to determine if it is significantly better than conventional Li-ion.

Acknowledgements

The authors would like to acknowledge support of the Army Research Laboratory.

References

[1] R.T. Carlin, H.C. De Long, J. Fuller, and P. Trulove, *J. Electrochem. Soc.*, **141** (7) L73 (1994)

[2] R. Santhanam, M. Noel, *J. Power Sources*, **66**, 47-54 (1997)

[3] R. Santhanam, M. Noel, *J. Power Sources*, **76**, 147-152 (1998)

[4] J.A. Seel and J.R. Dahn, *J. Electrochem. Soc.*, **147** (3) 892-898 (2000)

[5] W.C. West, J.F. Whitacre, N. Leifer, S. Greenbaum, M. Smart, R. Bugga, M. Blanco, and S.R. Narayanan, *J. Electrochem. Soc.*, **154** (10) A929 (2007)

[6] T. Ishihara, M. Koga, H Matsumoto, and M. Yoshio, *Electrochem. Solid State Lett.* , **10** (3), A74 (2007)

[7] N. Gunawardhana, G-J Park, N. Dimov, A. K. Thapa, H. Nakamura, H. Wang, T. Ishihara, M. Yoshio, *Journal of Power Sources*, **196**, 7886 (2011)

[8] T. Placke, O. Fromm, S.F. Lux, P. Bieker, S. Rothermel, H-W Meyer, S. Passerini, M. Winter, *J. Electrochem. Soc.*, **159** (11) A1755-A1765 (2012)

[9] D. Billaud and A. Chénite, *J. Power Sources*, **13**,1 (1984)

[10] A. Jobert, Ph. Touzain and L. Bonnetain, *Carbon*, **19**, 193 (1981).

[11] Z. Zhang and M Lerner, *J. Electrochem. Soc.*, **140**(3) 742 (1993).

[12] F.P. McCullough, A. Levine, and R.V. Snelgrove, U.S. Patent 4,830,938 (1989).

[13] F.P. McCullough and A.F. Beale, U.S. Patent 4,865,931 (1989).

[14] F.P. McCullough, U.S. Patent 5,518,836 (1996).

[15] F.P. McCullough, U.S. Patent 5,532,083 (1996).

[16] J.R. Dahn and J.A. Seel, *J. Electrochem. Soc.*, **147** (3) 899 (2000)

[17] J.A. Seel, *Doctoral Thesis*, Dalhousie University Halifax N.S. July 2004,

[18] J.A. Read, A. v. Cresce, M.H. Ervin, and K. Xu , *Energy Environ. Sci.*,7,617(2014).

[19] I. Gyuk, M. Johnson, J. Vetrano, K. Lynn, W. Parks, R. Handa, L. Kannberg, S. Hearne, K. Waldrip, R. Braccio Grid Energy Storage Report, U.S. Department of Energy, December 2013

[20] A.A. Akhil, G. Huff, A.B. Currier, B.C. Kaun, D.M. Rastler, S.B. Chen, … , W.D. Gauntlett, (2013). DOE/EPRI 2013 Electricity Storage Handbook in Collaboration with NRECA. Sandia National Laboratories Report, SAND2013-5131, Appendix B, Table B-31.

[21] P.A. Nelson, K.G. Gallagher, I. Bloom, and D.W. Dees, (2012), "The Performance and Cost of Lithium-Ion Batteries for Electric-Drive Vehicles", Argonne National Laboratory Report ANL-12/55, Table 5.1.

Potassium-Doped Lithium Manganese Spinel Cells for Use in Energy Harvesting Applications

Yakira J. Kirzner and Terrill B. Atwater
US Army-RDECOM-CERDEC-CPI-Power Division
5100 Magazine Road
Aberdeen Proving Ground, MD 21005

Abstract: *Lithium manganese oxide doped with potassium forms a spinel with the potential to pair well with electromagnetic energy harvesting devices. Synthesized with the stoichiometric formula $LiK_xMn_2O_4$, where $X = 0.075$ to 0.125, the spinels act as the active material for cathodes in rechargeable lithium cells. In order to sink pulses of power from energy harvesting devices, the doped-potassium allows for cell overcharge without affecting overall reversibility. Varying amounts of potassium were added to optimize the rate capabilities necessary to meet demands of an energy harvesting device. It was shown through pulse charging tests that $Li//LiK_xMn_2O_4$ cells are able to successfully maintain reversibility and exhibit great potential for maximizing energy recovery in energy harvesting devices.*

Keywords: Lithium-ion batteries; $LiK_xMn_2O_4$; Energy harvesting; Rechargeable batteries; Rechargeable lithium cells

Introduction

Lithium ion batteries have emerged from the field of electrochemistry as an exciting power solution due to their high energy density and ability to recharge. Improved battery performance over the past few decades has allowed new types of lithium ion batteries to be customized for a wide variety of applications.[1] Varying the chemistry, form factor, and fabrication method of the batteries has led to their utilization in portable devices, electric vehicles, and many other commercial and military technologies.

New energy harvesting devices being developed call for a customized energy storage system that can hold the power generated by the device until it is needed for rapid release. Lithium ion batteries were examined as a promising option to pair with energy harvesting systems due to their lightweight nature and conformal packaging abilities.[2] Specifically, potassium-doped manganese spinel cells were developed because of their unique ability to sink pulses of power and maintain overall reversibility.[2]

Using $LiK_xMn_2O_4$ as the cathode material, rechargeable cells were synthesized with X varying between 0.075 and 0.125. Batches of differing potassium concentrations were characterized and compared in order to best optimize the rate capabilities of the cells. Comparison was done by using intermittent pulse charge tests to simulate the batteries being paired with energy harvesting devices. After the cells were analyzed for their ability to meet high energy demands, they were additionally cycled before and after pulse charging to ensure reversibility.

Background

Electrochemical energy harvesting devices require a specific energy storage system that is capable of sinking pulses of energy and releasing that energy on demand. Since these devices generally only capture low levels of ambient energy, small batteries or capacitors are often the right choice for pairing. $LiMn_2O_4$ cathode batteries have demonstrated over 96 percent cycling efficiency at low currents, which is of the utmost importance for energy harvesting and scavenging. However, the major challenge facing batteries of this chemistry is damage caused by prolonged overcharge or overdischarge.[3,4]

When cycled, lithium ion batteries exchange lithium ions between the positive and negative electrodes upon charge and discharge. This can cause mechanical stress within the electrode as the ions are continuously inserted and extracted. Using $LiMn_2O_4$ as the cathode material, lithium will diffuse in and out of the spinel and can cause stress on the lattice structure through the constant breaking and forming of bonds.[5] The lithium gets inserted into the cathode during discharge and causes the crystal structure to undergo phase transitions which increasingly disrupt lattice stability each time the cell is discharged.[2] This is a particular challenge when being paired with an energy harvesting device, which forces intermittent cycling and thus a large potential for spinel degradation. One promising solution to this problem is doping the $LiMn_2O_4$ with potassium. The added Potassium ions in the crystal structure can improve lattice stability by creating a larger space from which lithium to enter and leave.[2]

To best improve the cathode material for energy storage in harvesting applications, different amounts of potassium were added to spinel material. The percentages of potassium chosen to add to the mixture were based off of previously demonstrated performance characteristics of $LiK_xMn_2O_4$ that would best optimize the capacity delivered.[2] The goal was to analyze the cell behavior and rate capabilities of each batch of doped spinel to best optimize the chemical composition for the challenging energy harvesting application. Additionally, the Army is investigating test protocol for kinetic energy harvesting devices under consideration.[6]

Experimental

$LiMn_2O_4$ was prepared by mixing LiOH with MnO_2 and doping the mixture with different concentrations of KOH. Heating in a box furnace for three days allowed for the chemical reaction yielding $LiK_xMn_2O_4$ to form the active material in the experimental cathodes. These cathodes were built by mixing the active material with carbon and the binder polytetrafluoroethylene (PTFE) and fabricated into button cells versus a metallic lithium anode. The cells were cycled, pulse charged, and re-cycled to evaluate the rate and reversibility capabilities of each batch of cells.

The cathode material was made from 20g of MnO_2 and 2.75g of LiOH, with 0, 0.48, 0.65, and 0.81g of KOH to make batches of $LiK_xMn_2O_4$ with X equaling 0, 0.075, 0.1, and 0.125, respectively. These stoichiometries were chosen to best optimize the theoretical capacity yields of the cells. The mixture was dry mixed in a Random Orbit Mixer Mill, heated at 800°C for 72 hours to facilitate the chemical reaction, and subsequently cooled down at 300°C to form the active ingredient of the cathodes. 2.5g of this material was then combined with 0.45g of Pure Black and 0.25g of PTFE using a mortar and pestle, and formed into a dough consistency using isopropanol. The newly mixed cathode material was calendared between Mylar sheets, punched into 1.25cm diameter discs, and dried in a vacuum oven yielding 0.12g cathodes.

Once the experimental cathodes were fabricated, button cells were constructed using metallic lithium as the anode. Additionally, aluminum screens and nickel screens were spot welded into the cathode and anode cans respectively, and three nonwoven glass separators were placed between the lithium manganese spinel material and the lithium. The electrolyte used was 1 molar $LiPF_6$ in proportional mixtures of diethyl carbonate, dimethyl carbonate and ethylene carbonate.

The button cells were put on three consecutive tests for overall cell behavior results. These tests were run on an ARBIN MSTAT4 Battery Cycler System. First they were put on a cycling test where they were charged and discharged for ten cycles, then they were pulse charged, and finally they were cycled according to the same profile as the first cycling test. For the two cycling tests, the cells were charged and discharged at a constant current of 2mA between 3.5 and 4.5V, with a 15 minute rest time between cycles for equilibration. The pulse charging tests were run at 4mA of constant current cycling between 3.5 and 4.5V, with the current pulsating between one minute of charge and 15 minutes of rest. This was to simulate the pulses of power that would be produced by an electrochemical energy harvesting device. These devices hit their storage systems with intermittent bursts of power that cause localized overcharging in the cells, while allowing them to relax between pulses. The one minute pulses of current in the pulse charging tests were designed to create the same localized overcharging effect, while the 15 minute rest period allow the cells to return to thermodynamic equilibrium between pulses.

Results from the two cycling tests run before and after the pulse charging regime can be analytically compared to evaluate the cells' ability to function under the stress of the challenging energy profile supplied by the energy harvesting devices.

Results

To compare the batches of $Li//LiK_xMn_2O_4$ cells with differing X values, their differential capacity per gram was plotted versus voltage on the same chart. The X values that were tested were 0.075, 0.1, and 0.125. Visually, it can be seen in **Figure 1** that the three curves line up evenly, though X=0.1 has the most defined peaks. The change in the amount of potassium added to the cathode effects the thermodynamics of how lithium gets inserted into the material. The lower values and more defined peaks in X=0.1 pinpoints more definitely the thermodynamics and kinetics of the first half lithium removed during charge.

The closer the charge peaks line up over the discharge peaks above and below the horizontal axis, the less energy loss is occurring. The shift in peaks that can be seen in **Figure 1** is due to activation energy and impedance. The slight extra peak that is additionally observed upon discharge is due to the lithium that is being inserted into the cathode changing sites from tetrahedral to octahedral. At the end of the discharge, all available tetrahedral sites are filled so the next lithium is forced to change the structure using more energy. The added potassium allows for this localized overcharge and maintains the reversibility of the cell for the next charge-discharge cycle. Since energy harvesting devices control the amount of energy their electrochemical storage components need to sink, this type of overcharge recovery allowed by the potassium is crucial.

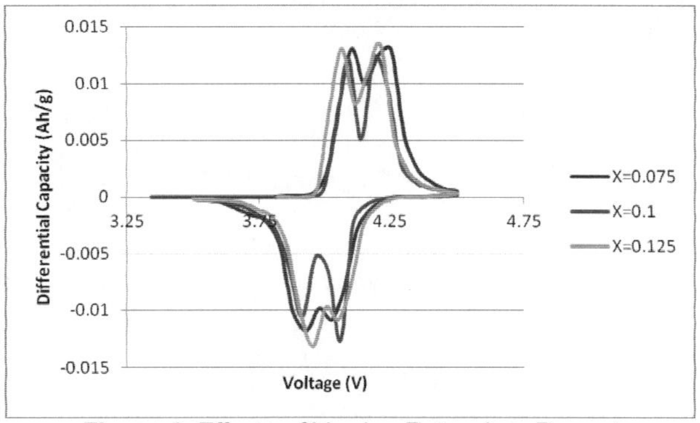

Figure 1. Effects of Varying Potassium Dopent Concentrations

To evaluate the performance of the potassium-doped lithium manganese spinel cells, they were cycled, pulse charged, and re-cycled. In **Figure 2** the cycle results of the cells with dopent stoichiometry X=0.075 are compared. The initial cycling test demonstrated good stability in the cathode material as demonstrated in **Figure 2**. Each cycle curve very closely overlays the other when graphed on a differential capacity versus voltage chart. **Figure 2** shows the performance of $LiK_{0.075}Mn_2O_4$ cells when cycled at 2mA between 3.5 and 4.5V and illustrates their good columbic efficiency.

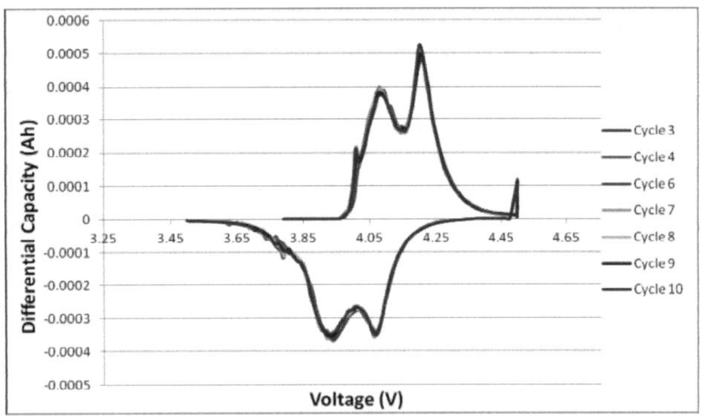

Figure 2. Differential Capacity of $Li//LiK_{0.075}Mn_2O_4$ Cells

The pulse charge tests simulated the energy pulses that would come from energy harvesting devices by sending bursts of current to the cell while cycling between 3.5 and 4.5V. The charge regime delivered the current in one minute increments to cause localized overcharging while allowing 15 minutes of rest time in between for the cells to thermodynamically equilibrate. **Figure 3** shows the current and voltage versus time for the $Li//LiK_{0.075}Mn_2O_4$ cells. The voltage curves representing voltage over time show favorable kinetics as the small distance between the bottom and top of the curve indicate minimal impedance. Additionally, the charge and discharge capacity lines line up at the end of each cycle demonstrating good columbic efficiency and no side reactions.

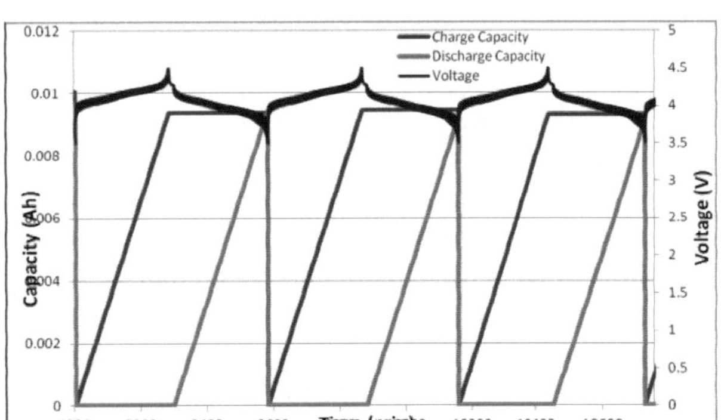

Figure 3. Pulse Charging of $Li//LiK_{0.075}Mn_2O_4$ Cells

The final cycling test was performed on the cells to evaluate their ability to recover from localized overcharging and bounce back to their original state. To effectively analyze this, the differential capacity curves were overlaid with the curves from the first cycle after the cells underwent the same charge regime. **Figure 4** shows that the before pulse and after pulse curves line up to indicate that the pulse charging caused no irreversible effects on the cells.

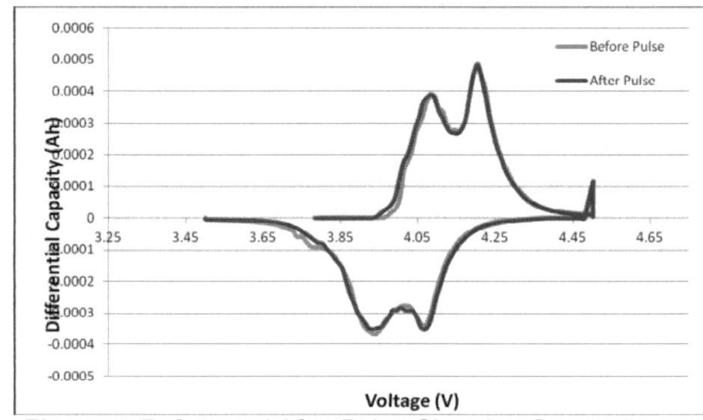

Figure 4. Before and After Pulse Charging Comparison on $Li//LiK_{0.075}Mn_2O_4$ Cells

Discussion

$Li//LiK_xMn_2O_4$ cells were fabricated in order to test their suitability as electrochemical storage for energy harvesting devices. The charge profile that the harvesting devices deliver causes localized overcharging on each burst of energy. Therefore, the storage system paired with the device must be capable of overcharge recovery with minimal losses so that it can continuously be utilized. The $LiK_xMn_2O_4$ chemistry demonstrated good reversibility before and after such a charge regime with very little capacity loss. The added potassium in the lithium spinel material acted to widen the MnO_2 sites for the lithium ions to exit and enter more easily upon charge and discharge. This acted to stabilize the spinel matrix so that there was minimal degradation during the demanding pulse charging tests.

Cells were tested with X values of 0.075, 0.1 and 0.125 to optimize the potassium dopent concentration. When cycled between 3.5 and 4.5V at 2mA, the $Li//LiK_{0.075}Mn_2O_4$ cells averaged a capacity between 0.009 and 0.011Ah, the $Li//LiK_{0.1}Mn_2O_4$ cells averaged between 0.013 and 0.014Ah, and the $Li//LiK_{0.125}Mn_2O_4$ cells averaged between 0.006 and 0.008Ah. With the most tests done on the $Li//LiK_{0.075}Mn_2O_4$ cells, the capacity remained relatively consistent throughout each ten-cycle batch of testing with minimal losses. With the theoretical capacity averaging around 0.012Ah, the cells performed between 75 percent and 91 percent of their potential. Future research will analytically compare the capacity results of the chemistries with varying K concentrations, optimize the fabrication method of the cells, and cycle the cells well beyond ten cycles to further evaluate performance. The ultimate goal of this research is to pair the $Li//LiK_xMn_2O_4$ cells with energy harvesting devices to act as their electrochemical storage system.

Conclusion

Energy harvesting devices are currently being developed as an effective way to generate power from ambient energy sources. Because the energy scavenged from different locations is both unpredictable and intermittent, it can subject its energy storage system to localized overcharging and mechanical wear. Potassium-doped lithium manganese spinel cells were examined for pairing with these devices in order to accept and release the energy captured while maintaining reversibility. The added potassium created space for the lithium to enter and leave without damaging the spinel matrix. Data showed successful overcharge recovery in the $Li//LiK_xMn_2O_4$ cells and complete reversibility when cycled repeatedly. This chemistry proved to be an exciting option for the electrochemical storage system for energy harvesting applications.

References

1. Reddy RB (Ed.), Linden's Handbook of Batteries 4ed., McGraw Hill inc, New York, NY, pp. 26.1-26,79, 2011.
2. Atwater TB and AJ Salkind, "Advanced Manganese Oxide Material for Rechargeable Lithium Cells," *Journal of Power Sources*, vol. 162, no. 2, pp. 773-779, 2006.
3. Dudney NJ, "Thin Film Micro-Batteries," *The Electrochemical Society*, vol. 17, no. 3, pp.44-48, 2008.
4. Priya S and DJ Inman (Eds.), Energy Harvesting Technologies, Springer Science+Business Media, LLC, 2009.
5. Vetter J, Novak P, Wagner MR, Veit C, Moller KC, Besenhard JO, Winter M, Wohlfahrt-Mehrens M, Vogler C and A Hammouche, "Ageing Mechanisms in Lithium-Ion Batteries," *Journal of Power Sources*, vol. 147, pp. 269-281, 2005.
6. Douglas JS, Atwater TB, Rawlings SL and J Collazo, "Optimization of Wearable Kinetic Energy Device Test Protocol," 46th Power Sources Symposium, 2014.
7. Etacheri V, Marom R, Elazari R, Salitra G and D Aurbach, "Challenges in the Development of Advanced Li-ion Batteries: A Review," *Energy and Environmental Science*, vol. 4, pp. 3243-3263, 2011.
8. Fergus JW, "Recent Developments in Cathode Materials for Lithium Ion Batteries," *Journal of Power Sources*, vol. 195, pp. 939-954, 2010.
9. Miller, JR and P Simon, "Electrochemical Capacitors for Energy Management," *Science Magazine*, vol. 321, pp. 651-652, 2008.
10. Sodano HA, Inman DJ and G Park, "Generation and Storage of Electricity from Power Harvesting Devices," *Journal of Intelligent Material Systems and Structures*, vol. 16, pp. 67-75, 2005.

Performance and Safety of Lithium-ion Capacitors

Judith A. Jeevarajan and Martin D. Martinez
Power Sources Branch, Propulsion and Power Division
NASA Johnson Space Center
Houston, Texas, United States, 77058

Abstract: *Lithium-ion capacitors (LIC) are a recent innovation in the area of supercapacitors and ultracapacitors. With an operating voltage range similar to that of lithium-ion batteries and a very low self-discharge rate, these can be readily used in the place of batteries especially when large currents are required to be stored safely for use at a later time.*

Keywords: lithium-ion capacitors; LIC, LICs, lithium-ion supercapacitor safety; high-voltage range capacitors.

Introduction

Lithium-ion capacitors are a hybrid between lithium-ion batteries and Electric Double Layer Capacitors (EDLC). Not much work has been carried out or published in the area of LICs. The cathode in the LICs is activated carbon and the anode is lithiated or lithium-ion doped carbon. The electrolyte is made up of a combination of organic solvents and a lithiated salt. The charge in the LIC is stored at the surface of the cathode in the electric double layer that develops between the cathode and the electrolyte. Figures 1 and 2 show the difference between the LIC and a lithium-ion battery [1]. The LICs described in this paper were manufactured by JSRMicro LLC. The voltage range provided by these LICs are higher than traditional capacitors, supercapacitors or ultracapacitors. The LICs have an operating voltage range of 3.8 V to 2.2 V. These can be charged to a voltage of up to 4.2 V, if needed, although this may reduce the cycle life of the LICs. The LICs tested under this program were of 1 Ah capacity. This paper will provide the details of the testing carried out on the LICs and will describe the performance and safety under a set of nominal and off-nominal conditions respectively.

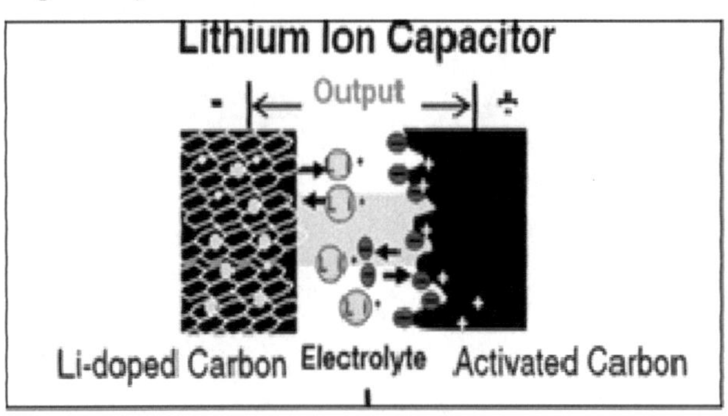

Figure 1. Schematic of Lithium-ion Capacitor (LIC). Courtesy: JSR Micro Inc.

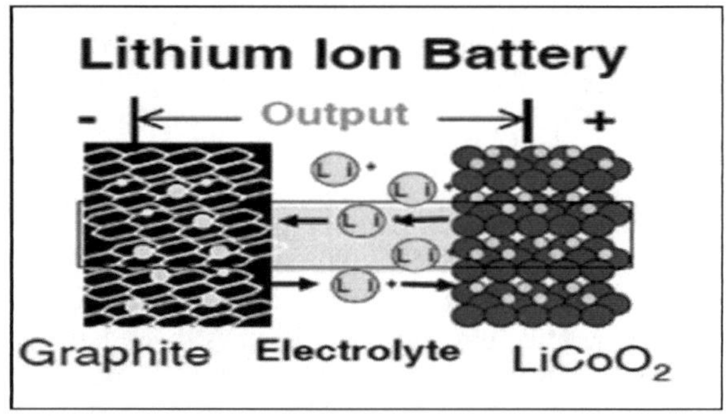

Figure 2. Schematic of a Lithium-ion battery. Courtesy: JSR Micro Inc.

Experimental

The tests carried out on the LICs to determine their performance testing included rate capability tests, performance at different temperatures, self discharge tests at different end-of-charge voltages, and high rate charge to nominal end of charge voltage. The safety tests included overcharge, overdischarge, external short, simulated internal short and heat-to-vent tests. The dimensions of the 1Ah LICs were 93mmX149.5mmX15.5mm and the mass was 370 g.

The rate capability tests included 100 cycles of charge and discharge between 3.8 V to 2.2 V, at various rates with currents of 1.5 A, 5.0 A, 7.5 A and 10 A charge currents and 1.5, 3.0 and 10A discharge currents in various combinations. A typical charge and discharge profile was used for a majority of the tests except the rate capability test which consisted of a charge current of 10 A to 3.8 V limit, hold at 3.8 V for 30 minutes and then discharge using a current of 10 A to 2.2 V. The performance at -30 ºC, -20 ºC, 0 ºC, 40 ºC, 60 ºC and 70 ºC was determined by charging and discharging at the stated temperatures using the typical charge and discharge profile. The self-discharge tests included storing the LICs at different end-of-charge voltages of 2.5 V, 3.0 V, 3.8 V and 4.2 V for more than 60 days. The change in open circuit voltage and the capacity retained were determined. The latter was carried out by discharging the LICs at a current of 1 A to 2.2 V. The high current charge test consisted of charging the LICs to 3.8 V at currents of up to 800 A. When the LIC was subjected to a high rate charge at 100 A, it was stored for seven days at the end of charge voltage and discharged using 10A current to determine the capacity retained under a high rate charge and short storage period.

The LICs were subjected to an overcharge test using a charge current of 1 A to a voltage limit of 20 V for a period of 6 hours. The overdischarge test consisted of discharging the LIC to 0 V using a current of 1 A. The external short test consisted of shorting the LIC using a load of less than 1 mohm (~0.85 mohm) with data collected at the rate of 1 kHZ for the first three seconds and then at the rate of 1Hz for the rest of the test. The simulated internal short was carried using a blunt rod and causing an indentation that would cause an internal short without penetrating the cell. The heat to vent test was carried out by heating the LIC at full state-of-charge at a rate of 3 ºC per minute until the LICs vented.

Results and Discussion

The Table 1 provides details of the various charge and discharge rates that the LICs were subjected to. It was observed that the capacity obtained under these various rates were greater than 1.4 Ah except for the 5.0 A charge and 10 A discharge protocol where capacities between 1.3 and 1.4 Ah were achieved. The capacity loss in all cases after the 100 cycles was insignificant with a maximum capacity loss recorded of less than 2 %. Figure 3 shows a typical charge and discharge profile for the LIC under the conditions described in the Experimental section.

Table 1. Results of Rate Capability Test on the 1 Ah LICs.

PCTest SAMPLE#	Test Number	Serial #	1st Cycle Capacity (Ah)	100th Cycle Capacity (Ah)	Capacity Change (%)	Capacity Change (Ah)
01	Protocol 1-1 (1.5A/10.0A)	3AL16-54	1.451	1.438	0.9%	0.013
02	Protocol 1-2 (1.5A/10.0A)	3AL16-56	1.469	1.463	0.4%	0.006
03	Protocol 1-3 (1.5A/10.0A)	3AL16-55	1.459	1.433	1.8%	0.026
04	Protocol 2-1 (5.0A/10.0A)	3AL16-57	1.314	1.310	0.3%	0.004
05	Protocol 2-2 (5.0A/10.0A)	3AK16-7	1.396	1.374	1.6%	0.022
06	Protocol 2-3 (5.0A/10.0A)	3AK16-9	1.413	1.399	1.0%	0.014
07	Protocol 3-1 (7.5A/10.0A)	3AK16-6	1.420	1.402	1.3%	0.018
08	Protocol 3-2 (7.5A/10.0A)	3AK16-8	1.424	1.425	-0.1%	-0.001
09	Protocol 3-3 (7.5A/10.0A)	3AK16-3	1.420	1.396	1.7%	0.024
01	Protocol 4-1 (10.0A/1.5A)	3AL16-54	1.491	1.488	0.2%	0.003
02	Protocol 4-2 (10.0A/1.5A)	3AL16-56	1.484	1.482	0.1%	0.002
03	Protocol 4-3 (10.0A/1.5A)	3AL16-55	1.496	1.494	0.1%	0.002
04	Protocol 5-1 (10.0A/3.0A)	3AL16-57	1.443	1.433	0.7%	0.010
05	Protocol 5-2 (10.0A/3.0A)	3AK16-7	1.458	1.456	0.1%	0.002
06	Protocol 5-3 (10.0A/3.0A)	3AK16-9	1.449	1.446	0.2%	0.003
07	Protocol 6-1 (1.5A/1.5A)	3AK16-6	1.456	1.451	0.3%	0.005
08	Protocol 6-2 (1.5A/1.5A)	3AK16-8	1.467	1.464	0.2%	0.003
09	Protocol 6-3 (1.5A/1.5A)	3AK16-3	1.459	1.458	0.1%	0.001

The performance at various temperatures indicated that at -30 ºC 1 Ah capacity was obtained, 1.2 Ah capacity was obtained at -20 ºC, 1.33 Ah capacity was obtained at 0 ºC, and 1.5 Ah capacity was obtained at 40 ºC, 60 ºC and 70 ºC. The maximum temperature increase observed through the discharge was 4 ºC. Figure 4 gives the charge and discharge profile at -30 ºC.

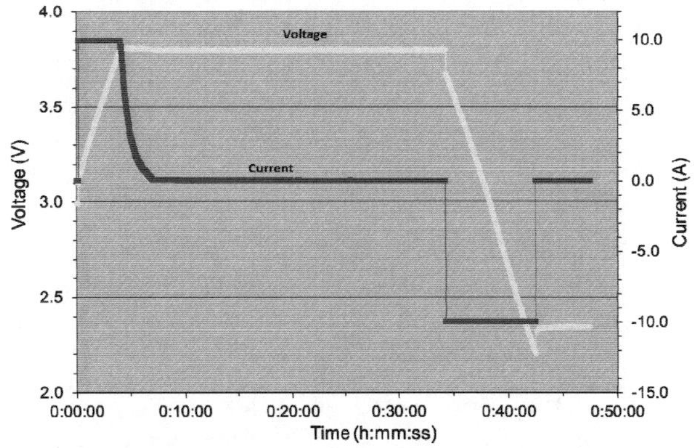

Figure 3. Typical charge and discharge profile for the Lithium-ion Capacitor (LIC) under a

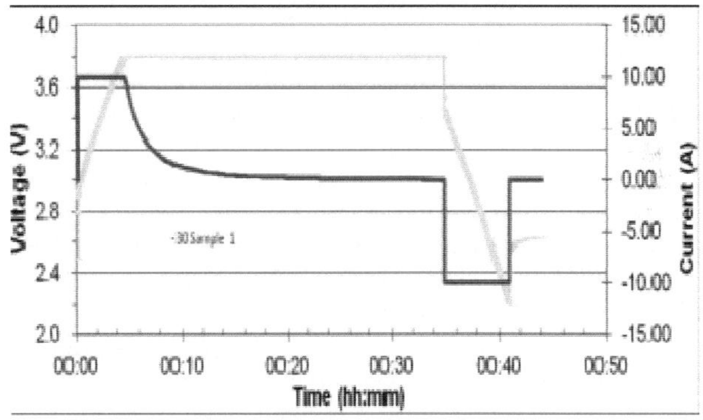

Figure 4. Performance of the LIC at -30 ºC.

The self-discharge test indicated that the maximum discharge occurred when the LICs were stored at 4.2 V displaying a loss in voltage of 7.4 % over the storage period where no change in voltage was observed when the LICs were stored at 2.5 V and 3.0 V. Table 2 provides the data on the voltage change and the capacity retained by the LICs after the storage period. Figure 5 provides the open circuit voltages (OCV) recorded once a day during the storage period.

Table 2. Results of the Self-Discharge Test on the 1 Ah LICs.

Sample #	Sample ID	Initial OCV (V)	Final OCV (V)	Capacity Retained (Ah)
1	16	4.183	3.868	1.724
2	17	3.784	3.698	1.425
3	18	2.996	2.984	0.675
4	19	2.524	2.540	0.306

The high-rate charge test with a charge current of 100 A and a storage period of even days after the charge provided up to 1.5 Ah capacity when discharged using a current of 10 A, after the storage period. Charging at currents of up to 800 A indicated that the maximum charge current accepted by the LIC was 140 A which is 140C rate for the 1 Ah LIC.

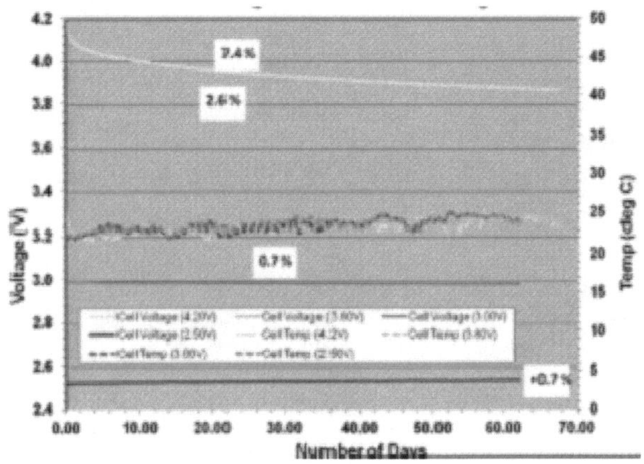

Figure 5. Self-Discharge tests showing OCV recorded each day for the Lithium-ion Capacitor (LIC) during the storage period.

The overcharge test resulted in the LICs swelling but no venting, fire or thermal runaway was observed. The maximum temperature observed was 40.7 ºC and the voltage plateaued at 4.77 V during the overcharge period. Figures 6 and 7 show the pictures of a typical LIC and one that was subjected to the overcharge test. The overdischarge test did not cause any venting or fire of the LICs but swelling of the LICs was observed and the maximum temperature recorded was 47 ºC. The external short test resulted in a maximum temperature rise of 29 ºC and currents of up to ~1900 A was recorded within the first few milliseconds after the short was applied. Figures 8 and 9 provide details of the external short test with data recorded at slow (1Hz) and fast (1kHz) data collection rates respectively. Under the simulated internal short test conditions, a maximum temperature of 97 ºC was recorded and the LICs exhibited venting and smoke but no fire. Similarly, when the LICs were subjected to the heat-to-vent test, the LICs vented at temperatures greater than 175 ºC and exhibited smoke but no fire.

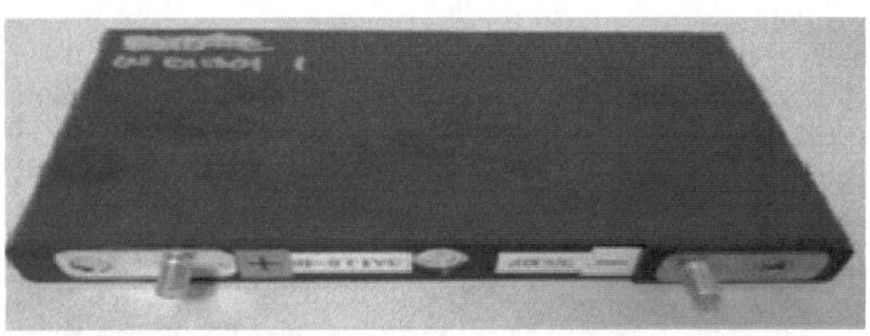

Figure 6. Photo of typical LIC.

Figure 7. Photo of LIC after the overcharge test showing swelling.

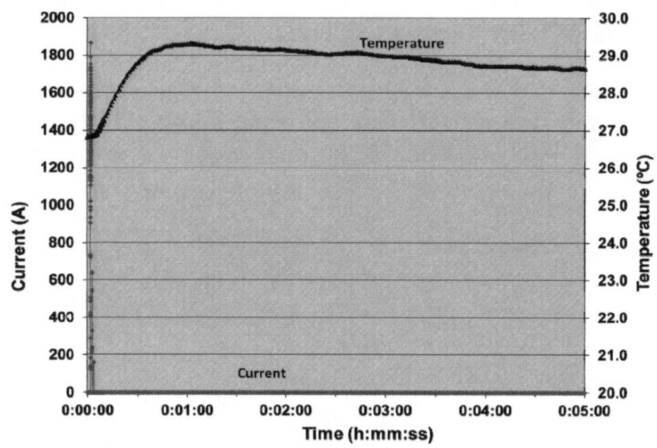

Figure 8. External Short Test on the LIC showing current and temperature recorded at 1Hz rate.

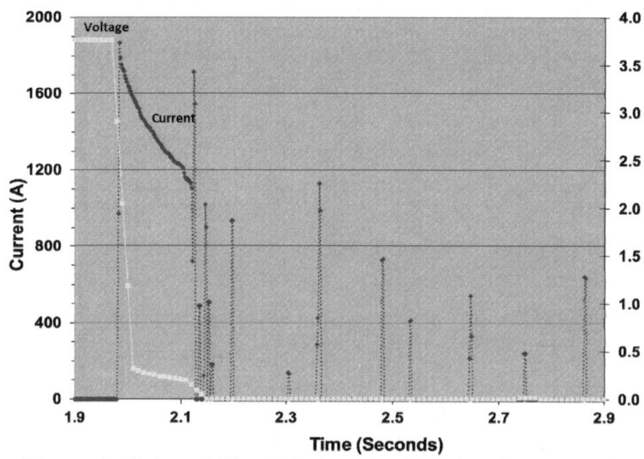

Figure 9. External Short Test on the LIC showing current and voltage recorded at 1kHz rate.

Summary

The performance of the LICs exceeded that stated in the specification sheet. At nominal discharge rates of 10 A, the capacity of the LICs was almost 50% more than the rated capacity. The LICs performed well at temperatures as low as -30 ºC providing the nameplate capacity of 1 Ah. No change in capacity was observed at 70 ºC compared to room temperature capacity. The LICs accepted charge of up to 140 A and although currents as high as 200A were accepted, the upper voltage limit of 3.8 V was reached instantaneously preventing nominal charge. The LICs did not show any fire or venting under conditions of overcharge and overdischarge as well as external shorts. The LICs showed venting and smoke under conditions of simulated internal short as well as high temperatures of greater than 175 ºC. The off-nominal tests indicate that the LICs have a higher tolerance to abuse than lithium-ion batteries.

Acknowledgements
The authors would like to thank JSR Micro Inc., for the collaboration in this work and providing significant guidance in determining the nominal test protocols. The authors would also like to express their gratitude to the test team at PCTest Engineering Inc., for carrying out the tests and providing flexibility to make changes to tests in order to obtain a greater understanding of the test results.

References

1. Technical Bulletin and communication, JSR Micro Inc.

In Situ Atomic Force Microscopy of Nanofabricated Amorphous Silicon for Lithium Ion Batteries

Collin R. Becker, Kenneth E. Strawhecker, Cynthia A. Lundgren
Electrochemistry Branch, U.S. Army Research Laboratory
2800 Powder Mill Rd., Adelphi, MD 20783

Abstract: *The use of silicon (Si) as an anode in lithium ion (Li-ion) secondary batteries can greatly increase energy density. However, the evolution of the solid electrolyte interphase (SEI), morphology, and mechanical properties of Si during lithiation and delithiation must be understood to effectively introduce Si into Li-ion batteries. Nanoscale Si has demonstrated the best performance in Li ion batteries as it is less susceptible to cracking compared to bulk Si anodes. To better understand the performance of nanoscale Si, in situ studies of Si during cycling are necessary. To this end, atomic force microscopy (AFM) is used to monitor precision-fabricated amorphous Si pillars. The pillars are fabricated using electron beam lithography and are 100 nm tall and range in diameter from 100 to 1000 nm. The AFM is able to monitor SEI formation, morphology changes, and mechanical properties during cycling in several electrolytes. Ex situ scanning electron microscopy (SEM) reveals that pillars that were not physically touched by the AFM probe appear to remain intact. However, pillars that were touched by the tip are eroded and indicate that the mechanical integrity of the pillars is degraded during cycling. Quantitatively, nanoindentation performed on pillars as small as 200 nm diameter, reveal that hardness and elastic modulus do not recover fully upon delithiation. The AFM therefore provides both valuable qualitative and quantitative information to guide experimental and computational research.*

Keywords: amorphous silicon; lithium-ion battery; silicon; anode; atomic force microscopy

Introduction

To meet the energy storage demands of the future for portable electronics, automobiles, and an electricity grid that relies on renewable energy sources, batteries with nearly 100% cycling efficiency and large energy densities are required. State of the art lithium ion (Li-ion) batteries are becoming the predominant choice for consumer electronics, but need further improvement as electronics become smaller and thinner and consumers demand cars with larger driving ranges[1]. To this end, if the graphite anode of a conventional Li-ion battery is replaced with silicon (Si), a significant improvement in energy density can be realized.

Unfortunately, Si is plagued by poor cycle life as it expands and contracts during lithiation and delithiation. Si expands up to 300% as it alloys with Li, so while it has a capacity of 3500 $mAhg^{-1}$, it is notorious for poor efficiency[2]–[4]. Nanoscale Si architectures have dramatically improved the cycle life of Si and help to overcome the degradation caused by mechanical stress in the material[5]. Still, significant gaps remain in understanding how nanoscale Si cycles, especially in regards to the solid electrolyte interphase (SEI). Several groups have performed *in situ* transmission electron microscope (TEM) studies that clearly show how Si nanoscale architectures can survive lithiation and delithiation[6]. While there have recently been TEM studies using specialized cells that can accommodate traditional electrolytes, most TEM studies use either a solid electrolyte or ionic liquid, which means that an SEI will not form[7].

In this study, we make use of an atomic force microscope (AFM) operating in a liquid electrolyte electrochemical cell to investigate how microfabricated Si structures cycle. This experiment is useful as it monitors the Si *in situ* in a conventional organic electrolyte. The Si is also fabricated so that changes in the precisely created geometry can be recorded easily. In addition, both qualitative and quantitative information can be gained from the interaction of the AFM probe with the Si. Specifically, elastic modulus can be resolved at several depths within the Si nanostructures to track the lithiation capacity of the material.

Experimental

Silicon Samples: To fabricate precision nanoscale Si structures we use electron beam lithography. We begin by coating a Si wafer with a metallic thin film to serve as a current collector. Next, we spin a bilayer of poly(methyl methacrylate) (PMMA) to serve as a resist for electron beam lithography. The resist is approximately 500 nm thick. Patterns are transferred to the PMMA to generate arrays of circles of 1000, 500, 300, 200, and 100 nm in diameter. The circles are then filled with 20 nm of nickel (Ni) followed by 100 nm of amorphous Si deposited by electron beam evaporation.

Critical to use of the AFM in this study, is the ability to have a very smooth substrate with which to reference the Si nanostructure. In prior work we used a titanium (Ti) thin film deposited by electron beam evaporation at a very slow rate of 0.05 nms^{-1} [8]. The (Ti) film however formed a native oxide after being removed from vacuum to perform electron beam lithography. Subsequently, the deposition of

Si to make nanostructures suffered from poor adhesion. We switched to nickel (Ni) and were able to avoid these problems. In addition we used an ion assist deposition and were able to evaporate at a reasonable 0.2 nms^{-1} and still have extremely smooth substrates.

Electrochemical Analysis: For electrochemical measurements, an electrolyte of propylene carbonate (PC) solvent with 1M lithium triflate was used. The sample is fixed in an electrochemical cell (Agilent) in a two electrode arrangement with a lithium foil serving as the counter and reference electrode. The active area of Si is very low so that the background current from the Ni substrate is large compared to intercalation of Li into Si. Therefore, potentiostatic methods are used to control the extent of lithiation of the samples. A Solartron SI 1287 is used and the experiments are performed in air in a dry room (dewpoint < -80C).

Characterization: An Agilent 5500 AFM is used for the morphological and indentation characterization. The experiments are conducted in contact mode with Bruker DNP, silicon nitride tips. A Zeiss SEM is used for *ex situ* analysis. For the *in situ* indentation studies, a sapphire cantilever with a spring constant of 604 Nm^{-1} and a diamond tip is used.

Results and Discussion

The as-fabricated pillars are shown in Figure 1 and show the smooth nickel substrate and ordered array of pillar sizes. By beginning with a precisely controlled structure morphological changes of the pillars can be tracked with relative ease and several of the exact same shape and size pillars can be monitored at the same time to ensure the results are reproducible within a sample set.

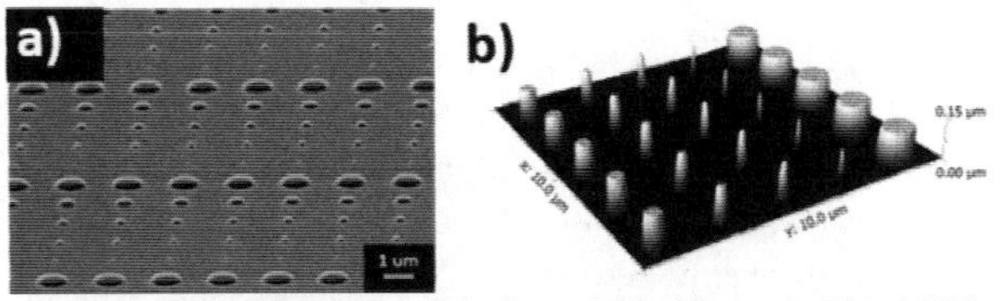

Figure 1. a) SEM of as-fabricated Si pillars and b) AFM image of as-fabricated Si pillars

In addition to the Si pillars, a set of Ni pillars was fabricated. The Ni will not lithiate and therefore the pillars should remain nearly the same shape and size unless the AFM tip is being modified during the electrochemical study. The electrochemical potential versus Li/Li^+ is decreased to set intervals from the open circuit and held for at least two hours to allow the pillars to equilibrate as monitored by a stable height and volume. The entire time the AFM probe is imaging the pillars. As evidenced in figure 2b), the Si pillars change shape. The sample that was composed of Ni pillars in figure 2a) on a nickel substrate was also tested as a control to verify the changes in height and volume were not just the buildup of an SEI. The Ni pillars do increase in height and diameter slightly, but when compared to the Si pillars the changes are minor therefore indicate the Si pillars are in fact lithiating and expanding. There is also a notable buildup of excess material on the Ni substrate, the exact composition of which is unknown.

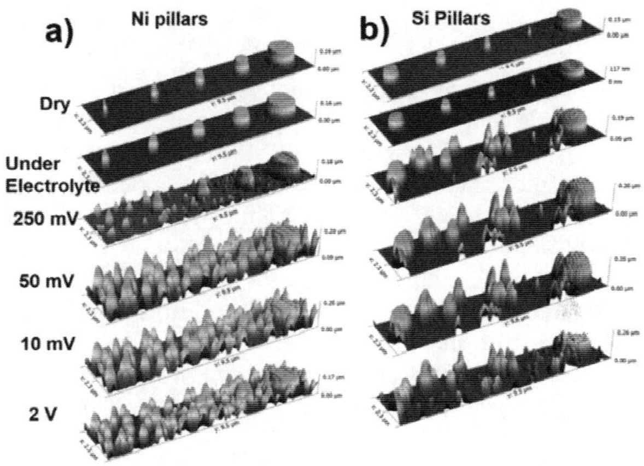

Figure 1. a) nickel pillars and b) silicon pillars during one charge and discharge cycle

By analyzing the AFM data, the change in heights and volumes of the pillars can be calculated. Figure 3 plots this data and reveals that the 1000 and 500 nm pillars behave quite similarly over two cycles and achieve volume expansion in the 350-400% range which is close to what the theoretical calculations predict. Since the volume is not dramatically greater than theory, two conditions may be present: the SEI layer in this PC based electrolyte is likely rather thin or the pillars may not fully be lithiating but a thick SEI film is forming to make the pillars appear to achieve the >300% theoretical volume increase. Our indentation results however do not indicate the presence of a thick SEI. The 100 nm pillars on the other hand reach a lower volume change than theory predicts except for the first charge (delithiation) cycle where a large volume is recorded. The 100 nm pillars are a challenging aspect ratio for the AFM tip to accurately record volume and the tip has been demonstrated to damage these fragile structures which may lead to underestimation of the actual volume[9]. Future work will explore the volume change of these small pillars in more detail.

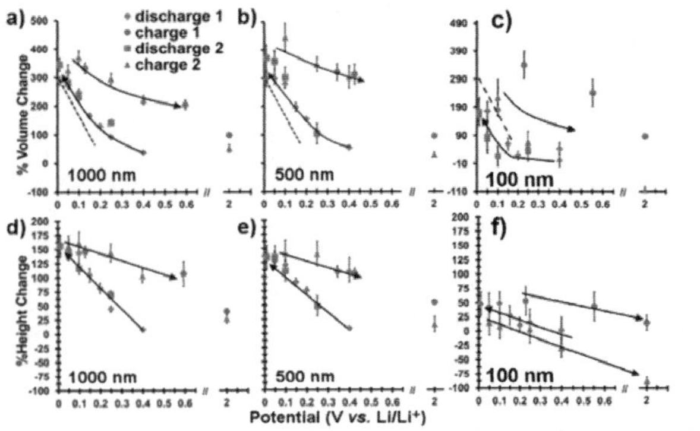

Figure 3. Plots of volume a)-c) and height d)-f) change of 1000, 500, and 100 nm pillars.

Using separate samples, experiments that cycled the pillars for 1 cycle and 5 cycles were performed and the pillars were examined *ex situ* using SEM. Figure 4 shows the SEM images of the pillars for a)-c) of the 1000 nm d)-f) the 300 nm and g)-i) the 100 nm pillar. After one cycle the pillars return to nearly the same dimensions as the as-fabricated pillars, but after 5 cycles the 1000 and 300 nm pillar have permanent deformation that results in a concave top. The 100 nm pillar on the other hand appears very similar to the as-fabricated dimension. Prior work however has shown that while the 100 and 200 nm pillar do not suffer distortion, the mechanical properties are severely degraded[9], [10].

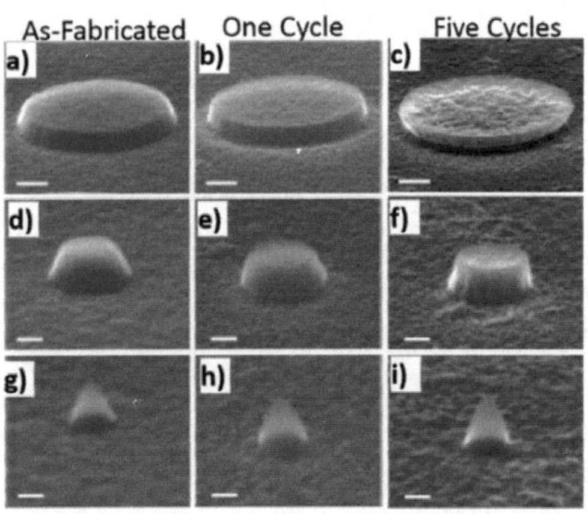

Figure 4. SEM images of the a)-c) 1000 nm pillars, d)-f) 300 nm pillars, and g)-i) 100 nm pillars as fabricated, after one cycle, and after five cycles.

In a separate study, utilizing the AFM to mechanically indent the pillars during lithiation and delithiation, the mechanical properties of the pillars were analyzed. In this study the pillars are indented prior to lithiation, then while holding the potential at 50mV, 10 mV, and finally when delithiating the pillars by returning the voltage to 2V vs Li/Li^+. Figure 5 shows the results of indenting the 1000 nm pillars. The primary finding here is that elastic modulus is unable to recover to the initial value after delithiation. Additionally, the modulus was able to be determined at three depths within the pillar. The data indicate that the elastic modulus of the pillar is higher at greater depths and therefore the pillar may not be fully lithiated.

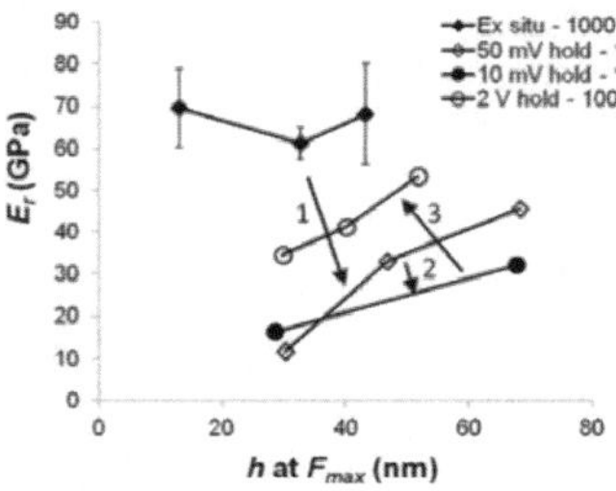

Figure 5. Plot of elastic modulus of pillars versus the depth (h) of the indent at the maximum force of the indent.

Conclusion

Using electron beam lithography, nanoscale Si pillars are fabricated with precisely controlled dimensions. *In situ* AFM is used to track the morphology and mechanical property changes during lithiation and delithiation. After one cycle the pillars return to nearly the initial dimensions. However, after 5 cycles the pillars have plastically deformed. The elastic modulus is also revealed to dramatically decrease during lithiation and unable to fully recover upon delithiation. Future work will investigate the SEI layer formation in different electrolyte compositions.

References

[1] U. Kasavajjula, C. Wang, and A. J. Appleby, "Nano- and bulk-silicon-based insertion anodes for lithium-ion secondary cells," *J. Power Sources*, vol. 163, no. 2, pp. 1003–1039, Jan. 2007.

[2] S. Iwamura, H. Nishihara, and T. Kyotani, "Fast and reversible lithium storage in a wrinkled structure formed from Si nanoparticles during lithiation/delithiation cycling," *J. Power Sources*, vol. 222, pp. 400–409, Jan. 2013.

[3] L. Y. Beaulieu, K. W. Eberman, R. L. Turner, L. J. Krause, and J. R. Dahn, "Colossal reversible volume changes in lithium alloys," *Electrochem. Solid State Lett.*, vol. 4, no. 9, pp. A137–A140, Sep. 2001.

[4] T. D. Hatchard and J. R. Dahn, "In situ XRD and electrochemical study of the reaction of lithium with amorphous silicon," *J. Electrochem. Soc.*, vol. 151, no. 6, pp. A838–A842, 2004.

[5] C. K. Chan, H. Peng, G. Liu, K. McIlwrath, X. F. Zhang, R. A. Huggins, and Y. Cui, "High-performance lithium battery anodes using silicon nanowires," *Nat. Nanotechnol.*, vol. 3, no. 1, pp. 31–35, Jan. 2008.

[6] M. T. McDowell, S. W. Lee, J. T. Harris, B. A. Korgel, C. Wang, W. D. Nix, and Y. Cui, "In Situ TEM of Two-Phase Lithiation of Amorphous Silicon Nanospheres," *Nano Lett.*, vol. 13, no. 2, pp. 758–764, Feb. 2013.

[7] Z. Zeng, W.-I. Liang, H.-G. Liao, H. L. Xin, Y.-H. Chu, and H. Zheng, "Visualization of Electrode–Electrolyte Interfaces in LiPF6/EC/DEC Electrolyte

for Lithium Ion Batteries via in Situ TEM," *Nano Lett.*, vol. 14, no. 4, pp. 1745–1750, Jan. 2014.

[8] C. R. Becker, K. E. Strawhecker, and J. Ligda, "Microfabricated Amorphous Silicon Nanopillars on an Ultrasmooth 500-nm-thick Titanium Adhesion Layer," US Army Research Lab, Adelphi, MD, ARL-TR-6209, 2012.

[9] C. R. Becker, K. E. Strawhecker, Q. P. McAllister, and C. A. Lundgren, "*In Situ* Atomic Force Microscopy of Lithiation and Delithiation of Silicon Nanostructures for Lithium Ion Batteries," *ACS Nano*, vol. 7, no. 10, pp. 9173–9182, Oct. 2013.

[10] Q. P. McAllister, K. E. Strawhecker, C. R. Becker, and C. A. Lundgren, "In situ atomic force microscopy nanoindentation of lithiated silicon nanopillars for lithium ion batteries," *J. Power Sources*, Jan. 2014.

Military Purpose Solid Oxide Fuel Cell Stack Technology

Scott L. Swartz, Gene B. Arkenberg, Chad T. Sellers, Joshua S. Emerick, Andrew P. Smith, and Lora B. Thrun

NexTech Materials, Ltd.
404 Enterprise Drive, Lewis Center, Ohio 43035

Abstract: *NexTech Materials is developing solid oxide fuel cell stacks in the 1 to 10 kW range, based on its patented "FlexCell" planar cell design. NexTech's SOFC stack technology has several unique attributes that make it attractive for military power applications. Sulfur tolerance enables operation with reformed logistic fuels without complete desulfurization. High single-pass fuel utilization capability enables high system efficiency without anode recycle. This paper will describe the current status of NexTech's military purpose SOFC stack technology.*

Keywords: solid oxide fuel cell; SOFC; sulfur tolerance; logistic fuels; JP-8; high efficiency; power and energy.

Introduction

Demand for electrical power by the U.S. military increases each year as enhanced communication and warfighting capabilities are implemented. Traditional power systems are becoming increasingly ineffective due to their size, weight and poor efficiency. Solid oxide fuel cells (SOFCs) offer a promising option to meet this growing demand. SOFCs have potential to provide quiet power at high specific power density while operating on sulfur-containing military logistic fuels (JP-8). The U.S. military has been evaluating SOFC technology for mission critical applications such as battery chargers, vehicle auxiliary power for silent watch, tent city combined heat and power, and primary power for unmanned vehicles (e.g., UAVs and UUVs). Successful development and deployment of SOFC power systems will enhance warfighting capabilities for all military branches.

NexTech Materials has been active in the development of SOFC technology since 1995 and has established state-of-the-art capabilities in the field. Over the past eight years, NexTech has been developing SOFC stack technology with potential to meet the demanding requirements of military applications. The core to NexTech's stack technology is the FlexCell™, a patented planar cell design that enables an unprecedented combination of performance, power density, efficiency and resistance to sulfur.

NexTech's *FlexCell* Platform

NexTech Materials has gained extensive experience in most SOFC cell designs, and used this experience to accelerate development of new cell architectures. Planar stacking configurations offer the advantages of simple cell interconnection, short interconnection paths and higher volumetric density. Tubular SOFCs offer simpler sealing and manifolding, but volumetric and gravimetric densities are limited for higher power systems. Thus, NexTech's cell design effort focused on planar SOFC stacks. Planar cells are typically manufactured with either the anode or the electrolyte as the load bearing component. Anode-supported cell designs have received considerable attention because of potential for lower temperature operation (due to a thin electrolyte layer), but suffer from challenges that limit durability and scalability. NexTech's planar FlexCell design overcomes these limitations; it is an electrolyte-supported planar element with a two-layer structure of a thin electrolyte layer mechanically supported by a thicker "honeycomb" mesh (Figure 1). With the FlexCell, more than 60 percent of the electrolyte membrane within the active area is thin (30 microns), and the periphery of the cell is dense (providing an optimum sealing surface). Anode and cathode layers are deposited onto opposite faces of the active cell region to complete fabrication of the FlexCell. These thin electrode features enable high single-pass fuel utilization without sacrificing performance.

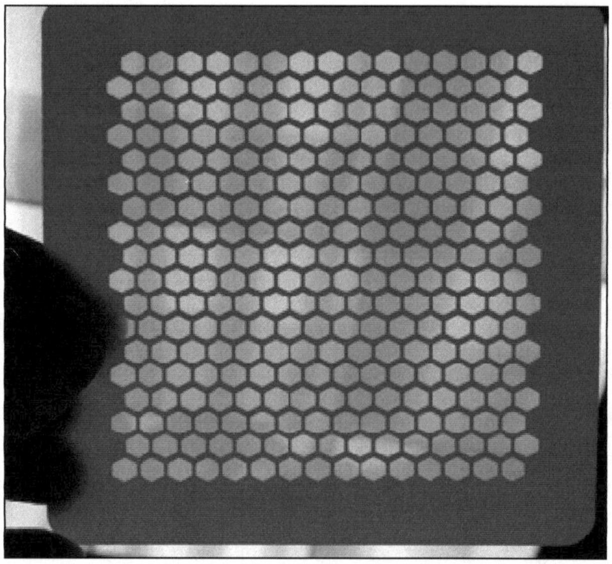

Figure 1. Most of the active area of the FlexCell membrane is very thin.

Status of SOFC Stack Development at NexTech

NexTech Materials has established and demonstrated two planar SOFC stack platforms: one based on 160-cm² active area cells for 1-3 kW scale power systems (see Figure 2), and one based on 300-cm² active area cells for 5-7 kW systems (see Figure 3). NexTech's stack design exploits the attributes of the FlexCell architecture and provides high gravimetric and volumetric power densities. The design capitalizes on the mechanical flexibility of the FlexCell and the gasketed sealing approach afforded by the dense cell perimeter. Another key advantage of the FlexCell design is that there is no intrinsic limitation to the size of cells that can be made. This scalability allows stacks to be designed without concerns related to the size and geometry of cells that can be made.

Figure 2. 24-cell stack of 160-cm^2 active area platform.

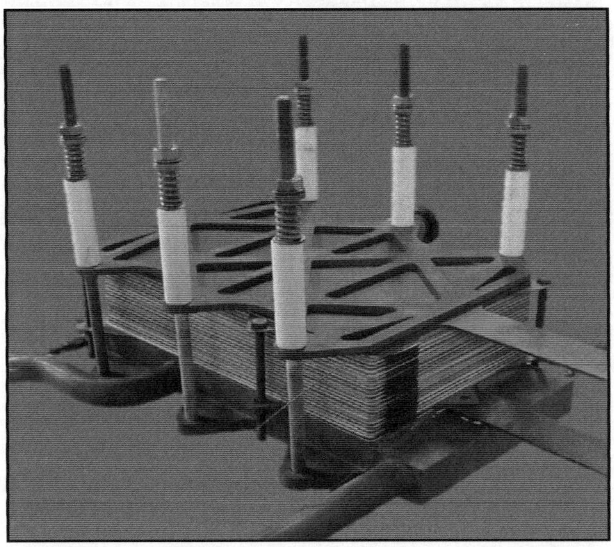

Figure 3. 20-cell stack of 300-cm^2 active area platform.

Recent work at NexTech has been aimed at improving performance, efficiency and reliability of its SOFC stacks. Approaches being pursued include optimizing seal gasket materials, improving design of stack compression means, and reducing resistive losses throughout the stack. These efforts not only led to improved stack performance, but also led to improved stack-to-stack performance reproducibility. Current performance levels of NexTech's stacks are shown by stack polarization curves in Figures 4 and 5 (tested at zero percent turndown). For the 160-cm^2 platform with diluted hydrogen fuel, a 12-cell stack delivers 356 mW/cm^2 at 80 percent fuel utilization (45 percent LHV efficiency). For the 300-cm^2 platform with simulated reformate fuel, a 10-cell stack delivers 355 mW/cm^2 at 80 percent fuel utilization (42 percent LHV efficiency).

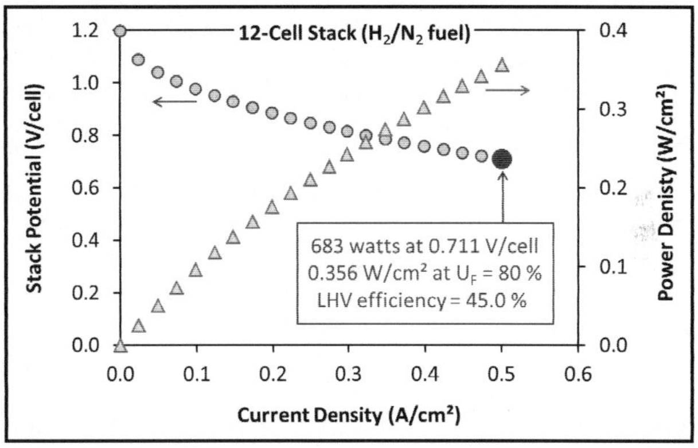

Figure 4. Polarization curve data obtained for a 12-cell stack of 160-cm² active area cells.

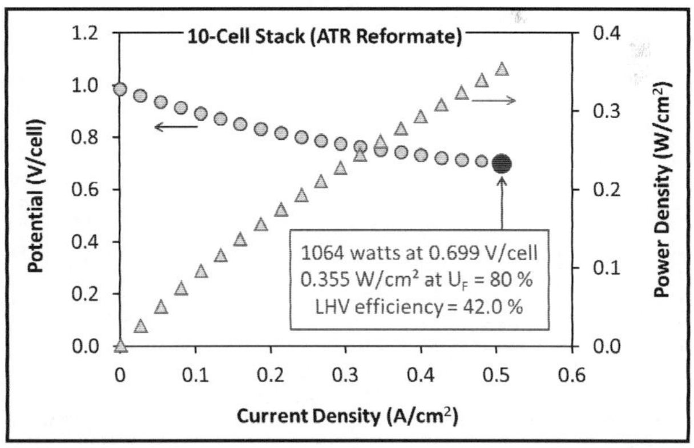

Figure 5. Polarization curve data obtained for a 10-cell stack of 300-cm² active area cells.

NexTech's Sulfur Tolerant SOFC Technology

One of the enabling attributes of NexTech's SOFC stack platform is unprecedented performance and stability in sulfur-containing fuels. At the single cell level, NexTech has demonstrated 500 hours of stable operation with simulated JP-8 reformate fuel containing 200 ppm H_2S. At the stack level, sulfur tolerance has been achieved in reformate fuels containing 100 ppm H_2S.

NexTech collaborated with Precision Combustion, Inc. (PCI) to demonstrate integration of a sulfur-tolerant SOFC stack with a sulfur tolerant JP-8 reformer. A 20-cell stack of 300-cm^2 active area cells was integrated with PCI's autothermal reformer. The reformer was configured with a desulfurizer that could be switched on or off with a few valve turns. More than 190 hours of testing was completed with JP-8 (350 ppmw sulfur) being fed to PCI's reformer and reformate being delivered to NexTech's stack. Data for the experiment are presented in Figure 6. A baseline was established with the reformer operating at 3.0 kW_{TH} and with sulfur being removed before the fuel entered the stack (point A in Figure 6). After 18 hours of steady state operation at 73.0 percent fuel utilization, the desulfurizer was bypassed and raw reformed JP-8 was sent directly to the stack (point B); the power dropped by approximately five percent but remained stable. At this point, the sulfur (H_2S +COS) content in the fuel was approximately 35 ppm. After 24 hours, fuel flow to the reformer was increased from 3.0 to 3.5 kW_{TH} (point C), so that the stack was operating at 62.5 percent fuel utilization. This condition was maintained for approximately 100 hours. During this steady-state operation segment, the desulfurizer was cycled on for four hours then off (points D and E) to assess the level of recovery after sulfur was removed from the reformate. After 160 hours, current was increased such that fuel utilization was increased to 75.3 percent, and power increased to 1120 watts (point F). Just prior to the conclusion of the test, the desulfurizer was cycled on and the power increased to 1160 watts (point G).

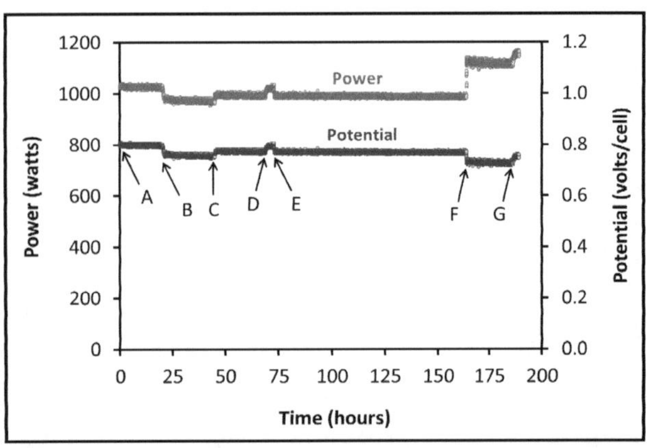

Figure 6. Results obtained with a PCI reformer delivering fuel to a NexTech stack (JP-8 fuel, 350 ppmw sulfur). Refer to text for an explanation of the specific conditions.

Stack efficiency, defined as the power output of the stack divided by the LHV of the reformate, ranged from 37 to 44 percent with desulfurized reformate and from 36 to 42 percent with non-desulfurized reformate. Total efficiency, defined as the power output of the stack divided by the LHV of the input JP-8 fuel, ranged from 29 to 34 percent with desulfurized reformate and from 28 to 32 percent with non-desulfurized reformate.

Also during the test, polarization curves were obtained with and without desulfurization of the reformate (see Figure 7). The pole curves retained linearity to high fuel utilizations (73 and 82 percent, respectively, for non-desulfurized and desulfurized reformate). These fuel utilizations correspond to stack electrical efficiencies of 41.5 and 47.4 percent, respectively (reformate basis). To our knowledge, these are the highest stack efficiencies ever obtained with reformed JP-8 as fuel at the kilowatt level.

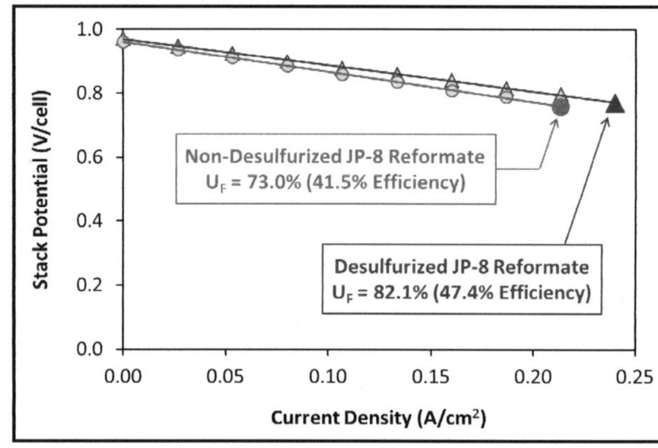

Figure 7. Polarization curves obtained with and without desulfurization of the JP-8 reformate during the integrated reformer/stack test (input JP-8 fuel at 3.0 kW_{TH}).

SOFC-Based UUV Energy System

NexTech Materials recently completed Phase I of an Office of Naval Research Future Naval Capability project aimed at design of an air-independent energy system for UUVs. NexTech and its team members (Northrop Grumman, ATK, PCI and pH Matter) designed an energy-dense power system for a 21-inch diameter UUV. The system, shown in Figure 8, is based on SOFC power generation using steam reformed JP-10 as fuel and liquid oxygen as oxidant, with batteries providing power during peak loads and being recharged at times of low loads.

To demonstrate required SOFC performance, a 26-cell stack of NexTech's 160-cm^2 platform was built and tested under design conditions (reactant flows corresponding to 33 percent turndown). Polarization curves were obtained with simulated JP-10 reformate as fuel, and with both air and pure oxygen as oxidant (see Figure 9). At 80 percent fuel utilization, stack power increased from 1024 to 1109 watts, and efficiency increased from 45.6 to 49.6 percent when air was replaced by oxygen.

To demonstrate stack durability with pure oxygen on the cathodes, a three-cell stack was tested for 250 hours under design conditions (simulated JP-10 reformate, 33 percent turndown, and 80 percent fuel utilization) for 250 hours (see Figure 10). No observable degradation was observed over the duration of this test. The stack also was subjected to a thermal cycle and a power outage, with no degradation caused by these transient events.

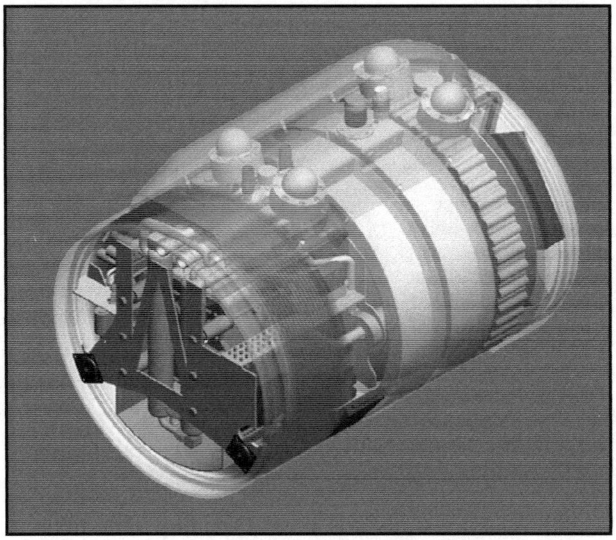

Figure 8. CAD model of SOFC-based UUV energy system.

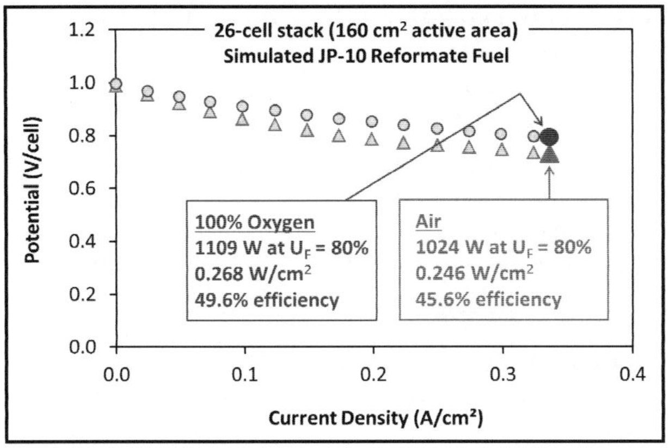

Figure 9. Pole curves obtained on a 26-cell stack with simulated JP-10 reformate and pure oxygen reactants at the 33 percent turndown condition.

Summary and Conclusions

NexTech Materials is developing military purpose solid oxide fuel cell stacks based on its patented electrolyte-supported planar *FlexCell* platform. These stacks have several important attributes that make them particularly attractive for military power systems. High single-pass fuel utilization enables stacks to be operated without complex anode recycling schemes. This capability has been demonstrated in stacks operating at 80 percent fuel utilization, with LHV efficiencies of 45 to 50 percent.

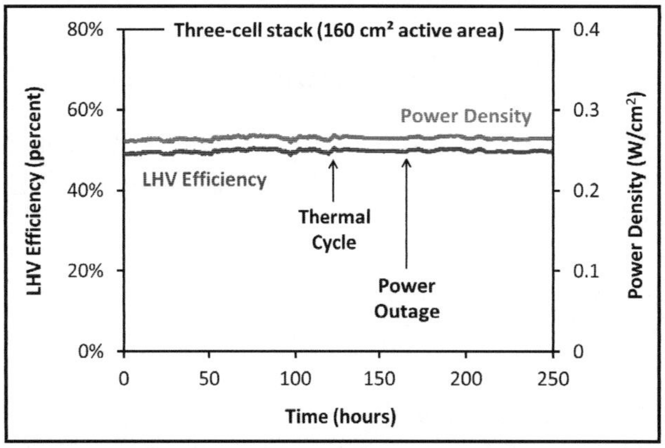

Figure 10. Steady-state testing of a three-cell stack with simulated JP-10 reformate and pure oxygen as reactants (80 percent fuel utilization, 50 percent efficiency).

NexTech's SOFC stacks also are tolerant to high levels of sulfur in reformate fuels (200 ppm H_2S in cells and 100 ppm H_2S in stacks). This sulfur tolerance is a key enabler for development of SOFC power systems designed for sulfur-containing military logistic fuels, by allowing the desulfurization components to be made smaller or eliminated. A first-of-its-kind demonstration was achieved by integrating a sulfur tolerant stack with a sulfur tolerant reformer and operating the stack with reformed JP-8 fuel without desulfurization.

Ongoing and planned stack development work at NexTech includes: (1) implementation of advanced materials and coating technology to improve thermal cycling capability; (2) material selection and component design work to reduce stack weight; (3) increasing the size and power generation scale of NexTech's stacks; and (4) application-specific demonstrations of SOFC power generation using military logistic fuels.

Acknowledgements

Financial support for this work was provided by the State of Ohio's Third Frontier Program, the Air Force Research Laboratory (Contract No. FA8650-08-C-2810), and the Office of Naval Research (Contracts N00014-11-C-0386 and N00014-12-D-0173). Collaborations with Precision Combustion, Northrop Grumman, ATK and pH Matter are gratefully acknowledged. Finally, the authors would like to thank their NexTech colleagues (Matt Seabaugh, Kellie Chenault, Neil Kidner, Mike Funk, Kari Smith, and Kay Tan) for their contributions to the work.

PPB-level Contaminant Adsorption for SOFC Cathode Protection

Peng Cheng & Bruce J. Tatarchuk*
Center for Microfibrous Materials Manufacturing
Department of Chemical Engineering
Auburn University
Auburn, AL, USA, 36849
* (334) 844-2023, tatarbj@auburn.edu

Abstract: *Contaminant gas removal is a critical process for current and future power supply systems including fuel cells, gas turbines (GT) or a combination on ships. Because of high energy efficiency, low emissions, and fuel flexibility, Solid Oxide Fuel Cells (SOFCs) are promising energy converting devices. Recently, however, researchers have shown that a significant degradation caused by SO_2 reacts with cathode side materials and thus hinder the active sites available for oxygen reduction. The major SO_2 source is the emission from marine fuels such as JP-5andJP-8 whose sulfur content can be up to 1200 ppmw. And even if the cell exposed to 100 ppbv of SO_2, there is a current loss during the test. Hence, it is necessary to remove cathode side SO_2. In this work, SO_2 was introduced at various initial concentrations. A packed bed consisting of mixed oxides ($MnOx/\gamma\text{-}Al_2O_3$, $CeO_2/\gamma\text{-}Al_2O_3$ and $Mn\text{-}CeO/\gamma\text{-}Al_2O_3$) was used as adsorbents operated at high space velocity. Concentrations of SO_2 upstream and downstream were collected by MultiRAE pro equipped with SO_2 sensor. The experiments for adsorption behavior (e.g. breakthrough capacity, saturation capacity) were carried out on different types of metal oxides with wetness impregnation. BET surface area, total pore volume and pore-size distribution were measured for supports with various pretreatment methods in order to characterize their surface morphology. Furthermore, by applying the H_2-temperature-programmed reduction technique, different oxygen species (surface oxygen and lattice oxygen) were identified, therefore explaining their functions in SO_2 oxidative adsorption.*

Keywords: Air filtration; Sulfur dioxide adsorption; Energy storage and conversion; Solid Oxide Fuel Cell power system.

Introduction

Due to the ability of converting chemical energy of fuel gas into electricity, over the last few decades, improvement of fuel cell performance becomes a major challenge for engineering scientists [1]. Nowadays, main research interest throughout the world has focused on the third generation fuel cell—SOFCs, which is able to meet the requirement of clean, high efficiency and zero/low emissions.

However, even though SOFCs have higher sulfur tolerance than Proton Exchange Membrane Fuel Cells (PEMFCs), cathode side SO_2 poisoning is still an issue, which is mainly caused by high sulfur content marine fuels combustion (e.g. JP-5 or JP-8). The tolerances for certain types of SOFC cathodes are summarized in Table 1. Much attention focuses on the development of sorbents with a high activity for sulfur dioxide destruction ($DeSO_x$ process) [2]. Furthermore, for logistical fuel cell system, the volume and weight are of critical concerns [3]. Therefore, optimizing the desulfurization efficiency and the size of the reactor is of vital importance.

Table.1 Sulfur dioxide tolerance of SOFCs.

Material of Cathode	Tolerance (ppbv)	Operation Temp. (°C)
$SmSrCoO_3$	10	n.m.
$LaSrCoFeO_3$	100	750

Owing to the much lower cost compared to the precious metals (Pt, Pd), Mn-Ce-Al mixed oxide materials have attracted considerable attention recently as a potential De-SOx sorbents [4, 5]. In this paper, we investigated SO_2 breakthrough performance of several binary or ternary regenerable adsorbents at 250 °C.

Experimental

In this study, $\gamma\text{-}Al_2O_3$ (493 m^2/g, 0.68 cc/g) was purchased from Sigma-Aldrich. $Mn(NO_3)_2 \cdot 4H_2O$, $Ce(NO_3)_3{\cdot}6H_2O$ and HNO_3 were purchased from Alfa Aesar. If not otherwise specified, all gases were purchased from Airgas South (Opelika, AL). The SO_2 source is 10 ppmv balanced in N_2 with ± 5% uncertainty from Airgas Inc (Durham, NC).

A series of supported $MnOx\text{-}CeO_2$ sorbents were separately prepared by impregnating $\gamma\text{-}Al_2O_3$ (125-180 μm) with corresponding metal nitrates at room temperature. The support were previously crushed and sieved to the desired size. Afterwards, the samples were dried on a hotplate at 323 K for at least 12 h, following aging for overnight. It was further placed in crucible with cover and calcined in stationary air at 823 K for 2 h by Lindberg/Blue furnace (Thermo Scientific Inc.). Various heating rates (5-20 K/min) were applied up to the final calcination temperature. For comparison, adsorbents were prepared by impregnating γ-Al_2O_3 with HNO_3 as well. All the samples were stored in 20 mL air tight vials and put in a desiccator until breakthrough test.

Breakthrough tests were carried out to evaluate the breakthrough capacity (B.T. Cap.) and breakthrough time for SO_2 removal. The adsorbents (0.1 g) were packed into a quartz tubular reactor (7.0 mm I.D) with quartz wool on both sides. Unless elsewhere stated, the breakthrough tests were maintained under the following conditions: atmospheric pressure, flow rate 1000 mL/min. Prior to each test, the upstream concentration was monitored for at least 30 min to ensure a constant SO_2 source was generated. The outlet SO_2 concentration was determined by MultiRAE pro equipped with SO_2 sensor (RAE Systems, CA), whose detection limit can be as low as 1 ppbv.

The surface area, pore volume and pore size distribution of adsorbents were measured by 50 points nitrogen adsorption-desorption analysis at its normal boiling point (77 K) with a Quantachrome Autosorb-1. The samples were outgassed at 473 K for at least 5 h under vacuum prior to physisorption measurements, if not otherwise noted. The surface area (S_{BET}) was calculated by the BET method; total pore volume (T.P.V.) was obtained at the point of 0.995 p/p°; the pore size distribution (P.S.D.) was calculated by applying the BJH method on the desorption branch of isotherm curve.

Temperature-programmed reduction in hydrogen (H_2-TPR) analysis was measured in a 4 mm I.D. straight quartz tube. Prior to each analysis, about 0.1 g of powder sample was loaded above a small amount of quartz wool and pretreated at 523 K for 1h under 15 mL/min ultra-high purity (UHP) argon flow in order to remove the moisture. After sample was cooled down to room temperature, the reduction gas mixture (5% H_2 in argon, 15 mL/min) was shifted. Effluent moisture during reduction was trapped in isopropanol slurry (195 K). The H_2 consumption was recorded ramping from 303 K to 1123 K (β=10 K/min) by online gas chromatograph (SRI 310C) equipped with thermal conductivity detector (TCD). The amount of hydrogen uptake was calibrated by CuO standard sample (>99.7%, Alfa Aesar).

Results and Discussion

Support evaluation: In a preliminary test, commercial γ-Al_2O_3 was selected as the support for adsorbent. Nitrogen adsorption-desorption isotherms of various pretreatment methods are shown in Figure 1. It needs to be pointed out here that 5-550-γ-Al_2O_3 denotes the support was heated up to 550 °C at a linearly heating rate of 5 °C/min from room temperature after drying. All of the three isotherms are type A hysteresis loop, which indicates a large amount of cylindrical pores [6]. The closure points of all the three hysteresis loops occurred at 0.4 p/p°. BET surface area, pore volume and mean pore size are listed in Table 2. It can be seen that after calcination, both the surface area and total pore volume were reduced drastically. Also, increasing the ramp rate shifted the pore volume from 0.68 cm^3/g for 5-550-γ-Al_2O_3 to 0.50 cm^3/g for 20-550-γ-Al_2O_3. The pore size distribution (P.S.D.) presented in Figure 2 shows that all these supports behaves a unimodal structure with pore size range from 1 nm to 8 nm. It also implies that pores around 2 nm contribute most to the total pore volume. And with calcinations, most pores around 2 nm reduced by c.a. 50%.

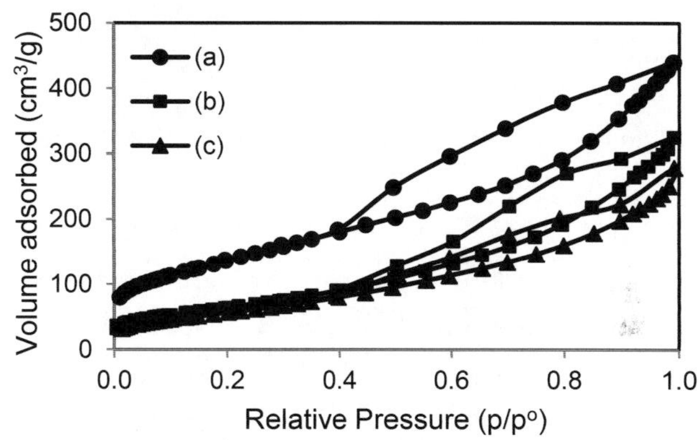

Figure 1. N_2 adsorption-desorption isotherms at 77 K of (a) Dried γ-Al_2O_3 (b) 5-550-γ-Al_2O_3 and (c) 20-550-γ-Al_2O_3.

Since surface area and total pore volume plays an important role in internal diffusion and mass transfer, ramping rate of 5 °C/min and final temperature 550 °C was kept for all the following wetness impregnation experiments.

Table 2. Surface area, pore volume and mean pore size of γ-Al_2O_3 support by different calcination methods.

Sample	S_{BET}[a] (m^2/g)	T.P.V.[b] (cm^3/g)	Pore size (nm)
Dried γ-Al_2O_3	493	0.682	2.77
5-550-γ-Al_2O_3	240	0.503	4.20
20-550-γ-Al_2O_3	211	0.430	4.08

a. Surface area was calculated by 7-point BET method range between p/p°=0.05~0.35.
b. Pore Volume was calculated at p/p°=0.995.

Breakthrough Performance of sorbents: The doped sorbents behaviors for SO_2 removal with a SO_2 challenge of 2000 ppbv (16.7% Oxygen and N_2 balance) are studied at 250 °C. The breakthrough point was defined at C/Co=0.05. The results are summarized in Table 3. Among the monometallic sorbents, 5 wt. % Mn doped on γ-Al_2O_3 shows the best performance. The stated results indicates that the optimal monometallic loading for low concentration SO_2 adsorption is 5 wt. % Mn on γ-Al_2O_3. It is possibly due to improved dispersed MnO_2 and Mn_3O_4

species, thus promoting the oxidation of SO_2 to SO_3 which further chemically adsorbed on the support [7, 8].

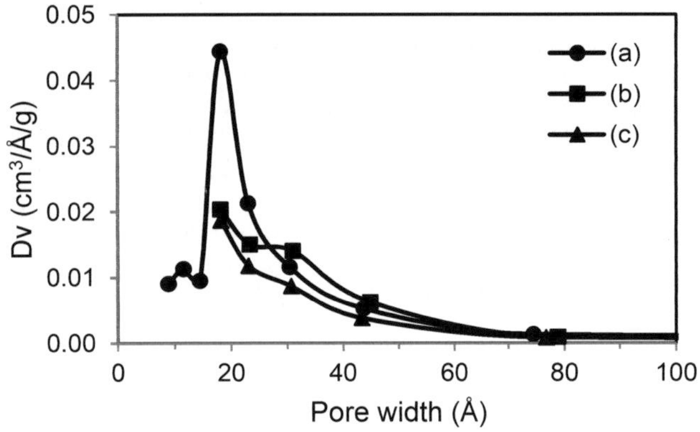

Figure 2. Pore size distributions of (a) Dried γ-Al_2O_3 (b) 5-550-γ-Al_2O_3 and (c) 20-550-γ-Al_2O_3.

Table 3. Sulfur dioxide capacities of various sorbents

Types of Sorbents[a]	B.T. Capacity, (mg of SO_2/ g of sorbent)
5Ce/γ-Al_2O_3	3.2
10Ce/γ-Al_2O_3	6.2
5Mn/γ-Al_2O_3	14.0
10Mn/γ-Al_2O_3	5.3
5Mn-5Ce/γ-Al_2O_3	17.8
5Mn-10Ce/γ-Al_2O_3	23.1

a. The number ahead of metal species denotes different metal loading. (e.g. 5Mn-5Ce/γ-Al_2O_3 means 5 wt. % Mn and 5 wt. % Ce doped on γ-Al_2O_3.)

For the bimetallic sorbents, by adding 5-10 wt. % Ce into MnOx/γ-Al_2O_3, they displayed an enhanced SO_2 breakthrough capacity over all the monometallic sorbents. Especially, doped sorbent 5 wt. % Mn-10 wt. %Ce/γ-Al_2O_3 shows a c.a. 65% increase in breakthrough capacity compared with the 5 wt. % Mn/γ-Al_2O_3, which is the best candidate for monometallic sorbents.

H_2-TPR studies: Figure 3 illustrates H_2-TPR profiles of doped and calcined samples. The α peaks appeared at 400 °C in curve (a) and (b) are attributed to the reduction of MnO_2 to Mn_2O_3; the corresponding β peaks appeared at 480 °C are ascribed to the reduction of Mn_2O_3 to Mn_3O_4; and the intensity of γ peaks (Mn_3O_4 to MnO) in this work is extremely weak compared to other researchers [7]. Hence, a mixture of manganese oxides are presented in the Mn doped adsorbents. Similar features were noticed for curve (a) and (b) except the intensity difference resulted from the Mn content. Since the α peak possesses the highest intensity, MnO_2 is a dominant species formed by calcination at 550 °C in static air.

By adding 5 wt. % Ce into Mn-Al oxides (curve d), a peak appeared at 370 °C (shifted about 30 °C to the lower temperature compared with the α peaks in curve a and b) with a shoulder on the higher temperature side around 450 °C was observed, which suggests strong interaction between active metal oxides and supports exist. This peak and shoulder are attributed to the reduction of surface oxygen and bulk oxygen [9]. Nevertheless, the previous peak and shoulder merged by further Ce addition (curve c).

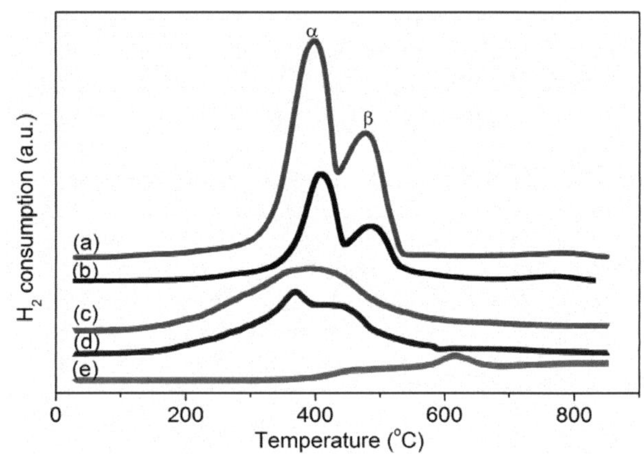

Figure 3. H_2-TPR profiles for (a) 10 wt. % Mn/γ-Al_2O_3, (b) 5 wt. % Mn/γ-Al_2O_3, (c) 5 wt. %Mn-10 wt. %Ce/γ-Al_2O_3, (d) 5 wt. %Mn-5 wt. %Ce/γ-Al_2O_3 and (e) 10 wt. % Ce/γ-Al_2O_3.

Reduction of 10 wt. %CeO_2/γ-Al_2O_3 is more difficult, and a peak appeared around 630 °C with a wide shoulder appeared at around 460 °C. It is worth noting that even the system was heated up to 850 °C, the 10 wt. %CeO_2/γ-Al_2O_3 sample was not reduced completely (curve e), which means the lattice oxygen is still not reduced thoroughly. It is obvious that mixing MnO_x and CeO_2 enhanced the surface oxygen species remarkably, thus promoting the breakthrough performance via providing more surface oxygen.

Conclusions

Lower heating rate (5 °C/min) possesses more surface area and pore volume, resulting in higher breakthrough capacity for sorbents and longer service time for SOFCs. By using $Mn(NO_3)_2{\cdot}4H_2O$ and $Ce(NO_3)_3{\cdot}6H_2O$ simultaneously as precursors, the performance of the sorbents are enhanced remarkably. The properties of the surface oxygen species were modified significantly once CeO_2 was impregnated onto γ-Al_2O_3. The decreased reduction temperature indicates that the Mn-Ce/γ-Al_2O_3 sorbents cause a reduction of the activation energy of SO_2 oxidative adsorption on the surface and thus improve the DeSOx ability.

Acknowledgements

This work was financially supported by Office of Naval Research (ONR) under the contract no. Navy-N00014-11-1-0388. The authors want to thank Dr. Hongyun Yang for technical assistance.

References

1. Stambouli, A. B., and Traversa, E., "Solid Oxide Fuel Cells: a Review of an Environmentally Clean and Efficient Source of Energy", *Renewable & Sustainable Energy Reviews*, Vol. 6, no. 5, pp. 433-455, October 2002.
2. Lu, Z.S., Muller, C., Yang, Z.X., Hermansson, K., and Kullgren, J., "SO_x on Ceria from adsorbed SO_2", *J. Chem. Phys.*, Vol 134, no. 18, pp. 184703, 2011.
3. Yang, H.Y., Lu, Y., Tatarchuk, B.J., "Glass Fiber Entrapped Sorbent for Reformates Desulfurization for Logistic PEM Fuel Cell Power Systems", *J. Power Source*, Vol 174, no. 1, pp. 302-311, November 2007.
4. Men, Y., Gnaser H., Ziegler, C., Zapf, R., Hessel, V., Kolb, G., "Characterization of $Cu/CeO_2/\gamma$-Al_2O_3 Thin Film Catalysts by Thermal Desorption Spectroscopy", *Catalysis Letter*, Vol 105, no. 1-2, pp. 35-40, November 2005.
5. Kylhammar, L., Carlsson, P., Ingelsten, H.H., Gronbeck, H., Skoglundh, M., "Regenerable Ceria-based SO_x Traps for Sulfur Removal in Lean Exhausts", *Applied Catalysis B: Environmental*, Vol 84, no. 1-2, pp. 268-276, October 2008.
6. Yuan, Z.L., Wang, L.N., Wang, J.H., Xia, S.X., Chen, P., Hou, Z.Y., Zheng, X.M., "Hydrogenolysis of Glycerol over Homogenously Dispersed Copper on Solid Base Catalysts", *Applied Catalysis B: Environmental*, Vol 101, no. 3-4, pp. 431-440, January 2011.
7. Qu, Y.F., Guo, J.X., Chu, Y.H., Sun, M.C., Yin, H.Q., "The Influence of Mn Species on the SO_2 Removal of Mn-based Activated Carbon Catalysts", *Applied Surface Science*, Vol 282, pp. 425-431, October 2013.
8. Mathieu, Y., Tzanis, L., Soulard, M., Pararin, J., Vierling, M., Moliere, M., "Adsorption of SOx by Oxide Materials: A review", *Fuel Processing Technology*, Vol 114, pp. 81-100, October 2013.
9. Watanabe, S., Ma, X.L., Song, C.S., "Characterization of Structural and Surface Properties of Nanocrystalline TiO_2-CeO_2 Mixed Oxides by XRD, XPS, TPR and TPD", *The Journal of Physical Chemistry C*, Vol 113, no 32, pp14249-14257, July 2009.

Fuel Processing Using Hydrogen Selective Palladium Composite Membranes

Zachary W. Dunbar and Deryn Chu
US Army Research Laboratory
Adelphi, Maryland 20705

Abstract: *Palladium metal membranes possess high selectivity for the separation and purification of hydrogen from other gaseous compounds. This characteristic is frequently exploited to aid in the generation of hydrogen in fuel processing systems – particularly those systems producing ultra high purity hydrogen needed for fuel cell applications. Unfortunately, the widespread adoption of palladium metal membranes has been stymied by their high cost and chemical sensitivity, particularly to sulfur.*

In this work, these challenges are addressed using microfabrication technology. This reduces the precious metal requirements of the membrane to sub micron levels, while maintaining high selectivity. The thin palladium membrane is mechanically supported with a nickel honeycomb structure. As a result, the completed membrane is completely metallic, allowing for superior sealability and thermal cycling durability relative to metallic/ceramic membranes. Membrane flux, chemical stability and mechanical durability will be presented and discussed.

Keywords: hydrogen purification; palladium membrane; fuel processing; reformation; fuel cell

Introduction

The US Army has growing demands for portable electrical power. Battery technology is well suited for low power applications, and conventional internal combustion generators work well at high power ranges. However there is an intermediate range loosely defined here as approximately 50 W to 5000 W, where neither technology is ideal. Batteries suffer from poor energy density, while internal combustion engines have poor efficiency in this power range, in addition to being noisy, maintenance intensive and producing toxic emissions. This power range is an ideal range where fuel cell technology can contribute in the near future [1-3].

For military applications, a major limiting factor for fuel cell deployment is the source of fuel[3-4]. Compressed hydrogen is a non-starter on the battlefield, for both logistical and safety reasons. Energy dense liquid hydrocarbon fuels, on the other hand, hold promise to enable fuel cell technology by providing a convenient, dense, and safe alternative to compressed hydrogen. JP-8, a kerosene-like mix of long chain hydrocarbons, is the ideal liquid fuel for the Army since it is readily available on the battlefield and is well understood from a fuel handling and safety perspective. Unfortunately, to make JP-8 useable by a fuel cell it must undergo several fuel processing steps to transform it into hydrogen-rich reformate gas [5]. The resulting gas is a high temperature mix of hydrogen and various reaction byproducts, some of which are detrimental to the fuel cell. Therefore, the reformate gas must be purified before being sent to the fuel cell for oxidation.

In this work, ARL continues its work on its microfabricated palladium membrane described in Power Sources 2012, as well as in the literature [7]. Long term stability, thermal cycling and sulfur tolerance are evaluated, and compared to the current state of the art methods for hydrogen purification.

Experimental Design

All microfabrication steps are conducted in the Adelphi Laboratory Center class 100 clean room.. Membrane fabrication begins with a commercial silicon wafer (Addison Engineering, 550 microns thick, SSP, test quality wafer). Palladium metal is deposited onto the polished side of the wafer to a thickness of 500 nm using a Kurt Lesker PVD75 thermal evaporator. The wafer is next moved to an automated wafer spinner/developer, and photoresist (AZ9245) is applied onto the palladium surface to a thickness of 10 microns. The photoresist acts as a mold for the electroplating procedure. After hard baking the photoresist, the wafer is patterned using a Karl Suss MA/BA6 contact aligner and a photomask from Photo Sciences, Inc. Next, it is developed using AZ400 developer solution for approximately 5 minutes. After the microfabrication steps, the wafer is ready for electroplating in order to build the nickel mechanical support. The wafer is placed in a nickel sulfamate plating solution (Transene Co.), and connected to a power supply. The wafer acts as the cathode, while nickel metal acts as the anode. The wafer is plated using constant current density. An SEM image of the final membrane (permeate side) is shown in **Figure 1**.

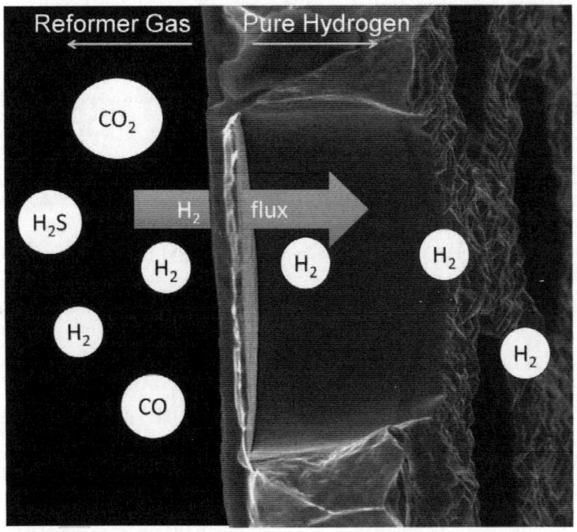

Figure 1. False-color SEM (scanning electron microscopy) cross-section of ARL's palladium membrane, with cartoon overlay demonstrating mechanism of purification.

Results & Discussion

ARL conducted a 350 hour life test of a sample membrane, measuring the hydrogen flux over time (**Figure 2**). The flux was remarkable stable, indicating no alloying of the palladium thin film and the structured nickel support. The palladium film was negatively influenced by the presence of carbon monoxide, as has been seen in other studies. However, the impacts were reversible when carbon monoxide was removed from the gas stream. Even with

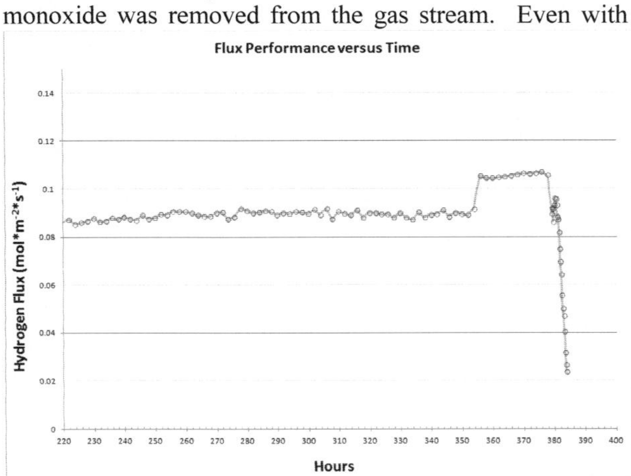

Figure 2. Membrane flux over time, for a 500 nm palladium membrane. The retentate atmosphere is 50% hydrogen, 29% carbon dioxide, 20% water and 1% carbon monoxide. After 345 hours operation, retentate atmosphere is switched to 50% hydrogen 50% helium. At 355 hours, retentate atmosphere is switched back to the original atmosphere, plus an additional 10 ppm hydrogen sulfide.

carbon monoxide present, the flux was at acceptable levels to theoretically provide sufficient hydrogen to a fuel cell. The palladium film was extremely sensitive to the presence of hydrogen sulfide, again as expected based on the literature. However, the effects of hydrogen sulfide were irreversible, and quickly deactivated the entire membrane.

The flux achieved in this study, combined with the relatively small amount of palladium used to fabricate the membrane, allows for the ARL membrane to compare very favorably with the state of the art membranes in the literature (**Figure 3**).

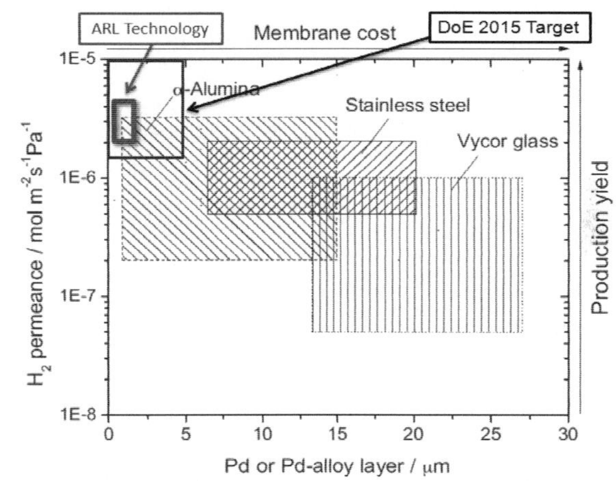

Figure 3. Comparison of ARL technology with the state of the art academic research using permeance and palladium thickness as metrics. From Yun, et al. [8]

Conclusions

The palladium composite membranes developed by the US Army Research Laboratory shows over 300 hours of long term stability in a synthetic reformate atmosphere. No alloying of the support and the palladium occurred, based on an XRD analysis. The membrane is stable over 12 aggressive thermal cycles, eventually developing leaks due to small hole formation, probably along grain boundaries. The membrane architecture is shown to easily scale to larger sizes, offering the possibility of simple mass production using existing microfabrication technology. The membrane shows little sulfur tolerance, as one would expect from a pure palladium membrane.

References

[1] D. Chu, R. Jiang, K. Gardner, R. Jacobs, J. Schmidt, T. Quakenbush, J. Stephens, Journal of Power Sources, 96 (2001) 174-178.

[2] S. Roychoudhury, M. Lyubovsky, D. Walsh, D. Chu, E. Kallio, Journal of Power Sources, 160 (2006) 510-513.

[3] A.S. Patil, T.G. Dubois, N. Sifer, E. Bostic, K. Gardner, M. Quah, C. Bolton, Journal of Power Sources, 136 (2004) 220-225.

[4] DOD 4140.25-M, DOD Directive 4140.25, (1993).

[5] K.L. Hohn, T. DuBois, Journal of Power Sources, 183 (2008) 295-302.

[6] V. Jayaraman, Y.S. Lin, J. Membr. Sci., 104 (1995) 251-262.

[7] Z.W. Dunbar, D. Chu, Journal of Power Sources, 217 (2012) 47-53.

[8] S. Yun, S.T. Oyama, J. Membr. Sci., 375 (2011) 28-45.

[9] P.L. Andrew, A.A. Haasz, Journal of Applied Physics, 70 (1991) 3600-3604.

Sea Salt Particles Filtration for SOFCs Using Pleated Filters via Various Nonwoven Filter Media in Newly Designed Packaging Configurations

Pengfei Zhao and Bruce J. Tatarchuk*
Department of Chemical Engineering
Auburn University
Auburn, AL, USA 36849
*tatarbj@auburn.edu

Abstract: *Solid Oxide Fuel Cells (SOFCs) are being considered for use onboard ships as power sources due to their high efficiency and lower waste emission. However, the exposure of several air contaminants like gaseous impurities and particulates is significantly detrimental to the performance of these fuel cells. In the marine environment, sea salt particles are the most common particulates and their removal from air stream fed into cathode side of fuel cell system is highly essential. To remove sea salt particles in a more efficient manner, our focus is on the design and optimization of a new pleated filter configuration (MESAs) and new nonwoven filtration media. Multi-Element Structured Arrays (MESAs) that developed by our group represent a new approach that can further increase the filtration area and reduce the pressure drop across the filter by integrating several pleated filters into a single unit. In this study, both single filter and MESAs were tested on a 24" × 24" test rig, which is built based on ASHRAE 52.2 standard, for the filtration performance, including particle removal efficiency and pressure drop across the system. After comparing the results, MESA's can reduce the initial pressure drop by ca. 70% and provide higher removal efficiency. The effects of varying media type, filter depth, pleat counts and MESA's counts were also experimentally investigated. The new nonwoven filter media consists of a three dimensional network of sinter-locked fibers. The diameter of the fibers is in the range of nano-scale to micron-scale. The effects of important media parameters like fiber diameter, solid volume fraction (SVF) of certain fiber material, total voidage and media thickness on filtration performance characteristics, including filtration efficiency, pressure drop and quality factor were studied in this work. Furthermore, loading capacity of salt particles, which is another significant parameter for filter media performance, was investigated as well. Various filter configurations and different types of filter media were experimentally tested. The results and discussion will be presented in depth.*

Keywords: Solid Oxide Fuel Cells (SOFCs); Sea salt; Air filtration; Pleated filters; MESAs; Nonwoven media.

Introduction

Nowadays, Solid Oxide Fuel Cells (SOFCs) are widely applied to provide electric power for ships and other ocean platforms with less harmful emissions or wastes. SOFCs are electrochemical devices that directly convert chemical energy from fuel into electricity by oxidizing the fuel, such as hydrogen or carbon monoxide. Usually, air is selected as the oxidizing agent. However, air always contains several different kinds of contaminants, including gases and particulates, which could cause severe degradation to the fuel cells [1,2]. At the ocean environment, sea salt particle (SSP) is the most harmful contaminant to the cells. Therefore, removal of SSP has significant influence on the operation of SOFCs. Those SSPs are usually generated from two sources, one is naturally from wind stresses over white caps and the other one is from either the wake or the bow spray. Sea salt particles mainly consist of size ranges from 0.01 to 10 microns [3]. The current approach is using coalescors or inertial separators to remove them. But these devices are only effective for particles larger than 8 microns in size. In order to remove much smaller particles in a more efficient manner, design and optimization of a new type of sea salt particles filter was developed and reported in this paper, including design of filter media and optimization of filter packaging configurations.

Experimental Setup

In this study, two different experimental setups were applied for tests of filter media and filter package configurations respectively, which are shown in Figures 1 and 2.

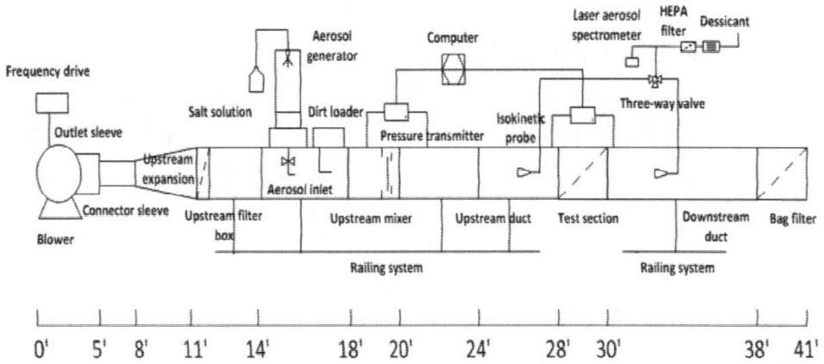

Figure 1. Schematic of full scale test rig for filter packaging configuration tests.

This full scale test rig was built based on ASHRAE 52.2 Standard (1992) [4] and several modifications were made to reduce the cost, simplify the overall design and remain compatible with purchased equipment. The whole system is about 41 feet long and 24 inches wide and can deliver up to 2000 cfm of air for evaluation of air filtration device in regards of pressure drop, particle removal efficiency and particles loading capacity. A blower driven by a 3 HP motor was applied to introduce room air into the test rig and could deliver air in 550 fpm face velocity according to the 24 inches by 24 inches test rig. Salt particles were generated by a TSI 8108 Large Particle Generator. A Kr-air ionizer and a drying air stream were used to neutralize any charges in the salt particles and dry the particles respectively [5]. To measure the pressure drop and particle removal efficiency across the tested filter, a differential pressure transmitter and a Laser Aerosol Spectrometer (LAS-XII) were applied for all the measurements.

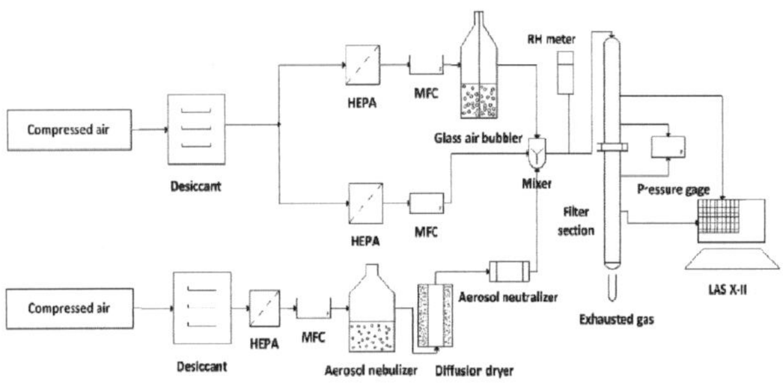

Figure 2. Schematic of setup for filter media tests.

This experimental setup was used for bench scale air filtration measurement. It is very helpful for filter media design. Compressed air was passed through silica gel desiccant to get rid of moisture and HEPA filter to eliminate contaminants in the air stream. Then, it flew into a nebulizer to generate aerosols from salt solution. Diffusion dryer (DD 250) from Air Techniques International (ATI) and an aerosol neutralizer body (Model-9000) from Brechtel manufacturing, Inc with two Polonium-210 strips (from NRD, LLC) were used to dry the salt particles and neutralize the particles into Boltzman equilibrium respectively. The same as the full scale test rig, pressure drop and particles removal efficiency were measured by a pressure transducer from Omega and Laser Aerosol Spectrometer (LAS-XII) from TSI.

Results and discussion

Two different types of tests were conducted, including pressure drop and removal efficiency. As for full scale test rig, different single filters were tested, like filter depth, filter pleat count and filter media type.

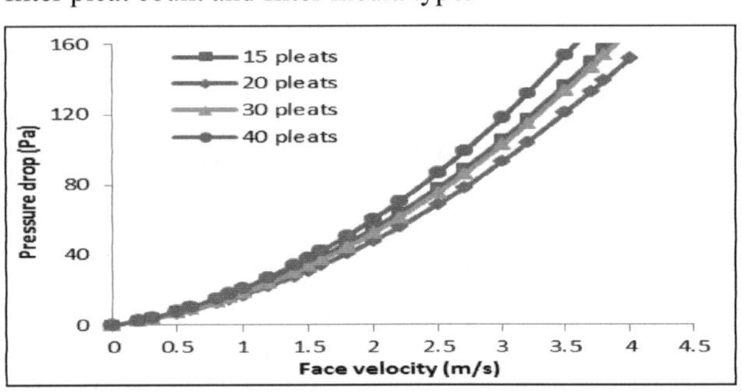

Figure 3. Pressure drop curves for 2 inch depth filter with different pleats.

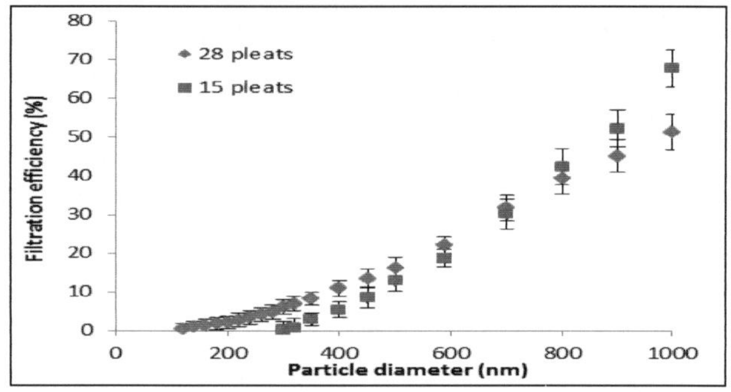

Figure 4. Filtration efficiency curves for 2 inch depth filter with different pleats.

Usually for a filter, higher particles removal efficiency means larger pressure drop. In order to judge if the filter is good on its filtration performance, a new term, quality factor (QF) is defined to measure of whether an increase in pressure drop is warranted by the increase in filtration efficiency [6,7].

$$QF = \frac{\gamma}{\Delta P / t} = \frac{\gamma t}{\Delta P} = \frac{\ln(1/P)}{\Delta P} = -\frac{\ln(1-E)}{\Delta P} \tag{2}$$

From the equation, larger of filtration efficiency and smaller of pressure drop can lead to higher quality factor, which means better filtration performance.

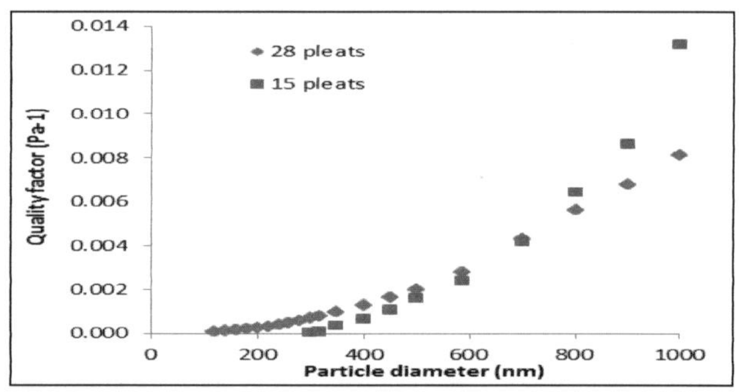

Figure 5. Comparison of quality factors for 2 inch depth filter with different pleats.

Experimental results have shown that filter pleats and filter depth have significant effect on filter performance. For single filters in same depth and different pleats, higher pleats has shown better performance for smaller particles and lower pleats has shown better performance for larger particles. The reason might be due to the different filtration mechanisms for small and large particles. For small particles, diffusion (Brownian motion) is the dominant mechanism and it is more significant at lower face velocity. On the contrary, inertial impaction is a dominant mechanism for large particles and higher the face velocity, the better of the filtration performance. Since higher pleats lead to larger filtration area and lower face velocity, according to diffusion mechanism, much more small particles are able to be captured and entrapped.

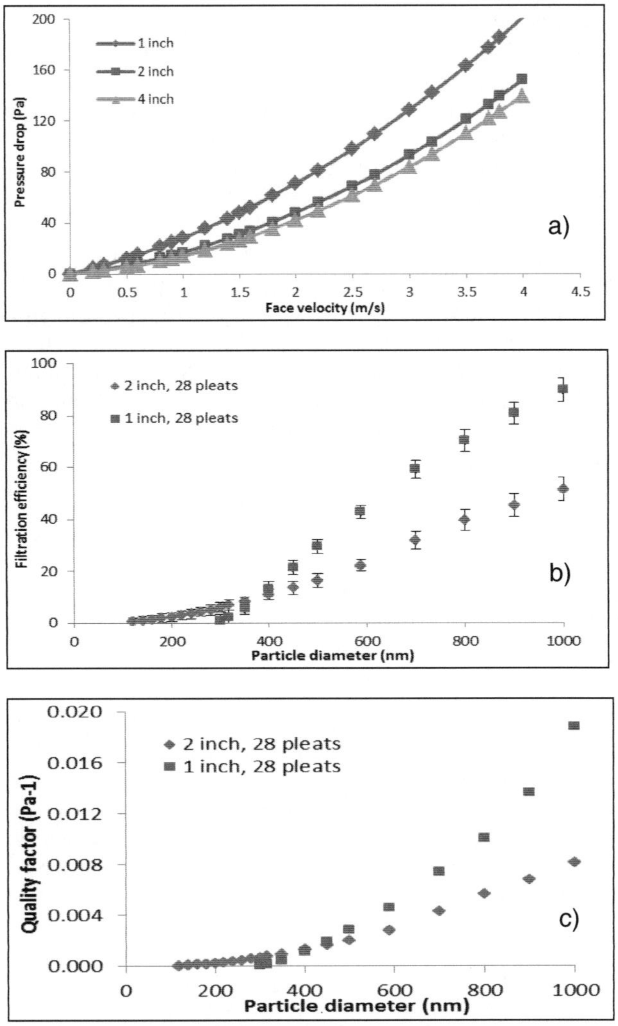

Figure 6. Comparisons of a) pressure drop, b) filtration efficiency, and c) quality factor between filters in different depth.

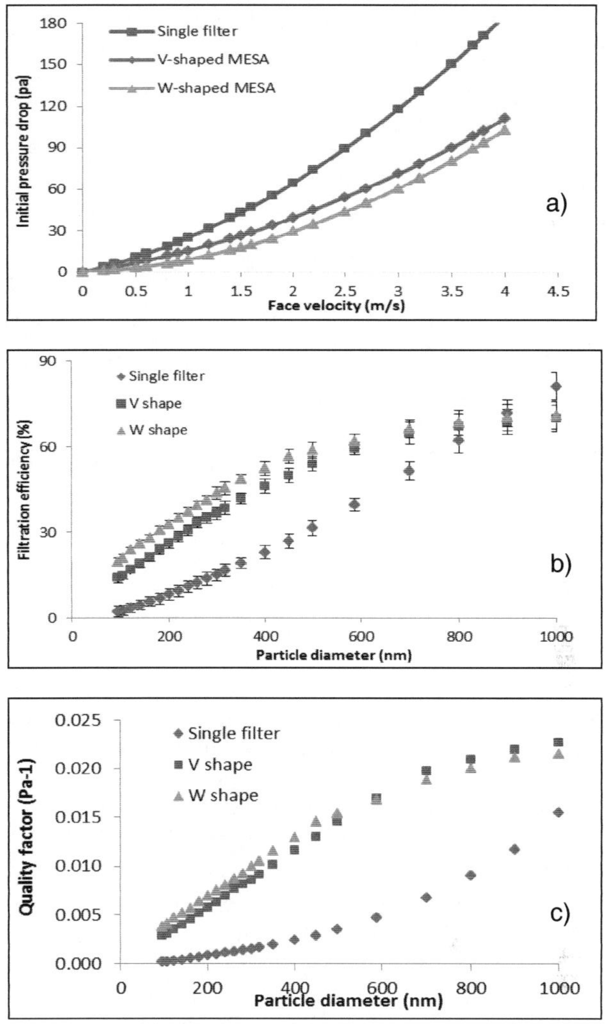

Figure 7. Comparisons of a) pressure drop, b) filtration efficiency, and c) quality factor between single filter and MESAs.

Besides single filters, multi-element structured arrays (MESAs) were tested as well in regard of their filtration performance and the comparisons between MESAs and single filter are shown in Figure 7.

The results indicate that MESAs significantly reduce pressure drop due to its lower face velocity and increase the filtration efficiency due to its larger filtration area, which leads to much higher quality factors compared to single filters. Although at 550 fpm, MESAs showed smaller filtration efficiency for particles larger than 800 nm, they still had greater quality factors. This suggests that the decrease of pressure drop for MESAs compensated the effect of decrease in filtration efficiency. Therefore, MESAs are able to enhance salt particles filtration performance significantly than single pleated filter and they can be applied into real circumstances, such as filtration system for SOFCs on ocean environment.

In terms of filter media design using a bench-scale test rig, several different types of filter materials were measured, including both nonwoven media, which were made by using wet-laid method and woven media. For nonwoven media, after entrapping carbon nano-scale fiber, filtration efficiency is improved significantly due to its much smaller fiber diameter since the smaller of the fiber size, the more particles are able to be trapped. Meanwhile, the increase of pressure drop after entrapping carbon nanofiber is not significant compared to that of particles collection efficiency due to the wet-laid method applied to manufacture the filter media. By this method, nanofiber is considered to be evenly dispersed into the depth of media instead of covering on the surface, which is able to make air pass through the media much easier and reduce the flow resistance. Therefore, filtration performance is improved after entrapping carbon nanofiber into nonwoven polymer media.

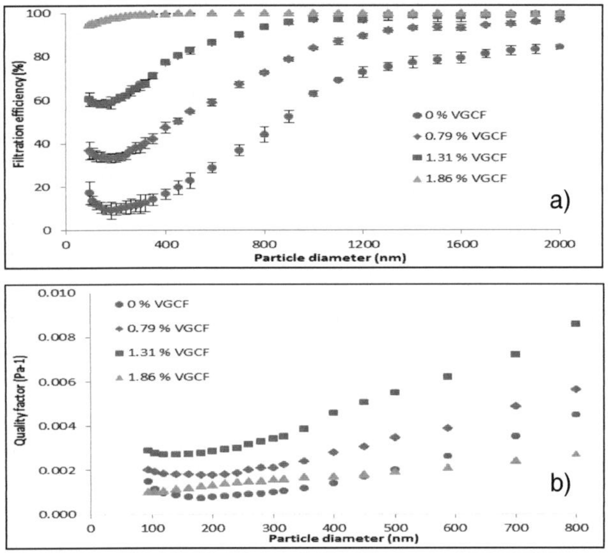

Figure 8. a) Filtration efficiency and b) quality factor of nonwoven polymer media entrapped with carbon nanofiber (VGCF).

For woven media, comparison of filtration performance was made with nonwoven media and the results indicate that nonwoven media has much better performance as filter media because of its homogeneous pore structure instead of inhomogeneous pore structure of woven media. Thus, for filtration purpose, nonwoven media has significantly higher performance than woven media.

Table 1. Comparison of filtration efficiency and pressure drop for nonwoven and woven media

	Number of layers	Thickness (mm)	Overall filtration efficiency (%)	Pressure drop per thickness (Pa/mm)
Nonwoven 19.07%	1	3.8	60.76	72.11
Knit	1	0.45	21.92	173.60
	2	1.0	36.59	152.20
	3	1.45	50.49	167.07
Single weave	1	0.5	12.02	85.60
	3	1.45	23.91	96.83
Felt	1	2.0	40.21	59.50

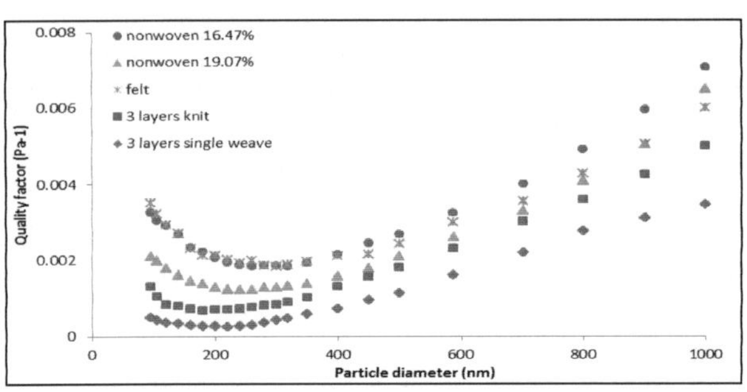

Figure 9. Comparison of quality factors between nonwoven and woven media.

Conclusions

This study mainly focuses on two aspects of salt particles filtration for SOFCs on ocean environment, one is packaging configuration design of pleated filters and the other is filter media design. The experimental results have shown that for single filter, 1 inch depth filter is better for large particles and 2 inch filter is better for small particles. According to different circumstances, different depth filter can be selected to achieve optimum performance. Also, Multi-element Structured Arrays (MESAs) designed by our research group have shown significantly higher filtration performance compared to single filters due to their larger surface area and lower air face velocity through the filters. Thus, MESAs are potentially widely applied as salt particles removal system for SOFCs during ocean platforms.

The study has also reported after entrapping nanofiber into polymer media, filtration performance can be enhanced due to its much higher particles collection efficiency and slightly higher pressure drop. The preliminary results have also demonstrated that the nonwoven media gives much better filtration performance for salt particles compared to woven media because of their different pore structures.

Overall, in order to reduce the amount of salt particles flowing into cathode side of SOFCs to a minimum, MESAs can be applied as filtration device for air stream and use nonwoven media as filter media. According to different situations, if ultra-pure clean air is needed, nonwoven media entrapped with carbon nanofiber can be considered as an option to improve filtration performance.

References

1. Yan, W.M., Chu, H.S., and Jang, J.H., "Effects of chlorides on the performance of proton exchange membrane fuel cells," *International Journal of Hydrogen Energy*, vol. 36, pp. 5435-5441, 2011.
2. Jing, F.N., Hou, M., and Yi, B.L., "The effect of ambient contamination on PEMFC performance," *Journal of Power Source*, vol. 166, pp. 172-176, 2007.
3. Majchrzak, R., Cole, T., and Cervi, M., "U.S. Navy Sea Salt Particle Removal Systems," *Carderock Division Naval Surface Warefare Center*, 1998.
4. ASHRAE 52.2, "Method of Testing General Ventilation Air-cleaning Devices Used for Removal Efficiency by Particle Size," *American National Standard*, GA, USA.
5. Sothen, R.A. and Tatarchuk, B.J., "A Semi-Empirical Pressure Drop Model: Part I-Pleated Filters," *Hvac&R Research*, vol. 14, pp. 841-860, 2008.
6. Spurny, K.R., "Advances in Aerosol Filtration," *Lewis*, 1998.
7. Brown, R.C., "Air Filtration: An Integrated Approach to the Theory and Application of Fibrous Filters," *Pergamon Press*, 1993.

Development and Applications of Logistics Fueled Solid Oxide Fuel Cell Systems with Novel Sulfur Mitigation Strategies for Man-Portable and Unmanned Systems

Thomas Westrich, Jon Rice
Ultra Electronics AMI
Ann Arbor, MI 48108

Abstract: *AMI has recently developed an integrated 250W JP8-fueled SOFC system which uses a novel sulfur mitigation strategy that does not require the use of a sulfur filter. The absence of a sulfur filter results in a smaller system size, lower weight, and zero deployed SOFC consumables. Through the use of a hydrogen-permeable membrane, the selective utilization of hydrogen at the fuel cell anode can be achieved. This paper will summarize recent developments of this technology and explore the existing development hurdles which impair logistics fueled SOFCs and the development path to unmanned systems, such as UAVs or UGVs.*

Keywords: Solid Oxide Fuel Cell; Sulfur; Logistics Fuel; JP-8; Membrane; Unmanned Vehicles.

Introduction

Individual warfighters require extremely lightweight, quiet, efficient, and reliable power sources for a variety of portable electronics and other applications in the modern battlefield without increasing the logistical burden. A solid oxide fuel cell (SOFC) fueled by JP-8 is considered a potential portable power system if it meets the requirements of future soldier missions; primarily safety, low weight, high power, and high energy density.

The JP-8 logistic fuel currently used in the battle field would be a logical choice as an energy source for SOFC fuel cell applications[1]. However, the heavy hydrocarbons in the logistic fuels have to be converted to hydrogen-rich reformate in order to generate electricity by a SOFC. Additionally, the large sulfur content in logistics fuels places demands on the sulfur tolerance or filtration requirements of the system[2]. Therefore, the SOFC power system should consist of an integrated system for logistic fuel processing and sulfur mitigation with a SOFC. The system integration of fuel processing and sulfur mitigation subsystems with the SOFC subsystem is an important development issue to be addressed, particularly for lightweight applications such as unmanned aerial or ground vehicles.

Ultra Electronics, AMI (UE-AMI) has been developing a sulfur-tolerant JP8-fueled SOFC system to meet this need. Through the use of a hydrogen-permeable membrane, the selective utilization of hydrogen at the fuel cell anode can be achieved[3]. The selective nature of the membrane prevents any other molecule from reaching the anode, specifically poisons, such as hydrogen sulfide and other sulfur compounds, and coke-forming small hydrocarbons, such as methane, ethylene and propylene. In addition, water generated as a product of electricity generation is recycled into the reformate, and in the presence of a catalyst, increases hydrogen production yields and reduces light hydrocarbon fractions. To date, UE-AMI has developed this technology into a prototype 15kg JP8-fueled system which has push-button start-up and shut-down, automated system control, and hybrid batteries to handle dynamic loads (shown in Figure 1).

Figure 1: JP-8 Fueled SOFC prototype system developed at Ultra Electronics AMI.

Experimental

Testing of individual subcomponents was accomplished prior to full system integration. Lab scale reformer endurance and thermal cycling tests were used to screen for reformer catalyst performance and assess catalyst lifetime performance. The palladium membranes used in this work were prepared and tested at UE-AMI facilities. Permeance and selectivity measurements as well as single cell power generation measurements were used to evaluate the performance of membrane formulations or single cell design concepts. The JP-8 used in this work was Mil-spec JP-8, containing 300ppmw sulfur.

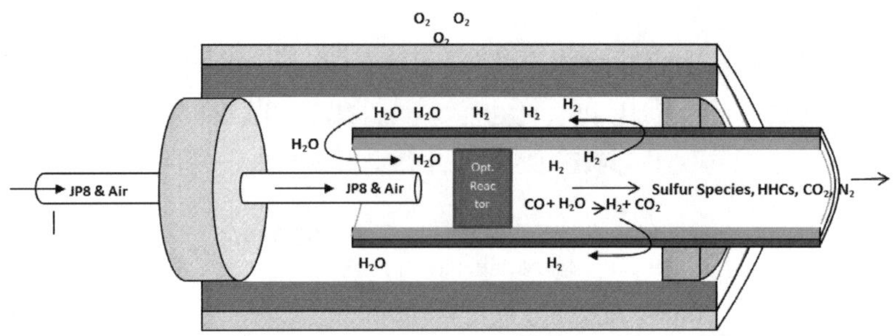

Figure 2: Schematic of the membrane-based JP-8 fueled SOFC cell design.

Results & Discussion

A schematic of the cell and membrane design used in this work is shown in Figure 2. Generally, sulfur-laden fuel species is introduced to the interior of the hydrogen-selective membrane, and can pass through the length of the SOFC tubular cell. As hydrogen is electrochemically consumed, a hydrogen partial pressure gradient is established across the membrane, causing a flow of hydrogen out of the fuel rich stream. As a result, further reforming and shift reactions are favorable within the membrane, leading to higher utilizations of light hydrocarbons. Additionally, electrochemically generated steam is driven into the fuel stream to aid in steam reforming or water-gas-shift reactions. During the course of technology developments, several improvements upon this design were made, however, the illustrated design represents the core technology.

Catalytic reforming experiments with 300ppmwS JP-8 were conducted with several catalyst formulations. The formulation with highest endurance performance was a Rhodium-loaded ceria catalyst[4]. Partial oxidation reforming endurance results are shown in Figure 3. The rhodium catalyst operated with near-equilibrium product distributions for most of the 450hr test. Catalyst deactivation near the end of the test resulted in the formation of additional light hydrocarbons, and the accumulation of heavy hydrocarbon tars near the reactor effluent.

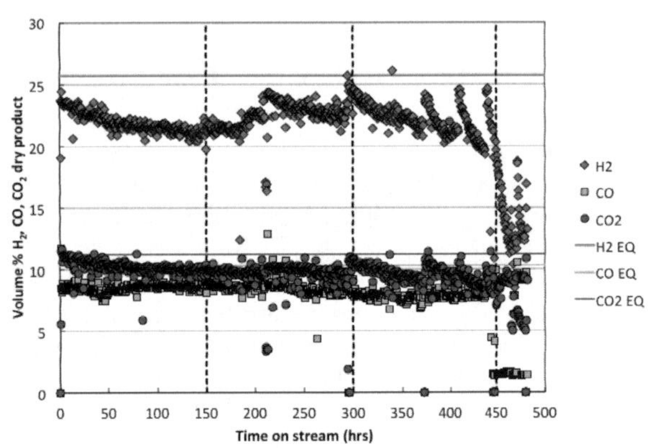

Figure 3: JP-8 Reformer product distribution during 450hr endurance test.

The palladium-based hydrogen permeable membranes were made with 3 thicknesses: 13.1μm, 17 μm, and 25 μm. The flux testing results are shown in Figure 4, along with the cell flux requirement for electrochemical performance.

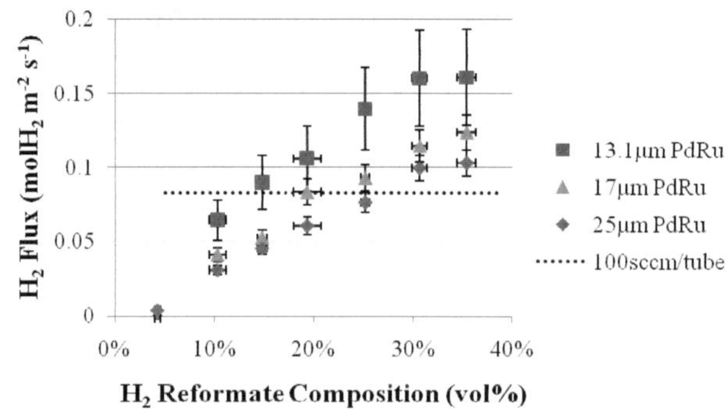

Figure 4: Hydrogen permeable palladium membrane flux results for membranes with varied thicknesses.

Qualitative membrane selectivity measurements were conducted using a single cell/membrane bundle. Upon exposure to H_2S concentrations in excess of 10ppb, the SOFC experiences significant performance degradation. A 2,800 hour experiment using a fuel source with 50ppm H2S in hydrogen successfully proved high membrane selectivity to hydrogen, and the endurance capability of the membrane (Figure 5).

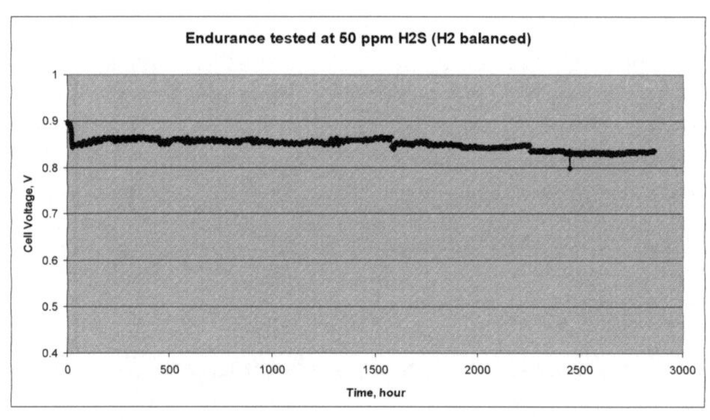

Figure 5: Demonstration of the performance of a SOFC cell and membrane bundle operating with 50ppm H2S in the fuel stream for nearly 3,000hrs.

Once the individual components were shown to meet performance requirements, a single cell/membrane bundle was tested with JP-8 reformate. Power curves for several cells operating on reformate are shown in Figure 6. For each cell, the thermal-to-electrical efficiency was calculated to be approximately 15%.

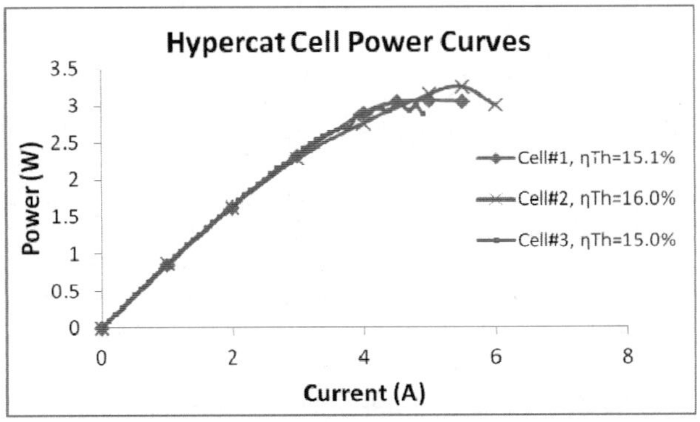

Figure 6: Single cell (SOFC tube and membrane bundle) power curve operating utilizing JP-8 reformate (approximately 40ppmv H_2S).

Low demonstrated thermal efficiencies of this technology are due to two prevailing factors. Firstly, an energy balance reveals that significant energy is not transferred across the current palladium membrane. This energy balance shows that nearly 50% of the thermal energy input to the system (in the form of JP-8) is not transferred across the membrane, either as a result of: sulfur-poisoned reforming reactions, low water recirculation rates, and sulfur-induced changes in hydrogen permeability. Secondly, the use of a primary catalytic partial oxidation reforming reaction significantly decreases the potential system efficiency; this strategy places a large burden on effective water recirculation within the cell/membrane bundle to return to autothermal reforming efficiency limits.

Further development of this technology into a high-TRL product will be required, specifically in the areas of JP-8 reforming (catalyst endurance), membrane manufacturing (low-cost, high-permeance, high-selectivity membranes), and improved system integration. The prototype units built for this effort experienced either lifetime or performance issues as a direct result of the aforementioned development opportunities. For example, significant developments have been made in the field of palladium-based hydrogen separation membranes over the past 40 years. Sulfur-tolerant[5] and very thin membranes[6] with high hydrogen permeance have been reported in literature and used in commercial hydrogen purification processes (albeit at significantly higher absolute pressures than used here). Use of this advanced membrane technology in the presented SOFC design would result in improved system performance, reliability and robustness – key criterion for unmanned vehicles.

This technology has the capability to significantly increase system specific power and energy relative to a comparable reformer/sulfur filtration/SOFC system. The use of a continuous and non-consumable sulfur filtration device, such as a hydrogen-selective membrane, results in the complete absence of large, heavy sulfur filtration beds. Therefore, this design approach is an excellent option for the demands of unmanned aerial or ground vehicles.

Acknowledgements

The authors would like to thank collaborators within Ultra Electronics AMI (Chris Schoeps, Tim LaBreche, and Dr. Aaron Crumm), as well as at the University of Michigan (Dr. Andrew Tadd and Professor Suljo Linic) for their help and support to this project. Funding was provided by DARPA (contract number: W911QX-09-C-0070-P00003).

References

1. Stangl, J. D., Wertz, R. O., Holcomb, F. H., "Military Requirements for JP-8 Reformers and Solid Oxide Fuel Cell Power Systems," US Army Corps of Engineers, ERDC/CERL TR-05-36, December 2005
2. Detail Specification: Turbine Fuel, Aviation, Kerosene Type, JP-8 (NATO F-34), NATO F-35, and JP-8+100 (NATO F-37) MIL-DTL-83133H
3. Lin, Y., Lee, G., Rei, M., "An Integrated Purification and Production of Hydrogen with Palladium Membrane-Catalytic Reactor," *Catalysis Today*, vol. 44, issues 1-4, pp. 343-349, 1998.
4. Tadd, A., "Deactivation of Noble-Metal Catalysts During Autothermal Reforming of Jet Fuel," 2011 AIChE Annual Meeting, Conference Proceedings.
5. Emerson, S., Dardas, Z., Hebert, R., Janowsky, G., Magdefrau, N., She, Y., Thibuad-Erkey, C., Wittenzeller, J., "Advanced Palladium Membrane Scale-Up for Hydrogen Separation," Report to the DOE Hydrogen Program (ID# PD011), 2011.
6. Li, Z. Y., Maeda, H., Kusakabe, K., Morooka, S., Anzai, H., Akiyama, S., "Preparation of Palladium-Silver Alloy Membranes for Hydrogen Separation by the Spray Pyrolysis Method," *Journal of Membrane Science*, vol. 78, issue 3, pp. 247-254, 1993.

Simple Approaches toward Superior Performance of Gel Polymer Electrolyte Lithium/Sulfur Battery

Sheng S. Zhang, and Dat T. Tran

U.S. Army Research Laboratory, RDRL-SED-C, Adelphi, MD 20783-1197

Abstract: *Lithium/sulfur (Li/S) battery is fundamentally a liquid electrochemical cell, in which long-chain lithium polysulfide (PS, Li_2S_n with $n \geq 4$) inevitably dissolves into a liquid electrolyte and serves as a liquid cathode (catholyte). As such, the chemical reaction between the dissolved PS and Li metal would be a major concern with the safety of Li/S battery at elevated temperatures. Gelling of the liquid PS catholyte is a simple approach toward the improved safety of Li/S battery. For this purpose, we developed three types of poly(ethylene oxide)-based polymer composite membranes, which allow the gel polymer electrolyte being formed in situ by activating the Li/S cell with a gel-forming liquid electrolyte. In this presentation, the advantages and disadvantages of each type of composite membranes will be discussed.*

Keywords: Lithium/sulfur battery, lithium polysulfide, catholyte, gel polymer electrolyte, separator.

Introduction

Lithium/sulfur (Li/S) battery is fundamentally a liquid electrochemical cell, in which long-chain lithium polysulfide (PS, Li_2S_n with $n \geq 4$) inevitably dissolves into liquid electrolyte and serves as the liquid cathode (or called as "catholyte") [1, 2]. Dissolution of PS transfers insulating sulfur species into the solution leading to high capacity and high rate capability. However, the dissolution meanwhile causes parasitic reactions between the dissolved PS and the Li anode, which has been identified to be the source for the thermal runway of Li/S battery at elevated temperatures. Gelling the PS catholyte provides an effective approach for reducing the PS reactivity and catholyte leakage. For manufacture convenience, the gel polymer electrolyte (GPE) is desired to be formed after the cell is sealed, which requires the employment of a porous polymer membrane. On the other hand, in view of the chemical stability, poly(ethylene oxide) (PEO) has been proven to be the most suitable polymer for the GPE of Li/S batteries [1]. Due to the difficulty to make a porous PEO membrane, the PEO-based GPEs are generally prepared either by a solution-casting method [3, 4] or by a melt-casting method [5, 6]. This means that the battery must be assembled in the "electrolyte activated" status, making the battery assembly unsafe. In order to facilitate the manufacture (assembly) of GPE Li/S batteries, a facile process that is suitable for in-situ formation of the PEO-based GPE is necessary to be developed.

When a porous polymer membrane is used to form the GPE in situ, the penetration of liquid electrolyte into the membrane is required to be fast sufficiently so that the liquid electrolyte can distribute throughout the membrane before the polymer is gelled. This can be achieved by incorporating significant amount of inorganic filler into the polymer membrane. Another benefit for the incorporation of inorganic filler is to dramatically enhance the dimensional stability of the GPE at elevated temperatures. In this work, we developed two simple processes for making of the PEO-based GPE Li/S battery, in which the GPE is formed in situ through either a PEO-SiO_2 composite membrane or a PEO composite modified separator. Unlike the inorganic PEO composites reported ever, where the content of the inorganic filler was not more than 30 wt.% [3-6], in our process significantly higher amounts of inorganic filler (>50 wt.%) were incorporated to promote the penetration of liquid electrolyte and enhance the mechanical strength of GPE. In this presentation, the advantages and disadvantages of these two approaches will be discussed.

Experimental

An electrode consisting of 77% sulfur, 10% Super-P carbon, 10% Ketjenblack EC-300JD carbon black and 3% poly(acrylonitrile-methyl methacrylate) by weight was coated onto a carbon-coated aluminum foil as the sulfur cathode. The sulfur cathode had an averaged sulfur loading of 2 mg cm^{-2}. A 0.5 mol Kg^{-1} LiTFSI tetraethylene glycol dimethyl ether (TEGDME) and a 0.25 mol Kg^{-1} LiTFSI-0.25 mol Kg^{-1} $LiNO_3$ 1:1 (wt.) dimethyl ether (DME)/dioxolane (DOL) were respectively used as the gel-forming electrolyte. A homogenous 50PEO-50SiO_2 (wt.) slurry in methanol was prepared using a 5100 Mixer Mill® machine (SPEX CertiPrep) and coated onto the sulfur cathode to form an electrode-supporting "electrode-membrane-assembly" (EMA), onto a Teflon substrate to form a free-standing composite membrane, or onto a commercial Celgard 3400 membrane to form a PEO-SiO_2 composite modified separator. Using the same procedure, the PEO-S slurry with different contents of sulfur was coated onto the Celgard 3400 membrane to form a PEO-S composite modified separator. The composite coatings had an averaged thickness of 25 μm.

Morphology of the PEO composite coatings was observed and photographed by a Nikon Eclipse LV100 microscope or a Quanta 200F scanning electron microscope. Cell's impedance was measured using a

Solartron SI 1287 Electrochemical Interface and a SI 1260 Impedance/Gain-Phase Analyzer. Using the sulfur cathode and the separator specified case-by-case in the discussion, coin cells were assembled by activating with 20 μL liquid electrolyte and heating the cell at 80 °C for 2 h to allow PEO gelling. The cells were galvanostatically cycled at room temperature (~22 °C) on a Maccor Series 4000 cycler.

Results and Discussion

The GPE is an electrolyte system with the liquid electrolyte completely plasticized into the polymer media, in which the liquid electrolyte dominates the ionic conductivity and the polymer contributes to the viscoelasticity. A challenge for the GPE as a battery separator is the loss of viscoelasticity with an increase of the temperature, which eventually results in the electrical circuit-shorting of battery. In order to overcome this disadvantage, we took two approaches of (1) incorporating significant amount of inorganic filler to form a composite gel polymer electrolyte (CGPE), and (2) coating the CGPE onto an existing separator, which are described and discussed below.

1. PEO-SiO_2 composite membrane: Two forms of PEO-SiO_2 composite membranes are prepared as: (1) coating composite membrane onto the sulfur cathode, and (2) coating the composite slurry onto a Teflon substrate and evaporating the solvent to form a free-standing membrane, as shown in Fig. 1a and Fig. 1b, respectively. The former, referred as to "electrode-membrane-assembly" (EMA), can have the content of SiO_2 as high as 95 wt.% without cracks. The EMA can be rolled into any diameters without creating cracks, which can be laminated directly with the Li anode without need of additional separator. The latter requires a relatively lower content of SiO_2 to remain the free-standing and flexible properties. The membrane shown in Fig. 1b has a composition of 50PEO-50SiO_2 (wt.), which is free-standing and very flexible.

The free-standing 50PEO-50SiO_2 membrane exhibits a network-like microstructure (see Fig. 1c), in which the dark networks and spots are the self-assembled SiO_2 networks and undispersed SiO_2 aggregates, respectively [7]. Normally, these SiO_2 networks and aggregates are embedded under a thin PEO film, which enables the fast penetration of liquid electrolyte over the membrane. As indicated by Fig. 1d, the 50PEO-50SiO_2 composite membrane can be instantly wetted by a wide range of electrolyte solvents, including the very viscous ionic liquid.

Upon absorption of a 0.5 mol Kg^{-1} LiTFSI TEGDME electrolyte, the liquid electrolyte is initially immobilized in the pores of SiO_2 networks and aggregates so that the ionic conductivity of the membrane has the same Arrhenius behavior as that of the liquid electrolyte, as suggested by the melting points between -30 °C and -40 °C of curves a-c in Fig. 2. With heating, the liquid electrolyte plasticizes into the PEO matrix, resulting in the disappearance of melting points of PEO at ~30 °C and TEGDME near -30 °C, as indicated by curve d in Fig. 2. This fact reveals that the CGPE can be formed in situ by employing the PEO-SiO_2 membrane and activating the cell with a gel-forming electrolyte. Probably because the CGPE forms better interface with the sulfur cathode than the liquid electrolyte, the CGPE cell does not experience a "capacity activation" period, and exhibits the same capacity and capacity retention as the liquid electrolyte cell after the capacity of the liquid electrolyte cell is stabilized (Fig. 3).

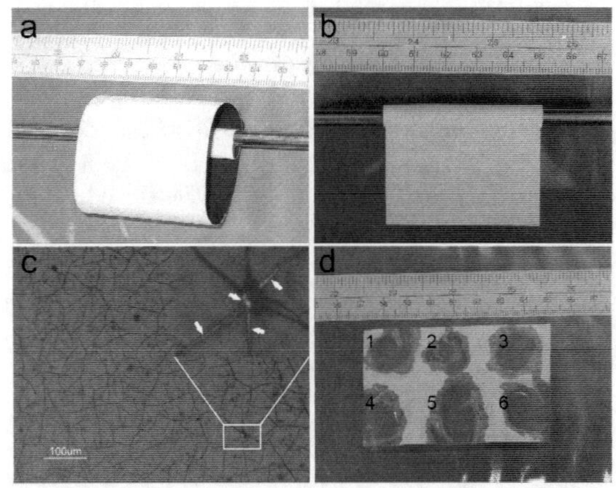

Figure 1. PEO-SiO_2 composite membrane. (a) EMA, (b) free-standing membrane, (c) microstructure of (b), and (d) wettability of various solvents on (b), where numbers 1-6 are DME, DOL, TEGDME, propylene carbonate, sulfolane, and N-methyl-N-butylpyrrolidinium bis(trifluoromethanesulfonyl)imide (an ionic liquid), respectively.

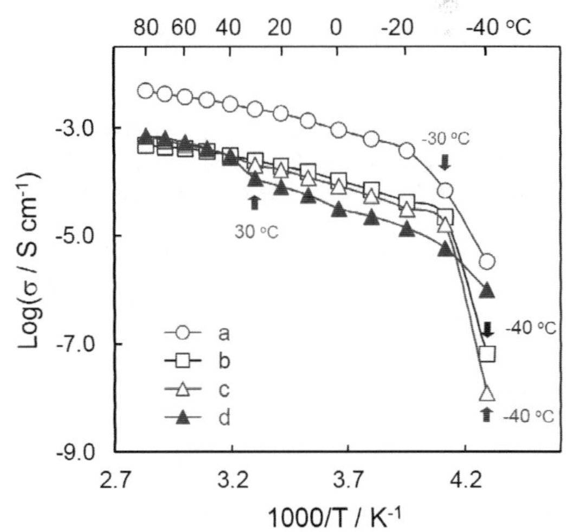

Figure 2. Arrhenius plots of the ionic conductivity. (a) 0.5 mol Kg^{-1} LiTFSI TEGDME liquid electrolyte, (b) Celgard membrane wetted with 80 wt.% liquid electrolyte, (c) composite membrane wetted with 62 wt.% liquid electrolyte and measured during heating, and (d) measured during the following cooling.

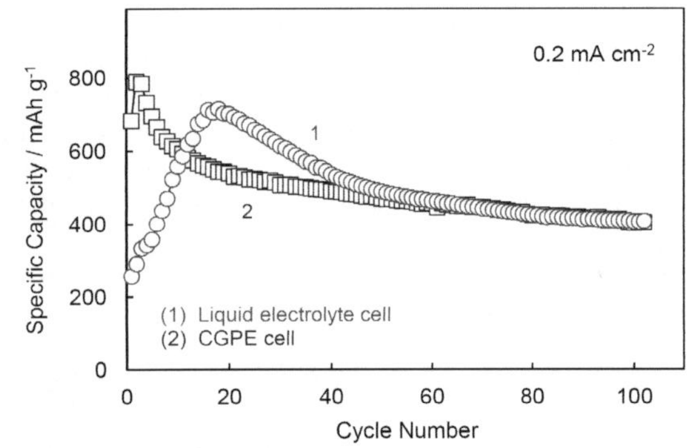

Figure 3. Cycling performance of Li/S cells. (1) Celgard separator wetted by 80 wt.% liquid electrolyte, and (2) GGPE formed with 62 wt.% liquid electrolyte.

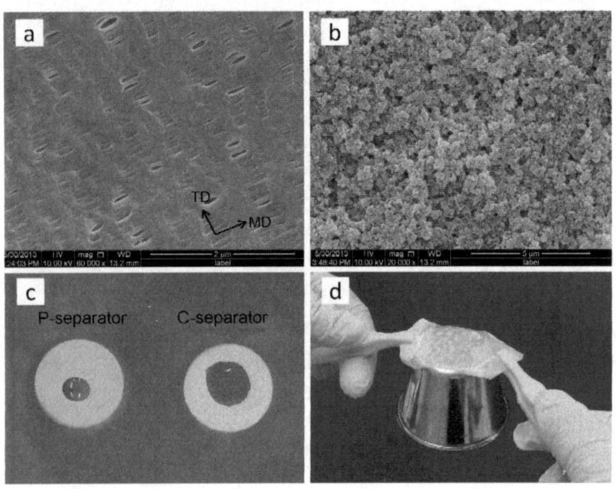

Figure 4. SEM image of P-separator (a) and C-separator (b), as well as the wettability of liquid electrolyte (c) and gluing ability of C-separator after gelled with a liquid electrolyte (d). The liquid electrolyte used was a 0.25 mol Kg^{-1} LiTFSI-0.25 mol Kg^{-1} $LiNO_3$ 1:1 (wt.) DME/DOL solution.

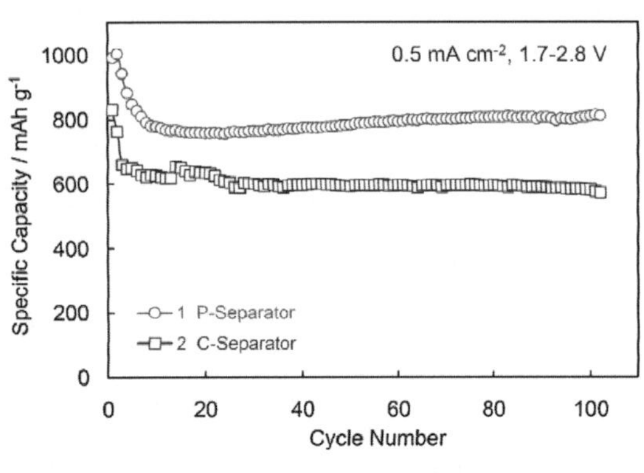

Figure 5. Capacity retention of the Li/S cells. (1) P-separator, and (2) C-separator.

2. PEO composite modified separator: An alternative approach to making the CGPE Li/S battery is to modify the existing separator with a PEO-SiO_2 composite. Fig. 4a and 4b show the SEM images of a Celgard 3401 separator before and after the coating of a 50PEO-50SiO_2 composite. It is shown that the surfaces of the composite coated separator (C-separator) are well covered by a layer of highly porous composite (Fig. 4b) and that the composite coating greatly enhances the wettability of liquid electrolyte on the separator (Fig. 4c). As an indication of the GPE formation, the separator shows strong gluing ability to a stainless steel cup after the PEO-SiO_2 composite is gelled (Fig. 4d).

Unlike the TEGDME-based electrolyte with which the CGPE and liquid electrolyte cells have nearly same capacities as indicated by Fig. 3, the C-separator Li/S cell with the DME/DOL based electrolyte is shown to suffer ~200 mA g^{-1} lower capacity as compared with the P-separator cell (Fig. 5). This is likely due to the relatively lower sulfur utilization in the highly viscous TEGDME electrolyte. As one can see by comparing the liquid electrolyte cells in Fig. 3 and Fig. 5, the TEGDME electrolyte makes the specific capacity of Li/S cell much lower because of its high viscosity. Ac-impedance analyses on Ni/Li_2S_9 catholyte soaked separator/Ni symmetric cells reveal that the PEO-SiO_2 composite absorbs and traps the dissolved PS within the CGPE matrix, making these PS electrochemically inactive [8]. This means that the benefits, such as increasing battery safety and reducing electrolyte leakage, of the CGPE are taken at the expense of specific capacity.

In order to compensate for the capacity loss of the GPE, we proposed electrochemically active sulfur particles as the inorganic filler to enhance the penetration of liquid electrolyte and to provide the additional surface source. As shown in Fig. 6a and Fig. 6b, the sulfur particles are completely embedded under a thick, net-like porous PEO film when the sulfur content is 20 wt.%, and almost exposed to the surface with a very thin and porous PEO film when the sulfur content increases to 60 et.%. As predicted, the penetration of the electrolyte solvent, triethylene glycol dimethyl ether (TG3), on the separator is increased with the content of sulfur in the PEO-S composite (see Fig. 6c and 6d), showing the ability of sulfur particles to serve as the wetting agent of liquid electrolyte for the filling process of liquid electrolyte in the Li/S battery assembly.

As shown in Fig. 7, after activated with the liquid electrolyte, the capacity of sulfur particles in the PEO-S composite can be slowly released to contribute to the overall capacity of the Li/S cells, and the release efficiency of sulfur capacity is greatly varied with the electrolyte/sulfur (E/S) ratio, which was also previously observed from the conventional liquid electrolyte Li/S cells [9]. Upon the capacity release (dissolution) of sulfur particles, resulting voids are closed and filled with a true PEO-based GPE.

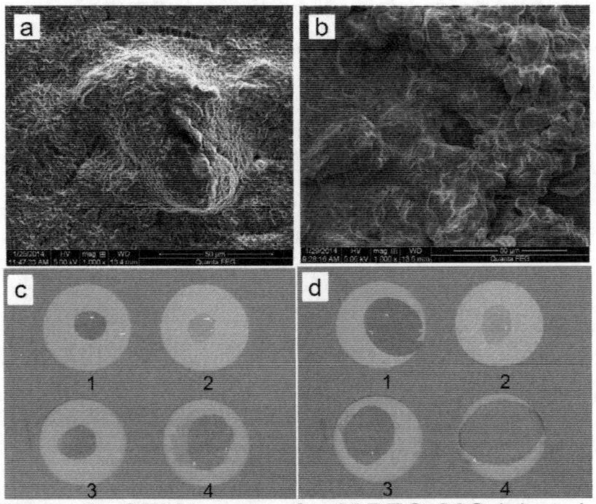

Figure 6. SEM image of a 80PEO-20S (a) and a 40PEO-60S (b) coated separator, as well as the wettability of TG3 on various separators after the solvent was applied for 2 minutes (c) and 20 minutes (d). In (c) and (d), (1) P-separator, (2) SC-separator with x=0%, (3) SC-separator with x=20%, and (4) SC-separator with x=40%.

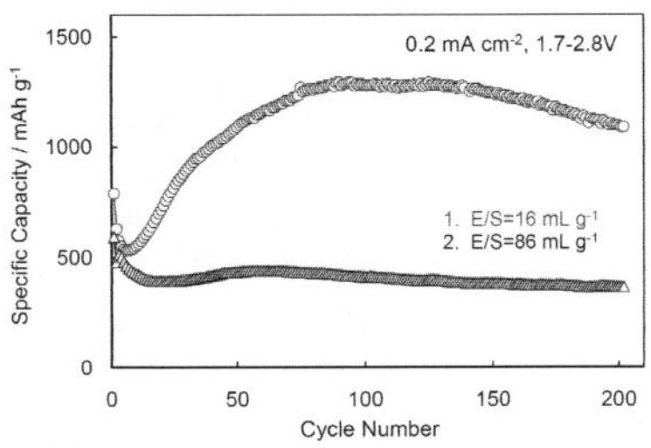

Figure 7. Release of sulfur capacity from a 40PEO-60S composite.

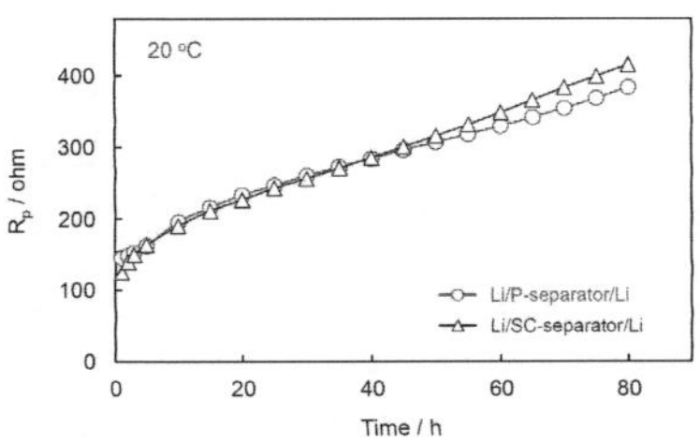

Figure 8. R_p growth in Li/Li symmetric cell.

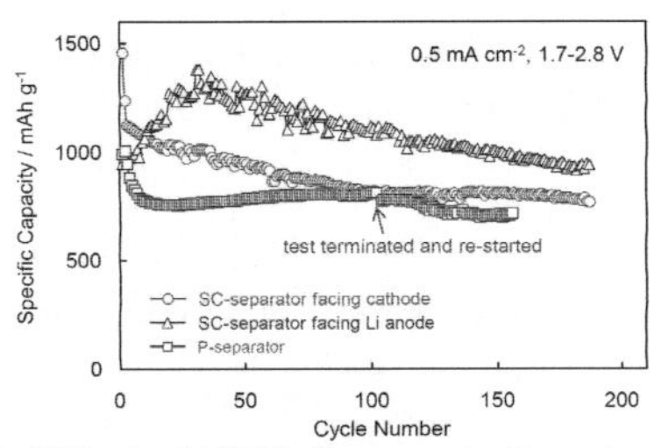

Figure 9. Effect of PEO-S composite orientation on cycling performance of Li/S cell.

The chemical stability of sulfur particles in the composite against the Li anode is evaluated by monitoring the ac impedance of a Li/Li symmetric cell, and the time dependences of the passivation resistance (R_p) for the P-separator and C-separator (coated with a 40PEO-60S composite) are compared in Fig. 8. It is shown that two separators have very similar R_p values and R_p growing rates with the storage time. These results verify that in contact with the sulfur particles, the stable passivation layer on the Li surface still can be formed, suggesting that the sulfur particles are chemically suitable for the wetting agent. Since the PEO-S composite provides extra capacity, the Li/S cells with the PEO-S composite coated separator exhibit even higher capacities than the liquid electrolyte Li/S cell (see Fig. 9), and the capacity increment varies with the orientation of PEO-S composite, which is attributed to the different capacity release mechanism of sulfur on the carbon surface and on the Li surface, respectively [10].

Conclusions

In order to take the advantages of GPEs, the PEO-based GPE Li/S battery can be conveniently assembled by employing a PEO composite membrane with significantly high content of inorganic filler. The high content of inorganic filler is the key to enabling the fast electrolyte filling and good dimensional stability at elevated temperatures. The PEO composite membrane can be directly coated onto the sulfur cathode to form an EMA, made into a free-standing membrane as the separator, or coated onto an existing separator. In particular, superior capacity to the liquid electrolyte Li/S cells can be obtained when sulfur particles are used as the wetting agent.

References

1. Zhang, S.S. , *J. Power Sources,* 231, 153, 2013.
2. Zhang, S.S., *J. Electrochem. Soc.,* 159, A1226, 2012.
3. Jeong, S.S., Lim, Y.T., Choi, Y.J., Cho, G.B., Kim, K.W., Ahn, H.J., Cho, K.K., *J. Power Sources*, 174, 745, 2007.
4. Tominaga, Y., Asai, S., Sumita, M., Panerob, S., Scrosati, B., *J. Power Sources*, 146, 402, 2005.
5. Aihara, Y., Appetecchi, G.B., Scrosati, B., *J. Electrochem. Soc.*, 149, A849, 2002.
6. Hassoun, J., Scrosati, Bruno., *Adv. Mater.*, 22, 5198, 2010.
7. Zhang, S.S., *J. Electrochem. Soc.*, 160, A1421, 2013.
8. Zhang, S.S., Tran, D.T., *Electrochim. Acta*, 114, 296, 2013.
9. Zhang, S.S., *Energies*, 5, 5190, 2012.
10. Zhang, S.S., Tran, D.T., *J. Mater. Chem. A*, 2, 7383, 2014.

Organosilicon-based Electrolytes with Enhanced Thermal and Electrochemical Stability to Enable High Energy Lithium Ion Batteries

Arthur Homa[1], Monica L. Usrey[1], Adrián Peña-Hueso[1], Michael Pollina[1], Peng Du[1], Xin Chen[2], Robert West[1,2], and Robert J. Hamers[1,2]

[1]Silatronix, Inc.
3587 Anderson Street, Suite 108
Madison, WI 53704

[2]Department of Chemistry
University of Wisconsin-Madison
Madison, WI 53705

Abstract: *Organosilicon (OS) electrolytes have been developed as a viable alternative to conventional carbonate electrolytes for Li-ion batteries.[1,2] A recent trend in the Li-ion industry toward adoption of new materials, including electrolytes, is driven by the desire to deploy larger capacity batteries under broader operating conditions. In addition, the development of new advanced Li-ion chemistries to meet these requirements often require electrolytes with enhanced thermal and electrochemical stability that provide performance across a wide temperature range. Silatronix has recently developed and synthesized new OS molecules to provide new (patent pending) solvents with superior thermal stability, enhanced high voltage stability, and improved resistance to fluorine attack, far beyond that of carbonates and previous generation OS solvents.[3] In addition, advanced generation OS-based electrolytes have demonstrated improved physical properties (such as viscosity, conductivity, and dielectric constant) that are very similar to electrolytes currently being used in commercial Li-ion applications. These advanced generation OS solvents represent a new opportunity to dramatically improve high temperature cycling stability, high voltage stability, and safety.*

Keywords: Li-ion batteries; organosilicon; electrolytes; enhanced stability; safety; high voltage

Introduction

Silatronix was founded in 2007 by Robert West (emeritus) and Robert Hamers, both highly recognized chemistry professors at the University of Wisconsin-Madison (UW-Madison). Dr. West had synthesized over 200 organosilicon compounds over three years with Argonne National Labs to identify an initial class of materials that function best as solvents ("Gen-1") for electrochemical energy storage. Since its founding Silatronix has developed two advanced generations of ultra-stable OS solvents ("Gen-2" and "Gen-3") to address the commercial needs of next generation Li-ion batteries by tailoring the solvent structure and electrolyte formulation to provide the physical characteristics required by specific applications.

For example, in this work, we seek to:

- Improve existing systems with better wide range temperature performance
- Enable ultra-high safety systems by reducing flammability and increasing thermal stability
- Enable high voltage (HV) advanced material systems with improved electrochemical stability

Review of Organosilicon Chemistry: Organosilicon chemistry involves the merging of a silane with a Li^+ coordinating functionality, such as ethylene oxide units, to produce solvents that retain the attractive properties of the organic fragment, like good conductivity and low toxicity, while the silicon atom improves stability and increases boiling point. This combination results in low molecular-weight solvents with unique properties including high thermal and electrochemical stability, high flash point, low vapor pressure and relatively low viscosity.

Since 2010, Silatronix has developed several advanced generation OS compounds, including "Gen-2" (e.g., 1S3M2, F1S3M2) and "Gen-3" (e.g., OS3 – patent pending) solvents whose thermal, chemical, and electrochemical properties surpass those of the original "Gen-1" OS solvents (e.g., 1ND2). The primary structural difference between the OS generations concerns the substituents on the Si atom, shown in Figure 1.

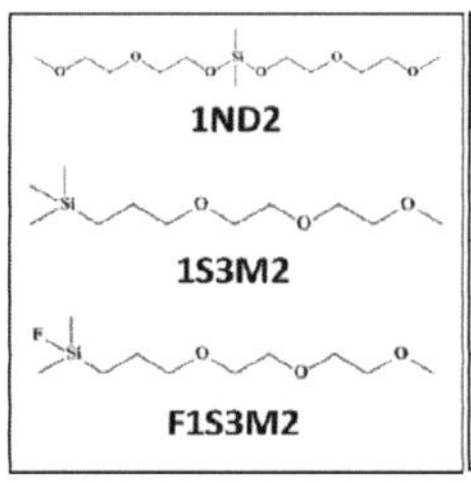

	Solvents (vol%)	Primary Salt
EOS-A	OS3 / EC / EMC 1:1:3	1M $LiPF_6$
EOS-B	OS3 / EMC 1:1	1M $LiPF_6$
EOS-C	OS3 / EC 4:1	1M $LiPF_6$

Figure 1. Structures of organosilicon solvents (right) and details for key OS3 formulations (left).

The "Gen-1" compounds are characterized by a Si-O bond, which is responsible for the excellent thermal stability of silicone polymers and enabled the production of OS electrolytes with high thermal stability. Encouraged by the successful results for "Gen-1" compounds, Silatronix performed mechanistic studies that identified advanced generation structural variants that provide even greater stability under more aggressive conditions. "Gen-2" and "Gen-3" OS solvents have thermal, chemical, and electrochemical properties that surpass those of the original compounds by introducing a less polar (i.e., more stable) Si-C bond, which is less susceptible to attack by fluorinated species, (e.g., HF and PF_5).[4] In addition, among the many substituents that can be placed on the silicon atom, fluorine

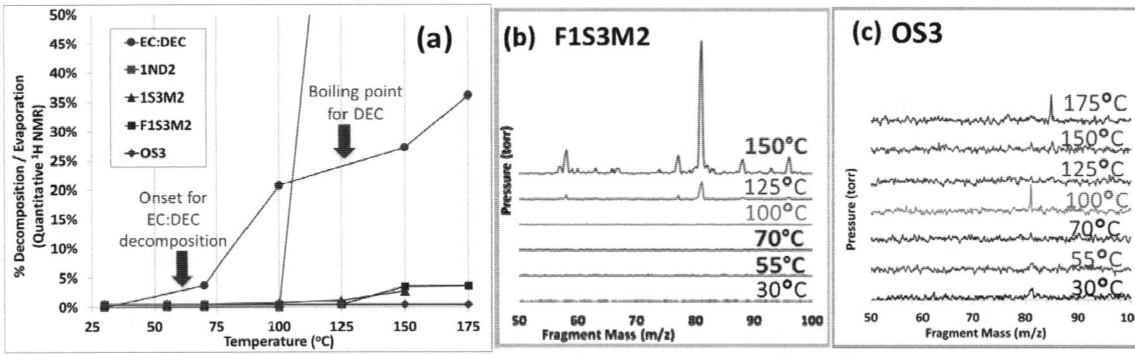

Figure 2. Thermal decomposition of 1M $LiPF_6$-based electrolytes including EC:DEC (5/5 v%) carbonate standard. (a) Degradation vs. temperature (by ^1H NMR). Gas phase EI-MS data for (b) F1S3M2 and (c) OS3 electrolytes.

could impart higher stability to the molecule, as the Si-F bond is the strongest of all single bonds formed by silicon.

In this work, we primarily focus on the characterization of a "Gen-3" OS compound with significantly enhanced thermal and electrochemical stability and abuse tolerance while maintaining comparable physical properties compared to commercial carbonate electrolytes (e.g., conductivity and viscosity). Coin cell performance is demonstrated across a wide temperature range (-10°C to 70°C) primarily in graphite/NCA full cells. Figure 1 summarizes key details for OS3 formulations developed during this study. Thermal stability and safety testing is also demonstrated for two "Gen-2" OS solvents.

Thermal Stability and Abuse Tolerance: Silatronix has conducted a number of studies to investigate the mechanisms of OS decomposition in the presence of industry-standard salts. Development of advanced generation OS compounds was driven by a mechanistic analysis of the thermal decomposition of "Gen-1" OS structures in the presence of $LiPF_6$. A custom atmospheric mass spectrometer (AMS) setup was developed to allow real-time identification of gas decomposition products evolved from a liquid sample under temperature control.

Figure 2 shows data showing the enhanced stability of "Gen-2" and "Gen-3" solvents compared to a "Gen-1" OS and a carbonate standard (all with $LiPF_6$) using the custom AMS setup. The extent of solvent decomposition as a function of temperature was determined by ^1H NMR (Figure 2a). The onset temperature for decomposition was identified by monitoring the cell head space using an argon purge leading to an electron ionization mass spectrometer (EI-MS). Sample data for F1S3M2 and OS3 are shown in Figures 2b and 2c. The EI-MS data also allows the identification of any gas phase decomposition products. For example, F1S3M2 (Figure 2b) produces Me_2SiF_2, the primary decomposition product of mono-fluorinated OS compounds reacting with $LiPF_6$ (confirmed by NIST ref.). We note that decomposition of the EC:DEC (5/5, v%) carbonate control begins at 55°C. The "Gen-1" OS (1ND2) does not decompose $\leq$ 100°C, but undergoes complete reaction at 125°C. The structural modifications of the "Gen-2" OS solvents results in a significant increase in thermal stability, as shown for 1S3M2 and F1S3M2. Neither "Gen-2" solvent show gas generation < 125°C and undergo only $\leq$ 5% total decomposition at 175°C. Even greater stability is observed with the "Gen-3" OS3 solvent, with no visible decomposition in the gas or liquid phase up to 175°C. No OS solvents studied to date undergo degradation when heated without salt or with a less reactive lithium salt (e.g., LiTFSI).

In order to confirm that the enhanced thermal stability observed in Figure 2 is maintained over the long term, electrolyte samples were sealed in glass NMR tubes. Teflon sleeves were used to line the tube in order to prevent reaction of the $LiPF_6$ (or its decomposition products) with the glass. The sealed tubes were placed in ovens at 70°C and 100°C. ^1H and ^{19}F NMR was used to quantify the decomposition over time. The F1S3M2 "Gen-2" OS electrolytes exhibited $\leq$ 0.6% decomposition after 140 days at 70°C and $\leq$ 3% decomposition after 202 days at 100°C. The "Gen-3" OS3 electrolyte showed no visible decomposition under any condition tested to date. In

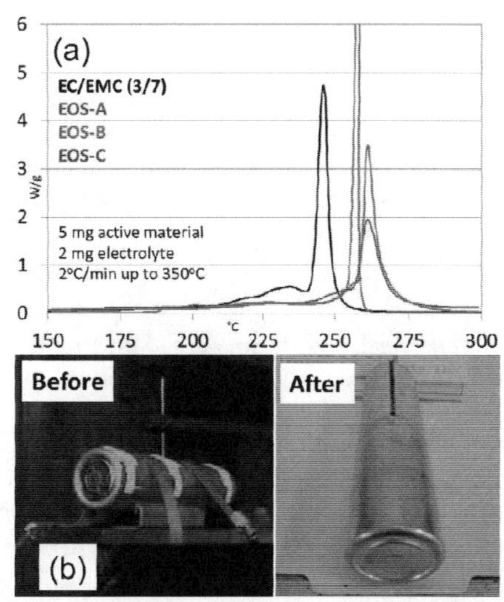

Figure 3. (a) Differential Scanning Calorimetry data for OS3 electrolytes with de-lithiated NCA cathode and (b) Nail penetration test for OS2 electrolyte with $LiFePO_4$.

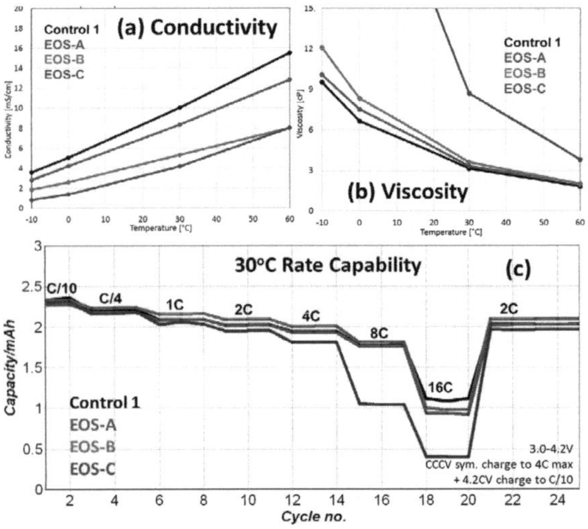

Figure 4. (a) Conductivity and (b) viscosity profiles and (c) 30°C coin cell cycling performance for OS3 electrolytes in graphite/NCA full cells.

contrast, all of the carbonate blends at 100°C ruptured before 28 days and all 70°C samples failed by 140 days. In multiple cases, CO_2 was observed in ^{13}C NMR for several failed carbonate samples that retained sufficient liquid for analysis indicating that degradation not evaporation was responsible for the rupture.

Differential Scanning Calorimetry (DSC) experiments with OS electrolytes show the fundamental enhanced thermal stability is preserved in the presence of energetic charged electrodes (Figure 3). All OS3-based formulations listed in Figure 1 show a higher onset temperature with de-lithiated NCA cathode material over an EC/EMC (3/7, vol%) carbonate blend (Figure 3a). Further evidence linking higher thermal stability to cell-level safety is demonstrated in a nail penetration test conducted under a NAVAIR SBIR contract. A charged 43 Ah cell with a commercial lithium iron phosphate cathode and an OS2 electrolyte with $LiPF_6$ showed no discernible venting of smoke or flames after fast nail penetration. Photographs of the OS2 cell prior to and after the nail penetration test (Figure 3b) clearly demonstrate this remarkable result. In contrast, the carbonate baseline cell reached a higher maximum temperature with production of both smoke and sparks. This test demonstrates the extraordinary safety benefit for a cell containing an OS electrolyte.

Physical Properties and Coin Cell Performance: The physical properties and coin cell cycling performance of the OS3 formulations listed in Figure 1 have been evaluated over a wide temperature range. Figure 4 shows the conductivity and viscosity data at -10°C, 0°C, 30°C, and 60°C. This data shows that all OS3 formulations have similar conductivity compared to the EC/EMC (3/7, vol%) + 1M $LiPF_6$ carbonate control. Figure 4b shows that all formulations containing the linear carbonate co-solvents match the carbonate control viscosity. Figure 4c shows 30°C rate capability data in NCA/graphite full cells

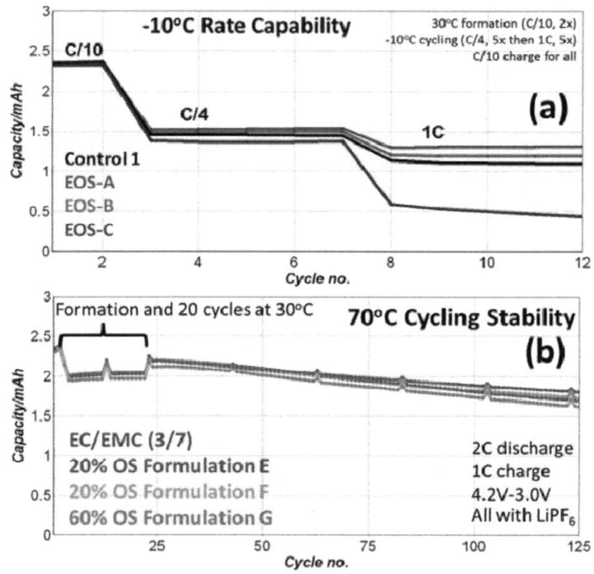

Figure 5. (a) -10°C and (b) 70°C coin cell cycling performance for OS3-based electrolytes in graphite/NCA full cells.

compared to an EC/EMC (3/7, vol%) control. All electrolytes contain the same additives. The discharge rates are shown for each 3 cycle step, with a symmetric charge up to 4C. All OS3 formulations tested match the carbonate up to a 4C rate and several OS3 formulations containing either EC/EMC or EMC alone as a co-solvent match the rate capability of the carbonate up to 16C.

The rate capability of the OS3 electrolytes in an NCA/graphite cell was also examined at -10°C, as shown in Figure 5a. Two formation cycles (C/10) were conducted at 30°C before cycling at -10°C. Both the charge and discharge were conducted at -10°C with a C/10 charge for each cycle. As with the 30°C data, all OS3 formulations match the carbonate discharge capacity up to C/4 at -10°C and several formulations perform as well as the EC/EMC control up to 1C. Figure 5b shows the 70°C cycling performance against the EC/EMC (3/7, vol%) control in NCA/graphite cells. Prior to 70°C cycling, two C/10 formation cycles and 20 cycles (1C charge / 2C discharge) were conducted at 30°C to ensure proper operation of the cell. In this data, the OS formulations (labeled E, F, and G) have comparable cycling stability to the carbonate control over 125 cycles. Historical 70°C data for EOS-A/B/C in the same NCA/graphite full cells demonstrated cycling stability comparable to or better than several carbonate blends under C/2 cycling.

Overall, the data shown in Figure 5 indicates that OS3 formulations are capable of operating across the wide temperature range required by many applications.

Electrochemical Stability: Recent technological developments to deliver higher energy and power density Li-ion batteries for electric vehicle applications have focused on increasing the operating voltage of the cells by

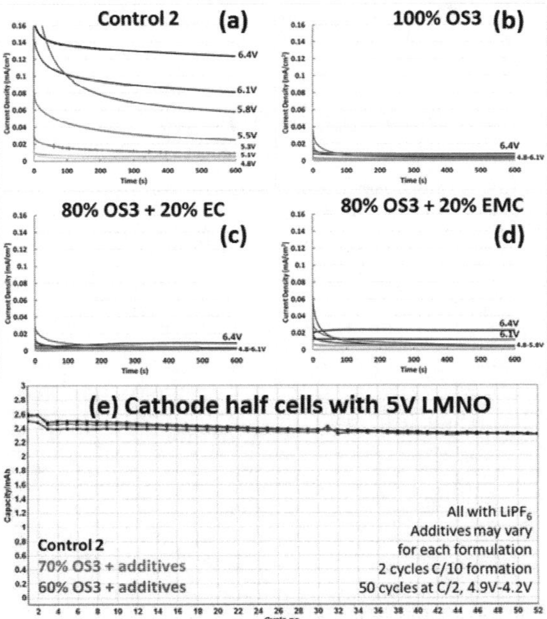

Figure 6. Parasitic current data for (a) EC/EMC (3/7, %v), (b) 100% OS3, (c) OS3/EC (8/2, %v), and (d) OS3/EMC (8/2, %v) in a Pt cell. (e) 30°C cycling in 5V LMNO cathode half cells.

using high voltage cathode materials. Currently limiting the utilization of several of these materials, including a 5V LMNO ($LiNi_{0.5}Mn_{1.5}O_4$) spinel cathode, is the instability of commercial electrolytes at voltages greater than 4.5V vs. Li/Li^+, with more aggressive degradation observed at elevated temperatures. Silatronix has been developing advanced generation OS solvents and formulations to provide the greater thermal and electrochemical stability required for these Li-ion batteries.

During the initial development of OS3 electrolytes for high voltage applications, in order to balance the high voltage stability with other key electrolyte performance criteria (e.g, conductivity/viscosity, safety/abuse tolerance, thermal stability), Silatronix has conducted chronoamperometric measurements on a suite of OS3-based formulations to evaluate the fundamental reactivity of the electrolytes at key voltages. In this experiment, the potential of a 3-electrode cell (WE: Pt, CE/RE: Li/Li^+) is increased from 4.8 to 6.4V in 0.1V steps and the current required to maintain that potential is measured for 10 minutes to allow the system to reach steady state. Electrolytes with more reactive (i.e., less stable) components will show a higher steady state current indicative of parasitic side reactions. Figure 6 compares data for the (a) EC/EMC (3/7, %vol, 1.2M $LiPF_6$) baseline carbonate to three OS3-based formulations with 1M $LiPF_6$ and (b) no co-solvent, (c) 20% EC, and (3) 20% EMC. All OS3 electrolytes showed superior stability at all potentials measured. Specifically, the current observed for the carbonate blend at 5.5V is higher than that observed for any OS3 formulation at 6.4V.

To further demonstrate the potential of OS electrolytes for high voltage applications, the cycling performance of OS3 electrolytes with the 5V LMNO spinel was evaluated in cathode half cells at 30°C, as shown in Figure 6e. In this testing, the voltage window was restricted to 4.2-4.9V to focus on evaluating the stability at the higher voltage without the capacity degradation associated with Mn dissolution. Optimization of the lower cutoff voltage is included in an ongoing program.

Conclusions: As shown above, OS solvents improve the overall electrolyte and battery stability across a number of performance metrics including: superior resistance to decomposition with $LiPF_6$, reduced side reactions at higher voltage, reduced reactivity between electrolyte and the active materials, and significantly reduced temperatures during safety testing. These benefits can be integrated into overall electrolyte formulations that deliver comparable or superior battery performance versus current commercial carbonate electrolytes. The advantages outlined in this work should allow the design of Li-ion batteries that exploit specific benefits of OS solvents in a number of applications across many active chemical systems.

Acknowledgements

The authors wish to acknowledge funding from NAVAIR SBIR contract #N68335-11-C-0401 and thank Saft America for providing electrode materials and large format cell performance and safety testing.

References

1. Rossi, N. A. A.; West, R., Silicon-containing liquid polymer electrolytes for application in lithium ion batteries. *Polymer International* **2009,** 58, (3), 267-272.

2. Zhang, L.; Zhang, Z.; Harring, S.; Straughan, M.; Butorac, R.; Chen, Z.; Lyons, L.; Amine, K.; West, R., Highly conductive trimethylsilyl oligo(ethylene oxide) electrolytes for energy storage applications. *Journal of Materials Chemistry* **2008,** 18, (31), 3713-3717.

3. Nitrile-Substituted Silanes and Electrolyte Compositions and Electrochemical Devices Containing Them. José Adrián Peña Hueso, David Osmalov, Jian Dong, Monica Usrey, Michael Pollina, Robert West. US Provisional 61/830,851. Filed 6/14/13.

4. Chen, X.; Usrey, M.; Pena-Hueso, A.; West, R.; Hamers, R. J., Thermal and electrochemical stability of organosilicon electrolytes for lithium-ion batteries. *Journal of Power Sources* 241, 1 November 2013, 311-319.

A Solid Electrolyte Interphase Layer Model for Simulating Lithium-Ion Cell Capacity Fade

Dr. Nicholas C. Propes[1], Mr. Rajiv Jaini[2], and Dr. Thomas F. Fuller[2]

[1]Global Technology Connection, Inc.
2839 Paces Ferry Rd. SE
Atlanta, GA, USA, 30339

[2]Georgia Institute of Technology
School of Chemical & Biomolecular Engineering
Atlanta, GA, USA, 30332

Abstract: *A physics-based model of lithium-ion cell performance degradation due to Solid Electrolyte Interphase (SEI) layer growth in the negative electrode is presented. An existing dual lithium-ion gProms model is used as the base model structure and expanded upon with SEI layer growth dynamics. Laboratory experiments were conducted on real cells to fit the model parameters to collected data. SEI layer growth affects the cycle life of cells as the lithium ions that shuttle between electrodes are permanently consumed by formation of the layer; and also as the SEI layer becomes thicker, the cell resistance increases. By incorporating SEI into the model, capacity fade can be accurately simulated.*

Keywords: lithium-ion cell, solid electrolyte interphase, physics-based model, capacity fade

Introduction

A decrease in discharge capacity over the lifetime of a lithium ion battery is characterized as capacity fade [1]. Several causes of capacity fade have been reported in recent years. This work focuses on understanding the effect of passive film formation on the surface of the negative electrode as a cause of capacity fade [2]. We aim to provide a physical interpretation of the solid electrolyte interphase (SEI) by simulating electrochemical impedance spectroscopy by mimicking the operation of a frequency response analyzer. This report provides background on the SEI, addresses electrochemical impedance spectroscopy (EIS), introduces battery modeling and frequency response analysis, and presents the obtained results and proposed future work for this project.

SEI Layer Formation: The SEI forms and grows as a result of electrolyte solution decomposition at the negative electrode and is most pronounced during the first few cycles [3]. The formation products typically are both organic and inorganic as a result of the electrolyte solution reduction. The SEI functions as a passivating, protecting film at the electrode-solution interface, which stabilizes the negative electrode during cycling.

A graphite negative electrode of the battery is delithiated on assembly, which requires that it be charged after assembly. At low potentials versus lithium, which are reached during charging, organic electrolyte solutions are out of their

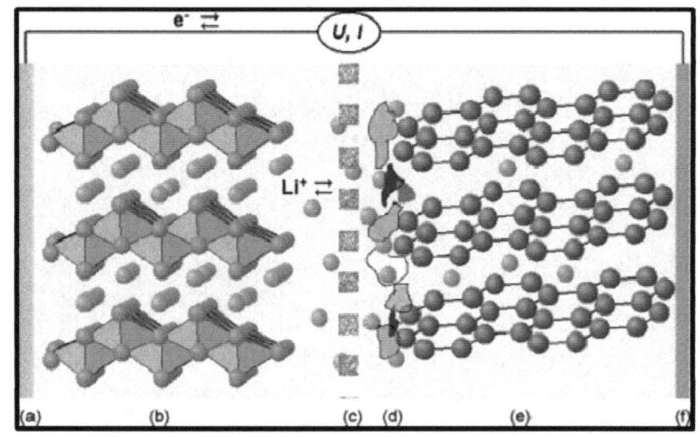

Figure 1. Schematic illustration of a typical Li-ion battery: (a) aluminum current collector; (b) oxide active material; (c) porous separator soaked with liquid electrolyte; (d) inhomogeneous SEI layer; (e) graphite active material and (f) copper current collector. Image and caption taken from [4].

electrochemical voltage window. The charging process then leads to a reduction of the solution phase components and deposition of insoluble components in the film that forms at the negative electrode surface. This SEI formation process continues but slows during subsequent cycles. Electrolyte and solution components are both reduced at the electrode surface, acting in parallel with each other, depositing a range of products at the electrode surface. Generally, the reduction process is speculated to begin from at least 2V, down to 0.8V versus lithium [5, 6].

The electrolyte-solution reduction process is both advantageous and detrimental to the lifetime of the cell. Initial decomposition of solution phase components slows reduction at the graphite electrode, all-the-while preventing intercalation of solution anions in the electrode [4]. The film is believed to be electronically insulating, thereby only allowing lithium ions to pass from and to the bulk solution to the electrode. The surface film formation reduces the intercalation of unwanted compounds, preventing swelling and thereby increasing battery lifetime [7]. Disadvantageously, the growing nature of the SEI during cycling causes an irreversible loss of lithium that reduces the lifetime of the cell [8].

The thickness of the SEI has been extensively reported for several negative electrodes in the literature [9]. Generally, thicknesses have been suggested to range from a few nanometers to several-hundred nanometers [6, 10, 11]. Additionally, because the film is an interphase, the SEI has both properties of the solution phase and negative electrode material. Several techniques have been used to experimentally measure the thickness of the SEI [9, 12]. Because of the dynamic nature of the SEI coupled with its relatively small thickness, electrochemical impedance spectroscopy is a useful technique in understanding the different physical phenomena, particularly if they respond with different characteristic times.

Electrochemical Analogies for Impedance: The equivalent circuit representation is a useful way to visualize the physical processes within the electrochemical cell. A Randles' type equivalent circuit is frequently found within the literature [13]. In this type of equivalent circuit, four physical processes are described by four electrical components. The equivalent circuit includes a solution resistance, R_s, representative of the potential drop through the solution between the electrodes. An ideal double layer capacitive component, C_{dl}, represents the double layer charging that occurs at the electrode-solution interface. In parallel with C_{dl}, a charge transfer resistance, R_{ct}, and Warburg constant phase element, Z_w, account for the electron transfer that occurs at the electrode-electrolyte interface and diffusion of ionic species within the cell, respectively.

A major drawback in attempting to fit EIS spectra to RLC circuit models, however, comes when assigning the specific circuitry to the spectra without supporting information, as many combinations of components could equally well reproduce a given spectra. Instead, we intend to develop a physics-based model, which eliminates the incorrect assignment of circuit elements to combinations of physical processes which could otherwise be misrepresented.

EIS Modeling Techniques: Several mathematical techniques have been proposed to model EIS spectra that are not based on arbitrarily assigning RLC networks to physical processes. Meyers et al. modeled the impedance by splitting system variables into steady and unsteady state variables to model the system perturbation. After deriving sets of governing equations for the important physical processes (charge transfer, double layer charging, etc.) that incorporated the perturbation, the authors solved the system of linear differential equations for the cases of single particles, then porous electrodes composed of the single particles. The model was able to provide insight on transport and kinetic parameters [14]. Sunde et al. simulated impedance and treated the electrode solid material as a mixed conductor, effectively treating both charge transport of electrons and holes. The model assumed dilute solution theory, coupled with sets of governing equations solved by Laplace transforms. The modeling results suggested the importance of introducing a Gerischer element at low frequencies to account for deviations of the diffusion coefficient of charged species [15]. These models simulated the impedance spectra but did not provide insight on the structure of the SEI, rather only attempted to fit transport and kinetic parameters to the output of their models.

Dual Lithium Ion Insertion Cell Model

A pseudo 2D model of the dual lithium ion insertion cell model was constructed in gPROMS with sub-models for the positive electrode, negative electrode, and separator. The separator and positive electrode follow the model equations presented by Fuller et al. [16]. The model includes mass balances and charge balances in the solution and SEI phases, transport equations in the solution, SEI, and solid phases, and interfacial kinetic expressions. The following equations apply in the negative electrode, where the SEI is believed to be formed. The flux of lithium in the solution phase is given as

$$N_+ = -D\nabla c + \frac{it_+^0}{z_+F} \tag{1}$$

where c is the concentration of lithium. A material balance on lithium in the solution phase is given as

$$\in \frac{\partial c}{\partial t} = \nabla \cdot N_+ + \frac{ai_{SEI}(x_{SEI}=0)}{F} \tag{2}$$

where i_{SEI} is the flux of charged species across the interface between the solution and SEI.

The current appears in the solution, SEI, and solid phases. The total current is the sum of the current in the electrolyte and the solid:

$$I = i_1 + i_2 \tag{3}$$

The current flowing in the solid is given as:

$$i_1 = -\sigma \nabla \phi_1 \tag{4}$$

where σ is the solid electronic conductivity and Φ_1 is the solid potential. The current in the solution phase is given by concentrated solution theory as:

$$i_2 = -\kappa \nabla \phi_2 + \frac{\kappa RT}{F}\left(1 + \frac{\partial \ln f_A}{\partial \ln c}\right)(1 - t_+^0)\nabla \ln c \tag{5}$$

where Φ_2, the solution potential, is set to zero at the end of the cell which acts as a reference lithium electrode.

Charge conservation that relates the interfacial solution-SEI flux to the solution phase current is given as

$$a\left(j_{SEI}(x_{SEI}=0) + \frac{dQ_{DL}}{dt}\right) = -\nabla \cdot i_2 \tag{6}$$

and to the solution phase current as

$$a\left(j_{SEI}(x_{SEI}=L_{SEI}) + \frac{dQ_{DL}}{dt}\right) = \nabla \cdot i_1 \tag{7}$$

where Q_{DL} is the double layer charge at the electrode-solution interface. The charge conservation equations account for the flux with respect to the thickness of the SEI.

The double layer charge is expressed as

$$Q_{DL} = C_{DL}(\phi_1 - \phi_{SEI}(x = L_{SEI})) \tag{8}$$

where Φ_{SEI} is the potential measured in the SEI.

The kinetics are expressed as a Butler-Volmer form as

$$j_{SEI}(x = L_{SEI}) = i_0 F(\exp(\frac{\alpha_a F}{RT}(\eta - U)) - \exp(-\frac{\alpha_c F}{RT}(\eta - U))) \quad (9)$$

where U is the open-circuit potential of the insertion material. The overpotential, □, is given as

$$\eta = \phi_1 - \phi_{SEI}(x = L_{SEI}) \quad (10)$$

and is the potential difference at the particle, SEI interphase.

The SEI is treated as a porous slab of finite thickness, with lithium flux to and from the solution to the solid particle. Transport in the SEI is governed by dilute solution theory as

$$j_{SEI} = -D_{SEI}\nabla c_{SEI} - \frac{i_{SEI}}{F} \quad (11)$$

A material balance on the SEI gives

$$\frac{\partial c_{SEI}}{\partial t} = -\nabla \cdot j_{SEI} \quad (12)$$

Charge transport in the SEI is governed by Ohm's Law as

$$i_{SEI} = -K_{SEI}\nabla \phi_{SEI} \quad (13)$$

The divergence of the SEI current is set equal to zero,

$$\nabla \cdot i_{SEI} = 0 \,. \quad (14)$$

Transport into the spherical particles of radius R_p is representative of the pseudo second dimension. Radial transport into the particle can be expressed as

$$\frac{\partial c_s}{\partial t} = D_s\left(\frac{\partial^2 c_s}{\partial r^2} + \frac{2}{r}\frac{\partial c_s}{\partial r}\right) \quad (15)$$

where c_s is the concentration of lithium in the solid particle.

Boundary Conditions: Several boundary conditions are required to solve the model equations. The boundary conditions for equations in this section requires that the ionic flux be zero at the electrodes,

$$N_+ = 0 \text{ at } x = 0 \text{ and } x = L \quad (16)$$

At the ends of the cell, the current is only in the solid phase and therefore,

$$i_2 = 0 \text{ at } x = 0 \text{ and } x = L \quad (17)$$

At the solution-SEI interfacial boundary, the concentrations in the solution and SEI are equal as

$$c = c_{SEI}(x = 0) \quad (18)$$

The potentials at the solution-SEI interfacial boundary are equal as

$$\phi_2 = \phi_{SEI}(x = 0) \quad (19)$$

Diffusion into the solid particle from the SEI is given as

$$j_{SEI}(x = L_{SEI}) = -D_s\frac{\partial c_s}{\partial r} \quad at \quad r = R_p \,. \quad (20)$$

Impedance Model

In addition to the dual lithium ion insertion cell model, a sub-model has been implemented to simulate EIS. The sub-model applies a sinusoidal current perturbation of frequency f over an integer number of cycles, N, and calculates the response. Unlike the models discussed previously, this model is not based on an equivalent circuit approach nor does it require assuming physical processes within the cell to develop analytical impedance expressions. Rather, the model is unique in that implementation only requires a transient, physical model of a system.

The real component of impedance, Z', is calculated [17] from the correlation between the measured cell potential, E_{Cell}, and the current excitation signal, using

$$Z' = 2\left(NI_{Amp}\right)^{-1}\int_0^{N/f} E_{Cell}(t)\sin(2\pi f t)\,dt \quad (21)$$

The imaginary component of impedance, Z'', is calculated in the same manner, but with a correlation that is out of phase by 90°,

$$Z'' = 2\left(NI_{Amp}\right)^{-1}\int_0^{N/f} E_{Cell}(t)\cos(2\pi f t)\,dt \quad (22)$$

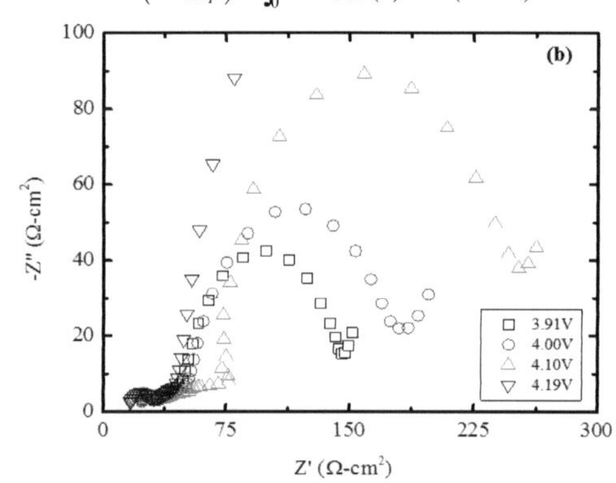

Figure 2. Full cell experimental data obtained by EIS for a range of states of charge. $LiNi_{0.8}Co_{0.15}Al_{0.05}O_2$ was used as the positive electrode active material.

Experimental data obtained by EIS is shown in Figure 2 for full cells (C/NCA). At high frequencies, the model outputs a single loop. Literature suggests that this loop is a result of a parallel SEI charging and resistive type process. The high frequency intercept is representative of the ohmic resistances within the cell. The second loop forms at mid-range frequencies and signals another resistive-capacitive type of process occurring in parallel with one another. Many attribute this loop to a parallel charge transfer and double layer charging phenomena. The tail end occurring at low frequencies is referred to as a Warburg impedance element, with slope of unity, representing diffusion in the electrolyte.

Simulation Results

The electrochemical spectra can be generated for combinations of model parameters. For each simulation, the SEI is treated as a layer of finite thickness, over which a distribution domain can be allotted. Figure 3 shows the impedance response to varying the SEI layer thickness.

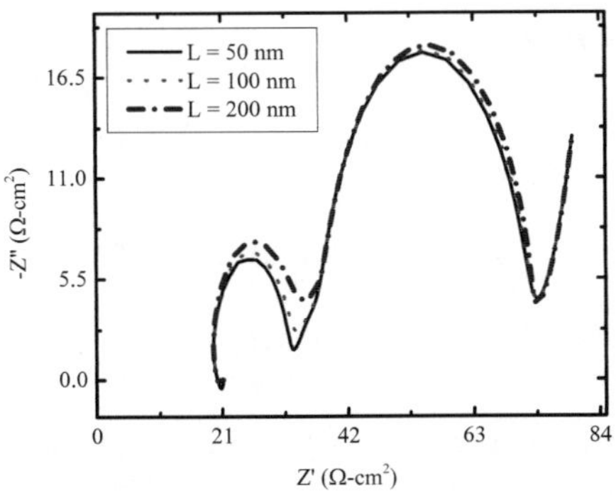

Figure 3. Simulated EIS spectra showing how variations in SEI layer thickness (L) affect the output.

The model equations, which account for transport through the SEI, do not cause the formation of a semicircle. If the SEI were to cause a semicircle, one would expect that changing the thickness, L, would influence the total impedance for that process. However, this relationship between thickness and impedance is not the case. The two semicircles are attributed to double layer charging that occurs at both the positive and negative electrodes. The time constants, therefore the capacitances, are chosen to illustrate the two processes. Further improvements to the model will require understanding the underlying transport of charged species and solvent within the SEI. Modeling the SEI as porous layer of finite thickness through which transport is governed by potential and concentration gradients is a strong starting point.

Acknowledgements

The authors wish to acknowledge funding received by the U.S. Missile Defense Agency for this work.

References

1. Spotnitz, R., *Simulation of capacity fade in lithium-ion batteries.* Journal of Power Sources, 2003. **113**(1): p. 72-80.
2. Arora, P., R.E. White, and M. Doyle, *Capacity fade mechanisms and side reactions in lithium-ion batteries.* Journal of the Electrochemical Society, 1998. **145**(10): p. 3647-3667.
3. Zhang, S.S., et al., *Understanding solid electrolyte interface film formation on graphite electrodes.* Electrochemical and Solid State Letters, 2001. **4**(12): p. A206-A208.
4. Verma, P., P. Maire, and P. Novák, *A review of the features and analyses of the solid electrolyte interphase in Li-ion batteries.* Electrochimica Acta, 2010. **55**(22): p. 6332-6341.
5. Aurbach, D., et al., *Failure and Stabilization Mechanisms of Graphite Electrodes.* The Journal of Physical Chemistry B, 1997. **101**(12): p. 2195-2206.
6. Edström, K., M. Herstedt, and D.P. Abraham, *A new look at the solid electrolyte interphase on graphite anodes in Li-ion batteries.* Journal of Power Sources, 2006. **153**(2): p. 380-384.
7. Besenhard, J.O., et al., *Filming mechanism of lithium-carbon anodes in organic and inorganic electrolytes.* Journal of Power Sources, 1995. **54**(2): p. 228-231.
8. Bryngelsson, H., et al., *How dynamic is the SEI?* Journal of Power Sources, 2007. **174**(2): p. 970-975.
9. Zaban, A. and D. Aurbach, *Impedance spectroscopy of lithium and nickel electrodes in propylene carbonate solutions of different lithium salts A comparative study.* Journal of Power Sources, 1995. **54**(2): p. 289-295.
10. Yoshida, T., et al., *Degradation mechanism and life prediction of lithium-ion batteries.* Journal of the Electrochemical Society, 2006. **153**(3): p. A576-A582.
11. Colclasure, A.M., K.A. Smith, and R.J. Kee, *Modeling detailed chemistry and transport for solid-electrolyte-interface (SEI) films in Li–ion batteries.* Electrochimica Acta, 2011. **58**(0): p. 33-43.
12. Zhang, H.L., et al., *New insight into the solid electrolyte interphase with use of a focused ion beam.* Journal of Physical Chemistry B, 2005. **109**(47): p. 22205-22211.
13. Liaw, B.Y., et al., *Modeling capacity fade in lithium-ion cells.* Journal of Power Sources, 2005. **140**(1): p. 157-161.
14. Meyers, J.P., et al., *The impedance response of a porous electrode composed of intercalation particles.* Journal of the Electrochemical Society, 2000. **147**(8): p. 2930-2940.
15. Sunde, S., et al., *An Impedance Model for a Porous Intercalation Electrode with Mixed Conductivity.* Journal of the Electrochemical Society, 2009. **156**(8): p. B927-B937.
16. Fuller, T.F., M. Doyle, and J. Newman, *Simulation and optimization of the dual lithium ion insertion cell.* Journal of the Electrochemical Society, 1994. **141**(1): p. 1-10.
17. Lasia, A., *Electrochemical Impedance Spectroscopy and its Applications*, in *Modern Aspects of Electrochemistry*, B.E. Conway, J.O.M. Bockris, and R. White, Editors. 2002, Springer US. p. 143-248.

Safety Considerations for Lithium-Ion Flight Batteries

Jeff Dermott[1] and James Bond[1]
[1]EaglePicher Technologies, LLC
Joplin, MO, USA
Jeff.Dermott@eaglepicher.com
James.Bond@eaglepicher.com

"This material is released to the public domain in accordance with ITAR 22 CFR 120.11"

Abstract: The desirability of Lithium-ion based flight batteries is supported mostly by the reduced footprint and mass that result from their much higher energy/power density than present SLA and NiCad implementations. However, the inherent sensitivities of this chemistry can yield catastrophic behavior if improper cell selection, cell integration (battery assembly), and operational oversight are not holistically approached during the battery design process. While DO-311 serves as a valid design guideline, recent media-covered events have highlighted these sensitivities. This paper will summarize the primary concerns with a Lithium-based battery implementation, and outline EaglePicher Technologies' multi-faceted design approach that integrates electro-chemical, mechanical and electrical methods to ensure the safe ongoing operation of the cells necessary to provide engine starting and emergency power needs for the airframe.

Key Words: Aircraft, Lithium-ion, BMS, Safety

Introduction: For the past several years, EaglePicher has been working to qualify a Lithium-ion battery for a very light jet application. The goal of the design effort has been to bring the benefits of Lithium-ion to the aircraft while preserving the safety of the aircraft.

Even though Lithium-ion represents a significantly safer system versus cells with a metallic lithium electrode they still suffer from the two safety issues that have historically plagued lithium based systems, (1) low resistance to abuse and (2) thermal runaway.

To mitigate these two safety concerns EaglePicher has the taken the following approach to the battery design.

1. Select a safe cell design
2. Design the battery to prevent internal and external propagation in the event of a cell failure
3. Protect the cells from abuse with a properly designed Battery Management System.

This Paper will describe EaglePicher's approach to the previously mentioned design considerations.

Cell Selection: It is common knowledge that there are the variety Lithium ion chemistries available and each one has its own unique performance characteristics. Thus the cell selection for a particular application must carefully weigh the pros and cons of each chemistry against the end application requirements.

To further complicate the cell selection process each chemistry can come in a variety of form factors from soft case pouch cells to hard case prismatic or cylindrical cells.

For EaglePicher the path to cell selection came from extensive cell level testing for both performance and safety. The goal was to maintain some amount of weight and cycle life advantage over traditional chemistries (NiCd, SLA) while meeting the safety requirements imposed by the aircraft industry via DO-311. The testing eventually led to the selection of a small format (26650), Lithium Iron Phosphate (LFP) cell. The wound cell design was packaged in a stainless steel container. The LFP chemistry offers a good compromise between safety and weight while the cell size and mechanical packaging provide added safety benefits that allowed the battery to pass the DO-311 abuse tests, in particular explosion containment testing.

Battery Design: After completion of cell level safety testing EaglePicher proceeded with battery level safety testing. This testing provided the final piece of data needed to show battery level compliance to the safety requirements of DO-311.

From the cell level testing, EaglePicher was confident that a thermal runaway event on a single cell would not propagate to adjacent cells. With this data in hand the driving requirement for the battery design was to thermally isolate the cells to prevent propagation to other battery components or to the exterior of the battery container. After several battery level tests it was determined that with proper placement of thermal barrier materials the battery container could contain a single cell event and also allow for the use of a light weight material, such as aluminum, for the battery container.

The Explosion Containment test is designed to create an internal cell short and drive the cell into thermal runaway. This test consists of fully charging an entire battery, then forcing a single cell in the interior of the cell pack into overcharge. During the over-charge of the single cell a spark-emitting device, placed next to the cell vent, is activated to assure that when the cell vents the electrolyte will be ignited.

Figure 1 below is a summary of the data taken during the battery explosion containment testing conducted on the EaglePicher battery design.

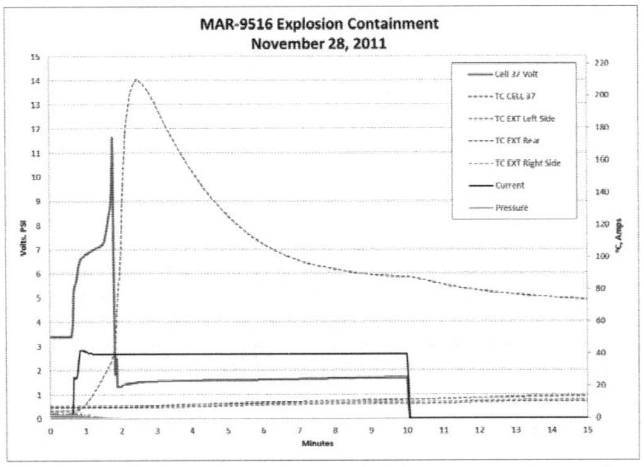

Figure 1. Explosion Containment Test

As can be seen in Figure 1 above the cell that is being overcharged eventually reaches nearly 12V (solid blue curve) at which time the internal short occurs. The short is indicated by a rapid rise in cell temperature (dotted red curve) and a corresponding rapid decrease in cell voltage. It should be noted that the cell which is being forced into thermal runaway reaches only about 200°C. This is consistent with the cell-level test data generated prior to selecting this particular cell design. Also significant is the fact that the two thermal couples placed on the exterior of the battery never exceed 20°C. During the test, battery internal pressure was also monitored. The pressure (solid red curve) is barely visible on the chart. The internal battery pressure rise from the event was less than 0.5 psi.

With these test results, EaglePicher was satisfied that the combination of cell selection and battery design would contain a single-cell thermal runaway event.

Battery Architecture: Special Condition(s) have been issued by the FAA and EASA for concerns with the application of lithium batteries into airframes. RTCA/DO-311 Addresses the Mitigation of Potential Failures of Lithium Battery Systems in a Layered Approach

- Communication / Notification of Battery Status to Avionics
- Integrated Battery Controls to Address Sensitivities of Lithium Cells
- Explosion Containment within Battery Casement

To address these requirements EaglePicher has developed a Lithium-ion battery architecture under the guidance of RTCA/DO-311 to serve the aviation industry. The battery design emphasizes safe cell operation with assurances to support ongoing discharge capability for emergency power needs.

EaglePicher's Lithium-ion battery consists of the following major subsystems. A block diagram of the aircraft battery is shown in Figure 2.

- Battery Management System (BMS)
- Redundant Protection Block (RPB)
- Peripheral Support Block (PSB)
- Current Limiter (bulk charge support)
- Isolation & Protection Switches (IPS)
- Terminal Filter Board (FBD)
- Cell Stack

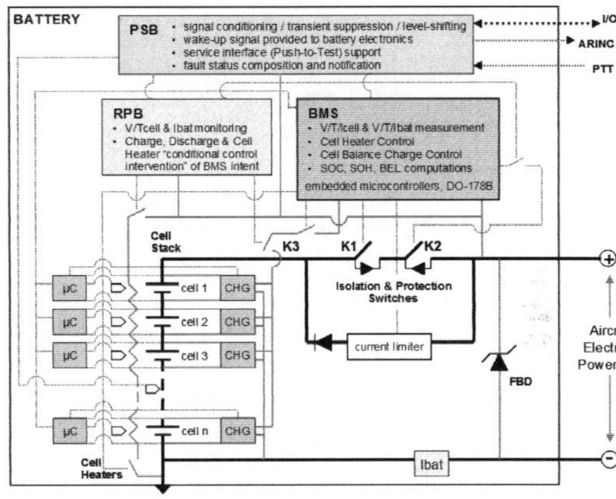

Figure 2. Aircraft Battery

The Battery Management System (BMS) contains an embedded controller which is the primary manager for the battery. Its functions are managing transition from bulk to cell balance charging, collection of cell data (voltage, current and temperature), heater control, safety protection, and battery health calculations. The controller utilizes software that is certified to DO-178B, Design Assurance Level "B".

EPT's patented isolated-source topology is used to balance each individual cell with an isolated, high-frequency DC-DC converter. The converter applies a constant current "bulk" charge to each cell until a specified voltage limit is reached. It then switches to a constant voltage taper until the lower current limit is reached. The current and voltage set-points are adjustable which make this arrangement easily adaptable to a multitude of chemistries, not just Lithium ion.

This approach assures maximum battery capacity is achieved and maximizes the cycle-life of each cell within the string. An additional benefit is the reduced need for elaborate and costly cell screening procedures prior to selecting cells for the battery. EPT's implementation of this approach achieves an overall net efficiency of about 90%.

The Redundant Protection Block (RPB) is comprised of fully independent and isolated monitoring circuits. It monitors cell voltage, cell temperature and battery current for compliance to safety limits. Its sole function is to provide a back-up safety net to the BMS. The RPB will intervene with BMS control of charge, discharge and cell heater functions if predetermined safety limits are breached. All fault and protection limits of the RPB are set outside the limits of those imposed by the BMS.

The RPB is a COTS-based hardware implementation and uses no software or firmware. Likewise it contains no custom or configurable devices.

The Current Limiter, implemented only on newer versions of the battery, supports bulk charge by limiting the maximum current (rate) delivered to cell stack. The advantages of the current limiter are the reduced size of the balance converters and the heat associated with bulk charging can be located away from the other electronics. Its operation is controlled by the BMS.

At the heart of the battery protection scheme is the Isolation & Protection Switches (IPS). These solid-state relays, K1 and K2, are capable of handling currents in excess of 1200A and are configured in a redundant implementation. They can isolate the cell stack from the bus and also prevent unwanted bulk charge. These two functions are critical for safe operation of the Lithium ion cells.

The battery communicates with the outside world via the Peripheral Support Block (PSB). The PSB handles the airframe I/O via discrete and analog signal conditioning. This block can be configured to meet the needs of a specific application. Its current configuration uses an ARINC 429 communications interface.

Additionally the PSB collects BMS/RPB/PSB status and it also contains an external watch-dog-timer which oversees BMS microcontroller operation.

Battery Performance: With a robust protection system in place EPT has been able to test the aircraft battery under a variety of environmental conditions and loads. Figure 3 below shows the battery voltage and current for a simulated aircraft starting sequence. This 30AH battery sustains a peak load of nearly 900A, at 10°C, for 3 consecutive start attempts while maintaining the battery voltage above 18V. This data emphasizes the excellent rate capability of the Lithium-ion power cells and the rate capability of the IPS.

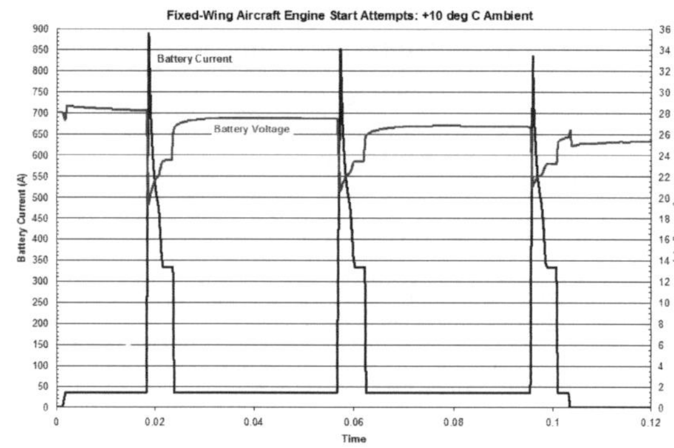

Figure 3. Aircraft Starting Simulation

Figure 4 illustrates one of the safety features of the battery. During bulk charge the heat produced by the DC/DC converters can result in a temperature rise in the battery electronics. The BMS will recognize this temperature rise, and at predetermined temperatures, will step the current down until the heat sink temperature stabilizes. This ensures that the battery electronics remain within their operating temperature limits.

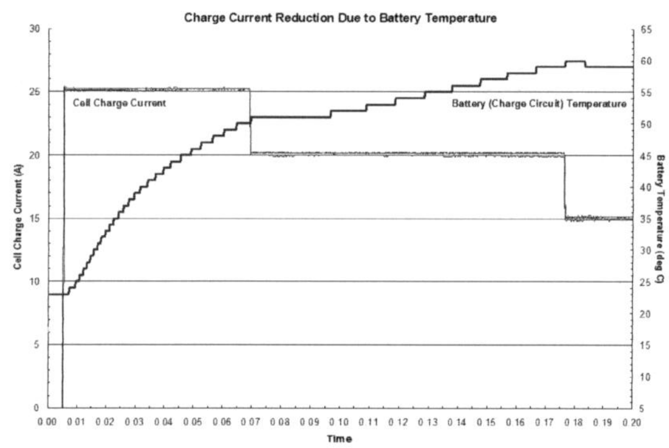

Figure 4. Battery Charge Current vs Temperature

The entire constant current – constant voltage charge scheme is illustrated in Figure 5. The charge begins at approximately 25A on each cell and as the individual cells rise to the cut-off voltage of 3.65V the balance circuits activate and the charge switches to constant voltage. The constant voltage charge is allowed to continue until the cell charge current reduces to approximately 1A. This allows all 8 cells in the battery to reach a similar state of charge and insures the maximum battery capacity can be obtained with each cycle.

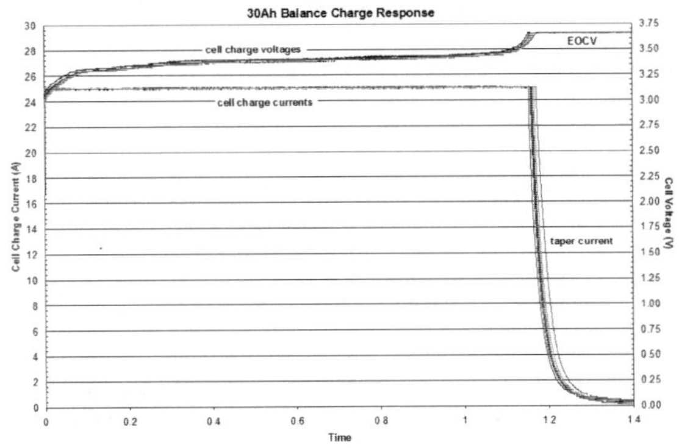

Figure 5. Cell Voltages During CC/CV Charge

Summary: In summary, EaglePicher's aircraft battery design utilizes a three-pronged approach to meet the demanding safety and performance requirements of DO-311. The battery design emphasizes safety, performance, and longevity of the Lithium ion cells.

Proper cell selection, based on rigorous cell level safety testing, has been used to overcome the safety concerns of the Lithium-ion chemistry that are not preventable with electronics. Additionally, proper battery design has been used to mitigate propagation from cell to cell and/or cell to other battery components in the event of a single cell thermal runaway event.

To protect against abuse and maximize cell life the battery employs a multi-function BMS. The BMS assure proper cell charging using EPT's patented isolated-source topology to balance each individual cell with an isolated, high-frequency DC-DC converter. Along with proper current and voltage regulation the BMS provides the cells and electronics with a proper thermal environment for safety and longevity.

This complete package of safety and performance provides an attractive replacement battery for many aircraft applications.

Acknowledgments: The authors wish to acknowledge the support of EaglePicher's management for the continued funding of this design effort and the efforts of the EaglePicher personnel who participated in the research, development and testing of the batteries.

Aqueous and Non-Aqueous Lithium-air batteries enabled by Water-Stable Lithium Metal Electrodes

Steven J. Visco, Vitaliy Nimon, Alexei Petrov, Kirill Pridatko, Nickolay Goncharenko, Eugene Nimon, and Lutgard De Jonghe,
PolyPlus Battery Company
2431 5th, Berkeley, CA, USA, 94707

Abstract: The extremely high theoretical energy density of the lithium-oxygen couple makes it very attractive for next generation battery development. However, there are a number of challenging technical hurdles that must be addressed for Li-Air batteries to become a commercial reality. In this article we demonstrate how the invention of water- stable, solid electrolyte protected lithium electrodes solves many of these issues, and paves the way for the development of aqueous and non-aqueous Li-Air batteries with unprecedented energy densities. We also show data for fully packaged Li-Air cells that achieve more than 800 Wh/kg.

Keywords: lithium; air; battery; solid electrolyte; LATP; protected lithium electrode; PLE.

Introduction: Although the exceptionally high theoretical energy density for the lithium-oxygen couple has attracted the attention of battery scientists for decades, reactivity of lithium metal with atmospheric moisture has precluded practical development of this intriguing technology. However, the invention of the water-stable, protected lithium metal electrode by PolyPlus Battery Company has enabled the development of a new generation of lithium battery technologies having aqueous electrolytes, including lithium-air and lithium-water batteries [1 - 5]. Protected lithium electrodes (PLEs) utilize water-stable, high Li+ conductivity solid electrolytes such as $Li_{1.3}Al_{0.3}Ti_{1.7}(PO_4)_3$ (LATP) to chemically isolate a lithium core from the external environment (fig.1). In this way lithium electrodes can be used in combination with aqueous and aggressive non-aqueous electrolytes, a practical necessity for both lithium-air and lithium-water batteries. Here we discuss the critical hurdles in lithium-air chemistry and our own progress in both aqueous and non-aqueous Li-Air systems.

Lithium-air Chemistry: Aqueous or Non-Aqueous? In conventional aqueous metal-air cells the products of the cell reaction are contained in the anode; in zinc-air cells the zinc suspension is converted to ZnO as the cell reaction proceeds whereas the structure and composition of the air electrode is essentially unchanged as the cell is discharged. This is fundamentally different in lithium-air technology since the lithium anode cannot accommodate the product of cell reaction. In a Li-Air cell the air electrode must facilitate oxygen reduction and evolution as well as accommodate a substantial amount of reaction product while still functioning as an air electrode throughout cell discharge. The engineering of such a structure is certainly non-trivial. There are also several types of lithium-air technology [6,7] which can be broadly divided by the choice of electrolyte, either aqueous or non-aqueous (Table 1). Although the choice of non-aqueous electrolyte allows the use of bare lithium foil, it also introduces a number of complex problems including the extremely low solubility of the cell reaction product, Li_2O_2, as well as reactivity of peroxide with most commonly used lithium battery electrolytes. For the case of non-aqueous Li-Air, most researchers use anhydrous oxygen to avoid corrosion of the bare Li electrode by ambient moisture. The use of bare unprotected lithium greatly limits the choice of electrolytes (due to reaction with lithium) and precludes the use of air due to rapid corrosion of the Li metal electrode by moisture. Some groups have reported ex situ passivation of lithium by carbonate electrolytes [8] or the use of oxidizing additives [9] like $LiNO_3$ to form a protective solid electrolyte interface (SEI) allowing the use of aggressive solvents like amides and sulfoxides. Although it is unclear that this approach is fully protective or that the SEI will survive extended cycling, preliminary results are interesting. PolyPlus invented and patented water-stable, protected lithium electrodes (PLEs) [2, 4]. We described PLEs and lithium-air primary and rechargeable batteries based on them publicly for the first time in Nara, Japan [10 - 12]. The essential concept is to use a dense, pinhole-free Li+ solid electrolyte to chemically isolate the lithium electrode (Li, LixC, LixSi, etc.) from the positive electrode (Fig. 2). In this way, lithium electrodes can be used in combination with aggressive solvents, including aqueous electrolyte. The ceramic electrolyte most commonly used is based on the lithium analog of NASICON (LISICON) with a composition of Li_{1+x+y}(M, Al, Ga)$_x$($Ge_{1-q}Ti_q$)$_{2-x}Si_yP_{3-y}O_{12}$, and typically is of the composition $Li_{1.3}Al_{0.3}Ti_{1.7}(PO_4)_3$ (LATP) produced in Japan by Ohara Corporation and in the U.S. by Corning. Although LISICON is stable to water, it is not stable to lithium, requiring the incorporation of an interlayer which can be solid state (i.e. Li_3N), polymeric, ionic liquid, or non-aqueous liquid electrolyte. Some groups prefer to call this a "dual electrolyte" system, but it all originates from the original PLE concept and patents. This advance now appears to be critical to the practical development of both non-aqueous and aqueous lithium-air, and lithium-sulfur batteries. The PLE also affords an elegant solution to the investigation and development of the air electrode for both aqueous and non-aqueous Li-Air chemistries. Among the key differences between the non-aqueous and aqueous air electrodes, is that for aqueous systems this electrode functions as a gas diffusion electrode with hydrophobic domains creating channels for O_2 gas transport whereas in the non-aqueous case the electrode is flooded. This fact highlights one of the key advantages of aqueous Li-Air over non- aqueous: the existence of 3-phase boundaries throughout the aqueous air electrode leads to much faster oxygen transport and better electrode kinetics, and therefore much higher sustained current densities. Another issue for the non-aqueous chemistry is solvent loss from the air electrode which would be unavoidable in a open system. Accordingly, any practical non-aqueous Li-Air battery would almost certainly need to be based on a closed system running on anhydrous oxygen, and such constraints may override the energy density advantages that Li-Air chemistry offers. We have studied both the non-aqueous and aqueous Li-Air chemistries in some detail to determine baseline performances for both approaches, and to initiate commercialization of ultralight weight rechargeable batteries. Assuming the use of commercially available components and reasonable values for components still in development, one can project Li-Air cell energy densities of about 1000 Wh/l and 600 Wh/kg for a reversible electrode capacity of 5 mAh/cm^2, implying that Li-Air cells should sustain current densities of at least 1 mA/cm^2 (C/5) in order to realize broad commercial application.

Non-Aqueous Li-Air: In the mid-2000's interest in Li-Air batteries rose tremendously as a number of research groups claimed to be on the path to batteries with an order of magnitude improved energy density, motivated by the extremely high energy density of the Li/O_2 couple. If one does not include the weight of the oxygen consumed as the discharge reaction progresses, the specific energy for the Li/O_2 couple is 11,600 Wh/kg. Although metal-air batteries gain weight as the cell reaction progress and O_2 is converted to lithium peroxide (yielding a theoretical maximum of 3450 Wh/kg), the average specific energy over the course of cell discharge is well over 7000 Wh/ kg, approaching that of gasoline, and providing ample motivation for cells developers.

The earliest work in non-aqueous Li-Air chemistry was reported by K.M. Abraham [13]. These studies were done with bare unprotected lithium, dry oxygen, and polymer electrolytes plasticized by organic carbonates. In fact most early studies of non-aqueous Li-Air batteries relied heavily on the use of electrolytes based on organic carbonate solvents typically used in Li-ion batteries. However, an early paper by Aurbach and Yeager [14] pointed out that carbonate electrolytes are unstable to nucleophilic attack by superoxide anion radical ($O^{2-\bullet}$), an intermediate in the reduction of oxygen. Consequently, early results that demonstrated extended cycling of $Li-O_2$ batteries and improvements due to electrocatalysts, were greatly affected by solvent degradation and oxidation of those degradation products. Since that time, a number of groups have conducted careful investigations of those degradation phenomena [15 - 16], followed by a search for stable non-aqueous electrolytes for $Li-O_2$ batteries [17].

In 2005, PolyPlus Battery Company expanded the exploration of a number of non-aqueous Li-Air chemistries based on the use of protected lithium electrodes (PLEs) in combination with solvents known to be stable to peroxide (and superoxide) but not necessarily to lithium metal including amides, sulfoxides and nitriles [18]. A schematic drawing of a non-aqueous Li-Air cell with a PLE is shown in figure 2. Although the theoretical energy densities for Li-Air chemistries are certainly large (Table 1), practical cell performance will not exceed that of commercial Li-ion batteries until Li-Air cells reach certain threshold current densities and capacities. Assuming commercially available components and reasonable values for components still in development, one can project Li-Air cell energy densities of about 1000 Wh/l and 600 Wh/kg for a reversible electrode capacity of 5 mAh/cm^2 at a current density of 1 mA/cm^2 (C/5). However, non-aqueous Li-Air performance is typically limited to much lower current densities, often below 0.1 mA/cm$_2$, and cycled capacity is typically less than 1.0 to 1.5 mAh/cm$_2$. Another concern for non-aqueous Li-Air technology is the irreversible and rapid reaction of lithium peroxide with carbon dioxide [Li_2O_2 (s) + CO_2 = Li_2CO_3 (s) + ½ O_2]. In fact the NASA space program proposed the use Li_2O_2 to scavenge CO_2 in spaceflight operations [19].

Aqueous Lithium-Air: The first examples of aqueous Li-Air batteries were reported by PolyPlus Battery Company [2, 10 - 12] enabled by the invention of the protected lithium electrode. One of the commonly recognized problems with aqueous metal-air chemistries is the high rate of self-discharge due to direct reaction of oxygen with the negative electrode. In stark contrast, the self-discharge rate of our aqueous Li-Air cell is effectively zero, due to the presence of a solid electrolyte membrane which chemically isolates the metal electrode from the positive electrode compartment (Fig. 3). The use of a Li+-conductive solid electrolyte in aqueous electrolyte also begs the question of stability of the ceramic LATP as a function of pH. In figure 4 we show the discharge profile for fully engineered Li-Air cells (800 Wh/kg at 0.3 mA/cm^2).

Table 1. Lithium-air cell types

Electrolyte	Theoretical Energy Density (end of discharge)	Anode	Type	OCV
Non-aqueous $Li + O_2 = Li_2O_2$	3450 Wh/kg 8000 Wh/l	Unprotected (bare Li)	Type A1	2.96 V
		Protected (PLE)	Type A2	
Aqueous $4Li + O_2 + 2\ H_2O =$ 4 LiOH (simplified)	3850 Wh/kg 7000 Wh/l	Unprotected (bare Li)	Not possible	3.45 V
		Protected (PLE)	Type B	

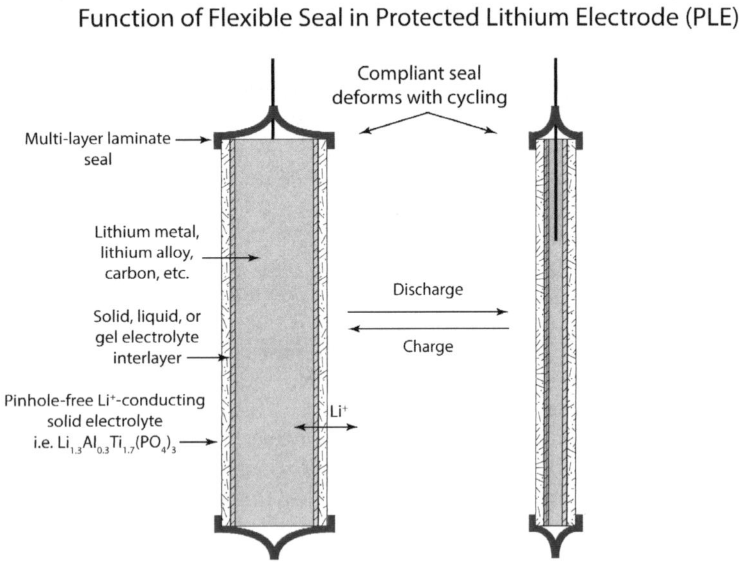

Figure 1: Schematic of protected lithium electrode

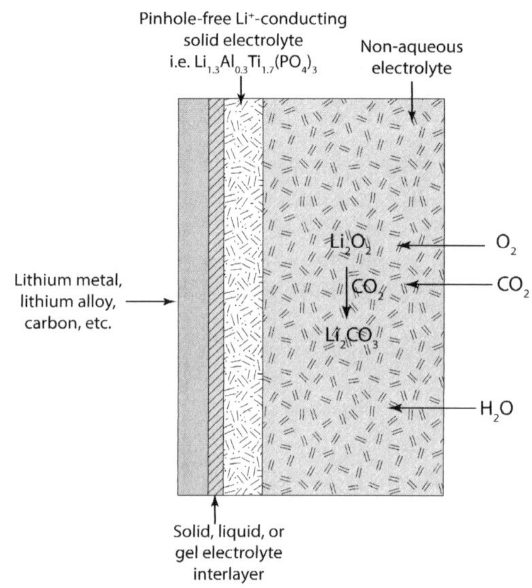

Figure 2: Non-aqueous PLE-based Li-Air

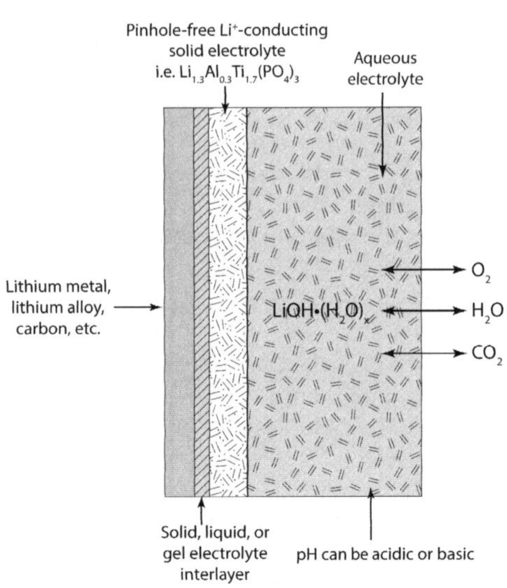

Figure 3. Aqueous PLE-Based Li-Air

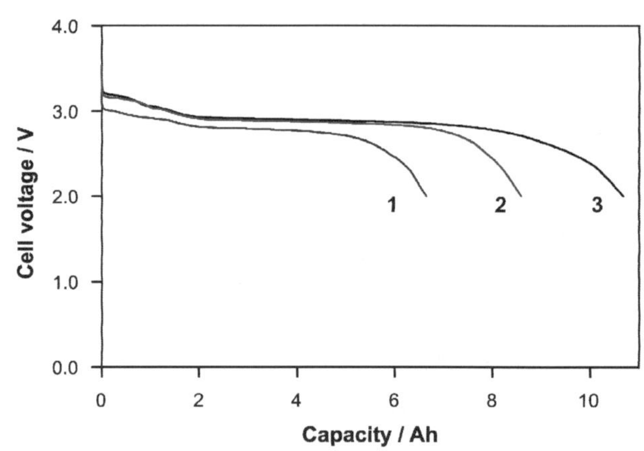

Figure 4: Discharge of fully engineered primary Li-Air cells with aqueous electrolyte comprising 2 M LiCl and 4 M NH4Cl; 1 - 1.0 mA/cm^2, 2 - 0.5 mA/cm^2, 3 - 0.3 mA/cm^2

References

1. Visco SJ, Nimon E, De Jonghe LC (2009) In: Garche J (ed) Encyclopedia of Electrochemical Power Sources. Elsevier, Amsterdam 4:376
2. Nimon YS, Visco SJ (2010) US Patent 7645543, filed Feb 3, 2004
3. Visco SJ, Katz BD, Nimon YS (2007) US Patent 7282295, filed Apr 14, 2004
4. Visco SJ, Nimon YS, Katz BD (2007) US Patent 7282296, filed Oct 14, 2003
5. Visco SJ, Nimon YS, Katz BD, Petrov A (2010) US Patent 7824806, filed Aug 8, 2006
6. Bruce PG, Freunberger SA, Hardwick LJ, Tarascon JM (2012) Nature Mater 11:19
7. Christiansen J, Albertus P, Sanchez-Carrera RS, Lohmann T, Kozinsky B, Leidtke R, Ahmed J, Kojic A (2012) J Electrochem Soc 159:R1-R30
8. Peng Z, Freunberger SA, Chen Y, Bruce PG (2012) Science 337:563-566
9. Walker W, Giordani V, Uddin J, Bryantsev VS, Chase GV, Addison D (2013) J Am Chem Soc 135:2076–2079
10. Visco SJ, Nimon E, Katz BD, De Jonghe LC, Chu MY (2004) In: Abstr Int Meet Lithium Batt. Nara, Japan 53
11. Visco SJ, Nimon E, Katz BD, De Jonghe LC, Chu MY (2004) In: Abstr Int Meet Lithium Batt. Nara, Japan 396
12. Visco SJ, Nimon E (2004) In: Abstr Int Meet Lithium Batt. Nara, Japan 397
13. Abraham KM, Jiang Z (1996) J Electrochem Soc 143:1-5
14. Aurbach D, Daroux M, Faguy P, Yeager E (1991) J Electroanal Chem 297:225-244
15. Mizuno F, Nakanishi S, Kotani Y, Yokoishi S, Iba H (2010) Electrochemistry 78:403-405
16. Freunberger SA, Peng Z, Hardwick LJ, Chen Y, Barde F, Bruce PG (2010) In: Proc 218th Electrochem Soc Meet, Las Vegas, Nevada
17. McCloskey BD, Bethune DS, Shelby RM, Girishkumar G, Luntz AC (2011) J Phys Chem Lett 2:1161–1166
18. Visco SJ, Nimon YS (2007) US Patent Application 20070117007, filed Nov 22, 2006
19. Dresser KJ, Prince RN (1969) NASA Contractor report In: Thermophys. Conf. Am. Inst. Aeronaut. San-Francisco, USA
20. Nimon VY, Visco SJ, De Jonghe LC, Volfkovich YM, Bograchev DA (2013) ECS Electrochem Lett 2:A33-A35
21. McCloskey BD, Speidel A, Scheffler R, Miller DC, Viswanathan V, Hummelshøj JS, Nørskov JK, Luntz AC (2012) J Phys Chem Lett 3:997-1001
22. Jung HG, Hassoun J, Park JB, Sun YK, Scrosati B (2012) Nat Chem 4:579-585
23. Visco SJ, De Jonghe LC, Nimon YS, Petrov A, Pridatko K (2012) US Patent 8323820, filed Jun 12, 2009
24. Visco SJ, De Jonghe LC, Nimon YS, Petrov A, Pridatko K (2013) US Patent 8455131, filed Jun 12, 2009
25. Visco SJ, De Jonghe LC, Nimon YS, Petrov A, Pridatko K (2013) US Patent 8389147, filed Jun 12, 2009
26. Visco SJ, Nimon YS, De Jonghe LC, Petrov A, Goncharenko N (2013) US Patent Application 20130045428, filed Aug 17, 2012

Electrolyte-Directed Reactions of the Oxygen Electrode in Lithium-air Batteries

K. M. Abraham[1]*, Iromie Gunasekara[1], Sanjeev Mukerjee[1], Edward J. Plichta[2] and Mary A. Hendrickson[2]

[1]Department of Chemistry, Northeastern University, Boston, MA 02115
Telephone: 781-444-8453; Fax: 781-445-6893;
E-mail: kmabraham@comcast.net

[2]US Army RDECOM CERDEC C2D, Army Power Division, RDER-CCA Aberdeen Proving Grounds, MD 21005

Abstract: *The oxygen reduction reactions (ORR) in the non-aqueous Li-air battery is influenced by the Lewis acidity of the Li^+ ions and the Lewis basicity of the solvent in the electrolyte through the formation of acid-base complexes of the type $Li^+(solvent)_n$, which lowers the acidity of the Li^+. Weakly acidic complexes formed between Li^+ and high donor number solvents, e.g. dimethyl sulfoxide, promotes the stabilization of the superoxide intermediate whereas strongly acidic complexes of Li^+ formed with low donor number solvents, e.g. tetraethylene glycol dimethyl ether, stabilize peroxide and monoxide. The acidity of Li^+ is further reduced by ion pair formation with the anion which complements the effect of the solvent. The basicity of the solvent also affects ORR catalysis as demonstrated with carbon cathodes catalyzed with cobalt phthalocyanine.*

Keywords: Li-air battery, non-aqueous electrolytes, donor nu9mber, HSAB concept

Introduction

A detailed understanding of the oxygen reduction (ORR) and evolution reactions (OER) in non-aqueous Li-air batteries is extremely important for the full development of these super high energy density batteries. It has become increasingly clear that the ORR mechanism and the stability of the ORR products are intimately connected with the acid-base properties of the non-aqueous solvents and the conducting cations present in the electrolyte[1-3]. The solvents influence the ORR mechanism and products through their electron donating properties defined by the Guttmann Donor Numbers (DN), and the salts influence these through the Lewis acidity of their cations. In Li^+-conducting electrolytes, the interplay of the basicity of the solvents and the acidity of Li^+ on ORR is demonstrated through the formation of solvated cations, ($Li^+(solvent)_n$), which lower the acidity of Li^+ in proportion to the basicity or the Donor Number of the solvent. The stability of the final ORR products formed in the non-aqueous Li-air battery is thus explained through a general theory based on the Hard Soft Acid Base (HSAB) concept.

We demonstrate that microelectrodes can be used to optimize the electrolyte properties and to unravel the influence of the lithium salt anion on the ORR through ion pair formation between Li^+ and the salt's anion. Finally, we show that the mechanism of ORR catalysis by transition metal complexes such as Cobalt phthalocycinine (CoPC) is also strongly influenced by the relative basicity of the solvent used for the electrolyte.

Results and Discussion

We have measured the relative acidity of a series of conducting cations using ^{13}C NMR chemical shifts and spin-lattice relaxation times (T1) in propylene carbonate (PC)[3], as depicted in Figure 1. The ^{13}C NMR spectra depicting the ^{13}C=O chemical shifts of PC with and without added salts

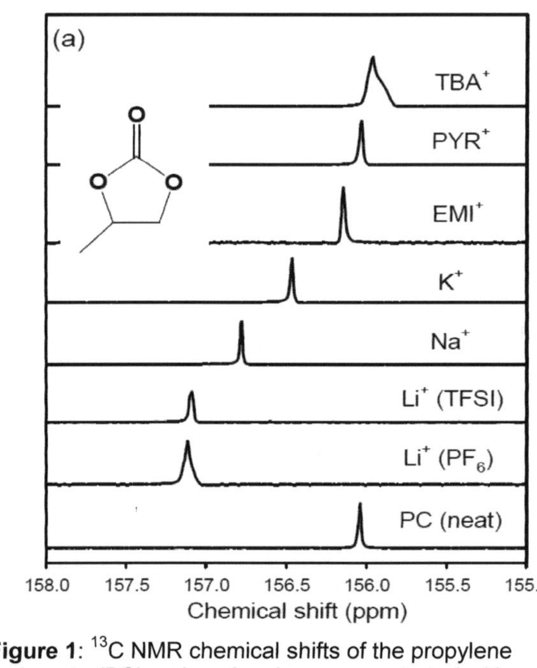

Figure 1: ^{13}C NMR chemical shifts of the propylene carbonate (PC) carbonyl carbon, concentrated with various 1M salt solutions. 1M $LiPF_6$ (Li^+), 1M LiTFSI (Li^+), $NaPF_6$ (Na^+), KPF_6 (K^+), EMITFSI (EMI^+), PYRTFSI (PYR^+), and $TBAPF_6$ (TBA^+). The structure of PC is shown in the inset.

including ionic liquids (EMITFSI and PYRTFSI) presented in Figure 1 show that in $LiPF_6$, LiTFSI and $NaPF_6$ salt solutions, Li^+ and Na^+ ions are strongly solvated to the carbonyl oxygen atoms of PC since they have the largest negative chemical shifts (less ^{13}C shielding) relative to PC, while K^+ and the three large cations, TBA^+, EMI^+, and PYR^+ are weakly coordinated.

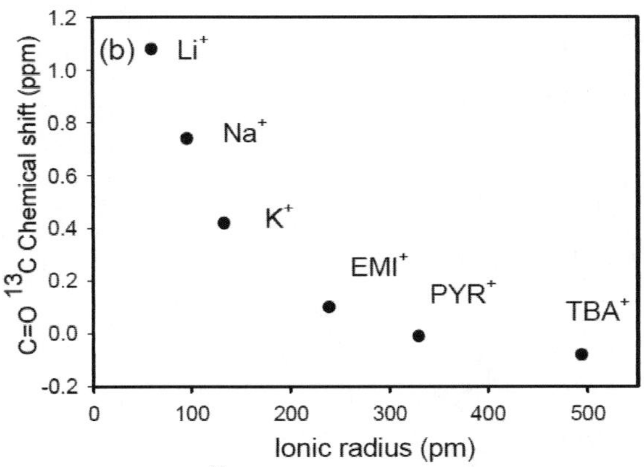

Figure 2: C(=O) ^{13}C chemical shifts relative to neat PC as a function of cation ionic radius.

The ^{13}C NMR chemical shifts of the C=O provide a measure of the complexing ability of the Lewis base C=O (by donating the electron pair on O) with the Lewis acid cations, and hence the measure of relative acidity of the cations. This effect is illustrated in Figure 2 with a cascading chemical shift as a function of the ionic radii of these cations. The larger the ionic radius of the cation the weaker is its complexing ability with the solvent and hence weaker is its Lewis acidity. The Lewis acidity of a cation is inversely proportional to the ionic radius of the cation since smaller ionic radius means higher positive charge density for the cation.

We have also correlated the Donor Number of several family of solvents used in preparing Li^+-conducting electrolytes with the solvation energy of the solvates formed between Li^+ and the solvents using Drago's equation, $-\Delta H = E_A E_B + C_A C_B + W$. In this equation[4], ΔH is the enthalpy (in cal/mole) of formation of a Lewis acid-base adduct, E_A, C_A and R_A are parameters characteristic of the acid and, and E_B , C_B and T_B are parameters characteristic of the base. These parameters for Li^+ are E_A = 11.72, C_A = 1.45 and R_A= 24.21 and for $(CH_3)_2SO$ these are E_B= 2.4, C_B= 1.47 and T_B=0.65, all values in kcal/mole. The enthalpy of formation calculated for a 1:1 adduct between Li^+ and DMSO is 46.0 kcal/mole whereas that for an adduct from Li^+ and CH_3CN is 40.34, about 12% lower. A similar trend should follow for adducts of Li^+ formed with a larger number of solvent molecules. Clearly, the higher solvation energy involved in the formation of the complex $Li^+(DMSO)_n$ translates into lower Lewis acidity for the Li^+ in this solvate than for the Li^+ in $Li^+(CH_3CN)_n$. The higher solvation energy calculated for the solvate formed between DMSO and Li^+ (see Table 1) is consistent with that expected from its high donor number of 29.8 compared with a donor number of 14.1 for CH_3CN.

Table 1: Donor Numbers of several solvents

Solvent	Donor Number of the solvent	Li^+-solvation Energy, k Cal/ mole
DMSO	29.8	46.00
MeCN	14.1	40.34
Diethyl ether	19.2	41.86

Microelectrode Study of the Role of Electrolyte on ORR mechanism and Products: We have studied the ORR in dimethyl sulfoxide (DMSO)-based electrolytes containing Li and tetrabutylammonium (TBA) salts at an 11μm diameter carbon microelectrode. Due to efficient mass transport of the electroactive species onto and the removal of reduction products from the microelectrode surface (radial diffusion), limiting current behavior is expected for ORR even at scan rates high as 500 mV s^{-1}. Indeed, we have observed steady state voltammograms with the characteristic limiting currents in all TBA salt-based electrolytes (Figure 3). This confirms that the reversible one-electron reduction product, superoxide (O_2^-), proposed by Cormac et al[1] , is soluble in TBA salt-based electrolytes. Oxygen transport parameters calculated from the Cottrell plots derived from chronoamperometric current-time transients on the microelectrode in $TBAPF_6$, $TBAClO_4$, $TBACF_3SO_3$, $TBAN(CF_3SO_2)_2$ in DMSO reveal that oxygen transport is not affected by the anions of these salts.

In contrast to the behavior of TBA salt solutions, peak-shaped (non-steady state) current-voltage profiles were observed in the electrolytes containing their Li salt counterparts (Figure 4). These voltammograms are attributed to electrode passivation by insoluble discharge products. As the microelectrode is passivized by insoluble ORR products, O_2 diffusion through the passivation film becomes increasingly inefficient and at the same time the effective area of the electrode available for ORR is greatly reduced. These two effects lead to a classical CV type current-voltage profile as the potential is scanned.

We have confirmed passivation film formation on the microelectrode from SEM/ EDAX and Raman spectroscopic data, which indicated that Li_2O and Li_2O_2 were formed at different reduction potentials[5]. A close look at the ORR mechanism and products in solutions of these various cations has clearly indicated that the strong Lewis acids Li^+ and Na^+ show a propensity to stabilize the strong base ORR products O_2^{2-} and O^{2-} while the weak Lewis acids TBA^+ and ionic liquid cations stabilize the one electron ORR product superoxide, O_2^-. When Li-conducting solutions in high DN solvents are used, the Lewis acidity of Li^+ is significantly decreased through the formation of solvates of Li^+. As a result the superoxide ion is stabilized more in these electrolytes than in electrolytes prepared using low Donor Number solvents such as the ethers. The Li^+-solvation energy calculated using Drago's equation, depicted in Table 1, for the various solvents further validate the overall HSAB concept.

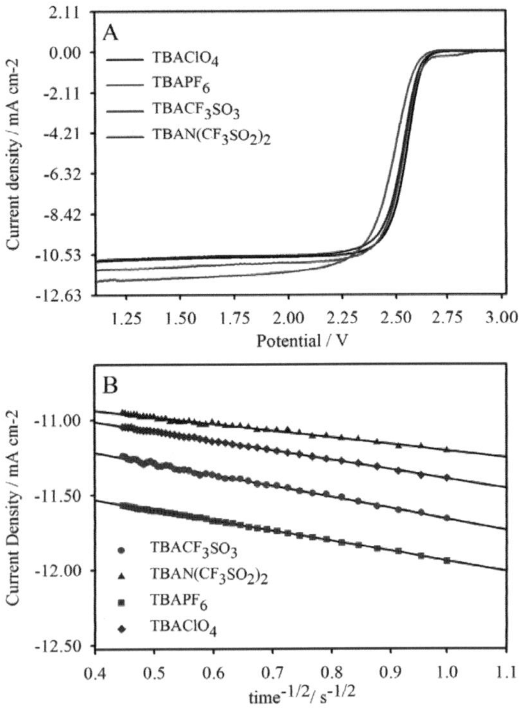

Figure 3 A): Current vs. potential scans at a microelectrode in 0.1 M TBA/DMSO. Scan rate 50 mV s^{-1} B): Cottrell plots calculated for the current- time transients obtained from potential jump chronoamperometry experiments.

The Li^+ is usually solvated by four solvent molecules to form solvent-separated ion pairs; e.g., $Li^+(DMSO)_4PF_6^-$ in $LiPF_6$/DMSO electrolyte. Despite its four oxygen atoms, the perchlorate ion (ClO_4^-) cannot form direct ion pair with Li^+ in high donor number solvents like DMSO. Trifluoromethanesulfonate ($CF_3SO_3^-$) (triflate) and bis (trifluoromethanesulfonyl) imide ($N(CF_3SO_2)_2^-$) (trflimide) anions can replace some of the solvent molecules and form direct ion pairs with Li^+ (Figure 5). Most stable coordination is calculated to be bi-dentate for bis(trifluoromethanesulfonyl)imide where the two oxygen atoms come from two different sulfur atoms of the anion. Mono-dentate coordination with Li^+ is the most stable for the trifluoromethanesulfonate anion in polar aprotic solvents. The negative charge on the bis(trifluoromethanesulfonyl)imide ion is delocalized onto

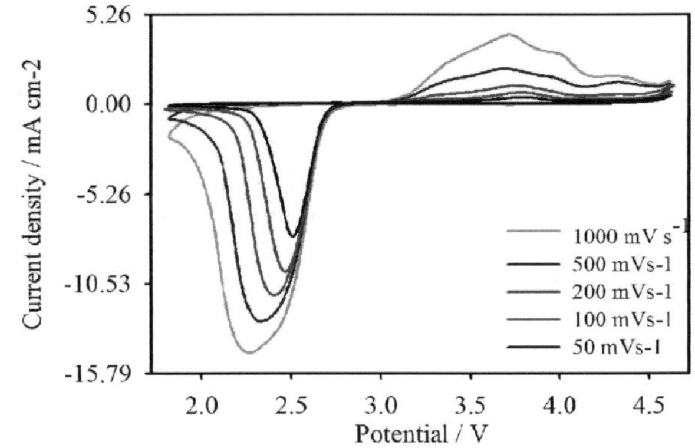

Figure 4: Current-voltage scans at the microelectrode in O2 purged 0.1 M LiPF6/ DMSO recorded at scan rates ranging from 50 - 1000 mV s^{-1}

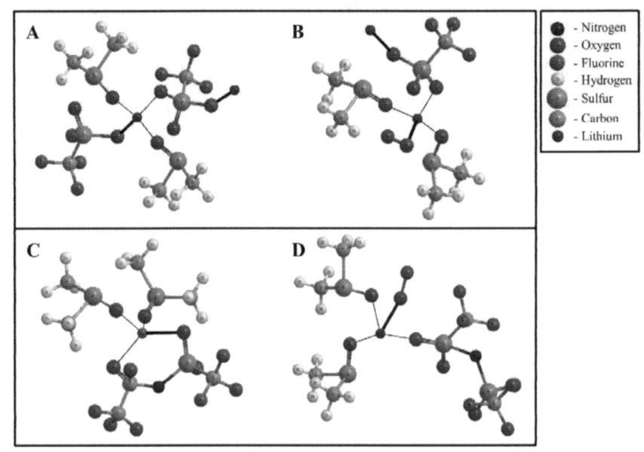

Figure 5: Solvation and contact ion pair formation in A) $LiCF_3SO_3$/DMSO and C) $LiN(CF_3SO_2)_2$/DMSO electrolytes. Ion pair between solvated Li^+ and superoxide ion in B) $LiCF_3SO_3$/DMSO, D) $LiN(CF_3SO_2)_2$/DMSO electrolytes

neighboring sulfonyl group and as a result it is less available for coordination with the Li^+. The Lewis basicity of the trifluoromethanesulfonate anion is higher than that of the bis (trifluoromethanesulfonyl) imide anion due to the three electron rich oxygen centers. Consequently, two triflate anions would have a more stable coordination with Li^+. In fact the donor numbers for anions presented in Table 2 lend further support for the ability of the triflate ion (with a high donor number of 16.90) to form strong internal coordination with Li^+. The high donor capability of the triflate anion has two possible advantages in the Li-air cathode reaction; it 1) stabilizes the superoxide ions by the softer $Li(triflate)_x^{(n-1)+}(solvent)_y$ cations and mitigates its chemical decomposition/ electrochemical conversion to peroxide, 2) possibly helps solvate the Li^+ in Li_2O_2 leading to some solubility for the peroxide in the $LiCF_3SO_3$/DMSO electrolyte and removing it from the electrode surface to mitigate

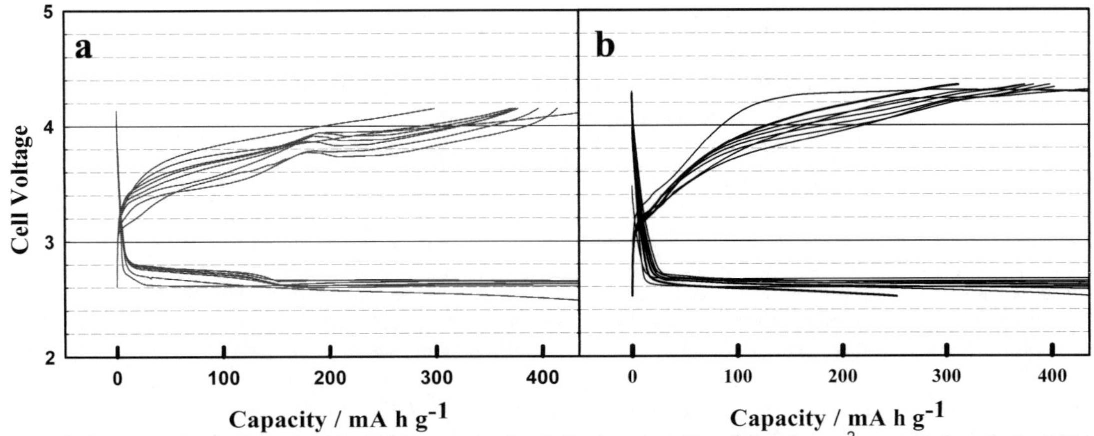

Figure 6: Galvanostatic cycling at 500 mAh/gram depth of discharge with a 0.1 mA cm-^{2} current density in 1 M $LiPF_6$ in TEGDME under oxygen flow for (a): CoPc-600 catalyzed Ketjenblack cathode and (b) uncatalyzed Ketjenblack cathode.

electrode passivation. Our experimentally observed trend in Columbic efficiencies suggests possible contributions from both of these effects. Note that on the microelectrode, soluble products would diffuse away quickly from the electrode surface making it unavailable for oxidation, while insoluble products that remain on the electrode surface are more efficiently oxidized. The results presented here indicate a unique role for the triflate anion on ORR in DMSO and point out the ability of microelectrode data to help diagnose the role of the Li salt on O_2 electrode reversibility in the Li-air cell.

Table 2: Donor Numbers of the anions

Solvent	Donor Number[6]
PF_6^-	2.5
$CF_3SO_3^-$	16.9
$N(CF_3SO_2)_2^-$	5.4
ClO_4^-	8.44

We have also found that the mechanism of ORR catalysis is strongly determined by the Donor Number of the solvents. In Li^+-conducting electrolytes using high Donor Number solvents such as DMSO, the ORR catalysis occurs through an outer Helmholtz layer process whereas in low Donor Number solvents catalysis occur via an inner Helmholtz layer process on the catalytic electrode. In the former case, the catalytic effect of the metal complex catalyst, Cobalt Phthalocyanine (CoPc), present in the porous carbon electrode is minimal whereas in the latter case strong adsorption of O_2 and its reduction products O_2^- and O_2^{2-} occur on the catalyst surface leading to the full (four electron) reduction of O_2 to O^{2-}. Galvanostatic cycling curves for a catalyzed and uncatalyzed lithium air cell are shown in Figure 6.

References

1. C.O.Laoire,S. Mukerjee,K. Abraham,E.J. Plichta and M. A. Hendrickson, *The Journal of Physical Chemistry C*, 2009, **113**, 20127-20134.
2. C. O. Laoire, S. Mukerjee, K. Abraham, E. J. Plichta and M. A. Hendrickson, *The Journal of Physical Chemistry C*, 2010, **114**, 9178-9186.
3. C. J. Allen, J. Hwang, R. Kautz, S. Mukerjee, E. J. Plichta, M. A. Hendrickson and K. M. Abraham, *The Journal of Physical Chemistry C*, 2012, **116**, 20755-20764.
4. R. S. Drago, D. C. Ferris and N. Wong, *Journal of the American Chemical Society*, 1990, **112**, 8953-8961.
5. I. Gunasekara, S. Mukerjee, E. J. Plichta, M. A. Hendrickson and K. M. Abraham, *Journal of The Electrochemical Society*, 2014, **161**, A381-A392.
6. W. Linert, A. Camard, M. Armand and C. Michot, *Coordination Chemistry Reviews*, 2002, **226**, 137-141.

Acknowledgement

The US Army RDECOM CERDEC C2D, Aberdeen Proving Grounds, MD, provided financial support for this work.

Recent Assessment of Metal-Air Systems for Commercial and Military Applications

Alexander P. Karpinski and Arthur Dobley
Yardney Technical Products, Inc.
2000 South County Trail, East Greenwich, Rhode Island 02818-1530 USA
Tel: 401-471-6580, e-mails karpinski@yardney.com and adobley@yardney.com

Abstract: It can be argued that the genesis for metal-air started with the work of Leclanche' in the mid to late 1800's while experimenting with MnO_2 electrodes. In the last 10 years metal-air has evolved to include a number of alkaline earth metal anodes which electrochemical equivalent energy densities are well beyond any traditional primary or rechargeable battery. Although zinc-air and a lesser extent aluminum-air are the dominant technologies that serve a number of applications, lithium-air (i.e., primary or secondary) is gaining a lot of traction due to its very high energy density and higher voltage potential.

In the past few years there have been some number of advancements that are starting to mainstream these electrochemistries on a variety of applications.

Keywords: metal-air; zinc-air; aluminum-air; lithium-air; magnesium-air; air cathode; gas diffusion electrode; oxygen; metal anode; electrolyte; air management

Introduction

Since the 1930s, Metal-air battery systems have been commercialized for an array of unique applications such as railway signaling, and navigation buoys. The interest level for metal-air power sources in these applications is somewhat cyclical based on the newer competing systems that solve some of the short comings associated with metal-air battery technology. Although these shortcomings are not fully resolved this system is still very attractive due to its very high specific energy. The metal anodes are electrochemically coupled to oxygen in the air through the air cathode. Oxygen gas, from the air, is essentially an unlimited cathode reactant source. Theoretically with oxygen as an unlimited cathode reactant, the capacity of the battery is limited by the metal anode and to a lesser extent, the electrolyte. Anodes commonly investigated are aluminum, lithium, magnesium and zinc. These would be paired with a tailored air cathode design to provide the most optimum performance in varying discharge conditions (e.g., for power or energy).

The desirable gas diffusion electrode (or air cathode) includes good polarization characteristics, mechanical integrity, low cost and long life. The electrode is typically composed of a combination of three different layers; a reactive carbon layer, a current collector, and a hydrophobic barrier film. The reactive carbon layer is the site of electrochemical activity and consists of finely divided activated carbon held together with hydrophobic binders, usually polytetrafluoroethylene (PTFE). Catalysts, such as platinum, silver or manganese, are incorporated into the carbon layer to increase the rate of oxygen reduction. The current collector is usually composed of an expanded metal mesh such as nickel. This layer also serves as a source of mechanical support. The barrier film is usually fluoropolymer or polyolefin, and is pressed or laminated on the air side of the cathode to provide an effective electrolyte barrier, while allowing oxygen to enter the carbon layer.

The metal-air battery usually offers a flat discharge voltage profile, environmental friendliness and long storage life.

Metal-air systems have also been formatted into hybrid systems which can augment the power portion of the system. These have included the addition of other batteries and/or capacitors.

Survey of Metal-Air Couples

Of all battery systems the metal-air system (i.e., uncommonly called a semi-fuel cell) is very unique in that it can be configured many different ways. Some designs utilize a jelled anode which is typically a mixture of zinc powder, caustic electrolyte and binder coupled with a catalyzed thin gas diffusion electrode. Some designs can be wound into a cylindrical cell[i] for higher rate applications. Some designs are simple prismatic cells whereas the electrodes are stacked as parallel elements and used either in a static or a flowing electrolyte system. Other designs use a hopper system where zinc pellets are feed into an electrolyte stream and pumped across the cathode. Another unique approach is a "dry" three foil system consisting of zinc foil, a solid electrolyte membrane and an air cathode in the form of a tape roll that is laminated into a common ply which results into a semi-fuel cell for an electric vehicle application. All these systems provide flexibility in packaging depending at the application. Refer to Table 1 for a cross section of these applications.

Table 1. Application Spectrum

Application	Organization	Couple	System	Comments
Electric Vehicle	Electric Fuel	Zn-air	Static; cartridges	hybrid power systems
Electric Vehicle	Phinergy	Al-air & Zn-air	Flowing Electrolyte	Range Extender
Electric Vehicle	Evionyx	Ni Zn & Zn-air		All electric hybrid
Electric Vehicle	Alupower/ Yardney	Al-Air	Flowing Electrolyte	Range Extender
Electric Vehicle	KIST*	Mg-Air	Static	Primary Power
Portable military	Arotech	Zn-air	Static	BA-8180/U & BA-8140/U
Portable military	Alupower/ Yardney	Al-air	Static	2.9kWh manportable
Grid Storage	EOS Technology	Zn Hybrid Cathode	Static and flowing	5 kW modules
Grid Storage	Powair	Zn-air	Flow battery	
Hearing Aid	Duracell, Energizer	Zn-air	Pasted anode	Button Cell
Portable Meters	Cegasa (Spain)	Zn-air	Static Prismatic	
Navigational aides/telecom	Automatic Power	Zn-air	Static Prismatic	
Oxygen sensors	Systech Illinois	Pb-air	Static	Electrochemi cal sensor

*Korea Institute of Science and Technology

Table 2[ii] provides a comparison of specific energy, energy density, and voltage for a range of common metals.

Table 2. Comparisons of Metals

Metal	Electrochemical Equivalent (Ah/g)	Theoretical Specific Energy (kWh/kg)	Theoretical* Cell Voltage	Typical Cell Voltage
Be	5.95	17.9	3.0	-
Li	3.86	13.0	3.4	2.4
Al	2.98	8.1	2.71	1.3
Mg	2.20	6.8	3.09	1.3
Ca	1.34	4.6	3.4	2.0
Cd[iii]	0.48	0.45	1.28	0.78
Fe	0.96	1.8	1.3	10
Pb	0.26	0.45	2.81	0.05
Ni	0.91	1.1	1.20	-
Si	3.92	8.5	2.16	1.15**
Zn	0.82	1.1	1.62	1.2

*Voltage with oxygen cathode and pH 14 electrolyte

**1-ethyl-3-methylimidazolium chloride and hydrogen fluoride (EMI·2.3HF•F) RTIL[iv]

The Metal-air system uses oxygen as the fuel and can be paired with a variety of anodes. The cathodic reactant (oxygen) can come in many forms such as the air we breathe, dissolved oxygen in the seawater, chlorate candles, (blood) plasma, hydrogen peroxide, or bottled oxygen.

Due to the construction of some metal air systems (e.g., physical gap between the anode and cathode) or the materials selected, inefficiencies can result in higher IR losses. Heat Generation of metal air cells[v] was calculated from the thermoneutral voltage and a typical operating voltage at a current density of 40 mA/cm^2. Refer to Table 3 which summarizes the ratio of heat generation to electrical power. This provides a measure to the inefficiency of the system whereas active thermal or enhanced air management may be required to prevent shutdown of the battery during operation. At higher rates the inefficiency becomes greater.

Table 3. Heat Generation Ratio

Couple	Thermoneutral Voltage	Heat Generation to Electrical Power
Aluminum-Air	2.93	1.15
Magnesium-Air	3.11	1.78
Zinc-Air	1.80	0.46
Lithium-Air	3.1	0.24

Lithium-Air: Lithium is the lightest of the metals, has the highest potential at over 3 volts, and a very high theoretical specific energy. There are two main types of Li-air chemistries; aqueous and non-aqueous. The aqueous cells can exhibit high power densities, but suffer from safety problems. For the non-aqueous cells the practical energy densities and especially power densities remain relatively low. The lithium-air systems is currently being developed as aqueous and non-aqueous systems (sometimes both) and a trade-off exists between performance and safety. There are two main discharge cell reactions:

$4Li + O_2 \rightarrow 2Li_2O$

$2Li + O_2 \rightarrow Li_2O_2$

This system currently attracts most of the research funding.

Zinc-Air: Considered one of the safest commercially available metal-air systems the primary zinc-air battery is the most widely used in terms of sales and volume. The dominating market is hearing aids but include many other relevant applications such as man-portable power for a host of military equipment. In addition to these there are so called boutique applications such as electric vehicles that leverage the unique forms/configurations of the zinc air active materials.

Although the main market is for primary cells, the zinc air battery has also been successfully developed as an electrically or mechanically rechargeable system. Electrically rechargeable systems have been successful with the development of bifunctional electrodes using perovskites[vi]. Mechanically rechargeable systems typically come in the form of replacement cartridges which also refreshes the electrolyte.

The anode can be metallic or in a mix with the electrolyte.

The overall net reaction can be expressed as follows:

Anode:
$Zn + 2OH^- \rightarrow Zn\ (OH)_2\ ^+ 2e^-$

$Zn\ (OH)_2 \rightarrow ZnO + H_2O$

Cathode: $O_2 + 2H_2O + 4e^- \rightarrow 4OH^-$

Magnesium-Air: There has been limited success in commercializing magnesium-air batteries. The corrosion of the magnesium is somewhat influenced by the direct reaction with the electrolyte thus forming magnesium hydroxide and a large amount of hydrogen. This in turn lowers the coulombic efficiency. The overall net reaction is as follows:

$Mg + ½O_2 + H_2O \rightarrow Mg\ (OH)_2$

Cathode: $O_2 + 2H_2O + 4e^- \rightarrow 4OH^-$

Over the years various electrolytes have been utilized in this couple with moderate success such as $LiClO_4$ and LiCl with seawater (NaCl) being the most common electrolyte used in commercial applications[vii].

Aluminum Air: Aluminum-air batteries exhibit both high energy density and operating voltage, and relatively easy to fabricate and operate safely. Although the discharge of aluminum anodes is irreversible it can be recharged mechanically by replacing the anode and the electrolyte.

The overall net reaction can be expressed as follows:

4 Al + 6H2O + 3(O) 2 → 4 Al (OH) 3

The electrolyte for aluminum air batteries can be either salt water or an alkaline. The conductivity of the salt water is lower than the alkaline with a corresponding energy reduction. These can be characterized as 0.0.5AH/ml for saline electrolyte and 0.4 AH/ml for alkaline electrolyte.

Although a saline electrolyte is safe, other challenges exist to achieve optimal performance. In order to minimize the voltage drop a narrower gap between the electrodes is required. As a consequence the byproducts of the anodic dissolution of aluminum reaction accumulate as a gelatinous product between the anode and cathode. This can cause anode passivation and the need for additional water since it binds the electrolyte. Some solutions include the use of flocculating agents to precipitate the aluminum hydroxide or the addition of 18% citrate in the NaCl solution. In either case these changes would impact energy density.

The use of alkaline electrolyte provides for excellent coulombic efficiency (e.g., from 60 to 98%) and increased voltage during discharge (e.g., 500mV). Depending on the electrolyte molarity the aluminum reaction product can be managed two ways. The first is to precipitate out the aluminum hydroxide (e.g., < 8M KOH) or operate as a solids-free design with a flowing electrolyte system. In both cases the electrolyte requires the addition of a low concentration (e.g., <1%) of tin (as a stannate) to control corrosion of the aluminum anode. The optimal operating temperature for the flowing electrolyte system is 60° to 80°C.

The stoichiometric rate for air reaction is 0.01 liters per minute per ampere or 10 cc/min.

Air Electrode: In simplistic terms, the gas diffusion electrode or air cathode is the site for three phase contact of a solid (carbons and catalyst), liquid (electrolyte) and gas (oxygen). An example of a cathode preparation would entail two layers of a carbon, binder, and catalyst mixture being deposited on both sides of a metal current collector (Figure 1). Carbon mats are impregnated with slurry of carbon, binder, and catalyst. Two of these impregnated mats are laminated around a current collector. All air cathodes would have a microporous PTFE layer added to the side exposed to the environment. This produces a double-sided air cathode.

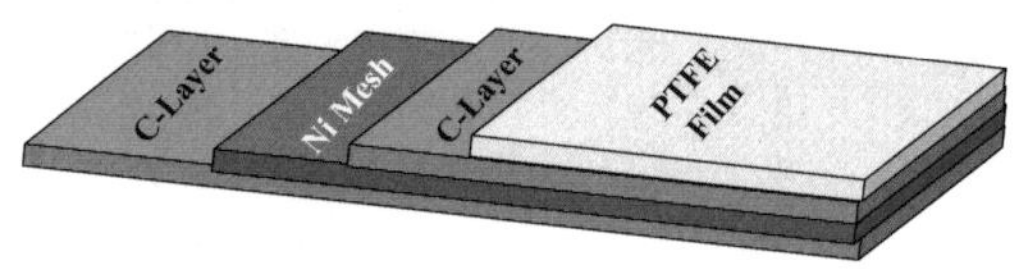

Figure 1. A diagram of a layered air cathode

Cells & Batteries

Metal-air cells come in a variety of physical configurations. The main specialty types are for man portable power and reserve power units being a prismatic or rectangular solid shape. The metal anode is either a slab or slurry. For separating the electrodes a physical space filled with electrolyte can be used or a sheet of separator. An example of a prismatic lithium-air cell is shown in Figure 2. The window in the center of the cell is the exposed air cathode that allows air to enter the cell. This cell was developed for a low rate, 12 volt battery system measuring 5 in. wide by 5 in. high by 5 in. long. Cells like this can be stacked together with electronics to for a man portable unit like the one shown in Figure 3 which depicts a 16 volt, 2.9 kWh aluminum air system for a man-portable application[viii].

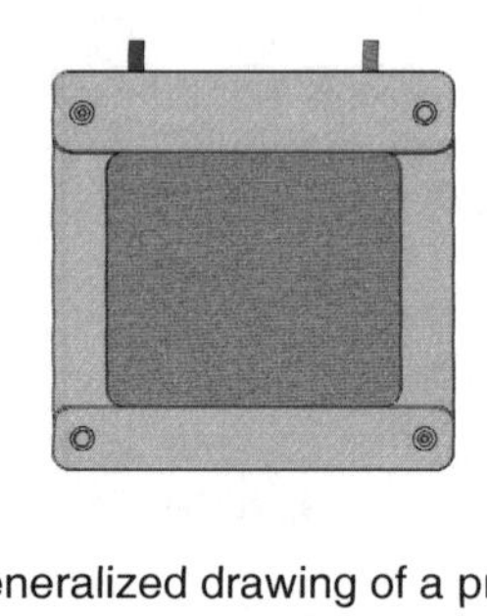

Figure 2. A generalized drawing of a prismatic lithium-air cell

Figure 3. A photograph of a 12/24 volt man portable aluminum-air battery (SOFAL)

Applications

The main commercial application of metal-air cells seen today is the use of Zn-air cells to power hearing aids. The majority of metal-air work is in research and development. Recent interest is in applying metal-air technology to automotive, grid storage and military applications. The automotive sector is focusing on Li-air cells as secondary systems, and also Al-air as primary batteries to be used as range extenders.

The grid storage area is focusing on many metal-air systems as both primary and secondary batteries to help provide peak power. Reserve power units, to be used during a power outage, are focusing on Al-air and Zn-air. The reserve power unit systems are primary and secondary. The military is an early adapter of metal-air systems (e.g., since the 1960's). They currently use Zn-air primary batteries due to the high specific energy. The military is interested in metal-air systems for man portable power to provide energy to sensors, communications, electronics, weapons, and computers. There is also military interest for providing power to the grid as a backup power sources, or for peak power demands as reserve power units.

Future Directions

With recent advancements in the battery industry involving materials, processing, instrumentation, and modeling, the metal-air systems are posed for a renaissance. Advancements in carbons, catalysts, and electrodes, will allow for increased voltages and energy. Newer processes will allow for lightweight cell and battery designs. Instrumentation and modeling will help increase knowledge into the fundamental properties of the metal-air chemistry and bring forth improvements. Due to the high theoretical specific energy, the metal-air batteries hold great promise to fill the energy requirements for military portable and reserve power.

Conclusions

This is an exciting time for metal-air batteries with their extremely high theoretical specific energy, and the worldwide interest in energy storage. A large amount of effort was dedicated to getting the Zn-air system into the commercial and military market. Several other metal-air systems hold the promise of greater performance than the Zn-air battery and should be investigated further. Metal-air batteries because of their high energy to weight ratio offer a great advantage to portable power and reserve power units.

---

[i] A.P. Karpinski et al, Progress on the Development of a Lightweight, Rechargeable Zinc-Air Battery, 6th Workshop for Battery Exploratory Development, Williamsburg, VA, June 1999

[ii] Alupower technical booklet

[iii] O. Wagner, Cadmium-Air Cell Studies, Research and Development Technical Report ECOM-3451, July 1971

[iv] G. Cohn et al, Silicon-air batteries, Electrochemistry Communications 11 (2009) 1916-1918

[v] K.F. Blurton, H.G. Oswin, Refuelable Batteries, Energetics Science Inc., NY, Symposium of Non-Fossil Chemical Fuels, Boston, 1972

[vi] W. Halliop et al, Bifunctional Electrodes for Electrically Rechargeable Zn/Air Cells, 197th Meeting of the Electrochemical Society, Toronto, Ontario, May 2000

[vii] A. Charkey, G Dalin, Metal-Air Systems, 20th Power Sources Proceedings, 1967

[viii] A.P. Karpinski et al, The SOFAL Aluminum-air Battery for Man-Portable Applications, 33rd IECEC, Colorado Springs, August 1998

Thin Component Thermal Battery Development and Process Scale-Up

Joe Edington and Julie Baumann
EaglePicher Technologies, LLC
Joplin, MO 64801
Phone: (417) 623-8000
Fax: (417) 206-4708
Joe.Edington@EaglePicher.com

Abstract
EaglePicher Technologies (EPT) has developed alternative manufacturing technologies to produce thin battery components for traditional and next-generation thermal batteries. This paper will discuss recent efforts to produce thin component battery designs, including; large diameter pulse batteries, small diameter high power batteries, and non-circular geometry thermal batteries. Additionally, this paper will describe the efforts made by EPT to scale-up tape casting capabilities to accommodate production-level manufacturing of thin component thermal batteries.

Introduction
Tape casting provides an enabling technology to produce thinner thermal battery components. Tape cast components provide the means of improving thermal battery energy density, reducing the weight penalties associated with pressed components for certain applications. Over the course of several years, EPT has developed tape casting techniques for manufacturing thermal battery components and has demonstrated these components in multiple battery designs.

Thin component technology fills a niche need in the market and is best suited for applications such as:

- Low capacity/high current draw (pulse batteries)
- High power/high voltage batteries
- Multi-stack or multi-battery designs
- Miniature batteries with very thin components
- Short life batteries
- Conformal shapes and geometries

Thin film batteries can be designed using solely thin film components or as a hybrid design incorporating thin film components with pressed components to meet the design needs of the battery. EaglePicher has demonstrated both design types using multiple battery configurations over the past several years. These efforts demonstrate that thin component technologies provide the design flexibility needed to meet a wide variety of demands for next-generation thermal batteries.

This paper details the efforts made by EaglePicher to scale up the tape casting process to support production level demands and discusses on-going development efforts to advance thin component battery technology.

Production Equipment
EaglePicher Technologies has purchased production equipment to scale up the manufacturing process for thin film components. This equipment includes a compact tape caster, an automated tape stacker, additional ovens for burn out, and more efficient cutting dies to increase throughput and product quality.

The production tape caster enables EPT to cast tape at a higher speed than the previous laboratory caster. The maximum casting speed is approximately 12 times greater and the automated slurry feeding systems allows for large batch sizes up to 6 gallons. The automated slurry feeder carefully controls the slurry level in the casting box throughout the casting run. The production caster can control the doctor blade gap to within one micron. The combined effects of these refinements produce tighter tolerances which improves tape quality over the laboratory caster.

Figure 1: Compact Tape Caster

The production stacker automates the tape cutting, stacking, and laminating processes which greatly improves throughput over the manual processes used on the laboratory scale. The stacker releases the green tape from the Mylar carrier then cuts the tape into 8" lengths. A vacuum head then picks up the individual segments and stacks the desired number of layer on a press block. The block is then conveyed to a heated press where the layers are laminated into a single sheet. These individual sheets are then ready for punching or cutting to produce the desired component size and shape for the battery design.

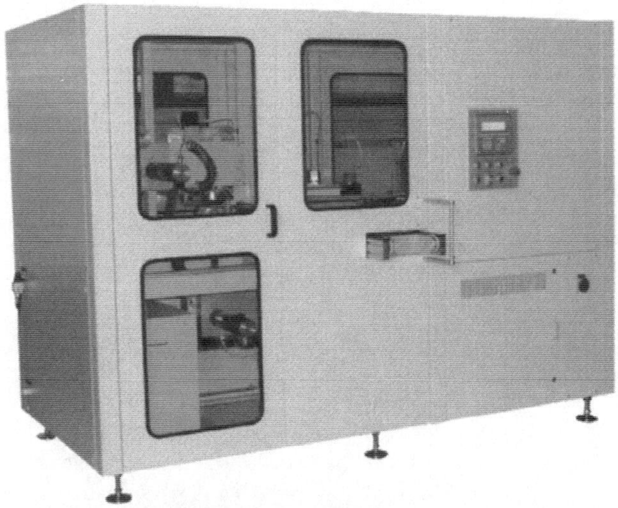

Figure 2: Automated Stacker

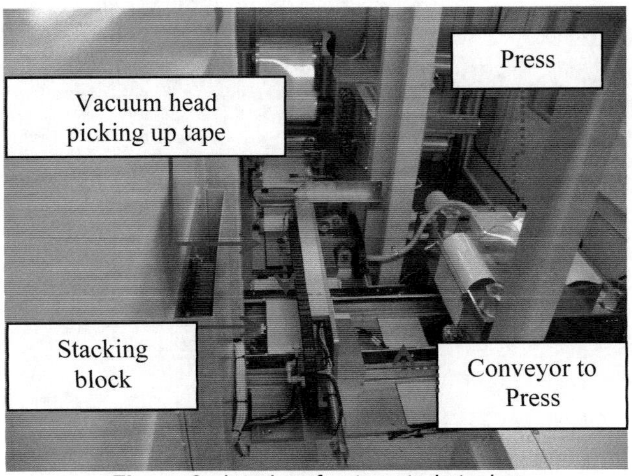

Figure 3: Interior of automated stacker

Inexpensive cutting dies are used to punch multiple parts from each 8" x 8" sheet in a single operation with the number of parts produced controlled by the size of the individual components. Additional oven capacity has been added to accommodate greater throughput. The number of components that can be produced in a burnout cycle is controlled by the size of the part. The added oven capacity has raised the daily throughput capability as described in the chart below. Programmable ovens allow for a reproducible burn out cycle, leading to reduced variability in battery components.

Table 1: Vacuum Oven Capacity

	Previous	**Current**
Diameter (inches)	**Capacity (parts/day)**	**Capacity (parts/day)**
0.5	660	11000
1	240	4000
2	61	1050
3	27	450

3-Inch Diameter Battery Development

EPT has been working to demonstrate thin film component technology in an existing production battery. The battery design is driven by a series of large current pulses (>300 amps), necessitating a cell diameter of 3 inches to support the current draw. The current production battery is manufactured using pressed component technology. The limitations of pressing technology produce a battery with 8X to 10X capacity margin, depending on the component. This results in a battery that is oversized to accommodate the current manufacturing process.

Tape cast components provide the capability to remove a large portion of this excess capacity, resulting in a smaller, lighter battery with improved safety characteristics. The tape cast version of this battery is approximately 28% smaller by volume than the current production design while meeting the performance requirements for the battery.

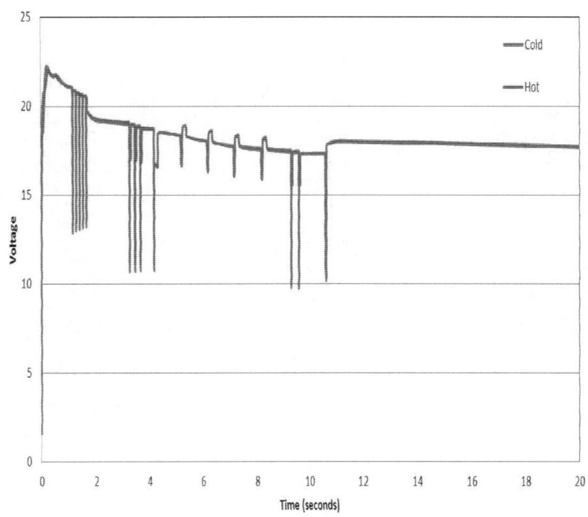

Figure 4: Prototype 3" Battery Test Data

This effort has progressed from 10-cell prototype batteries used during the development cycle to validate the battery design to the full scale 160 volt battery required to meet the performance specification. Early prototype batteries were manufactured using tapes produced on a laboratory-scale caster with manual processing techniques to produce components. These processes were then tailored for use with the production equipment and additional prototypes were built to demonstrate equivalence with the laboratory-scale performance. After successful completion of this step, the production equipment was used to cast and process tapes to build full scale batteries. These batteries met the design specification for this battery design across the full temperature range.

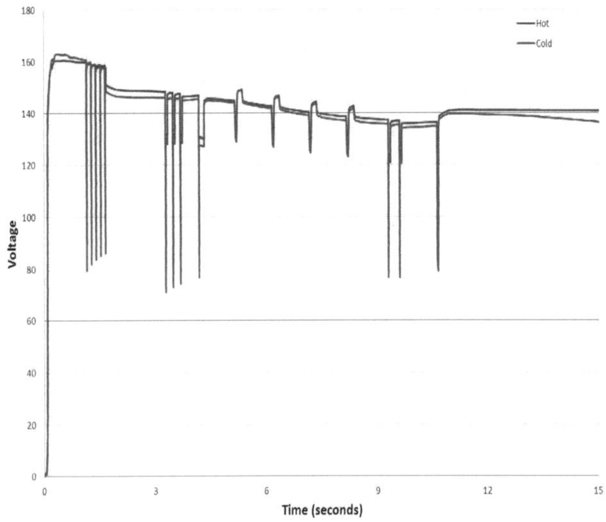

Figure 5: Full Scale 3" Battery Test Data

Figure 6: Production battery compared with thin component equivalent.

Non-Circular Battery Development

Thin film batteries with non-circular geometry were manufactured and tested to demonstrate the capability and to provide comparative data with equivalent circular cross-section batteries. A D-shaped geometry was chosen for this effort. Batteries were manufactured using thin film anodes, cathodes, and electrolyte/separators for both the circular and D-shaped configurations. The batteries were sized such that the surface area of the active components was equivalent for both shapes. Additionally, the cell heat balance and insulation design was the same for both designs to provide a fair comparison. Each battery contained ten cells.

The batteries were tested to two different load profiles to provide performance comparisons for high current/short life conditions and longer life/lower current conditions. The high current load profile included a ramp to 35 amps for approximately the first second of rise followed by a ramp down to the 6 amp base load. A 1.5 second excursion of 22 amps was included in the load profile. The low current profile included a one amp base load with five amp pulses every ten seconds to provide impedance checks.

Figure 7: D-Shaped Thermal Batteries

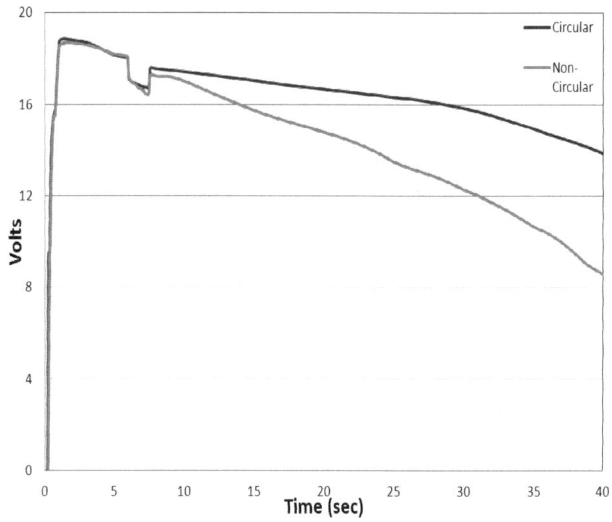

Figure 8: Test data for high current load profile

In both cases, the non-circular geometry batteries performed in an approximately equivalent manner to the circular equivalents for short time periods before tailing off much more rapidly. A portion of this effect is due to faster cooling at the corners of the D-shaped battery which effectively reduces the cross-sectional area of the cell. This effect does not account for all of the voltage reduction, however. It appears that some of this effect is likely due to build related issues, such as, edge alignment and other build quality issues that would need to be addressed before such a battery could be made for production purposes.

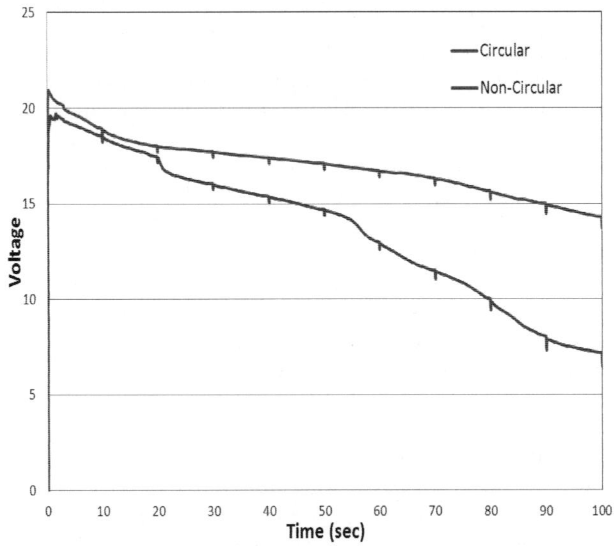

Figure 9: Test data for low current load profile

While non-circular geometry batteries may produce inferior performance to right circular cylinders of equivalent cross sectional area, there still could be applications where these designs are attractive. For instance, a non-circular geometry may allow for a larger cross-sectional area within the available space for the battery. This could provide enhanced performance, particularly early in life.

Other Efforts

EaglePicher is currently under contract to develop multiple thin film battery designs, primarily for space-limited, high power draw applications. These battery designs are primarily hybrid batteries containing thin film electrolyte with pressed components elsewhere or thin film electrolyte and cathode with pressed components elsewhere. Lessons learned from these development contracts coupled with our expanded manufacturing capabilities position EaglePicher to support production-level quantities of thin film batteries for demanding applications.

Summary

EaglePicher Technologies has continued its efforts to develop thin film thermal battery technology. These efforts have included scaling up and tailoring the existing laboratory-scale processes to function using production-scale equipment and demonstrating battery performance using multiple battery configurations including non-circular geometries.

Acknowledgments

EaglePicher would like to acknowledge the Missile Defense Agency and Marc Kenton of Erigo Technologies for support for these efforts through MDA contract HQ0147-13-C-7111.

Developing NanoFoil-Heated Thin-Film Thermal Battery

Michael Ding, Frank Krieger, and Jeffrey Swank
U.S. Army Research Laboratory
2800 Powder Mill Road, Adelphi, Maryland, USA, 20783
Michael.s.ding.civ@mail.mil

Abstract: *This report describes and discusses a series of experiments in which aluminum-nickel NanoFoil materials were used as the heat source for other thermal battery components, such as cathode, anode, and electrolyte, in the form of coated thin films, to develop a NanoFoil-heated thin-film thermal battery technology. This work culminated in the design, construction, and characterization of a complete, fully functional 12-cell NanoFoil-heated thin-film thermal battery prototype, which demonstrated a much faster rise in working voltage, a much lower internal gas pressure, a much shorter stack height, and a much greater flexibility in form factor, than the traditional pressed-pellet thermal batteries.*

Keywords: thermal battery; thin-film; NanoFoil; heat source; heat-sink; insulation; temperature; prototype; initiation; rise time; resistance; performance.

Introduction

Modern munitions require an increasing amount of onboard power and energy for enhanced functionality with diminishing volume and mass that can be allocated for the provision of such power and energy. This requirement poses a serious challenge to traditional thermal batteries, which have been one of the dominant means of meeting that requirement for the past half century [1, 2]. Current traditional thermal batteries are based on pressed pellet technology, being manufactured by cold pressing electrochemical and pyrotechnic powders into pellets and then assembling these pellets into a thermal battery stack, which is then sealed in a steel can with proper insulation. This technology allows only incremental improvements in term of volume, mass, and energy/power density, and does not provide packaging flexibility. The next generation of thermal battery technology centers around the thin-film approach, which would allow for the fabrication of much thinner and flexible battery components that can be cut and conformed to a wide variety of shapes. It also promises thin-film thermal battery devices with a faster rise, higher power, and smaller volume.

To develop thin-film thermal battery technology, cathodes, anodes, and electrolytes in the form of coated films on substrates have been developed, and electrochemical cells made of these films cut to the desired shapes have been tested. But to build complete, fully functional thin-film thermal battery devices, a compatible new heat source is required with drastically different traits from those of traditional pyrotechnic pressed heat pellets. One answer to this requirement is the adapted application of NanoFoil [3, 4], a trademarked metal foil made of alternating layers of aluminum and nickel, each with thickness typically of 100 nm or less [5, 6]. This foil material has been shown to possess many inherent advantages as a new heat source material for thermal batteries, especially for thin-film thermal batteries. These advantages include rapid propagation of reaction front, fast heat delivery, flexible form factor, mechanical integrity, inherent conduction of electricity, and safety against accidental initiation. It also presents many new technical challenges, such as reliable initiation, control of peak skin temperature, reduction of stack resistance, and thermal insulation and management [7–9]. This work aims at developing techniques and measures for realizing the potentials of the NanoFoil material as the new heat source for thin-film thermal batteries and overcoming its inherent technical barriers, with the ultimate goal of building a complete, fully functional NanoFoil-heated thin-film thermal battery prototype.

Experimental

NanoFoil discs for this work were custom-made by Indium Corporation according to our specification from a braze-free, sputtered aluminum (Al)-nickel (Ni) NanoFoil of 150 μm thickness, cut into 0.75-in-diameter discs with a special die. The delivered NanoFoil discs had an average weight of 0.22 g per disc, a reasonably smooth edge, somewhat limited flexibility, and metallic silver color. Thin-film components of anode/electrolyte and cathode were prepared by a coating method by the Advanced Power Sources Group at Sandia National Laboratories. These coated sheets, ranging from 5 to 11 mils in thickness, were cut with a precision die into discs of 0.75 in diameter. The assemblage and testing of the NanoFoil-heated thin-film thermal battery stacks from the above components was carried out at ARL, in a dry room with a typical dew point of –56 °C (0.074% relative humidity).

Figure 1 depicts the experimental setup for a 2-cell NanoFoil-heated thin-film battery stack, its initiation, its discharge, and the monitoring and recording of its rise time and temperature. The rise time value is determined as the difference between the time the battery voltage becomes stable under the load and the time the power is supplied to the match wire. Electrical discharge and testing was done with a Maccor 4300 system, with a discharge schedule of a constant current, typically 142 mA, superimposed with a –42-mA, 10-ms current pulse every second. The current pulse was applied so that the internal resistance of the battery could be calculated from the current pulse and the voltage response. The voltage changes on the match wires, the battery terminals, and the thermocouple terminals were measured and recorded with a high-speed data acquisition system at the sampling rate of 10,000 S/s.

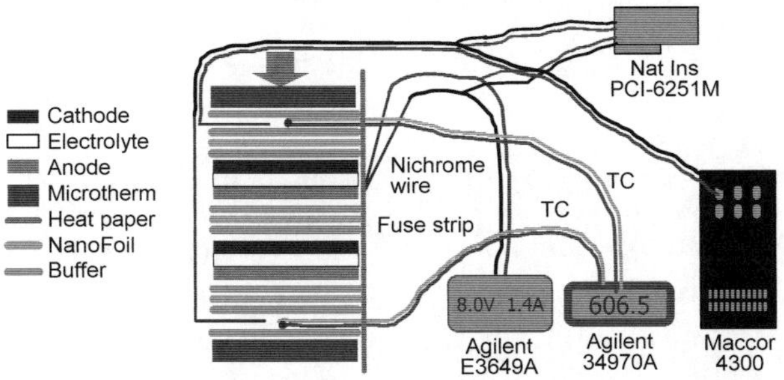

Figure 1. A schematic for the discharge setup and the electrical and thermal characterization of a 2-cell NanoFoil-heated thin-film thermal battery stack

Collection of gases generated by a 12-cell NanoFoil-heated thin-film thermal battery stack was carried out in a specially designed test fixture. The hermetic seal was achieved by using silicone gaskets between the fixture cover and body for passing the match wire leads and battery leads from inside the fixture to the outside. A copper tube was then connected to the connecting port, the other end of which was connected to a manifold for fixture evacuation, gas collection, and pressure monitor. After evacuating the fixture, the battery stack was initiated and gas samples were collected at different times, which were subsequently removed and analyzed using gas chromatography.

The making of the prototype NanoFoil-heated thin-film thermal battery proceeded according to the following procedure. The electrode was made from 3-mil-thick, 0.75-in-diameter stainless steel disc by spot-welding to it a strip of stainless steel of same thickness as the electrode lead. After attaching a match wire with a piece of heat paper at the top of the stack, the whole stack was transferred to a mechanical press and compressed with a pressure of about 100 lb. A piece of heat paper was then attached to the side of the stack with a piece of glass tape, the upper end of the fuse strip in firm contact with the piece of heat paper in touch with the match wire. The whole stack was then wrapped tightly with about 10 layers of glass tape for thermal insulation and mechanical stability. The pair of battery electrode leads and the pair of match leads were then connected to the properly designated posts on the header by spot-welding. The battery stack was then lowered into the battery can, the header was pushed into the can until the tops of the header and the rim of the can were flush, and the case was hermetically sealed with a Miyachi Unitek laser welder.

Results and discussion

Heat-Sink Effects and Their Mitigation: As shown in figure 2, conditions of thermal insulation on the stack ends have pronounced effects on the performance of the battery stacks. This is mainly due to the geometric nature of the thin-film thermal battery stacks, which in most cases will have much higher values of diameter-to-thickness ratio than the conventional pressed-pellet thermal battery stacks. As shown in figure 2 (top plot), provision of end-heating by the addition of one more NanoFoil heating stack to each end of the 12-cell NanoFoil-heated thin-film thermal battery stack prolonged the runtime of the stack to about 50 s from 30 s for a similar stack without the end-heating. The bottom plot of figure 2 plots stack resistance values calculated from the current-voltage pulses in the top-plot curves, which shows the two stacks to have similar stack resistances in their respective operation ranges.

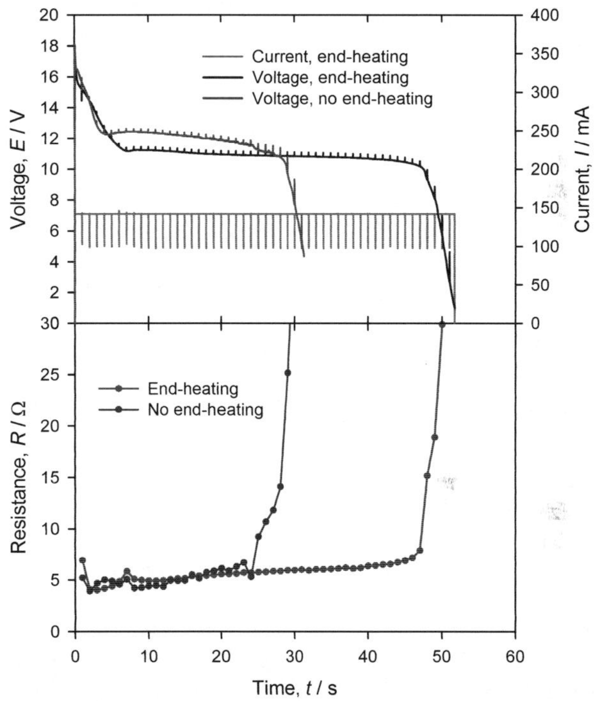

Figure 2. Comparison of voltage-time (top plot) and resistance-time (bottom plot) curvesfor two 12-cell NanoFoil-heated thin-film thermal battery stacks, one with end-heating and one without, as differentiated by the legends in the plots

Gases Generated by a 12-Cell NanoFoil-Heated Thin-Film Thermal Battery Stack: Gases generated inside the case of a thermal battery are known to be detrimental to the operation of the thermal battery. Moderate amounts of generated gases, especially the lighter components such as H_2, contribute to the heat conduction from stack core to the case, thus shortening the runtime of the battery. Higher amounts would generate excessive pressure to deform or bulge the case. Excessively high amounts would even rupture a glass-to-metal seal around an electrode and cause the battery to vent, thus creating a hazardous situation. The gases generated by a 12-cell NanoFoil-heated thin-film thermal battery stack were less than moderate. As shown in table 1 for the results of gas analysis for the stack, the total pressure inside the fixture was around 100 Torr, which is much lower than that inside thin-film thermal batteries of other technologies, even lower than that inside a typical traditional pressed-pellet thermal battery. This low pressure of gas is not expected to contribute greatly to the heat loss mechanisms of the thermal battery, even though the main component of the generated gas was H_2 according to the analysis. Furthermore, this low pressure is reflected in the completely un-deformed, un-bulged battery case after the initiation and discharge of the battery, as was visually observed.

Table 1. Gases generated by a 12-cell NanoFoil-heated thin-film thermal battery stack

Sample	Total Pressure /Torr	H_2	O_2, N_2	CO	CH_4
First	100.7	80.6	0	17.2	2.2
Second	100.2	68.6	13.1	14.0	4.3

A NanoFoil-Heated Thin-Film Thermal Battery Prototype: All the efforts described in the preceding sections eventually led to the design and construction of a prototype 12-cell NanoFoil-heated thin-film thermal battery. The selection of the 12-cell design for the prototyping was a compromise between limiting the material cost of the prototype stacks and demonstrating the benefits of building multi-cell stacks with thin-film electrochemical components and NanoFoil as the heat source.

As plotted in figure 3, the prototype battery performed well under the current load of 142 mA (equivalent to 50 mA/cm^2). The runtime of 50 s was satisfactory considering the limited heat contents of the NanoFoil discs and the short-time nature of the targeted applications. The other discharge properties, such as stack resistance, voltage plateau, and the ability to carry the current load, were also good. The voltage-time curves of figure 3 give a rise time of about 130 ms, a significant improvement over the earlier 12-cell stacks and over other technologies. This can be clearly seen in figure 4, which plots together the rise time curves of the prototype battery with two other batteries, one with the pressed-pellets for the anode and cathode-electrolyte and a pyrotechnic heat source, and one with anode and cathode-electrolyte pellets and NanoFoil discs as the heat source.

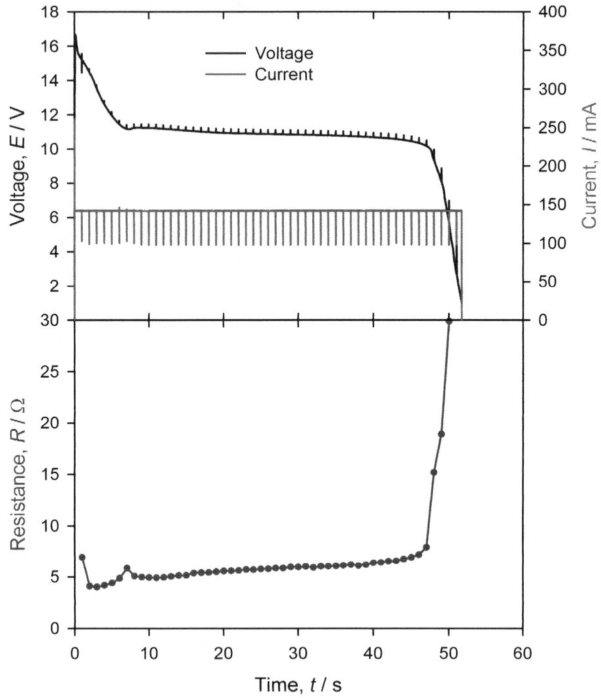

Figure 3. Discharge performance (top plot) of the prototype NanoFoil-heated thin-film thermal battery device and its stack resistance-time curve (bottom plot)

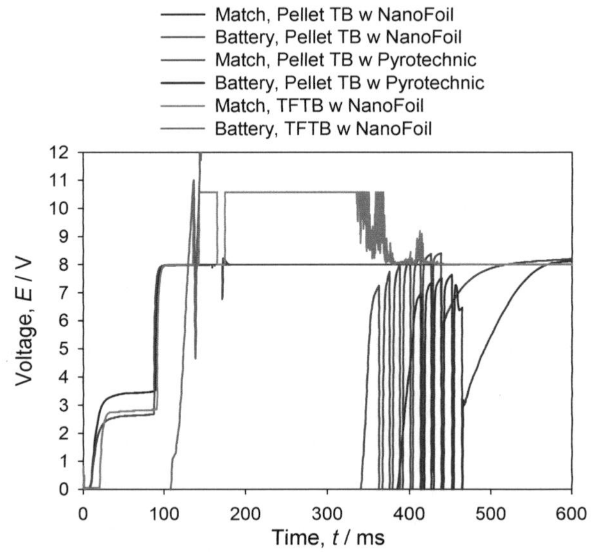

Figure 4. Improvements in rise time of the prototype NanoFoil-heated thin-film thermal battery device over a traditional pressed-pellet thermal battery and a NanoFoil-heated pressed-pellet thermal battery

Conclusions

A 12-cell NanoFoil-heated thin-film thermal battery was prototyped for the first time, which upon initiation and discharge demonstrated good operational performance. The rise time of the prototype was 130 ms, a significant improvement over the earlier 12-cell stacks and over other technologies. The runtime of 50 s was reasonably long considering the limited heat contents of the NanoFoil discs and the short-time nature of the targeted applications. The other discharge performance properties were also satisfactory, such as stack resistance, voltage plateau, and the ability to carry the current load.

A number of factors in the design of the prototype were found to be critical for the performance of the battery device. End-heating was found to significantly prolong the runtime by efficiently reducing the heat-sink from the stack into the end insulation on account of the high diameter-to-thickness ratios of the thin-film thermal batteries. The position of the match wire on the heat paper fuse strip was found to be effective in affecting the overall rise time of the stack; the shorter length of the reaction path in the fuse strip invariably led to a shorter rise time, as the reaction propagation speed in the heat paper is about two orders of magnitude smaller than in the NanoFoil.

The gases generated by the NanoFoil-heated thermal battery stack were found to be in much lower quantities than those generated by the traditional thermal batteries and by batteries with other technologies. Other benefits of the NanoFoil-heated thin-film thermal battery technology included flexibility in form factor, as all the components in the stack—cathode, anode/electrolyte, NanoFoil, and buffer—can be cut into any desired shapes, and reduced height of the stack, as all the necessary components in a NanoFoil-heated thin-film thermal battery stack are significantly thinner than their counterparts in the traditional pressed pellet thermal battery stack.

Acknowledgements

We thank the Office of the Secretary of Defense and the Joint Department of Defense (DOD)/Department of Energy (DOE) Munitions Technology Development Program for their financial and programmatic support, and Mr. Chris Janow in particular for his vision, efforts, and encouragement in the formulation, setup, and management of this program. We thank the Advanced Power Sources Group of Sandia National Laboratories for their collaboration in this program and the quality materials and components they supplied to us. We also thank many people at the U.S. Army Armament Research, Development, and Engineering Center for their support and collaborations, both past and present, which have helped the inception and growth of this program.

References

1. Lamb, C. M. in: Linden's Handbook of Batteries, 4th ed.; Reddy, T. B.; Linden, D., eds.; McGraw-Hill Companies, Inc., New York, 2011, p. 36.1.
2. Guidotti, R. A., and Masset, P. J., Power Sources 2006, 161, 1443.
3. Ding, M. S., Krieger, F. C., Swank, J. A., Poret, J. C., McMullan, C. W., and Chen, G., "Use of NanoFoil as a New Form of Heat Source in Thermal Batteries," ARL-TR-6141; U.S. Army Research Laboratory: Adelphi, MD, 2012.
4. Ding, M. S., Krieger, F. C., Swank, J. A., Janow, C. W., Delnick, F. M., and Branson, E. D., Proc. 45th Power Sources Conference, Las Vegas, NV, June 11–14, 2012, p. 623.
5. Jayaraman, S., Knio, O. M., Mann, A. B., and Weihs, T. P., J. Appl. Phys. 1999, 86, 800.
6. Gavens, A. J., Van Heerden, D., Mann, A. B., Reiss, M. E., and Weihs, T. P., J. Appl. Phys. 2000, 87, 1255.
7. Ding, M. S., Krieger, F. C., Swank, J. A., Poret, J. C., Chen, G., and McMullan, C. W., Proc. 43rd Power Sources Conference, Philadelphia, PA, July 7–10, 2008, p. 635.
8. Ding, M. S., Krieger, F. C., Swank, J. A., Poret, J. C., McMullan, C. W., and Chen, G., Proc. 43rd Power Sources Conference, Philadelphia, PA, July 7–10, 2008, p. 615.
9. Ding, M. S., Krieger, F. C., Swank, J. A.; McMullan, C. W., Chen, G., and Poret, J., Proc. 43rd Power Sources Conference, Philadelphia, PA, July 7–10, 2008, p. 377.

New Macroporous Ceramic Separator Pellets for Use as Thermal Battery Separator Layers

Christine Roberts, Lisa Mondy, Anne Grillet, Melissa Soehnel, David Barringer, Christopher Diantonio, Tom Chavez, Lindsey Evans, David Ingersoll
Sandia National Laboratories
PO Box 5800, Albuquerque, NM, USA, 87185-0346

Abstract: *We show that it is possible to manufacture strong macroporous ceramic films that can be backfilled with salt electrolyte to form rigid separator pellets suitable for use in thermal batteries. Two new ceramic tape casting processes are developed to mass-produce sintered magnesium oxide scaffolds with connected porosities of over 80% by volume. The effects of processing parameters on quality measures such as porosity and mechanical strength are quantified. These sintered ceramics have sufficient mechanical strength for battery applications and large porosities to allow efficient ionic transport. Methods to imbibe molten salt electrolyte into the sintered ceramic scaffold are also demonstrated. Discharge profiles of single cells including the new ceramic separators show that our first generation pellets perform as well or superior to traditional pressed separators. We believe that these separators are an improvement over traditional technology in terms of production cost and mechanical and discharge performance.*

Keywords: Molten salt batteries; Separator; Magnesium oxide; Porous ceramics

Introduction

Porous, permeable and mechanically robust ceramic scaffolds are useful for a wide variety of applications including catalyst supports, filters for liquid metals, and high temperature thermal insulation [1,2]. Our intent is to demonstrate the feasibility of using a rigid, sintered magnesium oxide ceramic scaffold backfilled with electrolyte as a battery separator. A separator is placed between the cathode and anode of a battery to prevent electrical contact of the electrodes but allow the transport of ionic charge carriers needed to complete the electrochemical circuit. Ceramic separators could allow safe operations of lithium ion batteries at higher temperatures. In molten salt batteries, a ceramic separator that is tape cast, sintered, and then backfilled with electrolyte will potentially have lower manufacturing costs and higher mechanical strength than current pressed-pellet technologies. Furthermore, the final shape of the separator could be versatile. The challenge is to create a highly porous ceramic scaffold that will meet the complex materials compatibility requirements of a battery system including wetting properties, dimensional stability, pore size and connectivity, and electrical resistance.

A quality battery separator has high electrical insulating properties to prevent short circuits, yet has high ionic mobility. Ionic resistance is both a function of the separator thickness and ionic transport through the material. Traditionally, the ionic resistance is measured using electrical impedance spectroscopy (EIS). The ratio of the resistivity of the separator to the resistivity of the electrolyte alone is termed the MacMullin number, N_m, which is a material property that takes into account both the tortuosity and the porosity of the material [3]. For perspective, common lithium ion battery separators have MacMullin numbers of 6-12 [4].

We report a method of producing highly porous MgO ceramics with commercially relevant MacMullin numbers by tape casting destabilized suspensions of MgO. When magnesium oxide is added to water, a hydrolysis reaction occurs producing magnesium hydroxide, also known as brucite, $Mg(OH)_2$, and increasing the pH of the suspension ($MgO + 2H_2O \leftrightarrow Mg(OH)_2 + OH^-$). As the suspension nears the brucite isoelectric point of pH 11 [5], the particles destabilize, aggregate, and form a fractal gel. When dried, this gel is a porous, open structure. Sintering strengthens the ceramic scaffold and dehydrates the brucite to MgO. Many processing parameters influence the amount of brucite formation such as pH [6], drying time, and surface-active additives, which in turn affect the porosity and ionic conductivity of the separator. Samples prepared in this manner will be referred to as "gelled".

Another more traditional method for tape casting porous ceramics is to add a sacrificial polymeric powder into the tape cast slurry. Here, nonaqueous slurries are used to prevent hydrolysis of the MgO. The slurry is coated, dried, stacked to the desired thickness, and sintered. Upon sintering, the polymeric species is burned away leaving a porous ceramic material. Samples prepared as described will be referred to as "poreformer".

Here we describe these two methods of producing porous ceramics and their final properties including strength, the ability be backfilled by the LiCl/KCl eutectic electrolyte, and MacMullin number. The best candidates were then tested in single cell battery stacks.

Materials and Methods

Gelled Sample Preparation: Aqueous dispersions of 2.5 – 17.5 vol% MgO particles (Fisher Scientific) are ball milled in 0.1 M hydrochloric acid (1N, Fluka Analytical) with 10 mm zirconium milling media to break up aggregates and disperse the particles. Variable durations of ball milling were explored, ranging from 1 to more than 20 hours. Polymer binder, either 0.01- 0.05wt% gellan (CP Kelco), or 0.01 wt% polyvinyl alcohol (PVA) (100,000 g/mol, 87% hydrolyzed, Fisher Scientific), is sometimes added to prevent cracking on drying. Samples are tape cast by hand on a silicone coated Mylar substrate using a blade coater with gaps of 2, 1, and 0.5 mm or cast into Teflon molds (3 cm diameter, 3-6 mm thick). The samples are either dried quickly at ambient conditions (drying time < 12 hr), or dried more slowly, either covered with a tray or dried in a desiccator over a saturated aqueous potassium chloride solution to control relative humidity at 84% at 25°C.

Once dry, the samples are removed from the substrate and sintered in a furnace (Thermolyne 46200) above a light dusting of MgO to aid in reducing shrinkage stress. Organic species burnout, including polymer binder and loss of chemically absorbed water is accomplished with a 2 hr hold at 650 °C, and then the samples are ramped to a final sintering temperature of 1400 °C over 12 hrs, with a 12 hr hold at temperature. Despite significant shrinkage during sintering, final tape cast samples are flat with thicknesses as low as 0.3 mm. Sample thickness was limited by the green sample strength. The sintered tape is then laser cut into circular disks with a 400 Watt 1060nm EDI CO2-Laser; model G-150 (Tucson, AZ).

Poreformer Sample Preparation: Porous MgO discs were prepared utilizing a sacrificial poreformer, poly-tetrafluoroethylene (Shamrock Technologies, Inc., MicroFLON 124-T4, mean particle size = 16-30μm) MgO (Alfa Aesar, Magnesium Oxide, 99.95%, -325 mesh powder) and Ferro B73305 binder system (Solvents: toluene/ethanol; Binder: 22.4% polyvinyl butyral terpolymer; Plasticizer: dioctyl phthalate) with KD-1 polyester/polyamine copolymer dispersant (Croda).

Several volume percent loadings of poreformer are prepared for comparison, including, 40 vol%, 50 vol%, and 70 vol% (percent ratio of total poreformer to total solids). The MgO and poreformer in the desired ratio is milled in a baffled Nalgene bottle with 5 mm diameter YSZ (yttria-stabilized zirconia) milling media and toluene using a turbula mixer. The milled mixture is then added to a pre-mix of the binder system, dispersant and milling media in a baffled Nalgene bottle and ball milled for at least 72 hours on a roller mill. The ball-milled slip is then passed through a three-roll mill, filtered through a sieve and de-aired in a vacuum chamber. The slip is then tape cast using a 14" wide aluminum double doctor blade fixed on a granite surface plate (HED International Inc., Labcast table top tape caster, Model TC-71LC). The underbed temperature controller and air-heater controller are maintained at 30°C. The slip is tape cast onto a silicone coated Mylar substrate using a doctor blade gap thickness of 356 μm for the reservoir blade and 279 μm for the casting blade at 10 cm/min. The initial dry green thickness of the tape is approximately 80-90μm. The sintered tape is laser cut into circular disks as above.

Sample Characterization: Both green and sintered ceramics are imaged with scanning electron microscopy (SEM) using a Zeiss Ultra Plus FESEM and a FEI Quanta 3d FEG. The final density of a sintered sample is measured by estimation of the sample dimensions and weight (Mettler Toledo, XS1003S). The fraction of open pore volume is estimated by an Archimedes test in which the fraction of pores that can be filled with water under a vacuum (-0.8 mPa gauge pressure) is measured. The strengths of sintered samples are tested with a TA.XTPlus texture analyzer (Texture Technologies) with a 2 mm diameter stainless steel punch. Additionally, particle size, degree of brucite conversion and slurry rheology were measured and are described in [7].

The ionic conductivity of the ceramic filled with an aqueous salt solution is measured using electrochemical impedance spectroscopy (EIS). Samples are filled with an aqueous electrolyte solution (0.85 M KCl conductivity standard, Fisher Scientific) and sandwiched between stainless steel electrodes. A Solartron SI 1287 potentiostat and a Solartron 1255B frequency response analyzer were used to impose an AC voltage (10mV amplitude) of varying frequency (0.01-300,000 Hz) across the separator. The resulting sinusoidal current is measured, and the complex impedance as a function of frequency is inferred. The resistance of the separator is measured at the frequency where the complex impedance is exactly in phase with the imposed AC voltage, with no detectable capacitance. Each resistance is measured more than three times and an average reported. The MacMullin number is calculated as the ratio between the resistivity of the separator and the electrolyte, and is always greater than one.

Samples are also filled with LiCl/KCl electrolyte (Alfa Aesar) by melting premeasured salt on top of the sample in a vacuum oven at 475 °C. Single cell stacks are then made containing one FeS_2 cathode, one LiSi anode and a novel ceramic separator. Stacks are discharged between heated metal platens within a dry and oxygen-free glove box. An 8 psi compressive pressure was added axially to the single cell during the test to simulate the expected pressure that the cell would experience in an activated battery. An Arbin Instruments BT2000 battery tester is used to apply either a constant current or a pulsed current load and monitor the resulting battery voltage. The constant current test consisted of an open circuit voltage hold for 60 seconds followed by a discharge at a 50 mA/cm^2 current density until the battery voltage was less than 0.5V. The pulse tests also started with a 60 second open circuit voltage hold followed by a current load of 50 mA/cm^2. Every two minutes the load is removed for 30 seconds, pulsed to a 200 mA/cm^2 load, rested at the open circuit voltage, and then returned to the steady current density of 50 mA/cm^2.

Results and Discussion:

Both gelled and poreformer samples are highly porous structures, as pictured in Figure 1. Gelled and poreformer samples have total porosities of up to 80 vol%. The pore size of the sintered poreformer samples is smaller than that of the gelled MgO samples. This is because in the poreformer samples the primary MgO particles make up the main network structure, whereas in the gelled MgO samples the network is made up of rod-shaped aggregates.

The poreformer sample porosity can be tailored by changing the amount of initial poreformer in the dispersion as well as the temperature that the samples were sintered. The sintering temperature also alters the percentage of porosity that is connected. The sintered porosity of gelled samples decreases with dispersion mill time and MgO dispersion concentration. These factors are discussed in [7].

As the total sintered porosity increases, the compressive strength of the sample decreases. Figure 2 shows the maximum load on a 2 mm diameter post that will not fracture the material. Each data point is the average of at least three measurements. Both gelled and poreformer samples are compared. In both cases, the fracture strength is a function of the sintered porosity of the material. Although the data are scattered, it seems as though gelled samples may have a greater fracture strength for a material of a given porosity.

A 2 kg load on a 2 mm diameter post corresponds to approximately 900 psi, which is above most closing forces that are used to package traditional thermal batteries. Therefore, it is unlikely that the sintered MgO network structures will collapse during battery activation. Furthermore, the addition of electrolyte salt to the magnesium oxide pore space will strengthen the samples at room temperature.

The permeability of the samples are first tested in simple EIS experiments using salt (KCl) water as the charge carrier. Figure 3 shows the MacMullin number of various samples with respect to the connected porosity of the sintered samples. These measured MacMullin numbers suggest that these materials are sufficiently permeable for battery separator applications.

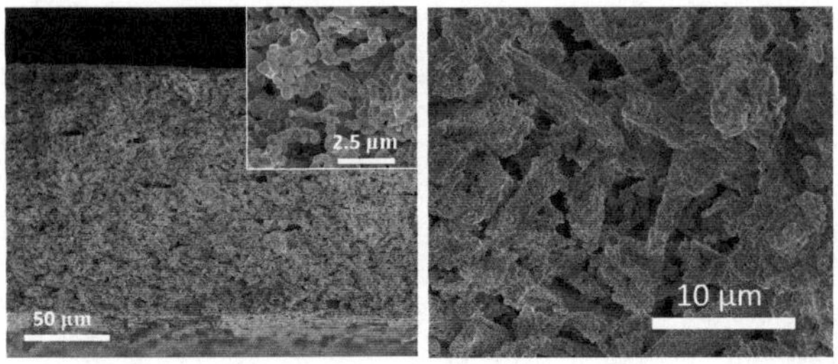

Figure 1. SEM images of cross sections of a 40% poreformer sample (left) and a gelled MgO sample (right)

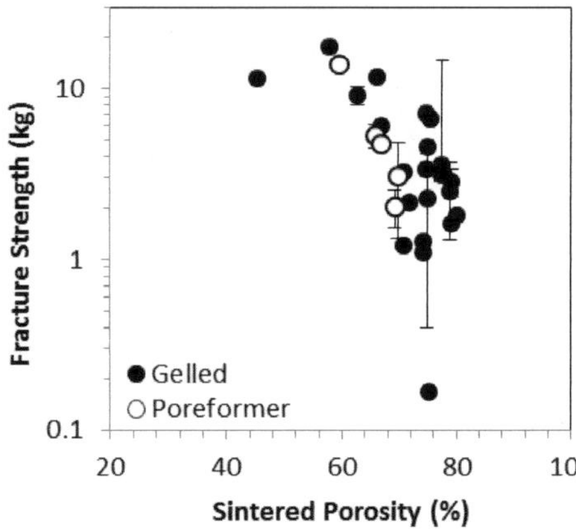

Figure 2. Fracture strength for porous MgO samples

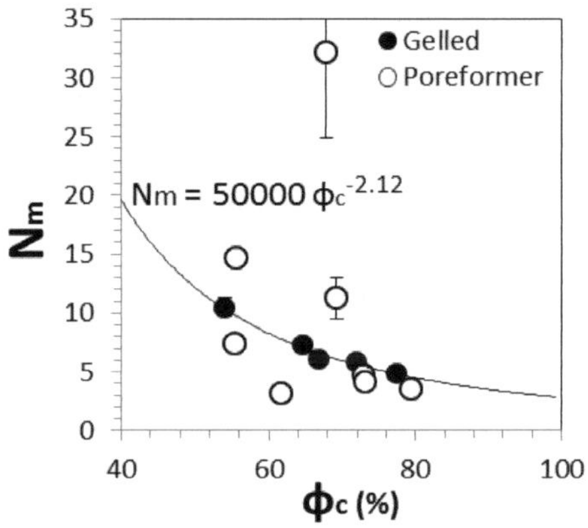

Figure 3. MacMullin numbers for porous MgO samples

Several methods for backfilling the samples with LiCl/KCl eutectic salt were explored, with the described method deemed to be the most effective. Approximately 70-100% of the connected porespace is filled with salt using this method. Occasionally excess salt remains on the top surface of the samples after filling, making definitive measurement of the fill amount by weight impossible.

Both constant current and pulsed current discharge profiles are measured for single cells of experimental separators as shown in Figures 4 and 5. A control, representing the performance of current pressed pellet technology, is also shown. The control single cells have the same anode and cathode formulations and dimensions.

In all materials, an initial voltage plateau at 1.9 V then decays to a second, lower voltage plateau. This is as expected for a thermal battery with the given chemistry. Large variation is seen in the performance of both the gelled and poreformer samples, primarily due to difficulties in filling the entire porespace with salt electrolyte.

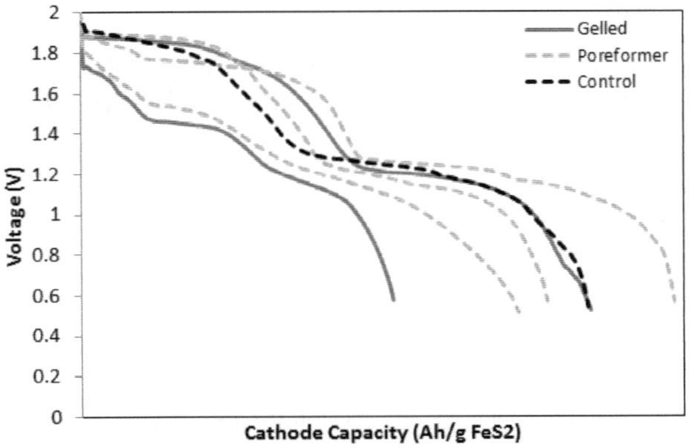

Figure 4. Constant current discharge at 500 °C for gelled and poreformer samples filled with LiCl/KCl electrolyte

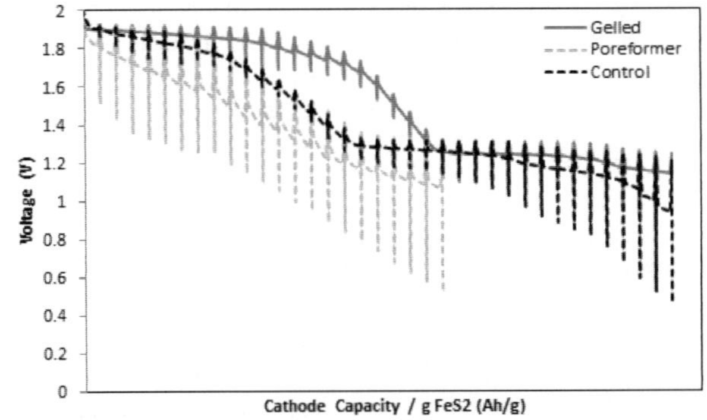

Figure 5. Pulsed current discharge at 500 °C for gelled and poreformer samples filled with LiCl/KCl electrolyte

Experimental separator thickness was also not controlled and varied between 0.45 and 1.5 mm, with the control separator having a thickness of 0.42 mm.

Examples of both novel ceramic separators were able to maintain an initial voltage plateau for a greater amount of cathode discharge as compared to the control separator. Pulsed current discharge curves indicate that the charge transport resistance of the poreformer samples is larger than the gelled MgO samples. This could be because the poreformer sample pore size is smaller and more tortuous. Gelled samples have a lower initial resistance than the control. This could be because although the control separator has a similar initial electrolyte volume fraction as the gelled sample, the unsintered control separators compress in thickness when activated, decreasing the amount of porespace in the MgO network available for charge transport. Further experiments are necessary to definitively report on the performance of these experimental ceramic separators.

Conclusions

Both gelled and poreformer ceramic separators are highly porous structures with porosities and permeabilities that allow charge transport sufficient for battery applications. Because these structures are sintered, their compressive strength is increased compared to current pressed pellet technology. Neither sintered ceramic separator is expected to compress upon activation, so the porespace in the MgO network will remain after melting of the electrolyte. Initial single cell discharge tests were promising, motivating future full-battery discharge experiments.

Acknowledgements

The authors would like to acknowledge helpful discussions with Karen Waldrip and Chris Apblett. Bob Fox, Michael Russell, Adrian Wagner, and Lindsey Hughes also provided laboratory help. This research is supported by the Laboratory Directed Research and Development program at Sandia National Laboratories. Sandia National Laboratories is a multi-program laboratory managed and operated by Sandia Corporation, a wholly owned subsidiary of Lockheed Martin Corporation, for the U.S. Department of Energy's National Nuclear Security Administration under contract DE-AC04-94AL85000.

References

1. Nettleship, I., "Applications of Porous Ceramics,"*Key Engineering Materials*, vol. 122-124, pp. 305-324, 1996.
2. Studart, A.R., U. T. Gonzenbach, E. Tervoort , L. J. Gauckler, "Processing Routes to Macroporous Ceramics: A Review," *Journal of the American Ceramic Society*, vol. 89, no. 6, pp. 1771-1789, 2006.
3. MacMullin, R.B., Muccini, G.A.,"Characteristics of porous beds and structures." AIChE J. vol 2, pp 393–403, 1956.
4. Arora, P., Zhang, Z.J., "Battery separators." Chem. Rev. vol 104,pp 4419–4462, 2004.
5. Pokrovsky, O.S., Schott, J., "Experimental study of brucite dissolution and precipitation in aqueous solutions: surface speciation and chemical affinity control." Geochim. Cosmochim. Acta vol 68, pp 31–45, 2004.
6. Phillips, V.A., Kolbe, J.L., Opperhauser, H., "Effect of pH on the growth of $Mg(OH)_2$ crystals in an aqueous environment at 60°C." J. Cryst. Growth vol 41, pp 228–234, 1977.
7. Mondy, L.A. et al., "New Composite Spearator Pellet to Increase Power Density and Reduce Size of Thermal Batteries", SAND2013-9787, Sandia National Laboratories, 2013.

Electrolyte Mobility within Molten Salt Batteries

Anne M. Grillet[*], Daniel E. Wesolowski[‡], Ashley N. Allen[‡], Christine C. Roberts[*], Lisa A. Mondy[*], Bonnie McKenzie[†], Richard P. Grant[†], Scott A. Roberts[*], Mario J. Martinez[*] & Jonathan R. Clausen[*]

[*]Engineering Sciences Center
Sandia National Laboratories
Albuquerque, NM 87185

[‡]Power Sources Technology Group
Sandia National Laboratories
Albuquerque, NM 87185

[†]Materials Science & Engineering
Sandia National Laboratories
Albuquerque, NM 87185

Abstract: *The movement of electrolyte during activation and operation of a molten salt battery is studied using bromine as a tracer element. Electron microscopy and spectroscopy measurements of bromine concentration within the single cell for various operating times are examined to track the movement of the electrolyte during activation and operation. We are able to elucidate the process of electrolyte transport from the separator into the electrodes and also probe the ionic permeability within the battery.*

Keywords: molten salt batteries; electrolyte; scanning electron microscopy; microprobe.

Introduction

The electrolyte within a molten salt battery is crucial to enable ionic conductivity of lithium ions while providing electrical separation of the battery electrodes [1]. Molten salt batteries are unusual power sources in that the electrolyte is solid during manufacture and storage of the batteries and is only allowed to distribute once the batteries are activated and the electrolyte melts.

Molten salt batteries are typically manufactured from pressed powder pellets [1]. The majority of the electrolyte begins in the separator layer but some is generally included in the cathode and sometimes also in the anode. Each of these layers contains some void space depending on the pressed density. On activation and melting of the electrolyte, molten salt batteries commonly experience stack relaxation [2]. An open question is what becomes of the electrolyte during this process. Infiltration of electrolyte into the electrodes reduces internal impedance of the battery, but excess electrolyte could cause collapse or shorting of the cells [2].

Performance of molten salt batteries has been extensively studied by measuring the internal resistance of the battery. One element of the internal resistance is due to the ionic conductivity of the electrolyte but other factors also contribute to the internal resistance. For example, only regions of the battery which are wetted by the electrolyte will be accessible to the ions. Regions which are fully saturated by electrolyte will have lower internal resistance than regions where residual voids remain. The internal structure of the battery electrodes means that the lithium ions must take a complex path as they move from the anode to the cathode. A significant fraction of the internal resistance of a molten salt battery is due to restriction of ion mobility. But direct measurement of the porous flow properties is challenging because the final structure is not set until after activation and stack relaxation and the environmental requirements (moisture sensitivity, high operating temperatures, etc.) are demanding.

A novel approach is to directly visualize and quantify the internal diffusion and movement of electrolyte and ions within molten salt batteries. Using several scanning electron microscopy (SEM) techniques, several key elements of electrolyte distribution and mobility can be investigated. The introduction of tracer ion into individual layers allows electrolyte movement to be tracked as a function of time. Ionic diffusion within the separator and electrodes can be quantified. These experiments will provide inputs for computational models being developed to predict the impact of electrolyte distribution on battery performance.

Methods and Materials

Studies were performed on a common molten salt battery configuration consisting of iron disulfide cathode, lithium silicon anode and a separator containing a magnesium oxide binder and electrolyte. Two electrolytes were used. The first was a eutectic of 45wt% lithium chloride and 55wt% potassium chloride with a melting point of 352˚C [3]. The second was a three component mixture of 12wt% lithium chloride, 36.5wt% lithium bromide and 51.4wt% potassium bromide with a melting point of 310˚C [4]. The cathode contained 25wt% of electrolyte binder mixture. For simplicity the anode was pressed without any added electrolyte ("dry"). Using scanning electron microscope (SEM) with energy dispersive spectroscopy (EDS), all of the elements except for lithium can be distinguished and their spatial distribution mapped.

Single battery cells were constructed and placed between the heated platens for specified amount of time ranging from 2 seconds to 900 seconds and then removed and placed on a brass block to quickly cool them. The metal platens were held at 500˚C within a dry and oxygen free glove box and a 12 psi compressive pressure was added axially to the single cell. A National Instruments high speed DAQ (USB-6251) was used monitor open circuit potential and temperature from a thermocouple placed in the center of the collector on the cell.

Quenched single cells were potted in polystyrene then epoxy for sectioning and water-free polishing in a dry room [5]. They were then imaged using a Zeiss Supra 55VP field emission gun scanning electron microscope (SEM). Energy dispersive spectroscopy (EDS) was performed with a Bruker quad Silicon Drift Detector with Bruker Esprit software to qualitatively map the distributions elements within the battery. Further analysis with a JEOL JXA-8530F HyperProbe Electron Probe Microanalyzer (EPMA) was performed to quantitatively measure chemical distributions. Data was taken using a 10μm beam size and spacing between points in the line scans was 10 μm. Samples were mounted in the SEM sample holder in a nitrogen purged glove bag and quickly transferred to the instrument chamber to minimize exposure to moisture in the air, but some water absorption was evident.

Results

Two series of tests will be reported varying the initial location of the bromine containing electrolyte. Figure 1 shows cross sections of several cells for various active times from these experiments. In the left column, the bromine containing electrolyte was placed in the separator and the cathode (right side) initially contained no bromine. In the right column, the bromine containing electrolyte was initially in the cathode and the separator started with no bromine. The anodes (left side) start with no electrolyte.

One early realization from these experiments regarded determination of an activation time for the single cell. Active times are reported relative to when the open circuit potential was reached (measured potential >1.8V) generally within 2 seconds of being placed on the heated platens. The open circuit potential is reached well before the thermocouple has reached the melting point of the electrolytes (c.f. Fig. 2). Thermocouple readings indicate that the single cells can take up to 100 seconds to reach thermal equilibrium with the preheated platens, but many of the tests were of shorter duration. Literature shows that molten salt viscosity is very low (similar to water) and only weakly dependent on temperature [3] so the non-isothermal effects will be neglected.

Figure 1b shows the single cell with a 2 second active time (The single cell was removed from the heated platens 2 seconds after achieving a voltage of 1.8V) but this portion of the single cell showed no evidence of the electrolyte having melted and all of the bromine was still located in the separator. All tests with active times greater than 12 seconds were fully melted as evidenced by separator shrinkage and lack of residual void space.

These images also provide a wealth of information about the mobility of the electrolyte. Looking at the transition from Figure 1b to c, there is a dramatic change in the

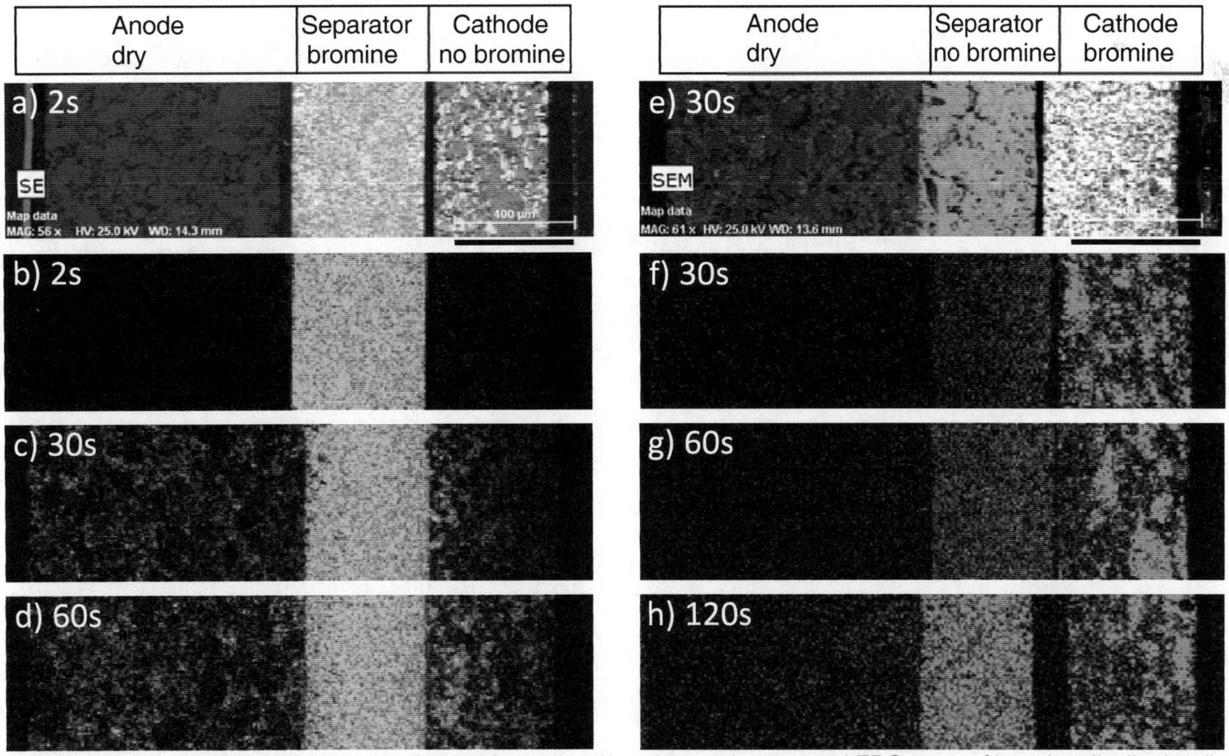

Figure 1: Images of single cells showing SEM (a&e) secondary electron images and EDS maps of bromine distribution (b-d & f-h). In left column, bromine was initially only in the middle separator. In column on right, bromine was initially only in the right cathode layer. Active times are: a) 2s, b) 2s, c) 30s, d) 60, e) 30s f) 30s, g) 60s, h) 120s. The bars represent 400microns.

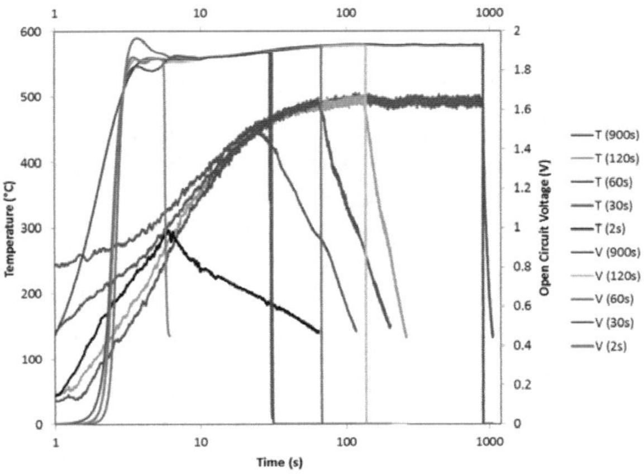

Figure 2: Temperature (left, darker lines) and open circuit voltage (right, lighter lines) as a function of time for 5 durations with bromine initially in the separator.

anode. Before the separator melts, there is no evidence of electrolyte in the anode as expected. After the separator melts, there is electrolyte throughout the anode. The anode was not fully flooded (there were still residual voids), but the electrolyte was evenly distributed across the entire anode. The distribution of bromine (as shown in Figure 1c-d) was similar to other electrolyte components such as potassium or chlorine. The dark regions apparent in in anode in in Figure 1c-d are due to the lithium silicon particles indicating the electrolyte does not penetrate the particles. The anode doesn't contain any electrolyte initially so these results suggest a fast wicking process of molten salt electrolyte drawn by capillary action to cover the surfaces of the anode. The wicking process draws enough electrolyte out of the separator to cause small voids (dark spots) in the separator. Inclusion of some electrolyte in the anode during manufacture would presumably reduce the wicking and not cause voids to form in the separator.

In addition to the fast wicking mechanism, there is also a slower diffusion process where the electrolyte in the separator and cathode mix together. In Figure 1c, the bromine has started to penetrate the cathode layer and the

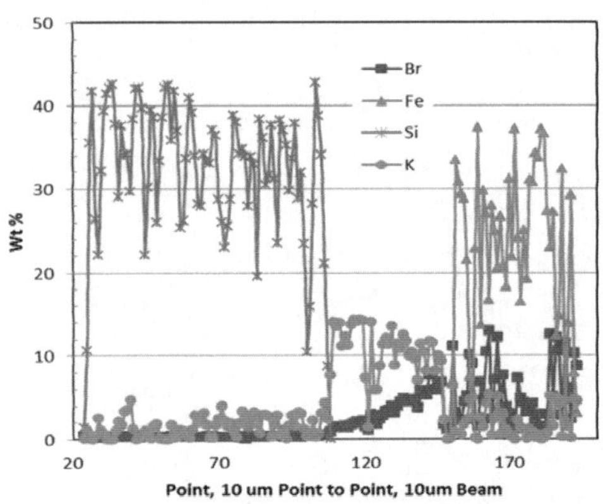

Figure 3: EPMA element concentrations across a cell with anode on the left. Bromine electrolyte is initially in the cathode on the right. Active time is 15s.

mixing progresses until the bromine is uniformly distributed throughout the battery. The converse is apparent in Figure 1f where the bromine has started to penetrate from the cathode into the edge of the separator. Once mixed into the separator layer, bromine also penetrates into the anode. Starting the bromine in the cathode allows separation of the wicking and diffusion transport into the anode.

Quantitative chemical element mapping across the single cells was performed using the Electron Probe Microanalyzer (EPMA). The analysis was complicated by the complex microstructure within the battery (c.f. Fig. 3) resulting in large spatial variations in measured elemental concentrations. As shown in Figure 1 a & e, both the anode and the cathode contain large particles and the electrolyte resides within the interstitial spaces. The cathode in particular is challenging because the blending of the iron disulfide and electrolyte is not uniform leaving electrolyte rich pockets and regions of primarily iron disulfide. The separator by contrast was reasonably uniform on the length scale of the EPMA measurement.

We have chosen to use a combination of line scans across the anode and separator (c.f. Fig. 3) and point-wise analysis in the electrolyte rich regions of the cathode to map the distribution of bromine and other elements. Additionally, the bromine concentrations were scaled with another component of the electrolyte in order to account for the variability in the fraction of electrolyte within the measurement volume. Potassium was selected for convenience. The bromine fraction is defined as $BF = \frac{\text{Br wt\%}}{\text{Br wt\%} + \text{K wt\%}}$. The starting value of the bromine fraction in the bromine rich electrolyte is 0.8.

Results showing the penetration of bromine into the neighboring layer are shown in Figure 4 with bromine moving from the separator into the cathode (a) and bromine moving from the cathode into the separator (b) as a function of distance from the interface between the two layers. Unfortunately the quantitative analysis for later times (120s-900s) in Figure 4a was troubled by water damage during transfer to the electron microscope which increased scatter in the data. We are able to see clear trends of bromine penetrating into the cathode (a) and separator (b). Once the battery activates and the electrolyte melts, the mixing in the interface region happens very rapidly. By 120s, there is no evidence of spatial gradients across the separator and cathode.

Figure 4 shows the average calculated bromine fraction as a function of time illustrating the rapid approach to equilibrium between the two layers. Within two minutes, the electrolyte between the two layers has completely mixed and the bromine is evenly distributed. Blue arrows on the right axis show the calculated final concentration

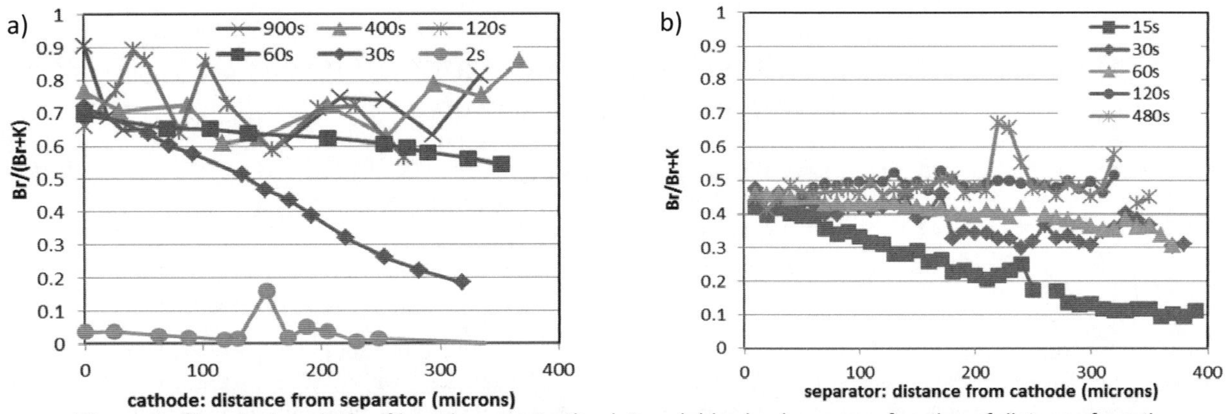

Figure 4: Chemical analysis of bromine penetration into neighboring layer as a function of distance from the cathode/separator interface: a) bromine penetrating into cathode; b) bromine penetrating into separator.

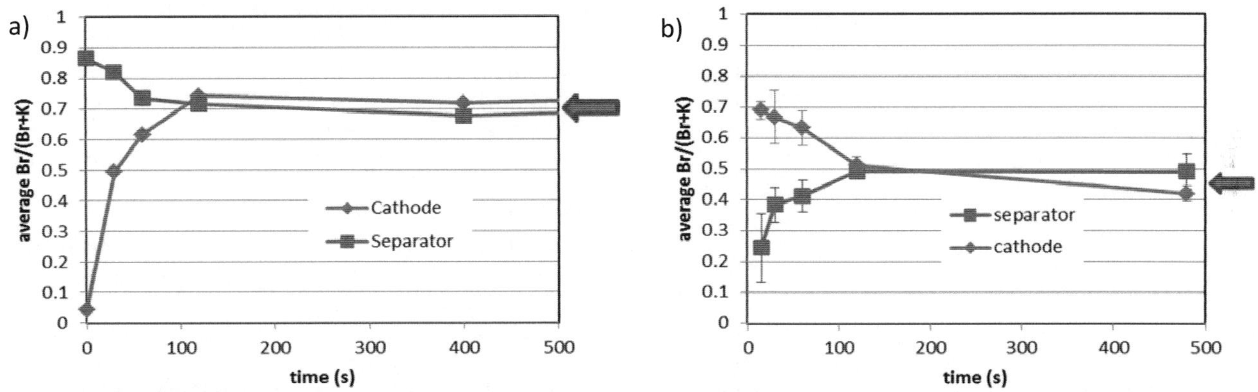

Figure 4: Average bromine fraction as a function of time: a) bromine starts in separator, b) bromine starts in cathode. The blue arrows show the expected final concentration and the error bars show one standard deviation.

after the electrolyte is well mixed. Both equilibrium concentrations measured agree well with the prediction.

Conclusions

We have presented a new method to analyze electrolyte mobility in molten salt batteries. There are clearly two mechanisms for electrolyte movement: 1) wicking where electrolyte is quickly drawn into the dry anode and 2) slower diffusion where electrolyte is mixed between layers. Despite the complex microstructure inside the battery elements, the electrolyte is well mixed within two minutes of activation due to the high permeability and high ionic conductivity of the molten salt electrolytes. These results will be used to populate porous flow models of thermal batteries in order to better understand their performance.

Acknowledgments

The authors gratefully acknowledge funding from the Joint Department of Defense/Department of Energy Munitions Technology Development Program. Sandia National Laboratories is a multi-program laboratory managed and operated by Sandia Corporation, a wholly owned subsidiary of Lockheed Martin Corporation, for the U.S. Department of Energy's National Nuclear Security Administration under contract DE-AC04-94AL85000.

References

1. Guidotti, R.A., and P. Masset, "Thermally activated ("thermal") battery technology: Part I: An overview," *Journal of Power Sources*, Vol. 161, pp. 1443-1449, 2006.
2. Masset, P., and R.A. Guidotti, "Thermally activated (thermal) battery technology: Part II: Molten salt electrolytes," *Journal of Power Sources*, Vol. 164, pp. 397-414, 2007.
3. Janz, G. J., R.P.T. Tomkins, C.B. Allen, J.R. Downey, Jr.,G.L. Gardner, U. Krebs, and S.K. Singer, "Molten Salts: Volume 4, Part 2, Chlorides and Mixtures," *Journal of Physical and Chemical Reference Data*, vol. 4, pp. 871, 1975.
4. Vissers, D.R., L. Redey, and T.D. Kaun, "Molten salt electrolytes for high-temperature lithium cells," Vol. 26(1-2), pp. 37-48, 1989.
5. Wesolowski, D.E., M.A. Rodriguez, B.B. McKenzie, and H.W. Papenguth. "Low-hazard metallography of moisture-sensitive electrochemical cells." Journal of Microscopy, 243, pp197–205, 2011.

Electrochemistry of the Lithium-Air Battery System Using Molten Nitrate Electrolytes

Melvin H. Miles
Department of Chemistry, University of LaVerne
LaVerne, CA USA 91750
Email: mmiles@laverne.edu

Abstract: The lithium-air battery system offers a theoretical energy density that rivals the energy density of gasoline. Nevertheless, many technological challenges block the road to the commercial development of this promising battery system. Most research on the lithium-air battery has centered on the use of organic liquid electrolytes as found in lithium-ion batteries. The use of low-melting molten nitrates such as $LiNO_3$-KNO_3 may solve major technological problems for lithium-air batteries as well as provide another pathway for the oxygen electrode reaction.

Keywords: electric automobile; electrode; melting point; oxygen; rechargeability; solubility; thermodynamics.

Introduction

The cell discharge reaction of the lithium-air battery involves the oxidation of lithium (Li) at the anode and the reduction of oxygen (O_2) at the cathode to form peroxide ($O_2^{=}$) or oxide ($O^{=}$) ions. The end products of the cell discharge are lithium peroxide (Li_2O_2) and/or lithium oxide (Li_2O). These cell discharge reactions can be expressed as $2\ Li + O_2 \rightarrow Li_2O_2$ and $2\ Li + ½O_2 \rightarrow Li_2O$. These two reactions yield standard cell potentials (E°) of 2.959 V and 2.908 V, respectively, and both cell reactions give high theoretical energy densities (11,425 Wh/kg and 11,231 Wh/kg, respectively) that rival the energy density of gasoline (1). The mass of oxygen is not included in these calculations because, as for the gasoline engine, oxygen is freely available from the atmosphere. The rechargeable lithium-air battery could extend the driving range of electric automobiles up to 500 miles between battery charges. Many technological challenges, however, block the road to the practical development of the lithium-air battery. These technical problems include the slow electrochemical kinetics for the reduction of oxygen at the cathode, the precipitation of insoluble lithium oxides in the pores of the air cathode, short battery lifetimes, and a low round-trip efficiency for the battery reactions (1).

The use of molten nitrate electrolytes such as $LiNO_3$-KNO_3 (eutectic mp=124°C) or $LiNO_3$-KNO_3-$CsNO_3$ (eutectic mp=97°C) may help to solve the major problems existing for lithium-air batteries. The higher operating temperatures alone will significantly increase the rate of the oxygen electrode reaction, the solubility of the lithium oxide products will likely increase, and the round trip efficiency is expected to improve. Another major advantage is that 60% of the atoms present in these nitrate melts are oxygen atoms, and these oxygen atoms can participate in the cathode reaction to form lithium oxides.

Molten Nitrate Systems

All types of batteries consist of three fundamental components: 1. an anode, 2. a cathode, and 3. a liquid or solid electrolyte. Any change in one of these three components results in a major change for the battery system. For example, a change in the electrolyte can completely change the chemistry and electrochemistry of the battery system as well as its operating temperature range and the electrochemical stability window.

Melt Composition: Previous work has shown that lithium nitrate ($LiNO_3$) must be a significant component of the nitrate melt in order to obtain a stable lithium anode (2). This is due to a protective Li_2O film that forms on the anode in nitrate melts that contain sufficient $LiNO_3$ (2). Recent studies have shown that sodium nitrate ($NaNO_3$) should be avoided due to the displacement reaction of sodium ions with lithium, $Na^+ + Li \rightarrow Na + Li^+$, to form the much more reactive sodium metal (3). Chloride ions in the melt should also be avoided because they can lead to an aggressive attack and corrosion of the protective oxide layer on the lithium anode (4). Furthermore, the use of molten nitrites such as KNO_2 in the electrolyte creates problems for the rechargeability of the lithium anode.

Various molten nitrate electrolytes have been investigated for possible applications in lithium cells (5). Molten nitrate electrolytes found to be suitable for use in the lithium-air battery system are presented in Table 1 .

Table 1 Molten Nitrate Eutectics Investigated.

Electrolyte	Mole %	Melting Point (°C)
$LiNO_3$-KNO_3-$CsNO_3$	37-39-24	97
$LiNO_3$-KNO_3	41-59	124
$LiNO_3$-$RbNO_3$-$CsNO_3$	64-29-7	145
$LiNO_3$-$CsNO_3$	60-40	170
$LiNO_3$-$RbNO_3$	66-34	180

Any of these listed compositions would be suitable for use as the electrolyte in the lithium-air battery, but the lower melting eutectics are preferable. Compositions other than these precise eutectic compositions can also be used. Note that the amount of $LiNO_3$ is at least 37 mole % and that no $NaNO_3$ is used. Nitrates of alkaline earth metals such as magnesium nitrate, $Mg(NO_3)_2$, and calcium nitrate, $Ca(NO_3)_2$, were also considered, but they offer no significant advantages in providing lower melting points or in most other properties for applications in lithium-air batteries. However, additions of small amounts of $Ca(NO_3)_2$ were found to increase the stability of the lithium anode.

Metal Oxide Solubilities: The protection of the lithium anode in molten nitrates depends on the low solubility of the oxides present on the lithium surface. Although experimental solubility measurements in molten nitrates are often lacking, ideal solubility calculations can yield useful predictions. Ideal solutions are found for liquids where all interactions are equal. This is a good approximation for oxides in molten nitrates where the metal cation is a component of the melt. Several ideal solubility calculations for metal oxides important for the molten nitrate electrolytes considered are presented in Table 2.

Table 2 - Ideal solubility of metal oxides in molten nitrates at 450 K (177°C).

Metal Oxide	X_1[a]	T_m(K)	ΔH_{fus}(kJ/mol)
CaO	$1.45x10^{-8}$	2886	80
Li_2O	$9.01x10^{-4}$	1711	35.6
K_2O	$1.81x10^{-2}$	1013	27
K_2O_2	$8.50x10^{-2}$	818	20.5
KO_2	$8.72x10^{-2}$	808	20.6
Rb_2O	$1.05x10^{-1}$	778	20
Cs_2O	$1.09x10^{-1}$	768	20

[a]Ideal solubility in mole fractions given by $\ln X_1=\Delta H_{fus}(T-T_m)/RTT_m$.

The required data was not available to include Li_2O_2 in Table 2, but the measured solubility of Li_2O_2 was significantly larger than for Li_2O in molten nitrates. Although the solubility of Li_2O is relatively small, the much smaller solubility of CaO would help to increase the stability of the lithium anode in molten nitrates, and this has been experimentally verified. The ideal solubility in molal units (moles/kg) is readily calculated from $m_1=11.374X_1/(1-X_1)$ for $LiNO_3$-KNO_3 at 450 K.

Thermal Stability of Molten Nitrates: Nitrate and nitrite based molten salts have been investigated as heat transfer fluids in high temperature solar power plants at operating temperatures above 500°C (6). Thermogravimetric measurements of single alkali nitrate salts including $LiNO_3$ and KNO_3 also show thermal stability up to 500°C (7). Therefore, excellent thermal stability is expected for molten nitrate electrolytes over the much lower proposed operating temperature range of 100°C to 200°C for the lithium-air battery system. It is interesting that the extensive research on solar thermal power plants has reported nitrate salt systems with melting points as low as 72°C (7), but these systems include $NaNO_3$ and $NaNO_2$ salts that would not be compatible with the lithium-air battery system.

Molten Nitrate Electrochemistry: The electrochemical reduction of molten nitrate mixtures containing $LiNO_3$ produces $LiNO_2$ and insoluble Li_2O as expressed by Equation 1.

$$2\,Li^+ + LiNO_3 + 2\,e^- \rightarrow LiNO_2 + Li_2O \qquad [1]$$

This reaction becomes blocked as insoluble Li_2O forms on the electrode surface. At more negative potentials, the reversible reduction of lithium ions occurs to form lithium metal

$$Li^+ + e^- \leftrightarrow Li \qquad [2]$$

The lithium formed is protected by a surface of lithium oxide that acts as a Solid Electrolyte Interface (SEI) and blocks further reaction of lithium with the molten nitrate electrolyte (2).

The electrochemical oxidation of molten nitrates produces colorless nitrogen monoxide (NO) and oxygen (O_2).

$$NO_3^- \rightarrow NO + O_2 + e^- \qquad [3]$$

This reaction has often been expressed with nitrogen dioxide (NO_2) as the product, but recent studies in an argon filled drybox did not show production of the brown NO_2 gas in contrast to experiments in an air atmosphere. Apparently, NO reacts with O_2 ($NO + \frac{1}{2}O_2 \rightarrow NO_2$) following the electrochemical reaction. It is interesting to note that the nitrogen atom is actually reduced in the anodic electrode reaction, but this is compensated by the loss of electrons for the oxygen atoms that form O_2 gas.

The electrochemical stability range for $LiNO_3$ is defined by Equations 2 and 3. The addition of these two reaction yields

$$LiNO_3 \rightarrow Li + NO + O_2 \qquad [4]$$

Thermodynamic calculations for this reaction at 450 K (177°C) yields $\Delta G° = 413.79$ kJ mol^{-1} and $E° = -4.2886$ V. This is close to the experimental electrostability window of about 4.5 V observed in molten $LiNO_3$-KNO_3 electrolytes (5).

The Lithium Anode in Nitrate Melts

The reversible performance of the lithium anode in molten nitrate electrolytes is critical for possible applications in a lithium-air battery system. The cyclic voltammogram trace presented in Figure 1 demonstrates the excellent reversibility of the lithium electrode reaction. This experiment used a cobalt wire working electrode (A=0.5 cm^2) and a Ni/NiO reference electrode in $LiNO_3$-KNO_3 at 200°C. The potential sweep rate was 50 mV/s. The reduction of $LiNO_3$ to form Li_2O (Equation 1) is the cathodic peak (B) at -1.1 V. The reversible lithium electrode reaction (Equation 2) is shown at the far left at a potential near -3.1 V. The rapid linear change in current with potential suggests that the current is controlled by Ohm's Law (E=IR) with an experimental resistance of 6.0 ohms. This resistance is close to the measured cell resistance. Although this experiment was conducted at a temperature above the melting point of lithium (mp = 180.50°C), the combination of the cobalt surface and the Li_2O protective film apparently immobilizes the liquid lithium. Electrochemical Impedance Spectroscopy (EIS) measurements indicate fast kinetics for the lithium electrode reactions with an exchange current density (i_o) of 10^{-2} A cm^2.

Similar studies were conducted on various electrode metals including Al, Ni, Fe, Mo, Ta, and Ti, and all gave good reversibilities for the lithium electrode reaction. For the Al electrode, the potential for the lithium electrode reaction was about 0.35 V more positive than with cobalt, and this suggests the formation of a Li-Al intermetallic compound with a ΔG of formation of about -34 kJmol^{-1} at 200°C. Lithium alloys and compounds with melting points
much higher than pure lithium are used in thermal batteries such as Li-Al and Li-Si. The Li-Al anode shows promise for use in the lithium-air battery because of its high melting point (718°C) and good stability.

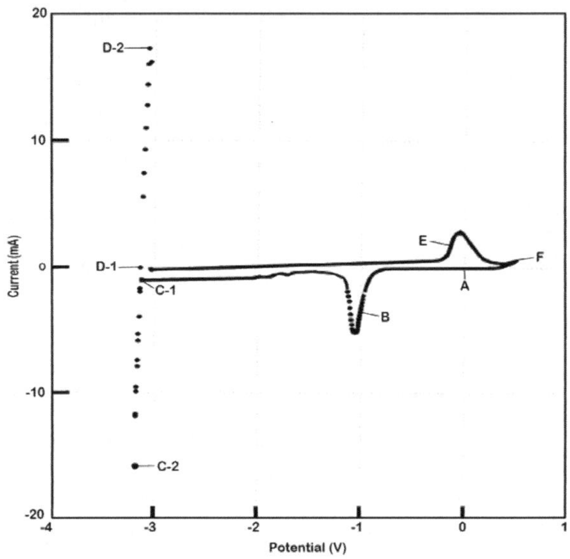

Figure 1. Cyclic voltammogram using a cobalt working electrode (A=0.5 cm^2) and a Ni/NiO reference electrode in $LiNO_3$-KNO_3 at 200°C.

The Oxygen Cathode in Nitrate Melts

Although more research is needed to fully characterize the oxygen electrode reaction in molten nitrates, it was observed in thermal battery studies that the reduction of oxygen created problems for electrode surfaces exposed to air. Therefore, most studies were conducted with fully submerged electrodes and with an atmosphere of argon. Other than expensive metals such as platinum, it is believed that nickel will provide the best catalytic surface for the reduction of oxygen in nitrate melts. The significantly higher temperatures of nitrate melts, in contrast to the use of organic liquids at room temperature, should greatly improve the kinetics for the oxygen electrode reaction. This may allow metal screens to be used as the cathode substrate rather than porous cathodes.

Another major advantage in using molten nitrate electrolytes is the fact that 60% of the atoms present in such electrolytes are oxygen atoms. These oxygen atoms may help to support the oxygen electrode reactions. The nitrate ions in these electrolytes exist in equilibrium with nitrite ions (NO_2^-) and oxygen (8), and this equilibrium, $NO_3^- \leftrightarrow NO_2^- + \frac{1}{2} O_2$, may help to support the oxygen electrode reaction. Carbon monoxide acts as a poison for electrode surfaces such as platinum and nickel, and this has been a problem for fuel cells. However, carbon monoxide reacts with nitrate melts to form the much less harmful carbon dioxide: $CO + LiNO_3 \rightarrow CO_2 + LiNO_2$.

Although the cyclic voltammogram shown in Figure 1 was obtained from an experiment using an argon atmosphere, it still provides insight regarding the oxygen electrode reaction. The anodic peak (E) near 0.0 V is the oxidation of Li_2O to form lithium ions and oxygen

$$Li_2O \leftrightarrow 2\,Li^+ + \tfrac{1}{2}O_2 + 2e^- \qquad [5]$$

The lithium oxide on the electrode surface is readily removed by this electrode reaction. It is expected that the reduction of oxygen, will begin at potentials slightly negative to the beginning of this anodic peak.

Nitrate Ion Pathway for Oxygen Reduction: Another major advantage for molten nitrate electrolytes for use in lithium-air batteries is that a completely different pathway for oxygen reduction is provided by the nitrate ions. This pathway is the reduction of $LiNO_3$ to form $LiNO_2$ and Li_2O (Equation 1) followed by the direct homogeneous reaction of the nitrite ion with oxygen represented by

$$LiNO_2 + \tfrac{1}{2}\,O_2 \rightarrow LiNO_3 \qquad [6]$$

The sum of Equation 1 and Equation 6 yields the oxygen reduction reaction at the cathode where Li_2O is the product (Reverse of Eq. 5). Although the thermodynamics of Equation 6 are favorable ($\Delta G° =$ -79.1 kJ mol^{-1}), catalysts may be needed to provide a sufficient reaction rate. Nitrogen dioxide has recently been reported as a catalyst for the conversion of $LiNO_2$ to $LiNO_3$ in the presence of oxygen (9). Also, a fast oxidation reaction of nitrite by dissolved oxygen has been reported in the tropospheric aqueous phase (10).

Summary

Although further research is needed, the use of molten nitrate electrolytes for the lithium-air battery system offers many advantages. These advantages include faster electrode kinetics, different solubilities for the lithium oxide products, a secondary source of oxygen contained in the electrolyte, and a novel nitrate ion pathway for the sluggish oxygen electrode reaction.

References

1. Jacoby, M., "Rechargeable Metal-Air Batteries", *Chemical and Engineering News*, Vol. 88, no. 47, pp. 29-31, 2010.

2. Miles, M.H., G.E. McManis, and A.N. Fletcher, "Effect of Temperature and Electrolyte Composition on the Lithium-Boron Alloy Anode in Nitrate Melts: Passivating Films on Solid and Liquid Lithium", *Electrochimica Acta*, Vol. 30, pp. 889-897, 1985.

3. Miles, M.H., A.A. Grumet, and K.W. Solomon, "Chloride-Free, Sodium Ion-Free, and Water-Free Thermal Battery Using Molten Nitrate Electrolyte", *U.S. Patent*, No. 8,039,138, October 18, 2011.

4. Miles, M.H., "Chloride-Free Thermal Batteries Using Molten Nitrate Electrolytes", *U.S. Patent*, No. 7,629,075, December 12, 2009.

5. Miles, M.H., "Electrochemistry of Molten Nitrate Electrolytes and Applications for High Voltages Lithium Cells", *Batteries and Supercapacitors*, Proceedings Vol. 2001-21, The Electrochemical Society, 2003, pp. 557-563.

6. Cordaro, J.G., "Chemical Perspectives on Alkali and Earth Alkaline Nitrate and Nitrite Salts for Concentrated Solar Power Applications", *Green*, Vol. 3, Issue 1, pp. 9-18, 2013.

7. Bauer, T., D. Laing, and R. Tamme, "Recent Progress in Alkali Nitrate/Nitrite Developments for Solar Thermal Power Applications", *Molten Salts Chemistry and Technology*, MS9, Trondheim, Norway, 5-9 June 2011, 10 pp.

8. Plambeck, J.A., "Fused Salt Systems", in *Encyclopedia of Electrochemistry of the Elements*, Vol. X, edited by A.J. Bard, Marcel Dekker, 1976, pp. 166-167 and 192-193.

9. Uddin. J., et al., "Lithium Nitrate as Regenerable SEI Stabilizing Agent for Rechargeable Li/O_2 Batteries", *Journal of Physical Chemistry Letters*, Vol. 4, pp. 3760-3765, 2013.

10. Takenaka, N., et al., "Fast Oxidation Reaction of Nitrite by Dissolved Oxygen in the Freezing Process in the Tropospheric Aqueous Phase", *Journal of Atmospheric Chemistry*, Vol. 29, Issue 2, pp. 135-150, 1998.

Wide Temperature and Safer Li-Ion Cell Development

Ramanathan Thillaiyan, Eric Quee, Wujun Fu, Jeff Dermott and Mario Destephen
EaglePicher Technologies LLC, an OMG company
3220 Industrial Road
Joplin, MO 64801
ramanathan.thillaiyan@eaglepicher.com

Abstract: *EaglePicher Technologies (EPT) has developed reduced flammable electrolyte without sacrificing the performance at higher rates while maintaining a wide operating temperature range. We demonstrated the electrolyte fire-retardant properties in bulk electrolyte as well as in vapor pressure tests. We demonstrated a wide-temperature Li-Ion cell with reduced flammable capability with superior cell performance in the operational temperature range from -40°C to +85°C. Further, we designed a safer Li-Ion cell and demonstrated cell safety under overcharge abuse conditions.*

Keywords: Li-Ion; safety; reduced flammable; electrolyte; wide temperature Li-Ion cell development

Introduction

One of the greatest challenges of modern society is to stabilize a consistent energy supply that will meet our growing energy demands [1]. Developing high-performance power generation and storage devices would be benefited in many industries such as consumer electronics, hybrid electrical vehicles and defense applications [2]. Li-Ion battery (LIB) technology is the front runner that provides high energy density rechargeable batteries as compared to conventional Ni-Cd and Ni-metal hydrides [3]. Rechargeable LIB with liquid electrolytes was developed by Sony Corporation in 1991 [4]. Since then LIB are extensively used in various portable power applications. However, its safety is key obstacle for high rate and high capacity applications. Several incidents such as fire and explosion of LIB have been reported [5].

Non-flammable electrolyte development [6] and overcharge protection additives [7] have been studied extensively by many research groups for LIB safety improvements. EPT has been focused on the development of reduced flammable electrolyte using fire-retardant additives in liquid organic electrolytes to improve the safety of the LIB. There are two mechanisms proposed to explain the flame retardation: (1) physical char-forming process, which buildup an isolating layer between the condensed and gas phases to stop combustion process [8] and (2) chemical radical-scavenging process, which terminates radical chain reactions responsible for the combustion reaction in the gas phases [9]. Numerous organic phosphate fire-retardant compounds have been investigated as electrolyte additives to reduce the flammability of the liquid electrolyte used in LIB [10].

Besides the safety concern of LIB, increasing its operation temperature range is critical especially for military and aircraft applications. The optimization of the electrolyte formulation to achieve extreme cold temperature performance while maintaining the cell safety is a complex issue in current LIB technology. The performance and stability of LIB at temperature extremes has been a challenge using conventional organic solvent based electrolytes. Several studies suggest that Ionic Liquid (IL) based electrolyte can improve the safety and high temperature cell performance but it adversely affects the low temperature cell performance. Therefore, the development of reduced flammable electrolyte which will allow LIB to operate temperature extremes is very important for various industries [11].

EPT has developed a unique electrolyte formulation with fire-retardant for wide temperature Li-Ion battery applications. We demonstrated the reduced-flammability of our proprietary electrolyte formulation. We studied the reduced flammable electrolyte performance in Li-Ion full cell and demonstrated good rate capability including a wide temperature operating range. The wide temperature range was tested from -40°C to +85 °C and cycled at 60°C, 71°C and 85°C. This paper will describe the development of reduced flammable electrolyte, its wide temperature performance and safer cell design.

Experimental

EPT reduced flammable electrolyte formulation (RF electrolyte) was developed with various flame retardant additive in the mixture of carbonate solvents. $LiNi_xCo_yMn_zO_2$ (NCM) cathode and graphite anode were prepared using standard industrial processes by mixing the active material mixed with carbon, poy(vinylidene fluoride) (PVDF) and N-methyl-2-pyrrolidinone (NMP). The resultant slurry was coated on the current collector.

Flammability of the RF electrolyte and baseline electrolyte was tested using open flash point test in bulk electrolyte and vapor pressure test. Thermal properties of the different electrolyte formulation were studied using Differential Scanning Calorimeter (DSC). The electrolyte performance was studied in a stacked pouch cell with a calculated capacity ~14 Ah and a hard case prismatic cell with a capacity of 30 Ah. Electrochemical tests were monitored with an Arbin battery cycler for rate and cycle life for the EPT-RF electrolyte, and the results were compared with baseline cell with same cell design. Advanced Li-ion pouch cell design was developed to improve the safety.

Results and Discussion

The bulk electrolyte flame test was carried out by taking 2 mL of electrolyte in a watch glass and igniting using a torch. Baseline electrolyte caught fire instantaneously. Several concentrations of the flame retardant additive were added into mixture of carbonate solvents and the test was repeated in the same manner as baseline electrolyte bulk fire retardant test. We identified the optimum amount of additive required for non-flammable electrolyte. Baseline and EPT proprietary electrolyte formulation fire-retardant result are shown in Figure 1. The pictures in Figure 1 were saved from the video in "save frame" mode using video editing software. Figure 1a shows the constant flame with baseline electrolyte upon ignition. The absence of fire after several attempts in Figure 1b and 1c shows the non-flammability of EPT RF electrolyte.

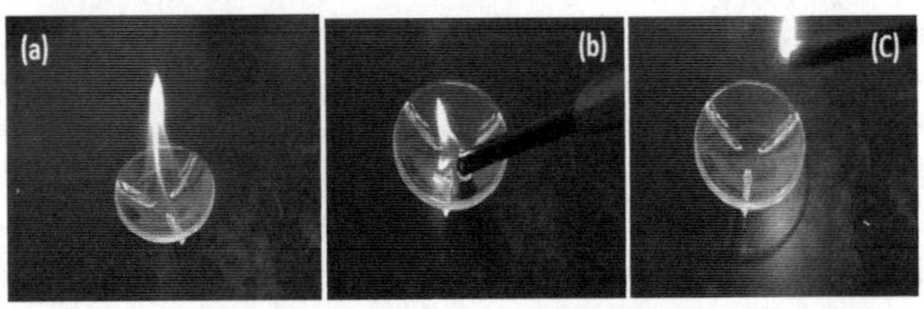

Figure 1. Bulk fire retardant test (a) baseline electrolyte catches fire instantaneously upon ignition and burnt continuously more than 2min; (b) and (c) EPT- RF electrolyte did not catch fire even after several attempts. The above photograph was saved as a picture frame mode from the video.

The bulk fire retardant test is a quick test, and was carried out in order to screen the optimum concentration of fire retardant additive to reduce the flammability of the electrolyte made at EPT. Furthermore, these electrolytes were tested for vapor pressure fire retardant which is shown in Figure 2. This test was carried out by heating electrolyte placed in a small aluminum pan using heating mantel. A gas torch was kept at a known fixed distance from the surface of the electrolyte in an aluminum pan in the heating mantel. The gas torch provides a continuous flame across the aluminum pan. The electrolyte temperature was increased through the heating mantel. The temperature corresponding to the first appearance of fire was determined for each electrolyte.

We found that baseline electrolyte caught fire at 44°C, whereas EPT-RF formulation only caught fire at 81°C. The test was repeated several times and found that ignition temperature for EPT- RF electrolyte is about 40°C higher than the baseline electrolyte formation.

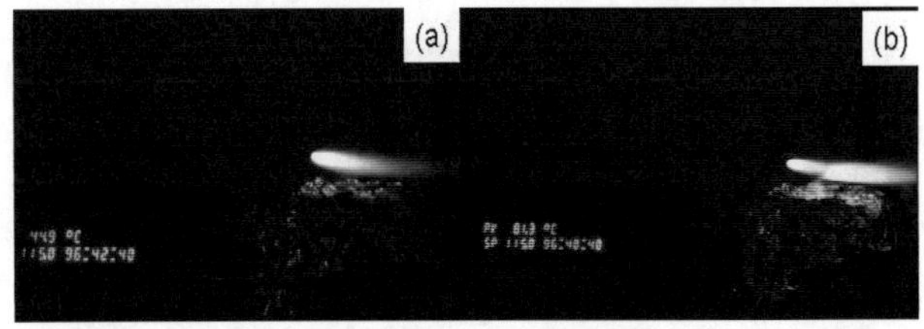

Figure 2. Vapor pressure flame retardant test (a) baseline electrolyte caught fire at 44°C; (b) EPT-RF electrolyte caught fire at 81°C at same heating rate. The gas torch flame was kept at the same distance above the electrolyte surface for both baseline and EPT-RF formulation.

The NCM/graphite pouch cells (calculated capacity 14Ah, is shown in Figure 3) were activated with baseline and EPT RF electrolytes respectively. Three cells for each formulation were tested. After formation cycles, these two sets of cells went through rate evaluation at different temperatures and thermal cycling tests. Figure 4 reveals that the rate capability of the baseline and EPT- RF formulation cells are similar at various discharge rates. There is no performance loss even at higher rate (4C), which is a significant achievement because the industry state of the art and the researcher usually observed performance loss with RF additive.

Figure 3. Photograph of EPT pouch full cell used for testing electrolyte formulations

It can be seen in Figure 5 that the EPT-RF electrolyte performance is very similar to the baseline electrolyte cells from temperature -40 °C to 50 °C. The cells were discharged at C/20 rate at sub-zero temperatures and at 1C discharge rate for higher temperatures. The cell capacity at -40°C is only ~38% of its room temperature capacity. However, this particular electrolyte was not developed to improve the low-temperature performance; it was developed to focus on the evaluation of reduced flammable additive in electrolyte at temperature extremes. This performance demonstrated that the flame retardant additive did not affect the cell performance over a wide temperature range whereas the literature has demonstrated that fire retardant additives affect the cell performance. At very low temperatures the electrolytes are frozen, which reduces Li ion diffusion into the electrode. This loss of performance at sub-zero temperature is similar to many literature results [12].

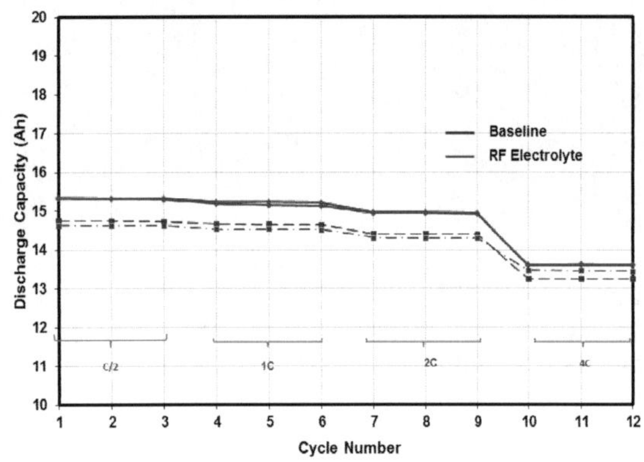

Figure 4. Comparison of rate capability of NCM/graphite full cell with baseline electrolyte and EPT-RF electrolyte.

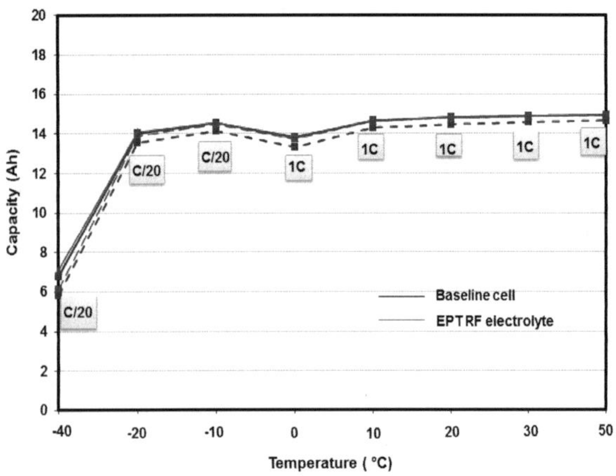

Figure 5. Temperature ramp tests of cells with baseline and EPT-RF electrolyte performance.

The reduced flammable electrolyte formulations were further optimized to improve the low temperature performance and high temperature stability. The cell performance is shown in Figure 6. Li-Ion cells using two different EPT formulations with reduced flammable electrolyte demonstrated superior performance over the baseline cell at the test temperature ranging from -40 °C and +50 °C.

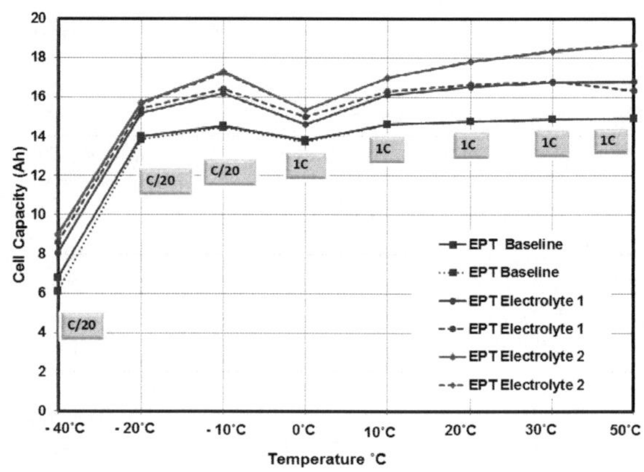

Figure 6. Wide temperature Li-Ion cell performances with reduced flammable electrolyte.

After the temperature characterization at 50°C, the cells were set to 60°C and cycle life tested for 100 cycles, and then the temperature was increased to 71°C for few cycles and again dropped to 60 °C for 25 cycles and then set to 85°C for few cycles. The high temperature cycle life stability of EPT Li-Ion cell performance is shown in Figure 7. The results in Figure 6 and Figure 7 demonstrated the EPT Li-Ion cell performance in a wide temperature range from -40°C to +85°C.

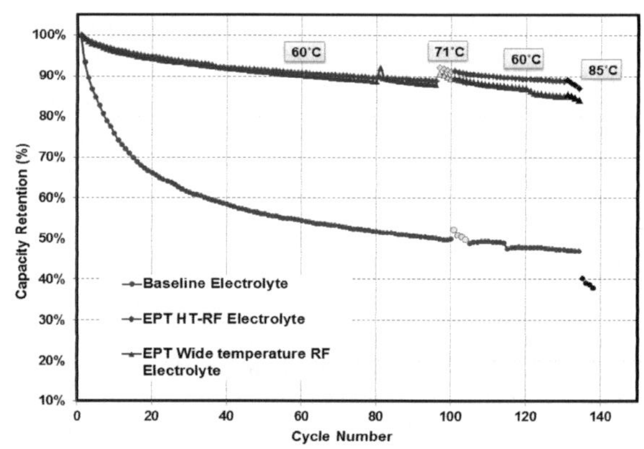

Figure 7 EPT Li-Ion Cell performances at higher temperature and compared with the baseline Li-Ion

A safer Li-Ion cell design was developed and the design was verified by an overcharge test carried out at 2C rate without any voltage control. Prior to the overcharge test, the cell was charge to 100% SOC.

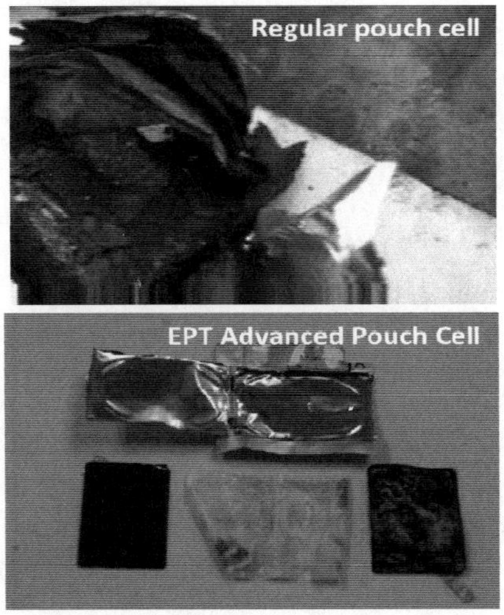

Figure 8. Photograph of overcharged test regular pouch cell after thermal runaway and EPT advanced pouch cell design which did not go through thermal runaway.

The regular pouch cell went to thermal runaway during the overcharge test within 20 min of overcharging at 2C rate. However, EPT advanced pouch cell design did not show any evidence of thermal runaway. The voltage profile in Figure 9 shows the cell voltage never goes to 0V even charging at 2C rate for more than 50 minutes. The DPA of the EPT advanced pouch cell in Figure 8 show that there is no evidence of fire inside the cell as we see a clean internal pouch materials and unburned separator. Figure 8 and Figure 9 confirm that the EPT Li-Ion cell design is safer.

Conclusion

EPT Li-Ion cell demonstrated superior performance over wide temperature range from -40°C to +85°C. EPT pouch cell design was safer than the regular Li-Ion cell under overcharge abused test. EPT proprietary electrolyte formulations performance in NCM/graphite full cell demonstrates that there is no performance loss by adding fire retardant additive. The literature demonstrates that the fire retardant additive usually has a negative impact on the rate capability of LIB. We successfully developed reduced flammable electrolyte with good rate capability and wide temperature range for Li-Ion battery applications. EPT has designed an advanced pouch cell and demonstrated that the cell did not go to the thermal runaway and improves the overall safety of the Li-Ion battery.

Acknowledgement

"This material is released to the public domain in accordance with ITAR 22 CFR 120.11"

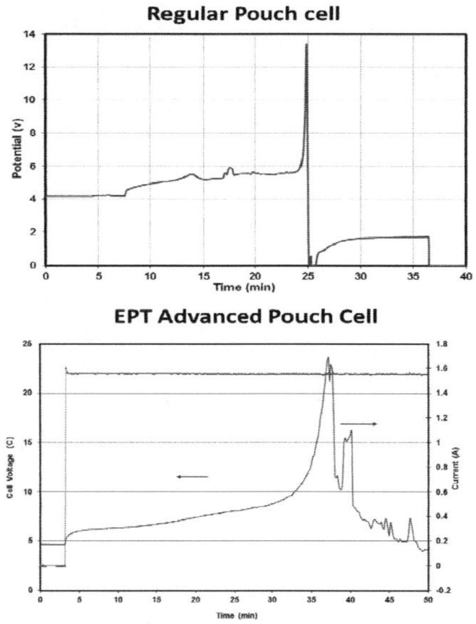

Figure 9. Overcharge test voltage and current profile of regular pouch cells show the regular pouch cell voltage went to 0V after thermal runaway and EPT advanced pouch cell did not go to 0V, showing no thermal runaway occurred.

Reference

1. Marom R, Amalraj,S. F., Leifer N, Jacob D and Aurbach D., *J Materials Chemistry*, 21, (2011), 9938

2. Stura E., Nicolini C., *Anal. Chim. Acta*, 568, (2006), 57-64.

3. Li X., Kang F., Shen W., *Carbon*, 44, (2006), 1334-1336.

4. Tarascon J. M and Armand M., Nature, 414, (2001), 359-367.

5. Abu-Lebdeh Y and Davidson Isobel., *J Electrochem. Society*, 156, (2009), A60-65.

6. Levan S.L., Winandy J. E., *Fire Materials*, 24, (2000), 277.

7. Wang X., Yasukawa E., Kasuya S., *J Electrochem. Society*, 148, (2001), A1058.

8. Granzow A., *Chem Res.*, 11, (1978), 177.

9. Xu K., Zhang S.S., Allen J.L, Jow R.T, *J Electrochem. Society*, 149, (2002), A1079.

10. Feng J. K.,M Cao Y.L., Ai X. P. and Yang H. X., *Electrochimca Acta*, 53, (2008) 8265-8268.

11. Zhao J., Buldum A. and Lu J. P., *Phys. Rev. Lett.* 85, (2000), 1706.

12. Zhang S.S, *J Power Sources*, 162, (2006), 1379-1394.

Modeling and Testing of Safer, High Power and High Energy Li-ion Cells and Batteries for Operation in Extreme Temperature Environments

Frank Puglia, Dr. Gregory J. Moore, Stuart Santee, Seth Cohen, Ryan Lawrence
Yardney Technical Products, Inc.
2000 South County Trail
East Greenwich, RI, United States of America, 02818

Abstract: *Yardney Technical Products/Lithion (YTP) is a company with 70 years of experience providing Silver-Zinc and Lithium battery solutions for high profile programs in the commercial and government markets. There is a distinct need within these markets for batteries that can operate at increasingly extreme rates and temperatures without the risk of catastrophic failure. The development of cells for these applications began with the comparison of several candidate chemistries for safer Lithium-ion (Li-ion) batteries optimized for applications with operating windows that exceed the requirements of commercial applications. This technology must provide an extended operating temperature range (-40°C to +85°C), high energy density, good cycle life, and long calendar life. Full size cells have been built and have undergone qualification testing on multiple programs and these results are presented.*

In the case of the development of very high power batteries, the low internal impedance results in new safety challenges that are not present, or are largely muted, with lower power batteries. In some failure modes (e.g. low rate internal and external shorting) the reduced specific energy of a high power cell improves the safety performance and the risk of fratricide is reduced. In failure modes involving low resistance internal or external shorts, the currents provided by the cell can quickly lead to thermal damage, mechanical damage and fratricide. A typical Li-ion energy type cell in 18650 format (3Ah) has a resistance around 60mΩ while a power cell in 18650 format (1.5Ah) has a resistance around 25mΩ. Yardney's 6Ah high power cell has an internal impedance of <0.8 mΩ and thus has about 8X lower impedance per Ah. This high power output in failure modes has a dramatic influence on the physical design requirements needed to maintain cell and battery level safety. This presentation reviews some of the thermal modeling and safety testing performed on cells designed to tolerate failure modes. It includes a thermal analysis of cells in series and parallel combinations in failure modes.

Keywords: Lithium; Li-ion; modeling; thermal; Yardney; High Power;

Introduction

As Li-ion battery quality improves and additional field results are collected the technology is gaining acceptance in an increasing number of applications that can benefit from the increased cycle life, power density and energy density of Li-ion batteries. However, these new applications are more environmentally demanding than the fairly benign environments of satellites, cell phones, laptops and most vehicles.

In applications where the environments are extreme, such as -40°C for an aircraft, -60°C for a deep space application or greater than 50°C for a vehicle application, many users are already experiencing lower than desired performance. The required operating range for military applications is often -40°C to 71°C (-40°F to 160°F) with storage excursions to 85°C (185°F). Operating at 71°C ambient can result in cell temperatures considerably higher. Assuming a 1kWh battery, a typical battery management system can produce on average 10 to 40+ watts in heat depending largely on state, isolation diodes and contactor configuration. Balancing resistors can result in considerably higher loads, often 1 watt per cell, but this balancing is only for a small portion of the cycle. The next heat source adding to ambient temperature is the inefficiency of the battery. Low rates such as a 5 hr discharge can be accomplished at 95-97% thermal efficiency at the cell level. High rates, such as a 40C discharge, typically achieve no more than 85% efficiency. The efficiency heuristics stated are for room temperature and warmer operation. Efficiency can be much lower for low temperature operation but this does not result in an over-temperature situation.

There are two areas in which the thermal performance of Li-ion batteries must improve. First, Li-ion batteries must expand the range of temperatures at which they can operate without degradation. Second, even batteries which can withstand 70°C ambient must be designed to maximize heat dissipation or they will be limited in power output because of inherent inefficiencies. In these cases there must be a cooling system to prevent the additive thermal effects from reaching undesirable temperatures. Advanced thermal designs for high power operation, passive and active, can have very dramatic benefits in enhancing both cell level safety (tolerance to failure) and battery level safety (tolerance to fratricide). Increased thermal stability and advanced thermal designs are discussed below.

Increased Thermal Stability

Most Li-ion cells operate within a voltage range of ~4.2 to 3.0V, whereas the range in which almost all of the energy is delivered is typically 4.2V-3.3V. Unless operating at high rates or low temperatures, there is very little capacity below 3.3V. This is evident in Figure 1, where the solid black line is at 3.3V. This range holds true for most metal-oxide (NCA, NCM) and spinel based Li-ion cells but it is not accurate for Iron Phosphate (FeP) based cells.

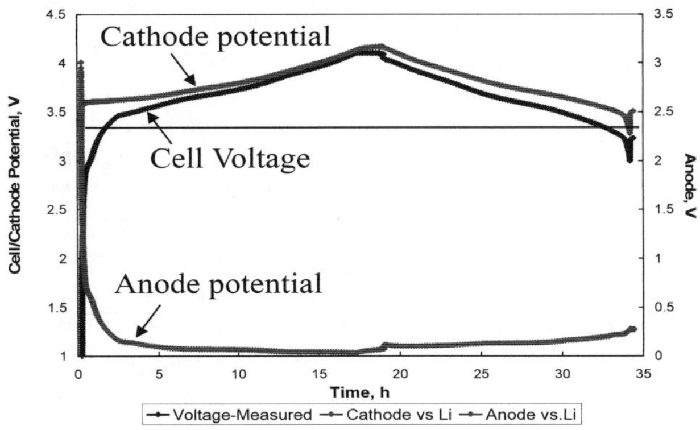

Figure 1. Generic graph of the anode, cathode and cell potential illustrating that most capacity is delivered above 3.3V for metal oxide (NCA, NCM) cells.

As the cell internal resistance grows the voltage curve can be depressed without there being a noticeable change in available capacity. This effect is evidenced in Figure 2. In this chart the cells are being cycled at both 40°C and -20°C. The capacity fade rate at 40°C is minor because the average discharge voltage is still very close to the ideal open circuit voltage. The suppression of the voltage on the -20°C discharge, due to increased internal resistance at low temperature, removes the 0.2V "margin" between the lower voltage cutoff and the open circuit potential curve. The increased degradation is only observed during the more stressful, low temperature discharges. The lower the temperature or the higher the rate, the more sensitive the system is to losses in deliverable energy.

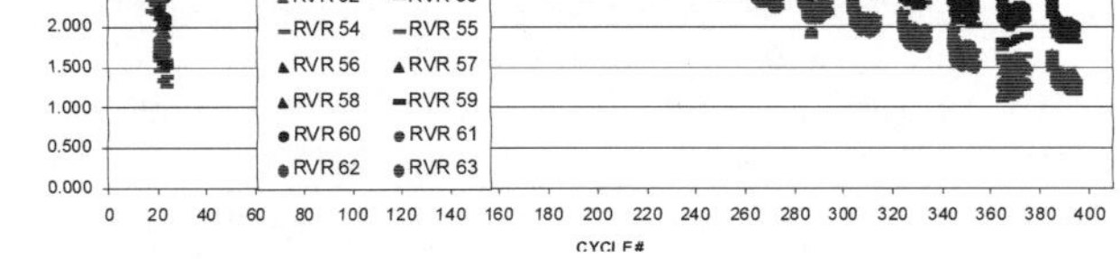

Figure 2. Example of variable temperature cycling (Ah vs. cycle number)

Yardney has a vested interest in minimizing the impedance growth of cells during cycling and temperature exposures since the applications for the military and aerospace that Yardney services require operation at both high rates and low temperatures

The results of cycling at variable temperatures are shown in Figure 3. The available discharge energy for the NCA and NCM (1:1:1) systems were essentially identical during initial room temperature (25°C) cycling. In this initial cycling each material was cycled to its recommended voltage cutoff. This was 4.1V, 4.2V and 3.65V for NCA, NCM and FeP respectively. At the start of the -20°C cycling, the voltage cycling range for each cell was adjusted to reflect the allowed battery voltage range for 24V Aircraft Batteries. This was 4.035V for NCA and NCM and 3.53V for FeP. This change in the voltage window accounts for the ~13% reduced capacity at 25°C for the NCM cells. The penalty associated with adjusting to the battery level voltage window will be different for each application and is generally lower for higher voltage batteries. The much larger reduction of capacity at low temperature is a result of reduced kinetics of the NCM chemistry versus the NCA chemistry. The comparatively reduced performance at low temperature discharge and at very high rates was confirmed by the material supplier. It is noted that the d50 particle size for the NCA and NCM were very similar. Iron phosphate is also known to be weak for low temperature discharge performance. In this case the weakness is attributable to both kinetics and the lower true and tap density of the cathode material that results in a thicker electrode for the same coulombic loading. Electrode thickness is a critical parameter for low temperature and high rate performance. With all parameters accounted for, the NCA based cells offer about twice the low temperature discharge energy as the FeP cells and about 50% more discharge energy than the NCM cells.

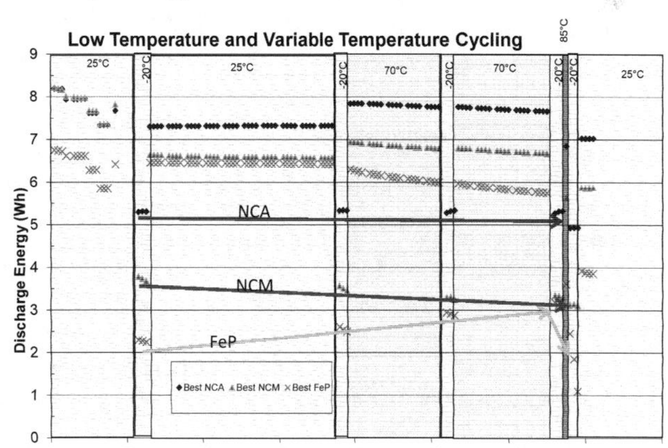

Figure 3. Available low temperature discharge energy for the best NCA, NCM and FeP systems identified.

The behavior of the Iron Phosphate cells was particularly interesting during this testing. An analysis of the discharge curves showed that the cell impedance had risen with the additional cycling. Each increase in impedance caused the cells to increase in temperature more than during previous low temperature cycles. This in turn resulted in increased capacity delivered despite the suppressed voltage. The available capacity began to decrease very rapidly once the voltage suppression due to increased impedance reached a critical level.

In addition to the variable temperature cycling, Yardney conducted testing to the multi-step profile association with the aircraft application of interest. This data for the NCA chemistry is shown in Figure 4. The voltage for the peak discharge pulse, a 2.5C load, is shown. After 350+ aircraft loading cycles, the voltage at the peak pulse is about 20mV lower at -20°C, 8mV lower at 25°C and 2mV lower at 43°C. Thus, while there is some impedance rise at the low temperature testing, the rate of voltage suppression after the first 100 cycles is only about 0.6mV per 20 cycles and thus the battery will easily support thousands of aircraft cycles before the low voltage is suppressed to 3.1V. At this time the 25°C and 43°C voltages for the 2.5V pulse will remain above 3.8V. No heater blankets were used at any time during this testing. Charging and discharging was conducted after soaking at each temperature.

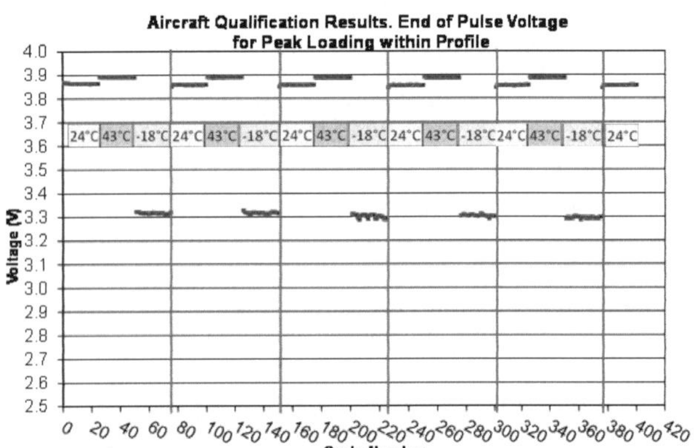

Figure 4. Variable temperature qualification testing.

The ability to withstand high operating temperatures is critical because of the wide operating range of military applications. The NCA based cells offer better temperature stability than any of the other cathode options evaluated. It is noted that the use of an NCA cathode must be done in conjunction with the realization that additional safety based thermal controls may be needed for NCA compared to other cathode options.

Designing for Thermal Control

As shown previously, low discharge rates such as a 5 hour discharge can be accomplished at 95-97% energy efficiency at the cell level. High rates, such as a 40C discharge, typically achieve no more than 85% efficiency. In this case, efficiency is defined as the energy delivered in the discharge cycle compared to that required to recharge the cell. For many high rate applications it is often more useful to approximate discharge efficiency in which the efficiency on discharge alone is approximated by the ratio of the Closed Circuit Voltage (CCV) to the Open Circuit Voltage (OCV) for each state of charge. This method may be appropriate when the charge and discharge cycles are thermally decoupled.

Yardney has calculated and measured that a typical Li-ion cell/battery heat capacity is ~0.95J g^{-1} $°C^{-1}$. For a 1 kWh battery, at 120Wh kg^{-1}, 97% discharge efficient, adiabatic operation will result in a temperature rise of ~14°C. This is a very acceptable value if the battery is at nominal conditions. However, adding 14°C to a battery starting at a temperature of 71°C, which is the high end of expected ambient temperatures for military aircraft, will result in accelerated battery aging. Achieving 97% energy efficiency on discharge is highly dependent on the cell design. Energy cells will often operate at 97% or lower energy efficiency for a C/5 discharge while a power cell can maintain this efficiency to a 2C or higher discharge rate. At these rates there is both ample time to spread the waste heat through the battery mass uniformly and to dissipate the heat through normal measures. Natural convection is often adequate at these low rates.

For a Directed Energy Application (DEW) high rate discharge, such as 40C-80C continuous, it is not unreasonable for the energy efficiency on the discharge to be less than 90%. This can result in an adiabatic temperature rise of the battery of 45°C. This greatly limits the ambient temperature allowed before an adiabatic discharge would result in temperatures that greatly accelerate aging. Further, as the entire discharge is limited in duration to perhaps less than 60seconds it is unlikely the heat will be uniformly distributed through the battery mass. Thus, the peak temperature as estimated by the heat capacity and battery mass will be significantly underestimated. The cell core will be considerably warmer.

To address this, Yardney's high power cell line is designed with a very high surface area to volume (A/V) ratio. A typical cylindrical cell may have an A/V ratio of 1.8:1 or lower. Yardney's cells are designed with an area to volume ratio of ~7. This creates a dramatically improved ability to reject heat from the cell. This is evidenced by Figure 5, in which three (A,B,C) cells with surface area to volume ratios (A/V) of 7, 3.5 and 2 respectively are modeled to a 150C discharge for 7 seconds. The cell with A/V ratio of ~2 is a good analog to a cylindrical cell. A 150C discharge rate is pushing the capability limits of Li-ion technology. The outside surfaces of the cells are held at a constant temperature to simulate an ideal cooling situation. A close analog to this would be the immersion of the cells in a flowing liquid. For the larger area to volume ratio cells this model is a reasonable approximation for having vigorous active cooling along the two large faces. The large faces account for over 90% of the area on the cell with the highest surface area to volume ratio. Figure 5 shows that for the thinnest cell, A/V ratio of 7, some of the heat is removed from the core of the electrode stack within the 7.5 seconds of the pulse. This is the reason that cell has a lower peak temperature than the other two cells. The cells with the lower A/V having approximately the same peak core temperature as the thermal path take too long for appreciable energy to be removed from the core within the duration of the pulse. However, the cell with an A/V ratio of 3 cools much faster and could thus support a higher duty cycle. Design C, the thickest cell with the A/V comparable to a cylindrical cell, takes close to 7 minutes to return to within 5°C of the starting temperature. This greatly limits the duty cycle that would be possible with this cell geometry. It is noted that in addition to a favorable A/V ratio, the total thickness should be no more than ~0.4" thick to achieve the best cooling. Figure 6 shows one of Yardney's aircraft cells manufactured with an A/V ratio of 7.5:1.

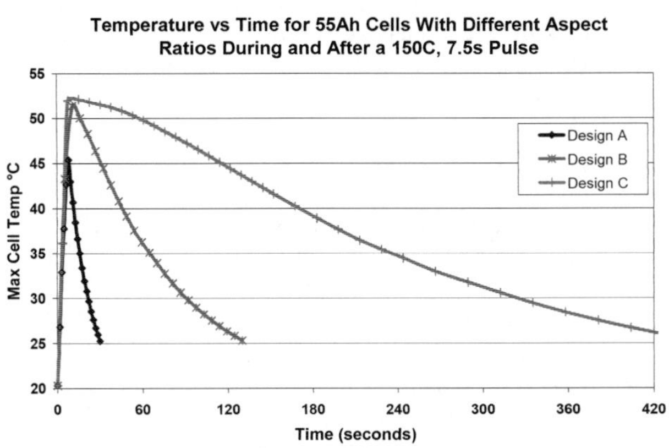

Figure 5. Rate of heating and ideal rate of cooling for various cell designs

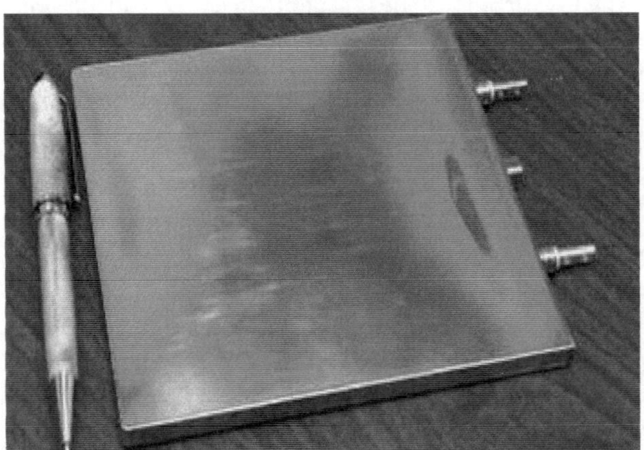

Figure 6. YTP Aircraft Cell with high A/V ratio

Yardney has also completed extensive safety testing and modeling of cells with high A/V ratios. As expected, the improved ability to move heat out of the cells resulted in increased tolerance to safety events. This includes internal shorts and overcharge events with the latter owing to delaying the rate of temperature rise that accompanies infinite overcharge.

The increased thermal management that is inherent within the cell also allows for dramatic enhancements in battery level thermal management. However, without a proper battery level thermal design, much of the thermal advantage at the cell level is lost. The reduced thickness of the cell, combined with the rectilinear shape, allows for the efficient use of traditional cooling methods. The cooling could be integrated through the battery pack, as is done with the Chevy Volt. Alternatively, highly conductive members could be added to the core of the battery pack, bringing the heat to the edges where the battery pack may be cooled with liquid or forced air. Pyrolytic graphite, heat pipes and graphene would all be excellent candidates for moving heat from the core of the battery to the edges. The rapid ability to remove heat from the cells also allows for the battery to be rapidly heated without generating large thermal gradients. Yardney has demonstrated battery level heating rates of several degrees Celsius per minute with min-max gradients remaining less than 1°C. This allows a cold soaked battery to come up to operating temperature in a faster and safer manner.

Conclusion

Li-ion chemistry, cell design and battery design needs to be improved as Li-ion technology is used in increasingly demanding applications. Yardney's previous work has shown that almost all components that comprise the Li-ion chemistry can contribute to temperature related aging and the current work demonstrates the high level of thermal stability that has been achieved on Yardney's latest generation of batteries. The cell geometries that worked for cells in laptop computers and many satellites have demonstrated thermal liabilities in high rate and high temperature environments as they result in higher core operating temperatures than cells specifically designed for the application.

Acknowledgements

Yardney would like to acknowledge Wright Patterson Air Force Base and NAVAIR, Patuxent River, for their recent help in the development of safer and higher power Li-ion batteries.

Dendrite-Suppression Electrolytes for Lithium-Metal and Lithium-Ion Batteries

Wu Xu,[a] Fei Ding,[a] Xilin Chen,[a] Yaohui Zhang,[a] Jiangfeng Qian,[a] Eduard Nasybulin,[a] Ruiguo Cao,[a] Mark H. Engelhard,[b] Ji-Guang Zhang[a]

[a] Energy and Environment Directorate, [b] Environmental Molecular Sciences Laboratory
Pacific Northwest National Laboratory (PNNL)
Richland, WA 99354, USA

Abstract: *Lithium (Li) dendrite formation is one of the critical challenges for rechargeable Li-metal batteries and Li-ion batteries, which has not been effectively solved by traditional methods. In this paper, we report the systematic investigation of a novel self-healing electrostatic shield (SHES) mechanism to change the Li deposition behavior by using low-concentration electrolyte additives whose redox potentials are close to that of Li^+. The SHES additive cations force Li to be deposited in the region away from protuberant tips due to their preferentially accumulation on the active sites of anode surface. Typical adsorption behavior rather than electrochemical reduction of the additive cation is observed. The existence of Cs^+ cations in the electrolytes does not change the components or structure of Li surface films, which is consistent with what the SHES mechanism predicts. The morphologies of deposited Li films on copper substrates are smooth and uniform during repeated deposition-stripping cycles and at various current densities (from 0.1 to 1.0 mA cm^{-2}) by adding only a small amount of Cs^+ additive in the electrolytes. Cs^+-additive also suppresses Li dendrite growth on carbon anode surface during overcharging, which should improve the safety of Li-ion batteries during abuse conditions. It does not affect the rate capability but improves the long-term cycling stability of Li metal anode, carbon anode and conventional Li-ion cathode materials.*

Keywords: Electrolyte; Dendrite-suppression; Coulombic efficiency; Li-metal battery; Li-ion battery

Introduction

Rechargeable Li metal batteries have high energy density because Li metal anode has a significantly high theoretical capacity of 3860 mAh g^{-1} and the lowest electrochemical potential at –3.040 V vs. standard hydrogen electrode. Unfortunately the development and application of rechargeable Li-metal batteries has been hindered in the past forty years due to two major problems—the Li dendrite growth on the Li anode during repeated charge/discharge processes and the low Coulombic efficiency (CE) [1]. As for the Li-ion batteries using carbonaceous anodes, Li dendrites grow on carbon anodes during several charging conditions such as overcharging, charging at low temperatures and fast charging. The formed Li dendrites can lead to serious safety hazards. During the past four decades, several approaches have been reported to suppress Li dendrite growth on Li metal and carbon anodes, including forming Li alloys [2], adding electrolyte additives [3,4], using blocking electrolyte membranes [5], and so on. However, the improvement on the suppression of Li dendrite growth so far is not satisfactory.

In this work, we first systematically investigated the effects of different electrolyte carbonate solvents and Li salts on Li deposition morphology and cycling efficiency [6]. Carbonate solvents were chosen for the study because they are the most common solvents used in electrolytes for the state-of-the-art Li-ion batteries and can be used with high voltage (>4 V) cathode materials where ether-based solvents are easily decomposed by oxidization. After that, we studied several new electrolyte additives to control Li dendrite growth based on a novel self-healing electrostatic shield (SHES) mechanism that fundamentally alters Li dendrite formation in all traditional approaches [7,8]. With the help of the SHES additives added to the conventional Li-ion battery electrolytes, Li dendrite formation and growth has been significantly suppressed. By optimizing electrolyte solvents, Li salts and other additives, the Li Coulombic efficiency has also been greatly improved to >97% with dendrite-free morphology. The long-term cycling stability and dendrite-free Li anode and carbonaceous anodes have been achieved. Further development of this approach will lead to long-term, safe operation of rechargeable Li-metal batteries and Li-ion batteries. Details of the investigations will be reported and discussed below.

Experimental

Electrolyte Preparation: The nonaqueous electrolytes were prepared inside an MBraun glovebox filled with purified argon where the moisture and oxygen content was less than 1 ppm. The solvent was selected from ethylene carbonate (EC), propylene carbonate (PC), dimethyl carbonate (DMC), ethyl methyl carbonate (EMC), vinylene carbonate (VC), monofluoroethylene carbonate (FEC), vinyl ethylene carbonate (VEC). Lithium salt was chosen from lithium hexafluorophosphate ($LiPF_6$), lithium hexafluoroarsenate ($LiAsF_6$), lithium tetrafluoroborate ($LiBF_4$), lithium perchlorate ($LiClO_4$), lithium bis(trifluoromethane-sulfonyl)imide (LiTFSI), lithium trifluoromethanesulfonate ($LiSO_3CF_3$), lithium bis(oxalato)-borate (LiBOB), lithium difluoro(oxalato) borate (LiDFOB) and lithium iodide (LiI). $CsPF_6$ was prepared by mixing stoichiometric CsI and $AgPF_6$ in PC solutions inside the glove box as described in ref. 7.

Li deposition. Li was electrodeposited on copper (Cu) foil substrates (10 mm × 10 mm) or carbon electrodes in different electrolyte solutions at the desired current densities inside the argon-filled glove box using a Solartron electrochemical interface (SI 1287). After deposition, the electrode was washed with DMC to remove the residual electrolyte and dried in the antechamber of the glove box under vacuum prior to characterization and analyses.

Electrochemical tests and cell cycling performance. The average CE of Li electrodes deposited in electrolytes with different carbonate solvents and/or different Li salts was measured in Li|Cu coin cells (type CR2032). The cells were charged (Li deposition) and discharged (Li stripping) on an Arbin battery testing system at a current density of 0.5 mA cm^{-2}. The battery performance was tested in $Li|Li_4Ti_5O_{12}$ coin cells.

Characterization. Surface morphologies of deposited Li films on Cu substrates or carbon electrodes were measured by scanning electron microscopy (SEM) and optical microscope. Surface element compositions were examined by energy dispersive x-ray fluorescence spectrometer (EDX) and inductively coupled plasma/atomic emission spectrometry (ICP/AES). The components of the surface layers on deposited Li electrodes were analyzed by X-ray photoelectron spectroscopy (XPS) and Fourier transform infrared (FTIR) spectroscopy. The adsorption tests were conducted by electrochemical methods.

Results and Discussion

Effect of carbonate solvents: The average CEs of Li electrodes in Li|Cu coin cells with the electrolytes of 1M $LiPF_6$ in different carbonate solvents are listed in Table I. It is seen that linear carbonate solvents (DMC and EMC) give much lower CEs of Li electrodes than cyclic carbonate solvents (the other five carbonates). The SEM images (not shown here) of the surface morphologies of deposited Li electrodes from these carbonate electrolytes all show randomly dendritic growth. The linear carbonate solvents lead to thin and poorly covered Li film on Cu foil, while cyclic carbonate solvents result in compact and even Li dendrites with greatly improved Li coverage on Cu foil. The cyclic carbonate solvents show high CE and good coverage because they can form a strong and flexible SEI layer by the reduction and polymerization on the Li surface, which has been demonstrated by XPS analysis [6]. Although PC has relatively lower CE than other cyclic carbonate solvents, it was chosen for the following studies due to its wide liquid state temperature range and the capability of forming high Li surface coverage during Li deposition.

Effect of lithium salts: Figure 1 shows the effect of salt anion on the surface morphologies of Li films deposited from electrolytes of different Li salts in PC. Li surface morphology from LiBOB is unique from those of other salts. It leads to the formation of fibrous rather than dendritic clusters found in other cases. Among the nine studied salts, LiBOB, $LiPF_6$, $LiAsF_6$, LiTFSI and LiI could result in compact Li films covered on Cu foil, but $LiBF_4$ gives poor Li deposition coverage. The latter is mostly related to the poor SEI formation capability of $LiBF_4$ salt.

Table I. Average Li Coulombic efficiency in 1 M $LiPF_6$ electrolytes with different carbonate solvents [6]

Carbonate solvent	Ave. Li Coulombic efficiency
EC	94.8%
PC	76.5%
DMC	23.6%
EMC	7.3%
VC	97.1%
FEC	98.2%
VEC	97.6%

Figure 1. SEM images of Li films deposited in electrolytes of 1 M (a) LiBOB, (b) $LiPF_6$, (c) $LiAsF_6$, (d) LiTFSI, (e) LiI, (f) LiDFOB, (g) $LiBF_4$, (h) $LiCF_3SO_3$, and (h) $LiClO_4$ in PC solvent. (Copied from ref. 6)

The effect of salt anion on the average Li CE is not as much as those between cyclic and linear carbonate solvents. When compared to $LiPF_6$ whose CE is 76.5% in PC, $LiAsF_6$, LiBOB and LiDFOB can greatly increase the CE to 95.2%, 92.5% and 85.7%, respectively because these three salts are able to be reduced before the reduction of PC solvent and to form good quality SEI layers on Li surface which then protect deposited Li film from side reactions between Li and PC electrolyte. The other salts slightly reduce the CE to 68.9~73.4%, probably because their SEI layers have poorer quality than that from $LiPF_6$. The results were confirmed by XPS analysis.

SHES mechanism and its effects on Li metal anode: The SHES mechanism is based on a non-Li cation (M^+) whose effective reduction potential ($E_{M/M+}$) is lower than that of Li^+ ($E_{Li/Li+}$) and the applied deposition voltage (V_a) is controlled as $E_{M/M+} < V_a < E_{Li/Li+}$. The suppression of Li dendrite growth by SHES mechanism is illustrated in Figure 2. During Li deposition, both Li^+ and M^+ cations preferably absorb to the surface of the initially formed Li protuberant tip, Li^+ gets the electron and deposits but the M^+ will not deposit. The additive M^+ forms a positively charged electrostatic shield around the Li protuberant tip, which expels the subsequent absorption and deposition of Li^+ on such a tip via the electrostatic repulsion effect and steric hindrance effect. The follow-up Li^+ has to absorb and deposit at other sites with lower M^+ coverage. By this way, the continuous growth of the Li tip is stopped, and then dendrite-free Li deposition films can be successfully obtained.

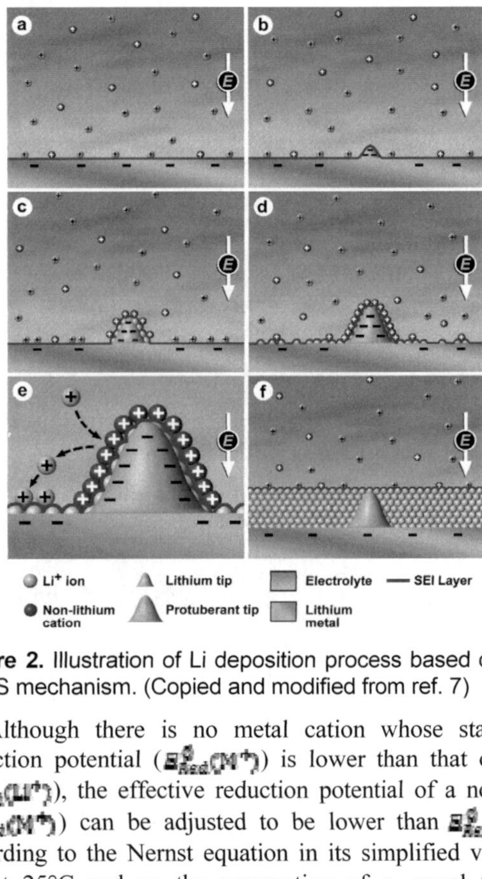

Figure 2. Illustration of Li deposition process based on the SHES mechanism. (Copied and modified from ref. 7)

Although there is no metal cation whose standard reduction potential ($E^{\phi}_{Red}(M^+)$) is lower than that of Li^+ ($E^{\phi}_{Red}(Li^+)$), the effective reduction potential of a non-Li^+ ($E_{Red}(M^+)$) can be adjusted to be lower than $E^{\phi}_{Red}(Li^+)$ according to the Nernst equation in its simplified version (1) at 25°C and on the assumption of α_x equal to the concentration c_x:

$$E_{\text{Red}} = E^{\phi}_{\text{Red}} - \frac{0.05916V}{z} \log_{10} \frac{1}{\alpha_{Ox}} \quad (1)$$

For example, the effective reduction potential (vs. SHE) of Cs^+ can be reduced from −3.026 V for 1.0 M concentration to −3.103 V for 0.05 M or −3.144 V for 0.01 M in the electrolyte, both are lower than the standard reduction potential of Li^+ (−3.040 V for 1.0 M). When using $CsPF_6$ as an additive in 1 M $LiPF_6$/PC electrolyte, distinguished change in deposited Li film morphology has been observed (Figure 3). Addition of 50 mM $CsPF_6$ can lead to smooth and mirror-like Li deposition film to the eye-view. When a dendritic Li film is formed, further deposition in the Cs^+-containing electrolyte can smoothen the needle-like and mossy morphology to form dense and spherical film. In addition, the SHES mechanism has also been demonstrated by computational simulations [7].

Figure 3. SEM morphologies of Li films deposited in 1 M $LiPF_6$/PC electrolyte with $CsPF_6$ of (a) 0 M, (b) 1 mM, (c) 5 mM, (d) 10 mM, (e) 50 mM, at 0.1 mA cm^{-2}. (From ref. 7)

With repeated Li deposition/stripping processes, 50m M Cs^+ additive in the electrolyte can still suppress Li dendrite formation although the morphology is not as good as that of the first deposition (Figure 4). Small bumps form after longer cycles.

Figure 4. SEM morphologies of Li films after repeated deposition/stripping cycles in the control electrolyte (a, b, c, and d) and electrolyte with Cs^+-salt additive (e, f, g, and h): (a, e) after first deposition, (b, f) after second deposition, (c, g) after third deposition, and (d, h) after 10th deposition. The deposition was done in beaker cells where no pressure was applied to Li surface. (Copied from ref. 8)

As shown in Figure 5, when the current density of the Li deposition increases from 0.1 mA cm^{-2} to 1.0 mA cm^{-2}, the deposited Li films still show a dendrite-free surface although more Li bumps are formed. It is demonstrated that the SHES additive and the mechanism work effectively at least at a current density up to 1.0 mA cm^{-2}.

The electrostatic adsorption instead of electrochemical reduction of the Cs^+ additive on Li surface or incorporation into Li surface film during deposition process has been demonstrated by electrochemical impedance spectroscopy, electrochemical quartz-crystal microbalance, XPS and ICP analyses. No Cs element was found in the deposited Li films. In addition, the effect of Cs^+ additive on the Li surface layer (i.e. SEI film) has also been studied by XPS and FTIR. The additive does not change the main components and structure of the Li SEI film but just slightly affect the compositions [8].

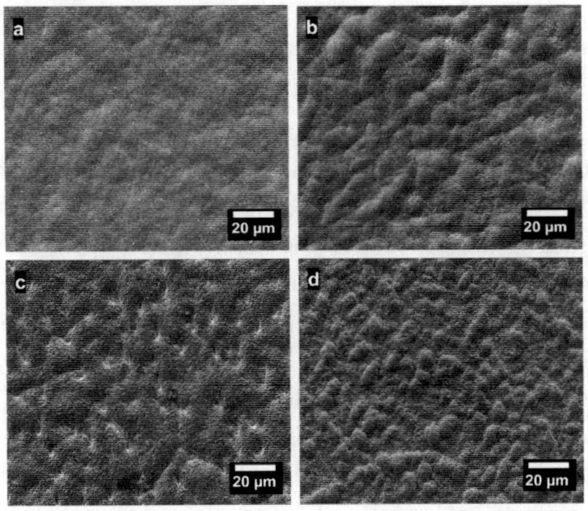

Figure 5. SEM morphologies of Li films at different current densities: (a) 0.1, (b) 0.2, (c) 0.5 and (d) 1.0 mA cm-2. The deposition was done in 1 M $LiPF_6$/PC + 50 mM $CsPF_6$. [8]

The effect of Cs^+-additive on the cycling stability and the rate capability of Li-metal batteries was tested in Li|$Li_4Ti_5O_{12}$ coin cells (Figure 6). The cells with Cs^+-additive exhibit excellent long-term cycling stability, while the cells with control electrolyte show capacity fading after 300 cycles. In addition, Cs^+-additive does not affect the rate capability of the cells. The post-analysis on the Li anodes after 100 cycles indicates that dendritic and mossy Li formed in the control cells but none was found for Cs^+-containing cells.

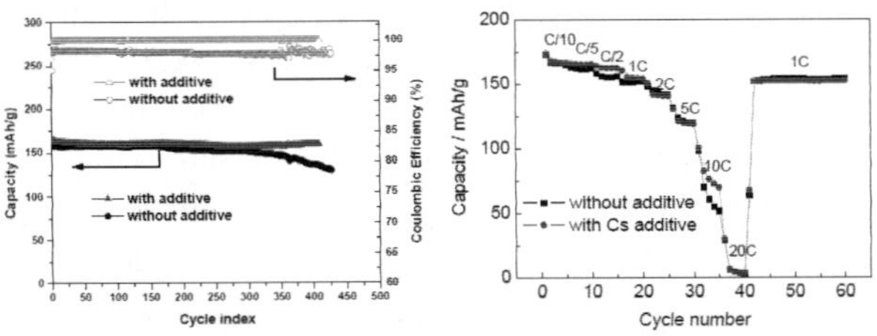

Figure 6. Effect of Cs^+-additive on battery performance of Li|$Li_4Ti_5O_{12}$ cells. The electrolytes were 1 M $LiPF_6$/PC with and without 50 mM $CsPF_6$. (Right figure from ref. 7 SI)

Figure 6 indicates that the electrolyte with the SHES additive can suppress Li dendrite formation and maintain long-term cycling of rechargeable Li-metal batteries. By optimizing electrolyte formulations, the Li CE has also been greatly improved to >97%. More work is needed to further improve the Li CE while to keep the dendrite-free morphology.

Effect of SHES additive on carbon anodes: Figure 7 shows the effect of Cs^+-additive on Li deposition morphology on hard carbon electrode surface during 200% overcharge, where the carbon electrode was prepared by hard carbon/SP/PVDF at 8:1:1 by weight. The overcharging test was conducted in a beaker cell inside the argon-filled glove box. A large amount of silver color Li dendrites are formed on the carbon electrode surface in the control electrolyte while no Li dendrites are found on carbon surface from the Cs^+-containing electrolyte, demonstrating that Cs^+-additive can prevent Li dendrite formation on carbon surface during overcharge stage, which should improve the safety of Li-ion batteries during abuse conditions. In addition, the addition of $CsPF_6$ into the electrolyte does not affect the rate capability (up to 10C rate) and the cycling stability of hard carbon electrode, respectively, in more than 250 cycles. The hard carbon even shows a little higher capacity in Cs-containing electrolyte than in the control electrolyte.

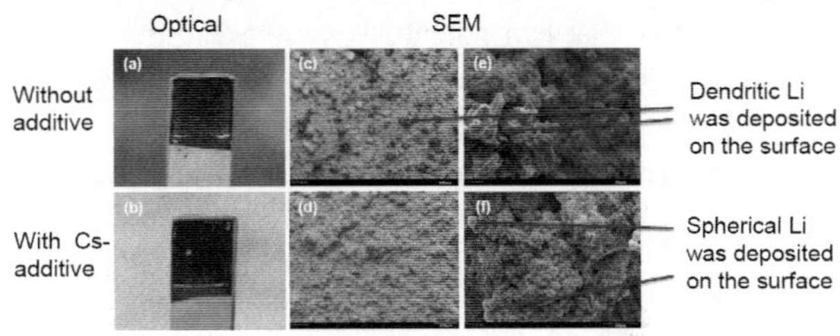

Figure 7. Surface morphologies of hard carbon electrodes after 200% overcharge in electrolytes of 1 M $LiPF_6$/PC with and without 50 mM $CsPF_6$.

Acknowledgements

This work was supported by the Assistant Secretary for Energy Efficiency and Renewable Energy, Office of Vehicle Technology of the U.S. Department of Energy (DOE). The XPS measurements were performed in the Environmental Molecular Sciences Laboratory, a national scientific user facility sponsored by the DOE's Office of Biological and Environmental Research and located at PNNL. This proceeding paper has been approved for public release and the distribution is unlimited.

References

1. D. Aurbach, E. Zinigrad, Y. Cohen, H. Teller, *Solid State Ionics*, **2002**, *148*, 405.
2. Y. Matsuda, *J. Power Sources*, **1993**, *43*, 1.
3. R. Mogi, M. Inaba, S. K. Jeong, Y. Iriyama, T. Abe, Z. Ogumi, Z. *J. Electrochem. Soc.*, **2002**, *149*, A1578.
4. Y. M. Lee, J. E. Seo, Y. G. Lee, S. H. Lee, K. Y. Cho, J. K. Park, *Electrochem. Solid-State Lett.*, **2007**, *10*, A216.
5. Y. Y. Lu, S. K. Das, S. S. Moganty, L. A. Archer, *Adv. Mater.*, **2012**, *24*, 4430.
6. F. Ding, W. Xu, X. Chen, J. Zhang, M. H. Engelhard, Y. Zhang, B. R. Johnson, J. V. Crum, T. A. Blake, X. Liu, J.-G. Zhang, *J. Electrochem. Soc.*, **2013**, *160*, A1894.
7. F. Ding, W. Xu, G. L. Graff, J. Zhang, M. Sushko, X. Chen, Y. Shao, M.H. Engelhard, Z. Nie, J. Xiao, X. Liu, P.V. Sushko, J. Liu, J.-G. Zhang, *J. Am. Chem. Soc.*, **2013**, *135*, 4450.
8. F. Ding, W. Xu, X. Chen, J. Zhang, Y. Shao, M. H. Engelhard, Y. Zhang, T. A. Blake, G. L. Graff, X. Liu, J.-G. Zhang, *J. Phys. Chem. C*, **2014**, *118*, 4043.

Development of Sodium-Iodine Battery

Andrew Mullenax, Mukul Bokil, Alexis Eccleston, Matthew Robins, Sai Bhavaraju
Ceramatec, Inc.

A critical barrier to power the military microgrids by renewable energy sources is the lack of cost-effective, reliable distributed energy storage. Another application where reliable and cost effective energy storage required is for powering military vehicles. Ceramatec, Inc., in partnership with Sandia National Labs is developing a novel, intermediate temperature (120 °C), sodium-based battery system that can potentially be the energy storage solution. This battery technology offers to address the safety & cost concerns associated with high temperature (> 300 °C) sodium batteries with ceramic electrolytes that are currently being used for large scale energy storage i.e. Sodium-Sulfur battery (Na-S). The low cycle life costs and long operational life of this battery should engender its widespread use on the military microgrid installations. This battery system will: 1) have better performance than Na-S, Li-ion and lead-acid, 2) have a maximum response time of less than 10 minutes, 3) have a target cost of less than $100/kWhr.

The key element in this proposal is the ceramic electrolyte, which is a proprietary sodium-ion conductor based on the NaSICON structure which has been developed by Ceramatec into a commercially-viable product. In this battery, we combined this NaSICON membrane with a sodium metal anode (one of the least expensive and energy dense metals) and iodine cathode. The present Na-I_2 batteries have high theoretical capacities (581 Wh/kg) and cell voltages (3.25 V) and are expected to have long cycle life (>5000 cycles). Consequently, fewer cells are required to reach the high voltages necessary for battery systems in comparison to other sodium battery chemistries. Since these batteries operate at significantly lower temperatures, the overall battery complexity and total cost through elimination of: cells, interconnect hardware, and charge control circuitry. Secondly, the lower temperature facilitates usage of many cheaper polymeric materials for battery construction. Also, the relative active material costs are low and can be acquired in commodity-size quantities with little or no additional processing required prior to incorporation into the battery.

As the first step, we have developed several aqueous, organic and molten salt catholytes containing sodium iodide/iodine that are stable at intermediate temperatures. Cyclic voltammetry studies were performed in 3 electrode cells on sodium iodide/iodine cathode that showed two distinct peaks (Figure 1) corresponding to iodide to tri-iodide and tri-iodide to iodine. Full cells were then designed and constructed with combination of steel and Teflon materials for operation at 120 °C . Figure 2 shows the discharge curves obtained using two distinct sodium iodide/iodine catholyte formulations, carbon cathode current collector, molten sodium anode, and a NaSICON separator. The data shows two distinct discharge curves corresponding to NaI to NaI_3 and NaI_3 to I_2 battery chemistries. Figure 3 are constant current charge/discharge curves obtained for one of these cathode formulations at a temperature of 118 °C. These data were collected with 115 mAh cells at C/3.5 charge/discharge rate and a current density corresponding to 10 mA per sq.cm. of membrane area. The cell was cycled 200 times at 50% Depth of Discharge (DOD) with energy efficiency of 87.5%. In summary, we have understood the redox electrochemistry of sodium iodide – Iodine cathode in aqueous and non-aqueous electrolytes and demonstrated long term and efficient performance of Na & I_2 full cells at practical DOD and C-rates. Initial cost estimates show that it is possible to fabricate these batteries at $200 per kWh making them attractive for renewable energy storage for military microgrids. This technology is also applicable for other intermediate temperature applications such as downhole batteries.

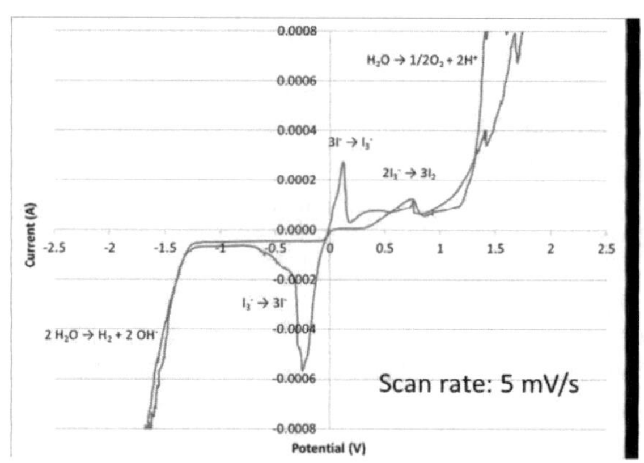

Figure 1. Cyclic Voltammograms for 0.2M NaI/0.1M I_2

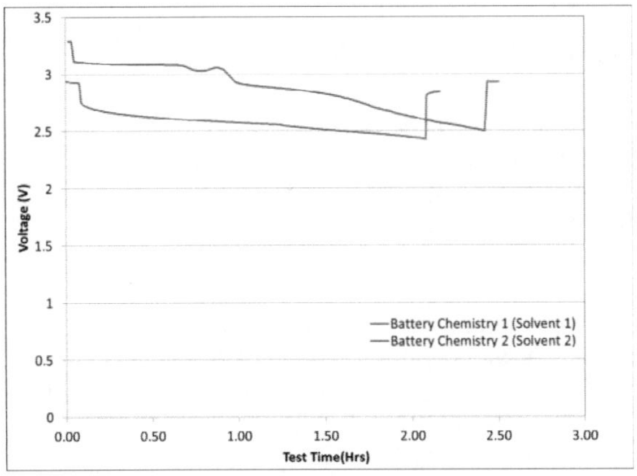

Figure 2. Two distinct high voltage battery chemistries observed for NaI/I_2 system

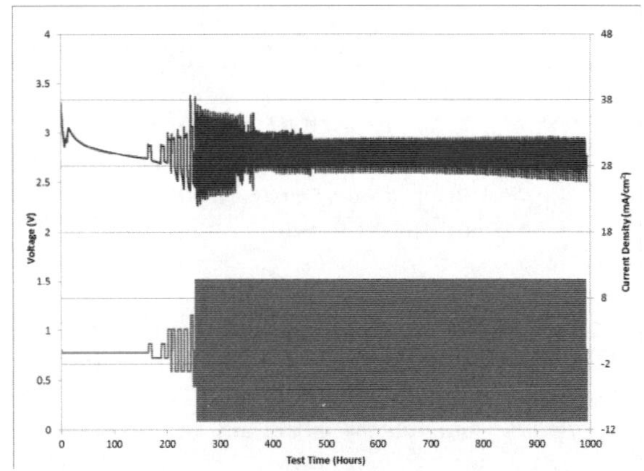

Figure 3. 200 cycle testing data for a Na-I_2 battery at C/3.5 rate

Life Performance of Large Electrochemical Capacitors

John R. Miller[a, b], Sue M. Butler[a], Seana McNeal[c]
[a]JME, Inc., 23500 Mercantile Road, Suite L, Beachwood, OH 44122
[b]Great Lakes Energy Institute, Case Western Reserve University, Cleveland, OH 44106
[c]Air Force Research Laboratory, Wright Patterson Air Force Base, Dayton, OH 45433

Abstract: *Six different electrochemical capacitor (EC) technologies were evaluated for performance and durability. Capacitor cells were held (aged) at a specified constant applied voltage and temperature and periodically removed from aging conditions for property measurements. Capacitors in this study were aged for more than 10,000 hours at rated temperature and two different voltages – rated voltage and rated voltage minus 0.1 V.*

Failure was defined as 30% loss of capacitance or doubling of DC resistance. The aging time required to reach each of these defined failure conditions was used to derive Weibull life distributions. Measured life for the Maxwell, Ioxus, Nippon Chemi-Con, and Yunasko capacitors exceeded manufacturer specifications. Properties of the JM Energy capacitors changed very little over the course of this study and life was not determined. This asymmetric electrochemical capacitor likely is affected by different stresses, for instance charge/discharge cycling or holding at low state of charge.

Keywords: electrochemical capacitor; ultracapacitor; supercapacitor; capacitor life; EDLC; reliability.

Introduction

Electrochemical capacitor (EC) technology has advanced considerably since the first components were introduced by Nippon Electric Corporation in 1978.[1] Today's products, on both a mass and a volume basis, store considerably more energy and deliver significantly higher power than earlier devices. They also provide much longer life. Today there are more than 50 companies throughout the world that manufacture EC products. Six different large-size (>1000 F) commercial or near-commercial ECs were selected for initial property and performance measurements and to perform a long-term aging evaluation. Photographs of these capacitor cells are shown in **Figure 1**. Twelve cells from each manufacturer were purchased for this study.

Test Capacitors and Initial Properties

The capacitors evaluated in this study are listed in **Table 1**. All are single cells. When the study began (late 2012), these were the newest models of capacitors available from each manufacturer.

Initial property measurements included electrochemical impedance spectroscopy (EIS) and charge/discharge measurements. EIS measurements were made using a Gamry Reference 3000 with cells at a bias of $0.75*V_{rated}$. Impedance results in the complex plane representation are shown in **Figure 2**. The equivalent series resistance (ESR) is the value of the impedance at the intersection with the real axis. Shown is an intersection with the real axis at 90-1000 μΩ for the different capacitor products. The asymmetric electrochemical capacitor cells (JM Energy) and the Nippon Chemi-Con (NCC) cells, both with carbonate electrolyte, showed higher ESR values partly because of the lower conductivity of such electrolytes. With porous electrodes, EIS data intersects the real axis at an angle of ~45°, which increases the real part of the impedance for all capacitor products except those from Yunasko.[2] The Yunasko cells have been designed to have minimum ESR and these cells have the lowest DC resistance and exhibit the highest charge/discharge efficiency. The JM Energy cells have been designed to maximize stored energy. And these cells have the highest DC resistance and exhibit the lowest charge/discharge efficiency.

Table 1. Electrochemical Capacitor products evaluated in this study.

Manufacturer	Model	Origin	Design	Electrolyte	Form Factor	Specifications
Maxwell	BCAP3000 (K2R2)	USA	Symmetric C-C	acetonitrile	60-mm-ϕ right cylinder	3000 F, 2.7 V, 65 °C
Ioxus	RSC2R7308LR	USA	Symmetric C-C	acetonitrile	60-mm-ϕ right cylinder	3000 F, 2.7 V, 65 °C
Nippon Chemi-Con	DXL Series	Japan	Symmetric C-C	carbonate	40-mm-ϕ right cylinder	1200 F, 2.5 V, 70 °C
JM Energy*	ULTIMO CLQ1100S1A	Japan	Asymmetric (LIC)*	carbonate	prismatic	1100 F, 3.8V, 65 °C
BatsCap	SC01911	France	Symmetric C-C	acetonitrile	62-mm-ϕ right cylinder	1200 F, 2.7 V, 65 °C
Yunasko	Pilot production	Ukraine	Symmetric C-C	acetonitrile	Prismatic	1200 F, 2.7 V, 60 °C

* Lithium-ion capacitor, minimum voltage 2.2 V

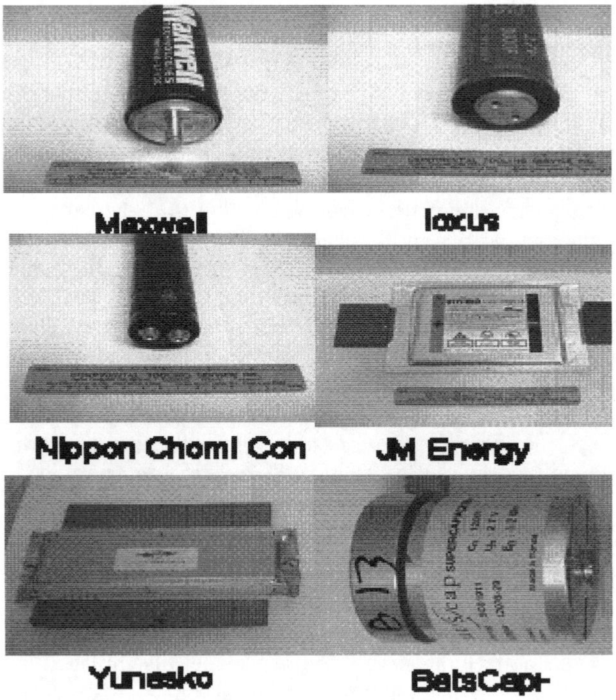

Figure 1. Photographs of the six different electrochemical capacitor technologies evaluated in this study.

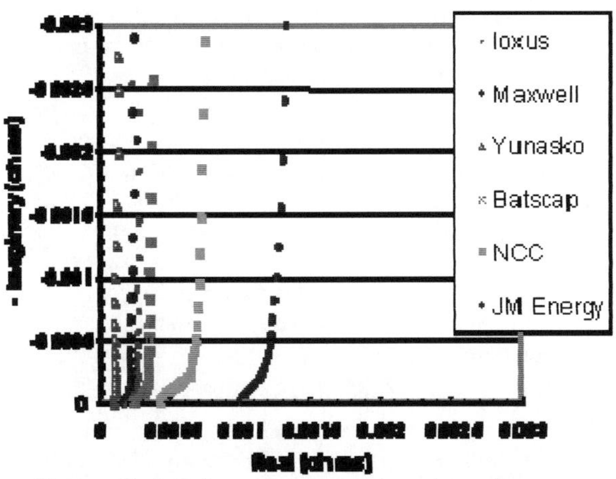

Figure 2. Initial room temperature impedance measurements of the six technologies in a complex plane format.

EIS phase angle results are shown in **Figure 3**. The frequency of the –45° phase angle can be used to judge the relative response times of the different capacitors. The Yunasko capacitor has the fastest response while the JM Energy capacitor has the slowest response. It is interesting to note that the Maxwell, Ioxus, and Nippon Chemi-Con capacitors have very similar response times even though the first two use acetonitrile-based electrolyte while NCC capacitors use propylene carbonate (PC) -based electrolyte. Generally capacitors with PC have slower response but the design of these capacitors has been optimized for power performance, thus giving them phase angle behavior comparable to the acetonitrile-based capacitors.

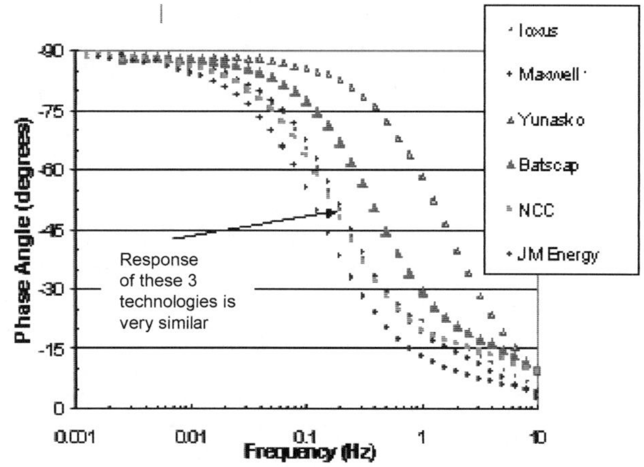

Figure 3. **Initial room temperature impedance phase angle of the six technologies. The phase angle allows direct and proper comparison of different size capacitors.**

Other measurements made before and during the aging study were charge/discharge measurements between rated voltage and half rated voltage (or for the full voltage window of the JM Energy cells). The DC resistance was derived by dividing the current-interrupt voltage change measured 5 seconds after the interruption by the discharge current. The current used for the capacitance measurement can influence its value, with the measured capacitance decreasing as measurement current increases. Generally current has little or no influence on the DC resistance values. Initial capacitance and resistance values are listed in **Table 2**. These measurements were made using relatively low currents (15 A for the 3000 F cells and 5 A for the other cells) while capacitance and resistance values used for the aging test were made using much higher currents (respectively 300 A and 150 A). Table 2 also lists ESR, specific energy, and the device response time calculated as the product of capacitance and DC resistance.

Aging Results

Voltage and temperature, not charge/discharge cycling, are generally the major stress factors that affect EC life.[3] Groups of ECs were aged at constant temperature and two different voltage levels. One group of 4 cells of each technology was aged at rated voltage and a second group of 5 cells was aged at 0.1 V below rated voltage, all at 65 °C temperature except 60 °C for the Yunasko cells (Table 1).

In this study, the time to reach failure for the capacitors in each group was fit to a Weibull distribution:

$$F(t) = 1 - e^{[-(\frac{t}{\alpha})^{\beta}]}$$

where F(t) is the fraction of the population failing by time t and α and β are both positive parameters. β has no units and is called the "shape factor," while α has units of time

and is called the "characteristic life." Values of $\beta < 1$ describe failure rates that are highest at short times. High values of β describe an ever-increasing failure rate with time. The parameter α, by definition, equals the time at which 63.2% of the cells have failed.(4)

Table 2. Initial properties of cells from the six electrochemical capacitor technologies evaluated in this study.

	Capacitance*,# (F)	DC Resistance* (μΩ)	ESR (μΩ)	Stored Energy# (Wh/kg)	Response Time^ (s)
Maxwell	3140 +/- 16	230 +/- 15	162	4.5	0.7
Ioxus	3100 +/-34	230 +/- 21	174	4.3	0.7
NCC	1090 +/- 22	860 +/- 26	420	2.8	1.1
Yunasko	1230 +/- 14	160 +/- 45	92	4.0	0.2
JM Energy	1090 +/- 2.3	2100 +/- 72	990	10	2.3
Batscap	1290 +/- 5.7	330 +/- 45	240	4.0	0.4

* The tolerances listed are one standard deviation of the twelve cells measured

Calculated assuming discharge to half rated voltage except JM Energy full voltage window

^ Calculated as product of the DC resistance and rated capacitance

Capacitor life may be defined in a number of ways: the time until the capacitor exhibits an explicit failure, such as a package rupture or internal short, or the time needed to reach poor performance. For this study, failure is defined when the EC exhibits a doubling of DC resistance or a 30% loss of capacitance or an explicit failure. Using these definitions, time to failure (life) for each capacitor in each group is used to derive Weibull life distributions at each test condition. Weibull shape and scale factors β and α were derived using Statgraphics software.

Weibull life models could be derived for the Maxwell, Ioxus, Nippon Chemi-Con, and Yunasko capacitors but not for the JM Energy or the Batscap products. Properties of the JM Energy capacitors changed very little over the course of aging. Defined failures were not observed. Three of the Batscap capacitors were damaged from improper handling during this study making the sample set too small for life distribution derivation.

As is usual for ECs during aging, the series resistance increased and capacitance decreased. Properties changed faster in the groups aged at the higher voltage. Life distribution derivations were made using the time needed to reach defined failures for capacitance and resistance measured at the highest test currents, 300 A for Maxwell and Ioxus and 150 A for Nippon Chemi-Con and Yunasko.

EC properties generally change most rapidly when voltage is first applied (primarily because impurities or active surface groups on an electrode undergo chemical reactions). In practice some capacitor manufacturers hold cells at maximum stress levels, i.e. "burn-in" the cells, to eliminate such rapid changes. For the purpose of determining capacitor life in this study, to reduce the effects from such possible early rapid change, we used measurements after 42 - 89 hours of aging as the initial property values. The exact time to failure with the above definitions was determined for each cell by graphical means with data smoothing. Because of the considerable scatter in the Yunasko resistance values, the time to reach the defined failure for each of these cells was determined by fitting the long-time results to a straight-line and extrapolating to the defined failure point.

Life data was well fit by a single straight line in each Weibull plot, suggesting a single failure mode was dominant for each group of cells. Weibull characteristic life and shape factors derived from the model fits are listed in **Table 3**. Note that all shape factors are much greater than one, signifying a "wear out" failure.

Figure 4 plots the life distributions for these four capacitor technologies using the Table 3 Weibull parameters. As shown, the Maxwell and Yunasko cells reached resistance failure before they reached capacitance failure. Ioxus and NCC cells failed the opposite way. For all of the technologies, cells aged at higher voltage failed sooner. A common rule-of-thumb for capacitor life is that it doubles with a 0.1 V reduction in applied voltage.(5,6) That relationship was found to be approximately correct for Maxwell and Ioxus cells but not for NCC and Yunasko cells, where life was not greatly extended with a 0.1 V reduction in applied voltage. Apparently another mechanism is interfering with the voltage stress impact on life.

Manufacturers generally rate their capacitors for 1000 to 2000 hours of life at rated conditions often using a definition of failure as used in this study. However, manufacturer capacitance values generally are determined using a low current discharge. Maxwell, Ioxus, and NCC capacitors meet the manufacturer's criteria for life. The Yunasko capacitors are in pilot production and the manufacturer has not assigned the criteria for their life. These capacitors would meet the standard criteria for life defined using capacitance loss. The initial resistance values for the Yunasko capacitors are extraordinarily low and when that resistance value is doubled, it is still substantially below the resistance of the other technologies when scaled to an equivalent size device. Thus, Yunasko capacitors remain fully functional with a much greater resistance increase than the other technologies. Thus the low characteristic life values listed in Table 3 do not represent true life.

Table 3. Weibull life distributions parameters derived using two different definitions of failure (end of life).

Technology, Aging conditions	Capacitance Failure: Characteristic Life (hr)	Capacitance Failure: Shape factor	Resistance Failure: Characteristic Life (hr)	Resistance Failure: Shape factor
Maxwell 2.6 V, 65°C	6500	5.5	5700	40
Maxwell 2.7 V, 65°C	3900	5.1	2400	12
Ioxus 2.6 V, 65°C	7500	14	10500	4.5
Ioxus 2.7 V, 65°C	4500	11	4600	9.5
NCC 2.4 V, 65°C	2700	4.9	8300	3.6
NCC 2.5 V, 65°C	1800	16	7200	3.2
Yunasko 2.6 V, 60°C	9600	4.5	560	1.7
Yunasko 2.7 V, 60°C	6500	2.3	380	1.8

Conclusion

Maxwell, Ioxus, and NCC capacitors exhibited long life at the accelerated aging conditions used in this study and can be expected to perform for many tens to hundreds of thousands of hours when operated at reduced voltage and/or lower temperatures. The pilot production Yunasko capacitors exhibited the longest life in terms of capacitance retention. Even with tripling of resistance these capacitors still have very low resistance values. Properties of the JM Energy capacitors changed very little over the course of this study with none reaching the failure definition. This asymmetric electrochemical capacitor apparently is stressed differently than symmetric ECs, for instance cycling or being maintained at a partial charge state.

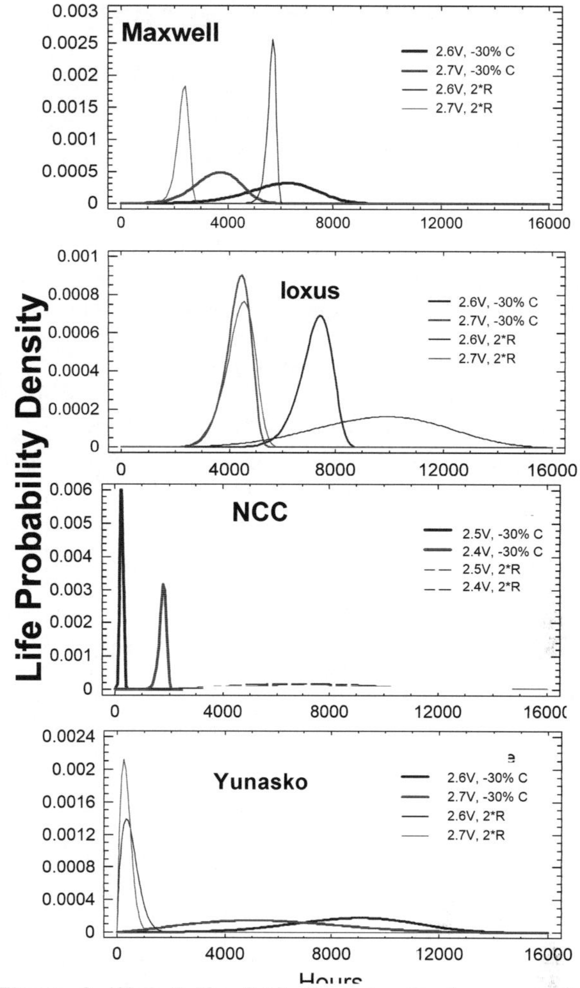

Figure 4. Weibull life distributions for the four capacitor technologies using the Table 3 parameters with failure defined by two criteria.

Acknowledgements

The authors thank the Wright Patterson AFB HESM team for discussions and helpful guidance.

References

1. Additional historic information can be found in: Miller, J.R. *"A Brief History of Supercapacitors"*, Battery + Energy Storage Technology (**BEST**) magazine, pp 61-78, Autumn issue, no. 18 (2007).
2. Conway, B.E., Electrochemical Supercapacitors: Scientific Fundamentals and Technological Applications, Chapter 14, pp377-416, *"Electrochemical Behavior of Porous Electrodes; Applications to Capacitors*", Kluwer Academic/Plenum Publishers, New York (1999).
3. Weingarth, D., Foelske-Schmitz, A., and Kotz, R., *"Cycle versus voltage hold -- Which is the better stability test for electrochemical double layer capacitors?"*, Journal of Power Sources **225,** pp84-88 (2013)
4. Beguin, F. and E. Frackowiak, editors, Supercapacitors: Materials, Systems, and Applications, Chapter 13 *"Reliability of Electrochemical Capacitors"*, pp 473-507, WILEY-VCH Verlag GmbH & Co, Weinheim, Germany (2013).
5. Miller, J.R., Goltser, I., and Butler, S., *"Electrochemical Capacitor Life Predictions Using Accelerated Test Methods"*, Proc. of the 42nd Power Sources Conference, Philadelphia, PA, pp581-584, (June 12-14, 2006).
6. Kotz, R., Ruch, P.W., and Cericola, D., *"Aging and failure mode of electrochemical capacitor during accelerated constant load tests"*, J. Power Sources **195**, pp923-928 (2010).

Saft Nickel-Carbon Capacitors for High-Power Applications

Ian Edward O'Connor & Carl Postiglione

ian.o'connor@saftamerica.com

Saft America, Inc.

701 Gil Harbin Industrial Blvd, Valdosta, Georgia, 31602

Abstract: *There is an increasing need for reliable and safe energy storage devices which can deliver high power. Supercapacitors have a unique capability to repeatedly deliver a significant amount of energy over a wide range of temperatures for an extended period of time. This is particularly important when it comes to critical applications as well as lifetime costs.*

In many applications a battery is utilized to provide both power and energy requirements. For example in a typical engine, a lead-acid battery is used to start the engine and also to run the electronics whilst the vehicle is operating. Starting an engine requires a large amount power, and a non-trivial amount of energy, however the battery size can be dramatically reduced when incorporating a supercapacitor into the starting system. A supercapacitor can guarantee the power to start, operate over a much wider temperature range and cost less over the long-term life of the vehicle.

Keywords: Supercapacitor; Nickel-Carbon Capacitor; Aqueous; Non-Flammable; Cold-Temperature Performance.

Introduction

Supercapacitors represent alternative devices for energy and power storage, especially for applications for which the energy is required for only a relatively short time-frame e.g. engine starting.[1] Saft America, Inc. currently provides an asymmetric aqueous supercapacitor with a Nickel oxyhydroxide electrode and an activated carbon electrode. The structure of the Saft Nickel-Carbon capacitor also called a NiCap is shown in Figure 1 compared to that of a standard symmetric set-up.

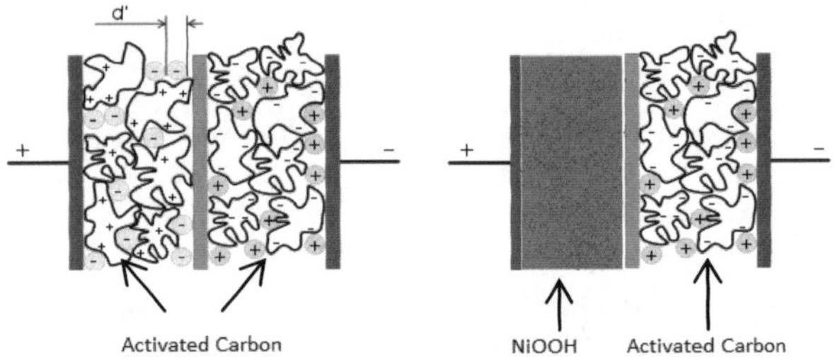

Figure 1. Symmetric versus asymmetric Saft Nickel-Carbon capacitor

Most supercapacitors on the market today contain organic electrolyte. Saft NiCaps contain aqueous electrolyte and this has a number of advantages including non-flammability, safe venting capability and no requirement for cell balancing. In addition to high flammability some organic electrolytes can have toxic decomposition products. In Figure 2 we can see the difference in the self-discharge of an organic system containing balancing equipment versus a Saft system without balancing equipment. This can be critical in some applications. As an example military vehicles need to be ready to go at very short notice. This currently requires maintaining the batteries at an optimal charge. Dead batteries mean loss of readiness. Supercapacitors that require cell balancing may also mean loss of readiness within a couple of weeks. Incoporation of a Saft NiCap can eliminate the need to maintain batteries for starting. It will hold its power for months and be able to crank an engine even if the vehicle shows no sign of life. In fact a 12 V Saft supercapacitor is able to maintain a voltage above 9 V for up to 4 years without any additional charge.

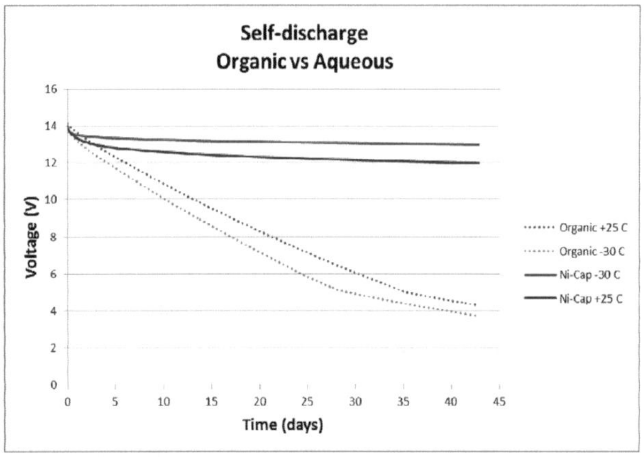

Figure 2. Discharge profile of an aqueous Nickel-carbon capacitor without electronic balancing requirements

In many other high power applications a supercapacitor can be a better choice than a battery, or reduce the battery requirements. The main reasons for this are the vastly superior cycle life and increased power capability that a supercapacitor can achieve. In figure 2 we can see the ease at which a Saft Nickel-Carbon capacitor can achieve 100,000 cycles. In a typical engine starting application a lead acid battery can achieve only 100's or a couple of thousand cycles before the performance is diminished.

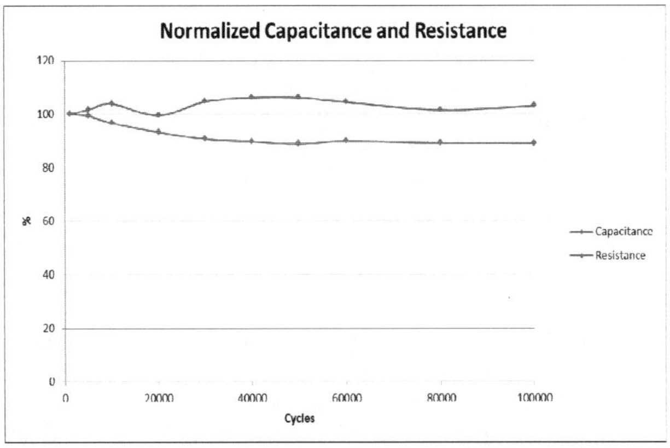

Figure 3. Cycling performance of Saft Nickel-Carbon capacitor

Due to the lack of a chemical reaction, supercapacitors not only have remarkable stability with the ability to charge and discharge for up to 1 million cycles but they also have superior low temperature capability.[2] A typical battery will lose significant performance capability below freezing and cease to function at all below around -20 °C, whereas Saft Nickel capacitors can continue to perform to -40 °C or below. In Figure 4 we can see the performance profile of a typical Saft supercapacitor across a wide temperature range.

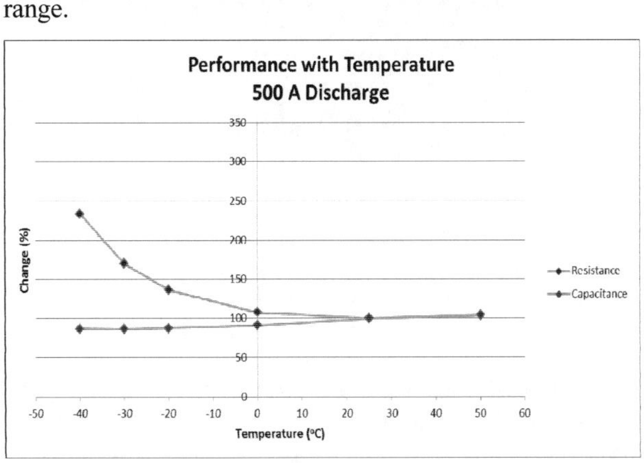

Figure 4. Performance of a Saft Nickel capacitor versus temperature

We believe that the market for using supercapacitors in engine starting will grow over the next few years considering the advantages they offer. The big 3 car companies are looking at using supercapacitors for start-stop applications. As mentioned previously a Supercapacitor can potentially start an engine up to 1 million times, so it is a good fit for applications like start-stop in which it could be required to start an engine several hundred times a day. Many commercial industries are specifying supercapacitors on new vehicles to prevent dead battery no-starts and save on lead acid battery replacement by reducing the number they use.

Penn State ARL is testing various engine starting technologies and has come to the determination that the optimal configuration is to utilize supercapacitors with low cost lead-acid batteries. They also felt that Saft technology was the best due to its aforementioned low self-discharge, better cold temp performance and safer electrolyte. For extreme cold weather starting conditions they recommend a system which uses a DC/DC converter to temporarily boost the NiCap's voltage by 20% and increase the energy available to start by 50%. In the course of Penn State ARL's testing they performed sequential engine start tests, without recharging, to evaluate the capability of Saft's NiCaps and this can be seen in Figure 5. A total of twenty starts were recorded far surpassing the requirements of a typical engine start protocol.

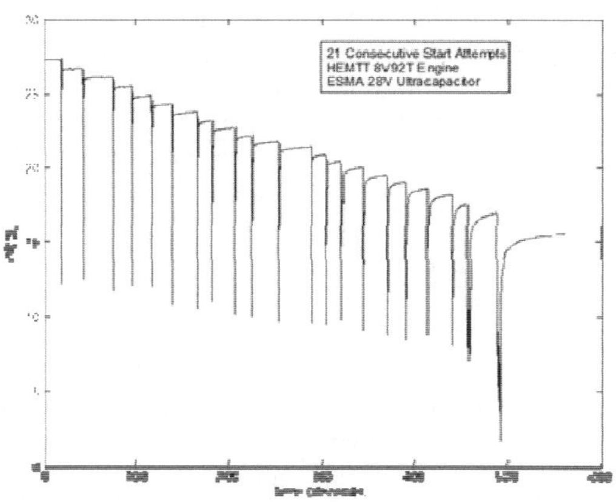

Figure 5. Saft Nickel capacitor perfomance under testing by Penn State ARL

Installation is a critical part of taking full advantage of this technology. Simply paralleling a Supercap with a vehicle's battery will gain substantial support in starting and an improvement in cycle capability. However, parasitic loads and self-discharge can drain the batteries, and therefore the supercapacitors, unless an isolation circuit is used. This ensures that the Nickel capacitor does not drain into dead batteries when the engine is off. This system engages the NiCap only when the engine is starting. Once it recharges the capacitor, it is isolated again until another start is needed. In figure 6 we can see a generic representation of the starting system.

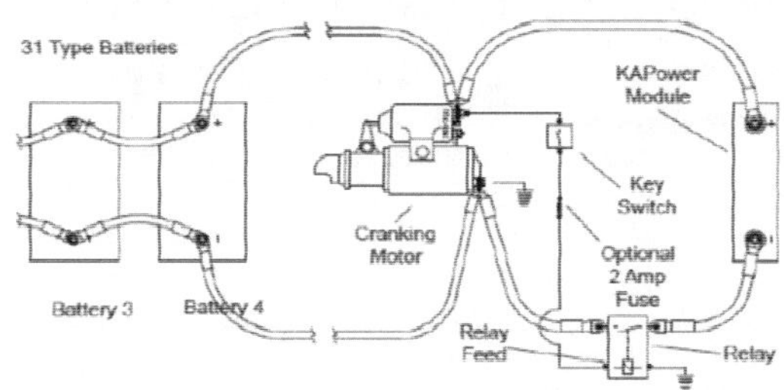

Figure 6. Schematic of an engine set-up incorporating a Saft nickel-carbon capacitor

Saft is currently supplying NiCaps into the transit bus market. These buses are a primary mode of transportation for people in cities and around the country. Dead batteries mean a loss of service resulting in reduced ridership as well as a significant inconvenience for passengers and driver. Many have begun using the NiCap with our partners Kold-Ban international in a starting module which is design to crank the bus regardless of the batteries' state of charge. Bus drivers are typically required to engage their battery cut-off switch the end of the day to keep the batteries isolated from any parasitic loads. However this often does not often happen and results in dead batteries the next morning. Also during breaks in the daily routes the lights and other accessories often remain on while the engine is off, draining the battery. Compounding this are parasitic loads that are never turned off, such as fire suppression and fare boxes. Since the battery may take hours to fully recharge, if not given the opportunity of doing so, they can fail en route. This can lead to no starts in the middle of the day stranding riders and costing the municipality thousands of dollars and hours of wasted time to pick up the riders with a new bus and get the dead bus back to the shop. Saft has over one thousand NiCap in the field with no dead battery no-starts reported thus far.

Saft has partnered with Kold Ban International[3] to develop an all in one Bus starting module. This includes isolation and control systems in a size that can fit in an 8D's space. Municipalities have reported an 80% drop in field calls because of this technology. In figure 7 we can see a unit installed in the lower battery tray of a transit bus in Tacoma WA.

Figure 7. Saft/KoldBan International unit installed in a transit bus

Not only do the NiCaps give reliable cranking in all weather conditions they can also be used to support voltage transient suppression. Many vehicles use electric fans and AC systems which when turned on require higher power levels for their electrical system to start. This requirement often creates a transient voltage spike that can cause harm or create error conditions. Using the NiCaps to absorb those transients is proving to be another application for this technology.

Saft is finishing the development of an 6T sized supercapacitor as can be seen in figure 8. This NiCap will be 24V 500F and 120kJ. In Engine starting applications it is designed to replace two 6T Lead Acid batteries but only require the space of one.

Figure 8. Prototype of a 6T nickel capacitor design

Saft will also have an isolation module that can be attached to the side of the capacitor or elsewhere in the vehicle. This module will allow the NiCap to start the vehicle and provide the required isolation for parasitic loads.

Saft's unique Nickel-Carbon asymmetrical design with simple aqueous electrolyte represents an economical and safe product that can be incorporated into a plethora of different applications with relative ease.

References

1. Beliakov, A., "Russian Supercapacitors to Start Engines", *Battery International*, 102, 1993
2. El Brouji, E.H., Briat, O., Vinassa, J.M. Bertrand, N. Woirgard, E. "Impact of Calendar Life and Cycling Ageing on Supercapacitor Performance", *IEEE Trans. Veh. Technol.*, 58, 3917 2009.
3. www.koldban.com

Millisecond-Pulse Electric Double Layer Capacitors

John R. Miller[1], Ronald A. Outlaw[2], Samuel G. Parler[3], and Sue M. Butler[1]
[1]JME, Inc, 23500 Mercantile Road, Suite L, Beachwood, OH 44122 USA
[2]College of William and Mary, Dept. of Applied Science, Williamsburg, VA 23185 USA
[3]Cornell Dubilier Electronics, Inc., 140 Technology Place, Liberty, SC 29657 USA

Abstract: *Electric double layer capacitors (EDLCs) fabricated using vertically-oriented graphene nanosheet electrodes and capable of efficiently delivering high-power millisecond-long pulses were developed. Two approaches are described for fabricating high-voltage EDLCs. Their volumetric advantage over aluminum electrolytic capacitor technology is shown. And their power levels and operating duty cycles can greatly exceed that provided by other capacitor technologies primarily because of the innovative planar design used to interconnect cells in series, which provides highly effective cooling.*

Keywords: electrochemical capacitor; electric double layer capacitor; graphene; Supercapacitor; Ultracapacitor; EDLC

Introduction

Electric double layer capacitors (EDLCs), sometimes referred to by the product names Supercapacitor or Ultracapacitor, have much higher energy density than other types of capacitors. They are increasingly being used because of their many attractive features including high cycle life and unexcelled reliability. Unfortunately, EDLCs do not offer a similar volumetric advantage for millisecond-pulse operation. That is because of their porous electrodes, which provide high surface area needed for charge storage, but at the expense of creating a multiple-time-constant electrical response. The typical response time is one second. To achieve efficient millisecond-pulse operation while retaining high capacitance density, a totally different electrode structure is needed than found in today's EDLCs.[(1)] It must have relatively high surface area concomitant with small electronic/ionic resistance values and minimal distributed charge storage.

We have developed an electrode structure that offers millisecond-pulse operation that also retains the major advantages of an EDLC[(2,3)]. Devices made with these electrodes offer up to a ten-fold reduction in volume over conventional aluminum electrolytic capacitor technology. Significantly, these devices, because they are EDLCs, have greatly enhanced reliability over aluminum electrolytic capacitors. Furthermore, heat generation is low and its dissipation exceptionally high compared with other types of capacitors, allowing these new EDLCs to operate at pulse-power levels and duty cycles heretofore not possible.

First discussed are EDLC electrodes made from vertically-oriented graphene nanosheet (VOGN) material that is grown on a metal current collector. The physical structure of these electrodes minimizes both electronic and ionic resistances and has minimal distributed charge storage. Then a cell design is described having improved volumetric efficiency. Third, two different approaches are presented for series connecting these cells to create high voltage EDLCs. Fourth, thermal management issues are discussed. Exceptional pulse-power performance is expected from these capacitors. And finally, applications most suitable for these millisecond-pulse EDLCs are identified.

Graphene Electrode

VOGN thin films are grown on bare nickel current collectors to form the EDLC electrodes. Radio frequency plasma enhanced chemical vapor deposition (RF PECVD) of CH_4/H_2 or C_2H_2/H_2 feed gases is used at power levels up to 1000 W. The substrate temperature is typically held between 550 and 850 °C during VOGN growth. No catalytic seed material is required or used. Growth proceeds by Volmer-Weber island impingement[(4)], which yields an upturned defect structure at carbon island boundaries followed by continued vertical growth controlled by sp2 bonding. During growth there is significant carbon dissolution into the nickel substrate as depicted in **Figure 1**. Generally the intensity ratio of the Raman D band to G band gradually decreases with growth time indicating the crystalline order of the VOGN increases with nanosheet height, which increases approximately linearly with time at rates of 70 nm/min using CH_4 and 190 nm/min using C_2H_2.[(5)] VOGN height was typically ~2 μm or less for the reported results. Electrode capacitance measured at 1 kHz typically was in the range of 100 to 300 μF/cm^2, depending on VOGN growth conditions and growth time.

VOGN Charge Storage Enhancement

As shown in **Figure 1d**, a typical 1-μm-tall VOGN structure is relatively open with >0.1 μm spacing between the vertical features. Such openings are much greater than necessary to allow efficient millisecond pulse operation with typical electrolytes. Thus it is possible to increase the electrode's geometric capacitance density by adding charge storage material on the surfaces of the VOGN structure. Carbon black, for instance, which can have relatively high surface area and thus have substantial double layer charge storage, has been shown to provide kHz-frequency-capacitance when in a ~1-μm-thick layer on a metal current collector.[(6)] Key requirements are: 1) electrically connect the charge storage material to the graphene nanosheets with minimal series resistance, and 2) prevent distributed charge

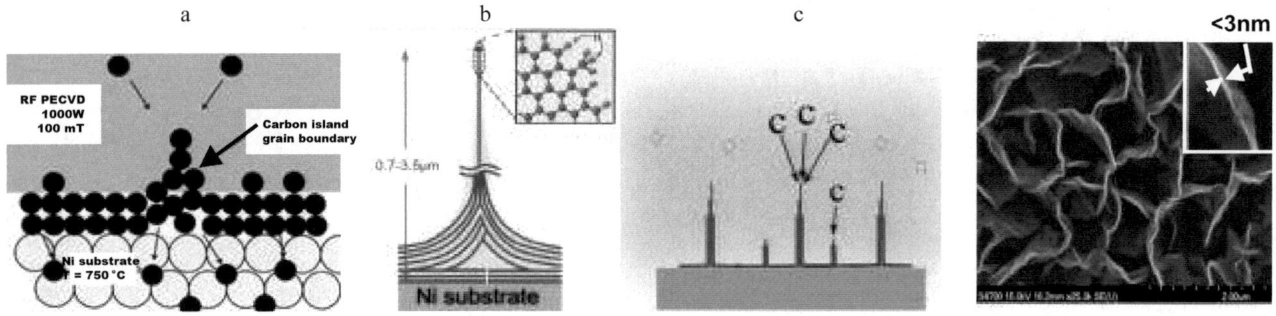

Figure 1. Mechanism of RF PECVD graphene growth on nickel. Some of the carbon deposited on the nickel dissolves into the lattice and forms a low-resistance ohmic connection (a). Graphene islands on the nickel grow primarily at their perimeter and expand in size until impinging another island to cause vertical growth via a Volmer-Weber mechanism, (b). and (c). Subsequent growth occurs predominantly on the top edges of the vertical structures, leading to the vertically oriented graphene nanosheet structure shown in the micrograph (d).

storage behavior from developing by not overpacking the voids since even rough surfaces[7] or densely packed solid metal spheres can exhibit porous electrode behavior.[8] Various processes have been used to apply the charge storage material, including electrospray deposition, ink jet printing, and dip-coating. A SEM micrograph of a VOGN electrode with carbon black charge storage material added using electrospray deposition is shown in **Figure 2**. Ten-fold or greater capacitance enhancements can readily be achieved using this approach.

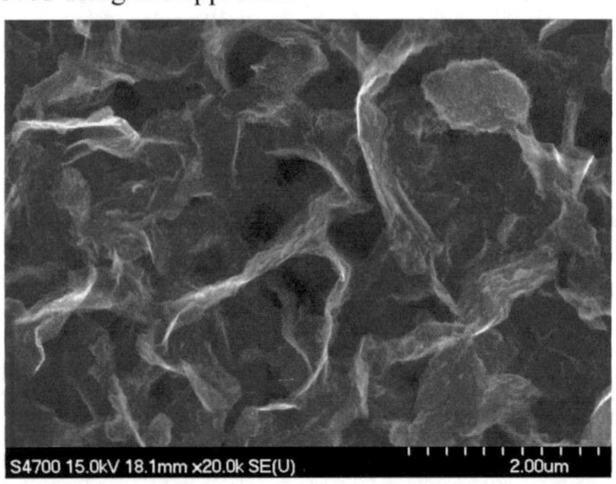

Figure 2. VOGN electrode covered with a thin coating of carbon black charge storage material. This can substantially increase geometric capacitance density and, if properly done, not adversely impact the frequency response of the electrode.

Cell Design

The conventional design for an EDLC cell (porous separator sandwiched between two electrodes inserted between two current collectors) is poorly suited for millisecond-pulse EDLC since the VOGN electrodes are typically only ~1 μm thick. With this electrode thickness and using a 25-μm-thick separator with two 50-μm-thick current collectors, active material occupies less than 2% of the total volume. Higher volumetric efficiency can be obtained using a planar design as shown in **Figure 3**, where the VOGN electrodes occupy more than 5% of the total volume, doubling the volumetric efficiency. Rather than relying on a separator to electronically isolate the two electrodes, this design separates the two electrodes by an insulating physical gap. The fabrication sequence is depicted in **Figure 3a**, where an interdigitated gap is cut (using a laser) through the VOGN layer and 1-μm-thick nickel underlayer down to the insulating substrate. This generates two electrically isolated electrodes, adjacent to each other. A single EDLC cell is created by overcoating the gap and fingers with electrolyte. The design shown in **Figure 3b** has 6-mm-long by 200-μm-wide fingers spaced using a 20-μm-wide gap. **Figure 3c** is a photograph of a planar EDLC fabricated having this design. An aqueous gelled or solid state electrolyte covers the two electrodes and gap.

Capacitor Design

EDLC cells, like battery cells, operate at low voltage. Thus cells must be series connected to create a high-voltage capacitor. **Figure 4** shows two approaches devised for interconnecting planar EDLC cells to create a high-voltage millisecond-pulse EDLC. The first approach (**Figure 4a**) involves stacking the Figure 3 planar cells then interconnecting them on opposite edges in an accordion-like fashion using, for example, solder. Volumetric efficiency of the planar design is maintained in this stack.

The second approach involves interconnecting planar EDLC cells using the metallization on the substrate. As shown (**Figure 4b**), interdigitated gaps are cut through the VOGN and nickel to create multiple electrically-isolated regions (six in the figure). The gaps are then individually covered with an electrolyte, making sure that each electrolyte band does not touch its neighbor. This is a "bipolar" design in two dimensions, with the substrate metallization serving as the bipolar plate. Connecting M cells in series each rated at voltage V_o with capacitance C_o and resistance R_o using either approach yields a capacitor with a voltage rating $M{\bullet}V_o$, capacitance C_o/M, and series resistance $M{\bullet}R_o$. The frequency response of this high-

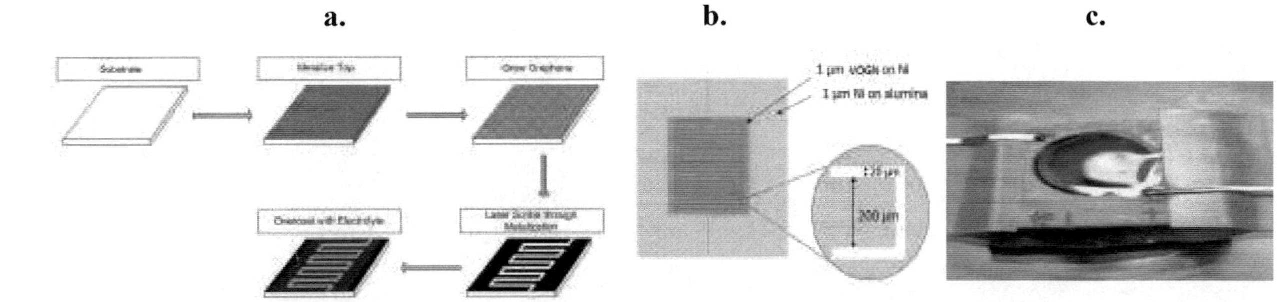

Figure 3. a.) Sequence of steps used to fabricate a planar EDLC cell, which has higher volumetric efficiency than a conventional "sandwich" design. Graphene is grown on a metallized insulating substrate, separated into two electrodes using a laser to cut a gap, then covered with an electrolyte to create a single EDLC cell. **b.)** Example pattern with 200-µm-wide fingers separated by 20-µm-wide gaps. and **c.)** Photograph of planar EDLC fabricated using this design coated with a gelled aqueous electrolyte.

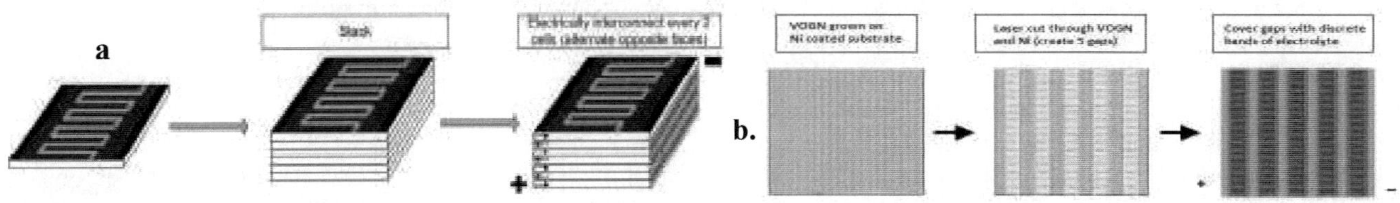

Figure 4. a.) Sequence of steps used to series-connect the Figure 3 cells using stacking. The last step involves electrically interconnecting every other cell on alternate sides of the stack. **b.)** Sequence of steps to series connect VOGN cells in a plane. Graphene is grown on a metallized insulating substrate, the surface segmented into N+1 electrically isolated regions, and then the gaps between each region covered with a band of electrolyte. This yields a capacitor having N series-connected EDLC cells. Electrolyte bands must be physically isolated from each other with this approach.

voltage capacitor will be nearly identical to that of one of its constituent cells. Voltage-balance resistors can be added to the planar design using, for instance, thick-film printing processes.

Capacitor Electrical Response

Figure 5 shows the impedance phase angle of three capacitors; a standard commercial EDLC, a pulse-optimized commercial EDLC, and a VOGN-electrode EDLC using an aqueous electrolyte. The –45°-phase-angle frequency values are ~0.2 Hz for the standard commercial EDLC, 10 Hz for the pulse-optimized EDLC, and ~10^4 Hz for our graphene-nanosheet-electrode EDLC. This means that the VOGN capacitor is 1000 times more responsive than the pulse-power-optimized commercial EDLC and 50,000 times more responsive than a standard commercial EDLC, remembering that charge or discharge times are indirectly related to this frequency. This clearly demonstrates that the VOGN electric double layer capacitor is well suited for efficient millisecond-pulse operation.

It is informative to compare the volume of a millisecond-pulse EDLC to that of a comparably-rated aluminum electrolytic capacitor since "lytics" are popular in pulse applications. High-voltage VOGN capacitors have not been produced but it is straight-forward to model their expected performance and make this comparison. Using the Figure 4b planar design with 3.0 V per cell operation, 25 mF/cm^2 areal capacitance density, 50 µm total thickness (substrate, VOGN capacitor, and protective cover), and ignoring gap capacitance loss and balancing resistor volume, the

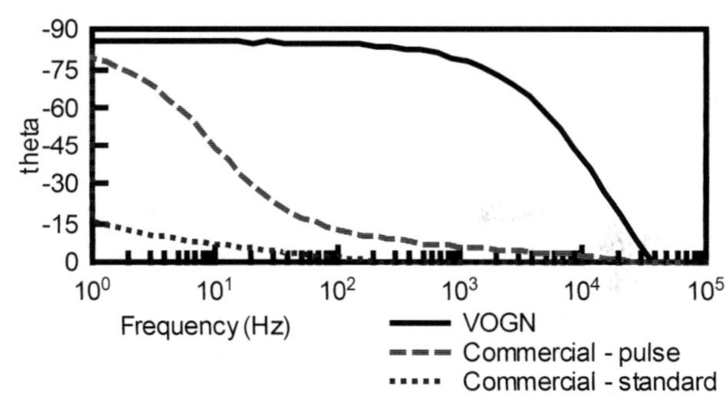

Figure 5. Impedance phase angle measurements from three capacitor cells; our VOGN-electrode EDLC, a pulse-power-optimized commercial EDLC, and a standard commercial EDLC. The VOGN-electrode EDLC shows capacitive behavior at frequencies above 1 kHz, orders of magnitude higher than the two commercial EDLCs.

calculated capacitance per volume (µF/cm^3) is 10.8/V^2 where V is the voltage rating. This equation is plotted in **Figure 6** along with values for commercial aluminum electrolytic capacitors. As shown, the volumetric advantage of the millisecond-pulse EDLC is clearly largest at low voltages. Significantly, the VOGN capacitor is predicted to have a capacitance density higher than present commercial aluminum electrolytic capacitors at all voltages.

Capacitor Thermal Management

The Figure 4b planar millisecond-pulse EDLC has unique power handling capabilities because heat extraction distances are small and uniform, i.e. directly through the

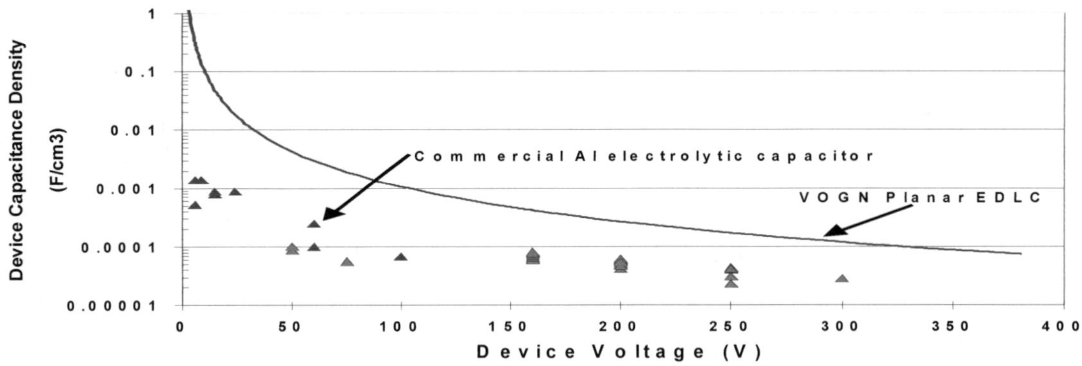

Figure 6. Comparison of the capacitance density of millisecond-pulse EDLCs (i.e. model predictions) with commercial aluminum electrolytic capacitors. EDLC technology clearly shows volumetric advantages that are greatest at low voltage but persist over the entire voltage range.

thin substrate (typically ≤50 μm), which for instance could be thermally anchored to a liquid-cooled heat sink. In contrast, aluminum electrolytic capacitor electrodes typically are wound into mm- to cm-diameter bobbins with heights of many cm. This geometry with these dimensions makes heat extraction problematic--power levels must be limited to prevent over-temperature conditions from occurring due to the self-heating.

Using 25 mF/cm^2 surface capacitance with 3.0 V/cell operation and assuming the R•C product is 1 ms, the maximum (matched-load) areal power density of the Figure 4b planar capacitor is 14 W/cm^2. At this peak level, power dissipation in the capacitor will be the same, i.e. 14 W/cm^2. Assuming such power pulses are delivered hundreds of times per second and the thermal resistance for the substrate and interface is 0.1 $^{o}C{\bullet}cm^2/W$, capacitor temperature rise will be less than 1.4 ^{o}C, which is negligible. Thus, the operating power level will not be limited by the EDLC temperature rise. In contrast, temperature rise is typically a major parameter with aluminum electrolytic capacitors. Other advantages of the millisecond-pulse EDLC over an electrolytic capacitor include its higher energy density, it does not suffer dielectric losses, and there is little gassing.

Suitable applications

Millisecond-pulse EDLCs can have electrical performance like an aluminum electrolytic capacitor. EDLC reliability is well established and this same high-reliability should transfer to the VOGN capacitors. A planar EDLC, because of its design, should offer unsurpassed power performance. Therefore, this EDLC appears well suited for a broad range of applications. It could serve as a substitute for a standard capacitor where an increase in system reliability is needed or where a higher level of power performance is required. Or the EDLC could help to conserve space since it likely will be smaller that the capacitor it replaces. Although not discussed, a VOGN capacitor could also offer higher operating temperature, perhaps to 200 C or higher, which may be important in some applications.

Conclusion

A high-voltage millisecond-pulse electric double layer capacitor was described that can be smaller and more reliable than a similar-rated aluminum electrolytic capacitor. Significantly, this EDLC can provide extremely high power operation.

Acknowledgements

This material is based upon work supported by the US Army Research, Development, and Engineering Command (RDECOM) under Contract No. W911QX-13-C-0056.

References

1. Many references discuss porous electrodes including:
(a) de Levie R, Electrochim Acta **8**, 751 (1963)
(b) Conway BE, Electrochemical Supercapacitors: Scientific Fundamentals and Technological Applications, (Chapter 14), Kluwer Academic/Plenum Publishers (1999).

2. Miller JR, Outlaw RA, Holloway BC, "Graphene double-layer capacitor with ac line-filtering performance", *Science* **329**, 1637-1639 (2010).

3. Miller JR, Outlaw RA, and Holloway BC, "Graphene electric double layer capacitor with ultra-high-power performance", *Electrochim Acta* **56**, 10443-10449 (2011).

4. Ohring M, Materials Science of Thin Films, 2nd ed., Academic Press, 745 (2002).

5. Cai M, Outlaw RA, Butler SM, and Miller JR, "A High Density of Vertically-Oriented Graphenes for Use in Electric Double Layer Capacitors", *Carbon* **50**, 5481–5488 (2012).

6. Kossyrev P, "Carbon black supercapacitors employing thin electrodes", *J. of Power Sources* **201**, 347–352 (2012).

7. Keiser H, Beccu KD, and Gutjahr M, "Evaluation of the Pore Structure of Porous Electrodes From Impedance Measurements", *Electrochim Acta* **21**, 539-543 (1976).

8. Candy JP and Fouillous P, "The characterization of porous electrodes by impedance measurements", *Electrochim Acta* **26**, 1029–1034 (1981).

Electrochemical Double-Layer Capacitors for Applications in Efficient Energy Storage and High Power Demand

Wenhua H. Zhu and Bruce J. Tatarchuk*

Center for Microfibrous Materials
Department of Chemical Engineering,
Auburn University, 212 Ross Hall, Auburn, AL 36849-5127
*tatarbj@auburn.edu, zhuwenh@auburn.edu

Abstract: *Battery packs are required to absorb and deliver energy and power quickly, especially for heavy-duty missions. The burden and thermal stress have significant negative impacts on the battery operating lifetime. Ultracapacitors have been shown to absorb and deliver power rapidly. The capacitors can polarize an electrolyte solution and store energy via charge separation at the electrode-electrolyte interface, i.e. the formation of an electrochemical double-layer capacitance. This non-faradic process has no chemical reaction and the energy is stored electrostatically. The structure of ultracapacitor combines the features (i.e. long cycle life and high charge/discharge rate) of a conventional capacitor with an enhanced energy storage capability due to high electrode surface area and low internal resistance. This unique feature reveals a solution to overcome the limited lifecycle concerns of current onboard energy storage using advanced battery technologies. To better understand these unique features, a NiOOH/C ultracapacitor power module with 300 F capacitance at an operating window from 4.0 volts to 14.5 volts, using 10 asymmetrical electrochemical capacitors connected in series, was tested and evaluated through electrical characterization. The ultracapacitor module was applied to form a hybrid power system with an advanced Pb-acid battery, and was then tested & evaluated for high power demands. The hybrid power system potentially provides efficient energy storage needs for fuel saving in various mission fields.*

Keywords: Ultracapacitor; hybrid power system; high power delivery; renewable energy; energy storage and conversion.

Introduction

Ultracapacitors have attracted more attention for various applications such as heavy-duty trucks, high-power pulsed lasers, armored car, tanks, or transit buses. These rapid power capture and proper energy delivery devices have been numerously built and quickly developed to increase energy efficiency, save fuels and reduce carbon dioxide emissions for pulse power and other strong power delivery fields [1-3]. For various electric vehicles including hybrid, plug-in hybrid, and fully electric-driven motor vehicles (HEVs, PHEVs, and EVs, respectively), the ultracapacitors are also considered to work in parallel with the battery packs in order to reduce the battery stress for long cycle life requirement [4]. The lifetime of energy storage systems is predictably prolonged because the ultracapacitor's rapid charge/discharge processes have no chemical reaction and only show low-level thermal production. The concept of hybrid power system combines high power capability of the ultracapacitor and high energy storage ability of the advanced rechargeable battery. This work focuses the understanding of a NiOOH/C ultracapacitor for rapid energy storage. The ultracapacitor module was electrically characterized. Its application in the hybrid power system together with an advanced Pb-acid battery was also tested and evaluated for high power and energy storage demands in order to save energy in the mission fields.

Experimental

The ultracapacitor module and its hybrid power system with a Pb-acid battery were set up for testing and evaluation. The ultracapacitor module is an internal bank of 10 individual capacitors connected in series (KBi/Kold-Ban International, Ltd., EC104). The module has a weight of 29.74 lbs and a dimension of 13.78 inch × 4.09 inch × 9.84 inch [5]. Its operating window of voltage is from 4.0 to 14.5 Volts. The module's leaking current is 5 mA at 14 Volts. The capacitor is an asymmetrical electrochemical double layer capacitor (EDLC), called as a NiOOH/C hybrid-capacitor. The capacitor module used activated carbon electrodes in conjunction with nickel electrodes, non-conducting separators, and an alkaline electrolyte (*ca.* 30% potassium hydroxide solution). The specific design of capacitor provides for a slight Faradaic process that creates high power and proper energy characteristics with good tolerance to cold temperature. It has a low self-discharge rate and a unique feature for a self-balancing effect of the voltage between the individual cells within the module without using complicate design of electronic circuitry. The Pb-acid battery is an advanced battery which provides double cranking power in comparison with the conventional ones. It uses rugged construction and AGM separator structure [6]. During the hybrid test, the ultracapacitor was installed in parallel with a Pb-acid battery to form as a hybrid power system. The hybrid power system was initially charged to a specified voltage level and then conducted tests at various loads operated in high pulse power modes.

Results and discussion

The need for rapid power capture and efficient energy delivery: Similar with a conventional capacitor, the positive and negative electronic charges on both of the EDLC electrodes increase with the energy storing process, and form the Helmholtz layers at the interface between the solid electrodes and electrolyte. The positive and negative ion charges balance the electronic charges at the solid electrode surfaces instead of the traditional dielectric polarization in the insulator. The thickness of the double layer depends on the ion dimension and the concentration of the electrolyte. For the concentrated electrolyte, it is estimated at 0.5-1.0 nm in thickness and the capacitance is *ca.* 10-20 $\mu F\ cm^{-2}$ for a smooth electrode [7]. The ions in a nanometer size are well distributed into high-surface porous carbon materials and formed the double layer charges in a nano-scale during the electric charge at the conductive carbon electrodes. The definition for the capacitance C is written as

$$C = \frac{\varepsilon_r \varepsilon_0}{d} A \quad (1)$$

where ε_r is the relative static permittivity (i.e. dielectric constant, ε_r =1 for vacuum), ε_0 is the electric constant, *ca.* 8.854×10^{-12} F m^{-1}, d is the distance between two conducting plate electrodes or thickness of the double layer, and A is the area of the conductor plate or the surface area around the double layer. The exceptional increase of the surface area significantly raises the capacitance due to a large amount of positive and negative electric charges on two electrodes. Therefore, the ultracapacitor based on the Helmholtz layers and porous structures improves the energy storage. The rapid electrostatic charge belongs to physical processes. The inorganic or organic electrolyte with proper ionic conductivity provides better performance than the conventional dielectric design. Without the limitation of chemical reactions, the ultracapacitor is able to be charged and discharged rapidly at a very low resistance without thermal management requirement. This concludes that the ultracapacitor exhibits its ability for high-power rapid capture and is also able to deliver proper energy stored in the double layer, especially for a short-time frame requirement such as heavy-duty battle-field missions.

The energy, E, stored in the capacitor at a potential difference of V between two electrodes is described as

$$E = \frac{1}{2} C V^2 \quad (2)$$

For the hybrid capacitor (asymmetric ultracapacitor) under testing in this work, the nickel electrode replaces the activated carbon in the positive electrode. For an assumed symmetric ultracapacitor, both of two high-surface-area electrodes equally supply a large double layer capacitance. The whole ultracapacitor can be viewed as two individual double-layer capacitors (C_d) connected in series [8] and the total capacitance is obtained as half of the single electrode capacitance, *i.e.* $C_d/2$. But for the asymmetric design, the positive electrode in the ultracapacitor uses the NiOOH electrode and it is basically comparable to that of the electrode applied in the battery system. This hybrid capacitor uses both of the battery and the ultracapacitor technologies. The activated carbon and nickel electrodes have unequal amounts of surface area and different mechanisms for capturing and storing regenerative energy. Consequently, the capacitor design forms an asymmetric structure. There is merely one negative electrode running as a double layer capacitor (C_d), and the nickel electrode (NiOOH) with a high specific capacitance allows the asymmetric design to exhibit a non-polarizable pseudocapacitive behavior through the Faradaic oxidation and reduction processes. The total capacitance of the hybrid NiOOH/C capacitor is approximately twice than that of the symmetric C/C capacitor.

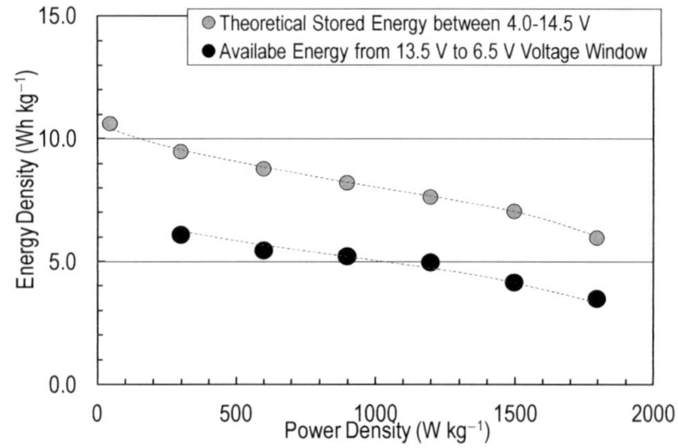

Figure 1. Ragone plots of the ultracapacitor. Theoretically, it has a maximum stored energy between 4.0 and 14.5 V. The actual available energy stored in the capacitor is based on the allowable or optimal voltage window.

From Eq.(2), the energy stored in the hybrid capacitor increases doubly with increase of the total capacitance value. In addition, this equation reveals that the energy stored in the capacitor is proportional to the voltage squared. The asymmetric ultracapacitor can be operated at up to 1.4 V instead of less than 1.2 V for the symmetric structure cell [9] in the aqueous electrolyte. Therefore, the hybrid capacitor using aqueous electrolyte and asymmetric structure increases the operating voltage window and exhibit *ca.* 3 times more available energy stored in the hybrid one than that of the comparable symmetric one. Using an organic electrolyte, the symmetric ultracapacitor may increase the operating voltage window in the region of discharge from 2.70 V down to 1.35 V. But the use of organic electrolyte also brings major disadvantages such as cell balancing, charge protection and thermal management requirement. Small amount of oxygen or hydrogen may be purged out or even recombined into water to maintain the concentration of the aqueous electrolyte, e.g. 30% KOH for the NOOH/C hybrid capacitor. The maximum power of the ultracapacitor is obtained when the load resistor (R_L) is equal to the equivalent series resistance (R_s) of the discharge capacitor [9]. The voltage drops from V_0 to $V_0/2$ and the maximum power output can be expressed as

$$P_{max} = V_0^2 / 4R_s \quad (3)$$

The above equation shows that the equivalent series resistance limits the maximum power output of the ultracapacitor. This value is related to the capacitor internal components such as ionic electrolyte, electrode structures, and current collectors.

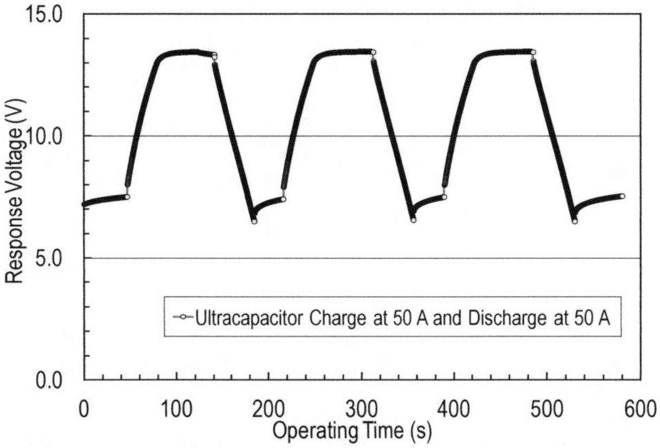

Figure 2. Charge and discharge characteristics of the ultracapacitor: 50A charge to a constant voltage of 13.5 V until the current is down to *ca.* 1.5 A, discharge at 50 A current to 6.5 V, rest for *ca.* 30 s, and then to the next cycle.

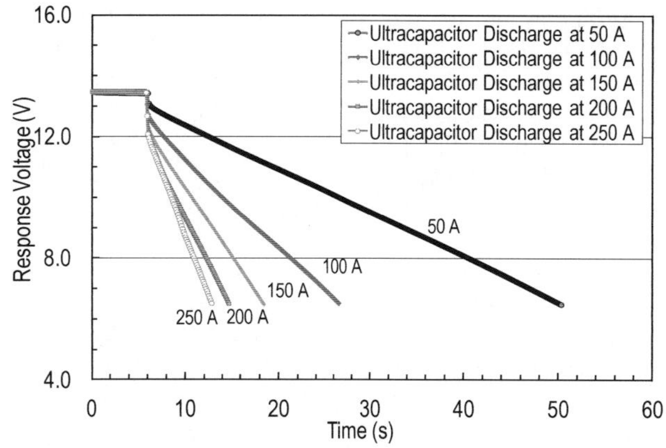

Figure 3. Discharge characteristics of the ultracapacitor versus different currents at the room temperature of *ca.* 23°C. The capacitor was charged at 50 A to a constant voltage of 13.5 V until the current was decreased to 1.5 A.

Characterization of the asymmetric ultracapacitor module: The hybrid capacitor was charged at a constant of 50 A to the upper limit of 14.5 V and 13.5 V until the current was down to 1.0 A, and then discharged at a constant power to 4.0 V and 6.5 V, respectively. Ragone plots of the ultracapacitor are shown in Figure 1. The data results show that the specific energy only slightly decreases with increase of the specific power in a wide operating range. The power module exhibits high-power output capability with proper energy storage. Figure 2 shows the charge & discharge characteristics of the ultracapacitor. The rapid energy storage module was charged at a constant current of 50 A to 13.5 V and maintained at this constant voltage (CV mode) until the current was reduced to *ca.* 1.5 A, discharge at 50 A current to 6.5 V, rest for *ca.* 30 sec, and then to next cycle.

The discharge characteristics of the ultracapacitor are shown in Figure 3. The response voltage is as a function of operating time at different discharge currents. The capacitor was first charged at 50 A to a constant voltage of 13.5 V until the current was decreased to 1.5 A, and the rest procedures are the same as the above test. It was discharged under different constant currents from 50 A to 250 A. At different ranges of currents, the discharge profile of straight lines reveals that the ultracapacitor module has an excellent steady capacitance. This is the vital characteristics for the capacitor to exhibit its energy output capability via its discharge profile. The test results reveal that the capacitor module has rapid energy storage capability and exceptional power output qualifications through its stable capacitance behavior. In order to reduce the thermal stress of the asymmetric ultracapacitor and store energy efficiently, it is preferred to be charged to the rate voltage (13.0 V, *i.e.* charging along with the linear voltage increase) and discharged to half of the rated voltage of 6.5 V. This is the normal use method to conduct the ultracapacitor evaluations.

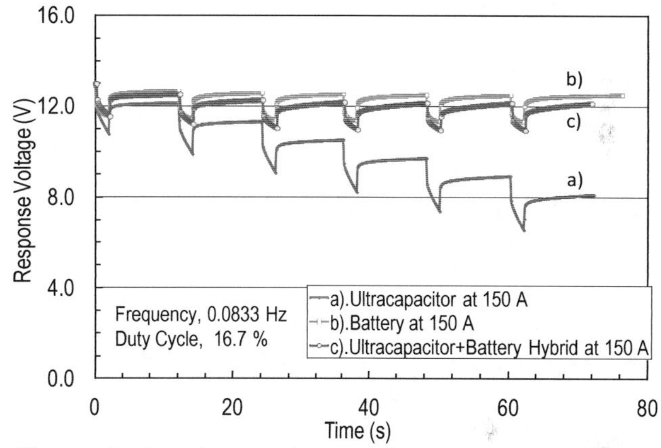

Figure 4. An ultracapacitor, a Pb-acid battery, and the energy-stored hybrid power system under pulse power testing using a modified cold cranking profile, operating under a frequency of 0.0833 Hz (12 sec), a duty cycle of 16.67%, and at a load current of 150 A. The power system was charged at 50 A to a constant voltage of 13.0 V until the current is down to *ca.* 1.0 A.

Hybrid power of the ultracapacitor module in parallel with a Pa-acid battery: For heavy-duty and frequent start-stop applications, the ultracapacitor is an excellent power source. For a mild duty such as personal HEV car, the Ni-MH and advanced Li-ion battery packs can satisfy the energy conversion and storage needs in order to get high energy efficiency, *i.e.* good mile-per-gallon (mpg) numbers, save fuels, and reduce CO_2 emissions. But in some particular situations, e.g. heavy-duty trucks, high-power pulsed lasers, armored car, or tanks in the battle fields, it is necessary to assure the power system to extend the mpg number for a certain limited amount of fuels. The hybrid power source concept can satisfy this heady-duty requirement, present exceptional energy storage capacity, and also provide appropriate low-temperature performance for guarantee of no power failure for various heavy-duty tasks such as the 72-hour mission or severe cold weather demand. In order to better understand the hybrid concept, two kinds of power sources were also connected in parallel to form a hybrid power system for testing and evaluations if necessary. As shown in Figure 4, it is a modified cold cranking profile – a constant current load for 2 seconds and a cycle for 12 seconds. The response voltage for the single ultracapacitor module decreases quickly during the 6-cycle cranking process. For the 1st and 2nd cycles, there is almost no difference between the single battery cranking and the hybrid power source. The rest four cycles, the battery cranking voltage during break periods and at 150 A loads is slightly higher than the hybrid one. The actual cranking current may increase to 580 A, 880 A, or even higher in the actual missions, the tremendous surge-power needs significantly increase the thermal stress or partial overpotentials due to mass transfer limitations. This process has large negative impacts on the battery lifetime. As a high power delivery device, the ultracapacitor module can drastically reduce the stress or partial overpotentials with slight voltage sacrifice.

The above cold ranking process is carried out without outside power input or energy storage addition during cycle periods. In the battle fields, it is favorable for capturing different kinds of regenerative energy during braking, decelerating or coasting processes. Here we use a modified hybrid pulse power characterization (HPPC) profile to evaluate the ultracapacitor and the hybrid power system consisting of an ultracapacitor module and the Pb-acid battery. The objective of the HPPC profile is to observe its discharge pulse and regenerative pulse power capabilities at a closely full charge state (*ca.* 100% SoC for battery) for both the minimum and maximum power-assist goals (10-sec discharge, 10-sec regeneration). The normal test protocol uses constant current at levels derived from the manufacturer's maximum rated discharge current. The modified characterization profile applies a load current for 10 sec in a total 60-sec cycle period. The single power source using the ultracapacitor under pulse power testing was also evaluated using the modified hybrid HPPC profile. The results are shown in Figure 5. The response voltage decreases with the energy consumption in the ultracapacitor, and the 1st charge pulse at 75 A is not in a good shape because the energy level stored in the capacitor is still too high for recapturing new electric energy. The rest pulses shows the energy capturing capability increases with proper consumption for the ultracapacitor. The noises for the pulse charge current is caused by the manual charge for circuit switching and potentially improved by a filtering device or the equipment update. The further results using this modified HPPC profile for testing and evaluation of the hybrid power source is to be included in the conference presentation section.

Summary and future work

The conventional dielectric capacitors function as the filtering device for frequency controls. The ultracapacitors

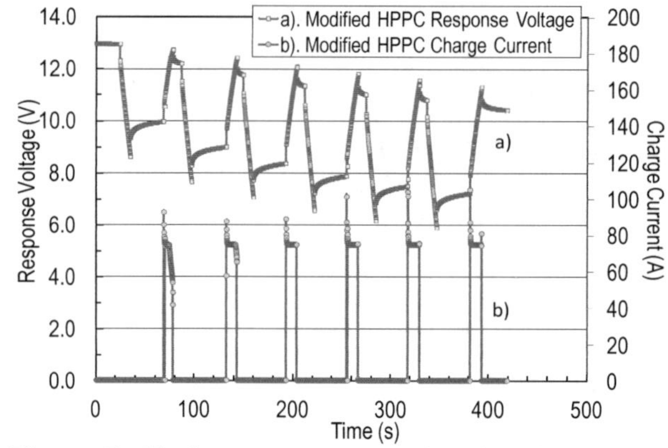

Figure 5. Single power source using the ultracapacitor under pulse power testing using a modified HPPC profile, operating under a frequency of 0.0167 Hz, a duty cycle of 16.67%, with a load current of 100 A for 10 sec, rest for 30 sec and then under a charge limit current of 75 A for 10 sec.

are developed for rapid energy storage and high power delivery. The rechargeable battery is an energy storage device using electroactive materials. For heavy duty and frequent start-stop applications, the ultracapacitor is an excellent power source. For a light duty such as HEV cars, the Ni-MH and advanced Li-ion battery packs can satisfy the energy conversion and storage needs in order to get high energy efficiency, *i.e.* good mile-per-gallon (mpg) numbers, save fuels, and reduce CO_2 emissions. However in particular situations such as heavy-duty trucks, high-power pulsed lasers, armored cars, or tanks in the battle fields, it is necessary to assure the power system to expand the mpg number for a limited amount of storage in the fuel tank. The hybrid power system is promising for the heavy-duty mission needs. It can deliver high power, has exceptional energy storage capacity, can guarantee no power failure, and can be applied in various tasks such as 72-hour missions or severe cold weather demands.

References

1. Lajnef, W., J. Vinassa, O. Briat, and E. Woirgard, *J. Power Sources*, vol. 168, pp. 553-560, 2007.
2. Tatarchuk, B. J., M. F. Rose, A. Krishnagopalan, J. N. Zabasajja, and D. A. Kohler, WO 9014224A1, 1990.
3. Tatarchuk, B. J., WO 9118698A1, 1991.
4. Burke, A. F., Annu. Battery Conf. Appl. Adv., 11th, Long Beach, Calif., Jan. 9-12, 1996, pp. 183-8, 1996.
5. KBi/Kold-Ban International, Ltd., Electrical Power Source, KAPower Installation - Operation Manual, Illinois, USA, 2003, pp. 1-14.
6. EnerSys Energy Products, Odyssey - The Extreme Battery: Application Manual, 2006, pp. 1-4.
7. Kotz, R., and M. Carlen, *Electrochim. Acta*, vol. 45, pp. 2483-2498, 2000.
8. O'Connor, I., M. Genicot, and H. Schuh, Introduction to Asymmetric Nickel Carbon Capacitors, Saft Batterien GmbH, 2012, pp. 1-11.
9. Burke, A., *J. Power Sources*, vol. 91, pp. 37-50, 2000.

Novel in Situ Experimental Techniques to Measure Internal Deformation, Force, Thermal Behavior, and Electrical Performance of Molten Salt Batteries

Kevin N. Long, Philip L. Reu, Enrico C. Quintana, Christine C. Roberts, Eric D. Branson Dennis K. Wong, Robert E. Fox, David Ingersoll, and Anne M. Grillet
Sandia National Laboratories
P.O. Box 5800, MS-0836, Albuquerque, NM 87185-0836

Abstract

We present two novel in situ *experimental approaches that record internal motion, thermal behavior, and electrical behavior of thermal batteries during ignition, rise time, and into the fully activated state. The purpose of this document is to briefly describe the two experimental methods and to present preliminary results. Our initial findings show non-axially symmetric deformation in as-received center-fired thermal batteries, a result we continue to investigate. Also, we report significant differences in stack force relaxation between two common insulation materials used to preload thermal batteries.*

Keywords: molten salt battery; mechanical deformation; battery stack force; in situ measurements; high speed imaging

Introduction

We are motivated both by the need to diagnose performance, design, and safety issues associated with battery production and aging as well as the need to obtain suites of validation data required to mature our long-term, multi-physics modeling efforts of thermal batteries. The test methods presented here address both of these needs. In the first method, high speed X-ray imaging and the Sampling Moiré Analysis technique [1][2] are combined to record internal cell displacements while the the power output of the battery can be simultaneously recorded as it is brought up under a desired impedance. The second method employs an open stack of electrochemical cells, current collectors, and heat pellets that are set to a target preload and subsequently ignited. High speed optical images of the stack deformation, stack force relaxation, flame front profiles, and battery power output are recorded during this test. Each method and associated preliminary results are presented respectively.

X-ray Experimental Setup and Sampling Moiré Analysis Analysis

A new Moiré analysis technique for high speed x-ray images has been developed to understand stack relaxation during activation of thermal batteries. Thermal batteries as received, were irradiated with a collimated X-ray source (Philips 225 kV, 2.5 kW) located approximated 2 meters away from the battery and oriented such that irradiation impinged orthogonally to the axis of the battery stack. See Figure 1 for an overview of the X-ray setup. Transmitted X-ray intensity varied spatially along the axis of the battery due to different absorption and scattering that arises from density variations between the layers. An intensified X-ray scintillator screen (Model Al-9448-F) converted transmitted X-rays to a grayscale visible image, which was subsequently recorded by a Phantom V9 camera with a K2 lens using a CF4 high magnification adapter. The camera resolution was 1632 x 1200 pixels, and frame rates of 500 and 1 frames-per-second (FPS) were used during ignition and rise time and later during the fully activated battery state respectively. The camera resolution exceed that of the scintillator screen, which allowed for 4 x 4 pixel averaging during post-processing to reduce noise without sacrificing the effective resolution. After preliminary results, we observed that internal motion of layers within the battery was slow relative to the 2 milli-second time step between images. Hence, 4 x 4 spatially averaged images were then averaged across 10 time points, which effectively reduced the maximum frame rate to 50 FPS. The secondary 1 FPS was not averaged in time.

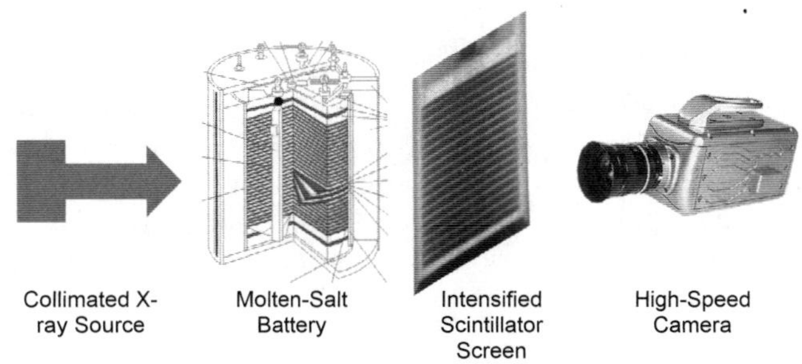

Figure 1. High speed X-ray experimental setup

We disclose here a few subtleties of the test setup. First, we assume that the 2 meters standoff between the X-ray source and battery (approximately 3 x 6 cm in diameter x height) was sufficient to produce a collimated source (parallel rays) orthogonal to the battery axis. Second, we note that the recorded optical image represents the net transmitted X-ray intensity, so that measured layer deformation is actually the average layer deformation along the X-ray path. Thus, if layers tilt, the recorded image will observe a net contrast reduction between adjacent layers. We have not fully explored this kind of behavior and its effects on the analyzed displacement field.

A common trigger was used to synchronize the battery activation and camera imaging. Thermal batteries are well suited for analysis by the Sampling Moiré technique as developed by Ri *et al.* [1]. The initial, nearly periodic array of electrochemical cells forms the specimen's one-dimensional grid. The Sampling Moiré technique tracks the phase shifting of Moiré interference fringes generated by the relative motion of the specimen grid (as the battery stack deforms) and the stationary, reference grid formed by the periodic array of CCDs in the camera. The ratio between the two grid periodic lengths plays an important role in the resolution of the calculated displacements, and we observed a displacement resolution of order 10 microns constrained largely by noise in the images. Only the vertical displacements can be measured given the 1D periodicity of the battery stack.

Xray Results and Discussion

Even at 50 FPS during the battery ignition and rise (after temporal averaging), a rich set of data is collected. We present a time lapse series of axial displacement field contours overlaid onto the reference image and a displacement field snapshot with axial displacements along vertical and horizontal cross-sections of the battery. Deformation data focuses on the battery's rise time. The batteries used were center hole fired, and

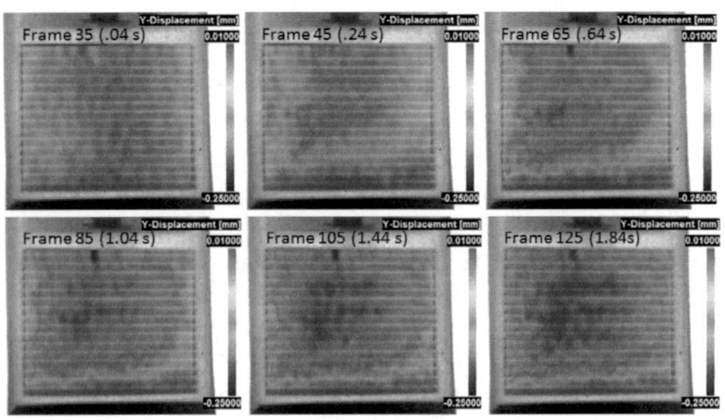

Figure 2. Time lapsed snapshots of axial (vertical) displacement field within the battery analyzed by the Sampling Moiré technique. The displacement field is superimposed on the reference (undeformed) image of the battery.

so we expect to see more deformation in the center compared with the edges, which are constrained by the wrapped insulation. More deformation is observed in the center as seen in Figs. 2 and 3, but the displacement field is not observed to be symmetric about the axis. We are still investigating to explain this behavior.

Open Stack Experimental Setup and Analysis Methods

We now present the second method which offers more diverse measurements and a customizable setup compared with the X-ray approach. Open battery stacks are held in a custom fixture which replicates the fixed height axial confinement experienced by a packaged battery, but allows imaging of the battery stack during activation and operation. Battery stacks are assembled within an Argon glove box and then mounted within the loading fixture as shown in the schematic in Fig. 4. Custom battery stacks were sandwiched between four layers insulation and then preloaded to nominally 500 lbs of clos-

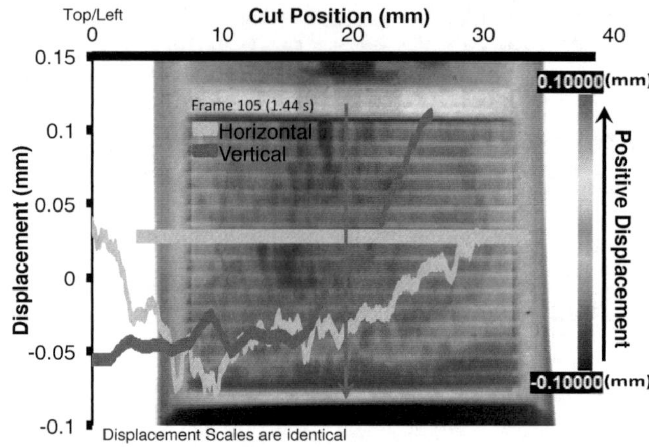

Figure 3. Axial (vertical) displacement along a vertical and horizontal cut at a specific snapshot in time near the fully activated state of the battery. The cuts (paths) are superimposed onto the displacement contours and reference image.

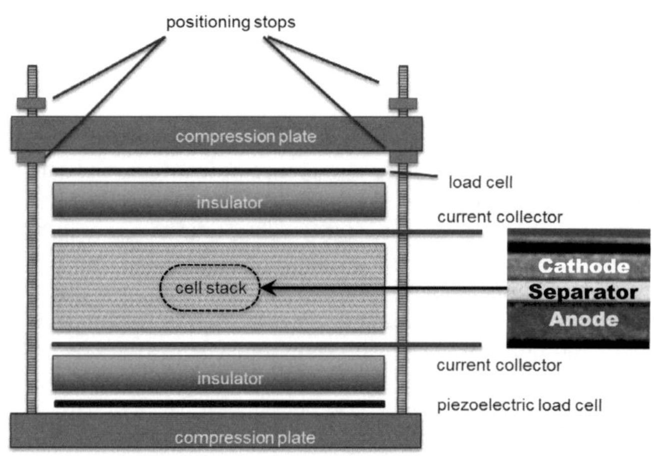

Figure 4. Open stack load fixture and battery experimental setup

ing force as measured by the load cell (LCKD-500 Omega). The preload was held and locked off with the positioning stops such that the force on the battery stack could be measured before, during, and after battery ignition. The battery stack was ignited from a single heat paper strip mounted to one side of the battery, which initiated the heat pellets in each of the cells. In each test, two layers of insulation were used on the top and on the bottom of the cell stacks (four layers total). Two types of insulation were used. Disks of Min-K (6.5 mm thickness) and Fiber Frax (FF) Board (1.6 mm thickness) were cut from sheets obtained from Morgan Advanced Materials PLC and Unifrax LLC respectively.

A desired number of electrochemical cells were assembled for each test. Each cell was nominally 1.61 mm total thickness and 44 mm in diameter. Material selection (anode, cathode, separator, and heat pellets) and manufacturing procedures follow standard press-pellet methods for thermal batteries; see references [3, 4, 5]. Pellet thicknesses were measured with fine calipers, and measurements were within 10% of specification dimensions. Outside of the electrochemical cells, stainless steel collectors were instrumented to an Arbin Battery Tester (BRT-2000 Arbin Instruments) to permit voltage and current measurement under a desired impedance.

The battery ignition pulse set the common zero time and triggered two high speed cameras, a wide view and tight view, setup outside the Argon glove box to record the cell stack deformation. Phantom V9 cameras mounted with Infinity K2 lenses were used. Once triggered, cameras recorded at 1000 FPS for 3 seconds, which was sufficient to image the batteries into their fully activated state. After 3 seconds, stills were taken once per minute to record the battery during cool down.

Given the number of measurement systems (electrical, optical, and mechanical), test integration and time triggering were challenging to realize. Moreover, initially, we intended to use Digital Image Correlation (DIC) to track clusters of material points within the separator and cathode layers, but this proved to be too difficult because the optical path between the battery surface and camera lens was often impeded by thermal waves (fluctuations in the index of refraction), smoke from the heat pellets, and occasionally aberrations in the glove box wall. Additionally, the natural contrast within layers changed as the electrolyte melted, and our efforts to supply artificial speckles to the separator and cathode layers did not prove fruitful. As such, we resorted to edge tracking within both the tight and wide views images to gather the displacement field of layer edges during the batteries' rise times. This method still suffered from impeded optical paths but not from the evolution of contrast within individual layers.

We pursued a test matrix that varied between 3, 5, and 10 electrochemical cells sandwiched between four layers of Fiber Frax Board and MinK respectively all preloaded to approximately 500 lbs, or 212 psi nominal stress. The preload was held for different lengths of time for different tests ranging from one hour to four days. Generally, the preload relaxed by 5 % prior to battery ignition for both types of insulation. For the majority of tests, electrical behavior, loads, and high speed imaging were simultaneously performed.

Open Stack Results and Discussion

We present selected results from the 3 and 5 cell Fiber Frax Board and MinK insulation tests and discuss the different electrical and mechanical behavior observed. Beginning with the voltage output comparison between the two insulations, one immediately notices that the battery stack freezes out substantially later with the MinK insulation compared with the FF Board as seen in Fig. 5. Recall that these battery stacks are not wrapped circumferentially, and fans are blowing transverse to the battery axis to mitigate smoke and thermal waves. Hence, we expect artificially early freeze-out times with this setup compared with an as-packaged battery. Figure 5 shows a significantly shorter battery life with double layers of Fiber Frax insulation compared with MinK, which is sensible given that MinK is thicker and assuming that their thermal resistances are similar. There is some chatter in the Fiber Frax stack measurement, which results from inadequate data sampling.

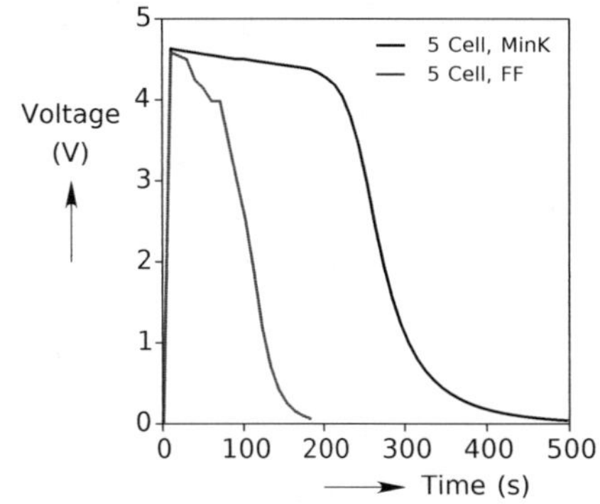

Figure 5. Voltage output for the 5 cell Fiber Frax Board and MinK insulation tests as measured by the Arbin BT-2000 Battery Tester

Next, we examine the net stack force vs. time during battery ignition for 3 and 5 cell stacks of Fiber Frax and MinK insulation layers respectively as shown in Fig. 6. Here, the load measurement was triggered at different times relative to battery stack ignition, such that in the case of the 5 cell Fiber Frax stack, the entire load relaxation curve was not captured. In each case, the measured load immediately prior to ignition was near 475 lbs or 202 psi for these tests provided the stack was allowed to relax pre-ignition for more than one hour approximately independent of the type of insulation. However, post-ignition, stack relaxation between corresponding FF and MinK stacks were different. For the stacks with Fiber Frax Board, the 3, 5, and 10 (not shown) cell stacks relaxed to less than 40 lbs as the separator layers compressed, indicates the displacement of the battery stack is enough to elastically unload the insulation. In contrast, the MinK stacks do not completely elastically unload during battery ignition so that a significant different is observed between the 3 and 5 cell config-

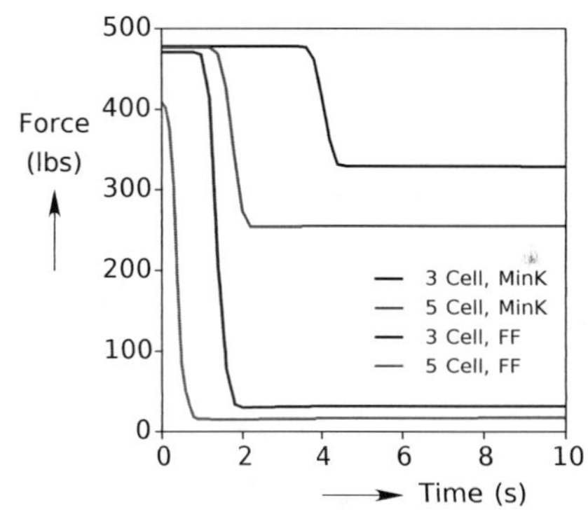

Figure 6. Stack force relaxation for both 3 and 5 cell configurations that use Fiber Frax Board and MinK insulation

urations. As expected, more unloading is observed with the 5 cell configuration in which there is more total separator layer to compress and relax the minK. These measured load relaxation trends have potentially important design implications for short and long life batteries.

In addition to stack force measurements, we attempted multiple methods of axial displacement measurement from the high speed images. Edge tracking proved most robust although it provides displacements only at discrete locations. An example of our analysis is shown in Fig. 7 for a single vertical slice through the battery. The load relaxation is also plotted for reference, and it is clear that once the stack load stabilizes, the battery layers also stop moving. There is a loss of data as the flame front moves across the cameras' field of view (smoke, heat waves, etc). While the image quality is sufficient to allow analysis, we see the individual cells moving towards the geometric center of the battery stack. The total displacement magnitude observed is approximately 0.2 mm between the top and bottom tracked edges, a magnitude similar to that observed in Fig. 2. Although only a single path was observed, we may build up data across the field of view by taking multiple parallel paths.

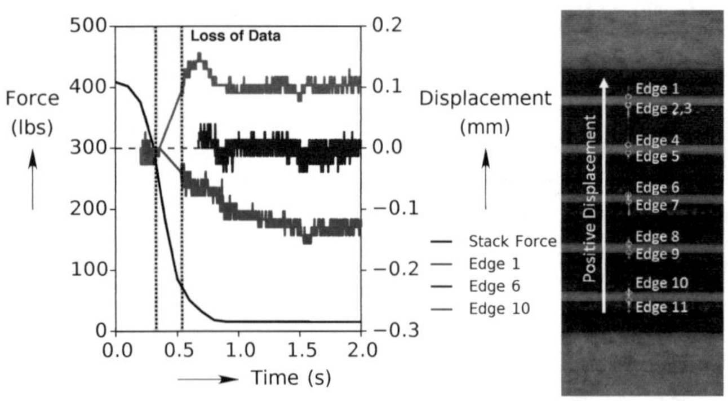

Figure 7. Axial displacement of specific edges from the 5 cell Fiber Frax Board test during battery ignition

Finally, we present initial efforts to characterize the burn front velocity. By manually tracking the burn fronts and linearly interpolating, we arrive at estimates of the burn front velocity as shown in Fig. 8. While crude, this method provides simple estimates of burn front speeds of approximately 75 $\mathrm{mm\,s^{-1}}$.

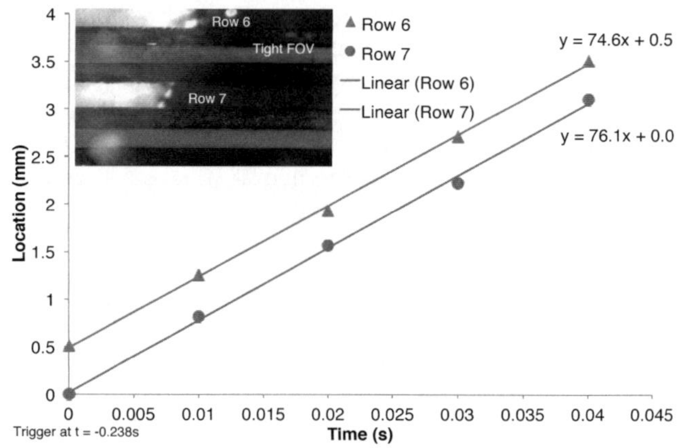

Figure 8. Flame front velocity measurement during battery ignition. A tight field of view is shown associated with the 5 cell MinK insulation test

Conclusion

We presented two novel methods for measuring thermal, electrical, and mechanical behaviors of thermal batteries before, during, and after battery ignition. The first method uses high speed X-ray imaging and the Sampling Moiré Analysis technique [1] to record internal cell displacements while the the power output of the battery is recorded as it is brought up under a resistive load or open circuit. This method offers a truly *in situ* approach to study batteries as manufactured. The second method employs an isolated battery stack of consisting of electrochemical cells, current collectors, and heat pellets, which are confined under a similar axial pressure as a full packaged battery would experience and then ignited. High speed optical images of the stack deformation, stack force relaxation, flame front profiles, and battery power output are recorded during this test. We observed spatial variations in the displacement fields from the X-ray test and distinct load relaxation signatures from the different types of insulations used in the open stacks. These represent new findings, and efforts continue to try to understand them.

Acknowledgment

Sandia National Laboratories is a multi-program laboratory managed and operated by Sandia Corporation, a wholly owned subsidiary of Lockheed Martin Corporation, for the U.S. Department of Energy's National Nuclear Security Administration under contract DE-AC04-94AL85000.

References

[1] Ri, S., M. Fujigaki, and Y. Morimoto. "Sampling Moiré, Method for Accurate Small Deformation Distribution Measurement." *Experimental Mechanics*, vol. 50, no. 4, pp. 501–508, 2010.

[2] Giraudeau, A. and F. Pierron. "Identification of material stiffness and damping in vibrating plates using full-field measurements." *Journal of Physics: Conference Series*, vol. 181, no. 1, p. 012063, 2009.

[3] Masset, P. J. and R. A. Guidotti. "Thermally activated ("thermal") battery technology Part IIIa: FeS2 cathode material." *Journal of Power Sources*, vol. 177, pp. 595–609, 2008.

[4] Guidotti, R. A. and P. J. Masset. "Thermally activated ("thermal") battery technology Part IV. Anode materials." *Journal of Power Sources*, vol. 183, pp. 388–398, 2008.

[5] Guidotti, R. A. and P. Masset. "Thermally activated ("thermal") battery technology Part I: An overview." *Journal of Power Sources*, vol. 161, pp. 1443–1449, 2006.

Assessing the Sensitivity of Thermal Battery Performance to Material Thermal Properties via Simulation

Edward S. Piekos, Anne M. Grillet, Nicholas D. Streeter, and Steven K. Showalter
Sandia National Laboratories
P.O. Box 5800
Albuquerque, NM, USA 87185

Abstract: *The response of various thermal battery performance parameters to changes in material properties are quantified via thermal simulations. Simulations of this type can help engineers prioritize measurements, set their required precision, and avoid unnecessarily stringent specifications for vendor-provided materials. Options for defining inputs and measuring responses are discussed. Examples of sensitivity studies on model batteries are used to demonstrate the utility of this approach.*

Keywords: thermal battery; thermal simulation; material properties; sensitivity.

Introduction

In a purely thermal analysis of a thermal battery (*i.e.* excluding electrochemical and mechanical effects), thermal conductivity and specific heat values are required for all materials. For pyrotechnic materials, burn rate and specific heat release are also required. Phase change materials add latent heat, as well as melting and solidification temperatures, to the list. Multiplying the number of required properties by the number of materials in a typical battery produces a large number of properties to be measured. Compounding the problem, all of these properties must be characterized at elevated temperature, many must be measured over a range of temperatures, and many present compatibility or safety issues in the measurement environment.

Sensitivity information can help engineers prioritize measurements, set their required precision, and avoid unnecessarily stringent specifications for vendor-provided materials. While the sensitivity of certain properties of individual thermal battery components to various parameters have been performed via measurement [1–4], studies of the type undertaken in this work would be prohibitively expensive and time consuming to perform in the physical realm.

Methodology

The simulations for this work were performed by solving the heat equation on an axisymmetric domain using the thermal/fluid finite element application [5] in the Sandia National Laboratories "Sierra" multiphysics suite [6].

Studies whose output measures are sensitive to activation, like rise time and peak temperature, employed the level set-based burn front model discussed in [7]. Those that examine long-time behavior employed a simpler model, where the pyrotechnics were subjected to a uniform volumetric heating during battery initiation. The time history of temperature for a center-fired battery under these models is compared in [7].

Baseline material properties were obtained from a database constructed by Sandia battery designers from various sources. Because many of these properties are temperature-dependent, with several represented by an unstructured table of values, a "fractional change" strategy was adopted for perturbing material properties. Under this strategy, all values for a particular property are multiplied by a constant factor of $1 + f_i$, where f_i is the desired fractional change in the input quantity. The simulation is then performed and f_o, the change in the output quantity normalized by its baseline value, is computed.

It should be noted that the sensitivity coefficients, formally defined as the rate of change of the output quantity of interest with respect to the rate of change in the input quantity, can be determined from the results presented herein, but they are not computed in this work. These coefficients were computed for 19 material properties, with respect to temperature at a given location, for an entire battery in [8]. Conversely, the presentation format chosen for the current work is intended to highlight the effect of relatively large changes in material properties, which can sometimes result from seemingly subtle manufacturing changes.

The hundreds of simulations required for this work were automated and parallelized by utilizing the open source DAKOTA [9] engineering optimization and uncertainty analysis toolkit.

Lifetime

In many applications, the duration of battery's ability to provide useful electrical power is a key design constraint. Unfortunately, the usual measures for defining "useful power" are not available to a thermal model without adding an electrochemical model. It is reasonable, however, to use the separator's state as a surrogate because a frozen thermal battery is, by design, unable to produce power.

Defining the "lifetime" as the time during which the electrolyte in the separator is in a liquid state is not as straightforward as it appears. First, because the internal resistance of a battery increases as its electrolyte begins to freeze,

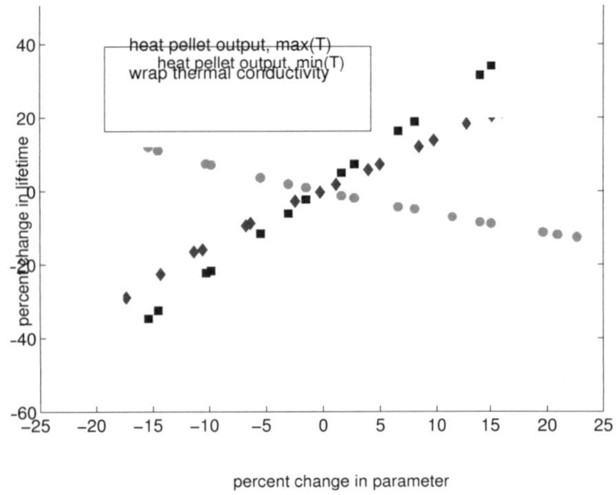

Figure 1. Sensitivity of battery lifetime to changes in wrap thermal conductivity and heat pellet output. The latter sensitivity is measured both in terms of when the maximum and minimum temperatures anywhere in any separator exceed the electrolyte melting temperature. The wrap thermal conductivity sensitivity was assessed with the *min(T)* condition.

a battery can become unusable before it actually freezes. Second, material composition gradients introduced by the discharge process can make the melting point location-dependent. Disregarding these complications, the question of "should all the electrolyte be melted during the lifetime, or can only some of it be melted?" must still be answered. The extremes for defining the end of life are 1) when the temperature anywhere in any separator drops below the electrolyte melting temperature, or $min(T) < T_{melt}$, which represents a conservative measure where any separator is partially frozen, and 2) when the maximum temperature across all separators drops below the melting temperature, or $max(T) < T_{melt}$, which represents a looser measure where all separators are fully frozen. For a battery with a design life of seven minutes, the difference between these measures was found to be more than three minutes at the baseline condition. Fortunately, as shown in Fig. 1, the difference is much smaller when viewing the results as a percent change from the baseline, with the *min(T)* condition proving to be somewhat more sensitive.

Figure 1 also shows the sensitivity of lifetime to the wrap insulation thermal conductivity, assessed with the *min(T)* condition. As commonly suspected, this quantity also has a strong effect on lifetime. It should be noted, however, that the enforcement of a room temperature isothermal boundary condition on the case exterior may have increased this sensitivity.

Rise Time

Similar to lifetime, the time required to reach an active state is also often a key design constraint. The considerations for defining rise time are very similar to those outlined in the

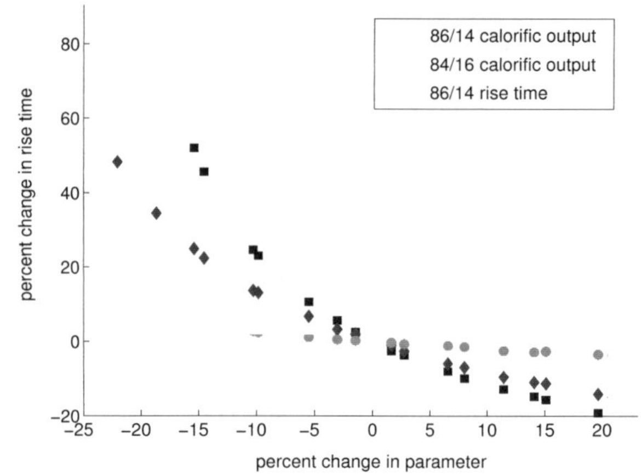

Figure 2. Sensitivity of the rise time of a small center-fired battery to to burn rate and calorific output for two heat pellet types.

previous section. In this case, $min(T) > T_{melt}$ represents a conservative measure where all electrolyte in all separators has melted and $max(T) > T_{melt}$ represents a looser measure where electrolyte has melted anywhere in any separator. Again, it was observed that plotting the data as a relative change cancels most of the difference between these measures, despite large differences in the unnormalized value.

Using the *min(T)* condition, the sensitivity to calorific output, for two heat pellet formulations (with 84/16 producing more heat), and burn rate are compared in Fig. 2 for the small, center-fired model battery examined in [7]. The immediately evident, and perhaps surprising, observation to be made from this figure is that the rise time is far more sensitive to calorific output than to burn rate. This effect is particularly strong when the calorific output is below the baseline value and with the less energetic heat pellet.

This result can be understood by noting that the time constant of the burn can be computed as the battery radius divided by the burn rate. The time constant of thermal diffusion through the materials between the heat pellet and the separator can be estimated as the thickness squared divided by the thermal diffusivity of the intervening materials (assuming no contact resistance at the interfaces). Because batteries designed for short rise times are often slender, it is often the case that thermal diffusion is the slower process. When limited by thermal diffusion, changing the driving temperature will change the time to reach a given temperature in the separator, thus creating the observed sensitivity to calorific output. The asymmetry is due to rise time being bounded below by zero, which it can never reach, and above by infinity, which it can easily reach if there is insufficient energy to melt the separator.

Given these observations, the sensitivity of rise time to the thermal diffusivity of the cell stack materials is of interest.

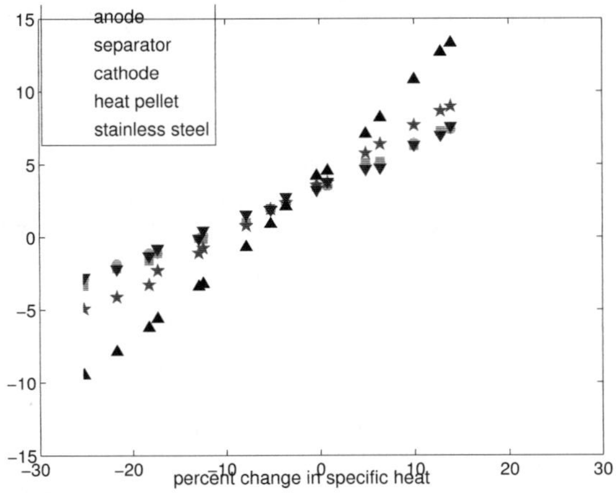

Figure 3. Sensitivity of rise time to the specific heat of materials used in the cell stack.

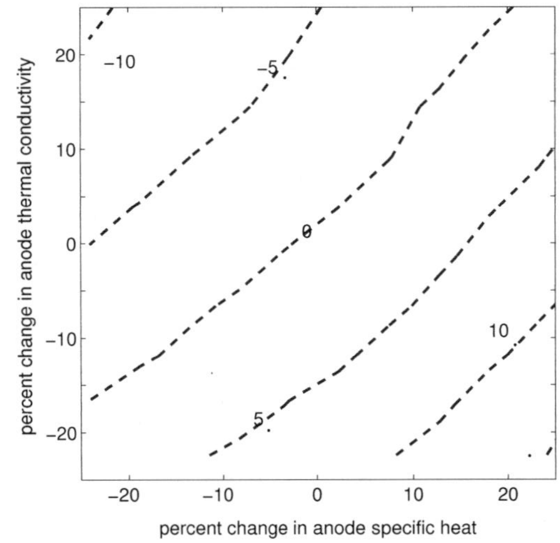

Figure 4. Contour plot of the percent change in rise time when the anode specific heat and thermal conductivity are varied concurrently.

Toward this end, Figure 3 presents the sensitivity of rise time to the specific heat of each material appearing in the cell stack. From this figure, it may be observed that the sensitivities are similar between materials, with the rise time somewhat more sensitive to the specific heat of the heat pellet and the cathode.

In the heat pellet's case, the higher sensitivity of rise time to its specific heat is derived from its larger mass, owing to a slightly larger thickness and a higher density than any of the battery materials, other than the stainless steel collector.[1] Also, because it is the heat source, its temperature must increase before heat can flow to any of the other materials.

Conversely, the sensitivity of the rise time to cathode specific heat is due to its *lower* mass compared to the other cell materials. This feature, combined with its position between the heat pellet and the separator, therefore makes it the rate-limiting step in thermal transport to the separator.

It is worth noting that the sensitivity to specific heat is reasonably linear out to the $\pm25\%$ perturbations applied in this work, thus a traditional sensitivity coefficient can be used for this parameter. This linearity was also observed when the study was repeated for thermal conductivity.

DAKOTA has the ability to sample multidimensional spaces, which is a useful feature in cases where the parameters under study may interact nonlinearly. To demonstrate this capability, a contour plot is presented in Fig. 4 where the thermal conductivity and the specific heat of the anode are both varied and the net effect on rise time is measured. In this case, the variables have a similar and nearly independent effect on rise time (due to their appearance as a quotient in the thermal diffusivity), so the contours are very close to diagonal lines.

Maximum Temperature

While both rise time and lifetime are improved by increasing the calorific output of the heat pellets, it is well known that this parameter cannot be increased freely. A primary concern is the danger of thermal degradation of battery materials, leading to reduced performance and possibly thermal runaway. For this reason, the sensitivity of the maximum anode temperature to the calorific output of the heat pellets was computed. The results of these simulations are shown in Fig. 5. Not surprisingly, the anode maximum temperature is positively correlated with heat pellet output and the dependence is strong. This relationship is reasonably linear, unlike the dependence of rise time or lifetime on heat pellet output.

In order to demonstrate the mediating influence of adjoining materials, the sensitivity of maximum anode temperature to the specific heat of stainless steel collectors placed on either side of the heat pellet is also shown in Fig. 5. In this case, there is a negative correlation, hence the buffering effect. As shown in Fig. 3, however, rise time would be negatively impacted by an increase in collector specific heat. Comparing Figures 3 and 5, the effect of collector specific heat on rise time is slightly stronger than its effect on anode maximum temperature, so modifying the collector to reduce an unacceptable anode peak temperature, caused by an attempt to reduce rise time by increasing the heat pellet output, would be counterproductive for this battery.

[1] Interestingly, because the collector sandwiches the heat pellet and its density is so high, the sensitivity of rise time to its specific heat is as large as that of the other materials, despite its relative thinness.

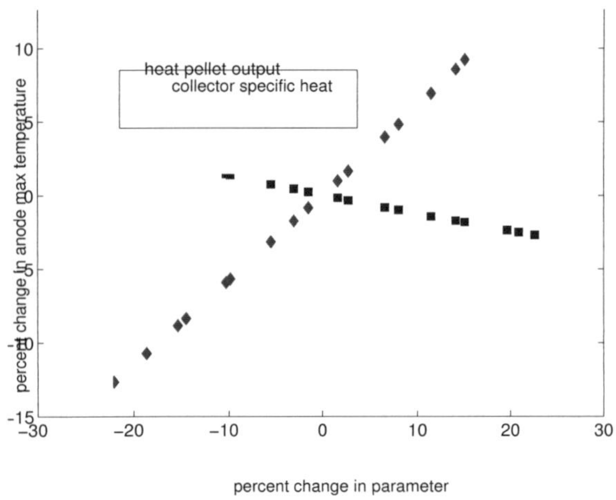

Figure 5. Sensitivity of the maximum anode temperature to changes in calorific output of the heat pellets and the specific heat of the collectors.

Conclusions

Sensitivity studies can provide useful information for battery designers in guiding decisions regarding battery geometry, material choice and characterization, and vendor requirements. Due to the large number of trials required to quantify these sensitivities, simulation is an indispensable tool for such studies. Automated execution and post processing, available through the DAKOTA toolkit, are extremely helpful when exploring a large parameter space.

Acknowledgments

Sandia National Laboratories is a multi-program laboratory managed and operated by Sandia Corporation, a wholly owned subsidiary of Lockheed Martin Corporation, for the U.S. Department of Energy's National Nuclear Security Administration under contract DE-AC04-94AL85000.

References

1. R.A. Guidotti, F. Reinhardt, and E.V. Thomas. "Deformation study of separator pellets for thermal batteries," Technical Report SAND90-2318, Sandia National Laboratories, May 1990.

2. J.W. Reed, R.R. Walters, R.A. Guidotti, and A.K. Jacobson. "Burn-rate studies with iron/potassium perchlorate heat pellets," In *Proceedings of the 35th International Power Sources Symposium*, pages 211–214, June 1992.

3. R.A. Guidotti and M. Moss. "Thermal conductivity of thermal-battery insulations," Technical Report SAND95-1649, Sandia National Laboratories, August 1995.

4. R.A. Guidotti, J. Odinek, and F.M. Reinhardt. "Characterization of Fe/$KClO_4$ heat powders and pellets," *Journal of Energetic Materials*, 24(4):271–305, 2006.

5. P.K. Notz, S.R. Subia, M.M. Hopkins, H.K. Moffatt, and D.R. Noble. "Aria 1.5: User Manual," Technical Report SAND2007-2734, Sandia National Laboratories, April 2007.

6. J.R. Stewart and H.C. Edwards. "A framework approach for developing parallel adaptive multiphysics applications," *Finite Elements In Analysis and Design*, 40(12):1599–1617, July 2004.

7. E.S. Piekos, A.M. Grillet, D. Ingersoll, N.D. Streeter, and D.R. Noble. "Modeling of thermal battery initiation using level sets," In *Proceedings of the 45th Power Sources Conference*, pages 595–598, 2012.

8. B.F. Blackwell, K.J. Dowding, R.J. Cochran, and D. Dobranich. "Utilization of sensitivity coefficients to guide the design of a thermal battery," In *Proceedings of the ASME Heat Transfer Division – 1998: Presented at the 1998 ASME IMECE*, volume 361-5, pages 73 – 82, Anaheim, CA, USA, November 1998.

9. B.M. Adams, L.E. Bauman, W.J. Bohnhoff, K.R. Dalbey, M.S. Ebeida, J.P. Eddy, M.S. Eldred, P.D. Hough, K.T. Hu, J.D. Jakeman, L.P. Swiler, and D.M. Vigil. "DAKOTA, a multilevel parallel object-oriented framework for design optimization, parameter estimation, uncertainty quantification, and sensitivity analysis: Version 5.4 user's manual," Technical Report SAND2010-2183, Sandia National Laboratories, December 2009, Updated November 2013.

Experimental and Mathematical Confirmation of Munitions Thermal Battery Heat Transfer Using FORTRAN and SIERRA Finite Element Thermal Models

Frank C. Krieger and Michael S. Ding
U.S. Army Research Laboratory, 2800 Powder Mill Road, Adelphi MD 20783
frank.c.krieger.civ@mail.mil
Mail Stop RDRL-SED-C; Phone 301-394-3115

Abstract: *Recent experiments (1–3) combined with mathematical modeling strongly suggest that simple and easily implemented methods of hydrogen gas removal can reduce required volumes or increase thermal lifetimes at specified volumes for many presently used vendor munitions thermal batteries by factors ranging from 1.5 to 3. ARL FORTRAN programs and Sandia SIERRA TABS (Thermally Activated Battery Simulator) finite element thermal optimization models independently confirm the importance of hydrogen gas presence in thermal battery operating gas atmospheres as well as the importance of the initial high rate transient heat transfer state that occurs immediately after thermal battery initiation. Results from ARL and Sierra models agree numerically and are further confirmed when using alternate mathematical methods (4–7) to analyze experimental results from operating Low Cost Competent Munition (LCCM) thermal batteries.*

Keywords: thermal battery life extension; gas control; transient heat transfer; FORTRAN; SIERRA TABS; finite element heat transfer model

Introduction

ARL FORTRAN and Sandia SIERRA TABS thermal battery heat transfer optimization programs both rely on numerical mathematical and parametric approximation methods to optimize thermal battery heat transfer and electrochemical performance. Many of the calculations required would be prohibitively difficult or impossible in a mathematically rigorous format.

Total required lifetimes for munitions thermal batteries vary widely, but typically range from 2 to 5 minutes for ARL applications. Calculations below show that the LCCM thermal cell stack will lose approximately 80 % of the heat required to establish a steady state temperature gradient into its thermal insulation package by 9 s after initiation if no extra pyrotechnic heating for the insulation package is in place. That amount of heat could prolong the present LCCM operating lifetime of nominally 110 s by approximately 150 s. Mathematical thermal models clearly show that significant thermal battery lifetime improvements are available for many applications if sufficient external pyrotechnic heat can be added to the thermal insulation to closely approach a steady state temperature gradient in the first few seconds after battery initiation. Heat loss rates both during and after the initial transient heat transfer state can be significantly reduced by hydrogen gas removal. SIERRA TABS finite element analyses employ more diverse mathematical methods than the ARL FORTRAN programs and deliver more parametric interaction information along with intuitive graphical interfaces. Comparison of the previously proven SIERRA TABS and ARL FORTRAN programs with other heat transfer analysis methods facilitates understanding of both the applicability of the numerical methods and the physical interactions of thermal battery operating parameters.

Experimental

Gas pressures in operating thermal batteries were recorded using an Agilent 34970A Data Acquisition/Switch Unit with MKS Baratron dual capacitance manometer pressure transducers. Gas compositions were analyzed using an Agilent 7890A gas chromatograph with a 50-µl sample loop and a thermal conductivity detector (1–3).

Finite Element Planar Model Using LCCM Constant Value Thermal Properties

Radiation and convection heat loss from operating munitions thermal battery cell stacks are nearly always insignificant because of the thermal insulation materials and packaging methods used. Thermal cell stack heat loss during battery operation is ordinarily modeled as being due only to conduction heat loss. During the normally short lifetimes of munitions thermal batteries, steady state conditions may be approached closely but are rarely reached. A combination of transient and steady state calculations can usually be applied to estimate the thermal lifetime of the battery to an accuracy of about ±15%. Closer accuracy can be achieved for specific applications if necessary. In most practical production situations, however, the calculated accuracy of thermal lifetimes will be limited to about ±15% by the uncertainty of geometric considerations such as the actual position of the cell stack in the battery case and the actual operating internal component dimensions after pyrotechnic initiation and electrolyte melting, as well as by the lack of high temperature thermal data for some components of the battery that may have been momentarily heated to temperatures as high as 1400 °C to 2000 °C by the pyrotechnic materials and melted or fused, or perhaps altered chemically as components of operating electrochemical cells.

Results from a simple Excel finite element model of heat flow into a planar wall made of a predominantly micro-porous LCCM thermal insulation package using constant heat transfer parameters with global thermal conductivity values (K) = 0.00045 (4.5 E–4), 0.00015 (1.5 E–4), and 0.000050 (5.0 E–5) cal/s-cm-°C, with density (ρ) = 0.34

g/cc, and with specific heat (Cp) = 0.2262 cal/g-°C are shown in Figures 1–3. The K values for Figures 1–3 are nominal values for munitions thermal batteries with (1) the experimental LCCM thermal battery operating gas atmosphere, (2) with an air atmosphere containing little or no hydrogen, and (3) with the one of the most efficient economically available thermal insulation packages using a low thermal conductivity gas (xenon) atmosphere. The only construction and material differences for the thermal insulation packages in Figures 1–3 are the gases enclosed in the porous thermal insulators. The constant value thermal properties for the individual walls are shown in the textboxes of Figures 1–3.

The steady state temperature gradient is closely approached by the uppermost linear curve in each of Figures 1–3. The steep initial temperature gradients immediately after time zero (To) illustrate the rapid heat transfer rates that occur early in the transient state when compared with the much slower heat loss rates that occur during steady state. The initial temperature gradient iterations for successively smaller K values in Figures 1–3 must occur at successively later times to insure mathematical stability if the node distances are held constant.

For the transient finite element calculations of Figures 1–3, the insulation was initially held at –40 °C. The top, bottom, and side faces of the insulation were adiabatic. At To, one face of the planar wall was suddenly (mathematically) exposed to and held at a constant temperature of 600 °C while the opposite face was held at –40 °C. At the LCCM experimental thermal insulation package thermal conductivity of 4.5 E–4 cal/s-cm-°C, theoretical calculations show that 81.56% of the heat required to establish a steady state temperature gradient in the planar wall will be transferred into the insulation wall by 9 seconds after initial exposure of one face of the wall to a constant temperature of 600 °C as shown in Figure 4. Using the thermal insulation package properties of Figure 1, calculations based on previously proven LCCM heat transfer optimizations (3) show that enough heat would be lost from the LCCM thermal cell stack by 9 seconds after battery initiation (327.6 calories) to prolong the operating lifetime during normal operation by 150.7 s if no pyrotechnic material at all had been placed within the thermal insulation. The measured lifetime of one of the most successful laboratory tested LCCM batteries was 112.9 s, with some heat paper placed within the thermal insulation (3). If the heat required for a steady state temperature gradient in the thermal insulation package is supplied to the thermal insulation using external pyrotechnic material such as heat paper or Nanofoil, that heat must be supplied quickly before significant amounts of heat can be lost into the thermal insulation from the operating thermal cells. Pyrotechnic material in the thermal insulation must therefore be placed near the thermal cells, increasing the chances of overheating and damaging the thermal cell components. Nanofoil is presently an expensive metallic material that could cause electrical short circuits. With further development effort to reduce costs and with appropriate battery construction methods, Nanofoil might become effective as an external insulation heat source because it has more rapid burn rates and better dimensional stability after initiation than heat

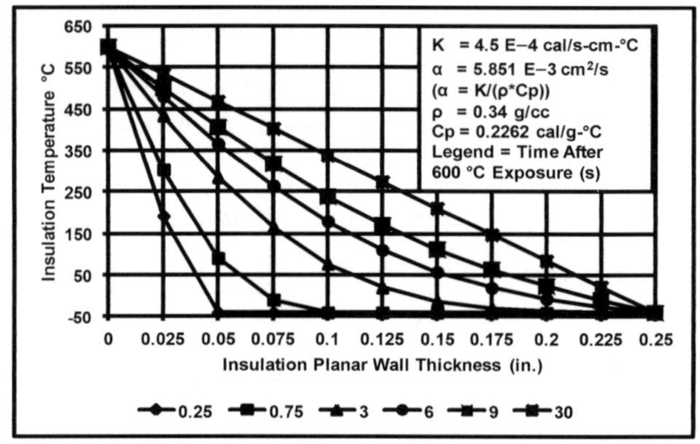

Figure 1. Finite element transient temperature gradients in a planar wall of the LCCM thermal insulation package when using the LCCM operating gas atmosphere.

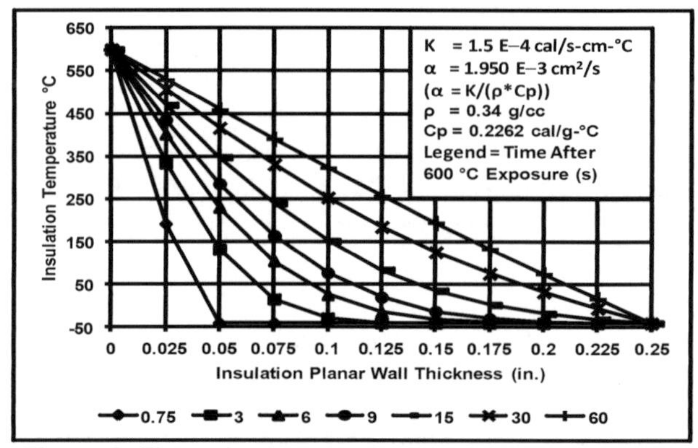

Figure 2. Finite element transient temperature gradients in a planar wall of the LCCM thermal insulation package when effectively using an air atmosphere with little or no hydrogen.

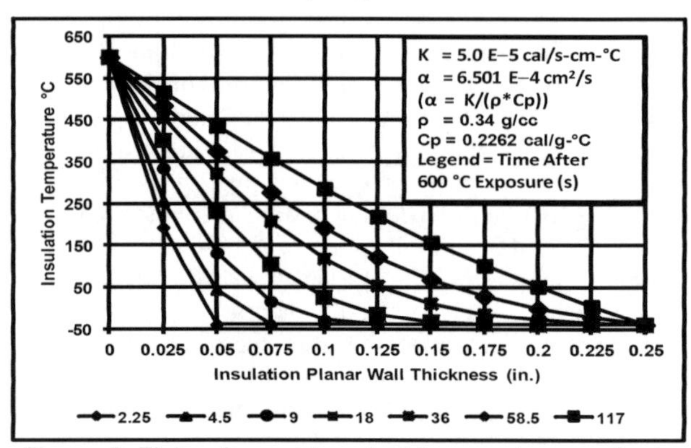

Figure 3. Finite element transient temperature gradients in a planar wall of the LCCM thermal insulation package when using a low thermal conductivity gas (xenon) atmosphere.

paper. ARL FORTRAN and Sandia SIERRA TABS analysis methods can be used to help determine the proper placement of pyrotechnic material in the thermal insulation.

Semi-infinite Planar Wall Theoretical Transient and LCCM Steady State Calculations Using Constant Value Thermal Properties

The total theoretically calculated amount of heat that will be transferred into a 1 cm^2 area of planar walls of semi-infinite length with the constant thermal properties shown in Figures 1–3 when the walls are initially at –40 °C after one face of the walls is suddenly exposed to and held at a temperature of 600 °C is shown in Figure 4.

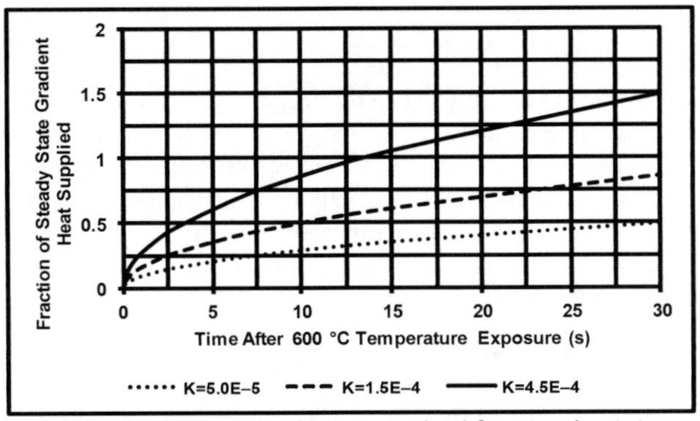

Figure 4. Fractions of heat required for steady state temperature gradients in the LCCM thermal insulation package finite element planar walls of Figures 1–3 that enter semi-infinite planes with the thermal properties of Figures 1–3 shortly after plane face exposures to 600 °C.

The heat quantities shown entering the semi-infinite planar walls in Figure 4 are expressed as fractions of the heat required to establish steady state temperature gradients in a 1 cm^2 area of the 0.25 in. thick LCCM finite element planar insulation package walls of Figures 1–3. The physical constructions of the three walls of Figures 1–3 differ only by the gas present in the porous thermal insulation, and each of the 3 walls requires a total of 15.63 calories for a steady state temperature gradient. For Figure 1 thermal properties with a K value of 4.5 E–4 cal/s-cm-°C, the theoretically calculated value agreed with the total amount of heat summed from individual elements in the finite element planar wall within 0.107% at 6 s after To (24 iterations), and within 3.99% at 9 s after To (36 iterations). The two methods will show less agreement immediately after To when there are fewer finite element iterations, and also after the temperatures of the semi-infinite planar walls at points 0.25 in. from the 600 °C surfaces rise far enough above –40 °C so that significant amounts of heat transferred into the semi-infinite walls from the 600 °C surfaces will have passed beyond the 0.25 in. finite element wall widths.

Tables 1 and 2 compare theoretically calculated transient heat transfer rates and quantities into the semi-infinite planar walls with steady state calculations across the walls shown in Figures 1–3 at selected times. The semi-infinite planar wall and steady state calculations shown in Tables 1 and 2 all used the constant LCCM thermal properties shown in the textboxes of Figures 1–3.

Table 1. Semi-Infinite Planar Wall Theoretical Transient (TT) and Steady State (SS) LCCM Thermal Insulation Package Heat Flow Rate Ratios*

Time After 600 °C Exposure	TT/SS Rate Ratio for K= 5.0E–5	TT/SS Rate Ratio for K= 1.5E–4	TT/SS Rate Ratio for K= 4.5E–4	TT dq/dt Rate for K= 4.5E–4
(s)				cal/s-cm^2
0.10	44.43	25.65	14.81	6.72
0.25	28.10	16.22	9.37	4.25
0.50	19.87	11.47	6.62	3.00
0.75	16.22	9.37	5.41	2.45
1.00	14.05	8.11	4.68	2.12
2.00	9.93	5.74	3.31	1.50
3.00	8.11	4.68	2.70	1.23
6.00	5.74	3.31	1.91	0.87
9.00	4.68	2.70	1.56	0.71
15.00	3.63	2.09	1.21	0.55
30.00	2.57	1.48	0.86	0.39
60.00	1.81	1.05	0.60	0.27
120.00	1.28	0.74	0.43	0.19
1200.00	0.41	0.23	0.14	0.06
12000.00	0.13	0.07	0.04	0.02

*Includes Calculated TT dq/dt Heat Flow Rate into the 600 °C Wall Surface (1 cm^2 Area) for K=4.5E–4 cal/s-cm-°C

The theoretical calculations for the semi-infinite planar walls used dq/dt = K*A*ΔT/SQRT(π*α*τ) for the heat transfer rates entering the 600 °C surface and Q = K*A*ΔT*2*SQRT(τ/(π*α)) for the total quantities of heat transferred into the insulation at time τ (s) after the face exposures to 600 °C where dq/dt = heat transfer rate (cal/s), K = thermal conductivity (cal/s-cm-°C), A = area (1 cm^2), ΔT = temperature difference (640 °C), SQRT = square root function, π = 3.14159, α = thermal diffusivity (cm^2/s), and Q = total heat (cal). The corresponding calculated steady state heat loss rates across the finite element planar walls of Figures 1–3 for 1 cm^2 wall areas of thickness ΔX = 0.25 in. (0.635 cm) are dq/dt = K*A*ΔT/ΔX = 0.4535, 0.1512, and 0.05039 cal/s for the three K values, respectively.

At shorter times, the transient heat loss rates and total heat loss quantities for the semi-infinite walls are much greater than the steady state heat loss rates and total quantities across the 0.25 in. thick walls because insulation portions near the 600 °C surfaces remain unheated. At longer times, the transient heat loss rates and total heat loss quantities into the semi-infinite planes become much less than the steady state heat loss rates and total quantities across the 0.25 in. thick finite element walls because the steady state cold surfaces at –40 °C and 0.25 in. from the 600 °C steady state hot surfaces constantly maintain a large temperature gradient for the steady state walls. The temperatures of the insulation in the semi-infinite planar walls, on the other hand, continue to increase at longer times and continue to reduce the temperature gradients at the planar wall 600 °C surfaces.

Table 2. Semi-Infinite Planar Wall Theoretical Transient (TT) and Steady State (SS) LCCM Thermal Insulation Package Total Heat Quantity Ratios*

Time After 600 °C Exposure	TT/SS Total Quantity Ratio for K= 5.0E−5	TT/SS Total Quantity Ratio for K= 1.5E−4	TT/SS Total Quantity Ratio for K= 4.5E−4	TT Total Heat Quantity for K= 4.5E−4
(s)				cal/cm^2
0.10	88.86	51.30	29.62	1.34
0.25	56.20	32.45	18.73	2.12
0.50	39.74	22.94	13.25	3.00
0.75	32.45	18.73	10.82	3.68
1.00	28.10	16.22	9.37	4.25
2.00	19.87	11.47	6.62	6.01
3.00	16.22	9.37	5.41	7.36
6.00	11.47	6.62	3.82	10.41
9.00	9.37	5.41	3.12	12.74
15.00	7.26	4.19	2.42	16.45
30.00	5.13	2.96	1.71	23.27
60.00	3.63	2.09	1.21	32.91
120.00	2.57	1.48	0.86	46.54
1200.00	0.81	0.47	0.27	147.16
12000.00	0.26	0.15	0.09	465.37
*Includes Calculated TT Total Heat Quantity for K=4.5E−4 with 1 cm^2 Area				

The planar model calculations discussed above clearly illustrate the potential effects of the rapid transient state heat flow that takes place during the first few seconds after thermal battery initiation. For cylindrical LCCM geometric dimensions with constant thermal conductivity values, cell stack heights L, and insulation cylindrical wall radii R_1 and R_2, steady state radial heat losses can be calculated as planar heat losses to an accuracy of ~ 2.2% by using a planar wall area of $2*\pi*L*0.5*(R_1+R_2)$ for the radial insulation walls (3, 4).

Thermal Battery Mathematical Models With Temperature Dependent Thermal Properties

Calculated LCCM and vendor thermal battery thermal lifetimes and dimensions with temperature dependent thermal properties were found to agree numerically within ±15% when ARL FORTRAN and SIERRA TABS thermal models were compared. Variable thermal properties were expressed as constant, polynomial, or power law values. Neither ARL FORTRAN nor SIERRA TABS calculations required excessive computer time or resources.

Summary and Conclusions

Numerical values from ARL FORTRAN and SIERRA TABS heat transfer calculations agreed and were confirmed by alternate heat transfer analysis methods. Calculations clearly show that many vendor thermal battery thermal lifetimes could be extended by factors ranging from 1.5 to 3 by removing hydrogen gas from the operating battery atmospheres. Many vendor thermal battery applications are heat limited. Simple placement of $BaCrO_4$ and $Zr/BaCrO_4$ heat paper made from low Zr percentage heat powder such as 22/78 weight percent $Zr/BaCrO_4$ in the thermal insulation for heat limited applications could remove hydrogen from the operating atmospheres and provide longer vendor thermal lifetimes with only minimal construction changes. Heat paper made from high Zr percentages of $Zr/BaCrO_4$ heat powder such as the 28/72 weight percent $Zr/BaCrO_4$ heat powder that was used to heat the thermal insulation in the LCCM flight test thermal batteries evolves large amounts of hydrogen gas and should be avoided (2).

Even partial removal of hydrogen gas from vendor thermal battery gas atmospheres can produce substantial thermal lifetime benefits. Significantly greater thermal lifetime benefits are available by incorporating experimentally verified enhanced gas control methods, battery construction changes, materials choices, and thermal modeling as has been outlined previously (1–3).

Acknowledgements

This work was funded in part by a Picatinny/Armament Research, Development, and Engineering Center (ARDEC) Technical Program Annex (TPA) under the supervision of Bradley Armstrong. Ed Piekos and Anne Grillet of Sandia provided knowledgeable assistance and support on the SIERRA TABS finite element models.

References

1. Krieger, F., and M. Ding., "Thermal Battery Operating Gas Atmosphere Control and Heat Transfer Optimization," *ARL-TR-6156,* U.S. Army Research Laboratory, Adelphi MD, (SEP 2012).
2. Krieger, F., et al, "Gas Control Experiments and Calculations for Pressed Pellet Thermal Batteries," *Proc. 45th Power Sources Conference,* p. 551, (June 2012).
3. Krieger, F., and M. Ding, "Heat Transfer in the LCCM Thermal Reserve Battery," *ARL-TR-4843,* U.S. Army Research Laboratory, Adelphi MD, (SEP 2009).
4. Jakob, M., "Heat Transfer," John Wiley & Sons Inc., New York, Vol. 1, Sixth Printing (1958).
5. Schneider, P. J., "Temperature Response Charts," John Wiley and Sons, Inc., New York, (1963).
6. Rohsenow, W., J. Hartnett, and Y. Cho, "Handbook of Heat Transfer," 3rd Ed., McGraw-Hill, New York, London, Sydney, etc., (1998).
7. Holman, J. P., "Heat Transfer," 9th Ed., McGraw-Hill Higher Education, New York, London, Sydney, etc., (2002).

Model Parameterization for Electrochemical Predictions of LiSi/FeS_2 Batteries

John Hewson, Harry Moffat, Victor Brunini
Sandia National Laboratories
P. O. Box 5800, Albuquerque, NM 87185-0836
E-mail: *jchewso@sandia.gov*

Abstract:

Predictive modeling of electrochemical phenomena relies on the determination of parameter values. Some parameters are easily determined from separate measurements like the electrochemical potential. Other quantities are more difficult to measure and must be inferred in the context of other uncertainties; reaction rate constants fall into this category. Uncertainties in parameter values lead to uncertainties in predictions. We discuss the predictive abilities and associated uncertainties in the context of data available for LiSi/FeS_2 batteries in this work. Results include sensitivity analyses, uncertainty quantification and parameter calibration. Results show that uncertainties in both kinetic and transport parameters can result in significant prediction uncertainty, although these uncertainties can be significantly reduced with careful measurements.

Keywords: Thermal battery; primary lithium cell; molten salt electrolyte; iron disulfide; computational modeling; parameter estimation; uncertainty quantification.

Introduction

Thermal batteries are employed in a range of applications where long-term battery storage must be followed by highly reliable operation. These batteries are characterized by a salt electrolyte that is inactive until it is heated above the salt melting point, after which discharge progresses with ion conduction through the molten salt. Important performance attributes such as active lifetime, voltage outputs and load (current) capabilities affect critical design considerations such as cathode, anode and separator dimensions and material characteristics and requirements for redundancy or overdesign. Battery designs have historically been based on design guides rooted in empirical build and test protocols. Predictive modeling and simulation tools can provide value by helping to identify constraints and optimize designs relative to these constraints. These predictive models require accurate physical and chemical representations to move beyond the direct empirical experience along with carefully determined parameter values that populate these models.

In this work, we outline the parameterization of a set of models based on the macrohomogeneous approximation [1] and highlight key parameters subject to uncertainties that influence the overall prediction uncertainty. We discuss the calibration of interphase reaction rates and solid-state diffusion coefficients, determined from cell-level measurements in the presence of both experimental uncertainty and uncertainty in other parameters. Finally, we quantify some of the more significant of these other parameter uncertainties.

Model

The battery is comprised of a porous Li-Si alloy anode, a porous FeS_2 cathode, and a porous MgO separator that prevents short circuits between the electrodes. Solid pore volumes are filled with a LiCl-KCl eutectic salt electrolyte. The overall geometry of a single cell is indicated schematically in Figure 1. Prediction of battery operation through a direct solution of the continuum conservation equations for potential and species composition is sought. These conservation equations describe the relevant ion and electron transport processes as driven by thermodynamic potentials. Between the electrode and electrolyte phases electrochemical reactions are responsible for charge transfer. In the current implementation, these are treated as elementary reactions satisfying detailed balance.

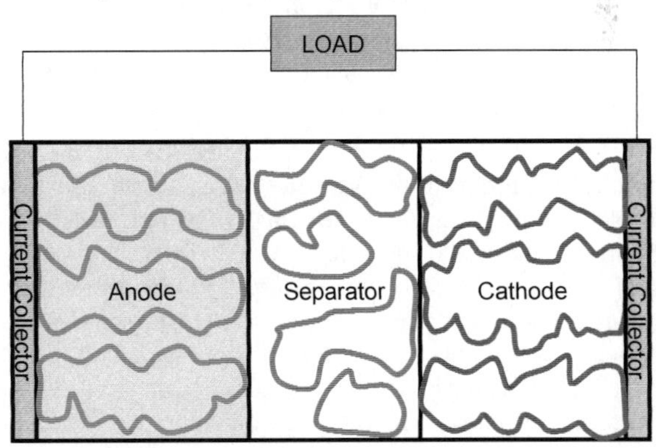

Figure 1. Single cell schematic indicating porous anode, separator and cathode.

Computational Framework. Conservation equations are implemented within the Sierra framework application code Aria, a code developed at Sandia National Laboratories to solve general thermal/fluid/electro/chemical transport problems on unstructured grids using finite-element methods. Material models for thermodynamic, kinetic and transport phenomena are implemented within the context of Cantera. Cantera is a constitutive modeling package that provides models for thermodynamics, kinetics and transport, written in C++.

Electrochemical parameters. Models and parameters are required for thermodynamic, kinetic and transport properties of relevance to the particular materials of concern. To the extent possible, models for these quantities are derived from fundamental measurements as described in the following.

The driving potential and open circuit voltages are determined by the thermodynamics of the electrode materials. These have been reasonably well characterized and multiple implementations are provided within the current models. Of interest is the implementation based on fundamental chemical phases described previously [2] used here for the anode materials and a simpler model of the cathode [3] used in the results presented here.

Given the thermodynamics-determined open-circuit voltage (OCV) the actual cell potential is determined by the cell current and internal losses from either transport or kinetic processes. For kinetic processes, this potential loss is the reaction overpotential and is determined by individual reaction rates. Potential losses can take the form of changes in either the reactant activity or the electrostatic potential of charged reactants. The latter is the overpotential associated with, for example, a Butler-Volmer form of the reaction rate. Transport limitations described below can also lead to changes in the reactant activity and this is incorporated into elementary chemical reactions that are used within the Cantera framework. (In the context of a simple Butler-Volmer reaction, these activity changes would lead to a varying equilibrium voltage.) In the present work, multiple cathode and anode phases lead to interphase reactions that occur both on active particle surfaces and internal to particles between phase boundaries. Either internal or particle-surface reactions can be rate limiting and both cases are considered below.

Current is produced through the transport of ions and electrons, and resistance to this transport results in important additional potential losses. For the current predictions, we consider three sources of transport-related potential loss: electron conductivity in solid phases, ion conductivity in the electrolyte phase and solid state diffusion of active species (Li atoms or ions) within electrode particles. Electron conductivity is generally described through Ohms law, but material resistivities are subject to uncertainty. Conduction of ions is described using the Stefan-Maxwell equations as described previously [4]. In the present we do not address uncertainties in the ion conduction except to note that uncertainties exist around the model of tortuosity; here the Bruggemann power law is used to express tortuosity in terms of the volume fraction, $\tau^2=\phi^{3/2}$. Solid-state diffusion within particles can also cause a loss of chemical potential as discussed below.

Results and Discussion

Calibration of electrode reaction rates and solid-state diffusion coefficients. Figure 2 shows predicted cell potentials as a function of the overall capacity for a low load condition and a pair of higher load constant current conditions together with measurements for the same conditions. These conditions were used to calibrate the rate-limiting interphase reaction rates together with the solid-state diffusion coefficient for lithium in the cathode particles. In this section, we discuss this calibration while subsequent sections address other interacting uncertainties affecting predictions and further discuss the tradeoff between potential losses associated with interphase reactions and solid-state diffusive losses.

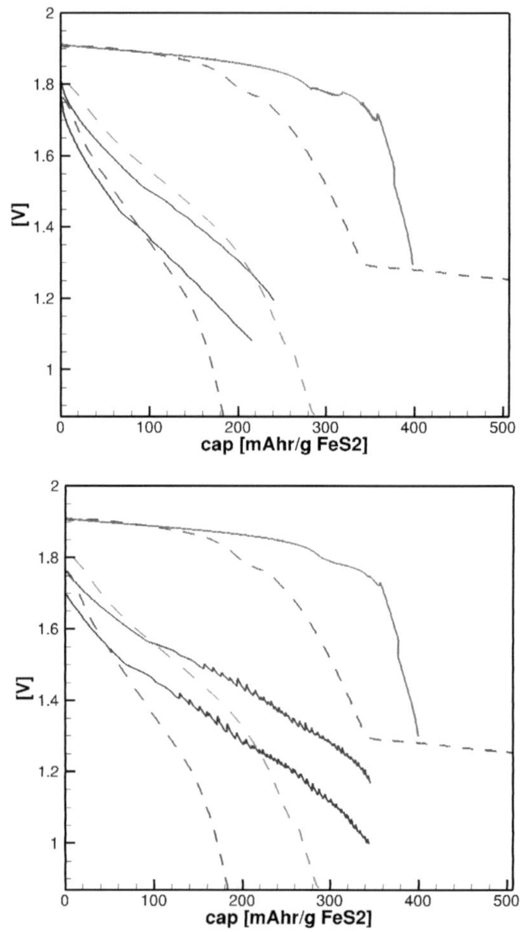

Figure 2. Predicted (solid) and measured (dashed) cell potential for low and high constant current loads. Predictions assume inner (upper plot) or outer (lower plot) reaction surface is rate limiting.

Based on measurements not presented here, we assume that the significant potential losses are associated with the cathode. Anode reaction rate constants are set large enough that anode-side potential losses associated with kinetics are negligible. In the absence of diffusive losses, the overpotential varies in a manner analogous to the familiar

Butler-Volmer expression. The exchange current density, i_0, depends on the forward and reverse reaction rate constants and the potential loss, η, is as required to drive the reaction forward to get a required net current flux.

Because the cathode and anode exhibit a series of distinct plateaus indicating separate phases, active particles take on a shell and core form with reactions occurring at the outer surface between the electrolyte and the particles along with reactions occurring at inner surfaces between a pair of phases. The outer reactions will generally produce a gradient of lithium defects that must diffuse to/from the inner surface, and the inner surface area will vary as the relative quantities of different phases changes. Rate-limiting reactions can occur at either the inner or outer reacting surfaces and the diffusion can reduce reaction potentials in between. If we assume that the reaction at the inner surface is fast and the outer reaction along with diffusion is rate-limiting, the rate can be expressed most simply (analogous to the Butler-Volmer form) as

$$S_{out} = \frac{i_0 r_{in}\left(e^{-(1-\alpha)F\eta/RT} - e^{\alpha F\eta/RT}\right)}{r_{in} + Da(r_{out} - r_{in})} \qquad (1)$$

where r_{in} and r_{out} are the radii of the inner and outer reacting surfaces, F is Faraday's constant. Da is a Damköhler number, the ratio of the kinetic rates to diffusive rates defined as $Da = i_0 r_{out} / DC_0F$ where D is the diffusion coefficient that is unknown and C_0 is a characteristic diffusing species concentration. If the inner reaction rate is limiting, the rate expression is similarly

$$S_{in} = \frac{i_0 r_{out}^2\left(e^{-(1-\alpha)F\eta/RT} - e^{\alpha F\eta/RT}\right)}{r_{out}^2 + Da(r_{out} - r_{in})r_{in}} \qquad (2)$$

In the same manner that an overpotential to drive a desired current can be determined given an exchange current density, it is possible to determine the additional overpotential required in the presence of diffusive losses.

For either Eq. (1) or (2) a reaction rate constant (or exchange current density) and a diffusion coefficient (or Damköhler number) were determined using measurements and a least squares calibration procedure over a series of measured values early in the evolution of the first plateau. As often occurs, a relatively narrow valley of near optimal conditions occurs as can be seen in Figure 3 where contours of the residual error (in voltage squared) are shown. The contours provide reasonable definition for the diffusion coefficient or Damköhler number, but a range of reaction rate constants are possible and a lower reaction rate constant coupled with larger diffusion coefficients also perform with only moderately more error.

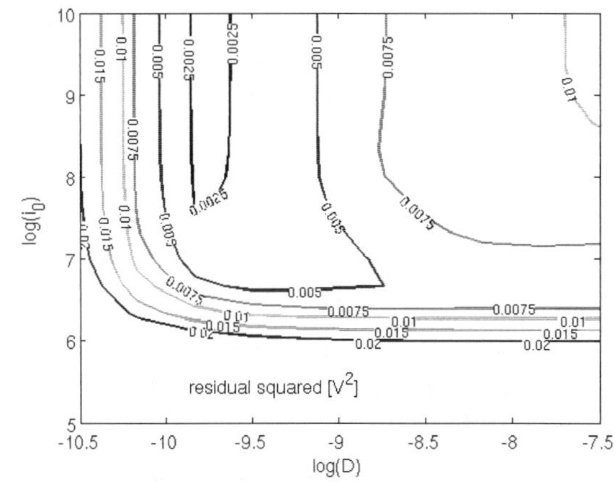

Figure 3. Residual mean square error for predictions versus exchange current density (normalized) and solid state diffusivity; minimal root mean square errors for this fitting approach are on the order of 50 mV.

Uncertainty quantification based on other uncertain parameters. The predictions shown in Figure 2 have additional uncertainty associated with other parameters in addition to those calibrated as described in the previous section. Here we focus on three diverse parameter uncertainties: the particle size distribution, the cathode electronic conductivity and the potential for capacity-reducing side reactions.

An uncertainty related to the kinetics is the active material particle size distribution. An approximate particle size range is known, but variations and uncertainties in particle size (and shape) affect the area over which interphase reactions occur. Reductions in interphase area require larger overpotentials to drive a required interphase current. The surface-to-volume ratio also affects the characteristic solid-state diffusion length scale discussed below. Here we allow the particle diameter to vary with a uniform distribution 50% above and below a nominal value.

Uncertainties exist in all material properties to some degree, and the electronic conductivity of the cathode material is particularly uncertain. The cathode material can be considered to be a semiconductor with relatively low conductivity subject to strong uncertainties associated with the levels of impurities; these uncertainties lead to reported cathode conductivities over nearly an order of magnitude at operating temperatures. Here we allow the cathode conductivity to vary uniformly by a factor of six.

The potential for side reactions is an additional uncertainty that needs to be addressed. Side reactions at high temperatures are known to reduce capacity, leading to more rapid depletion of plateaus. Here we allow the number of electrons lost in side reactions to vary from none to one half electron per FeS_2.

The combined prediction variation across these three parameters is measured by applying a Monte Carlo process to select parameter values with Latin hypercube sampling using Dakota [5]. The resulting root mean square variance (one standard deviation) for cell potential is approximately 50 mV at low loads and 100 mV at high loads. Figure 4 shows scatter plots of the predicted cell potential for these low and high load conditions as a function of each of the variables. The correlation between the variance of the inputs and output is also measured and given in Table 1. These uncertainties add to the uncertainty around the ca!ibration of rate constants and diffusion coefficients, but the overall uncertainties do not increase dramatically.

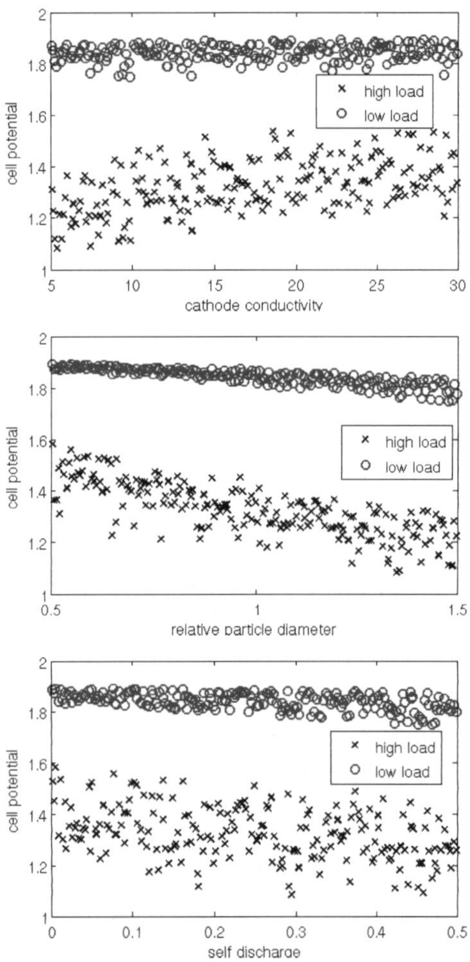

Figure 4. Scatter plots showing uncertainty in cell potential predictions with varying (top) cathode electical conductivity, (middle) relative cathode particle diameter and (bottom) degree of self discharge at low and high loads.

Table 1: Correlation coefficient between varied model parameters and cell potential predictions.

	Side reaction (e^- loss)	*Cathode particle diameter*	*Cathode conductivity*
Low load	-0.46	-0.84	0.11
High load	-0.38	-0.76	0.49

Summary

A suite of physics-based models for prediction of thermal battery performance characteristics is implemented for cell level predictions. Some model parameters and material properties that are the necessary input to the physics models have significant uncertainty while others are essentially unknown. In the latter category are interphase reaction rates and solid-state diffusion coefficients that are fit to cell-level data here. Approximate uncertaintites associated with other input parameters are estimated through variance-based sampling.

Acknowledgements

Sandia is a multiprogram laboratory operated by Sandia Corporation, a Lockheed Martin Company for the United States Department of Energy's National Nuclear Security Administration under contract DE-AC04-94AL85000. The authors gratefully acknowledge funding from the Joint Department of Defense/Department of Energy Munitions Technology Development Program and from the Physics and Engineering Models component of the Advanced Simulation and Computing Program at Sandia.

References

[1] R. Pollard and J. Newman, "Transport Equations for a Mixture of 2 Binary Molten Salts in a Porous Electrode," *J. Electrochem. Soc.,* vol. 126, pp. 1713-1717, 1979.

[2] J. C. Hewson, H. K. Moffat, C. Lueth, and D. Ingersoll, "Predicting Electrochemical Phenomena in Lithium Molten Salt Batteries," in *45th Power Sources Conference*, Las Vegas, NV, 2012.

[3] D. Bernardi and J. Newman, "Mathematical Modeling of Lithium (Alloy), Iron Disulfide Cells," *J. Electrochem. Soc.,* vol. 134, pp. 1309-1318, Jun 1987.

[4] J. C. Hewson, H. K. Moffat, C. Lueth, and D. Ingersoll, "Predicting Electrochemical Phenomena in Lithium Molten Salt Batteries," in *44th Power Sources Conference*, Las Vegas, NV, 2010, pp. 529-532.

[5] B. M. Adams, L. E. Bauman, W. J. Bohnhoff, K. R. Dalbey, M. S. Ebeida, J. P. Eddy, *et al.*, "DAKOTA, A Multilevel Parallel Object-Oriented Framework for Design Optimization, Parameter Estimation, Uncertainty Quantification, and Sensitivity Analysis: Version 5.4 User's Manual," December 2009. Updated April 2013.

Towards a Coupled Multiphysics Model of Molten Salt Battery Mechanics

Scott A. Roberts, Kevin N. Long, Jonathan R. Clausen, Mario J. Martinez, Edward S. Piekos, and Anne M. Grillet
Sandia National Laboratories
P.O. Box 5800, MS-0836, Albuquerque, NM 87185-0836

Abstract: *When molten salt batteries activate, a number of mechanical processes take place over a very short time span. First, electrolyte that is originally located in the separator wicks into the porous anode and cathode materials under capillary forces, enabling the electrochemical activation of the battery. Second, typically the stack axially compresses by 10 to 20 percent due to the melting of the electrolyte and rearrangement of the solid network, also leading to additional electrolyte flow. These mechanical behaviors influence battery performance, and a number of open questions remain as to how the mechanical behavior depends on processing and operational parameters.*

In this work, we develop a computational model based on the finite element method to study these mechanical behaviors. This model couples heat transport, two-phase porous flow, and solid deformation to study the battery activation process. We demonstrate a custom constitutive model for the solid stress, explore how it behaves with and without the presence of the liquid electrolyte, and compare simulations to experimental measurements. We also demonstrate the interplay between capillary wicking and deformation-driven flow.

Keywords: molten salt battery; multiphysics model; thermal transport; porous flow; mechanical deformation

Introduction

The electrochemical cells that comprise typical molten salt batteries consist of individual layers that are manufactured by pressing the constituent materials into pellets. These pellets are stacked into a case, often including other materials such as insulation, and sealed under a significant axial closing force. When the battery is activated, the solid electrolyte that was pressed into the separator and cathode, and sometimes the anode, melts and flows throughout the battery, enabling the closure of the electrochemical circuit. The result of this electrolyte flow is a rearrangement of the granular network of the pellets, particularly the separator, that can lead to an axial compression of 10 to 20 percent. This process is illustrated schematically in Figure 1.

Details of the cell consolidation process are important to battery performance for a number of reasons. First, the detailed timing of the electrolyte melting and flow governs the cell electrochemical potential rise time behavior of the battery. Previous modeling efforts to understand rise time have only focused on the thermal problem, assuming that the battery is active as soon as any section of the separator melts. However, this approach neglects the kinetics inherent in electrolyte flow and how the properties of the porous medium evolve as a function of temperature and the pressure distribution in the battery. Secondly, the axial deformation of the separator is critical to performance. Too much deformation can cause electrolyte to leak out of the separator, potentially causing a short circuit. Too little deformation could cause poor contact between the pellets, which inherently have non-planar surfaces, resulting in a contact resistance [1].

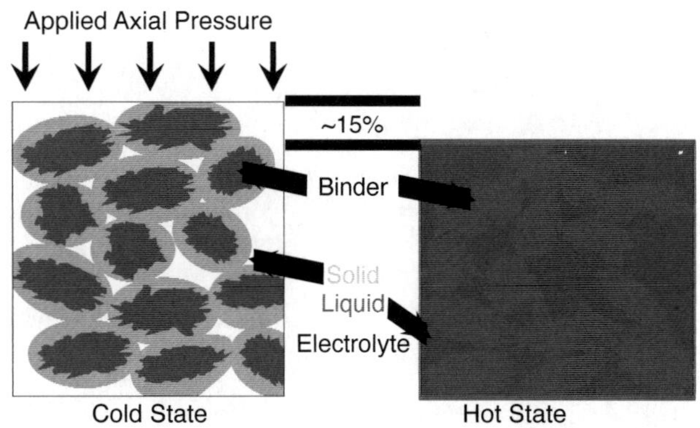

Figure 1. Schematic of the separator pellet in the cold state (left) compared to the hot state (right), showing axial compression upon melting of the electrolyte.

Historically, computer models of molten salt battery performance have focused on thermal transport (for rise time and lifetime) and the electrochemistry (for understanding voltage response and lifetime as a function of the current draw). However, in this paper we discuss the development of a multiphysics model of molten salt battery performance that includes solid deformation, electrolyte transport, and thermal transport, with future couplings to a detailed electrochemistry model. We begin by discussing models for the additional physics of solid deformation and electrolyte flow. We then discuss our vision for a fully-coupled computational simulation framework, then demonstrate some of the physics models individually.

Model

In this paper, we discuss the development of a computational model for thermal battery performance that couples thermal transport, electrolyte transport (porous flow), solid mechanics, and electrochemistry. This model is developed within the Sierra mechanics framework [2], primarily in Sierra/Aria [3], and is based on the finite element method. All simulations are done in the three-dimensional wedge shown in Figure 2.

In the following sub-sections, we discuss the models for thermal transport, electrolyte transport, and solid mechanics.

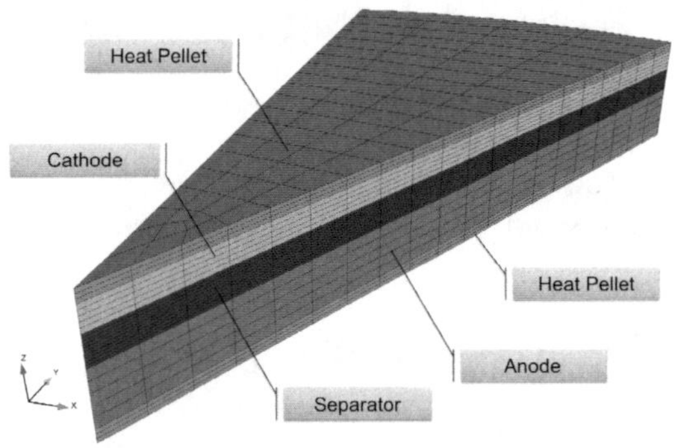

Figure 2. Schematic of a generic wedge-like section of a single battery cell used for simulations. Blue is the heat pellet, yellow is the cathode, red is the separator, and green is the anode.

Since electrochemistry is only considered here in the context of a future coupling, the models for that are omitted. We conclude by discussing options for multiphysics coupling.

Thermal transport: For thermal transport, a standard Fourier-diffusion governing equation is used,

$$\rho C_p \frac{\partial T}{\partial t} = \boldsymbol{\nabla} \cdot \kappa \boldsymbol{\nabla} T + S_E, \tag{1}$$

where ρ is the density, C_p is the heat capacity, T is temperature, t is time, κ is the thermal conductivity, and S_E is a volumetric energy source. The critical energy source is from the burning of the heat pellets. This burning process is tracked using a level-set method based on a fast-marching algorithm, with the burn speed of the heat pellet specified a-priori [4].

Fluid transport: Transport of the molten electrolyte through the battery cell is captured using a two-phase porous flow formulation,

$$\frac{\partial(\phi \rho_a S_a)}{\partial t} = \boldsymbol{\nabla} \cdot \left(\frac{\rho_a k_{r,a}}{\mu_a} \boldsymbol{K} \cdot (\boldsymbol{\nabla} p_a - \rho_a \boldsymbol{g}) \right). \tag{2}$$

Here, the subscript a means that a property is evaluated for phase a, ϕ is the porosity, S_a is the saturation, $k_{r,a}$ is the relative permeability, μ_a is the viscosity, $\boldsymbol{K}$ is the intrinsic permeability tensor (isotropic here, $\boldsymbol{K} = K\boldsymbol{I}$), p_a is the pressure, and $\boldsymbol{g}$ is the gravitational vector. This equation is solved twice; once for the wetting phase ($a = w$), which represents the electrolyte, and once for the non-wetting phase ($a = n$), which represents the gas phase.

In (2), there are two equations, but four unknowns (S_w, S_n, p_w, and p_n). The saturations are related by a summation rule, $S_n = 1 - S_w$, leaving three unknowns. The wetting and non-wetting pressures are related by $p_n = p_w + p_c$, where p_c is the capillary pressure, which represents the pressure jump across a fluid-gas interface within the pore space. This capillary pressure is typically captured using an empirical model. In this case, we employ the popular van Genuchten formulation [5], which provides functional forms for $p_c = f(S_w, S_n)$ and $k_{r,a} = f(S_w, S_n)$. These closure equations reduce the number of unknowns to two, consistent with the two equations we will solve.

Typically, porous flow codes solve for p_n and S_w as their degrees of freedom, using the closure equations to calculate p_w and S_n. However, this poses a challenge for simulations with sharp changes in the material properties as in a battery, where the porosity and permeability differ between the anode, separator, and cathode. This causes a discontinuity in the saturation across an interface between two layers, which is difficult to capture using a continuous finite element formulation. To overcome this obstacle, we modified our code to solve for p_n and p_w, which are both continuous across material boundaries. This modification enables the stable solution of two-phase porous flow in a battery cell.

Solid mechanics: Deformation of the pellets is captured using a standard quasi-static conservation equation,

$$\boldsymbol{\nabla} \cdot \boldsymbol{T} = 0, \tag{3}$$

where $\boldsymbol{T}$ is the solid stress tensor. For all materials except the separator, a simple linear elastic constitutive model for the stress is used, $\boldsymbol{T} = \lambda \text{tr}(\boldsymbol{E})\boldsymbol{I} + 2G\boldsymbol{E}$, where $\boldsymbol{E} = \frac{1}{2}(\boldsymbol{\nabla d} + \boldsymbol{\nabla d}^T)$, λ and G are the moduli of the composite separator, and $\boldsymbol{d}$ is the displacement vector.

To capture the large deformation of the separator upon melting, we have developed a phenomenological constitutive model that takes into account the load state during the melting transformation to create the volumetric and axial strains that are observed with experiments. In this model, we multiplicatively decompose the deformation gradient associated with the cold state combined material and hot state solid skeleton into three components associated with different phenomena:

- $\boldsymbol{F}^{\Theta}$, volumetric deformation due to thermal expansion of each phase, the specific volume changes associated with melting of the electrolyte, the loss of void (air) space, and transport of the electrolyte phase
- $\boldsymbol{F}^{X}$, permanent shape and volume change of the solid skeleton during the cold-to-hot phase transition
- $\boldsymbol{F}^{M}$, elastic deformation experienced by the cold state solid and hot state solid skeleton

Various rules for flow, deformation, and phase change are used to calculate these decomposed quantities, but this model is too complicated to discuss here. Instead, we refer to the reader to a detailed report that is currently in preparation [6].

Multiphysics coupling: The critical path towards a useful performance model is coupling the various physics described previously into a single simulation. A key challenge in this path is determining which models need to be coupled to accurately capture the physics, and how those models are going to be coupled, i.e. what variables will be shared between the models and how they will be included in the appropriate constitutive equations. While ideally one may wish to fully-couple all of

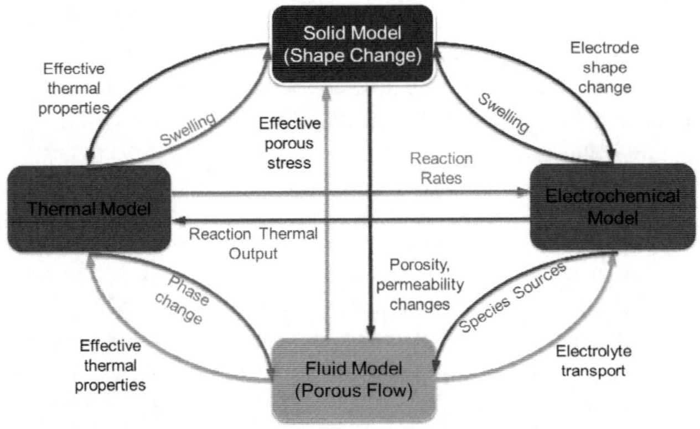

Figure 3. Representation of the various physics models and potential couplings between each of them. The colored text and arrows represent information belonging to a certain set of physics (of the same color) being transferred to another set of physics.

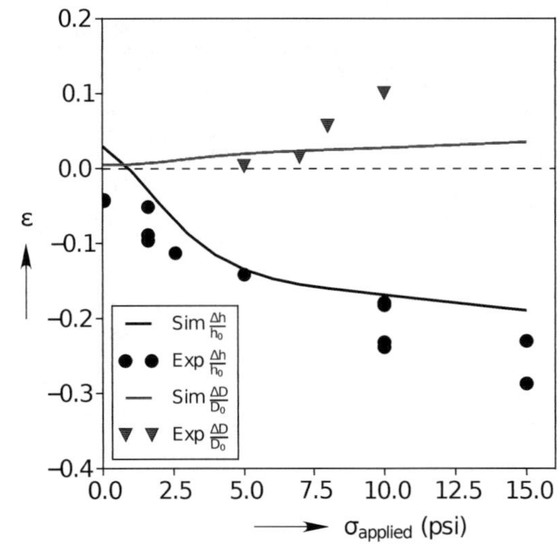

Figure 4. Fit and predicted axial and diameter strains under bonded boundary conditions. Experimental data courtesy of C. C. Roberts.

the physics, this is often not computationally practical. Figure 3 shows how physical phenomena from one model may potentially influence the behavior of the other models. Each additional coupling increases the complexity of the governing equations, thereby increasing the nonlinearity of the problem and drastically increasing solve times. Therefore, care must be taken to only couple physics where necessary.

In addition to correctly choosing which models are coupled, there are options on how tightly coupled the models are in the computational framework. If the relevant physical timescales are on the same order of magnitude and the coupling between the physics are strong, then the equations should be solved simultaneously in the same equation system. This is likely the case for the electrolyte transport and solid mechanics; deformation of the solid will immediately lead to a large change in the pressure and flow of the electrolyte. Alternatively, if the relevant time scales are disparate and the coupling is more weak, then the equations can be solved in a segregated fashion, where at any given time the degrees of freedom from one model can be considered fixed to the other model allowing solution in separate linear systems. This is most likely the case for the thermal and solid models, where the thermal transport is not strongly influenced by small deformations in the solid.

The segregated framework is highly preferred, as it drastically improves model performance, at the risk of lower stability and additional errors. However, Sierra/Aria allows for easy exploration of the effects of coupling, and when the models are fully integrated, various coupling schemes will be evaluated. Our expected outcome is that the solid and fluid mechanics will be solved simultaneously, while the thermal transport and electrochemistry will be segregated.

Results and Discussion

In this section, we demonstrate simulations of two separate physics models. First we show the results of preliminary validation simulations for the custom constitutive model for solid mechanics. Second, we test the two-pressure formulation for porous flow on a model battery cell.

Constitutive model for solid mechanics: In an effort to validate the solid mechanics constitutive model, our collaborators have performed a number of experiments quantifying the axial and transverse strains under a number of different axial stress conditions. In these experiments, a separator was placed between two platens and a constant axial force was applied. The system was then heated to above the melting point of the electrolyte, and the strains were measured [6]. The solid mechanics model for the separator was also run under similar conditions, with the assumption that the separator was bonded to the platens, which is similar to the observed conditions. The unknown material properties in the constitutive equations were then fit (calibrated) to the experimental data, and the results of this calibration are shown in Figure 4.

The model results in Figure 4 show reasonable agreement with the experimental data, particularly in the axial strain results. The simulation results show two regimes of behavior, one for pressures < 5 psi and one for pressures > 5 psi. It is arguable if the experimental data shows these two regimes distinctly. Conversely, the diameter strain experimental data clearly shows two regimes, with no strain at lower pressures and significant strain at higher pressures. This behavior is consistent with our mechanistic understanding that during the early stages of compression, the separator is simply losing "void", or gas, space, causing the material to respond with an effective Poisson's ratio of near zero. However, once all of the void space is removed, the material is a fully saturated solid, acting like an incompressible liquid, and responds with a Poisson's ratio near 0.5. Unfortunately, the current constitutive model is unable to capture these two regimes. This this an area for future improvement of the model.

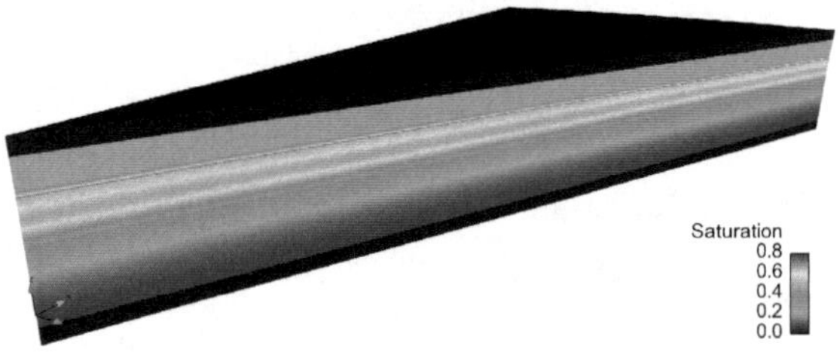

Figure 5. Snapshot of a simulation of two-phase porous flow with static geometry. Colors shown are the electrolyte saturation in each layer.

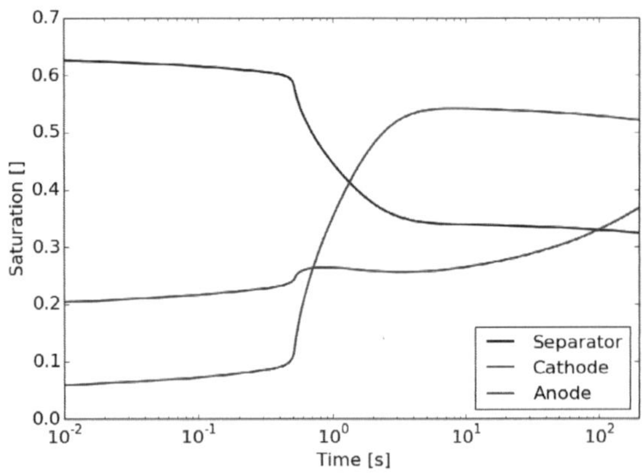

Figure 6. Volume average saturation for individual material layers throughout time. The abrupt change at ~0.5 s is correlated to the point in time that the electrolyte in the separator begins to melt.

Two-phase flow of electrolyte: The new two-pressure formulation for porous flow was tested in the single cell geometry shown in Figure 2. Each material was initialized with a porosity and saturation consistent with the real materials. In order to model the melting of the solid electrolyte, the viscosity of the electrolyte was artificially increased by three orders of magnitude to prevent flow prior to melting. The porous flow was coupled to the thermal model, including an advancing burn front in the heat pellet.

The results of this simulation are shown in Figures 5 and 6. Figure 5 shows the saturation state throughout the stack just after melting. You can see the sharp jump in saturation that appears between the separator and the cathode, which would not have been possible with the standard pressure-saturation formulation. In Figure 6, The volume average saturation for each of the active layers is shown as a function of time. Here, the melting transition can be clearly seen at ~0.5 s, followed by rapid wicking into the relatively dry anode and then a slower transport process into the cathode, all the the while depleting the electrolyte in the separator.

In this simulation, the separator is depleted of electrolyte because it is not allowed to compress, as it does in reality. This is because we have not coupled the fluid flow to the solid mechanics in this simulation. When the separator compresses, void space is removed, leading to an increase in the saturation. This will be improved in future simulations that will couple the thermal, fluid, and solid transport.

Conclusions

In this paper, we presented a concept for a multiphysics model of molten salt battery performance that includes thermal, solid, and fluid transport coupled to electrochemistry. Models for the relevant physics were shown, and we discussed the impact of coupling physics and the different solution strategies. Finally, we demonstrated both the solid and fluid models, discussing areas of future coupling and improvement.

Acknowledgments

The authors wish to thank the thermal battery engineers and scientists of Sandia's Power Sources and Metrology Group, who continually provide useful insight and feedback into the operation of molten salt batteries. We also appreciate the experimental support of many of our colleagues, including Christine C. Roberts and Lisa A. Mondy, who have provided data to populate these models.

The authors gratefully acknowledge funding form the Joint Department of Defense/Department of Energy Munitions Technology Development Program. Sandia National Laboratories is a multi-program laboratory managed and operated by Sandia Corporation, a wholly owned subsidiary of Lockheed Martin Corporation, for the U.S. Department of Energy's National Nuclear Security Administration under contract DE-AC04-94AL85000.

References

[1] Masset, P. and R. A. Guidotti. "Thermal activated (thermal) battery technology: Part II. Molten salt electrolytes." *Journal of Power Sources*, vol. 164, no. 1, pp. 397–414, 2007.

[2] Stewart, J. R. and H. C. Edwards. "The SIERRA framework for developing advanced parallel mechanics applications." In *Large-Scale PDE-Constrained Optimization*, pp. 301–315. Springer, 2003.

[3] Notz, P., S. Subia, M. Hopkins, H. Moffat, and D. Noble. "ARIA Manual Aria 1.5: User's Manual." Tech. Rep. SAND2007-2734, Sandia National Laboratories, 2007.

[4] Piekos, E., A. Grillet, D. Ingersoll, N. Streeter, and D. Noble. "Modeling of Thermal Battery Initiation Using Level Sets." In *Proceedings of the 45th Power Sources Conference*, pp. 595–598, 2012.

[5] van Genuchten, M. T. "A Closed-form Equation for Predicting the Hydraulic Conductivity of Unsaturated Soils." *Soil Science Society of America Journal*, vol. 44, pp. 892–898, 1980.

[6] Long, K. N., C. C. Roberts, S. A. Roberts, and A. M. Grillet. "The Mechanics of Pressed-Pellet Separators in Molten Salt Batteries." Tech. rep., Sandia National Laboratories, 2014. *in preparation.*

Hybrid Pack Design to Enable Safe 230 Wh/kg Soldier Portable Power

Chris Silkowski[1], Mike Wixom[1], Hongxia (Jane) Zhou[1], Pu Zhang[1], Brian Glomski[1], Jim Ockers[2], Trung Nguyen[3]

[1]Navitas Advanced Solutions Group
4880 Venture Drive
Ann Arbor, MI 48108
csilkowski@navitassys.com

[2]Preissner Engineering & Consulting, LLC
1925 Timber Trail
Ann Arbor, MI 48103

[3]EIC Laboratories, Inc.
111 Downey Street
Norwood, MA 02062

Abstract: *The hybrid high energy cell—high power cell lithium-ion battery concept is discussed and bench test data is presented. In the hybrid battery, main energy storage and power delivery functions are separated into optimized high energy density and high power density cells, resulting in an energy-dense battery system featuring improved abuse tolerance and electrical performance.*

Keywords: Navitas; hybrid battery; lithium-ion; abuse tolerance; high energy; BB2590.

Introduction

Conventional lithium-ion battery systems are assemblies composed of a single type of lithium-ion cell. The component cell is designed to meet the energy, rate capability, and power capability requirements of the intended application. In other words, the cell possesses a high energy density and can generally discharge that energy at a significant rate. This represents a safety risk—the combination of concentrated stored energy and the ability to deliver or dissipate that energy at a rate high enough to heat the cell to unsafe temperatures or otherwise excite failure modes.

Navitas Advanced Solution Group's battery-battery hybrid device concept seeks to decouple the interactive risk of the battery's energy storage and power storage/delivery functions into separate, cooperating lithium-ion cells optimized either for high energy density or for high power density. The general electrical circuit of a hybrid battery is shown in Figure 1.

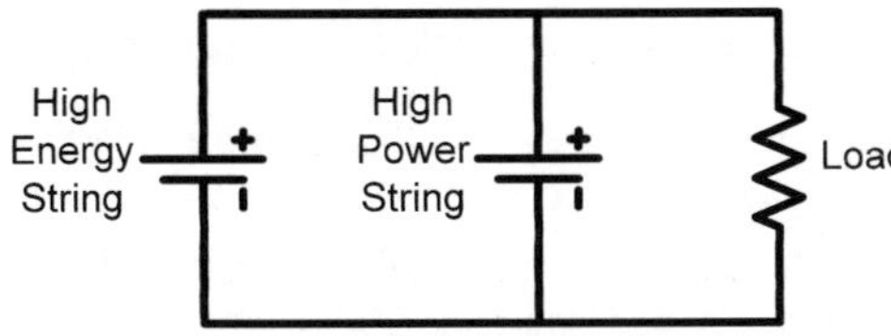

Figure 1. A general hybrid battery circuit.

The goal of hybridization is to reduce the discharge rate capability of the high energy density cell element—increasing abuse tolerance—and move the high discharge rate and power capability to an essentially safe low energy density cell featuring high power:energy ratio. This concept is illustrated in Figure 2.

In a hybrid battery arrangement, the high energy cell element provides continuous low-rate discharge power, but pulses and transient events requiring higher levels of power are assisted (load leveled) by the high power element. This action becomes particularly valuable as additional safety enhancement modifications are considered for high energy cells. Modified organic electrolytes, ionic liquid electrolytes, heat-resistant layers, ceramic-coated active material powders, and other safety enhancements can impede lithium ion transport and reduce cell power and rate capability. The hybrid battery system allows the inclusion of these beneficial features at minimum impact to system electrical performance.

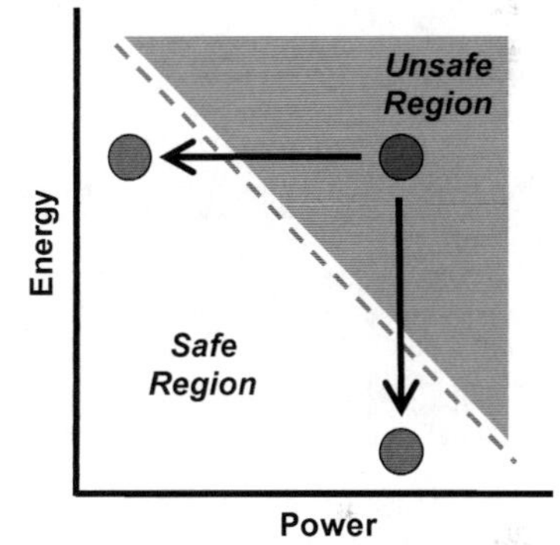

Figure 2. Hybrid battery systems potentially improve abuse tolerance by separating main energy storage and power storage functions into optimized cooperating cells.

The hybrid arrangement also benefits battery service life. Stresses on the high energy element—high C-rate pulses and the resistive heating and active material expansion/contraction that accompany them—are reduced by the load leveling action of the high power strings. With heating and mechanical stresses reduced on the high energy cells, battery service life is increased.

Hybrid battery systems can be classified as "passive" and "active" hybrids. A passive system contains no electronics coupling the high energy and high power elements—only a straightforward parallel electrical connection. In a passive hybrid, the voltage of the high power cell (or string) must be selected carefully to assist the high energy cell across a wide state of discharge (SOD) range, and ideally concentrate that assistance in the SOD region where the high energy cell is least efficient.

Lithium Iron Phosphate (LFP) chemistry cells are well-suited to high power cell duty in a hybrid battery system. The nominal voltage of a graphite/LFP cell is 3.3V, while high energy density metal oxide cells run at 3.7V nominal. In a hybrid arrangement, this voltage relationship insures that following discharge load leveling work, the LFP cell is recharged to a high state of charge (SOC), where its impedance is lowest and power capability is highest. The voltage relationship is pictured in Figure 3. This voltage relationship is preserved over 80% of the hybrid battery's SOD range, though in practice significant load leveling operation occurs over a more limited SOD range. The bulk of load leveling assistance occurs at >60% SOD, where high energy cell impedance is rising, efficiency drops, and cell self-heating increases.

An active hybrid makes use of a DC-DC converter circuit or the like to recharge or otherwise regulate or control the high power element. An active hybrid increases design flexibility and allows the use of a wider variety of high power cell chemistries and series arrangements; however, some drawbacks exist. System complexity is increased, additional volume is required by the electronics, cost is increased, and the circuit consumes energy. As such, active hybrid designs are selected only when a passive design cannot meet application requirements.

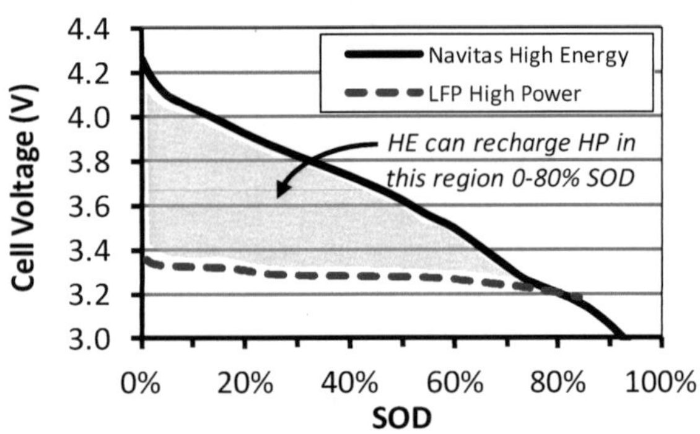

Figure 3. Example of the component cell voltage relationship required for passive hybrid battery operation.

Navitas ASG has demonstrated a high energy cell with specific energy of 270-300 Wh/kg[1]. Integrating this cell into a hybrid battery system with the Navitas-made LFP power cell enables continuous current output of 14A and pulse power exceeding 90 A (>1.2 kW) from a BB2590-equivalent battery pack. The hybrid battery delivers this performance with high power cells requiring less than 10% mass and volume claim in the pack—i.e., most of the pack is available for high density energy storage. As a consequence of the improved cell and pack energy density, the total stored energy in the 24Ah hybrid BB2590 is 340 Wh—a 60% improvement in energy content over a state of the art 211 Wh BB2590. Elements of this hybrid battery design are patent pending.

Bench testing shows that in addition to high battery energy density, the passive hybrid battery configuration assists Navitas BB2590 electrical performance as tested under communications pulse profiles. This paper discusses experimental conditions and test data.

Experimental

Test Profiles: BB2590 communications test profiles DARPA 1, 2, 3 are shown in Figure 4. Cells or assemblies were charged at low rate (C/5), then discharged under the repetitive pulse profiles until the lower voltage limit was reached.

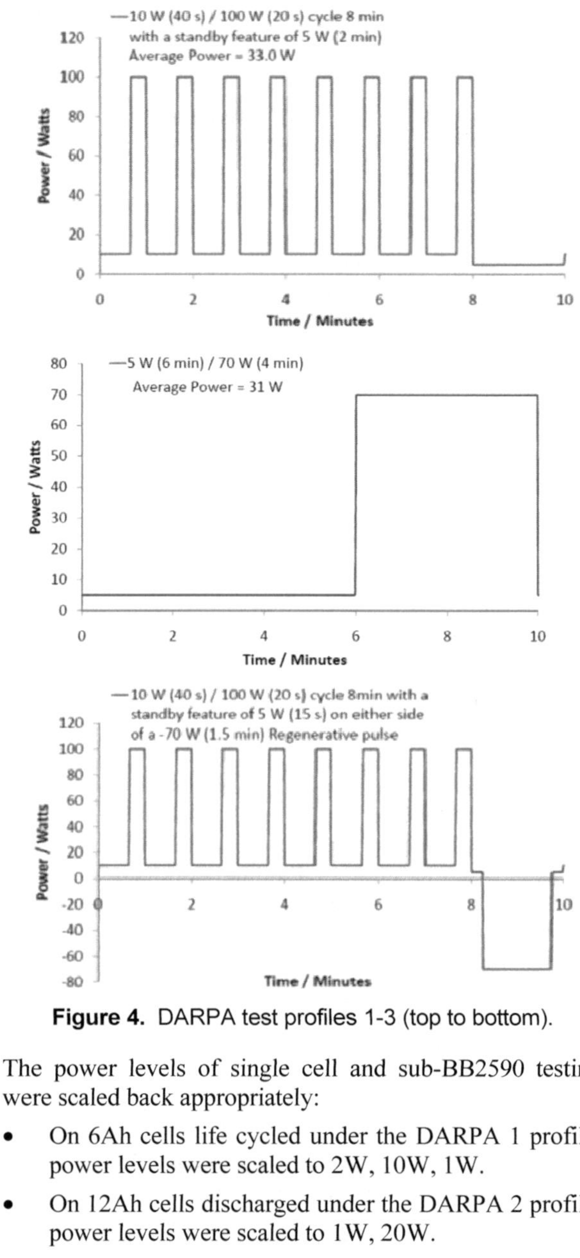

Figure 4. DARPA test profiles 1-3 (top to bottom).

The power levels of single cell and sub-BB2590 testing were scaled back appropriately:

- On 6Ah cells life cycled under the DARPA 1 profile, power levels were scaled to 2W, 10W, 1W.
- On 12Ah cells discharged under the DARPA 2 profile, power levels were scaled to 1W, 20W.

Cells: 6 Ah and 12 Ah, 270-300 Wh/kg metal oxide high energy and 350 mAh, 60 Wh/kg, 4.5 kW/kg LFP high power prismatic lithium ion cells were fabricated by Navitas ASG. The 12 Ah and 350 mAh cells and their sizes relative to one another are shown in Figure 5. Cells were tested individually, as cell-level hybrid assemblies, or assembled into 4S strings appropriate for 15V hybrid BB2590-type operation.

Figure 5. Left: 350 mAh LFP high power cell.
Right: 12 Ah high energy metal oxide cell.

Test Hardware: Electrical testing was conducted with a Maccor, Inc. Series 4000 Automated Test System outfitted with auxiliary temperature (thermocouple) and voltage sensors for synchronized data acquisition. Precision shunts (25A, 50 mV) were used to measure current flow between high energy and high power elements. Temperature control was provided with a Tenney TUJR environmental chamber.

Results and Discussion

DARPA 1 Profile Testing: A BB2590-equivalent bench assembly of high energy and high power cells was constructed and tested. The battery consisted of eight 12 Ah high energy cells (4S2P strings) set in parallel with eight 350 mAh high power LFP cells (4S2P strings). The assembly was instrumented and the DARPA 1 test profile was performed. The battery delivered 10– 11.2 hours of run time under this profile. Figure 6 shows the battery voltage profile under discharge and also the current output of one 4S high energy and one 4S high power string.

The load leveling action of the hybrid configuration was most pronounced in the 7-10 hour region; little significant interaction between high energy and high power strings was observed before ~7 h. Figures 7 and 8 examine the pulse discharge data in greater detail. Figure 7 examines the 7.7–7.8 h region. Here, both discharge load leveling and recharging between pulses was observed. Approximately 15% of the pulse discharge current is supplied by the high power strings in this region. Figure 8 examines the 8.5–8.6 h region. Here, battery voltage is 13V (3.3V/cell, the plateau voltage of the LFP cell) and significant load leveling is observed: 25–30% of the pulse current is supplied by the high power strings. Recharging is slower here as the battery voltage is close to the high power string voltage and driving force is diminished.

DARPA 1 Profile Life Cycle Testing: Cell-level tests were conducted to assess the cycle life of the hybrid battery system. Single 6 Ah high energy cells were cycled with and without a 350 mAh high power cell in parallel. Cells were cycled against the scaled version of the DARPA 1 profile (10W maximum). The cycle life of the hybrid device is increased relative to that of a single 6 Ah cell. Figure 9 shows the cycle life of single and hybrid 6 Ah devices under pulse discharge.

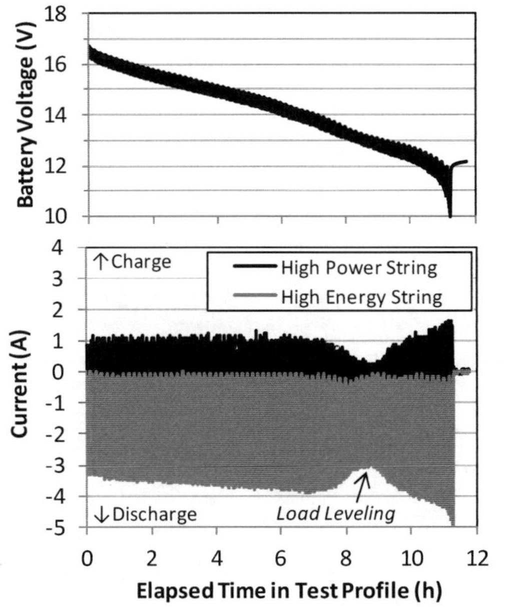

Figure 6. Hybrid battery voltage and high energy/high power string current output under DARPA 1 profile.

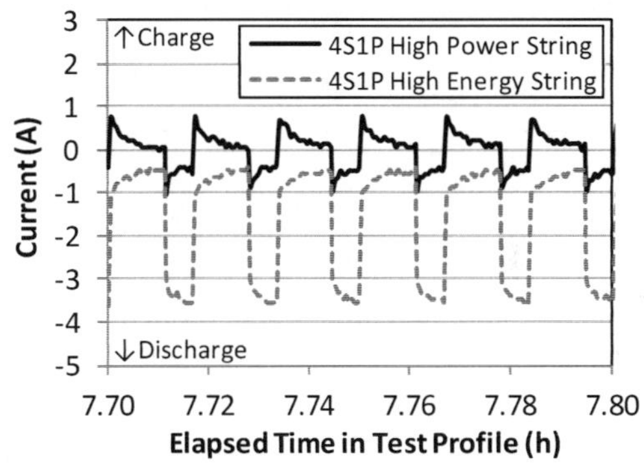

Figure 7. High energy and high power string current output under DARPA 1 profile.

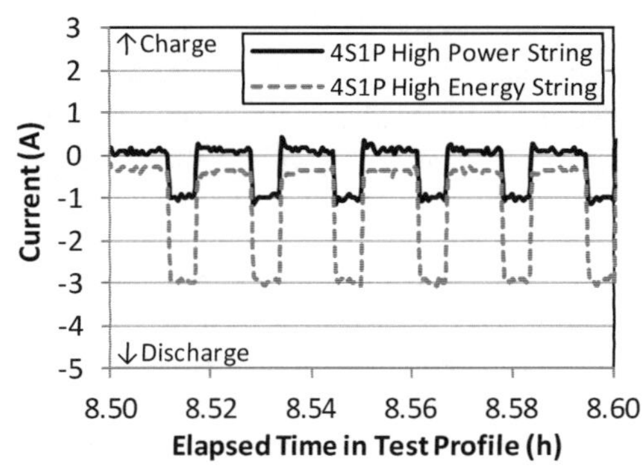

Figure 8. High energy and high power string current output under DARPA 1 profile.

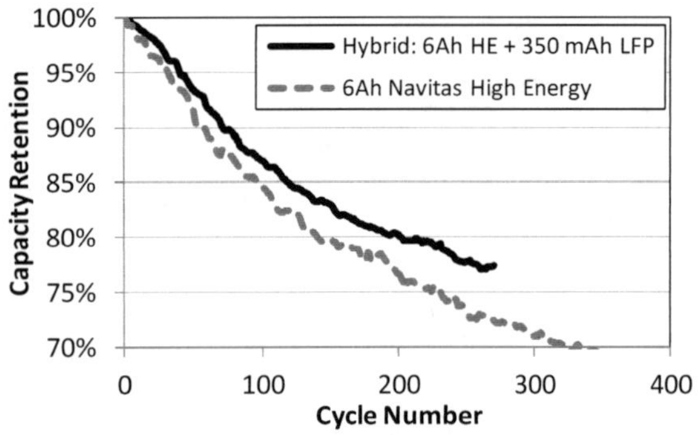

Figure 9. DARPA1 profile (10W max power level) life cycling at room temperature.

DARPA 2 Profile Testing: The DARPA 2 test profile was conducted on the BB2590-equivalent bench assembly of high energy and high power cells. The battery delivered 11.9 hours of run time under this profile.

DARPA 2 Profile Testing on Single Cells: Cell-level tests were conducted to determine the heating behavior of the hybrid battery system. Single 12 Ah high energy cells were discharged with and without a 350 mAh high power cell in parallel. Cells were discharged against the scaled version of the DARPA 2 profile (20W max). The temperature rise of the high energy cell is substantially reduced in the hybrid configuration. Figure 10 shows the temperature rise of the single and hybrid 12 Ah devices under pulse discharge.

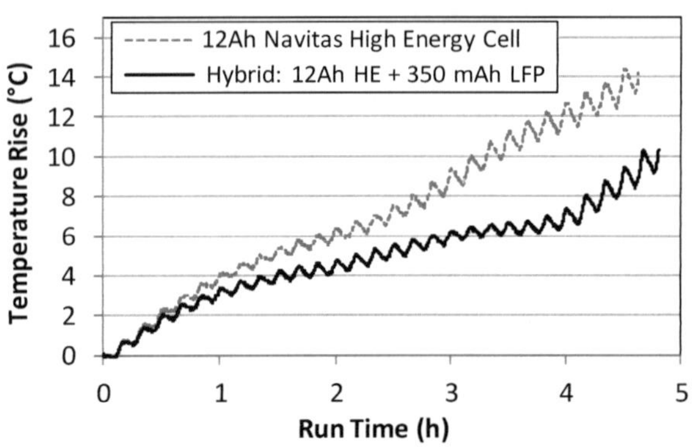

Figure 10. Temperature rise of cells discharged under scaled DARPA 2 profile.

The hybrid device runs cooler. Transference of thermal burden to the LFP cell increases battery abuse tolerance and service life. Battery run times under heavy loads will also be increased, as it will take longer to reach cut-off temperature.

DARPA 3 Profile Testing: The DARPA 3 test profile was conducted on the BB2590-equivalent bench assembly of high energy and high power cells. The battery delivered 16.5 hours of run time under this profile. The high power strings were able to accept the profile's 70W regeneration pulses and extend the battery's run time.

Summary: Table 1 summarizes the performance of the Navitas BB2590-equivalent hybrid battery and compares it to state of the art BB2590. The high energy hybrid BB2590 delivers a 60-140% improvement over state of the art. The greatest improvement is realized against profiles containing a high incidence of pulses.

Table 2 summarizes discharge performance of the BB2590-equivalent hybrid battery under a variety of test profiles and soak temperature conditions. The hybrid battery shows high performance down to -40°C. Temperature rise of the high energy strings is below 5°C under room temperature (23°C) discharge.

Table 1. Run times of Navitas hybrid BB2590-type battery vs. state of the art BB2590.

Test Profile	Run Time, Navitas Hybrid	Run Time, SOA BB2590	Improvement
DARPA 1	10.0 h	4.5 h	+120%
DARPA 2	11.9 h	6.7 h	+60%
DARPA 3	16.5 h	6.8 h	+140%

Table 2. Electrical performance of Navitas hybrid BB2590-type battery.

Test	Capacity (Ah)	Energy (Wh)	Run Time (h)	HE Cell Temp. Rise (°C)
DARPA 1 (23°C)	24.1	331	10.0	2.4
DARPA 1 (-20°C)	22.6	285	8.6	7.5
DARPA 1 (-30°C)	19.8	227	6.9	9.5
DARPA 2 (23°C)	26.4	369	11.9	2.4
DARPA 3 (23°C)	26.5	362	16.5	2.2
-2A (23°C)	24.6	346	12.3	2.2
-2A (-30°C)	22.7	281	11.3	5.4
-2A (-40°C)	18.5	210	9.3	5.7
Packbot (23°C)	26.2	363	6.1	3.4

Conclusions

Navitas Advanced Solutions Group's high energy cell—high power cell hybrid battery system concept has been demonstrated in bench testing. A hybrid battery increases battery energy density, run time, and cycle life. A hybrid BB2590-type battery possesses 60% higher energy than a state of the art BB2590 and shows 60–140% run time improvements under communications profiles. Service life and abuse tolerance are increased by reducing high energy metal oxide cell heating and sharing the thermal burden with highly safe, thermally stable LFP high power cells.

Acknowledgements

Navitas thanks the U.S. Defense Advanced Research Projects Agency (DARPA) and the U.S. Army RDECOM Communications Electronics Research, Development and Engineering Center (CERDEC) for their partnership and funding of this work. Navitas thanks Viet Vu for his technical vision and guidance in this program.

References

1. P. Zhang, et. al., "Novel Chemistry for High Energy 600 Wh/L Lithium Ion Cells," *Proc. 46th Power Sources Conference*, 2014.

Tadiran High Power Rechargeable Lithium Ion Cell For Extreme Temperature Conditions

Hersel Yamin and Chen Menachem
Tadiran Batteries Ltd.
P.O. Box 1 K.Ekron, 76950 Israel

Abstract
Several types of a new family of AA size high power rechargeable lithium ion cells was developed. This family consists of 3 members having the AA size diameter and various cell lengths. Their internal design consists of high surface area carbon anode and lithiated NCA cathode. The electrolyte is based on the carbonate solvent mixture. The cells were designed to deliver high power density in a continuous and a pulse mode of operation. They are capable to be charged and discharged at extreme temperature conditions from -40°C to 72°C . The cells show excellent long term stability during accelerated storage and while on long term operation. Thousands of full charge and discharge cycles can be delivered before cell capacity drops to 80% of their initial value. The cells have relatively low self discharge rate of about 1% per month at room temperature. The electrical performance and the long term charge/discharge data at various environmental conditions will be presented.

Introduction
The current Lithium ion battery is one of the most widely used rechargeable battery for portable electronics. The battery has high energy density, good power capability, high number of cycles, fair long term stability and safety level. One of the main drawback of the lithium ion cells is their limited operation under high and low temperature condition. Consumer grade lithium ion battery cannot be charged at below zero degree centigrade and above 45°C. Charging at low temperatures leads to permanent plating of metallic lithium on cell anode that cannot be removed during cycling. The aim of this work is to present the electrical performance and the operating life characteristics of the TLI cells. Operating life model for long term usage under extreme temperature conditions will be presented.

Experimental
The electrochemical cells are standard AA size cells . The anode is based on low surface area carbon, cell cathode consists of lithium intercalated nickel cobalt aluminum compound (NCA) . The electrolyte is based on LiPF6 salt dissolved in carbonate solvents mixture. Electrode surface area is approximately 360cm2 . Cells are hermetically sealed by laser welding and glass to metal joint. Charge /discharge cycles were conducted by Maccor 96 channels cycler. Long term trickle charge was conducted by connecting the rechargeable cell to primary Li/SOCl2 cell at 3.65 volt or to Li/SO2Cl2 cell at 3.90 volt. Test at various temperatures were carried out after cell stabilization at the test temperature for at least 16 hours

Results and Discussion
Power capability
The discharge curves of TLI cells at various currents are presented in Figure 1. At low discharge current of 100mA (about C/4) cell capacity is 380mAh while under 5A (about 14C rate) the cell delivers 320mAh or 85% of its low rate capacity.

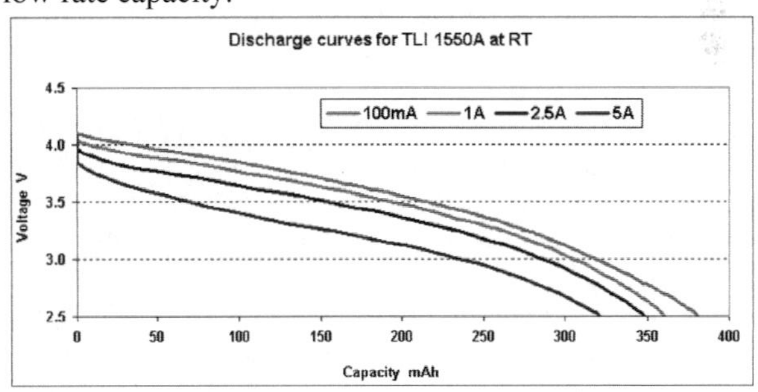

Figure 1: Discharge curves of TLI AA cell at various currents

Figure 2 describes discharge curves at constant current of 2A at various temperatures between -40°C and 85°C. As can be seen at 85ºC cell capacity is identical to the room temperature capacity while only 40% of the capacity is obtained at -40°C at 2A rate

.

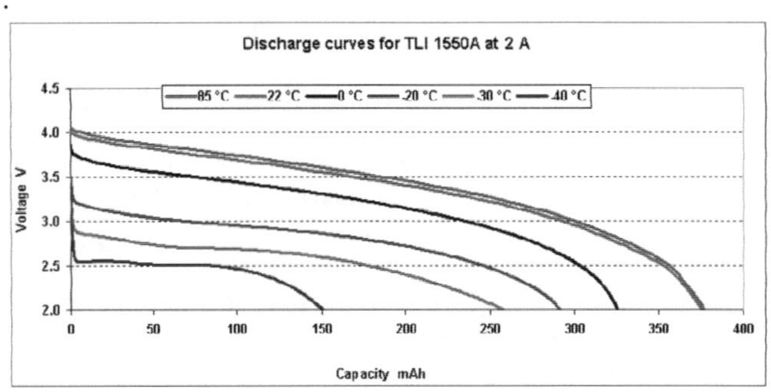

Figure 2: Discharge curves of TLI AA Cell at 2A @ various temperatures

Charge discharge cycles

Charge discharge cycles were conducted at constant current of 440mA to a given voltage of 4.1 V, 3.9V and 3.65V followed by 20mA charge current at the end of charge. The charge time was approximately 1 hour. Discharge tests were conducted at constant current of 250mA to 2.5V cut off. Figure 3 describes typical voltage time curve and charge current at 4.1V.

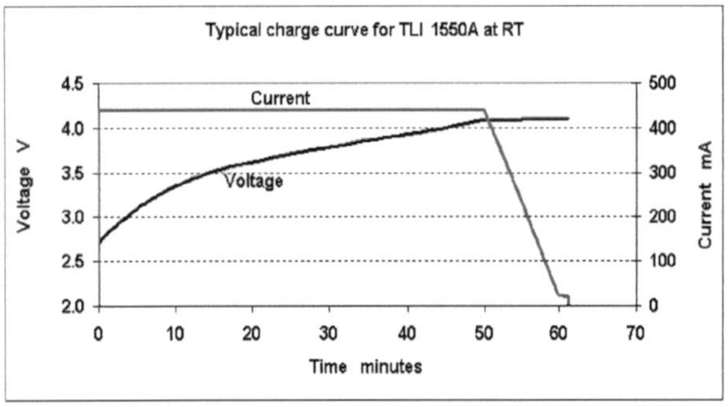

Figure 3: typical voltage time curve and charge current at 4.1V.

Capacity versus charge cycle for the first 5000 cycles is given in Figure 4. Cell impedance measured at 1Khz is indicated in the figure. It can be seen that cell impedance increases from 40mΩ for the first cycle to 45mΩ after 2500 cycles and stabilized at this value for another 2500 cycles. The calculated capacity loss is about 0.004% per cycle. This value is significantly decreased during the last 2500 cycles. Similar results were obtained at charging voltage of 3.9V but with much more cycles.

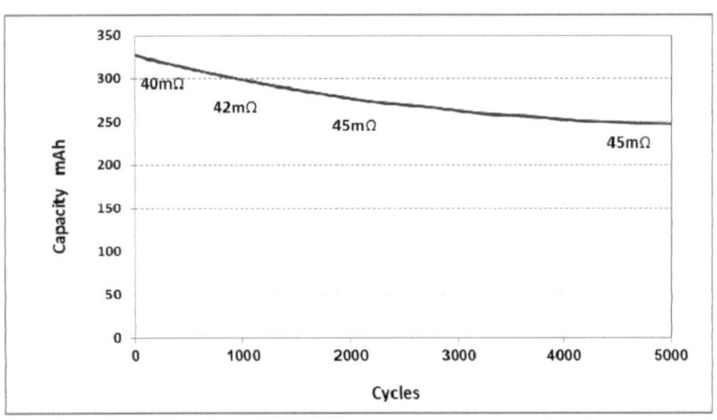

Figure 4: typical capacity versus cycle number at charge regime given in figure 3

At charging voltage of 3.9V capacity loss is calculated to be 1% per each 1000 cycles. At lower charging voltage of 3.65 Volt the cell delivers about 40% of its full capacity. The calculated capacity loss for the first 40000 cycles is 9.5%. Cell capacity vs. cycle number at various charge voltage of 3.67V , 3.9V and 4.1V is given in figure5. The initial reduction of the capacity under various charge voltage shows the same type of behavior with the cycle number It decreases rapidly during the first 1000 cycles and more slowly later on.

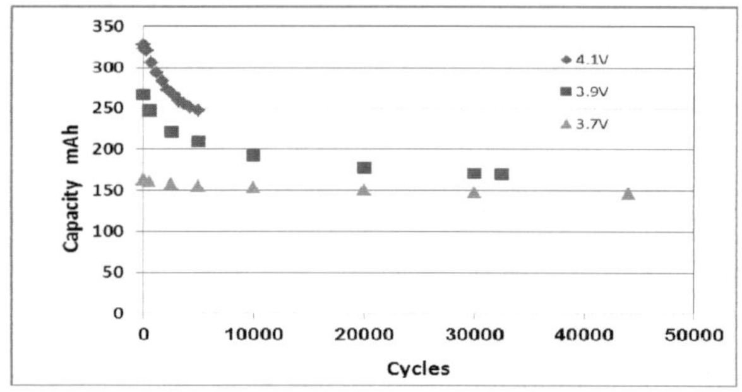

Figure 5: capacity vs. cycle number at 3 voltage levels

One of the most remarkable characteristic of the TLI cell is its capability to be charged and discharged at extreme temperature condition. Figure 6 describes cell capacity vs. the first 100 cycles at various temperatures ranging from -40°C to 85°C. The capacity loss at 85°C is approximately 0.13% per cycle during the first 100 cycles. The capacity loss decreases with the increase of the cycle number . As can be seen capacity loss decreases to 0.015% for the last 50 cycles.

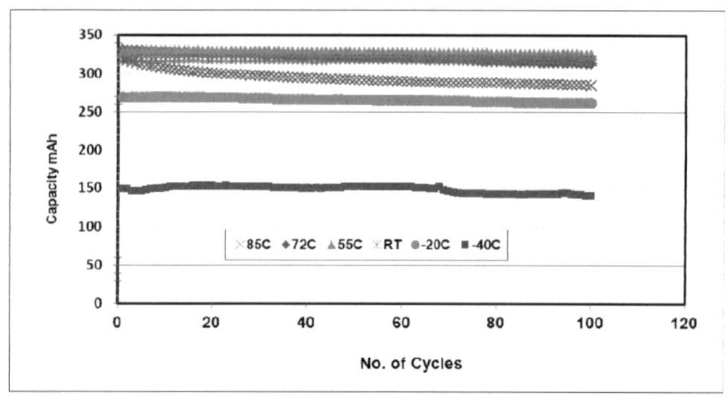

Figure 6: capacity vs. cycle number at various temperatures

As the initial capacity is a temperature dependent we have normalized the y axis to 100% for each temperature as indicated in the graph.

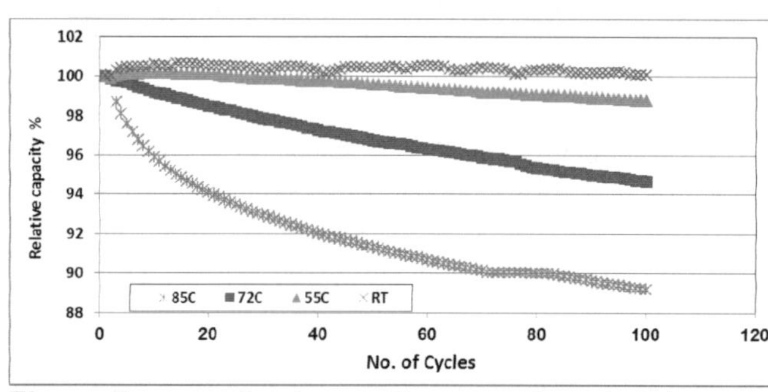

Figure 7: normalized capacity vs. cycles at various temperatures

Accelerated storage and life test

Capacity degradation during cycling and during storage is a function of several parameters like charge and discharge end voltage, cycling rate, operating and storage temperature etc. The contribution of each parameter to the overall capacity loss and to the impedance rise can be determined by appropriate study. Figure 8 describes cell impedance measured at 1khz during charge and discharge cycling tests at constant power at 72°C, 65°C and 21°C. Cycle rate is one cycle per day ,10 cells per test .As can be seen after 150 days at 72C cell impedance increases from 55mΩ to 82mΩ after 150cycles (150days of operation).

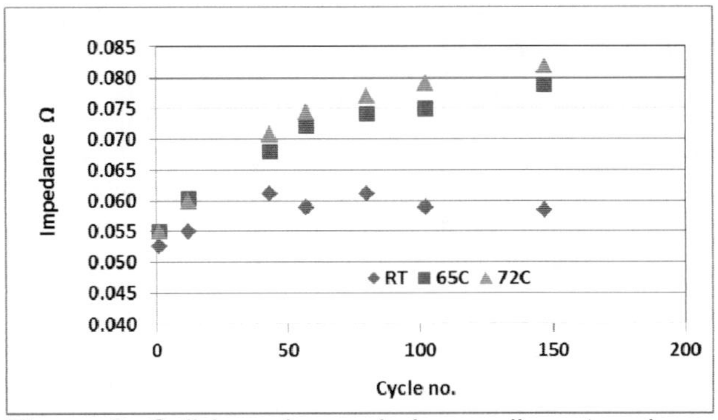

Figure 8: Cell impedance during cycling at various temperatures

Accelerated cycling test was studied at temperature of 72°C , 65°C and 21°C at constant power of 1.33 Watt . The average discharge capacity of 10 cells at 72C is given in figure 9. At room temperature a minor change in cell capacity was observed during the first 190 cycles. During cycling at 65°C cell capacity decreases from 250mAh at the first cycle to 230mAh after 150 cycles. At temperature of 72°C cell capacity decreased from 250mAh to 215mAh after 150 cycles

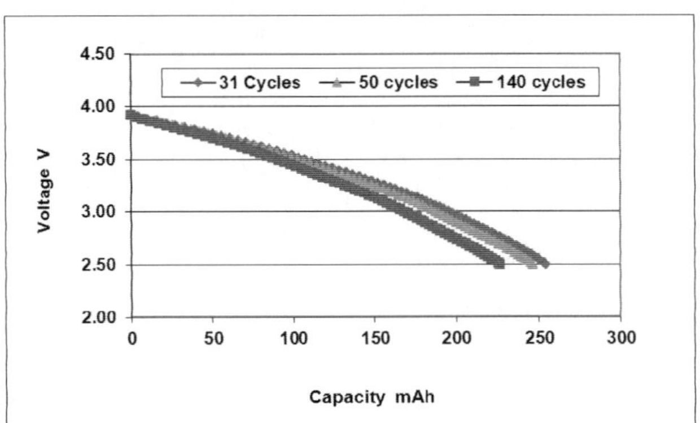

Figure 9: Discharge capacity at 72 C for various cycles

Exponential curve fitting under the tested temperature show correlation factor of 0.92 for 72°C and 0.95 for the 65°C (see figure10). Arrhenius plot of capacity loss versus 1/T after 150 days of cycling test predicts acceleration factors of 45 and 30 for 72°C and 65°C respectively in comparison to room temperature cycling. This means that cell capacity is expected to decrease to 80% of its intial value after 18 years of continuous cycling at room temperature. During this period 6750 cycles are expected

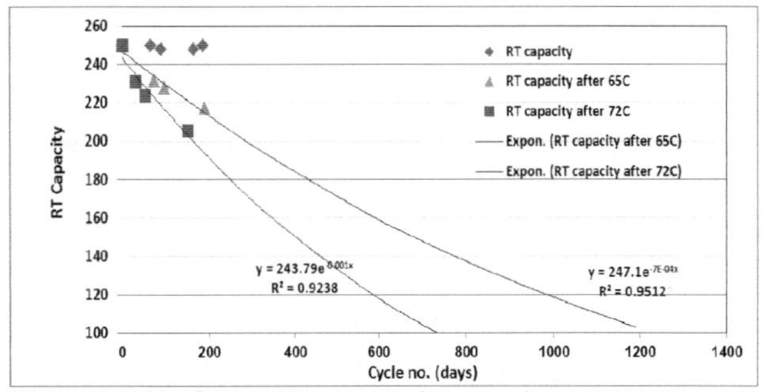

Figure 10: Capacity vs cycle number at constant power of 1.33 Watt at various temperatures

Storage at constant voltage

The effect of charging voltage on the irreversible loss of cell capacity was studied at two different charging voltage levels : 3.65V and 3.9V. For the 3.65 V the cells were trickle charged by connection to Li/SOCl2 cells and for 3.9 volt by connection to Li/SO2Cl2 cells. After a predetermined storage time the capacity loss in comparison to non-stored cell was calculated from the discharge curves. At 3.65V the irreversible capacity loss on storage was found to be about 4% during 10 years while at 3.9V the rate of capacity loss is 40% higher. The self-discharge rate during room temperature storage was studied by two different techniques : (a) measurement of cell OCV versus time using titration curve of OCV versus capacity and (b) by a micro calorimetric measurement of the heat out put. Figure 11 describes micro calorimetric measurement of TLI AA cell stored under trickle charge of 3.65 V for 5 years . The calculated self-discharge value is 2.6μA. For first approximation the thermo neutral potential was taken as cell OCV

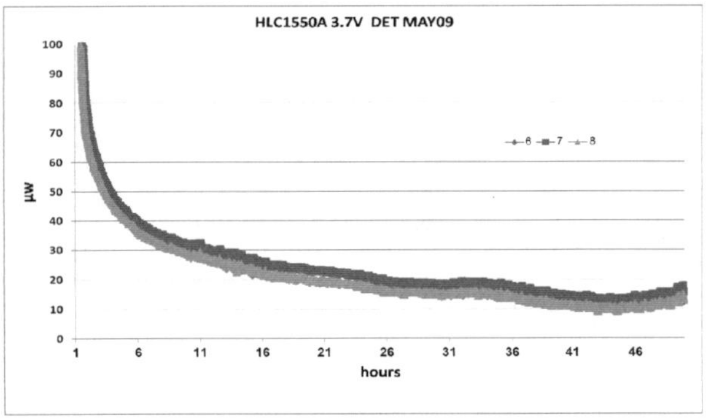

Figure 11: Microcaloremetry of 3 cells after 5 years at 3.65V

Figure 12 describes voltage time curve of 1550A during long term storage. Cell voltage decreases from 3.9V to 3.78V after 2 years of storage and to a value of 3.70 volt after 5 years. Capacity loss during the first 2 years and the first 5 years of storage at 3.9V is 54.4mAh and 86.5mAh respectively. The calculated self-discharge rate from these values are 3.2 and 1.9 μA respectively. This value is in a fair agreement with heat output of about 12μWatt (about 3.0μ A) found by micro calorimeter after 2 years of storage at 3.9V.

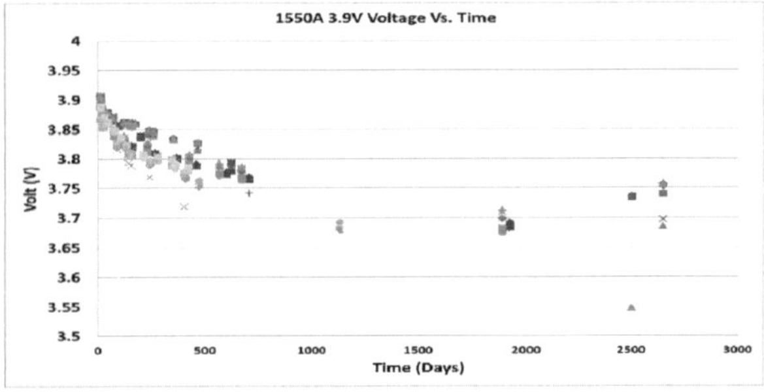

Figure 12: Voltage time curves of TLI cells charged to 3.9 V

Charge and discharge tests performed after 5 years of storage at 3.9V at room temperature show reversible capacity of 243mAh in comparison to 250mAh for non-stored cell. This indicates that the irreversible loss on storage is about 0.6% per year at 3.9V. During 8.5 years of charge /discharge cycling (10-11 cycles per day) the irreversible capacity loss is about 36% (see figure 4).

One possible way to predict life under less frequent cycles than 11 cycles per day is to take into account both the number of cycles and the operating period. For the TLI cell under charge and discharge end voltage of 3.9 V and 2.5V the empirical equation for capacity loss is found to be :

$$Q = 0.6Y + 0.95N$$

Where Q is the total irreversible capacity loss in percent , Y is the operating time in years and N is the total number of cycles given in thousands. For example: The TLI cell is capable to be charged and discharged 3 times per day for 18 years continuously at 3.9 volt. Cell capacity under these conditions will be reduced to 70% of its initial capacity after this period of operation

Saft High Power Lithium Titanate Cells

Thomas A. Greszler*, Y. Yvonne Chen, Bridget Deveney
Saft America
107 Beaver Court, Cockeysville, MD 21030
*Thomas.Greszler@saftamerica.com

Abstract: *SAFT has successfully applied Li-ion electrochemistry to defense and space applications which require very high power. In fact, by optimizing both the electrochemical and electro-mechanical cell design, Saft has developed a range of Li-ion products that can deliver very high power. There are, however, still inherent limitations for high power applications with traditional Li-ion chemistry. Particularly, even with an optimized cell design, cycle life can be limited for applications which require very rapid charging due to both lithium plating and electrolyte decomposition on the graphitic negative electrode. Lithium titanate oxide (LTO), due to operation above both the lithium plating and solvent reduction potentials, minimizes (or eliminates) these phenomenon and can potentially provide extremely long cycle life. Saft has recently developed, with DOE/USABC funding, LTO based technology for high power applications. The cell provides ~2,500 W/kg at room temperature (charge and discharge) and nearly 700W/kg at -30°C. Impedance growth is shown to occur mainly on the positive electrode and is largely mitigated by improved electrode processing and optimized electrolyte. Saft intends to commercialize this LTO technology and believes it to be a good match for a number of applications in the defense market.*

Keywords: Lithium-ion; Titanate; Impedance Growth; High Power; LTO.

Introduction

Saft has been manufacturing Li-Ion batteries for more than 30 years and is a world leader in providing state of the art lithium ion systems for demanding applications in commercial, defense and space markets. Our products have evolved to match the requirements of the market with a focus on high performance over a wide temperature range, long life, high quality and reliability, and rugged systems that can operate in uncontrolled and abusive environments. Recently Saft has investigated the use of LTO as a replacement to traditional graphite as the negative of a Li-ion battery. LTO has the benefit of enabling symmetric charge/discharge plus extremely long cycle life but reduces the energy density and has historically suffered from high impedance growth at elevated temperatures. Here we present the results of Saft's research including energy density, impedance as a function of temperature, and cycle life. Much of this research was funded by USABC and the DOE to develop a cell capable of meeting the stringent performance and cost targets of the USABC 12V Start-Stop system.

Cell Chemistry

Saft LTO cell is based on an Lithium Nickel Manganese Cobalt Oxide (NMC) positive paired with an LTO negative. This provides the open circuit potential shown in figure 1.

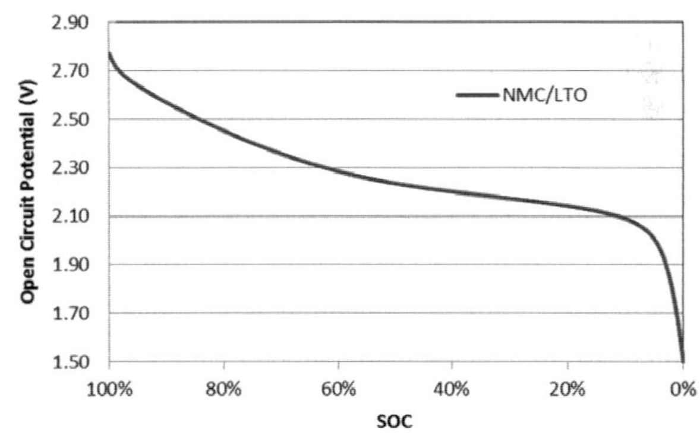

Figure 1. Open circuit potential of NMC/LTO cell.

Separators and electrolytes have been chosen to enable operation at low temperature (-30°C) while minimizing cost. Electrodes were designed to provide high power but other configurations are possible with higher energy density.

Cell Format, Capacity, and Power Capability

Prototype cells have been produced in a prismatic format with properties shown in table 1.

Table 1. LTO/NMC prismatic cell properties

Cell	LP10P-LTO
Nominal Voltage (V)	2.3
Nominal Capacity at C rate (Ah)	11
Specific Energy (Wh/kg)	41
Energy Density (Wh/L)	70
Specific Pulse (2s) Power at 25°C 100% SOC (W/kg)	2460
Specific Pulse (2s) Power at -30°C 100% SOC (W/kg)	676

Power capability as a function of depth of discharge (DOD) for both charge and discharge is shown in figure 2. The cell is capable of ~2,000W of charge at high DOD and ~1,500W of discharge at low DOD.

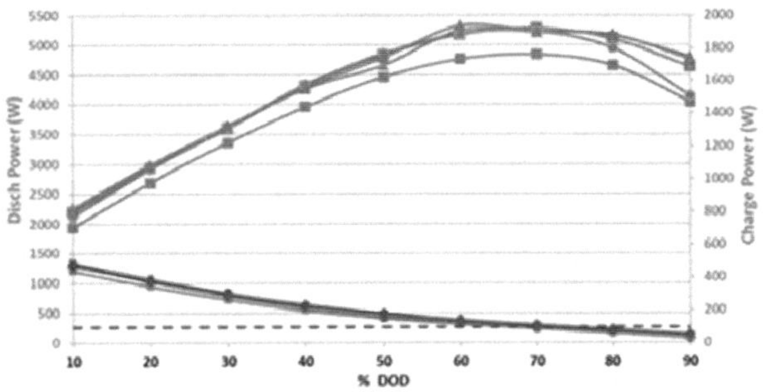

Figure 2. Charge and discharge power capability of 11Ah (nominal) prismatic cell utilizing NMC/LTO chemistries. Each line is results from an individual cell. The red dotted line indicates scaled discharge power requirement for USABC 12V start-stop applications.

Cycle Life

Cycle life was tested utilizing the USABC 12V Start-Stop cycling protocol which is shown schematically in figure 3.

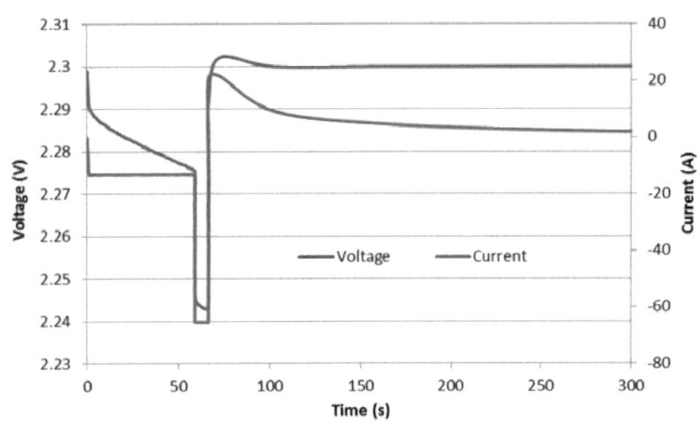

Figure 3. USABC Start-Stop profile scaled to 10Ah cell.

Cycling performance of two generations of cells is shown in figure 4. Generation 2 was modified from generation 1by altering the electrode fabrication process conditions and by changing the electrolyte (type and additives) resulting in dramatically improved impedance growth. Further improvements are possible via further optimization of the electrolyte and processing conditions. Capacity degradation (not shown) is minimal for both generations with less than 5% decay over 15,000 cycles (which corresponds to over 1,500 hours on test). Impedance growth at room temperature (not shown) is very low with less than 5% growth after 15,000 cycles. Figure 5 shows cell internal pressure (measured with a pressure transducer mounted in the fill port) for one of the generation 2 cells. Internal pressure is low, even after 15,000 cycles indicating that gassing is largely mitigated for this design. This is especially impressive since this cell was not vented post formation, so the internal pressure includes all formation gasses. In fact, of the ~16 psi of total internal pressure, ~8 psi is from formation. The total pressure (~16 psi or 1.1 bar) is a very typical result for NMC/graphite cells – further indicating that the LTO with the generation 2 design is not inducing any excessive gas formation.

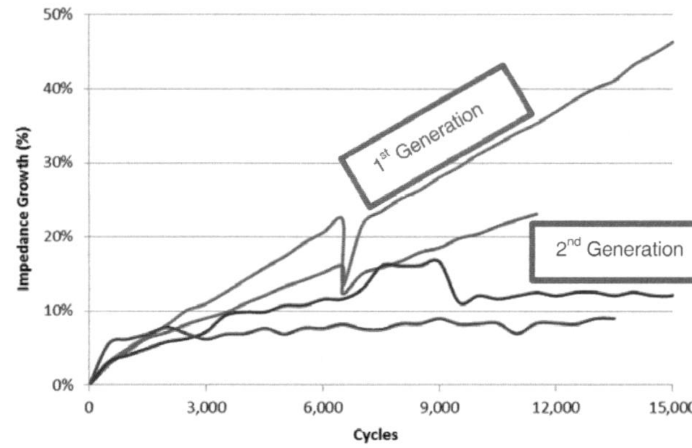

Figure 4. Cycle life impedance growth (2 second) at 45°C under USABC Start-Stop cycling protocol showing significantly improved cycle life for 2nd generation cells.

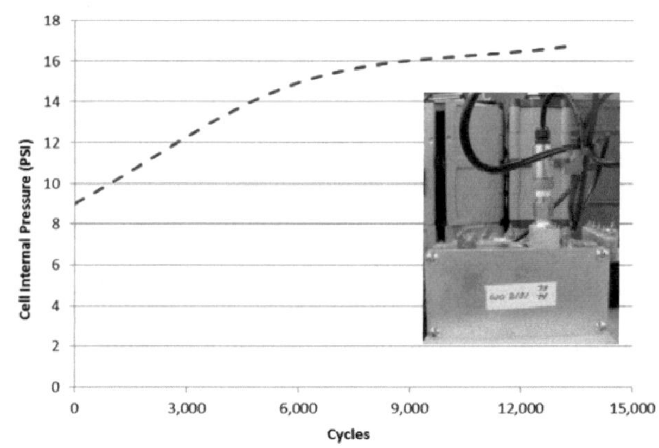

Figure 5. Cell internal pressure for one generation two cell. Internal pressure is low and stabilizing.

Understanding of Impedance Growth

To determine the source and location of the impedance growth, electrodes from generation one and generation two cells were harvested after ~12,000 cycles and rebuilt into half cells with lithium counter electrodes. Fresh (non-cycled) electrodes were also included for reference. The half cells were cycled at low rate (C/10) and impedance was estimated from the total potential difference between the charge and discharge curves at 50% SOC. In addition, the half cells were pulsed at 1C at various SOCs. The negative electrode cycling is shown in figure 6 and the positive electrode cycling is shown in figure 7. Figures 8 shows the calculated impedance from the cycle results. At the time of publication, the pulse results were not yet available but will be presented during the conference.

Results indicate that the cell impedance growth occurs on the positive electrode. Since this impedance growth is not observed for graphite/NMC cells, it is strongly indicative of an interaction with the LTO negative. Generation 2 cells, which show significantly less cell impedance growth, show practically no impedance growth on the positive in half-cell configuration. There is, however, a small increase in impedance on the negative for generation two cells (as opposed to generation one which shows no negative impedance growth vs. the control). This is very likely due to the formation of a protective SEI-like film on the negative which is the cause of the reduced impedance growth on the cathode and for the cell overall.

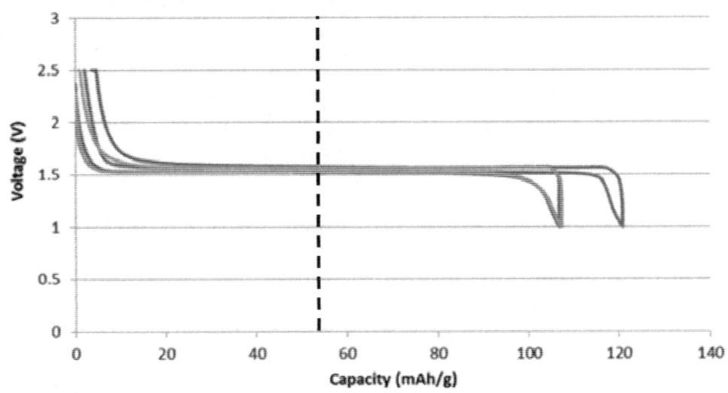

Figure 6. Negative electrode half cells built from recovered electrodes post 12,000 Start-Stop cycles (green is generation one, red is generation two, and blue is not cycled). Little impedance growth is observed.

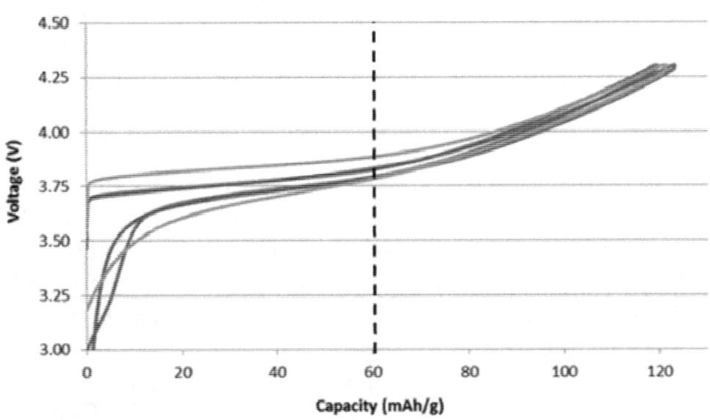

Figure 7. Positive electrode half cells built from recovered electrodes post 12,000 Start-Stop cycles (green is generation one, red is generation two, and blue is not cycled). Significant impedance growth is observed for the generation one electrode while the generation two electrode is nearly identical to the non-cycled control.

The exact cause of the impedance growth is not yet understood but it is suspected that electrolyte partially reacts on the negative surface creating species which are oxidized on the cathode to form an insulating layer. This theory is currently being confirmed with XPS analysis and is bolstered by gas analysis which found no passivation gases (CO and CO_2) on fresh cells but significant amounts post cycling. In contrast, the electrode and electrolyte changes for generation two cells formed a stable SEI-like film on the surface of the negative electrode particles, which prevents further electrolyte degradation and mitigates impedance growth.

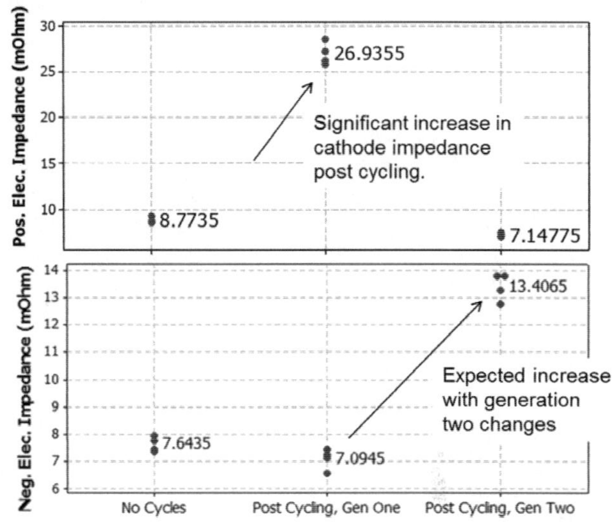

Figure 8. Impedance of half-cells calculated from the cycle test. Cell impedance growth occurs on the positive electrode.

Next Steps for LTO Development at Saft

LTO based cells based on the improved design are being industrialized at Saft. In addition, Saft is investigating a 12V start-stop battery consisting of five cells in series in a single injection-molded thermoplastic polymer (IMTP) mono-block designed for direct replacement of the current lead-acid cell but with full start-stop functionality. A schematic representation of the cell is shown in figure 9.

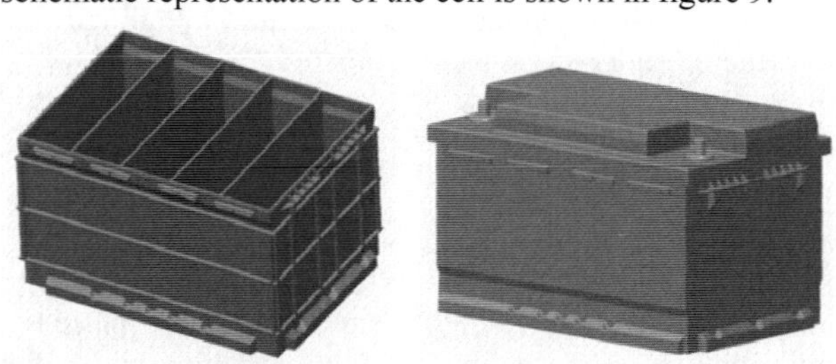

Figure 9. Schematic of the proposed mono-block 12V start-stop battery.

Acknowledgements

The authors kindly acknowledge the support from the DOE and USABC. Analysis and discussion is also gratefully acknowledged from Saft colleagues in Bordeaux, France including F. Fischer, D. Germond, L. El Ouatani and C. Tessier.

Very High Rate, Wide Temperature Range LTO-LMO Battery

Michael Erickson, Konstantin Tikhonov, and Marc Juzkow
Leyden Energy
46840 Lakeview Blvd, Fremont, CA, USA, 94538

Abstract: *Leyden Energy has developed a high power, wide temperature range LTO/LMO battery chemistry with long cycle life and excellent safety. Rates of up to 40C with 78% capacity retention have been demonstrated. Cold crank performance at -30 °C exceeds USABC targets, while USABC shallow cycle life is also expected to exceed the 500k cycle requirement. Leyden Energy LTO/LMO cell power capability, thermal performance, longevity, and safety is presented.*

Keywords: Start-Stop, high rate, lithium titanate, lithium manganese oxide

Introduction

Increasing vehicle electrification allows OEM's to reach fuel efficiency and emissions targets. Incremental approaches to electrification (vs. full EV) are lower cost solutions. In particular, start-stop and energy recuperation cost much less to implement than a mild or full hybrid and together can contribute from 2 to 6% improvement in fuel consumption[1].

Most lithium-ion batteries, however, cannot meet the combined demands for high power, cold cranking, regen at low temperatures and cycle life. Some designs therefore pair batteries with supercapacitors to divide the workload for high power requirements and high energy requirements. Another design pairs a lead-acid battery for cold-cranking with a lithium-ion battery for energy storage. This adds cost and complexity to the system.

Leyden Energy has developed a single battery solution for automotive start-stop applications based on lithium titanate (LTO) / lithium manganese oxide (LMO) chemistry that handles all loads, providing dynamic charge acceptance for recuperation, cold cranking at -30°C and high power for starting a vehicle hundreds of thousands of times over a wide temperature range. Leyden Energy's high power lithium ion battery cell chemistry provides similar power capability to supercapacitors but with approximately 10X energy density.

Figure 1. Example Leyden Energy 20 Ah pouch cell

LTO/LMO Couple

LTO and LMO active materials form an attractive redox couple that yield an average operating voltage of 2.5 V. Both materials have spinel crystal structures known to enable fast charge/discharge kinetics and stable cycle life. Each material is also known for excellent safety characteristics. LTO's operating voltage is 1.55 V vs Li, thus avoiding SEI formation and Li plating. LTO is less exothermic than graphite when subjected to temperatures from 100 to 400°C[2], while LMO has a higher oxygen release onset temperature (~400°C) than other common cathodes[3]. Also, LMO, when combined with the no SEI forming LTO, mitigates known LMO-electrolyte interfacial stability issues[4]. An additional attractive feature of this couple is that LMO is a known low cost active material and LTO is becoming more cost competitive with graphite.

Figure 2 shows discharge voltage profiles for LTO vs LMO and LTO and LMO vs Li. A fairly flat full cell voltage profile is generated from the narrow operating voltage ranges of the LTO and LMO.

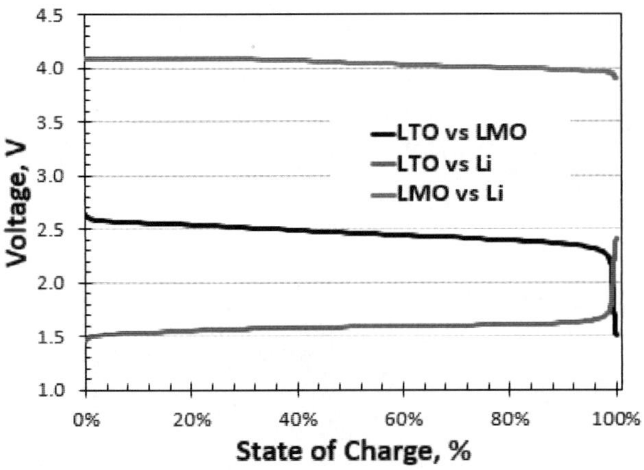

Figure 2. Voltage profiles LTO vs LMO, LTO, vs Li, and LMO vs Li

Cycle Life

Representative cycle life at 100% DOD from 25 to 75°C for LTO/LMO is presented in Figure 3. Excellent capacity retention from this couple is observed from 25 to 60°C. At 75°C and 200 cycles, capacity retention is over 90%.

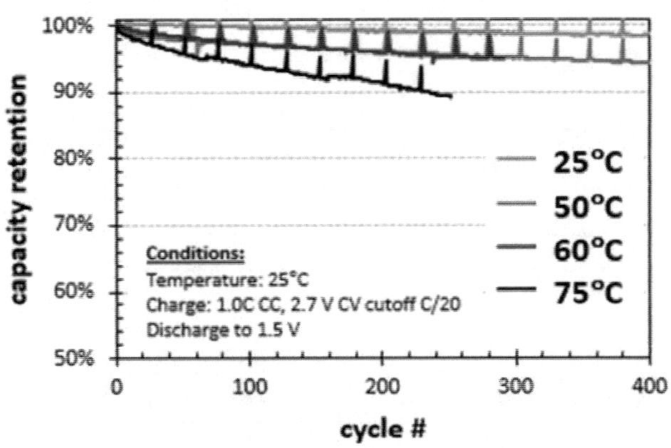

Figure 3. Cycle life data from 25 to 75°C

Shallow cycle life testing at 30 and 50°C was performed in accordance to the United States Advanced Battery Consortium (USABC) Battery Test Manual for 12 Volt Start/Stop vehicles (Figure 4)[5]. Using 100% DOD capacity checks performed every 1,440 shallow cycles to monitor capacity loss, there is only a 2% capacity loss over 16,000 cycles at 30°C and a 4% capacity loss over 23,000 cycles at 50°C.

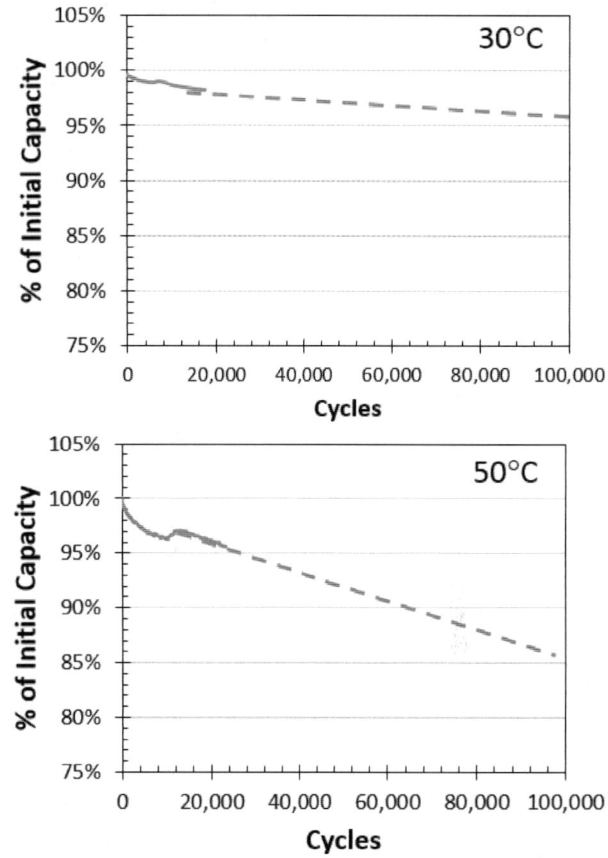

Figure 4. Shallow cycle life testing at 30 and 50°C

Power Capability

LTO/LMO discharge power capability from -30 to 50°C at a constant power discharge (approximate average 1.6C) is shown in Figure 5. Significant energy is available at -30°C.

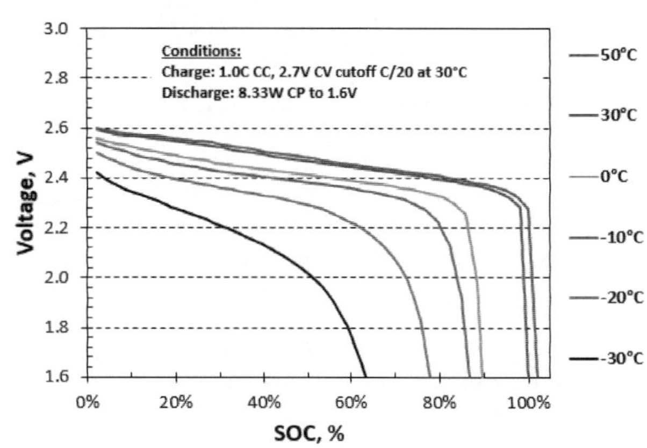

Figure 5. Discharge power capability from -30 to 50°C

Figure 6 shows the rate capability of this LTO/LMO design at rates to 40C. Retention of 1C capacity through 40C is just under 80%.

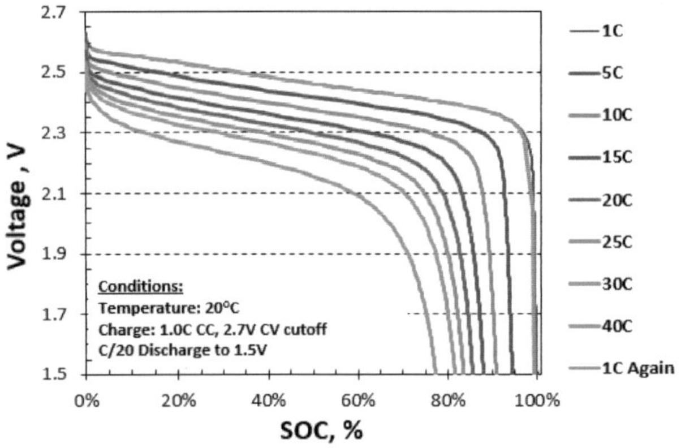

Figure 6. LTO / LMO rate capability at room temperature

The Hybrid Pulse Power Characterization test (HPPC) results scaled as indicated in the USABC Start-Stop Manual are shown in Figure 7. The BOL results significantly exceed the USABC 12V Start/Stop requirements[5].

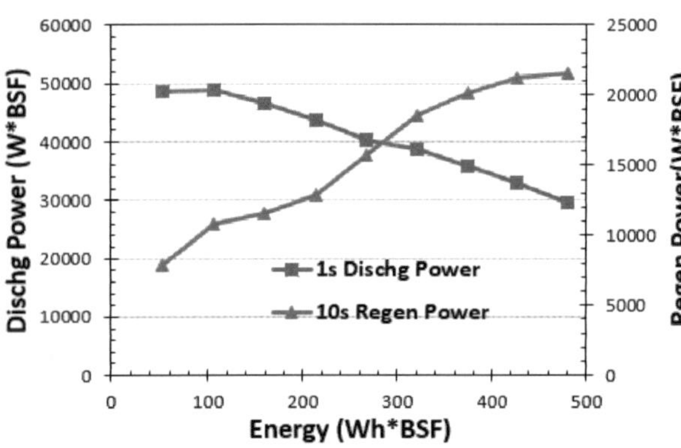

Figure 7. HPPC data for LTO / LMO cell

Results from a charge acceptance test using the indicated charge C-rates and a 1C discharge are shown in Figure 8. At 10C charge rate, cells can be charged to 80% of full capacity without going into CV mode. Fast charge capability is sustainable over hundreds of thousands of cycles, which is an important feature for a variety of applications requiring energy recuperation.

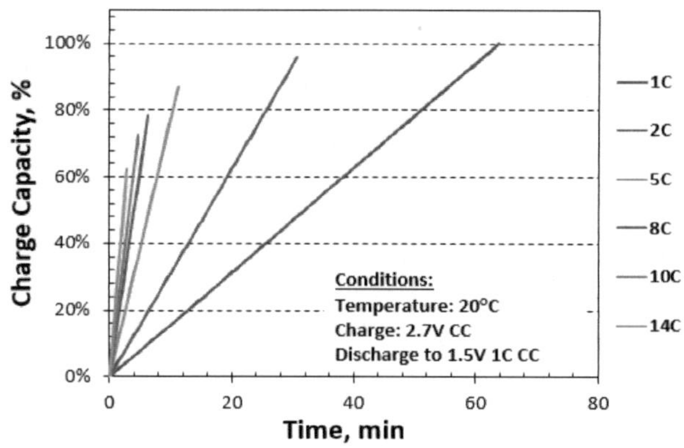

Figure 8. LTO / LMO charge acceptance as a percentage of 1C capacity at room temperature

Cold Crank at -30°C

Excellent low temperature power capability is illustrated by results of the -30°C USABC Cold Crank test at 100, 50 and 30% SOC and shown in Figure 9. The Leyden Energy LTO/LMO design exceeded the scaled USABC voltage requirement of 8 V (1.6V/cell) even at 30% SOC[5]. The test for a complete pack requires 3 consecutive pulse sequences of 6kW for 0.5 sec and 4kW for 4 sec.

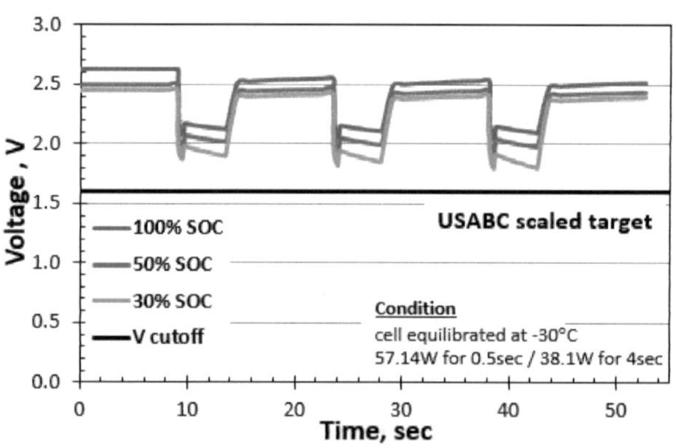

Figure 9. Cold crank (-30°C) test result at 100, 50, and 30% SOC

Safety

The LTO/LMO chemistry has been evaluated in 2 and 20 Ah pouch cells and passes critical UL, UN, and custom safety tests. Figure 10 shows the result of a nail penetration test performed on a 20 Ah pouch cell. Maximum temperature during the test stayed below 36°C.

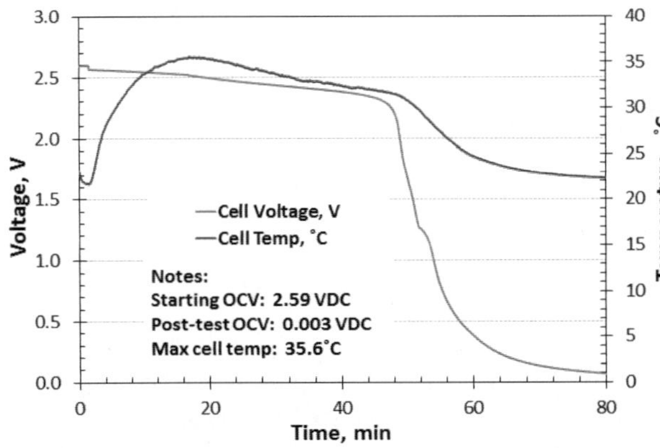

Figure 10. Nail penetration test result for 20 Ah cell

Figure 11 shows the result of a 150°C heating test. After 30 min at 150°C, no thermal runaway was observed. After the 30 minute exposure, the oven temperature was increased to 200°C. No thermal runaway was observed.

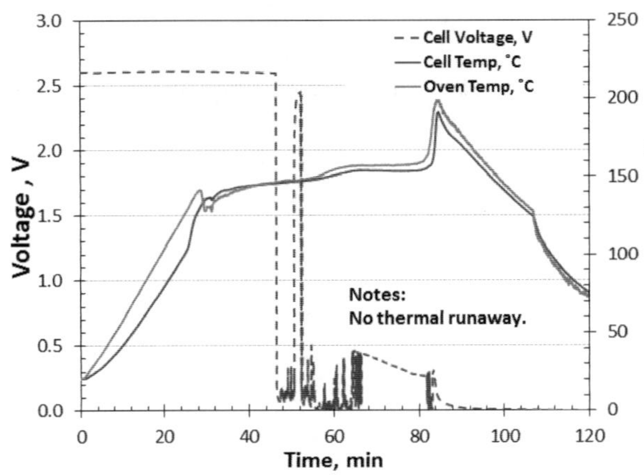

Figure 11. Heat test result at 150°C for 20 Ah cell

Improving High Temperature Performance

Leyden Energy is developing solutions to expand the operating range of the LTO-LMO batteries. The development approach is focused on the surface treatments of LTO material in-house and builds upon Leyden's experience with the surface treatments over the past 3 years. Leyden is in progress of developing the next generation of LTO chemistry to extend the operating temperature range from the present 45°C to 75°C (Figure 12) and survival temperature to 100°C.

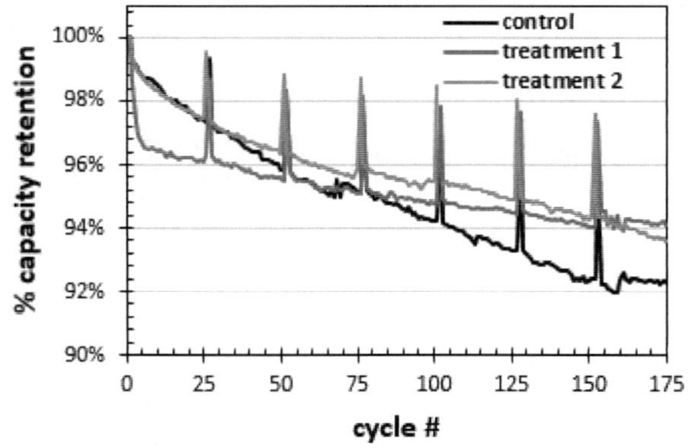

Figure 12. Cycle life results at 75°C for LTO/LMO cells with bare LTO and two surface treated LTOs

Conclusion

Leyden Energy LTO/LMO cells have a wide operating temperature range and a discharge and regen power comparable to that of a supercapacitor. The LTO/LMO couple enables extremely long cycle life beyond conventional Li-ion cells with a graphite anode while also having unmatched safety characteristics.

Acknowledgements

The authors wish to thank the United States Advanced Battery Consortium for funding USABC Start/Stop contract 13-2123-ABC.

References

1. Tataria, H., Gross, O., Bae, C., Cunningham, B., Barnes, J. A., Deppe, J., Neubauer, J. "USABC Development of 12 Volt Battery for Start-Stop Application," *EVS27 International Battery, Hybrid and Fuel Cell Electric Vehicle Symposium,* conference proceedings, 2013.
2. Dahn, J. R., Fuller, E. W., Obrovac, M., von Sacken, U., "The Thermal stability of Li_xCoO_2, Li_xNiO_2, and λ-MnO_2 and consequences for the safety of Li-ion cells," *Solid State Ionics*, vol. 69, pp. 265-270, 1994.
3. Belharouak, I., Koenig Jr, G.M., Amine, K., "Electrochemistry and safety of $Li_4Ti_5O_{12}$ and graphite anodes paired with $LiMn_2O_4$ for hybrid electric vehicle Li-ion battery applications," *Journal of Power Sources*, vol. 196, pp. 10344-10350, 2011.
4. Cho, I. H., Kim, S., Shin, S. C., Choi, N., "Effect of SEI on Capacity Losses of Spinel Lithium Manganese Oxide/Graphite Batteries Stored at 60°C," Electrochemical and Solid-State Letters, vol. 13, pp. A168-A172, 2010.
5. U.S. Department of Energy Vehicle Technologies Program Batter Test Manual for 12 Volt Start/Stop Vehicles, Revision 0, Nov. 2013.

CAM-7/LTO Lithium-Ion Cells for a 6T Battery with Excellent Low-Temperature Performance

David Ofer, Daniel Kaplan, Oksu Han, Shawn Montgomery, Yoo-Eup Hyung, Brian Barnett, and Suresh Sriramulu
TIAX LLC
35 Hartwell Avenue
Lexington, MA 02421

Abstract: *TIAX is developing laminated prismatic lithium-ion (Li-ion) cells capable of charging at low temperature (to -50 °C) to replace current lead-acid cells in 6T vehicle batteries. The novel cells target cell-level energy content of 90 Wh/kg and 250 Wh/l and are based on TIAX's high energy, high power CAM-7 cathode material, high rate capability lithium titanate (LTO) anode material, and a low-temperature-capable electrolyte formulation. Tests of pouch cells ranging up to 3 Ah in size show excellent performance at -46 °C and robust cycle life at ambient temperature.*

Keywords: laminate packaging; lithium-ion; low-temperature electrolyte, CAM-7; lithium titanate.

Introduction

Military applications can require rechargeable batteries to operate in extreme environments with temperatures as low as -50 °C or as high as 70 °C, e.g., the Silent Watch application, which is driving development of vehicle batteries with increased run times. However, these temperature extremes extend beyond the operational temperature range of current commercial Li-ion technology,, hindering the replacement of low energy density lead-acid technology used in current military vehicle 6T batteries with more energy dense and deep-cycling-tolerant Li-ion cells.

Operational temperature limitations of Li-ion batteries are related to their electrolytes and he active materials. At low temperatures, performance is hampered by low electrolyte conductivity and poor electrochemical kinetics associated with ion-desolvation processes.[1] Low-temperature charge acceptance capability is particularly poor because the graphitic carbon anodes used in Li-ion cells are prone to plating lithium metal when charged rapidly or at low temperature: a condition giving rise to rapid fade and serious safety concerns. At high temperatures, Li-ion battery lifetime is compromised by thermal instability of the electrolytes and of electrode surface films they form, and by the electrolytes' reactivity with the charged electrode materials; in particular by decomposition reactions at the graphitic carbon anode.[2] Furthermore, decomposition reactions of Li-ion electrolytes at high temperature can yield gaseous products that may limit the use of laminated prismatic pouch cell designs, which are otherwise very advantageous for their light weight and easy form factor reconfiguration.

In an Army TARDEC-sponsored program, TIAX is developing low-temperature-capable (to -50 °C) laminated prismatic lithium-ion cells employing TIAX's high-energy, high-power CAM-7 cathode material, a high rate capability lithium titanate (LTO) anode material, and a novel low-temperature-capable electrolyte formulation. Although LTO anode material yields lower energy density cells than graphite anode materials, LTO offers performance, life and cell design advantages that better facilitate meeting Army performance targets, and the use of high energy content CAM-7 cathode material enables LTO anode to be used with the least possible cost to cell energy content. The novel TIAX cells are targeting implementation in a 6T-format battery, with cell-level energy content of about 90 Wh/kg and 250 Wh/l, and capability for charge and discharge at temperatures approaching -50 °C.

Cell Chemistry

CAM-7: CAM-7 is a dopant-stabilized $LiNiO_2$-class cathode material with a unique combination of high energy content and power capability as shown in Figure 1.

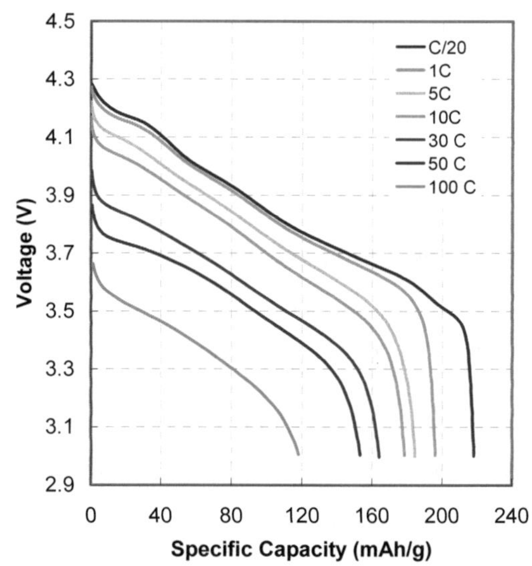

Figure 1. Capacity and rate capability of CAM-7 measured in a low loading (~2 mg/cm^2) electrode in a coin cell vs. a Li metal counter electrode. The cell was charged in CCCV mode to 4.3 V, and discharged at rates shown on basis of 200 mAh/g 1C rate.

CAM-7 also delivers outstanding low-temperature performance as shown by Figure 2, which compares the discharge performance of CAM-7 relative to commercially available NCA ($LiNi_{0.8}Co_{0.15}Al_{0.05}O_2$) and NCM ($LiNi_{1/3}Co_{1/3}Mn_{1/3}O_2$) cathode materials at -20 °C. CAM-7 has higher discharge capacity at a higher average voltage.

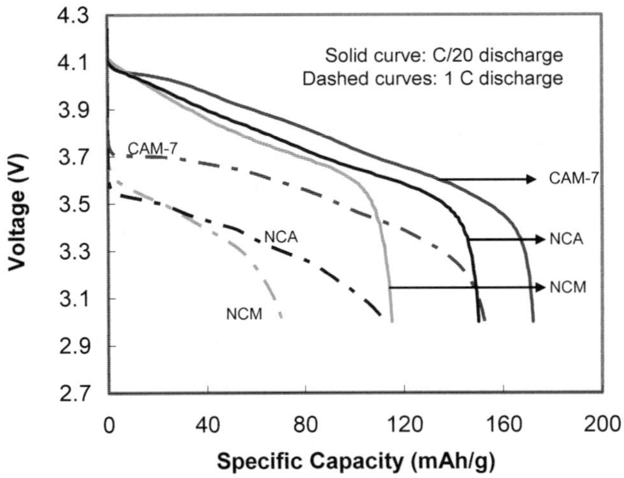

Figure 2. Discharge voltage profiles of CAM-7 and competing cathode materials at -20 °C, measured for 10-11 mg/cm^2 electrodes vs. Li metal in coin cells. Cells were charged to 4.2 V at RT, equilibrated at -20 °C, and discharged at C/20 and 1C on basis of 200 mAh/g 1C rate.

CAM-7 is produced by a readily scalable solid-state synthetic process. A separate company, CAMX Power, has been established to commercialize CAM-7, and has installed and is operating a 50 t/y plant for producing CAM-7 in Rowley, Massachusetts.

LTO: Graphitic carbon, the predominant Li-ion anode active material, can not be lithiated (charged) at low temperatures without a high probability of undesirable Li metal plating. Nano-structured $Li_4Ti_5O_{12}$ or LTO anode material has exceptionally high rate capability and can be lithiated very rapidly as shown in Figure 3, because its potential is far positive of Li metal (~1.55 V vs. Li), which also prevents high impedance SEI films from forming on its surface.

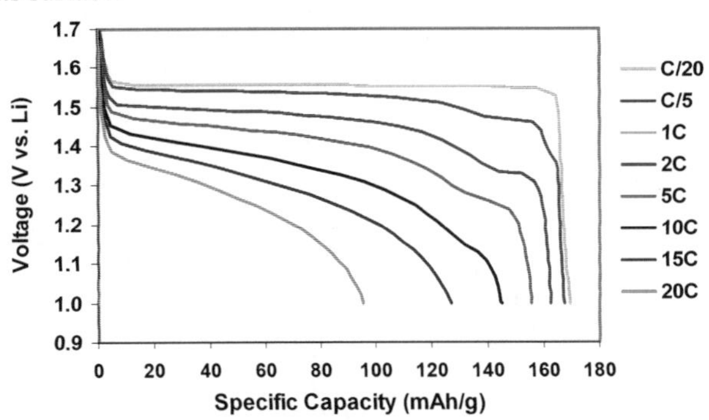

Figure 3. Ambient temperature half cell lithiation profiles as function of C-rate (1C = 170 mA/g) for LTO electrodes with 0.7 mAh/cm^2 active material loading.

Low-temperature electrolyte: Current commercial Li-ion electrolytes consist almost exclusively of $LiPF_6$ salt in mixtures of cyclic ethylene carbonate (EC) with various linear carbonates, these having emerged as providing the best overall balance of properties for Li-ion batteries in consumer electronics.[3] However, cells with these electrolytes generally do not have acceptable performance below -20 °C because of the high freezing point and viscosity of EC as well as its high activation energy for lithium ion desolvation.

Reducing the electrolyte EC content, and replacing linear carbonates with alternative higher dielectric constant, low viscosity, low freezing point cosolvents has been shown to greatly improve Li-ion low-temperature performance.[4] A comparison of the properties of alternative cosolvents to those of standard carbonate solvents is shown in Table 1. Nitriles or esters can offer a better combination of high polarity with low viscosity and extended liquid temperature range than linear carbonates do.

Solvent	Abb.	Molecular Formula	Melting Point (ºC)	Dielectric constant (20 ºC)	Viscosity (cp @ 25 °C)
Ethylene Carbonate	**EC**	$C_3H_4O_3$	38	90 (40 °C)	1.86 (40 °C)
Diethyl Carbonate	**DEC**	$C_5H_{10}O_3$	-43	2.8	0.75
Dimethyl Carbonate	**DMC**	$C_3H_6O_3$	4	3.1	0.59
Ethyl Methyl Carbonate	**EMC**	$C_4H_8O_3$	-55	2.9	0.65
Butyronitrile	**BN**	C_3H_7CN	-112	20.7	0.52
Methyl Acetate	**MA**	$CH_3CO_2CH_3$	-99	6.7	0.37
Methyl Butyrate	**MB**	$C_3H_7CO_2CH_3$	-85	5.6	0.58

Table 1. Comparison of electrolyte solvent physical properties.

Initial development of this CAM-7/LTO/low-temperature electrolyte cell chemistry has taken place in coin cells, and it is now being tested in stacked-electrode laminate pouch cells ranging from 1 Ah to 3 Ah in size.

Laminate Pouch Cell Performance

Ambient temperature: The CAM-7/LTO cell chemistry cycles very stably. This cycling stability was demonstrated by initial ~1 Ah pouch cells built with electrode loading of 1.3 mAh/cm^2 in an anode-limited design (cathode utilization limited to ~85%) and conventional all-carbonate-solvent electrolyte. Cells of this type cycled over their full depth of discharge (DOD) 1,000 times with no decrease in capacity or increase in area specific impedance (ASI), as shown by Figure 4. Cycling was conducted at ambient laboratory temperature conditions at 1C/1C (1A) charge/discharge rate between limits of 1.4V and 2.75V, with interruptions at 100 cycle intervals for a C/5 cycle and a 1C pulsed current characterization of impedance at 1 second and 10 seconds pulse duration as a function of state of charge (SOC).

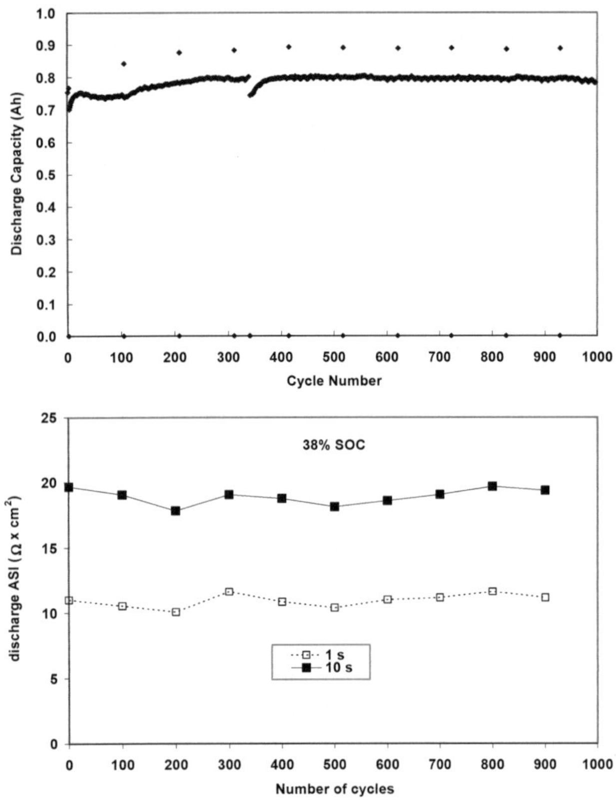

Figure 4. Top: 1C discharge capacity of 1 Ah CAM-7/LTO pouch cell vs. cycle number, and C/5 discharge capacity measured at 100-cycle intervals. Bottom: 1 second and 10 second ASI for the 1 Ah pouch cell at 38% SOC measured at 100-cycle intervals during 1C/1C cycling.

1 Ah cells filled with ester-based low-temperature electrolyte formulation had good power capability at -46 °C. They also had good ambient temperature performance, as shown by Figure 5 which compares ASI measured as a function of SOC for cells filled with conventional electrolyte and low-temperature electrolyte.

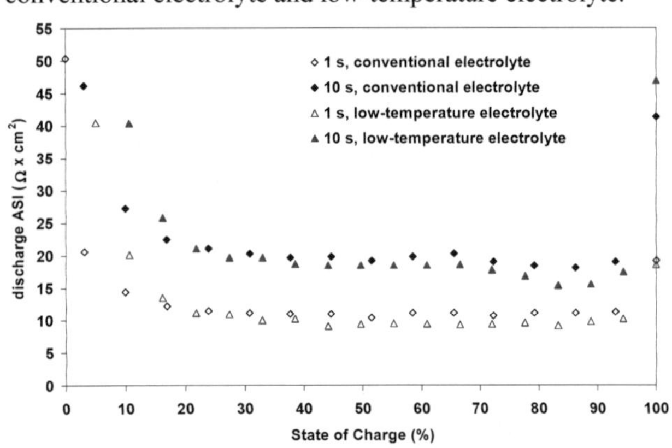

Figure 5. 1 second and 10 second ASI dependence on SOC for 1 Ah pouch cells filled with conventional all-carbonate-solvent electrolyte and low-temperature electrolyte.

The low loading electrodes used in these initial 1 Ah cells projected to yield scaled-up pouch cells with energy content of ~80 Wh/kg and ~220 Wh/l, which are below the targets. Therefore, subsequent larger pouch cells employed electrodes having 1.7 mAh/cm^2 loading and projecting to meet the 90 Wh/kg and 250 Wh/l targets in 10 Ah cells.

Figure 6 shows data for ambient laboratory temperature characterization of a 3 Ah pouch cell built with 1.7 mAh/cm^2 loading electrodes and an ester-based low-temperature-capable electrolyte formulation. This unoptimized cell weighs 81g and delivers about 7 Wh energy at C/20, i.e., yielding 86 Wh/kg. The Figure 6 data show that the cell has high rate capability, with only ~100 mV polarization measured for charge or discharge at the 3C rate relative to the C/20 rate, and also demonstrate the cell's suitability for rapid charging. More extended cycling tests are in progress.

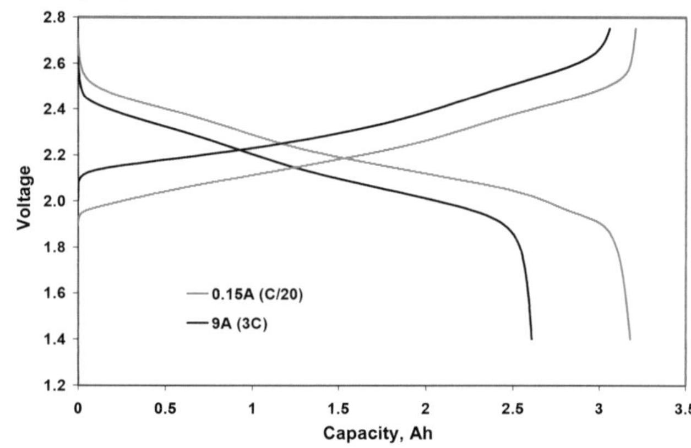

Figure 6. Ambient temperature charge and discharge voltage characteristics for a 3 Ah CAM-7/LTO pouch cell built with low-temperature electrolyte.

Low temperature (-46 °C): CAM-7/LTO pouch cells filled with low-temperature-capable electrolyte demonstrate outstanding performance at -46 °C, as illustrated by Figure 7 which shows -46 °C data for a 2.5Ah pouch cell built with 1.7 mAh/cm^2 loading electrodes.

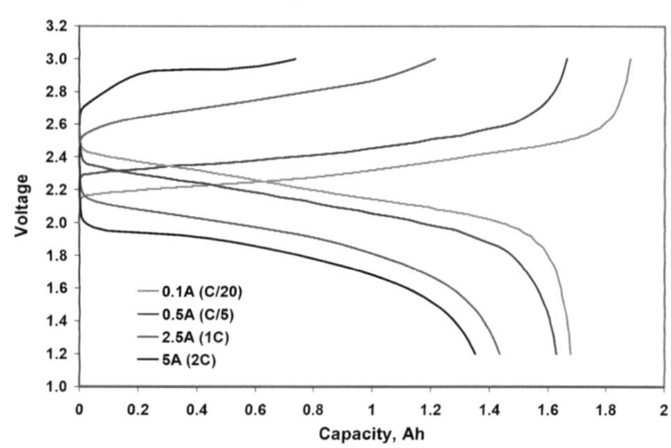

Figure 7. Voltage characteristics at -46 °C for a 2.5 Ah CAM-7/LTO/ low-temperature electrolyte pouch cell.

The -46 °C cycling shown in Figure 7 was performed between 1.2V to 3V voltage limits that are expanded relative to the 1.4V to 2.75V limits used for ambient temperature cycling shown in Figure 6. These expanded voltage limits are enabled by the use of LTO anode which avoids Li metal plating concerns, and which therefore also enables anode-limited cell design, preventing cathode excursion to excessively high overcharge potentials. As Figure 7 shows, the expanded voltage limits facilitate these cells' remarkable ability to be effectively charged at very low temperature at reasonable rates.

Figure 7 also suggests that the cell's rate capability benefits from some amount of self-heating at rates above 1C. The 2C charge and discharge curves both show large and rapid initial polarization, but then flatten. Most significantly, the 150-200 mV polarization between the 2C and 1C curves is much less than the 300-500 mV polarization between the 1C and C/20 curves. Higher rate tests are in progress.

Cold cranking capability is an important attribute for vehicle batteries. Specification MIL-PRF-32143B, which governs testing and qualification of the 6T battery, calls for measurement of the battery's ability to sustain a 3.33C pulse (400 A for a 120 Ah battery) for 30 seconds at -40 °C before its voltage reaches 50% of the charge voltage. CAM-7/LTO pouch cells perform well when subjected to a scaled version of this test at -46 °C. Cells were first charged to 2.75 V at the C/50 rate at -46 °C, and then discharged by repeating the sequence of a 30 second 3.5C pulse followed by a 30 minute rest at open circuit, until the cell voltage reached 1.35 V. Figure 8 shows results of the scaled MIL-PRF-32143B cold cranking test performed on 2.5 Ah and 3 Ah CAM-7/LTO pouch cells built with 1.7 mAh/cm^2 loading electrodes.

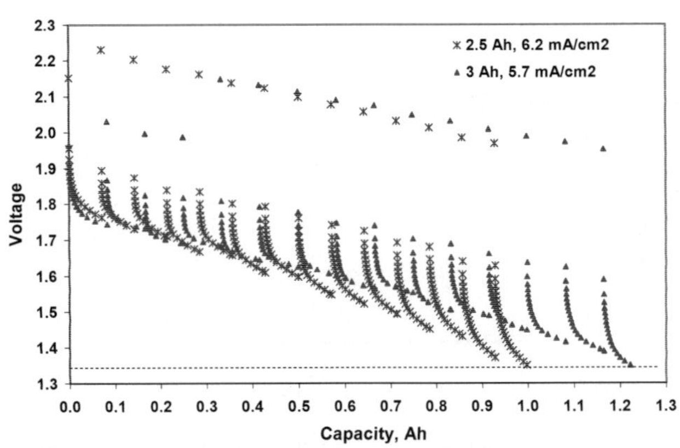

Figure 8. Scaled MIL-PRF-32143B-based cold cranking tests at -46 °C for 2.5 Ah and 3 Ah CAM-7/LTO pouch cells built with ester-based electrolyte.

Figure 8 shows that at -46 °C, the CAM-7/LTO pouch cells can support the 30 second pulsing at ~3.5C discharge rate over about 40% of their capacity range, substantially exceeding the requirements of MIL-PRF-32143B.

Testing of cycle and storage life of CAM-7/LTO/low-temperature-capable electrolyte pouch cells at ambient and elevated temperatures is being initiated. Cell gassing will be studied as an important element of these efforts.

Conclusions

Li-ion pouch cells based on CAM-7 cathodes, LTO anodes and low-temperature performance-enhancing electrolyte offer great promise for improving the specific energy and the low-temperature performance of the 6T battery. Ambient temperature tests show that this chemistry has potential to be very stable and long-lived, particularly with respect to high depth-of-discharge cycling. Further assessment of this technology's potential awaits results of more aggressive testing at elevated temperatures.

Acknowledgements: This material is based upon work supported by the United States Army under Contract No. W56HZV-11-C-0065.

References

1. Kang Xu, "Charge-Transfer" Process at Graphite/Electrolyte Interface and the Solvation Sheath Structure of Li$^+$ in Nonaqueous Electrolytes," *Journal of the Electrochemical Society*, Vol. 154, no. 3, pp. A162-A167, 2007.
2. Michel Broussely in "Advances in Lithium-Ion Batteries," W. van Schalwijk and B. Scrosati, eds., Chapter 13, Kluwer Academic/Plenum, 2002.
3. Kang Xu, "Nonaqueous Liquid Electrolytes for Lithium-Based Rechargeable Batteries," *Chemical Reviews*, Vol. 104, pp. 4303-4417, 2004.
4. M.C. Smart, B.V. Ratnakumar, K.B. Chin and L.D. Whitcanack, "Lithium-Ion Electrolytes Containing Ester Cosolvents for Improved Low Temperature Performance," *Journal of the Electrochemical Society*, Vol. 157, pp. A1361-A1374, 2010.

Lithium-Ion Cells with Ultracapacitor Performance

David Ofer, Celine Yang, Leah Nation, Christopher McCoy, Brian Barnett, and Suresh Sriramulu
TIAX LLC
35 Hartwell Avenue
Lexington, MA 02421

Abstract: *TIAX is developing Li-ion cells capable of very high charge and discharge power acceptance/delivery based on TIAX's high energy, high power CAM-7 cathode material and high rate capability lithium titanate (LTO) anode material. This Li-ion technology can provide much higher energy density than ultracapacitors for pulsed or continuous charge or discharge at the 5 kW/l power density level, while also meeting the life requirements of energy storage applications.*

Keywords: ultracapacitor; lithium-ion; usable energy; CAM-7; lithium titanate.

Introduction

Existing battery technologies have difficulty meeting electrical energy storage (EES) requirements for accepting and delivering high power associated with load leveling and power conditioning while also having significant energy density storage, or meeting similar requirements for certain emerging vehicular applications. For example, the high rate charging capability (dynamic charge acceptance) needed by micro-hybrid (start-stop) vehicle batteries is proving challenging even for lead-acid batteries. Military EES applications can be even more demanding, for example, requiring capability to power pulsed energy weapons. The bidirectional (charge and discharge) power densities required in such applications are not available in present batteries, but can be provided by electrochemical double-layer capacitors, which are often referred to as ultracapacitors.

Ultracapacitors function by charge and discharge of electrochemical double layers at high surface area electrodes. Their lack of discrete electron transfer and associated chemical changes results in extremely fast kinetics (i.e., high power) and very long cycle life. However, ultracapacitors have much lower energy densities than batteries, up to only about 10 Wh/l, for fundamental reasons including that their ultimate source of charge is the relatively low concentration ionic content of the electrolyte solution.[1] For example, a typical 1M organic electrolyte solution of ~1 g/cc density contains ~27 Ah of charge (cations or anions) per kg electrolyte. If half that charge can be separated and capacitively stored by a 3 V charging voltage (an aggressive assumption), upon discharge to 1.5 V the electrolyte alone will have delivered only ~15 Wh/kg, before the masses of electrodes, packaging, and other cell components are even considered. In order to achieve high energy density, electrochemical energy storage devices must therefore employ at least one Faradaic (i.e., battery-type as opposed to capacitive) electrode that serves as the high capacity (high charge density) source of the charge-compensating ions involved at **both** electrodes.[2]

Accordingly, in a Navy-sponsored program, TIAX is developing a lithium-ion cell technology that provides the energy density of batteries and the cell-level power density of electrochemical double layer capacitors, targeting 70 Wh/l usable energy within which the cell can sustain charge and discharge pulsing at 5 kW/l power density for 1 second duration. This novel Li-ion technology, based on TIAX's proprietary CAM-7 cathode material, a nano-structured $Li_4Ti_5O_{12}$ (LTO) anode material and high power-capable electrolyte and separator, is directed towards meeting NAVFAC EES targets for 200 Wh/l overall energy density and 25,000 full depth of discharge cycle life.

Cell Chemistry and Design

CAM-7: TIAX's CAM-7 is a stabilized $LiNiO_2$-based cathode material offering an outstanding combination of high capacity and high rate capability as shown in Figure 1.

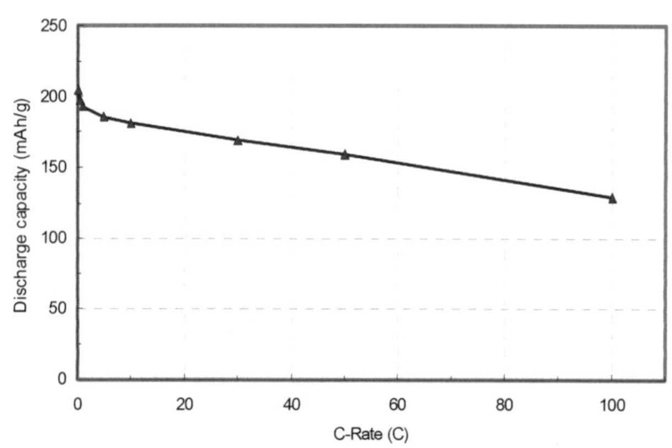

Figure 1. Discharge rate capability of CAM-7 in low loading (~2 mg/cm^2) Li metal half cells on basis of 200 mAh/g 1C rate.

TIAX has installed a 50 metric ton per year CAM-7 pilot plant in Rowley, Massachusetts. CAM-7 is being sampled to many of the prominent domestic and foreign battery manufacturers and developers for both vehicle and consumer electronics applications.

LTO: Although graphitic carbon is the predominant Li-ion anode active material, it can not be lithiated (as occurs in Li-ion cell charging) at high rates without a high probability of undesirable Li metal plating because its potential is close to that of Li. LTO anode material was first noted for its negligible volume change during electrochemical cycling, earning it designation as a "zero strain material,"[3] and giving it exceptional cycling stability. Nano-structured LTO is capable of exceptionally high rate capability and can be lithiated (charged) very rapidly without danger of Li plating because of its high potential (~1.55 V vs. Li). LTO's high potential also means that high impedance films of electrolyte reduction products (SEI) do not form on its surface, enabling high surface area material to be used without incurring high 1st cycle irreversible capacity loss. LTO's ability to sustain high rate charging is illustrated by half cell data shown in Figure 2.

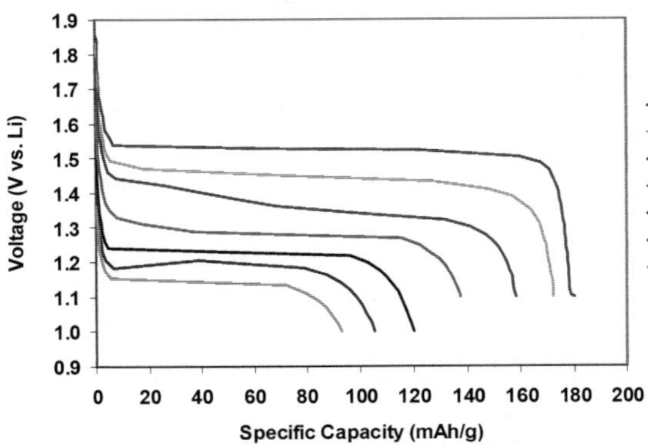

Figure 2. Half cell lithiation profiles as function of C-rate (1C = 170 mA/g) for LTO electrodes with 0.07 mAh/cm^2 active material loading. Commercially available LTO was fabricated into electrodes at TIAX.

Although LTO has very attractive attributes with respect to stability and charging rate capability, its low capacity and high potential impose significant sacrifice of Li-ion cell energy. However, LTO remains the only commercially available Li-ion anode alternative to carbon materials and is the only material capable of being charged at very high rates and low temperatures, and thus the use of a cathode material having the highest possible energy content (CAM-7) along with suitable high rate capability helps offset the loss of cell-level energy content that comes with use of LTO.

Separator: Separator selection can be a very important factor determining the power capability of Li-ion cells. Separator properties vary greatly depending on the applications for which they are intended, with high power-capable separators tending to be thin with high porosity and low tortuosity.[4] TIAX has sourced and evaluated various commercial and experimental separators from the leading separator manufacturers. Figure 3 summarizes capacity data for discharge of Li metal half cells employing identical CAM-7 electrodes (~7.5mg/cm^2 active material loading; C/5 capacity of ~ 1.5 mAh/cm^2) and electrolyte (1M $LiPF_6$ in 1:1:1 EC:DMC:EMC) but different separator materials, showing how strongly the separators impact the cells' rate capability. Commercially available, very high power capability separators are being used in this high power Li-ion technology.

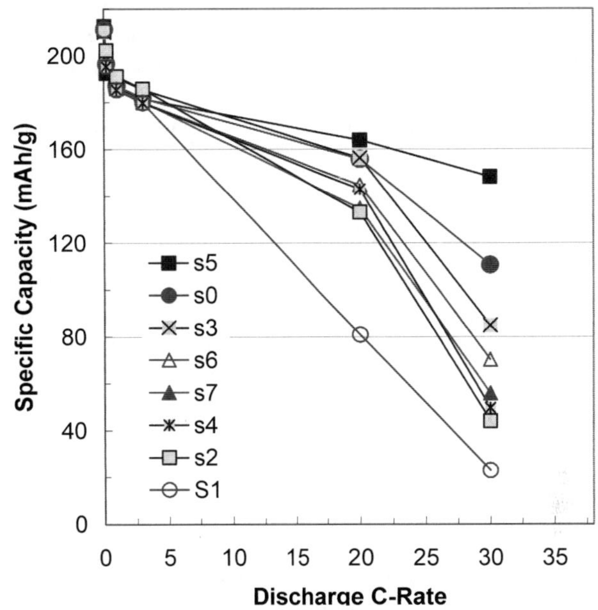

Figure 3. Discharge rate capability of ~7.5 mg/cm^2 CAM-7 electrodes in Li metal half cells dependence on separator type. Rates on basis of 200 mAh/g 1C rate.

The high power CAM-7/LTO cell chemistry is being implemented and tested in 2 cm^2 coin cells using electrode design parameters (formulations, loadings and balance; i.e., anode to cathode ratio) that specifically target high power density and long life. An 18650 cell (1.8 cm diameter, 6.5 cm height cylindrical format) engineering model based on these electrode designs is used to derive test conditions for the coin cells that scale to 5 kW/l in 18650 cells made with identically designed electrodes, and then uses the same model to project 18650 cell performance from the coin cell results. State-of-the-art commercial 3F ultracapacitors are tested in parallel under similarly-scaled test conditions that have been derived by the same approach of measuring the ultracapacitor's electrode design parameters and inputting them in the 18650 engineering model.

Cell Performance

Continuous 5 kW/l cycling energy acceptance & delivery: Direct comparison of the continuous 5 kW/l power acceptance or delivery capabilities of a CAM-7/LTO cell to those of an ultracapacitor demonstrates the enormous energy advantage of the Li-ion system, as shown in Figure 4. The 5 kW/l charge to 2.85 V and discharge to 1.0 V data were obtained at ambient temperature following low rate discharge of the cells to 1.4 V and low rate charge of the cells to 2.75 V, respectively. The Li-ion cell's electrodes employ a low-loading (1.7 mAh/cm^2), high power design that projects to ~200 Wh/l (low rate) in an 18650 cell. The actual power densities used to generate the Figure 4 data (i.e., scaling to 5 kW/l in an 18650 cell design) were 90 mW/cm^2 of face-to-face electrode area for the Li-ion cell and 140 mW/cm^2 for the ultracapacitor, reflecting the different design parameters of the relatively thinner Li-ion and thicker ultracapacitor electrodes. Even under these very high power charge and discharge conditions, the Li-ion cell accepts or delivers more than 5 times the energy density of the ultrapacitor (i.e., operates for over 5 times as long).

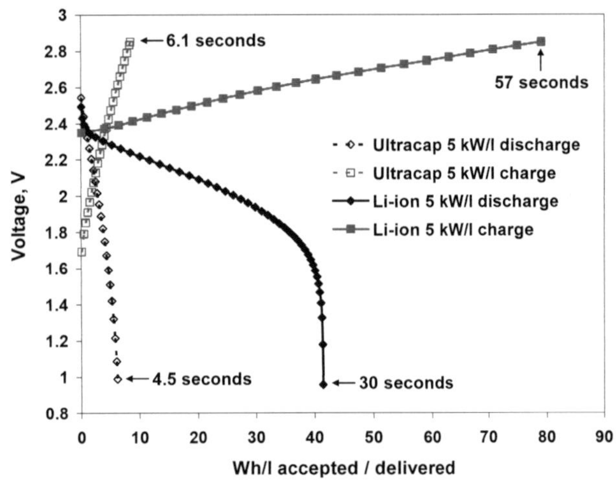

Figure 4. Voltage curves for a CAM-7/LTO Li-ion coin cell and a commercial 3F ultracapacitor charged and discharged at powers scaling to 5 kW/l in 18650 cell designs.

Although they fade more rapidly than ultracapacitors, high power CAM-7/LTO cells nevertheless maintain superior energy acceptance and delivery for continuous 5 kW/l charge and discharge over many thousands of cycles, as shown in Figure 5 below.

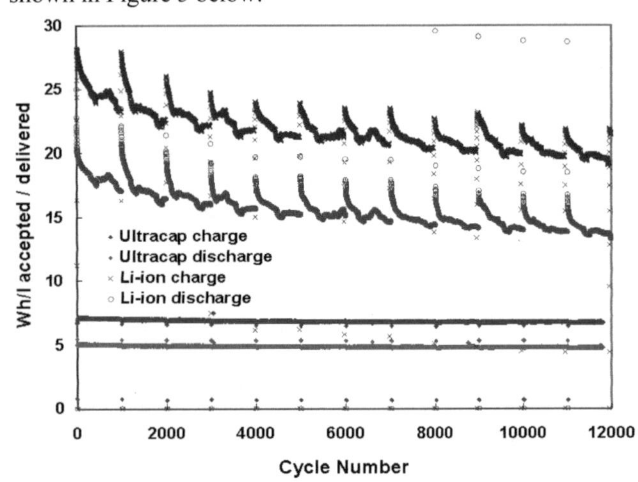

Figure 5. Charge and discharge energies for continuous 5 kW/l constant power cycling of a CAM-7/LTO Li-ion coin cell between 1.0 V and 2.65 V and a 3F ultracapacitor between 1.0 V and 2.85 V scaled to 18650 cell-level energy density.

Continuous cycling shown in Figure 5 is interrupted at 1000 cycle intervals in order to measure 5 kW/l pulse power capability across the cells' full state of charge (SOC) range. During continuous 5 kW/l cycling, the Li-ion cell is cycled across only ~10% of its SOC range (although the energy density accepted or delivered is still about 3 times that of the ultracapacitor). However, the Li-ion cell's SOC cycling range and energy accepted/delivered are higher at 1,000 cycle intervals immediately following the pulse power characterization because the pulse power characterization ends with the cells at 100% SOC (fully charged), and thus in subsequent 5 kW/l continuous cycling, the cell's SOC cycling range gradually narrows as the upper limit adjusts back to an intermediate value. Other fluctuations in the cell's energy acceptance and delivery are due to variations in laboratory temperature. Importantly, the Li-ion cell cycles with approximately the same energy efficiency as the ultracapacitor, that being ~70%. The narrow SOC cycling range also results in low cycling-induced degradation of the Li-ion cell; it maintains capability for high energy density acceptance and delivery of high power (~20% decline as compared to ~5% decline for the ultracapacitor). The Li-ion cell's high power capability retention is also demonstrated by measurements of 5 kW/l pulse power capability, discussed below.

Usable energy for pulsed 5 kW/l acceptance & delivery: For the 5 kW/l pulse power capability evaluation (conducted at 1,000 cycle intervals), 5 kW/l charges or discharges are repeated across the cell's full SOC range. Li-ion cells are charged to 3 V cutoff and discharged to 1 V cutoff at the scaled 5 kW/l power level beginning at 100% state of charge (SOC) (for discharge power) or 0% SOC (for charge power), and when the cutoff voltage is reached, the cell is allowed to rest, and the SOC is decremented (discharge) or advanced (charge) by 5% at the C/5 rate (i.e., for 36 seconds). The 5 kW/l, rest, C/5 sequence is repeated until the C/5 discharge or charge steps reach 1.4 V or 2.75 V, respectively, these being the respective 0% and 100% SOC voltages. An analogous procedure is applied to ultracapacitors with the difference being that the 5 kW/l cyling voltage limits are 2.85 V and 1.0 V.

Figure 6 shows results for the full 5 kW/l pulse charge and discharge capability testing of a 3F ultracapacitor at different 1,000 cycle intervals during the continuous 5 kW/l cycling. The triangular region formed under the intersection of the charge and discharge energy vs. SOC curves defines the SOC range over which an electrode/cell design can both accept **and** deliver a given amount of energy for charge and discharge at 5 kW/l constant power. In practical applications requiring the ability to either source or sink power at any given time, such as in hybrid electric vehicle batteries and load leveling batteries, the ability to accept and deliver a given level of power and energy can define the allowable operational SOC range, and thus the usable energy of an electrical energy storage device.

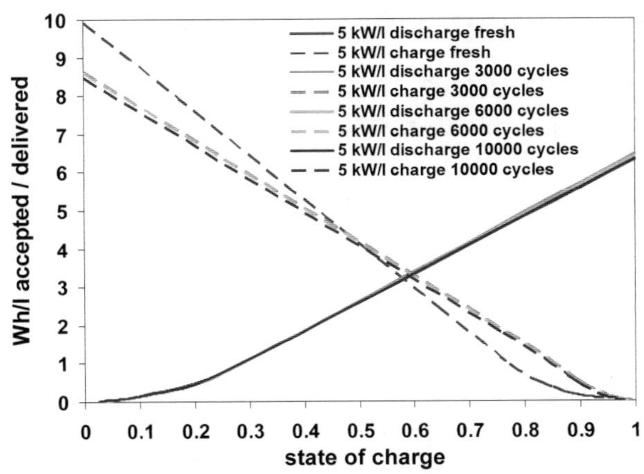

Figure 6. 5 kW/l pulse capability as a function of SOC for a 3F ultracapacitor.

Figure 7 compares the dependence of usable energy on cycle number for the ultracapacitor and the CAM-7/LTO Li-ion cell. The figure illustrates how the boundaries of the usable energy range are set by the length of time for which a given level of bidirectional (charge or discharge) power must be sustained.

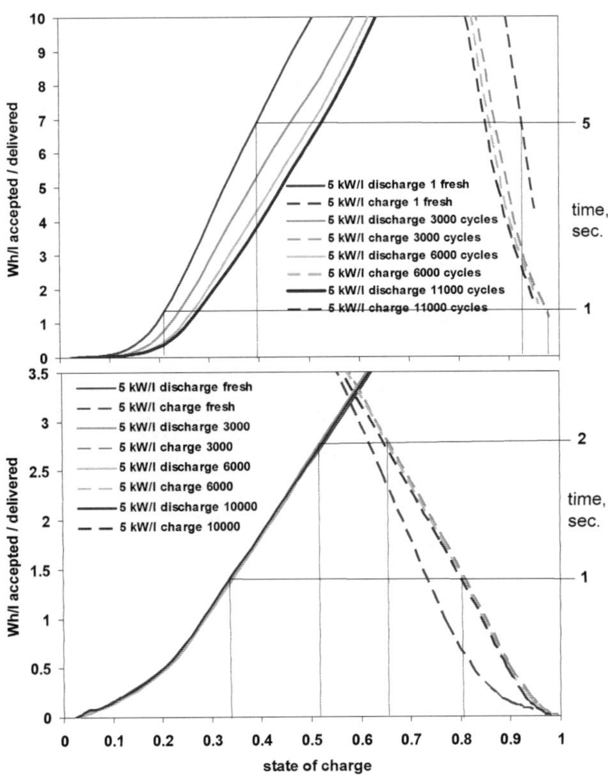

Figure 7. 5 kW/l pulse capability as a function of SOC at intervals during 5 kW/l constant power cycling. Top: CAM-7 LTO Li-ion cell. Bottom: 3F ultracapacitor.

Like Figures 4 and 5, Figure 7 shows the energy advantage that Li-ion cells can provide over ultracapacitors, even in high power applications. Li-ion cells have the potential to sustain 5 second long 5 kW/l charge or discharge pulses over a broad usable energy range (~50% of the SOC range, or ~100 Wh/l), whereas ultracapacitors can not do so at all. The total projected energy density of an ultracapacitor-based 18650 cell is ~8 Wh/l, and thus the projected usable energy density for 1 second duration bidirectional 5 kW/l pulse power capability shown in Figure 6 does not exceed 5 Wh/l, whereas that for a Li-ion cell is ~150 Wh/l. The usable energy of the ultracapacitor is unchanged after 10,000 continuous 5 kW/l constant power cycles, while the 5 sec. duration and 1 sec. duration usable energies of the Li-ion cell decline ~38% and ~12%, respectively, after 11,000 cycles (but with almost all this loss occurring in the first 6,000 cycles). Even with these losses, the Li-ion technology's usable energy density still remains far greater than the ultracapacitor usable energy density.

Conclusions

Suitably designed CAM-7 cathode, LTO anode Li-ion technology can sustain cell-level power density comparable to that of ultracapacitors for both discharge and charge. The approximately 150 Wh/l usable energy range within which bidirectional 5kW/l power can be sustained by this Li-ion technology for 1 second is more than 20 times higher than that of ultracapacitors. The novel cell technology is robust, and shows promise to retain usable energy density for high power acceptance/delivery superior to that of ultracapacitors for over 10,000 cycles.

Acknowledgements: TIAX thanks the US Navy NAVFAC for funding under Phase I SBIR contract # N39430-13-P-1246.

References

1. J.P. Zheng, J. Huang, and T.R. Jow, "The Limitations of Energy Density for Electrochemical Capacitors" *Journal of the Electrochemical Society*, Vol. 144, no. 6, pp. 2026-2031, 1997.
2. Jim P. Zheng, "High Energy Density Electrochemical Capacitors without Consumption of Electrolyte" *Journal of the Electrochemical Society*, Vol. 156, no. 7, pp. A500-A505, 2009.
3. Tsutomu Ohzuku, Atsushi Ueda, and Norihiro Yamamoto, "Zero-Strain Insertion Material of $Li[Li_{1/3}Ti_{5/3}]O_4$ for Rechargeable Lithium Cells," *Journal of the Electrochemical Society*, Vol. 142, no. 5, pp. 1431-1435, 1995.
4. K.M. Abraham, "Directions in Secondary Lithium Battery Research and Development," *Electrochimica Acta*, Vol. 38, no. 9, pp. 1233-1248, 1993.

Supercapacitors for Wide Temperature Operation

Marshall C. Smart, William C. West, Abhijit V. Shevade, Keith J. Billings, Keith B. Chin, Ratnakumar V. Bugga and Erik J. Brandon*

Jet Propulsion Laboratory, California Institute of Technology
4800 Oak Grove Drive, Pasadena, CA 91109
*erik.j.brandon@jpl.nasa.gov

Abstract: Options for rechargeable energy storage technologies capable of operating at extreme temperatures (-55 to +125°C) are limited. However, recent developments in new electrode and electrolyte materials, as well as new cell architectures, are expanding the potential operating temperatures for practical rechargeable batteries. Supercapacitors are limited to operation between -40°C and +65°C, constrained by the melting and boiling points of the electrolytes as well as the materials used in cell construction. This presentation will focus on new systems designed to further expand the temperatures limits of these supercapacitors.

Keywords: Supercapacitors, ultracapacitors, double-layer capacitors

Introduction

Developing rechargeable energy storage technologies capable of operating over wide temperature ranges remains a challenge. Lithium ion batteries offer high specific energies of >150 Wh/kg and are ideal for portable applications where long cycle life is required. Typical operational temperature limits are in the range of -20°C to +60°C during cell discharge. A variety of markets could benefit from cell technologies offering wider operational limits, including "under the hood" applications such as electric and plug-in/hybrid vehicles, robotic aerial/underwater/space vehicles and distributed sensing in harsh environments.

Supercapacitors [1,2] are one type of energy storage technology being pursued for wide temperature applications. Traditional supercapacitors store energy at the interface between a liquid electrolyte and solid electrolyte (i.e., at the electrochemical double-layer). This charge storage mechanism is well suited for both low and high temperature operational conditions, particularly where high power pulses are required. Since charging and discharging the capacitor involves only a rearrangement of the double-layer, and not the more temperature sensitive electrode intercalation/insertion processes, lower temperature operation is possible.

Moderate to high temperature operation can also be targeted, since there is no change in phase of the electrode during operation, and no solid electrolyte interphase (SEI) is required such as for Li-ion batteries. The stability of this SEI at elevated temperatures makes high temperature operation more difficult to achieve. In both cases the choice of supercapacitor electrolyte is critical, as traditional electrolytes based on an acetonitrile solvent cannot be employed over wide temperatures. This is based on the melting point of acetonitrile of -45°C, and its boiling point of +82°C, which sets the rated limits of most commercially available supercapacitors to -40°C to +65°C. The current focus of research is on supercapacitors with either a lower or higher operational temperature, and future efforts will focus on the more significant challenge of developing a single cell capable of operating at both extremes.

Low Temperature Operation

One approach to extending the operation of supercapacitors at low temperatures and maintaining adequate performance is to suppress the melting point of the acetonitrile (AN) solvent used in standard electrolytes [3-6]. We have reported the addition of several low melting point co-solvents to the baseline AN systems, which typically employ a tetraethylammonium tetrafluoroborate salt, or TEATFB (Table 1).

One previous study we reported focused on the use of 1,3-dioxolane (DIOX) as a co-solvent. DIOX was evaluated in the past as a lithium ion battery electrolyte solvent, and has a melting point of -95°C [4,5]. More recent studies have focused on alternative electrode materials, based on zeolite templated carbons, which can provide for a higher capacity than standard activated carbons [6].

Table 1. Characteristics of electrolyte solvent systems.

Solvent	Melting Point (°C)	Dielectric Constant (ε)	Viscosity (cP)
Acetonitrile (AN)	-45.7	37.5	0.345
1,3-dioxolane (DIOX)	-95	7.3	0.6
Methyl formate (MF)	-100	8.5	0.319

In addition to the DIOX modified electrolytes, recent work has shown that methyl formate (MF) modified electrolytes exhibit excellent behavior at low temperatures. This is due to the combination of a very low melting point (-100°C) and a viscosity even lower than acetonitrile (see Table 1).

One of the main challenges is maintaining salt solubility in AN:MF blended electrolyte formulations. Typically supercapacitor electrolytes utilize a >1 M concentration of the quaternary ammonium salt, to achieve high ionic conductivity and low equivalent series resistance at the cell level.

However, due to the low dielectric constant of MF, lower salt concentrations must be employed or there is a risk of salt precipitation at reduced temperatures. Coin cells (2032 form factor) using high surface area carbon electrodes (PACMM203, Material Method) and a polyethylene separator (Tonen-Setella) were used to evaluate these electrolyte blends. Electrodes were punched from a larger sheet. Electrolytes were prepared using different TEATFB concentrations, in 1:1 vol/vol% blends of AN:MF. Electrochemical Impedance Spectroscopy (EIS) measurements were performed using a Princeton Applied Physics VMP2 instrument. The equivalent series resistances (ESR) extracted from the EIS data are shown in Fig. 1 as a function of temperature.

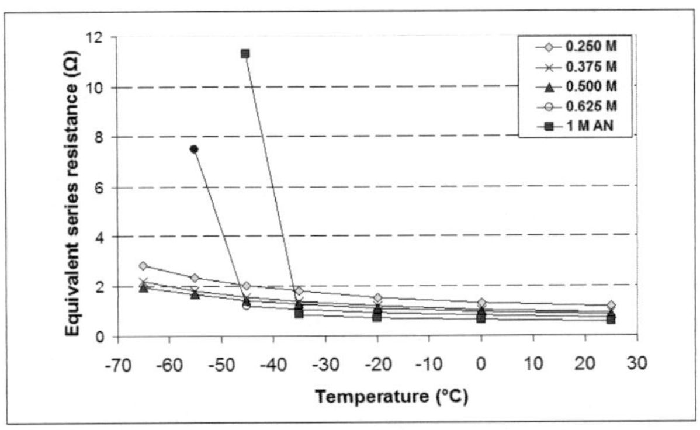

Figure 1. ESR vs. temperature for supercapacitor cells using five different salt concentrations: 0.250, 0.375, 0.500 and 0.625 M TEATFB 1:1 AN:MF, and a baseline 1 M TEATFB cell in pure AN.

As seen in Fig. 1, the baseline 1 M electrolyte in pure AN provides the lowest ESR down to the -35 to -40°C range. However, below this temperature, the ESR rises significantly. Modified AN:MF electrolytes show comparable ESR values, and for electrolytes ≤0.5 M, operation can be extended to -65°C. DC discharge data is shown in Fig. 2. The dc data were collected using constant current discharging at various temperatures. Capacitance was extracted from the linear portion of the voltage vs. time curve.

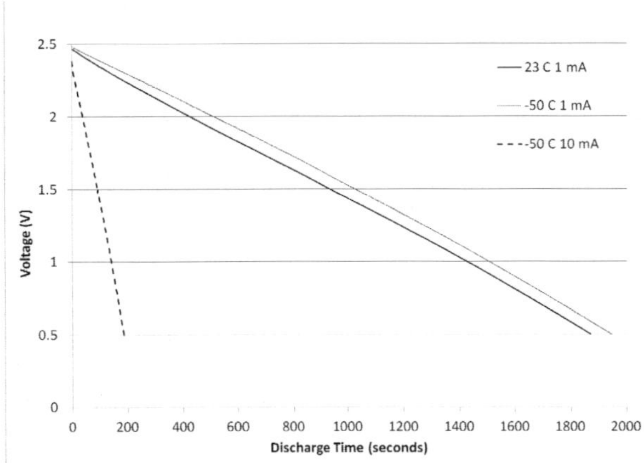

Figure 2. DC discharge data for 0.5 M TEATFB in 1:1 AN:MF cells at +23°C (0.5 mA/cm^2) and at -50°C (0.5 and 5 mA/cm^2).

As seen in Fig. 2, these modified electrolytes show excellent discharge characteristics over a range of current densities (0.5 and 5 mA/cm^2). Also, capacitance measured at room temperature (~1 F for these coin cells, utilizing ~2 cm^2 high surface area carbon electrodes) is maintained at low temperature. The combination of low ESR and capacity retention at low temperatures makes 1:1 AN:MF blends very attractive for extending the low temperature limit of supercapacitors.

High Temperature Operation

At the high temperature end, operation is limited by the boiling point of acetonitrile (+82°C). However, based on the relatively high volatility of the solvent, operation is effectively limited to much lower temperatures. Therefore, the rated limit of commercially available cells is typically +65°C. Operation at higher temperature requires the choice of a solvent system with low volatility and high thermal stability. Ionic liquids have been pursued in recent years as high temperature electrolyte systems (Table 2).

Table 2. High temperature ionic liquid electrolyte candidates.

Ionic Liquid Name	Molecular Structure
1-ethyl-3-methylimidazolium bis (trifluoromethylsulfonyl) imide (EMIM)	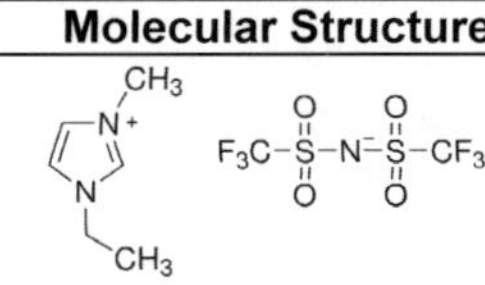
1-butyl-3-methylimidazolium bis (trifluoromethylsulfoyl) imide (BMM)	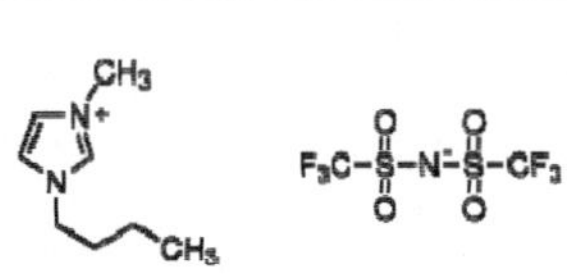
1-butyl-1-methylpyrrolidinium bis (trifluoromethylsulfony) imide (BMPYR)	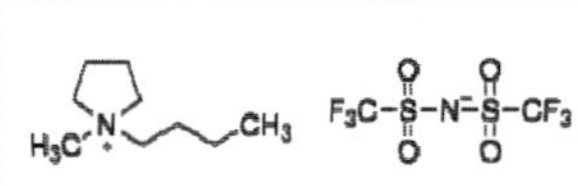

Thermogravimetric analysis of these three electrolytes is shown in Fig. 3 (up to a temperature of 550°C). As seen from these data, virtually no mass loss is observed up to approximately +300°C. The key consideration in choosing a candidate electrolyte is to maintain sufficient margin below this decomposition temperature, for the operating limit. Although this limit has not yet been evaluated, tests reported here were performed to +100°C.

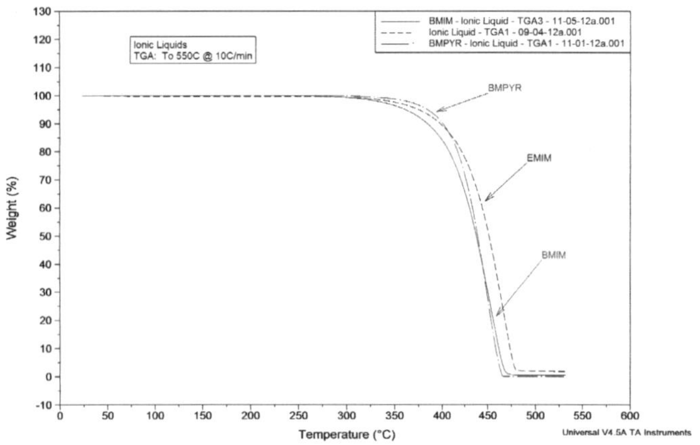

Figure 3. Thermogravimentric analysis for ionic liquids given in Table 2.

A prototype Swagelok-type cell made from stainless steel was used to evaluate ionic liquids in a supercapacitor configuration. High surface area electrodes were punched from larger sheets (Valqua, 0.95 cm^2 area). A zirconia based separator was used, along with the BMPYR electrolyte. Representative data at 100°C are show in Fig. 4 (constant current charging and discharging). Smaller electrodes were used relative to the low temperature coin cells, but the high temperature capacitance at 550 mF compares favorably to the room temperature value.

Conclusions

Supercapacitors capable of charging and discharging over wide temperatures are currently under development. Careful consideration of the electrolyte is required. For low temperature operation, the melting point of the electrolyte system must be sufficiently below the service conditions, and solubility of the electrolyte must be maintained. This can be achieved by careful selection of an appropriate co-solvent. For high temperature operation, electrolytes with low volatility and high thermal degradation limits must be selected. Ionic liquids can meet both of these criteria.

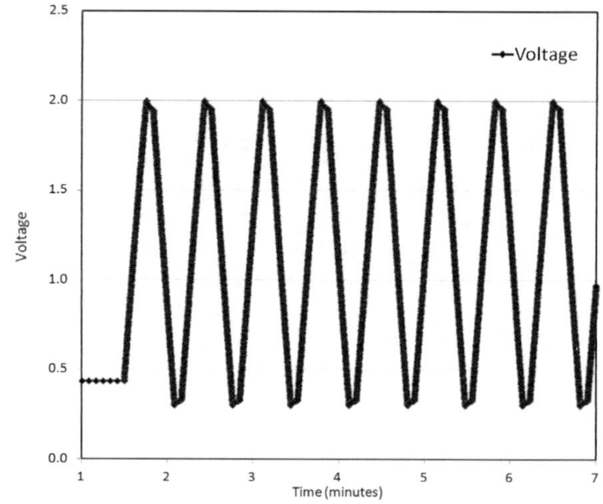

Figure 4. Constant current charging and discharging of high temperature cell (1 mA current at +100°C). Cell capacitance is ~550 mF.

Acknowledgment

The work described here was carried out at the Jet Propulsion Laboratory (JPL), California Institute of Technology, under contract with the National Aeronautics and Space Administration (NASA). The authors wish to thank Greg Chase of Liox (Pasadena, CA) for guidance in developing the high temperature test cell.

References

1. F. Beguin and E. Frackowiak, *Supercapacitors,* Wiley-VCH, Weinheim, 2013.
2. A. Yu, V. Chabot, J. Zhang, *Electrochemical Supercapacitors for Energy Storage and Delivery*, CRC Press, New York, 2013.
3. Brandon, E.J., West, W.C., Smart, M.C., Whitcanack, L.D. and G.A Plett., "Extending the Low Temperature Operational Limit of Double-layer Capacitors," *J. Power Sources,* Vol. 170, pp.225-232, 2007.
4. West, W.C., Smart, M.C., Brandon, E.J., Whitcanack, L.D. and G.A. Plett, "Double-layer Capacitor Electrolyte Using 1,3-Dioxolane for Low Temperature Operation," *J. Electrochem. Soc.,* Vol. 155, pp. A716-A720, 2008.
5. US Patent 8081418, "Low Temperature Double-Layer Capacitors", Dec 20, 2011.
6. Korneblit, Y., Kajdos, A., West, W.C., Smart, M.C., Brandon, E.J., Kvit, A., Jagiello, J. and G. Yushin, "Electrochemical Studies of Dual-Solvent Supercapacitors involving Microporous Electrodes at Ultra-Low Temperatures," *Adv. Ener. Mater.* Vol. 22, pp. 1655- 1662.

A Novel Mediator All-Solid-State Supercapacitor for Low-Temperature Applications

Xiangyang Zhou, Jinshu Cai, Daniel Gu
Department of Mechanical and Aerospace Engineering
University of Miami
Coral Gables, FL 33146

Azzam N. Mansour
Materials and Power Systems Branch, NSWC, Carderock Division
West Bethesda, MD 20817-5700

Abstract: *Aqueous, non-aqueous, and solid-state electrolyte supercapacitors suffer from significant performance degradation below freezing temperatures mainly due to: 1) reduction in ionic conductivity and 2) increase in liquid viscosity and, hence, immobility and inaccessibility of the ions in highly porous electrodes. In order to mitigate these problems, the membrane separator is cast with a PVDF/LiTFS polymer electrolyte doped with a low concentration of $K_3Fe(III)(CN)_6$ and $K_4Fe(II)(CN)_6$ mediators. At the low concentration, electron exchanges between the neighboring mediators result in local breakdowns of electro-neutrality and consequently displacements of ions, thereby promoting ionic conduction. Electrochemical measurements indicate that the SC with mediators in the separator and electrodes possesses good capacitance retention of 87.3% when the temperature is reduced from 20°C to -20°C.*

Keywords: Supercapacitor; low temperature; solid-state electrolyte; mediator.

Introduction

Commercial SCs may have to be deployed over a wide temperature range from -30°C to 90°C [1]. However, almost all SCs including aqueous, non-aqueous, and solid-state electrolyte SCs suffer from performance reduction due to low temperatures [2-10]. For aqueous electrolyte based SCs at below 0°C, the specific capacitance may decrease by 45% while the internal resistance may increase by 45% right [7]. Non-aqueous electrolytes including acetonitrile (ACN) based electrolytes [3, 4], organic carbonate, and ester based electrolytes [5, 8, 9] showed much less reduction of performance at temperatures as low as -10°C. However, when temperature decreases from 25°C to -30°C, the specific energy decreases by two orders of magnitude [11].

In order to mitigate the problem, it is proposed to add small amount of mediators (redox pairs) into the polymer electrolyte. The electron transfer among closely located mediators will promote local charge imbalance and disturbance of local electric field thereby promoting ionic conduction at low temperatures. In fact, there are two different electron transfer routes between two mediators: diabatic (Figure1a) and adiabatic (Figure1.2 b) [12]. In both cases, there are two states, which are before and after electron transfer (R the reactant state), (P the product state). The relation between energy and nuclear coordinate length in the diagram (Figure1) provides the framework for the dependence of energy on vibrational state, thus on temperature. For the diabatic reaction, the reactant R along with the reaction path (arrow marked), climbs over the energy barrier at point B and then it becomes product state P. As the temperature is decreased, the decreased vibrational energy of reactant R cannot overcome the energy point B and the reaction is hindered. While in an adiabatic process, quantum tunneling permits electron transfer even when the vibration energy is very low.

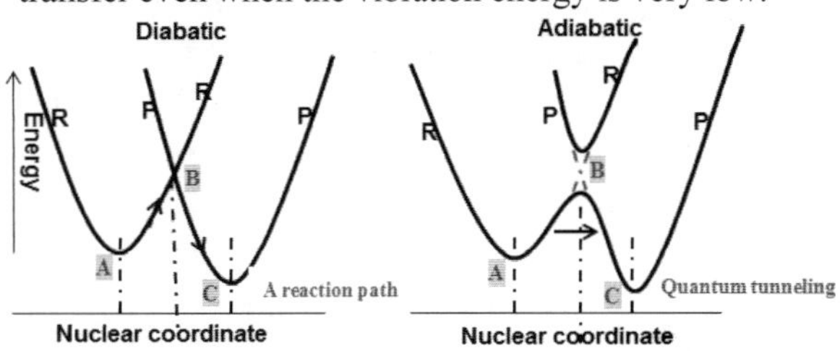

Figure 1 Parabolic curve of relation on energy and nuclear coordinate length.

When low concentration mediators are contained in the membrane, the membrane is assumed as a micro-heterogeneous system. If there is no continual connectivity of occupied sites/mediators, the electronic conductivity could only locally exist, but could not globally exist. This involves a geometrical model called percolation, which is a continuous geometrical phase transformation. Thus, addition of the mediators in polymer electrolyte may achieve high power, energy, ideality and reversibility of all-solid-state SCs at the low temperature. The reduction of capacitance due to low temperature may be mitigated and the reduction of specific power and energy due to low temperature can also be diminished. Due to the very low concentration of mediators, the self-discharge could be in an acceptable range.

Experimental

PVDF powder (M.W. = 534,000, Sigma–Aldrich) was uniformly dispersed in acetone (99.9%, Sigma–Aldrich) and stirred at 60°C till dissolved homogeneously as the transparent gel, then add LiTFS powder (99.995%, Sigma–

Aldrich) in PVDF polymer gel with a mass ratio of PVDF to LiTFS from 1:0.2-1:2 list in Table 3.2. The mixture was stirred for approximately 6 h at room temperature till presented a homogeneous translucent gel. The gel was cast into evaporation dishes with covers and dried in ambient atmosphere for 12 h to form transparent PVDF/LiTFS membrane with uniform thickness. For the mediator-containing membranes, specific amounts of $K_3Fe(CN)_6/K_4Fe(CN)_6$ were added to make the electrolyte with different concentrations as given in Table 1.

Table 1 Mediator concentrations in PVDF /LiTFS membranes

wt%	$K_4Fe(CN)_6$	$K_3Fe(CN)_6$	PVDF	LiTFS
0%	0	0	50	50
1.3%	0.65	0.65	49.3	49.3
2.0%	1.0	1.0	49	49
3%	1.5	1.5	48.5	48.5
4%	2	2	48	48
5%	2.5	2.5	47.5	47.5
6%	3	3	47	47
7%	3.5	3.5	46.5	46.5
8%	4	4	46	46
9%	4.5	4.5	45.5	45.5
10%	5	5	45	45
12.5%	6.25	6.25	43.75	43.75

Results

Conductivity of the membrane

As shown in Figure 2, at mediator concentrations of 1.3 and 3.0 wt%, the electronic conductivity is as low as 10^{-6} S/cm whereas the ionic conductivity is 10^{-2} S/cm at 20°C or $>10^{-4}$ S/cm at -20°C.

These results demonstrate that if the concentration of mediators in the membrane is lower than 3 wt%, the electronic conductivity is at a very low level similar to that of a mediator free membrane at both 20° and -20°C. However, the ionic conductivity at 20°C is high and the ionic conductivity at -20°C is two folds of that for the mediator free membrane. This means that addition of mediators does improve the ionic conductivity at -20°C. It is believed that the large steps in the electronic and ionic conducties are due to percolations of the local mediator clusters. Surely for the high concentrations the electronic conductivity is significant and the membranes cannot be used as the separators in the all-solid-state supercapacitors.

Cyclic voltammetry

All-solid-state supercapacitors (SCs) were fabricated according to the method in Ref. 7. SCs with mediator containing and mediator free membranes are evaluated using the cyclic voltammetry (CV) method. There are four SCs: SC1, no mediator in separator and porous carbon electrodes; SC2, with mediator in electrodes but without mediator in the separator; SC3 without mediator in electrodes and with mediator in separator; and SC4 with mediator in electrodes and separator. The concentration of mediators in separator is 2.6 wt%.

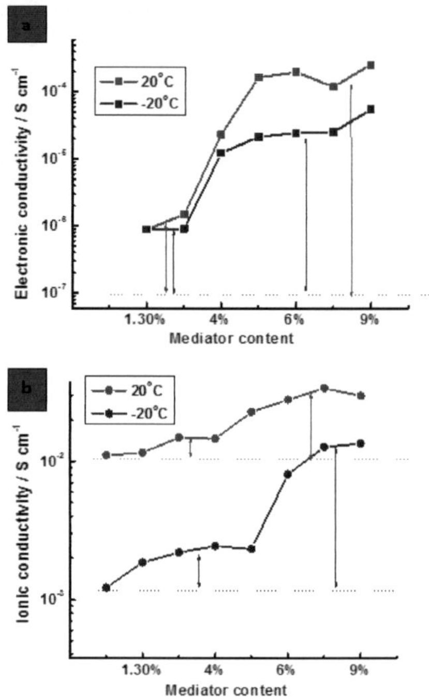

Figure 2 Electronic (top) and ionic (bottom) conductivity as functions of mediator concentration at 20°and -20°.

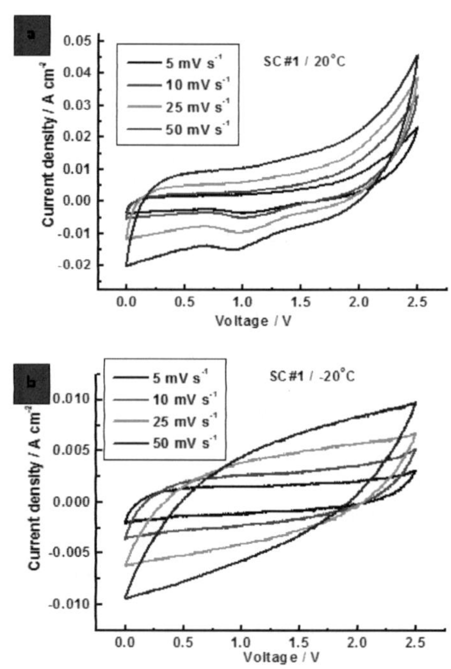

Figure 3 CVs for a mediator free SCs (SC1) at 20°and -20°.

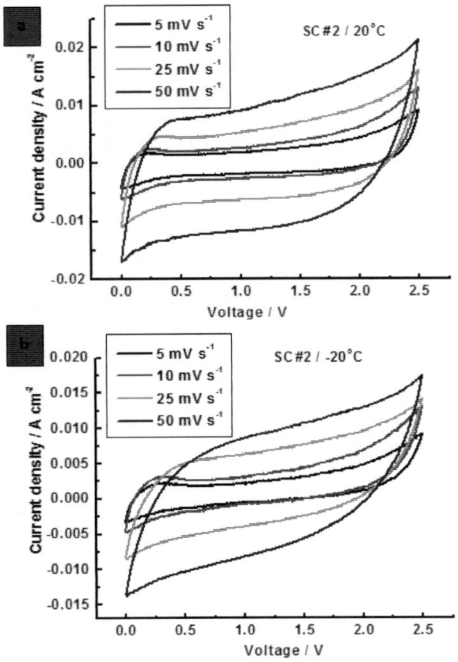

Figure 4 CVs for SC2 with mediator in electrodes but without mediator in the separator at 20°and -20°.

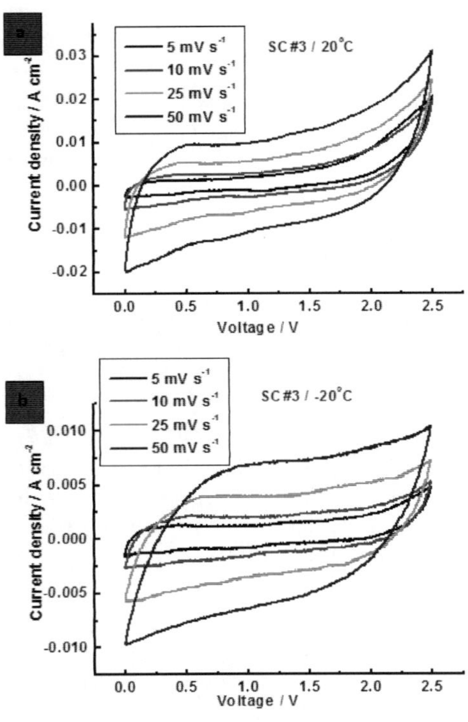

Figure 5 CVs for SC3 without mediator in electrodes but with mediator in the separator at 20°and -20°.

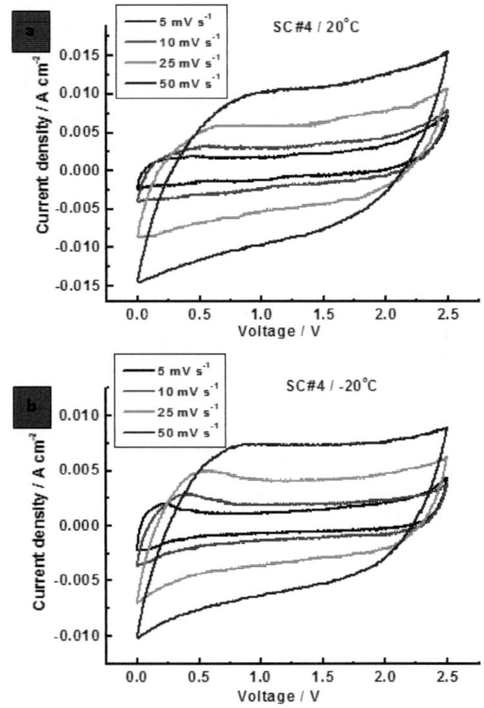

Figure 6 CVs for SC3 with mediator in electrodes and the separator at 20°and -20°.

It is clear from these results that the CVs at -20°C in Figures 3 and 4 are inclined indicating the effect of a high internal resistance. The CVs in Figures 5 and 6, however, show the high internal resistance is largely mitigated. As shown in Figure 6, when there are mediators in the electrodes and the separator, the shapes of the CVs are similar for the 20° and -20°C.

Figure 7 illustrates the galvanostatic charge discharge (GDC) curves and the corresponding specific power vs. specific energy curves for the SCs. It is clear that SC4, which is made from two mediator-containing electrodes and a mediator containing membrane, provides the highest specific energy at 20°C, which is reduced only little at -20°C.

Conclusions

Mediator-containing all-solid-state SCs are designed and fabricated. According to the experimental results the following conclusions can be drawn:

1) The addition of mediators mitigates the increases in the resistance of the PVDF membrane separator and the PEO/$LiClO_4$ solid-state electrolyte. Furthermore, the increase in the internal resistance of the SC was mitigated from 17 folds to 5.3 folds and the increase in the charge transfer resistance was mitigated from 8.2 folds to 2.8 folds at -20°C.
2) The addition of the mediators also improves performance of the ideality or reversibility of all-solid-

state SCs at the low temperature, which is showing a significant enhancement effect of the mediators in comparison with mediator free SC.

3) The reduction of capacitance due to low temperature can be diminished by the addition of the mediators. The highest capacitance retention reached at -20°C relative to 20°C is 87.3%.
4) The reduction in specific power and energy due to the low temperature is also diminished by the addition of the mediators in the polymer membrane (2.6 wt%) and electrode (12 wt%), respectively.

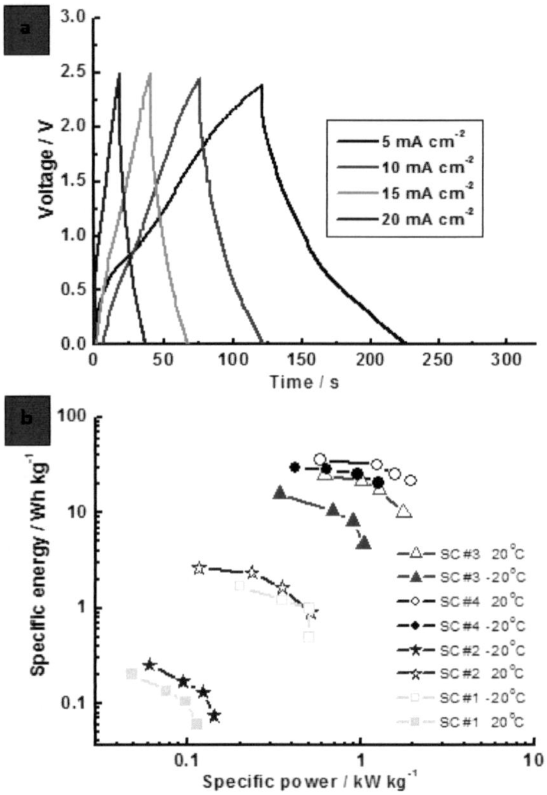

Figure 7 GDCs for SC1, SC2, SC3, and SC4 at 20 and -20°C.

Acknowledgement

The authors would like to thank Office of Naval Research (ONR) for financial support under award numbers N00014-08-1-0332 and N00014-08-WX-20797.

References

1. Conway, B.E., *Electrochemical Supercapacitors*. 1999, New York: Klumer/Plenum Publishers.
2. Liu, P., M. Verbrugge, and S. Soukiazian, *Influence of temperature and electrolyte on the performance of activated-carbon supercapacitors.* Journal of Power Sources, 2006. **156**(2): p. 712-718.
3. Iwama, E., et al., *Characterization of commercial supercapacitors for low temperature applications.* Journal of Power Sources, 2012. **219**: p. 235-239.
4. Hung, K.S., et al., *Wide-temperature range operation supercapacitors from nanostructured activated carbon fabric.* Journal of Power Sources, 2009. **193**(2): p. 944-949.
5. Brandon, E.J., et al., *Extending the low temperature operational limit of double-layer capacitors.* Journal of Power Sources, 2007. **170**(1): p. 225-232.
6. Wang, J.G., et al., *Effect of temperature on the pseudo-capacitive behavior of freestanding MnO2@carbon nanofibers composites electrodes in mild electrolyte.* Journal of Power Sources, 2013. **224**: p. 86-92.
7. Zhou, J.J., et al., *Development of all-solid-state mediator-enhanced supercapacitors with polyvinylidene fluoride/lithium trifluoromethanesulfonate separators.* Journal of Power Sources, 2011. **196**(23): p. 10479-10483.
8. Janes, A. and E. Lust, *Use of organic esters as co-solvents for electrical double layer capacitors with low temperature performance.* Journal of Electroanalytical Chemistry, 2006. **588**(2): p. 285-295.
9. Lin, R.Y., et al., *Capacitive Energy Storage from -50 to 100 degrees C Using an Ionic Liquid Electrolyte.* Journal of Physical Chemistry Letters, 2011. **2**(19): p. 2396-2401.
10. Bendler, J.T., J.J. Fontanella, and M.F. Shlesinger, *A new Vogel-like law: Ionic conductivity, dielectric relaxation, and viscosity near the glass transition.* Physical Review Letters, 2001. **87**(19).
11. Nohara, S., et al., *Self-discharge characteristics of an electric double-layer capacitor with polymer hydrogel electrolyte.* Research on Chemical Intermediates, 2006. **32**(5-6): p. 491-496.
12. Grampp, G. and W. Jaenicke, *Kinetics of Diabatic and Adiabatic Electron Exchange in Organic-Systems Comparison of Theory and Experiment.* Berichte Der Bunsen-Gesellschaft-Physical Chemistry Chemical Physics, 1991. **95**(8): p. 904-927.

Supercapacitor Electrode Material from a Copolymer, Poly (Acrylonitrile-co-vinylimidazole) with Incorporation of Ammonium Bicarbonate as a Porogen

Sahila Perananthan[a], Jeliza S. Bonso[a], Samsuddin Faisal Mahmood[a], Lissa King Magel[b], and John P. Ferraris*[a]

[a]Department of Chemistry, The University of Texas at Dallas, 800 West Campbell Road, Richardson, Texas, USA, 75080

[b]Solarno, Inc. Coppell, Texas, USA, 75019

Abstract: In order to achieve high energy density, electrodes used in supercapacitors should have high surface area that is accessible to the electrolyte. In this study, porous carbon nanofiber electrodes were prepared by electrospinning a solution of copolymer poly(acrylonitrile-co-vinylimidazole), (PAN-VIM) with and without incorporation of ammonium bicarbonate (ABC) as a porogen. The copolymer, PAN-VIM was synthesized and characterized by ATR-FTIR, ^{1}H NMR and gel permeation chromatography (GPC). Incorporation of ABC as a porogen produces pores when it decomposes during subsequent thermal treatments. As-spun nanofibers were thermally stabilized, carbonized, and CO_2 activated. Coin cells were constructed and the electrochemical behavior of the devices was characterized by cyclic voltammetry (CV), galvanostatic charge/discharge, and EIS measurements. The energy density obtained for the electrodes prepared without the porogen is 70 Wh/kg @ 1 A/g and 60 Wh/kg @ 10 A/g. With the addition of porogen the energy density is 68 Wh/kg @ 1 A/g and 66 Wh/kg @ 10 A/g. The addition of the porogen lead to a greatly reduced drop of energy density with increasing current (power) density.

Keywords: Supercapacitors; porogen; electrospun copolymer; PAN; Polyacrylonitrile-co-vinylimidazole; nanofibers.

1.Introduction

Supercapacitors, also known as electrochemical capacitors, are energy storage devices that store the energy electrostatically within the electrochemical double-layer that is formed at the electrode and electrolyte interface.[1] Since the charge storage mechanism is electrostatic, no or negligibly small chemical charge transfer reactions are involved, so supercapacitors are expected to have a much longer cycle life than batteries. Supercapacitors can store much more energy than conventional capacitors and offer much higher power density than batteries, which is useful in applications that require high power such as hybrid electric vehicles, telecommunication devices, and stand-by power systems. Electrospinning is a versatile, simple and efficient technique to produce nonwoven nanofiber mats of polymers[2] which can be subsequently converted to carbon nanofibers by heat treatment. Carbon nanofibers have garnered much attention in recent years because of their large surface area and relatively high conductivity, which makes them attractive electrode materials in high performance supercapacitors.[3] Polyacrylonitrile (PAN) is a widely studied carbon precursor polymer due to its spinnability, high carbon yield and fiber strength.[4] Prior to carbonization, PAN fibers are thermally cyclized into a stabilized ladder polymer. However, the high crystallinity of the PAN precursor polymer can impede the cyclization, resulting in a non uniform microstructure of the carbon fiber. It is reported that introducing imidazole comonomer could reduce the interaction between nitrile groups in PAN and thus facilitate conversion to the ladder polymer. Earlier work from this group on steam activated PAN-VIM nanofibers with a surface area of 1120 m^2/g showed an energy density of 47.4 Wh/kg and a power density of 7.2 W/kg.[5] In this work we have added thermally labile ammonium bicarbonate (ABC) to the polymer solution as a porogen, to enhance the porosity and surface area of the resulting carbon fibers.

2. Experimental

2.1 Synthesis of copolymer

PAN-VIM copolymer with a AN:VIM ratio of 90:10 was synthesized according to the reported procedure.[5]

2.2 Electrospinning

A solution of copolymer and a saturated solution of ammonium bicarbonate were prepared separately in dimethylformamide (DMF) and mixed together so that the concentration of copolymer is 10 wt%. This solution was electrospun under an applied voltage of 18 kV (Gamma High Voltage Research, Inc.). Electrospun nanofiber mats were stabilized at 280 °C for 1.5 hours under air flow, and then carbonized and activated using CO_2 in a single step for 1 hour at 1000 °C under helium. All the chemicals used for synthesis and electrospinning were purchased from Aldrich Chemical Co.

2.3 Characterization

The surface morphology of as-spun and carbonized nanofibers was observed by scanning electron microscopy (SEM, Zeiss SUPRA 40 SEM) after gold and palladium sputtering. The ratio of disordered to graphitic carbon was measured by Raman spectroscopy using a HORIBA Jobin Yvon high-resolution LabRam Raman microscope system with 633 nm helium-neon laser. Surface area and pore volume were obtained using N_2 gas after degassing at 200 °C (Micromeritics ASAP2020).

2.4 Electrochemical measurements

CR 2032 coin cells were assembled using electrodes punched out from the carbonized and activated mat. Ethylmethylimidazolium bis(trifluoromethylsulfonyl) imide (EMITFSI, IoLiTec, Inc,) was used as the electrolyte, the separator was GORE™ polytetrafluoroethylene (W.L. Gore & Associates, Inc.), and carbon coated aluminum was used as the current collector. Cyclic voltammetry (CV) and galvanostatic charge–discharge curves were obtained using an Arbin Supercapacitor Testing System. Electrochemical impedance spectroscopy was measured using a PARSTAT 2273 Galvanostat (Princeton Applied Research) in the frequency range of 100 kHz to 10 mHz.

3. Results and discussion

Surface morphology of the electrospun and carbonized fibers of PAN-VIM and PAN-VIM-ABC are shown in Fig 1. The SEM image shows that the as-spun PAN-VIM fibers have diameters of 828±108 nm and PAN-VIM-ABC fibers have diameters of 548±114. After heat treatment, the fiber morphology was retained with a reduced fiber diameter of 278±35 and 383±48, respectively. The surface of the porogen-containing fiber appears somewhat rougher.

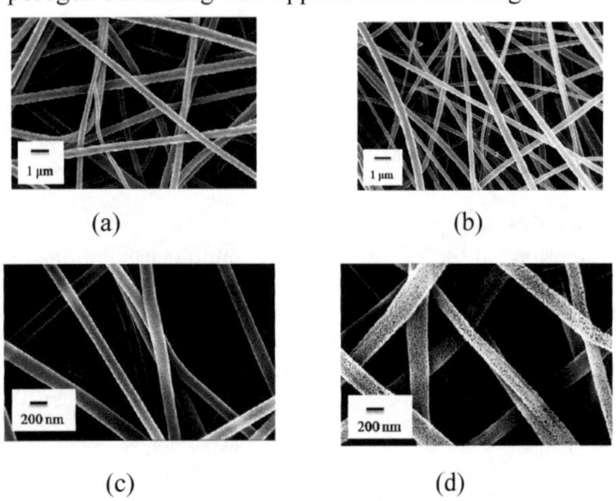

Figure 1. SEM images of (a) electrospun (c) carbonized PAN-VIM (b) electrospun (d)carbonized PAN-VIM-ABC.

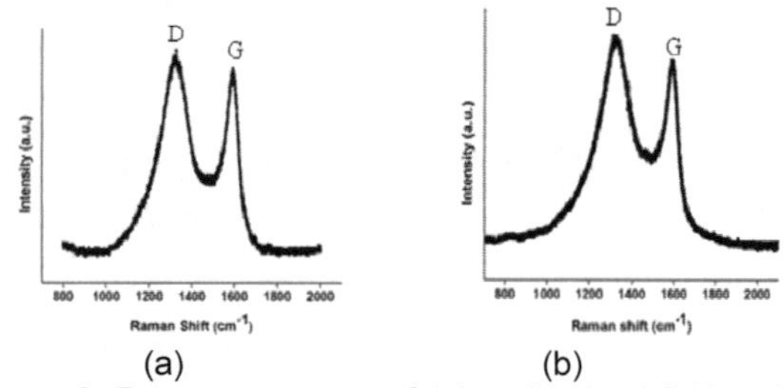

Figure 2. Raman spectrum of (a) carbonized PAN-VIM (b) carbonized PAN-VIM-ABC.

Fig. 2 shows the Raman spectra of the two carbonized fiber mats. There are two broad overlapping peaks centered around 1360 and 1590 cm^{-1}. The first is the well-known D band which corresponds to structure defects and disordered carbon and the second is the G band attributed to graphitic carbon.[6] The ratio of the integrated intensity of D peak to G peak, denoted by (I_D/I_G) PAN-VIM had an I_D/I_G of 3.10 and it increased to 3.12 with the incorporation of ABC, which is consistent with slightly increased disorder.

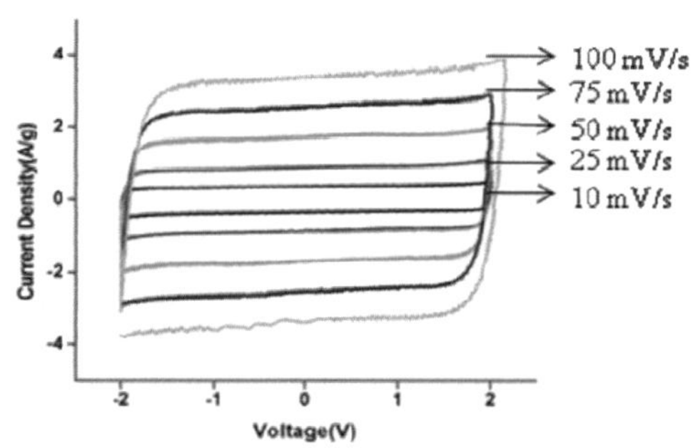

(a)

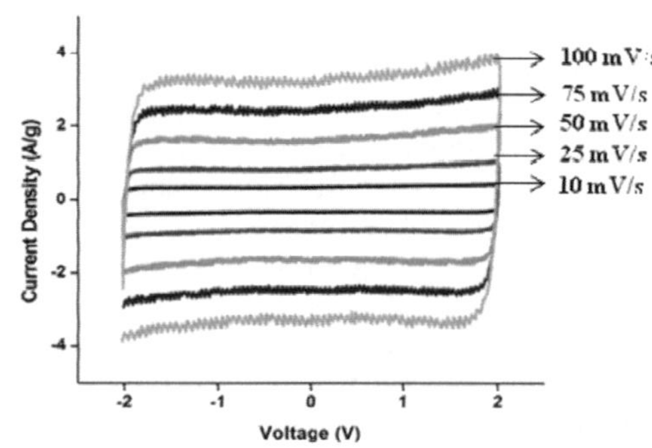

(b)

Figure 3. Cyclic voltammograms of (a) PAN-VIM (b) PAN-VIM-ABC at different scan rates.

EMITFSI was selected as the electrolyte because of its large voltage window compared to aqueous and organic electrolytes (4V) since energy density is quadratically related to the voltage ($E = \frac{1}{2} CV^2$).[7] The electrochemical performance was studied using cyclic voltammetry (CV), galvanostatic charge–discharge testing at 3.5 V and EIS. Fig. 3 shows CV plots of both (a) PAN-VIM and (b) PAN-VIM-ABC electrodes. In both cases box like CVs were obtained, which is typical for double layer capacitors. The specific capacitance of PAN-VIM decreased from 141 to 136 F/g while PAN-VIM-ABC remained unchanged at143 F/g as the scan rate increased from 10 to 100 mV/s.

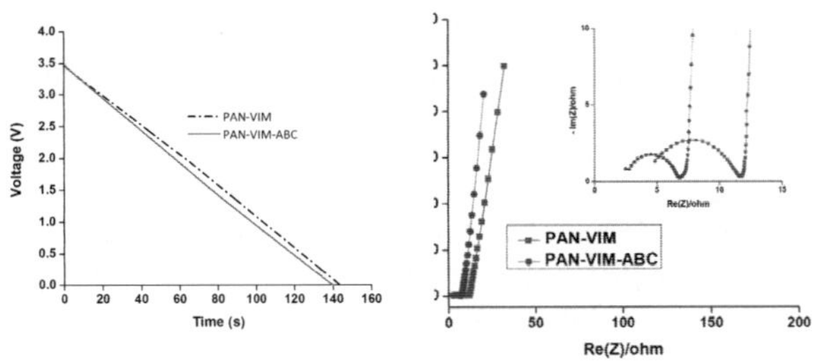

(a) (b)

Figure 4. (a) discharge curves at 1 A/g, and (b) Nyquist plot

The galvanostatic discharge plots in Fig. 4(a) show that both are linear with small initial voltage drops of 0.02 V and 0.01 V for PAN-VIM and PAN-VIM-ABC, respectively. Electrochemical impedance spectroscopy (Fig 4(b)) shows that PAN-VIM-ABC has a lower charge transfer resistance (diameter of the semicircle) of 4.4 Ω, compared to PAN-VIM with 7.6 Ω.

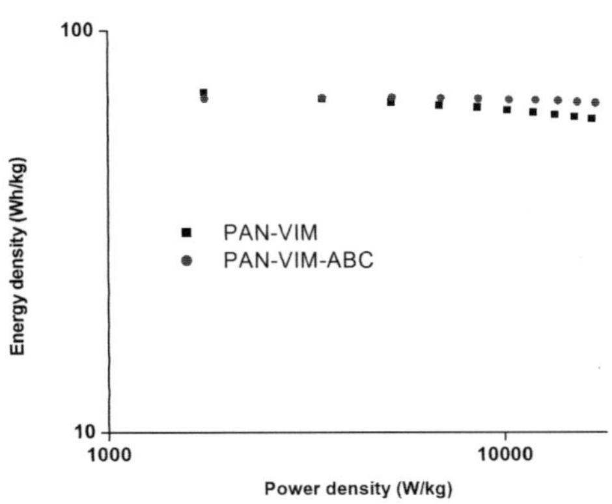

Figure 5. Ragone plot of PAN-VIM and PAN-VIM-ABC.

The Ragone plot in Fig. 5 shows the energy and power density values at discharge rates from 1 A/g to 10 A/g. PAN-VIM-ABC retained 97% of its initial energy density at the higher discharge rate compared to 86% for the PAN-VIM.

Fig. 6 shows the pore size distribution for the two carbon materials.

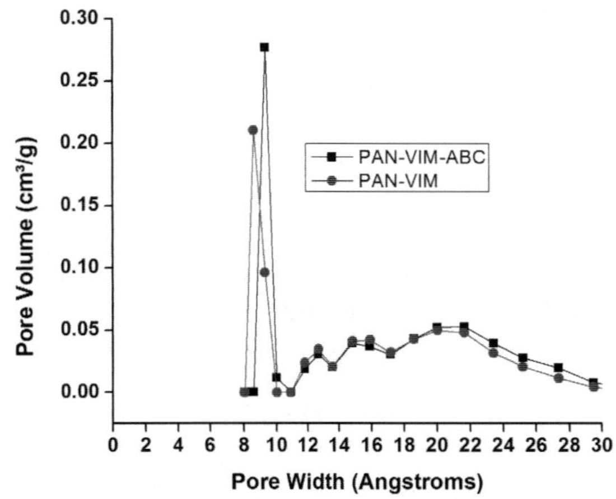

Figure 6. Surface area and pore size analysis of PAN-VIM and PAN-VIM-ABC.

Table 1 shows the surface area of both samples. There is a small increase in pore volume for PAN-VIM-ABC compared to PAN-VIM and its pore width in the 8 to 10 Angstrom range is shifted to slightly larger values, which may better accommodate the size of the EMI (7.6 Å) and TFSI (7.9 Å) ions.

Table 1. Surface area and pore size analysis data

	BET SSA (m^2g^{-1})	**DFT TPV (cm^3g^{-1})**	**V_{micro} (cm^3g^{-1})**	**V_{meso} (cm^3g^{-1})**
PAN-VIM	1754	0.726	0.559	0.167
PAN-VIM-ABC	1777	0.753	0.592	0.161

4. Conclusions

PAN-VIM and PAN-VIM-ABC nanofibers were electrospun, and then stabilized, carbonized and CO_2 activated. PAN-VIM-ABC had a high specific capacitance of 143 F/g, which was invariant over a scan rate range of 10 mV/s to 100 mV/s. In addition, it retained 97% of its initial energy density (68 Wh/kg) when the current density increased from 1 A/g to 10 A/g.

Acknowledgments

We would like to acknowledge financial support from NSF (IIP-1127564). We also thank NSF (CHE-1126177) grant for providing the Bruker AVANCE III™ 500 NMR facility and Dr. Ron Smaldone and Dr. Christina Thompson for their help with the surface area analysis.

References

1. Conway B. E., "Transition from Supercapacitor to Battery Behavior in Electrochemical Energy Storage" *J. Electrochem. Soc.*,, vol. 138, pp. 1539–1548, 1991.

2. Reneker D. H, Yarin AL. "Electrospinning jets and polymer nanofibers",*Electrospinning jets and polymer nanofibers. Polymer*, vol. 49, pp. 2387–425, 2008.

3Sarmadi AM, Noel C.J, Birch J.B. "Effects of heat treatment on dyeability, glass transition temperature, and tensile properties of poly(acrylonitrile) fibers", *Ind Eng Chem Res,* vol. 29, pp. 1640–6, 1990.

4. Deng, W.J., A. Lobovsky, S.T. Iacono, T.Y. Wu, N. Tomar, S.M. Budy, T. Long, W.P.Hoffman, D.W. Smith, "Poly (acrylonitrile-co-1-vinylimidazole): A new melt processable carbon fiber precursor",*Polymer.*, vol. 52, pp. 622, 2011.

5. Kyung-Hye, J, W.Deng , D. W. Smith Jr. J. P. Ferraris, "Carbon nanofiber electrodes for supercapacitors derived from new precursor polymer: Poly(acrylonitrile-co-vinylimidazole) ",*Electrochemistry Communications*, vol 23, pp. 149–152, 2012.

6. Ruiz-Rosas,R., J. Bedia, M. Lallave, I. G. Loscertales, A. Barrero, J. Rodr´ıguez-Mirasol and T. Cordero "Characterization of co- electrospun lignin/alumina microfibers And tubes", *Carbon*, vol. 48, pp. 696–705, 2010.

7. Largeot, C.; Portet, C.; Chmiola, J.; Taberna, P.; Gogotsi, Y.; Simon, P. "Relation between the Ion Size and Pore Size for an Electric Double-Layer Capacitor", *J. Am. Chem. Soc*, vol. *130*, pp. 2730–2731, 2008.

Hydrothermally Derived Activated Carbons for Electrochemical Capacitors

Stephen M. Lipka, Christopher Swartz, Rong Chen, Fon Rogers, Uschi M. Graham
Electrochemical Power Sources Group, Center for Applied Energy Research
University of Kentucky
2582 Research Park Drive, Lexington, KY 40511
e-mail: steve.lipka@uky.edu

Abstract: Spherical, high-performance activated carbons have been produced at the University of Kentucky as electrode materials for electrochemical capacitors. The carbon spheres are produced through the hydrothermal dehydration/degradation of carbohydrate precursors, including mono- and disaccharides. Careful manipulation of synthesis conditions, including reactant concentration, reaction temperature and dwell time, allows for control of product yield and sphere diameter. The spheres were then carbonized, and subjected to various physical and chemical activation schemes to produce materials with high surface areas (2000-3000 m^2/g). The electrochemical performance of the activated carbon spheres was then characterized in aprotic electrolytes.

Keywords: Carbon spheres; activated carbons; hydrothermal synthesis; electrochemical capacitor.

Introduction

Electrochemical capacitors are low-maintenance electrochemical energy storage devices that are complementary to batteries, and typically feature high power densities (rapid charge/discharge capabilities), long cycle life (hundreds of thousands of cycles) [1], and low equivalent series resistance (ESR). Power densities for electrochemical capacitors typically range from 10-100 times greater than for batteries, while batteries feature significantly higher energy densities than electrochemical capacitors. Electrochemical capacitors are starting to find widespread utility in a variety of applications, including hybrid electric vehicles (capturing energy from regenerative braking), hybrid buses, and various consumer applications, including cordless electric screwdrivers, portable speakers, and power sources for flashes in portable cameras. Numerous potential military applications have also been identified for electrochemical capacitors, including both symmetric and asymmetric designs [1].

Activated carbons are currently used as electrode materials in electrochemical capacitors, and are attractive electrode materials for several reasons, including high conductivity, high specific surface areas (1000-3000 m^2/g), tunable pore structures, and good thermal and electrochemical stability [2]. The development of new carbon-based electrode materials with improved energy and power densities relative to activated carbon is ongoing, and materials such as graphene, carbon aerogels, carbon nanotubes, and conducting polymers have been examined as suitable replacements for activated carbon.

Previous reports have demonstrated the utility of activated spherical carbons as active materials in electrochemical capacitors [3,4], and fluorinated carbon spheres have been employed as energy-dense cathodes in primary Li-CF_x batteries [5]. Sulfur-impregnated carbon spheres have also been successfully demonstrated as cathodes for rechargeable lithium-sulfur batteries [6]. Carbon microspheres have also been examined as suitable materials for adsorbents and catalyst supports [7,8]. Efficient packing of spherical carbons has led to enhanced volumetric energy densities in energy storage applications [3,5].

Spherical carbons have been synthesized through an array of methods, including hydrothermal synthesis, chemical vapor deposition, ultrasonic spray pyrolysis, and by pyrolysis of polymer microspheres [7]. Hydrothermal synthesis is a particularly attractive synthetic method for the production of carbonaceous spheres, due to the use of low cost precursors (i.e. carbohydrates), aqueous-based solvents, and relatively benign reaction conditions (temperatures < 200 °C.) This paper discuss the preparation of activated carbon spheres using hydrothermal synthesis, and used as capacitive energy storage electrodes in symmetric carbon/carbon electrochemical capacitors in organic electrolytes. SEM images of activated carbon spheres are shown in Figure 1.

Figure 1. SEM images of activated carbon spheres.

Synthesis of spherical carbons

A laboratory-scale 2L Parr pressure vessel was used for the synthesis of spherical carbons. Xylose was used as the carbohydrate precursor, and was dissolved in deionized water at a certain concentration. Other additives, including KOH, were added to the reaction mixture at various concentrations to assist with the control of particle size. The pressure vessel was then heated to 200 °C for 5 hours. The pressure vessel was then cooled to room temperature, and the solid product was isolated by vacuum filtration. The solid product was then dried in a vacuum oven at 120 °C for 12 hours. Typical product yields were 45%, and yields were calculated by (mass of carbon spheres)/(mass of carbohydrate precursor) x 100%.

Carbonization/Activation of spherical carbons

Carbonization of the as-produced carbon spheres was performed at 500 °C for 60 minutes, in a nitrogen atmosphere. Typical carbonization mass losses are 40%. Physical activation (CO_2) was performed in a tube furnace at 950 °C for 18 hours (mass loss = 76%). Chemical activation was performed by mixing the carbonized spherical carbons with NaOH (4:1 NaOH/carbon), in a solid-state activation. The mixture was then heated to 400 °C for 3 hours, and then to 800 °C for 30 minutes. The chemical activation mass loss was 53%. The mixture was then rinsed with DI water and dilute acid to neutralize the residual NaOH. The activated carbon was then dried in a vacuum oven overnight.

Physical Characterization of spherical carbons

Scanning electron microscopy was performed using a Hitachi S-4800. The average particle size for the activated carbon spheres ranged from 2-5 microns (Figure 1). BET surface area data was generated using a Micromeritics ASAP 2020, and density functional theory was used to calculate the pore size distribution of the activated carbon spheres. As-produced, "green" carbon spheres have surface areas < 10 m^2/g, while carbonized samples have surface areas approaching 200 m^2/g. Table 1 is a summary of the BET surface area data and pore size distributions for the physically activated sample 1, and chemically activated sample 2. The chemically activated carbon spheres had a much higher surface area and total pore volume than physically activated spheres, and also featured a significantly higher degree of mesoporosity, and lower degree of microporosity than the physically activated carbon spheres.

Table 1. Summary of BET surface area and pore size distribution for activated carbon spheres.

sample	BET surface area (m^2/g)	Total pore volume (cm^3/g)	% micro	% meso	% macro
1 (CO_2)	2154	1.032	77.8	21.4	0.8
2 (NaOH)	2982	1.491	47.7	51.9	0.4

Electrochemical characterization

Symmetric carbon/carbon electrochemical capacitors were fabricated and tested. Activated carbon (92%) was mixed with 5% KS6 graphite, and 3% Teflon 6C, and Teflon-bonded sheets were constructed. Electrodes of 12 mm diameter, and 60-80 microns in thickness were used in the symmetric capacitors. For electrochemical testing in certain electrolytes, the electrodes were pressed onto 14 mm titanium mesh, and testing was performed using an EL-CELL test cell. The separator used in the cell is CELGARD® 3501. The carbon electrodes and separator were both wetted with electrolyte during cell assembly. Electrochemical characterization was evaluated using cyclic voltammetry (sweep rate = 20 mV/s), constant current charge/discharge, and electrochemical impedance spectroscopy. Galvanostatic charge/discharge experiments were performed at various current densities based on active mass of carbon (mA/g). Electrolytes used for electrochemical screening include 1.8M triethylmethylammonium tetrafluoroborate ($TEMABF_4$) in propylene carbonate (PC); 1M tetraethylammonium tetrafluoroborate ($TEABF_4$) in CH_3CN, and 0.5M lithium bis(trifluoromethanesulfonyl imide) (LiIm) in 1-ethyl-3-methylimidazolium bis(trifluoromethanesulfonyl imide) (EMIIm).

The cyclic voltammetry data and DC data for CO_2-activated sample 1 and NaOH-activated sample 2 in 1.8M $TEMABF_4$ in PC is shown in Figure 2. Sample 2 featured a significantly higher gravimetric and volumetric capacitance (188 F/g, 63 F/cm^3) than the physically activated sample 1 (127 F/g, 48 F/cm^3). Both samples exhibited pure double layer charge storage, as seen by the linear charge and discharge profiles in Figure 2b.

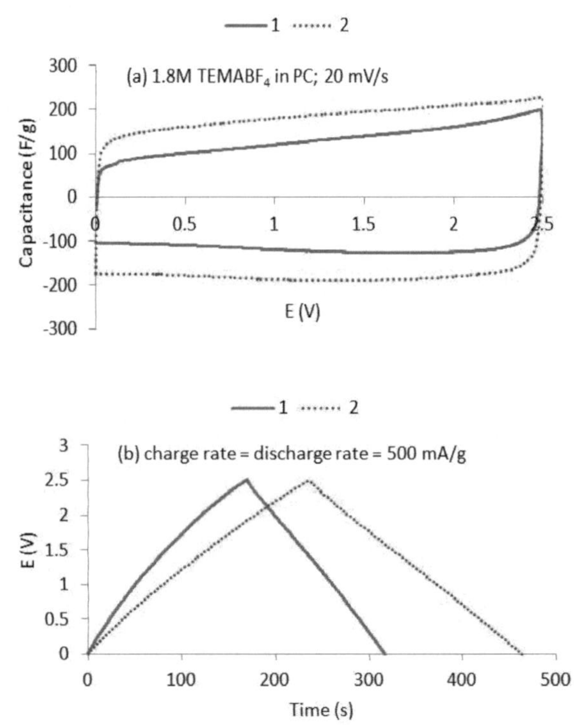

Figure 2. (a) Cyclic voltammetry data; (b) constant current charge/discharge data for activated carbon spheres.

The electrochemical impedance spectroscopy data for both activated carbon sphere samples in 1.8M $TEMABF_4$ in PC is shown in Figure 3. The average electrode thickness in both cells is ~ 60 microns.

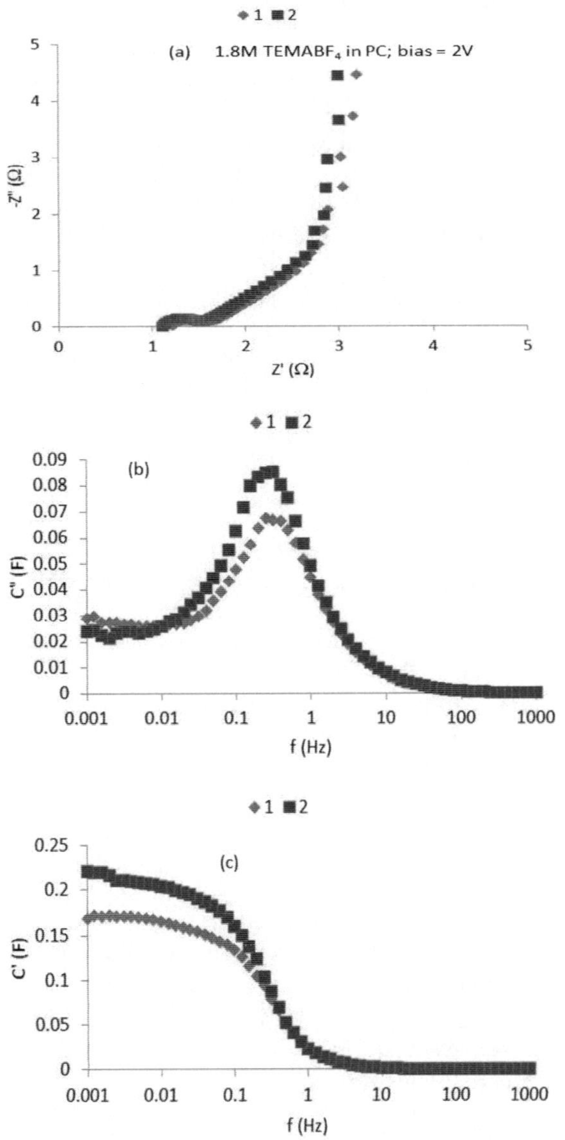

Figure 3. EIS data.(a) Nyquist plot; (b) C" (F) vs. frequency (Hz); (c) C' (F) vs. frequency (Hz).

The solution resistance for both samples is 1.1-1.2 Ω in PC, as seen in the Nyquist plot in Figure 3a. The plot of imaginary capacitance (C"(F)) vs. frequency (Hz) is seen in Figure 3b. The imaginary part of the capacitance reaches a maximum at a frequency f_0, and the RC time constant for the entire system is defined as $\tau_0 = 1/f_0$ [9]. Physically activated sample 1 has an f_0 of 0.39811 Hz (τ_0 = 2.51 s), while chemically activated sample 2 has an f_0 of 0.31623 Hz (τ_0 = 3.16 s). The plot of real capacitance (C' (F)) vs. frequency (Hz) in Figure 3c indicates that the cell capacitance for sample 1 is 0.168 F (123 F/g), while the cell capacitance for sample 2 is 0.220 F (191 F/g), with both capacitance measurements taken at 0.001 Hz.

The cylic voltammetry data and constant current charge/discharge data for the activated carbon spheres in 1M $TEABF_4$ in CH_3CN is shown in Figure 4. Both samples featured rectangular voltammograms, and linear charge/discharge profiles, indicative of pure double layer charge storage. The CO_2-activated sample 1 had a capacitance of 131 F/g, 58 F/cm^3, and the NaOH-activated sample 2 had significantly higher capacitance in acetonitrile (186 F/g, 61 F/cm^3).

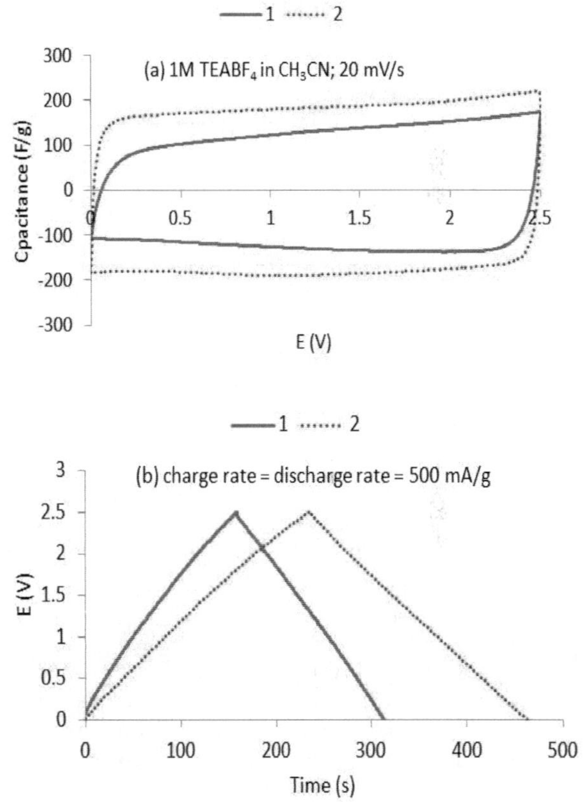

Figure 4. (a) Cyclic voltammetry data; (b) constant current charge/discharge data for activated carbon spheres in acetonitrile.

The electrochemical performance of chemically activated sample 2 was also screened in an ionic liquid based electrolyte (0.5M LiIm in EMIIm). Figure 5 shows the cyclic voltammetry data and constant current charge/discharge data in 0.5M LiIm in EMIIm. The chemically activated carbon spheres had a gravimetric capacitance of 185 F/g, and a volumetric capacitance of 59 F/cm^3 in the ionic liquid based electrolyte.

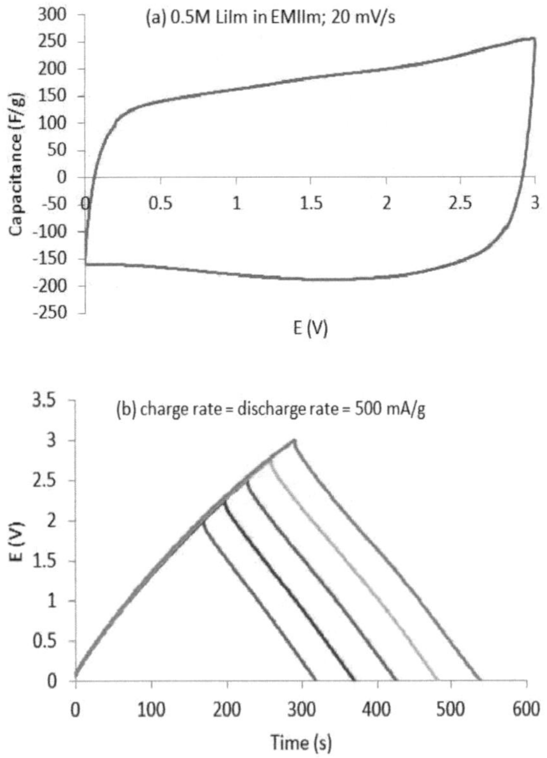

Figure 5. (a) Cyclic voltammetry data; (b) constant current charge/discharge data for chemically activated carbon spheres in 0.5M LiIm in EMIIm.

Conclusions

Spherical carbons were produced hydrothermally using xylose as a precursor, and had an average particle size of 2-5 microns. The spheres were then carbonized, and subjected to both physical and chemical activations using CO_2 and NaOH, respectively. The activated carbon spheres had high surface areas (> 2000 m^2/g), and total pore volumes > 1 cm^3/g. The electrochemical performance of the activated spheres was examined in various aprotic electrolytes, with the chemically activated carbon spheres featuring gravimetric capacitance > 180 F/g, and volumetric capacitance > 60 F/cm^3.

Acknowledgements

The authors wish to acknowledge Ifedi Anyaegbunam and Artashes Ter-Isahakyan for assistance with the preparation of spherical carbon materials.

References

1. Long, J. W., "Opportunities for Electrochemical Capacitors as Energy-Storage Solutions in Present and Future Navy and Marine Corps Missions." Naval Research Laboratory, Report no. NRL/MR/6170--09-9227.
2. Pandolfo, A. G.; Hollenkamp, A. F., "Carbon properties and their role in supercapacitors," *Journal of Power Sources*, vol. 157, pp. 11-27, 2006.
3. Lipka, S., Kunadian, I., Chen, R., Swartz, C., Rogers, F., "Spherical High Performance Activated Carbon Materials for Electrochemical Capacitors," Proceedings of the 45th Power Sources Conference, pp.607-610, 2012.
4. Wang, J., Shen, L., Ding, B., Nie, P., Deng, H., Dou, H., Zhang, X., "Fabrication of porous carbon spheres for high-performance electrochemical capacitors," *RSC Adv.*, vol. 4, pp. 7538-7544, 2014.
5. Loth, M. A., Kunadian, I., Chen, R., Graham, U., Swartz, C., Lipka, S. M., "Fluorinated Carbon Nanospheres for Primary Lithium/CF_x Batteries," Proceedings of the 45th Power Sources Conference, pp.29-32, 2012.
6. Loth, M. A., Rogers, F., Chen, R., Swartz, C., Graham, U., Lipka, S., "Spherical carbon/sulfur composite cathodes for rechargeable lithium batteries," Abstract #338, Honolulu PRiME 2012.
7. Ju, M., Zeng, C., Wang, C., Zhang, L., "Preparation of Ultrafine Carbon Spheres by Controlled Polymerization of Furfuryl Alcohol in Microdroplets," *Ind. Eng. Chem. Res.*, vol. 53, pp. 3084-3090, 2014.
8. Graham, U., Jacobs, G., Gnanamani, M., Lipka, S., Shafer, W., Swartz, C., Jermwongratanachai, T., Chen, R., Rogers, F., Davis, B. H., "Fischer Tropsch Synthesis: High Oxygenate-Selectivity of Cobalt Catalysts supported on Hydrothermal Carbons," manuscript in review.
9. Taberna, P., Simon, P., Fauvarque, J. "Electrochemical characteristics and impedance spectroscopy studies of carbon-carbon supercapacitors," *Journal of the Electrochemical Society*, vol. 150, p. A292, 2003.

Physical and Electrochemical Characterization of Promising Carbides and Nitrides for Supercapacitors Applications

***Abdoulaye Djire*[a], *Olabode T Ajenifujah*[a], *Alice E. S. Sleightholme*[a], *Paul Rasmussen*[ab], *Levi T Thompson**[ab]**

[a] Department of Chemical Engineering
[b] Hydrogen Energy Technology Laboratory
University of Michigan, Ann Arbor, MI 48109-2136, USA

Abstract: *Phase-pure, nanostructured W, Ti and Nb carbides and nitrides were synthesized using a temperature -program reaction method, and were characterized electrochemically in aqueous KOH and H_2SO_4 electrolytes. The materials were observed to be electrochemically stable in both electrolytes. With the exception of NbC, capacitances for most of the materials exceeded those expected for double-layer charging and suggested a pseudocapacitive-storage mechanism. The capacitance as function of scan rate was logarithmic, and reached a maximum value at low scan rate.*

Keywords: Energy storage; early transition-metal nitrides and carbides; electrochemical capacitor; supercapacitor; double layer; pseudocapacitance.

Introduction

Due to their high power densities (up to 15 kW kg^{-1}), moderate energy densities (5 Wh kg^{-1}), and long cycle life (e.g. >1,000,000), electrochemical capactiors (or "supercapacitors") are receiving increased interest stimulated by their potential use in applications such as memory back-up devices, portable electronics, uninterruptible power supplies, hybrid systems and large industrial equipment [1-3]. In terms of their specific energy and specific power, they fill the gap between conventional capacitors and batteries, and can be used in hybrid configurations to manage short, high power pulses, thereby minimizing stresses on the primary energy-storage devices.

Currently, the high cost and moderate energy density of supercapacitors limits their use. Research in this field has focused on increasing energy density without sacrificing cycle life or power density [4]. In order to increase the energy density, either the capacitance and/or the operating voltage must be increased. Supercapacitors are classified into two major types based on their charge-storage mechanisms: electrostatic double-layer (accumulation of charges at the electrode/electrolyte interface) and pseudocapacitive (fast and reversible surface redox reactions) [5]. The material used most often in commercial supercapacitors is activated carbon which is relatively expensive and has limited capacitance (100–125 Fg^{-1}) [6]. The mechanism of charge storage for these materials is electrostatic double layer and energy densities for the corresponding devices can reach 5 Wh kg^{-1} [7,8]. Over the past few years, significant emphasis has been placed on finding lower-cost, better performing materials.

Materials that exhibit pseudocapacitance include conducting polymers like polyaniline, polypyrrole, polythiophene and their derivatives, and the oxides of Ru, and Mn based materials [4, 9-13]. Hydrous RuO_2 is currently the benchmark pseudocapacitive material with capacitances up to 1300 F g^{-1} [14, 15] and energy densities in excess of 8 Wh kg^{-1} [2.9]. However, the high cost of Ru and its toxicity limits its large-scale use. Other pseudocapacitive oxides have advantages over RuO_2 with respect to the cost, environmental safety, and theoretical capacitances, however lower electronic conductivity, poor compatibility with organic electrolytes and short cycle life have limited their applications as supercapacitor materials[12-14].

Early transition-metal carbides and nitrides represent another class of materials that have been reported to exhibit pseudocapacitance behavior in aqueous electrolytes [16-19]. These materials have high electronic conductivities, can be produced with high surface areas and are inexpensive to synthesize. In particular, VN and Mo_2N have been the most studied for supercapacitor applications [18, 19]. There are fewer reports on the pseudocapacitive properties of other carbides and nitrides. In the present work, we explore both physical and electrochemical characteristics of early transition metal carbides and nitrides including tungsten carbide (WC_{1-X}), titanium nitride (TiN), and niobium nitride and carbide (NbN, NbC) in both aqueous base and acid electrolytes.

Experimental

Material Synthesis

High-surface-area W, Nb, and Ti carbides and nitrides were prepared from their oxide precursors, WO_3 (Alfa Aesar), Nb_2O_5 (Alfa Aesar) and TiO_2 (Alfa Aesar), respectively, by temperature-programmed reaction (TPR) synthesis with 15% CH_4 in H_2 (Cryogenic Gases) or NH_3 (Cryogenic Gases), respectively. The oxide precursors were supported on a quartz-wool plug in a quartz tube reactor.

After synthesis, the materials were quenched to room temperature and then passivated using a flowing mixture of 1% O_2/He (Cryogenic Gases) to form an oxygen-rich protective layer that prevents oxidation of the bulk material when exposed to air.

Physical Characterization

The physical surface areas and pore size distribution of the passivated materials were determined by N_2 physisorption using a Micrometrics ASAP 2010 analyzer with the Brunauer–Emmett–Teller (BET) method and Barrett-Joiner-Helenda (BJH) method, respectively. Prior to analysis, the materials were degassed in vacuum at 350 ºC for 24 hours. The materials were then characterized by X-ray diffraction (XRD) using a Rigaku Miniflex Diffractometer with Cu Kα (λ=0.15404nm) source. The XRD was carried out at a scan rate of 5.0° min^{-1} with a step size of 0.1° over a 2θ range of 10° to 90°. The JADE 10.0 software was used for peak identification.

Electrochemical Characterization

The electrochemical measurements were carried out in 0.1 mol dm^{-3} H_2SO_4 and 0.1 mol dm^{-3} KOH electrolytes using cyclic voltammetry (CV). These experiments were performed using a glass three-electrode cell with an Autolab PGSTAT302N potentiostat. The working electrode was prepared by mixing the as-prepared material (80 wt. %), carbon black (10 wt. %, Super PLi (TIMCAL) and polyvinylidene fluoride (10 wt. %, Kynar) in N-methylpyrrolidione solvent (Alfa Aesar). The resulting slurry was coated onto a Ti foil and then dried in vacuum at 80°C for 8 hours. A flowing stream of N_2 was bubbled through the aqueous electrolytes for at least 30 min before the experiments and maintained as a blanket over the solution during experiments in order to eliminate oxygen. A Pt plate was used as the CE, and Hg/$HgSO_4$ (Sat. K_2SO_4, Radiometer Analytical) and Hg/HgO (0.1 mol dm^{-3} KOH, Radiometer Analytical) were used as the RE in acid and base, respectively. The specific capacitances, C, were estimated by integrating the area under the cyclic voltammograms using equation [1]:

$$C = \int i dv / \square . m . \Delta V \qquad (1)$$

where i is the current, m is the mass of active material, v is the voltage scan rate and ΔV is the operating voltage window.

Results and Discussion

Fig. 1 shows the X-ray diffraction patterns of the synthesized TiN, WC_{1-x}, NbC and NbN. The peaks matched the standard peaks of model compounds. This confirmed that the bulk materials were phase pure.

Fig. 2 shows the current as function of applied voltage for all synthesized materials. To determine the stable operating windows, each material was cycled 50 times in 0.1 mol dm^{-3} H_2SO_4 and 0.1 mol dm^{-3} KOH at 50 mVs^{-1} within an initial potential window that was expanded from the open circuit potential (OCP) to more negative and positive potentials in increments of 100 mV until the material showed evidence of H_2 or O_2 evolution, or other reaction.

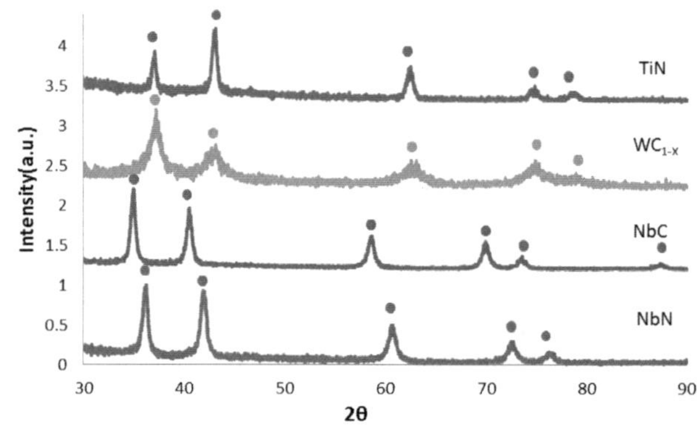

Fig. 1. X-ray diffraction patterns of the synthesized nitrides and carbides.

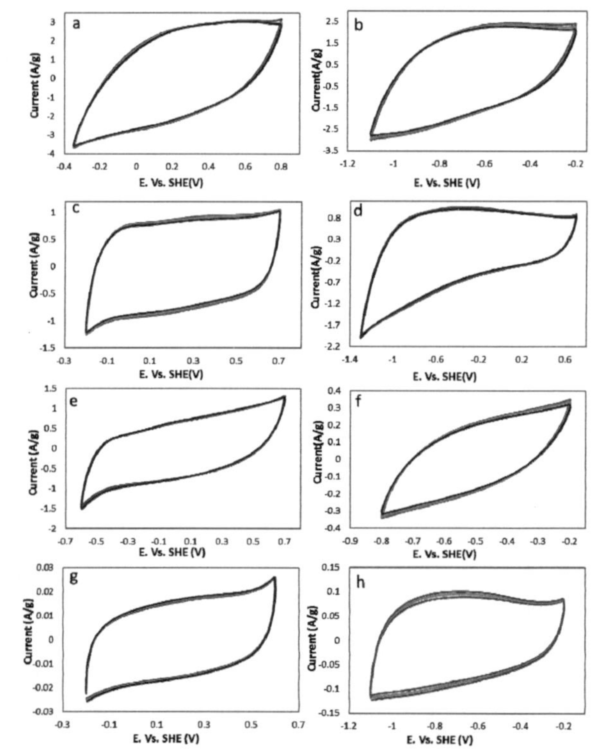

Fig. 2. Cyclic voltammetry of WC_{1-x} in 0.1M H_2SO_4 (a) and 0.1M KOH (b); TiN in 0.1M H_2SO_4 (c) and 0.1M KOH; NbN in 0.1M H_2SO_4 (e) and 0.1M KOH (f); NbC in 0.1M H_2SO_4 (g) and 0.1M KOH (h). All measurements were performed using a scan rate of 50 mV/s and at room temperature. The scans shown are the 10th, 50th and 100th.

^{3} H_2SO_4 and 0.1 mol dm^{-3} KOH at 50 mVs^{-1} within an initial potential window that was expanded from the open circuit potential (OCP) to more negative and positive potentials in increments of 100 mV until the material showed evidence of H_2 or O_2 evolution, or other reaction. Once a stable window was identified, the materials were scanned continuously for 100 cycles. As shown in Fig. 2, the cyclic voltammograms of multiple scans, 10, 50 and 100 overlapped, this indicates material stability.

Table 1 lists the electrochemical stability windows, surface areas and capacitances for all materials in aqueous media. All of these materials have wide operating voltage window except for NbN in base electrolyte. In particular, the voltage window of TiN and NbN in base and acid, respectively, have exceeded the thermodynamic voltage window of pure aqueous electrolyte. This indicates that these materials have high over potentials. WC_{1-x} had the highest surface area. The relatively low surface areas for TiN and NbC were due to the high final soak temperature (1000 □C and 900 □C, respectively) required during synthesis. The capacitance recorded at 50 mV/s for all materials are also listed in Table 1. With the exception of NbC, all of the materials had specific capacitances higher than the expected double layer capacitance. This suggests the presence of pseudocapacitive mechanisms in these materials.

To understand the mechanism for the pseudocapacitance, promising materials including WC_{1-X}, TiN and NbN were further studied by means of capacitance dependence on scan rate [20]. Fig. 3 shows the capacitance as function of scan rate in 0.1 mol dm^{-3} H_2SO_4 and 0.1 mol dm^{-3} KOH aqueous electrolytes from 2000 mV/s to 2mV/s. For all of the materials, the capacitances were logarithmically correlated with scan rate. This is expected for pseudocapacitive materials [21-22]. For materials exhibiting only double-layer charge storage, varying scan rate does not change significantly the capacitance. At higher scan rate (2000 mV/s), the capacitance is negligible. This is due to the cell resistance and transport limitations occurring at fast scan rate. Capacitances for TiN in both electrolytes increased rapidly as the scan rate was reduced, which indicates the superior electronic conductivity of TiN over WC_{1-x} and NbN. At low scan rate, the plots of capacitance reached a plateau. This region indicates the maximum capacitance of the materials. The increase of capacitance with scan rate indicates the ability of electrolytes ions to diffuse into pores. Electrolyte ions have sufficient time to travel the Debye length scale and fill out the pores structures of the materials. Table 2 summarizes the electrochemical performance of the promising electrodes in both acid and base media. As mentioned previously, the specific capacitance for all promising electrode materials is much higher than the expected double-layer capacitance. These values are somewhat close to the specific capacitances reported for VN and Mo_2N in the literature [14, 17, 19]. However, there were no prominent peaks observed in the voltammograms shown in Fig. 2. This indicates that the materials were charged and discharged at a pseudo-constant rate over the entire potential window.

Conclusion

Phase pure novel W, Ti and Nb carbides and nitrides were synthesized using a temperature program reaction method, and characterized electrochemically in aqueous KOH and H_2SO_4 electrolytes. All of the materials were electrochemically stable in both aqueous acid and base electrolytes. Capacitances for most of the materials exceeded the expected double layer charging and suggested a pseudocapacitive storage mechanism. TiN and WC_{1-x} were among the most promising electrode materials with specific capacitances close to those reported specific capacitances for VN and Mo_2N in aqueous media. Overall, the capacitances for all materials was found to vary logarithmically with scan rate and reach a maximum value at lower scan rate.

Table 1. Physical and electrochemical properties of synthesized carbides and nitrides in aqueous media.

Material	Surface Area (m^2g^{-1})	Voltage window (V)	Gravimetric capacitance (Fg^{-1})[a]	Areal capacitance (μFcm^{-2})[b]
WC_{1-X}	65	1.15(H2SO4)	43	66
		0.9(KOH)	143	220
TiN	18	0.9(H2SO4)	24	133
		1.6(KOH)	27	150
NbN	34	1.3(H2SO4)	11	32
		0.6(KOH)	7.6	22
NbC	16	0.8(H2SO4)	0.69	4.3
		1.1(KOH)	3.5	22

[a] Gravimetric capacitances estimated using equation 1 at 50mVs^{-1}, scan 100

[b] Specific areal capacitance determined from gravimetric capacitance

Table 2. Electrochemical performance of promising carbides and nitrides in aqueous media.

Material	Gravimetric capacitance(Fg^{-1})[a]	Areal capacitance(μFcm^{-2})[b]
WC_{1-X}	124	191
	229	352
TiN	39	217
	41	228
NbN	39	115

[a] Gravimetric capacitances estimated using equation 1 at $2mVs^{-1}$, scan 5

[b] Specific areal capacitance determined from gravimetric capacitance

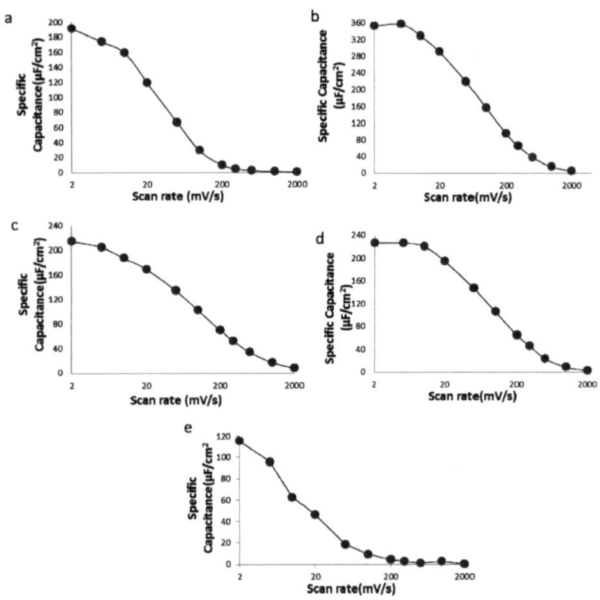

Fig. 3. Plot of specific capacitance vs. scan rate for WC_{1-x} in (a) 0.1M H_2SO_4 (b) 0.1M KOH; TiN in (c) 0.1M H_2SO_4 (d) 0.1M KOH; NbN in (e) 0.1M H_2SO_4.

Acknowledgments

The authors acknowledge financial support from the Automotive Research Center, Army Tank Command and Army Research Office (W911NF-11-1-0465).

References

1. Pech, D., Brunet, M., Durou, H., Huang, P., Mochalin, V., Gogotsi, Y., Taberna, P. L., Simon, P., Nature Nanotechnology, 5, 651-654, 2010.
2. Conway, B. E; Electrochemical Supercapacitors; Kluwer Academic/ Plenum Publishers, 1999.
3. Linsen Zhang et al.; International Journal of Hydrogen Energy 34, 4889-5899, 2009.
4. Simon, Patrice; Gogotsi, Yury; Nature Materials 7, 845, 2008.
5. P. Simon, A. Burke, the Electrochemical Society: Interface Spring, p. 38, 2008.
6. Burke, Int. J. Energy Res. 34, 133, 2010.
7. M. Mastragostino, C. Arbizzani, F. Soavi, Solid State Ionics 148, 493, 2002.
8. Rudge, J. Davey, I. Raistrick, S. Gottesfeld, J. Power Sources 47, 89, 1994.
9. C.-C. Hu, K.-H. Chang, M.-C. Lin, Y.-T. Wu, Nano Lett. 6 (12) ,2690, 2006.
10. C.-C. Hu, T.-W. Tsou, Electrochem. Commun. 4, 105, 2002.
11. T. Brousse, M. Toupin, R. Dugas, L. Athouel, O. Crosnier, D. Belanger, J. Electrochem. Soc. 153 (12), A2171, 2006.
12. C. Xu, F. Kang, B. Li, H. Du, J. Mater. Res. 25 (8), 1421, 2010.
13. M. Toupin, T. Brousse, D. Bélanger, Chem. Mater. 16 (16) 3184, 2004.
14. L. Volpe, M.J. Boudart, Solid State Chem. 59, 332, 1985.
15. Levy, R. B., Boudart M., Science, 181, 547, 1973.
16. Cladridge, J. B., York, A. P. E., Brungs, A. J., Green Malcolm, L. H., Chem. Mater., 12, 132, 2000.
17. Wixom, M.R., Tarnowski, D. J., Parker, J. M., Lee, J.Q., Chen, P. L., Song, I., L. Thompson. T., Mat. Res. Soc. Symp. Proc, 496, 643,1998.
18. Choi, D. W., Blomgren, G. E., Kumta, P. N., Adv. Mater., 18, 1178, 2006.
19. P. Pande, P. Rasmussen, L. Thompson, J Power sources, 207, 212-215, 2012.
20. W. Sugimoto, T. Kizaki, K. Yokoshima, Y. Murakami, Y. Takasu, Electrochemica Acta, 49, 313-320, 2004.
21. J. Chang, C. Huang, W. Tsai, M. Deng, I. Sun, P. Chen, Electrochimica Acta, 53, 4457-4453, 2008.
22. S. Pang, B. Wee, S. Chin, International Journal of Electrochemistry, 10, 4061, 2011.

Investigation of Defects Generated in Vertically Oriented Graphene-based Electrochemical Double-layer Capacitors

Ronald A. Quinlan[1], Minzhen Cai[2], Ronald A. Outlaw[2], Sue M. Butler[3], John R. Miller[3], and Azzam N. Mansour[1]

[1]Naval Surface Warfare Center, Carderock
Materials and Power Systems Branch
9500 MacArthur Blvd., Bldg. 60, Code 616, West Bethesda, MD 20817-5700
Office: 301-227-0446 | Fax: 301-227-5480 | E-mail: ronald.quinlan@navy.mil

[2]The College of William and Mary
Department of Applied Science
325 McGlothlin-Street Hall, 251 Jamestown Rd., Williamsburg, VA 23185

[3]JME Capacitor, Incorporated and Great Lakes Energy Institute, Case Western Reserve
Cleveland, OH 44106

Abstract: *Energy and energy storage have recently become a primary focus for civilian and defense communities. Electrochemical capacitors do not require the bulky dielectric layers of conventional capacitors and make use of high surface area electrode materials to achieve increased energy densities compared to conventional capacitors and higher rates than batteries. Due to their availability, ease of processing, tunable properties and environmental friendliness, carbon materials have become an area of intense interest for use in electrochemical capacitors. Early carbon-based electrochemical double-layer capacitors (EDLCs) have performed poorly at filtering voltage ripple, possessing RC time constants around 1 s, which is too long for 120 Hz filtering (8.3 ms period). Initial investigations indicate that porosity, including size and distribution of the pores, is the apparent limitation. Recently, vertically oriented graphene nanosheets (VOGN) were shown to perform very well as a result of their open morphology, which allows efficient ingress and egress of the electrolyte, as well as providing large, external surface areas for electrolyte contact and charge separation. Furthermore, it was shown that by increasing the sheet height, the capacitance could be increased as well. Though there was a linear correlation between surface area and capacitance, the slope of the response was one half, which suggests that another mechanism could be contributing to the observed performance.*

The effect of intentionally generated defects has on the capacitance and overall performance of vertically oriented graphene based EDLCs will be presented. Our results suggest an optimized defect structure for the VOGN and that the defect structure may be responsible for the increased capacitance of the material. These results could significantly impact further development of the material for increased capacitance and other concerns for EDLCs, such as cycle life and self-discharge.

Keywords: graphene; electrochemical double-layer capacitor; defect; NEXAFS

Introduction

As the demands for safe, efficient and reliable energy increase, energy storage technologies have been pushed to the forefront of civilian and defense communities. Electrochemical capacitors have drawn a lot of attention in recent years because of their high power densities, stability, and low environmental impact. Based on the mechanism of charge storage, electrochemical capacitors can be classified as electrochemical double-layer capacitors (EDLCs), which store energy at the electrode/electrolyte interface due to ion adsorption[1,2], or pseudocapacitors, which generate energy as a result of fast Faradaic reactions.[2] EDLC electrodes are typically comprised of activated carbon and surface area, pore structure, and electrical conductivity of carbon material are very important.[3] The two main functions of capacitors are to store charge and to filter voltage ripple. However, early carbon-based EDLCs have performed poorly at filtering, possessing RC time constants around 1 s, which is too long for 120 Hz filtering.[4] Initial investigations indicate that porosity, including size and distribution of the pores, is the limiting factor.[3] Carbon nanotubes were investigated for use as EDLC electrodes[5] and while these electrodes were not capable of filtering at 120 Hz due to ionic resistance (created as a result of the inherent porosity of the nanotube paper) and electronic resistance with the current collector, they showed that by using materials with external surface area rather than internal surface area the frequency response could be improved. Chemically modified graphene has also been investigated, but access to the surface area was restricted due to porous electrode behavior.[6] Previous efforts by Miller et al.[4] showed that vertically oriented graphene nanosheets (VOGN) based EDLCs were capable of filtering at 120 Hz with an impedance phase angle approaching -90°. The success of the material was attributed to the high

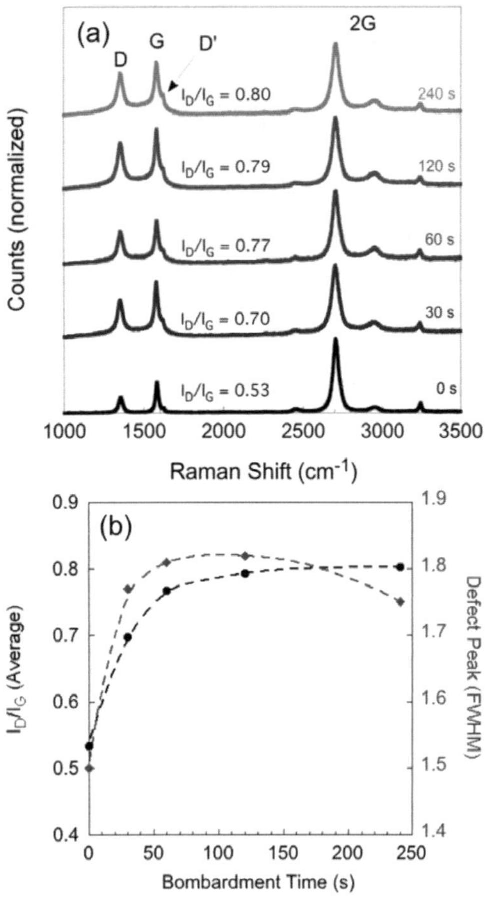

Figure 1: Raman spectra of VOGN after ion bombardment (a) showing retention of the graphene structure, but with a growing defect density and the ID/IG ratio plotted versus bombardment time (black circles), which shows a leveling off of the I_D/I_G ratio (b, left axis). The full-width-half-maximum of the defect peak of the C 1s photoemission region is plotted (b, right axis) (red diamonds) to emphasize the correlation of the increasing FWHM with bombardment time.

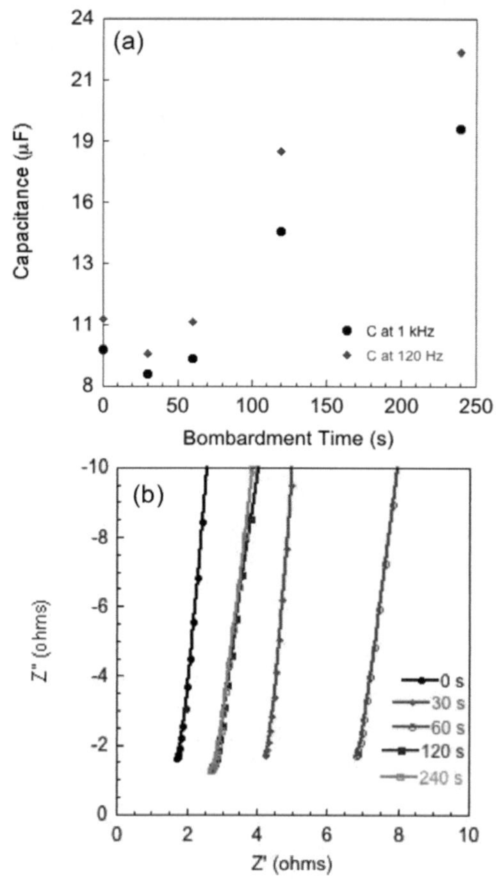

Figure 2: Capacitance values from the series-RC circuit of EIS results (a) at 1 kHz (black circles) and at 120 Hz (red diamonds). Complex plane plot of the EIS data (b) for ion bombarded samples in half-cell configurations.

conductivity of the graphene nanosheets, the large edge density, and the open morphology of the material, which allows for efficient egress and ingress of the electrolyte with easy access to the edge planes. Cai et al. [7] recently showed that grounding the substrate during the growth process provides better crystallinity, better verticality, and a higher density of sheets. They were also able to show a linear response for the decrease in defect density as measured by Raman spectroscopy and an increase in specific capacitance. While the increase in specific capacitance was proportional to the increase in surface area, the slope was only one half, indicating an additional mechanism besides surface area having an effect on the double-layer charge storage. In an effort to better understand the mechanism, the effects of intentionally created defects in the vertical graphene sheets via Ar^+ ion bombardment were correlated to device performance and the material characterized using X-ray photoelectron spectroscopy (XPS) and near-edge X-ray absorption fine-structure (NEXAFS) spectroscopy.[8]

Experimental

Growth: Vertically oriented graphene nanosheets (VOGN) were grown on p-type Si substrates by radio frequency (RF) plasma-enhanced chemical vapor deposition (PECVD).[9,10] Briefly, the Si substrates were plasma etched in 40% Ar/60% H_2 plasma, heated to 720 °C in a 60 mTorr hydrogen atmosphere and then grown with a mixture of methane and hydrogen (40/60) in a 100 mTorr atmosphere. Growth time was approximately 20 min in a 1000 W plasma.

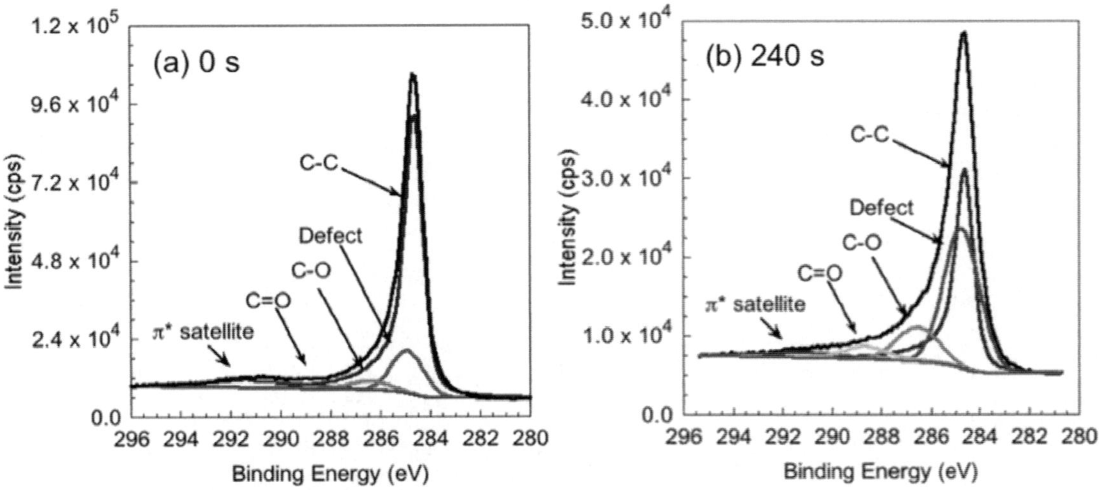

Figure 3: The C 1s photoemission region of the pristine vertically oriented graphene nanosheets (a) and the 240 s ion bombarded vertically oriented graphene nanosheets (b).

Characterization: Scanning electron microscopy (SEM) was performed using a Hitachi S-4700. Raman measurements were taken using a Renishaw in Via spectrometer at 514 nm. Test cells were fabricated in beakers using 38 wt% sulfuric acid electrolyte. XPS measurements were made using a Physical Electronics 5400 (Mg Kα X-rays, 1253.6 eV), equipped with a standard Ar^+ ion sputter gun and operated at ~1 x 10^{-9} Torr.

Results and Discussion

Raman spectroscopy shows increasing I_D/I_G ratios with increasing ion bombardment time (Figure 1a), which correlates well to the measured defect density increase as measured by XPS (Figure 1b).

Capacitance values increased from 10.8 μF (0 s) to 22.5 μF (240 s) at 120 Hz and from 9.6 to 19.2 μF at 1KHz (Figure 2a). The samples showed a capacity retention of 85% at high frequency and the complex plane plot revealed no porous electrode behavior (Figure 2b).

The C 1s and O 1s photoemission regions were analyzed before and after ion bombardment using HOPG (SPI Grade 2, cleaved in atmosphere) to determine a baseline. The C 1s spectra were deconvoluted to include the C-C (sp^2), C-C (defect), C-O, C=O, and π* satellite (Figure 3a,b). The O 1s spectra were deconvoluted into two subpeaks, a high binding energy subpeak associated with O*C(=O) and a lower binding energy subpeak associated with OC(=O*), O=C, or O-C (Figure 3c,d). The area of the defect peak (in the C 1s spectra) increased sharply between 0 and 30s and followed the trend observed in the Raman spectra (Figure 1b). Though the trend observed in the O 1s spectra did not appear to agree with assignments in the C 1s region, it has been previously shown that the oxygen energies can vary greatly depending on the aromaticity of the carbon structure.[11]

The C K-edge NEXAFS (Figure 4) of the bombarded samples reveals a splitting of the π* resonance at 285.5 eV. As the bombardment time increases, the resonance broadens into two, possibly three, distinct subpeaks. The shape of the resonance has been related to core-hole screening [12,13] and also distortion of the sp^2 hybridization.[14] The appearance of these peaks suggest that the density of states above the Fermi energy has been altered, creating mid-gap states and moving the Fermi energy away from the Dirac zone. A more complete deconvolution of the resonance is needed to determine if it is a shift in unoccupied states or occupied states.

Summary

VOGN with increased defect density showed an increase in capacitive behavior compared to the as-deposited materials. Characterization by XPS with subpeak deconvolution showed an increase in the FWHM of the "defect peak" for carbon materials that corresponds to the trend observed with Raman spectroscopy. The oxygen signal increased with ion bombardment time suggesting decoration of the created defects with oxygen functional groups. The observed capacitance trend was similar to the trends observed via Raman and XPS, but with a slight decrease observed for the initial defect creation period, which suggest an optimized defect structure is generated after 30 s of bombardment, but before 240 s. Characterization by NEXAFS spectroscopy showed splitting of the graphitic 1s → $\pi^*_{C=C}$ resonance into potentially three peaks, which may indicate small morphological changes in the graphene plane and increased charge carriers at the surface of the material.

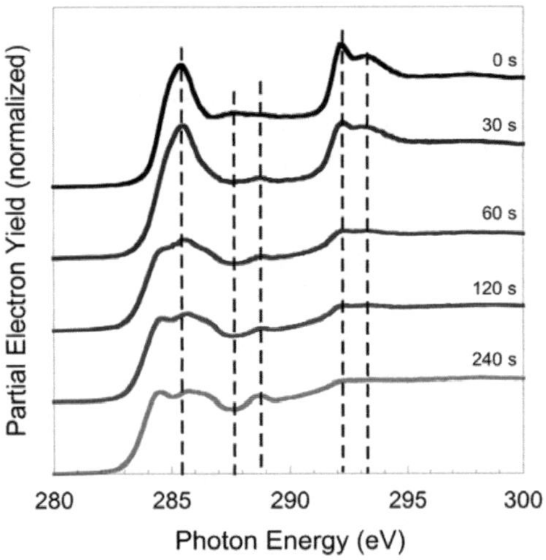

Figure 4: Stacked C K-edge NEXAFS of pristine (black), 30 s (blue), 60 s (green), 120 s (red), and 240 s (orange) bombarded samples.

References

[1] E. Frackowiak and F. Beguin, Carbon **39**, 937 (2001).

[2] L.L. Zhang, R. Zhou, and X.S. Zhao, Journal of Materials Chemistry **20**, 5983 (2010).

[3] E. Frackowiak, Phys Chem Chem Phys **9**, 1774 (2007).

[4] J.R. Miller, R.A. Outlaw, and B.C. Holloway, Science **329**, 1637 (2010).

[5] C. Niu, E.K. Sichel, R. Hoch, D. Moy, and H. Tennent, Appl. Phys. Lett. **70**, 1480 (1997).

[6] M.D. Stoller, S. Park, Y. Zhu, J. An, and R.S. Ruoff, Nano Lett. **8**, 3498 (2008).

[7] M. Cai, R.A. Outlaw, S.M. Butler, and J.R. Miller, Carbon **50**, 5481 (2012).

[8] R.A. Quinlan, M. Cai, R.A. Outlaw, S.M. Butler, J.R. Miller, and A.N. Mansour, Carbon (2013).

[9] J.J. Wang, M.Y. Zhu, R.A. Outlaw, X. Zhao, D.M. Manos, B.C. Holloway, and V.P. Mammana, Appl. Phys. Lett. **85**, 1265 (2004).

[10] J. Wang, M. Zhu, R.A. Outlaw, X. Zhao, D.M. Manos, and B.C. Holloway, Carbon **42**, 2867 (2004).

[11] D. Briggs and G. Beamson, Analytical Chemistry **65**, 1517 (1993).

[12] P.A. Bruhwiler, A.J. Maxwell, C. Puglia, A. Nilsson, S. andersson, and N. Martensson, Physical Review Letters **74**, 614 (1995).

[13] O. Wessely, M. Katsnelson, and O. Eriksson, Physical Review Letters **94**, 167401 (2005).

[14] C. Lenardi, P. Piseri, V. Briois, C.E. Bottani, A.L. Bassi, and P. Milani, Journal of Applied Physics **85**, 7159 (1999).

Manufacturing and Temperature Effects on Heat Pellet Ignition Sensitivity

Emilee L. Reinholz and Daniel E. Wesolowski
Power Sources Technology Group
Sandia National Laboratories
Albuquerque, NM, USA, 87185-0614
Contact Author Email: elreinh@sandia.gov

Abstract: *Reliable ignition of $Fe/KClO_4$ heat pellets is essential for thermal battery performance. Pellet density and exposure to humidity strongly affect heat pellet ignition sensitivity, but other factors may affect performance. Experiments were performed using a 20-Watt 810 nm (IR) solid-state laser in a pulse mode. Pulse width at peak power was varied to adjust energy input. Variables tested include age, surface finish, $Fe/KClO_4$ composition, manufacturer, temperature, and TNT thin film deposition. A 25% increase in ignition energy was observed for a reduction in test temperature from 25°C to -55°C. TNT deposition exacerbated the energy increase at cold temperature but had no effect at room temperature. Significant ignition sensitivity differences were also observed by heat powder manufacturer and pellet pressing technique. The ignition energy was independent of calorific output or burn rate.*

Keywords: ignition sensitivity; heat pellet; thermal batteries; $Fe/KClO_4$; iron/potassium perchlorate.

Introduction

Heat pellets provide the heat source essential for thermal battery activation and performance. Without consistent and predictable heat pellet ignition, thermal battery performance is unreliable. Thus, characterization of heat pellet ignition sensitivity (the energy required to ignite a heat pellet [1]) is critical for the design and development of thermal batteries.

Previous authors have investigated the effects of manufacturing and environmental parameters upon $Fe/KClO_4$ heat pellet burn rate and ignition sensitivity. Increased temperature and decreased particle size increase the burn rate [2]. The burn rate also increases with pellet density, but at a certain point the density becomes so high that combustion is self-quenched and ignition is prevented [2,3]. Rittenhouse shows a significant increase in energy for ignition when heat pellets are exposed to greater than 33% relative humidity for two days, or 42% for 16 hours (at 25°C). Short periods of exposure to higher relative humidity affect pellets more negatively than months of exposure to lower humidity levels [4]. Pellet thickness was not shown to affect burn rate [2]. With respect to ignition sensitivity, exposure to humidity [4], greater pellet density, increased iron particle size, and higher ratios of $Fe/KClO_4$ require increased heat pellet ignition energy [5].

Other important factors that may prevent reliable ignition have not yet been investigated. Laser ignition sensitivity tests were used in this study to measure the energy threshold required for heat pellet ignition. Variables included age, temperature, surface finish, pellet manufacturer, $Fe/KClO_4$ composition, and presence of a TNT thin film.

Experimental Procedures

Table 1 indicates the experimental variables in these tests. Heat pellets consisting of $Fe/KClO_4$ were pressed to a

Table 1. Heat pellet experimental test conditions. Highlighted cells within each column indicate tests to compare.

Type	Powder Year	$Fe/KClO_4$ Composition	Surface Finish	Temperature (°C)	Vendor	TNT film
A	1972	88/12	pristine	25	A	N
B	1979	86/14	pristine	25	A	N
C	1984	88/12	pristine	25	A	N
D	1991	86/14	pristine	25	A	N
E1, E2	1999	88/12	pristine	25	A	N
F	2007	88/12	pristine	25	A	N
G1, G2	1999	88/12	pristine	-55	A	N
H	1999	88/12	pristine	75	A	N
I	1999	88/12	pristine	25	A	Y
J	1999	88/12	pristine	-55	A	Y
K	Unknown	88/12	pristine	25	B	N
L	Unknown	88/12	carbon paint	25	B	N

constant density of 3.35 g/cc. Heat powder was supplied by two commercial vendors (A and B) and manufactured over a span of nearly four decades. All pellet types were manually pressed except for type F, which were pressed on automated systems. $Fe/KClO_4$ ratios in the heat powders included 86/14 and 88/12.

Pellet types E, G, H, K, and J were pressed into pellets from the same powder, but at different times. Types E1, G1, and H were pressed into pellets in 2011. Types E2, G2, I, and J were pressed in 2013. Types E1 and E2 served as the 88/12 reference materials.

Reference 88/12 material was used to determine if the emissivity of the heat pellets has a significant impact on ignition sensitivity. Reference heat pellets were painted with carbon spray and tested for surface finish comparison.

Thin TNT films of 14-20 μm thickness were deposited onto one side of pellet types I and J using an evaporation system. IR measurements confirmed that no TNT was present on the backside of these pellets despite the high porosity of heat pellets.

All heat pellets were stored in a dry room, a laboratory with a very low, well-controlled humidity level. Pellets were moved individually from the dry room prior to testing to minimize exposure to ambient humidity levels.

Ignition sensitivity tests were performed with a 20-Watt 810 nm (IR) solid-state laser in pulse mode. The laser was built by Quantic Industries, Inc. Pulse width at peak power was varied to adjust energy output, where pulses varied from 100 to 700 ms. The pulse amplitude range was maintained at 0 to 5 V. The laser spot size was 2 to 3 mm. The laser was calibrated before, after, and periodically between tests using an Ophir calorimeter. The glass window of the microscope stage cover was integrated during calibration to maintain the same optical path used during testing. Linear calibration curves were calculated to determine the relationship between pulse width and output energy in Joules.

Samples were placed in an airtight, temperature-controlled microscope stage with fine X and Y plane control. The X and Y knobs adjusted the sample position after each pulse to ensure adequate spacing between each pulse. No spot was hit more than once. A liquid nitrogen cooled microscope stage was used to control the heat pellet temperature. Samples were maintained within 1°C of either 25°C, -55°C, or 75°C during testing. Pellets tested at -55°C were placed in the sample stage at room temperature, and the stage was cooled only after samples were sealed inside to protect them from water condensation. Following ignition of each pellet, the stage was returned to room temperature and opened for sample removal. The glass window of the sample stage was cleaned between ignitions.

A modified Bruceton method was applied to determine the correct pulse width for each pulse. The first pulse's energy for each pellet type was very low (i.e. 200 ms pulse width) and increased with a uniform 25 ms step size until ignition occurred. The first pulse of subsequent pellets of the same type was three steps lower than the previous ignition (75 ms lower). Again, each pulse thereafter increased with a uniform 25 ms step size until ignition occurred. The result of each pulse was recorded as either a 0 (no ignition) or a 1 (ignition). A minimum of ten pellets of each type were tested. These results and the calibration data were then analyzed to determine the ignition sensitivity of each pellet type.

Results and Discussion

Periodic sensitivity tests of type E pellets established the baseline ignition sensitivity. The mean ignition energy for E1 pellets was 5.1±0.9 J, averaged over five tests with a ±95% confidence interval (Figure 1). Anomalous tests on 7/30/13 indicated lower ignition energy, possibly due to temporary use of a different pulse generator. With those results excluded, the mean ignition energy was 5.4±0.6 J. The mean ignition energy for E2 pellets was similar, 5.7±0.6 J, averaged over 3 tests. Since both averages are within one standard deviation of each other, the ignition sensitivity baseline data compares well to pellets pressed from the same powder at different times. It also supports consistent laser output energy over time. However, previous tests performed on similar equipment show an ignition sensitivity of 1 to 3 J. This is substantially lower than the energy levels reported here. The setup used here was from a previous system and was modified prior to testing for the addition of temperature control. It is believed that the laser system was slightly defocused during modification. Though the consistent post-modification results indicate quantitative comparisons are possible, the absolute values are not directly comparable to other testing techniques, such as static sensitivity testing.

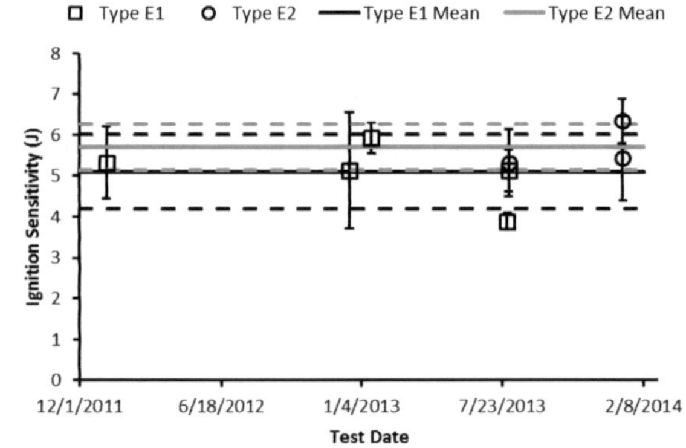

Figure 1. Baseline ignition sensitivity of type E pellets.

Pellets were tested to ensure the laser energy was effectively absorbed. Pellets with carbon paint ignited at 7.5±1.0 J, compared to 7.1±1.4 J for unpainted, pristine pellets (from a different lot than the baseline pellets). This indicates that laser energy absorption is excellent in the untreated pellets and justifies the use of plain pellets in the laser system.

Supplier variability was tested by comparing results from pellet types E1 and K. Comparison demonstrates a substantial difference in ignition sensitivity for pellets, which were pressed by two different vendors, but in the same manner. Pellets from Vendor B required a mean 7.1±1.4 J, whereas the reference E1 pellets from Vendor A required a mean 5.1±0.9 J, nearly 40% less energy. Though the specific differences between these powders and pellets have not yet been investigated, Guidotti et al., reported that manufacturing differences such as iron particle size can strongly affect ignition sensitivity [5].

The effect of temperature upon mean ignition sensitivity revealed a 25% increase for pellets tested at -55°C (7.5±0.2 J) when compared to tests conducted at 25°C (5.9±0.3 J) and 75°C (5.7±0.5 J). Tests at 75°C required slightly less energy than tests at 25°C, but this difference was not statistically significant, as seen in Figure 2. This indicates that at lower temperatures, ignition sensitivity may depend on the competition between self-quenching, caused by cooling, and flame propagation, similar to the observation made by both Reed et al., and McCarthy et al. [2,3].

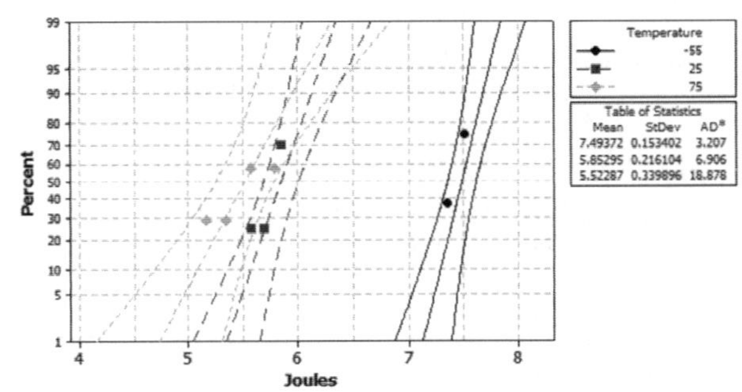

Figure 2. Probability plot for energy threshold showing the effect of temperature on ignition sensitivity.

TNT may have been present on heat pellets exposed to certain primer compositions for long periods of time [6]. TNT deposition on heat pellets required a slight increase in ignition energy compared to identical control pellets for tests conducted at 25°C, for which the ignition sensitivity was measured to be 6.3±2.0 J versus 5.6±1.8 J, respectively. At -55°C, however, the difference was significant. Control pellets ignited at 8.3±1.5 J, but because only one of ten heat pellets with TNT ignited, no mean ignition sensitivity could be established for comparison. Each pellet that failed to ignite was tested at the maximum pulse width three times in three different spots. Because this energy output tested the limits of our laser, either the maximum energy output for the laser was just slightly below the ignition sensitivity of these pellets, or at cold temperatures, the effects of TNT deposition compete with heat pellet burn front propagation. The reasons for this outcome have yet to be established.

No observable trend occurred from differences in $Fe/KClO_4$ composition. 86/14 and 88/12 heat pellets were tested. This indicates $Fe/KClO_4$ composition and ignition sensitivity are not related, which is contrary to results reported by Guidotti et al. [5], although the correlation found by Guidotti was weak. A lack of correlation is expected because ignition is dependent upon local effects between iron and potassium perchlorate. This chemical reaction requires the same activation energy independent of the overall composition, and once activated, quenching is unlikely.

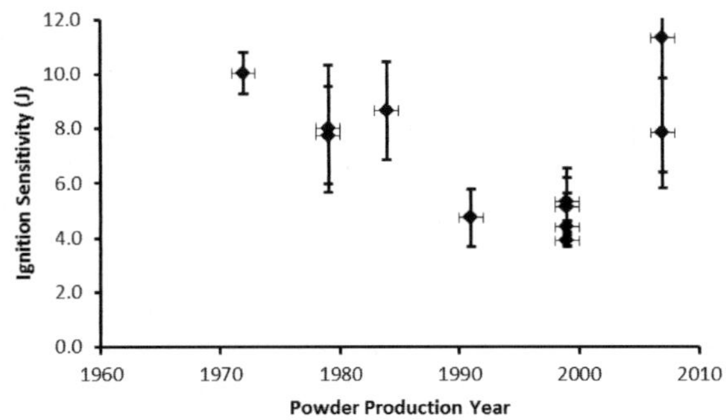

Figure 3. Aging effects upon ignition sensitivity.

Pellet types A through F were extracted from thermal batteries fabricated between 1972 and 2007. All pellets were fabricated from heat powder made by the same manufacturer. Figure 3 shows what appears to be a nearly linear trend between powder production year and ignition energy. This suggests a previously unsuspected aging trend in heat pellets. It is possible to speculate as to the source of such an aging trend, but more data is necessary to confirm this unexpected result.

The pellets from 2007 did not follow the apparent aging trend, however, as they required greater energy to ignite and also demonstrated greater variability. The 2007 pellets

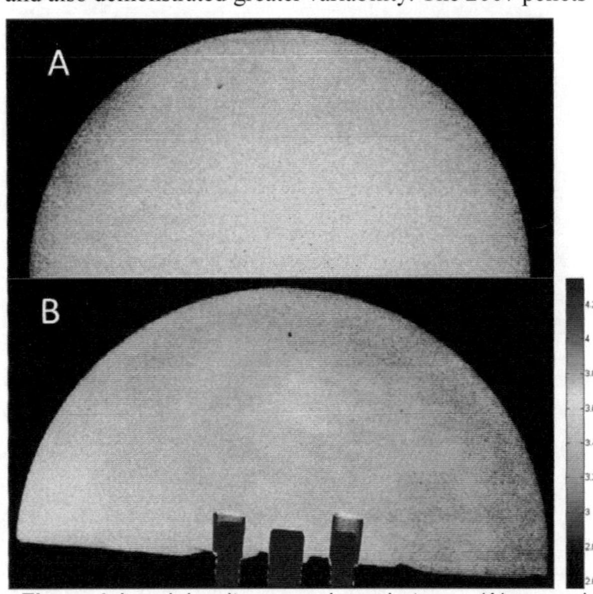

Figure 4. Local density comparisons between (A) manual and (B) automated pellet pressing processes.

do not dismiss the aging hypothesis because manufacturing effects may explain the difference. Automated presses were employed to create the 2007 pellets, while manual presses were used to form all the earlier pellets. The spot size of the laser system is less than 3 mm. Local density variation was measured using an X-ray system calibrated with a density standard. The results (Figure 4) show the local density varies from approximately 3.1 to 3.9 g/cc, even with a nominal pellet density. This is a significant density variation. Previous ignition sensitivity efforts suggest that the highest density areas may require two times more energy to ignite than the optimal density area [7].

The magnitude of density variation is larger in automated presses and the form is different. The automated presses show signs of powder clumping and tend to have higher density on one side than the other, as might be expected from a single sweeping action to smooth the powder in the die. Manually pressed pellets tend to be more homogenous, but with lower density around edges. This is consistent with loading in the center of the die and spreading to the edges.

Conclusions

Systematic testing of vendor, temperature, TNT deposition, age, $Fe/KClO_4$ composition, and surface finish, demonstrated parameters that can significantly affect heat pellet ignition sensitivity. Little or no observable effects resulted from changes to surface finish, composition, or coating with TNT at ambient temperature. Ignition sensitivity was substantially affected by cold temperature. This sensitivity was heightened with TNT coating. Manufacturing effects are also important for ignition sensitivity. Specifically, differences across powder vendors and pressing modes (manual vs. automated) were observed. Finally, the present work suggests a previously unidentified aging trend that will be explored in future work.

Acknowledgements

Many thanks to Ed Thomas for his assistance in our statistical analysis, and to Alex Tappan and Michael Marquez for conducting the TNT thin film deposition for these experiments.

Sandia National Laboratories is a multi-program laboratory managed and operated by Sandia Corporation, a wholly owned subsidiary of Lockheed Martin Corporation, for the U.S. Department of Energy's National Nuclear Security Administration under contract DE-AC04-94AL85000.

References

1. Thomas, E. V. Evaluating the Ignition Sensitivity of Thermal-Battery Heat Pellets. *Technometrics.* **1994**, *36*, 273-282.
2. Reed, J. W.; Walters, R. R.; Guidotti, R. A.; Jacobson, A. K. Burn-Rate Studies with Iron/Potassium Perchlorate Heat Pellets. Proceedings of the IEEE 35th International Power Sources Symposium, Cherry Hill, NJ, June 22-25, 1992; IEEE Publishing: 1992; 211-214.
3. McCarthy, D. K.; Leslie, W. B.; Dietzel, R. W. *Burn Front Velocity as a Function of Pellet Density in Iron/Potassium Perchlorate Heat Powders*; Report No. SAND83-1025; Sandia National Laboratories: Albuquerque, NM, May 1985; 1-20.
4. Rittenhouse, C. T. *Evaluation of Humidity Effects on Iron/Potassium Perchlorate Heat Pellets, Progress Report No. 1*; Report No. MTR-219; Unidynamics Phoenix, Inc.: Phoenix, AZ, Feb. 1981; 1-18.
5. Guidotti, R. A.; Odinek, J.; Reinhardt, F. W. Characterization of $Fe/KClO_4$ Heat Powders and Pellets. *J. Energ. Mater.* **2006**, *24*, 271-305.
6. Dellinger, J. G.; Loyola, V. M.; Alam, M. K. Sandia National Laboratories: Albuquerque, NM. Internal communication, 2010.
7. Evans, T. P. *Ignition Sensitivity Testing: A Preliminary Approach*; Report No. GEPP-TM-814; General Electric Company Neutron Devices Department: St. Petersburg, FL, June 1984; 1-22.

Copper Vanadates as High Voltage Cathodes for Thermal Batteries

Tomer Hillel[1] and Yair Ein-Eli[*1,2]
1. Department of Materials Science & Engineering; 2. The Nancy & Stephen Grand Technion Energy Program, Technion-Israel Institute of Technology, Haifa 32000, Israel
Ofer Raz[3]
3. Power Sources Department, Rafael Ltd., P.O.B 2250 Haifa 31021. Israel

Abstract: *Thermal batteries are primary batteries which operate at elevated temperatures. Novel cathode materials for thermal batteries are needed in order to improve the thermal stability, capacity, current density as well as cell voltage. In order to develop such cathode materials, a series of CuO-V_2O_5 based oxides were synthesized using a solid state reaction processes. The structure and morphology were determined and the electrochemical properties at room temperature and elevated temperatures (500^0C) were investigated. In this study, the effects of current densities and temperature on the electrochemical behavior are reported. It was found that at high temperature a 2.5V voltage plateau at a current load of 100 mA/cm^2 was achieved, while a voltage plateau of 2.2V was recorded with a higher current load of 310 mA/cm^2.*

Keywords: Thermal batteries; Cathodes; *CuO-V_2O_5 oxide*

Introduction

V_2O_5 is a promising cathode for batteries due to its high capacity, high discharge rates and low cost. In the last two decades vanadium oxides and metal vanadates have been tested as cathodes in thermal batteries application [1-9] Gibbard [1] stated that LiV_2O_5 is a promising cathode for replacing FeS_2 due to its thermal stability and low polarization at high current densities. Li investigated the discharge mechanism of vanadium oxides and metal vanadates synthesis and discharge characteristics [2, 3] followed by a description of V_2O_5 discharge mechanism [4]. The main drawback V_2O_5 exhibited was the low electrical conductivity of its discharge product, Li_3VO_4, disabling high current density discharge [4]. To overcome this problem, a combination of metallic copper as an electrical conductivity enhancer that is extracted during discharge from each LiV_2O_5 particle was presented by Ein-Eli [5]. This mechanism was previously presented for room temperature copper vanadets discharge by Tarascon at.al. [6]. Dai presented $Cu_3V_2O_8$ and $Cu_5V_2O_{10}$ cathodes materials and the evaluation of the first $Cu_3V_2O_8$ cathode incorporated in a thermal battery [7-9]. The results showed a high voltage and capacity compared to FeS_2. Also, Ein Eli at el studied CuV_2O_6, $Cu_2V_2O_7$ cathode [5]. The results showed a high voltage of 3.2 vs. Li with low capacity.

*Corresponding author's e-mail address: eineli@tx.technion.ac.il

Dual phase V_2O_5-CuV_2O_6 was not previously investigated at elevated temperatures. Material compositions in this dual phase V_2O_5 – CuV_2O_6 area is characterize by two phases, obeying the liver role. Poor oxygen atmosphere during V_2O_5:CuO synthesis results in oxygen deficiency, forming $Cu_xV_2O_5$ and V_2O_5. The V_2O_5 $Cu_xV_2O_5$ phase diagram at elevated temperature is characterized by 3 phases: α β' and ε in compositions of 0-0.02, 0.26-0.64, and 0.85-1 respectively, as shown in Figure 1.

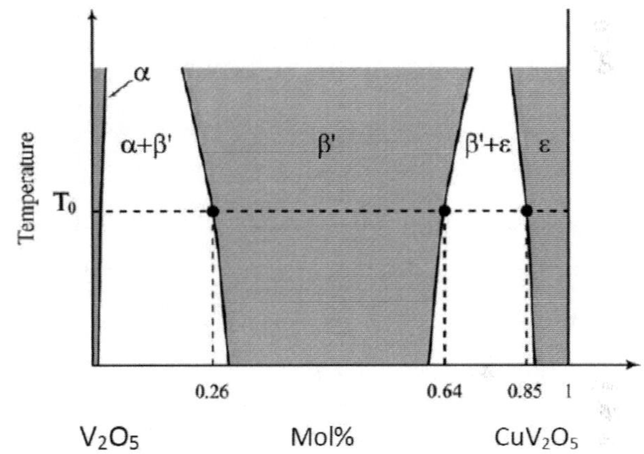

Figure 1: Schematic phase diagram V_2O_5-CuV_2O_5 (T_0=600°C) [10].

In this work we investigated and characterized the structure and electrochemical properties of multiple phases in the V_2O_5 to CuV_2O_5 Range.

Experimental

Copper vanadates [$Cu_xV_2O_5$] host cathodes materials in several compositions (X= 0.2, 0.25. 0.33, 0.4, 0.5) were synthesized by a solid state reaction from CuO and V_2O_5 powders. The materials were mixed and grounded using a planetary ball mill, pressed into pellets and dried at 200°C for one hour. Synthesis of $Cu_xV_2O_5$ was conducted in a tube furnace under Ar atmosphere. The temperature was increased slowly at a constant rate of 1 °C/min to 620°C and was maintained for 72 hours. Afterwards, a slow cooling at a constant rate of 1 °C/min to room temperature was processed.

X-Ray diffraction analysis was conducted in order to examine the cathode phases using a conventional X-ray powder diffractometer (Philips X'Pert Diffractometer, Eindhoven, The Netherlands) with a CuKα tube, operated at 40 mA and 40 kV. High resolution scanning electron microscopy (HRSEM, LEO 982 Gemini microscope equipped with a field emission gun (FEG–SEM)) was used to study the morphology of the cathode powder subsequent to different processing.

Elevated temperatures discharge measurements were performed at 525°C using a custom made system. The cell was assembled from a pelletized cathode material 1-1.5 mm in thickness, LAN (80 weight % Fe) anode and a separator composed of eutectic KCl-LiCl mixed with MgO. To prevent spillage, all 3 components comprising anode, separator and cathode were circled by a ceramic ring and mechanically isolated (top and bottom) with Mica. The measurements were conducted under a dry air atmosphere (2-3% humidity). The cell was introduced to a pressurized and preheated oven and heated to the test temperature. For stabilization, the cell was maintained at its OCP for a short duration of 30 sec and only then a current load was applied.

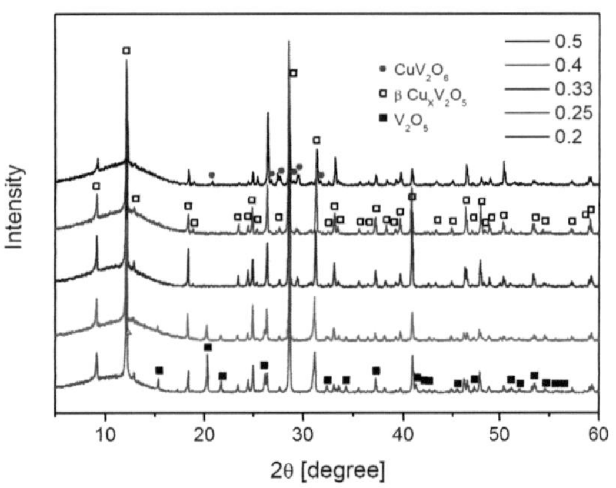

Figure 2: XRD Pattern of synthesized compositions of $Cu_xV_2O_5$ having x= 0.2, 0.25. 0.33, 0.4 and 0.5.

Results and Discussion

Cathode Material Characterization

The synthesized **compositions $Cu_xV_2O_5$ (X= 0.2, 0.25. 0.33, 0.4, 0.5)** materials were studied by powder x-ray diffraction (Figure 2). Materials were identified as a dual phase composed of $Cu_xV_2O_5$ and V_2O_5 or CuV_2O_6. Phase ratio in each composition was calculated from the X ray diffraction by "match" program and presented in Table 1along with the theoretical composition. A good correlation between the molar fractions of CuO in the synthesis with the calculated $Cu_xV_2O_5$ molar fraction was achieved. A minor contamination of a second phase is present and can be described as unfinished oxygen deficiency process in spite of the long synthesis time.

The morphologies of the materials were evaluated by SEM and are presented in Figure 3. The morphology of $Cu_xV_2O_5$ in compositions of x= 0.2, 0.25, 0.33, 0.4 and 0.5 is similar and contains mainly rectangular rods. It is clearly shown in Figure 3 a-c that only a single phase composition is formed. Dual phase morphology composed of rods $Cu_xV_2O_5$, and rounded V_2O_5 head particles, [11] are shown in Figure 3 d & e.

CuO fraction	Phase	Analysis %	Theoretical %	Phase	Analysis %	Theoretical %
0.5	$Cu_{0.47}V_2O_5$	92.9	100	CuV_2O_6	7.1	0
0.4	$Cu_{0.4}V_2O_5$	97.6	100	CuV_2O_6	2.4	0
0.33	$Cu_{0.34}V_2O_5$	95.7	100	CuV_2O_6	4.3	0
0.25	$Cu_{0.261}V_2O_5$	88.8	96	V_2O_5	11.2	4
0.2	$Cu_{0.261}V_2O_5$	74.4	77	V_2O_5	25.6	23

Table 1: XRD analyzed data including both phase formula and phase fraction, as calculated by match program and theoretical fraction, as expected by a phase diagram.

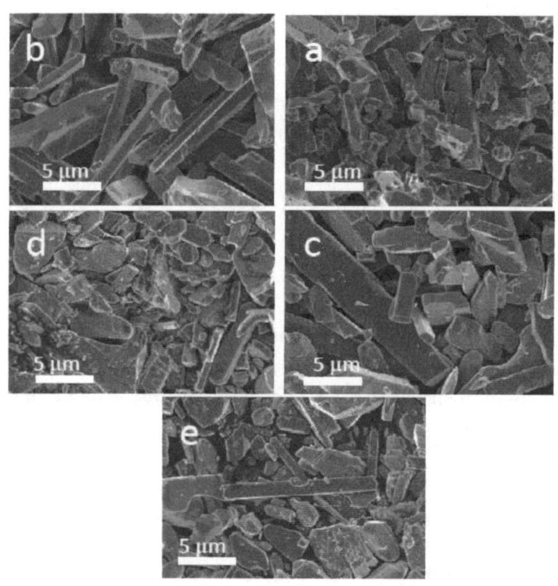

Figure 3: SEM (SE) photograph of $Cu_xV_2O_5$ particles having x=0.5 (a); 0.4 (b); 0.33 (c); 0.25 (d) and 0.2 (e).

Discharge at elevated temperature

Discharge behavior can be divided into two distinctive sections as shown in Figure 4. In section I, gradual potential decrease with a few plateaus takes place from 3.1 down to 2.5V. $Cu_xV_2O_5$ is reduced to LiV_2O_5 and a metallic copper. The switch point is at ~ one Li per formula. Section II represents LiV_2O_5 discharge, having a long plateau from 2.5 V with a light slope to 2.15 V, with a rather large capacity, reaching up to ~ 600 mAh/g above the potential of 2.1V. This explains the similarity of discharge behavior of the different compounds. LiV_2O_5 discharge mechanism at room temperature is described in detailed by Galy [12].

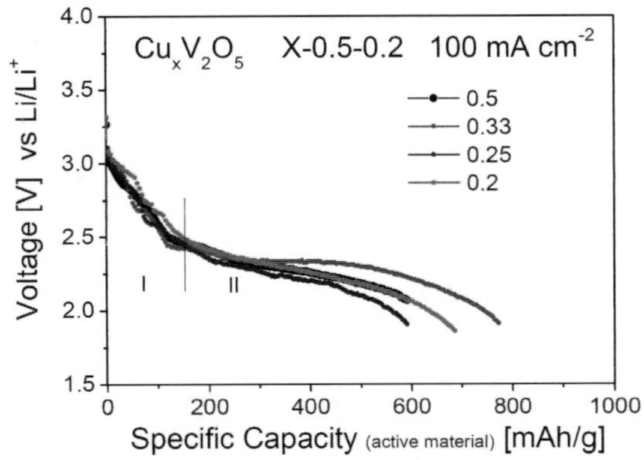

Figure 4: High temperature galvanostatic discharge curves of a $Cu_xV_2O_5$ having x=0.2-0.5 performed at a current density of 100 mA/cm^2. Conditions: Cathode limited, LiCl KCl electrolyte LAN anode.

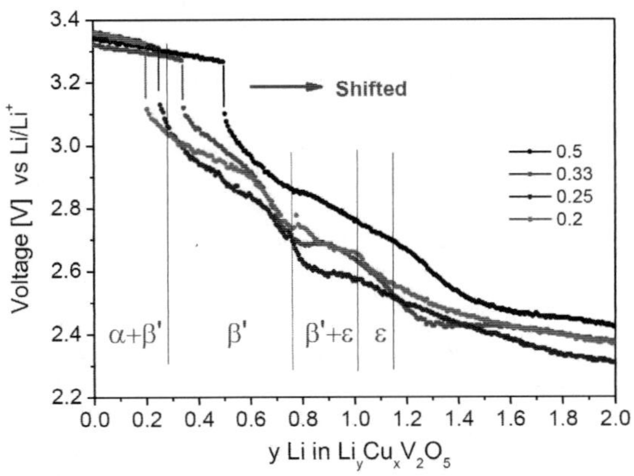

Figure 5: shifted high temperature galvanostatic discharge curves of section I. The shift is correlated to Cu molar fraction (x). Discharge conditions: current density of 100 mA/cm^2, cathode limited, LiCl-KCl electrolyte, LAN anode.

Discharge behavior of section I is in correlation with V_2O_5: CuV_2O_5 phase diagram. It can be divided into two stages, as described in Figures 5-6. The oxidation states of $Li_yCu_xV_2O_5$ when (y=0) is $Cu_x^{1+}\ V_{(x)}^{4+}\ V_{(2-x)}^{5+}\ O_5$ [13]. In the first stage, up to y=1-x V^{+5} is reduced to V^{+4} up to the point which V^{+4}/V^{+5} ratio is equal to one. This reduction process is similar to the mechanism studied at room temperature accompanied by a phase transformation α+β' → β' → β'+ε → ε [14]. The phase transformation is reflected in the galvanostatic discharge. In order to reveal this behavior, the discharge starting point was shifted to a higher Li molar content correlated to Cu molar fraction X, as seen in Figure 5.

Stage 2 (1-x<y<1) in $Li_yCu_xV_2O_5$ is characterized by Li insertion and copper extraction. In this process copper is reduced from Cu^{+1} to a metallic Cupper [Cu^0]. At the end of stage 2, LiV_2O_5 is formed, and a metallic Copper particles are spread in the cathode bulk material [14].

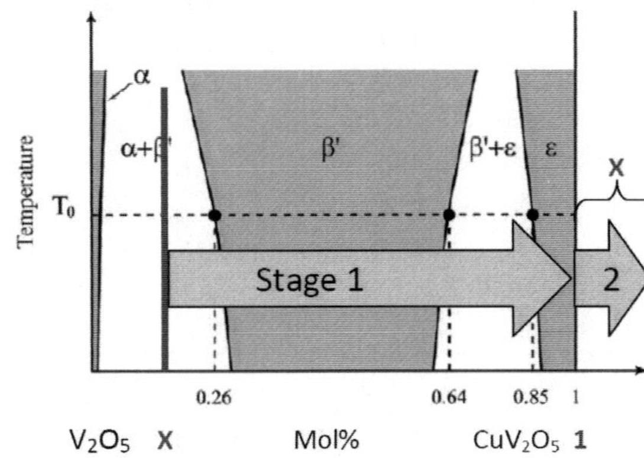

Figure 6: section I discharge mechanism of $CuxV_2O_5$.

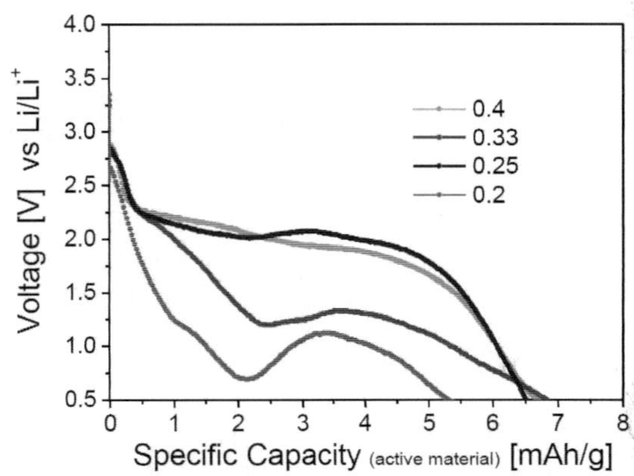

Figure 7: High temperature galvanostatic discharge curves of a $Cu_xV_2O_5$ having x=0.2-0.4 performed at a current density of 310 mA/cm^2. Cathode limited, LiCl KCl electrolyte, LAN anode.

Discharge experiments were also performed at high current density of 310 mA/cm^2. Two distinct behaviors of 0.2, 0.33 and 0.25, 0.4 x copper content were detected. The first two compositions of 0.2 and 0.33 suffer from decrease in cell potential at y~2. In this discharge stage, low electric conductivity reduction product Li_3VO_4 [4] is at its maximum content. The rise in cell voltage for y>2 is correlated to the decrease in Li_3VO_4 and increase in $V_nO_{n\pm1}$ products that have a higher electrical conductivity [4]. Discharge behavior of the 0.2 composition tracks the discharge mechanism published by Galy [12] and presented in Table 2.

The second behavior, especially in the 0.25 composition, seems to overcome this obstacle of low electronic conductivity and presents a steady discharge plateau with only traces of the low electric conductivity Li_3VO_4 product at y~2.

X in $Li_xV_2O_5$	phase %	Li Vanadate	V^X	phase %	oxide	V^X
1	100	LiV_2O_5	5+, 4+			
1.14	89	$LiVO_3$	5+	11	V_6O_{11}	4+, 3+
1.33	80	$LiVO_3$	5+	20	V_2O_3	3+
1.85	73	Li_3VO_4	5+	27	V_6O_{11}	4+, 3+
2.4	57	Li_3VO_4	5+	43	V_2O_3	3+
3	25	Li_3VO_4	5+	75	$LiVO_2$	3+
4	33	Li_2O	3+	67	$LiVO_2$	3+

Table 2: Phase content and vanadium valance as a function of Li intercalation into LiV_2O_5 [12]

Conclusions

$Cu_xV_2O_5$ is a promising cathode material for thermal batteries. Compositions containing x values between 0.2-0.5 produce high voltage and high capacity cathode material.

Copper addition to V_2O_5 in these compositions results in an increase of the electric conductivity.

Low current densities of 100 mA/cm^2 do not show the effects of Li_3VO_4 ohmic polarization. However, at high current density of 310 mA/cm^2 cell resistant increases significantly and ohmic polarization affects some compositions.

It is also shown that the discharge mechanism at elevated temperature is similar to the reported room temperature process. This mechanism is composed of two distinct sections, $Cu_xV_2O_5$ up to 1 Li and LiV_2O_5 from there.

1 Gibbard, H.F., *High temperature, high pulse power lithium batteries.* Journal of Power Sources, 1989. 26(1-2): p. 81-91.

2. Li, Z.Y., Huang, B. Y., Tang, C. F., Liu, Z. J. Qu, X. H., *Synthesis of β-$M_XV_2O_5$ (M=Li, Na, K) by sol-gel method and their cathodically discharging behavior at high temperature.* Gongneng Cailiao/Journal of Functional Materials, 2001. 32(2): p. 184-186.

3. Cao, D.M., Z.Y. Li, and K.C. Zhou, *Influence of doping Mo on $Li_{1+x}V_3O_8$ phase and cathodical discharge behaviors at elevated temperature.* Zhongnan Daxue Xuebao (Ziran Kexue Ban)/Journal of Central South University (Science and Technology), 2005. 36(5): p. 766-770.

4. Li, Z.Y., D.M. Cao, and K.C. Zhou, *Discharge mechanisms of vanadium-lithium oxide cathodes for thermal cell.* Zhongguo Youse Jinshu Xuebao/Chinese Journal of Nonferrous Metals, 2008. 18(1): p. 59-66.

5. Hillel, T. and Ein-Eli, Y. *Copper vanadate as promising high voltage cathodes for Li thermal batteries.* Journal of Power Sources, 2013. 229(0): p. 112-116.

6. Morcrette, M., Rozier, P., Dupont, L., Mugnier, E., Sannier, L., Galy, J., Tarascon, J. M., *A reversible copper extrusion-insertion electrode for rechargeable Li batteries.* Nat Mater, 2003. 2(11): p. 755-761.

7. Dai, J., R.M. LaFollette, and D. Reisner, *Thin Film $Cu_5V_2O_{10}$ Electrode for Thermal Batteries.* Meeting Abstracts, 2010. MA2010-02(6): p. 346.

8. Dai, J., Lai, M., LaFollette, R.M., Reisner, D., *Thin Film Copper Vanadium Oxide Electrodes for Thermal Batteries.* ECS Transactions, 2011. 33(27): p. 3-9.

9. Dai, J., M. Lai, and J. McKee, *Evaluation of a LiSi/$Cu_3V_2O_8$ Thermal Battery.* ECS Transactions, 2012. 41(11): p. 11-16.

10. Monchoux, J.P. and J. Galy, *Diffusion and phase transformations in spark plasma synthesized and sintered Cu-V_2O_5 couples.* Journal of Solid State Chemistry, 2008. 181(4): p. 693-699.

11. Glushenkov, A.M., et al., *A novel approach for real mass transformation from V_2O_5 particles to nanorods.* Crystal Growth and Design, 2008. 8(10): p. 3661-3665.

12. Rozier, P., J.M. Savariault, and J. Galy, *A new interpretation of the LixV2O5 electrochemical behaviour for 1 < x < 3.* Solid State Ionics, 1997. 98(3-4): p. 133-144.

13. Galy, J., Darriet, J., Casalot, A., Goodenough, J. B., *Structure of the MxV_2O_5-β and $M_xV_2-yTyO_5$-β phases.* Journal of Solid State Chemistry, 1970. 1(3–4): p. 339-348.

14. García-Alvarado, F. and J.M. Tarascon, *New vanadium bronzes MyV_2O_5 (M=Cu or Ag; 0<y<0.85): Structure and lithium intercalation.* Solid State Ionics, 1993. 63-65(C): p. 401-406.

Enhanced Nanostructuring of Iron Disulfide for Thermal Battery Cathode Materials

Giuseppe L. Di Benedetto
Ryan R. Carpenter
Advanced Materials Technology Branch
U.S. Army Armament Research, Development and Engineering Center
Picatinny Arsenal, NJ, USA, 07806
E-mail: giuseppe.l.dibenedetto.civ@mail.mil

David B. Swanson
Brian D. Wightman
EnerSys Advanced Systems, Inc.
104 Rock Road, Horsham, PA, USA, 19044
E-mail: david.swanson@enersys.com

Abstract: *For the U.S. Army, the power requirements for guided precision munitions are increasing. Thermal batteries will need to supply a significantly higher level of power to the electronics, fuze, and actuation components of future munitions, while at the same time occupying less volume. The use of Nanomaterials offers the potential to produce batteries with performance improvements, such as higher voltages and increased current densities. Thermal batteries manufactured today can benefit from performance improvements. Understanding the potential and capabilities of nanoscale materials in thermal batteries is critical in pushing the state-of-the art. In this study, nanoscale iron disulfide (FeS_2) was synthesized using a fully scalable method, and characterized utilizing SEM, XRD, XRF, BET, EDS, and other techniques. Current FeS_2 powder used in thermal battery cathodes has nominal particle size of 44 microns in diameter. By reducing this size to the nanoscale, performance improvements are expected. However, the challenge in synthesizing nanoscale FeS_2 is maintaining the proper stoichiometric ratio for optimal performance. This study successfully used high energy milling to produce kilogram quantities of acceptable FeS_2 powder for cathode use in thermal batteries, and can be applied to other potential nanoscale cathode material candidates.*

Keywords: nanomaterials; thermal battery; molten salt battery; cathode; nanoscale; iron disulfide; milling.

Introduction

A thermal battery is a highly reliable primary power source used in critical military applications, such as precision munitions and missiles. It consists of a series of solid anode, separator, and cathode pellets, and also employs internal pyrotechnic pellets that provide an on demand heat source. These batteries can remain dormant for decades until the pyrotechnic is activated on demand, melting the separator pellet and creating a high power source for a limited time in expendable weapons systems.

In an effort to extend the operating performance, this study aims to explore the use of Nanoparticles in the electrode pellets of an existing qualified thermal battery design. Previous researchers have completed preliminary work on Nanostructured Iron Disulfide (FeS_2) for thermal battery designs. Nano-sized particles have been prepared by chemical hydrothermal synthesis at high temperature and pressures [1, 2] and by high energy ball milling particle size reduction [3]. These powders have been reported to have enhanced properties when used in thermal batteries [4]. This enhancement is believed to come from the very small particle size (<100 nanometers average particle size) which results in an extremely large surface area per volume of active cathode material. Enhanced material properties also reported were increases in mechanical robustness of electrode pellets, increased thermal stability, and overall power density.

This study aims to use a fully scalable high energy milling method to produce kilogram quantities of FeS_2 powder for cathode use in thermal batteries.

Experimental

Synthesis of FeS_2 nanoparticles: Nanoscale FeS_2 was synthesized through mechanical attrition using horizontal high-energy milling equipment. The starting powder was micron sized (~20 micron) and obtained commercially. Dry milling was performed under an inert gas environment, and all powders, as-is and processed, were stored in argon glovebox at <5ppm O_2 to minimize oxygen contamination. Previous experiments were performed with different milling media types, and Yttria Stabilized Zirconia (YSZ) was used instead of chrome steel in order to minimize iron contamination in the processed powder. After performing a previous processing time study, it was determined that processing at 6h can produce nanoscale FeS_2 powder.

Powder Characterization: The powder properties were characterized using multiple techniques. Scanning Electron Microscopy (SEM) was performed using a Zeiss Supra V40 @ 10kV with In-Lens detector. Surface area analysis was done through the Barret-Emmet-Teller (B.E.T.) method using a Quantachrome Nova 4000e. Two different X-Ray techniques were utilized, X-Ray Diffraction (XRD) and X-Ray Fluorescence (XRF), with Rigaku Ultima and ZSX Primus II equipment used respectively. Thermo-gravimetric analysis (TGA) & Differential thermal analysis (DTA) was performed using a Netzsch Jupiter STA449C.

Laser Diffraction particle size analysis was completed using a Horiba LA-950v2, and Oxygen content was tested using a Horiba EMGA-620W.

Catholyte Powder & Cathode Pellet Fabrication: Under inert conditions, the Nano-sized Iron Disulfide was mixed with Electrolyte powder and blended. After standard processing, pulverizing, sieving and drying under vacuum, the Catholyte was pressed into Cathode pellets.

Cathode pellets were prepared by hand die and were pressed in dry room conditions (<3% RH). Pellets were made from each type of Catholyte powder: standard Catholyte powder with micron-sized Iron Disulfide and Nano Catholyte powder with Nano-sized Iron Disulfide. All the pellets produced were uniform and robust, with no cracks. Nano Cathode pellets were darker in coloration than Micron Cathodes as shown in Figure 1.

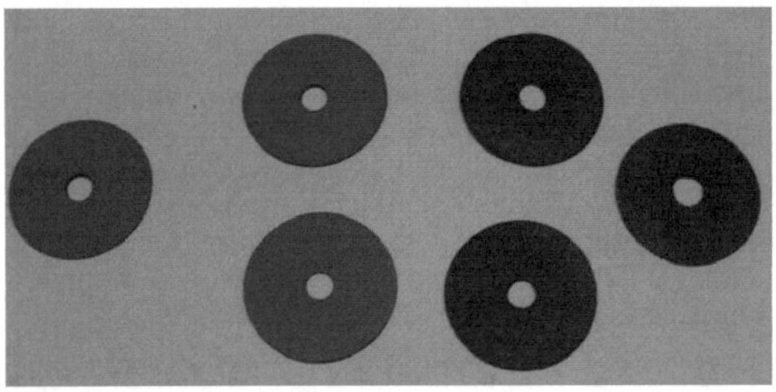

Figure 1. Comparison of Nano Catholyte pellets (right) and Micron Catholyte pellets (left). Pellets were pressed by hand die.

The Nano Cathode pellets produced were the same dimensions, including thickness and density as the Micron Cathode pellets. It was expected that the Nano particles would compact more efficiently than Micron sized particles, resulting in a pellet that weighed the same but was slightly thinner. It is speculated that the reason for the equal pellet thickness could be due to an interaction with the Electrolyte mixture.

Single Cell Testing: A Single Cell Thermal Battery (SCTB) testing device clamps thermal battery pellets between two thermostatically controlled metal platens at pressure, and allows voltage and currents to flow between metal current collectors on each side of a Cathode-Separator-Anode pellet "sandwich". The cell is held at a constant temperature throughout testing.

Results and Discussion

Scanning Electron Microscopy: Scanning Electron Microscopy was used to identify the particle morphology as well as to gain a general idea of particle size. A comparison of the as-received powder to the milled powder is shown in Figure 2. A comparison to steel media is also included to confirm that similar particle size results could be obtained while changing the milling media used. A magnified view of the powder processed for 6h with YSZ media is shown in Figure 3. Particles range from <50nm to micron sized agglomerate particles. A visual indication of the differences between nanoscale and micron FeS_2 is shown in Figure 4. The nanoscale FeS_2 (left) is noticeably darker.

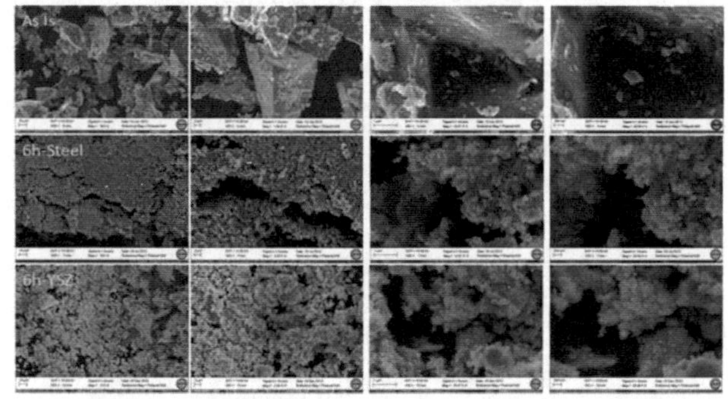

Figure 2. Scanning Electron Microscope (SEM) images. Top row: as received Iron Disulfide (FeS_2), shown magnified from 500X, 1,000X, 15,000X, 30,000X; Second row: FeS_2 milled for 6 hours from 500X, 2,000X, 15,000X, 25,000X; Third row: FeS_2 milled for 6 hours (YSZ), from 500X, 2,000X, 15,000X, 25,000X.

Figure 3. 50kx magnification of FeS_2 Powder

Figure 4. Comparison of Nanoscale (left) and Micron-sized (right) Iron Disulfide powders.

X-Ray Diffraction: X-Ray Diffraction was performed using Cu-Kα source. The patterns are shown in Figure 5. (as received) and Figure 6. (milled). Both patterns match the known reference for FeS_2 (98-000-0087). The processed powder did not show any other major peaks due to contamination. Peak broadening is apparent in the milled XRD pattern, and is an indication of a reduction in particle size. Using the Scherrer equation, the average crystallite size for the milled power was determined to be 57nm.

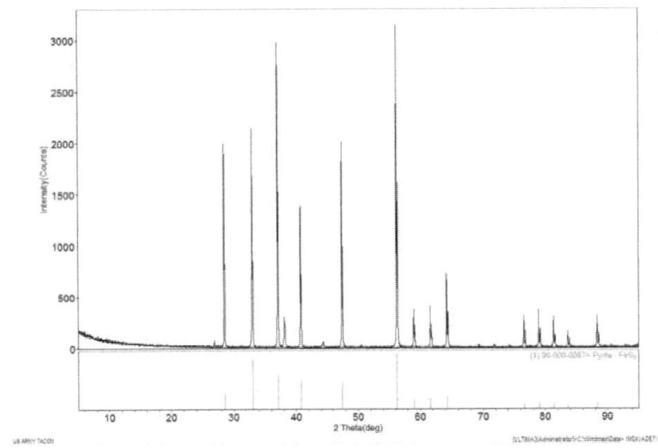

Figure 5. X-Ray Diffraction (XRD) Spectrum of As Received Iron Disulfide powder.

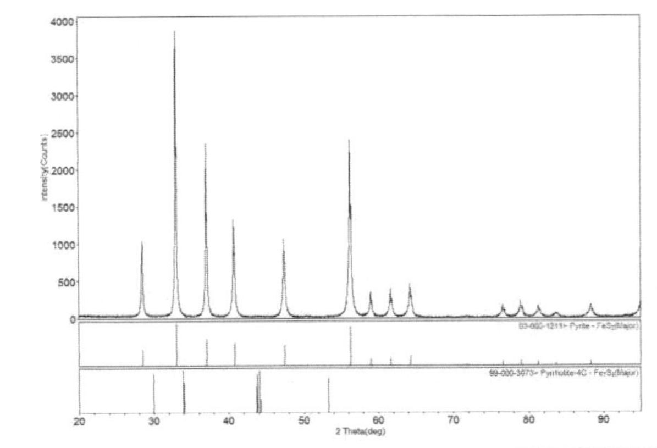

Figure 6. X-Ray Diffraction (XRD) Spectrum of Nanoscale Iron Disulfide powder after 6hr milling time.

Barret-Emmet-Teller Analysis: BET analysis was performed as an additional technique to determine particle size. The multi-point plot for the milled power is shown in Figure 7., and correlates to Table 1. which is the connected data summary. The nanoscale FeS_2 had a surface area measurement of 20.637 m^2/g which correlates to 62nm particle size through a derivation calculation assuming all particles are spherical.

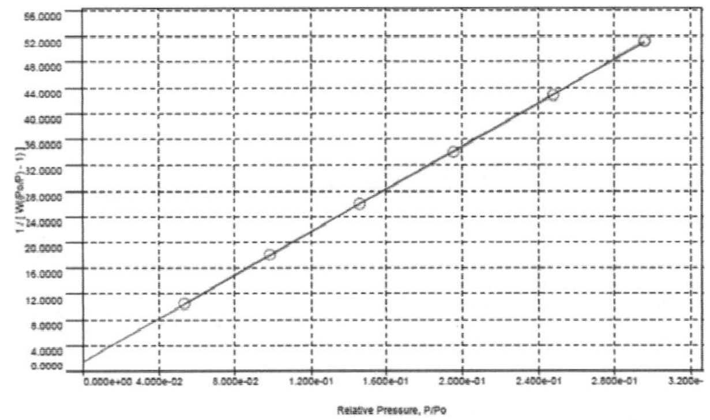

Figure 7. BET Plot

BET Summary	
Slope	167.214
Intercept	1.53E+00
Corellation Coefficient	0.999925
C constant	110.034
Surface Area	20.637 m^2/g

Table 1. BET Data of Nanoscale Iron Disulfide powder after 6hr milling time.

Single Cell Testing: Figure 8 below is a comparison of SCTB test results for cells made up with standard Micron Catholyte and with Nano Catholyte. The current density is the same in this test as in the full scale G3190B2 Thermal Battery, with the output voltage from one cell only. The Micron Catholyte cell shown is typical for this type of Cathode (Cell 1D). It is compared with three cells (Cells 1A, 1B and 1C) made with Nano Catholyte. Each Nano Catholyte cell achieved a slightly higher voltage plateau shown by the Micron Cathode cell, and stayed on each plateau longer. The overall average run time for Nano Catholyte cells is almost twice the run time of the Micron Catholyte cell. A comparison of maximum voltages, run times, and capacities for Nano and Micron Catholyte cells at this discharge rate is shown in Table 2 below. This longer runtime and higher capacity trend is maintained at higher current densities up to 200 mA/cm^2 as shown in Figure 9. It seems clear that Nano Iron Disulfide particles show marked rate improvement in Single Cell Thermal Battery testing.

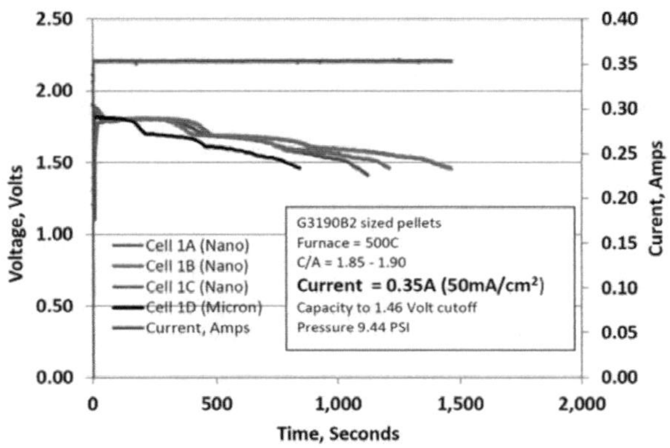

Figure 8. Single Cell Thermal Battery test at 500°C and 0.350 amps (50 mA/cm^2 current density).

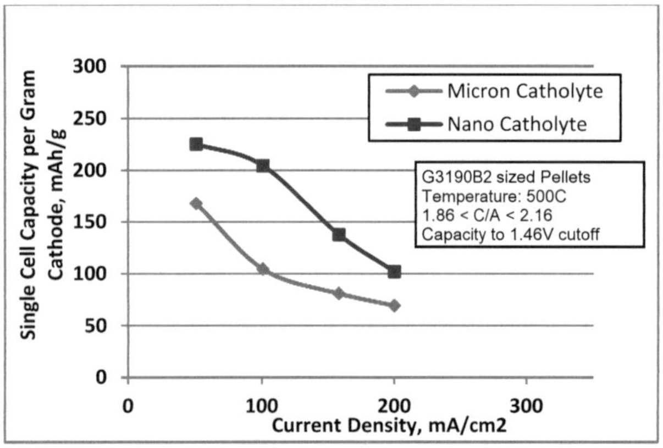

Figure 9. Average Capacity per Unit Mass Active Cathode as a Function of Current Density, for Single Cell Thermal Battery testing results.

	Cell Maximum Voltage, Volts	Cell Run Time to 1.46V Cutoff*, seconds	Cell Capacity to 1.46 V Cutoff* mAhr
Micron Single Cell	1.897	843	82.0
Avg. Nano Single Cell	2.016	1249	121.4
Average Improvement	6.3%	48.2%	48.0%

Table 2. Cell performance values for Single Cell Thermal Battery testing at 500°C: comparison between Micron Catholyte and Nano Catholyte at 0.350 Amps (50 mA/cm^2 current density).

Conclusion

Nanoscale FeS_2 particles were successfully produced through the high energy milling processing of micron-sized particles for use in thermal batteries. The milling parameters required for this size reduction were determined, and the particle size and purity were optimized. This high energy milling method is fully scalable, and kilogram quantities of nanoscale FeS_2 were produced. The nanoscale powders were successfully characterized using SEM, XRD, XRF, BET, EDS, and other techniques. Catholyte mixtures were made with nanoscale FeS_2, and thermal battery electrode pellets were fabricated from this material. Single cell thermal battery testing was completed using these pellets and they have been characterized for voltage, capacity and rate performance. Nano Catholyte single cell testing has shown a significant performance improvement over the test results of Micron Catholyte cells. The techniques and methods utilized in this study can be applied to other potential nanoscale cathode material candidates.

Acknowledgements

This work was partially funded through the Life Cycle Pilot Process (LCPP) of Project Director for Joint Services (PD JS) under Contract W15QKN-11-C-0152.

References

1. Guidotti, R. A., F. W. Reinhardt, J. Dai, and D. E. Reisner, "Preparation and Characterization of Synthetic Pyrite for Thermal-Battery Cathodes," *Proceedings of 40th Power Sources Conference*, p. 339, 2002.
2. Guidotti, R. A., P. J. Nigrey, F. W. Reinhardt, and J. G. Odinek, "Evaluation of Nanoparticulate Metal Disulfides in Thermal Batteries," *Proceedings of 40th Power Sources Conference*, p. 250, 2002.
3. Au, M., "Nanostructured Thermal Batteries with High Power Density," *Journal of Power Sources*, vol. 115, pp. 360-366, 2003.
4. Au, M., Y. Lei, and T. Yaday, *NASA Tech Briefs*, April, 1999.
5. Swift, G. A., "Cathode Materials for Use in Thermal Batteries," *Proceedings of 44th Power Sources Conference*, p. 581, 2010.
6. Masset, P. J., and R. A. Guidotti, "Thermal activated (thermal) battery technology Part IIIa: FeS2 cathode material." *Journal of Power Sources*, vol. 177, pp. 595-609, 2008.

Thermal Battery Improvements

Geoffrey A. Swift
EaglePicher Technologies, LLC
Joplin, MO 64801

Abstract
Ongoing efforts to improve thermal battery performance are presented. Anode improvements include investigating novel alloys. Cathode improvements include alternate active materials and flooding electrolytes. Results will compare performance between industry standard materials and improved materials in terms of voltage, capacity, and impedance.

Keywords: Thermal Batteries; Cathode; Anode

Introduction
Thermal batteries operate in hostile environments, both from their use as power source for various weapons systems, and from their intrinsic nature. Unlike most batteries, which operate at ambient or intermediate temperatures, thermal batteries require high temperature to operate. Thermal battery electrolytes are typically some combination of two or more halide salts and an inert binder material. The electrolyte formulation is chosen to remain solid, and therefore non-conductive, at temperatures below its melting point. This allows long-term storage of the batteries, since self-discharge is greatly inhibited by the solid electrolyte. High temperature is required to melt the electrolyte, which is usually incorporated into the anode and cathode in addition to the separator. The battery is activated via a pyrotechnic ignition which inputs sufficient heat to melt the electrolyte, but without exceeding the temperature at which the anode and cathode materials melt, deflagrate, or decompose. With the electrolyte molten, the battery may be discharged.[1-2]

Thermal battery anodes must also be compatible with the electrolytes and also be suitable for operation at temperatures approaching 600°C. Most often, the anode is Lithium-Silicon (Li-Si) or Lithium-Aluminum (Li-Al), chosen with a composition whose liquidus temperature is higher than that of the halide electrolyte. Alternate alloy compositions including Mg, B, Fe, Sb, Bi, Sn, and Ge have been reported, in binary and ternary compositions. For typical anode pellet preparation, the alloy must be one brittle enough that it can be reduced to a powder for pressing. A newly-developed alloy has been shown to possess a higher voltage than Li-Si (1.9V), but less than that of Li metal (2.2V). The new alloy can be easily reduced to a powder and is compatible with all relevant materials for inclusion in a thermal battery. Results are presented for initial testing of the new alloy.[3]

Thermal batteries often use pyrite-based cathodes. This limits the operating temperature to below 600°C, the decomposition temperature of FeS_2. The low cost and easy availability of FeS_2 has kept it the primary thermal battery cathode material for decades. Other disulfide materials have been demonstrated to perform adequately in thermal batteries, including CoS_2 and NiS_2. These offer various advantages over FeS_2. Higher maximum operating temperature, lower impedance under pulsing, and greater voltage stability are cited as justification for the much higher costs associated with materials that typically must be manufactured as opposed to mined. Potential cathode improvement avenues include using alternate active materials, different type and amount of flooding electrolyte, and incorporation of conductive additives. Previous reports have demonstrated marked improvement over industry standard cathode formulations.[4-5]

Two different improvement efforts are described. The first effort seeks to replace a silver oxide-zinc (SOZ) battery with a thermal battery, and the other to develop a new, higher-voltage cathode. SOZ batteries have excellent capacity, rate capability and voltage stability, but also high cost due to the market price variation of silver. Replacing an SOZ battery with a thermal battery can be a difficult proposition, as SOZ batteries often have very tight voltage regulation requirements. This requires a thermal battery with very low impedance to avoid failing minimum voltage during discharge. Results are presented from battery test data comparing standard cathode performance and improved cathode performance under the loading conditions of an SOZ battery.

The second cathode improvement effort focused on increased cell voltage. The industry-standard Li-Si/FeS_2 couple operates at 1.9V under load. Increasing the cell voltage would enable smaller envelopes or greater voltage in existing envelopes. To that end, a new cathode material was developed to provide higher cell voltage. Obtaining a different voltage requires altering the chemistry. However, it was desired that any new cathode material be compatible with already-existing thermal battery components, which is to say a drop-in replacement. Thus, the new material must be compatible with the electrolytes used in thermal batteries, while also surviving the temperature and other environmental conditions associated with thermal batteries. Thus, the active material was the only factor to be changed in the cathode. Results are presented from initial testing of this new material.

Experimental Procedure

New Anode Alloy

The new alloy was prepared by co-melting components in an inert atmosphere glove box. The melt was cooled and ground to a powder. The alloy powder was mixed with electrolyte in a dry room and pressed into pellets for single cell testing.

Single cells were discharged in an inert atmosphere glove box at 500°C. A base load of 1A was applied, with 5A pulses occurring every 60s. A duplicate single cell was run using Li-Si for comparison.

SOZ replacement battery

The new cathode formulation was prepared using standard methods. All preparation took place in a dry room (RH<3%). Mixture of active material with electrolyte was carried out via turbula blender for 30 minutes. The powders were sieved after mixing to ensure no aggregation had occurred. Pellets were pressed and stacked in order with anode, electrolyte, and heat pellets, in order to obtain the required voltage for the battery. A battery built using typical FeS_2-based cathode pellets was also constructed, for comparison with the new formulation's performance. The batteries were activated using an externally activated squib, with the voltage rise occurring within specified limits. The discharge began immediately, including a high base load and very high pulses (>300A).

Higher Voltage Cathode

A novel cathode material was prepared for testing in the typical manner of thermal battery materials. The cathode material was mixed with electrolyte in a dry room and pressed into pellets for single cell testing. Single cell tests were carried out under the same conditions as for the new anode alloy, as described above. A single cell using a standard cathode was run under the same conditions to provide a comparison. Finally, a single cell using the new alloy and the higher voltage cathode was run to demonstrate the combination.

Results and Discussion

New Anode Alloy

Single cell discharge traces are shown in Figure 1 for both a production Li-Si anode and the new alloy anode. Of particular note is the early discharge behavior, up to about 400s. In this region, the new alloy delivers a higher voltage than the Li-Si anode, even though both use the same type and lot of separator and cathode powders, pressed to the same weight and thickness. Beginning around 400s, the voltage of the new alloy single cell rolls off. The second plateau is very similar to that of the Li-Si anode. However, while the Li-Si cell experiences its own voltage roll-off at around 600s, the new alloy anode does not roll-off from its second plateau until around 1000s. This indicates a clearly superior performance for the new alloy, especially for a longer life battery with somewhat forgiving minimum voltage requirements.

Beyond the higher voltage and longer life, the new alloy also exhibits a reduced impedance under pulsing. Figure 2 shows the impedance under the pulses for the single cells of Figure 1. Even though both cells use the same FeS_2-based cathode, the new alloy experiences less polarization during discharge. Both cells still show the typical high-impedance second phase that forms during FeS_2 discharge, but the increase for the new alloy is both delayed in its effects and of lower magnitude. Only when the Li-Si cell discharges past that point and begins to reduce earlier than the new alloy cell does it show a lower impedance. However, the Li-Si cell shows its second impedance increase due to exhaustion of capacity earlier than the new alloy.

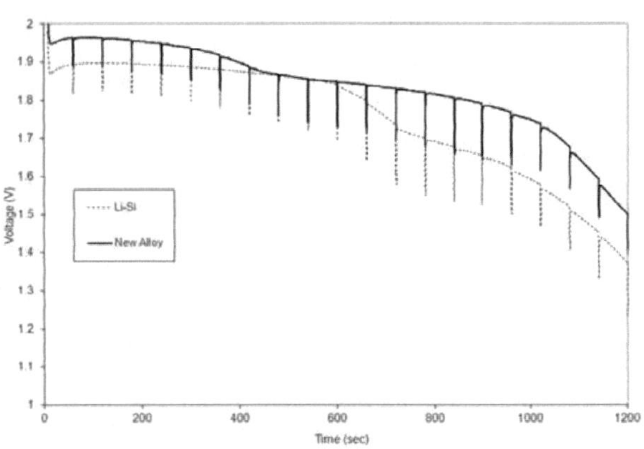

Figure 1. Discharge traces for single cells using new anode alloy and Li-Si, using the same cathode and separator materials. Test conducted at 500°C in inert atmosphere, with 1A base load and 5A pulses.

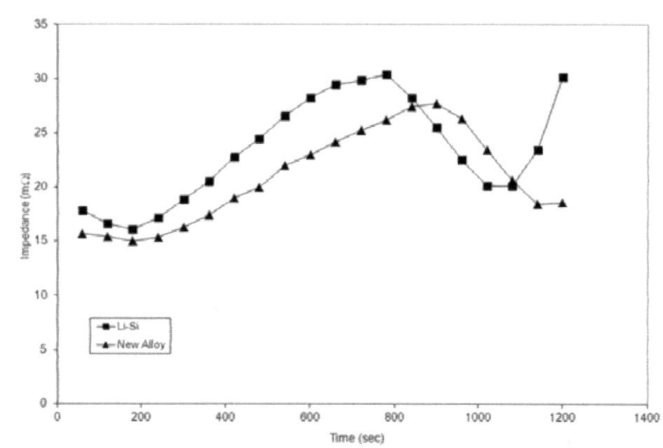

Figure 2. Impedance under pulsing for single cells shown in Fig. 1, using new anode alloy and Li-Si, using the same cathode and separator materials. Test conducted at 500°C in inert atmosphere, with 1A base load and 5A pulses.

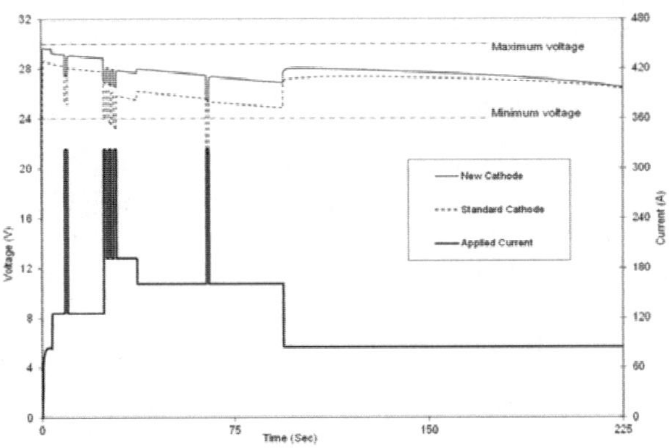

Figure 3. Discharge for SOZ replacement thermal battery. Dashed lines indicate minimum and maximum voltages, while bold line indicates applied current. Dotted line shows standard cathode discharge, while solid line indicates discharge of new cathode formulation.

Thus, the new alloy has several features to recommend it. First, it delivers a higher cell voltage early in life, rolling off to a similar voltage as industry-standard anodes. Second, the second plateau appears to last as long as Li-Si's first plateau, meaning the capacity and thus the life of the new alloy is superior to Li-Si. Third, even though the anode is not considered especially to factor into cell impedance, the new alloy measurably decreases the impedance of cells during pulsing. All these factors motivate additional effort for the new alloy, including type and amount of flooding electrolyte to optimize performance.

SOZ replacement battery

Figure 3 shows the discharge of batteries built using standard and new cathode formulations. The minimum and maximum voltages are indicated by dashed. The standard cathode shows performance expected for such materials. While the maximum voltage was not exceeded, the minimum voltage was violated on the third pulse. Return to the varying base load (80-120A) got the discharge back within the operating limits, but the final pulse again violated the minimum voltage. Thus, this battery would have failed to meet the operating requirements which the SOZ battery could deliver.

The new cathode formulation, however, performed much more admirably. The discharge remained with the upper and lower voltage limits, even during the five pulses. This result is due to both the new formulation's lower impedance and its superior pressability. Higher-density pellets allowed for more cells in the same envelope, thus the higher initial voltage. Further, batteries with the new formulation were subjected to—and passed—all the operating and non-operating environments (e.g, shock, vibration, high- and low-temperature, humidity) for this program.

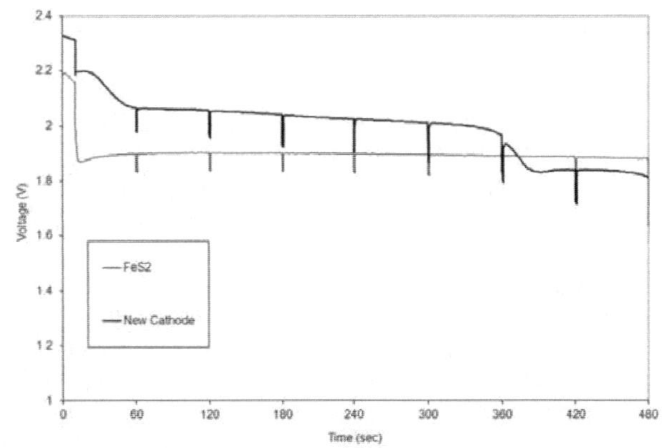

Figure 4. Discharge traces for single cells using FeS2 and new material as cathodes, using the same anode and separator materials. Tests were conducted at 500°C in inert atmosphere, with 1A base load and 5A pulses.

Higher Voltage Cathode

Figure 4 shows single cell discharges for a typical FeS_2 cathode and for a new cathode material. Both cells used the same Li-Si anode and all-Li^+ electrolyte materials. The new cathode maintained a voltage 10% higher than the FeS_2 cathode for 6 minutes. At that time, the new cathode rolled off to a lower voltage plateau just under the FeS_2 plateau. The new cathode was compatible with the electrolytes and tolerated the 500C test temperature without any side reactions or other failure mechanisms. The impedance under the 5A pulses was slightly higher than for FeS_2, but not excessively so. Additional effort is underway for this new cathode, from optimizing the type and amount of flooding electrolyte to attempting to reduce the impedance under pulsing.

Conclusions

EaglePicher's efforts to improve thermal battery performance have yielded multiple successes. First, a novel alloy for anodes was developed that delivers higher voltage versus FeS_2 than Li-Si. Second, a new cathode formulation designed for low impedance was used to qualify a thermal battery to replace a silver oxide-zinc battery. Third, a novel higher voltage cathode is capable of delivering cell voltages versus Li-Si 10% higher than FeS_2. This cathode, when combined with the new anode alloy, delivers a cell voltage of 2.13V, nearly that of pure lithium metal versus FeS_2. Additional effort

Acknowledgments

Thanks are offered to Trudy Harris and Eric Petersen for sample preparation and data collection. This material is released to the public domain in accordance with ITAR 22 CFR 120.11.

References

1. V. Klasons and C.M. Lamb, "Thermal Batteries," in *Handbook of Batteries*, 3rd ed., eds. D. Linden and T.B. Reddy, pp. 21.1-21.22, McGraw Hill, New York, NY, 2002
2. P. Masset, R.A. Guidotti, "Thermal Activated (Thermal) Battery Technology Part II: Molten Salt Electrolytes", *J. Power Sources*, **164**, pp. 397-414 (2008)
3. R.A. Guidotti, P. Masset, "Thermally Activated ("Thermal") Battery Technology: Part IV. Anode Materials", *J. Power Sources*, **183**, pp. 388–398 (2008)
4. P. Masset, R.A. Guidotti, "Thermal Activated ("Thermal") Battery Technology: Part IIIa: FeS_2 Cathode Material", *J. Power Sources*, **177**, pp. 595–609 (2008)
5. P. Masset, R.A. Guidotti, "Thermal Activated ("Thermal") Battery Technology: Part IIIb: Sulfur and Oxide-based Cathode Materials", *J. Power Sources*, **178**, pp. 456–466 (2008)

Improvements to $LiCoPO_4$ Based Li-ion Cathodes

Jan L. Allen, Joshua L. Allen, Samuel A. Delp
Jeff Wolfenstine and T. Richard Jow
U.S. Army Research Laboratory
Adelphi, Maryland, USA 20783

Abstract: *$LiCoPO_4$ is a promising cathode material to enable high energy, abuse tolerant Li-ion batteries. However unmodified $LiCoPO_4$ shows a severe loss of discharge capacity upon multiple charge – discharge cycles owing to structure deterioration and electrolyte decomposition. Recent advances in chemical substitution of $LiCoPO_4$ and high voltage stabilizing electrolyte additives now show that capacity fade can be significantly reduced. Additionally, the modifications lead to improved discharge capacity and power, thereby increasing interest in $LiCoPO_4$ as a Li-ion cathode. In particular, Fe substitution of $LiCoPO_4$ leads to much improved cycling as well as improved rate of discharge. Our study of transport through electrochemical impedance spectroscopy and DC polarization suggests that Fe substitution increases the ionic and electronic conductivity of the material relative to $LiCoPO_4$. These improvements are in agreement with first principle modeling calculations. We have developed new modifications of $LiCoPO_4$ beyond simple Fe substitution which have further increased cycle life, discharge capacity, rate of discharge and coulombic efficiency. The synthesis and measurements of electrochemical properties and electronic and ionic transport of substituted $LiCoPO_4$ are discussed and compared to $LiCoPO_4$.*

Keywords: Li-ion; battery; cathode; $LiCoPO_4$; phospho-olivine; phosphate; rechargeable; positive electrode

Introduction

Olivine-structured $LiFePO_4$ [1] is a commercialized cathode material with excellent safety under abuse conditions. It has a relatively low energy density owing to its relatively low voltage (3.4 V) of Li insertion. It would therefore be highly desirable to find a next generation cathode material with a similar safety profile but higher energy density. Manganese, cobalt and nickel form $LiMPO_4$ structures with the olivine structure with cell voltages of 4.1, 4.8 and 5.1 V, respectively [1-3].

We used a combination of experimental data (XPS) and first principles calculations to understand the potential of these materials to replace $LiFePO_4$ for higher energy applications. The experimentally confirmed model shows that $LiCoPO_4$ is the most promising material to replace $LiFePO_4$ [4]. In particular, $LiCoPO_4$ is of interest as a Li-ion cathode owing to its high energy (up to ~800 Wh / kg) and the potential for enhanced abuse tolerance owing to the strong covalent bonding of the PO_4 network. In general, at the same voltage a phosphate based cathode will be less likely to release oxygen than an oxide cathode under abuse such as overcharge. The commercialization of $LiCoPO_4$ has been hindered by the lack of suitable electrolytes that can operate near 5 V and its capacity fade which results from structure deterioration [5-7]. Recent advances in electrolyte [8] and substitutions that enhance the stability of the material [9] and the transport properties [10] have increased interest in this material as a next generation, high energy, high voltage (~4.8V) cathode material.

Experimental

$LiCoPO_4$ samples were prepared via a citrate complexation route [5]. $Co(OH)_2$, LiH_2PO_4, and citric acid, 1, 1.01, 1.02, molar ratio, respectively, were mixed into deionized water until all solids were dissolved. The resulting solution was evaporated to dryness via a microwave oven. The resulting dried mass was removed, ground lightly with mortar and pestle and heated in air at a rate of 10 °C min^{-1} to 600 °C and the reactant mixture was held at this temperature for 12 h.

Fe-substituted $LiCoPO_4$ was synthesized via an aqueous mixture that was produced through the 1 M HNO_3 (aq) dissolution of $Co(OH)_2$, LiH_2PO_4, $FeC_2O_4.2H_2O$ in a molar ratio of 1:1:1.01:1, respectively. The solution was evaporated rapidly in a microwave oven. The resulting precipitate was lightly ground with a mortar and pestle and then heated in a flow of N_2 at a rate of 10 °C min^{-1} to 600 °C and subsequently held at 600° C for 12 hours.

Next generation substituted $LiCoPO_4$ was synthesized via a solid state method. The starting components LiH_2PO_4, $Co(OH)_2$, $FeC_2O_4.2H_2O$ and proprietary substituents were ball milled in a Spex mill 8000 for 90 minutes and the resulting powder was heated at a rate of 10° C per minute to 700°C under N_2 and held at that temperature for 12 hours.

For transport measurements, dense discs of $LiCoPO_4$ and $Li_{1-x}Co_{0.9}Fe_{0.1}PO_4$ were prepared by hot-pressing of the powders at 1073 K at 62 MPa pressure for 0.5 h in graphite dies under Ar. Rectangular parallelepipeds were cut from the disc perpendicular to the pressing direction using a low-speed diamond saw and polished under mineral oil for density, micro-structural and electrical property measurements. The relative density values (~98%) of the samples were determined by dividing the bulk density determined from the weight and volume by the theoretical density. Phase purity was confirmed using X-ray powder diffraction. Data were collected using a Rigaku Ultima III diffractometer (Cu Kα radiation).

Electrical conductivity measurements were performed on the hot-pressed $LiCoPO_4$ and $Li_{1-x}Co_{0.9}Fe_{0.1}PO_4$ samples using the two probe method. Pt was sputter coated on to the top and bottom surfaces of the specimens. Electrochemical impedance spectra (EIS), 0.1–10^6 Hz frequency range, 100 mV AC amplitude, 480 – 680 K temperature range and DC Polarization measurements, 2V bias, 330 - 620 K temperature range were obtained using a Solartron 1260. The bulk, grain boundary and electrode contribution to the impedance were separated by fitting the spectra using ZView (Scribner Associates, Inc.). The DC polarization steady-state current and 2 volt potential were used to determine the resistance which was converted to electronic conductivity using the specimen dimensions.

Carbon coating to improve electronic conductivity was done by ball milling the samples of $LiCoPO_4$ and Fe-substituted $LiCoPO_4$ for 30 min with 5% by mass acetylene black followed by heating for 1 h at 600 °C under N_2. In the case of next generation $LiCoPO_4$, the 5 wt. % acetylene black was added directly to the starting mix.

For electrochemical testing, a composite electrode was fabricated by a slurry coating method. Using N-methylpyrrolidone (NMP) as solvent, a slurry was used to coat an Al foil substrate to produce a composite electrode of 80 wt.% active, 10 wt.% polyvinylidene fluoride (PVDF) and 8 wt.% super-P carbon and 2 wt.% conductive carbon nanotube composite (CheapTubes.com). The electrode film was cut into small discs with an area of 0.97 cm^2, dried under an infrared lamp in air before use. In a dry room (Dew point < -80 °C), Li/active coin cells (Hohsen Al-clad CR2032) were assembled using Celgard® 2400 as the separator and a 1.0 molal $LiPF_6$ solution in a 3:7 (wt.%) mixture of ethylene carbonate (EC) and ethyl methyl carbonate (EMC) electrolyte with and without 1 wt.% tris(hexafluoroisopropyl)phosphate (HFiPP). Electrochemical testing was performed using a Maccor Series 4000 tester. For calculation of C-rate, a capacity of ~170 mA h g^{-1} was assumed.

Results and Discussion

$LiCoPO_4$ based cathodes presents several challenges. One challenge is the low electronic conductivity of $LiCoPO_4$. The insulating nature will prevent the transfer of electrons from the cathode to the current collector necessary for its function as a Li-ion battery positive electrode. In figure 1, the conductivity of $LiCoPO_4$ and $Li_{1-x}Co_{0.9}Fe_{0.1}PO_4$ is shown as a function of temperature. The partial substitution of Fe for Co increases the room temperature electronic conductivity about 4 orders of magnitude. However, it is still too low at around 2 x 10^{-12} S cm^{-1}. The addition of a carbon coating is thus needed to reach a reasonable electronic conductivity for use in a Li-ion battery.

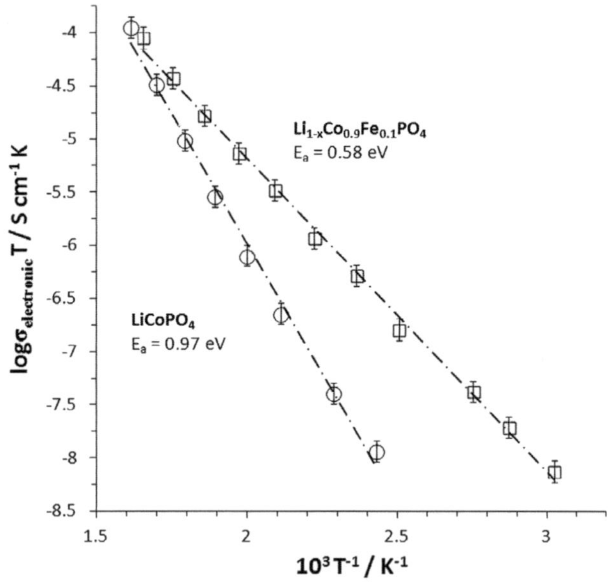

Figure 1. Electronic conductivity of $LiCoPO_4$ and $Li_{1-x}Co_{0.9}Fe_{0.1}PO_4$ as a function of temperature.

The ionic conductivity on the other hand is quite sufficient for use as a Li-ion battery.

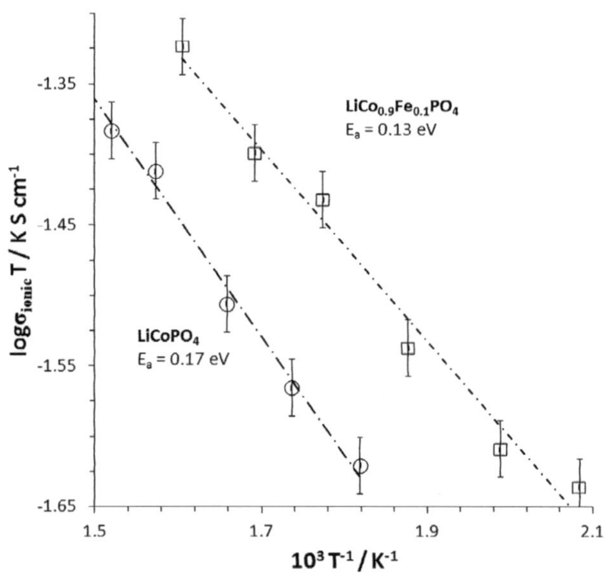

Figure 2. Ionic conductivity of $LiCoPO_4$ and $Li_{1-x}Co_{0.9}Fe_{0.1}PO_4$ as a function of temperature.

The Li-ion conductivity of $LiCoPO_4$ was found to be about 4 x 10^{-6} S cm^{-1} and $Li_{1-x}Co_{0.9}Fe_{0.1}PO_4$ has a Li-ion conductivity of 1 x 10^{-5} S cm^{-1} (Figure 2). Therefore, the substitution by Fe for Co increases the Li-ion conductivity as well as the electronic. The increased electronic conductivity of Fe-substituted $LiCoPO_4$ relative to $LiCoPO_4$ is in agreement with first principle calculations of the electronic structure of these materials [4].

Other challenges to the use of $LiCoPO_4$ are the instability of the electrolyte and the instability of the $LiCoPO_4$ electrode material itself at 5 V. These are addressed through the use of electrolyte additives [8] and through substitutional chemistry of $LiCoPO_4$ [9]. Figure 3 shows the comparison of using $LiCoPO_4$ with a state of the art electrolyte versus an Fe-substituted $LiCoPO_4$ cycled with an electrolyte containing a stabilizing additive.

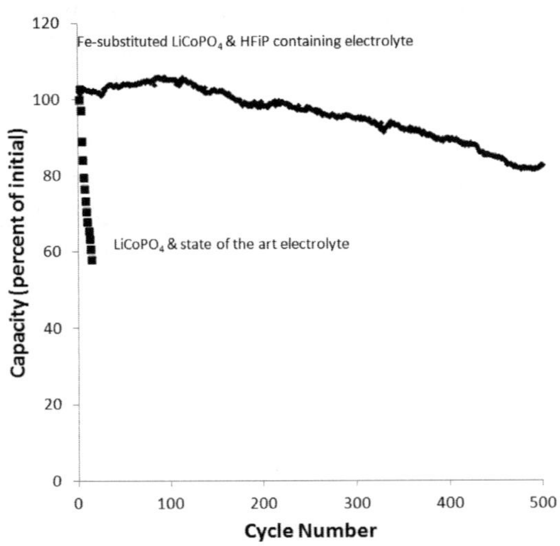

Figure 3. Comparison of Fe-substituted $LiCoPO_4$ with HFiP containing electrolyte and $LiCoPO_4$ cycled in standard electrolyte. The "standard electrolyte" is 1 m $LiPF_6$ in EC:EMC, 3:7. The HFiP electrolyte is 1 m $LiPF_6$ in EC:EMC, 3:7 with 1% HFiPP electrolyte additive.

With the dramatic improvement in capacity retention demonstrated in Figure 3, further efforts were made to increase the capacity and the stability of the electrolyte through new substitutional chemistry. These next generation substituted $LiCoPO_4$ materials have higher discharge capacity, more stable capacity, higher rate and higher coulombic efficiency.

Figure 4 compares the discharge capacity of the next generation material to the Fe-substituted $LiCoPO_4$ demonstrating the improvements in discharge capacity and the stabilization of the capacity during charge / discharge cycling. The Fe-substituted $LiCoPO_4$ has an initial capacity of about 110 mAh g^{-1}. This capacity fades over time but still maintains about 80% of the initial capacity over 500 cycles. The next generation substituted $LiCoPO_4$ shows a capacity of about 130 mA g^{-1} and throughout the first 500 cycles maintains a higher capacity than its predecessor generation.

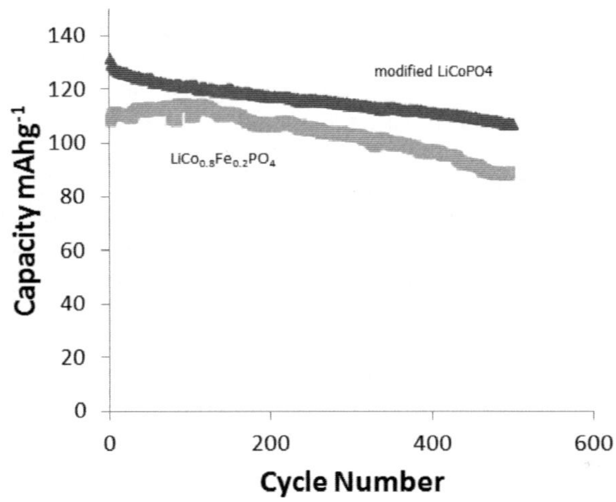

Figure 4. Comparison of the discharge capacity as a function of cycle of next generation (modified) $LiCoPO_4$ to Fe-substituted $LiCoPO_4$.

The next generation modified $LiCoPO_4$ also exhibits improved coulombic efficiency. The coulombic efficiency of Fe-substituted $LiCoPO_4$ is about 97.8%. The next generation $LiCoPO_4$ material has a coulombic efficiency of greater than 99%. The coulombic efficiency and discharge capacity of next generation $LiCoPO_4$ is shown in Figure 5.

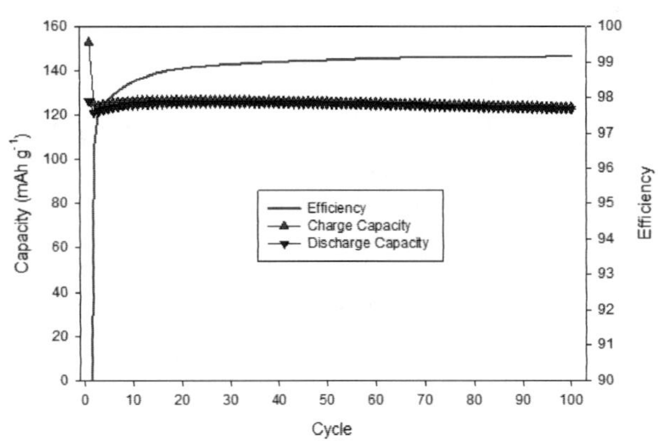

Figure 5. Demonstration of the coulombic efficiency of next generation substituted $LiCoPO_4$.

Conclusions

$LiCoPO_4$ is a 5 V Li-ion battery offering the potential of a high energy safe Li-ion battery system. $LiCoPO_4$ is the most likely replacement for $LiFePO_4$ as a higher energy cathode. Fe substitution of $LiCoPO_4$ has led to much improved cycle life and discharge capacity. Next generation substitutions of $LiCoPO_4$ lead to even higher capacity, improved cycle life and coulombic efficiency. $LiCoPO_4$ is a promising cathode material for the development of higher energy, safe Li-ion battery systems to meet the requirements of the military and commercial sectors. Further substitutional studies for enhanced perfomance as well as studies to find an improved electrolyte formulation are underway.

Acknowledgements

Authors acknowledge funding provided by the Army Research Laboratory. Hot pressing was performed by T. Thompson & J. Sakamoto at Michigan State University.

References

1. Padhi, A.K., Nanjundaswamy, K.S., Goodenough, J.B., "Phospho-olivines as positive electrode materials for rechargeable lithium batteries, " *J. Electrochem. Soc.*, vol. 144, pp. 1188-1194, 1997.
2. Amine, K., Yasuda, H., Yamachi, M., "Olivine $LiCoPO_4$ as 4.8 V electrode material for lithium batteries," *Electrochem. Solid State Lett.*, vol. 3, pp. 178-179, 2000.
3. Wolfenstine, J., Allen, J.L., "Ni^{3+}/Ni^{2+} redox potential in $LiNiPO_4$," *J. Power Sources*, vol. 142, pp.389-390, 2005.
4. Johannes, M.D., Hoang, K., Allen, J.L., Gaskell, K, "Hole polaron formation and migration in olivine phosphate materials," Phys. Rev. B, vol. 85, pp. 115106-11512, 2012.
5. Tadanaga, K., Mizuno, F.,Hayashi, A., Minami, T., Tatsumisago, M., "Preparation of $LiCoPO_4$ for lithium battery cathodes through solution process," *Electrochemistry*, vol. 71, pp. 1192-1195, 2003.
6. N.N. Bramnik, K.G.Bramnik, T. Buhrmester, C. Baehtz, H. Ehrenberg and H. Fuess, "Electrochemical and structural study of $LiCoPO_4$-based electrodes," *J. Solid State Electrochem.* vol.8, pp. 558-564, 2004.
7. Wolfenstine, J., Lee, U., Poese, B., Allen, J.L., "Effect of oxygen partial pressure on the discharge capacity of $LiCoPO_4$," *J. Power Sources*, vol. 144, pp. 226-230, 2005.
8. Cresce, A.V., Xu, K., "Electrolytes in support of 5 V Li ion chemistry," *J. Electrochem. Soc.* vol. 158, pp. A337-A342, 2011.
9. Allen, J.L., Jow, T.R., Wolfenstine, J., "Improved Cycle life of Fe-substituted $LiCoPO_4$," *J. Power Sources*, vol. 196, pp. 8656-8661, 2011.
10. Allen, J.L., Thompson, T., Sakamoto, J., Becker, C.R., Jow, T.R., Wolfenstine, J., "Transport properties of $LiCoPO_4$ and Fe-substituted $LiCoPO_4$," *J. Power Sources*, vol. 254, pp. 204-208, 2014.

High Energy Density Li-ion Cell Development

Hyun Joo Bang, Owen Crowther, Mai Tucker, and Mario Destephen
Research and Development
EaglePicher Technologies, LLC
3220 Industrial Road, Joplin, MO 64801
Email: Hyun.Bang@eaglepicher.com

Abstract: *Demand for a high energy Li-ion battery has been intensively increased. To meet high energy density requirement, development of new lithium ion chemistries is inevitable due to limitation of energy density from convention lithium ion chemistry. Therefore, employment of new Li-ion chemistry for next generation Li-ion cells is necessary for high energy density.*

EaglePicher Technologies has been developing new high energy Li-ion chemistry targeting more than 250Wh/kg of energy density for the next generation applications. The developed Li-ion cells utilizing silicon-carbon anode material and high specific capacity cathode material demonstrate the target performance as designed.

Keywords: Li-ion battery; high energy density; silicon carbon anode; high specific capacity cathode;

Introduction

Intensive technical efforts have focused on developing high energy density lithium ion (Li-ion) cell with reliable cell performance over a decade due to high demands of Li-ion cell on a wide spectrum of applications. Current Li-ion cell chemistry uses conventional $LiCoO_2$ or $LiNi_xCo_yMn_xO_2$ as cathode active material and graphite as anode material. This demand will necessitate development of new cathode and anode materials with higher specific capacity. In addition, improvement in electrode density by advanced processing methods, suitable electrolyte for high rate applications, and improved cell design are also required. A development of alternative cathode material with higher specific capacity is one of the most urgent technical tasks for the higher energy density lithium ion cell [1]. At the same time, multiple development pathways are in progress to develop higher energy anodes. Beyond incremental improvements in conventional graphite anode, new materials such as Silicon (Si), Si-Carbon composite of various types (including Si coated on CNF or CNT), SiOx, and mixed metal oxide have been developed [2-4]. Table 1 shows the comparison of various anode materials in terms of specific capacity and their operation voltage.

Among them silicon has received extensive attention due to high specific capacity (~4200mAh/g). However, silicon material intrinsically undergoes severe volume changes during cycling; expansion and contraction during the insertion and extraction of lithium ions. These changes can cause fracture of the Si crystal structure, resulting in poor contact between Si particles, and eventually the loss of its electronic pathway. Poor electronic contact between Si particles and other components in anode after cycling leads to most of the capacity loss [5]. Common approaches to overcome the volume expansion of silicon material are introduction of carbon material partially in anode structure at the expense of capacity for improving good cycling performance. Various carbonaceous materials, such as graphite, multiwall carbon nano-tubes, and pyrolyzed carbon, have been used to form nanostructure as an active buffering matrix to alleviate the volume expansion and contraction of Si particle during cycling.

Table 1 Comparison of various candidate anode materials

Material	Average potential	Specific capacity
Graphite	0.1-0.2 V	372 mA·h/g
Titanate	1-2 V	160 mA·h/g
Sn ($Li_{4.4}Sn$)	0.1 ~ 1.0 V	994 mA·h/g
Si ($Li_{4.2}Si$)	0.5-1 V	4212 mA·h/g

Electrode preparation and Cell Construction

The selected cathode was prepared using a typical slurry mixing process and film casting (web coating) process which consist of a continuous mixing of the powders (active material, conductive carbon and binder) with solvent (NMP), producing slurry mixture. The mixed slurry is coated on the metal substrate (Aluminum) followed by drying process. Adhesion of the coated electrode onto the metal substrate is an initial technical challenge to obtain good electrochemical contact and mechanical integrity of the electrode while the electrode loading and thickness should meet the design requirements. The selected anode material to match the cathodes is silicon-graphite composite material, and also prepared by web coating process. An aqueous binder (carboxyl methyl cellulose: CMC) was used instead of conventional PVDF-NMP binder system for anode processing to enhance anode integrity. The rapid volume change of silicon material during cycling requires enhanced mechanical integrity of the anode to prevent loss of contacts between particles in anode. CMC binder is reported to have better adhesion to silicon powder due to particle shape morphology, compared to PVDF binder. Several optimization efforts were carried out to find optimal binder amounts for good adhesion of silicon-graphite material on the current collector, while achieving good electronic and ionic conductivity of the anode.

Cell tests were performed in both coin type cells and pouch cells. Coin cells were constructed with the electrode containing the candidate active material (cathode or anode) and lithium metal as a counter electrode for material evaluation. Pouch cells were used to evaluate overall cell performance. Pouch cell construction started from bagging the electrode with separator. Stacks of the bagged electrodes were integrated into prismatic multi-layered pouch material packaging. The cell was hermetically sealed after electrolyte injection into a cell. Constructed cells were placed into oven with constant temperature for initial cell formation which utilized low current level cycling profile. After formation cycling, cells were tested with different test profiles to evaluate overall cell performance.

Chemistry development

Anode chemistry development

The development of high energy density lithium ion cell chemistry started with anode development.

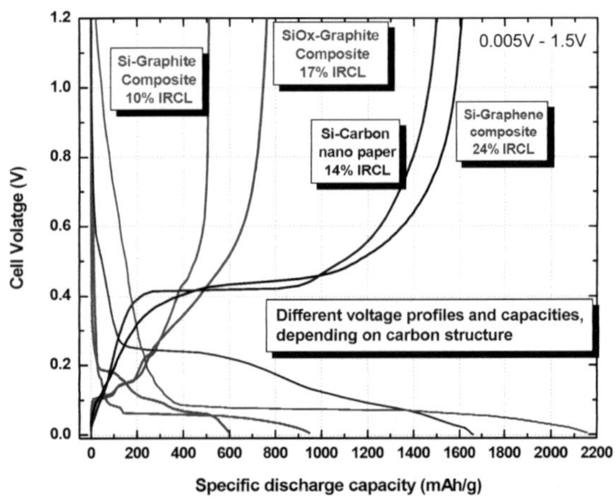

Figure 1. Charge and discharge curves of various silicon-carbon anode materials tested with Li metal as a anode. Tested voltage range is from 5 mV to 1.5V at C/30-rate

Several silicon-carbon materials were evaluated to select a candidate anode material for further development. Figure 1 shows initial charge and discharge curves of the tested silicon-carbon anodes at low C-rate to determine reversible specific capacity, irreversible capacity loss and overall voltage profile of each materials. Table 2 summarizes the test results shown in Figure 1.

Criteria of screening the anode material for development are 1) sustainable specific capacity that meet the design requirement, 2) low irreversible capacity loss, 3) low voltage profile for high cell voltage, and 4) good discharge rate capability.

Silicon-graphite system was selected a primary candidate chemistry among several silicon-carbon materials for further anode development since the selected silicon-graphite material showed the lowest irreversible capacity loss, relatively low and flat voltage profiles, and compatible capacity to the selected cathode on the design parameters.

Table 2. Comparison of various anode chemistries

Chemistry	Specific Capacity	Irreversible capacity loss
Si-graphite composite	550 mAh/g	10%
SiOx graphite composite	790 mAh/g	17%
Si-nano porous carbon paper	1350 mAh/g	14%
Si-Graphene composite	1600 mAh/g	24%

Further electrode optimization was carried out to maximize the selected silicon-graphite composite anode. Stabilization of silicon-graphite anode during cycling is one of the biggest technical challenges to achieve good cycling performance. As shown in Figure 2, the maximum reversible capacity of the optimized anode was ~626 mAh/g at C/20 discharge rate. The anode was also tested at different discharge C-rates. The test anode delivered discharge capacity of 552 mAh/g at C/5 and 502 mAh/g at 1C discharge rate that corresponded to 88.2% and 80.1% capacity retention. The improvement of anode was achieved through homogenous particle distribution and mechanical integrity by improving slurry mixing process and coating process.

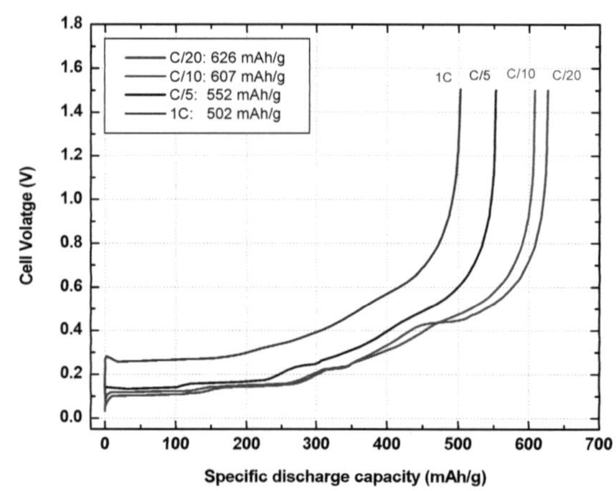

Figure 2. Rate performance of the optimized silicon-graphite composite anode tested at different C-rates (vs. Li Metal)

Cathode chemistry development

Several electrode formulas were prepared to determine the optimum electrode formulation for candidate cathode materials evaluation. The formulas had different active masses and carbon mixtures. The loading of electrode of all formulation was the same based on the tentative cell design. Table 3 shows the different formulations. The processed cathodes were tested first in coin cell configuration with Li metal anode. Among the tested cathodes, the electrodes with formula 3 and 4 delivered the highest discharge capacity at C-rate of C/20 to C/2. The discharge capacities of those electrodes were close to 200 mAh/g at C/20 and decreased to ~178 mAh/g at C/2 rate. At 1C discharge rate, the electrode made of the formula 3 was superior to the other 3 electrodes, delivering the discharge capacity of 160 mAh/g. The test result implied that the highly conductive carbon in the formula 3 was effective to utilize the candidate cathode material.

Table 3. Comparison of various anode chemistries

Cathode	Cathode formulation
Formula1	High active mass ratio conventional carbon mixture
Formula 2	High active mass ratio with conventional carbon mixture and high conductive carbon
Formula 3	High active mass ratio high conductive carbon only
Formula 4	Same as the formula 2 but low active mass ratio

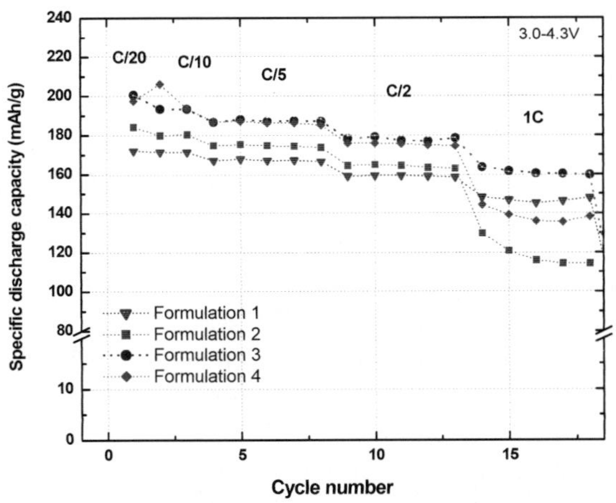

Figure 3. Discharge Capacity of Several Cathodes with Different Compositions; Tested at Different C-rates.

Another method to maximize the cathode specific capacity or increase the utilization cathode material was to use wide voltage window (high charge cutoff voltage). The specific capacity of lithium ion cathode material depended on utilization of lithium in cathode that was determined by charge cutoff voltage. However, excess utilization of lithium can deteriorate stability of cathode material, resulting in poor cycling performance. The optimal charge cutoff voltage needed to be determined under consideration of specific capacity and cycling performance.

Prior to determination of optimal charge cutoff voltage, surface modification was performed for the candidate cathode material to enhance stability of the cathode material for higher charge voltage cutoff. The modified cathode materials were tested in different charge cutoff voltage range. Table 4 shows the test results.

Table 4 summary of specific capacity of the optimized cathode tested at different charge cutoff voltage.

	Modified cathodes		
Cutoff V	4.5 V	4.4 V	4.3 V
C/20 Discharge, mAh/g	205	187.4	189.3
C/10 Discharge, mAh/g	199.7	188.9	186.7
C/5 Discharge, mAh/g	188.9	181.9	179.2
1C Discharge, mAh/g	175.9	170.8	165.1
1C-Rate retention, % Based on capacity of C/10	88.1 %	90.4 %	88.4 %

As shown in table 4, the specific capacity of the tested cathode increased as the charge cutoff voltage increased for most tested C-rates. The surface modification did not affect the rate capability of the cathode.

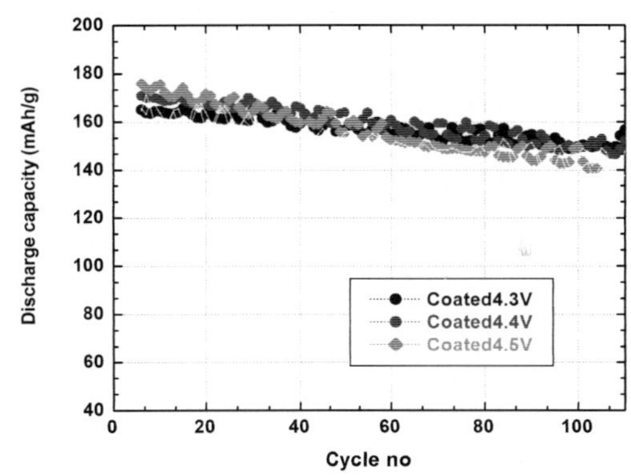

Figure 4. Comparison of cycling performance for the surface modified cathode; cycled in different charge cutoff voltage (ex: 4.3V, 4.4V and 4.5V) 1C discharge rate was applied for cycling.

The cathodes were cycled 1C discharge rate with different cutoff voltage to determine optimal or maximum charge voltage cutoff for an acceptable cycling performance. Figure 4 shows cycling performance of the surface modified cathode with different charge voltage cutoff conditions (4.3V, 4.4V and 4.5V). At the beginning of cycling, the discharge capacity of the surface modified cathode increased corresponding to increase of charge cutoff voltage. There was no significant difference in capacity fade between the electrodes cycled to 4.3V and 4.4V charge cutoff voltage. The cathode with 4.5V charge cutoff voltage condition demonstrated faster capacity fade than the cells cycled with 4.3V and 4.4V charge cutoff.

Performance and Discussion

The test pouch cell with the developed cathode and the anode were constructed for overall cell performance evaluation and confirming the compatibility of the cathode and anode. Figure 5 shows the test results of the constructed pouch cell performance. The pouch cell delivered the cell discharge capacity close to the estimated capacity at C/20 discharge rate based on the active mass of cathode material with the projected specific capacity in the optimized charge voltage range. The cell capacity and the voltage profile gradually decreased as the applied current level (or C-rate) increased. The highest C-rate applied was 1C discharge. The capacity obtained at 1C-rate was 85% of the maximum capacity which validates the overall cell design and the compatibility of the cathode and the anode chemistry.

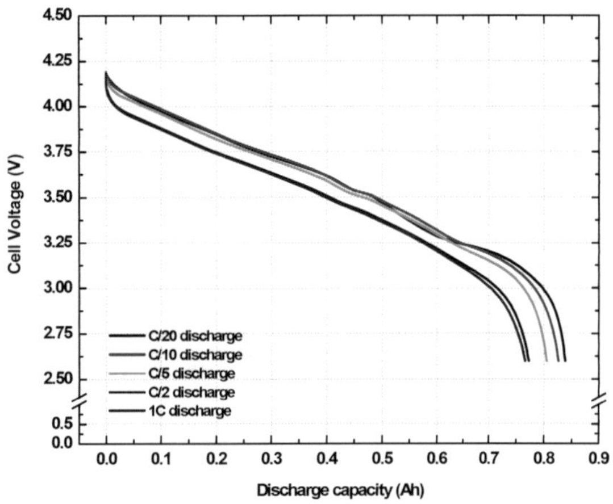

Figure 5. Discharge Capacity of the constructed pouch cell with the optimized cathode and anode at different discharge rates.

After validation of the cell design and chemistry in the test pouch cell format, the large format pouch cells were constructed to evaluate the energy density of the developed Li-ion chemistry. Prior to the test for the energy density estimation, further optimization of the large format cells assembly was carried out to maximize the cell performance. Figure 6 showed the performance a series of the large pouch cells after the cell assembly optimization. The series of the cells initially were formatted with mild current level cycles which consist of multi-steps cycling profile. The estimation of the energy density was performed at 1C discharge rate. The energy density from the tested pouch cells were > ~250 Wh/kg at 1C discharge rate which matched with the design target and also previous results of evaluation.

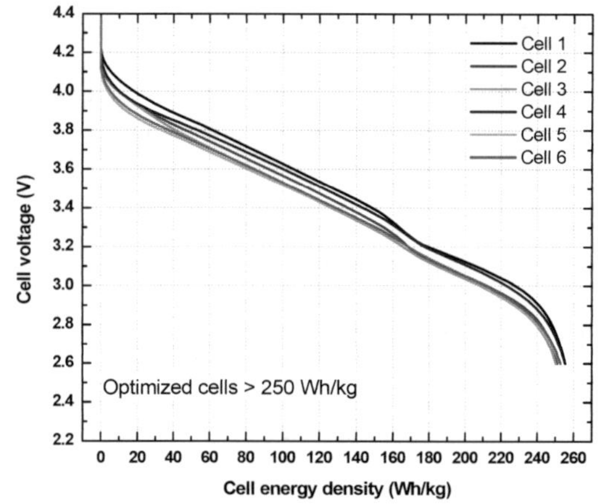

Figure 6. Energy Density plots of a set of the optimized cells; tested at1C-rate discharge (5.5A)

Summary

EPT has developed high energy density Li-ion cells (>250 Wh/kg at 1C discharge). The developed Li-ion cells showed the matching cell performance to the designed cell performance. The developed high specific capacity cathode and the silicon carbon anode demonstrated higher energy density than conventional lithium ion chemistry.

Acknowledgement

"This material is released to the public domain in accordance with ITAR 22 CFR 120.11"

References

1. Bloom, I., S.A. Jones, V.S. Battaglia, G.L. Henriksen, J.P. Chrsitophersen, R.B. Wright, C.D. Ho, J.R.Belt, and C.G. Motloch, "Effect of cathode composition on capacity fade, impedance rise", *Journal Power Sources* vol. 124, pp. 538-550, 2003.
2. Obrovaca, M. N., and L. J. Krauseb, "Reversible cycling of crystalline silicon powder", *Journal of Electrochem Soc.,* ,vol. 154, pp. A103-A108, 2007.
3. Morita T., and N. Takami, " Nano Si cluster-SiOx-Ccomposite material as high capacity anode material forrechargeable lithium batteries". *Journal of Electrochem Soc.*, vol. 153, pp. A425-A430, 2006.
4. Poizot, P., S. Laruelle, , S. Grugeon, L. Dupont, and J. M. Tarascon, "Searching for new anode materials for the Li-ion technology: time to deviate from the usual path", *Journal Power Sources,* vol. 97-98, pp. 235-239, 2001.
5. Li J., and Dahn , J. R., "An in situ X-ray diffraction study of the reaction of Li with crystalline Silicon", *Journal of Electrochem Soc,*, vol.154, A156-A161, 2007

Novel Chemistry for High Energy 600 Wh/L Lithium Ion Cells

Pu Zhang, Hongxia Zhou, Patrick Hagans, Christopher Silkowski, and Michael Wixom
Navitas Advanced Solutions Group
4880 Venture Drive, Ann Arbor, MI 48108
pzhang@navitassys.com

Abstract: *As new and more powerful combat systems are developed, there is an increasing need for rechargeable electrical power. High energy density lithium batteries are attractive power sources for vehicle propulsion, portable power units, and other battlefield applications. One of the main issues with increasing need for power and energy is the available volume. There is not enough room in the existing systems to increase power without sacrificing the vital system and space. This paper will demonstrate high energy lithium cells at 300 Wh/kg and 600 Wh/L based on high energy metal oxide cathode and Si composite anode chemistry. With development of advanced electrode materials, performance-enhanced electrolyte, and novel cell design, such high energy cells have shown >300 cycles at 80% capacity retention. All the electrodes were prepared using mass production slurry casting formulations and processing. Prismatic pouch cells have been built in pilot scale and demonstrated for portable power BB2590 and UAV applications. Next generation of cells are under development for enhanced safety and abuse tolerance. Performance data are presented for both cells and pack levels.*

Keywords: lithium ion; silicon anode; high energy; BB2590; UAV

Introduction

There is a motivation to increase lithium ion cell energy density for mobile and stationary applications. Lithium-ion batteries have high energy density and long cycle life. They are flexible in design and one of the most promising energy storage devices. The specific energy and energy density of lithium ion cells today are 200 Wh/kg and 500 Wh/L respectively. However, the ever-growing need for higher capacity and higher power, especially for increasing number of emerging new applications, has further prompted widespread research efforts towards developing electrodes and other materials with more appropriate properties for higher energy, longer life and lower cost.

Silicon-based materials have emerged as the anode of the future for lithium ion batteries, due to the high theoretical capacity of Si (4200 mAh/g, much higher than traditional graphite anode at 372 mAh/g). However, the enormous volume change of Si upon repeated lithium insertion and extraction leads to severe particle segregation and loss of particle–particle electronic contacts. Therefore pure silicon anodes suffer large capacity fading due to pulverization during cycling, which have prevented them from being commercially used. Significant efforts have been made to improve the cycling reversibility of Si-based anodes by improving the micro-structural stability and connect-ability. One generally accepted strategy is to prepare Si composite materials.

The work at Navitas has demonstrated the benefit of Si-carbon composites for cycle life and the presence of silicon for high lithium-storage capacity to improve the overall electrochemical performance of lithium ion anodes.

Navitas has also optimized a metal oxide cathode configuration for the high energy density lithium ion battery. The cathode has high specific capacity with good cycle life.

It is known that the electrolyte plays an important role for the cell performance, especially for the cell containing Si-based anode. Certain types of additives help to form stable solid electrolyte interphase (SEI) film on the Si anode. We have developed an advanced electrolyte for Si anode with significantly improved cycle life and reduced gas evolution.

Conventional electrolyte for lithium-ion battery is a liquid and contains flammable organic solvents. It is found that the vapor and/or aerosol of the solvents are the main contributor to the cell flammability during abuse conditions. A polymer-electrolyte with low vapor pressure has been developed to address the safety concern.

In this paper, we will demonstrate >300 cycles to 80% capacity retention in a high energy cell of 600 Wh/L, through a novel chemistry design including a Si composite anode, a high energy cathode, and an advanced electrolyte. The pack level performance for BB2590 and UAV applications is also reported.

Experimental

Electrode Development

The cathode is a high nickel content lithium metal oxide and the anode is a silicon carbon composite. Both the electrodes were fabricated by mixing the slurry containing active material, conductive additive, and binder in a planetary mixer. The prepared slurry was coated on to Al foil (cathode) or Cu foil (anode) using a continuous slot die coater. The coated electrode was then calendered to a desired thickness (porosity).

Half Cell and Li Ion Full Cell Fabrication

Half cells were built in the form of CR2025, with lithium as counter electrode. Li ion pouch cells were assembled in a dry-room at <2% moisture.

Cell and Battery Pack Test

Both cells and pack were tested on MACCOR. Environmental chambers were used for high and low temperature test condition.

Gassing Measurement

The volume change of single-layer-pouch cells (SLP) was measured by water immersion method. The cells were charged to 4.3V and stored at 60 °C for certain period of time.

Open Cup Ignition Test

For each electrolyte, a gram of sample was added to an aluminum open cup that is sitting on a 60°C hot plate. The ignition source was set at 1 cm above the cup. The duration of the open flame was recorded.

Results and Discussion

Electrode Development

The lithium metal oxide cathode shows a reversible specific capacity of 200 mAh/g when cycled at 4.3 - 3.0V in a half cell and the Si composite anode is 550 mAh/g at 0.01 - 0.7V. The electrode loading is 4 mAh/cm^2.

Electrolyte Development

The application of Si anode is limited mainly due to the short cycle life, which is attributed to the large volume expansion and contraction of Si during cycling. The SEI continues to decay and re-form due to the new exposed surfaces, which causes cell capacity degradation and cell swelling (gassing).

We have developed an electrolyte that addresses both cycle life and gas evolution issues. Figure 1 shows the improvement of cycle life from the new electrolyte over a conventional electrolyte in lithium ion cells. It should be noted that the cycle life was obtained with only partially optimized laboratory cells. In an optimized system, a cycle life of 300 has been demonstrated (Figure 5 on next page). Figure 2 compares the volume change of the new electrolyte containing cell to the baseline cell when charged to 4.3V and stored at 60°C for up to 30 days. Most of the volume change happened during the first 2 weeks. The volume change of the new electrolyte cells is 40% of the baseline cells (i.e., 60% reduction of gas generation).

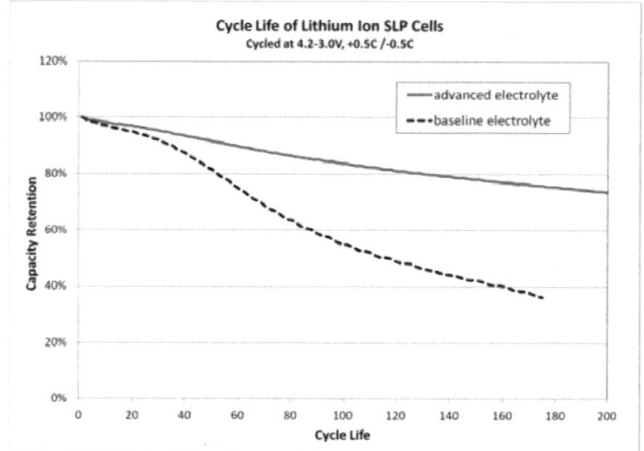

Figure 1. Cycle life of Li ion pouch cells with different electrolytes (4.2 – 3.0V; +0.5C/-0.5C)

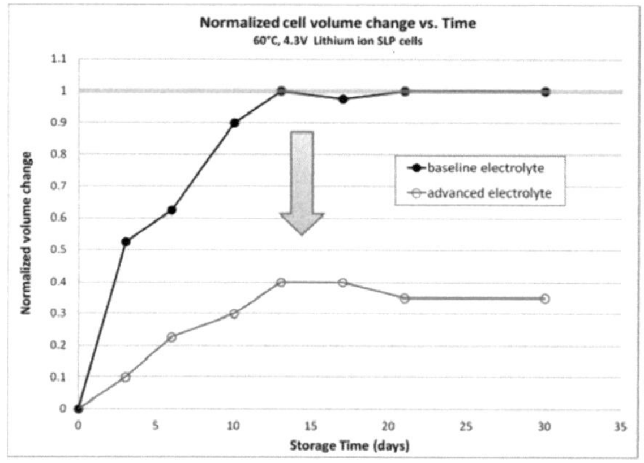

Figure 2. Cell Volume Increase vs. Time (stored at 4.3V and 60°C); lithium ion SLP cells; the volume change is normalized (baseline = 1)

To improve the safety of the cell, we have also developed a gel electrolyte that reduces the vapor pressure of the organic solvent, thus reducing flammability. A proprietary in-situ polymerization process overcomes technical challenges of low ionic conductivity of gel electrolytes and poor wetting ability (US patent pending).

In the open cup ignition test, the gel electrolyte shows much less flammability than the liquid electrolyte, indicating lower vapor pressure and potential safety advantage from this gel electrolyte (see Table 1).

Table 1. Open cup ignition test on electrolytes

Electrolyte	Duration of Flame (second)
Liquid electrolyte	40
Gel electrolyte	15

The cycle life of the cells with gel electrolyte is comparable to the baseline cells with liquid electrolyte (Figure 3).

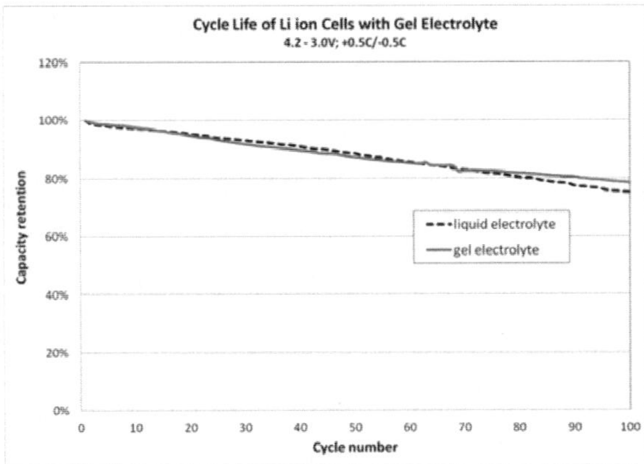

Figure 3. Cycle life comparison of Li ion pouch cells with gel electrolyte and liquid electrolyte (4.2 – 3.0V; +0.5C / -0.5C)

Prismatic Pouch Cell Development

Prismatic cells were demonstrated in two sizes for the high energy chemistry and are described in Table 2. The achievable specific energies were 270-300 Wh/kg with pulse power capability of >500W/kg. Figure 4 shows an example of a 6 Ah pouch cell. Table 3 summarizes the performance characteristics of Navitas' high energy cells, ranging from 2 Ah to 15 Ah.

Table 2. Parameters of prismatic pouch cells

Cell Model	HEC-6	HEC-12
L x W x H (mm)	95x54x6.5	95x54x3.4
Capacity (Ah)	6	12
Specific Energy (Wh/kg)	280	300
Energy Density (Wh/L)	705	730
Voltage Range (V)	4.3 – 3.0	4.3 – 3.0

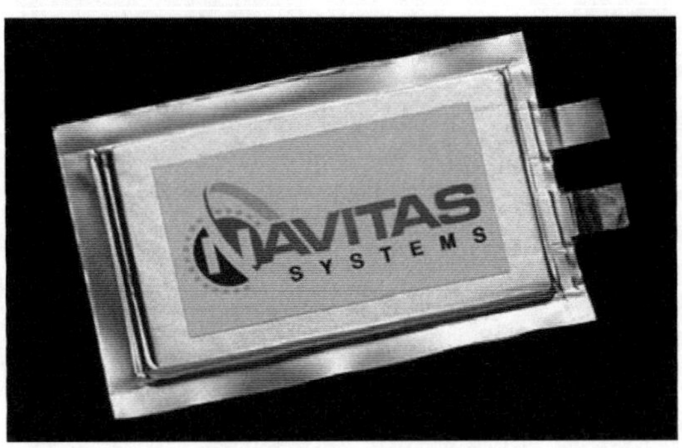

Figure 4. Navitas prototype HEC-6 pouch cell. It has capacity of 6 Ah and energy density of 700 Wh/L.

The cycle life of a 6Ah cell was tested at +0.5C/-0.5C between 4.3V – 3.0 V. This cell was developed with optimized cell configuration and processes. The cell attains >300 cycles to 80% capacity retention (Figure 5).

As a technology platform, high energy chemistry is adaptable to multiple cell form factors.

Table 3. Navitas high energy pouch cells (2 Ah - 15 Ah)

Operating Voltage	3.6 V
Max Voltage	4.3 V
Min Cut-off Voltage	3.0 V
Specific Energy	260-300 Wh/kg
Energy Density	550-730 Wh/L
Max continuous current	1C
Cycle life	>300 to 80% retention

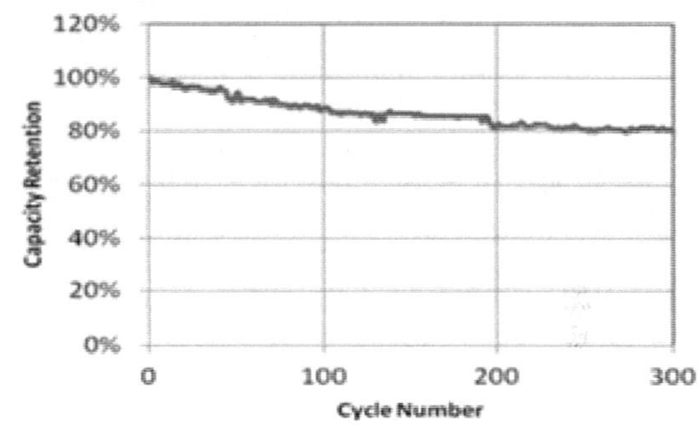

Figure 5. Cycle life of a 6Ah prototype cell (HEC-6) between 4.3 - 3.0 V at +0.5C/-0.5C and room temperature

Pack Development for BB2590 and UAV Applications

Navitas' High Energy Chemistry (HEC) cell technology has been applied in rechargeable BB 2590 batteries, which is the most common military battery, and other military systems including long endurance unmanned aerial vehicles (UAV). The UAV markets are limited to thousands of vehicles in the present fleet, but the market is growing rapidly.

BB2590 is a 5 inch tall soldier-portable Li-ion battery used primarily for US/NATO communications equipment and tactical robotics. BB2590 based on Navitas' HEC-6 cells (5.5Ah version) possesses 40-50% greater specific energy than COTS battery based on graphite/metal oxide cells (Figures 6 and 7).

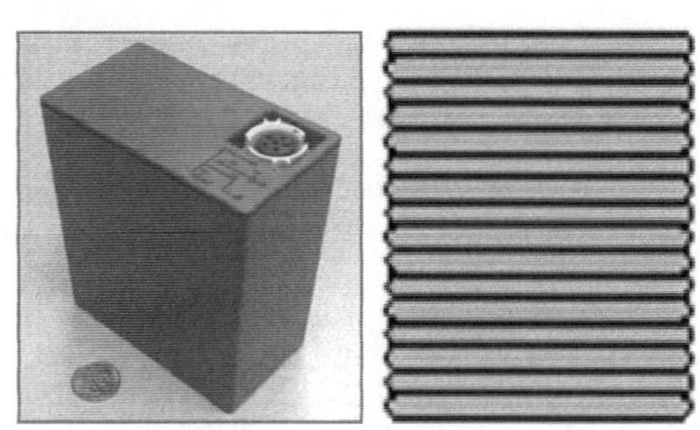

Figure 6. Configuration of Navitas BB2590: 16 parallel cells of HEC-6, 1.47 kg, 317 Wh, 215 Wh/kg, and 368 Wh/L

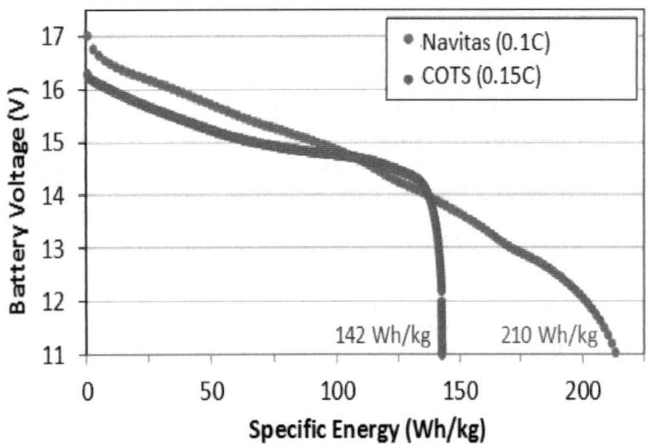

Figure 7. Comparison of specific energy of Navitas' BB2590 battery vs. COTS battery

In the UAV application, a Navitas 6Ah prototype cell delivers 280 Wh/kg and 525 Wh/L. Its cycle life meets 100 cycle target at +0.5C/-0.5C between 4.3 - 3.0V. The flight time in AeroVironment Raven was tested under "Standard" and "350g + Large Fairing" (heavy load) profiles:

- Standard Profile (~0.3C avg., 1.1C peak):
  - 57% increase in flight time vs. SOA
- 350g + Large Fairing Profile (~0.5C avg., 1.7C peak):
  - 76% increase in flight time vs. SOA

The Raven flight profiles under standard load and heavy load are shown in Figures 8 and 9, respectively.

Conclusion

Navitas has demonstrated high energy lithium cells at 300 Wh/kg and 600 Wh/L based with high energy metal oxide cathode and Si composite anode chemistry. With development of advanced electrode materials, performance-enhanced electrolyte, and novel cell design, the cell attains a cycle life of >300 to 80% capacity retention. Navitas BB2590 battery based on the high energy cells possesses 40% - 50% higher specific energy than COTS battery. Navitas UAV prototype cell delivers 60% - 80% increase in flight time.

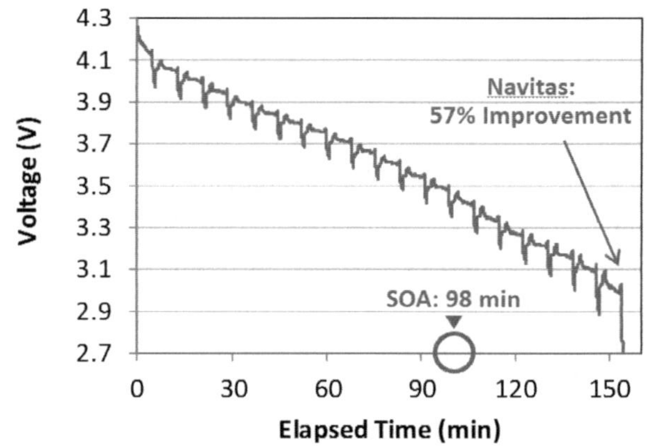

Figure 8. Navitas 6Ah UAV Cell Prototype Raven Flight Profile under standard load

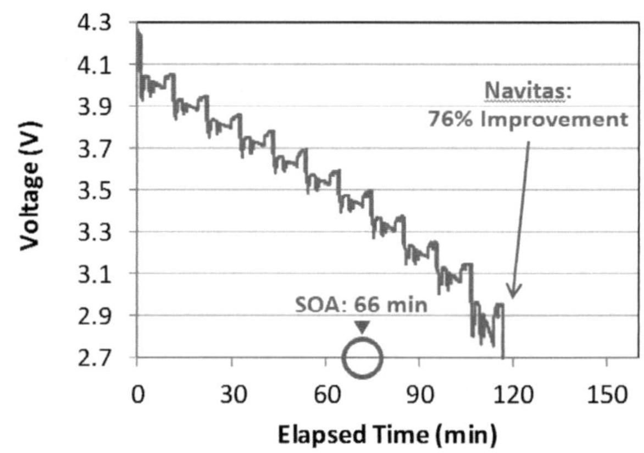

Figure 9. Navitas 6Ah UAV Cell Prototype Raven Flight Profile under heavy load

Acknowledgement

This work was supported by the DARPA-LOTS program.

Advanced Li/S Technology Development

Ramanathan Thillaiyan, Wujun Fu, Ernest Ndzebet, Umamaheswari Janakiraman and Mario Destephen
EaglePicher Technologies, LLC, an OMG company
3220 Industrial Road
Joplin, MO 64801

Abstract: *As an alternative power source for advanced electronic devices and vehicles, Li/S cells are receiving significant attention in recent years. However, the poor cycle life and low system efficiency have plagued Li/S and prevented the commercial realization. Herein, we reported systematic technical approaches including cathode, electrolyte and separator development to address the complex challenges involved in the Li/S chemistry. EPT high loading cathode confines the polysulfides by using suitable and low-cost carbon material. By modifying the physicochemical properties of electrolytes, EPT proprietary electrolyte effectively prevent the solid Li_2S deposition on the anode side and further improve the cell performance. EPT proprietary separator alleviates the diffusion of polysulfides and promotes the cycle life. Intermittence, shelf life performance and safety evaluation of EPT advanced Li/S cell will also be discussed. The technology advancement for Li/S system demonstrated herein strongly suggests a substantial opportunity for the development of Li/S battery for various industrial and defense applications including medical, portable power, unmanned aircraft and surveillance usage.*

Keywords: lithium; sulfur; Li/S battery; alternative power source; energy storage; cathode; separator; electrolyte.

Introduction

The strong demand for sustainable, clean energy technologies is one of the most critical concerns in current and upcoming decades. Electrical energy storage system not only can reduce the consumption of fossil fuel, but also allow widespread application of intermittent renewable energy storage from solar and wind. Among all rechargeable batteries, lithium ion batteries (LIBs), which have been proven successful in the portable electronics market, still represent the state-of-the-art energy storage technology.[1-2] However, LIBs based upon insertion cathodes have reached their limitation in energy density of ~ 200 Wh/kg. In addition, safety concerns arising from the chemical instability of the oxide cathodes under abuse conditions of overcharge/high temperature, and the high cost associated with expensive transition metals are key limiting factors of LIBs. To meet the increasing demand of electrical energy, alternative cathode materials, with a significantly increased capacity and energy density, reduced cost, and enhanced safety are highly desired.

Sulfur, one of the most abundant elements on earth, is a very attractive cathode material because of its extremely high theoretical capacity (1675 mAh/g).[3] Through redox-driven phase-transformation chemistry instead of the conventional insertion chemistry involved in LIBs, the combination of lithium metal as the anode and elemental sulfur as the cathode provides a specific energy density of 2500 Wh/kg assuming of complete reaction of Li with S to form Li_2S. In addition, elemental sulfur is inexpensive and environmentally friendly. Thus, the Li/S chemistry has been considered as one of the most promising battery chemistries for the next generation of high energy batteries.[3]

However, despite considerable advantages of sulfur chemistry, the commercialization of Li/S battery still remains as a huge challenge because of some major issues involved in Li/S chemistry. First, elemental sulfur is electrically and ionically insulating ($5x10^{-30}$ S cm^{-1} at 25°C), leading to the poor electrochemical contact and low utilization of active material in the cathode.[4] The second challenge lies in the intermediate discharge products, lithium polysulfides, which are highly soluble in most organic electrolyte solutions. The dissolved polysulfide intermediates can migrate through electrolytes to the Li anode to form insoluble Li_2S or Li_2S_2 on the anode surface inhibiting the transportation of Li ions. The reduced products can also diffuse back to the cathode during cycling. The polysulfides species shuttling between the anode and cathode during the cycle process, accompanied with a series of side reduction reactions with lithium anode and reoxidation reactions with the sulfur cathode result in the permanent loss of active materials, and therefore lead to the low coulombic efficiency and poor cycle life of Li/S battery.[3]

To address those intrinsic issues involved in Li/S chemistry, extensive studies have been devoted to improve the conductivity of the sulfur cathode and prevent polysulfide dissolution and shuttling. One approach is the addition of various conductive carbon materials to form carbon/sulfur composites to improve the overall electrode conductivity. Another approach is to protect the lithium anode to block the chemical reaction path at the anode side. For example, lithium nitrate ($LiNO_3$)[5] reacts with lithium anode to form a stable passivation film on its surface. The anode passivation layer blocks any further chemical reactions of polysulfides species with the lithium anode;

hence, this greatly improves the cycling efficiency of the Li/S battery. Other approaches, including introduction of the novel Li/S cell configuration, synthesis of sulfur-polymer hybrid cathode and application of efficient electrolyte, have also been reported by a number of publications from different research groups.[6-7] Apparently, there is no simple approach which can allow us to address all these complex problems. In order to radically promote the Li/S technology, a more holistic research approach is needed. Herein, we reported a systematic technical approach including high loading C/S cathode development, electrolyte formulation and novel separator synthesis to overcome the interlinked issues within Li/S chemistry. By incorporation of overall technical development into EPT advanced Li/S prototype cell, we demonstrated an improved Li/S technology with increased capacity and energy density, improved intermittence discharge performance, prolonged storage life as well as the enhanced safety performance. The overall improvement represents a promising future for industrial scale of Li/S batteries.

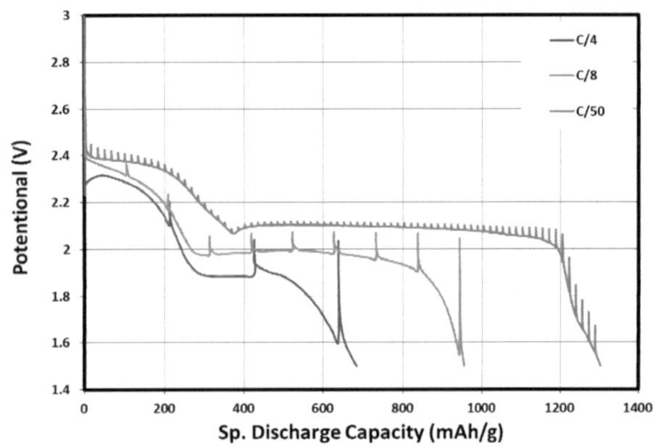

Figure 1. Discharge of high loading C/S cathode with baseline electrolyte at different C-rates.

Experimental

Sulfur and conductive carbon were mixed thoroughly with suitable ratio. Through heat treatment, the sulfur was encapsulated within carbon to form the C/S composite. The slurry was prepared by mixing C/S composite, the binder poly(vinylidene fluoride) (PVDF) and the solvent N-methyl-2-pyrrolidinone (NMP). Then the slurry was coated onto aluminum foil to obtain C/S cathode.

The baseline electrolyte is composed of 1M lithium bis(trifluoromethane sulfone)imide (LiTFSI) in equal volumes of dioxolane and diglyme. EPT proprietary electrolyte was prepared by dissolving LiTFSI in organic solvents with addition of various additives. EPT proprietary separator was prepared via a conventional solution casting method.

The Li/S pouch cells were assembled by using lithium anode, C/S cathode, celgard 2325/EPT proprietary separator and the baseline/EPT proprietary electrolyte. The Li/S cells were evaluated by using Arbin battery test system between 2.7 V and 1.5 V (vs. Li+/Li) at room temperature. The intermittent discharge test was performed at the following procedures: the cells were discharged from OCV to 2.1V initially, then stored at ambient conditions for 3 days, and followed by continuing to discharge to 1.5 V. The shelf life performance was evaluated at room temperature (RT) and 45 °C. The cells were stored up to one month at these temperatures.

Results and Discussion

Due to the insulating nature of sulfur, conductive materials must be involved for the sulfur cathode preparation. Carbon is an ideal electronic conduit to enable redox accessibility of sulfur and act as a framework to encapsulate the polysulfides species as well. By selecting commercially available, low cost carbon material, we synthesized C/S composite via mechanical mixing and subsequent heat treatment. The loading of the resulting cathode was increased up to ~ 16 mg/cm^2, which is significantly higher than any values reported in literature. In addition, the high loading C/S cathode exhibited high initial discharge capacity and impressive rate capability as well. As shown in Figure 1, the first discharge capacity of EPT high loading cathode can reach 1301 mAh/g at C/50, which is around 78% of the theoretical capacity. Even at C/4 discharge rate, the capacity still remain at 686 mAh/g, indicating the good rate capability of the high loading cathode, which is due to the intimate contact between sulfur and carbon and well distribution of S in the carbon matrix.

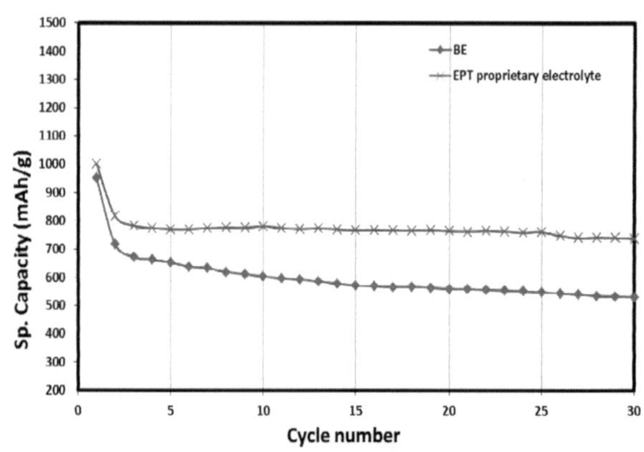

Figure 2. Cycling performance of Li/S pouch cell containing baseline electrolyte and EPT proprietary electrolyte.

A mixture of cyclic or linear ethers containing LITFSI salt is commonly used as the electrolyte for Li/S battery. Additives can have significant effect on Li/S battery performance by modifying the physicochemical properties of the electrolyte. EPT proprietary electrolyte for Li/S system was formulated with several additives and co-solvents in order to: 1) adjust the physical properties of electrolytes, such as viscosity and conductivity, to retard the polysulfides diffusion and migration within the electrolyte; 2) to remove the deposition of insoluble Li_2S/Li_2S_2 on the lithium anode surface to ensure the good transportation of lithium ions and avoid the active materials loss.

Figure 2 showed the cycling performance comparison of the Li/S pouch cell with baseline electrolyte and EPT proprietary electrolyte. As can be seen, the EPT electrolyte formulation not only enhances the active material utilization but also significantly improves the cyclability of the Li/S cell. After 30 cycles, the Li/S cell with EPT electrolyte remained the capacity of 737 mAh/g, which is around 38% increase compared to the cell with baseline electrolyte.

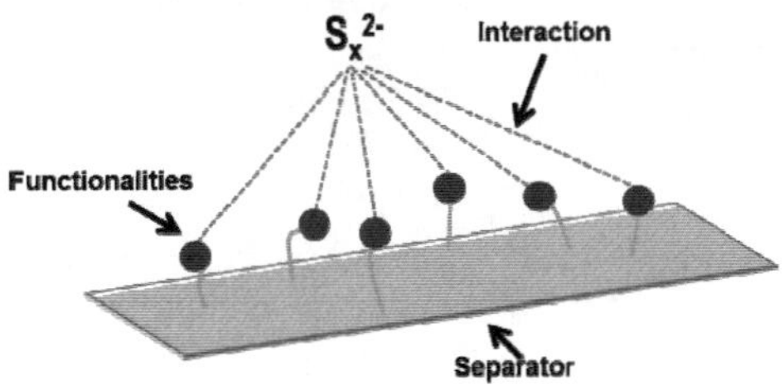

Figure 3. Schematic of the interaction between polysulfides and nanoclay functionalities polymer film separator.

To further promote Li/S technology, EPT introduced the nanoclay functionalized polymer film as separator, which is specifically designed for Li/S system. Since polysulfides shuttle involves the migration of the polysulfides through the separator, the modification of the polymer separator and creation of the interaction between polysulfides and separator will slow down the migration and diffusion of polysulfides to the lithium anode thus inhibiting the polysulfides shuttle. The schematic mechanism illiustrated in Figure 3.

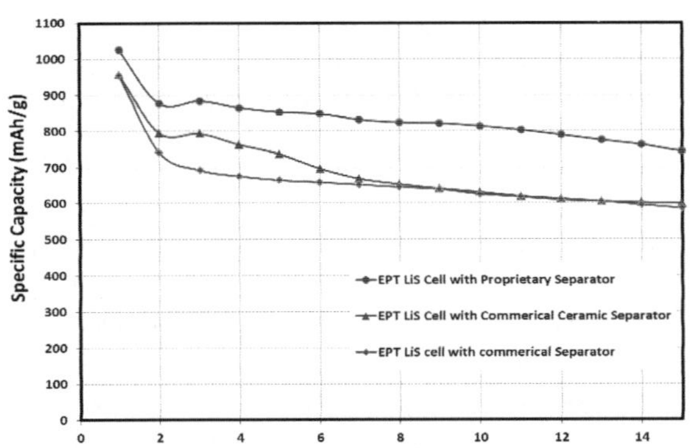

Figure 4. Cycling performance of Li/S pouch cell containing commercial celgard/ceramic separators and EPT proprietary separator.

The cycling performances of the Li/S cells containing three different separators, two commercially available separators (celgard and ceramic) and EPT proprietary separator were showed in Figure 4. The initial discharge capacity of the Li/S cell with EPT proprietary separator displayed a slightly higher than the cells with commercial separators. However, the cycling performance significant improved. Indeed after 15 cycles, the capacity of Li/S cell with EPT proprietary separator is around 755 mAh/g, which is around 16 % and 35 % higher than the cells with ceramic and celgard separators respectively. Thus, the results suggest that to use specifically designed separator in Li/S system instead of conventional separators generally applied in lithium-ion batteries.

Figure 5. Digital photo of EPT Li/S stack pouch prototype cell.

By combining EPT high loading C/S cathode, lithium anode, EPT proprietary electrolyte and separator, we systematically demonstrated the improvements of Li/S technology. Those improvements were consolidated in our prototype stack pouch cell, as shown in Figure 5. To fully evaluate our advanced Li/S battery, several key characters, such as intermittent discharge performance, shelf life performance at various temperatures and safety performance, were also tested.

Figure 6 reveals the intermittence and shelf life performance of EPT advanced Li/S cell and cell with baseline electrolyte/baseline electrolyte with $LiNO_3$ in it. Compared with the corresponding continuous discharge capacity, the capacity loss between continuous and intermittent discharge of EPT advanced Li/S cell was 2.1%, much lower than other cells with baseline electrolyte (11.2 % and 8.1 % with $LiNO_3$), indicating the EPT Li/S cell has a better intermittent performance than regular Li/S cells. In addition, EPT advanced Li/S cell also exhibited higher discharge capacity after storage at various conditions than other cells. In particular, for the cell stored at 45 °C for one month, the capacity of the EPT cell still remained at 1038 mAh/g, significantly higher than other two cells. The improved shelf life performance could be attributed to the better stability towards the self-discharge because of the involvement of EPT proprietary electrolyte and separator in EPT advanced Li/S cell.

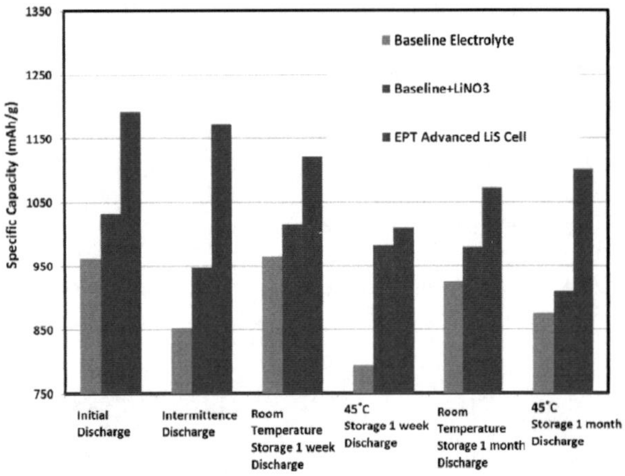

Figure 6. Comparison of initial discharge, intermittence discharge and shelf life performance of Li/S cells with baseline electrolyte, baseline electrolyte with $LiNO_3$ and EPT advanced LiS cell.

Safety testing was carried out in EPT advanced Li/S stack pouch cell using nail penetration and overcharge testing. The nail penetration test was carried out on a fully discharged cell. As shown in Figure 7, after the nail puncture, the cell did not cause fire or smoke, even after several hours with the nail remaining inside. Overcharge evaluation was also carried out on a fully-charged cell, and was continuously charge at 1C without applying any limitation to the maximum voltage 8V. The cell started swelling at around 5V, and a small amount of smoke observed at 8V while no fire observed during the whole test period. The safety evaluations strongly suggested EPT Li/S cell is safe for overcharge and nail penetration.

Conclusion

EPT systematic approach to the Li/S technology to address the intrinsic challenges involved in Li/S chemistry provides an opportunity to develop Li/S battery for various industrial applications. By combining high loading C/S cathode development, EPT proprietary electrolyte formulation and novel separator design, EPT have successfully delivered the EPT advanced LiS prototype cell, which not only showed the good utilization of active material, but also displayed the enhanced intermittent and shelf life performance. In addition, safety evaluation was also consolidated in our cell design. We believe that technical advancement realized herein will make Li/S battery a commercially viable technology in the near future.

Acknowledgements

This material is released to the public domin in accordance with ITAR 22 CFR 120.11.

Figure 7. Nail Penetration test before and after nail penetrate through the EPT advanced Li/S cell.

References

1. Armand, M., Tarascon, J. M. "Building Better Batteries," *Nature*, vol 451, pp. 652-657, 2008.
2. Jung, H. G., Jang, M. W., Hassoun, J., Sun, Y. K., Scrosati, B. A high-rate long-life $Li_4Ti_5O_{12}/Li[Ni_{0.45}Co_{0.1}Mn_{1.45}]O_4$ lithium-ion battery," *Nature Communication*, vol 2, pp. 516, 2011.
3. Evers, S., Nazar, L. F. "New Approaches for High Energy Density Lithium-Sulfur Battery Cathodes," Accounts of Chemical Research, vol 46, pp. 1135-1143, 2013.
4. Liang, C., Dudney, N. J., Howe, J. Y. "Hierarchically Structured Sulfur/Carbon nanocomposite material for High-Energy Lithium Battery," *Chemistry of Materials*, vol 21, pp. 4724-4730, 2009.
5. Aurbach, D., Pollak, E., Elazari, R., Salitra, G., Kelley, C.S., Affinito, J. "O the Surface Chemical Aspects of Very High Energy Density, Rechargeable Li-Sulfur Batteries," *Journal of Chemical Society*, vol 156, pp. A694-A702, 2009.
6. Su, Y., Manthiram, A. "A new Approach to Improve Cycle Performance of Rechargeable Lithium-Sulfur Batteries by Inserting a Free-Standing MWCNT Interlayer," *Chemical Communication*, vol 48, pp. 8817-8819, 2012.
7. Manthiram, A., Fu, Y., Su, Y., "Challenges and Prospects of Lithium-Sulfur Batteries," Accounts of Chemical Research, vol 46, pp. 1125-1134, 2013.

Charge Optimization of BB-2590 Military Batteries Using Solar Power Regulated By a Dynamically Switching Converter

Nnamdi Ibeka and Jonathan Novoa
US ARMY RDECOM, CERDEC, CP&I
Aberdeen Proving Ground, MD 21005

Abstract: *DC-DC converters are used to regulate the output voltage from a power source to meet the voltage requirement of a peripheral receiving power using buck (step-down), boost (step-up), or buck-boost (combination) conversion methods. It is best to identify the most favorable converter type on an application basis. The research at hand will explore the voltage conversion methods used to charge BB-2590 military batteries in 16 volt or 32 volt mode using emulated power scavenged from a source representing solar energy. The voltage output capabilities from solar panels will vary with respect to the quality of the energy available. Therefore, a buck-boost converter would be most favorable for this application due to the necessity of a charge-controller to be able to step-up or step-down the input voltage provided by the source to the required output voltage to the peripheral. The data resulting from this study will determine the practicality of a DC-DC buck-boost converter dynamically switching its output voltage between 16 V and 32 V with respect to fluctuating source input voltages in order to increase the charge efficiency of BB-2590 military batteries in the field using solar power.*

Keywords: Charging Techniques; Charge-Controllers; BB-2590; DC-DC Converter; Solar Charge Optimization; Dynamically Switching Converter.

Introduction

In regards to leveraging solar energy, it is imperative that proper controller mechanisms are implemented in order optimize the transfer of solar energy from the source to the load or storage medium. The current state-of-the-art solar charge-controller technologies use Maximum Power Point Tracking (MPPT) algorithms which automate the selection of a solar panel's operating voltage such that the power output of the panel is maximized. The implementation of the MPPT algorithm in charge-controllers effectively minimizes the power wasted in energy harvesting using solar panels. Various MPPT methods have been developed such as, the perturb-and-observe method, open and short-circuit method, incremental conductance algorithm, fussy logic, and the artificial neural network. Maximum Power Point Tracking effectively optimizes solar charging from a supply intensive stand-point. The purpose of this study is to investigate whether the optimization of solar charging techniques can be improved further by introducing a demand or load intensive algorithm into a solar charging mechanism. For peripherals that are capable of accepting multiple charge voltages it would be advantageous to exploit the usage of all possible charge voltages based on maximum efficiency, thereby optimizing charge-controller efficiency from a demand intensive stand-point.

The BB-2590 military battery is an example of an energy storage unit that can accept charges at multiple voltages, more specifically, 16 V or 32 V. The charge efficiency of BB-2590 military batteries using solar power can be optimized by examining the correlation between the variance in conversion efficiency of a buck-boost DC-DC converter to the fluctuation in input voltage of a source representing a solar panel. A trend or correlation is defined as it pertains to the fixed output voltage received by a BB-2590 in 16 V and 32 V modes. Comprised of two cell arrays, it is standard practice to charge the unit at 16 V in a parallel configuration which lends to maintaining the balance of the cells. There are potential cases where charging at 32 V in a series circuit configuration may be more advantageous which this experiment serves to investigate. Charging a BB-2590 using 32 V introduces an increased risk of the cell arrays becoming unbalanced which would subsequently deplete the health and degrade the safety of the battery. Therefore, it is assumed that in any full adaption of a final system, the capability to exchange data with the charge-controller will be present, and may override the charging system in order to preserve the health of the battery.

Experimental

Efficiency Profiling and Characterization: The purpose of the efficiency characterization experiment is to obtain and analyze efficiency data for a DC-DC buck-boost converter in order to determine the most efficient method to charge a BB-2590 military battery while using solar power as the primary energy source. The most efficient method for charging the aforementioned batteries using solar power will be identified by generating a profile which depicts when it is more advantageous to convert to a 16 V output as opposed to a 32 V output, and vice versa depending on the input voltage from the source as well as the load requirement. Upon conclusion of this experimentation, the practicality or lack thereof, of developing an algorithm to be integrated into a solar charge-controller which would enable a converter to switch output voltages dynamically, such that the charging efficiency of a BB-2590 would be optimized would be determined. The DC-DC converter used in the experimentation had an input voltage constraint of 9-40 volts, a maximum output constraint of 40 V, and a maximum current output limitation of 7.5 amps. As depicted in Figure 1, the converter was configured with a programmable DC power supply attached to the input terminals and a programmable DC load bank attached to the output terminals of the converter. A 50 mV, 5 amp rated shunt was integrated between the converter and both supply and load peripherals for data measurement and acquisition. The voltage output of the converter was manipulated by adjusting tunable resistors attached on a circuit from the voltage trim pin to the voltage (-) output pin on the converter. The purpose of implementing this mechanism was to provide means to manually manipulate the output voltage of the converter in order to obtain data for a specific charging scenario of 16 V or 32 V output. The resistive values required to obtain the specified output voltages for the converter being evaluated were calculated using the generalized equation in Figure 2.

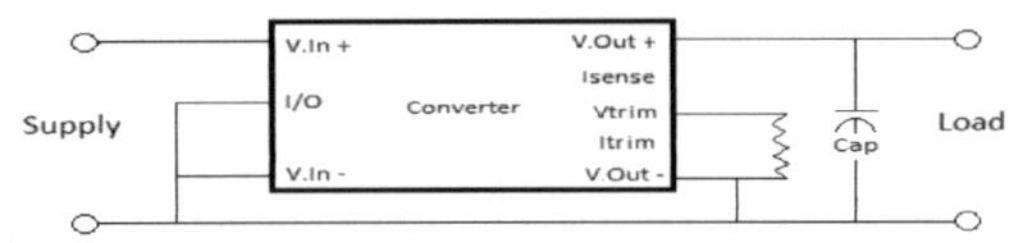

Figure 1. Converter Configuration with Resistor Trim

$$R_{trim}(V_{out}) = \left(\frac{K_1 * V_{max}}{V_{out} + (K_2 * V_{max})}\right) - K_3$$

Figure 2. Resistor Trim Equation

Therefore, in order to obtain an output of 16 V a resistive value of 15.28 kΩ should be applied across the voltage output (-) and voltage trim pins. To obtain a 32 V output, 3.02 kΩ of resistance should be applied across the respective pins.

The pertinent data points needed to complete this experiment are input voltage, input current, output voltage and output current. These data points are used to calculate the converter power input and output and subsequently, the efficiency of the converter. The profiles generated by the efficiency testing are dependent upon a varying input voltage, a set output voltage, and constant load. Therefore, the test was conducted for 16 V and 32 V fixed outputs using a voltage input range of 11-36 volts at loads of 20, 40, 60, 80 and 100 watts. The input voltage constraints for this experiment were set to reflect a typical solar panel operational voltage range within the performance constraints of the converter, while the load step was capped at a 100 watt nominal maximum to represent the maximum power a BB-2590 could potentially draw during a charge cycle. Each individual test requires the user to set the input voltage on the power supply, set a constant power requirement on the load bank, and manipulate the resistive circuit on the voltage trim pin to obtain the desired output voltage (16 V or 32 V). Using these settings to operate the converter, voltage and current data is recorded using a data acquisition unit hardwired via shunts in the test setup. For each voltage output setting and load step, the voltage input is increased for each test by an increment of 0.5-volts starting from the lower limit voltage, 11 V to the higher limit, 36 V and then decreases to 11 V by the same increment. A total of 100 data points were collected at five second intervals for each test.

Dynamic Switching Proof of Concept: The purpose of this experiment is to validate the hypothesis that implies that it is plausible to charge BB-2590 batteries by implementing an automated process that enables the converter to switch the acceptable output voltage to optimize charge efficiency when using solar power based on a conversion efficiency profile. In this experiment a micro-controller is introduced into the configuration. The purpose of this controller is to automate the switching process of the converter by reading input and output data from the converter using analog signals and implementing the programming logic as shown in Figure 3.

The voltage output is manipulated automatically by the micro-controller which applies a specified voltage to the voltage trim pin as opposed to manipulating the output voltage manually using tunable resistors across the voltage trim and voltage output (-) pins as proposed in the previous experiment. See Figure 4. The voltage that must be applied to the voltage trim pin for the converter being evaluated is calculated using the generalized equation in Figure 5 and must be implemented into the programming logic of the micro-controller. Therefore, in order to obtain an output voltage of 16 V, 1.452 volts should be applied to the voltage trim pin and to obtain a 32 V output, 0.539 volts should be applied to the voltage trim pin.

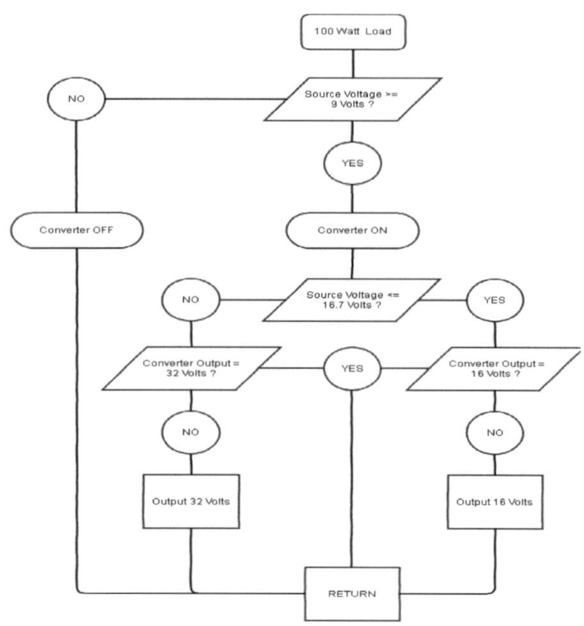

Figure 3. Micro-controller Logic for a 100 Watt Load Profile

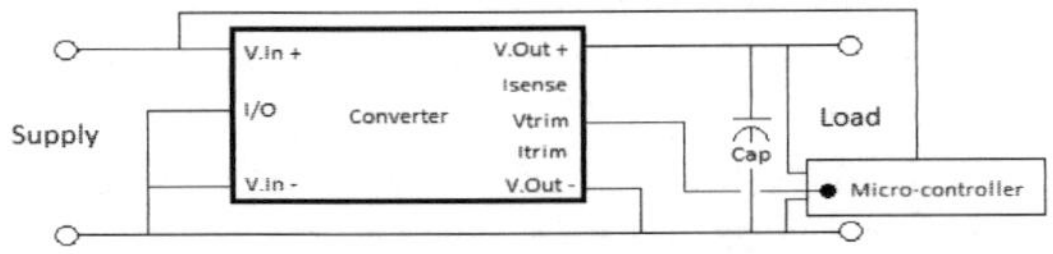

Figure 4. Converter Configuration with Micro-controller

$$V_{trim}(V_{out}) = K_1 - K_2 * \left(\frac{V_{out}}{V_{max}}\right)$$

Figure 5. Voltage Trim Equation

The proposed experiment will compare the efficiency of the converter with an output voltage fixed at 16 V over the entire previously specified range of input voltages and a fixed load (100 watts) to that of the same converter with the dynamic switching capability implemented under the same experimental constraints. The input voltage profile, load, and time duration constraints will be held constant in both tests. The dynamic switching test will utilize the applicable efficiency characterization profile in order to determine the optimal output voltage. The input voltage step will be changed automatically in 0.5-volt steps using a programmable power supply. Input and output voltage, current, and power data as well as temperature data will be collected and used to characterize the efficiency of the cited charging methods being compared. This experiment was designed to be executed using a singular charge profile intentionally, in this case the 100 watt efficiency profile, in order to simplify the programming logic required prove the concept. A full-scale model of this concept would require the micro-controller to interpret both voltage and current data in order to calculate and differentiate between loads, thereby enabling the capability to switch between multiple load profiles dynamically.

Results

The data obtained from the conversion profile shown in Figure 6, for a 100 watt load depicts a clear point at which it is more efficient to convert to 16 V as opposed to 32 V output and vice versa for a range of inputs ranging from 11 V to 36 V. For a peripheral drawing 100 watts, it is more efficient to convert to a 16 V output when the source is providing power within a voltage range of 11 V to 16.5 V. When utilizing a source providing 17 V to 36 V it is more efficient to convert to an output voltage of 32 V. A compilation of the results from the conversion efficiency tests conducted for 20, 40, 60, and 80 watt loads in Figure 7 also depicts clear points at which it is more ideal to convert to one voltage over another.

Temperature data in Figure 8 shows the fluctuation in temperature over time during the comparative efficiency testing of the converter. Temperature profiles were recorded for the test while the output was fixed to 16 V constantly as well as while the output was programmed to switch between 16 V and 32 V dynamically depending on the source voltage provided to sustain a 100 watt load. The temperature profiles for both conversion methods are noticeably similar during the beginning of the conversion cycle, but deviate from each other as time progresses, followed by a period of time where they begin to converge again at the end of the cycle. The divergence of the temperature profiles from one another is a direct correlation to the variation in efficiency between the conversion methods. Waste energy is dissipated in the form of heat. Therefore, given that higher temperatures were reached during the conversion test conducted under 16 V constant

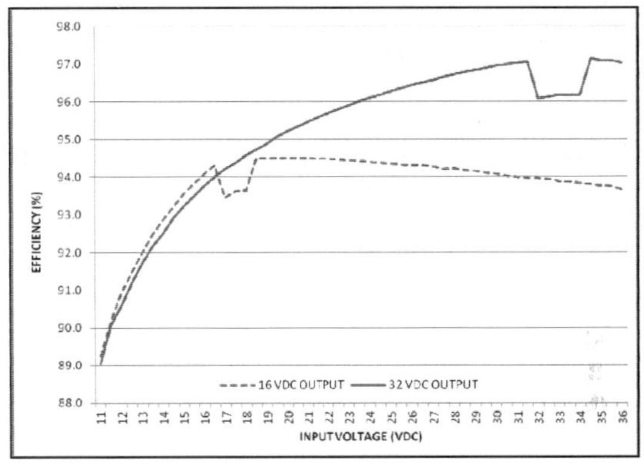

Figure 6. 100 Watt Load Converter Efficiency Profile

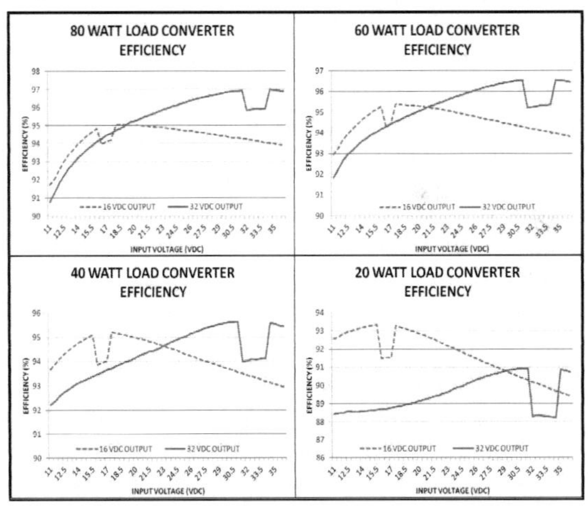

Figure 7. Profiles for 80, 60, 40, and 20 Watt Loads

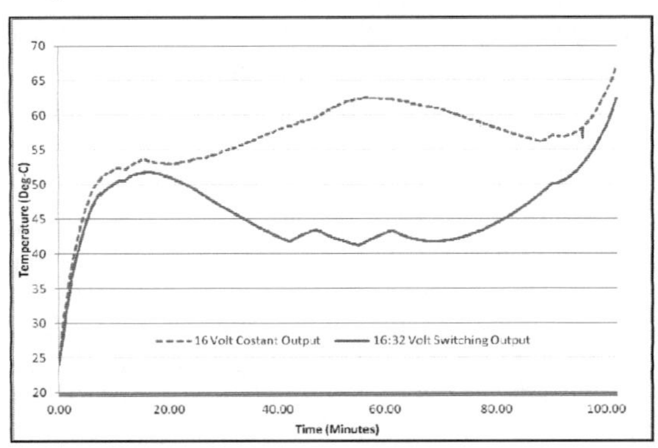

Figure 8. Temperature Profile Comparison

output conditions over the span of the test cycle as compared to the 16V or 32 V switching test cycle, the dynamic switching conversion method is more efficient as evidenced by the average operating efficiencies and temperatures of the test cycles tabulated in Table 1.

Table 1. 100-Watt Profile Conversion Summary

Output	Energy In (Whrs)	Energy Out (Whrs)	Avg. Efficiency (%)	Avg. Temp. (°C)
16 VDC Constant	182.56	170.16	93.20	56.63
16:32 VDC Switching	178.70	169.56	94.88	45.90

Table 1 is a summary of the overall performance of both conversion tests conducted using the 100 watt conversion profile. The tabulated values of energy into and out of the converter reflect the cumulative amount of energy in and out of the converter at the conclusion of the respective tests. The energy data was used to calculate the average efficiency of the converter for each of the tests.

Discussion

Efficiency data obtained from conversion profiles depicted in Figure 6 and Figure 7 show that in most test scenarios included in this experiment the overall peak efficiencies of the converter were reached while converting to a 32 V output as opposed to 16 V. For example, during the 100 watt profile characterization test, the peak efficiency reached while converting to 16 V was 94.51 percent for a source voltage ranging from 19 V to 21 V. The respective efficiencies while converting to 32 V for the same range of source voltages spanned from 94.89 to 95.46 percent. The peak efficiency obtained while converting to 32 V was 97.13 percent when converting from a 34.5 V input. The variance seen in efficiencies clearly highlights the benefits of switching output voltages of the converter based on the source voltage and load demand.

The aforementioned figures in this section consistently show distinctive dips in efficiency while converting from source voltages that are relatively close to the set output voltage which recover once outside of the voltage ranges depicted in figures 6 and 7. The dips in efficiency are assumed to be a physical limitation of the converter, better described as the inability of the converter to adequately buck or boost voltages that are within a certain range of the desired output which consequently results in the additional losses seen for those respective source voltage ranges.

The areas of convergences and divergences of temperatures in the profile in Figure 8 can be explained by the design of the input voltage profile for the 100 watt load test. The profile as described in the experimental section begins with a source voltage of 11 V and increases to 36 V by increments of 0.5 volts and then returns back to 11 V by the same increment; a pyramid step design. As evidenced in the 100 watt profile, from source voltages of 11 V to 16.5 V it is more efficient to convert to an output of 16 V. This discovery is consistent with the convergent temperatures seen in profiles of both conversion methods shown in the data. In the beginning and ending stages of the input voltage step profile, based on the efficiency characterization the switching conversion method would yield a conversion to 16 V. Therefore, the operating temperature from the dynamic switching profile should converge to that of the 16 V constant profile since both methods yield the same output voltage during those instances.

Conclusion

As evidenced by the data provided in this study, the capability for a solar charge-controller to switch dynamically between multiple output voltages in order to charge a peripheral more efficiently is both plausible and beneficial. More specifically, implementing an algorithm that would facilitate the ability of a solar charge-controller to charge a BB-2590 military battery in both 16 V and 32 V depending on the voltage provided from the source would be a beneficial military application given that solar energy is extremely variant and this capability has the potential to make battery charging more efficient by adapting to those changes. It was discovered that at higher loads, a 32 V output is preferential for the majority of input voltages examined in the profile. The examination of smaller loads profiles showed that the preferable output voltage is more evenly distributed across the spectrum of input voltages examined in the profile. The concept of dynamically switching the output of a converter automatically from an algorithm derived from a conversion profile was achieved successfully and shows technological promise to enhance the charging efficiencies of BB-2590 batteries as well as other military peripherals that can accept multiple charge voltages.

Acknowledgements

The authors wish to thank Terrill B. Atwater, Ph.D for his assistance in troubleshooting the test setup for this experiment and Darren Z. Stephens for his contributions to the development of the prototype for this experiment.

References

1. MIL-PRF-32383/3, "Performance Specification Sheet: Battery, Rechargeable, Sealed, BB-2590()/U, BB-390()/U, and BB-3590()/U." June 16, 2011. http://www.assistdocs.com
2. Liu, C., Wu, B., and Cheung, R. "Advanced Algorithm for MPPT Control of Photovoltaic Systems," *Canadian Solar Buildings Conference,* Montreal, Canada, Aug. 20, 2004.
3. Rosu-Hamzescu, M. and Oprea, S., "Practical Guide to Implementing Solar Panel MPPT Algorithms," *Microchip Technology Inc.*, vol. AN1521, 2013.

Recent Advances in Highly Resonant Wireless Power Transfer Technology for Soldier Power Applications

Morris Kesler, Jeff Muhs, Ky Sealy, Ryan Bohm, and Volkan Efe
WiTricity Corporation; 149 Grove Street, Watertown, MA 02472

Kailash C. Shukla and Frank Ashe
US Army Natick Soldier RDEC; 15 Kansas Street; Natick, MA 01760

1. Introduction

In a typical 72-hour mission, dismounted warfighters carry as many as 7 types of batteries, 70 primary cells, and over 20 pounds of batteries[1]. In addition to the physical burden of carrying batteries, the reliance on several different batteries introduces a complex supply chain and the possibility of user error and power-depleted devices. To address these challenges, the Natick Soldier Research and Development Engineering Center (NSRDEC) is directing a research and development effort by Protonex and WiTricity to develop wireless power transfer systems for soldier-based applications. This paper reviews preliminary modeling and experimental results from two proof-of-concept HRWPT systems being developed by WiTricity. The first system transfers power wirelessly from a Stryker™ seatback to a soldier-worn Improved Outer Tactical Vest (IOTV), illustrated in *Figure 1*. The second system transfers power from the IOTV to an Advanced Combat Helmet (ACH) for similar purposes, also illustrated in *Figure 1*. By distributing power wirelessly from a Stryker seat to a central power source integrated into a IOTV and by transferring power to equipment mounted on both IOTVs and ACHs, initial estimates based on statistical modeling suggest the potential to significantly reduce battery weight and the number of cells while better ensuring equipment availability, eliminating errors, and putting more hours back into the fight.

[1] Dr. Ed Shaffer; ARL Battery Technology Industry Day, McClean, VA; 2/16/11.

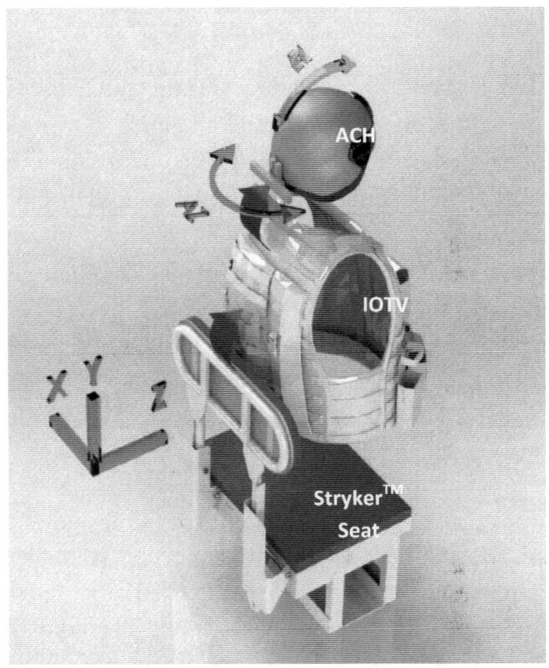

Figure 1: Illustration of Stryker™-to-IOTV and IOTV-to-ACH highly resonant wireless power transfer systems.

2. Technology Overview

In recent years, researchers at the Massachusetts Institute of Technology invented a technique for transmitting power over "mid-range" distances using a non-radiative approach that utilizes resonance to enhance the efficiency of the energy transfer[2]. High

[2] A.B. Kurs, A. Karalis, R. Moffatt, J.D. Joannopoulos, P.H. Fisher, and M. Soljacic, "Wireless Power Transfer via Strongly Coupled Magnetic Resonances", *Science*, **317**, pp. 83-86, (2007).

quality factor resonators – now being commercialized by WiTricity – enable efficient energy transfer at lower coupling rates, at greater distances, and with more positional freedom than is otherwise possible. The design of the resonators is optimized to provide the best coil-to-coil efficiency over the required range of relative resonator offsets, as well as to minimize system size and weight. From an overall system perspective, highly efficient source and device electronics are key, as well as detailed modeling to determine the power level that can be safely transferred in a given application.

HRWPT technology provides several advantages over traditional magnetic induction. First, it works over much larger distances. Magnetic induction, the technology in cordless toothbrushes and other civilian applications, requires source and capture devices to be within millimeters of one another. In contrast, HRWPT works with a high degree of energy transfer efficiency over distances several times the size of the devices themselves, and can even transfer energy through non-metallic materials such as plastic, ceramics, textiles, concrete, wood, and glass.

Second, HRWPT is safe for people and animals. Magnetic fields of the levels needed for most wireless energy transfer applications are intrinsically safe for people and animals. Systems based on HRWPT can be designed to meet the strictest military and civilian regulatory standards for human exposure to electric and magnetic fields.

Third, HRWPT can work in the tiniest device, or the biggest vehicle. The scalability of HRWPT designs enables solutions to be developed at any level. Reference designs and prototypes already have been produced at power levels from milliwatts to kilowatts, while flexible geometries allow HRWPT systems to be embedded in vests, helmets, weapons, cameras, sensors, and more.

Fourth, HRWPT can be highly efficient. Even taking into account the variables related to source and device size, orientation and distance from one to another, HRWPT is efficient. For example, in electric vehicle charging, end-to-end efficiencies in excess of 90 percent are achievable over gaps of 15 cm.

3. System Description

Wireless energy transfer systems based on HRWPT have a common set of functional blocks, see *Fig. 2.*

The input power to HRWPT systems is usually either wall power (AC mains), which is converted to DC in an AC/DC rectifier block, or alternatively, a DC voltage directly from a battery or other DC supply, as is the case in the two proof-of-concept systems described in this paper. A high-efficiency switching amplifier converts the DC voltage into an RF voltage waveform used to drive the source resonator. An impedance matching network (IMN) is used to efficiently couple the amplifier output to the source resonator while enabling efficient switching-amplifier operation. Class D or E switching amplifiers are suitable in many applications and generally require inductive load impedance for highest efficiency. The IMN serves to transform the source resonator impedance, loaded by the coupling to the device resonator and output load, into such impedance for the source amplifier. The magnetic field generated by the source resonator couples to the device resonator, exciting the resonator and causing energy to accumulate. This energy is coupled out of the device resonator to do useful work, for example, directly powering a load or charging a battery. A second IMN is used to efficiently couple energy from the resonator to the load. It may transform the actual load impedance into effective load impedance seen by the device resonator, which more closely matches the loading for optimum efficiency. For loads requiring a DC voltage, a rectifier converts the received AC power back into DC. The overall system efficiency can vary widely depending on a number of parameters and is the product of the efficiencies of each element shown in *Figure 2*. Because of this, modeled and experimental data is limited to the source resonator-to-device resonator efficiency.

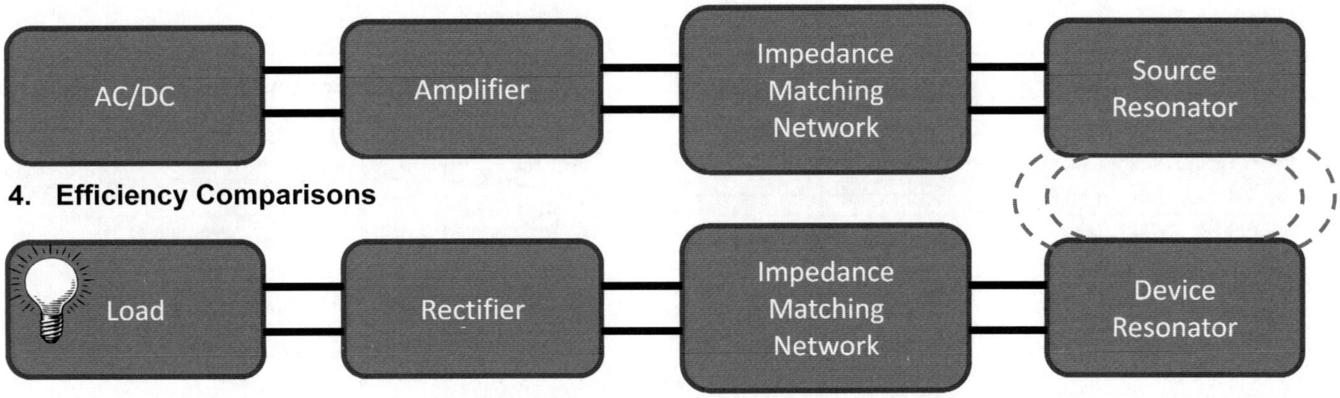

Figure 2: Block diagram of HRWPT system

4. Efficiency Comparisons

Resonator design simulations and measurements were performed for the Stryker seat-to- IOTV and IOTV-to-ACH systems. For the two configurations evaluated, the optimal resonator-to-resonator efficiency (both modeled and measured) are shown in Figures 3 and 4, respectively. In general, the plots show good agreement between the measured results and the model predictions. Differences are attributed to measurement accuracy and variations between the actual configurations tested and those used in the simulations.

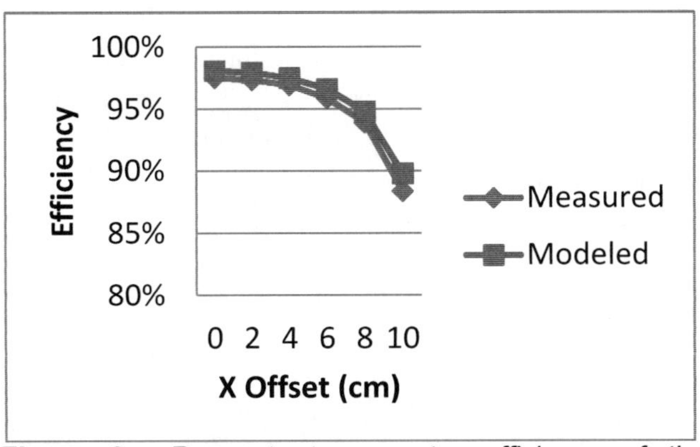

Figure 3a: Resonator-to-resonator efficiency of the Stryker seat-to-IOTV system as function of x offset.

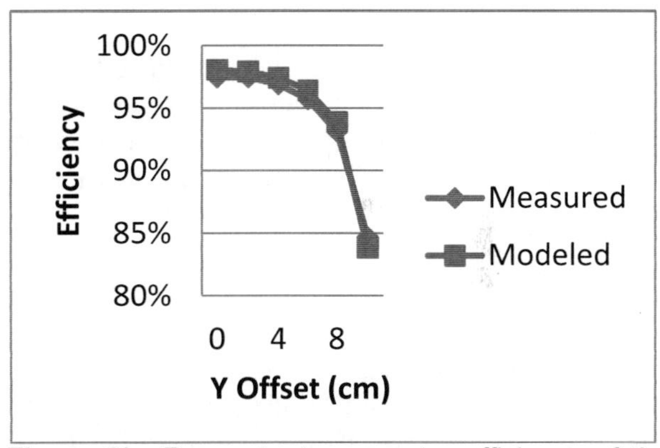

Figure 3b: Resonator-to-resonator efficiency of the Stryker seat-to-IOTV system as a function of y offset.

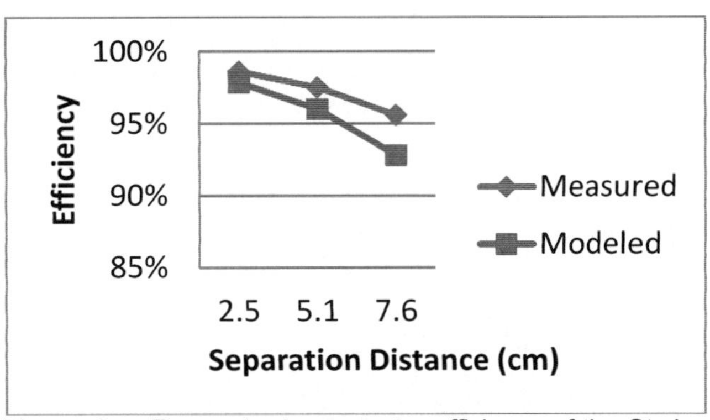

Figure 3c: Resonator-to-resonator efficiency of the Stryker seat-to-IOTV system as a function of separation distance (z).

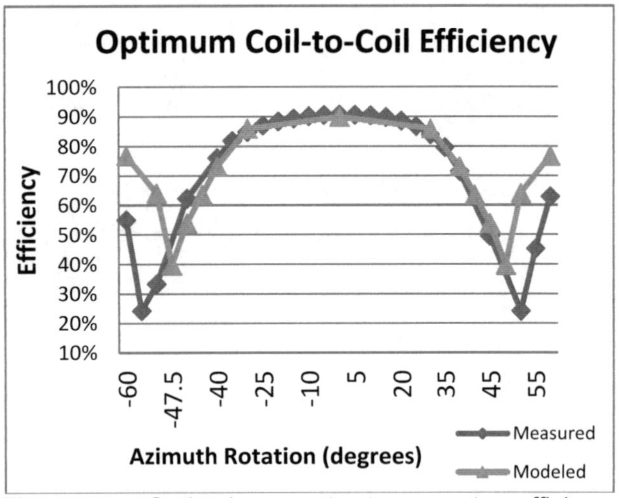

Figure 4a: Optimal resonator-to-resonator efficiency for IOVT-to-ACH system as a function of ACH azimuth rotation relative to IOTV position (in degrees).

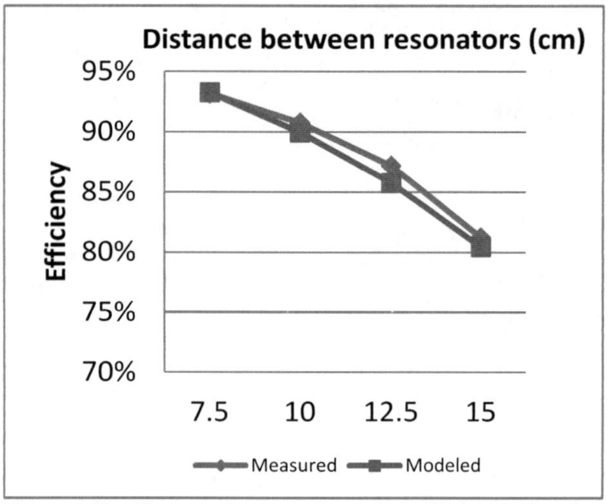

Figure 4b: Resonator-to-resonator efficiency for the IOVT-to-ACH system as a function of distance between resonators.

5. Summary

This paper has reviewed preliminary modeling and experimental results from two proof-of-concept HRWPT systems being developed by WiTricity. The first system transfers power wirelessly from a Stryker seat to a soldier-worn IOTV. The second system transfers power from the IOTV to an ACH. The modeled and measured resonator-to-resonator efficiencies correlated well and suggest that wireless soldier power distribution is both feasible and has the potential to significantly reduce battery weight and the number of cells while better ensuring equipment availability, eliminating errors, and putting more hours back into the fight.

State of Charge Indicator (SOCI) Design for Li/CFx Battery

Prof. Herbert L. Hess*, Vishu Gupta*, Dumidu Wijayasekara*,
Dr. Edward J. William*, Matthew C. Huff*, Ondrej Linda', Mason Krei',
Dr. Milos Manic', Dr. Ash Thakker^, Dr. Freeman Rufus^, Clint Justin Govar"

*University of Idaho, Moscow, ID, USA 83843
'University of Idaho, Idaho Falls, ID, USA 83401
^Global Technologies Inc., Atlanta, GA, USA 31126
"US Marine Corps, Quantico, VA, USA 22134
Contact e-mail: hhess@uidaho.edu

***Abstract*— The lithium polycarbon monofluoride (LiCFx) battery is sensitive to a number of dynamic environmental conditions, such as the ambient temperature. The flat discharge profile typical of the LiCFx battery current State of Charge Indicator (SOCI) technology poses a challenge to obtaining accurate estimates using conventional, voltage-based SOCI technology.**

To monitor this LiCFx discharge state of charge, an Artificial Neural Network (ANN) algorithm provides a nonlinear solution. The underlying technology is charge counting with nonlinear ANN-based compensation for temperature, rate of charge, and charge history. This paper explains the design of an ANN algorithm and its training. Measurement error for this ANN-based solution is estimated to be within 2-3%. Initial cost estimates are under USD $30 in bulk quantities. Drain on the battery is less than 1.5% per year, with a 10-year shelf life for the SOCI. This paper describes the performance of a sequence of prototypes based on this ANN technology. Appropriate testing results support the accuracy estimate.

***Index Terms*— LiCFx, Lithium batteries, Artificial Neural Network, State of Charge, Embedded System**

INTRODUCTION

SEVERAL batteries provide a reliable source for the numerous hand-held devices utilized throughout the world today. The cell provides a relatively flat voltage discharge curve for a majority of the discharge profile, for a continuous discharge current at a specific temperature shown in Figure 1.

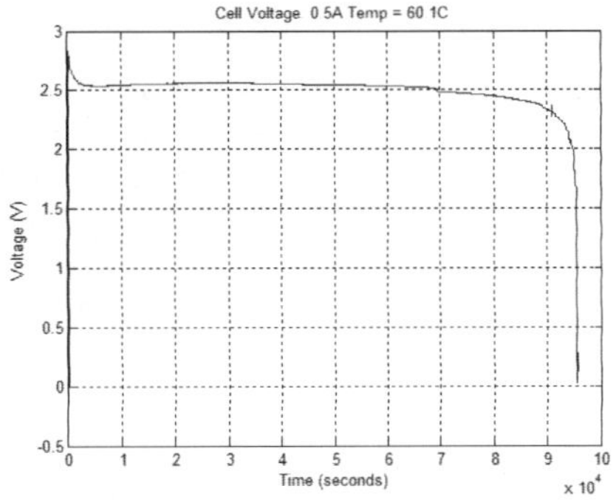

Figure 1: Discharge curve of D-sized LiCFx cell [1,2].

The discharge curve of battery was taken at 60°C and 0.5A. Moreover, the flat discharge curve, with a sudden drop toward the end, makes it challenging to indicate the SOC of the battery accurately.

Thus, the flat discharge curve of the battery, along with the nonlinear change in battery performance due to variation in temperature, proves difficult to use Colomb Counting alone to calculate the SOC.

For the LiCFx battery, in order to increase the accuracy and accommodate the flat discharge curve of the battery, an Artificial Neural Network (ANN) is being used as the main evaluator.

SOCI DESIGN OVERVIEW

The SOCI has been designed to take voltage, discharge current and ambient temperature inputs from the battery count. These values are collected from the respective sensors that are present on the board (shown in Figure 2).

Figure 2: SOCI prototype board [1]

The output of these sensors is sent to the MSP430 series microcontroller, where all of the evaluation is performed. The data is converted using the A/D converter on the MSP430. This converted data is sent to the ANN, which uses these parameters to calculate the SOC along with the usual SOC calculating method.

This display is read from left to right, and the number of lit LEDs indicates the range of SOC of the battery. Table 1 presents the range of values for each LED.

Table 1: LED Indication of SOC of Battery [5]

No. of Lit LEDs	% of Battery Capacity Remaining
5	90% - 100%
4	70% - 89%
3	50% - 69%
2	30% - 49%
1	10% - 29%

The designed SOCI was required to meet the following specifications [5]:

- Accuracy > 95%
- User-activated LED display using 5 LEDs [5]
- Operation under extreme temperatures (-40°C to 80°C)
- Low cost, small size, low current consumption
- Available sleep mode
- SMBus capabilities

Several prototypes of a SOCI meeting these requirements have been developed. The performance of the SOCI has been improved over the different versions to better meet these requirements.

ARTIFICIAL NEURAL NETWORK

Artificial neural networks (ANNs) are computational intelligence architectures based on biological neural networks. They are capable of "learning" interdependencies and trends in data [5].

The basic unit of an ANN is a neuron, which is functionally similar to a biological neuron and has a set of inputs and produces an output based on those inputs. Thus it creates an interconnected network of neurons that combines to produce an output based on a number of weights, aggregations and comparisons.

An artificial neuron aims to achieve the same goal by using weights and a threshold value, and by producing an output vector for a given input vector. An input vector, which is fed to an artificial neuron, with *n* dimensions can be expressed as:

$$\vec{X} = \{x_1, x_2, ..., x_n\} \quad (1)$$

In an artificial neuron, for each input x_q a weight w_q is assigned. The neuron calculates the weighted sum *z* as:

$$net = \sum_{q=1}^{n} w_q x_q \quad (2)$$

The output of the neuron is governed by the activation function, which acts as a threshold. The output is given by:

$$o = f_s\left(\sum_{q=1}^{n} w_q x_q\right) \quad (3)$$

where $f_s(x)$ is an activation function, and the sigmoid activation function is used typically:

$$f_s(x) = \frac{1}{1 + e^{\lambda_s x}} \quad (4)$$

An ANN consists of multiple interconnected artificial neurons, arranged in several layers. The neurons are arranged in layers: one input layer, one output layer, and multiple hidden layers. The neurons in the input layer have the activation function $f_s(x) = x$.

A. ANN First Implementation

The ANN implemented is called a "feed forward" network. This consists of two layers of neutrons, in which one of the layers evaluates the synaptic weight of each input and sums the weights as input for the second layer. The second layer evaluates the weight of the input from the first layer. The second layer also calculates the final output [4,5].

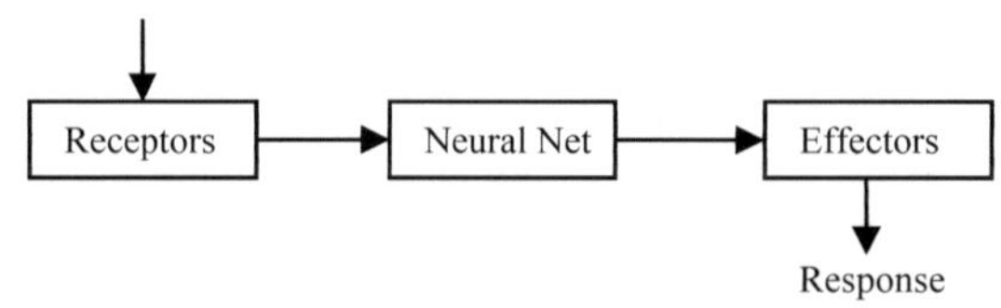

Figure 3: Generalized operation of a feed forward neural network system [1].

The implemented ANN consists of the stimuli/inputs to the receptors which process the input. The input to the ANN consists of 5 values:

- The battery capacity (Ah)
- The voltage/current over three time steps (t_1, t_2 and t_3)
- Operational temperature

The output is assigned a value between 0 and 1 and represents 0% and 100% effective capacity, respectively, of the SOC at that time.

B. ANN Revised Implementation

The data collected from testing batteries [1] and MATLAB simulated math model data are being used to train the ANN for various discharge current and temperature conditions. As shown in Figure 4, the ANN is a Tansig/Linear Neural Network (NN), which consists of 5 inputs, 14 hidden neurons and 1 output. The voltage, current and temperature data was processed into 5 different time-varying features that hold a strong relationship with the SOC [3]:

- Ampere-hour (Ah) discharged
- Time average current voltage and temperature
- Cumulative average of duty cycle.

The data used has been modeled using a constant load with five degree increments from -40°C to 80°C [3]. Figure 4 shows the overview of the feed forward network.

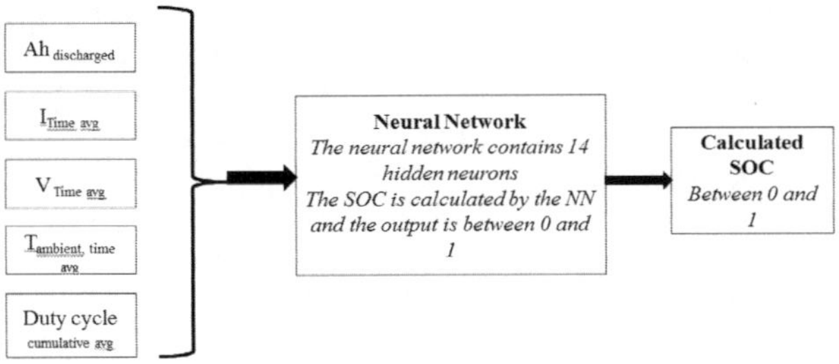

Figure 4: Feed forward ANN [3]

For each set of data at specified conditions, the training process was performed by using 60% of the data to train the network, 20% to validate the training, and 20% to test the ANN. The ANN has been tested using MATLAB.

Figure 5 shows the evaluation of the SOC algorithm with respect to the training data. In this case, the SOC has been trained with 60% of the data available for certain input conditions and then tested for 20% of that data [3]. As indicated below, the estimated and the true SOC values are nearly identical.

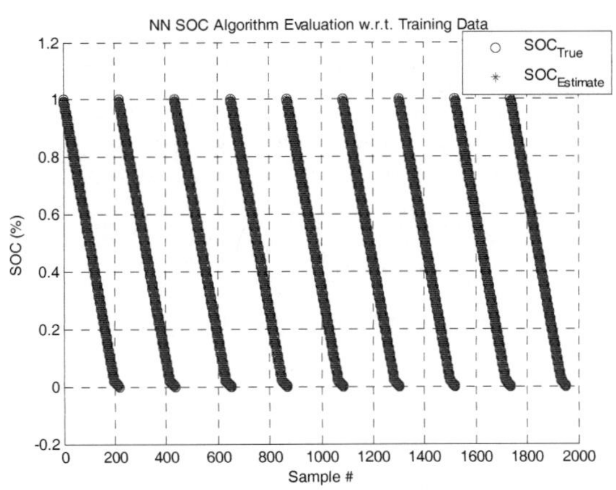

Figure 5: NN SOC Algorithm Evaluation for Training Data [3]

When calculating the percent error from Figure 5, the value was less than 1%.

The ANN has also been programmed onto the MSP430 and has been tested on the SOCI design as well by being a part of the system.

For the SOCI, the ANN was trained with temperatures from 24°C to 80°C [1]. The extreme cold temperatures were excluded in this case.

SOCI PERFORMANCE

The performance of the SOCI has improved over several versions. Contributing factors here are improvements in the hardware design, and increases in the accuracy of both the control software and the evaluating software.

C. Size

As shown in the figure below, the size of the board has been reduced significantly. The width of the SOCI has been brought down from 2.5" to 2.0". The horizontal white line on Version 5 indicates the space above which the circuit for the SOCI resides.

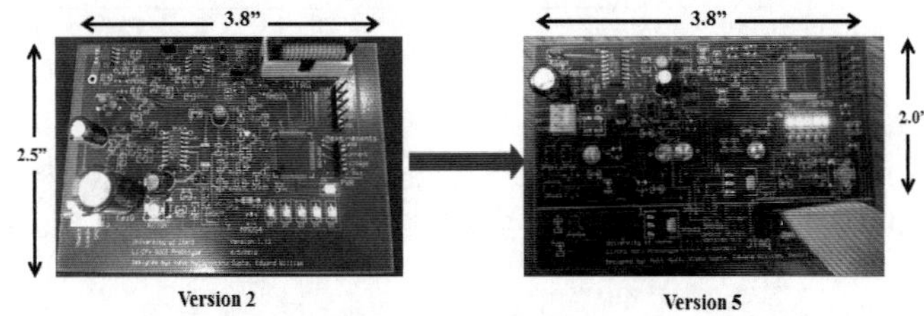

Figure 6: Sizes of Versions 2 and 5 [4,2].

D. Current Consumption

Table 2 provides an overview of the current consumption of the SOCI in various stages of operation, over different versions of the board. This is the current that the SOCI consumes from the LiCFx battery in different modes of operation [5].

Table 2: Comparison of current consumption of the SOCI board in different versions [1]

Mode	Requirement	Version 2	Versions 3 /4	Version 5
Sleep mode	$I_{SOCI} \leq 50\mu A$	2.52mA	52.0μA	50.1μA
Storage mode	$I_{SOCI} \leq 20\mu A$	2.52mA	52.0μA	50.1μA
ON mode	Not specified	34.98mA	11mA	5.1mA

Overall current consumption has decreased and, in all but one case, the set requirements are met.

E. Component Count

To help reduce the size, designs and number of components have been modified. Table 3 provides an overview of these changes.

Table 3: Component comparison [1]

Component	Version 2 board	Version 3 /4 board	Version 5 board
MSP430	YES	YES	YES
Buck Converter	YES	YES	YES
Boost Converter	YES	NO	NO
Current Sensor	YES	YES (modified)	YES (modified)
Voltage Sensor	YES	YES	YES
Temperature Sensor	YES	YES	YES
LED Display	YES	YES (modified)	YES (modified)
User Button	YES	YES	YES
SMBus	NO	NO	YES
3.3V Coin Cells	NO	YES	YES

F. Cost Analysis

Table 4 provides a cost comparison of the different versions. The SOCI design has significantly cut down on the total price of the board.

Table 4: Cost Analysis of the Different Versions

	Version 3 /4		Version 5	
	Initial Cost/Unit	Bulk Cost/ Unit	Initial Cost/Unit	Bulk Cost/Unit
Total Price (minus board)	$63.58	$26.94	$49.53	$23.96
Total Price	$100.82	$34.54	$85.48	**$31.56**

G. Accuracy

For the SOCI, accuracy is the most important feature. With the use of traditional methods and the ANN, the accuracy of the SOCI has increased. Table 5 provides the Accuracy Error of the sensors and the ANN.

Table 5: Accuracy Error [2,4,5]

	Version 2	Version 5 board
Voltage Sensor	<1.5%	<0.5%
Current Sensor	<1.5%	<0.5%
ANN accuracy	2%	<1.2%

The temperature sensor accuracy is not shown above, as it was unchanged.

CONCLUSION

This paper presented an overview of the use of Artificial Neural Networks to determine the SOC of a high-performance, flat-discharge-curve LiCFx battery. It also presented test results over multiple prototypes of the board. By utilizing the ANN, along with improved hardware and software, the overall accuracy of the board ranges from 96% - 98%. The accuracy error has been reduced to less than 1% in the final version (Version 5) of the board. The sensor accuracies have been brought under 0.05% for the current and the voltage sensors.

The ANN also provides an extra feature of making this SOCI trainable for other battery chemistries. As observed from the data, using the ANN technology on the SOCI board, the performance and the accuracy of the design have improved across several parameters such as cost, current consumption and the overall space used by the design.

Future work needs to be conducted to further improve the performance and utility of the SOCI board.

ACKNOWLEDGEMENTS

The authors would like to express their gratitude to Clint Justin Govar for sponsoring this research under US MARCOR contract number M67854-08-C-653.

REFERENCES

[1] Gupta, Vishu, et al. (June 2012). "Design of a State of Charge Indicator (SOCI) for Lithium Polycarbon Monofluoride (LiCFx) Batteries," Army Power Sources Conference 2012, Las Vegas, NV, USA.

[2] Rufus, F, et al. (Eds.), (2009). *SBIR Phase II Report.*US MARCOR SBIR#: N06-11 Contract#: M67854-08-C-6530.

[3] Huff, Matthew C. (2010). Embedded System Development for the lithium polycarbon monofluoride (Li/CFx) Battery's State of Charge Indicator (SOCI). University of Idaho.

[4] William, Edward J. (2010). State of Charge Indicator (SOCI) Design for the Lithium Polycarbon Monofluoride (Li/CFx) Battery. University of Idaho.

Neural Network Models for Battery Management Systems

John Olson
TDA Research, Inc.
Wheat Ridge, CO 80305
jolson@tda.com

John Heinzel
Naval Surface Warfare Center
Philadelphia, PA 19112
john.heinzel@navy.mil

Abstract: *Accurate diagnostics and prognostics are important features desired in battery management systems (BMS). TDA Research is developing battery models based on neural networks (NN) that are ideal for use in a BMS. Although collecting the appropriate training data sets and creating accurate models can be involved, the resulting models are run with minimal computation time and power, ideal for a BMS application. The NN models also operate well with noisy data typical of BMS collected data. Batteries often have multiple failure mechanisms and age at different rates, factors that again are easily handled with NN models.*

Keywords: neural network; model; battery management system; BMS; state of charge; state of health; diagnostic; prognostic; conditional awareness

Introduction

The Navy is developing advanced electric power and propulsion technologies for their fleet to increase the electrical power for sensors and weapons and decrease the use of fossil fuels [1, 2]. Advanced systems maybe composed of a variety of energy storage packs of differing chemistries. Further, battery packs may be changed out across the platform's lifecycle, causing costly certification and control systems changes to accommodate. The Navy has indicated an interest in standard, sophisticated battery management systems [3]. Given cost, complexity and lifecycle of energy storage systems versus ship lifetime, it may be of great use to the Navy to have a universal BMS that will allow for common diagnostics and prognostics regardless of the pack size and type. In addition, because of the keen sensitivity to safety and long-term performance of large systems, advancements in the capabilities of prognostics to allow full conditional awareness to support both safety (understand degradation far before the onset of failure) as well as condition-based maintenance and system design are highly desirable and an active are of investment and research [4,5].

As part of this effort, TDA Research is developing models based on neural networks (NN). NN was one of the first artificial intelligence (AI) algorithms, and has become one of the most utilized AI algorithms for a wide variety of applications [5]. Although the use of NN for battery models is mentioned in the scientific and patent literature, no accounts of its implementation in a BMS have been found.

NN are a form of algorithms which are adept at evaluating non-linear and noisy data having complex relationships. They were originally fashioned after biological neuron models, with their multiple interconnected neurons. A simple graphic describing their basic structure is shown in

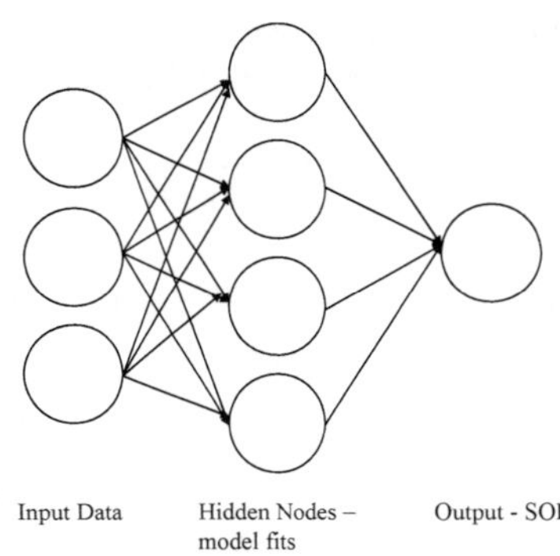

Figure 1. Neural networks create multi-dimensional models that can solve complex non-linear problems. Input data is computed at each hidden node.

Figure 1. Note that the number of input nodes, hidden nodes and output nodes are fully adaptable depending on the model under development. The NN models are a learning algorithm, where training data (typically large data sets) are used to create the model. The science of creating the NN models and solving them is mature and a variety of software packages are available commercially.

NN models are particularly well suited for use with BMSs. Although collecting the appropriate training data sets and creating and testing functional models can be involved, the resulting models are capable of computation with minimal time and power, ideal for a BMS application. NN models have no 'equation' describing their calculations, or for that matter any real insight into how the model mechanistically functions, but these are not limitations for a typical BMS application. The NN models operate seamlessly with noisy data typical of battery acquisition data. Batteries often have multiple failure mechanisms and age at different rates, factors that are readily embraced with NN models.

TDA is developing NN models for calculation of state of charge (SOC), state of health (SOH) and fault detection. Our training data set is primarily comprised of parametric laboratory battery life cycle data with variables of discharge/charge rates and temperature. In this paper we will describe our initial efforts to develop NN models for BMS. We will discuss the development of the training data, describe the process of creating the models and provide two NN model examples, one of SOC and the other of SOH.

Training Data

The development of the training data is the first step in creating NN models. Our training data is based on cycle life testing of four different cells: two types of lithium-ion batteries (lithium cobalt oxide (LCO) and lithium iron phosphate (LFP)), sealed lead-acid (SLA) batteries and ultracapacitors. The testing was designed to support the three major NN models under development, namely SOC, SOH and faults. We aged the cells by cycling at three different temperatures, 23° C, 40° C and 60° C using computer automated cycling equipment (Maccor) and a variety of temperature regulating devices. We also used current pulses during charge and discharge to allow calculation of the cell resistance. We periodically characterized the cells for rate performance versus temperature (-40° C - 60° C).

As an example, we show the capacity fade of the LCO cells versus temperature in Figure 2. The initial capacity

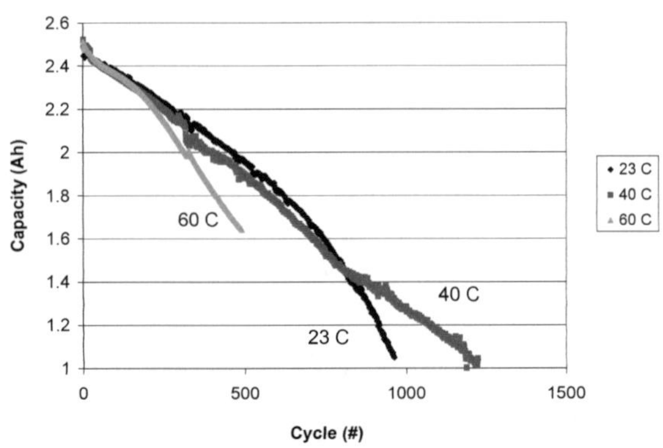

Figure 2. LCO cycle life for three cells cycled at different temperatures.

fade of the three cells was very similar, irrespective of temperature. Then around 300 cycles, the 60° C cell showed a steeper capacity decline, likely a change in degradation mechanism [6]. The 40° C cell also showed a change in capacity fade at about 750 cycles. The 23° C cell did not show a capacity fade change. The average discharge resistance is shown in Figure 3. Resistance data is collected by current pulse periodically during each

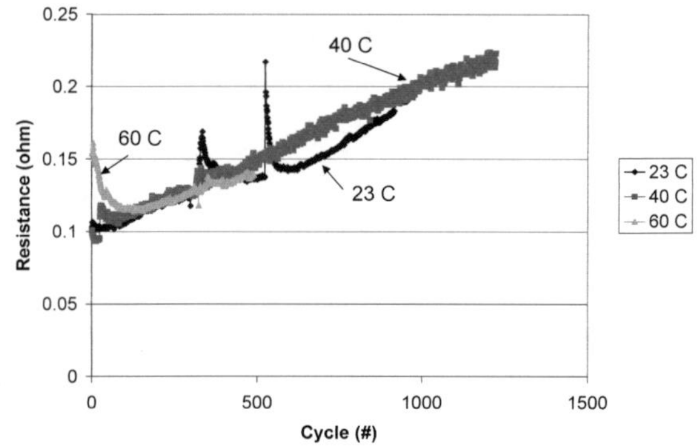

Figure 3. Resistance of three LCO cells cycled at three different temperatures determined with current pulses.

charge and discharge. The resistances were averaged across each discharge. In general, all three cells show an increasing resistance of about the same rate. However, a concern for the use of resistance data directly in the training data set is the variability observed. In particular the 23° C cell had two spikes which were related to pauses in the cycling, while the 60° C cell initially had a higher resistance which eventually declined. We have observed similar variability in resistance for the other cell chemistries, even more extreme. Since laboratory cycling is much more uniform than the cycling expected in the field, these results indicate that resistance data may not be reliable as input data for the NN models, either as training data or for NN calculation.

SOC NN Model

We will start with a simple SOC model to demonstrate the utility of the NN algorithms. The training data consisted of four discharges of an 18650 LFP cell at currents of 2 A, 1 A, 0.5 A and 0.25 A all taken at room temperature (Figure 4).

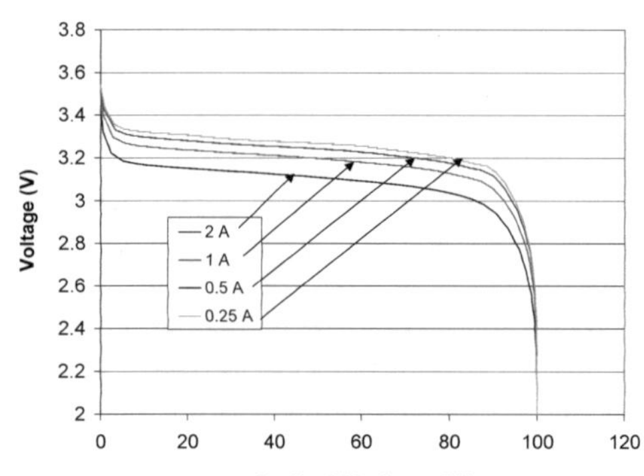

Figure 4. Training data for the simple SOC NN model consisted of 4 discharges at different rates of LFP cells at room temperature.

LFP chemistry is known for having a flat discharge profile, which is evident in the training data. This is not ideal from a modeling perspective and therefore we have been looking at improving the fidelity of the training data by using the first derivative of the Ah with voltage, or dQ/dV [7]. The same discharge data expressed as dQ/dV is shown in Figure 5. This data shows a large peak for all discharge rates with a maximum at about 40% depth of

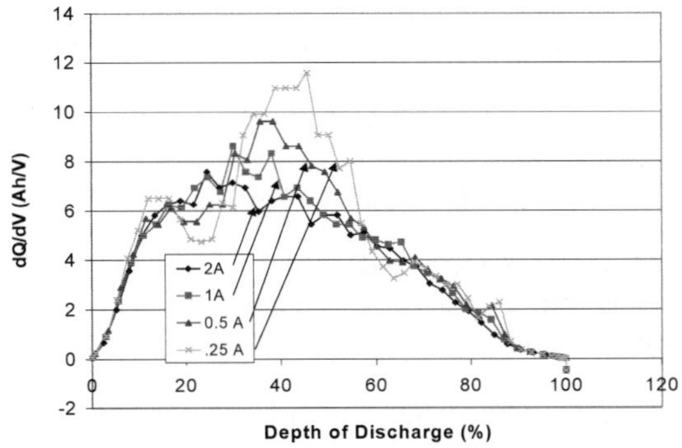

Figure 5. The same discharge data expressed as dQ/dV has much greater response showing the maximum variability during the flat point of the discharge curve.

discharge. This is where the discharge profiles are the most flat.

We experimented with different combinations of training data and ultimately selected the discharge rate, discharge voltage and dQ/dV. The output data consists of one parameter, namely SOC. For the training, we give the SOC data 'answer', while during use of the model it will calculate the SOC based on our input data from the BMS (same form as the training data).

The next step is to use NeuroShell2 (Ward Systems Group) to create the NN model. NeuroShell2 offers 15 different NN architectures, which is ideal for evaluating different data sets. We found by trial and error that using recurrent algorithms were the most effective NN architectures for this data set. Recurrent networks mix results from previous input, and thus are known to be effective for time trended data.

The next step is to train the model. We created a test set consisting of 20% of the training data randomly selected for a supervised training. This is a key part of training, because if you under train the model you lose accuracy while overtraining will prevent the model from responding flexibly to new input data [8]. Using a test set is a particularly clever way of training the data to prevent under or overtraining. During the training, the test set is used periodically to evaluate the fit to the model. As the model is trained, the fits get better until the model starts to over train and the fits then get worse. This is where the training is stopped. The training for this simple data set took a little over a minute to perform.

Now the NN model is complete and ready to make predictions. For this model our correlation coefficient was 0.9959. This is basically a measure of how well the model can fit the training data used to create it. Overall, the fit is quite good, but suffers somewhat during early times. This is often the case with recurrent models - they require a few iterations to lock into the best fits.

Although the fit of the model to the training data is useful, especially for evaluating the gross ability of the model to fit, a more relevant test is to use new independent data to verify the model. We created a data set to verify the model based on a multi-rate discharge of the same LFP cell again at room temperature (Figure 6). The discharge

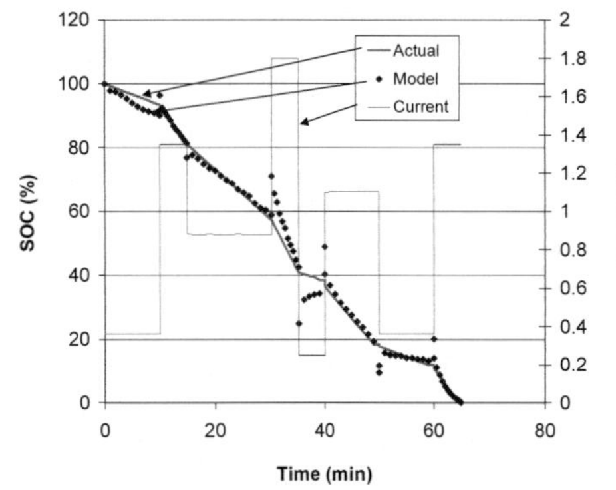

Figure 6. Verification of the NN model using a multi-rate discharge demonstrates the quality of the fit.

rates varied from a high of 1.8 A to a low of 0.25 A. The pink data are the actual SOC and the blue data are the model results. The fit is quite good, but suffers during periods when the current is changed. You can see the impact of the recurrent network, because when the current shifts from a lower level to a higher one, the SOC prediction is high, while when the current shifts from a higher current to a lower one, the SOC prediction is low.

SOH NN Model

We will now demonstrate the same modeling principles with a simple SOH NN Model. We will start by defining SOH, which we define as the full discharge in Ah divided by the initial capacity $Ah/Ah_{Initial}$. The $Ah_{Initial}$ is the name plate capacity of the cell and does not change. So in effect, our NN SOH model is actually predicting the Ah capacity of a full discharge. We convert it to SOH for clarity. This makes sense, since although cell resistance, self-discharge or other battery characteristics are certainly indicators of SOH, the key battery characteristic is capacity.

The SOH NN model was developed using the cycle life data for the LCO cell at 40° C as shown in Figure 7. Thus, we did not use temperature and rate as input into our model, but we have now extended our models to include

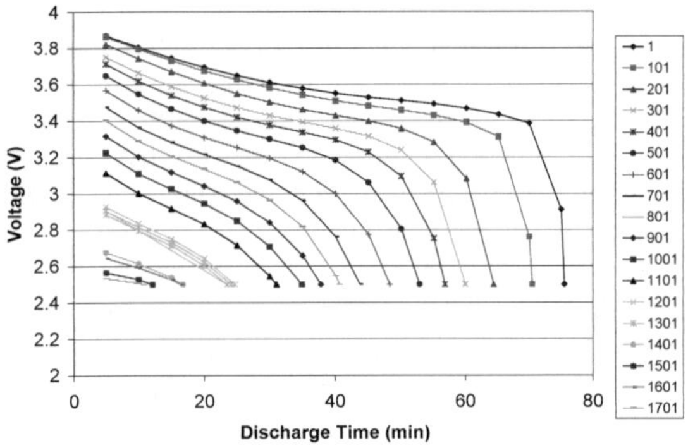

Figure 7. Training data from LCO cell at 40° C. Discharge curves were selected at 100 cycle intervals.

these key inputs. Our first fits using just voltage and dQ/dV were rather poor. Then we added number of cycles to the input data. This fit was much improved; however, cycle life is dependent on both the number of cycles and the depth of discharge. While our cycle life data was determined with 100% discharges, in a real application this won't be the case; partial discharges will more likely be the norm. We then evaluated use of Ah Throughput which gave us a very good fit. We recognize that life is highly correlated with depth of discharge and that use of Ah Throughput doesn't reflect this dependence. However, the use of the other input data effectively compensates for the shortcomings of the Ah Throughput input. This is a demonstration of the power of the use of multiple input data.

To verify the NN model with independent data, we used cycle life data from the same data set. We selected four discharges that spanned the training set range, yet did not duplicate any data in the training set. We ran the SOH NN model with the results shown in Figure 8. The fit is quite

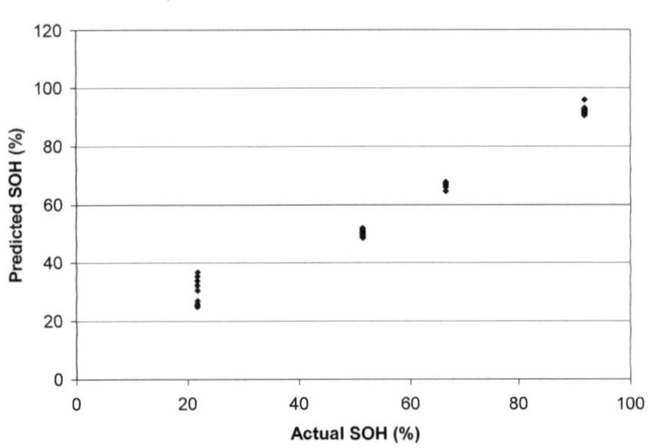

Figure 8. Verification of SOH NN model using data independent of the training set data. The fit degrades slightly as the SOH decreases.

good, although getting poorer at the lower SOH. Each grouping of data represents every data point in the discharge for the four cycles used for verification. In other words, the NN model creates a SOH output for each input data consisting of points on a discharge curve.

Conclusions

NN models have been shown to be useful for the modeling of batteries and other energy storage for use in BMS applications. When compiled, they require minimal computational power and work well with noisy or incomplete data often present in BMS data. Our NN models are trained with parametric laboratory cycle life data. Use of dQ/dV as an input parameter adds fidelity to the models, particularly for batteries like LFP that have flat discharge profiles. We demonstrate the ability of the NN models on a simple SOC model and SOH model. Both are shown to have excellent accuracy.

More development is underway to create full and robust models. However, there are no indications that use of NN models has any significant shortcomings for use on BMS applications. It is anticipated that the implementation of NN approaches into scalable BMS systems will enable common approaches to interfacing energy storage systems to control systems and interface equipment, offering operational benefit and cost savings across the lifecycle of installed energy storage systems, particularly as battery systems are replaced over time.

Acknowledgments

This paper is based upon work supported by the Naval Sea Systems Command under Contract No. N00024-14-C-4011. Any opinions, findings and conclusions or recommendations expressed in this material are those of the authors and do not necessarily reflect the views of the Naval Sea Systems Command.

References

1. http://greenfleet.dodlive.mil/files/2010/04/Adv-Energy-Storage.pdf
2. http://energy.gov/videos/arpa-e-2011-keynote-ray-mabus-secretary-navy
3. http://www.navsea.navy.mil/Media/Naval Power Systems Technology Development Roadmap - Distribution A – 14 May 2013 - Final.pdf
4. John Heinzel (author), personal communication, 2014.
5. http://www.arpa-e.energy.gov/sites/default/files /documents/files/Day_1_Gur.pdf
6. http://uhaweb.hartford.edu/compsci/neural-networks-definition.html
7. Bloom, I., Jones, S., Bastaglia, V., Henriksen, G., Christophersen, J., Wright, R., Ho, C., Belt, J., Motloch, C., *J. Power Sources*, 124, 538-550, 2003.
8. Atwater, T.,Tavares, P., Marzocca, L., "Proceedings of the 44th Power Sources Conference" (2010)
9. NeuroShell2 Manual, Ward Systems, Fredrick MD.

The Value of Battery Diagnostics and Prognostics

Bor Yann Liaw*, Arnaud Devie and Matthieu Dubarry
Hawaii Natural Energy Institute, SOEST
University of Hawaii at Manoa
Honolulu, Hawaii, USA 96822

Abstract: *Battery diagnostic and prognostic techniques are often being underused and their value undermined because of the lack of adequate communication tools to transfer the understanding between the material scientists and cell engineers, that understand the inner working of the battery, and the engineers that need to manage the battery functions from the real usage of the cells. Even with the complex postmortem analyses, it is often very difficult to correlate what happened in the practical use versus those phenomena observed in the laboratory testing, especially in a quantitative manner with temporal resolution. Here we explain a simple yet practical diagnostic and prognostic technique that could transfer such knowledge quantitatively with temporal variations to enable battery diagnostics and prognostics for better BMS operation.*

Keywords: Battery diagnosis and prognosis, dQ/dV, SOC estimation, SOH estimation, mechanistic model, degradation mechanisms.

Introduction

In the last two decades batteries have become an important part of our lifestyle, from portable electronics, electrified vehicles, to recent integration of renewable electric grid. The art of battery design and performance engineering (BDPE) follows a conventional wisdom of "design, build, and test" paradigm to deliver products that could meet the design goals and specifications for a specific use. To keep up and warrant such performance specifics and to ensure safety and reliability, battery management systems (BMS) are developed and implemented in battery systems to monitor and control the battery performance. In general, battery diagnostics and prognostics (BDP) are supposed to provide the communication between BDPE and BMS to permit quantifiable information and knowledge transferred. However, engineers who design BMS usually have little understanding of the electrochemical processes involved in the batteries. It is particularly true when Li-ion batteries (LIB) operate with more complicated chemistries than Ni-MH or lead-acid ones and require much more delicate and sophisticated controls. Such a complicated operation with LIB posts demanding needs for better quantification that renders those conventionally favored black box, empirical models (derived from empirical correlations) dysfunctional in the BMS for a proper control of the battery performance, including the SOC and SOH tracking. Almost all empirical models work well within the specification of a battery. But, when duty-cycle-induced degradation becomes severe, the model often fails when it is needed the most. There exists a great disconnect between real life situations and laboratory test results. To mitigate this problem, a new strategy needs to be developed to overcome the issues raised from empirical models and approaches. We believe a more mechanistic approach using basic principles would be a better solution.

There must be a tool to translate the phenomena observed in the laboratory testing quantitatively to engineers in the field to facilitate them diagnose a battery system in order to execute proper control and management.

Here we present such an interesting approach for BDP. The intent is to establish a quantitative, coherent and consistent understanding of battery degradation in a time-resolved, quantifiable manner. Namely, this approach can translate physical phenomena into quantifiable parameters to assist BMS engineers perform BDP. It shall positively impact the next-generation BMS design for emerging applications.

Battery degradation is influenced by many "factors," either extrinsic or intrinsic, and their effects are often inter-related. As the system being scaled up from single cells to modules and packs, the types of stress factors increase and their coupling intensifies. It is thus critical to resolve them as much as we can in the BDP approach. Here we outlined some comments regarding these factors to help deciphering and distinguishing them in the approach:

Intrinsic factors: In a chemical system such as a battery, the intrinsic factors are those related to the thermodynamics and kinetics due to variations in the internal compositions of the active materials in the cell chemistry, including those variations in the degradation. In other words, these factors are the intrinsic properties of the compositions in the cell. The variations of these properties are affected by the extrinsic factors as exhibited by the environment (e.g., temperature or pressure) and duty cycle (e.g., voltage, rate, and magnitude of the external load that consumes energy).

Extrinsic factors: Extrinsic factors are those imposed by the environment and operating conditions. In addition to those common ones mentioned previously, they include events, such as overcharging, thermal excursions or exposures to temperature extremes, and other abusive incidents that can compromise battery's safety, reliability and capability in performing certain functions.

Depending on the aging and abusive conditions (from the extrinsic factors), the degree of degradation (variations in the intrinsic factors) and likely the underlying mechanisms could vary. There may be more than one extrinsic factor varied and several intrinsic factors affected in the cell. For example, a cell may experience concurrence of corrosion at the current collector, cracking in the active material grains, dissolution of the active materials, and the formation of passivation layers [1,2], as a result of the impacts from the extrinsic factors.

Extended to large cell assemblies such as a battery pack for a vehicle or grid energy storage application, additional factors need to be considered with a large number of cells in a topological arrangement. For instance, cell quality and its variability, presence of an internal temperature gradient or heat distribution, imbalance among the cells caused by the extrinsic factors are all critical considerations in BMS. Other extrinsic factors include the contact resistance that may vary with time and other conditions due to vibration or corrosion. Although not a topic in this work, these extrinsic factors play a critical role in a battery system's reliability. Interested readers should refer to Refs. [3,4] regarding the impacts on battery performance from cell variability. The imbalance issue and quantifying the effect on performance of a battery assembly is currently under investigation in our laboratory. A study on how to properly define and estimate SOC from a cell to a battery pack has been published [5].

One of the most critical aspects in applying practical BDP tools in our method is the ability to categorize and quantify contributions from different attributes of the degradation processes. **Figure 1** is a schematic of all major degradation mechanisms that could occur in a typical Li-ion cell [1]. These mechanisms have been reported in the literature by various authors. However, most of the observations are phenomenological, difficult to quantify over the entire cell. They are hardly detectable by any physical measurements or characterization techniques. Even if it were possible, it is probably cost prohibitive to implement.

Electrochemical measurements remain the most effective method to monitor the battery condition. Analyzing the voltage, current, and temperature of the battery is direct and essential for BMS. Extracting useful information from such measurements is key to successful BMS. We have shown that it is possible to classify these degradation mechanisms by their effects on the electrochemical behavior of the cell [2]. Every degradation mechanisms could belong to at least one of three classifications of attributes to degradation: i.e. (1) loss of active materials (LAM), including (2) loss of lithium inventory (LLI), and (3) change in reaction kinetics as often indicated by the cell impedance (**Figure 1**).

Using such simple classifications, we take great advantages in conducting battery diagnostics and prognostics. We were able to translate those degradation phenomena observed qualitatively into quantifiable contributions from the three classifications of degradation. Two methods to achieve the quantification are vital here. One is tracking the SOC of the cell using the open circuit voltage (OCV) measurements. The other is tracking the SOH using the incremental capacity (dQ/dV) analysis during aging. To facilitate dQ/dV analysis, we also developed a model to simulate degradation losses based on the attributes for validation [2,6]. Such a capability allows the handling of the aging-pathway dependence in BDP with great flexibility.

Identifying and quantifying the intrinsic factors to cell degradation

The essence of classifying three attributes of degradation is to identify and quantify intrinsic factors and their variations in aging. It is in compliance with tracking SOC and SOH. A typical discharge curve spells the variations of voltage (which indicates what reaction is taking place) as a function of charge released (i.e. capacity, which depicts the extent of the reaction). Since battery is a chemical system, the state of the battery is only defined when all compositions in the system are in equilibrium. The OCV in equilibrium shall be the indicator of the SOC, which is the principle of tracking SOC in aging process. Knowing the SOC changes in the

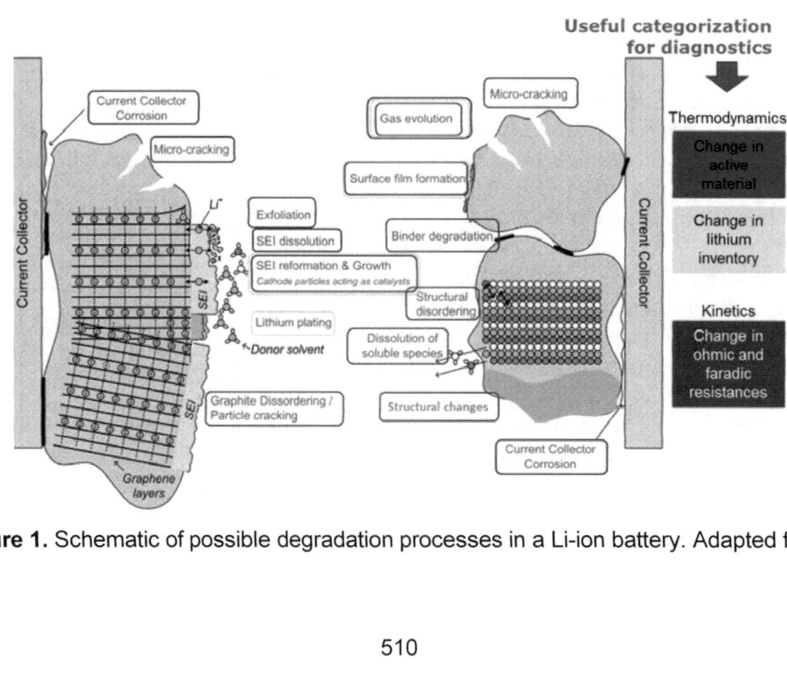

Figure 1. Schematic of possible degradation processes in a Li-ion battery. Adapted from [4]

process and the corresponding capacity, one can estimate the changes in composition in the cell, which is the basis for SOH tracking [7]. The dQ/dV analysis takes a refined step to estimate the capacity released in each increment of voltage change in the reaction. Such a subtle differentiation takes the full advantage of a sensitive measurement in detecting changes in SOH. Our mechanistic model allows us to quantify such an effect.

Figure 2 presents an example of a successful mapping of the degradation attributes of a commercial cell, made of graphite intercalation compound (GIC) anode and layered NMC and spinel (LMO) composite cathode, using these SOC and SOH tracking techniques. The effect of the three attributes was quantified. This cell mainly suffered from a linear LLI, coupled with the contributions from LAM and kinetic degradation [8]. This diagnostic illustration is useful to demonstrate the degradation in the intrinsic factors under the influence of the extrinsic factors, in this case primarily the 2C cycle aging at room temperature.

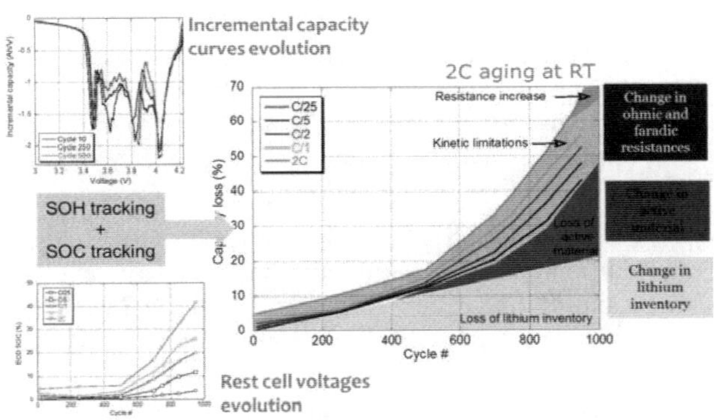

Figure 2. Example of diagnosing variations in the intrinsic factors for a commercial GIC||{NMC+LMO} cell cycled a 2C at room temperature.

The main difficulty of this analysis lies in the interpretation of the incremental capacity (dQ/dV) curve and its evolution with aging (graph in the upper left corner). These curves are often complicated to interpret by experienced battery researchers and a fortiori for engineers.

Interpretation of incremental capacity curves: **Figure 3** presents an example of a typical incremental capacity curve for the same commercial cell illustrated in **Figure 2** with the associated peak indexed [9]. Each peak is indexed with two numbers to depict the corresponding reaction in the cathode (open circle) and anode (solid circle) respectively, because each comprises the capacity released from cathode and anode simultaneously. An easy way to comprehend the convolution of the reactions in each electrode is to imagine the battery charge-discharge behavior as a clepsydra, i.e. a water clock, with two connected bulbs filled with a given amount of water. In this analogy, as exhibited in the lower illustration of **Figure 3**, each electrode is represented by its incremental capacity curve with reactions indexed. The two curves serve as the bulbs in the clepsydra and the lithium in the inventory is the amount of water held in the clock (the yellow area). The upper one is the anode and the lower one the cathode. When a battery is discharging, the lithium ions flow from the anode to the cathode; thus, in the clepsydra analogy, the yellow area in the upper bulb is decreasing, while an increasing yellow area commensurate to the loss in the upper one is showing up in the lower bulb. Using this illustration, every peak on the incremental capacity curve can be indexed by looking at the lithium level in each bulb during the progression of the discharge or charge process. The voltage is the difference in the liquid levels between the two bulbs.

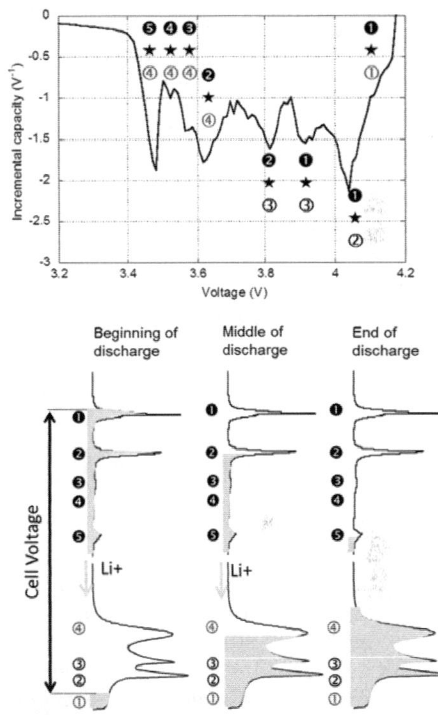

Figure 3. Example of an incremental capacity curve for a commercial cell and of the peak indexation using the clepsydra analogy.

Interpretation of degradation on the incremental capacity curves: using the clepsydra analogy, we enticed to illustrate the effects of the three classifications of attributes on the incremental capacity curves. For a simple case involving cell impedance change, it shall create a farther separation of the two bulbs. For the cases of LLI and LAM, it shall create more complicated alterations in the incremental capacity curves; e.g. changing the peak positions and shape. Sometimes, it may change the index of the peak. **Figure 4** illustrates how LAM and LLI affect the clepsydra settings. In the case of LAM on one of the electrodes, the associated bulb shall become smaller, so the rate of filling the peaks will change. In the case of LLI, the bulbs size shall remain the same, but the amount of available lithium ions will be lowered; thus, the relative level of the yellow area in the bulbs will shift.

Using this technique, one can diagnose the degradation of lithium ion cells, while an in-depth understanding of the underlying electrochemical reactions is not necessary. Being able to diagnose the possible mechanisms involved in degradation, we hope that the communication among the researchers and engineers could prevail to improve the cell performance, reliability and safety.

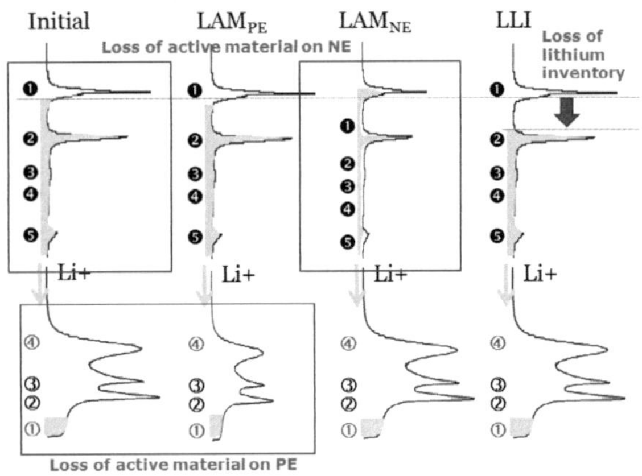

Figure 4. Illustration of the effect of loss of active material (LAM) and loss of lithium inventory (LLI) on incremental capacity curves.

Conclusion

Here we presented a simplified, yet practical, approach for battery diagnostics and prognostics. It offers a coherent and consistent understanding of the battery behavior in a neat and quantifiable manner, and it has been incorporated into a mechanistic model [2,6] that has been applied successfully to commercial cells of different chemistries [10,11]. It is important to recognize that this mechanistic approach is fundamentally different from the conventional empirically based BDP. It offers the possibility to translate quantitative information of battery degradation among researchers and engineers, bridging the knowledge gap between the BDPE and BMS communities.

Acknowledgements

The funding support was provided by the Idaho National Laboratory (INL) under the U.S. Department of Energy, EERE Office, Developmental and Applied Diagnostic Testing (DADT) program (Contract No. DE-AC07-05ID14517). We are grateful to Timothy Murphy and Kevin Gering (INL) for their support. The authors are also grateful to Karim Zaghib of IREQ (Hydro-Quebec), Michael Spahr of TIMCAL, and Michael Coleman of Altairnano for providing LFP, GIC, NMC and LTO data for the model, respectively.

References

1. J. Groot, "State of health estimation of Li ion batteries cycle life test methods", *Licentiate thesis, Chalmers University of Technology*, 2012.
2. M. Dubarry, C. Truchot and B.Y. Liaw, "Synthesize battery degradation modes via a diagnostic and prognostic model", *Journal of Power Sources*, vol. 219, pp. 204-216, 2012.
3. M. Dubarry, N. Vuillaume and B.Y. Liaw, "Origins and accommodation of cell variations in Li-ion battery pack modeling", *International Journal of Energy Research*, vol. 34, no. 2, pp. 216-231, 2010.
4. M. Dubarry, N. Vuillaume and B.Y. Liaw, "From single cell model to battery pack simulation for Li-ion batteries", *Journal of Power Sources*, vol. 186, no.2, pp. 500-507, 2009.
5. C. Truchot, M. Dubarry and B.Y. Liaw, "State-of-charge estimation and uncertainty for lithium-ion battery strings", *Applied Energy*, vol. 119, pp. 218-227, 2014.
6. M. Dubarry, C. Truchot and B.Y. Liaw, "A Unique Mechanistic Model for Battery Diagnosis and Prognosis", *Proceedings of the 45th Power Sources Conference*, p. 127, 2012.
7. M. Dubarry, V. Svoboda, R. Hwu and B.Y. Liaw, "Incremental Capacity Analysis and Close-to-Equilibrium OCV Measurements to Quantify Capacity Fade in Commercial Rechargeable Lithium Batteries", *Electrochemical. Solid State Letters*, vol.9, no. 10, pp. A454-457, 2006.
8. M. Dubarry, C. Truchot, B.Y. Liaw, K. Gering, S. Sazhin, D. Jamison and C. Michelbacher, "Evaluation of Commercial Lithium-ion Cells Based on Composite Positive Electrode for Plug-in Hybrid Electric Vehicle (PHEV) Applications. Part II. Degradation Mechanism under 2 C Cycle Aging", *Journal of Power Sources*, vol. 196, no. 23, pp. 10336-10343, 2011.
9. M. Dubarry, C. Truchot, M. Cugnet, B.Y. Liaw, K. Gering, S. Sazhin, D. Jamison and C. Michelbacher, "Evaluation of Commercial Lithium-ion Cells Based on Composite Positive Electrode for Plug-in Hybrid Electric Vehicle (PHEV) Applications. Part I. Initial Characterizations", *Journal of Power Sources*, vol. 196, no. 23, pp. 10328-10335, 2011.
10. M. Dubarry, C. Truchot and B.Y. Liaw, "Cell Degradation in Commercial $LiFePO_4$ Cells with High-Power and High-Energy Designs", *Journal of Power Sources*, vol. 258, pp. 408-414, 2014.
11. A. Devie, M. Dubarry and B.Y. Liaw, "Diagnostics of Li-Ion Commercial Cells - Experimental Case studies", *ECS Transactions*, in print, 2014.

Development of Sealed, Large-Format Silver-Zinc Batteries and Cells for Department of Defense Applications

Dr. Bryan D. Hirschorn, Michael A. Solis, Thomas T. Terjesen
BST Systems, Inc.
78 Plainfield Pike Rd. Plainfield, CT, USA, 06374

Abstract: *BST Systems, Inc. has developed smart, sealed, safe large-format silver-zinc cells (100-365 Ah) that operate continuously at low, sub-atmospheric internal pressure. The patent-pending technology for smart sealed silver-zinc, and other aqueous batteries, utilizes a conventional recombination catalyst in conjunction with an automatic gas balancer (AGB) that enables stoichiometric recombination of all the hydrogen generated during cell operation. The AGB is incorporated in the cell, is electrically reversible, is powered by the cell, and is controlled by a sensor-regulated algorithm. Prototype cells and batteries have demonstrated continuous operation without releasing gas within a pressure range of -10 psig to +10 psig over typical silver-zinc lifetimes without maintenance. Negative gauge pressures have been observed on every cycle. In addition, the operation of the AGB has a <1% impact on the energy delivered by the cells and batteries.*

Keywords: silver; zinc; safe; sealed; hydrogen; aqueous; rechargeable; maintenance; aerospace; underwater vehicles.

Introduction

Rechargeable silver-zinc batteries are a safe, high energy-dense power source used in a variety of Department of Defense and aerospace applications. Conventional silver-zinc cells can release hydrogen gas during operation when cell relief valves open. For applications with an enclosed battery compartment, such as underwater vehicles, the accumulation of combustible gas mixtures is managed through use of evacuation and backfill (with inert gas) procedures and, requires costly purging equipment and maintenance schedules. The development of a sealed silver-zinc battery would be a significant advancement in silver-zinc technology, as a maintenance-free cell would reduce operational cost, extend cycle-life, and broaden the silver-zinc market into applications where silver-zinc batteries are not employed due to potential hydrogen release. In addition, a sealed silver-zinc battery would allow for factory activation of cells rather than the standard practice of end-user activation. The objective of the effort is to develop the first smart, maintenance-free, sealed, safe large-format silver-zinc cells and batteries that can be charged *in situ* (inside an undersea vehicle, for example). The development of sealed silver-zinc cells, and other aqueous batteries, have been attempted in the past through the use of stoichiometric hydrogen/oxygen recombination catalysts within cells [1-4]. Such recombination catalysts are not in use in silver-zinc cells because they are not effective with the non-stoichiometric gas generation, which leads to hydrogen gas accumulation within the cell and unacceptable pressures. Unfortunately, thus far a completely maintenance-free (for the lifetime of the battery), sealed silver-zinc battery has been unattainable due to the inability of the recombination catalyst to consume the gas mixtures produced by the cells for the entire duration of the cell's practical life. As such, state-of-the-art, large-format silver-zinc cells and batteries periodically release gases when cell relief valves open. To overcome the release of gases, BST Systems, Inc. has designed a sealed silver-zinc cell that incorporates a replaceable catalyst allowing for sealed operation of silver-zinc batteries between maintenance cycles of the undersea vehicle they power [5].

During the development of the sealed cell referred to above, there were ideas to achieve sealed operation throughout the life of the cell or battery. Accordingly, BST Systems, Inc. has developed a Smart Sealed Cell System (SSCS) for silver-zinc batteries. The SSCS comprises a hydrogen/oxygen gas recombination catalyst (GRC), an automatic gas balancer (AGB), and a Smart Management System (SMS) based on microprocessor control through a proprietary algorithm driven by a sensor. The SSCS includes a power supply that draws needed energy from the cell/battery. The components of the SSCS are located within the cell or battery and effectively remove gases generated during operation, such that, the battery can operate without releasing gas.

Method

Hydrogen gas is generated non-synchronously and non-stoichiometrically (in excess) compared to oxygen gas during normal operations (discharge, charge, open-circuit stand) of a silver-zinc battery. Recombination catalysts are ineffective for the purposes of sealing silver-zinc batteries and other aqueous battery systems. Replaceable catalyst

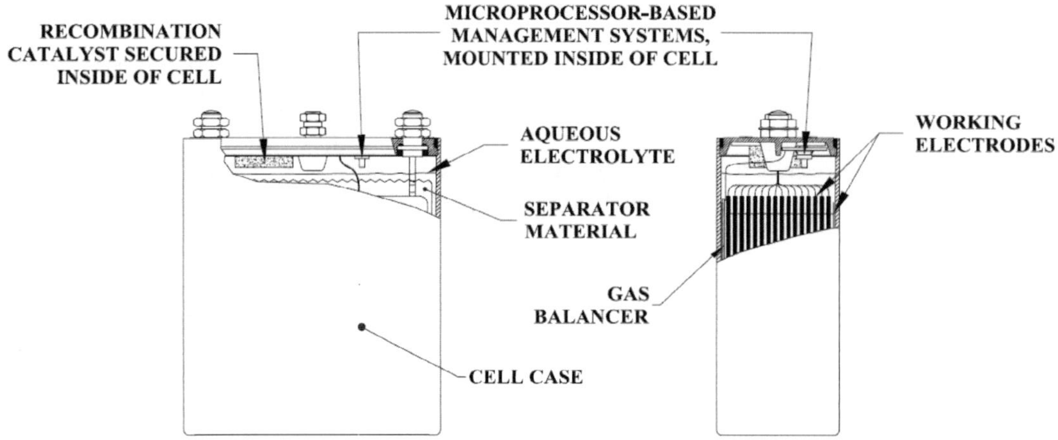

Figure 1: A schematic of the Smart Sealed Cell System (SSCS) at the cell level.

cartridges from BST Systems, Inc. provide limited periods of sealed operation, but will not support sealed operation throughout the life of the cell or battery. BST Systems, Inc. has developed an automatic gas balancer (AGB) that is implemented within the electrode pack and is electrically controlled by a proprietary sensor-regulated control algorithm.

The AGB supplies oxygen automatically when there is insufficient oxygen, on a stoichiometric basis, inside the cell or battery module. Oxygen gas generated from the operation of the AGB mixes with hydrogen gas produced during normal operation of the battery. The stoichiometric hydrogen/oxygen mixture recombines at a catalyst surface in the headspace, forming water or water vapor, which results in a low and sustainable pressure maintained within the sealed cell or battery.

Configuration of the Smart Sealed Cell System

The Smart Sealed Cell System (SSCS) can be configured at the cell level or the battery/module level.

SSCS at the Cell Level: As shown in Figure 1, the SSCS can be configured at the cell level, where all of its components (AGB, SMS, and GRC) are internal to the envelope of the cell. In such a configuration, each cell within a battery is independently sealed. In cell-level SSCS, recombined water is returned to the electrolyte. A prototype of the cell-level SSCS is shown in Figure 2.

SSCS at the Battery/Module level: As shown in Figure 3, the SSCS can be configured at the battery/module level, where its AGB component resides in each cell of the battery, and the other components (SMS and GRC) are located in a collection chamber within the battery housing. In such a configuration, a group of cells, assembled in a battery module, are sealed. Although plumbing connections between the individual cells and a collection chamber are required, for the SSCS at the battery/module level only one set of SMS and GRC is required, thus, there is lower costs associated with the SSCS at the battery/module level than the cell level.

Experimental

Two of BST's production cells, 365Ah and 140Ah, were modified for performance testing of the SSCS at the cell level (2 cells of 365 Ah) and at the battery/module level (4 cells of 140 Ah).

The 365 Ah cells were cycled individually following a protocol similar to the Acceptance Test method for applications for this cell size. A vented formation cycle was performed and the cells were vacuumed and sealed under vacuum prior to cycling. The discharges were performed at 60 A both timed (to 300 Ah) and full discharge. Full discharges to 1.20 V were performed on cycles 1, 2, 4, 5, 15, 25, 35, 45, 50. All other cycles were timed discharges to 300 Ah. Charges were performed at 10 A to a 2.02 V cut-off. Open-circuit periods were a minimum of 8 hours. The cycles with full discharges required up to 60 hours.

Figure 2: A prototype 365 Ah sealed, silver-zinc cell with SSCS at the cell level.

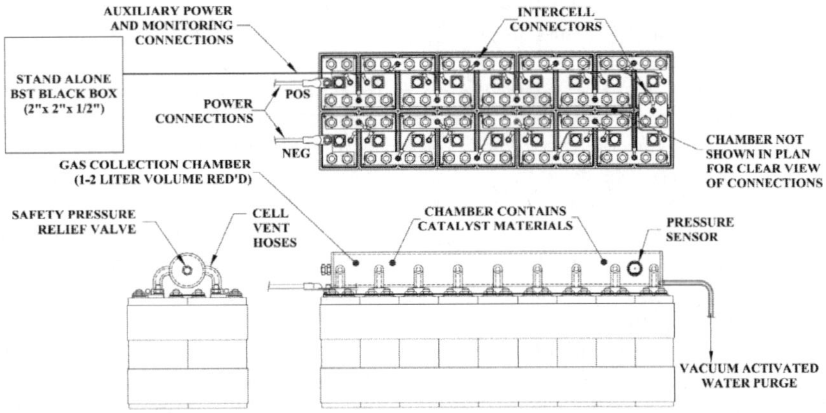

Figure 3: A schematic of the Smart Sealed Cell System (SSCS) configured at the battery/module level.

The cycles timed to 300 Ah required at least 50 hours.

A string of four 140 Ah cells were used to evaluate the SSCS at the battery/module level. As shown in Figure 4, vacuum tubing was used to connect the four-cell string to the collection chamber, which housed the recombination catalysts, sensor, and microprocessor. The system was vacuumed and sealed under vacuum prior to cycling. Full discharges at 50 A were performed every cycle. Charges were at 7 A to 2.02 V cut-off. Open-circuit periods were a minimum of 8 hours. The cycles required up to 40 hours.

Figure 4: A prototype sealed, 140 Ah four-cell string with SSCS at the battery/module level.

Results and Discussion

The SSCS at the cell level (365 Ah) and the battery/module level (140 Ah string) were evaluated in terms of internal pressure and capacity retention as a function of cycling.

Cell-level SSCS: The internal cell pressure of the sealed, 365 Ah cell as a function of cycle number is shown in Figure 5. It is seen that the pressure within the cell has remained at negative, vacuum pressures for over 40 cycles (3 months). The cell has operated continuously without gas release well below the safety relief valve threshold of 30 psig. Power required to operate the SSCS is supplied by the cell, thus the cell is self-contained.

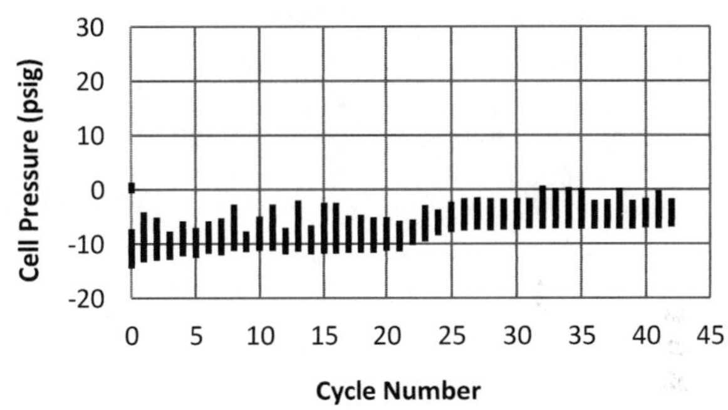

Figure 5: Internal pressure as a function of cycle number for a sealed, 365 Ah cell. The bars represent the pressure range over the complete cycle (charge/discharge/open-circuit).

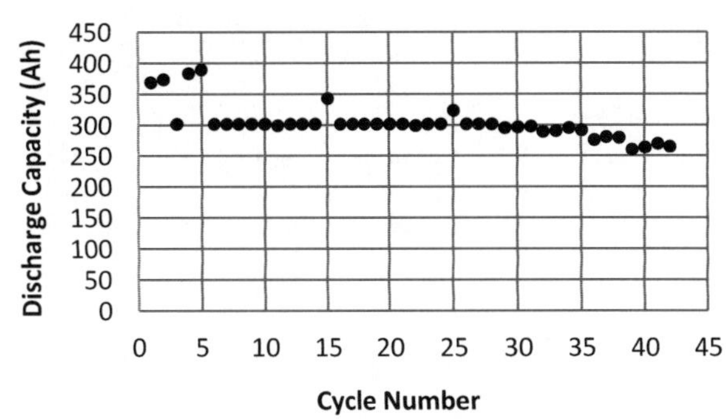

Figure 6: Discharge capacity as a function of cycle number for a sealed, 365 Ah cell.

The discharge capacity of the sealed, 365 Ah cell as a function of cycle number is shown in Figure 6. In order to accommodate the SSCS hardware, the initial capacity of the sealed, 365 Ah prototype was lower than BST Systems' conventional 365 Ah cell which delivers over 400 Ah initial and over 300 Ah on cycle 50. Future prototypes will incorporate SSCS hardware with decreased size, thus a sealed cell with the capability to achieve these targets is anticipated. The initial energy densities of the sealed, 365Ah cell prototype were 155 Wh/kg and 285 Wh/l.

Battery-level SSCS: The internal system pressure of a sealed, 140 Ah four-cell string as a function of cycle number is shown in Figure 7. It is seen that the pressure within the battery string has remained less than 5 psig for 70 cycles (5 months). For cycles 1-50, open-circuit periods were 8 hours. For cycles 50-70, open-circuit periods were 24 hours. As shown in Figure 7, rapid cycling (8 hour open-circuit periods) resulted in a higher pressure range than cycling following 24 hour open-circuit periods.

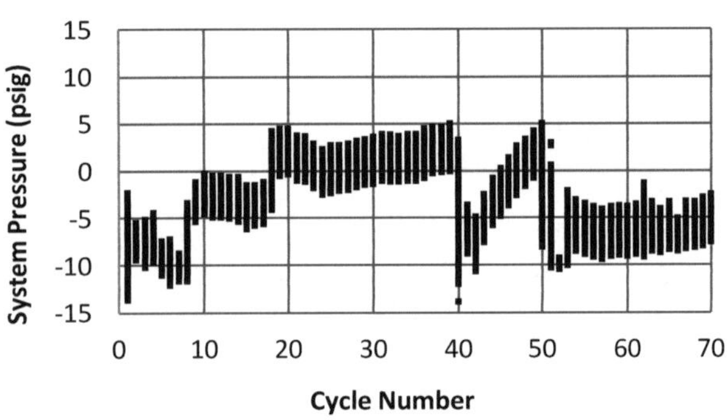

Figure 7: Internal pressure as a function of cycle number for a sealed, 140 Ah four-cell string. The bars represent the pressure range over the complete cycle (charge/discharge/open-circuit).

The discharge capacity of the sealed, 140 Ah four-cell string as a function of cycle number is shown in Figure 8. It is seen that the capacity retention was approximately 70% at cycle 20, typical of the 140 Ah cell, which is designed for low-cycle number applications. Extended cycling past 20 cycles was performed for the purpose of sealed operation evaluation. The initial energy densities of the sealed, 140 Ah cells were 135 Wh/kg and 263 Wh/l.

Conclusions and Future Work

BST Systems, Inc. has demonstrated lifetime sealed, safe operation of prototype silver-zinc cells and batteries by utilizing its patent-pending Smart Sealed Cell System technology. The sealed, silver-zinc technology enables safe, large-format, high-energy dense batteries for demanding applications in confined spaces, such as underwater vehicles. The Smart Sealed Cell System technology can be applied to other aqueous battery systems, beyond silver-zinc, where operation without gas release is desired.

The Smart Sealed Cell System technology is currently in the prototype phase. BST Systems, Inc. is in the process of progressing from prototypes to products, optimizing the control algorithm, and demonstrating performance on operational platforms.

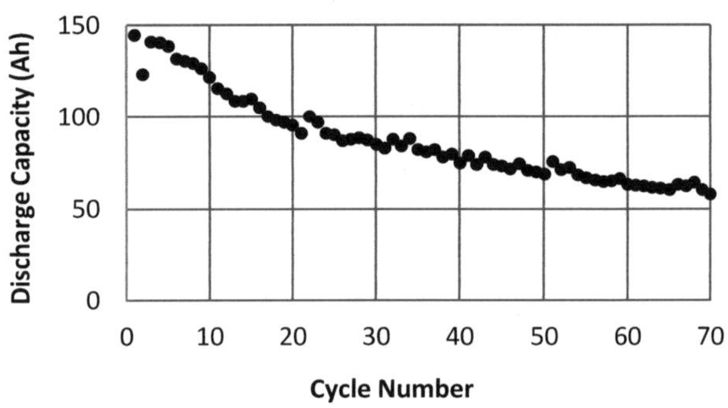

Figure 8: Discharge capacity as a function of cycle number for a sealed, 140 Ah four-cell string.

Acknowledgements

The authors wish to thank and acknowledge the BST team for their support on this project.

References

1. Gaines, L., "Secondary Silver-Zinc Battery Technology," *Journal of the Electrochemical Society*, vol. 13, no. 2, pp. 61C-67C, 1969.
2. Misra S.S., T.M. Noveske, S.L. Mraz, and A.J. Williamson, "The Role of Recombination Catalyst in VRLA Cells," *Journal of Power Sources*, Vol. 95, pp. 162-173, 2001.
3. Levy I., A. Charkey, "Gas Recombination Assembly for Electrochemical Cells," *Energy Research Corporation,* US Patent 4810598, 1989.
4. Charkey A., "Sealed Zinc Secondary Battery and Zinc Electrode Therefor," *Energy Research Corporation,* US Patent A 5460899A, 1995.
5. Hirschorn B., T.T. Terjesen, P.V. Imhof, "Novel Methods to Improve the Operation and Performance of Silver-Zinc Batteries," *Proceedings of the 46th Power Sources Conference,* 2014.

Three-Dimensional Zinc Electrode Architectures for Rechargeable Alkaline Batteries

Joseph F. Parker,[1] Irina R. Pala,[2] Matthew D. Wattendorf,[3] Debra R. Rolison,[1,*] and Jeffrey W. Long[1,*]

[1]Surface Chemistry Branch – Code 6170
U.S. Naval Research Laboratory
Washington, DC 20375, USA
*jeffrey.long@nrl.navy.mil
*debra.rolison@nrl.navy.mil

[2]National Research Council
Washington, DC 20001, USA
Post-doctoral associate
residing in Code 6170
U.S. Naval Research Laboratory

[3]Thomas Jefferson High School
for Science & Technology
Alexandria, VA 22312, USA
Student Volunteer in Code 6170
U.S. Naval Research Laboratory

Abstract: *Since the invention of the Leclanché cell in 1866, zinc has remained one of the most common and trusted electrode materials for commercial primary batteries. Broader implementation of zinc-based batteries is currently hindered by poor rechargeability—a consequence of the complex dissolution/precipitation processes that accompanies* Zn/Zn^{2+} *cycling and the ad hoc construction of conventional powdered-bed Zn anodes. We fabricate Zn "sponge" electrodes from emulsion-cast, consolidated Zn powders that are thermally treated to produce rugged monolithic forms. With this Zn sponge architecture, a highly conductive scaffold wired in 3D, we are now able to achieve Zn utilization up to ~90% (720 mA h* g_{Zn}^{-1}*) when discharged in primary Zn–air cells and dendrite-free cycling in symmetric Zn–Zn test cells and prototype Ag–Zn cells, up to 328 mA h* g_{Zn}^{-1}*. This paper describes the role of precursor Zn particle size on the physical and electrochemical characteristics of the resulting Zn sponge.*

Keywords: zinc–air; battery; rechargeable; three-dimensional; capacity

Introduction

Zinc-based batteries (*e.g.*, Zn–air, Ag–Zn, Ni–Zn, etc.) have inherent characteristics that overcome some of the drawbacks of Li-ion batteries in terms of safety concerns associated with toxic and flammable electrolytes and high materials and manufacturing costs. Zinc–air batteries also provide significantly higher specific energy (400 W h kg^{-1}) than typical Li-ion batteries. Broader implementation of Zn-based batteries is hindered by limited electrochemical rechargeability and modest capacity utilization (typically <60% of the 820 mA h g_{Zn}^{-1} theoretical discharge capacity). The non-ideal cycling and poor utilization of Zn in these batteries arises from the complex dissolution/precipitation dynamics that accompany Zn redox in alkaline electrolytes.

During discharge, metallic zinc is oxidized and reacts with hydroxide in the contacting electrolyte to form soluble zincate ions. Dissolved zincate, primarily as $Zn(OH)_4^{2-}$, diffuses from its point of electrogeneration until it supersaturates and then rapidly dehydrates and precipitates to form semiconducting zinc oxide (ZnO). Upon electrochemical recharge, ZnO is reduced back to Zn metal, concomitant with a second dissolution step, but with Zn often deposited at locations other than where initially oxidized. With progressive discharge–charge cycling, morphological changes become more pronounced, particularly at points of high current density, eventually electrogenerating dendrites that can pierce the separator and cause the battery to short. Such deleterious shape change is exacerbated in Zn electrodes that are fabricated as a powder-bed comprising a loosely connected composite of metal particles, gelling agents, binders, and other additives.

We have recently described a 3D architectural approach to redesign Zn anodes,[1] focusing on a monolithic "sponge" form factor in which the solid metal 3D network is interpenetrated by a co-continuous network of solid and void. The 3D wired network supports a more homogeneous current distribution throughout the electrode structure, minimizing local current hot spots that would otherwise spur formation of dendrites during cycling. The confined volume of void spaces within a porous 3D structure promotes more rapid saturation of zincate upon discharge and subsequent dehydration to ZnO, thereby abating shape change. Our initial studies demonstrate that this combination of structural properties results in high capacity utilization and dendrite-free cycling in rechargeable Zn cells (symmetric Zn–Zn and asymmetric Ag–Zn). In this paper, we fabricate Zn sponges from precursor Zn powders of varying particle size and examine how such parameters impact mechanical integrity and discharge capacity in primary Zn–air cells.

Experimental

Zn Sponge Fabrication: The preparation of Zn sponge electrodes follows the general protocol previously reported.[1] Briefly, an emulsified suspension of Zn powder and emulsion stabilizers is poured into cylindrical molds, followed by drying overnight at room temperature.[2] The mold-released monoliths are fragile, and therefore require an additional treatment that involves heating under Ar to

410 °C ($m.p._{Zn}$: 419.5 °C) to achieve greater particle–particle cohesion, followed by heating in ambient air to 665 °C to stabilize the porous structure of the monolith with a thin coating of ZnO, decompose the carbonaceous emulsifiers, and fuse the inner core of Zn. The heat-treated Zn sponges are immersed in additive-free 6 M KOH and held at a negative potential to electrochemically reduce the thermally generated ZnO coating, while still maintaining the intermetallic Zn core of the sponge.[1] The Zn particle sizes used in this study are summarized in Table 1.

Table 1. Summary of Zn particle sizes used in this study

Zn sponge formulation	size range	structural integrity
Z38	10–38 μm	high
Z63†	10–63 μm	high
Z88	53–88 μm	medium
Z170	75-425 μm (d_{50} ≈ 170 μm)	low

†Reference 1.

Preparation of Zn–air cells: The reduced Zn sponge electrodes are infiltrated with 6 M KOH, dipped in gel electrolyte (6 M KOH plus poly(acrylic acid)), and then placed atop a tin current collector. A single aqueous compatible separator (Freudenberg or Celgard) is placed between the Zn sponge and air cathode ("E-4," Electric Fuel Technologies). Nickel mesh is used as the positive current collector and attached to the positive external terminal via Pt-Rh wire. The constant-current single-discharge experiments are performed using a current density of 5 mA cm^{-2}, applied until the cell voltage falls below 0.9 V; note that this rate is ca. 5× higher current than that typical of hearing-aid cells and was chosen to stress the connectivity of the 3D wiring in the sponge.

Results and Discussion

The dried, pre-thermally treated Zn sponges vary in their mechanical integrity and are qualitatively ranked according to their ability to be handled as Z170 < Z88 < Z63 < Z38. The difference between sponges prepared from Z63 and Z38 is minor, with very little crumbling of either upon transfer to the furnace for the heat treatment. Z88 remains structurally intact, yet exhibits noticeable Zn particle loss when handled. Z170 is difficult to manipulate after casting in the plastic mold, readily breaking upon routine handling. After thermal treatment all Zn sponge formulations are robust enough for routine handling (Figure 1).

Figure 1. Photographs of the four formulations of Zn sponges from smallest (Z38) to largest (Z170) particle size. The increase of porosity with particle size is visible by eye.

Before transferring Zn sponges to the Zn–air cell, the sponges are electroreduced in bulk 6 M KOH until the open circuit potential versus a Zn wire quasi-reference electrode indicates conversion to the all-metal state. The changes in the handleability of the Z38, Z63, and Z88 sponges post-reduction are negligible when compared to their pre-reduced counterparts. The Z170 sponge is unusable after electroreduction due to complete structure breakdown. Any full-cell experiments using the Z170 sponge require direct transfer of the sponges to the Zn–air cell, without the removal of thermally induced ZnO. The initial open circuit voltage of each Zn–air cell is >1.4 V, and cell resistance is 0.5–2 Ω. Zinc–air cells are discharged at 5 mA cm^{-2} (Figure 2) until breaching a voltage cutoff of 0.9-V, which occurs at 32 h, 37 h,[1] 37 h, and 7 h for cells containing the Z38, Z63, Z88, and Z170 electrodes, respectively. The corresponding Zn-normalized capacity and utilization is summarized in Figure 3.

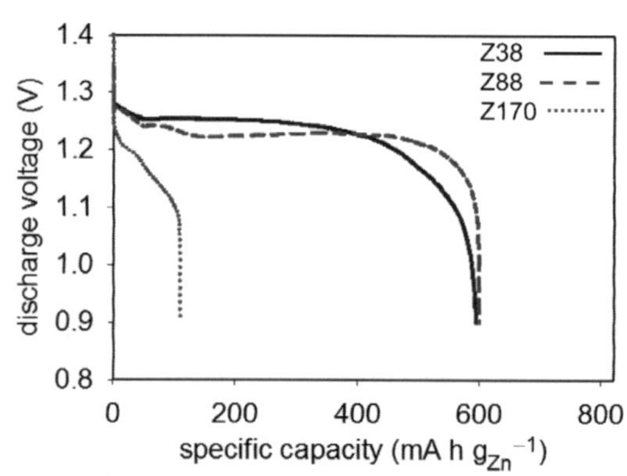

Figure 2. Zinc-normalized capacities in primary Zn–air cells using 3D Zn sponge electrodes prepared with varying particle sizes. See reference 1 for Z63 data.

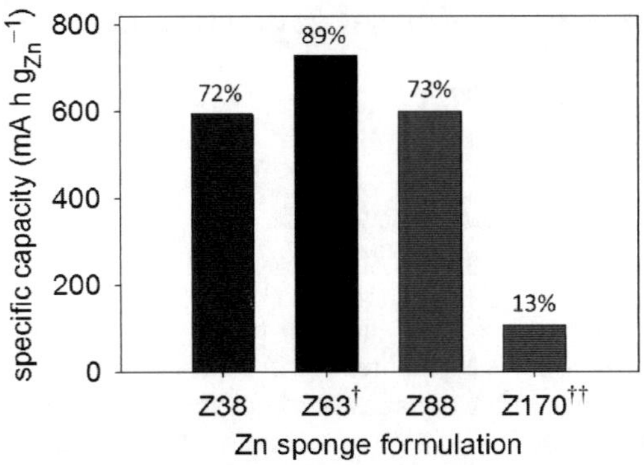

Figure 3. Measured capacities in primary Zn–air cells prepared with varying particle size (3D Zn sponge electrodes). †Reference 1. ††Z170 sponges were too fragile to undergo the electroreduction step, so these cells were prepared by simply infiltrating thermally-treated Z170 with 6 M KOH.

Commercial battery manufacturers generally prefer to use coarse Zn powder (100s of μm)[3] versus fine particles (< 50 μm) because the rate of hydrogen evolution decreases as the particle size increases. In examples where smaller particles are used to slightly increase the discharge capacity,[4] the gassing associated with self-discharge is often managed by the addition of mercury[5] and lead to the Zn particles. As battery manufacturers continue to reject nontoxic additives, they must resort to either using larger particles or using nontoxic additives, such as Bi and In. The Zn alloy we use to formulate our Zn sponges (Grillo-Werke GmbH) contains 300 ppm In and 300 ppm Bi (gas evolution rate of 1.55 mL h^{-1}, as reported in the Grillo-Werke specification sheet, lower than historic mercury amalgamations[5]). Therefore, when choosing the appropriate formulation for a specific Zn application, one must consider a combination of factors including mechanical integrity, specific capacity, and gassing rate. In the case of our 3D Zn sponge electrodes, the use of coarse Zn particle sizes greatly reduces the structural integrity, yielding Zn electrodes that are virtually unusable in high depths-of-discharge experiments or long-term cycling.

Conclusions

The discharge performance of Zn–air cells using Zn sponge anodes formulated from four different Zn particle distributions revealed a trend of increasing specific capacity of Z170<Z38≤Z88<Z63. The mechanical integrity of the synthesized sponges increases with decreasing particle size as expected: Z170<Z88<Z63<Z38. In applications for high depth-of-discharge, Z63 is the desired formulation of the systems investigated. In applications where mechanical integrity for high-impact or long term cycling, Z38 or Z63 would be the electrodes of choice.

Acknowledgements

The information, data, or work presented herein was funded in part by the Advanced Research Projects Agency–Energy (ARPA–E), U.S. Department of Energy, under Award Number DE-AR-0000391 and has been Approved for Public Release, Distribution Unlimited. The views expressed are those of the authors and do not reflect the official policy or position of the Department of Defense, Department of Energy, or the U.S. Government. I.R.P. is a National Research Council–Naval Research Laboratory Postdoctoral Associate (2011–2014).

References

1. Parker, J. F., Chervin, C. N., Nelson, E. S., Rolison, D. R., and J. W. Long, "Wiring zinc in three dimensions re-writes battery performance–dendrite-free cycling," *Energy & Environmental Science*, vol. 7, pp. 1117–1124, 2014.
2. Drillet, J.-F., Adam, M., Barg, S., Herter, A., Koch, D., Schmidt, V. M., and M. Wilhelm, "Development of a novel zinc/air fuel cell with a Zn foam anode, a PVA/KOH Membrane and a MnO_2/SiOC-based Air Cathode," *ECS Transactions*, vol. 28, pp. 13–21, 2010.
3. Phillips, J., Mohanta, S., Geng, M., Barton, J., McKinney, B., and J. Wu, "Environmentally friendly nickel-zinc battery for high rate applications with higher specific energy," *ECS Transactions*, vol. 16, pp. 11–17, 2009.
4. J. Daniel-Ivad and J.-Y. Huot, "Mercury- and Lead-free rechargeable Zn/MnO_2 cells," *Electrochemical Society Proceedings,* vol. 95-14, pp. 109–120, 1996.
5. R. N. Snyder and J. J. Lander, "Rate of hydrogen evolution of zinc electrodes in alkaline solutions," *Electrochemical Technology*, vol. 3, pp. 161–466, 1965.

Battery Deterioration Mechanism Analysis for Nickel-Metal Hydride Batteries

Wenhua H. Zhu and Bruce J. Tatarchuk*
Center for Microfibrous Materials
Department of Chemical Engineering,
Auburn University, 212 Ross Hall, Auburn, AL 36849-5127
*tatarbj@auburn.edu, zhuwenh@auburn.edu

Abstract: *The Ni-MH power system for efficient energy storage and delivery has numerous advantages including system safety, high gravimetric and volumetric energy density, long battery lifetime, proper overcharge and over-discharge protection, flexible cell design and packaging, lower cost for pack production, quick charge acceptance, and large operating windows both of voltage and temperature. Many hybrid electric vehicles are dependent on the nickel-metal hydride battery packs. Although the cost of the battery power system for onboard energy storage is quickly reduced due to large volume production, the operational lifetime is still the most important concern of this energy-storage technique. The battery performance deterioration primarily includes electrode degradations, separator weakening, and electrolyte-saturation-level changes. The Ni-MH battery characteristics and performance were experimentally examined according to the energy storage requirement. The battery state-of-charge performance was also evaluated at different charge and discharge rates for the energy storage applications. The self-discharge rate was calculated based on its actual capacity measured at a certain period of time. AC impedance data were collected for analysis on the battery's physical process and its reaction mechanism at a specified charge-input level. The battery system deterioration was analyzed from the electrode structure, electrode side-reactions, and separator aging. This indication provides significant essentials for cycle lifetime improvement of the battery pack and potentially increases energy-storage efficiency for the Ni-MH battery power system.*

Keywords: Nickel-metal hydride battery; Ni-MH electrode degradation; battery deterioration mechanism; onboard energy storage.

Introduction

The battery packs and ultracapacitor modules, applied separately or served as a hybrid power system, are mostly efficient way for on-board energy storage, power capturing and delivery[1]. The Li-ion battery and its packs have been quickly made visible progress at least for high-density energy storage for PHEVs, although the consumers still hesitate on the battery reliability, aging, and replacement cost[2]. However, the Ni-MH batteries as one of the major rechargeable (Pb-acid, Ni-MH, and Li-ion) batteries have been successfully developed for on-board energy storage needs in the HEV applications [3]. The Ni-MH battery packs are currently operated onboard with good abuse tolerance, proper cost, and acceptable low temperature performance. It is still valuable to get more information back from the Ni-MH battery long-term energy storage and road services. This makes further product improvement possible if the Li-ion battery technologies are hard to make any further breakthrough in the cycle lifetime, aging, and thermal management. In this work, we conducted the electrical characterization on different types of single Ni-MH batteries. The results are obtained from extensive testing & evaluations. The deterioration mechanism are analyzed and discussed for potentially improving product quality.

Experimental

Sealed cylindrical Li-ion and Ni-MH cells can be formed as a module for the HEV or PHEV applications [3, 4]. In this work, the cylindrical Ni-MH batteries of D-size with a diameter of 32 mm and the height of 60 mm were applied for testing and evaluations of the batteries. Experimental data were collected during their operation at full and partial state-of-charge. In details, two types of the NiMH-A1/B2 and NiMH-C3/D4 batteries were applied to the performance tests. The batteries have capacities of 3702 mAh (A1), 4362 mAh (B2), and *ca.* 3000 mAh (C3/C4), respectively. The new type of the NiMH-C3/C4 batteries exhibits a slow self-discharge rate. The above capacity was measured at a 0.2C charge rate up to 115% or 120% RoC. The rated capacity was obtained by discharging the battery to 1.00 V cut-off voltage at a 0.2C rate. The term of RoC refers to the **r**atio **o**f the **c**harge input to the rated capacity after the battery is fully discharged as 100% DoD, i.e. 0% SoC. The Arbin battery tester was applied to battery tests and measurement. All work was performed at room temperature. The batteries were charged to a certain level of RoC at a 0.2C rate and then conducted impedance tests. The Gamry FC350^{TM} system with an electronic load is applied to the battery impedance tests. Due to relatively high energy Ni-MH cells applied in the tests, the short-term changes of the physical processes and the electrochemical reactions are neglected at certain of load current via small *ac* signal disturbance. Hybrid measurements compensate for the change in cell impedance as frequency is varied by changing *ac* current amplitude to keep measured *ac* voltage at a set of value. The previously measured impedance point is used in determining the new current amplitude, as the scan proceeds from 10 kHz to 10 μHz. In this work, the hybrid EIS mode was applied for the experiments in order to obtain the impedance data of the rechargeable battery at various frequencies. Small amount of the consumed capacity and energy of the Ni-MH battery was approximately calculated and charged back after each impedance measurement. The battery was ready for the impedance test at another RoC (or SoC) level. The computer system collects these impedance data for analyzing and understanding of the battery energy-storage mechanisms.

Results and discussion

On-board energy storage challenges: Both of Ni-MH and Li-ion Battery packs have been rapidly developed for HEV or PHEV applications for fuel saving, reduction of CO_2, SO_2, and NO_x emissions. The full/med hybrids (150 V-350 V, possible 15-50 kW to power-assisted HEVs) using Ni-MH and Li-ion packs have been developed on the real road services. And the hybrid power systems through the ultracapacitor power modules and the NiMH or Li-ion battery energy storage packs are potentially applied to the on-board energy storage system to significantly increase the battery service lifetime. For the 20-50 kW power requirements on the PHEV on-board energy storage, the recent Li-ion battery systems are capable of delivering power and energy for the system needs. The hybrid energy systems through the ultracapacitor power modules and the Li-ion battery energy storage packs are also to be expected to provide proper energy and power for prolonging the battery service lifetime[5]. The cost of Li-ion batteries is higher than the Ni-MH battery packs, due to raw materials & processing, battery module packaging, and related manufacturing costs. The difficulties of the Lithium battery system take account of a power loss when discharging at low temperatures and also have power deterioration even standby over time and for the duration of cycle missions. Many Ni-MH batteries and their packs are on the markets and also provide the HEV on-board energy storage needs. The battery performance deterioration has great impact on its cycle life target. It is still valuable to explore the mechanisms of the capacity decay and theoretical explanation for the power loss during various cycle missions.

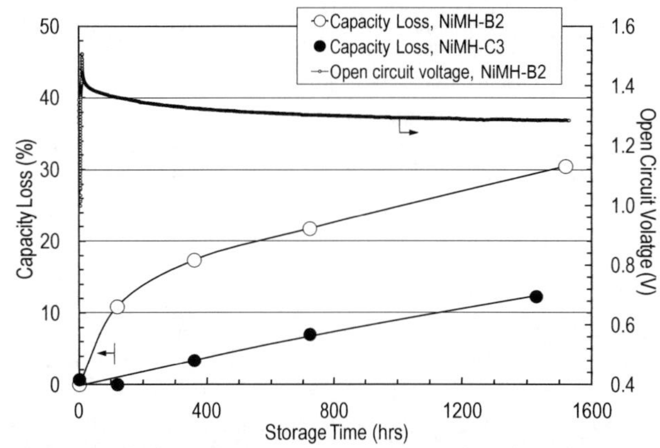

Figure 1. Self-discharge voltage versus a function of time at open circuit. The Ni-MH batteries were discharged to 1.0 V cut-off voltage at a 0.2C rate after charged to 120% RoC.

Self-discharge and capacity losses: Voltage data were gathered during the battery storage tests (Figure 1). The capacity was obtained after the battery was discharged to 1.00 V cut-off voltage at a 0.2 C rate. The capacity losses and voltage degradation rates are shown in Table 1. The batteries NiMH-A1/B2 are the traditional Ni-MH battery and the NiMH-C3/D4 is differently designed for a slow self-discharge rate[6]. At the Week-4, the NiMH-B2 voltage decay is 35% faster than the slower NiMH-C3 one. The capacity degradation for the NiMH-B2 one is 10.61 mAh/day faster than the NiMH-C3 type battery. The capacity decay of the traditional battery is averagely two-times faster than the slower designed one.

Energy efficiency and state-of-charge as a function of charge input: The NiMH-C3 battery was charged to a certain level of RoCs and then discharged to 1.00 V cut-off voltage at the same rate. The parameter of the state-of-charge value (SoC) was obtained after the capacity was measured. The Coulomb and energy efficiency are shown in Figure 2. The battery RoC line linearly increases with the charge input. The SoC line gradually separates from the RoC line after the SoC value exceeds 80% because the

Table 1. Self discharge measurement and capacity degradation of the Ni-MH batteries. Discharged down to 1.00 V cut-off after fully charged at 120 % RoC at a 0.2C rate

Storage Time (days)	NiMH-B2 Voltage Drop (mV/day)	NiMH-B2 Capacity Degradation[a] (mAh/day)	NiMH-C3 Voltage Drop (mV/day)	NiMH-C3 Capacity Degradation[a] (mAh/day)
0-7 (Week 1)	19.86	76.0	17.9	–[b]
8-14 (Week 2)	3.43	28.3	1.93	10.71
15-21 (Week 3)	1.86	14.9	1.13	11.43
22-28 (Week 4)	1.14	12.9	0.743	2.29
29-35 (Week 5)	1.00	11.7	0.529	5.29
36-63 (Weeks 6-9)	0.50	11.5	0.532	4.98

[a] The degradation rate is defined as the average capacity change during the storage period of measurement.
[b] The battery capacity had a very small amount of change in the first 7 days due to its low self-discharge design. This small capacity loss was neglected in this period of test.

oxygen evolution is started to happen during increase of the charge input. At the initial charge stage, the inefficient charge is considered to be caused by higher resistance of the $Ni(OH)_2$ active material. The optimal voltage window is narrowed due to the burst energy absorption in considering of the battery electrode overpotentials and mass transport limitations.

Impedance data analysis of two types of Ni-MH batteries: As mentioned earlier, the hybrid EIS mode was applied for the experiments to collect the impedance data of the rechargeable battery at various frequencies. Small amount of the consumed capacity and energy of the Ni-MH battery was approximately calculated and charged back after each impedance measurement. For two types of batteries from Figures 3&4, the slow self-discharge NiMH-C3 battery has a twist on the phase angle data at *ca.* 1 Hz frequency. This phenomenon is not clear for its relationship to the self-discharge rate of the battery at a slow capacity loss. After charged to various RoC levels, the Nyquist plots of the NiMH-B2 battery are obtained as shown in Figure 5. The equivalent series resistance is slightly changed (small increase from 14.3 mΩ to 18 mΩ) from 20% to 80% RoC level. It shows a small decline from 18 mΩ to 16.3 mΩ if the RoC value continuously increases to 100%. This likely results from temporary changes of the electrolyte saturation level. Similar results are obtained for the NiMH-C3 battery.

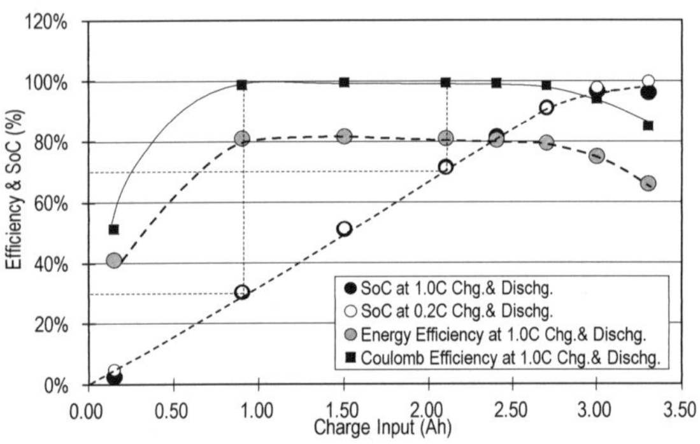

Figure 2. The NiMH-C3 battery energy, coulomb efficiency, and state-of-charge as a function of charge input.

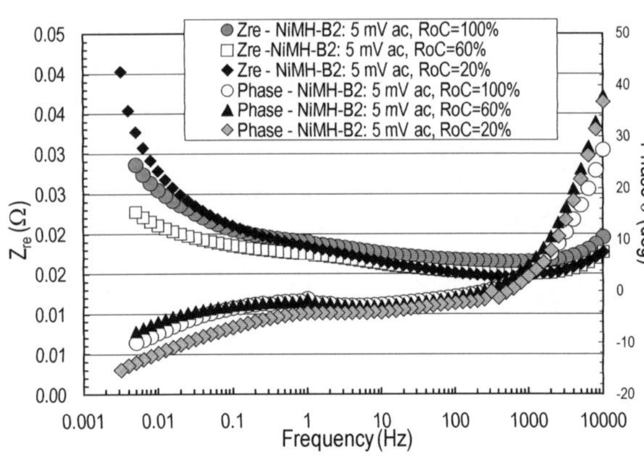

Figure 3. Bode plots of the NiMH-B2 battery from impedance data via 5 mV *ac* at different charge input levels.

The starved electrolyte and its tolerance effects on battery resistance, performance deterioration, cycle life, and storage efficiency need further assessments in the future work.

Mechanism analysis of self-discharge and performance deterioration: It is of significant importance for reducing the self-discharge rate and prolonging the battery service life in order to increase energy-storage efficiency for fuel savings. For the cell self-discharge as shown in Table 2, the charged material of NiOOH is thermodynamically instable and self-decomposed leading to oxygen release [7]. This oxygen consumes hydrogen stored inside the MH hydride alloys. Nitrite/Nitrate ions, and/or organic impurities dissolved from the separator formed as NO_2^-/NH_4OH redox shuttles [8, 9]. This greatly increases the self-discharge rate. Two major factors on the performance decay are contributed from both of the electrodes after use of stable separators. As shown in Table 3, the swelling of the positive electrodes, the structure changes of the hydride alloys, separator crumble or deposits can be further contributions to performance deterioration. The impedance tool is a powerful technique for battery failure analysis and further product improvement through understanding of the capacity loss and battery deterioration mechanisms.

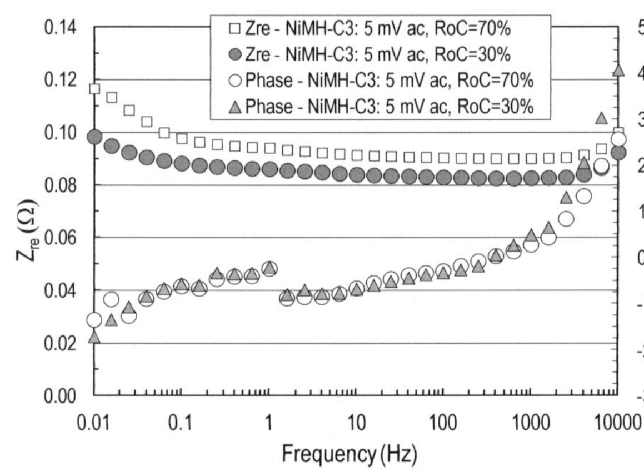

Figure 4. Bode plots of the NiMH-C3 battery from impedance data via 5 mV *ac* at different charge input levels.

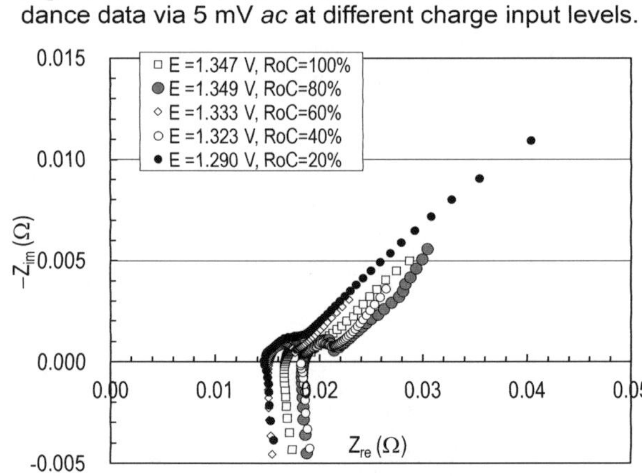

Figure 5. Nyquist plots of the NiMH-B2 battery after charged to various RoC levels. Impedance data were uncompensated values at an initial loading of 0.1C 436 mA current, 5 mV *ac*.

Table 2. Battery deterioration due to self-discharge inside the Ni-MH batteries

At the Positive Electrode	In the Separator	At the Negative Electrode
• Self-decomposition (Thermodynamic instability) of the charged positive material (NiOOH)* leading to oxygen release. $NiOOH + \frac{1}{2}H_2O \rightleftharpoons Ni(OH)_2 + \frac{1}{4}O_2$ — This oxygen consumes hydrogen stored inside the MH alloys. • Reduction of the positive electrode by hydrogen gas coming from the MH electrode, and impurities of redox shuttles. $NiOOH + \frac{1}{2}H_2 \rightleftharpoons Ni(OH)_2$ $NH_4OH + 6NiOOH + OH^- \rightarrow 6Ni(OH)_2 + NO_2^-$	• Nitrate ions, metal ions and/or organic impurities dissolved from the separator — Accelerated by ammonia and amine ions. • Microscopic short circuit in the separator — Particle deposits migrated from the positive and negative electrode elements such as zinc, cobalt, aluminum, and manganese. — Redox shuttle reaction suppressed by using sulfonated and grafted polypropylene separators — Use of stable polyolefin separators	• Hydrogen gas evolution at the hydrogen-absorbing alloy electrode $MH + 3H_2O \rightleftharpoons M(OH)_3 + \frac{3}{2}H_2$ • Hydrogen oxidation with oxygen from the positive electrode. $2MH_{ads} + \frac{1}{2}O_2 \rightarrow 2M + H_2O$ • Oxidation of nitrite impurities of redox shuttles. $NO_2^- + MH_x \rightarrow NH_4OH + MH_{x-6} + OH^-$

Table 3. Battery deterioration mechanism analysis inside a Ni-MH cell

At the Positive Electrode	Deterioration in the Separator	At the Negative Electrode	Battery Electrolyte and Structure
• Loss of active material especially in sintered electrode structure. • Electrode expansion due to charge/discharge. • Migration of Al from the negative electrode to the positive electrode	• Microscopic short circuit in the separator by deposits. • Impurities dissolved from the separator or separator degradation * Principally improved by stable-structured separators.	• Oxidation of the hydrogen-absorbing alloy • Alloy metal ions dissolved in the electrolyte • Increase of the negative resistance * Largely improved by using a hydrogen-absorbing alloy with higher oxidation resistibility	• Pressure release of the electrolyte with the inner gas from the cell operation. • Consumption of electrolyte due to the hydride alloy oxidation. * Decrease of the electrolyte in the separator – a dominant factor of the deterioration.

Summary

Many HEVs and other needs for on-board energy storage are dependent on the Ni-MH battery packs, because this type of power system has features of longer cycle lifetime, proper tolerance mechanism for overcharge and over-discharge, lower cost for battery pack production, quick charge acceptance, and large operating windows both of voltage and temperature. The battery performance deterioration mainly includes electrode degradations, separator weakening, and level changes of electrolyte saturation in the electrodes. The self-discharge rate can be further reduced by improvement on electrode structures and enhancement of the metal hydride alloys. The *AC* impedance technique is recognized as a powerful tool for diagnostics and analysis on the electrochemical reactions and other related physical processes for the battery packs. The battery system deterioration can be further understood from analyzing the electrode structure, electrolyte saturation levels, and separator aging. This indication provides significant essentials for cycle lifetime improvement of the battery pack and potentially increases energy storage efficiency of the Ni-MH battery power system. The quality improvement and assurance on the battery packs potentially give more confidence for rapid energy storage onboard and proper power delivery in order to get high energy efficiency, i.e. good mile-per-gallon (mpg) numbers, fuel saving, CO_2, SO_2, and NO_x emissions' reduction.

References

1. Lajnef, W. J., M. Vinassa, O. Briat, S. Azzopardi, and E. Woirgard, *J. Power Sources*, vol.168, pp.553-560, 2007.
2. Zhang, J., and J. Lee, *J. Power Sources*, vol. 196, pp. 6007-6014, 2011.
3. Taniguchi, A., N. Fujioka, M. Ikoma, and A. Ohta, *J. Power Sources*, vol. 100, pp. 117-124, 2001.
4. Mastali, M., J. Vazquez-Arenas, R. Fraser, M. Fowler, S. Afshar, and M. Stevens, *Journal of Power Sources,* vol. 239, pp. 294-307, 2013.
5. Pesaran, A. A., "Choices and Requirements of Batteries for EVs, HEVs, PHEVs," NREL/PR-5400-51474, National Renewable Energy Laboratory, April 21, 2011.
6. Zhu, W. H., Y. Zhu, Z. Davis, and B. J. Tatarchuk, *Appl. Energy*, vol. 106, pp. 307-313, 2013.
7. Yang, X.-G., and B. Y. Liaw, *J. Electrochem. Soc.*, vol. 151, pp. A137-A143, 2004.
8. Leblanc, P., P. Blanchard, and S. Senyarich, *J. Electrochem. Soc.,* vol. 145, pp. 844-847, 1998.
9. Kritzer, P., *J. Power Sources*, vol.137, pp.317-21, 2004.

Solving Critical Military Battery Industrial Base Challenges with Title III: A User's Perspective

Keith DeVries
Naval Surface Warfare Center
Crane, IN, USA 47522

Abstract: *Mr. Keith DeVries will be discussing the applicability of Defense Production Act (DPA) Title III authorities to solve industrial base issues associated with energy storage devices (batteries) required for military applications. Though many military applications can use commercially available batteries/battery cells other applications such as missile, space and submarine main storage batteries have requirements that lead to unique battery designs and usage profiles. When the industrial base is unable to provide cost effective solutions to meeting those unique National Security requirements program offices should consider Title III authorities as an effective alternative to augment their efforts in solving those industrial base issues. Through the development of a set of programmatic and technical plans incorporating resources from the DoD Program Office(s), Title III and cost share by the vendors, solutions can be developed that meet national security requirements and improve profitability of the vendors. This presentation will discuss, from a program office perspective, how to engage the Title III process to solve military battery challenges.*

Keywords: Battery; Power Systems; VRLA; Lead Acid; Silver Zinc; Defense Production Act; Title III; Industrial Base; Industrial Mobilization; Investment; DoD; NAVSEA; AFRL; Executive Agent; Sustainment.

Introduction

The Department of Defense (DoD) often finds itself dependent upon vendors with manufacturing equipment/processes, technology, or quality control challenges that fail to meet DoD requirements. One of the main drivers that determine plant or process investment by the vendors is the demand for the assets by the DoD. If the demand is the low the investment is harder for the vendor to justify the investment. To ensure the vendors remain motivated and available to support the DoD needs, programs such as the Title III are available and used where needed This becomes especially important to Small Business where the product line is mainly focused on the DoD requirements. Without out Programs like Title III the small vendors do not have the capital to make the investments needed in equipment, the processes or technology improvements. If these types of investments do not occur it slows the platform technology improvements because of the lack energy improvements.

.

This situation can present itself when the military's product comes from a unique industrial base. In the case of batteries, this could manifest as unique chemistries, size, or designs when no existing commercial or other military product/chemistry can meet the National Security need. In some cases safety can be a major consideration where dealing with certain weapons systems.

In other scenarios, the military application could be a non-standard configuration of chemistries available for commercial use. The cells could be oversized; the battery configuration of cells could be to an unconventional requirement not offered in a commercial listing.

The last common military requirement involves the application of Commercially-available Off The Shelf (COTS) technology, applied to military needs. In this scenario, if the commercial volume far exceeds the military demand, the industrial provider may not realize enough return on investment to make the changes required to meet military technical and safety demands.

In scenarios where military programs require investment that industry isn't able to justify through internal capital improvements, the Defense Production Act Title III authorities may be utilized to provide solutions.

Defense Production Act Authorities

The Defense Production Act (DPA) was enacted in 1950 and provides the President with unique opportunities to maintain and enhance the defense industrial and technological base. The DPA requires reauthorization on a periodic basis. The DPA was most recently reauthorized in October 2009 and is scheduled to expire September 30, 2014—pending action from Congress to renew the authorization.

The DPA is further broken down into seven sections, Titles I through VII. Titles II, IV, V, and VI are no longer active, and have been retired by Congress since their inception. The remaining active Titles are:

Title I provides the ability to prioritize Defense contracting requirements, commonly referred to DO or DX ratings for contracts.

Title VII provides administrative authority relating to Defense Production Act contracting activities and industrial base support.

Title III – enables the expansion of productive capacity and supply by aiding manufacturers in meeting the national security demand of the DoD.

Production capabilities that would otherwise be inadequate to meet DoD requirements are transformed to support the material requirements of defense programs in a timely and affordable manner. Title III focuses on materials and components that could be used in a broad spectrum of defense systems. The direct and indirect benefits to defense programs resulting from Title III initiatives are substantial. Moreover, Title III projects create numerous economic and technological benefits for domestic industries and consumers.

Within the Title III authorities, there are three principal opportunities for industrial intervention.

Section 303a – Purchases provides funding for engineering support to improve quality and yield, test quantities for process validation and qualification testing, and costs to develop business and marketing plans.

Section 303e – Installation of Equipment in Industrial Facilities provides funding for capital investments in equipment and facilities to improve capacity, capability, or quality of delivered product. At the end of the program, title transfers from government ownership to industrial partner, to be used for commercial and DoD production.

Section 303g – Development of Substitutes provides funding for the investigation and maturation of technological alternative technologies for strategic and critical components, critical technology items, and other industrial resources.

Industrial Applications

The most recent applications of this authority for DoD energy storage applications have been in the Valve Regulated Lead Acid (VRLA) industry and the Silver Zinc (AgZn) industry.

Valve Regulated Lead Acid: The Navy uses Valve Regulated Lead Acid technology in several critical applications, and has experienced performance below requirements in the larger cell and battery designs. After investing significant resources over several years by both government and industry, the products provided still did not meet key performance requirements. An identified area for improvement is the ability to consistently control the manufacturing process and allow data collection that would verify the process with real time data available to the process operators. Part of this effort is to update the equipment that allows better control and monitoring of the processes.

Silver-Zinc: These types of efforts are critical in providing the Navy with the silver zinc technology cells and batteries in the future. The use of silver zinc technology has seen a decline over the last several years because of the decommissioning of vehicles including the NR-1 and the DSRV. The two primary providers of this technology are small business set aside sources. With the current decline in budgets and resources it has come to the point where Title III may be the only source for technology and process improvement that in turn could enhance the applications that could benefit. The lithium ion technology when first introduced was considered to be a technology that would drastically reduce the need for silver zinc battery technology. This was mainly due to longer cycle life of lithium ion, but safety concerns with lithium ion technology developed and more systems are now considering the use of silver zinc technology. However, even with the decline in silver zinc use the technology remains a critical part of several systems. The manufacturing processes and equipment has seen little change over the last several years and would potentially benefit from help with formation equipment, pasting, and other automation such as data collection and testing. Developing automated equipment and processes could potentially expand the cycle life, reduce the cost of the technology and provide the DoD with a more stable manufacturing base.

Process Map

In approaching a Title III investment for an energy storage application, there is a recommended process to follow to maximize the success of the endeavor. Industry can't pursue an investment without buy-in from the DoD programs it supports, and DoD can't realize benefit without coordination and buy-in from industry. This is a partnership from start to finish, and will provide benefits to both DoD and the manufacturing base.

Phase 1 – Socialization: Upon identification of the opportunity to make a Title III investment that will benefit the DoD end-user, there will be several informal conversations between industry and government.

Where there are several industrial providers competing in the same DoD requirements-space, it is essential to socialize the planned improvements across the markets to provide opportunities to improve the industrial base while maintaining market competition. It is critical that vendors are approached early in the process to determine the areas that should be considered for improvement since they understand the processes and equipment used in the individual plants. It should be understood going in that vendors may provide the same product built to the same specification, but may use different manufacturing equipment and processes. Since Title III is being sought in cases where the market isn't naturally providing the solutions, similar capability gaps should be present in all active industry partners. To estimate and communicate the level of investment required, preliminary estimates of process improvements or capital investments should be developed. The vendors will need to determine if space is available, environmental impact, upper management buy in, equipment cost and lead time that would allow limited interruptions in the commercial lines.

There are several government entities that will need to be in agreement before using Title III. The DoD Program Office should be aware, and the technical authority for the technology should concur that investment is necessary and should provide benefit. The technical authority should include the Technical Warrant Holder and the In-Service Engineering Agent (ISEA) for the chemistry/application. In addition, initial discussions should include the DPA Title III office, to provide awareness of the challenge and the approaches being taken to address it.

When coordination is complete and there is agreement that the Title III project should proceed, it is vital to capture the national security implications. There should be correspondence from the senior management of the affected Program Offices, highlighting the need, its impact on the nation's security, and the fact that industry isn't positioned to solve the problem. At this point it must be clear that this is a national security issue supported by the top level of management in the DoD.

Stage 2 – Education: At this point, there are often several opportunities to engage industry and the DoD components affected by the Title III process. Title III is a non-standard process, and often both the government partners and industry will be unfamiliar with the process, the requirements for the program, and the potential outcomes. DPA Title III representatives and DoD ISEAs can provide additional information and coordinate meetings as necessary to ensure all questions are answered. These meetings can be with the entire community—industry, Program Offices, ISEAs—or with individual groups as appropriate.

Stage 3 – Selection: When the letters of intent have been received, the DPA Title III office will make an evaluation of the program's merit and the definition of successful outcomes. The Title III office will then task its Executive Agent to begin detailed requirements generation in coordination with the program office and ISEA communities. This will lead to a formal Request for Procurement (RFP), though the specific contracting vehicle to be used will be exercised at the discretion of the Title III Executive Agent's Contracting Officer.

In parallel, work will begin on DPA Title III's official program designation, the Presidential Determination. This document provides the structured description of the problem to be solved, the approaches being taken, and the anticipated benefit to the DoD. This PD will highlight the National Security benefits of the project and will be signed by the Under Secretary of Defense for Acquisition, Technology, and Defense (USD, AT&L) as delegated by the President. The document is then provided to the US Congress for awareness and comment.

Conclusion

The authorities granted within the Defense Production Act, specifically within Title III, can be of great value to both DoD programs and the industrial partners on whom they depend. The ability to effect win-win change in a scenario where there is little commercial incentive for industry can provide increased technical value to the DoD end-users and can bolster commercial viability by accelerating improvements in the commercial products manufactured in the same plant. Title III's authorities will be best suited to technologies and products that are vital to the Nation's defense, underscoring the need to pursue non-standard technological investments.

A Title III program must have consistent buy-in from all stakeholders. Industry and DoD user communities must be committed to the program's success to ensure the technical requirements are accurately captured and addressed.

As the program progresses, communication will be critical. Clear, consistent capture of emerging challenges will ensure all stakeholders maintain understanding of the end objectives and the hurdles to overcome in order to succeed.

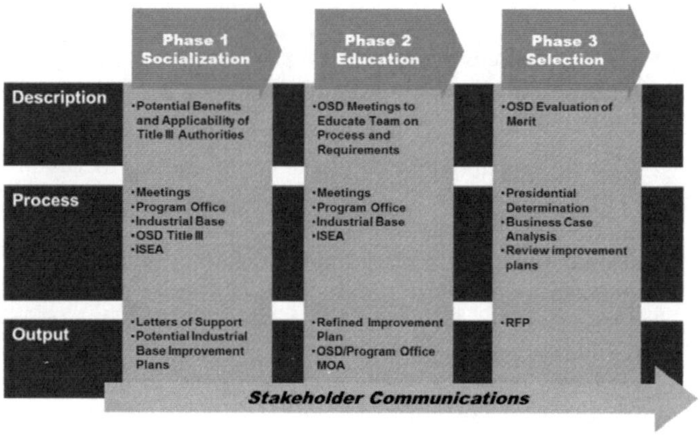

Figure 1 - Typical DPA Title III Process Flow

Acknowledgements

I would like to acknowledge the support of the Naval Sea Systems command for their outstanding support in endorsing the VRLA Project as a top level National Security issue. The support from top management of the Program Office, PM392, the critical support offices including George Drakeley, Dave Cherry and the Commander Naval Sea Systems Command were vital in elevating this program as a top priority. We would also like to recognize the OSD Title 3 Program Office, Mark Buffler, and the Title 3 Executive Agent, Jeff Smith, for prioritizing the Program at the top of new programs and developing the business case for the Program. OSD and the EA developed and fast-tracked the Presidential Determination, the most important part of the Title 3 process. The outstanding dedication and support of all involved in this program has contributed to solution of a top level national security issue.

References

1. Defense Production Act – Title III
   http://www.dpatitle3.com

Saft LEO Cells Development

Chengsong Ma*, Robert Staniewicz* Albert Zimmerman**
* SAFT America Inc, 107 Beaver Court, Cockeysville, MD 21030
** The Aerospace Corporation, 2310 E. El Segundo Blvd, El Segundo, CA 90245-4691

Saft America, Inc. Space and Defense Division, located in Cockeysville, Maryland is the world leader in providing state of the art lithium ion systems for the demanding defense and space markets. Saft has been manufacturing batteries at its Cockeysville location for more than 30 years. Our research and development and our production facilities are focused within the defense and space markets working with all of the major contractors in the market. Our products have evolved to match the requirements of all branches of the military/space with a focus on high performance over a wide temperature range, long life, high quality and reliability, and rugged systems that can operate in uncontrolled and abusive environments.

Saft has developed a space cell which showed excellent energy density and specific energy with nearly 100% columbic efficiency. The cells are hermetically sealed and completely maintenance free. The cells have shown 15 year GEO life at 80% DOD and 25,000 LEO cycles at 20% DOD

.

Fig.1 Saft VL48E cell

Fig.1 is the image of Saft VL48E cell

Table 1 is the technical information of VL48E. The nominal voltage is 3.6V and cell can deliver 48Ah at C/2 discharge rate when cells charged to 4.1V as end of charge voltage.

Cell electrical characteristics	
Nominal voltage	3.6 V
Nominal capacity at C/2 rate at 4.1 V/3 V & 25° C	48 Ah
Maximum discharge current at 25° C:	
Continuous	100 A
~2 s pulse	300 A
Specific energy	150 Wh/Kg
Energy density[1]	300 Wh/l
Cell mechanical characteristics	
Diameter max	54 mm
Height max[1]	245 mm
Mass max	1.15 kg
Volume max[1]	0.56 l
Cell operating conditions	
Lower voltage limit for discharge:	
Continuous (0° C to + 45° C)	2.5 V
Charging method	Constant current/constant voltage (CCCV)
Charging voltage (max)	4.1 V
Recommended continuous charge current	
GEO	C/10
LEO (20% DOD)	C/5
Operating temperature:	
Charge	+ 10° C to + 35° C
Discharge	0° C to + 40° C
Storage and transportation temperature	- 40° C to + 65° C

Table 1. Technical SPEC of VL48E

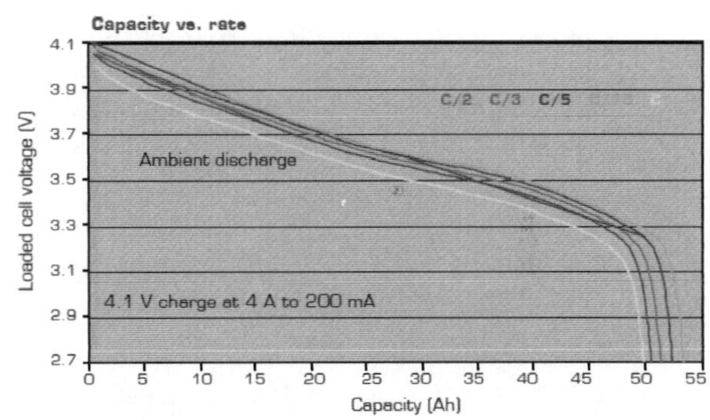

Fig 2 Capacity of Vl48E at different rate

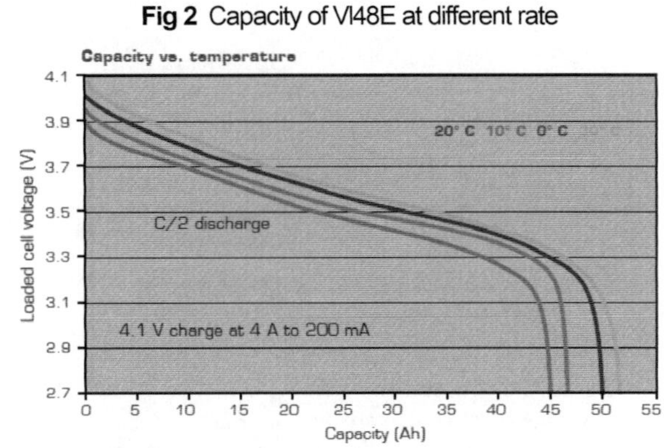

Fig .3 Capacity of Vl48E at different temperature

VL48E has excellent rate performance up to C discharge rate at ambient temperature. This cell also has good C/2 discharge behavior at 0°C.

Saft delivered VL48E cells to NASA Glenn for testing under LEO conditions. The battery experts at NASA Glenn used 46Ah as the rated capacity for the VL48E cells. A design of experiments incorporated: three temperatures (10, 20 and 30°C); three DOD (20, 30 and 35% DOD); and three EOC voltages (3.85V, 3.95V and 4.05V).

Temp. (ºC)	End-of-charge Voltage (V)	DOD (%)	Saft		
			Ah out	Charge Current (A)	Discharge Current (A)
30	3.85	35	16.07	19.28	27.55
20	3.95	20	9.18	11.02	15.74
10	4.05	30	13.77	16.52	23.61
30	3.85	20	9.18	11.02	15.74
30	4.05	20	9.18	11.02	15.74
10	3.85	35	16.07	19.28	27.55
10	3.85	20	9.18	11.02	15.74
20	4.05	35	16.07	19.28	27.55
30	3.95	30	13.77	16.52	23.61
20	3.85	30	13.77	16.52	23.61

Table 2 NASA GRC DOE of LEO test

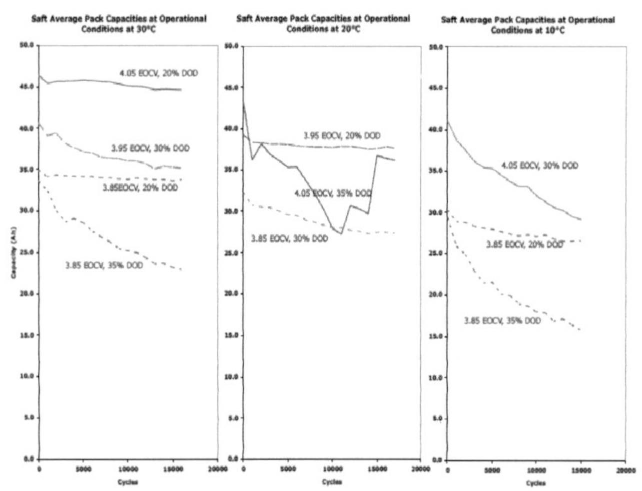

Fig.4 Pack capacity at different DOE

Table 2 indicates the testing matrix. Batteries composed of four cells in series (4S) were tested. Each 4S battery had balancing electronics to minimize the impact of cell divergence due to slight differences in self-discharge rates.

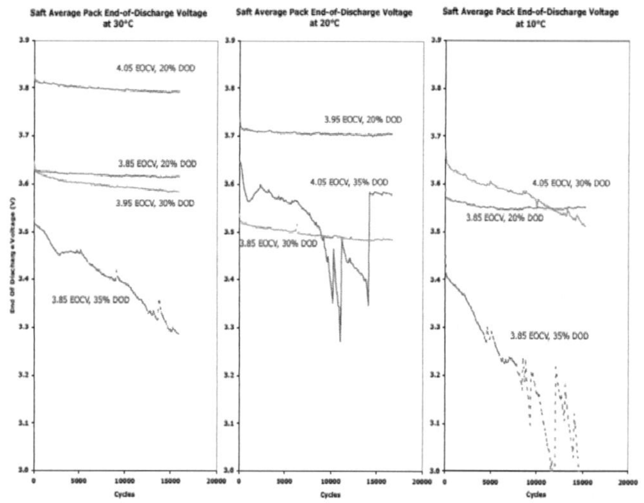

Fig.5 Pack end of discharge voltage at different DOE

NASA's results indicate that 35% DOD is less stable than 30% DOD and 20% DOD is considerably more stable than 30% DOD. When the DOD is 20%, then other factors such as varying EOCV or temperature appear to have little effect on the stability of the cycling batteries.

Figure 4 shows the diminution in a diagnostic capacity check as a function of cycle number for the three test temperatures while Figure 5 has EODV plotted in a slightly condensed and summarized format.

The stability of the EODV is excellent. At most, the EODV for each cell in the 4s battery has declined by ~ 0.03 V. If we take a first order hypothesis that the decline in voltage at constant current is due to an impedance increase of the cell, then $\Delta R = \Delta V / I$ or $\Delta R = 0.03/15.74 = 1.9m\Omega$. The starting impedance of the cells would have been about $3m\Omega$, this means 66% increase in the total impedance over 16,000 cycles. While the percentage increase sounds high, the absolute impedance is relatively low. For 6,000 cycles the impedance increase of cells will be ~ $0.7m\Omega$ ($3.7\ m\Omega$ at 6000 cycles compared to $3m\Omega$) or an increase in impedance of 24% for 6,000 cycles. Furthermore, as shown in Figure 4, the operational capacity decrease of the cells at 20% DOD is very low over the 16,000 cycles, supporting the hypothesis that impedance increase is the main factor leading to decline in EODV at 20% DOD.

The operation temperature to be selected is between 10° to 30°C. The EODV of the cells in the battery cycling at 20% DOD and10°C show more variability and a higher impedance increase. The result is not surprising. At colder temperature the electrolyte impedance is higher and the electrodes covered with a solid state ionic conductor follow a logarithmic response to temperature.

Saft also produces a medium energy cell called "high power LEO cell". These cells are tab-less design and provide less impedance. We delivered cells to Aerospace for LEO testing.

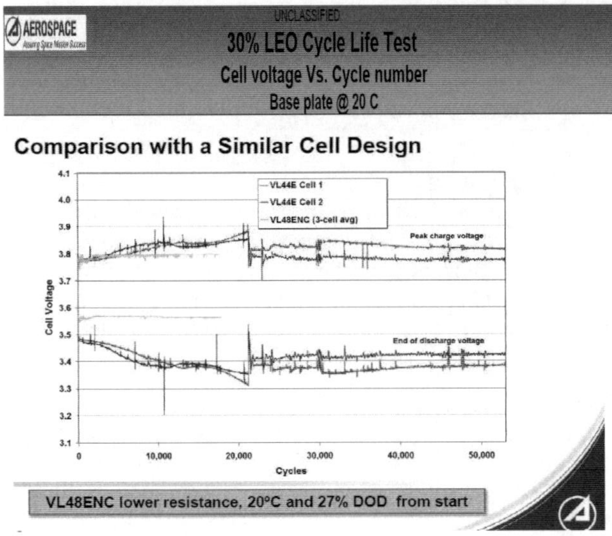

Fig.6 Aerospace Corporation Testing of Saft VL44L Cell

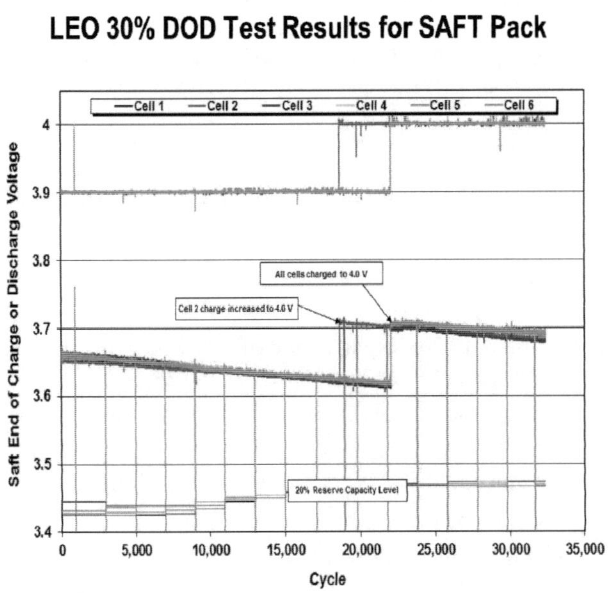

Figure 6 demonstrates the cycle performance of the VL44L cell. Aerospace de-rated the capacity to 5/6 or called the cell a 36.67Ah cell, this means the 30% DOD is really 25% DOD based on the real capacity of 44Ah per cell. The cell was initially tested against an EOCV = 3.9V, later Aerospace changed the EOCV to 4V cutoff without any ill effect. The charge rate was 12.17A to the limit and then tapered for a total time of 61 minutes in charge. For 25% DOD the discharge current was 18.84A for 35 minutes at 20°C.

The loss in energy is less than 10% over >31,000 cycles.

Conclusion.

Saft space cells demonstrated 31,000 LEO cycles with stable cycle life and projected approximately 70,000 LEO cycles based on on-going test by customers. With Saft high energy cell a battery system will require less number of cells for given energy requirement, thus can reduce the complexity of battery management system. Saft's technical experience and high competence in electrochemistry design combine to provide excellent batteries meeting the needs of space cells in both industry and government.

Acknowledgment

Saft greatly appreciate that NASA-GRC shared and interpreted the testing data of VL48E cells.

Solvent Free Flexible Lithium Ion Manufacturing Process

Michael D. Eskra and Paula K. Ralston
Eskra Technical Products, Inc.
Saukville, WI, USA, 53080

Abstract: *Under a DLA BATTNET Short Term Project (STP) Eskra Technical Products, Inc. (ETP) developed a dry process for the manufacture of lithium electrodes, successfully eliminating the use of solvents and/or liquids. Presently, lithium-ion (Li-ion) rechargeable battery manufacturing processes use environmentally harmful and toxic solvents, such as methyl ethyl ketone (MEK) and n-methyl pyrolidine (NMP). This adds significant costs to the manufacture of Li-ion batteries, which in turn precludes their use in some instances. In some cases, water soluble binders are used, however, drying lines and processes also impact efficiency and cost effectiveness. The ETP process involves the use of powder coating subsequent layers of active material and PVDF binder and thermal processing. This novel coating system can be used with all common active materials for both anodes and cathodes, as well as differing particle sizes for the production of Li-ion electrodes. The ETP dry process totally eliminates the use of solvents and/or liquids enabling a reduction in processing steps required such as slurry preparation, wet-coating, drying, and solvent reclaiming. Product line changeovers are simplified, enabling fast change over from anode to cathode pairs using a web based process. This simplification also allows more cost effective small run production. Significant cost savings are possible along with reduction in organic contamination. Development is also underway for using this same process with a novel ceramic separator.*

The ETP process and equipment developed produced Li-ion cells for validation testing. The resulting electrodes perform similar to conventionally solvent cast electrodes in life and exhibit a significant increase in power compared to solvent cast electrodes. Ten second pulses of 100 to 300 C-rate were demonstrated using this process with common active materials.

Keywords: Lithium ion; low cost lithium ion manufacturing; just-in-time manufacturing; solventless; solvent free; lithium ion manufacturing; dry process; batteries.

Introduction

Under DLA BATTNET Short Term Project, (STP), ETP Inc. was tasked to develop an electrode manufacturing process for Lithium Ion batteries, which would enable just-in-time capability and small order delivery for the Defense Community. Under the STP task ETP was to demonstrate a laboratory scale, proof-of-concept process for a totally dry, solvent free manufacture of electrodes in 12 months and \$414,000.

Existing Issues

Existing Lithium Ion manufacturing is normally dedicated to one cell type, and changes in active loadings and chemistries can be expensive due to capitalization costs and implementation time. The majority of existing manufacturing is product specific; one machine = one product.

The US has lost jobs and quality of product due to the expense of Lithium Ion manufacturing. The significant majority of cells being purchased for government and military applications are manufactured in, and purchased from Japan and China. Many of these cells are them packaged by various vendors to supply the needs of the government. Recently counterfeit batteries have been introduced into mainstream portable electronics and could therefore find their way into the defense supply chain. This situation would likely become much more significant if the supply chain was interrupted by such things as a blockade or political unrest. In any case there is a distinct lack of US control when purchasing from foreign manufacturers, as well as vendor turnover and running changes to active material and hence variable product is being introduced to the supply chain which these problems would escalate, during war time.

Goals

Goals for this project:

- Ability to Produce Multiple Electrode Chemistries and Designs from the same Equipment
- Allow Small Lots of Different Types of Batteries from the Same Line
- Reduce Level of Work in Process and Scrap
- Rapid and Inexpensive Change-Over
- Minimization of Capital Requirements, Enabling Sustainable Business Decisions for the Manufacturer
- Eliminate the Use of Solvents (NMP and MEK, Known Carcinogens)
- 100% Dry Process
- Process Should be Independent of Active Materials
- Uniform Porosity
- Lower Operational Costs

Concept Development

ETP believed that there was a better alternative to the solvent based casting system to make electrodes that would be more cost effective for short run manufacturing, but also economical for large ongoing manufacturing operations. Intuitively putting materials into a process and having to extract them back out seemed unnecessary if a method could be developed to eliminate the need for the step.

Compounding the difficulty in developing a dry process is the complexity and variety of the PVDF (polyvinylidene flouride) material. There are many types of PVDF available and several are used in the lithium ion battery electrode. The melting temperatures in the literature are somewhat confusing, due to the relatively wide ranges. Initial trials were run to determine if the PVDF could be fibrillated similar to dry PTFE (polytetrafluoroethylene). ETP thought this might be possible due to the similarities of the molecular structure. However that was process was quickly abandoned because of PVDF's poor fibrillating qualities.

The concept of using a fluidized bed and a heated target initially showed very poor results. Material would be sprayed onto the target, apparently making good electrodes, only to have the material fall off the current collector. These early trials were done in a laboratory hood using hot plates and household cooking utensils. Sometimes however, the active material adhered.

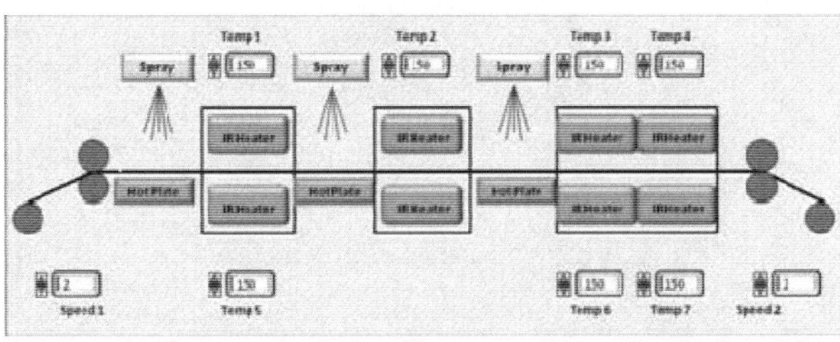

Figure 1. Concept of Dry Process Manufacturing Line

To be commercially viable ETP believed it had to develop a process that was workable and low cost. To that end ETP purchased Eastwood powder coating guns to regulate the flow of material onto the target current collector. Trials indicated that powder coating multiple layers, with proper temperature control would provide suitable electrodes.

A decision was made to move the process from out of the lab hood and onto a structure that would allow web to web simulation and proper temperature control. Using material left over from other projects the team assembled a proof of concept demonstration machine. This allowed us to do process studies and build full cells to test the results.

The process studies indicate that the process operational range of most active material is 50°F or 27°C. Within this window of operation, electrodes can be made that can be twisted, bent or folded without material loss. The machine presently has three stages and with those three stages electrodes from 0.5mil to 0.025" have been successfully made.

This layering concept would allow for varying active material characteristics throughout the thickness of the electrode if warranted. The compositions of the individual active materials are sprayed as the final mixture. The results have been very encouraging with exceptional power and capacity as compared to both commercial and laboratory solvent cast electrodes.

Figure 2. Proof-of-Concept Manufacturing Line

Achievements

ETP, Inc. developed a proof-of-concept manufacturing line and demonstrated a 100% dry process for lithium ion electrode manufacturing.

The ETP process is based upon the concept of a charged fluidized bed, depositing onto a grounded electrode current collector. Active materials, conductive (and any other) additives, and PVDF binder, are sprayed onto a heated current collector, and subsequently processed.

The elimination of the solvents normally used to make electrodes, has distinct advantages, both economic and environmental. Expensive solvent recovery processes are eliminated, resulting in savings in capital costs, energy consumption, and labor demands. Long term health and environmental concerns are eliminated from the use of carcinogenic solvents. Also, performance improvements in electrodes are, in principle, possible, as more optimum binder distribution in electrodes can be accomplished. This process, initially developed in the laboratory, was also validated in a proof of concept machine built to make electrodes. Electrodes prepared in this manner have been shown to have excellent performance in actual cells.

Manufacturing costs are lowered as the process allows for the total elimination of solvents, slurry preparation, drying and solvent recovery. Facility costs are lowered as the method requires a much smaller footprint compared to conventional manufacturing techniques. Our estimates are that the ETP dry process will produce a savings of 25-35%

in the overall cost of manufacturing lithium batteries. This game-changing improvement could signal a revival in the US domestic lithium battery industry, allowing domestic battery producers to compete successfully with overseas battery producers.

The same binder and active materials as conventional lithium ion batteries are used in manufacturing the electrode leaving no issues with non-compatible components being added to the cell to limit life or hinder performance.

This concept line has successfully produced both cathodes and anodes for lithium ion batteries. Performance of test cells have been as good as, or better than that of commercially made electrodes.

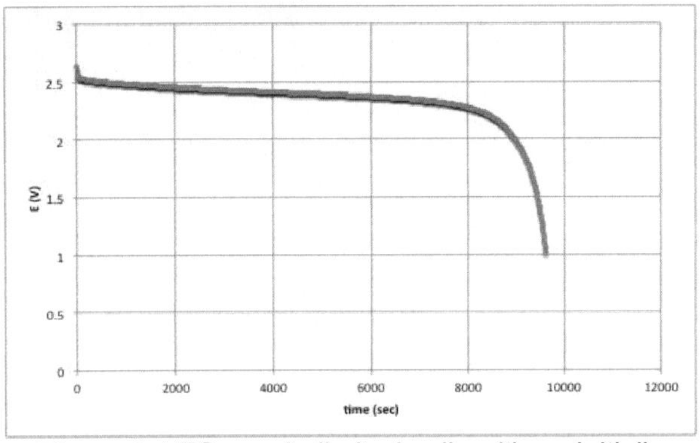

Figure 3. LTO anode-limited cells with an initially specific capacity of 0.485 mAh/cm^2

The ETP process applies to all common active materials and particle sizes for both cathodes and anodes. The adhesion was found to be as good, if not better than conventional coating methods.

Figure 4. Electrode strip manufactured on ETP's proof-of-concept machine

Figure 5. Physical Testing of Electrodes

Acknowledgements

ETP, Inc. would like to acknowledge SVE, Inc. and MEGTEC Systems for their participation and Matt Hutchens of DLA BATTNET for his support through DLA BATTNET contract SP4701-09-D-0049.

Flaw Detection and Characterization of a Nanocomposite Ceramic Separator (NCS) for Li Ion Batteries

Patrick Hagans[a], Susan Babinec[b], William Hicks[a], L. Curt Maxey[c], Ralph Dinwiddie[c], Beth L. Armstrong[c], David L. Wood III[c] and Claus Daniel[c]
[a]Navitas Systems ASG, 4880 Venture Dr., Suite 100, Ann Arbor, MI 48106
[b]ARPA-E, U.S. Dept. of Energy, 1000 Independence Ave., SW, Washington, DC 20585
[c]Oak Ridge National Laboratory, One Bethel Valley Rd., Oak Ridge, TN 37831

Abstract: The use of a nanocomposite of silica and PVDF as a full separator in Li ion batteries is illustrated. Sophisticated tools for the detection of flaws in the NCS coating are presented that have possible application to online deployment. This separator reached pilot stage before being discontinued for business reasons.

Keywords: Lithium ion battery; separator; HiPot; silica; PVDF; nanocomposite.

Introduction

Thin (~20 µm) porous polyolefin (PO) sheet is the material of choice as separator material for use in lithium ion battery cells. Although the porosity and tortuosity is conducive to high ionic conductivity these materials are not optimal from a safety perspective due to shrinkage that occurs at lower temperatures (1). The resulting electrode shorting that can occur during a thermal event can easily lead to a thermal runaway event. For this reason a low cost composite of small particle size silica (SiO_2) and polyvinylidene difluoride (PVDF) has been developed for use as a separator (2). The separator can be applied to either electrode using a conventional slot die coating process. Two main impediments exist to the transition of this process into mass production: (1) How to protect the electrode edges since they are no longer covered with wrapped separator, and (2) How to prevent and/or detect the formation of flaws or defects in a porous coating applied to a somewhat rough surface at thickness of 10 – 20 µm. It is this last point that is the focus of this paper.

Nanocomposite Separator Properties and Capability

Figure 1A is an SEM image of the as received silica powder. Even though the particle sizes are relatively large, the surface area is also large due to high surface roughness and porosity of each of the particles. Figure 1B is a surface image of a 65:35 (SiO_2:PVDF, by weight) hand cast NCS film on to a glass plate with a doctor blade to a thickness of 37 µm. The glass plate enables the film to be easily peeled away intact for imaging of the interfacial surface. The silica particles in the NCS are now very well defined with considerably less surface roughness compared to the as-received material. This is caused by a relatively uniform coating of PVDF that has formed on the surface of each particle as verified by an elemental fluorine EDS map obtained in the SEM (data not shown). In addition, a web-like structure of PVDF is also visible on the surface that provides both cohesive adhesion between particles and adhesion to the current collector. Both the surface and the interface have identical structures including a uniform silica particle size distribution suggesting that the coating and drying processes used do not promote binder or particle migration.

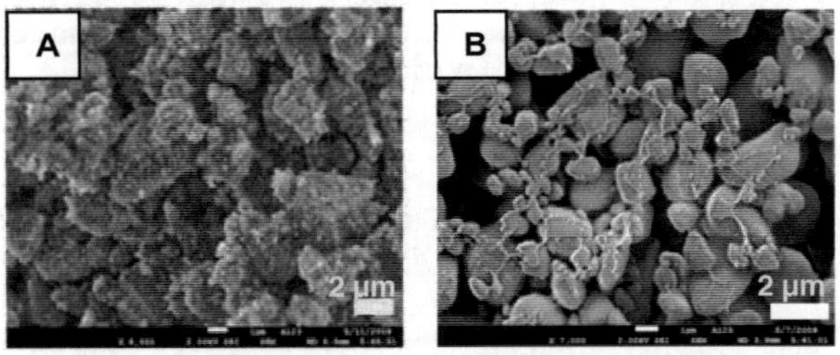

Figure 1. A: SEM image of as-received SiO_2. B: SEM image of the surface of 65:35 silica:PVDF coating.

Due to the silica content and the NCS porosity the wettability of the NCS layer to carbonate electrolytes is expected to be very good. This was confirmed with dynamic Sessile-drop contact angle measurements of coated and NCS coated anode and cathode using three different solvents (water, formamide and diiodomethane). Data for NCS coated anode is shown in Figure 2. Interestingly, all three contact angles for the coated anode were ≥ those for the cathode suggesting differences between the two NCS coatings even though compositionally they are the same. Droplet volumes during each measurement dropped to near zero indicating that wetting could be primarily attributed to penetration. In every case the contact angle for uncoated electrode was larger than that for the same NCS coated electrode and, for a given solvent, anode contact angle > cathode contact angle (data not shown).

Both Hg and H_2O porosimetry measurements were conducted on the same electrodes in Figure 2. Hg porosimetry data for uncoated and NCS coated anode and cathode are shown in Figure 3. A trimodal pore-size distribution is observed for anode while it is more unimodal for cathode. The smallest anode pores appear to be filled in during NCS coating while this does not appear to be the case for cathode. Discrete NCS porosity for the anode is visible in the range 0.3 to 2 μm while for cathode NCS porosity is observed in the range 0.04 to 4 μm.

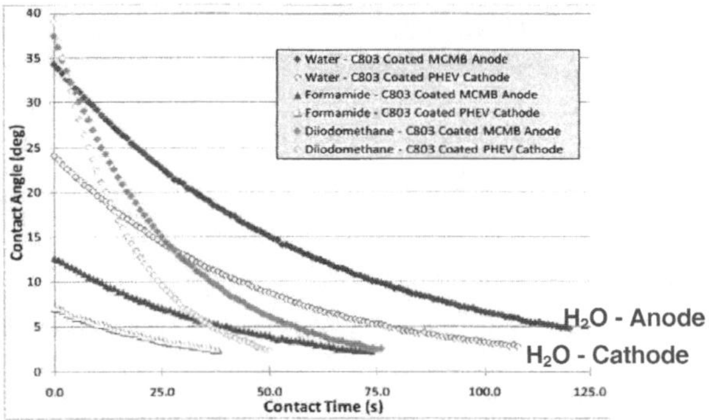

Figure 2. Dynamic Sessile-drop contact angle measurements as a function of contact time for NCS coated anode and cathode using water, formamide and diiodomethane droplets. NCS thickness: 30 μm anode, 19 μm cathode.

Figure 4 shows a plot of conductivity vs. separator thickness for PO separator and various compositions of silica:PVDF. The conductivities are not true separator conductivities. Instead, they were calculated using the high frequency intercept on the Z' axis of an electrochemical impedance scan of individual single layer pouch cells with each thickness of separator. In all cases, the SOC, electrodes, electrolyte and cell compression were the same; the only difference was the separator layer. As shown the cells having NCS with high silica content (65:35, 75:25. 85:15) have conductivities similar to that for the polyolefin separator (polyethylene based) at a thickness of 20 μm.

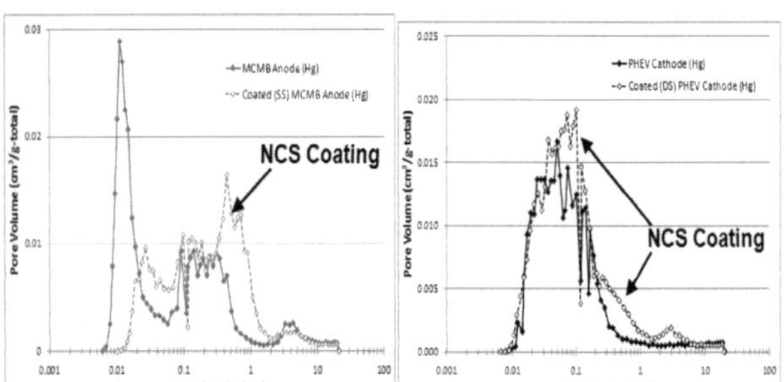

Figure 3. Plot of pore volume vs. pore diameter from Hg porosimetry measurements of uncoated and NCS coated anode (left) and cathode (right).

The cycling capability of a 500 mAh full NCS Li ion cell is illustrated in Figure 5. Each anode contained a 17 μm NCS layer. The cycling was conducted at room temperature at a charge/discharge rate of 1.5C/-2.5C. The cathode was LFP (Lithium Iron Phosphate) and the anode was MCMB (MesoCarbon MicroBeads). As observed, the retained capacity is 85% at 6800 cycles with very low DCR growth.

Detection of Defects

During the early stages of development of NCS a number of different types of flaws were visually or microscopically

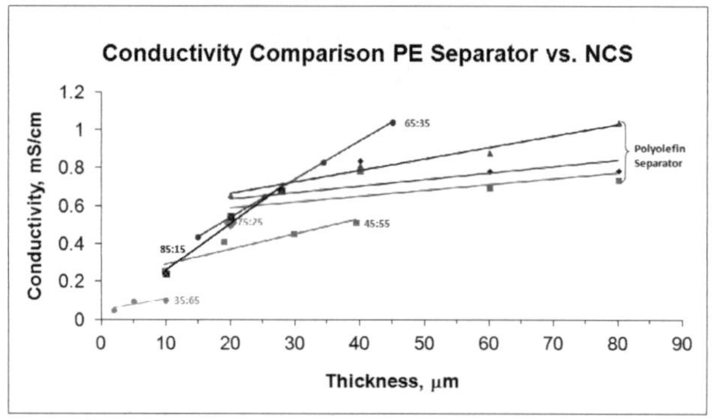

Figure 4. Cell conductivity as measured from the high frequency intercept of the real impedance axis of an electrochemical impedance scan of single layer pouch cells with various thicknesses of NCS and polyolefin separators. Electrodes: LFP and graphite.

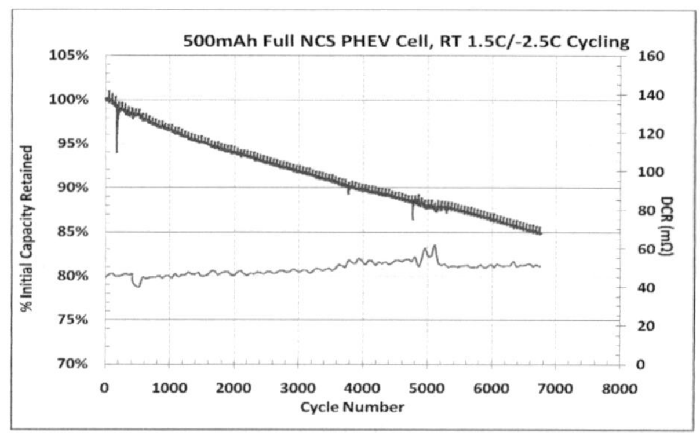

Figure 5. Capacity retention of a 500 mAh cell containing a 17 um thick nanocomposite separator coated onto each MCMB anode. The anode edges were sprayed separately with NCS to prevent shorting. Note that this cell contains only a NCS separator.

observed including blisters, cracks, holes/voids, agglomerates, local thickness variation and indentations/gouges caused by mishandling and loose particles. Many of these were eliminated through mixing, coating and drying process changes. The coating process details and substrate characteristics were found to be substantial contributors to the difficulty to coat, defect content and resulting performance. However, cells still occasionally failed HiPot testing when subjected to 500 V for 1 s. Testing was then initiated on individual electrodes in an attempt to determine the cause of these failures. HiPot testing of individual electrode samples was started where the voltage was ramped slowly (0.83 V/s) while at the same time monitoring the leakage current. Shown in Figure 6 and Table 1 are HiPot results for various configurations of uncoated and NCS coated electrodes where the NCS coating thickness is either 10 or 15 μm.

Two important conclusions resulted from this study: 1. The NCS anode is the weakest link, and 2. Neither 10 or 15 µm of NCS on just the cathode is sufficient to prevent HiPot failure. The NCS quality also affected the cycling capability as illustrated in Figure 7. As shown, 30 um of NCS on just the cathode produced excellent capacity retention while NCS on just the anode or on both the anode and cathode demonstrated decreased cycling capability. Electrochemical impedance scans for the same cells at beginning of life (not shown) indicated a much larger charge transfer resistance of the cell with NCS only on anode. Again, the anode is proven to be the weakest link.

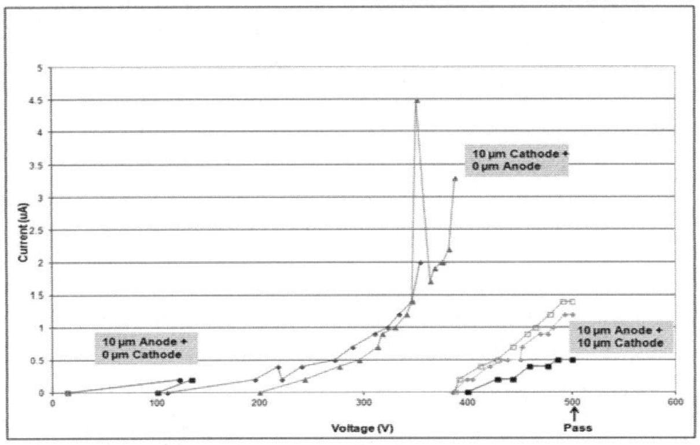

Figure 6. Leakage current vs. voltage for a HiPot scans of single 3450 electrodes with and without NCS.

Table 1. HiPot results for various configurations of NCS coated anode and cathode.

NCS Coated Anode vs. NCS Coated Cathode (Both ~15 µm)	Fail 250-300V
NCS Coated Cathode vs. NCS Coated Cathode	Pass (500V)
NCS Coated Anode vs. NCS Coated Anode	Fail ~ 240V
NCS Coated Cathode vs. Bare Anode	Fail ~135V

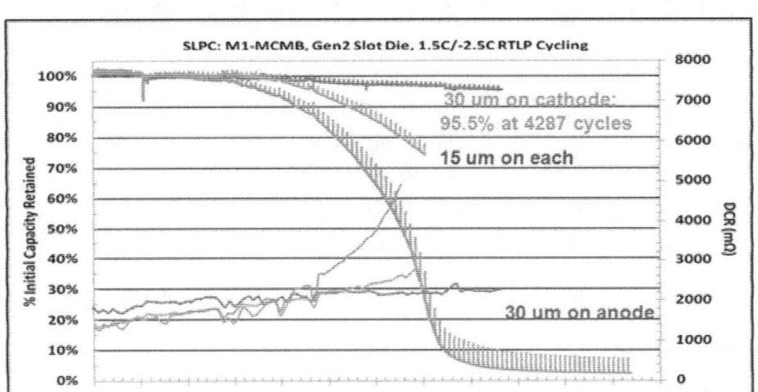

Figure 7. Capacity retention and DCR of LFP-MCMB cells with 30 um total NCS separator thickness.

Both macro and micro defects in the anode NCS layer were blamed for the poor HiPot and cycling results. Shown in Figures 8A and 9 are the HiPot failure points on NCS coated anodes. Figure 8A shows the HiPot failure point occurs at a NCS stress crack near the anode edge. Figure 8B shows a polished SEM cross section view of a similar crack indicating that the crack has a direct path to the anode surface. Given that that the dielectric strength of air is 3 V/µm it is not surprising that anodes with severe crack defects will fail early in the HiPot test. Figure 9 shows another NCS coated anode HiPot failure spot (right image; left image is bare cathode that faced the anode during the HiPot test. In this example it is not clear why the failure point occurred at this position. It should also be pointed out that not all defects result in HiPot failures. The dielectric strength of the material at the defect point (which depends on thickness, structure and composition) determines if HiPot failure occurs or not.

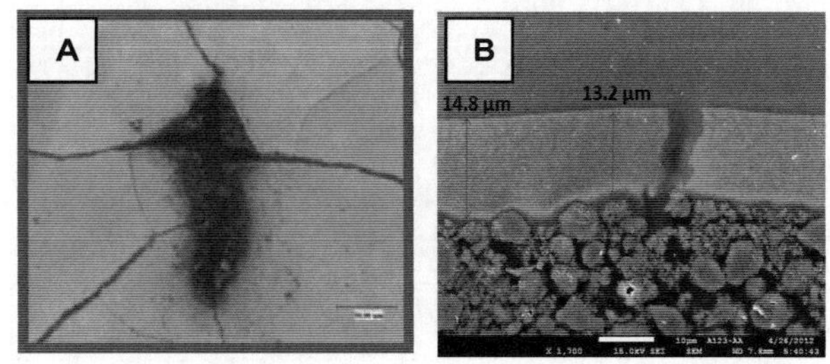

Figure 8. A: HiPot failure point at stress crack near the edge of NCS coated anode. B: SEM image of a polished cross section of NCS coated anode showing that stress crack travels from NCS to anode surface.

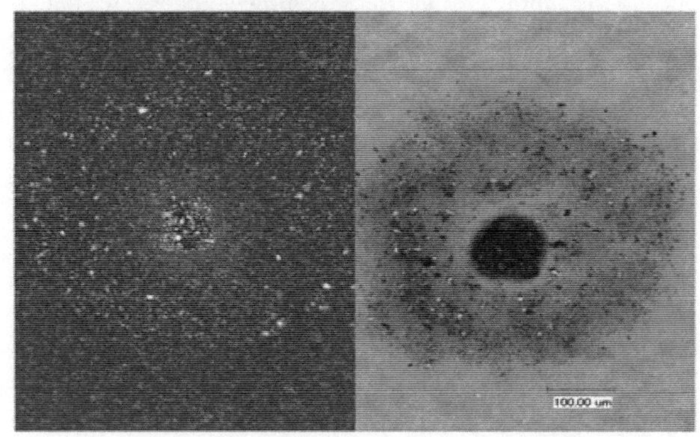

Figure 9. Light microscope images of HiPot failure point on NCS coated anode (right) and the same position on the uncoated cathode (left) that faced the anode during the HiPot test.

Alternate Defect Detection Methods

Two separate techniques were explored for detection of NCS flaws that have the possibility of implementation into high volume, on-line production process control: IR imaging as a non-destructive tool and a continuous dielectric breakdown test.

For IR imaging an Indigo Phoenix IR camera with 320 by 256 detectors in the focal plane array was used. This camera uses indium antimonide as the detector material and can take approximately 240 images per second. The sensitivity of the camera to temperature differences is on the order of 0.012°C. The typical techniques for non-destructive evaluation (NDE) using an IR camera involve thermally stimulating the material under test and observing the resulting temperature profiles as a function of time. A specimen's flaws are often revealed since heat flow is affected by microstructure, composition, porosity, density, delamination, cracks and other structural and chemical factors. In this case the substrate was pulse heated from the rear using a xenon flash-lamp. Flaws, such as divots and blisters, are clearly visible in the IR images shortly after the flash occurs. Figure 10 shows a visible image of an NCS coated cathode with several types of noticeable defects and an IR image of the same sample after the heat pulse. The maximum contrast between the flaws and background substrate appears at approximately 8 ms after the flash.

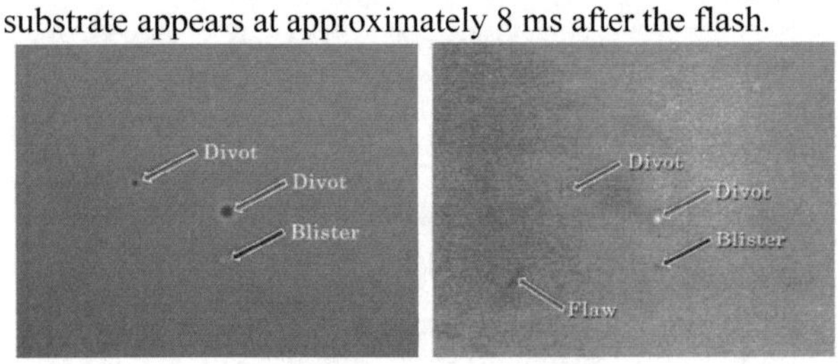

Figure 10. Proof-of-concept IR imaging of visible NCS defects on a cathode substrate. Visible image left, IR image right. Note possible flaw (lower left in IR image) not visible in the left image.

On-line imaging of the NCS coating process was also conducted on a proto-type size slot die coater. The IR camera was positioned in several different locations in order to identify the area most sensitive to flaw detection. The slot die and drying were conducted so as to produce two obvious defects in the NCS film: Blisters and dry or uncoated regions. These flaws were easily detected with the camera since the energy absorbed by the coating during drying persists longer in the coating over the areas with flaws. In addition to flaw detection, the IR camera was also able to provide useful information on temperature distributions both along the substrate, in the direction of travel and across the substrate, perpendicular to the direction of travel.

A second on-line method which involved the development of test methodologies for measuring the dielectric breakdown of lithium-ion battery electrodes with an NCS coating was investigated. The research efforts focused on the use of a highly specialized custom electrode adapted to the manufacturing processes for these materials.

An 8" x 12" granite surface plate was chosen for the test surface to provide a very stable platform onto which the specimens could be mounted for testing. An adhesive aluminum electrode was placed on the granite surface plate to provide the low-voltage contact with the specimen. A current sense resistor was placed in series with that electrode and connected to ground potential. This resistor provided the means for obtaining a current signal. An oscilloscope was used in the initial tests to monitor the current signal. A high-voltage laboratory power supply was connected to the custom electrode, which was placed in contact with the test specimen (see Figure 11).

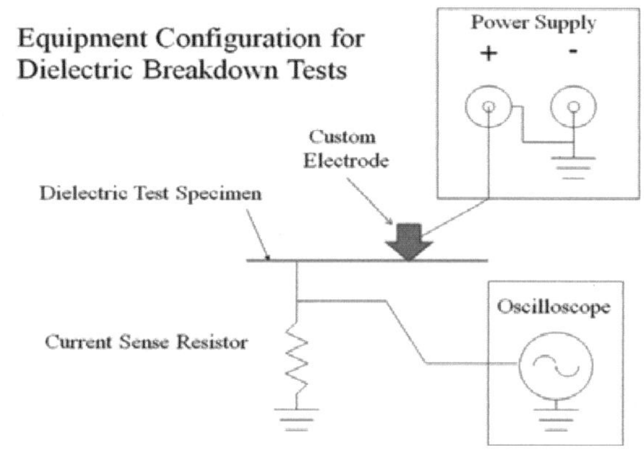

Figure 11. Initial experimental setup for the automated dielectric breakdown test.

Due to the sensitivity of dielectric breakdown of the NCS to water content the entire unit was enclosed in a humidity controlled dry box. A LabVIEW software operated motion control system for the custom electrode was also added. Testing at near 0% humidity on NCS coated samples produced leakage currents that were observed to be nil. In most cases, breakdown events were limited in their occurrence, but highly repeatable when observed.

Further improvements as a result of on-line testing of this unit have produced a system whose capability includes the ability to run a series of tests on a specific material at a variety of voltages under a variety of humidity conditions in a fully automated sequence of tests over the course of many hours.

Acknowledgements

The research at Oak Ridge National Laboratory, managed by U T Battelle, LLC, for the U. S. Department of Energy (DOE) under contract DE-AC05-00OR22725, was sponsored by the Advanced Manufacturing Office for the Office of Energy Efficiency and Renewable Energy.

References

1. Orendorff, C. A., "The Role of Separators in Lithium-Ion Cell Safety, *The Electrochemical Society Interface*, Summer 2012, pp. 61-65.

2. Babinec, S. J., Hagans, P., Hicks, W. and Chiang, Y-M., "Composite Separator for Electrochemical Cell and Method for its Manufacture," *U. S. Patent Application 2013/0183568,* July 18, 2013.

Electrochemical Capacitor Materials Evaluations using Sealed Cells: Case Western Reserve University Capacitor Prototyping Facility

Susannah Butler[1], Robert F. Savinell[2], Mirko Antloga[2], John Dix[1], and John R. Miller[1,2]
[1]JME, Inc, 23500 Mercantile Road, Suite L, Beachwood, OH 44122 USA
[2]Case Western Reserve University, 10900 Euclid Ave, Cleveland, Ohio 44106

Abstract: *Case Western Reserve University created a Capacitor Prototyping Facility for the evaluation of advanced electrochemical capacitor materials in sealed packages. We describe this facility and discuss its capabilities, then discuss how outside users may evaluate their materials using this facility.*

Keywords: Electrochemical capacitor; Supercapacitor; Ultracapacitor; EDLC; electric double layer capacitor; prototype capacitor; user facility.

Introduction: An active area of energy storage research is focused on electrochemical capacitor materials including electrodes, electrolyte, separator, additives, and package-seal materials. Often the first material evaluation step uses laboratory-level beaker-cells, pouch cells, or button cells. Such testing approaches are typically unsuitable for scaling performance to commercial-size capacitors and further, they generally do not allow reliable life performance evaluations.

Our objective was to create a facility to produce electrochemical capacitors in a repeatable manner that can be used to test new materials and designs. This entails making sealed devices that can be used for performance measurements and life studies on materials relevant to commercial products as well as to explore compositions of advanced new materials. The Case facility provides the opportunity to test capacitor materials without having to approach commercial organizations.

The capacitor prototyping laboratory is located at Case Western Reserve University (Case) in Cleveland Ohio and is available to outside users. Contact any of the authors for more information on the various ways this facility can be used to help advance your materials.

Experimental: The process for making the sealed devices is similar to the process used by commercial capacitor manufacturers. A flow diagram is shown in **Figure 1**. The steps include mixing of electrode materials and binder, coating the current collector, calendaring and tabbing the electrodes, and winding electrode bobbins. Then the electrodes are dried at elevated temperature under vacuum before transfer to a drybox and the electrolyte is added and the package sealed. At each step data is logged for the individual experiment and each capacitor is labeled with a bar code that contains experimental and fabrication parameters. Details follow.

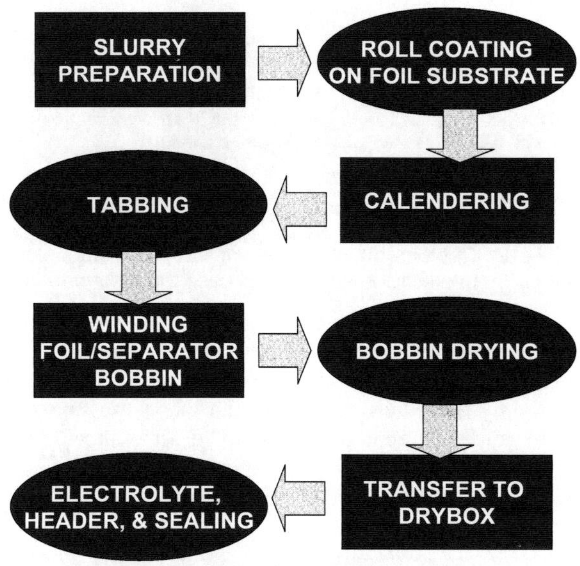

Figure 1. Capacitor fabrication flow diagram.

Electrode materials are typically mixed in an aqueous slurry (though other solvents can be used). Mixing is performed under vacuum using a Ross mixer or an Ultra-Turrax dispersing machine. The slurry is prepared with a viscosity suitable for use in the subsequent coating step, generally between 800 and 2000 cps. Coating is done using an Eager knife-roller coating machine. It is capable of single-sided coating on 15-cm-wide roll-to-roll foils. The electrode slurry mixture is transferred to the delivery trough and coated on the current collector, generally a pretreated aluminum foil. The electrode material is applied to one side of the current collector at a time. The coater is adjusted for the desired coating thickness, roller speed, and temperatures of each of the two heated drying zones. Coating thickness is monitored throughout a coating run using a hand-held micrometer with adjustments made to meet thickness tolerances.

After both sides of the current collector are coated, individual electrodes are prepared by cutting to the desired dimensions, removing the coating on an area for subsequent tabbing, and calendering. A series of calendering steps is usually performed, using a MTI model HR-01 hot roll press with adjustable temperature, speed, and thickness settings. This increases the electrode density. After calendaring, aluminum tabs are ultrasonically welded to the electrode on the strip where the coating has been removed. A photograph of an electrode strip with welded tab is shown in **Figure 2**. The tabs later are mechanically connected to the bottom posts of the terminals penetrating the capacitor header.

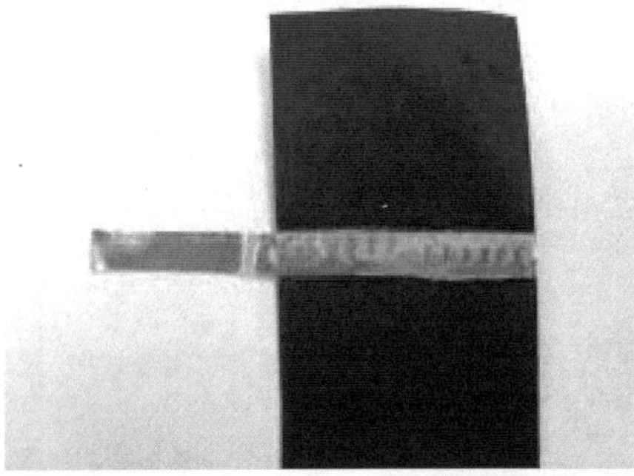

Figure 2. Photograph of the aluminum tab ultrasonically welded to an electrode strip. In this case the electrode is 30 mm wide.

The next step involves winding two electrodes and two separators into a bobbin using a custom winder. The result is a tightly wound electrode bobbin as shown in **Figure 3**. Tape is applied around the bobbin to hold it as shown in the figure. A photograph of the equipment items described in the preceding steps is shown in **Figure 4**.

Figure 3. Wound electrode bobbin. The height of the bobbin without the aluminum tabs is approximately 32 mm. At the left of the bobbin is a capacitor header. Tabs are attached to terminal posts penetrating the header.

The wound bobbins are placed into identifiable locations on a carousel, which is then inserted into a vacuum drying chamber as shown in **Figure 5.** This chamber is heated in a laboratory oven. After drying, the chamber is removed from the drying oven while still under vacuum and transferred to the dry box for subsequent operations. Posts on the bottom of the header below each terminal are connected to the two welded tabs using a "staking" operation. The bobbin is placed in the can, electrolyte is added, and the package is crimp-sealed against the header using a pneumatic press. Each finished device is visually inspected, placed in the same bobbin location, and removed from the dry box. Finally, barcode labels are affixed to each capacitor for identification. A photograph of a finished capacitor is shown in **Figure 6.**

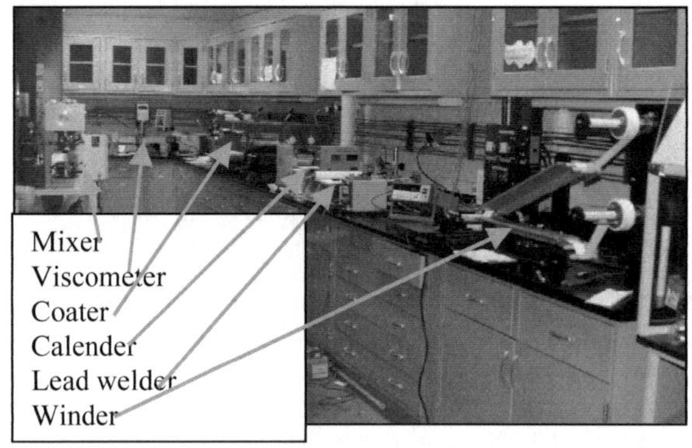

Figure 4. Fabrication equipment located in the Case capacitor prototyping facility.

Figure 5. A carousel with electrode bobbins (left) is inserted in the vacuum chamber (right) that is heated to dry the bobbin before packaging.

Results: Batches of capacitors have been fabricated at the Case prototyping facility that are suitable for durability studies at voltage and elevated temperature. Measurements on three nominally identical capacitors aged at 2.5 V and 65 °C are shown in **Figure 7**. Their aging behavior is nearly identical. The large initial property changes are typical for electrochemical capacitors and are due to irreversible reactions. Similar behavior is typical for commercial electrochemical capacitors but often not observed due to use of a "burn in" procedure that is imposed after fabrication.

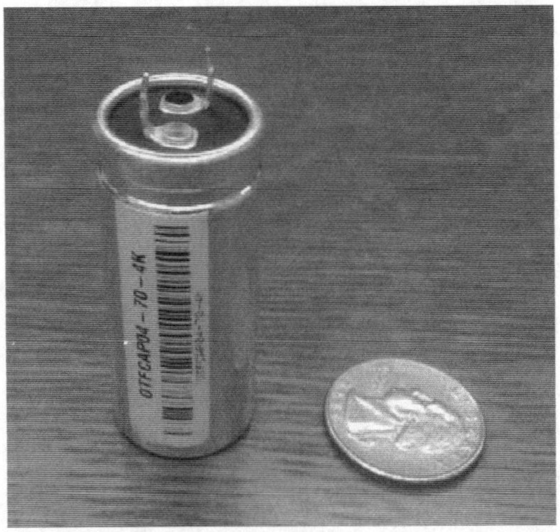

Figure 6. Photograph of a capacitor fabricated at the Case prototyping facility. Package dimensions are 22 mm diameter by 46 mm tall (not including terminal posts).

Conclusion: A specialized laboratory was created at Case Western Reserve University in Cleveland Ohio to fabricate prototype electrochemical capacitors. These capacitors allow performance and life evaluation of new materials or new designs. They also offer the advantages of similarity to commercial products and allow prediction of performance of materials in commercial-size devices. This compliments much of the research ongoing in electrochemical capacitors today. The laboratory is available for use by outside researchers under a variety of arrangements. Proprietary work can be performed.

Acknowledgements: The Case Western Reserve University capacitor prototyping laboratory was supported by the Ohio Department of Development under a Third Frontier grant. Additional support has been provided by:

- Calgon Carbon Corporation (activated carbon and grant support)
- Maxwell Technologies (grant support)
- BASF (electrolyte)
- Ioxus (packaging)
- Nippon Kodoshi Corp (separator)
- Nippon Chemi-Con (Al foil and tabs)
- Kuraray Chemical (activated carbon)
- Zeon (binder)
- A123 (18650 cell winder)

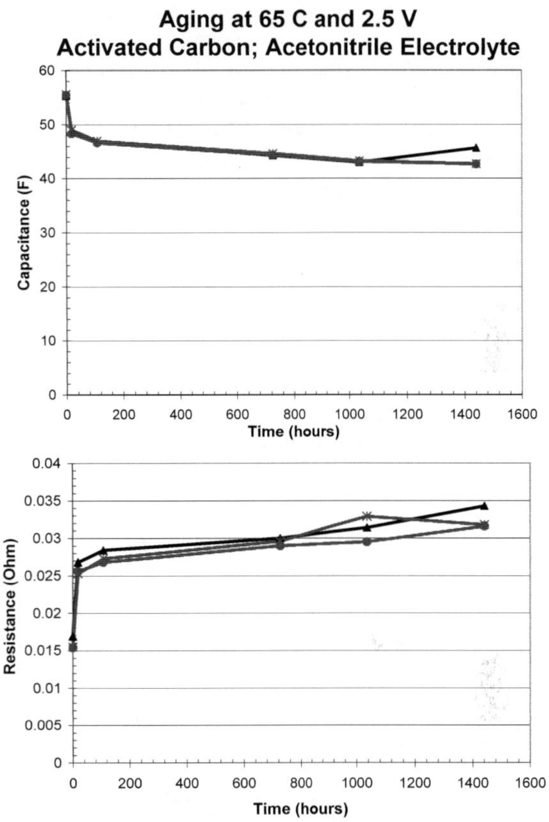

Figure 7. Capacitance and resistance of three Case prototype capacitors aged at 65 °C and 2.5 V for 1400 hours.

High Performance Recycled Materials

Kyle A. Kotaich and Steven E. Sloop
OnTo Technology LLC
63221 Service RD STE F, Bend, Oregon 97701

Abstract: *The metals refining industry is technically mismatched for recycling lithium-ion batteries. They may return no material for the manufacture of new batteries. While increased capacity is a way to achieve lower manufacturing cost in electric drive applications, at end-of-life, an increased feedstock through today's metal refineries just increases the amount of lithium containing residue, which is 5x more costly to purify than salt-brine-lithium. To address the fundamental technical mismatch, OnTo developed innovative advanced battery recycling that can reduce lifetime costs and return critical material to battery manufacturing, as well as recover high-energy metals such as aluminum. This poster summarizes direct recycling of lithium cobalt oxide, nickel-cobalt-manganese oxide, and lithium manganese oxide mixed formulations.*

Keywords: advanced battery recycling; lithium-ion recycling; high energy, high power materials cost reduction; critical materials.

Introduction: Y2013 demand for lithium-ion cathodes was 90,000T, \$2.1B, with CAGR of 16%. Lithium cobalt oxide (LCO) demand was 32,000T [1]. Recycling of lithium-ion batteries is small in comparison to the manufacturing tonnage. The single largest industry sponsored collection effort gathered less than 1% of the manufacturing tonnage in 2013. This shows the advanced battery recycling industry is still in its infancy. In the near term, recycling will grow faster than the battery industry [2], and is ultimately limited by the battery market growth rate. The rapid growth rate expected in the next several years is a concern in light of the inability for recycling infrastructure to produce any value from advanced battery feedstock.

The manufacturing market is trending away from LCO to NMC and other cobalt diminimis chemistries. They require fees for recycling based upon smelting or hydrometallurgy, which cannot produce a product from them. For example, recovery of lithium from smelting residue is five times more costly than production of lithium from salt brines [2]. This paper demonstrates the ability of OnTo to produce marketable cobalt diminimis cathodes as well as LCO and mixed metal oxide sourced from recycle feedstock; that flexibility and efficiency is the foundation for disruption of the growing recycling market.

Experimental

Recycle scrap material was obtained for three chemistries, LCO, NMC and LMO (lithium mixed metal oxide); with LCO sourced from consumer electronic recalled batteries from LGChem/Apple, NMC from electric vehicle grade batteries, and LMO from a Nissan prototype hybrid electric vehicle battery. The systems were well used in each case and summarized as follows.

LCO: The LCO cells were sourced from computer packs with an average of 116 cycles, with visible heat-damage and with an average capacity of 50% of normal 2.2Ah/cell. The average capacity of the cells is detailed in Figure 1.

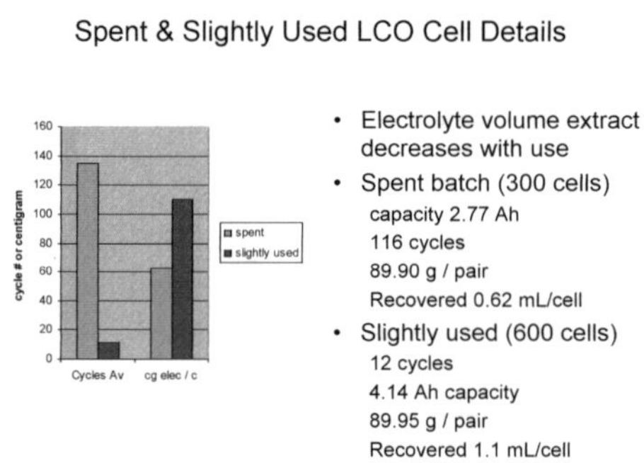

Figure 1. Used LCO cell details. The cells used as feedstock show approximately 50% capacity fade.

NMC: These were sourced from cells with 50% of the original manufacturing capacity, which as verified by measurement using a relatively low current density. The assessment of capacity is shown in Figure 2.

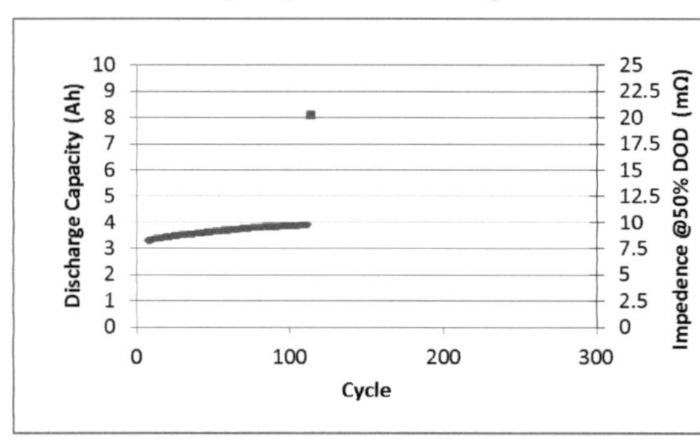

Figure 2. Used NMC cell details. The cell has approximately 50% capacity fade from the original 8Ah cell.

LMO: These modules were cycled in house until the capacity faded to 80% of original. An accelerated fade method was used in which the modules were cycled at 1C in a controlled temperature of 45°C. The cycle number vs. capacity is shown in Figure 3.

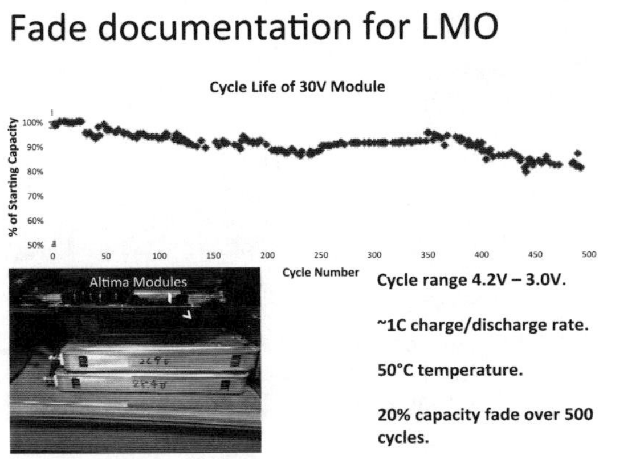

Figure 3. Used LMO cell details. The module has approximately 20% capacity fade from the original capacity.

The cells and modules were recycled using OnTo's patented and patent pending processes described elsewhere [3]. The recycled, refurbished cathode material was first prequalified in lithium/cathode half cells, and then manufactured into full cells against graphite. The performance of the recycled materials is summarized herein.

Results and Discussion

Manufacturing Qualification for LCO: Recycled LCO has specific capacity of 150 mAh/g as measured in a half-cell against lithium at room temperature. Typically, standard LCO has a specific capacity of 140 mAh/g under the same circumstances. The recycled material shows an increased capacity capability in the half cell. The discharge profile of cell voltage vs. specific capacity is shown in Figure 4 for recycled LCO.

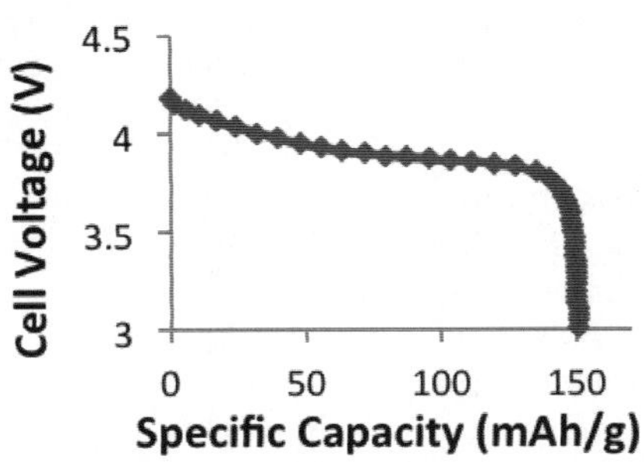

Figure 4. Specific capacity of recycled LCO. The specific capacity of recycled LCO is shown to be 150 mAh/g at a discharge rate of C/20.

The recycled product forms high quality, uniform electrode coating on aluminum, as is expected for commercial grade LCO in a manufacturing setting. Figure 5-6 shows the progress of recycled LCO in coating, cell build, and comparative cycling behavior. Recycled and standard LCO behave similarly in the full cell test, which includes a self-discharge evaluation at cycle 15 in Figure 7.

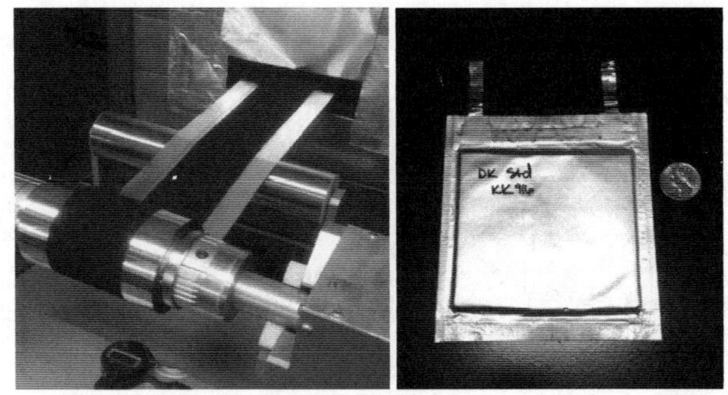

Figure 5 & 6. Manufacturing with recycled LCO. The recycled product coats standard current collectors in typical double sided mode producing a roll of cathode tape for manufacturing batteries. A full cell manufactured from recycled LCO against graphite is shown on the left.

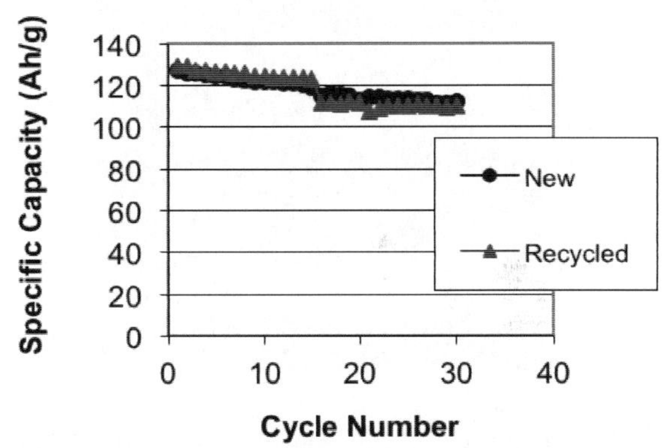

Figure 7. Specific capacity vs. Cycle number for new and recycled LCO. The discharge rate is C/12 for these cells. The recycled material maintains high capacity with cycling and self-discharge testing.

Manufacturing Qualification for NMC: Recycled NMC has specific capacity of 150 mAh/g at a cycle rate of C/2, which matches standard material. The high rate capability is a feature for power delivery in electric drive applications, i.e. NMC has the same capacity as LCO with ten-fold increase in current density (comparing Figures 4 & 8). The discharge profile of the recycled NMC and new NMC half-cell voltage vs. specific capacity is shown in Figure 8.

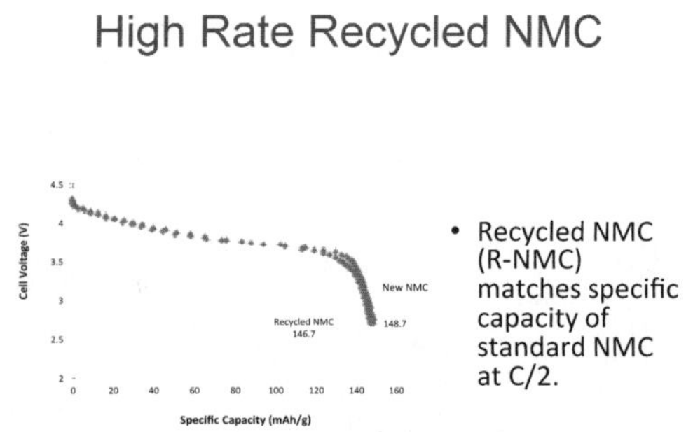

Figure 8. Specific capacity of recycled and new NMC. The recycled material maintains high specific capacity at a high discharge rate.

The morphology of recycled NMC has a nodular, rosette structure. This characteristic morphology is maintained through the recycling process. An example of a scanning electron micrograph taken from recycled NMC is shown in Figure 9.

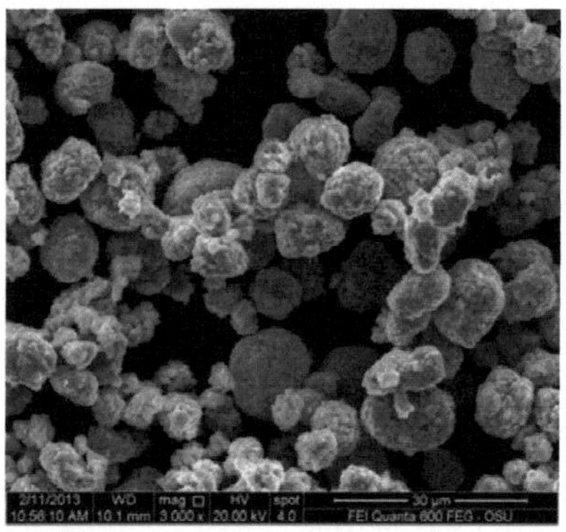

Figure 9. Micrograph of recycled NMC. The recycled material maintains the rosette-structured morphology typically observed with any standard NMC.

A commercial partner was utilized to manufacture full cells from recycled NMC. The sample cells are shown in Figure 10. These are the first cells ever manufactured utilizing recycled NMC in a commercial setting. The cycle life testing is underway.

Manufacturing Qualification for LMO: Recycled LMO has specific capacity of 130 mAh/g at a cycle rate of C/20, which matches standard material. The discharge profile of cell voltage vs. specific capacity is shown in Figure 11.

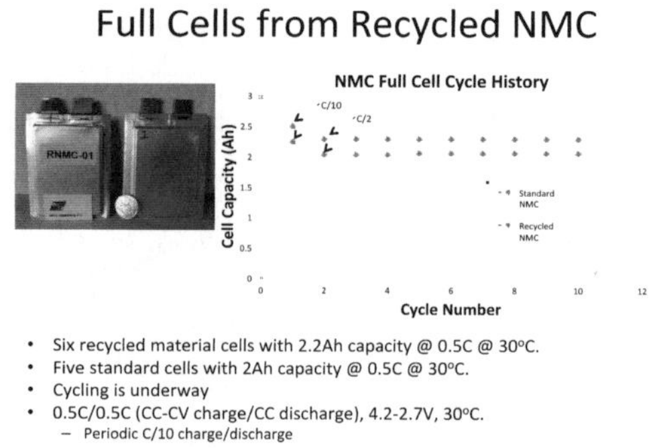

Figure 10. Full cells of new and recycled NMC. The full cell has capacity of 2.2Ah at room temperature and is undergoing cycle life testing.

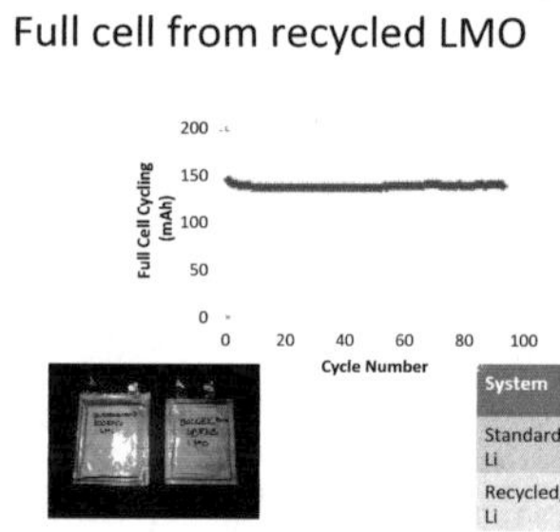

System	mAh/g	Rate
Standard/ Li	130	C/20
Recycled/ Li	130	C/20

Figure 11. Specific capacity and full cell cycling for LMO. The recycled material maintains high capacity with cycling at a rate of C/15.

Conclusion: OnTo Technology has developed a recycling process that produces manufacturing grade material from various lithium-ion chemistries. The process also recovers aluminum and copper, representing a high degree of overall energy efficiency in comparison to hydrometallurgy and smelting. The technology has potential to reduce and eliminate life-cycle costs. Department of Defense electric drive systems are good candidates to utilize OnTo's recycling technology to maintain use and reuse of critical materials such as lithium and cobalt.

Acknowledgements

Author S.E. Sloop acknowledges SBIR grant funding from NSF 0750552 and DOE DE-SC0006336.

References

1. Pillot, Christophe, "The Rechargeable Battery Market and Main Trends 2013-2025" *31st International Battery Seminar & Exhibit*, March 2014
2. Frost and Sullivan Report, M5B6-18, "Global Electric Vehicle Lithium-ion Battery Second Life and Recycling Market Analysis", November 2010.
3. Sloop, Steven E., US Patent 7,198,865 and application: 12/390,364 (approved 4/2014)

Influence of Submicron-sized FeS_2 Cathode Powder on Single Cell Discharge Performance of Thermal Batteries

Jungmin Lee, Seung-Ho Kang, Tae-Uk Hur and Hae-Won Cheong
The 4th R&D Institute
Agency for Defense Development
Daejeon, Korea, 305-600

Abstract: *Thermally activated batteries are used for military power sources that require robustness and long storage life such as missiles and torpedoes. FeS_2 powder is currently used for cathode materials because of its high specific energy density, environmental non-toxicity and low cost. However, large particle size of conventional FeS_2 has deterred its high power applications. In order to improve the power density, high energy ball milling of FeS_2 powder has been introduced to crush the micron-sized FeS_2. Discharge performances of the single cells fabricated with submicron-sized and conventional FeS_2 powder were evaluated.*

Keywords: thermal batteries; FeS_2; high energy ball milling; discharge characteristic.

Introduction

Thermally activated batteries are used for primary power sources of military applications [1-2]. Li(Si)/FeS_2 system is the most popular couple in thermal battery [3]. And the FeS_2 meets the most of the requirements for the cathode materials to be used in thermal batteries such as high specific energy density, long storage life, environmental non-toxicity and low cost [4-5]. Researches on fine particles of FeS_2 powder have been done to improve electrochemical performances of thermal batteries. Recently, M. Au reported that thermal batteries with nano-sized FeS_2 cathode material have better electrochemical performances than those with the micron-sized FeS_2 cathode material [6]. Y. Shao-Horn also reported that nano-sized FeS_2 electrodes are superior to FeS_2 electrodes with an average crystal size of 10μm [7]. In this article, we adopted high energy ball milling technique to fabricate submicron-scale FeS_2 particle. In addition we analyzed the FeS_2 particles with materials characterization methods and evaluated discharge performances of single cells.

Experimental

Preparation of Electrode Materials: The submicron-scale FeS_2 cathode was made by high energy ball milling process from its micron-sized precursors. Ball-to-powder weight ratio (BPR) was 5:1, milling speed is 600 rotation per minute (RPM) and milling tine was 2 hour. The cathode consists of 73.5 wt.% submicron and micro-scale FeS_2, 25 wt.% eutectic salt mixture (LiCl-KCl-MgO) and 1.5 wt.% Li_2O. And anode consists of 75 wt.% Li(Si) alloy and 25 wt.% eutectic mixture (LiCl-KCl). And electrolyte of LiCl-LiBr-LiF composition was used for single cell discharge performances [8-9].

Preparation of Electrode Pellets: Thirty millimeter diameter pellets of electrodes were prepared by conventional cold press process. Li(Si) alloy powders with eutectic salt and electrolyte salt were pressed to pellet under 2.94g/cm^2 and 2.47 g/cm^2 static pressure for anode and electrolyte, respectively. Cathode pellet was also fabricated by cold press of 5.89 g/cm^2 static pressure.

Characterization of FeS_2 powders: Morphologies and phases of FeS_2 powders were characterized by Scanning Electron Micrograph (SEM) and X-Ray Diffraction (XRD) respectively. Thermal properties of FeS_2 were analyzed by Thermo gravimetric Analysis (TGA).

Characterization of Discharge Performance: Li/FeS_2 couples are adopted for the single cell discharge performances. Consecutive pulse current with current 5.5-7.5A for 0.5s each were applied.

Results and discussion

Materials Characterizations:

High energy ball milling was applied to crush as-received FeS_2 cathode material. Fig. 1 shows that the particle size of micron-sized FeS_2 decrease with milling time and milling condition. Particle size of FeS_2 decreased from 100μm to 266nm in wet condition (■). For the dry mill process (●) small amount of graphite (~4wt.%) was added

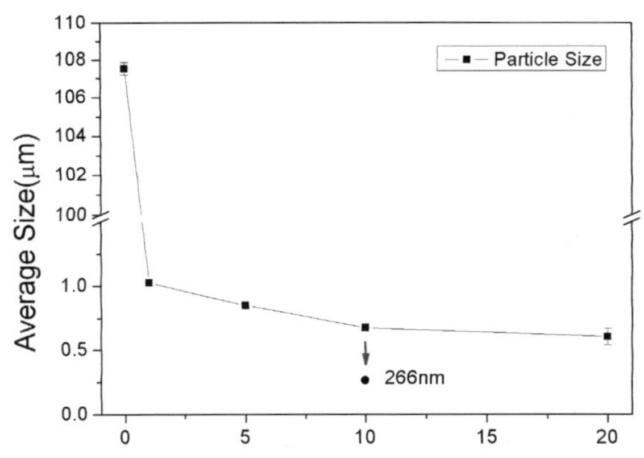

Figure 1 Particle size analysis of FeS_2 powders produced by high energy ball milling

as milling media to the FeS_2 material. Fig. 2 shows SEM micrographs of FeS_2 cathode powders. (a,c) and (b,d) were micron-sized and submicron-sized FeS_2 materials respectively. (a,b) and (c,d) were before and after powder processing respectively. After high energy mill and powder processing, particle size decreased and LiCl-KCl eutectic salt was homogeneously coated around FeS_2 materials.

Figure 2 Raw FeS_2 (a-c) and FeS_2+Graphite nano composite powder (b-d) produced by high energy ball milling, before (a-b), after (c-d) powder processing

TG analysis of micron and submicron-sized FeS_2 were shown in fig. 3. As-received FeS_2 has stable phase, it did not has any thermal decompositions until it reached 550℃. Contrary to the behavior, the weight of submicron-sized FeS_2 decrease consistently with temperature. And thermal decomposition temperatures of micron and submicron-FeS_2 materials decreased from 634℃ to 516℃. High energy mill process might generate severe impact on the FeS_2 material ensuing unstable phases.

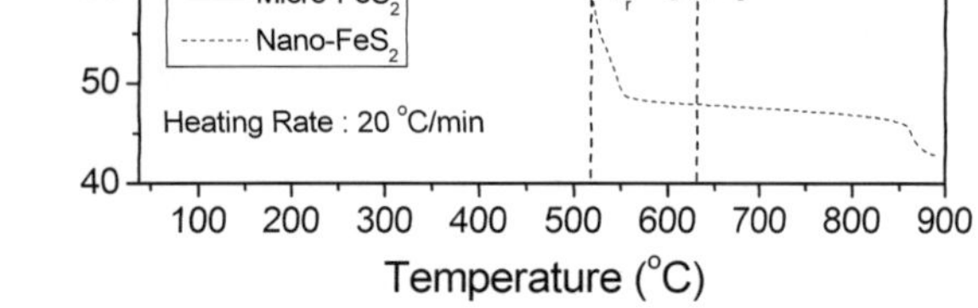

Figure 3 TG analysis of micron and submicron-sized FeS_2 powders

XRD analysis of micron and submicron-sized FeS_2 were shown in fig. 4. From the FWHM(Fall Width Half Maximum) of (200) miller index in the XRD results, crystalline sizes of micron and submicron-FeS_2 can be calculated by Scherrer equation. Crystalline sizes of micron and submicron-sized FeS_2 decreased from 55.23nm to 39.45nm. Crystalline size reductions of FeS_2 materials might come from the high energy impact during milling process.

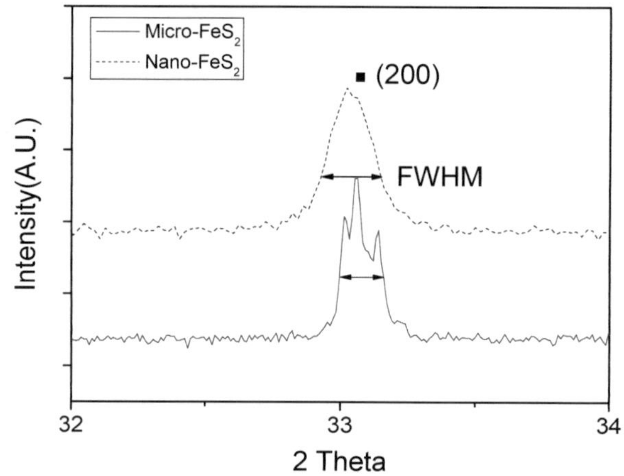

Figure 4 XRD analysis of micro and submicron-sized FeS_2 powders

Discharge Performances:

Fig. 5 shows discharge performances and polarizations of single cells. Red line is discharge property from single cell produced by micron-sized (100μm) FeS_2 powder. Blue line is by submicron-sized (200nm) FeS_2 powder. Same amount of FeS_2 cathode materials were used for preparation of electrode pellets. From the discharge performances, we can derive the followings. First, open circuit voltage (OCV) of single cell with submicron-sized FeS_2 (2.4V) is higher than those with micro-sized FeS_2 (1.9V). Second, before it reached 1.0eq. Li/mol FeS_2 capacity, single cell with submicron-sized FeS_2 has higher voltage. This might be due to the fact that submicron-sized FeS_2 has higher surface area for electrochemical reactions than the micro-sized FeS_2. Therefore electrochemical reactions of single cell with submicron-sized FeS_2 have occurred actively than those with the micro-sized FeS_2. After the electrochemical reaction passed 1.0eq. Li/mol FeS_2 capacity, single cell with submicron-sized FeS_2 degraded severely than those with micro-sized FeS_2. This phenomenon can be explained by exhaustion and phase decompositions of submicron-sized FeS_2 materials at the final stage of discharge performances.

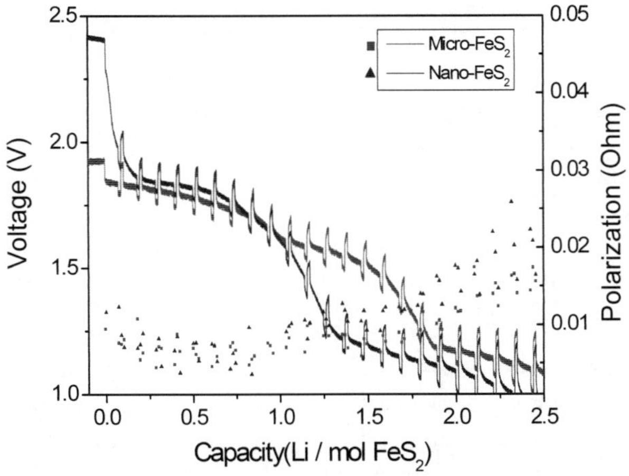

Figure 5 Discharge performances and polarizations of single cells produced by micro and submicron-sized FeS_2 powders

Polarizations of single cells with submicron-sized FeS_2 (▲) and micro-sized FeS_2 (■) were calculated by the pulsed current. At initial state of discharge, i.e. before 1.0eq. Li/mol FeS_2 capacity, polarizations of single cell with submicron-sized FeS_2 were slightly lower than those with micro-sized FeS_2. However, after 1.0eq. Li/mol FeS_2 capacity, these tendencies changed abruptly. At final stage of discharge, polarizations of single cell with submicron-sized FeS_2 were higher than the micro-sized FeS_2. These also might be due to the fact that the submicron-sized FeS_2 had higher usage rate at initial discharge stage. In addition submicron-sized FeS_2 was unstable phases, so it could easily decompose during electrochemical reaction.

Conclusions

Single cells for thermal battery applications were fabricated with submicron-sized and micron-sized FeS_2 materials. From the experimental and analytic results, we can derive followings.

1. At initial stage, discharge performances of single cell with submicron-sized FeS_2 were superior to those with micro-sized FeS_2. This can be explained that the submicron-sized FeS_2 has higher surface area for electrochemical reactions than the micro-sized FeS_2.

2. Contrary to the initial stage, at final stage, discharge performances of single cell with submicron-sized FeS_2 degraded severely. This might be due to the fact that the exhaustion and phase decompositions of submicron-sized FeS_2 materials.

Acknowledgements

This work was supported by the ADD (Agency for Defense Development) research project of "Nano-composite electrode technology using meso-porous incorporator". The authors gratefully acknowledge the use of the services and facilities at Vitzromiltech Co., Ltd.

References

1. Guidotti, R. A. and P. Masset, "Thermally activated ("thermal") battery technology: Part I: An overview," *Journal of power sources*, vol. 161, no. 2, pp. 1443-1449, 2006
2. Masset, P. and R. A. Guidotti, "Thermal activated (thermal) battery technology: Part II. Molten salt electrolytes," *Journal of power sources*, vol. 164, no. 1, pp. 397-414, 2007
3. Masset, P. J. and R. A. Guidotti, "Thermal activated ("thermal") battery technology: Part IIIa: FeS2 cathode material," *Journal of power sources*, vol. 177, no. 2, pp. 595-609, 2008
4. Feng, X., X. He, W. Pu, C. Jiang and C. Wan, "Hydrothermal synthesis of FeS2 for lithium batteries," *Ionics*, vol. 13, no. 5, pp. 375-377, 2007
5. Pemsler, J., R. Lam, J. Litchfield, S. Dallek, B. Larrick and B. Beard, "Discharge behavior and thermal stability of synthetic FeS2 cathode material," *Journal of the Electrochemical Society*, vol. 137, no. 1, pp. 1-7, 1990
6. Au, M., "Nanostructured thermal batteries with high power density," *Journal of power sources*, vol. 115, no. 2, pp. 360-366, 2003
7. Shao-Horn, Y., S. Osmialowski and Q. C. Horn, "Nano-FeS2 for commercial Li/FeS2 primary batteries," *Journal of the Electrochemical Society*, vol. 149, no. 11, pp. A1499-A1502, 2002
8. Cheong, H.-W., S.-H. Kang, J.-M. Kim and S.-B. Cho, "Enhanced salt coating on FeS2 surface with the addition of Li2O," *Journal of Ceramic Processing Research*, vol. 13, no. pp. S198-S201, 2012
9. Cheong, H.-W., S.-H. Ha and Y.-S. Choi, "Surface modified ceramic fiber separators for thermal batteries," *Journal of Ceramic Processing Research*, vol. 13, no. pp. S308-S311, 2012

Integrated Energy Storage and Generation in Support of Very Isolated Data Collection

Derek C. Neal, Herbert L. Hess, Doug Frome, Kathleen Kavanagh
Dept of Electrical and Computer Engineering
University of Idaho
Moscow, ID, USA, 83844

Abstract: *The design of a power system for remote mountainous research sites presents similar unique challenges as a military deployment to a remote area. In the case at hand, a Mountainous Ecosystem Sensor Array (MESA) consists of 78 sensors divided into three micro-networks that span 600 meters of elevation change in the isolated mountains of the Frank Church Wilderness Area of central Idaho. This exceptionally remote location offers a unique benchmark for identifying the important issues for such a remote data gathering and communications load, identifying and applying environmental constraints such as three-dimensional terrain, forest canopy, and creative sensor dispersion. The communication problem at hand is transmitting data packets through a self-creating and self-healing mesh communication network from Idaho to a server that stores the data in California.*

Keywords: environmental sensor network; mesh network; micro solar power; micro wind power, rechargeable battery; battery charge controller

Introduction

Deep in the Frank Church Wilderness Area of central Idaho, the Mountainous Ecosystem Sensor Array (MESA) was designed and deployed in late 2012. Sensors in the MESA network will gather "atmospheric, hydrologic, geospheric, and biological processes" in a "pristine natural site with limited human impact" to act as an "indispensable benchmark for comparison with human dominated sites [1]." Models derived from sensor array data will "allow for better predictions of vegetation changes, impacts of changing temperature and precipitation patterns and the consequences of human use on terrestrial and aquatic ecosystems...Models will enhance cross disciplinary understanding of natural and anthropogenic influences on climate change and ultimately inform decision making. Paradoxically what makes [the remote wilderness] challenging to sense is what makes [it] unique for climate research [1]." There exists no support structure except for Taylor Wilderness Research Station (TWRS) which provides a satellite internet link to transfer data to the web and a base station for deployment. Only accessible by small light aircraft or by foot, the research station remains extremely remote and presents unique challenges for large installations. Because of the isolated nature of the location and the strict regulations governing wilderness areas, the sensor network must be transparent to its pristine surroundings. This not only means utilizing small devices, but also creative deployment and camouflaging of the network and its support structure.

Design Overview

The MESA system consists of three micro-networks each containing 26 sensors and 10 network devices. Sensors and devices are mounted on one of four trees as pictured in Figure 1. Most are on the main tree powered by a large central 12V lead acid battery bank at the base of the tree. Generation sources include a 123W 12V solar panel and small 12V wind turbine. Network devices inside of weatherproof enclosures are represented with squares. These devices, made by Intelesense™, make up the nodes of the mesh network that provide power and sample the sensors connected to them. They transmit data using mesh network protocols to form a self-creating and self-healing topology. The peripheral trees 1-3 are powered by small 10W solar panels and 3.3V lithium-ion battery packs. The three micro-networks span 2 km of horizontal distance and over 600 m of elevation change (See Figure 2). The lower site resides on TWRS property at 1170 m MSL and will stay as a permanent installation. The other two sites are in the wilderness area and received a five year permit. The data propagates through the mesh network to the gateway device connected to the satellite internet link at the research station. Data travels to the Intelesense™ server where it is stored and presented for analysis.

Energy Storage

The MESA team evaluated eight different chemistries against several desired characteristics. Lithium iron phosphate and lead acid AGM batteries became the chemistries of choice, mainly due to their lower operating temperature. Table 1 shows the average measured current and amp-hour (Ah) demand per day for each location in the micro-net. The Amp-hour capacity was multiplied by five days based on the weather data analysis to ensure continued operation through obscuration weather systems. To avoid deep discharge, the bank was further oversized such that it only discharges to 40% of capacity by the end of the obscured days. Battery performance is degraded in low temperatures decreasing the nominal cell voltage and capacity. This equates to a 1.5 winter correction factor which was applied to all battery types. After applying these factors, the bank size requirement for the main tree equals 118.7 Ah while the peripheral trees require 10.1 Ah or less. Small packs of 4 parallel 3.3V 26650 $LiFePO_4$ cells (9.6Ah) made by A123 Systems were selected for the storage requirement for the peripheral trees. Although slightly less than the stated requirement, the MESA team traded battery capacity for an oversized panel. The A123 Systems™ batteries have an operating temperature range of -30°C-55°C [2]. For the main tree, the team selected a bank of three solar specific Deka™ 8A22NF 55Ah lead acid AGM batteries made by East Penn Manufacturing Company. This 165 Ah bank can operate to temperatures as low as -40°C and only costs $430 [3].

Figure 2. MESA micro-net locations from TWRS

Energy Harvesting

Common realistic electrical power sources for an isolated system are solar, wind and hydroelectric. Due to the isolated nature of the Frank Church, many generation techniques would be prohibited or too complex to implement. Only the low elevation site has water that can be used to generate hydroelectricity, and water rights to utilize the water for power generation are difficult to obtain. The micro-network sites were chosen partially because they are all located on the south face of the mountain ridge and receive ample sunshine almost year round. The MESA team selected solar power as the primary source of generation mainly because it is the most commercially available and is the least invasive medium to minimize the impact on the sensitive location.

Solar: Great effort was taken to minimize the power supply footprint while still providing the needed energy in the worst of winter weather. Using extrapolated solar radiance data from Mountain Microclimate Simulator (MTCLIM) for TWRS, the MESA team estimated a conservative winter value of available radiance [4]. After sorting the data by Julian date, and averaging the solar radiance values in December for the past decade, the results yield an average of 1042 Wh/m^2/day. The more efficient the solar cell, the smaller the panel may be to deliver a given amount of power. Therefore, the MESA team utilized monocrystalline photovoltaic cell technology [5], [6]. Warner Energy™ makes a 0.84 m^2 flexible panel for the military which has camouflage matting as well as an antiglare coating on the solar cells while maintaining a panel efficiency of 14.7% [7]. Given the average December radiance, this panel can supply 128.7 Wh/day which exceeds the main tree power requirement of 113.9 Wh/day from Table 1. A small monocrystalline SolarTech™ SPM010P-R panel powers each of the peripheral trees. Assuming the same radiance, and an efficiency of 9.5%, the panel can supply 10.4 Wh/day, which is almost 4 times the requirement for Tree #1 from Table 1 [8]. This large buffer helps offset the small battery bank deficit mentioned previously.

Because of the isolated nature of the MESA system, it must operate autonomously and the panels must be fixed at one angle year round. At TWRS, the solar altitude on the winter equinox at solar noon is 21.45° [9], [10]. Rather than fix the panels for one particular day in winter, they were angled at 26° from the vertical plane to maximize production during the entire winter season [11].

Table 1. Measured system power requirements

Locatio n	Bus	Averag e mA	Ah/day	Oversized Ah/5 days	Wh/day
Main Tree	12V	395.6	9.5	118.7	113.9
Tree 1	3.3V	33.7	0.8	10.1	2.7
Tree 2	3.3V	22.8	0.6	6.8	1.8
Tree 3	3.3V	13.8	0.3	4.1	1.1

To integrate the solar production with the system necessitates a charge controller to regulate the current and voltage applied to the battery bank. MPPT controllers attempt to control the operating point of the panel to extract maximum power [12], [13]. Manufacturers use various methods to identify the knee point in the I-V curve (see Figure 3) such as perturb and observe (P&O), incremental conductance (IC), and constant voltage (CV). These methods track the maximum power voltage (V_{MP}) for any given photovoltaic current output (I_{PV}). Typically, highly efficient DC-DC converters then step this voltage down to the appropriate charging voltage while boosting the current to conserve maximum power [14]. Controllers for 12V lead acid or lithium-ion batteries are widely available from a myriad of vendors. However, 3.3V solar chargers are much less common and required a bit of searching. Solar Converters Inc™ (SCI) based out of Ontario Canada offers chargers that boast 94% efficiency in a wide range of voltages including 3.3V lithium-ion cells [15]. The peripheral trees use the SCI PT12-5 B3.3, a MPPT 3.3V controller for the lithium iron phosphate cells. The MESA team used the SCI PT12-15, a MPPT 12V charge controller, for the lead-acid battery system on the main tree. It includes a temperature compensation sensor to adjust the set point voltage in a dynamic outdoor environment.

Additionally the PT12-15 includes an automatic low voltage disconnect feature to interrupt current to the load if battery voltage falls below 11.0V to protect against deep discharge [16].

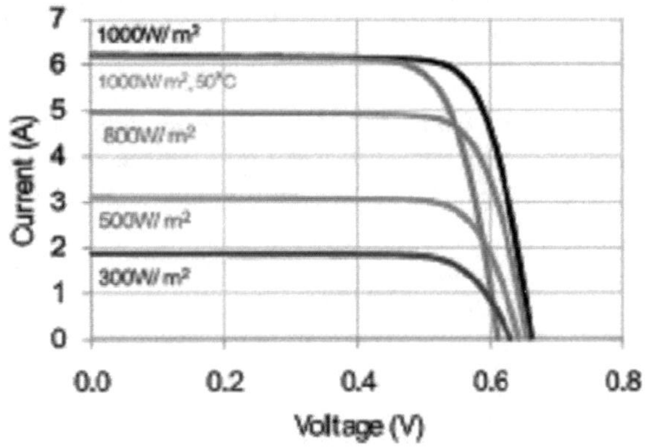

Figure 3. STAR123 I-V curve [7]

Wind: Besides solar power, another viable and realistic renewable energy resource available at all the MESA deployment sites is wind. However, the terrain that covers the central Idaho mountains, does not lend itself well for a stereotypical wind turbine installation. The network spans a steep canyon subject to dynamic airflow patterns affected by multiple variables. Again, much like solar panels, a difficult paradox is presented where an object that does not function well when obstructed must be concealed. Therefore, in order to diversify the power generation system, a wind turbine was specified and sized that could function in a transient environment and also could be realistically mounted and concealed in the evergreen mountain forest. The MESA team favored vertical axis turbines as more compatible for tree installation. The Forgen500™ is a very small multi-bladed Savonius drag based vertical axis turbine. The rotor blades are made of light durable aluminum. It weighs only 15 lbs, and is virtually silent during operation. Case studies of the Forgen turbine show its success in harsh environments including high turbulent winds in non-traditional mounting locations [17]. Direct battery coupling allows the turbine to be directly in parallel with the solar charger eliminating potential controller conflicts [18].

Mesh Network

The entire MESA system consists of 30 wireless network devices, or motes (10 per micro-network) which use a mesh protocol to synchronize, discover optimal communication paths, and transfer data packets in minimal time [19]. Intelesense™, based out of California, manufactures wireless network motes that quickly became the preferred choice for the MESA system due to their superb technical support, user-friendly interface, robust hardware, and flexibility. Furthermore, they had solved and provided a large piece of the system design: data storage and presentation. Many of the MESA sensors already had drivers available and Intelesense™ wrote the remaining drivers. Such customer service was absent from all other explored companies. Their network design resides on two main hierarchal levels using two separate devices. The Intelecell (Figure 5) houses a microcontroller, three digital sensors ports, three analog sensor ports, and two radios [20]. All Intelecells in the network mesh together using the 900 MHz Digi International XTend radio controlled by a proprietary Intelesense™ protocol called Intelenet. The second radio, the 900 MHz Digi International XBeePro, uses the Digimesh protocol to network with a lower level of devices called Intelemotes shown in Figure 5 [21]. Intelemotes are smaller and less expensive devices with only one analog and one digital sensor ports. These two layers form a hierarchal system where motes strive to send their data to the higher level XTend network and the XTend network seeks the final gateway destination. The gateway is simply another Intelecell that has access to the internet via satellite internet at TWRS.

Figure 4. Forgen500 on main tree above the canopy

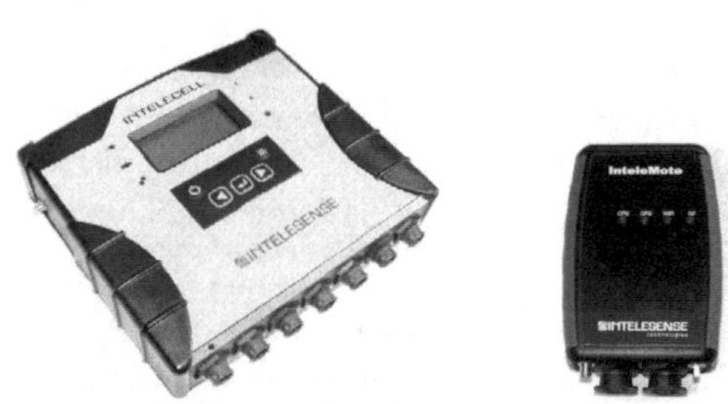

Fig 5. Intelecell (.19x.17x.05m); Intelemote (.12x.08x.03m)

Data Storage

The MESA network monitors over 200 environmental parameters at three different sites with 78 sensors, most sampling every two minutes. Having chosen the Intelesense™ mesh network devices for the MESA system opened the door to using this manufacturer's medium for organizing and presenting this massive amount of sensor data. Their provided solution saved the MESA team significant time and money. Intelesense™ has provided two forums for viewing data. First is a user account activated website *www.intelesense.net* that displays data from each mote in graphical or tabular format which can then be downloaded to PC based spreadsheet programs [22]. Second is a scientific forum called *www.colaborate.org* where networks are geographically displayed through a Google Earth™ based program called Inteleview. Information from other organizations and data centers can be layered on top of the base network information. Summaries, comments and updates can be posted to inform of current status and future intentions. It can be used to share files, communicate with fellow team members, and even collaborate with other groups. Ultimately, the goal of *collaborate.org* is to make data available from multiple fields of study and from various projects to researchers all over the world [23].

Conclusion

The Mountainous Ecosystem Sensor Array is a pioneer project in remote system design. Utilizing available commercial technology, the MESA team assembled a one of a kind environmental sensor network. Lessons can be drawn from this project to a myriad of different fields such as off-grid power production, mesh network implementation, and data transmission and storage. Significant contributions of the MESA project include: interface methods between sensors and motes, system concealment techniques, low irradiance PV sizing considerations, and field testing of mesh networks and small hybrid power supplies.

Acknowledgements

The MESA team would like to thank our technician Paul Robinson, Professor Tim Link, and tree climber Pete Gäg for their technical expertise, and back breaking labor. The project wouldn't have been possible without the TWRS care takers, Arnold and Interstate Aviation and animal pack teamsters Jim Akenson and Pete Volk.

References

1. K. Kavanagh *et al.*, "MRI: Development of a smart 3-D wireless sensor network for terrain-climate research in remote mountainous environments," University of Idaho, ID, MRI NSF 10-529, Apr. 21, 2010.
2. *Nanophosphate EXT: Optimizing Lithium Ion Battery Performance over an Expanded Operating Temperature Range*, A123 Systems, 2012, pp. 7.
3. *Valve-Regulated Lead-Acid Technical Manual*, East Penn, Anaheim, CA, 2004, pp. 1.
4. R. D. Hungerford et al., "MTCLIM: A Mountain Microclimate Simulation Model," Research Paper INT-414, Intermountain Research Station, Fort Collins, CO, 1989
5. S. R. Wenham et al., "Semiconductors and P-N Junctions," in *Applied Photovoltaics*, London, Earthscan, 2007, ch. 2, sec. 2.2, pp. 34-36.
6. Engineering.com. *Photovoltaics* [Online]. Available: http://www.engineering.com/SustainableEngineering/RenewableEnergyEngineering/SolarEnergyEngineering/Photovoltaics/tabid/3890.aspx.
7. *STAR 123-Foldable Solar Panel*, Warner Energy Technologies, 2012, pp. 1.
8. SolarTech Power, Inc. *M-Series Solar Panels* [Online]. Available: http://www.solartechpower.com/MSeries.html
9. B. K. Hodge, *Alternative Energy Systems and Applications*, Hoboken, John Wiley & Sons, 2010, ch. 4, ch. 6, ch. 9.
10. Earth System Research Laboratory. *NOAA Solar Calculator* [Online]. Available: http://www.esrl.noaa.gov/gmd/grad/solcalc
11. C. R. Landau. (2012). *Optimum Tilt of Solar Panels* [Online]. Available: http://www.macslab.com
12. D. P. Hohm and M. E. Ropp, "Comparative Study of Maximum Power Point Tracking Algorithms," *Prog. Photovolt: Res. Appl.*, vol. 11, pp. 47-55, Apr. 2003.
13. R. Faranda and S. Leva, "Energy comparison of MPPT techniques for PV systems," *WSEAS Transactions on Power Systems*, issue 6, vol. 3, pp. 446-454, Jun. 2008.
14. Wind & Sun. *What the heck is an MPPT??* [Online]. Available: http://www.windsun.com
15. Solar Converters Inc. *PT Charge Controllers* http://www.solarconverters.com/products/80-power-tracker-chargers/pt-charge-controllers
16. *Manual Rev. H Model: PT 12/24-15*, Solar Converters Inc., pp. 1-5.
17. Forgen Renewables. (2011). *Wind Turbines* [Online]. Available: http://forgenrenewables.com/products/wind-turbines
18. *AirX Owner's Manual*, Southwest Windpower, Inc., 2008, pp. 13-23.
19. *XBee-Pro 900/900 DigiMesh RF Modules*, Digi International Inc., 2011, pp. 6-38.
20. *Intelecell Field Router-User Guide*, Intelesense™ Technologies, 2013, pp. 1-34.
21. *Intelecell Mote-User Guide*, Intelesense™ Technologies, 2013, pp. 1-24.
22. Intelesense™. (2013). *Groups* [Online]. Available: http://www.Intelesense™.net/groups
23. Intelesense™. (2013). *Inteleview* [Online]. Available: https://universityofidaho.collaborate..org.

VSP Products Alternative Power System

Dusko Jovicic
AZ Defense Solutions LLC
John Von Stach
VSP Products

VSP GENERATORS

Design and installation of hybrid solar and wind energy generation projects just got much easier! The VSP Generator combines a complete energy management system with a battery management system all in one easy-to-use, turnkey, compact unit. This "one cart solution" is really five solutions in one:

1. **An uninterrupted power source** – one use of the VSP Generator is as an uninterrupted power source (UPS) to facilities such as data centres, cell phone towers that require a guaranteed source of clean pure sine wave , uninterrupted power with built in spike and surge protection. Or very simply if the homeowners is going away and is worried that the basement may flood if the grid power fails, you can use the VSP generators to supply power to a sump pump when the grid power fails. Once grid power becomes available the VSP generator switches back over to grid power and any energy that was used gets instantly restored via its on board charging system keeping the VSP generator at 100% full at all times ready for the next power outage. Completely maintenance free!

2. **Portable generator** – a second use is as portable generator. The VSP Generator is the world's first portable electric generator. Until now, if someone wanted a portable generator only a gas or diesel unit was available. The VSP generator not only is portable but also propels itself under its own power. Its auto drive system allows the unit to go forward and reverse. When compared to gas or diesel portable generator to get 8-10hrs of power out of a gas or diesel unit it would cost about $30.00-$40.00 for fuel. To get the same out of the VSP GENERATOR wouldn't, cost a dime if you connected it to our portable solar charge kits or our portable wind turbines. If you just simply plugged it into grid power to recharge it,it would take 6 hours to fully recharge and would only cost $ 2 -$3 on you power bill and ready to go for the next day. No smoke ,no smell, no pollution, no maintenance, no fuel. Simply flip the switch to turn it on and off, no starting issues like a gas or diesel. Clean pure sine wave electricity with built in surge and spike protection.

3. **Back-up residential generator** – a third use is as a back-up residential generator. The VSP Generator can be connected directly to the home's electrical panel.

4. **Renewable energy power station** – a fourth use is as a renewable energy power supply. The VSP generator can be connected to both solar PV panels and small wind turbines. This is a perfect solution for locations without a grid source of electricity, such as remote areas, developing countries, portable hospitals, remote offices, or for military camps on foreign soil.

5. **Control centre** – a fifth use is as a control centre. In situations where a home is both connected to the grid and has renewable energy whether it is an existing rooftop solar array or a wind turbine the VSP generator allows the homeowner to choose if they want to sell their power or use the power. It puts the homeowner in control and takes the monopoly away from the power company. Now the homeowner can be in charge and can use the grid as there back up power. Most importantly by having the VSP Generator you can now use your existing solar array or wind turbine when the grid shuts down. When a storm hits and the grid gets shut down for weeks on end anyone who currently has a solar array or wind turbine cannot even access the power they are making. They are completely disconnected from the grid. Now with the VSP GENERATOR the homeowner very simply just flips a switch and the solar and wind power gets fed directly to the VSP generator and the generator feeds the power to the home.

The VSP Power Station includes the following features and benefits:

- **Simplified & efficient power electronics** – all required electronics built right in including the latest in solar charge controllers and sine wave technology for wind conversion. The VSP's inverting systems only consume 2% of the stored battery power to operate the unit, whereas, the less expensive square wave inverter systems consume 40% of the stored battery power just to convert the power.

- **Simple to use** – its plug and play design is simple to understand and work with for both installer and end-user

- **Much cheaper to operate than diesel** – to get 10 hours of power with a portable gas or diesel generator costs about $40 in fuel. To get 10 hours of power with the VSP Power Station costs about 80 cents in power, if recharged by grid electricity. The VSP's inexpensive operation is a key reason why it is an excellent alternative to a gas or diesel generator set.

- **Automatic grid backup** – the VSP includes built-in transfer switches, which allows the VSP Power Station to act as backup power to the grid. The VSP Power Station is simply plugged into an electrical outlet. Whenever the grid power shuts off the VSP Power Station turns on automatically and continues the power supply to whatever you have plugged into the VSP unit. When the grid power resumes, the VSP Power Station provides a buffer of two minutes to ensure the incoming grid power is safe and without harmful spikes. Once this two minutes passes the VSP Power Station automatically shuts off and power is now supplied to whatever is plugged into the VSP unit by grid power. Any energy that was used from the generator gets instantly restored through its on board AC charging system.

- **Dual Voltage** – the VSP inverting system is selectable dual voltage 120 or 220 volts. Competitor invertors provide just one voltage alternative.

- **Maintenance free batteries** – the VSP comes included with maintenance-free, sealed lead acid batteries in a flameproof case that do not emit gases. Safe for indoor use. No weekly top up of batteries required.

- **Produces safe power** – the VSP Power Station supplies pure sine wave electricity, which is the cleanest form of electricity available, even cleaner than the cleanest of grid power. The VSP produces consistent, reliable and safe power, which eliminates damaging electrical events such as brown-outs and spiking. Safe for all medical devices and sensitive electronics.

- **Remote monitoring** – with an online monitoring and computer system built-in, both energy input and output can be monitored and managed remotely by internet.

- **Advanced metering** – the VSP Power Station is the only machine in the world to have a watt meter showing how much power is being consumed from the VSP Power Station and a second watt meter on the input side showing how much power is flowing into the Power Station from solar and/or wind generation. Having accurate metering on the input allows the operator to fine tune the solar PV setup for maximum solar power.

- **Safe for indoor use** – its quiet operation, no fumes, no fuel use and no moving parts allow for safe indoor use.

- **Maintenance free** - very important for remote locations or where budgets are tight

- **Flexible** – operates 120 V AC /220VAC or 12 V DC products anywhere. Can be connected to solar, wind and electrical grid. Interchanges easily between single and three phase.

- **Proven technology** – thousands of units sold, many in developing countries

- **Cost effective** – price of VSP solar solution with VSP Battery Pak included competitive with traditional grid-tied inverter-based solar systems without batteries.

- **Seamless integration** – easily configures with existing diesel generator set technology to offset use.

Whether a site wishes to lessen its dependence on the grid, lessen its dependence on a gas or diesel generator set, or create electricity where there is no other source the many benefits of the VSP Power Station make it an attractive solution. VSP - bringing a little bit of tomorrow here today!

MANAGEMENT TEAM:

Dusko Jovicic serves as President of AZ Defense Solutions LLC and has served as a contractor to the US military in Bosnia, Kosovo, Iraq, and Afghanistan in various capacities . Through this experience, Dusko recognized the ongoing energy challenges faced by the US military. As a result, he formed a partnership with John Von Stach, President of VSP Products, Inc, to offer solutions to the energy challenges faced by the Department of Defense.

John Von Stach founded VSP Products to develop and manufacture specialty green energy electronic products. The idea for these products was conceived by us as a result of numerous attempts to make green products that will provide clean, low priced energy. John was involved in various retail, wholesale, and manufacturing businesses for the past 20 years and he has 10 years retail experience and also owning a very successful motorcycle and snow machine shop. With this experience, he has gained a great deal of knowledge in modifications, such as electricity, gas and diesel engines.

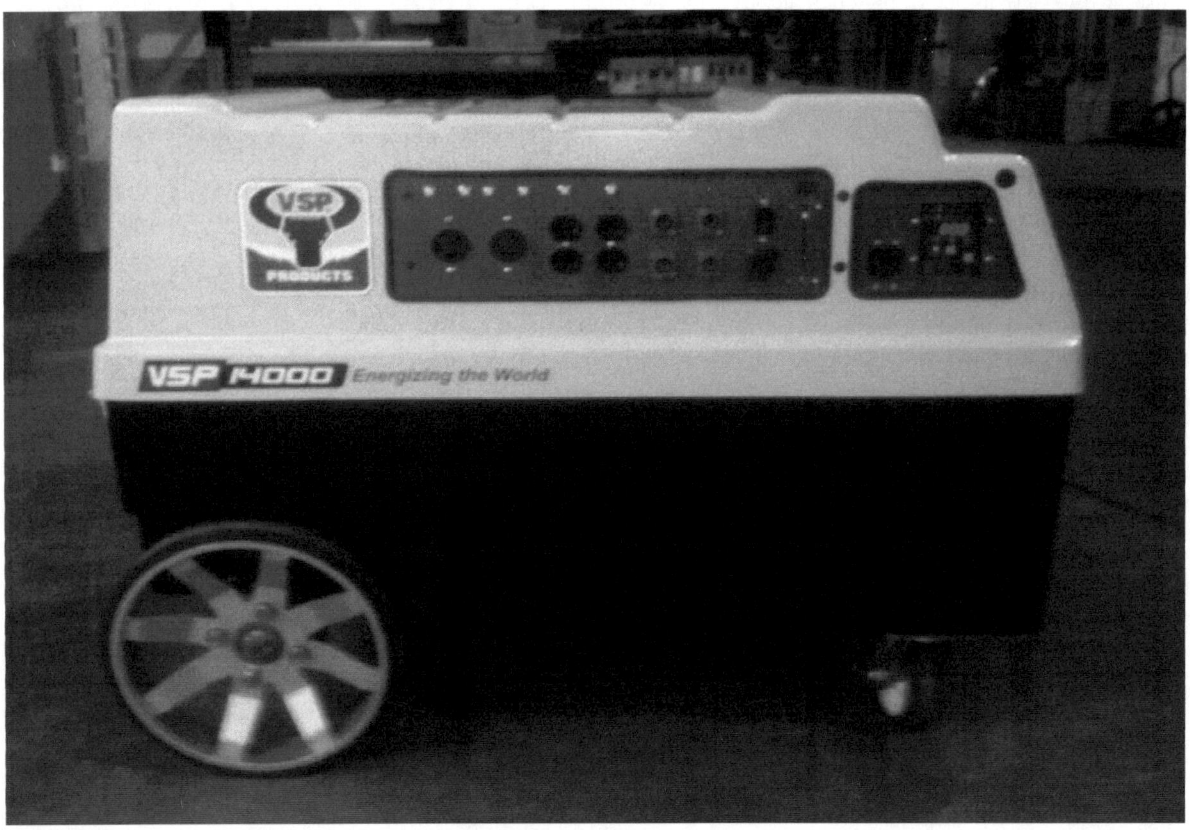
VSP
PRODUCTS
VSP 14000
Energizing the World

Electrochemical Properties of Lithium-based Anodes with Metal Foams for Thermal Batteries

Yu-Song Choi, Hye-Ryeon Yu and Hae-Won Cheong[+]
Agency for Defense Development
Yuseong P.O. Box 35, Daejeon, 305-600, Korea

Abstract: Lithium based anodes were prepared by the impregnation of lithium to the molten salt coated nickel metal foam. The open circuit voltage of lithium impregnated anode was 2.05 V, which is fairly higher than that of the Li(Si) (1.95V). The specific capacity of lithium impregnated anode (2,913 $As \cdot g^{-1}$) showed two times higher than that of the Li(Si) anode (1,050 $As \cdot g^{-1}$). These improvements could be attributed to the impregnation into the high porosity (90%) nickel foam which enhances lithium content drastically. Due to their excellent electrochemical properties, lithium impregnated anodes could be new anode for thermal batteries with enhanced energy and power density.

Keywords: thermal batteries; metal foam; molten salt; lithium anode; impregnation

Introduction

Due to their excellent mechanical robustness, reliability, and long shelf life, thermal batteries have been used as the primary power sources for guided weapons [1]. Thermal batteries are activated by the melting of solid electrolyte to molten salt at the high temperature of 500°C. Li(Si) and FeS_2 (pyrite) are the typical anode and cathode materials for thermal batteries, respectively [2,3]. FeS_2 is naturally abundant and Li(Si) is inexpensive and has a high electromotive force (emf), compared to the other anode materials. The low emf and the low lithium content of Li(Si), however, has limited the high capacity application of thermal batteries. The pure lithium shows the highest specific energy and power density, however, which melts at around 180°C far below the operating temperature of thermal batteries, 500°C. In order to use pure lithium for anode, considerable amount of fine iron powder was applied to hold the molten lithium which is well known as Lithium anode (LAN). But, LAN shows lower specific capacity than the theoretical one because of the extensive weight fraction of heavy iron powder.

In this study, we attempted to fabricate and characterize the lithium based anode, lithium impregnated metal foam, as an alternative way to hold the molten lithium.

Experiment

Lithium impregnation: The nickel foams (porosity: 90%, pore size: 800 μm, thickness: 0.5 mm) were coated with molten salt as lithium impregnation agent. In a vacuum furnace purged with argon (Ar), metallic lithium foils were placed on top of the salt coated nickel foam. The prepared samples were heated up to 500°C for 4h under Ar atmosphere (50 sccm)[4]. A schematic drawing of the lithium impregnation method is shown in Figure 1.

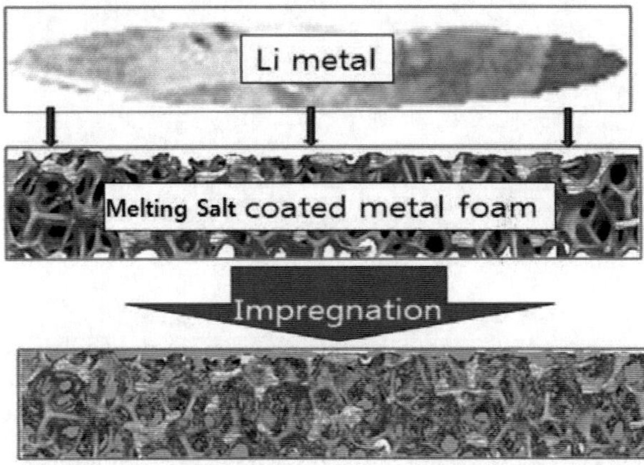

Figure 1. Lithium impregnated metal foam anode.

Preparation of Single Cells: The prepared single cells are listed in Table 1 and shown in Figure 2. Li(Si) was fabricated with following ratios and methods. The anode was prepared with the mixture of 75 wt.% of the commercial Li(Si) (Li 44 wt.%, Si 56 wt.%) and 25 wt.% of LiCl-KCl eutectic salts. Then, the anode was prepared by melting the mixture followed by grinding and pressing. And then, the FeS_2 particles (average size of 98 μm) as cathode were mixed with Li_2O, a voltage regulator, and then melted followed by grinding and sieving. The pyrite cathode pellets were made by pressing with a density of 3 g $\bullet cm^{-3}$. LiF-LiCl-LiBr eutectic salt was mixed with the MgO binder (99%) and then melted followed by grinding [5].

Table 1. The composition of prepared single cells

Sample	Anode	Electrolyte	Cathode
Sample A	Li(Si)	LiF-LiCl-LiBr	FeS_2
Sample B	Li-impregnated metal foam		

Figure 2. The image of prepared single cells.

Electrochemical test: The single cells were discharged at 500°C with pulse current (4 A, 1 sec → 2 A, 4 sec → 0 A, 1 sec). The cell discharge was terminated when the voltage dropped below 1.00V. Figure 3 depicts a single cell discharge test process. The discharge test equipment consists of pressing device of single cell, DC electronic load, shunt, and data acquisition system.

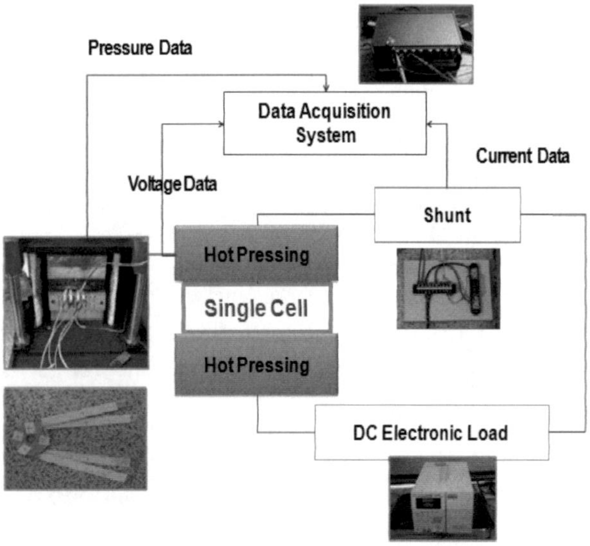

Figure 3. Single cell discharge test process.

Results and Discussion

The SEM image of as-received nickel foam is presented in Figure 4. The nickel foam has uniform pores, large surface area and pore volume.

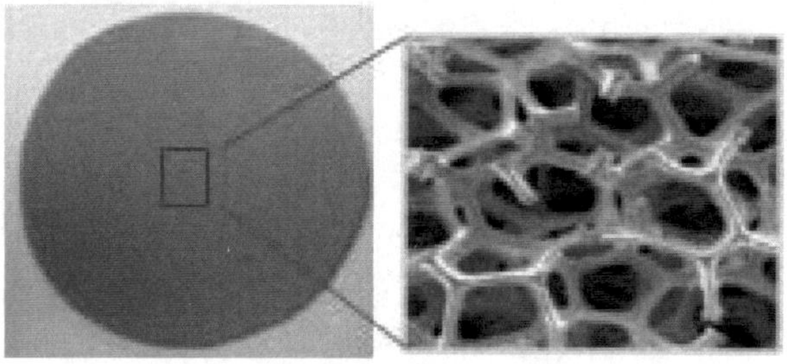

Figure 4. The SEM image of as-received nickel foam.

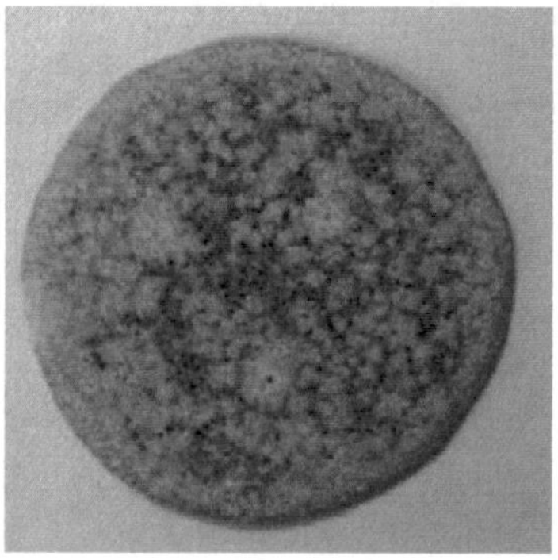

Figure 5. The image of salt coated nickel metal form.

Figure 5 indicates the nickel metal foam impregnated with lithium. The coated salt enhances the lithium impregnation into the porous metal foam. The poor interfacial affinity between the surface of nickel metal foam and molten lithium results in poor impregnation due to the high viscosity and surface tension of molten lithium. The effect of salt coating is presented in Figure 6. As mentioned before, when lithium impregnated without salt coating, the infiltration of molten lithium into the porous structure of nickel metal foam is restricted. As shown in left image of Figure 6, the lithium was not impregnated into the nickel metal foam and just shrunk on the surface of metal foam. The residual on the metal foam was agglomerated and discolored. On the other hand, the lithium impregnated nickel metal foam with salt coating (right image of Figure 6) was made up without discoloration. Moreover, the lithium placed on the top of the nickel metal foam is perfectly impregnated into the metal foam. Hence, the salt coating on the nickel metal foam is useful method for improvement of interfacial affinity between melted lithium and surface of the metal foam.

Figure 6. The image of lithium impregnation without (left) and with salt coating (right).

The discharge performance of 2 samples is depicted in Figure 7. These graphs indicated the change of voltage according to the induced current profile.

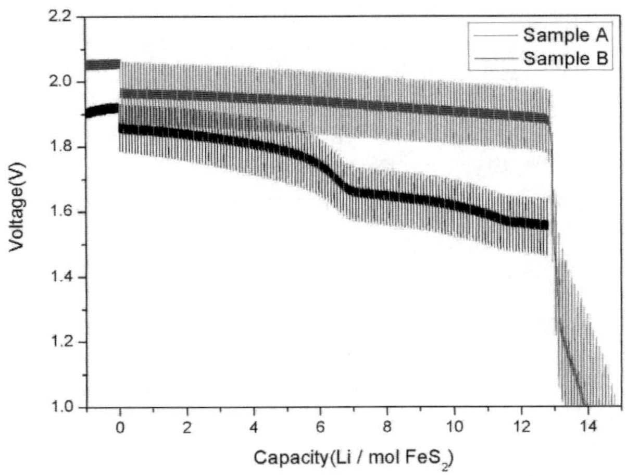

Figure 7. Discharge performance of the prepared samples

The specific capacities of two samples are calculated based on the data (Figure 7). As a result, The sample B(lithium impregnated anode) showed over two times higher specific capacity than the conventional Li(Si). This improvement can be attributed to the higher lithium content in the pores of lithium impregnated metal foam anode. The open circuit voltage of sample B was 2.05 V, which is fairly higher than that of the sample A, 1.95V. Due to their excellent electrochemical properties, sample B impregnated with molten lithium could be the new anode for thermal batteries with enhanced energy density and power capability.

Conclusion

In summary, this study investigated the new anode instead of conventional Li(Si) anode. The specific capacity of lithium impregnated metal foam anode was over two times higher than that of the Li(Si) anode. These improvements could be attributed to the sound impregnation into the high porosity (90%) nickel metal foam which enhances lithium content drastically, compared to the Li(Si). Due to their excellent electrochemical properties, lithium impregnated metal foam anodes could be a new anode for thermal batteries with enhanced high energy and power density.

References

1. R.A. Guidotti and R. Masset, "Thermal Activated ("thermal") Battery Technology: Part I: An Overview", *Journal of Power Sources*, vol.161, no.1, pp1443–1449, 2006.
2. R.A. Guidotti and R. Masset, "Thermal Activated ("thermal") Battery Technology: Part IV: Anode Materials", *Journal of Power Sources*, vol. 183, no.1, pp 388–398, 2008.
3. P.J. Masset and R.A. Guidotti, "Thermal Activated ("thermal") Battery Technology: Part IIIa: FeS_2 Cathode Material:", *Journal of Power Sources*, vol.177, no.2, pp 595–609, 2008.
4. T. Hao, M. matsuo, Y. Nakamori, and S.I. Orimo, "Impregnation method for the synthesis of Li–N–H systems", *Journal of Alloys and Compounds*, vol. 458, L1–L5, 2008.
5. Y. Choi, S. Cho, and Y.S. Lee, "Effect of the addition of carbon black and carbon nanotube to FeS_2 cathode on the electrochemical performance of thermal battery", *Journal of Industrial and Engineering Chemistry*, *In Press, Corrected Proof*, 2014.

Ozone Removal using New Structure of Matter for High Performance Heterogeneous Catalysis at Short Contact Time

Qiang Gu, Bruce Tatarchuk
Chemical Engineering
Auburn Univeristy
Alabama, USA, 36849

Abstract: *In this research, ozone has been used as model compound. MFEC reactors were investigated under aircraft bleed air conditions of high temperature (100-200℃) and high face velocity (10-30 m/s) resulting an interlayer contact time of 67-200 μsec. Precious metal (Pd, Ag) and transition metal (Mn) catalysts were impregnated on entrapped particles (e.g. γ-Al_2O_3) using incipient wetness method. Ozone test concentration was set at a high-demanding 1.5 ppmv. Results showed that a high level of ozone decomposition was achieved with a significant reduction of catalyst consumption. Because the entrapped small particles (150-250μm) improve the contact efficiency significantly, this kind of reactor has shown high catalytic activity even though the contact time for the reactant has been shortened to 100 μs range due to the high face velocity. This feature has enabled MFEC to be used at high mass flow conditions, including fuel cell cathode air. Besides, several other aspects including humidity, system pressure been investigated for affection on the reaction.*

Keywords: Nickel Fiber, Ozone, Reaction, Fuel Cell, Cathode Air

Introduction

The demand for improved aircraft cabin air quality has led to adaptation of readily available catalytic reaction systems. Ozone contamination has been addressed by using monoliths similar to those used in automobile exhaust systems operating at temperatures of 100-200ºC. The high contacting efficiency of microfibrous entrapped catalyst and sorbent materials allow minimization of the system size and weight required to address these significant challenges.

Photochemical conversion of oxygen creates ozone in the atmosphere. Ozone is usually found in the earth's upper atmosphere (10~30 miles above the earth's surface). The concentration increases with latitude and changes with seasons and weather. The Global Atmosphere Sampling Program conducted ozone concentration measurement in and out of the cabin of a B-747-100 in 1977. It indicated that the outside ozone concentration can be well over the limit set by FAA in 1985. According to FAA, cabin air ozone level should not be over 0.25 ppm at any time above 32,000 ft flight. 0.10 ppm should not be exceeded for any 3-hour flight over 27,000 ft. If the aircraft cabin air has been left untreated, it will cause a series of health problems, including coughing, throat irritation and uncomfortable chest feelings.

Ozone is also created by common equipment, including copiers, pool cleaners, and water purification systems. Catalytic ozone decomposition has been widely applied to these situations to protect human health. Today, most ozone releasing equipment has installed ozone filters. But some of have been adapted in a non-optimized way. For instance, packed bed style converters have been popular in most situations. But in situations like aircraft filter, pressure drop has been a great issue in packed bed converters. Microfibrous materials filters have been developed as a high contact-efficiency and low pressure drop alternative for these situations.

Microfibrous entrapped sorbents and catalyst materials have been manufactured from many types of metal fibers entrapping various sorbents and catalyst supports. Micro scale pictures of four different materials taken by SEM are shown as Figure 1. Figure 1A shows a material made from activated carbon fiber and two micron stainless steel fibers. The size reference on Figure 1A, B and C is thirty micron in length. Figure 1B shows 55-88 micron BPL carbon entrapped by a mixture of 2, 4 and 8 micron nickel fibers. Figure 1C shows spray dried titania particles entrapped by two micron stainless steel fibers. Figure 1D shows γ-alumina particles entrapped in a mesh of four and eight micron nickel fibers. Several catalyst supports have been entrapped in copper fibers as well. These materials are especially useful for applications in reducing environments at high temperatures.

Figure 1. Various Metal Fiber Based Microfibrous Materials

Sintered microfibrous entrapped catalysts or sorbent particulates (MFEC) are a high contacting efficiency composite material prepared using traditional high speed and low cost paper making equipment and techniques. In the preparation process, μm diameter metal, polymer or ceramic fibers are slurried in an aqueous suspension with cellulose fibers and other selected particulates and/or fibers. The resulting mixture is then cast into a perform sheet using a wetlay process and dried to create a sheet or roll of perform material. Subsequent sintering of the preform at elevated temperatures (ca. 1000ºC) removes the cellulosic binder and entraps the selected particulates/fibers within a sinter-locked network of fibers. The wetlay process is a self-correcting filtration mechanism, so uniform basis weights of components result from this process. The microfibers used are typically cut to lengths of 3-6 mm resulting in high aspect ratios of the fibers (i.e. 250-3000). The effective channel size in these materials can be designed almost independently from the particle diameter, since it also depends on voidage and the mixture of fiber diameters chosen to design the MFEC. This allows small particles with high surface to volume ratios to be entrapped in a very open material. Higher mass and heat transfer rates employing the small particles are accomplished without acquiring the penalty of high pressure drops that would ensue from using packed beds of small particulates.

The physical properties of these composite materials are approximately averaged contributions of the properties of the components. Mixtures with different sizes of fibers and particle sizes of very different material densities can be combined in this process. For chemical processing applications the high void volume of the metallic binder/carrier (i.e. 80-99%) facilitates intralayer heat and mass transport while the ability to entrap very small particulates (using the novel pore size-void volume relationship of microfibrous carrier) greatly reduces intraparticle heat and mass transport. In the wetlay process fibers tend to form layers stacked on top of each other with some fibers interconnecting the layers. This produces a structure that has less resistance to flow in the horizontal plane than in the vertical plane. For applications employing these materials as a fixed bed of catalyst or sorbent this causes the radial transport properties to be larger than those in the axial direction.

Testing and Evaluation on Microfibrous Materials and Related Pressure Drop

A. Testing system design

Figure 2 shows novel design system for testing microfibrous material at millisecond contact time. A variable frequency drive is used to control the system speed, which can reach over 30 meters per second in face velocity. Heaters as well as purging air are used to control temperature, which can reach as high as 200ºC. Pollutants are mixed at the outlet of the blower to meet the required concentration level required for tests. System speed is acquired by differential pressure across a bare section of the test rig. Pollutant concentration level and temperature are both monitored upstream and downstream of the reactor section.

Figure 2. Ozone decomposition test rig

The unique attribute of the system is the short contact time of the reactant with catalyst surface. For a millimeter thickness of MFEC, a system speed of over 30 meters per second shortened the contact time to less than 0.1 micro second. Due to entrapment of small particles, the mass transfer rate to the catalyst was increased enough to meet the test requirement for ozone reduction.

B. Pressure Drop of Pleated Structures

Pressure drop has played a significant role in aircraft filter performance. Since lower pressure drop help with energy saving and reduces the operating cost of commercial aircraft, microfibrous material has shown a great improvement compared with packed bed reactors. Kalluri et al. has performed a comparison between microfibrous material reactors and monoliths. Results showed that microfibrous material has only a slight higher pressure drop than monolith. Considering the much better performance in conversion, microfibrous material has shown great capability in aircraft filters.

Pressure drop modification by adding fairing to the filter has also been performed. 6 inch long triangular and round-top fairing has been investigated under the same condition as aircraft engine bleed air. Results showed that triangular fairings performed better than round-top fairings, since triangular fairings helped the air flow change more smoothly than round-top ones.

Results and Discussion

Activated carbon and zeolites can be made into adsorbent filters, but they face the disadvantage of frequent replacement. Common methods of ozone removal include catalytic decomposition of ozone to oxygen. Due to the large surface to volume ratio provided by microfibrous material, it enables a high conversion rate at a low contact time within the reactor.

Five Ozone Catalysts were tested at 373K, 423K, 473K at face velocities ranges from 10~30 m/s for conversion. Catalysts are listed in table 1.

Table 1. Ozone Decomposition Catalysts

Catalyst	Weight Percent
Pd/Al_2O_3	1% wt Pd
Pd/SiO_2	1% wt Pd
Ag/Al_2O_3	1% wt Ag
MnO_2/Al_2O_3	10% wt Mn
$Pd-MnO_2/Al_2O_3$	1% wt Pd 10% wt MnO_2

The decomposition of ozone depends on catalyst, contact time and running period. The relationship between face velocities and conversion rates are shown in Figure 3. Linear trends are observed in the figures. Quederni et al. found that the ozone decomposition over porous media follows the first order reaction. We applied the first order model with Arrhenius temperature dependence to analyze the ozone conversion data.

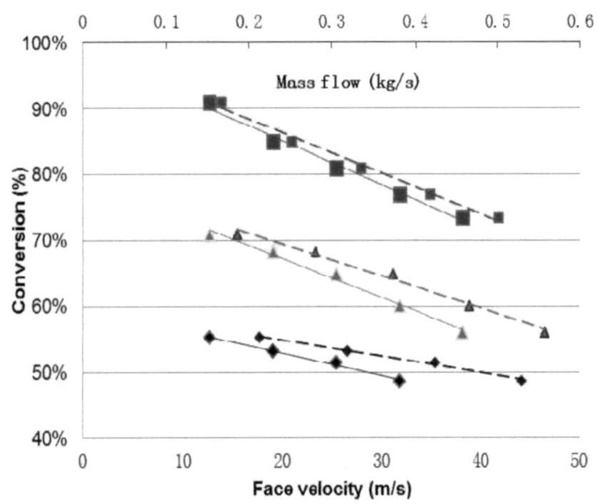

Figure 3. Ozone conversions at different temperatures and face velocities

The Arrhenius fit for 1% Pd/Al_2O_3 catalyst is shown in Figure 4 as a sample of the analysis. Comparison of rate constant and activation energy were listed in Table 2. As we observe, activation energy for each catalyst were small, the activity of each catalyst would depend on the catalyst property. Reaction constant, k, was calculated for both per weight of precious metal and per precious metal atom. As seen, mixture of Pd and MnO2 has the highest per atom reaction constant. This is consistent with its best performance in terms of ozone decomposition among catalysts.

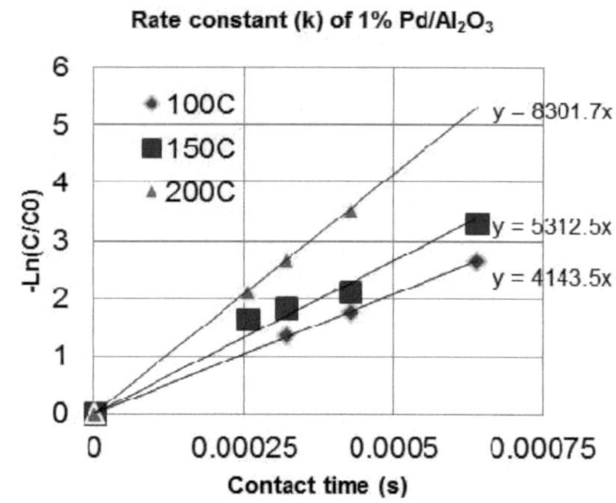

Figure 4. Arrhenius fit for 1% Pd/Al_2O_3

Ozone concentration is of key importance to on board passengers, especially to airline employees who log far more hours than typical passengers. Therefore, ozone converter aging performance should be tested carefully. An MFEC ozone converter aging has been performed at a worst case situation of 10 ppmv concentration, which is reported as the highest ambient ozone concentration at altitude. In this test, after a 42-day continuous run, MFEC showed a decrease in catalytic performance. However, the final conversion rate meets health restrictions by most organizations.

Table 2. Ozone Decomposition Catalysts

Catalysts	**Rate constant k (1/s)**			**Ea (kJ/mol)**	**k per wt. of PM (1/s*gram PM)**
	100C	150C	200C		
1% Pd/Al_2O_3	885	1640	4530	23.6	31,701
1% Pd/SiO_2	574	1463	4403	29.7	30,812
1% Ag/Al_2O_3	1921	3001	4527	12.5	31,679
10% MnO_2/Al_2O_3	3801	4304	4710	3.2	3,296
1% Pd-10% MnO_2/Al_2O_3	4144	5313	8302	10.0	5,810

Conclusion

Microfibrous material, as a novel heterogeneous catalytic converter, has shown great promise in improving aircraft cabin air quality. Microfibrous material has provided a large surface area to volume ratio of entrapped catalyst. This attribute helps with the demand of volume of air handling system in a limited space. Meanwhile, microfibrous catalytic converters guarantee high conversion rate of common cabin pollutant, including ozone, CO, VOC and other vapor phase toxic chemical. By further engineering design, microfibrous entrapped catalyst and sorbent (MFEC/S) materials can be applied as a compact system for the benefit of aircraft cabin air.

Acknowledgements

This work is supported by U.S. Army Tank-Automotive Research, Development and Engineering Center (TARDEC). Contract No. W56HZV-05-C-0686. The author would like to thank Mr. Ronald Putt and Troy Barron for technical assistance.

Reference

1. Harris, D., D. Cahela, and B. Tatarchuk, "Wet layup and sintering of metal-containing microfibrous composites for chemical processing opportunities," *Composites Part A: Applied Science and Manufacturing,* 32(8):1117-26, 2001.
2. R. Sothen and B. Tatarchuk, "A semi-empirical pressure drop model: part I- pleated filters," *HVAC&R Research*, 11: 14-6, 2008.
3. National Research Council, "The airliner cabin environment and health of passenger and crew," *National Academy Press,* Washington, DC, 2002. R.
4. R. Kalluri, D. Cachela and B. Tatarchuk, "Comparative heterogeneous contacting efficiency in fixed bed reactors: opportunities for new microstructured systems," *Applied Catalysis B: Environmental* 90 (2009) 507-515.
5. R. B. Bird, W.E Stewart and E.N. Lightfoot, "Transport Phenomena," pg 200, John Wiley & Sons, 1960.
6. G. F. Froment and K. B. Bischoff, "Chemical Reactor Analysis and Design," pg 181, John Wiley & Sons, 1979.
7. R. M. Heck and R.J. Farrauto, Catalytic Air Pollution Control: Commercial Technology, Van Nostrand Reinhold, New York, 1995.
8. E. Tronconi and A. Beretta, Catal. Today 52 (1991) 249-258.
9. E. H. Hunt, D. R. Space, "The airplane cabin environment-issues pertaining to flight attendant comfort," *International in-flight service management organization conference*, Canada, November, 1994
10. R. Kalluri, D. Cachela, and B. Tatarchuk, "Microfibrous entrapped small particle adsorbents for high efficiency heterogeneous contacting," *Separation and Purification Technology* 62(2008)304-316.
11. R. K. Duggirala, C. J. Roy, S. M. Saeidi, J. Khodadadi, D. R. Cahela, and B. J. Tatarchuck, "Pressure Drop Predictions for Microfibrous Flows using CFD," *Journal of Fluids Engineering,* Vol. 130, July 2008, 13 pages (DOI: 10.1115/1.2948363).
12. R. R. Kalluri, R. K., Duggirala, D. R. Cahela, C. J. Roy, and B. J. Tatarchuk, "CFD Analysis of Mass Transfer Enhancement Due to Inert Structures Present in Fluid Flow Paths in Heterogeneous Contacting Systems," manuscript submitted to *Computers and Chemical Engineering*, June 2008.
13. R. K. Duggirala, C. J. Roy, R. Kalluri, H. Yang, D. R. Cahela, and B. J. Tatarchuk, "Computational Fluid Dynamics Simulations of Desulfurization using Catalytic Particles Embedded in a Matrix of Sinter-Bonded Microfibers," manuscript in preparation for submission to *Chemical Engineering Science*.
14. NASA GASP (Global Atmospheric Sampling Program) Aircraft Observations, 1975Mar-1979Jul

Enhanced Electrochemical Performance of Li-ion Batteries With Cu-SPB as Conductive Agent

***Umer Farooq*[1, 2], *Adnan Yaqub*[1, 2], *Syed Atif Pervez*[1, 2], *Chil-Hoon Doh*[1, 2]**
[1]University of Science and Technology, Daejeon,305-333,South Korea
[2]Korea Electrotechnology Research Institute, Changwon, 642-120, South Korea.

Abstract: *Lithium-ion batteries are considered to be the best available energy storage technology in today's electronics, upcoming EVs and high energy storage grid stations. These commercially used Li-ion batteries have graphite as negative electrode material but it offers limited theoretical capacity of 372mAh/g. Therefore some alternative anode materials are required to replace traditional graphite. In recent years, an impressive research has been conducted to introduce the Silicon (Si) as anode material in lithium ion batteries on commercial level. Many factors like electrolyte, binder, electrode composition ratio etc play a key role in electrochemical performance of an electrode [1].*

In this work, we conducted a comprehensive study to examine the electrochemical performance of Si based anode material with a novel Cu-SPB conductive material. Nanosized Si/Graphite composite was synthesized in first step by using solid state method. Afterwards, this nanosized Si/Grpahite powder was tested for battery application with Cu-SPB. We examined structural dimensions of electrode composite using field emission electron microscopy (FESEM) and elemental mapping using energy dispersive x-ray spectroscopy (EDS). Phase analysis was carried out using x-ray diffraction (XRD). Introduction of Cu-SPB showed improvement in all electrochemical parameters and this improvement is attributed to high conductive nature of Cu.[2]

In conclusion, the electrochemical performance of an electrode highly depends on selection of conductive material in electrode. Cu-SPB exhibited remarkable improvement with Si as anode active material in terms of all electrochemical properties like specific discharge capacity, columbic efficiency and stable capacity retention.

References

1. H. Wu, Y. Cui, *Nano Today* 7, 414, 2012.

2. M.Yoshio, T.Tsumura, N.Dimov, *J. of power sources* 163, 215, 2006.

Analysis of Durability of Monolithic Catalyst for Reforming Gasoline Using Accelerated Aging

Sung-Baek Cho, Jae-In Lee, Hyunjin Ji
The Energetics and Defense Materials R&D Institute
Agency for Defense Development
Yuseong P.O Box 35, Dae-Jeon, 305-600 Korea

Abstract:

Because of popularization of the fuel cell, generation and supply technology of the hydrogen becomes more important. The gasoline reforming technology has many merits such as good mobility, availability, serviceability in comparison with other technologies and the catalyst for reforming is one of the most important things for this technology. For developing the new catalyst, to evaluate the performance is easily conducted by analyzing reforming gas, but to evaluate the durability is difficult because the catalyst generally has the durability of several thousand hours. Although various reasons can cause degradation of catalyst, thermally deactivation is the most dominant point because of very high operation temperature. Therefore, in this study, the monolithic catalyst was acceleratedly aged by applying excessive high temperature so that long time aging can be simulated during short time and then analyzed to know the dominant reason. The surface state and specific surface area were analyzed by using SEM, BET and the dominant reason of degradation was found. From this analysis, we were able to expect the durability easily during short time and confirmed degradation of catalyst performance and durability through reforming test during long time.

Keywords: reforming; gasoline; catalyst; durability; accelerated aging

Introduction

Various electronic devices such as personal communication equipment, operation computer are used for effective modern warfare. The stable energy supply for these devices is very important and winning of warfare is impossible without stable energy sources. The small diesel electric generators have been used for main energy sources of military[1]. Small diesel generator has many advantages because it is small and light to move and fuel supply is so easy. However, it has also fatal disadvantages as military power sources because it makes tremendous noise of 90~100dB when it operates and it has low fuel efficiency of 30%[1,2]. These two disadvantages were more stressed in real battle field. The tremendous noise makes application difficult and can induce emotional distress of our forces. In addition, it can increase detection rate of a location of our forces remarkably. Low efficiency can also cause a distress as using electric devices when the supply is breaking. Recently, Proton Exchange Membrane Fuel Cell(PEMFC) power sources for military becomes highlight as a substitute for the diesel generator[1,2]. PEMFC power source generates very low noise and has good fuel efficiency in comparison with the diesel generator. Therefore, it can decrease detection rate and improve safety. However, it has serious problem to need the hydrogen gas as fuel in battle field. In case of civil installation PEMFC power source, it is supplied with the hydrogen gas easily through structured infra, but it is impossible to supply hydrogen gas to mobile PEMFC power source through infra in battle field. To solve this problem, fuel processor technology to convert fuel to into the hydrogen gas has been researched and various catalysts have been developed for it [3]. We find the degradation of the catalyst during performance test as shown figure 1. This means that the durability is as important as the performance. However, to evaluate the durability is difficult and needs very long time. Therefore, in this study, we analyzed main factors of the degradation using accelerated aging during short time.

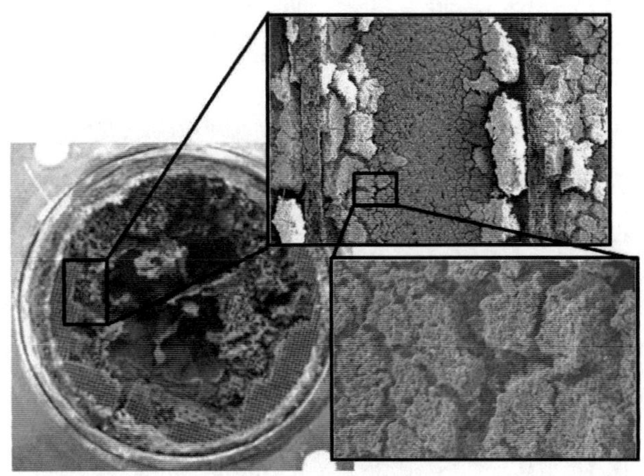

Figure 1. The degradation of catalyst during performance test.

Experiment

Accelerated aging: The rate of chemical reactions is usually expressed by a Arrhenius relationship as shown equation (1).

$$\mathrm{Re}\,actionRate = \frac{\Delta}{t} = Ke^{-E_a/RT} \quad (1)$$

Here, t is the reaction time, Δ the chemical variation, K the proportional constant, R the gas constant(1.986 calories per mole), Ea the energy of activation of the reaction, and T the temperature in degrees Kelvin(273 plus the degrees Centigrade). If the chemical variation at temperature, T1 during time, t1 is same with the chemical variation at temperature T2 during time t2, the equation (2) is induced from equation (1).

$$\Delta = t_1 e^{-E_a / RT_1} = t_2 e^{-E_a / RT_{21}} \quad (2)$$

Therefore, t2 is described as equation (3)

$$t_2 = t_1 e^{-\frac{E_a}{R}(\frac{1}{T_1} - \frac{1}{T_2})} \quad (3)$$

Experiment: Cordierite monoliths with a cell density of 900 cpsi were cut to obtain samples with 144 channels/cross section as shown figure 2. Monoliths were wash-coated with alumina by repeated dipping in slurry of finely grounded alumina powder, diluted nitric acid solution, and pseudobohemite. La_2O_3 was added to the wash-coat by impregnation, followed by calcinations at 600°C for 3h. The mixtures with Pt, Rh, Pd and mixed metal oxide were added to the monolith using the novel DP method with urea. Several cycles were needed to reach a target loading of 20 wt% of perovskite. After each cycle, the monolithic samples were calcined at 600°C for 3h [4].

Figure 2. The samples which have a cell density of 900 cpsi and 144 channels/cross section.

The prepared samples were accelerated aged in the condition of table 1 using electric furnace as shown figure 3. Each 5 samples were used for each test condition.

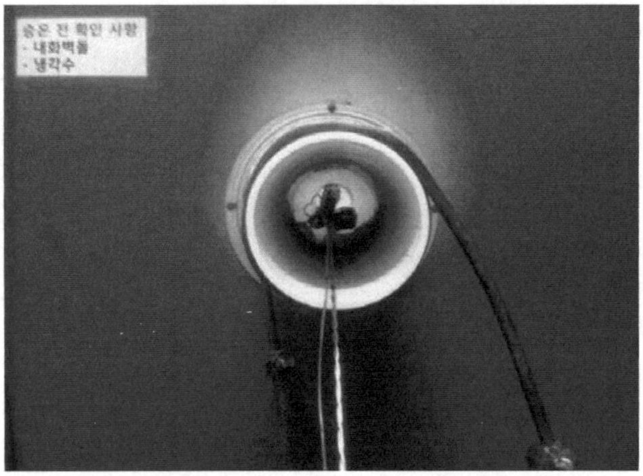

Figure 3. The samples were accelerated aged in the electric furnace at atmosphere

Table 1. The conditions of aging

No.	Temperature (°C)	Time (hour)
1	650	1
2	650	2
3	650	4
4	650	8
5	800	1
6	800	2
7	800	4
8	800	8
9	1000	1
10	1000	2
11	1000	4
12	1000	8

Experiment Results

Thermally induced degradation of catalysts results from loss of catalytic surface area due to crystallite growth of the catalytic phase, loss of support area due to support collapse and of catalytic surface area due to pore collapse on crystallites of the active phase, and chemical transformations of catalytic phases to non-catalytic phases[5]. These degradations take place at high reaction temperatures and are generally accelerated by the presence of water vapor.

Figure 4(a) shows the results of SEM analysis carried out over the fresh catalyst. The fresh catalyst has absolutely uniform surface coated by the mixture and there are no crack due to support collapse and no chemical transformation of the catalytic phases.

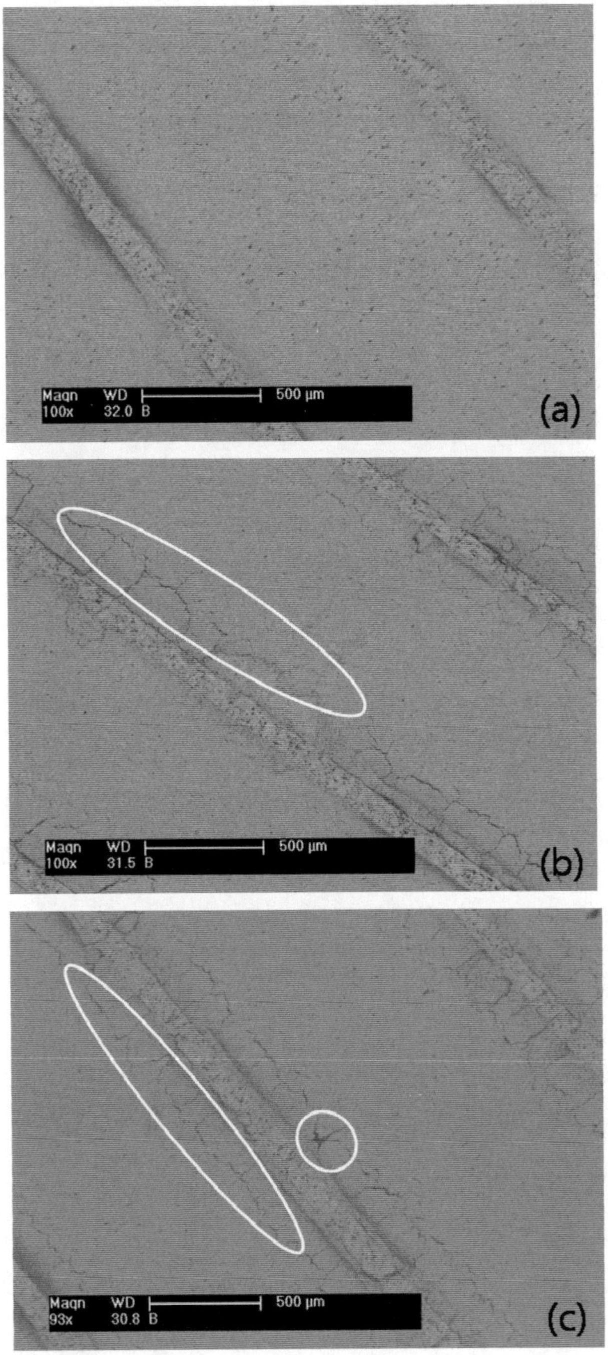

Figure 4. SEM images of (a) fresh catalyst, (b) catalyst aged 4 h at 1000℃ and (c) catalyst aged 8 h at 1000℃

In contrast, figure 4(b) shows the results of SEM analysis carried out over the catalyst aged 4 h at 1000 °C. This catalyst has non-uniform surface due to chemical transformations of catalytic phase to non-catalytic phase and there are some cracks due to support collapse. Figure 4(c) shows the results of SEM analysis carried out over the catalyst aged 8 h at 1000 °C. This catalyst has excessively non-uniform surface due to extensive chemical transformations and there are many cracks and some pore without catalytic mixture due to support collapse. These results of SEM analysis are confirmed by results of the BET SSA measurements as shown figure 5.

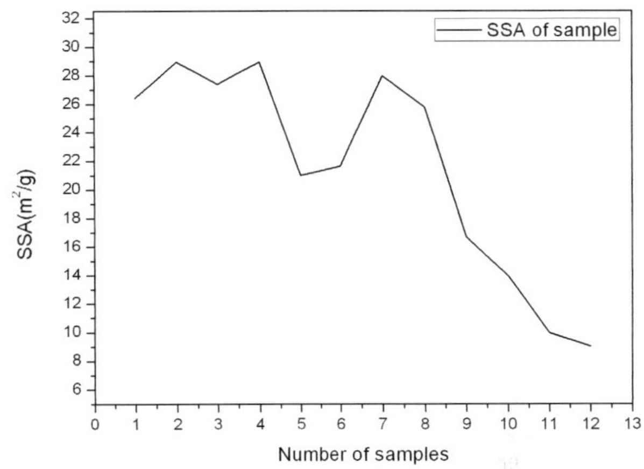

Figure 5. BET SSA measurements of the aged catalysts

The catalysts which were aged 1h, 2 h, 4 h, 8 h at 650 °C, and 1h, 2 h, 4 h, 8 h at 800 °C maintains the normal SSA level between 20 m^2g^{-1} and 30 m^2g^{-1}. However, the catalysts which were aged 1 h at 1000°C have the SSA of 16.7 m^2g^{-1}, the catalysts which were aged 2 h at 1000 °C have the SSA of 13.985 m^2g^{-1}, the catalysts which were aged 4 h at 1000 °C have 9.994 m^2g^{-1}, and finally the catalysts which were aged 8 h at 1000 °C have the SSA of 9.0 m^2g^{-1}. Therefore, these results mean that this catalyst can operate normally under 800 °C, but have degradation above 1000 °C. This decrement of SSA is caused by active area loss of catalysts due to chemical transformation of catalytic phase and support collapse.

Conclusion

We used the accelerated aging to analyze the durability and the main reasons of degradation of the catalyst in short time. As a result, we confirmed the main condition and reasons of degradation and we could decide the operation condition of the catalyst for longer use.

References

1. J. C. Amphlett, R. F. Mann, B. A. Peppley, P. R. Roberge, A. Rodrigues, J. P. Salvador , "Simulation of a 250kW diesel fuel processor/PEM fuel cell system," *Journal of Power Sources*, vol. 106, pp. 16-20, 2002.
2. Ashok S. Patil, Terry G. Dubois, Nicholas Sifer, Elizabeth Bostic, Kristopher Gardner, Michel Quah, Christopher Bolton, "Portable fuel cell systems for America's army : technology transition to the field," *Journal of Power Sources*, Vol. 136, pp. 220-225, 2004.

3. J. Mathiak, A. Heinzel, J. Roes, Th. Kalk, H. Kraus, H. Brandt, "Coupling of a 2.5 kW steam reformer with a 1 kW PEM fuel cell," *Journal of Power Sources*, vol. 131, pp. 112-119, 2004.
4. Stefano Cimino, Raffaele Pirone, Gennaro Russo, "Thermal Stability of Perovskite-Based Monolithic Reactors in the Catalytic Combustion of Methane," *Ind. Eng. Chem. Res.*, Vol. 40, no. 1, pp. 80-85, 2001.
5. Calvin H. Bartholomew, "Mechanisms of catalyst deactivation," *Applied Catalysis A : General*, Vol. 212, pp. 17-60, 2001.

A Study on Automatic Control Algorithms for Military Fuel Cell Power Source System Using a Fuel Processor

Jae-In Lee, Hyunki Yoon, Sang-Hyeon Ha, Sung-Baek Cho
The Energetics and Defense Materials R&D Institute
Agency for Defense Development
Yuseong P.O Box 35, Dae-Jeon, 305-600 Korea

Abstract:

The Pure hydrogen gas was used for the nonmilitary proton exchange membrane (PEM) fuel cell system which is installed in the building. However, in case of military, the hydrogen is not suitable for the PEM fuel cell system due to the difficulty of supply and storage. Therefore, the fuel processing technology which generates the hydrogen gas from various kind of fuel was being gradually applied to the military PEM fuel cell system. In addition, the nonmilitary PEM fuel cell system was connected with the huge power system so that load dynamics of it was not important problem. However, the military PEM fuel cell system was not connected with another power system and operated independently in the warfare field so that low load dynamics of it becomes important problem and the hybrid system between the fuel cell and secondary battery was needed to solve this problem. Thus, the military PEM fuel cell must need various automatic controls essentially. In this paper, we researched and developed various algorithms to control fuel processor, fuel cell stack operation, hybrid operation of secondary battery, various BOP and system. Finally, we applied these algorithms to the military PEM fuel cell power source system and demonstrated automatic control algorithms.

Keywords: Automatic control algorithm, Military PEM fuel cell power system, Fuel processor

Introduction

The diesel electric generators have been used for military power source. However, it has some disadvantages as military power sources such as tremendous noise of 90~100 dB and low fuel efficiency of 30 %[1-3]. The tremendous noise makes application difficult as shown figure 1.

The Proton Exchange Membrane Fuel Cell(PEMFC) has better energy conversion efficiency and makes less noise than the diesel electric generator. Therefore, a mobile PEMFC system can become safe and effective power source for battle field[1-3]. However, there is a serious problem to apply PEMFC system to mobile power source for military because it needs the hydrogen gas as fuel. It is remarkably difficult to store and carry the hydrogen gas unlike fossil fuels such as diesel and gasoline. Thus, to solve this problem, we researched and developed PEMFC system which has a fuel processor to convert a gasoline into the hydrogen gas[4]. Using gasoline is good solution because it was generally used for military vehicle and easy to store and carry. However, it is difficult to set temperature conditions of gasoline fuel processor and the heat generated at fuel processor influences other components such as secondary battery, DC/DC converter and balance of plant(BOP). A lot of BOP are added to system to solve and it makes system complex. In this study, we developed automatic control algorithm and program to operate the complex system[4,5].

Figure 1. Military Diesel generator operation

Fuel Cell power system

Fuel cell system consists of the fuel processor, high temperature PEMFC module, power control system and a lot of BOPs such as pump, blower, pre-heater and glow plug as shown figure 2.

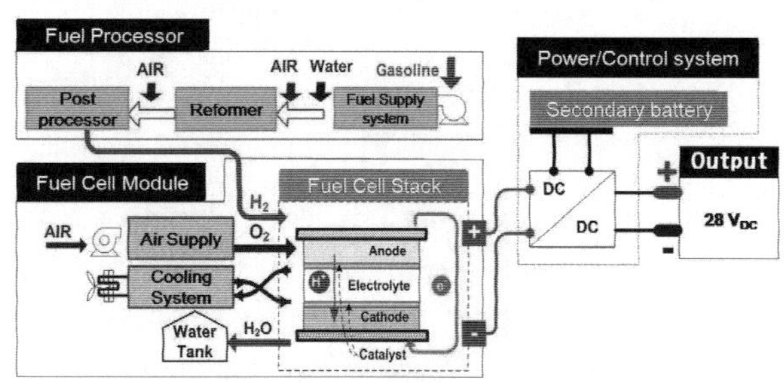

Figure 2. Concept diagram of fuel cell power system for military

After a heater heats a reformer of the fuel processor to the level of catalytic combustion, gasoline is supplied to reformer and causes combustion. After catalytic combustion, partial oxidation(POX) reaction is occurred and then, auto thermal reaction(ATR) is followed to convert gasoline into H2. After that, a postprocessor increases the purity of H2 gas. While fuel processor goes to ready, HT-PEMFC is also heated to normal operation temperature by pre-heater. After fuel processor and HT-PEMFC are ready, the HT-PEMFC is linked with the fuel processor and generates the electricity. The generated electricity charges a secondary battery through input DC/DC converter and charged secondary battery is discharged through output DC/DC converter. This control sequence is realized and optimized by using test bench as shown figure 3.

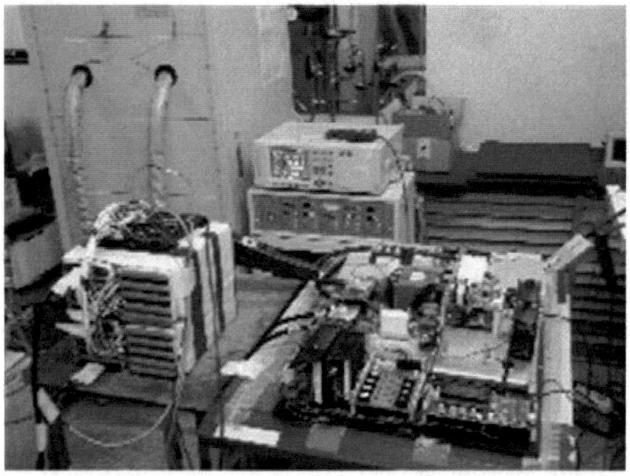

Figure 3. Test bench for optimizing automatic control sequence of fuel cell power system

Algorithm Development

Main Algorithm: Figure 4 shows the main algorithm of system. After start signal input, system checks BOPs and communication through initializing and then, it becomes stand-by state. After stand-by, the fuel processor and HT-PEMFC are heated to become ready state. After the fuel processor and HT-PEMFC become ready-state, two components are linked together and generate electricity. After generating, the system stops to operate through stop procedure.

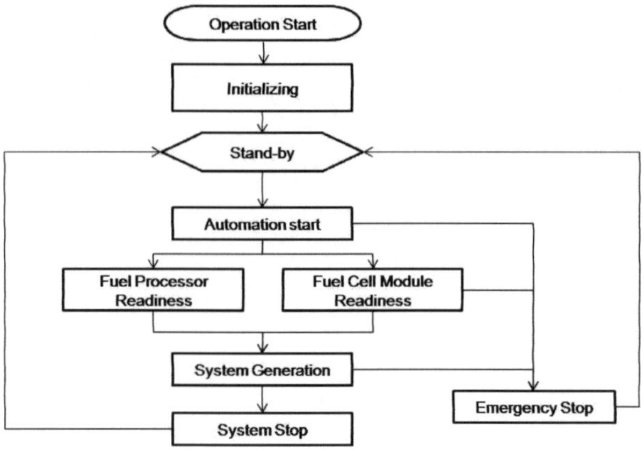

Figure 4. Algorithm diagram for the main sequence

Fuel Processor: Figure 5 shows the algorithm for the fuel processor. After start signal of processor input, a gasoline evaporator is heated to gasoline combustion temperature, and then a glow plug start to turn on/off repeatedly. After the temperature of evaporator increase to enough level, gasoline and air are supplied to the reformer and catalytic combustion is occurred. After catalytic combustion, the fuel of POX condition is supplied and POX is occurred. After the temperature of a postprocessor increase to DI water supply condition, the DI water is supplied to the reformer and ATR mode is started. After temperatures of all components are stable and ready-state, the fuel processor sends ready signal to system.

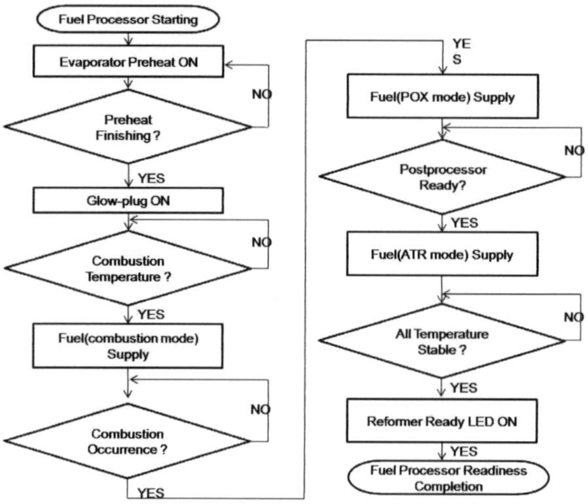

Figure 5. Algorithm diagram for the fuel processor control

HT-PEMFC Module: Figure 6 shows the algorithm for the HT-PEMFC Module. HT-PEMFC module is controlled by using 4 modes of ready, heat-up, normal operation and cool down modes. In the beginning, the system distinguishes a state between the first operation and ready on the basis of a temperature of stack outlet, and then if the state is the first operation, the module starts heat-up mode. After the stack is heated enough, the module becomes the ready mode and sends the link signal to the system. After linking with the fuel processor, the module operates under the normal operation mode and generates stable electricity. After stop signal is inputted, the module is operated under cool down mode to prevent the stack degradation and finally stopped.

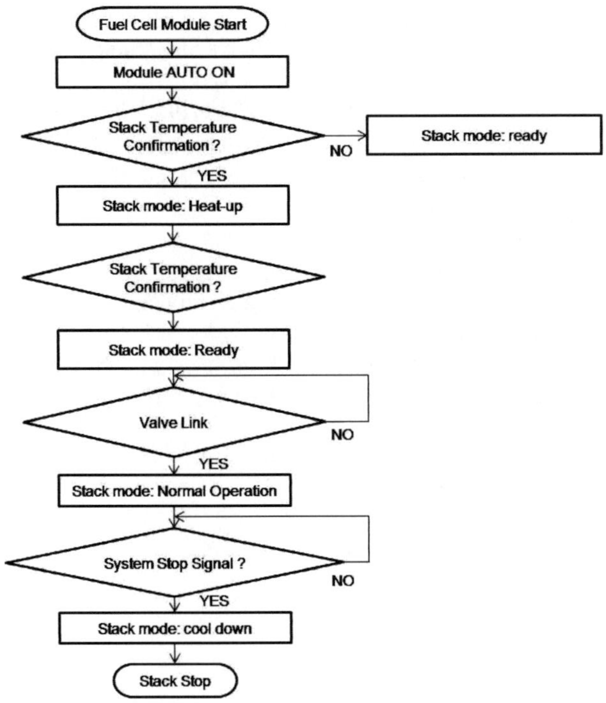

Figure 6. Algorithm diagram for the fuel cell module

Generation: Figure 7 shows the algorithm for generation. If the fuel processor and fuel cell module are ready, two components are linked together to generate. After a link valve becomes open to supply the fuel cell module with H2 gas and the electric switch turns on, the system can confirm the voltage of the stack. If the voltage of the stack is the normal state, input DC/DC converter turns on and the system confirms if the stack can be capable of the initial load. After the temperature of the stack increased to normal state through generation, the system generates stable electricity and charges secondary battery.

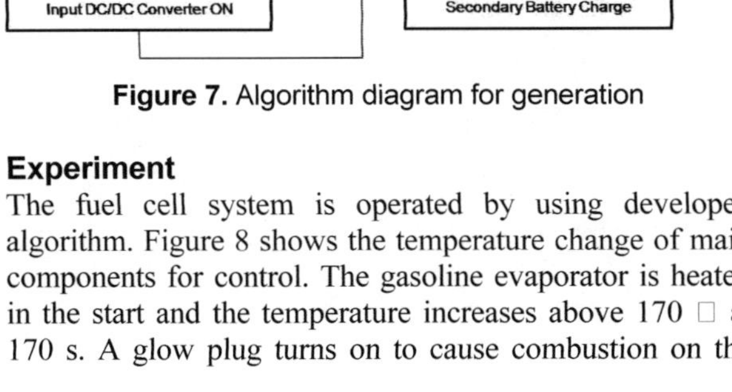

Figure 7. Algorithm diagram for generation

Experiment

The fuel cell system is operated by using developed algorithm. Figure 8 shows the temperature change of main components for control. The gasoline evaporator is heated in the start and the temperature increases above 170 □ at 170 s. A glow plug turns on to cause combustion on the reformer from this time. The combustion on the reformer starts at 190 s and the temperature rapidly increases to maximum 770 □. After combustion, the system supply the reformer with the fuel of POX mode and the temperature decrease to 500 □ and increase slowly again. The temperature of the postprocessor increases above 400 □ at 510 s and the reformer turns to ATR mode and the system supplies the reformer with DI water. After supply of DI water, the temperature of postprocessor decreases to 300 □ and becomes stable, and the temperature of reformer stops to increase and becomes stable at 700 □ level. Every components of the fuel processor becomes stable and the fuel processor becomes ready state at 900 s. While the fuel processor turns to ready state, the pre-heater of fuel cell module is ignited and start to heat the module at 480 s. After the module is heat above 130 □ and becomes ready at 1550 s, the module is linked with the fuel processor and generates electricity.

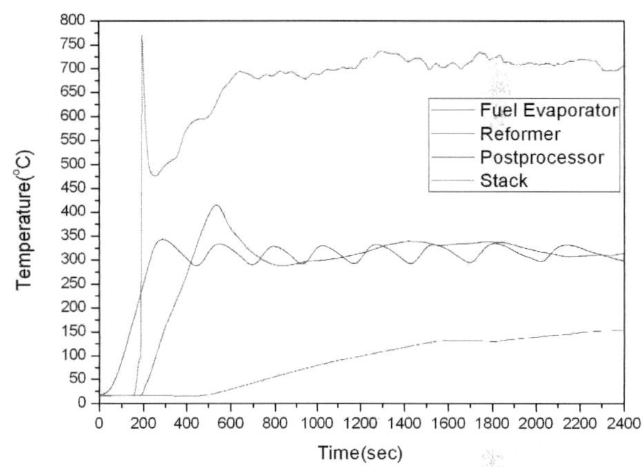

Figure 8. Temperature change of main components for control

Figure 9 shows the discharge result of the system. The system shows stable operation on the various conditions such as regular power, alternative power, and maximum power.

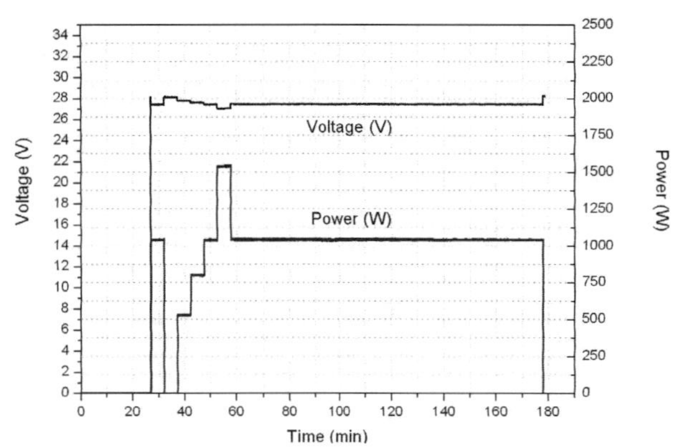

Figure 9. The discharge result of the system

Conclusion

We developed the auto control algorithm of the PEMFC power system for military which has the fuel processor. After we developed the main algorithm, we researched the algorithms of each component and combined them. As a results, we confirmed that the fuel cell system operate and generate stable electricity.

References

1. Jon M. Moore, J. Barry Lakeman, Gary O. Mepsted, "Development of a PEM fuel cell powered portable field generator for the dismounted soldier," *Journal of Power Sources*, vol. 106, pp. 16-20, 2002.
2. Ashok S. Patil, Terry G. Dubois, Nicholas Sifer, Elizabeth Bostic, Kristopher Gardner, Michel Quah, Christopher Bolton, "Portable fuel cell systems for America's army : technology transition to the field," *Journal of Power Sources*, Vol. 136, pp. 220-225, 2004.
3. J. C. Amphlett, R. F. Mann, B. A. Peppley, P. R. Roberge, A. Rodrigues, J. P. Salvador , "Simulation of a 250kW diesel fuel processor/PEM fuel cell system," *Journal of Power Sources*, vol. 106, pp. 16-20, 2002.
4. J. Mathiak, A. Heinzel, J. Roes, Th. Kalk, H. Kraus, H. Brandt, "Coupling of a 2.5 kW steam reformer with a 1 kW PEM fuel cell," *Journal of Power Sources*, vol. 131, pp. 112-119, 2004.
5. Jay T. Pukrushpan, Huei Peng, Anna G. Stefanopoulou, "Control-Oriented Modeling and Analysis for Automotive Fuel Cell Systems,"*Transactions of the ASME*, Vol. 126, pp. 14-25, March 2004.

Evaluation of Membrane Electrode Assembly Materials for High-Temperature Proton Exchange Membrane Fuel Cells

Lung-Yu Sung [a*], Kan-Lin Hsueh [a,b], Reiko Ohara [c], Chao-Ho Lan [c], Wen-Sheng Chang [a]

[a] Green Energy and Environment Research Labs, Industrial Technology Research Institute, Hsinchu 310, Taiwan
[b] Department of Energy Engineering, National United University, Miaoli 360, Taiwan
[c] Green Energy & Ecology Research Labs., Industrial Technology Research Institute, Tainan 734, Taiwan

Abstract: *The cell performances of three commercial high-temperature MEAs (membrane-electrode assemblies) based on phosphoric acid-doped polymer membranes (PBI, ABPBI, Pyridine) were studied in the temperature range of 120~190 °C without humidification. These MEAs have a five-layer structure with an active area of 25 cm^2. The results of the cell performance tests indicated that the best operating temperature was between 180 °C and 190 °C. The maximum output power density was obtained in the voltage range of 0.45~0.5 V. The cell current densities of these MEAs under the conditions of 180 °C, 0.6 V, and H_2/air, were 215 mA/cm^2, 380 mA/cm^2, and 370 mA/cm^2. From the electrochemical impedance spectroscopy (EIS) analysis, we found that the charge transfer resistance and the cell internal resistance were decreased as the cell temperature increased. These MEAs can reach steady state after a 24-hour activation process, as indicated from the current-voltage polarization curve. The best cell assembly pressure was 60 kgf-cm, which can provide good performance and sealing of the cell. The cell current-voltage curve was not affected by using gaskets of different thicknesses (300 μm and 500 μm).*

Keywords: High-temperature PEM fuel cell; polymer membrane; Membrane-electrode assembly; Phosphoric acid.

Introduction

The low-temperature proton exchange membrane fuel cell (LT-PEMFC) has an operating temperature in the range of 60~80 °C. At these temperatures, the fuel cell can be quickly started. However, many technical challenges are also encountered in low temperature operation [1]. For example, a LT-PEMFC faces complicated thermal-water management, low CO tolerance (CO < 10 ppm), complex fuel processing, and slow oxygen reduction reaction (ORR) at the cathode. These technical barriers have hindered the commercialization of LT-PEMFC. Recently, the R&D direction of PEMFC is towards high temperature (> 100 ℃). The high temperature PEM fuel cell (HT-PEMFC) is operated in the range of 140~200 °C. Many technical problems associated with LT-PEMFCs can be overcome by using HT-PEMFCs. The application areas for HT-PEMFCs are wider than those for LT-PEMFCs. Currently, the membrane materials used in HT-PEMFCs can be classified into four categories: (1) modified perfluorosulphonic acid (PFSA) membranes [1,2], (2) alternative membranes based on partially fluorinated and aromatic hydrocarbon polymers [3], (3) organic-inorganic composite polymer membranes [4], and (4) acid-base polymer membranes [5,6]. The zip-unzip movement of the H^+ proton migration inside the acid-base polymer membrane is due to the hydrogen bonding or ionic bonding of the acidic functional groups. Hydrogen protons can be transferred without water. This mechanism is the so-called hopping mechanism. Because the membrane water content is reduced, the proton conductivity of HT-PEM is not decreased as low as LT-PEM, Nafion. The acid-base polymer has good thermal stability, chemical stability, and mechanical strength. Therefore, acid-base polymer membranes have been widely used in HT-PEMFCs.

The purpose of this study was to evaluate the cell performance of three commercial high-temperature MEA materials (PBI, ABPBI, and Pyridine) using the current-voltage polarization curve (IV) / current-power curve (IP) and electrochemical impedance spectroscopy (EIS) techniques and to determine the best operating conditions for HT-PEMFCs (e.g., activation procedure, assembly pressure, and operating temperature).

Experimental setup and procedures

A single HT-PEMFC (25 cm^2) was used for all the experiments (Fig. 1a). The flow-field plate with serpentine flow channels was POCO graphite (Fig. 1b). The key component of the fuel cell, HT-MEA, had a five-layer structure (one proton exchange membrane, two catalyst layers, and two gas diffusion layers). The active catalyst area was of dimensions of 5 cm × 5 cm. Two types of gas diffusion layers (GDLs), carbon paper and carbon cloth, were tested. Three types of polymer membranes were tested. This study is focused on PBI, ABPBI, and Pyridine membrane, as depicted in Fig. 2. The details and specifications of the HT-PEMFC are listed in Table 1.

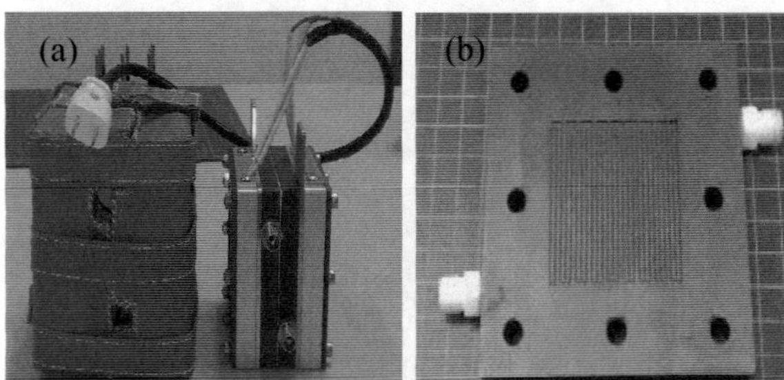

Figure 1. (a) High temperature PEM fuel cell (active area: 25 cm^2); (b) flow-field plate and serpentine flow channels.

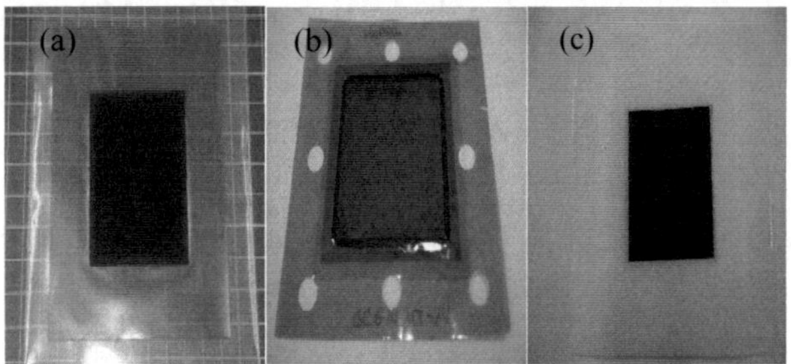

Figure 2. Five-layer membrane electrode assembly with different types of membrane: (a) PBI; (b) ABPBI; (c) Pyridine.

Table 1. Components and specifications of HT-PEMFC

Items	**MEA-1**	**MEA-2**	**MEA-3**
Structure of MEA	5 layer	5 layer	5 layer
Active area	5cm x 5cm	5cm x 5cm	5cm x 5cm
PEM membrane	PBI/H_3PO_4	ABPBI/H_3PO_4	Pyridine/H_3PO_4
Thickness of membrane	40 μm	20-80 μm	60-80 μm
Types of GDL	Carbon cloth	Carbon paper	Carbon cloth
Flow field plate	POCO		
Configuration of flow channels	Serpentine, 65 cm (length)		
Flow channel width/depth/interval	1 mm/1 mm/1 mm		

A fuel cell testing station (HEPHAS, HTS-125) was used for this study (Fig. 3). The reacting gases (H_2, air) were used without humidification. The flow rates of the gases were controlled by mass flow controllers (Brooks 5850e). The cell operating temperature (120~190 °C) was controlled by four heating rods (40 W). The cathode and anode current collectors were connected to an electronic load (Scribner model 890e). This testing system can measure the IV/IP curves either at constant current mode or at constant voltage mode. The system also can measure in-situ EIS (Scribner model 880). The details of the testing conditions for HT-PEMFC are listed in Table 2.

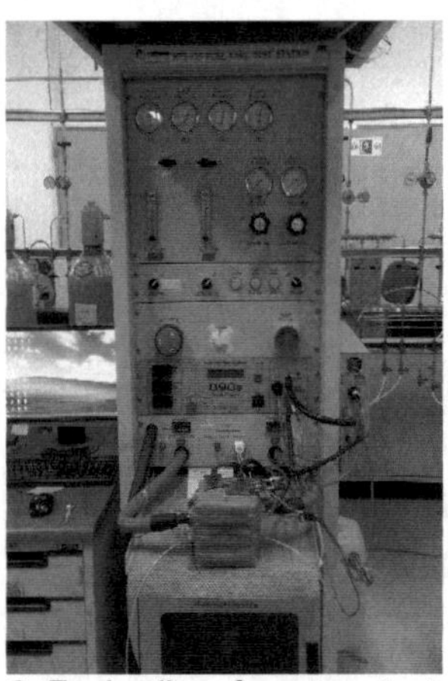

Figure 3. Fuel cell performance test station.

Table 2. Test conditions of the HT-PEMFC

Items	Test conditions
Cell camping pressure	20~120 kgf-cm
Cell operation temp.	120~190 °C
Cell operation voltage	OCV~0.4 V
Gasket thickness	300 μm, 500 μm
Stoich. ratio	1.5 X (H_2), 3.0 X (air)
Humidity of H_2, air	Without humidification
Pressure of H_2, air	Ambient pressure
AC impedance measurement (EIS)	Frequency range (10 kHz ~ 0.1 Hz), Amplitude (5 mV)

Results and discussion

1. Cell activation and gasket thickness

For the cell to reach a steady state quickly, a series of activation steps was applied after cell assembly. This study used constant current mode (@ 200 mA/cm^2, 180 °C, H_2/air, and 24~64 hrs) in the activation procedure. The cell testing and analysis were started after the activation procedure.

Fig. 4 shows the IV polarization curves at different activation durations (24 hr and 64 hr). No significant difference was observed. The output current densities of both cells were 330 mA/cm^2 (@ 0.6 V). Although a longer activation period was recommended by the supplier, the cell reached its steady state after 24 hrs of activation. This achievement of steady state could be verified from the IV curves. A short activation period is beneficial to fuel savings and the reduction of operating cost.

Fig. 5 shows the IV polarization curves of cell with two different gasket thicknesses (300 μm and 500 μm) operated at 140 °C and 180 °C. No significant difference was observed. This lack of difference may be due to the gasket being soft PTFE. Although the gasket thickness was different, a similar contact resistance was obtained at fixed assembly pressure.

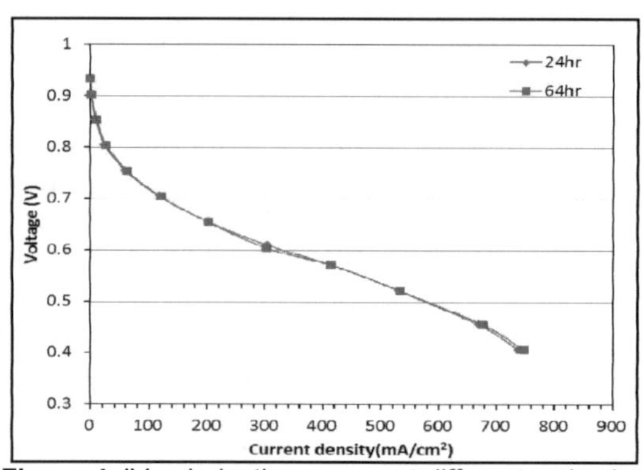

Figure 4. IV polarization curves at different activation periods (24 hr and 48 hr).

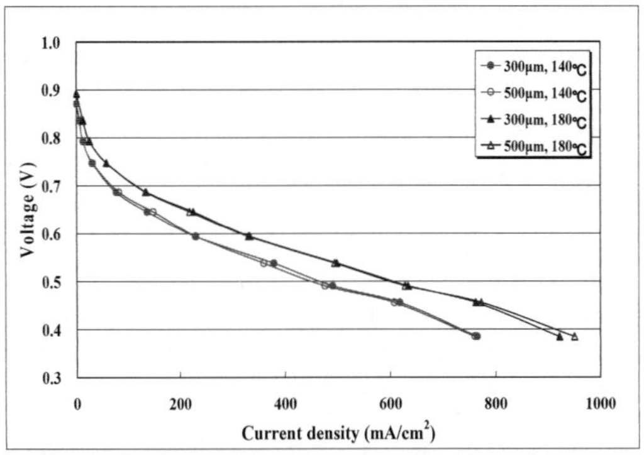

Figure 5. IV polarization curves at different thicknesses of the gasket (300 μm and 500 μm).

2. Effects of cell assembly pressure

The single cell used in this study was assembled in the order of end plate, current collector, flow plate, gasket, five-layer MEA, gasket, flow plate, current collector, and end plate. The assembly pressure applied on the cell significantly affects the contact resistance inside the cell. The contact resistance can be greatly reduced by increasing the assembly pressure. However, the excess pressure may change the porosity of the GDL, damage cell components, and reduce the cell performance. Figs. 6 and 7 are the IV curve and Nyquist plots at different cell assembly pressures. The cell output current density is closely related to the assembly pressure. The current densities were increased as the assembly pressures increased. At a cell voltage of 0.55 V, the current density was 420 mA/cm^2 (20 kgf-cm), 505 mA/cm^2 (40 kgf-cm), and 530 mA/cm^2 (60 kgf-cm). However, when the assembly pressure is greater than 60 kgf-cm, the current densities were decreased as the assembly pressure increased. The current density at high assembly pressure was 520 mA/cm^2 (80 kgf-cm), 510 mA/cm^2 (100 kgf-cm), and 485 mA/cm^2 (120 kgf-cm). A similar trend was observed from the Nyquist plot in Fig. 7. The optimal assembly pressure was 60 kgf-cm. At this pressure, a minimum charge transfer resistance (16.5 mΩ) was obtained. The cell internal resistance exhibited little variation (~4 mΩ) when the assembly pressure> 40 kgf-cm.

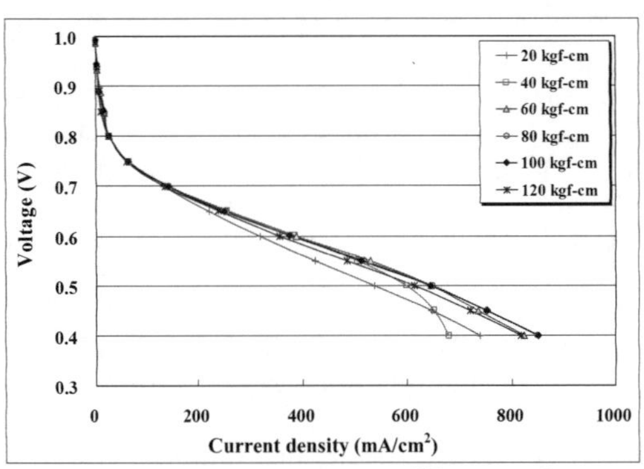

Figure 6. IV polarization curves at different cell assembly pressures (20~120 kgf-cm).

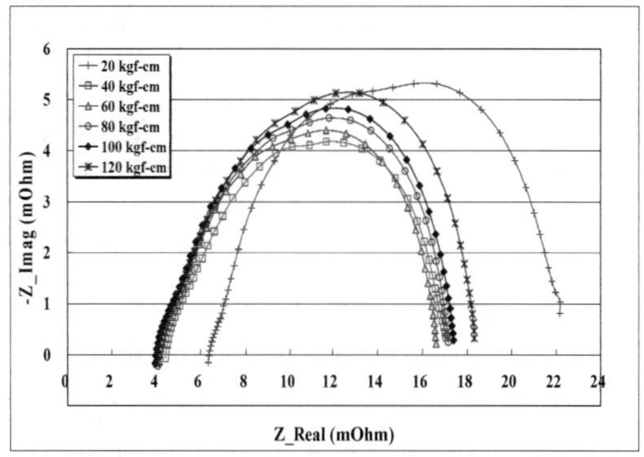

Figure 7. Nyquist plots of EIS measured at different cell assembly pressures (20~120 kgf-cm).

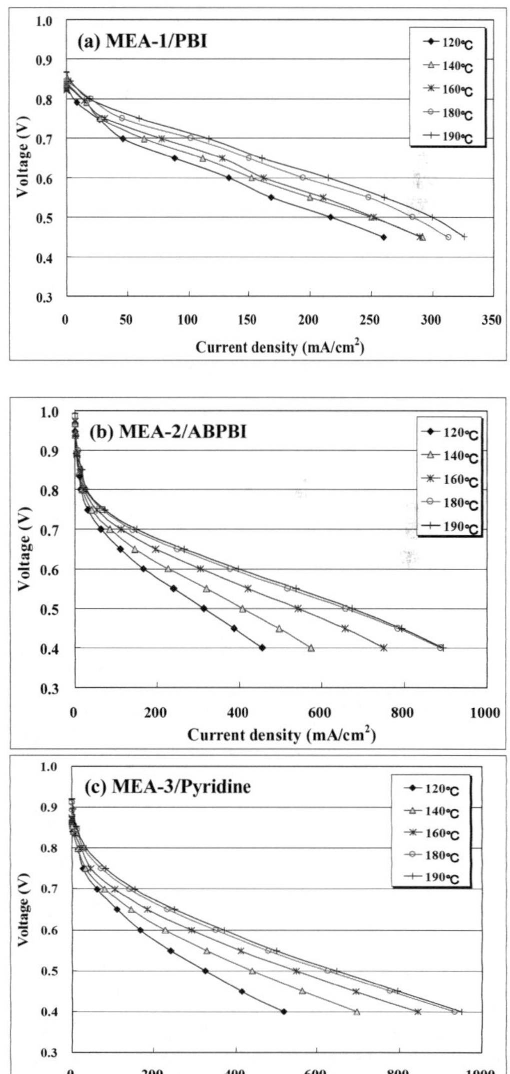

Figure 8. IV polarization curves at different cell temperatures (120~190 ℃) with three types of membrane: (a) PBI; (b) ABPBI; (c) Pyridine.

3. Effects of temperature on fuel cell performance

Figs. 8 and 9 show the IV curve and the Nyquist plot of the high-temperature fuel cell with three different membranes (PBI, ABPBI, and Pyridine). The cell operating temperatures considered were 120, 140, 160, 180, and 190 °C. The reacting gases (H_2/air) were not humidified. The scanning frequency of EIS ranged from 0.1 Hz to 10 kHz (amplitude: 5 mV). From Fig. 8, the IV curve of the HT-PEMFC had following characteristics. (1) A large activation over-potential was observed at low current density region (< 100 mA/cm^2). (2) No mass transfer limiting current density region was observed. This may be because the cell was operated at a high temperature (> 100 °C). At this temperature, no liquid water was accumulated (flooding) on the cathode. (3) The cell performance was increased as the cell temperature increased. The optimal cell temperature was between 180 °C and 190 °C. From the EIS curve shown in Fig. 9, the charge transfer resistance and cell internal resistance were observed to decrease as the cell temperature increased. No mass-transfer-related resistance was observed in the low frequency region. This behavior was consistent with the results shown in Fig. 8.

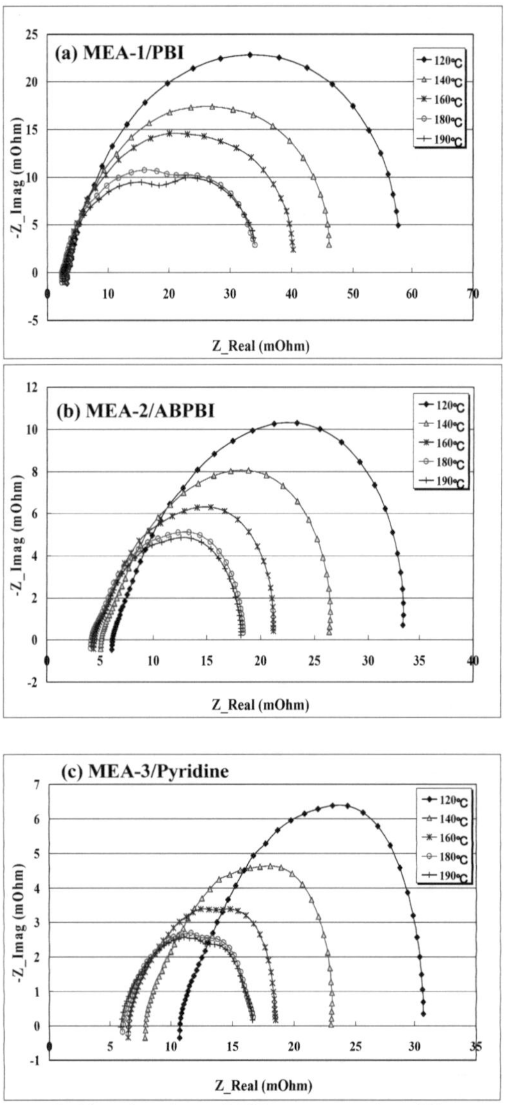

Figure 9. Nyquist plots of EIS measured at different cell temperatures (120~190 ℃) with three types of membrane: (a) PBI; (b) ABPBI; (c) Pyridine.

Concluding remarks

Important findings of this study are summarized as follows:

1. The optimal cell operating temperature was between 180 °C and 190 °C. The maximum output power was obtained in the cell voltage region of 0.45~0.5 V. Although better cell performance was obtained at high temperature, the aggregation of catalyst was also accelerated. This aggregation may seriously affect cell life. There is a tradeoff between the cell operating temperature and the cell life.
2. Both the charge transfer resistance and cell internal resistance decreased as the cell temperature increased. The minimum resistance was obtained for cell temperatures in the range of 180~190 °C. This behavior is consistent with the IV results.
3. The output current density of the cells (MEA-1, MEA-2, and MEA-3) was 215, 380, and 370 mA/cm^2, respectively, under conditions of 180 ℃, 0.6 V, and H_2/air. The measured result was slightly different from the data provided by the manufacturer.
4. The optimal cell assembly pressure was 60 kgf-cm, which can provide a good performance and sealing.
5. The thickness of the soft PTFE gaskets (300μm and 500μm) had little effect on the IV curve.
6. The cell activation period (24 hr and 64 hr) had little effect on the IV curve.

Acknowledgements

We gratefully acknowledge the financial support of the Bureau of Energy (BOE), Ministry of Economic Affairs (MOEA), Taiwan.

References

[1] Q. Li, R. He, J.O. Jensen, N.J. Bjerrum, Chem. Mater., 15, pp. 4896-4915 (2003).
[2] C. Yang, P. Costamagna, S. Srinivasan, J. Benziger, A.B. Bocarsly, J. Power Sources, 103, pp. 1-9 (2001).
[3] W.L. Harrison, M.A. Hickner, Y.S. Kim, J.E. McGrath, Fuel Cells, 5, pp. 201-212 (2005).
[4] T. Ogoshi, Y. Chujo, Compos. Interf., 11, pp. 539-66 (2005).
[5] Y.-L. Ma, J. S. Wainright, M. H. Litt, and R. F. Savinell, J. Electrochem. Soc., 151, pp. A8 (2004).
[6] Z. Qi, S. Buelte, J. Power Sources, 161, pp. 1126-1132 (2006).

Ceramic Fuel Cell Modules in Li-145 Form Factor

Simon S. Ang[1], Tom Cannon[2], Ryan Tian and Jingyi Chen
University of Arkansas, High Density Electronics Center (HiDEC)
700 W. Research Center Blvd., Fayetteville, Arkansas 72701
Siang@uark.edu [1] Tcannon@uark.edu [2] (479) 575-5031

Abstract: The Li-145 battery form factor fuel cell module has been developed based on microsystem-integration technology using a low-temperature co-fired ceramic (LTCC) technology. Three-dimensional interconnects and cavities, afforded by the LTCC technology, enable fuel cells to be completely integrated within a ceramic thin-slab to reduce footprint and to take advantage of the physical properties of LTCC. This leads to smaller cell size and faster response time, enables operation in extreme environments, and paves the way for integration of additional electrical power management devices or mechanical on-board functions. In each such module, many miniaturized fuel-cells can be integrated, connected in series or parallel configurations and controlled through the internal module interconnections. When connecting the modules to a central power bus, a "power pack" system is formed that can be scaled up or down, like playing Lego, in order to meet the customer's changing needs of current-outputs from 100s to 1,000s of amperes. LTCC gives us the flexibility of current collector cavity sizes from smaller than 0.5"x0.5" all the way through 8"x8". In this way the active area of the fuel cell can be tailored to a wide range of power source applications. For this LTCC-145 fuel cell design, three 24-cell LTCC modules are being used to form a power pack size that fits into the Li-145 battery form factor delivering similar energy density requirements with room for onboard fuel storage, super capacitors and control electronics. The expected power from the LTCC-145 is 25 Watts at an output voltage of 18.9V. While Nafion and platinum loaded carbon cloth are used as the membrane electrode assemblies (MEAs) for these ceramic fuel cell modules, nanostructured membranes and catalysts are being developed to improve the efficiency, life span and allow alternate fuel sources for these fuel cell modules.

Topic: Fuel Cells, Fuel Processing and Storage

Keywords: Ceramic fuel cell modules; miniaturized fuel cells; power pack; LTCC; Li-145 battery; nanostructures; nanostructured membranes; bimetallic catalysts; alternate fuel sources.

Introduction

Three dimensional interconnects and cavities afforded by low-temperature co-fired ceramic (LTCC) technology enable fuel cells to be completely integrated within a ceramic structure. This leads to smaller package size, enables operation in extreme environments, and paves the way for integration of additional electrical power management devices or mechanical on-board functions. A polymer electrolyte membrane fuel cell (PEM-FC) module in '3D Cube Form' was designed, fabricated and fully tested using the LTCC technology [1]. The membrane electrode assembly (MEA) functions to separate electrons at a conductive anode and to conduct the electrons to an external circuit. This must be done while allowing the hydrogen ion to pass through a gas barrier to the cathode so that it may recombine with electrons and ultimately balance the reaction. The structure of the LTCC-based MEA consists of gas channels and anode/cathode current collectors embedded in the LTCC structure. Two halves are mated to form the assembly that houses the gas diffusion layer and the gas barrier membrane. Many variables affect cell performance including gas channeling methods, diffusion layer construction, electrode-to-diffusion layer interface, and electrode conducting material [2].

Fuel Cell Construction

DuPont 951 Green Tape with a 10 mil thickness was used for fabrication of the cells. This tape is available in multiple thicknesses and is designed for use as an insulating layer [3]. As seen in Figure 1, both the anode and cathode plates have a similar build sequence. Each begins with a four-layer tape base. An AutoCAD software was used to design the artwork used for fabrication. The artwork was converted to run on an automatic tape-punching tool, where layers were then punched individually. Following this, the four layers were laminated together to form 40 mil-thick unfired end plates. The LTCC surfaces were then metallized by applying a paste mixture of silver and palladium. This conductive paste was used to form the current collectors and the conductors that connect to the outside of the cell. Following this step, extra layers of tape were laminated to the structure to form the MEA sealing lip.

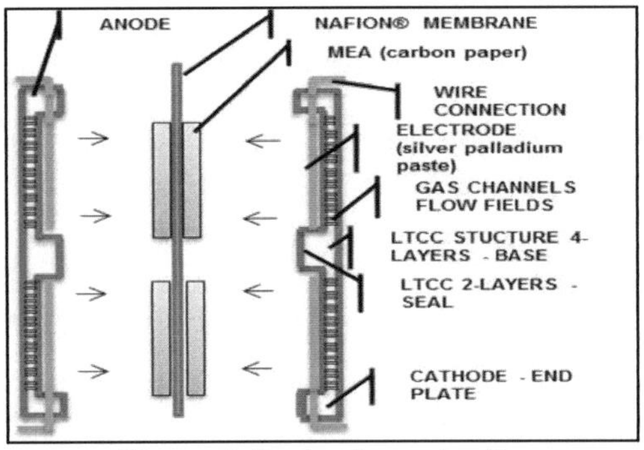

Figure 1. Fuel cell construction

The ceramic pieces were then fired in a furnace. Cell construction began with MEAs built using carbon cloth on carbon cloth doped with 0.5 mg/cm^2 of a platinum/ruthenium (Pt/Ru) in a 1:1 ratio. Fuel channel size was the first variable taken into consideration when designing the cells. It is already know that channel shape and size has a significant effect on output levels [4]. In order to establish a starting point, 20 mil round holes were selected using a 0.5 mm x 0.5 mm grid layout for the gas flow fields. A ceramic structure was designed that anchors four MEAs, channels the fuel, integrates the electrodes, and provides the necessary electrical interconnect for multiple cell configurations. Figure 2 shows the completed 4 x 4 fuel cell plates with fuel

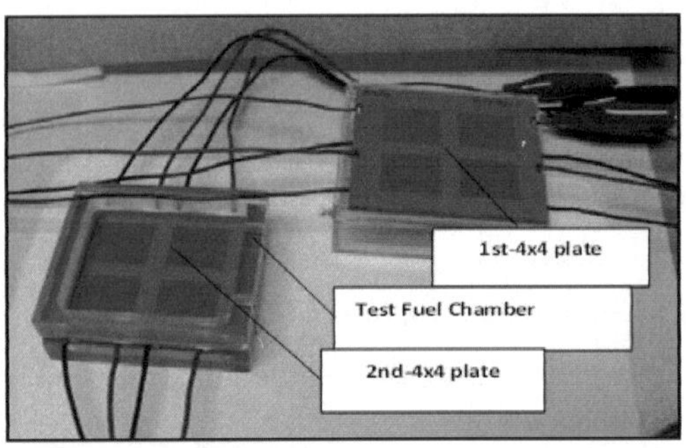

Figure 2. 8-cell fuel cell module with fuel storage.

storage to form the 8-cell fuel cell module.

The next step was to design a 12-cell plate and add the MEA's. A completed 12-cell place is shown in Figure 3. (45mm x 135mm x 1.5mm) A filter medium is used on the cathode of each of the three modules, to remove dust and particles and hold water vapor to help hydrate the fuel cell membranes. The fuel distribution chambers are designed with gas flow tubing to allow the fuel to flow in only one direction allowing full coverage of each of the 24 cells in the module as shown in Figure 4. The chambers also incorporate water collection capillaries to direct the water away from the anodes keeping the cells from becoming flooded. The output of water is redirected to the cathode air filters to hydrate the fuel cells. A sensor can be used to control the flushing of the chamber.

Adding the fuel chamber and a second 12-cell plate forms the 24-cell module. By connecting three 24-cell modules (45mm x 135mm x 8mm each) with fuel distribution chambers, the overall size will fit into the Li-145 form factor and still allow room for changeable fuel supply canister and controls, as seen in Figure 5-A & B.

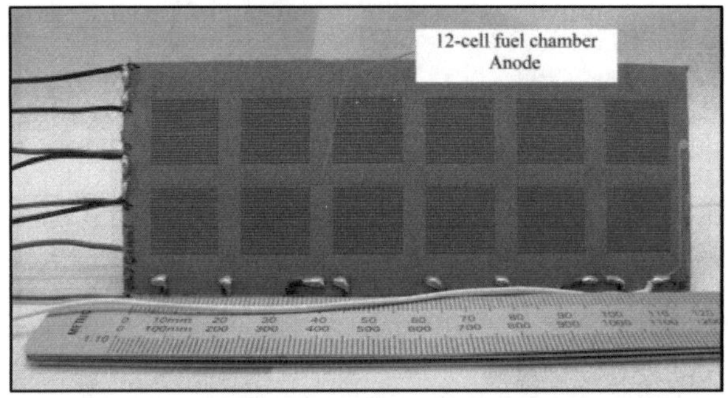

Figure 3. 12-cell Fuel Cell Plate

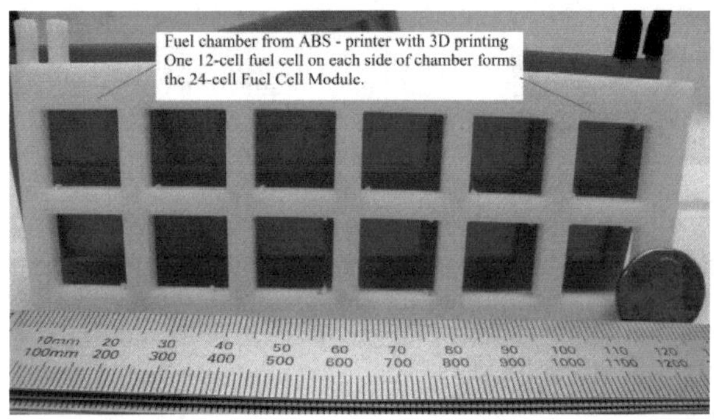

Figure 4. Fuel distribution chamber

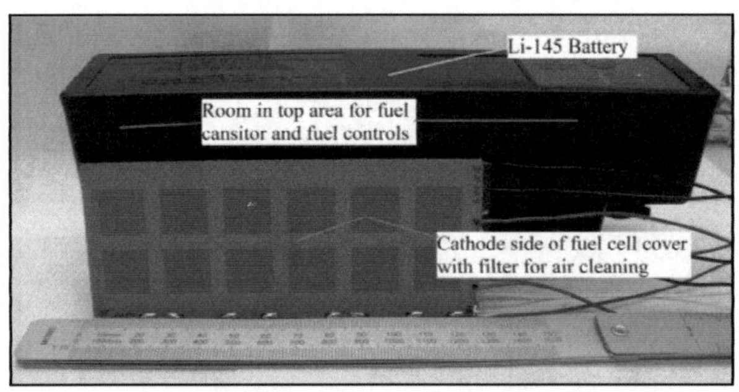

Figure 5A-B. LTCC 24-cell fuel cell with Li-145 battery – Depth and Thickness

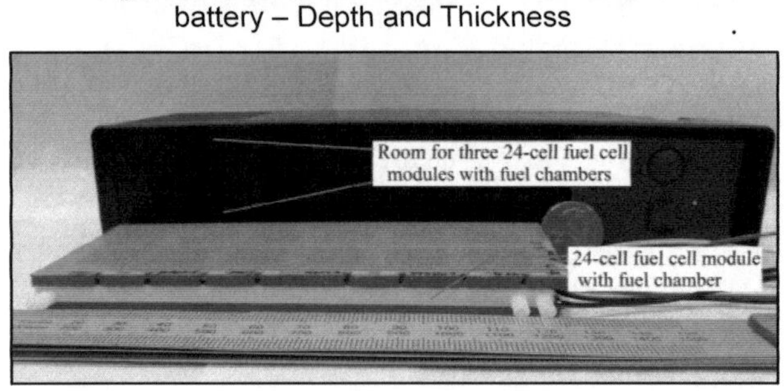

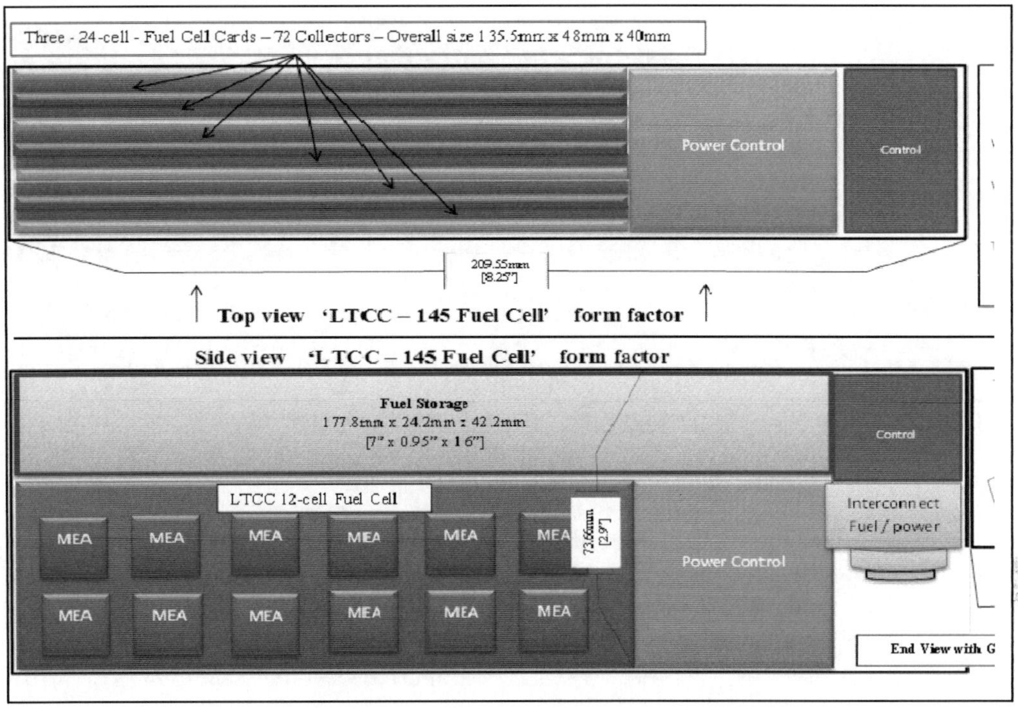

Figure 6. The LTCC-145 concept drawing

LTCC-145 Concept

This design of three 24-cell modules (45mm x 135mm x 8mm each) with fuel distribution chambers, has the overall size of 135mm x 45mm x 35mm, placed in the form factor of the Li-145 allows room for solid hydrogen fuel storage and electronic management, as seen in Figure 6. Since one liter of hydrogen will produce 2.89 Wh of work. (3.2–3.5 Wh per liter, deregulated due to temperature changes) [5], the canister volume size of 178mm x 24.2mm x 42.2mm that holds 60 liters of hydrogen in solid form can be expected to yield 173Wh (i.e., 2.89 x 60 = 173.4Wh). With an average power draw of 6.5W, the fuel cell is expected to run for over 26 hours before changing the fuel canister, this is based on a potential application with the Falcon AN/PRC-150 radio, with average operation times of 60%(I)30%(R)10%(T).

Testing

Current-voltage (I-V) performance data was collected by using a test circuit consisting of a two voltmeters. One voltmeter was set to measure the cell's output voltage, while the other was used to measure voltage across a 0.1 ohm precision current-sense resistor in series with a variable resistance. [6] Multiple current and voltage measurements were taken from open-circuit to short circuit condition using a purely resistive load. Before testing the performance of the 8-cells, we first characterized individual cells within each of the 4-cell plates. This was followed by the testing of various series and parallel cell combinations. Hydrogen was fed from a gas cylinder with back pressures of 1psi created by running the output gas port through a needle valve into a 500 ml beaker of water. The 8-cell module (45mm x 45mm x 8mm), with fuel storage and 0.5mg/cm² Pt loading, produces 2,448mV @ 1,042mA for 2.55Watts at 70% of Nernst Voltage as shown in Figure 7. On this basis, one 24-cell module (45mm x 135mm x 8mm), is three times that of the eight cell module, with the fuel storage and has a projected output power of 7.65Watts. When integrating 3 such 24-cell modules (i.e., 72 cells) to a central power bus, a compact FC "power pack" (45mm x 135mm x 35 mm) is formed that can produce an average output power of over 23Watts. At the time of this writing the 24-cell modules were undergoing testing for power, fuel consumption and cycle duration for 1,000 cycles.

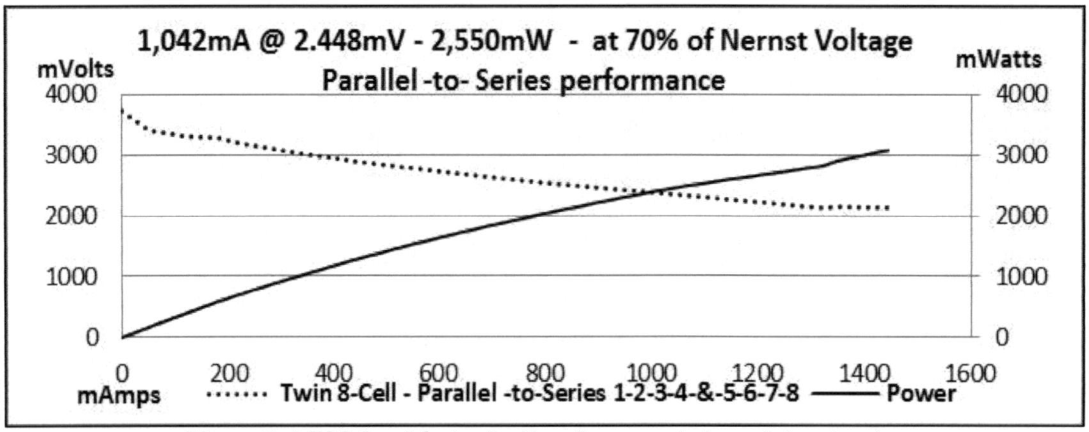

Figure 7. LTCC 8-cell fuel cell with cells connected parallel and series

Nanostructure Membranes and Catalysts

While Nafion and platinum loaded carbon cloth are used as the membrane electrode assemblies (MEAs) for these ceramic fuel cell modules, nanostructured membranes [7] and catalysts are being developed to improve the efficiency and life span of these fuel cell modules and to allow use of alternate fuels, like Natural Gas. [8] A high proton conductivity nanofiber with tunable pore structures and proton passage across the PEM is also being developed, for operations in hotter environments. [9]

Conclusion

A ceramic fuel cell module LTCC-145, in Li-145 form factor, has been fabricated for a direct replacement of the Li-145 battery.

References

[1] T. Cannon, S.S. Ang, M. Steger, K. Porter, E.V. Porter, and M Glover, "A Ceramic "Power Cube" Fuel Cell," 45th Power Sources Conference, Las Vegas (NV), June 11-14, 2012. Pg. 215-218.

[2] Colleen Spiegel, PEM Fuel Cell Modeling and Simulation, 84 Theobaid's Road London, Elsevier 2008 pp. 49-165.

[3] "LTCC Product Technical Information : DuPont Microcircuit Materials." [Online]. Available:http://www2.dupont.com/MCM/en_US/tech_info/products/ltcc.html#951.

[4] Uwe Partach, Adrian Goldberg, Michael Stelter, LTCC - Based Micro-Scale PEM Fuel Cell, IEEE Electronics System Integration Technology Conference, 1st Vol. 1, 2006 pp. 544-549

[5] Energy Density - facts and equations on hydrogen density and volumes. http://hypertextbook.com/facts/2005/MichelleFung.s www.siei.org/usefulequations.htm

[6] Shannon C. Page, Adnan H. Anbuky, Susan P. Krumdieck, and Jack Brouwer - Test Method and Equivalent Circuit Modeling of a PEM Fuel Cell in a Passive State, IEEE Transactions on Energy Conversion, Vol. 22, No. 3, September 2007 pp. 764-773.

[7] Novel Path to Nanocomposite Cathodes and Anodes Enabling High Power Li-ion and Next-Generation Batteries (Page 99) Daniel E. Morse, Hong-Li Zhang, Jon von Bulow, Lyle Kaplan-Reinig, Christie Reji, Nick Whelan, *LifeCel Technology Inc. & University of California, Santa Barbara,* 45th Power Sources Conference, June 2012

[8] J. Chen, B. Yao, C. Li, and G. Shi, "An improved Hummers method for eco-friendly synthesis of graphene oxide," Carbon, Volume 64, November 2013, pg. 225–229.

[9] W. Dong, Z. Shi, J. Ma, C. Hou, Q. Wan, S. Feng, A. Cogbill, Z.R. Tian, "One-pot redox syntheses of heteronanostructures of Ag nanoparticles on MoO_3 nanofibers," *J. Phys. Chem. B.* 2006, 110, 5845-5848.

Safe Li-Ion Technology for Micro and Mild Hybrid Application based on CEA Bipolar $LiFePO_4/Li_4Ti_5O_{12}$ Technology

M. Chami, C. Leys, Y. Reynier, F. Fusalba, S. Martinet, S. Jouanneau[1]

[1] Séverine Jouanneau, Head of Service - Commissariat à l'Energie Atomique – Direction de la Recherche Technologique, 17, rue des Martyrs – 38054 Grenoble Cedex 9 - FRANCE, severine.jouanneau@cea.fr

Abstract

The bipolar design consists in identical cells stacked together. This technology offers several advantages because it simplifies cell-to-cell connections and so offers a lowering internal resistance for the whole battery. The bipolar battery can be designed to present a large capacity with high voltage and appreciable flexible form factor.

The CEA's patented bipolar battery developed for the Hybrid Electric Vehicle (HEV) is based upon the use of $Li_4Ti_5O_{12}$ anode material (allowing the use of a common bipolar aluminium current collector [1], and high power application) and $LiFePO_4$ cathode material (cycle life, safety [2], low cost). The main target has been first to achieve a sealed system with no electrolyte leakage, and then to demonstrate the advantage of the $Li_4Ti_5O_{12}$ / $LiFePO_4$ couple (1.9V) for high power Li-ion bipolar battery [3]. To increase the battery cycle life, a new design (Figure 1) has been elaborated and has allowed to develop standard energy battery of 15Wh (24V, 0.65 Ah), with stable performances at high rate cycling.

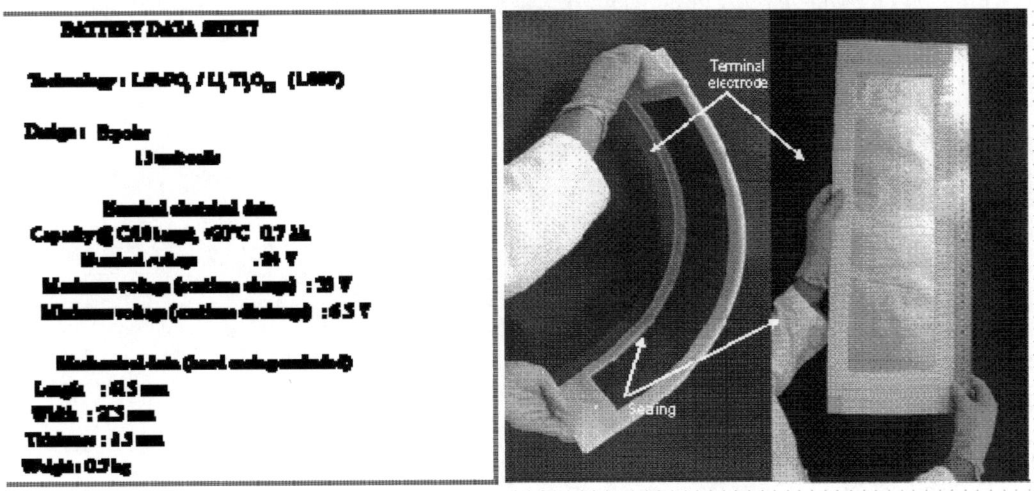

Figure 1 : CEA 15Wh Li ion bipolar cell data sheet and photography.

At high cycle rate (5C), capacity loss is less than 20% after more than 1000 cycles (Figure 2). The cycle life obtained for scale 1 battery at 24V with 13 bipolar cell compartments fits well with result on conventional 1.9V button cells.

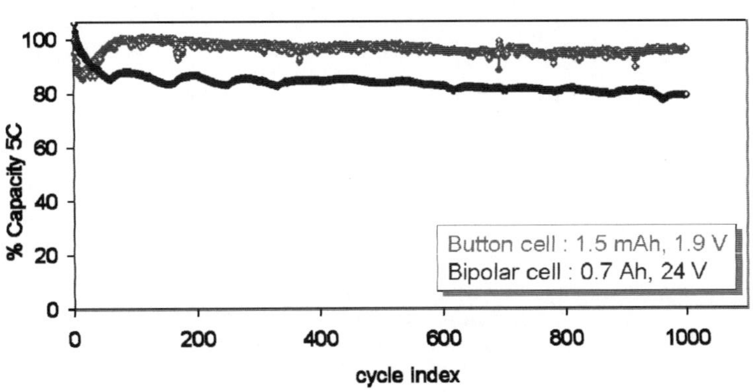

Figure 2 : 24V bipolar cell, 0.7 Ah high rate cycling @5C, 20°C. Capacity loss versus cycling.

A 15Wh bipolar cell was tested during HEV profiles. An HEV profile corresponds to a micro cycle made of discharge at max. current 60 A and 6 V cut-off voltage -60 A (1s) ⇔ 80 C rate- with a charge at max. current 30 A and 30 V cut-off voltage -30 A (3s) ⇔ 40 C rate- being repeated to simulate an accelerated duty profile -100 µcycles ~ 1 week of actual operation. It is thus reported more than 35,000 HEV profiles performed by the 15Wh bipolar cell.

Acknowledgment

ADEME (financial support), Renault, VALEO and PSA are acknowledged for discussions and their part of this work under contract ADEME n° 05 66 C0080. The authors thank all their colleagues at CEA-LITEN for their contribution to the bipolar technology during the last 10 years.

References

[1] US 7 326 493 Patent

[2]"Development and Test of Safe, High Power Lithium Ion Main Batteries for General Aviation Aircraft"http://www.sae.org/technical/papers/2008-01-2884

[3] K.Nakahara, R.Nakajima, T. Matsushima and H. Majima, J. Power Sources 117 (2003) 131-136

Keywords: *"Battery" Lithium-ion" "bipolar" "Power" "Safety" "High cycle life" "Low cost"*

A High Voltage Thermal Battery with High Capacity Cathodes

Pyoungho Choi,[1] Ivy Mills,[1] Sameer Singhal,[1] and Mohan Sanghadasa[2]
[1]CFD Research Corporation, 701 McMillian Way, Huntsville, AL 35806
[2]US Army RDECOM AMRDEC, Redstone Arsenal, AL 35898

The current thermal battery technology needs significant improvement in power density and energy density to meet various future space and defense requirements.

CFD Research Corporation, in collaboration with the U.S. Army, is developing a next-generation "high capacity thermal battery" made of lithium-silicon anode, molten salt electrolyte, and transition metal-based high capacity cathodes. The electrodes are engineered to provide fast kinetics and high rate of discharge through structural and compositional modifications. Several new high capacity cathode materials have been investigated and they have shown high open circuit voltage (>3V) and operating voltage (>2.2V). The performance of the thermal battery with the cathode depends strongly on the electrolyte used as it should be electrochemically stable at the high voltage, and compatible with the high capacity cathodes. As the traditional electrolytes are not suitable for the high voltage operation due to their low electrochemical windows (<3V), we have developed new molten salt electrolytes with high ionic conductivity and electrochemical stability. The batteries were tested over wide range of discharge rate and they have shown substantial increase in power and energy densities. The size of thermal battery will be reduced dramatically with the development of high voltage cathode materials. The effect of electrolyte, ball milling time, and discharge rate on the performance will be presented.

The performance of the battery will be compared with that of the current state of the art LiSi/FeS_2 and LiSi/CoS_2 thermal batteries.

Power Sources Conference
Palisades Convention Management
411 Lafayette Street, Suite 201
New York, NY 10003

ISBN 978-1-5108-5234-1

9 781510 852341

CURRAN ASSOCIATES INC.
proceedings.com